California

[handwritten] MARK, JASON
RORY + SAM

JULY 03

MARK + TRACY 3-17 SEPT 05

written and researched by

JD Dickey, Nick Edwards, Mark Ellwood and Paul Whitfield

with additional contribution from

Greg Ward

[handwritten] July 03 Jason, Rory Sam + Mark
3-17 Sept 05 Mark + Tracy

ROUGH GUIDES

www.roughguides.com

[handwritten] Jason's Book.

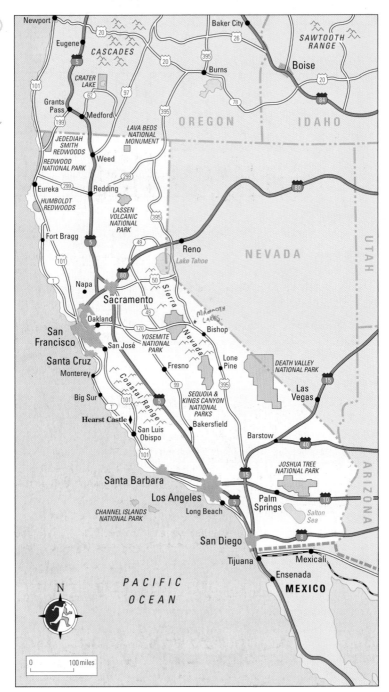

Introduction to

California

California is America squared. It's the place you go to find more America than you ever thought possible.

What's Wrong with America by Scott Bradfield

Perhaps no region of the world has been as idealized as California, and few, if any, actually manage to live up to the hype to the same degree. Justly celebrated for its sun, sand, surf, and sea, it has a whole lot more besides, such as high mountain ranges, Gold Rush ghost towns, glitzy cities, deep primeval forests, and hot, dry deserts.

California doesn't dwell too much on the past, and, in some ways, represents the ultimate "now" society, with all that entails. Urban life is very much lived in the fast lane, and conspicuous consumption is often emphasized to the exclusion of almost everything else. But this is only one side of the coin, and the deeper sense of age here often gets skimmed over. Once you get out of the cities, however, it is readily apparent in the landscape: dense groves of ancient trees, primitive rock carvings left by the aboriginal Native American culture, and the eerie ghost towns of the Gold Rush pioneers. A land of superlatives, California really is full of the oldest, the tallest, the largest, the most spectacular – all of which go far beyond local bravura.

It's important to bear in mind, too, that the supposed "superficiality" of California and Californians is largely a myth, one grounded in LA's position as entertainment, theme park, and beach culture capital of America, as well as the perception that San Francisco – or, just as much, nearby cities

Fact file

- California is known as the "Golden State," a nickname that derives from the Gold Rush days of the 1840s and 50s and is perpetuated by the golden poppy, or *Eschscholzia californica*, which appears all over California each spring and is the state flower.

- California raised the flags of Spain, England, Mexico, and the short-lived Bear Republic before it was admitted to the Union on September 9, 1850, as the thirty-first state.

- Each year, California becomes home to more immigrants than any other state, most settlers hailing from Latin America and Asia. Almost a third of all immigrants to the US settle in the state.

- The third largest state in the US (after Texas and Alaska), California boasts an almost 700-mile-long coast along the Pacific and around 25,000 square miles of desert.

- Based on agriculture and such industries as electronic components, aerospace, film production, and tourism, the state's economy is the strongest in the US. Indeed, if it were a country, California's economy would rank as seventh largest in the world.

like Berkeley and Santa Cruz – serves as some sort of bastion of the lunatic fringe. But this is an image promoted as much by Americans on the East Coast as visitors to the state, even if the area's endeavors to gain cultural credibility can sometimes seem brash.

Politically, California's probably the USA's most schizophrenic state, home to some of its most reactionary figures – Ronald Reagan and Richard Nixon to name but two – yet also the source of some of the country's most progressive political movements. Some of the fiercest protests of the Sixties emanated from here, and in many ways this is still the heart of liberal America. Consider the level of environmental awareness, which puts the smoky East to shame,

> A land of superlatives, California really is full of the oldest, the tallest, the largest, the most spectacular – all of which go far beyond local bravura.

and the fact that California has helped set the standard for the rest of the US (if not the world) regarding gay pride and social permissiveness. The region is economically crucial as well, with the cash-flush entertainment field dominated by California's film industry and ascendant music business; even in the increasingly important financial markets, Los Angeles has become a major player.

Where to go

California covers nearly 160,000 square miles: keep in mind that distances between the main destinations can be huge, and that you won't, unless you're here for an extended period, be able to see everything on one trip.

In an area so varied, it's hard to pick out specific highlights, and much will depend on the kind of vacation you're looking for. You may well start off in **Los Angeles**, far and away the biggest and most stimulating Californian city: a maddening collection of freeways and beaches, seedy suburbs and high-gloss neighborhoods, and extreme lifestyles that you should see at least once, even if you make a quick exit for more relaxed locales.

Among the oldest European settlements in California, its 21 **missions** were established by the Spanish in the late eighteenth century in a burst of supposedly religious zeal aimed at christianizing the local heathens. The truth, of course, is more complex: each mission was accompanied by a *pueblo*, or secular settlement, and, most importantly, a *presidio*, or military fortress. Masterminded by Franciscan Father Junípero Serra, the entire network ran largely along what was known as the *Camino Real*, or Royal Road, from San Diego to Solano, just north of San Francisco, ensuring that every mission was one day's ride or hard walk from the next. This proximity enabled easy commerce and communication along the chain.

The missions flourished for more than a hundred years, converting and killing thousands of locals through a combination of evangelism and smallpox. Eventually, when the missions were secularized under Mexican rule in 1834, much of the land was given not to the indigenous peoples, but to the Spanish-speaking *californio* ranchers.

The largest and most populous settlement of all, was **San Luis Rey** (p.238) – its huge *lavanderia,* or washing area, is now an impressive sunken garden; while arguably the most famous is **San Juan Capistrano** (p.157), which welcomes migrating swallows every March. Visitors will find the most evocative sense of early settler life at the restorations at **San Antonio de Padua** (p.467) and **La Purisima** (p.453).

From Los Angeles you have a number of choices. You can head south to **San Diego**, the seventh-largest city in America, complete with broad, welcoming beaches and a handy position close to the Mexican border, or you could push inland to the Californian **desert** areas, notably **Death Valley** – as its name suggests, a barren inhospitable landscape of volcanic craters and windswept sand dunes that in summer (when you can fry an egg on your car bonnet) becomes the hottest place on earth. From here, it's a logical trip across into Nevada to the **Grand Canyon** via **Las Vegas**; though not actually in California, both spots are accessible from it and are, as well,

California cuisine and wine

In much of rural California, the diner is king, and the tuna melt and diet soda the last word in culinary sophistication. Nothing wrong with that, but the state also offers just about every gastronomic diversion imaginable, as well as a wide range of ethnic cuisines, which exploit the fabulous array of fruit, vegetables, and dairy produce grown here. This abundance, along with Mexican and Asian influences, led in the Eighties to the creation of California cuisine, a style with an almost obsessive devotion to the freshest local ingredients, simply prepared to bring out the natural goodness and look great on the plate. This may not sound so novel now, but at the time it was revolutionary, and the spread of such dishes as blackened ahi tuna layered with sesame, and mesclun salads with goat cheese and toasted walnuts only attests to California cuisine's enduring vitality.

The state's culinary rise has been matched by the improvement in its wines. Bulk wines for everyday quaffing are still the mainstay of California's industrial winemakers (California produces more than 17 million gallons of wine each year), but an ever increasing acreage is being planted by boutique wineries, particularly in the Napa (see p.717) and Sonoma (see p.722) valleys north of San Francisco. Growers are forever experimenting with different varieties and applying modern winemaking techniques to produce wines that challenge almost any in the world for both quality and price.

among the star attractions in the US – and thus covered in the Guide. An alternative is to make the steady journey up the **Central Coast**, a gorgeous run following the shoreline north through some of the state's most dramatic scenery, and taking in some of its liveliest small towns, notably Santa Barbara and Santa Cruz.

The Central Coast makes the transition from Southern to Northern California – a break that's more than just geographical. **San Francisco**, California's second city, is quite different from LA: the coast's oldest, most European-looking metropolis, it's set compactly over a series of steep hills, with wooden houses tumbling down to water on both sides. San Francisco also provides access to some of the state's most extraordinary scenery, not least in the national parks to the east, especially **Yosemite**, where powerful waterfalls cascade into a sheer glacial valley, immortalized by Ansel Adams – and countless others – in search of the definitive landscape photograph. Yosemite marks the high (not altitude-wise) point of the Sierras; south from it are the worthy national parks of **Sequoia** and **Kings Canyon**, and north an interesting mix of quaint towns like Nevada City and resort spots such as Lake Tahoe.

North of San Francisco, the population thins and the physical look changes yet again. The climate is wetter up here, the valleys that much greener, flanked by a jagged coastline shadowed by mighty redwoods, the tallest trees in the world. Though many visitors choose to venture no further than the **Wine Country** and the Russian River Valley on weekend forays from the city, it's well worth taking time out to explore the state's northernmost regions, which are split rather distinctly in two. The coastline is rugged and peaceful; the interior, meanwhile, makes the coastline look positively overdeveloped – it's a volcano-scarred desolation that's as different from the popular image of California as it's possible to be.

National parks and monuments

California really packs a punch when it comes to dramatic scenery, much of it protected in a fabulous array of national parks and monuments. If you're looking for challenging but rewarding hikes, ideal camping, or just cataloging various types of trees and wildlife, you can't do much better than these. Superlatives abound: Death Valley (see p.325) has the lowest point in the Western Hemisphere and is the driest area in the US; the Bristlecone Pine Forest (see p.344) contains the world's most ancient trees; Mount Whitney (see p.338) is the highest peak in the 48 contiguous states and forms the eastern boundary of Sequoia National Park (see p.395), which in turn produces the largest trees in the world (the sequoias); and the north coast provides ideal conditions for growing the planet's tallest trees – the redwoods. Elsewhere, huge rock piles and an outlandish form of yucca dot the desert of Joshua Tree National Park (see p.276), volcanic cones and lava tubes pepper Northern California, and the wondrous domes and spires of Yosemite (see p.409) are only rivaled for scenic wonder by Nevada's Grand Canyon (see p.312).

On shaky ground

California's a seismic timebomb. The state is bisected by the most famous faultline in the world, the San Andreas, which runs from San Francisco to Los Angeles and marks where the Pacific and North American tectonic plates meet. However, it's not the most active fault at the moment – that honor goes to one of its tributaries, the Hayward. Each

year, an estimated 500,000 seismic tremors are detected in California. While the San Francisco earthquake of 1906 is the most famous, it wasn't actually the quake itself that leveled the city, but a careless homeowner cooking breakfast on a gas stove at the time; the ensuing fire raged for four days, razed 28,000 buildings, and left at least 3000 dead. Since then, there have been several significant shocks, most notably in 1989, when San Francisco again shook during the Loma Prieta. That quake occurred during the World Series, and was seen by millions watching on television. Of course, everyone's waiting for the Big One, a massive earthquake that, it's feared, could wipe out Los Angeles. Gossip has intensified recently, since experts have pegged the interval between major ruptures in the southern reaches of the San Andreas at 140 years: the last such quake was Fort Tejon in 1857.

When to go

California's climate comes close to its subtropical ideal. In **Southern California** in particular, you can count on endless days of sunshine from May to October, and warm dry nights – though LA's notorious **smog** is at its worst when the temperatures are highest, in August and September.

Right along the **coast**, mornings can be hazily overcast, especially in May and June, though you can still get a suntan – or sunburn – even under grayish skies. In winter temperatures drop somewhat, but more importantly it can rain for weeks on end, causing massive mudslides that wipe out roads and hillside homes. Inland, the deserts are warm in winter and unbearably hot (120°F is not unusual) in summer; desert nights can be freezing in winter, when, strangely but beautifully, it can even snow. For serious **snow**, head to the

mountains, where hiking trails at the higher elevations are blocked from November to June every year: skiers can take advantage of well-groomed slopes along the Sierra Nevada mountains and around Lake Tahoe.

The coast of **Northern California** is wetter and cooler than the south, its summers tempered by sea breezes and fog, and its winters mild but wet. **San Francisco**, because of its exposed position at the tip of a peninsula, can be chilly all year, with summer fogs tending to roll in to ruin what may have started off as a pleasant sunny day. Head a mile inland, and you're back in the sun.

Daytime temperatures (max & min F)

	Jan	April	July	Oct
San Diego				
	66	69	76	73
	46	54	63	58
Las Vegas				
	60	81	103	84
	29	45	68	47
Los Angeles				
	65	72	83	77
	47	53	63	57
San Francisco				
	56	62	65	68
	45	49	54	54
Death Valley				
	65	91	116	91
	37	61	87	51

things not to miss

It's not possible to see everything that California has to offer in one trip – and we don't suggest you try. What follows is a selective taste of the state's highlights: from its vibrant cities to its serene deserts. They're arranged in five colour-coded categories, which you can browse through to find the very best things to see and experience. All highlights have a page reference to take you straight into the guide, where you can find out more.

01 **The Third Street Promenade** Page **138** ● Sooner or later, all visitors to LA visit this Santa Monica pedestrian mall for its people watching, swinging nightlife, and fine dining options.

02 **Cholla Cactus Garden** Page **280** • One of the high points of any trip to Joshua Tree National Park is this cactus garden, a circular hike that takes in the unique jumping cholla.

03 **Bodie Ghost Town** Page **362** • Well past its 1880s gold-mining heyday, when it was the second largest town in the state, Bodie is now an intriguing time capsule of some 150 atmospheric wooden buildings.

04 Buck Owens' Crystal Palace

Page **372** • Catch the strains of the Bakersfield Sound at this country music hotspot – if you're lucky, maybe Buck himself will take the stage.

05 The Grand Canyon Page **312** • Whether you stand at its rim and gaze at the brilliant multicolored rock strata, view it via helicopter tour, or take a hike or mule ride into the Inner Gorge, you'll find the world's largest canyon lives up to every bit of hype.

06 Klamath Basin Wildlife Refuge Page **790** • Each year, tourists from the avian world rest up in the gigantic sanctuary of the Klamath Basin before resuming their journeys along the Pacific Flyway.

07 Redwood National Park Page **754** • The tallest trees in the world – some close to 400 feet high – preside over this dramatic national park.

08 Riding a cable car Page **526** • No visit to San Francisco is complete without a ride on one of the city's cable cars, the best means of scaling the city's hills and enjoying the views.

09 **Casa de Balboa** Page **217** • Built for the 1915 Panama–California International Exposition, the Casa de Balboa contains an eclectic troika of museums – the Museum of Photographic Arts, San Diego Historical Society Museum, and the Model Railroad Museum.

10 **Red Rock Canyon petroglyphs** Page **349** • Once used as a backdrop in Spielberg's *Jurassic Park*, the canyon's rock formations present a panoply of aboriginal carvings.

11 **Rafting on the Kern River** Page **374** • The Kern River offers some of the most thrilling whitewater rafting anywhere in the States.

13 Cruising Sunset Boulevard Page **131** • The Sunset Strip has long been a choice LA place to hang out, jammed with groovy bars and clubs, swanky hotels, and towering billboards selling fashion, liquor, and starlets.

12 SeaWorld Page **225** • Killer whales, walruses, sharks, and manatees display their prodigious talents at this state-of-the-art marine theme park in San Diego's Mission Bay.

SIGHTS | NATURE | EVENTS | CONSUME | ACTIVITIES

14 La Purisima Mission Page **453** • Just east of Lompoc, La Purisima reveals a faithful glimpse of late-eighteenth-century mission life.

16 Nevada City Page **669** • One of the best preserved of the Gold Country towns, charming Nevada City is full of antique stores and quaint old buildings.

15 Big Sur Page **471** • Eyeball the secluded beauty of Big Sur's approximately ninety miles of rocky cliffs and crashing waves along the Pacific. *Done*

18 The Mojave National Preserve Page **297** • The Mojave Desert can be shocking in its extremes, and should not go unappreciated – some of the imposing sand dunes of the preserve, in the desert's eastern portion, rise as high as 4000 feet.

17 Skiing Lake Tahoe Page **689** • Hit the renowned slopes around lovely Lake Tahoe, home to unbeatable downhill skiing. *Done*

Done

19 **Gay Pride parade** Page **579** • In late June, the Gay Pride parade takes over the streets of San Francisco's Castro district in exuberant fashion.

20 **Surfing on Swami's Beach** Page **237** • This consummate California pastime can be enjoyed year-round on the state's southern beaches.

21 **Wine tasting** Page **710** • Sip California's finest vintages on a trip to Wine Country, in Sonoma, Napa, Russian River, or Anderson valleys.

22 **Mexican food** Page **43** • Duck in most any roadside taqueria or burrito joint to enjoy what's more or less the state's signature cuisine.

23 **Ride the Coast Starlight** Page **441** • While most visitors take to the highways, the best way to see the hundred-mile-long coast between Santa Barbara and San Luis Obispo is on the Coast Starlight train.

DONE

24 **Tufa towers of Mono Lake** Page **360** • See the fluffy, sandcastle-like tufa
spires that have frothed up from below the surface of this fast-shrinking body of water.

25
Berkeley's bookstores
Page **603** • The radical town holds a wide range of first- and second-hand bookstores, which make for an excellent day's browsing.

26 **Lava Beds National Monument** Page **785** • Explore this striking chain of volcanic caves, lava flows, and craters in the Modoc National Forest, a natural monument to the 1872 war between the US and Modoc Indians.

27 **Hearst Castle** Page **463** • Of all California's lavish dreams, none quite rivals William Randolph Hearst's monument to himself, which boasts a Mudejar cathedral facade and a private cinema.

28 **Whale watching** Page **642** • Springtime is your best chance of seeing gray whales during their annual migration in the Pacific.

29 Bridalveil Falls Page **424** • There's much stunning geology up and down the state, but nothing surpasses Yosemite Valley, where the awe-inspiring Bridalveil Falls cascade over six hundred feet of sheer rock.

31 The Chinese Theatre Page **117** • A cherished relic of the Twenties, the Chinese Theatre recalls the glory years of Hollywood cinema, both with its Art Deco interior and the celebrity hand- and footprints pressed into the pavement outside.

30 The Getty Center Page **134** • High above West LA, this celebrated museum holds an impressive collection – featuring excellent period furniture and priceless paintings such as Van Gogh's *Irises* – in its funky modern building, complemented by the lovely gardens outside.

32 Centro Cultural Page 245 •
The eye-catching golf ball of a building in downtown Tijuana makes a good case for choosing culture over hedonism in the seedy town; while there, admire the impressive exhibits on Mexican culture and history.

33 Viva Las Vegas Page 300 •
Just a patch of desert a century ago, Vegas has grown into the world's casino and resort capital, with replicas of whole cities in themed hotels like the *Venetian* along its famed Strip.

34 Hiking Mount Whitney Page 341 • Hike the tallest mountain in the continental US, which sits right on the edge of Sequoia National Park.

Contents

Using the Rough Guide

We've tried to make this Rough Guide a good read and easy to use. The book is divided into five main sections, and you should be able to find whatever you want in one of them.

Color section

The front color section offers a quick survey of California. The **introduction** aims to give you a feel for the state, with suggestions on where to go. We also tell you what the weather is like and include a basic regional fact file. Next, our authors round up their favorite aspects of California in the "things not to miss" section – whether it's great food, amazing sights, or a special activity. Right after this comes a full contents list.

Basics

The Basics section covers all the **pre-departure** nitty-gritty to help you plan your trip. This is where to find out which airlines fly to your destination, what paperwork you'll need, what to do about money and insurance, Internet access, food, public transport, car rental – in fact just about every piece of **general practical information** you might need.

Guide

This is the heart of the Rough Guide, divided into user-friendly chapters, each of which covers a major city or a general region. Every chapter starts with a list of **highlights**, a practical **map**, and an **introduction** that helps

you to decide where to go. Chapters then move on to **detailed coverage** of your destination. Introductions to the various cities, towns, and smaller regions within each chapter should help you plan your itinerary. We start most **town accounts** with information on arrival and accommodation, followed by a tour of the sights, and finally reviews of places to eat and drink, and details of nightlife. Longer accounts also have a directory of practical listings.

Contexts

Read Contexts to get a deeper understanding of what makes California tick. We include a brief history, articles about the state's wildlife, and a detailed further reading section that reviews dozens of **books** relating to the country.

Index + small print

Apart from a **full index**, which includes maps as well as places, this section covers publishing information, credits, and acknowledgments, and also has our contact details in case you want to send in updates and corrections to the book – or suggestions as to how we might improve it.

Chapter list and map

Contents

x = DoNE

Contexts

793–844

Index and small print

845–857

CONTENTS

Map symbols

maps are listed in the full index using coloured text

Interstate	
U.S. Highway	
Highway	
4WD track	
Unpaved road	
Path/trail	
Railway	
Ferry route	
International border	
State border	
Chapter division boundary	
River	
✈ Airport	
◉ Hotel	
▣ Restaurant	
Ski resort	
Golf course	
⚠ Campsite	
🌲 Picnic area	
Church (regional maps)	
🏛 Historic house	
Museum	
Entrance gate	
Lighthouse	
Ruins	

Caves	
Oasis	
Spring/spa	
Viewpoint	
Mountain range	
▲ Mountain peak	
Pass	
Gorge/cutting	
Waterfall	
Marshland	
General point of interest	
(i) Information centre	
✉ Post office	
Telephone	
@ Internet café	
★ Public transport stop	
P Parking	
One-way street	
Building	
Church	
Cemetery	
National Park	
Park	
Military Base	
Beach	

Basics

Basics

Getting there

The second largest state in the continental US, California presents an easy target for both domestic and international visitors. All the main airlines operate daily scheduled flights to San Francisco and LA from all over the world, and the state is easily accessible by road or rail throughout the year. £372 EACH ←Loos WWW. THOMASCOOK. COM

Generally, the most expensive time to fly is **high season**, roughly between June and August and around Christmas. April–May and September–October are considerably less pricey, and the rest of the year is considered low season and is cheaper still.

You can often cut costs by going through a **specialist flight agent** – either a consolidator, who buys up blocks of tickets from the airlines and sells them at a discount, or a **discount agent** who, in addition to dealing with discounted flights, may also offer special student and youth fares and a range of other travel-related services such as travel insurance, rail passes, car rentals, tours, and the like. Some agents specialize in **charter flights**, which may be cheaper than anything available on a scheduled flight, but again departure dates are fixed and withdrawal penalties are high. For some destinations, like Los Angeles, San Francisco, and Las Vegas, you may even find it cheaper to pick up a bargain **package deal** from one of the tour operators listed below and then find your own accommodation when you get there. A further possibility is to see if you can arrange a courier flight, although you'll need a flexible schedule, and preferably be traveling alone with very little luggage. In return for shepherding a parcel through customs, you can expect to get a deeply discounted ticket. You'll probably also be restricted in the duration of your stay.

Booking flights online

Many airlines and discount travel websites offer you the opportunity to book your tickets online, cutting out the costs of agents and middlemen. Good deals can often be found through discount or auction sites, as well as through the airlines' own websites.

Online booking agents and general travel sites

www.cheapflights.com Bookings from the UK and Ireland only. Flight deals, travel agents, plus links to other travel sites.

www.cheaptickets.com Discount flight specialists.

www.etn.nl/discount.htm A hub of consolidator and discount agent Web links, maintained by the nonprofit European Travel Network.

www.expedia.com Discount airfares, all–airline search engine and daily deals.

www.flyaow.com Online air travel info and reservations site.

www.gaytravel.com Gay online travel agent, concentrating mostly on accommodation.

www.hotwire.com Bookings from the US only. Last-minute savings of up to forty percent on regular published fares. Travelers must be at least 18 and there are no refunds, transfers, or changes allowed. Log-in required.

www.lastminute.com Offers good last-minute holiday package and flight-only deals.

www.priceline.com Name-your-own-price website that has deals at around forty percent off standard fares. You cannot specify flight times (although you do specify dates) and the tickets are non-refundable, non-transferable, and non-changeable.

www.travelocity.com Destination guides, hot web fares, and best deals for car hire, accommodation and lodging, as well as fares. Provides access to the travel agent system SABRE, the most comprehensive central reservations system in the US.

www.travelshop.com.au Australian website offering discounted flights, packages, insurance, and online bookings.

From elsewhere in North America

Getting to California from anywhere else in North America is never a problem, for the region is well served by air, rail, and road networks. Flying remains the best but most expensive way to travel; taking a train comes a slow second. Traveling by bus is the least expensive method, but again is slow, and is much less comfortable than either train or plane.

By air

If you are flying to Los Angeles, most domestic flights land at the city's international **LAX** airport, though some touch down at the smaller airports at Burbank, Long Beach, Ontario, and John Wayne in Orange County. Visitors to San Francisco will probably use the main **San Francisco International Airport** (known as SFO), as well as two others, both in the Bay Area: **Oakland International** (OAK), across the Bay, is easily accessible and **Mineta San Jose International** (SJO), forty miles south, is a bit out of the way but has good connections with the western US, especially LA. Some carriers also fly to **San** Diego's Lindbergh Airport non-stop.

As airlines tend to match each other's prices, there's generally little difference in the quoted fares. Published round-trip prices start at around $400 from New York and other eastern seaboard cities, slightly less from Midwest cities (and slightly more from Toronto and Montréal), although regular airline promotions and savers can almost halve that price at slack times. What makes more difference than your choice of carrier are the conditions governing the ticket – whether it's fully refundable, the time and day, and, most importantly, the **time of year** you travel. Least expensive of all is a non-summer-season midweek flight, booked and paid for at least three weeks in advance, but keep in mind that one-way tickets are sometimes more expensive than round-trip tickets. Also, while it's good to call the airlines directly to get a sense of their official fares, it's also worth checking with a reputable **travel agent** to find out about any **special deals** or student/youth fares that may be available.

In addition to the big-name scheduled airlines, a few lesser-known carriers run no-frills flights, which can prove to be very good value, especially if you have a flexible schedule

Airlines in the US and Canada

Aer Lingus ℡1-800/223-6537, ⓦwww.aerlingus.ie
Aeromexico ℡1-800/237-6639, ⓦwww.aeromexico.com
Air Canada ℡1-888/247-2262, ⓦwww.aircanada.ca
Air France in the US ℡1-800/237-2747, ⓦwww.airfrance.com; in Canada ℡1-800/667-2747, ⓦwww.airfrance.ca
Alaska Airlines ℡1-800/252-7522, ⓦwww.alaska-air.com
America West ℡1-800/235-9292, ⓦwww.americawest.com
American Airlines ℡1-800/433-7300, ⓦwww.aa.com
British Airways ℡1-800/247-9297, ⓦwww.britishairways.com
Continental ℡1-800/523-3273, ⓦwww.continental.com
Delta Airlines ℡1-800/221-1212, ⓦwww.delta.com
Hawaiian Airlines ℡1-800/367-5320, ⓦwww.hawaiianair.com

Iberia ℡1-800/772-4642, ⓦwww.iberia.com
Icelandair ℡1-800/223-5500, ⓦwww.icelandair.com
JetBlue ℡1-800/538-2583, ⓦwww.jetblue.com
Lufthansa in the US ℡1-800/645-3880; in Canada ℡1-800/563-5954, ⓦwww.lufthansa-usa.com
Northwest/KLM ℡1-800/225-2525, ⓦwww.nwa.com, ⓦwww.klm.com
SAS ℡1-800/221-2350, ⓦwww.scandinavian.net
Southwest ℡1-800/435-9792, ⓦwww.iflyswa.com
United Airlines ℡1-800/241-6522, ⓦwww.ual.com
US Airways ℡1-800/428-4322, ⓦwww.usair.com
Virgin Atlantic Airways ℡1-800/862-8621, ⓦwww.virginatlantic.com

and can put up with a few delays. JetBlue has flights from New York to Long Beach and Oakland for under $300 round-trip. Southwest flies from a host of Midwestern and Western cities at rock-bottom prices; four daily flights leave Salt Lake City for Oakland (they don't go directly to San Francisco) from $154 round-trip ($126 one-way). Their lowest fare out of Seattle to Oakland is $126 round-trip ($125 one-way), while LA to Oakland goes for as low as $114 round-trip ($95 one-way).

Travelers intending to fly from **Canada** are likely to find that, with less competition on these routes, fares are somewhat higher than they are for flights wholly within the US. You may well find that it's worth the effort to get to a US city first, and fly on to California from there.

By train

If you have a bit more money and hanker after a few more creature comforts (all the trains have private cabins and dining cars), or simply have the time and inclination to take in some of the rest of the US on your way to California, then an Amtrak **train** may be just the ticket for you. The most spectacular train journey of all has to be the **California Zephyr**, which runs all the way from Chicago to San Francisco (53 hours; departs 2.45pm daily) and comes into its own during the ride through the Rockies west of Denver. After climbing alongside raging rivers through gorgeous mountain scenery, the route drops down the west flank of the Rockies and races across the Utah and Nevada deserts by night, stopping at Salt Lake City and Reno. The next day the train climbs up and over the mighty Sierra Nevada, following the route of the first transcontinental railroad on its way into Oakland, where you change to a bus for the ride into San Francisco.

The major southern route, the 3000-mile **Sunset Limited**, originates in Miami and stops at New Orleans, Houston, San Antonio, and Flagstaff (where a connecting bus heads to the Grand Canyon) before eventually arriving in Los Angeles.

Amtrak **fares** can be more expensive than flying, though off-peak discounts and special deals can make the train an economical as well as an aesthetic choice. A one-way

> For all information on **Amtrak fares and schedules,** and to make reservations, use the toll-free number ☏1-800/USA-RAIL or website ⊛www.amtrak.com. Do not call individual stations.

cross-country ticket from New York to Oakland costs $314 on the day of travel, though it is only $177 if booked a week in advance. International travelers can take advantage of **rail passes** (see p.34 for a summary), while special deals and weekly **rail sales** for all comers are advertised on Amtrak's website (see box above). Although Amtrak's basic fares and passes are reasonable value, if you want to travel in a bit more comfort the cost rises quickly. **Sleeping compartments,** which include meals, small toilets, and showers, start at around $150 per night for one or two people.

By bus

Bus travel is the most tedious and time-consuming way to get to California, but, if you don't mind the discomfort, can save you a lot of money. **Greyhound** (☏1-800/231-2222, ⊛www.greyhound.com) is the sole long-distance operator and has an extensive network of destinations in California. A one-way ticket from New York to San Francisco, bought seven days in advance, costs $99, while tickets purchased on the day of travel go for $156.

The best reason to go Greyhound is if you're planning to visit a number of other places en route; Greyhound's **Discovery Pass** is good for unlimited travel within a certain time, and costs $199 for seven days, $299 for fifteen days, $389 for thirty days, and $549 for sixty days. **Foreign visitors** can buy better-value **Ameripasses** before leaving home; see p.34 for details.

An alternative, in every sense, is the San Francisco-based **Green Tortoise** bus company; see p.36 for details.

By car

Driving your own car gives the greatest freedom and flexibility, but if you don't have one (or don't trust the one you do have), one option worth considering is a **driveaway**. Companies operate in most major cities, and are paid to find drivers to take a customer's car from one place to another – most commonly between California and New York. The company will normally pay for your insurance and your first tank of gas; after that, you'll be expected to drive along the most direct route and to average 400 miles a day. Many driveaway companies are keen to use foreign travelers, but if you can convince them you are a safe bet they'll take something like a $250 deposit, which you get back after delivering the car in good condition. It makes obvious sense to get in touch in advance, to spare yourself a week's wait for a car to turn up. Look under "Automobile transporters and driveaway companies" in the *Yellow Pages* and phone around for the latest offers; or try one of the ninety branches of Auto Driveaway, based in Chicago (☎312/341-1900).

Renting a car is the usual story of phoning your local branch of one of the majors (Avis, Hertz, Budget, Thrifty, etc – listed on p.31), of which Thrifty tends to be the cheapest. Most have offices at destination airports, and addresses and phone numbers are comprehensively documented in the *Yellow Pages*.

Also worth considering are **fly-drive deals**, which give cut-rate (and sometimes free) car rental when buying an air ticket. They usually work out cheaper than renting on the spot and are especially good value if you intend to do a lot of driving.

Package tours

Many operators run all-inclusive **packages** that combine plane tickets and hotel accommodation with (for example) sightseeing, wining and dining, or excursions to tourist sites. Even if the "package" aspect doesn't thrill you to pieces, these deals can still be more convenient and sometimes even work out to be more economical than arranging the same thing yourself, provided you don't mind losing a little flexibility. With such a vast range of packages available, it's impossible to give an overview – major travel agents will have brochures detailing what's available.

Tour operators

Abercrombie & Kent ☎1-800/323-7308 or 630/954-2944, ⍟www.abercrombiekent.com.

Adventure Center ☎1-800/228-8747 or 510/654-1879, ⍟www.adventure-center.com. Hiking and "soft adventure" specialists.
Backroads ☎1-800/GO-ACTIVE or 510/527-1555, ⍟www.backroads.com. Cycling, hiking, and multi-sport tours.
Holidaze Ski Tours ☎1-800/526-2827 or 732/280-1120, ⍟www.holidaze.com.
Mountain Travel Sobek ☎1-888/MTSOBEK or 510/527-8100, ⍟www.mtsobek.com.
REI Adventures ☎1-800/622-2236, ⍟www.rei.com/travel. Climbing, cycling, hiking, cruising, paddling, and multi-sport tours.

From Britain and Ireland

Though flying to California is pretty straightforward, choosing the best route can be more complicated than you might think, with prices fluctuating wildly according to how and when you go. The majority of budget options involve non-stop services from Britain, although many others turn out to be so-called "direct" flights, which can land several times, waiting an hour or so at each stop – a flight is called direct as long as it keeps the same flight number throughout its journey. The first place the plane lands is your point of entry into the US, which means you'll have to collect your bags and go through customs and immigration formalities there, even if you're continuing on to California on the same plane. This can be a real pain after a ten-hour journey, so it's worth finding out before you book a ticket.

Fares, routes, and agents

Although you can fly to the US from many regional airports, the only **non-stop flights** from Britain to California are from London. Most land in LA; fewer travel non-stop to San Francisco, and only British Airways flies non-stop to San Diego. The non-stop **flight time** is around eleven hours from London to San Francisco or LA; add an hour at least for each intervening stop on direct flights, twice that if you have to change planes.

Britain remains one of the best places in Europe to obtain flight bargains, though **fares** vary widely according to season, availability, and the current level of inter-airline competition. The comments that follow can only act as a general guide, so be sure to shop around carefully for the best offers by checking the

Sample airfares from Britain

The prices given below (in £ sterling) are a general indication of the minimum transatlantic round-trip **airfares** currently obtainable from specialist companies; youth discount fares are cheaper. Remember to add £60–70 airport tax to these figures. Each airline decides the exact dates of its seasons. Prices are for departures from London to LA or San Francisco

low	Nov–Mar (except Christmas)	200
shoulder	April, May, Sept, Oct	250
high	June–Aug, Christmas	492

travel ads in the weekend papers, on the **holiday pages** of ITV's *Teletext* and, in London, scouring *Time Out* and the *Evening Standard*. Giveaway magazines aimed at young travelers, like *TNT*, are also useful resources. The **Internet** is another valuable resource, and you'll often find good deals on any of the travel-based sites shown in the box p.11.

Stand-by deals (open-dated tickets you pay for and then decide later when you want to fly – if there's room on the plane) are few and far between and don't give great savings: in general you're better off with an **Apex** ticket. The conditions on these are pretty standard whomever you fly with – seats must be purchased seven days or more in advance, and you must stay for at least one Saturday night; tickets are normally valid for up to six months. Some airlines also do less expensive **Super-Apex** tickets, which fall into two categories. The first are approximately £150 cheaper than an ordinary Apex but must be bought 21 days in advance and require a minimum stay of seven days and a maximum stay of one month; the second are around £100 less than an Apex, must be purchased fourteen days in advance and entail a minimum stay of a week and a maximum stay of two months – such tickets are usually non-refundable or changeable. "Open-jaw" tickets can be a good idea, allowing you to fly into LA, for example, and back from San Francisco for little or no extra charge; fares are calculated by halving the return fares to each destination and adding the two figures together. This makes a convenient option for those who want a fly-drive holiday (see below).

For an overview of the various offers, and unofficially discounted tickets, go straight to

an **agent** specializing in low-cost flights (we've listed some on p.16). Especially if you're under 26 or a student, they may be able to knock up to thirty percent off the regular Apex fares when there are no special airline deals. Agents will usually offer non-stop flights, or "direct" flights via another airport in the USA, although you may be offered other, stranger combinations (London–Los Angeles via Amsterdam, Manchester–Los Angeles via Paris for example) – all worth considering if the price is right.

Finally, if you've got a bit more time, or want to see a bit more of the USA, it's often possible to stop over in another city – **New York** especially – and fly on from there for little more than the cost of a direct flight to California. Also, with increased competition on the **London–Los Angeles** route, thanks to Virgin Atlantic among others and price wars between US carriers, the cost of a connecting flight from LA to San Francisco has been brought down to less than £40. Many airlines also offer **air passes**, which allow foreign travelers to fly between a given number of US cities for one discounted price. For more details on long-distance travel within the US, see p.30.

One word of **warning**: it's not a good idea to buy a **one-way** ticket to the States. Not only are they rarely good value compared to a round-trip ticket, but US immigration officials usually take them as a sign that you aren't planning to go home and may refuse you entry. With increased airport checks, you are unlikely to be allowed to board your flight to begin with.

Flights from Britain

The following carriers operate **non-stop flights** from London to California (all from Heathrow unless otherwise stated):

Air New Zealand daily from Heathrow to Los Angeles.
American Airlines daily to Los Angeles.
Continental daily to Los Angeles and San Francisco.
British Airways daily to Los Angeles, San Francisco, and San Diego.

United Airlines daily to Los Angeles and San Francisco.
Virgin Atlantic daily to Los Angeles and San Francisco, and in summer five times a week from Gatwick to San Francisco.

The following carriers operate **one-stop direct flights** from London to California (all from Gatwick unless otherwise stated):

American Airlines daily via Dallas to San Francisco, and daily from Heathrow via New York, Chicago, or Los Angeles to San Francisco.
Continental daily via Denver, Miami, Houston, or Newark to Los Angeles, San Francisco, and San Diego.

Delta daily via Cincinnati or Atlanta to Los Angeles, San Francisco, and San Diego.
Northwest daily via Detroit or Minneapolis to Los Angeles and San Francisco.

Airlines

Air New Zealand ☎ 020/8741 2299, 🖳 www.airnz.co.nz
American Airlines ☎ 0345/789 789, 🖳 www.aa.com
British Airways ☎ 0345/222 111, 🖳 www.britishairways.com
Continental ☎ 01293/776 464, 🖳 www.flycontinental.com
Delta ☎ 0800/414 767, 🖳 www.delta-air.com
Northwest ☎ 01424/224 400, 🖳 www.nwa.com
United ☎ 0845/844 4777, 🖳 www.ual.com
Virgin Atlantic ☎ 01293/747 747, 🖳 www.fly.virgin.com

Travel agents

Bridge the World 47 Chalk Farm Rd, London NW1 8AN ☎ 020/7916 0990, 🖳 www.b-t-w.co.uk
Destination Group 14 Greville St, London EC1N 8SB ☎ 020/7400 7045, 🖳 www.destination-group.com
London Flight Centre 131 Earls Court Rd, London SW5 9RH ☎ 020/7244 6411, 🖳 www.topdecktravel.co.uk
STA Travel 86 Old Brompton Rd, London SW7 (with branches nationwide) ☎ 0870/160 6070, 🖳 www.statravel.co.uk
Trailfinders 42–50 Earls Court Rd, London W8 ☎ 020/7628 7628, 🖳 www.trailfinders.com; branches nationwide.

Travel Bug 597 Cheetham Hill Rd, Manchester M8 5EJ ☎ 0161/721 4000; 125 Gloucester Rd, London SW7 ☎ 020/7835 2000, 🖳 www. flynow.com
Travel Cuts 295a Regent St, London W1 ☎ 020/7255 2082, 🖳 www.travelcuts.com.
USIT Campus 52 Grosvenor Gardens, London SW1 ☎ 020/7730 2101, national call center 0870/240 1010, 🖳 www.usitcampus.co.uk
USIT Now Fountain Centre, College St, Belfast BT1 6ET ☎ 028/9032 4073, 🖳 www.usitnow.com

Tour operators

Airtours Wavell House, Helmshore, Rossendale, Lancs BB4 4NB ☎ 0870/241 2567, 🖳 www.airtours.co.uk. Multi-center holidays including combinations of Los Angeles, San Francisco, and Las Vegas.
American Adventures 64 Mount Pleasant Ave, Tunbridge Wells, Kent TN1 1QY ☎ 01892/512 700, 🖳 www.americanadventures.com. Small-group touring and adventure holidays on the West Coast; also hosteling with Road Runner International (see below).
Bon Voyage 18 Bellevue Rd, Southampton, Hants SO15 2AY ☎ 0800/316 3012, 🖳 www.bon-voyage.co.uk. Flight-plus-accommodation deals in San Francisco, Los Angeles, and Palm Springs.
Bridge Travel Service Bridge House, Broxbourne, Herts EN10 7DT ☎ 01992/456 600, 🖳 www.bridgetravel.co.uk. City breaks in Los Angeles; accommodation only.

British Airways Holidays Astral Towers, Bettsway, London Road, Crawley, West Sussex RH10 2XA ☏0870/242 4245, ⓦwww.baholidays .co.uk. City breaks in Los Angeles, San Diego, and San Francisco, and fly-drive deals (including motorhomes).

Connections 10 York Way, Lancaster Rd, High Wycombe, Bucks HP12 3PY ☏01494/473 173, ⓦwww.connectionsworldwide.net. Tailor-made vacations, including short breaks in Los Angeles and San Francisco.

Contiki Travel Wells House, 15 Elmfield Rd, Bromley, Kent BR1 1LS ☏020/8290 6777, ⓦwww.contiki.co.uk. West Coast coach tours, aimed at 18–35-year-olds.

Destination Group 14 Greville St, London EC1N 8SB ☏020/7400 7045, ⓦwww.destination-group .com. Tailor-made holidays; can arrange accommodation and fly-drive deals.

Explore Worldwide 1 Frederick St, Aldershot, Hants GU11 1LQ ☏01252/760 000, ⓦwww.explore.co.uk. Small-group walking tours, camping, or staying in hotels.

Flydrive USA PO Box 45, Bexhill-on-Sea, East Sussex TN40 1PY ☏01424/224 400. Flight-plus-accommodation and fly-drive combinations.

Kuoni Kuoni House, Dorking, Surrey RH5 4AZ ☏01306/742 888, ⓦwww.kuoni.co.uk. Multi-center flight-plus-accommodation-plus-car deals featuring Los Angeles, San Francisco, and San Diego.

North America Travel Service 7 Albion St, Leeds LS1 5ER ☏0113/246 1466; also branches in London, Nottingham, Manchester, and Barnsley. Tailor-mades: flights, accommodation, car hire, and so on.

Premier Holidays Westbrook, Milton Road, Cambridge CB4 1YQ ☏01223/516 516, ⓦwww.premierholidays.co.uk. Flight-plus-accommodation deals throughout California.

Road Runner 64 Mount Pleasant Ave, Tunbridge Wells, Kent TN1 1QY ☏01892/512 700, ⓦwww.americanadventures.com. Hosteling version of American Adventures touring and adventure packages (see above).

Top Deck Travel 131 Earls Court Rd, London SW5 ☏020/7370 4555, ⓦwww.topdecktravel .co.uk. Agents for numerous adventure touring specialists.

TrekAmerica Malvern House, 4 Waterperry Court, Middleton Road, Banbury OX16 4QB ☏01295/256 777, ⓦwww.trekamerica.com. Touring adventure holidays (see above).

United Vacations Heathrow Airport ☏0870/606 2222, ⓦwww.unitedvacations.co.uk. City breaks, tailor-mades, and fly-drives.

Virgin Holidays The Galleria, Station Road, Crawley, West Sussex RH10 1WW ☏0870/220 2788, ⓦwww.virginholidays.co.uk. Packages to a wide range of California destinations.

Courier flights

It's still possible – though not as common as it used to be – for those on a very tight budget to travel as **couriers**. Courier firms offer opportunities to travel at discounted rates (for example £200 return to the West Coast) in return for delivering a package or escorting a cargo. There'll be someone to check you in and to meet you at your destination, which minimizes any red-tape hassle. You may have to travel light (but not necessarily, if you're escorting a cargo of several tons), and accept tight restrictions on travel dates. The best place to contact in Britain is the UK branch of the **International Association of Air Travel Couriers** (☏0800/074 6481, ⓦwww.aircourier.co.uk), which has an annual membership fee of £32; or check your phone directory for local operators, which are more likely to come and go.

Packages

Packages – fly-drive, flight-accommodation deals, and guided tours (or a combination of all three) – can work out cheaper than arranging the same trip yourself, especially for a short-term stay. The obvious drawbacks are the loss of flexibility and the fact that most schemes use hotels in the mid-range bracket, but there is a wide variety of options available. Travel agents have plenty of brochures and information about the various combinations.

Fly-drive

Fly-drive deals, which give cut-rate (sometimes free) car rental when buying a transatlantic ticket, always work out cheaper than renting on the spot and give especially great value if you intend to do a lot of driving. On the other hand, you'll probably have to pay more for the flight than if you booked it through a discount agent. Competition between airlines (especially Northwest and TWA) and tour operators means that it's well worth phoning to check on current special promotions.

Northwest Flydrive offers excellent deals for not much more than an ordinary Apex fare; for example, a return flight to LA or San Francisco and a week's car rental (including insurance) might cost less than £300 per person in low season. Several of the other companies listed in the box on p.16 offer similar, and sometimes even cheaper, packages. It's also well worth checking what's on offer at Getaway (☎020/7797 3007) or Holiday America (☎01424/224 400, ⊛www.holiday-america.net).

Watch out for hidden extras, such as local taxes, "drop-off" charges, which can be as much as a week's rental, and Collision Damage Waiver insurance (see p.31). Remember, too, that while you can drive in the States with a British license, there can be problems renting vehicles if you're under 25. For complete car-rental and driveaway details, see "Getting around California" (p.31).

Flight and accommodation details

There's really no end of combined **flight and accommodation deals** to California. Drawbacks include the loss of flexibility and the fact that you'll probably have to stay in hotels in the mid-range to expensive bracket, even though less expensive accommodation is almost always available.

A handful of tour operators (see box) offer quite deluxe packages, of which Virgin Holidays are among the least expensive: for example, seven nights in San Francisco plus return flight costs around £550 in low season, £830 per person in high season. Discount agents can set up more basic packages for under £500 each. Pre-booked accommodation schemes, under which you buy vouchers for use in a specific group of hotels, are not normally good value.

Touring and adventure packages

A simple and exciting way to see a chunk of California's extensive wilderness, without being hassled by too many practical considerations, is to take a specialist **touring and adventure package**, which includes transportation, accommodation, food, and a guide. Some of the more adventurous carry small groups around on minibuses and use a combination of budget hotels and camping (equipment, except a sleeping bag, is provided). Most also have a food kitty of around £25 per week, with many meals cooked and eaten communally, although there's plenty of time to leave the group and do your own thing.

TrekAmerica (see above) is one UK-based company to offer such deals; a typical package would be ten days in California and the "Wild West" for £425 or so excluding flights. Other operators are listed opposite. If you're interested in **backcountry hiking**, the San Francisco-based Sierra Club (see p.56) offers a range of tours that take you into parts of the state that most people never see.

Flights from Ireland

Aer Lingus and Delta both fly daily **direct** to Los Angeles from Dublin and Shannon. The **cheapest flights** from Ireland – if you're under 26 or a student – are available from USIT. Student-only return fares to San Francisco or Los Angeles direct range from €500 to €780. Flights via London may cost less, but you pay slightly more tax. Ordinary Apex fares are only marginally higher.

USIT can be contacted at Aston Quay, O'Connell Bridge, Dublin 2 (☎01/677 8117, ⊛www.usitnow.ie). Aer Lingus is at 40 O'Connell St, Dublin 1 and Dublin Airport (☎01/886 8888, ⊛www.aerlingus.ie), and Delta Airlines is at 24 Merrion Square, Dublin 2 (☎01/676 8080).

From Australia and New Zealand

If you are coming from Australia and New Zealand, there's very little price difference between airlines and no shortage of flights, either via the Pacific or Asia, to Los Angeles and San Francisco. Crossing the Pacific most flights are non-stop, with traveling time between Auckland/Sydney and LA twelve to fourteen hours, though some allow stopovers in Honolulu and a number of the South Pacific islands. If you go via Asia (a slightly more roundabout route that can work out a little cheaper), you'll usually have to spend a night, or the best part of a day, in the airline's home city.

Various **coupon deals** – available with your international ticket for discounted flights within the US – are good value if California is part of a wider US trip. A minimum purchase of three coupons usually applies and should cost under US$400. Tickets purchased directly from the airlines are usually at published rates, which are often more expensive than a round-the-world fare. Travel agents offer the best deals on fares and have the latest information on limited special offers, such as free stopovers, fly-drive-accommodation and Disneyland packages. Flight Centres and STA (which offer fare reductions for ISIC cardholders and under-26s) generally offer the lowest fares.

Airfares vary throughout the year, with seasonal differences generally working out between A/NZ$200. For most airlines, **low season** is from mid-January to the end of February and October to the end of November; **high season** mid-May to the end of August and December to mid-January; **shoulder seasons** cover the rest of the year, though all of this is complicated by periodic high prices during school holidays. Seat availability on most international flights out of Australia and New Zealand is limited, so it's best to book several weeks ahead.

Traveling from **Australia**, fares to LA and San Francisco from eastern cities cost the same, while from Perth they're about A$400 more. There are daily non-stop flights from Sydney, to LA and San Francisco on United Airlines and to LA on Qantas, for around A$1800 low season. In addition there are several airlines that fly via Asia, which involves either a transfer or stopover in their home cities. The best deal is on JAL (A$1600–1900), which includes a night's stopover accommodation in Tokyo or Osaka in the fare. If you don't want to spend the night, Cathay Pacific and Singapore Airlines can get you there, via a transfer in the home cities of Hong Kong and Singapore, for around A$1750, and Korean Air (via Seoul) are sometimes a few dollars cheaper. Look out for special deals from agents (see box below) at slack times, which can see tickets to Los Angeles from Sydney go for as little as A$1279.

From **New Zealand**, most flights are out of **Auckland** (add about NZ$200–250 for Christchurch and Wellington departures). The best deals are on Air New Zealand, to Los Angeles either non-stop or via Honolulu, Fiji, Tonga, or Papeete, or United Airlines, also non-stop to LA or San Francisco (both cost around NZ$2100–2500). Air Pacific via Fiji, and Qantas via Sydney (though direct is cheaper) both start around NZ$1800–2000. Via Asia, Singapore Airlines offers the best connecting service to LA and San Francisco from NZ$2099, while the best value for money (around NZ$1850–2250) is on JAL via either a transfer or stopover in Tokyo.

If you intend to take in California as part of a world trip, a round-the-world (**RTW**) ticket offers the greatest flexibility. In recent years, many of the major international airlines have aligned themselves with one of two globe-spanning networks: the "Star Alliance," which links Air New Zealand, Ansett Australia, United, Lufthansa, Thai, SAS, Varig, and Air Canada; and "One World," which combines routes run by American, British Airways, Canadian Airlines, Cathay Pacific, LAN Chile, and Qantas. Both offer RTW deals with three stopovers in each continental sector you visit, with the option of adding additional sectors relatively cheaply. Fares depend on the number of sectors required, but start at around A$2500 (low season) for a US–Europe–Asia and home itinerary. If this is more flexibility than you need, you can save $200–300 by going with an individual airline (in concert with code-share partners) and accepting fewer stops.

Airlines

Air New Zealand Australia ☎ 132 476, New Zealand ☎ 0800/737 000, ⊛ www.airnz.co.nz
Air Pacific Australia ☎ 1-800/230 150, New Zealand ☎ 0800/800 178, ⊛ www.airpacific.com
Cathay Pacific Australia ☎ 131 747, New Zealand ☎ 09/379 0861, ⊛ www.cathaypacific.com
Delta Air Lines Australia ☎ 02/9251 3211, New Zealand ☎ 09/379 3370, ⊛ www.delta-air.com
JAL Japan Airlines Australia ☎ 02/9272 1111, New Zealand ☎ 09/379 9906, ⊛ www.japanair.com
Korean Air Australia ☎ 02/9262 6000, New Zealand ☎ 09/914 2000, ⊛ www.koreanair.com.au
Qantas Australia ☎ 131 313, ⊛ www.qantas.com.au; New Zealand ☎ 09/357 8900, ⊛ www.qantas.co.nz
Singapore Airlines Australia ☎ 131 011, New Zealand ☎ 09/303 2129, ⊛ www.singaporeair.com

United Airlines Australia ☎131 777, ⓦwww.unitedairlines.com.au; New Zealand ☎09/379 3800, ⓦwww.unitedairlines.co.nz

agency incorporating YHA travel and your first stop for ISIC student cards.

Travel agents

Anywhere Travel Australia ☎02/9663 0411, ⓔanywhere@aussiemail.com.au. Local agency specializing in cheap airfares to anywhere.
Budget Travel New Zealand ☎0800/808 480, ⓦwww.budgettravel.co.nz. Major countrywide flight discounter.
Flight Centre Australia ☎133 133, ⓦwww.flightcentre.com.au; New Zealand ☎0800/243 544, ⓦwww.flightcentre.co.nz. Near-ubiquitous high-street agency frequently offering some of the lowest fares around.
Northern Gateway Australia ☎1-800/174 800, ⓦwww.northerngateway.com.au. Local discount agent.
STA Travel Australia ☎1300/733 035, ⓦwww.statravel.com.au; New Zealand ☎0508/782 872, ⓦwww.statravel.co.nz. A major player in student, youth, and budget travel with branches in many universities.
Trailfinders Australia ☎02/9247 7666, ⓦwww.trailfinders.com.au. Knowledgeable staff skilled at turning up odd itineraries and good prices.
Travel.com.au Australia ☎02/9290 1500, ⓦwww.travel.com.au. Youth-oriented center with an efficient travel agency offering good fares, a travel bookshop, and Internet café.
Usit Beyond New Zealand ☎0800/788 336, ⓦwww.usitbeyond.co.nz. Youth-oriented travel

Specialist agents

Adventure Specialists Australia ☎02/9261 2927. A good selection of adventure treks and tours.
Adventure World Australia ☎02/8913 0755, ⓦwww.adventureworld.com.au; New Zealand ☎09/524 5118, ⓦwww.adventureworld.com.nz. Individual and small-group exploratory tours and treks.
Journeys Worldwide Australia ☎07/3221 4788, ⓦwww.journeysworldwide.com.au. All US travel arrangements.
Peregrine Adventures Australia ☎03/9662 2700, ⓦwww.peregrine.net.au. With offices in Brisbane, Sydney, Adelaide, and Perth, Peregrine offers small-group active holidays from short walking and camping to longer overland trips through California.
Sydney International Travel Centre Australia ☎1-800/251 911 or 02/9299 8000, ⓦwww.sydneytravel.com.au. Individually tailored holidays, Disneyland passes, flights, and bus and rail tours.
Travel Plan Australia ☎02/9438 1333, ⓦwww.travelplan.com.au. Ski holiday packages in the Lake Tahoe region.
Wiltrans Australia ☎02/9255 0899 or ☎1-800/251 174. Five-star all-inclusive escorted Californian sightseeing holidays.

Red tape and visas

Under the Visa Waiver Program – designed to speed up lengthy immigration proce-dures – citizens of Andorra, Australia, Austria, Belgium, Brunei, Denmark, Finland, France, Germany, Iceland, Ireland, Italy, Japan, Liechtenstein, Luxembourg, Monaco, the Netherlands, New Zealand, Norway, Portugal, San Marino, Singapore, Slovenia, Spain, Sweden, Switzerland, the United Kingdom, and Uruguay visiting the United States for a period of less than ninety days only need a passport and a visa waiver form. The latter will be provided either by your travel agency, or by the airline before check-in or on the plane, and must be presented to immigration on arrival. The same form covers entry across the land borders with Canada and Mexico as well as by air. However, those eligible for the scheme must apply for a visa if they intend to work, study, or stay in the country for more than ninety days.

Prospective visitors from parts of the world not mentioned above require a valid passport and a **non-immigrant visitor's visa**. How you'll obtain a visa depends on what country you're in and your status when you apply, so telephone the nearest US embassy or consulate (listed below). You'll need a passport valid six months beyond your intended stay, two passport photos, and will be charged the equivalent of $65. Expect it to take up to three weeks, though it could be substantially quicker. More information can be found at ⓦwww.travel.state.gov/visa_services.

In **Britain**, only British or EU citizens, and those from other countries eligible for the Visa Waiver Program, can apply by post – fill in the application form available at most travel agents and send it with your passport and a SAE to the nearest US embassy or consulate. Expect a wait of ten days to three weeks before your passport is returned – longer if they have even the slightest reason to think you might be involved with terrorists. All others must apply in person at the embassy or consulate, making an appointment in advance.

Australian and **New Zealand** passport holders staying less than ninety days do not require a visa, providing they arrive on a commercial flight with an onward or return ticket. You'll need an application form, available from a US embassy or consulate (see box opposite), one signed passport photo and your passport, and either post it or personally lodge it at one of the US embassies or consulates. Processing takes about ten working days for postal applications; personal lodgements take two days – but check details with the consulate first.

Whatever your nationality, visas are not issued to convicted felons and anybody who owns up to being a communist, fascist, or a drug dealer.

US embassies and consulates abroad

Australia

Canberra Moonah Place, Yarralumla, ACT 2600 ☎02/6214 5600, ⓕ6214 5970, ⓦusembassy-australia.state.gov
Melbourne 553 St Kilda Road, PO Box 6722, Vic 3004 ☎03/9526 5900, ⓕ9510 4646
Sydney MLC Centre, 59th floor, 19–29 Martin Place, NSW 2000 ☎02/9373 9200, ⓕ9373 9125

Perth 16 St George's Terrace, 13th floor, WA 6000 ☎08/9202 1224, ⓕ9231 9444

Canada

Ottawa 490 Sussex Drive, ON K1N 1G8 ☎613/238-5335, ⓦwww.usembassycanada.gov
Calgary 615 Macleod Trail SE, Room 1000, AB T2G 4T8 ☎403/266-8962, ⓕ264-6630
Halifax Suite 910, Purdy's Wharf Tower II,1969 Upper Water St, NS B3J 3R7 ☎902/429-2480, ⓕ423-6861
Montréal 1155 St Alexandre St, PQ, H3B 1Z1 ☎514/398-9695, ⓕ398-0973
Toronto 360 University Ave, ON M5G 1S4 ☎416/595-1700, ⓕ595-0051
Vancouver 1075 W Pender St, BC V6E 2M6 ☎604/685-4311, ⓕ685-5285

Denmark

Copenhagen Dag Hammerskjöld Allé 24, 2100 ☎3555-3144, ⓕ3543-0223, ⓦwww.usembassy.dk

Ireland

Dublin 42 Elgin Rd, Ballsbridge ☎01/668-8777, ⓕ668-9946, ⓦwww.usembassy.ie

Netherlands

Den Hague Lange Voorhout 102, 2514 EJ ☎070/310-9209, ⓕ361-4688, ⓦwww.usemb.nl.
Amsterdam Museumplein 19, 1071 DJ ☎020/575-5309, ⓕ575-5310.

New Zealand

Wellington 29 Fitzherbert Terrace, Thorndon ☎04/462 6000, ⓕ478 1701, ⓦusembassy.org.nz
Auckland 3rd floor, Citibank Building, 23 Customs St ☎09/303 2724, ⓕ366 0870

Norway

Oslo Drammensveien 18, 0244 ☎2244-8550, ⓦwww.usa.no

South Africa

Pretoria 877 Pretorius St, Arcadia 0083 ☎012/342 1048, ⓕ342 2244, ⓦusembassy.state.gov/pretoria
Cape Town 7th floor, Monte Carlo Building, Heerengracht, Foreshore ☎021/421 44351, ⓕ425 3014
Durban 2901 Durban Bay Building, 333 Smith St ☎031/304 4737, ⓕ301 0265.
Johannesburg 1 River St, Killarney ☎011/644 8000, ⓕ646 6913.

UK

London 24 Grosvenor Square, W1A 1AE
☏020/7499 9000; visa hotline (£1.50 a minute)
☏09061/500 590, ⓦwww.usembassy.org.uk
Belfast Queen's House, 14 Queen St, BT1 6EQ
☏028/9032 8239, ⓕ9024 8482.
Edinburgh 3 Regent Terrace, EH7 5BW
☏0131/556 8315, ⓕ557 6023.

Embassies and consulates in California

Australia

Los Angeles 2049 Century Park E, CA 90067
☏310/229-4800

Canada

Los Angeles 300 S Grand Ave, CA 90071
☏213/346-2701
San Francisco 50 Fremont St, CA 94105
☏415/541-3900

Denmark

San Francisco 601 Montgomery St, Suite 400,
CA 94111 ☏415/391-0100

Ireland

San Francisco 44 Montgomery St, CA 94104
☏415/392-4214

Netherlands

San Francisco 1 Maritime Plaza, CA 94111
☏415/981-6454

Norway

San Diego 6240 Brynwood Court, CA 92120
☏619/582-5586

South Africa

Los Angeles 6300 Wilshire B, Suite 600, CA
90048 ☏323/651-0902

Sweden

San Diego 530 Broadway, CA 92101 ☏619/233-
1106

UK

Los Angeles 11766 Wilshire Blvd, Suite 400, CA
90025 ☏310/477-3322, ⓕ575-1450
San Francisco 1 Sansome St, Suite 850, CA
94101 ☏415/981-3030, ⓕ434-2018

Immigration controls

The standard immigration regulations apply to all visitors, whether or not they are using the Visa Waiver Program. During the flight, you'll be handed an **immigration form** (and a customs declaration), which must be given up at immigration control once you land. The form requires you cite your proposed **length of stay** and to list an **address**, at least for your first night. Previously "touring" was satisfactory, but since **September 11**, controls have become more stringent and they require a verifiable address. If you have no accommodation arranged for your first night, pick a plausible-sounding hotel from the appropriate section of the Guide and list that.

You probably won't be asked unless you look disreputable in the eyes of the official on duty, but you should be able to prove that you have a return air ticket (if flying in), and enough money to support yourself while in the US; anyone revealing the slightest intention of working while in the country is likely to be refused admission. Around $300–400 a week is usually considered sufficient – waving a credit card or two may do the trick. You may also experience difficulties if you admit to being HIV positive or having AIDS or TB. Part of the immigration form will be attached to your passport, where it must stay until you leave, when an immigration or airline official will detach it.

> **Canadian citizens** are in a particularly privileged position when it comes to crossing the border into the US. Though it is possible to enter the States without your passport, you should really have it with you on any trip that brings you as far as California. Only if you plan to stay for more than ninety days do you need a visa. Bear in mind that if you cross into the US by car, trunks and passenger compartments are subject to spot searches by Customs personnel. Remember too, that without the proper paperwork, Canadians are legally barred from seeking gainful employment in the US.

Customs

Customs officers will relieve you of your customs declaration and check if you're carrying any fresh foods. You'll also be asked if you've visited a farm in the last month – if you have, you may well have your shoes taken away for inspection. The duty-free allowance if you're over 17 is 200 cigarettes and 100 cigars, a liter of spirits (if you're over 21), and $400 worth of gifts, which can include an additional 100 cigars. As well as foods and anything agricultural, it's prohibited to carry into the country any articles from Afghanistan, Cuba, Iran, Libya, Serbia, and Sudan, or obscene publications, drug paraphernalia, lottery tickets, chocolate liqueurs, or pre-Columbian artifacts. Anyone caught carrying drugs into the country will not only face prosecution, but be entered in the records as an undesirable and probably denied entry for all time. There are more details on the US Customs website at Ⓦ www.customs.treas.gov/travel/travel.

Extensions and leaving

The date stamped on your passport is the latest you're legally allowed to stay. Leaving a few days later may not matter, especially if you're heading home, but more than a week or so can result in a protracted, rather unpleasant interrogation from officials, which may cause you to miss your flight and be denied entry to the US in the future.

To get an **extension** before your time is up, apply at the nearest **US Immigration and Naturalization Service** (Ⓦ www.ins.usdoj.gov) office; the address will be under the Federal Government Offices listings at the front of the phone book. The service will automatically assume that you're working illegally, and it's up to you to convince them otherwise. Do this by providing evidence of ample finances and, if you can, bring along an upstanding American citizen to vouch for you. You'll also have to explain why you didn't plan for the extra time initially.

Information, websites, and maps

California's official tourism website (Ⓦ www.visitcalifornia.com) is a reasonable starting point for advance information. Much of the same material is available in their "tourism information packet," which can be ordered online, by calling ☏1-800-GOCALIF, or by contacting the California Office of Tourism, 801 K St, Suite 1600, Sacramento, CA 95814-3520 ☏916/322-2881 or 1-800/862-2543. Once you've arrived in the state, you'll find most towns have visitor centers of some description – often called the Convention and Visitors Bureau (CVB) or Chamber of Commerce: all are listed in the guide. These will give out detailed information on the local area and can often help with finding accommodation. Free newspapers in most areas carry news of events and entertainment.

Most bookstores will have a range of local trail guides, the best of which we've listed in Contexts, p.833.

Websites

Nowhere is more net-savvy than California and almost anything you might wish to know (and a lot more besides) is available online.

We've included the most useful websites throughout the guide, and have listed a few sites below which should inspire further exploration.

Ain't it Cool News ⓦ www.aint-it-cool-news
.com. Self-confessed geek Harry Knowles offers up
rambling film reviews and Hollywood insider secrets.
Backcountry Resource Center ⓦ pweb.jps.net
/~prichins/backcountry_resource_center. Superb
non-commercial site laden with valuable information
on backcountry skiing, climbing, and general outdoor
interest with plenty of useful links.
The California Beerpage ⓦ www.beerpage.com.
Accessible guide to California's microbreweries and
beer festivals.
**Caltrans: The California Department of
Transportation** ⓦ www.dot.ca.gov. Straightforward
and informative, the Caltrans homepage contains
current highway conditions, public transit schedules,
information on traveling by bike, and more.
E! Online ⓦ www.eonline.com. Breathless,
gossipy, and visually gorgeous site with pages full of
star profiles and movie reviews.
LA Times ⓦ www.latimes.com. California's largest
circulating newspaper and good source of current
state news.
Rough Guides ⓦ www.roughguides.com.
Post any of your pre-trip questions – or post-trip
suggestions – in Travel Talk, our online forum for
travelers.
Surf Scene Magazine & Surf Report
ⓦ www.surfscene.net. Hot California surfing news,
with daily surf reports, as well as surfing links and a
photo gallery.
Variety ⓦ www.variety.com. The daily morning
read of Hollywood insiders, full of news, reviews,
previews, and the latest Tinseltown tales.

Maps

Tourist offices throughout the state supply
good **maps**, either free or for a small charge,
and, supplemented with our own, these
should be enough for general sightseeing
and touring. Rand McNally (see below) produces a decent low-cost ($3.95) map of the
state and its *Road Atlas* ($11.95), covering
the whole country plus Mexico and Canada,
is a worthwhile investment if you're traveling
further afield. For driving or cycling through
rural areas, the *Atlas & Gazetteer: Northern
California* and *Atlas & Gazetteer: Southern
and Central California* ($19.95 each; pub-
lished by DeLorme, ⓦ www.delorme.com)
are valuable companions, with detailed city
plans, marked campsites, and reams of
national park and forest information. **Hikers**
should visit ranger stations in parks and
wilderness areas, which all sell good-quality
local topographic maps for around $4, and

camping stores generally have a good selection too. The **American Automobile
Association** (☎ 1-800/272-2155 in Northern
CA, ☎ 1-800/678-3839 in Southern CA,
ⓦ www.aaa.com), has offices in most large
cities and provides excellent free maps and
travel assistance to its members, and members of affiliated organizations elsewhere.

Map outlets

In the US and Canada

Adventurous Traveler Bookstore 102 Lake St,
Burlington, VT 05401 ☎ 1-800/282-3963,
ⓦ www.adventuroustraveler.com.
Book Passage 51 Tamal Vista Blvd, Corte
Madera, CA 94925 ☎ 1-800/999-7909,
ⓦ www.bookpassage.com.
Distant Lands 56 S Raymond Ave, Pasadena, CA
91105 ☎ 1-800/310-3220,
ⓦ www.distantlands.com.
Elliot Bay Book Company 101 S Main St,
Seattle, WA 98104 ☎ 1-800/962-5311,
ⓦ www.elliotbaybook.com.
Forsyth Travel Library 226 Westchester Ave,
White Plains, NY 10604 ☎ 1-800/367-7984,
ⓦ www.forsyth.com.
Get Lost 1825 Market St, San Francisco, CA
94103 ☎ 415/437-0529,
ⓦ www.getlostbooks.com.
Globe Corner Bookstore 28 Church St,
Cambridge, MA 02138 ☎ 1-800/358-6013,
ⓦ www.globercorner.com.
GORP Travel ☎ 1-877/440-4677,
ⓦ www.gorp.com/gorp/books/main.
Map Link 30 S La Patera Lane, Unit 5, Santa
Barbara, CA 93117 ☎ 805/692-6777,
ⓦ www.maplink.com.
Phileas Fogg's Books & Maps 87 Stanford
Shopping Center, Palo Alto, CA 94304 ☎ 415/327-
1754.
Rand McNally ☎ 1-800/333-0136,
ⓦ www.randmcnally.com. Around thirty stores
across the US; dial ext 2111 or check the website
for the nearest location.
Sierra Club Bookstore 6014 College Ave,
Oakland, CA 94618 ☎ 510/658-7470,
ⓦ www.sierraclubbookstore.com.
The Travel Bug Bookstore 2667 W Broadway,
Vancouver, BC V6K 2G2 ☎ 604/737-1122,
ⓦ www.swifty.com/tbug.
World of Maps 1235 Wellington St, Ottawa, ON
K1Y 3A3 ☎ 1-800/214-8524,
ⓦ www.worldofmaps.com.

In the UK and Ireland

Blackwell's Map and Travel Shop 50 Broad St, Oxford OX1 3BQ ☎ 01865/793 550, ⓦ http://maps.blackwell.co.uk/index.

Easons Bookshop 40 O'Connell St, Dublin 1 ☎ 01/873 3811, ⓦ www.eason.ie.

Heffers Map and Travel 20 Trinity St, Cambridge CB2 1TJ ☎ 01865/333 536, ⓦ www.heffers.co.uk.

Hodges Figgis Bookshop 5658 Dawson St, Dublin 2 ☎ 01/677 4754, ⓦ www.hodgesfiggis.com.

James Thin Booksellers 5359 South Bridge, Edinburgh EH1 1YS ☎ 0131/622 8222, ⓦ www.jthin.co.uk.

The Map Shop 30a Belvoir St, Leicester LE1 6QH ☎ 0116/247 1400, ⓦ www.mapshopleicester.co.uk.

National Map Centre 2224 Caxton St, London SW1H 0QU ☎ 020/7222 2466, ⓦ www.mapsnmc.co.uk, ⓔ info@mapsnmc.co.uk.

Newcastle Map Centre 55 Grey St, Newcastle-upon-Tyne NE1 6EF ☎ 0191/261 5622.

Ordnance Survey Ireland Phoenix Park, Dublin 8 ☎ 01/8025 349, ⓦ www.irlgov.ie/osi, ⓔ osni@osni.gov.uk.

Ordnance Survey of Northern Ireland Colby House, Stranmillis Ct, Belfast BT9 5BJ ☎ 028/9025 5755, ⓦ www.osni.gov.uk.

Stanfords 1214 Long Acre, London WC2E 9LP ☎ 020/7836 1321, ⓦ www.stanfords.co.uk, ⓔ sales@stanfords.co.uk. Maps available by mail, phone order, or email. Other branches within British Airways offices at 156 Regent St, London W1R 5TA ☎ 020/7434 4744 and 29 Corn St, Bristol BS1 1HT ☎ 0117/929 9966.

The Travel Bookshop 1315 Blenheim Crescent, London W11 2EE ☎ 020/7229 5260, ⓦ www.thetravelbookshop.co.uk.

In Australia and New Zealand

The Map Shop 610 Peel St, Adelaide, SA 5000 ☎ 08/8231 2033, ⓦ www.mapshop.net.au.

Mapland 372 Little Bourke St, Melbourne, Victoria 3000 ☎ 03/9670 4383, ⓦ www.mapland.com.au.

MapWorld 173 Gloucester St, Christchurch, New Zealand ☎ 0800/627 967 or 03/374 5399, ⓦ www.mapworld.co.nz.

Perth Map Centre 1/884 Hay St, Perth, WA 6000 ☎ 08/9322 5733, ⓦ www.perthmap.com.au.

Specialty Maps 46 Albert St, Auckland 1001 ☎ 09/307 2217, ⓦ www.ubdonline.co.nz/maps.

Insurance

Even though EU health care privileges apply in America, residents of the United Kingdom would do well to take out an insurance policy before traveling to cover against theft, loss, and illness or injury. Before paying for a new policy, however, it's worth checking whether you are already covered – some all-risks home insurance policies may cover your possessions when overseas, and many private medical schemes include cover when abroad. In Canada, provincial health plans usually provide partial cover for medical mishaps overseas, while holders of official student/teacher/youth cards in Canada and the US are entitled to meagre accident coverage and hospital in-patient benefits. Students will often find that their student health coverage extends during the vacations and for one term beyond the date of last enrolment.

After exhausting the possibilities above, you might want to contact a specialist travel insurance company, or consider the travel insurance deal Rough Guides offers (see box). A typical travel insurance policy usually provides cover for the loss of baggage, tickets and – up to a certain limit – cash or checks, as well as cancellation or curtailment of your journey. Most of them exclude so-called dangerous sports unless an extra premium is paid: in America, this can mean scuba-diving, white-water rafting, windsurfing, and trekking,

Insurance

Rough Guides offers its own travel insurance, customized for our readers by a leading UK broker and backed by a Lloyd's underwriter. It's available for anyone, of any nationality and any age, traveling anywhere in the world.

There are two main Rough Guide insurance plans: **Essential**, for basic, no-frills cover; and **Premier** – with more generous and extensive benefits. Alternatively, you can take out **annual multi-trip insurance**, which covers you for any number of trips throughout the year (with a maximum of sixty days for any one trip). Unlike many policies, the Rough Guides schemes are calculated by the day, so if you're traveling for 27 days rather than a month, that's all you pay for. If you intend to be away for the whole year, the Adventurer policy will cover you for 365 days. Each plan can be supplemented with a "Hazardous Activities Premium" if you plan to indulge in sports considered dangerous, such as skiing, scuba diving, or trekking. For a policy quote, call the Rough Guide Insurance Line on UK freefone ☏0800/015 0906; US toll-free ☏1-866/220-5588, or, if you're calling from elsewhere ☏+44 1243/621 046. Alternatively, get an online quote or buy online at ⊛www.roughguides.com/insurance.

though probably not kayaking or jeep safaris. Many policies can be chopped and changed to exclude coverage you don't need – for example, sickness and accident benefits can often be excluded or included at will. If you do take medical coverage, ascertain whether benefits will be paid as treatment proceeds or only after return home, and if there is a 24-hour medical emergency number. When securing baggage cover, make sure that the per-article limit – typically under £500 – will cover your most valuable possession. If you need to make a claim, you should keep receipts for medicines and medical treatment, and in the event you have anything stolen, you must obtain an official theft report from the police.

Health

Foreign travelers should be comforted that if you have a serious accident while you're in California, emergency services will get to you sooner and charge you later. For emergencies, dial toll-free ☏911 from any phone. If you have medical or dental problems that don't require an ambulance, most hospitals will have a walk-in emergency room: for your nearest hospital, check with your hotel or dial information at ☏411. The same is true for dental work.

Should you need to see a doctor, lists can be found in the *Yellow Pages* under "Clinics" or "Physicians and Surgeons." Be aware that even consultations are costly, usually around $75–100 each visit, which is payable in advance. Keep receipts for any part of your medical treatment, including prescriptions, so that you can claim against your insurance once you're home.

For minor ailments, stop by a local pharmacy, many of which are open 24 hours. Foreign visitors should note that many medicines available over the counter at home – codeine-based painkillers, for one – are **prescription-only** in the US. Bring additional supplies if you're particularly brand loyal.

By far the most common tourist illness in California is **sunburn**: south of Santa

Barbara and in the state's interior, the summer sun can be fierce, so plenty of protective sunscreen (SPF 15 and above) is a must. Surfers and swimmers should also watch for strong currents and **undertows** at some beaches: we've noted in the text where the water can be especially treacherous. Note that despite the media's frenzied circling around the story of man-eating **sharks**, it's still a blip on beach safety compared with sunburn and swimming difficulties.

Travelers from Europe, Canada, and Australia do not require inoculations to enter the USA.

Costs, money, and banks

Despite the recent slowing of the US economy and the slight weakening of the dollar, the United States remains a fairly expensive place to travel and, with its large urban population, California is one of the pricier states. It is true that car rental, gas, clothes, and consumer goods are usually somewhat cheaper than in Western Europe and Australasia, but the benefit is often less than it seems once you've factored in the additional sales tax or added in the cost of rental-car insurance. At first, eating and drinking seem a bargain (and fast-food joints are), but in more upscale establishments, you'll be adding close to 25 percent to your expected total to cover taxes and tips. It soon mounts up.

For museums and similar attractions, the prices we quote are generally for adults; you can assume that **children** (typically aged 5–12 or 14) get in half-price. Generally youth and **student cards** are of little benefit; take it if you have one, but don't make any special effort to get one.

Naturally, costs will increase slightly overall during the life of this edition, but the relative comparisons should remain valid.

Costs

Accommodation is likely to be your biggest single expense. A few hotel or motel rooms cost under $40, but it's more usual to pay between $50 and $80 for anything halfway decent in a city, though rates in untouristed rural areas can be appreciably cheaper. Hostels offering dorm beds – usually for $15–23 – are reasonably common in the big cities, but they are sparsely scattered around the state, besides which they save little money for two or more people traveling together. Camping, of course, is cheap and convenient around the national parks (ranging from free to about $18 a night per site), but is rarely practical in or around the big cities.

As for **food**, $15 a day is enough to get an adequate life-support diet if you are eating cheap and preparing some meals yourself, but $30 is more realistic if you are eating out at diners and budget Mexican places. For around $45 a day, you can dine pretty well. Beyond this, everything hinges on how much sightseeing, taxi taking, drinking, and socializing you do. Much of any of these – especially in the major cities – and you're likely to go through upwards of $75 a day.

The rates for **traveling around**, especially on buses and, to a lesser extent, on trains and even planes, may look inexpensive on paper, but the distances involved mean that costs soon stack up. For a group of two or more, **renting a car** can be a very good investment, not least because it enables you to camp or stay in the ubiquitous budget motels along the interstate highways instead of relying on expensive downtown hotels.

Remember that a **sales tax** of 7.25 percent is added to virtually everything you buy except for groceries and prescription drugs; it is seldom included in the quoted price.

27

Exchange rates and US currency

Regular upheaval in the world money markets causes the relative value of the US dollar to vary considerably against the currencies of the rest of the world. Generally speaking, one Canadian dollar is worth between 65¢ and 70¢; one Australian dollar is worth between 50¢ and 55¢; one New Zealand dollar is worth between 45¢ and 50¢; and one euro roughly equivalent to a dollar. Over the last few years, the dollar/sterling rate has remained remarkably stable at between $1.50 and $1.60 to the pound.

Bills and coins

US banknotes (typically $1, $5, $10, $20, $50, and $100) are all the same color and size so be sure to check what you are handing over; anyone frequently dealing with money usually states the denomination of the bill they have just received. The dollar is made up of 100 cents with coins of 1 cent (known as a penny, and regarded as worthless), 5 cents (a nickel), 10 cents (a dime), and 25 cents (a quarter). Quarters are very useful for buses, vending machines, parking meters, and telephones, so always carry plenty.

Plastic money and cash machines

If you don't already have a **credit card**, you should think seriously about getting one before you set off. For many services, it's simply taken for granted that you'll be paying with plastic. When renting a car (or even a bike) or checking into a hotel, you may well be asked to show a credit card to establish your creditworthiness – even if you intend to settle the bill in cash. **Visa**, **MasterCard**, **Diners Club**, **American Express**, and **Discover** are the most widely used.

With MasterCard or Visa (including those issued by foreign banks), it is also possible to **withdraw cash** at any bank displaying relevant stickers, or from appropriate automated teller machines (ATMs). Remember that all cash advances are treated as loans, with interest accruing daily from the date of withdrawal; there is generally a transaction fee on top of this. However, you may be able to make withdrawals from ATMs in California using your debit card, which is not liable to interest payments, and the flat transaction fee is usually quite small – your bank will be able to advise you on this. Make sure you have a personal identification number (PIN) that's designed to work overseas.

A compromise between travelers' checks and plastic is **Visa TravelMoney**, a disposable pre-paid debit card with a PIN which works in all ATMs that take Visa cards. You load up your account with funds before leaving home, and when they run out, you simply throw the card away. You can buy up to nine cards to access the same funds – useful for couples or families traveling together – and it's a good idea to buy at least one extra as a backup in case of loss or theft. There is also a 24-hour toll-free customer assistance number: ☏1-800/847-2911. The card is available in most countries from branches of Thomas Cook and Citicorp. For more information, check the Visa TravelMoney website at ⊛www.usa.visa.com/personal/cards/visa_travel_money.

Overseas visitors should also bear in mind that fluctuating **exchange rates** (see box) may result in spending more (or less) than expected when the item eventually shows up on a statement.

Banks and travelers' checks

It is worth carrying a second major credit card as a backup, but you may feel more comfortable with a wad of **US dollar travelers' checks**. These are the best way for both American and foreign visitors to carry money; they offer the great security of knowing that lost or stolen checks will be replaced. You should have no problem using the better-known checks, such as American Express and Visa, in the same way as cash in shops, restaurants, and gas stations (don't be put off by "no checks" signs, which only refer to personal checks). Be sure to have plenty of the $10 and $20 denominations for everyday transactions.

With credit cards, cash cards, and travelers' checks, you may never need to visit **banks**, which are generally open from 9am until 5pm Monday to Thursday, and 9am to 6pm on Friday. Most major banks **change foreign travelers' checks** and **currency**; though exchange bureaus, always found at airports, tend to charge less commission: Thomas Cook or American Express are the biggest names. Rarely, if ever, do hotels change foreign currency. **Emergency phone numbers** to call if your checks and/or credit cards are stolen are on p.57.

To find the nearest bank that sells a particular brand of travelers' check, or to buy checks by phone, call the following numbers: American Express ☎1-800/673-3782, Citicorp ☎1-800/645-6556, MasterCard ☎1-800/223-9920, Thomas Cook ☎1-800/223-7373, and Visa ☎1-800/227-6811.

Financial emergencies

Having money wired from home using one of the companies listed below is never convenient or cheap, and should be considered a last resort. It's also possible to have money wired directly from a bank in your home country to a bank in California, although this is somewhat less reliable because it involves two separate institutions. If you go this route, your home bank will need the address of the bank branch where you want to pick up the money, and the address and telex number of the bank's head office; money wired this way normally takes two working days to arrive and costs around $40 per transaction.

Foreign travelers in difficulties have the final option of throwing themselves on the mercy of their nearest national **consulate**, which will – in worst cases only – repatriate you, but will never, under any circumstances, lend you money. See p.22 for the addresses of consulates in LA and San Francisco.

Money-wiring companies

Thomas Cook US ☎1-800/287-7362, Canada ☎1-888/823-4732, UK ☎01733/318 922, Republic of Ireland ☎01/677 1721, ⊛www.us.thomascook.com.

Travelers Express Moneygram US ☎1-800/926-3947, Canada ☎1-800/933-3278, ⊛www.moneygram.com.

Western Union US and Canada ☎1-800/325-6000, Australia ☎1-800/501 500, New Zealand ☎09/270 0050, UK ☎0800/833 833, Republic of Ireland ☎1-800/395 395, ⊛www.westernunion.com.

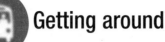

Getting around

Although distances can be great, getting around California is seldom much of a problem. Certainly, things are always easier if you have a car, but between the major cities there are good bus links and a reasonable train service. The only regions where things are more difficult using public transportation are the isolated rural areas, though even here, by adroit forward planning, you can often get to the main points of interest on local buses and charter services, details of which are in the relevant sections of the guide.

By car

Driving is by far the best way to get around California. Los Angeles, for example, grew up and assumed its present shape after cars were invented, sprawling for so many miles in all directions that your hotel may be fifteen or twenty miles from the sights you came to see. Away from the cities, points of interest are much harder to reach without your own transportation; most national and state parks are only served by infrequent public transportation as far as the main visitor center, if that much. What's more, if you are planning on doing a fair amount of camping, renting a car can save you money by allowing access to less expensive, out-of-the-way campgrounds.

Drivers wishing to **rent** cars are supposed to have held their licenses for at least one year (though this is rarely checked); people under 25 years old may encounter problems, and will probably get lumbered with a higher than normal insurance premium. Car rental companies will also expect you to have a credit card; of the major companies renting new cars (see opposite), only Enterprise still accepts a hefty cash **deposit** ($500) as an alternative. The likeliest tactic for getting a good deal is to phone the major firms' toll-free numbers and ask for their best rate – most will try to beat the offers of their competitors, so it's worth haggling.

In general, the lowest rates are available at the airport branches – $149 a week for a subcompact is a fairly standard budget rate. Always be sure to get free unlimited mileage and be aware that leaving the car in a different city to the one in which you rent it will incur a **drop-off charge** that can be $200 or more. However, many companies do not charge drop-off fees within California itself, so check before you book if you plan a one-way drive. If you are planning to venture outside California, inquire if there are any limitations; some companies don't allow travel beyond Reno or into Mexico, while others simply ramp up their insurance charges. Also, don't automatically go for the cheapest rate, as there's a big difference in the quality of cars from company to company; industry leaders like Hertz, Avis, and Budget tend to have newer, lower-mileage cars, often with air-conditioning and stereo cassette decks or CD players as standard equipment – no small consideration on a 2000-mile desert drive.

Alternatively, various **local** companies rent out new – and not so new (try Rent-a-Heap

Road conditions

The California Department of Transportation (CalTrans) operates a toll-free **24-hour information line** (☏1-800/427-ROAD) giving up-to-the-minute details of road conditions throughout the state. On a touch-tone phone, simply input the number of the road ("5" for I-5, "299" for Hwy-299, etc) and a recorded voice will tell you about any relevant weather conditions, delays, detours, snow closures and so on. From out of state, or without a touch-tone phone, road information is also available on ☏916/445-1534. Nevada Highways has a similar system on ☏775/793-1313.

or Rent-a-Wreck) – vehicles. They are certainly cheaper than the big chains if you just want to spin around a city for a day, but you have to drop them back where you picked them up, and free mileage is seldom included, so they can work out more costly for long-distance travel. Addresses and phone numbers are listed in the *Yellow Pages*.

When you rent a car, read the small print carefully for details on the **Collision Damage Waiver (CDW)** – sometimes called a Liability Damage Waiver (LDW) or a Physical Damage Waiver (PDW) – a form of insurance which usually isn't included in the initial rental charge but is well worth considering. Americans who have their own car insurance policy may already be covered (check before you leave home), but foreign visitors should definitely consider taking this option. It specifically covers the car that you are driving, as you are in any case insured for damage to other vehicles. At $9–13 a day, it can add twenty to forty percent to the daily rental fee, but without it you're liable for every scratch to the car – even those that aren't your fault. Some credit card companies offer automatic CDW coverage to anyone using their card; read the fine print beforehand in any case. Smaller companies may offer low-cost CDW that still leaves you liable for, say, the first $500 of any claim. Before stumping up for their optional Personal Accident Coverage (or similar), consult your travel insurance policy, which may cover you for a certain amount of rental vehicle excess, eliminating the need for this extra cost.

You should also check your **third-party liability**. The standard policy often only covers you for the first $15,000 of the third party's claim against you, a paltry sum in litigation-conscious America. Companies strongly advise taking out third-party insurance, which costs a further $10–12 a day but indemnifies the driver for up to $2,000,000.

If you **break down** in a rented car, there will be an emergency number pinned to the dashboard or tucked away in the glove compartment. You can summon the highway patrol on one of the new emergency phones stationed along freeways (usually at half-mile intervals) and many other remote highways (mostly every two miles) – although since the highway patrol and state police cruise by regularly, you can just sit tight and wait. Raising your car hood is generally recognized as a call for assistance, although women traveling alone should be wary of doing this. Another tip is to rent a **mobile telephone** from the car rental agency (or from outlets at major airports) – you often only have to pay a nominal amount until you actually use it, and in larger cities they increasingly come built into the car. Having a phone can be reassuring at least, and a potential lifesaver should something go terribly wrong.

One variation on renting is a **driveaway**, whereby you drive a car from one place to another on behalf of the owner, paying only for the gas you use. The same rules as for renting apply, but look the car over before you take it, as you'll be lumbered with any repair costs, and a large fuel bill if the vehicle's a big drinker. The most common routes are between California and New York, although there's a fair chance you'll find something that needs shifting up the coast, from Los Angeles to San Francisco. See p.14 for further details.

Car rental companies

Alamo ☎1-800/522-9696,
ⓦ www.alamo.com
Avis ☎1-800/331-1084;
in Canada ☎1-800/272-5871,
ⓦ www.avis.com
Budget ☎1-800/527-0700,
ⓦ www.budgetrentacar.com
Dollar ☎1-800/800-4000,
ⓦ www.dollarcar.com
Enterprise ☎1-800/325-8007,
ⓦ www.enterprise.com
Hertz ☎1-800/654-3001;
in Canada ☎1-800/263-0600,
ⓦ www.hertz.com
Kemwell Holiday Autos ☎1-800/422-7737,
ⓦ www.kemwel.com
National ☎1-800/227-7368,
ⓦ www.nationalcar.com
Payless ☎1-800/729-5377,
ⓦ www.paylesscar.com
Rent-A-Wreck ☎1-800/535-1391,
ⓦ www.rent-a-wreck.com
Thrifty ☎1-800/367-2277,
ⓦ www.thrifty.com

[handwritten annotations near Hertz entry: £180 HYUNDAI SONATA — 2006 MODEL — AA DISCOUNT — 3·3L V6]

Driving for foreign visitors

UK nationals can **drive** in the US on a full UK driving license (International Driving Permits are not always regarded as sufficient). It's probably best to book in advance if you want to **rent a car** or an **RV**. For the most savings do the former from a major company; meanwhile, most travel agents who specialize in the US can arrange RV rental – and usually do it cheaper if you book a flight through them as well. Once you have a vehicle, you'll find that **petrol** (US "gasoline") is fairly cheap, though California is one of the more expensive states for it; a self-served US gallon (3.8 liters) of **unleaded** – which most cars use – costs between $1.60 and $1.90, depending on the location of the gas station. In California, most gas stations are self-service; full-service pumps often charge upwards of $0.30 extra per gallon.

American **miles** are the same as British miles but very occasionally **distances** are given in **hours** – the length of time it should take to drive between any two places. There are obviously other differences between driving in the US and in Britain, such as the need in the US to **drive on the right**. This can be remarkably easy to forget – some people draw a cross or tie a ribbon on their right hand to remind them.

There are several **types of road**. The best for covering long distances quickly are the wide, straight, and fast **interstate highways**, usually at least six-lane motorways and always prefixed by "I" (eg I-5) – marked on maps by a red, white, and blue shield bearing the number. Even-numbered interstates usually run east–west and those with odd numbers north–south. Drivers **change lanes** somewhat frequently; in California, you are also permitted to stay in the fast lane while being overtaken on the inside, although common courtesy dictates that slower drivers stay to the right.

A grade down, and broadly similar to British dual carriageways and main roads, are the **state highways** (eg Hwy-1) and the **US highways** (eg US-395). Some major roads in cities are technically state highways but are better known by their local names. Hwy-2 in Los Angeles, for instance, is better known as Santa Monica Boulevard. In rural areas, you'll also find much smaller **county roads**; their number is preceded by a letter denoting their county. In built-up areas **streets** are arranged on a grid system and labeled at each junction.

Renting an RV

Besides cars, Recreational Vehicles or **RVs** (camper vans) can be rented from around $450 a week (usually with no or limited free mileage), although outlets are surprisingly rare, as people tend to own their RVs: El Monte RVs (℡1-888/337-2214, ☻www .elmonte.com) has a dozen or so California locations, mostly in the LA and Bay Area regions. The Recreational Vehicle Rental Association, 3930 University Drive, Fairfax, VA 22030 (℡703/591-7130 or 1-800/336-0355, ☻www.rvra.org), publishes a directory of rental firms in the US and Canada ($10, $15 outside North America) or you can get details of their many members online. Two of the larger companies offering RV rentals are Cruise America (℡1-800/327-7799, ☻www .cruiseamerica.com) and Moturis (℡1-

877/668-8747, ☻www.moturis.com).

On top of the rental fees, take into account the cost of gas (some RVs do twelve miles to the gallon or less) and any drop-off charges, in case you plan to do a one-way trip across the country. Also, it is rarely legal simply to pull up in an RV and spend the night at the roadside – you are expected to stay in designated parks that cost around $20 or more per night.

By plane

A **plane** is obviously the quickest way of getting around California, and much less expensive than you may think. By keeping up to date with the ever-changing deals being offered by airlines – check with your local travel agent, read the ads in local newspapers, or search the Internet – you may be able to take advantage of heavily discounted fares.

Although the law says that drivers must keep up with the flow of traffic, which is often hurtling along at 75mph, the maximum **speed limit** in California is 70mph, with lower signposted limits – usually around 35–45mph – in built-up areas, and 20mph near schools when children are present. If given a ticket for **speeding**, your case will come to court and the size of the fine will be at the discretion of the judge; $90 is a rough minimum. If the **police** do flag you down, don't get out of the car, and don't reach into the glove compartment as the cops may think you have a gun. Simply sit still with your hands on the wheel; when questioned, be polite and don't attempt to make jokes.

As for other possible violations, US law requires that any **alcohol** be carried unopened in the boot (US "trunk") of the car, and it can't be stressed enough that **driving under the influence (DUI)** is a very serious offense. At **junctions**, one rule is crucially different from the UK: you can turn right on a red light (having first come to a halt) if there is no traffic approaching from the left, unless there is a "no turn on red" sign; otherwise red means stop. Stopping is also compulsory, in both directions, when you come upon a school bus disgorging passengers with its lights flashing and not doing so is regarded as a serious infraction. Blinking red lights should be treated as a stop sign, and blinking yellow lights indicate that you should cross the intersection with caution, but do not need to come to a complete stop. And at any intersection with more than one **stop sign**, cars proceed in the order in which they arrived; if two vehicles arrive simultaneously, the one on the right has right of way.

Once at your destination, you'll find in cities at least that **parking meters** are commonplace. Charges for an hour range from 25¢–$1. **Car parks** (US "parking lots") charge up to $20 a day. If you park in the wrong place (such as within 10ft of a fire hydrant) your car is likely to be towed away or **wheel-clamped**; a ticket on the windshield tells you where to pay the fine. Watch out for signs indicating the **street cleaning** schedule, as you mustn't park overnight before an early-morning clean. **Validated parking**, where your fee for parking in, say, a shopping mall's lot is waived if one of the stores has stamped your parking stub (just ask), is common, as is **valet parking** at even quite modest restaurants, for which a small tip is expected.

Airlines with a strong route structure in the state include Alaska, American, Continental, Delta, Northwest, Reno Air, Southwest, TWA, and United. Phone the airlines for routes and schedules, then buy your ticket from a travel agent using the computerized Fare Assurance Program, which processes all the available ticket options and searches for the lowest fare, taking into account the special needs of individual travelers. One agent using the service is Travel Avenue (☎1-800/333-3335).

At **off-peak times**, flights between Los Angeles and San Francisco can cost as little as $50 one-way (slightly less than the equivalent train fare), though may require a booking to be made 21 days in advance.

By train

Unlike elsewhere in the US, traveling on the Amtrak **rail** network is a viable way of getting about California, thanks in great measure to the growing number of Amtrak Thruway buses, which bring passengers from the many rail-less parts of the state to the trains. Traveling by train is slightly more expensive than Greyhound, $53 one-way between Los Angeles and San Francisco, for example, but unlike on a bus, a smooth journey with few if any delays is a near certainty. All the major cities are connected and the carriages clean, comfortable, and rarely crowded. Probably the prettiest route is the Coast Starlight, which winds along the coast between Santa Barbara and San Luis Obispo, a 100-mile coastline ride during which it's not unusual to see seals, dolphins, or even whales in the waters offshore. The other LA-to-SF Amtrak routes head inland, by bus to Bakersfield then by rail north through the dull San Joaquin Valley. Avoid these unless you are making for Yosemite National Park.

Rail, bus, and air passes

Amtrak rail passes

Foreign travelers have a choice of four rail passes that cover California; the National Pass allows travel over the entire system, whereas the Coastal Pass permits unlimited train travel on the east and west coasts, but not between the two.

	15-day (June–Aug)	15-day (Sept–May)	30-day (June–Aug)	30-day (Sept–May)
Far West	$245	$190	$320	$265
West	$325	$200	$405	$270
Coastal	–	–	$285	$235
National	$440	$295	$550	$385

On production of a passport issued outside the US or Canada, the passes can be bought at travel agents, or at Amtrak stations in the US. In the **UK**, you can buy them from Destination Marketing, 14 Greville St, London EC1N 8SB (℡020/7400 7099); in **Ireland**, contact Usit Now (℡01/602 1600); in **Australia**, Amtrak Rail USA, 4 Davies St, Surry Hills (℡02/9318 1044); and in **New Zealand** passes can be purchased from almost any travel agent.

In addition, foreigners and US citizens alike can find great deals on the weekly **Rail Sale** promotions or invest in one of the new **California Rail Passes**: the Statewide pass allows 7 days of travel in a 21-day period for $159, while the Northern and Southern passes allow 5 days travel out of 7 in their respective areas for $99.

Greyhound Ameripasses

Foreign visitors and US and Canadian nationals can all buy a **Greyhound Ameripass** or **Discovery Pass**, offering unlimited travel within a set time limit: most travel agents can oblige or you can order online at ⊛www.greyhound.com. They come in several durations and the fare for international visitors is slightly less. A seven-day pass costs $184 for foreign visitors ($199 for North Americans), ten days go for $234 ($249), fifteen days for $274 ($299), thirty days for $364 ($389), forty-five days for $404 ($439), and the longest, a sixty-day pass, is $494 ($549). All kids under 12 go half price, and there are discounts of around seven percent for North American students and seniors (62+). No daily extensions are available. The first time you use your pass, it will be dated by the ticket clerk (which becomes the commencement date of the ticket), and your destination is written on a page that the driver will tear out and keep as you board the bus. Repeat this procedure for every subsequent journey.

Air passes

All the main American airlines (and British Airways, in conjunction with its partners) offer **air passes** for visitors who plan to fly a lot within the US. These must be purchased in advance, and comprise between three and eight **coupons**, each valid for a flight of any duration in the US, though in many cases only one flight can be transcontinental. Rates start at around US$400 for three coupons, and $60 for each additional coupon; a little more if you are not traveling to the States with that airline.

There are also **Visit USA** fares only available to non-US residents. These can be substantially less than the standard fare for that flight, and it is certainly worth asking your travel agent, but in many cases there are discount fares available which undercut the Visit USA fare. If you just plan to buy one flight, good low-season fares from New York, Washington, and Boston to California are $300–350 round trip; LA is marginally less expensive than San Francisco.

B

BASICS | Getting around

For all information on Amtrak fares and schedules in the US, use the toll-free number ☎1-800/USA-RAIL, or use the reservation facility on their website ⊛www.amtrak.com; do not phone individual stations.

If California is part of wider travels, it may be economic to buy one of Amtrak's rail passes (see opposite).

By bus

If you're traveling on your own, and making a lot of stops, **buses** are by far the cheapest way to get around. The main long-distance service is **Greyhound** (⊛www .greyhound.com), which links all major cities and many smaller towns. Out in the country, buses are fairly scarce, sometimes appearing only once a day; as a result, you'll need to plot your route with care. But along the main highways, buses run around the clock to a fairly full timetable, stopping only for meal breaks (almost always fast-food dives) and driver changeovers. Greyhound buses are slightly less uncomfortable than you might expect, and it's feasible to save on a night's accommodation by traveling overnight and sleeping on the bus – though you may not feel up to much the next day.

It used to be that any sizeable community would have a Greyhound station; in some places, the post office or a gas station now doubles as the bus stop and ticket office, and in many others the bus service has been canceled altogether. Note that advance reservations, either in person at the station or on the toll-free number, are useful for getting cheaper tickets but do not guarantee a seat, so it's still wise to arrive in good time and join the **queue** at busy stations – if a bus is full you may be forced to wait until the next one, sometimes overnight or longer, although there is a policy that if more than ten people are unseated they will put on an extra bus.

Fares average 10¢ a mile, which can add up quickly; for example, $42 ($35 if pur-

chased seven days in advance) from Los Angeles to San Francisco one way. For long-trip travel, riding the bus costs about the same as the train; considering the time (75 hours coast-to-coast, if you eat and sleep on the bus) it's not that much cheaper than flying. However, the bus is the best deal if you plan to visit a lot of places, and Greyhound's **Ameripasses** (see opposite) can work out to be good value. There are also assorted three-, seven- fourteen-, and twenty-one-day advance purchase discounts, which can be useful for longer trips, though they seldom offer savings within California.

Greyhound produces a condensed **timetable** of major country-wide routes, but does not distribute it to travelers; to plan your route, pick up the free route-by-route timetables from larger stations, or consult Greyhound's website.

Smaller companies catering specifically to tourists come and go with alarming frequency. One currently operational is **AmeriBus** (☎954/923-1480, ⊛www .ameribus.com), which uses buses and minivans on a circuit from LA up the coast to San Francisco, inland to Yosemite, down to Las Vegas and then back to LA. Services leave the major cities daily, so if you fork out $129 you've got unlimited travel around this loop for one month.

Bear in mind that fair distances can be covered for very little money – if also very slowly – using **local buses**, which connect neighboring districts. It's possible, for example, to travel from San Diego to Los Angeles for around $5, but it'll take all day and at least three changes of bus to do it. And of course, there's always the hippyish Green Tortoise, which runs between the major Californian cities (see box).

Greyhound's nationwide toll-free **information service** can give you routes and times, plus phone numbers and addresses of local terminals. You can also make reservations: ☎1-800/231-2222.

Green Tortoise

One alternative to long-distance bus hell is the slightly countercultural **Green Tortoise**, whose buses, furnished with foam cushions, bunks, fridges, and rock music, ply the major Californian cities, running between Los Angeles, San Francisco, and on into the Pacific Northwest. (In summer, they also cross the country to New York and Boston, transcontinental trips which amount to mini-tours of the nation.) Other Green Tortoise trips include excursions to the major national parks (in 16 days for $629), south to Mexico and Central America, and north to Alaska.

Main office: 494 Broadway, San Francisco, CA 94133 ☎415/956-7500 or 1-800/867-8647, ⊛www.greentortoise.com.

Cycling

In general, **cycling** is a cheap and healthy method of getting around all the big **cities**, some of which have cycle lanes and local buses equipped to carry bikes, strapped to the outside. In **country areas**, certainly, there's much scenic and largely level land, especially around Sacramento and the Wine Country.

Bikes can be **rented** for $15–30 a day, and $90–120 a week from most bike stores; the local visitor center will have details (we've listed rental options where applicable throughout the guide). Apart from the coastal fog, which tends to clear by midday, you'll encounter few **weather** problems (except perhaps sunburn), but remember that the further north you go, the lower the temperatures and the more frequent the rains become.

For **long-distance cycling**, you'll need maps, spare tires, tools, panniers, a helmet (not a legal necessity, but a very good idea), and a good quality multi-speed bike. Don't immediately splurge on a mountain bike, unless you are planning a lot of off-road use – good road conditions and trail restrictions in national parks make a touring bike an equally good or better choice. A route avoiding the interstates – on which cycling is illegal – is essential, and it's also wise to cycle north to south, as the wind blows this way in the summer and can make all the difference between a pleasant trip and a journey full of acute leg-ache. The main **problem** you'll encounter is traffic: wide, cumbersome recreational vehicles spew unpleasant exhaust in your face and, in Northern California, enormous logging trucks have slipstreams that will pull you towards the middle of the road. Be particularly careful if you're planning to cycle along Hwy-1 on the central coast since, besides heavy traffic, it has tight curves, dangerous precipices, and is prone to fog.

If you're camping as well as cycling, look out for **hiker/biker campgrounds** ($3 per person per night), which are free of cars and RVs, dotted across California's state parks and beaches. Many of them were set up in 1976 as part of the **Pacific Coast Bicentennial Bike Route**, running 1825 miles from the Mexican border to Vancouver, Canada. Sites are allotted on a first-come-first-served basis, and all offer water and toilet facilities but seldom showers. For more information, call ☎1-800/444-7275 or write to Hostelling International – USA (see p.39); the Adventure Cycling Association (formerly Bikecentennial), PO Box 8308, Missoula, MT 59807 (☎406/721-1776 or 1-800/755-2453, ⊛www.adv-cycling.org) or the Sierra Club (details on p.56).

Hitching

The usual advice given to **hitchhikers** is that they should use their common sense; in fact, common sense should tell anyone that hitchhiking in the US is a **bad idea**. We do not recommend it, though it is practiced commonly enough by hikers seeking access to Sierra trailheads.

Accommodation

Generally $59.99 double room for two. 2005.

Motel 6 Mainly Motel6.Com.

Accommodation standards in California – as in the rest of the US – are high, and costs inevitably form a significant proportion of the expenses for any trip to the state. It is possible to haggle, however, especially in the chain motels, and if you're on your own, you can possibly pare costs down by sleeping in dormitory-style hostels, where a bed will generally go for $13–20. However, groups of two or more will find it only a little more expensive to stay in the far more plentiful motels and hotels, where basic rooms away from the major cities typically cost around $40 per night. Many hotels will set up a third single bed for around $5 to $10 on top of the regular price, reducing costs for three people sharing. By contrast, the solo traveler will have a hard time of it: "singles" are usually double rooms at an only slightly reduced rate. Prices quoted by hotels and motels are almost always for the actual room rather than for each person using it.

However, with the exception of the budget Interstate motels, there's rarely such a thing as a set rate for a room, most applying **seasonal rates**. A basic motel in a seaside or mountain resort may double its prices according to the season, while a big-city hotel which charges $200 per room during the week will often slash its tariff at the weekend when all the business types have gone home.

Since cheap accommodation in the cities, on the popular sections of the coast and close to the major national parks is snapped up fast, **book ahead** whenever possible, using the suggestions in this book.

Reservations are only held until 5pm or 6pm unless you've told them you'll be arriving late. Most of the larger chains have an advance booking form in their brochures and will make reservations at another of their premises for you.

Wherever you stay, you'll be expected to **pay in advance**, at least for the first night and perhaps for further nights too, particularly if it's **high season** – generally summer, but most likely winter in desert and ski areas – and the hotel expects to be busy. Payment can be in cash or travelers' checks, though it's more common to give your credit card number and sign for everything when you leave.

Accommodation price codes

All the **accommodation** listed in this book has been categorized into one of nine **price codes**, as set out below. The prices quoted are for cheapest available room for two people in the high season. You can expect many places to jump into the next highest category on Friday and Saturday nights, and almost all lodging (except state and federally run campgrounds) is subject to additional local hotel taxes, which are generally around ten percent but may soar to twenty percent. For campgrounds, and hostels that offer individual beds or bunks, we have given the per-person price (excluding tax) along with a code for any private rooms.

① up to $40   **④** $70–90   **⑦** $150–200
② $40–55   **⑤** $90–120 **⑧** $200–250
③ $55–70   **⑥** $120–150 **⑨** $250+

Hotels and motels

Hotels and **motels** are essentially the same thing, although motels tend to congregate along the main approach roads to cities, around beaches, and by the main road junctions in country areas. High-rise hotels predominate along the popular sections of the coast and are sometimes the only accommodation in city centers.

In general, there's a uniform standard of comfort everywhere, with all rooms featuring one or more double or queen beds, plus bathroom, cable TV, phone, refrigerator, and a coffee maker. The budget places (costing around $40) will be pretty basic and possibly run down, but an extra $10–15 will get you more space, modern fittings, and better facilities, such as a swimming pool. Paying over $100 brings you into the realms of the in-room hot tub.

Microwaves are fairly common, but only rarely will you find full cooking facilities in your room. Instead, an increasing number of hotels (and the better motels) provide a **complimentary breakfast**. Sometimes, this will be no more than a cup of coffee and a sticky bun, but it may be a sit-down affair and likely to comprise fruit, cereals, muffins, and toast. In the pricier places, you may also be offered made-to-order omelets.

Enormous roadside signs make finding cheap hotels and motels pretty simple, and you'll soon become familiar with the numerous chains. Common budget-priced **chains**, including *Econolodge*, *Days Inn*, and *Motel 6*, offer rooms costing $30–45. For mid-priced options ($50–100) try *Best Western*, *Howard Johnson*, *Travelodge*, and *Ramada*, though if you can afford to pay this much there's normally somewhere with more character to stay – when it's worth blowing a hunk of cash on somewhere really atmospheric we've said as much in the guide. Bear in mind that the most upscale establishments have all manner of services which may appear to be free but for which you'll be expected to **tip** in a style commensurate with the hotel's status – ie big.

Discounts and reservations

During **off-peak periods**, many motels and hotels struggle to fill their rooms, and it's worth **haggling** to get a few dollars off the asking price. Staying in the same place for more than one night will bring further reductions, and motels in particular offer worthwhile discounts (usually ten percent) for seniors and members of various organizations, particularly the American Automobile Association (AAA). Members of sister motoring associations in other countries may also be entitled to such discounts. Additionally, pick up the many **discount coupons** which fill tourist information offices and look out for the free *Traveler Discount Guide*. Read the small print, though – what appears to be an amazingly cheap room rate sometimes turns out to be a per-person charge for two people sharing, and limited to midweek.

B&B inns and hotels

Bed and breakfast in California is a luxury – even the mattresses have to conform to a standard of comfort far higher than those in hotels. Typically, the bed-and-breakfast inns, as they're usually known, are restored buildings and grand houses in the smaller cities and more rural areas although the big cities also have a few, especially San Francisco. Even the larger establishments – often distinguished by being called B&B Hotels – tend to have no more than ten rooms, often without TV and phone but with plentiful flowers, stuffed cushions, and a sometimes contrived homely atmosphere. Others may just be a couple of furnished rooms in someone's home, or an entire apartment where you won't even see your host. Victorian and Romantic are dominant themes; while selecting the best in that vein, we've also gone out of our way to seek out those that don't conform.

While always including a huge and wholesome breakfast (five courses are not unheard of), prices vary greatly: anything from $70 to $250 depending on location and season. Most fall between $85 and $125 per night for a double, a little more for a whole apartment. Bear in mind, too, that they are frequently booked well in advance, and even if they're not full, the cheaper rooms that determine our price code may be already taken.

As well as the B&Bs listed in the *Guide*,

there are hundreds more throughout the state, many of them listed on various **accommodation websites** such as California B&B Travel (ⓦwww.bbtravel.com), the California Association of B&B Inns (ⓦwww.cabbi.com), and B&B Inns of North America (ⓦwww.inntravels.com).

Hostels

At an average of $16 per night per person (though over $20 in LA and San Francisco), **hostels** are clearly the cheapest accommodation option in California other than camping. There are two main kinds of hostel-type accommodation in the US: the internationally affiliated HI-AYH hostels, and a growing number of independent hostels variously aligned with assorted umbrella organizations.

Altogether California has around twenty **HI-AYH** hostels (the prefix is shortened to HI in "Listings"), mostly in major cities and close to popular hiking areas, including national and state parks. Most urban hostels have 24-hour access, while rural ones may have a curfew and limited daytime hours. HI also operates a couple of small "home hostels" in the state; though similar to other hostels you need to reserve in advance or there may be no one there to receive you.

Rates at HI hostels range from $13 to $25 for members. Non-members generally pay an additional $3 per night, so becoming a member will quickly pay off. Membership is international, but you are expected to join in your home country (see box below for contacts), something which will cost the equivalent of $15–25 annually.

Details of all hostels are listed in the *USA Hostel Directory*, available free to members (otherwise $3): pick one up at a hostel, order online, or request a copy from the HI National Office (☎202/783-6161, ⓦwww.hiayh.org). HI hostels don't allow sleeping bags though some will provide sheets as a matter of course. Otherwise, you'll need to rent a **sheet sleeping bag** (typically $2 a night) or bring your own. Few hostels provide meals, but most have **cooking** facilities. Alcohol and smoking are banned.

Particularly if you're traveling in high season, it's advisable to make **reservations**, either by contacting the hostel directly, booking online (at least 48 hours in advance), or by dialing toll-free (within North America) on ☎1-800/909-4776, followed by the first three letters of the city you are headed for. When booking from outside North America it is easiest to book online (at ⓦwww.hiayh.com), which allows you to reserve at any California hostel. There's also the IBN booking service (ⓦwww.yhabooking .com), which helps you book certain big city and gateway hostels through your home organization (see box for numbers). Santa Monica in LA and all the San Francisco hostels can be booked this way.

Independent hostels now number around forty and are concentrated in the big cities. They're usually a little less expensive than their HI counterparts, and have fewer rules, but the quality is not as consistent; some can be quite poor, while others, which we've included in the book, are absolutely wonderful. In popular areas, especially LA, San Francisco, and San Diego, they compete fiercely for your business with airport and train station pick-ups, free breakfasts, and free bike hire. There is often no curfew and, at some, a party atmosphere is encouraged at barbecues and keg parties. Their independent status may be due to a failure to measure up to the HI's (fairly rigid) criteria, yet often it's simply because the owners prefer not to be tied down by HI regulations. Many have now loosely affiliated themselves under an assortment of bodies, mostly designed to encourage you to move on to a sister hostel.

All the information in this book was accurate at the time of going to press; however, hostels are often shoestring organizations, prone to changing address or closing down altogether. Similarly, new ones appear each year; check the noticeboards of other hostels for news or consult hostel websites, particularly ⓦwww.hostels.com.

Youth hostel contacts

Australia Australia Youth Hostels Association, 422 Kent St, Sydney ☎02/9261 1111, ⓦwww.yha.com.au

Canada Canadian Hostelling Association, Room 400, 205 Catherine St, Ottawa, ON K2P 1C3 ☎1-800/663-5777 or 613/237-7884, ⓦwww.hostellingintl.ca

England Youth Hostel Association, Trevelyan House, 8 St Stephen's Hill, St Albans, Herts AL1 2DY ☏0870/870 8808, Ⓦwww.yha.org.uk
New Zealand New Zealand Youth Hostels Association, 173 Gloucester St, Christchurch ☏0800/278 299 or 03/379 9970, Ⓦwww.yha.co.nz
Northern Ireland Hostelling International Northern Ireland, 2232 Donegall Rd, Belfast BT12 5JN ☏028/9032 4733, Ⓦwww.hini.org.uk
Republic of Ireland An Óige, 61 Mountjoy St, Dublin 7 ☏01/830 4555, Ⓦwww.irelandyha.org
Scotland Scottish Youth Hostel Association, 7 Glebe Crescent, Stirling FK8 2JA ☏0870/155 3255, Ⓦwww.syha.org.uk
USA HI National Office, 733 15th St NW, Suite 840, Washington DC 20005 ☏202/783-6161, Ⓔhiayhserv@hiayh.org, Ⓦwww.hiayh.org

Camping

California **campgrounds** range from the primitive – a flat piece of ground that may or may not have a pit toilet and water tap – to others that are more like open-air hotels, with shops, restaurants, and washing facilities. In major cities, campgrounds tend to be inconveniently sited on the outskirts, if they exist at all.

When camping in national and state parks, as well as national forests, you can typically expect a large site with picnic table and fire pit, designed to accommodate up to two vehicles and six people. It is usually a short walk to an outhouse and drinking water. Note that sites fill up quickly and it's worth reserving well in advance (see list below for contact numbers).

Naturally enough, prices vary accordingly, ranging from nothing for the most basic plots, up to $20 a night for something comparatively luxurious, and more like $22–30 if you want to hook your **RV** up to electricity, water, sewage, and cable TV. For comprehensive listings of these check out Ⓦwww.californiacampgrounds.org and Kampgrounds of America (Ⓦwww.koa.com).

There are plenty of campgrounds but often plenty of people intending to use them as well: take care over plotting your route if you're intending to camp in the big national parks, or anywhere at all during national holidays or the summer, when many grounds will be either full or very crowded. Vacancies often exist in the grounds outside the parks

– where the facilities are usually marginally better – and by contrast, some of the more basic campgrounds in isolated areas will often be empty whatever time of year you're there. Often rural campgrounds have no one in attendance (though a ranger may stop by), and if there's any charge at all you'll need to pay by posting the money in the slot provided; save your small bills.

Look out too for **hiker/biker** or **walk-in** campgrounds, which, at $1 per person per night, are much cheaper than most sites but only available if you are traveling under your own steam.

Much of California is in the public domain, and, if you're backpacking, you can **camp rough** pretty much anywhere you want in the gaping **wilderness areas** and **deserts**. However, in the more heavily hiked areas (we've indicated the relevant areas in the text), you must first get a **wilderness permit** (almost always free), and usually a free **campfire permit** (even if you are using a cooking stove). Campfire permits are available from park rangers' offices and once obtained are usually valid for a year. You should also take the proper precautions – carry sufficient food and drink to cover emergencies, inform someone of your travel plans, and watch out for bears and rattlesnakes, as well as the effect *your* presence can have on *their* environment; see "Backcountry Camping, Hiking, and Wildlife" on p.53.

Camping reservation contacts

National Parks (except Yosemite) ☏1-800/365-2267, Ⓦreservations.nps.gov. Operational 7am–7pm Pacific Time.
National Forests National Recreation Reservation Service ☏518/885-3639 or 1-877/444-6777, Ⓦwww.reserveusa.com.
State Parks California State Parks Reservations ☏1-800/444-7275 or 916/638-5883, Ⓦwww.reserveamerica.com.
Yosemite National Park ☏1-800/436-7275, Ⓦreservations.nps.gov. Operational 7am–7pm Pacific Time.

Long-term accommodation

Excluding San Francisco, **apartment-hunting** in California is not the nightmare it is in, say, New York: accommodation is plentiful and not always expensive, although the absence of housing associations means that there is very little really cheap accommodation anywhere except in very isolated country areas. Accommodation is almost always rented unfurnished, so you'll have to buy furniture; expect to pay at least $700 a month for a studio or one-bedroom apartment and upwards of $2000 per month for two to three bedrooms in Los Angeles or San Francisco. Most landlords will expect one month's rent as a deposit, plus one other month in advance.

By far the best way to find somewhere is to ask around – particularly near universities or college campuses, where apartment turnover is usually frequent. Otherwise rooms for rent are often advertised in the windows of houses, and local papers have "Apartments For Rent" sections. In **Los Angeles** the best source is the *LA Weekly* (ⓦ www.laweekly.com), although you should also scan the *LA Times* classifieds. In **San Francisco** check out the *Chronicle* (ⓦ www.sfchron.com) and the free *San Francisco Bay Guardian* (ⓦ www.sfbg.com), *SF Weekly* (ⓦ www.sfweekly.com), and the *East Bay Express* (ⓦ www.eastbayexpress .com).

Eating and drinking

It's not too much of an exaggeration to say that in California – its cities, at least – you can eat whatever you want, whenever you want. On every main street, a mass of restaurants, fast-food places, and coffee shops try to outdo one another with bargains and special offers. Be warned, though, that in rural areas you might go for days finding little more than diners and cheap Mexican joints.

California's cornucopia stems largely from its being one of the most agriculturally rich parts of the country. Junkfood is as common as anywhere else in the US, but the state also produces its own range of highly nutritious goodies: apples, avocados, dates, grapes, kiwi fruit, melons, oranges, and peaches are everywhere, plus abundant seafood, high-quality meat, and dairy goods. You'll rarely find anything that's not fresh, be it a bagel or a spinach-in-Mornay-sauce croissant (California's mix'n'match food concoctions can be as anarchic as its architecture), and even fast food won't necessarily be rubbish.

California is also one of the most **health-conscious** states in the country, and the supermarket shelves are chock-full of products which if not fat-free, are low-fat, low-sodium, caffeine-free, and dairy-free. Much the same ethic runs through the menu of most restaurants, though you needn't worry about going hungry: portions are universally huge, and what you don't eat can always be "boxed up" for later consumption.

Breakfasts

For the price, on average $5–8, breakfast is the best-value and most filling meal of the day. Go to a diner, café or coffee shop, all of which serve breakfast until at least 11am, with some diners serving them all day.

The breakfasts themselves are pretty much what you'd find all over the country. **Eggs** are the staple ingredient, served in a variety of styles and, in omelet form, with the occasional exotic filling (avocado, for instance). There is usually also some form of **meat** available: ham, bacon, or sausages. Some sort of toast or muffin invariably accompanies this.

If you wish, you can add **waffles**, **pancakes**, or **French toast** to the combination, consumed swamped in butter with lashings of sickly-sweet syrup, flavored to mimic the more delicate and expensive maple syrup. A concession to California's love of light food is the option of **fruit**: typically apple, banana, orange, pineapple, or strawberry, wonderfully styled and served on their own or with pancakes, though costing as much as a full-blown fry-up.

Lunch and snacks

Between 11am and 3pm you should look for the excellent-value **lunchtime set menus** on offer – Chinese, Indian, and Thai restaurants frequently have help-yourself buffets for $5–8, and many Japanese restaurants give you a chance to eat sushi much more cheaply ($8–12) than usual. Most Mexican restaurants are exceptionally well priced all the time: you can get a good-sized lunch for $5–8. In Northern California, watch out for seafood restaurants selling **fish'n'chips**: the fish is breaded and then fried, and the chips are chunky chipped potatoes rather than the matchstick french fries you normally find. A plateful is about $6. Look as well for **clam chowder**, a thick, creamy shellfish soup served almost everywhere for $4–5, sometimes using a hollowed-out sourdough cottage loaf as a bowl ($5–8).

As you'd expect, there's also **pizza**, available from chains like *Pizza Hut*, *Round Table*, and *Shakey's*, or local, more personalized restaurants. Most are dependable and have a similar range of offerings; count on paying around $12 for a basic two-person pizza. If it's a warm day and you can't face hot food, delis (see below) usually serve a broad range of salads for about $4.

For **quick snacks**, you'll find many **delis** do ready-cooked meals for $4–6 as well as a range of **sandwiches** which can be meals in themselves: huge French rolls filled with a custom-built combination of meat, cheese, and vegetables; **bagels** are also everywhere, filled with anything you fancy. **Street stands** sell hot dogs, burgers, tacos, or a slice of pizza for around $2, and most shopping malls have ethnic fast-food stalls, often pricier than their equivalent outside, but usually edible and filling. Be a little wary of the grottier **Mexican fast-food** stands if you're buying meat, although they're generally filling, cheap, and more authentic than the Tex-Mex outlets. There are chains, too, like *El Pollo Loco*, *Del Taco*, and *Taco Bell*, which sell swift tacos and burritos from $1 up. And of course the **burger chains** are as ubiquitous here as anywhere in the US: best to seek out the few In-n-Out burger chain if possible, all made to order and as delicious as you'll find.

Restaurants

Even if it often seems swamped by the more fashionable regional and ethnic cuisines, traditional **American cooking** – juicy burgers, steaks, fries, salads (invariably served before the main dish), and baked potatoes – is found all over California. Cheapest of the food chains is the California-wide *Denny's*, although you'll rarely need to spend more than $12 for a solid blowout anywhere.

By contrast, though, it's **California cuisine**, geared towards health and aesthetics, that's raved about by foodies on the West Coast – and rightly so. Basically a development of French *nouvelle cuisine*, using the wide mix of fresh, locally available ingredients, California cuisine is based on physiological efficiency – eating only what you need to and what your body can process. Vegetables are harvested before maturity and steamed to preserve a high concentration of vitamins, with a strong flavor – and to look better on the plate. Seafood comes from oyster farms and the catches of small-time fishermen, and what little meat there is on the menu tends to come from animals reared on organic farms. The result is small but beautifully presented portions, and high, high prices: it's not unusual to spend $40 a head (or much more) for a full dinner with wine. To whet your appetite, starters (perhaps $8–10) include mussels in jalapeño and sesame vinaigrette, snails in puff pastry with mushroom purée, and, among main courses, roasted goat cheese salad with walnuts, swordfish with herb butter, and ahi tuna with cactus ratatouille.

Restaurants serving California cuisine build their reputation by word of mouth; if you can, ask a local enthusiast for recommendations, or simply follow our suggestions in the guide, especially in Berkeley, the recognized birthplace of California cuisine. Of other American regional cooking, **Cajun** remains in vogue. Also known as "Creole," it originated in Louisiana as a way of saving money by cooking up leftovers. It is centered on black beans, rice, and seafood, and is always highly spiced. There are a few relatively inexpensive places to find it (charging around $12 a dish, but its cachet has generally pushed prices up.

Although technically ethnic, **Mexican** food is so common that it often seems like (and, historically, often is) an indigenous cuisine, especially in Southern California. What's more, day or night, it's the cheapest type of food to eat: even a full dinner with a beer or margarita will rarely be over $12 anywhere except in the most upmarket establishments. Californian Mexican food is generally different from what you'll find in Mexico, making more use of fresh vegetables and fruit, but the essentials are the same: lots of rice and pinto beans, often served refried (ie boiled, mashed, and fried), with variations on the **tortilla**, a thin maize or flour-dough pancake. You can eat it as an accompaniment to your main dish; wrapped around the food and eaten by hand (a **burrito**); filled and folded (a **taco**); rolled, filled and baked (an **enchilada**); or fried flat and topped with a stack of food (a **tostada**). One of the few options for vegetarians in this meat-oriented cuisine is the **chile relleno**, a green pepper stuffed with cheese, dipped in egg batter, and fried. Veggie burritos, filled with beans, rice, lettuce, avocado, cheese, and sour cream are another prevalent option for those averse to meat.

Other ethnic cuisines are plentiful too. **Chinese** food is everywhere, and during lunchtime can often be as cheap as Mexican. **Japanese** is more expensive and fashionable – sushi is worshipped by some Californians. **Italian** food is very popular, but can be expensive once you leave the simple pizzas and pastas to explore the specialist Italian regional cooking that has caught on in the last few years. **French** food, too, is widely available, though always pricey, and the cuisine of social climbers and power-lunchers, rarely found outside the larger cities. **Thai**, **Korean**, **Vietnamese**, and **Indonesian** food is similarly city-based, though usually cheaper; **Indian** restaurants, on the other hand, are thin on the ground just about everywhere and often very expensive – although as Indian cuisine catches on the situation is gradually changing for the better, with a sprinkling of moderately priced Southern Indian food outlets.

Drinking

In freeway-dominated Los Angeles, the traditional neighborhood bar is as rare as the traditional neighborhood. There are exceptions, but LA bars tend to be either extremely pretentious or extremely seedy, neither good for long bouts of social drinking. On the other hand, San Francisco is the consummate boozing town, still with a strong contingent of old-fashioned, get-drunk bars that are fun to spend an evening in, even if you don't plan to get legless. Elsewhere in the state you'll find the normal array of spots in which to imbibe.

To **buy and consume alcohol** in California, you need to be 21, and could well be asked for ID even if you look much older. **Licensing laws** and **drinking hours** are, however, among the most liberal in the country (though laws on drinking and driving are not). Alcohol can be bought and consumed any time between 6am and 2am, seven days a week in bars, nightclubs, and many restaurants. Some restaurants only have a beer and wine license, and many allow you to take your own bottled wine into a restaurant, where the corkage fee will be $5–10. You can buy beer, wine, or spirits more cheaply and easily in supermarkets, many delis, and, of course, liquor stores.

American beers fall into two distinct categories: wonderful and tasteless. The latter are found everywhere: light, fizzy brands such as Budweiser, Miller, Schlitz, and so on. The alternative is a fabulous range of **micro-brewed beers**, the product of a wave of backyard and in-house operations that swelled about ten years ago and has now matured to the point that many pump out over 150,000 barrels a year and are classed as "regional breweries." Head for one of the **brewpubs** (many are listed in the guide along with breweries you can visit; see also the California Beerpage website listed on p.24) and you'll find handcrafted beers such as crisp pilsners, wheat beers, and stouts on tap, at prices only marginally above those of the national brews. Bottled microbrews, like

Chico's hoppy Sierra Nevada Pale Ale and the full-bodied, San Francisco-brewed Anchor Steam Beer, are sold throughout the state, while Red Tail Ale is found throughout Northern California. **Imported beers** are of course available in most places as well. Expect to fork out $3–4 for a glass of draught beer, about the same as for a bottle of imported beer.

If you're partial to the internationally known **Californian wines**, like Gallo and Paul Masson, you may be surprised to learn that they are held in low regard on the West Coast, and are produced in plants resembling oil refineries. Most people prefer the produce of California's innumerable as well, invariably good, smaller wineries. The Napa and Sonoma valleys – which produce predominantly dry wines made from French-strain grapes – are widely, and rightly, regarded as the cradle of the Californian wine industry. Wines are categorized by grape-type rather than place of origin: the heavy and fruity Cabernet Sauvignon is probably the most popular red, along with the lighter Merlot and Pinot Noir. Among the whites, Chardonnay is very dry and flavorful, and generally preferred to Sauvignon Blanc or Fumé Blanc, though these have their devotees. The most unusual is the strongly flavored Zinfandel, which comes in white (mocked by wine snobs, but popular nonetheless), red, or rosé.

You can learn a lot about Californian wine by taking a **winery tour**, mostly including free tastings (although some charge $4–5 for a full glass or two), a number of which we've mentioned in the guide. Alternatively, the visitor centers in popular wine-producing areas produce informative regional directories. The best lesson of all, of course, is simply to buy the stuff. It's fairly inexpensive: a decent glass of wine in a bar or restaurant costs $4–6, a bottle $10–20. Buying from a supermarket is better still – a tolerable bottle can be purchased for as little as $7.

Cocktails are extremely popular, especially during **happy hours** (usually any time between 5pm and 7pm) when drinks are half-price and there's often a buffet thrown in. Varieties are innumerable, sometimes specific to a single bar or cocktail lounge, and they cost anything between $3 and $6.

An increasing alternative to drinking dens, **coffee shops** (look out for any joint with "Java" in the title) play a vibrant part in California's social scene, and are havens of high-quality coffee far removed from the stuff served in diners and convenience stores. In larger towns and cities, cafés will boast of the quality of the roast, and offer a full array of espressos, cappuccinos, lattes, and the like, served straight, iced, organic, or flavored with syrups. Herbal teas and light snacks are often also on the menu.

Communications

$22 a minute in Luxor Vegas to UK!

You'll have no trouble keeping in touch while in California. In rural areas the nearest public phone may be miles away, but phones are generally plentiful, mobile phone coverage is good, there is Internet access all over the place, and post offices are abundant.

Telephones

Californian **telephones** are run by a huge variety of companies, many of which were hived off from the previous Bell System monopoly – the successor to which is the nationwide AT&T network.

Public telephones generally work, and – in cities at any rate – can be found nearly everywhere. They take 5¢, 10¢, and 25¢ coins. The cost of a **local call** from a public phone (generally one within the same area code) is typically 35¢–50¢; when necessary,

Telephone area codes

Central Los Angeles 213
Hollywood and inner East Los Angeles 323
West Los Angeles 310
Outer East Los Angeles and Long Beach 562
Pasadena and the San Gabriel Valley 626
Burbank and the San Fernando Valley 818
Northern Orange County 714
Southern Orange County and Newport Beach 949
San Bernardino and Riverside 909
San Diego 619
Owens Valley and Southeastern California 760

Santa Barbara and San Luis Obispo 805
Monterey, Santa Cruz, and Big Sur 831
Bakersfield and the southern San Joaquin Valley 661
Fresno and the central San Joaquin Valley 559
San Francisco and Marin County 415
East Bay and Oakland 510
The San Mateo Peninsula 650
San Jose 408
Wine Country and North Coast 707
Sacramento 916
Gold Country, Stockton, and Yosemite 209
Lake Tahoe and northeastern California 530

a voice comes on the line telling you to pay more.

Some numbers covered by the same area code are considered so far apart that calls between them count as non-local (zone calls) and cost much more. Pricier still are long-distance calls (ie to a different area code and always preceded by a 1), for which you'll need plenty of change. Non-local calls and long-distance calls are much less expensive if made between 6pm and 8am – the cheapest rates are after 11pm and at weekends – and calls from private phones are always much cheaper than those from public phones. Detailed rates are listed at the front of the telephone directory (the *White Pages*, a copious source of information on many matters).

Rates are much cheaper using **phone cards** – typically in denominations of $5, $10, and $20 – bought from general stores and some hostels. These provide you with a temporary account (just tap in the number printed on the card), and are a lot cheaper than feeding coins into a payphone, especially if calling abroad. There are many brands, some quoting long-distance rates as low as five cents a minute, but beware of the 50¢ connection fee only mentioned in the fine print. Making telephone calls from **hotel rooms** is usually more expensive than from a payphone, though many hotels offer free local calls from rooms – ask when you check in.

Many government agencies, car rental firms, hotels and so on have **toll-free numbers**, which always have the prefix ☎1-800, ☎1-888, ☎1-877, or ☎1-866. Within the US, you can dial any number starting with those digits free of charge, though some numbers only operate inside California: it isn't apparent from the number until you try. Numbers with the prefix ☎1-900 are pay-per-call lines, generally quite expensive and almost always involving either sports, phone psychics, or phone sex.

Phone numbers throughout this book are given with the area code followed by the local number: for local calls just dial the seven-digit local number; for anywhere more than a few miles away dial 1 followed by the area code and local number. For international calls dial the country's international access number, then 1 and the area and local numbers (see box, p.46).

Calling home

One of the most convenient ways of phoning home from abroad is via a **telephone charge card** from your phone company back home. Using a PIN number, you can make calls from most hotel, public, and private phones that will be charged to your account. Since most major charge cards are free to obtain, it's certainly worth getting one at least for emergencies; but bear in mind that rates aren't necessarily cheaper than calling from a public phone.

In the **US and Canada**, AT&T, MCI, Sprint, Canada Direct, and other North American long-distance companies all enable their customers to bill credit-card calls to their home number.

In **the UK and Ireland**, British Telecom (☎0800/345 144, ⊛www.chargecard.bt .com) will issue free to all BT customers the BT Charge Card, which can be used in 116 countries; AT&T (dial ☎0800/890 011, then 888/641-6123 when you hear the AT&T prompt to be transferred to the Florida Call Center; free 24 hours) has the Global Calling Card; while NTL (☎0500/100 505) issues its own Global Calling Card, which can be used in more than sixty countries abroad, though the fees cannot be charged to a normal phone bill.

To call **Australia and New Zealand** from California, telephone charge cards such as Telstra Telecard or Optus Calling Card in Australia, and Telecom NZ's Calling Card can be used to make calls, which are charged back to a domestic account or credit card. Apply to Telstra (☎1800/038 000), Optus (☎1300/300 937), or Telecom NZ (☎04/801 9000).

Useful numbers

Emergencies ☎911; ask for the appropriate emergency service: fire, police, or ambulance
Directory information ☎411
Directory inquiries for toll-free numbers ☎1-800/555-1212
Long-distance directory information ☎1-(area code)/555-1212
International operator ☎00

Calling home from California

Australia 00 + 61 + city code
Canada 1 + area code
New Zealand 00 + 64 + city code
UK and Northern Ireland 00 + 44 + city code
Republic of Ireland 00 + 353 + city code

Email and Internet access

One of the best ways to keep in touch while traveling is to sign up for a **free Internet email address** that can be accessed from anywhere, for example via YahooMail or Hotmail – accessible through ⊛www.yahoo.com and ⊛www.hotmail.com. Once you've set up an account, you can use these sites to pick up and send mail from any Internet café, or hotel with Internet access. Internet cafés are found in most towns of any size, but many travelers prefer the **free Internet access** provided by almost all public libraries. Generally, you just reserve a half-hour slot and away you go. If neither of these options fit the bill, or you just need a fast machine with assorted peripherals, then find a commercial photocopying and printing shop (look under "Copying" in the *Yellow Pages*). They'll charge around 20¢ a minute for use of their computers, but you're guaranteed fast access. Most upscale hotels also offer email and Internet access – though again at a price.

If you are traveling with a laptop and want to get connected, browse ⊛www.kropla .com, which gives details of how to plug your laptop in when abroad, phone country codes around the world, and information about electrical systems in different countries.

Mail services

Post offices are usually open Monday to Friday from 9am until 5pm, and Saturday from 9am to noon (sometimes 4pm), and there are blue **mailboxes** on many street corners. **Ordinary mail** within the US costs 37¢ for letters weighing up to an ounce; addresses must include the **zip code**, and a return address should be written in the upper left corner of the envelope. **Airmail** from California to Europe generally takes about a week. Aerograms and letters weighing up to half an ounce (a single sheet) cost 60¢, and postcards cost 55¢.

The last line of the address is made up of the city name, an abbreviation denoting the state (in California "CA") and a five-digit number – the **zip code** – denoting the local post office. Letters which don't carry the zip code are liable to get lost or at least delayed; if you don't know it, phone books carry a list for their service area or check at ⊛www.usps.com.

Letters can be sent c/o **General Delivery**

(what's known elsewhere as **poste restante**) to the one relevant post office in each city, but must include the zip code and will only be held for thirty days before being returned to sender – so make sure there's a return address on the envelope. If you're receiving mail at someone else's address, it should include "c/o" and the regular occupant's name, or it is likely to be returned.

Rules on sending **parcels** are very rigid: packages must be sealed according to the instructions given at the start of the *Yellow Pages*. To send anything out of the country, you'll need a green **customs declaration form**, available from the post office. **Postal rates** for sending a parcel weighing up to 1lb to Europe, Australia, and New Zealand are $10–11.

The media

Every major urban center in California has its own newspaper, from the politically obsessed *Sacramento Bee* to the Hollywood hype of the *Los Angeles Times*. You'll also be able to pick up *USA Today,* the moderate if rather toothless national daily, while such East Coast stalwarts as the *New York Times*, the *Washington Post*, and the *Wall Street Journal* should be available in most towns, with a slight price premium. Until recently, the *San Francisco Chronicle* was arguably the most highly regarded of California's newspapers; however, since it became embroiled in a nasty ownership spat with its major competitor, the *San Francisco Examiner*, a couple of years ago, it's rather stumbled.

As in any North American town, the best place to turn for entertainment listings – not to mention an irreverent take on local government and politics – is one of the many freesheets available on most street corners. Since nightlife venues, clubs, and bars open and close so rapidly, they're the best source of up-to-date listings available. We've noted local titles in relevant towns throughout the text; note that many have online editions, too, so you can check them out before you travel.

Television

In California, you'll have access to all the usual stations: from major networks like ABC, CBS, and NBC to smaller netlets like the WB and UPN. Expect talk shows in the morning, soaps in the afternoon, and marquee name comedies and dramas during primetime. If that's all too maddeningly commercial-heavy, there's always PBS, the rather earnest, ad-free station, which fills its schedule with news, documentaries, and imported period dramas. The precise channel numbers vary from area to area.

There's a wider choice on cable, including CNN for news and music on MTV; well-regarded premium channels like HBO and Showtime are often available on hotel TV systems, showing original series and blockbuster movies.

Radio

Listening to the radio – and how its mix of stations changes during your travels (for example, a rapid increase in Christian pop stations) – is often one of the smartest ways to gauge the character of the local area. And as the land of the roadtrip, it's not surprising that California is well served by diverse radio stations. It's best to skip most specialty stations on the AM frequency – although AM chat shows, with their often angry, confrontational callers and hosts can be hilarious and illuminating, if not in the intended sense. On FM, you'll find the usual mix of rock, Latin and R'n'B: stations are too numerous to list, although all pop-rock stations KLLC (97.3 FM, known as 'Alice') in San Francisco and KROQ (106.7 FM) in Los Angeles are especially well known. Expect commercials interrupted by an occasional tune during drive time (6–9am and 4–7pm); also note that many stations have an astonishingly limited playlist – and songs in heavy rotation will often be played half a dozen times a day.

In Southern California, you'll also often come across Mexican stations (some local, others broadcasting from over the border),

which can be enjoyable even for non-Spanish speakers.

A safe harbor if you're struggling to find satisfying local news is to tune to National Public Radio (NPR), the listener-funded talk station with a refreshingly sober take on news and chat (FM frequencies vary). To check for local frequencies for the World Service log on to the BBC, (⊛www.bbc.co.uk/worldservice), Radio Canada (⊛www.rcinet.ca), or the Voice of America (⊛www.voa.gov).

Public holidays and festivals

Someone, somewhere is always celebrating something in California, although apart from national holidays, few festivities are shared throughout the entire state. Instead, there is a disparate multitude of local events: art and craft shows, county fairs, ethnic celebrations, music festivals, rodeos, sandcastle building competitions, and many others of every hue and shade.

Among California's major annual events are the **gay and lesbian freedom** parades held in June in LA and, particularly, San Francisco; the **Academy Awards** in LA in March, and the world-class **Monterey Jazz Festival** in September. These and other local highlights are covered in the text. In addition, California tourist offices can provide full lists, or you can just phone the visitor center in a particular region ahead of your arrival and ask what's coming up.

Public holidays

The biggest and most all-American of the **national festivals and holidays** is **Independence Day** on the Fourth of July, when the entire country grinds to a standstill as people get drunk, salute the flag, and take part in firework displays, marches, beauty pageants, and more, all in commemoration of the signing of the Declaration of Independence in 1776. **Halloween** (October 31) lacks any such patriotic overtones and is not a public holiday despite being one of the most popular yearly flings. Traditionally, kids run around the streets banging on doors

demanding "trick or treat," and are given pieces of candy. These days that sort of activity is mostly confined to rural and suburban areas, while in bigger cities Halloween has grown into a massive gay celebration: in West Hollywood in LA and San Francisco's Castro district, the night is marked by mass

January 1 **New Year's Day**
January 15 **Martin Luther King Jr's Birthday**
Third Monday in February **Presidents' Day**
Varies (usually early April) **Easter Monday**
Last Monday in May **Memorial Day**
July 4 **Independence Day**
First Monday in September **Labor Day**
Second Monday in October **Columbus Day**
November 11 **Veterans' Day**
Fourth Thursday in November **Thanksgiving Day**
December 25 **Christmas Day**

cross-dressing, huge block parties, and general licentiousness. More sedate is **Thanksgiving Day**, on the last Thursday in November. The third big event of the year is essentially a domestic affair, when relatives return to the familial nest to stuff themselves with roast turkey, and (supposedly) fondly recall the first harvest of the Pilgrims in Massachusetts – though in fact Thanksgiving was already a national holiday before anyone thought to make that connection.

On the national **public holidays** listed below, banks and offices are liable to be closed all day, and shops may reduce their hours. The traditional **summer season** for tourism runs from **Memorial Day to Labor Day**, though California's benign weather extends that considerably, and the desert areas have their peak season through the winter.

Sports and outdoor pursuits

Nowhere in the country do the various forms of athletic activity and competition have a higher profile than in California. The big cities generally have at least one team in each of the major professional sports – football (though LA lost its last football team to Oakland in 1995), baseball, and basketball – as well as supporting teams in soccer, volleyball, ice hockey, wrestling, and even roller derby.

For foreign visitors, American sports can appear something of a mystery; one unusual feature is that in all the major sports the divisions are fixed, apart from the occasional expansion, so there is no fear of relegation to lower leagues. Another puzzle is the passion for **intercollegiate sports** – college and university teams, competing against one another in the Pacific-10 Conference, usually with an enthusiasm fueled by passionate local rivalries. In Los Angeles, USC and UCLA have an intense and high-powered sporting enmity, with fans on each side as vociferous as any European soccer crowd, and in the San Francisco Bay Area, the rivalry between UC Berkeley and Stanford is akin to that of Britain's Oxford and Cambridge.

And in California, where being physically fit and adventurous often appears to be a condition of state citizenship, the locals are passionate about their outdoor pursuits; the most popular include surfing, cycling, and skiing. When and where to enjoy any of California's most popular outdoor pursuits are detailed in the relevant chapters of the guide, along with listings of guides and facilities.

Football

Professional football in America attracts the most obsessive and devoted fans of any sport, perhaps because there are fewer games played – only sixteen in a season, which lasts throughout the fall and culminates in the **Super Bowl** at the end of January. With many quick skirmishes and military-like movements up and down the field, it's ideal for television, and nowhere is this more apparent than during the **televised games** which are a feature of many bars on Monday nights – though most games are played on Sunday afternoons and evenings.

The game lasts for four fifteen-minute quarters, with a fifteen-minute break at half-time. But since time is only counted when play is in progress, matches can take at least three hours to complete, mainly due to interruptions for TV advertising. Commentators will discuss the game throughout to help your comprehension, though they use such a barrage of statistics to illustrate their remarks that you may feel hopelessly confused. Not that it matters – the spectacle of American football is fun to experience, even if you haven't a clue what's going on. Players tend to be huge, averaging about six foot five and weighing upwards of three hundred pounds; they look even bigger when they're suited up for battle in shoulder pads and helmets. The best players become nationally known celebrities, raking in millions of dollars in fees for product endorsements on top of astronomical salaries.

Teams and tickets

All major teams play in the **National Football League** (NFL), the sport's governing body, which divides the teams into two conferences of equal stature, the **National Football Conference** (NFC) and the **American Football Conference** (AFC). In turn, each conference is split into four divisions, North, East, South, and West. For the end-of-season playoffs, the best team in each of the eight divisions, plus two wildcards from each conference, fight it out for the title.

The Californian teams are the Oakland Raiders, who have promised much but delivered little of late; the San Diego Chargers, on the up and up as the 2002–3 season started; and the San Francisco 49ers, who nearly always make the play-offs and have won five Super Bowls (a record shared with the Dallas Cowboys) but are currently trying to rejuvenate their team.

Tickets are usually in excess of $50 for professional games and can be very hard to come by, while college games can be as low as $5 and are more readily available – check at the respective campuses covered in the text.

Booking tickets

NFL ☎ 212/450-2000, ⊛ www.nfl.com
Oakland Raiders ☎ 510/864-5000,
⊛ www.raiders.com
San Diego Chargers ☎ 619/280-2112,
⊛ www.chargers.com
San Francisco 49ers ☎ 415/656-4900,
⊛ www.sf49ers.com

Baseball

Baseball is often called "America's pastime," though the players' strike in 1994 left its image tarnished. The lustre has more or less come back, and after the threat of

another image-shattering strike was averted at the last minute in 2002, home-run king Barry Bonds led the **San Francisco Giants** to their first World Series in thirteen years in an all-California match-up against the **Anaheim Angels**. The Angels, having never appeared in the showpiece before, came from behind to clinch the championship in the seventh game.

Games are played – 162 each season – all over the US almost every day from April to September, with the division and league championships, followed by the World Series (the final best-of-seven play-off) lasting through October. Watching a game, even if you don't understand what's going on, can be at the very least a pleasant day out, drinking beer and eating hot dogs in the bleachers (unshaded benches) beyond the outfield; tickets in this area are cheap and the crowds usually friendly and sociable.

Teams and tickets

All major league baseball teams play in either the **National League** or the **American League**, each of equal stature and split into three divisions, East, Central, and West. For the end-of-season playoffs and the World Series, the best team in each of the six divisions plus a second-place wildcard from each league fight it out for the title. The 2002 Giants v Angels World Series was unique in being the first time both league's wildcards had reached the final stage.

In addition to the Anaheim Angels and San Francisco Giants, California's other major league clubs are the **Oakland Athletics** (A's), **Los Angeles Dodgers**, and **San Diego Padres**. There are also numerous **minor league** clubs, known as **farm teams** because they supply the top clubs with talent.

Tickets for games cost $7–70 per seat, and are generally available on the day of the game.

Booking tickets

The Major Leagues ☎ 212/931-7800,
⊛ www.majorleaguebaseball.com
Anaheim Angels ☎ 1-888/796-4256,
⊛ www.angelsbaseball.com
Los Angeles Dodgers ☎ 323/224-1500,
⊛ www.dodgers.com

Oakland Athletics ☎510/638-4900,
🌐www.oaklandathletics.com
San Diego Padres ☎619/881-6500,
🌐www.padres.com
San Francisco Giants ☎415/972-2000,
🌐www.sfgiants.com

Basketball

Basketball is one of the few professional sports that is also actually played by many ordinary Americans, since all you need is a ball and a hoop. The men's professional game is governed by the **National Basketball Association** (NBA), which oversees a season running from November until the playoffs in June. It is played by athletes of phenomenal agility; seven-foot-tall giants who float through the air over a wall of equally tall defenders, seeming to change direction in mid-flight before slam-dunking the ball (smashing it through the hoop which such force that the backboard sometimes shatters) to score two points. Games last for an exhausting 48 minutes of actual playing time, around two hours total.

The women's professional game is run by the **WNBA**; the season goes through the summer.

Teams and tickets

California's professional men's basketball teams consist of the **Los Angeles Lakers**, the **Golden State Warriors** (who play in Oakland), the **Sacramento Kings**, and the **Los Angeles Clippers**. The Lakers have ruled the NBA roost in recent seasons, collecting three consecutive titles up to 2002. LA's **UCLA** once dominated the college game, winning national championships throughout the 1960s; they emerged to win again in 1995. **USC**, **UC Berkeley**, and **Stanford** also field perpetually competitive intercollegiate teams, the last being the predominant force in the Pac-10 athletic conference in recent years.

Local women's basketball teams are in LA and Sacramento; tickets (beginning at about $8) are much more reasonable.

Tickets for NBA teams

The NBA ☎212/407-8000, 🌐www.nba.com
Golden State Warriors ☎510/986-2200,

🌐www.nba.com/warriors
Los Angeles Clippers ☎310/426-6001,
🌐www.nba.com/clippers
Los Angeles Lakers ☎310/419-3100,
🌐www.nba.com/lakers
Sacramento Kings ☎916/928-0000,
🌐www.nba.com/kings

Tickets for WNBA teams

WNBA ☎212/688-9622, 🌐www.wnba.com
Los Angeles Sparks ☎310/330-2434,
🌐www.wnba.com/sparks
Sacramento Monarchs ☎916/928-3650,
🌐www.wnba.com/monarchs

Ice hockey

Despite California's sun and sand reputation, **ice hockey** enjoys considerable popularity in the state, although most of the players are imported from more traditionally hockey-centric regions in Canada, Eastern Europe, and Scandinavia. A considerable rivalry has developed over the years between players from the United States and Canada, owing largely to Canada's fear of losing their long-time claim as the world's premier hockey nation. After the overconfident US and Canadian national teams were both humiliated by the Czech Republic, Russia, and Finland in the 1998 Winter Olympics, they returned to contest the 2002 Olympic Final in Salt Lake City, and the Canadians retained North American bragging rights with a convincing win. The domestic title is the **Stanley Cup**, contested by the playoff winners of the two **NHL** (National Hockey League) conferences (Eastern and Western), each comprised of three divisions of five teams. The season runs from October to June and, amazingly for such a fast and physical sport, each team plays several times a week.

Teams and tickets

California boasts three **NHL** (National Hockey League) teams, and although none has achieved any major success, they still manage to draw considerable crowds; the **San Jose Sharks** sell out nearly every game and have started to mount a serious challenge in the new millennium, reaching the last four of the Stanley Cup in 2002. **Tickets** start at about $20.

Booking tickets

NHL ☎212/789-2000, ⓦwww.nhl.com
San Jose Sharks ☎408/287-7070,
ⓦwww.sj-sharks.com
Los Angeles Kings ☎310/419-3160,
ⓦwww.lakings.com
Anaheim Mighty Ducks ☎714/704-2700,
ⓦwww.mightyducks.com

Soccer

In the main, the traditional American sports rule, but **soccer** is quickly gaining ground, especially as a participation sport for youngsters of both sexes. At the professional level, the successful US bid to host the **1994 World Cup** led to the establishment of **Major League Soccer** (ⓦwww.mlsnet.com) in 1996. The game continues to get injections of exposure with the national men's team qualifying for the finals of the **World Cup** both times since they hosted it and surprising everyone by making a spirited run to the quarter-finals in Japan/Korea 2002, where they narrowly lost to Germany. The US women's team have done even better, beating China in a nail-biting penalty shoot-out to win the **1999 Women's World Cup** in Anaheim. President Clinton was in the stands, and the win made the headlines across the nation, assuring a high profile, which led to the inauguration in 2001 of **WUSA** (Women's United Soccer Association; ⓦwww.wusa.com), the sport's first professional league for women.

Teams and tickets

The **Los Angeles Galaxy** and **San Jose Clash** both play in the Western Conference of the MSL; having each reached the MSL Cup final, only to be beaten by DC United on both occasions, the Galaxy finally triumphed in 2002 with an overtime win versus the New England Revolution. The season runs through the summer and tickets cost $10–30.

Of the eight teams in WUSA, two are based in California: the **San Jose Cyber Rays** and the **San Diego Spirit**. Ticket prices are similar to the men's game.

Booking tickets

Los Angeles Galaxy ☎1-888/657-5425,
ⓦwww.lagalaxy.com

San Jose Clash ☎408/985-4625,
ⓦwww.clash.com
San Diego Spirit ☎619/692-9872,
ⓦwww.sandiegospirit.com
San Jose Cyber Rays ☎408/260-3900,
ⓦwww.bayareacyberrays.com

Outdoor pursuits

Surfing is probably the best-known Californian pastime, immortalized in the songs of the Beach Boys and Frankie Avalon. The Southern California coast up to San Francisco is dotted with excellent surfing beaches. Some of the finest places to catch a wave, with or without a board, are at Tourmaline Beach near San Diego, Huntington Beach and Malibu in Los Angeles, along the coast north of Santa Barbara, and at Santa Cruz – where there's a small but worthy surfing museum.

Cycling is an extremely popular outdoor pursuit, with California home to some highly competitive, world-class road races, particularly around the Wine Country. The heavy-duty, all-terrain **mountain bike** was invented here, designed to tackle the slopes of Mount Tamalpais in Marin County. Weekend enthusiasts now put their knobby tires to use on the countless trails that weave throughout California's beautiful backcountry. Special mountain bike parks, most of them operating in summer only, exploit the groomed, snow-free runs of the Sierra ski bowls of Lake Tahoe and Mammoth. In such places, and throughout California, you can rent bikes for $15–30 a day; see "Getting Around," p.36, for more on general cycling.

Skiing and **snowboarding** are also wildly popular, with downhill resorts all over eastern California – where, believe it or not, it snows heavily most winters. In fact, the Sierra Nevada mountains offer some of the best skiing in the US, particularly around Lake Tahoe, where the 1960 Winter Olympics were held (see p.684). You can rent equipment for about $25 a day, plus another $40 to $60 a day for lift tickets.

A cheaper option is **cross-country skiing**, or ski-touring. A number of backcountry ski lodges in the Sierra Nevada offer a range of rustic accommodation, equipment rental and lessons, from as little as $20 a day for skis, boots and poles, up to about $200 for an all-inclusive weekend tour.

California also has some of the world's best **rafting** rivers, the best of which cascade off the western side of the Sierra Nevada. Most rivers are highly seasonal, normally running best from mid-April to the end of June. Rivers and rapids are classed according to a grading system, ranging from a Class I, which is painstakingly easy, to a Class VI, which is literally dicing with death. Trips can be as short as a couple of hours, taking in the best a river has to offer (or just the most accessible section), or can extend up to several days, allowing more time to hike up side canyons, swim, or just laze about on the bank. You might typically expect to pay around $100 for a four- to six-hour trip, going up to $130–150 a day for longer outings, including food and camping equipment rental.

Backcountry camping, hiking, and wildlife

California's landscape is one of *the* compelling reasons for visiting the state, with some of the most fabulous backcountry and wilderness areas in the US, coated by dense forests and capped by great mountains. While there are huge areas reachable only on foot, the excellent road system makes much of it easily accessible, aided by well-equipped and beautiful campgrounds right where you need them.

Unfortunately, it isn't all as wild as it once was, and the more popular areas can get pretty crowded. If you're thinking of joining the throngs, you can help preserve the special qualities of the environment by observing a few simple rules. For practical information on traveling through the deserts, see the box on p.254.

The US's protected backcountry areas fall into a number of potentially confusing categories. Most numerous are California **state parks** (@www.parks.ca.gov), which include state beaches, state historic parks, and state recreational areas, often around sites of geological or historical importance and not necessarily in rural areas. Daily fees (halved by Governor Davis in 2000) are usually $24, though a $35 **annual pass** (available at most parks and through @www.store.parks.co.gov) gives free access to most sites for a year.

National parks – such as Yosemite, Death Valley, and Joshua Tree – are large, federally controlled, and preserved areas of great natural beauty comprising several different features or ecosystems; entry fees are generally $10 per car (valid seven days), though Yosemite costs $20. These are supple-mented by the smaller **national monuments** (free to $5), like Devil's Postpile, with just one major feature, and **national seashores**. If you plan on visiting a few of these, invest in a **National Parks Pass** ($50 from any national park entrance), which grants both driver and passengers (or if cycling or hiking, the holder's immediate family) twelve months' access to all the national parks across the country. The **Golden Eagle Pass** ($65) additionally provides nationwide access to national monuments, historic sites, recreation areas, and wildlife refuges, though as few of these charge a significant entry fee it is usually better to buy the National Parks Pass and upgrade (for $15) if needed.

Excellent free **ranger programs** – such as guided walks, slide shows, and campfire talks – are held throughout the year. The federal government also operates **national recreation areas**, often huge hydro dams where you can jetski or windsurf free of the necessarily restrictive laws of the national parks. Campgrounds and equipment-rental outlets are always abundant.

California's eighteen **national forests** cover twenty percent of the state's surface area.

You're likely to meet many kinds of **wildlife** and come upon unexpected **hazards** on your travels through the wilderness, but only a few are likely to cause problems. With due care, many potential difficulties can be avoided.

Hiking in the **foothills** should not be problematic, but you should check your clothes frequently for **ticks** – pesky bloodsucking burrowing insects that are known to carry Lyme disease. If you have been bitten, and especially if you get flu-like symptoms, get advice from a park ranger. Also annoying around water are **mosquitos**; carry insect repellent or candles scented with citronella to keep them at bay.

Other than in a national park, you're highly unlikely to encounter a **bear**. Even there, it's rare to stumble across one in the wilderness, and if you do it will be a black bear – the last California grizzly was shot in 1922. To reduce the likelihood of an unwanted encounter, make noise as you walk. If you see a bear before it detects you (they've got poor eyesight but an acute sense of smell), give it a wide berth; but if a bear visits your camp, scare it off by yelling and banging pots and pans. Basically, the bear isn't interested in you but in your food, and you should do everything you safely can to prevent them from getting it – bears who successfully raid campsites can become dependent on human food. Bears within state and national parks are protected, but if they spend too much time around people the park rangers are, depressingly, left with no option but to shoot them. Some campgrounds are equipped with steel **bear lockers**, which you are obliged to use for storing food when not preparing or eating it. In the backcountry, you are strongly advised to store food in your pack within a hard plastic **bear-resistant food canister**. These can be purchased ($75–85) or rented (usually $3 a day, but sometimes $3 per trip) from camp stores in Yosemite, Kings Canyon, and Sequoia national parks. The alternatives are far inferior. Hanging food in a tree is a disaster, as Sierra bears simply chew through the supporting rope. The recommended variation is the **counterbalance method** (where food is balanced over a high tree branch in two equally weighted sacks on the opposite ends of a rope – see park literature for more information), but your chances of finding a suitable tree after a long day's hike are slim. Finally, never feed a bear or get between a mother and her cubs. Cubs are cute; irate mothers are not.

Rattlesnakes, which live in the desert areas and drier foothills up to around 6000ft, seldom attack unless provoked: do not tease or try to handle them. Rattlesnake bites are rarely fatal, but you might suffer severe tissue damage (see p.255 for advice on what to do if bitten).

Mountain lions (aka cougars, panthers, or pumas) are being hard hit by increasing urban expansion into former habitats (from deserts to coastal and sub-alpine forests). Sightings are rare in the newly suburbanized areas, and there

Most of them border the national parks, and are also federally administered (by the US Forest Service), but with much less protection. More roads run through national forests, and often there is some limited logging and other land-based industry operated on a supposedly sustainable basis.

All the above forms of protected land can contain **wilderness areas**, which aim to protect natural resources in their most native state. In practice, this means there's no commercial activity at all; buildings, motor-ized vehicles, and bicycles are not permitted, nor are firearms or pets. Overnight camping is allowed, but **wilderness permits** (usually free, though there's often a booking fee for advance reservations) must be obtained from the land management agency responsible. In California, Lava Beds, Lassen, Death Valley, Sequoia-Kings Canyon, Joshua Tree, Pinnacles, Point Reyes, and Yosemite all have large wilderness areas – 94 percent of Yosemite, for example – with only the regions near roads, visitor centers, have been few attacks on pedestrians. But to reduce the already slim chance of an unwanted encounter, avoid walking by yourself, especially after dark, when lions tend to hunt. Make noise as you walk, wield a stick, and keep children close to you. If you encounter one, don't run. Instead, face the lion and make yourself appear larger by raising your arms, or holding your coat above you, and it will probably back away. If not, throw rocks and sticks in its vicinity. If it attacks, fight back. Its normal prey doesn't do this and it will probably flee.

Campground critters – ground squirrels, chipmunks, and racoons – are usually just a nuisance, though they tend to carry diseases and you should avoid contact. Only the marmot is a real pest, as it likes to chew through radiator hoses and car electrics to reach a warm engine on a cold night. Before setting off in the morning from high-country trailheads, check the motor for gnawed components, otherwise you might find yourself with a seized engine and a cooked or, at best, terrified marmot as a passenger. Boots and rucksacks also can fall prey to marmot scrutiny.

Poison oak is one thing that isn't going to come and get you, though you may come up against it. Recognized by its shiny configuration of three dark-green-veined leaves (turning red or yellow in the fall) that secrete an oily juice, this twiggy shrub or climbing vine is found in open woods or along stream banks throughout much of California. It's highly allergenic, so avoid touching it. If you do, washing with strong soap, taking frequent dips in the sea, and applying cortisone cream usually helps relieve the symptoms in mild cases; in extreme cases, see a doctor.

In the mountains, your biggest dangers have nothing to do with the flora or fauna. Late **snows** are common, giving rise to the possibility of avalanches and meltwaters, which make otherwise simple stream crossings hazardous. **Drowning** in fast-flowing meltwater rivers is the single biggest cause of death in the Kings Canyon and Sequoia national parks. The riverbanks are strewn with large, slippery boulders – keep well clear unless you are specifically there for river activities.

With much of the High Sierra above 10,000ft, **Acute Mountain Sickness** (aka altitude sickness) is always a possibility. Only those planning to bag one of the 14,000-foot peaks are likely to have to contend with much more than a slight headache, but it pays to be on the alert and to acclimatize slowly. Try to limit your exertions for the first day or so, drink plenty of fluids, eat little and often, and note any nausea, headaches, or double vision. If you experience any of these symptoms, the only solution is to descend until they ease, then ascend more gradually.

For more on the hazards of snakes and spiders, see Chapter Three, p.255, and for more on Californian wildlife generally, see p.806 of Contexts.

and buildings designated as less stringently regulated "front country."

Camping

When **camping rough**, check that fires are permitted before you start one; if they are, use a stove in preference to local materials – in some places firewood is scarce, although you may be allowed to use deadwood. No open fires are allowed in wilderness areas, where you should also try to camp on previously used sites. Where there are no toilets,

bury human waste at least four inches into the ground and a hundred feet from the nearest water supply and camp. Always **pack out what you pack in** (or more if you come across some other inconsiderate soul's litter), and avoid the old advice to burn rubbish; wildfires have been started in this way. A growing problem is giardia, a water-borne protozoan causing an intestinal disease, symptoms of which are chronic diarrhea, abdominal cramps, fatigue, and loss of weight. To avoid catching it, **never**

B

drink directly from rivers and streams, no matter how clear and inviting they may look (you never know what unspeakable acts people – or animals – further upstream have performed in them). **Water** should be boiled for at least five minutes, or cleansed with an iodine-based purifier (such as Potable Aqua) or a giardia-rated filter, available from camping and sports shops.

Finally, don't use **soaps or detergents** (even special ecological or biodegradable soaps) anywhere near lakes and streams; people using water purifiers or filters downstream won't thank you at all. Instead carry water at least a hundred feet (preferably two hundred) from the water's edge before washing.

Camping equipment

Choose your tent wisely. Many Sierra sites are on rock with only a thin covering of soil, so driving pegs in can be a problem; free-standing dome-style tents are therefore preferable. Go for one with a large area of mosquito netting and a removable fly sheet: tents designed for harsh European winters can get horribly sweaty once the California sun rises.

Most developed campgrounds are equipped with fire rings with some form of grill for cooking, but many people prefer a **Coleman stove**, powered by white gas (a kind of super-clean gasoline). Both stoves and white gas (also used for MSR backcountry stoves) are widely available in camping stores. Other camping stoves are less common. Equipment using butane and propane – Camping Gaz and, to a lesser extent, EPI gas, Scorpion and Optimus – is on the rise, though outside of major camping areas you'll be pushed to find supplies: stock up when you can. If you need methylated spirits for your Trangia, go to a hardware store and ask for denatured alcohol.

Hiking

No special permits are required for **day hikes**. Simply front up at the trailhead of your choice with the appropriate gear – map, raincoat, comfortable boots, etc – and head off into the wilderness. **Overnight trips** require **wilderness permits** (see above), which operate on a quota system in popular areas in peak periods. If there's a hike you specifically want to take, obtain your permit well ahead of time (at least two weeks, more for popular hikes). When completing the form for your permit, be sure to ask a park ranger for weather conditions and general information about the hike you're undertaking.

Hikes covered in the guide (usually appearing in boxes) are given with length and estimated walking time for a healthy, but not especially fit, adult. **State parks** have graded trails designed for people who drive to the corner store, so anyone used to walking and with a moderate degree of fitness will find their ratings conservative.

In California, the **Sierra Club** (85 2nd St, 2nd Floor, San Francisco, CA 94105-3441 ☎415/ 977-5500, ⓦ www.sierraclub.org) offers a range of backcountry hikes into otherwise barely accessible parts of the High Sierra wilderness, with food and guide provided. The tours are mostly in the summer, and are heavily subscribed, making it essential to book at least three months in advance: check the website for availability and to make reservations. You can expect to pay $400–600 for seven to ten days and will also have to pay $39 to join the club.

Crime and personal safety

No one can pretend California is trouble free, although away from the urban centers, crime is often remarkably low key. Even the lawless reputation of Los Angeles is far in excess of the truth, and most of the city, by day at least, is fairly safe; at night, though, a few areas – notably Compton, Inglewood, and East LA – are completely off limits. Members of the notorious LA gangs are a rare sight outside their own territories (which are usually well away from where you're likely to be), and they tend to kill each other rather than tourists. By being careful, planning ahead, and taking care of your possessions, you should have few real problems.

Mugging and theft

The biggest problem for most travelers is the threat of **mugging**. It's impossible to give hard and fast rules about what to do if you're confronted by a mugger. Whether to run, scream, or fight depends on the situation – but most locals would just hand over their money.

Of course, the best thing is simply to avoid being mugged, and a few obvious **basic rules** are worth remembering. Don't flash money around; don't peer at your map (or this book) at every street corner, thereby announcing that you're a lost stranger; even if you're terrified or drunk (or both), try not to appear so. Avoid dark streets, especially ones you can't see the end of; and in the early hours, stick to the roadside edge of the pavement so it's easier to run into the road to attract attention. If you have to ask for directions, choose your target carefully. Another idea is to carry a wad of cash, perhaps $50 or so, separate from the bulk of your holdings so that if you do get confronted you can hand over something of value without it costing you everything.

If the worst happens and your assailant is toting a gun or (more likely) a knife, try to stay calm: remember that he (for this is generally a male pursuit) is probably scared too. Keep still, don't make any sudden movements – and hand over your money. When he's gone, you should, despite your shock, try to find a phone and dial ☏**911**, or head to the nearest police station. Here, report the theft and get a reference number on the report to claim insurance and travelers' check refunds. If you're in a big city, ring the local Travelers Aid (their numbers are listed in the phone book) for sympathy and practical advice. For specific advice for women in case of mugging or attack, see p.65.

Another potential source of trouble is having your **hotel room burglarized**. Always store valuables in the hotel safe when you go out; when inside, keep your door locked and don't open it to anyone you don't trust. If they claim to be hotel staff and you don't believe them, call reception to check.

Stolen travelers' checks and credit cards

Keep a record of the numbers of your **travelers' checks** separately from the actual checks; if you lose them, ring the issuing company on the toll-free number below.

They'll ask you for the check numbers, the place you bought them, when and how you lost them, and whether it's been reported to the police. All being well, you should get the missing checks reissued within a couple of days – and perhaps an emergency advance to tide you over.

Emergency numbers and websites

American Express (TCs) ☏1-800/221-7282; (credit cards) ☏1-800/528-4800;
🌐www.travel.americanexpress.com
Citicorp ☏1-800/645-6556,
🌐www.citibank.com
Diner's club ☏1-800/234-6377,
🌐www.dinersclub.com
MasterCard ☏1-800/307-7309,
🌐www.mastercard.com
Thomas Cook ☏1-800/223-7373,
🌐www.us.thomascook.com
Visa ☏1-800/227-6811; 🌐www.visa.com

Car crime

Crimes committed against tourists driving **rental cars** in the US have garnered headlines around the world in recent years. In major urbanized areas, any car you rent should have nothing on it – such as a particular license plate – that makes it easy to spot as a rental car. When driving, under no circumstances stop in any unlit or seemingly deserted urban area – and especially not if someone is waving you down and suggesting that there is something wrong with your car. Similarly, if you are "accidentally" rammed by the driver behind you, do not stop immediately but drive on to the nearest well-lit, busy area and **phone ☏911** for assistance. Keep your doors locked and windows never more than slightly open. Do not open your door or window if someone approaches your car on the pretext of asking directions. Hide any valuables out of sight, preferably locked in the trunk or in the glove compartment (any valuables you don't need for your journey should be left in your hotel safe).

Living and working in California

Gone are the days when foreigners might snag an illicit summer job in the Californian sun without a problem: immigration laws (and the penalties for breaking them) have sharpened recently, especially since the terrorist attacks of September 11, 2001. The following suggestions for finding work are basic and, if you're not a US citizen, represent the limit of what you can do unless you have a social security number, which is technically essential for any kind of legal employment.

Recent increases in the fines for employing illegal workers (now $10,000) have lessened the appeal of illegal labor to bar and restaurant owners. If you do manage to get hired, you're more likely than ever to be hidden out of sight, in lower paid jobs (think dishwasher rather than waiter). The one exception, where papers are rarely checked, is in the agricultural industry: California's vast farms are always in need of fresh, fit labor and it's worth dropping in if you see a harvest in progress. Although this kind of work may seem initially appealing, think carefully before you take it on: most farms are miles from major centers, and the long hours in scorching weather are grueling. In return for the back-breaking work, though, expect surprisingly good wages and often bed and board as well.

Useful publications and websites

Another pre-planning strategy for working abroad is to get hold of *Overseas Jobs* *Express* (Premier House, Shoreham Airport, Sussex BN43 5FF; ☏01273/699 611, ⓦwww.overseasjobs.com), a fortnightly publication with a range of job vacancies, available by subscription only. Vacation Work also publishes books on summer jobs abroad and how to work your way around the world; call ☏01865/241 978 or visit ⓦwww.vacationwork.co.uk for their catalogue. Travel magazines like the reliable *Wanderlust* (every two months; £2.80) have a Job Shop section that often advertises job opportunities with tour companies. ⓦwww.studyabroad.com is a useful website with listings and links to study and work programs worldwide.

Au pair work

For young women (in most cases) working as an **au pair** is a viable option. Applicants for au pair visas to the US who will be looking after babies under two will have to prove that they have at least 200 hours' experience with infants, 24 hours' training in child development, and 8 hours' child safety training. Applicants will also have to undergo testing to provide a personality profile. The prospective employers must provide a written description of the job they expect their au pair to perform, so there is protection on both sides. Au Pair in America (see below) can arrange visas and placements.

Study and work programs

From the UK and Ireland

British Council 10 Spring Gardens, London SW1A 2BN ☎020/7930 8466. Produce a free leaflet that details study opportunities abroad. The Council's Central Management Direct Teaching (☎020/7389 4931) recruits TEFL teachers for posts worldwide (check ⊛www.britishcouncil.org /work/jobs for a current list of vacancies), and its Central Bureau for International Education and Training (☎020/7389 4004, publications ☎020/ 7389 4880, ⊛www.centralbureau.org.uk) enables those who already work as educators to find out about teacher development programs abroad.
BTCV 36 St Mary's St, Wallingford, Oxon OX10 0EU ☎01491/839 766, ⊛www.btcv.org.uk. One of the largest environmental charities in Britain, with branches across the country, also has a programme of national and international working holidays (as a paying volunteer), ranging from dry-stone walling in Japan to turtle monitoring in Turkey; comprehensive brochure available.
BUNAC (British Universities' North America Club) 16 Bowling Green Lane, London EC1R 0QH ☎020/7251 3472, ⊛www.bunac.org. Organizes working holidays in the US for students, typically at summer camps or training placements with companies.
Camp America/Au Pair in America 37 Queen's Gate, London SW7 5HR. Camps ☎020/7581 7373, ⊛www.campamerica.co.uk; au pairs ☎020/7581 7311, ⊛www.aupairamerica.co.uk. The Camp America scheme is similar to that of Camp Counselors USA (see below). The Au Pair scheme is open to both men and women aged 18–26, though women are mostly preferred. There is a placement fee of £40, a £67 contribution towards insurance, and a good faith deposit of £268; the combined amount includes the interviewing and selection process, visa (covering you for 13 months, 12 months working plus optional one month travel at the end), and flight to the US.
Camp Counselors USA Green Dragon House,

64–70 High St, Croydon CR0 9XN ☎020/8688 9051, ⊛www.campcounselors.com. Volunteer summer work (9 weeks from any time in June) for over-18s; you need to have experience with children (except for support staff, who must be full-time students) and be a specialist in an area like arts and crafts, drama, or sports. Also runs a work experience program (see below).
Council Exchange 52 Poland St, London W1F 7AB ☎020/7478 2000. International study and work programs for students and recent graduates; notably recruits for Internship USA.
Earthwatch Institute 57 Woodstock Rd, Oxford OX2 6HJ ☎01865/311 600, ⊛www.earthwatch.org. Long-established international charity with environmental and archeological research projects worldwide (130 projects in around 55 countries). Participation mainly as a paying volunteer but fellowships for teachers and students available.
Field Studies Council Overseas (FSCO) Montford Bridge, Shrewsbury SY4 1HW ☎01743/852 150, ⊛www.fscoverseas.org.uk. Respected educational charity with over 20 years' experience of organizing specialized holidays with study tours visits worldwide. Group size is generally limited to 10–15 people. *Overseas Experiences* brochure available.
Work Experience USA Green Dragon House, 64–70 High St, Croydon CR0 9XN ☎020/8688 9051, ⊛www.campcounselors.com. For full-time students only, a chance to live and work in a regular job in the US. £695 covers flights, insurance, guaranteed job offer, orientation, and help with tax forms and other paper work. Minimum 10 weeks, maximum 4 months, plus one month's travel. They also offer a scheme as above but you find your own job in the USA for £595 – check the website for details.

From Australia and New Zealand

Australian Volunteers International 71 Argyle St, Fitzroy, Melbourne ☎03/9279 1788, ⊛www.ozvol.org.au. Postings for up to 2 years in developing countries.
Australians Studying Abroad 1/970 High St, Armadale, Melbourne ☎1800/645 755 or 03/9509 1955, ⊛www.asatravinfo.com.au. Study tours focusing on art and culture.
Council on International Educational Exchange 91 York St, Level 3, Sydney ☎1300/135 331 or 02/8235 7000, ⊛www.councilexchanges.org.au, ⓔinfo@councilexchanges.org.au. International student exchange programs.

Travelers with disabilities

Travelers with mobility problems or other physical disabilities are likely to find California – as with the US in general – to be much more in tune with their needs than anywhere else in the world. All public buildings must be wheelchair-accessible and have suitable toilets; most city street corners have dropped curbs; subways have elevators, and most city buses are able to kneel to make access easier and are built with space and handgrips for wheelchair users. Most hotels, restaurants, and theaters (certainly any built in the last ten years or so) have excellent wheelchair access.

Getting to and from California

Most airlines, transatlantic and within the US, do whatever they can to ease your journey, and will usually let attendants of people with serious disabilities accompany them at no extra charge. The Air Carriers Access Act of 1986 obliged all domestic air carriers to make the majority of their services accessible to travelers with disabilities.

Almost every **Amtrak train** includes one or more coaches with accommodation for disabled passengers. Guide dogs travel free, and Amtrak will provide wheelchair assistance at its train stations, adapted seating on board, and a fifteen percent discount on the regular fare, all provided 24 hours' notice is given. Passengers with hearing impairment can get information on ☎1-800/523-6590.

Traveling by **Greyhound** and **Amtrak Thruway** buses, however, is not to be recommended. Buses are not equipped with lifts for wheelchairs, though staff will assist with boarding (intercity carriers are required by law to do this), and the "Helping Hand" scheme offers two-for-the-price-of-one tickets to passengers unable to travel alone (carry a doctor's certificate). For assistance on Greyhound, call ☎1-800/752-4841 at least 48 hours before you intend to travel.

The major **car rental** firms can, given sufficient notice, provide vehicles with hand controls (though these are usually only available on the more expensive models, and you'll need to reserve well in advance). The American Automobile Association (see p.30) produces the *Handicapped Driver's Mobility Guide* for **drivers with disabilities** (available

free from AAA, Traffic Safety Dept, 150 Van Ness Ave, San Francisco, CA 94102; ☎415/565-2012). There are no longer differences in state **parking regulations** for disabled motorists; the Department of Transportation has decreed that all state licenses issued to disabled persons must carry a three-inch square international access symbol, and each state must provide placards bearing this symbol to be hung from the rear-view mirror – the placards are blue for permanent disabilities, red for temporary (maximum of six months). More information can be obtained from state motor vehicle offices.

As in other parts of the world, the rise of the **self-service gas station** is unwelcome for many disabled drivers. The state of California has addressed this by changing its laws so that most service stations are required to provide full service to disabled drivers at self-service prices.

Information

The California Office of Tourism's free *California State Visitor's Guide* (available at ⌾www.gocalif.ca.gov) lists handicapped facilities at places of accommodation and attractions. The *San Francisco Lodging Guide* (free from the San Francisco CVB, 900 Market St, San Francisco, CA 94103 ☎415/391-2000, ⌾www.sfvisitor.org) lists many wheelchair-accessible properties – hotels, motels, apartments, B&Bs, hostels, RV parks – in the city and surrounding counties; as always, travelers should call to confirm details. The Center for Independent Living, 2539 Telegraph Ave in Berkeley

(☎510/841-4776, ☻www.cilberkeley.org) has long been one of the most effective organizations for people with disabilities in the world; it has a variety of counseling services.

National organizations facilitating travel for people with disabilities include SATH, the Society for the Advancement of Travelers with Handicaps (347 Fifth Ave, Suite 610, New York, NY 10016 ☎212/447-7284, ☻www.sath.org), a nonprofit travel-industry grouping which includes travel agents, tour operators, hotel and airline management for people with disabilities. They will pass on any inquiry to the appropriate member; allow plenty of time for a response. Mobility International USA (PO Box 10767, Eugene, OR 97440 ☎541/343-1284, ☻www.miusa .org) answers transportation queries and operates an exchange program for people with disabilities.

Other useful resources are *Travel for the Disabled*, *Wheelchair Vagabond*, and *Directory for Travel Agencies for the Disabled*, all produced by **Twin Peaks Press**, PO Box 129, Vancouver, WA 98666 (☎360/694-2462 or 1-800/637-2256). Information-packed websites include Access-Able at ☻www .access-able.com and Accessible San Diego at ☻www.accessandiego.org.

Accommodation

The big motel and hotel chains are often the safest bet for accessible **accommodation**; there are plenty of excellent local alternatives, of course, but with a chain at least you'll know what to expect. At the higher end of the scale, *Embassy Suites* (☎1-800/362-2779, voice; 1-800/458-4708, TDD; ☻www.embassysuites.com) have been working to implement new standards of access which meet and exceed ADA requirements, involving both new construction and the retrofitting of their one hundred existing hotels, and providing special training to all employees. Although the president of **Hyatt International Corporation** (☎1-800/233-1234, ☻www.hyatt.com) summed up the hotel industry's initial reaction to the ADA as "the end of the world as we know it," Hyatt has also committed itself to extensive redesign to improve accessibility.

The great outdoors

Citizens or permanent residents of the US who have been "medically determined to be blind or permanently disabled" can obtain the **Golden Access Passport**, a free lifetime entrance pass to those federally operated parks, monuments, historic sites, recreation areas, and wildlife refuges which charge entrance fees. The pass must be picked up in person, from the areas described, and it also provides a fifty percent discount on fees charged for facilities such as camping, boat launching, and parking. The **Golden Bear Pass** (free to the disabled) offers similar concessions to state-run parks, beaches, and historic sites.

For visitors to **national and state parks** the somewhat outdated *California Parks Access: A Complete Guide to the State and National Parks for Visitors With Limited Mobility* (Cougar Pass Pub Co) is a great buy, with detailed descriptions of trails, sights, and their access limitations.

Yosemite National Park (PO Box 577, Yosemite, CA 95389, ☎209/372-0200, voice; 209/372-4726, TDD; ☻www.nps.gov /yose) can supply general information direct, and wheelchairs are available to rent at the medical clinic (☎209/372-4637).

The **state parks** service also offers reduced rates for permanently disabled people who apply by mail for a Disabled Discount Pass ($3.50 once-only payment) to the California State Parks Store, PO Box 942896 Sacramento, CA 94296 (☎916 /653-4000). The pass gives a fifty percent discount on all parking and camping fees above $3, except at Hearst Castle.

Packages

Many US **tour companies** cater for disabled travelers or specialize in organizing disabled group tours. State tourist departments should be able to provide lists of such companies; failing that, ask the National Tour Association, 546 E Main St, PO Box 3071, Lexington, KY 40596 (☎606/226-4444 or 1-800/755-8687, ☻www.ntaonline.com). They can put you in touch with operators whose tours match your needs.

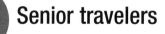

Senior travelers

The greatest advantage most retired people have over other travelers is date flexibility: off- and shoulder-season rates in hotels can be significantly lower than peak rates; there may even be senior-specific discounts. Winter is often a cheap, choice time to visit the Californian coast, since that's when it's least susceptible to chilling morning fogs. As for travel, Amtrak, Greyhound, and many US airlines offer percentage discounts to anyone who can produce ID that proves they're over 62: don't expect hefty price breaks, but it's always worth checking. Museums and art galleries are better, and most will charge a reduced student/seniors rate, often to those 55 or older.

Any US citizen or permanent resident aged 62 or over is entitled to free admission for life to all national parks, monuments, and historic sites, using a Golden Age Passport, for which a once-only $10 fee is charged; it can be issued at any such site. This free entry also applies to any accompanying car passengers, or for those hiking or cycling, the passport holder's immediate family. It also gives a 50 percent reduction on fees for camping, parking, and boat launching.

Contacts and resources

American Association of Retired Persons 601 E St NW, Washington, DC 20049 ☎202/434-2277 or 1-800/424-3410, ⊛www.aarp.org. AARP can provide discounts on accommodation and vehicle rental. Membership open to US and Canadian residents aged 50 or over for an annual fee of US $10 or $27 for three years. Canadian residents only have the annual option.

Elderhostel 75 Federal St, Boston, MA 02110 ☎1/877-426-8056, ⊛www.elderhostel.com. Runs an extensive worldwide network of educational and activity programs, cruises, and homestays for people over 60 (companions may be younger). Programs generally last a week or more and costs are in line with those of commercial tours.

Saga Holidays 222 Berkeley St, Boston, MA 02116 ☎1-877/265-6862, ⊛www.sagaholidays .com. Specializes in worldwide group travel for seniors, with a few domestic trips. Saga's Road Scholar coach tours and their Smithsonian Odyssey Tours to US parks have a more educational slant.

Traveling with children

There's plenty to occupy kids in California, from Disneyland in Los Angeles to the miles of beach coastline, so you're unlikely to encounter major problems when traveling as a family.

Hotels and motels will usually allow kids under a certain age (14, or sometimes 18) to stay free in the same room as their parents; most will add extra cots at nominal charges. Restaurants are equally amenable with children's menus and play areas. Museums and attractions should offer discounts for kids, or even family packages; many towns have children's museums, too, and we've listed the pick of sights in appropriate places in the text.

Contact the California State Tourist Office (see above) for excellent, free brochures that can answer most questions. Specific guide-books for those traveling with children include the *Unofficial Guide to California* ($17) and *Trouble-free with Children* ($9); there are guides in the *Kidding Around* series for San Francisco and Los Angeles.

Getting around

When flying, children under 2 are normally carried free – although don't expect a sepa-rate seat for them as they'll have to travel on your lap. Standard practice for airlines is to charge half-price for kids under 12.

However, once they arrive here, most peo-ple opt to get around by car. If that's your plan, check with the rental company in advance about car seats – they're usually available for around $4–5 extra per day; if not, you'll have to bring your own. Otherwise, be aware that distances in California are large, so journeys can be tedious for younger kids. Bring plenty of sen-sible snacks and games, and make regular rest stops; don't travel through major cities during rush hour and be realistic about the distance you can cover in a day (it's best to plan to arrive at your destination well before sunset). Older kids will sometimes enjoy playing "navigator" for the driver – which is not only useful, but a way to help them understand the time and distance until arrival and keep complaints to a minimum.

Contacts for travelers with children

Families Welcome 92 N Main St, Ashland, OR 97520 ☎ 541/482-6121 or 1-800/326-0724. Vacations for parents and kids.
Rascals in Paradise 2107 Van Ness Ave, Suite 403, San Francisco, CA 94109 ☎ 415/921-7000 or 1-800/872-7225, ⊛ www.rascalsinparadise.com. Can arrange scheduled and customized itineraries built around activities for kids.
Travel With Your Children 40 Fifth Ave, New York, NY 10011 ☎ 212/477 5524 or 1-888/822-4388. Publishes a regular newsletter, *Family Travel Times* (⊛ www.familytraveltimes.com), as well as a series of books on travel with children including *Great Adventure Vacations with Your Kids.*

Gay and lesbian travelers

California's easy-going attitude is evident in its vibrant gay and lesbian scene. The heart of gay California (and, arguably, of gay America) is San Francisco, which has been almost synonymous with gay life since World War II, when sus-pected homosexuals, purged by the military at their point of embarkation, stayed put rather than going home to face stigma and shame. This, and the advent of gay liberation in the early 1970s, nurtured a gay community with powerful politi-cal and social connections.

San Francisco's gay, lesbian, bisexual, and transgender scene is easy to find; but there are also strong communities in Los Angeles, centered in West Hollywood, Palm Springs, and Santa Cruz, which has become some-thing of a lesbian mecca in recent years. Be aware, though, that outside major urban centers and particularly in the deserts of interior California, attitudes may be more conservative and openness about your sex-uality may provoke uneasiness from locals.

For a complete rundown on local resources, bars, and clubs, see the relevant headings in individual cities.

Contacts for gay and lesbian travelers

In the US and Canada

Damron Company PO Box 422458, San Francisco, CA 94142 ☎ 1-800/462-6654 or

415/255-0404, ⓦ www.damron.com. Publisher of the *Men's Travel Guide*, a pocket-sized yearbook full of listings of hotels, bars, clubs, and resources for gay men; the *Women's Traveler*, which provides similar listings for lesbians; the *Road Atlas*, which shows lodging and entertainment in major US cities; and *Damron Accommodations*, which provides detailed listings of over 1000 accommodations for gays and lesbians worldwide.

Gayellow Pages PO Box 533, Village Station, New York, NY 10014 ☎ 212/674-0120, ⓦ www.gayellowpages.com. Useful directory of businesses in the US and Canada.

International Gay & Lesbian Travel Association 4331 N Federal Hwy, Suite 304, Fort Lauderdale, FL 33308 ☎ 954/776-2626 or 1-800/448-8550, ⓦ www.iglta.org. Trade group that can provide a list of gay- and lesbian-owned or -friendly travel agents, accommodation, and other travel businesses.

In the UK

Dream Waves Redcot High St, Child Okeford, Blandford DT22 8ET ☎ 01258/861 149, ⓔ dreamwaves@aol.com. Specializes in exclusively gay holidays, including skiing trips and summer sun packages.

Madison Travel 118 Western Rd, Hove, East Sussex NN3 1DB ☎ 01273/202 532, ⓦ www.madisontravel.co.uk. Established travel

agents specializing in packages to gay- and lesbian-friendly mainstream destinations, and also to gay/lesbian destinations.

ⓦ **www.gaytravel.co.uk** Online gay and lesbian travel agent, offering good deals on all types of holiday. Also lists gay- and lesbian-friendly hotels around the world.

In Australia and New Zealand

Gay and Lesbian Travel ⓦ www.galta.com.au. Directory and links for gay and lesbian travel in Australia and worldwide.

Gay Travel ⓦ www.gaytravel.com. The site for trip planning, bookings, and general information about international travel.

Parkside Travel 70 Glen Osmond Rd, Parkside, SA 5063 ☎ 08/8274 1222, ⓔ parkside @herveyworld.com.au. Gay travel agent associated with local branch of Hervey World Travel; all aspects of gay and lesbian travel worldwide.

Silke's Travel 263 Oxford St, Darlinghurst, NSW 2010 ☎ 02/8347 2000 or 1800/807 860, ⓦ www.silkes.com.au. Long-established gay and lesbian specialist, with the emphasis on women's travel.

Tearaway Travel 52 Porter St, Prahan, VIC 3181 ☎ 03/9510 6644, ⓦ www.tearaway.com. Gay-specific business dealing with international and domestic travel.

Women travelers

Practically speaking, though a woman traveling alone is certainly not the attention-grabbing spectacle in California that she might be elsewhere in the world (or even elsewhere in the US), you're likely to come across some sort of harassment. More serious than the odd offensive comment, rape statistics in the US are high, and it goes without saying that, even more than anyone else, women should never hitchhike alone – this is widely interpreted as an invitation for trouble, and there's no shortage of weirdos to give it. Similarly, if you have a car, be careful whom you pick up: just because you're in the driver's seat doesn't mean you're safe. If you can, avoid traveling at night by public transportation – deserted bus stations, while not necessarily threatening, will do little to make you feel secure, and where possible you should team up with another woman. On Greyhound buses, follow the example of other women traveling alone and sit as near to the front – and the driver – as possible.

Californian **cities**, especially San Francisco, can feel surprisingly safe, and **muggings** are an uncommon occurrence. But as with anywhere, particular care has to be taken at night, and a modicum of common sense can often avert disasters. Walking through unlit, empty streets is never a good idea, and you should take cabs wherever possible. The advice that women who look confident tend not to encounter trouble is, like all home truths, grounded in fact but not written in stone; those who stand around looking lost and a bit scared are prime targets, but nobody is immune. Provided you listen to advice, though, and stick to the better parts of a town, going into **bars** and **clubs** alone should pose no problems, especially in San Francisco and LA, where there's generally a pretty healthy attitude towards women who choose to do so and whose privacy will be respected. Only extremely unevolved specimens will assume you're available. If in doubt, gay and lesbian bars are usually a trouble-free alternative.

Small towns in rural areas are not blessed with the same liberal attitudes toward lone women travelers that you'll find in the cities.

If you have a **vehicle breakdown** in a country area, walk to the nearest house or town for help; don't wait by the vehicle in the middle of nowhere hoping for somebody to stop – they will, but it may not be the kind of help you're looking for. Should disaster strike, all major towns have some kind of rape counseling service available; if not, the local sheriff's office will make adequate arrangements for you to get help, counseling, and, if necessary, get you home.

The National Organization for Women (@www.now.org) is a women's issues group whose lobbying has done much to affect positive social legislation. NOW branches, listed in local phone directories and on their website, can provide referrals for specific concerns, such as rape crisis centers and counseling services, feminist bookstores, and lesbian bars. Further back-up material can be found in *Women's Travel in Your Pocket* ($14; Ferrari Publications, PO Box 37887, Phoenix, AZ 85069 ☎602/863-2408), an annual guide for (lesbian) women travelers. Specific women's contacts are listed where applicable in the city sections of the guide.

Directory

Addresses Generally speaking, roads in built-up areas are laid out to a grid system, creating "blocks" of buildings: addresses of buildings refer to the block, which will be numbered in sequence, from a central point usually downtown; for example, 620 S Cedar will be six blocks south of downtown. In small towns, and parts of larger cities, "streets" and "avenues" often run north–south and east–west respectively; streets are usually named (sometimes alphabetically), avenues generally numbered.

Cigarettes and smoking Smoking is a much-frowned-upon activity in California, which has banned smoking in all indoor public places, including bars and restaurants. Cigarettes are sold in virtually any food shop, drugstore, or bar, and also from vending machines. A packet of twenty

costs around $2.50, much cheaper than in Britain, though many smokers buy cigarettes by the carton for around $18.

Departure tax All airport, customs, and security taxes are included in the price of your ticket.

Drugs Possession of under an ounce of the widely consumed marijuana is a misdemeanor in California, and the worst you'll get is a $200 fine. Being caught with more than an ounce, however, means facing a criminal charge for dealing, and a possible prison sentence – stiffer if caught anywhere near a school. Other drugs are, of course, completely illegal and it's a much more serious offense if you're caught with any.

Electricity 110V AC. The insubstantial two-pronged plugs have now largely been replaced by a more sturdy three-pronged affair. Foreign devices will need both a plug adapter and a transformer, though laptops usually automatically detect and cope with the different voltage.

Floors In the US, what would be the ground floor in Britain is the first floor, the first floor the second floor, and so on.

ID Should be carried at all times. Two pieces should diffuse any suspicion, one of which should have a photo: driving license, passport, and credit card(s) are your best bets.

Measurements and sizes The US has yet to go metric, so measurements are in inches, feet, yards, and miles; weight in ounces, pounds, and tons. American pints and gallons are about four-fifths of Imperial ones, so a US gallon is only 3.8 liters rather than 4.5. Clothing sizes are always two figures less what they would be in Britain – a British women's size 12 is a US size 10 – while British shoe sizes are half a size below American ones for women, and one size below for men.

Time California runs on Pacific Standard Time (PST), which is eight hours behind GMT, and jumps forward an hour in summer (the last Sunday in April to the last Sunday in October), largely in step with the UK. In summer, when it is noon Monday in California it is 3pm in New York, 8pm in London, 5am Tuesday in Sydney, and 7am Tuesday in Auckland.

Tipping You really shouldn't leave a bar or restaurant without leaving a tip of at least fifteen percent and about the same should be added to taxi fares. A hotel porter should get roughly $1 for each bag carried to your room; a coatcheck clerk should receive the same per coat. When paying by credit card you're expected to add the tip to the total bill before filling in the amount and signing.

Videos and DVDs The standard format used for video cassettes in the US is different from that used in Britain and Australasia, though many modern VCRs will play both formats. DVDs also work to different formats around the world so when buying make sure that the disc will play on your machine back home.

Guide

Guide

Los Angeles

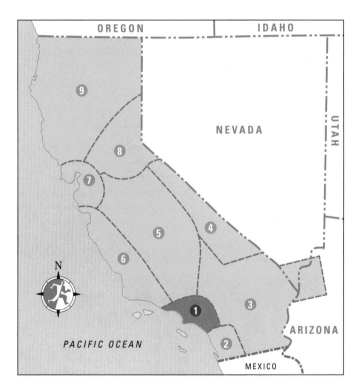

CHAPTER 1 # Highlights

* **Pacific Coast Highway** This sinewy stretch of Highway 1 winds around coastal cliffs and legendary beaches from Santa Monica to Malibu, where the views are stunning. See p.136

* **Getty Center** A colossal, modernist arts center, the Getty is stuffed with treasures of the Old World and does much to help the city shake off its reputation as a culture-free zone. See p.134

* **Musso and Frank Grill** This classically dark and moody watering hole has long been a favorite hangout for movie stars of the Golden Age and today's brattier celebrities. See p.172

* **Golden Triangle/Rodeo Drive** For high-end consumers (and avid window shoppers), this compact section of downtown Beverly Hills, featuring jewelry, fashion, and beauty merchants, is the main reason to visit Los Angeles. See p.131

* **Disneyland** This monumental corporate resort offers pricey hotels, monorails, and family-oriented rides of the original 1950s-era theme park and the newer California Adventure. See p.150

* **Rose Parade** If you are here on New Year's Day, check out this Pasadena procession of grand floral floats and marching bands, culminating in a momentous football game. See p.160

Los Angeles

The sprawling metropolis of **LOS ANGELES** spreads across a great desert basin in a colorful jangle of fast-food joints, shopping malls, palm trees, and swimming pools, bordered by snowcapped mountains and the Pacific Ocean and stitched together by an intricate network of freeways crossing a thousand square miles of architectural, social, and cultural anarchy. It's an extremely visual city, colorful and brash in countless ways, and famously hard to make sense of – simply put, this maddening patchwork is like nowhere else on earth.

For all that, LA seems very familiar. The entertainment industry has been popularizing the city ever since filmmakers arrived in the 1910s, attracted by a climate that allowed them to film outdoors year-round, plenty of open land on which to build elaborate sets, nearby landscapes varied enough to form an imaginary backdrop to just about anywhere in the world, and of course, the ever popular lures of cheap labor and low taxes. Since then, the money and glitz of Hollywood have lured countless thousands of would-be actors, writers, designers, and other budding celebrities to cast their lot in this hard-edged glamour-town, their triumphs and (more often) failures becoming intrinsic to the city's accumulated mythology. In recent years, so too has the threat of sudden disaster: floods, fires, and earthquakes are facts of life here, and the coexistence of both extremes – spectacle and tragedy – lends a perilous, almost unhinged personality to the city.

Some history

Originally settled by Chumash and Tongva peoples about a thousand years before the arrival of Spanish settlers in 1781, Los Angeles was named for the Spanish phrase for "**Our Lady Queen of the Angels**," a religious honorific. The village later became a link in Junípero Serra's lengthy chain of 21 Franciscan missions (see p.vii), as well as a staging ground for Spanish military expeditions. In 1821, Mexico gained control of California, and the entire terrain was subdivided into huge **ranchos** under the control of politically powerful land bosses, only to be swallowed up again during the Mexican-American War in 1847 by the US, which did everything it could to eradicate the social and governmental structures created by Spain and Mexico.

Up until the Civil War, LA was a multicultural community of white American immigrants, poor Chinese laborers, and wealthy Mexican ranchers, with a population of under fifty thousand. It wasn't until the completion of the **transcontinental railroad** in the 1870s that the city really began to grow, consistently doubling in population every ten years. Hundreds of thousands descended upon the basin, drawn by the prospect of living in a Mediterranean-style paradise.

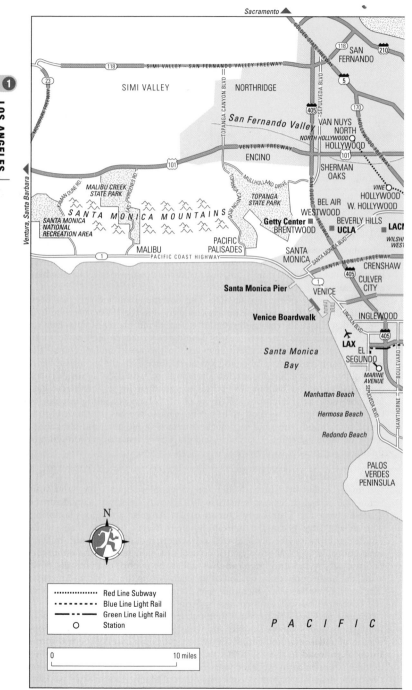

Sacramento ▲

Ventura, Santa Barbara ◄

118 SIMI VALLEY - SAN FERNANDO VALLEY FREEWAY

SIMI VALLEY

NORTHRIDGE

San Fernando Valley

VAN NUYS
NORTH
NORTH HOLLYWOOD
HOLLYWOOD

VENTURA FREEWAY

ENCINO

SHERMAN
OAKS

MULHOLLAND DRIVE

VINE
HOLLYWOOD
W. HOLLYWOOD

TOPANGA
STATE PARK

MALIBU CREEK
STATE PARK

BEL AIR
WESTWOOD

BEVERLY HILLS
UCLA

LACI

S A N T A   M O N I C A   M O U N T A I N S

Getty Center
BRENTWOOD

WILSHI
WEST

SANTA MONICA
NATIONAL
RECREATION AREA

PACIFIC
PALISADES

SANTA
MONICA

MALIBU

PACIFIC COAST HIGHWAY

CRENSHAW

CULVER
CITY

Santa Monica Pier

VENICE

INGLEWOOD

Venice Boardwalk

LAX

Santa Monica
Bay

EL
SEGUNDO

MARINE
AVENUE

Manhattan Beach

Hermosa Beach

Redondo Beach

PALOS
VERDES
PENINSULA

N

	Red Line Subway
	Blue Line Light Rail
	Green Line Light Rail
O	Station

P A C I F I C

0   10 miles

Santa Catalina Island ▼

SAN
FERNANDO

GOLDEN STATE FREEWAY

SEPULVEDA BLVD

TOPANGA CANYON BLVD

KANAN DUME RD

LAS VIRGENES RD

TOPANGA CANYON RD

SAN DIEGO FREEWAY

SANTA MONICA BLVD

SANTA MONICA FREEWAY

LINCOLN BLVD

SEPULVEDA BLVD

HAWTHORNE BLVD

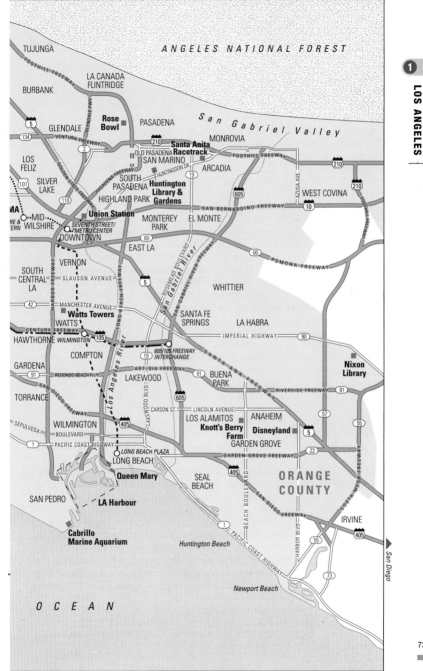

TUJUNGA

ANGELES NATIONAL FOREST

LA CANADA
FLINTRIDGE

BURBANK

FOOTHILL FREEWAY

GLENDALE

VENTURA FREEWAY

Rose
Bowl

PASADENA

San Gabriel Valley

MONROVIA

LOS
FELIZ

SILVER
LAKE

210

Santa Anita
Racetrack

OLD PASADENA

SAN MARINO

SOUTH
PASADENA

HIGHLAND PARK

HUNTINGTON DR

ARCADIA

WEST COVINA

210

Huntington
Library &
Gardens

605

AZUSA AVE

PASADENA FREEWAY

GOLDEN STATE FREEWAY

GLENDALE FWY

210

2

134

5

101

MA

RE &
ERN

MID-
WILSHIRE

110

SEVENTH STREET/
METRO CENTER

Union Station

DOWNTOWN

MONTEREY
PARK

EL MONTE

SAN BERNARDINO FREEWAY

10

VERNON

SLAUSON AVENUE

60

EAST LA

ROSEMEAD BOULEVARD

San Gabriel River

SOUTH
CENTRAL
LA

60

POMONA FREEWAY

42

MANCHESTER AVENUE

Watts Towers

WATTS

SAN GABRIEL RIVER FREEWAY

HAWTHORNE

CENTURY FREEWAY

WILMINGTON

105

GARDENA

91

REDONDO BEACH FWY

COMPTON

ARTESIA FREEWAY

605/105 FREEWAY
INTERCHANGE

SANTA FE
SPRINGS

WHITTIER

LA HABRA

IMPERIAL HIGHWAY

90

HARBOR FREEWAY

LONG BEACH FREEWAY

Los Angeles River

LAKEWOOD

91

BUENA
PARK

RIVERSIDE FREEWAY

91

Nixon
Library

TORRANCE

SAN DIEGO FREEWAY

SEPULVEDA

WILMINGTON

BOULEVARD

405

LAKEWOOD BLVD

605

CARSON ST.

LINCOLN AVENUE

LOS ALAMITOS

Knott's Berry
Farm

ANAHEIM

Disneyland

GARDEN GROVE

57

55

5

22

SANTA ANA FREEWAY

1

PACIFIC COAST HIGHWAY

19

Long Beach Plaza

LONG BEACH

Queen Mary

GARDEN GROVE FREEWAY

ORANGE
COUNTY

SAN PEDRO

LA Harbour

SEAL
BEACH

405

BEACH BOULEVARD

SAN DIEGO FREEWAY

Cabrillo
Marine Aquarium

Huntington Beach

1

PACIFIC COAST HIGHWAY

HARBOR BLVD

55

COSTA MESA FREEWAY

IRVINE

405

73

San Diego

Newport Beach

O C E A N

Ranches were subdivided into innumerable suburban lots, and scores of new towns, like San Pedro and Santa Monica, sprang up. Meanwhile, land speculators marketed an enduring image of Los Angeles, epitomized by the family-sized suburban house (with a swimming pool and a two-car garage) set amid the orange groves in a glorious land of sunshine.

More **boom years** followed World War II, when veterans, many of whom had passed through on their way to the South Pacific, came back to stay, buying government-subsidized houses and finding well-paid jobs in the mushrooming defense and aeronautics industries, along with other work for oil, steel, and automotive companies. Despite an ongoing undercurrent of racial strife and increasingly dreadful pollution, in many ways the 1940s through the 1970s were LA's historic peak. Along with heavy manufacturing, the entertainment and real estate sectors drew ever-increasing numbers of people from around the country, and LA's population exploded, eventually turning the city into the nation's second-largest metropolis.

After the Cold War, though, Southern California was hit very hard by cutbacks in defense spending, particularly in the aeronautics industry. Unemployment reached a peak of ten percent in the early 1990s, resulting in a spike in crime and a shameless paranoia growing in the suburbs. The **riots of 1992** (see p.105) exacerbated tensions, which were only increased by a pair of earthquakes and various floods and fires in Southern California during the same period. With economic, social, and racial troubles rampant, the city entered one of its darkest periods, with abundant cynicism and anger among many residents. Intolerant attitudes fueled much of the drive for the 1994 passage of **Proposition 187**, a state measure (later invalidated by the courts) denying access to health and education services to illegal – largely Latino – immigrants, and, more recently, for ballot measures designed to undercut Affirmative Action programs and Spanish-language instruction.

In spite of the hostility, **Latino immigration** has continued to increase dramatically, especially in Santa Ana and Garden Grove, and once entrenched suburbanites now seek new refuges in distant "edge cities" like Rancho Cucamonga and Palmdale, where their only neighbors are state prisons stocked with LA convicts whom they once fled. Even in South Central, long the center of African-American culture in LA, massive sociological upheaval is taking place with traditional black neighborhoods becoming majority-Latino, and many of those newcomers arriving from some of the most impoverished regions of Central America.

Unfortunately, LA's abiding racial animosities (and often outright hostility) are nothing new, having been with the city ever since its first settlement, and continuing in the barbaric misbehavior of some local police and the historic inability of LA's leaders even to acknowledge or respond to it. One recent bright spot, though, has been the appointment of New York police reformer William Bratton to head the long-troubled LAPD, offering hope that the entrenched ills of the department can finally be addressed, perhaps even solved. However, for many neighborhood residents, from the San Fernando Valley to the Harbor Area, this change is too little and too late. Their one perverse solution to LA's troubles has been to push for **secession**, arguing that Balkanizing

Because the Los Angeles region has eight telephone area codes – ☎213, ☎310, ☎323, ☎562, ☎626, ☎714, ☎818, and ☎949 – we have included the code before each number.

this already fractious city will solve all the region's problems – and gambling that it won't make them worse instead.

At the same time, LA has made progress in the last six years or so to regain its economic footing, focusing on entertainment and real estate once more. About the only symbol of the hard-working old days is the port of LA and Long Beach, which handles over sixty percent of the ocean-going cargo coming into the West Coast and remains the one economic dynamo for the southern part of the city. In LA proper, numerous glossy **museums**, many built during the last two decades, maintain the city as an international center of visual art, and the forest of Downtown skyscrapers attests to its key position as the high-finance gateway between America and the Far East. But the extent of the contradictions involved in dwelling in – or even visiting – a metropolis that contains at least 100,000 homeless alongside some of the highest standards of living in the world are never far away.

Arrival

Arriving in LA is potentially one of the most nerve-wracking experiences you're likely to have. However you get to the city, and especially if you're not driving, you're faced with an unending sprawl that can be a source of bewilderment even for those who've lived in it for years. Provided you don't panic, however, this ungainly beast of a city can be managed and even navigated, if not necessarily tamed.

By plane

All European and many domestic **flights** use Los Angeles International Airport – always known as **LAX** – sixteen miles southwest of Downtown LA (T310/646-5252, Wwww.los-angeles-lax.com). If you're on a budget, and not planning to rent a car (in which case see "Driving and car rental," p.79), the cheapest option is to take the free **"C" shuttle bus** (not "A" or "B," which serve the parking lots), running 24 hours a day from each terminal, to the LAX Transit Center at Vicksburg Avenue and 96th Street. From here, local **buses** (the citywide MTA and individual lines to Santa Monica, Culver City, and Torrance) leave for different parts of LA – see "City transportation" on p.80 for more details.

The most convenient way into town is to ride a minibus service such as **LAX Chequer Shuttle** (T1-800/545-7745, Wwww.laxchequer.com) or **Super Shuttle** (T310/782-6600 or 1-800/554-3146, Wwww.supershuttle.com), which run to Downtown, Hollywood, West LA, and Santa Monica (the SuperShuttle also goes to Long Beach and Disneyland) and deliver you to your door; most have flashing signs on their fronts advertising their general destination. If you're heading to Santa Monica or the South Bay, another possibility is **Coast Shuttle** (T310/417-3988). Fares vary depending on your destination, but are generally around $25–30, plus tip. The shuttles run around the clock from outside the baggage reclaim areas, and you should never have to wait more than fifteen or twenty minutes; pay the fare when you board.

Taxis from the airport charge at least $25 to Downtown and West LA, $30 to Hollywood, and $90 to Disneyland. Unlicensed taxi operators may approach you and offer flat fares to your destination; generally, such offers are best avoided. Don't even consider using the **Metro** system to get to your destination from LAX. The nearest light-rail train, the Green Line, stops miles from the airport, and the overall journey involves three time-consuming transfers (very difficult with luggage) before you even arrive in Downtown Los Angeles. Other destinations are completely inaccessible by rail.

Most flights into LA use LAX, but if you're arriving from elsewhere in the US or Mexico, you can land at one of the **smaller airports** in the LA area – at Burbank, Long Beach, Ontario, or Orange County's John Wayne Airport in Costa Mesa. These are similarly well served by car rental firms; if you want to use public transportation phone the MTA Regional Information Network on arrival (Mon–Fri 6am–7pm, Sat 8am–6pm; ☏1-800/COMMUTE, outside LA 1-800/2LA-RIDE, or 213/626-4455, ⓦwww.mta.net), and tell them where you are and where you want to go.

△ Traffic on the Harbor Freeway

By bus

The main **Greyhound** bus terminal, at 1716 E 7th St (☎213/629-8401, Ⓦwww.greyhound.com), is in a seedy section of Downtown – though access is restricted to ticket holders and it's safe enough inside. There are other Greyhound terminals elsewhere in LA handling fewer services: in Hollywood at 1715 N Cahuenga Blvd (☎323/466-6384); in Pasadena at 645 E Walnut St (☎626/792-5116); North Hollywood at 11225 Magnolia Blvd (☎818/761-5119); Long Beach at 1498 Long Beach Blvd (☎562/218-3011); and Anaheim at 101 W Winston Rd (☎714/999-1256). Only the Downtown terminal is open around the clock; all have toilets and left-luggage lockers.

By train

Arriving in LA by **train**, you'll be greeted with the expansive Mission Revival architecture of Union Station, on the north side of Downtown at 800 N Alameda St (☎213/624-01710), from which you can also access the nearby Gateway Transit Center, which offers connections to bus lines. Amtrak trains also stop at outlying stations in the LA area; for all listings, call Amtrak (☎1-800/USA-RAIL, Ⓦwww.amtrak.com).

By car

The main routes by **car** into Los Angeles are the interstate highways, all of which pass through Downtown. From the east, I-10, the San Bernardino Freeway, and I-210, the Foothill Freeway, have replaced the legendary Route 66; from the north and south, I-5 connects LA with Sacramento and San Diego. Of the non-interstate routes into the city, US-101, the scenic route from San Francisco, cuts across the San Fernando Valley and Hollywood into Downtown; Hwy-1, or the Pacific Coast Highway (PCH), follows the entire coast of California and takes surface streets through Santa Monica, the South Bay, and Orange County; and US-60, the Pomona Freeway, parallels I-10 through the eastern suburbs, providing a less hair-raising interchange when it reaches Downtown.

Information

For free maps, accommodation suggestions, and general information, the **Convention and Visitors Bureau** (**CVB**) operates two **visitor centers**: Downtown at 685 S Figueroa St (Mon–Fri 8am–5pm, Sat 8.30am–5pm; ☎213/689-8822, Ⓦwww.lacvb.com), and in Hollywood at the Janes House, 6541 Hollywood Blvd (Mon–Fri 9am–5pm; ☎323/689-8822 or ☎1-800/228-2452).

Other LA suburbs have their own bureaus. In Santa Monica at 1400 Ocean Ave (daily 10am–4pm; ☎310/393-7593, Ⓦwww.santamonica.com); Anaheim near Disneyland at 800 W Katella Ave (daily 9am–5pm; ☎714/999-8999, Ⓦwww.anaheimoc.org); Beverly Hills, 239 S Beverly Drive (☎310/248-1015, Ⓦwww.beverlyhillscvb.com); and Long Beach, 1 World Trade Center, Suite 300 (☎562/436-3645, Ⓦwww.visitlongbeach.com).

All the centers offer free **maps** of their area, but you'd do better to purchase Gousha Publications' fully indexed *Los Angeles City Map* ($2.95), available from

1

vending machines in visitor centers and most hotel lobbies. If you're in LA for a considerable period of time, consider investing in the thick, comprehensive *LA County Thomas Guide* ($31.95), the city's definitive **road atlas**, used by tourists and locals alike to navigate the bewildering maze of LA streets. It's no good if you're absolutely lost and have no idea of the city compass – use a free-way map, local street guides, and ring ahead to your destination for directions instead – but for a meticulous, up-to-date guide of hard-to-find streets in unfa-miliar neighborhoods, every driver in the city should have one. There are also similarly good *Thomas Guides* covering Orange, Riverside, and San Bernardino counties.

Newspapers and magazines

LA has just one **daily newspaper** of consequence: the *Los Angeles Times* (Ⓦwww.latimes.com), available from street-corner racks all over Southern California (35¢). The Sunday edition ($2.50) is huge, and its "Calendar" section contains the most complete listings of what's on and where, as well as reviews and gossip of the city's arts and entertainment worlds. Of the city's many **free papers**, the fullest and most useful is the free *LA Weekly* (Ⓦwww.laweekly.com), with over a hundred pages of news, reviews, and listings with an alternative bent. Numerous small local papers covering individual neighborhoods, musical scenes, and political activism are available all over LA, especially at cafés and record- and bookstores, and if all else fails, the touristy *Where LA* public-relations magazine can be found for free inside many hotel rooms.

To get a sense of how style-conscious LA sees itself, pick up a copy of the monthly *Los Angeles* magazine ($2.95; Ⓦwww.lamag.com), packed with gos-sipy news and profiles of local movers and shakers, as well as reviews of the city's trendiest restaurants and clubs. There are also dozens of less glossy, more erratically published zines – including *Spunk* and *The Edge* – focusing on LA's diverse gay and lesbian culture and nightclubs.

City transportation

The only certainty when it comes to **getting around** LA is that wherever and however you're going, you should allow plenty of time to get there. Obviously, this is partly due to the sheer size of the city, but the confusing entanglements of freeways and the gridlock common during rush hours can make car trips lengthy undertakings – and the fact that most local buses stop on every corner hardly makes bus travel a speedy alternative.

Driving and car rental

Not surprisingly, the best way to get around LA – though by no means the only way – is to **drive**. Despite the traffic being bumper-to-bumper much of the day, the **freeways** are the only way to cover long distances quickly. The sys-tem, however, can be confusing, especially since each stretch can have two or three names (often derived from their eventual destination, however far away) as well as a number. Out of an eye-popping, four-level interchange known as "The Stack," four major freeways fan out from Downtown: the Hollywood Freeway (a section of US-101) heads northwest through Hollywood into the

San Fernando Valley; the Santa Monica Freeway (I-10) connects the northern edge of South Central LA with West LA and Santa Monica; the Harbor Freeway (I-110) runs south to San Pedro – heading northeast it's called the Pasadena Freeway; and the Santa Ana Freeway (I-5) passes Disneyland and continues through Orange County. **Other area freeways** include the San Diego Freeway (I-405), roughly following the coast through West LA and the South Bay; the Ventura Freeway (Hwy-134), linking Burbank, Glendale, and Pasadena to US-101 in the San Fernando Valley; the Long Beach Freeway (I-710), a truck-heavy route connecting East LA and Long Beach; the Foothill Freeway (I-210), skirting the suburbs at the base of the San Gabriel Mountains; and the San Gabriel River Freeway (I-605), linking those suburbs with Long Beach. For **shorter journeys**, especially between Hollywood and West LA, the wide avenues and boulevards are a better – and sometimes the only – option, not least because you get to see more of the city.

All the major **car rental** firms have branches throughout the city (simply look in the phone book for the nearest office or call one of the toll-free numbers listed on p.31), and most have their main office close to LAX, linked to each terminal by a free shuttle bus. A number of smaller rental companies specialize in everything from Gremlins to Bentleys. The best-known is *Rent-a-Wreck* (☎310/826-7555 or 1-800/995-0994), at 12333 W Pico Blvd in West LA and also near Pasadena and in Reseda in the San Fernando Valley, offering mid-1960s Mustang convertibles and other, less appealing, vehicles. Expect to pay in the region of $50 per day.

Parking is a particular problem Downtown, along Melrose Avenue's trendy Westside shopping zone, in downtown Beverly Hills and in Westwood. Anywhere else is less troublesome, but watch out for restrictions – some lampposts boast as many as four placards listing dos and don'ts. Sometimes it's better to shell out $5 for valet parking than get stuck with a $30 ticket for parking in a forbidden residential zone.

Public transportation

The bulk of LA's public transportation is operated by the LA County Metropolitan Transit Authority (**MTA** or **"Metro"**). Its massive **Gateway Transit Center**, to the east of Union Station on Chavez Avenue at Vignes Street, may eventually serve 100,000 commuters a day traveling by Metrorail, light rail, Metrolink commuter rail, Amtrak, and the regional bus systems. The Center comprises **Patsaouras Transit Plaza**, from which you can hop on a bus; the glass-domed **East Portal**, through which you can connect to a train; and the 26-story **Gateway Tower**, at which you can find an MTA customer service office on the ground floor.

Metrorail and Metrolink

Hampered by construction scandals and budget difficulties, LA's **Metrorail** subway and light-rail system has been struggling even to come into partial use. A successful local ballot measure ensures the system will not expand beyond its current plans, which are narrowly limited in scope and only involve three lines. The underground **Red Line** stretches only from the Gateway Transit Center northwest to Hollywood and then North Hollywood in the San Fernando Valley, providing some minimal relief for visitors charting that simple course in their travels. Of more use to residents than tourists, the **Green Line** runs between industrial El Segundo and colorless Norwalk, along the middle of the

MTA offices and information

For **MTA route and transfer information**, phone ☏213/626-4455 or 1-800-COM-MUTE (Mon–Fri 7.30am–3.30pm); be prepared to wait, and be ready to give precise details of where you are and where you want to go. Otherwise, you can visit MTA on the Web at ⊛www.mta.net or go in person to Downtown's Gateway Transit Center, Chavez Ave at Vignes St (Mon–Fri 6am–6.30pm), or to three other centrally located offices: at 515 S Flower St, on level C of Arco Plaza (Mon–Fri 7.30am–3.30pm); 5301 Wilshire Blvd (Mon–Fri 9am–5pm); or 6249 Hollywood Blvd (Mon–Fri 10am–6pm).

Century Freeway. Tantalizingly close to LAX, but in practical terms absolutely useless if you are in a hurry, the placing of the line has attracted much just criticism. Currently the most complete route, the **Blue Line**, leaves Downtown and heads overland through South Central to Long Beach. It's a fairly safe journey through some of the most economically depressed areas of the city, and highlights the normality of everyday commuters' lives rather than the gangs and guns of media repute. **Fares** on all journeys are $1.35 one way, with one-hour-long transfers available for 25¢. Peak-hour trains run at five- to six-minute intervals, at other times every ten to fifteen minutes. Don't bring take-away refreshments on the trains – the fines start at $250.

As one rail alternative, **Metrolink** commuter trains operate primarily inter-suburban to Downtown routes on weekdays, though can be useful if you find yourself in any such far-flung districts, among them cities in Orange, Ventura, Riverside, and San Bernardino counties. Although casual visitors may find the service useful mainly for reaching the more outlying corners of the San Fernando Valley, the system does reach as far as Oceanside (see p.238) in San Diego County, from which you can connect to that region's transit system and avoid the freeways altogether. One-way fares range from $3–10, depending on when you're traveling (most routes run during daily business hours) and how far you're going. For information on specific routes and schedules, call ☏1-800/371-LINK or visit on the Net at ⊛www.metrolinktrains.com.

Buses

Car-less Angelenos not lucky enough to live near a train route are most at ease with **buses**. Although initially bewildering, the MTA bus network is really quite simple: the main routes run east–west (ie between Downtown and the coast) and north–south (between Downtown and the South Bay). Establishing the best transfer point if you need to change buses can be difficult, but with a bit of planning you should have few real problems – though you must always allow plenty of time.

Area brochures are available free from MTA offices, and you can pick up diagrams and timetables for individual bus routes, as well as regional bus maps showing larger sections of the metropolis. Buses on the major arteries between Downtown and the coast run roughly every fifteen minutes between 5am and 2am; other routes, and the **all-night services** along the major thoroughfares, are less frequent, usually every thirty minutes or hourly. At night be careful not to get stranded Downtown waiting for connecting buses.

The standard **one-way fare** is $1.35, except for night routes (9pm–5am), when the cost is only 75¢; **transfers**, which can be used in one direction within the time marked on the ticket (usually three hours), cost 25¢ more; and

MTA bus routes

MTA's **buses** fall into six categories, as shown below. Some of the routes can be characterized by their passengers: the early morning east–west route along Wilshire Boulevard is full of Latin American service workers, whereas tourists dominate the route west along Santa Monica Boulevard to the beach and pier. Whatever bus you're on, if traveling alone, especially at night, sit up front near the driver. Try and sit near a ventilation hatch, too, as the air conditioning can emit a rather sickly-sweet odor.

#1–99 – local routes to and from Downtown

#100–299 – local routes to other areas

#300–399 – limited-stop routes (usually rush hours only)

#400–499 – express routes to and from Downtown

#500–599 – express routes, other areas

#600–699 – special service routes (for sports events and the like)

Major LA bus services

From LAX to:
Downtown #42, #439
Long Beach #232
San Fernando Valley/Getty Center #561
San Pedro #225
Watts Towers #117
West Hollywood #220 (for Hollywood change to #4 along Santa Monica Boulevard)

To and from Downtown:
Along Hollywood Blvd #1
Along Sunset Blvd #2, #3, #302
Along Santa Monica Blvd #4, #304
Along Melrose Ave #10, #11
Along Wilshire Blvd #20, #21, #22, #320

From Downtown to:
Santa Monica #20, #22, #320, #322, #434
Venice #33, #333, #436
Forest Lawn Cemetery, Glendale #90, #91
East LA #68
Exposition Park #38, #81
Huntington Library #79, #379
Burbank Studios #96
San Pedro #445, #446, #447, transfer to DASH #142 for Catalina
Manhattan Beach/Hermosa Beach/ Redondo Beach #439
Palos Verdes #444
Long Beach #60
Orange County, Knott's Berry Farm, Disneyland #460

express buses (a limited commuter service), and any others using a freeway, are usually $1.85, but can be as much as $3.85 depending on length of trip and the number of zones you pass through, as shown on station maps. Put the correct money (coins or notes) into the slot when getting on. If you're staying a while, you can save some money with a **weekly** or **monthly pass**, which cost $11 and $42, respectively (with monthly student passes for $30), and also give reductions at selected shops and travel agents. If you're staying about two weeks, consider a **semi-monthly pass**, sold for $21.

There are also the mini **DASH** buses, which operate through the LA Department of Transportation, or LADOT (☎808-2273 for area codes 213, 310, 323, and 818, ⓦ www.ladottransit.com), with a flat fare of 25¢. Six routes run through Downtown every five to ten minutes between 6.30am and 6pm on weekdays, and every fifteen to twenty minutes between 10am and 5pm on Saturdays and Sundays. Other DASH routes travel widely throughout the metropolis, including the mid-Wilshire area, Pacific Palisades, Venice, and

Guided tours of LA

One quick and easy way to see different sides of LA is from the window of a **guided bus tour**, which can vary greatly in cost and quality. The **mainstream tours** carry large busloads around the major sights and generally don't cover anything that you couldn't see for yourself at less cost. **Specialist tours**, tailored to suit particular interests, usually carry smaller groups of people and are often better value. **Studio tours** of film and TV production areas are covered on day-trips by most of the mainstream operators, though again you'll save money by turning up independently.

Mainstream tours

By far the most popular of the mainstream tours is the half-day **"stars' homes"** jaunt. Usually including the Farmers Market, Sunset Strip, Rodeo Drive, the Hollywood Bowl and, of course, the "stars' homes," this is much less enjoyable than it sounds – frequently no more than a view of the gate at the end of the driveway of the house of some has-been TV or celluloid celebrity. These tours are typically the most visible, and the area around the Chinese Theatre is thick with tourists lining up for tickets. Other programs include tours around the Westside at night, to the beach areas, the *Queen Mary*, day-long excursions to Disneyland, and shopping trips to the Mexican border city of Tijuana.

Costs are $30 minimum per person; assorted leaflets are strewn over hotel lobbies and visitor centers. You can make reservations at – and be picked up from – most hotels. Otherwise contact one of the following booking offices:

Casablanca Tours 6362 Hollywood Blvd (☏323/461-0156, ⊛www.casablancatours .com).

Hollywood Fantasy Tours 6671 Hollywood Blvd (☏323/469-8184).

Starline Tours 6925 Hollywood Blvd (☏323/463-3333, ⊛www.starlinetours.com).

Specialist tours

The specialist tours listed are also generally $30+ per person. For more suggestions, pick up the free *LA Visitors Guide* from hotels and visitor centers.

Black LA Tours ☏323/750-9267. Black historical and entertainment tours of once renowned Central Avenue and important sites for African-American society and culture. Prices vary.

---

several sections of South Central LA, usually every fifteen to thirty minutes on weekdays, more erratically on Saturdays, and not at all on Sundays.

Other **local bus services** include: Orange County (OCTD; ☏714/636-7433, ⊛www.octa.net), Long Beach (LBTD; ☏562/591-2301, ⊛www.lbtransit .org), Culver City (☏310/253-6500, ⊛www.culvercity.org/depts_bus), and Santa Monica (☏310/451-5444, ⊛www.bigbluebus.com).

Taxis

You can find **taxis** at most terminals and major hotels. Otherwise call – among the more reliable companies are Independent Cab Co (☏1-800/521-8294), LA Taxi (☏1-800/200-1085), and United Independent Taxi (☏1-800/411-0303). The typical fare is $2, plus $1.60 for each mile, with a $2.50 surcharge if you're picked up at LAX: the driver won't know every street in LA but will know the major ones; ask for the nearest junction and give directions from there.

The California Native 6701 W 87th Place ☎310/642-1140 or 1-800/926-1140, ⓦwww.calnative.com. Tour uninhabited islands off the coast of California, go sea kayaking, and take adventure hikes for $195 and up.

Googie Tours ☎323/980-3480. Pilgrimages to Southern California's remaining space-age glass and formica diners, quirky cocktail lounges, classic fast-food joints and other jewels of Pop Architecture. $40.

Haunted Hearse Tours PO Box 461145, Hollywood ☎323/782-9652. Two-and-a-half hours in the back of a 1969 Cadillac hearse pausing at the scene of many, though by no means all, of the eventful deaths, scandals, perverted sex acts and drug orgies that have tainted Hollywood and the surrounding area. $40.

Neon Cruises 501 W Olympic Blvd, Downtown ☎213/489-9918, ⓦwww.neonmona .org/cruise. Three-hour-long, eye-popping evening tours of LA's best remaining neon art, once a month on Saturdays, organized through the Museum of Neon Art. Very popular tours often must be booked months in advance. $45.

Off 'n Running Tours 1129 Cardiff Ave ☎310/246-1418. Curious four- to six-mile jogging tours of the stars' homes and various jaunts around Beverly Hills and West LA. $50.

SPARC tours: the Murals of LA 685 Venice Blvd, Venice ☎310/822-9560, ⓦwww.sparcmurals.org. Public art in LA is alive and well in the tradition of Diego Rivera, and this is a thoroughly enlightening tour of the "mural capital of the world." Along with being an excellent resource center, SPARC conducts two-hour mural tours ($400), personalized to your interests and sometimes including discussions with the artists.

Studio tours

For some small insight into how a film or TV show is made, or just to admire the special effects, there are guided tours at Warner Bros Studios ($33; ⓦwww.burbank.com/warner_bros_tour), NBC Television Studios ($7) and Universal Studios ($45; ⓦwww.universalstudioshollywood.com), all in or near Burbank (see p.164). If you want to be part of the **audience** in a TV show, Hollywood Boulevard, just outside the Chinese Theatre, is the major solicitation spot: TV company reps regularly appear handing out free tickets, and they'll bus you to the studio and back. All you have to do once there is be willing to laugh and clap on cue.

Cycling

Cycling in LA may sound perverse, but in some areas it can be one of the better ways of getting around. There is an excellent beach bike-path between Santa Monica and Redondo Beach, and from Long Beach to Newport Beach, and many equally enjoyable inland routes, notably around Griffith Park and the grand mansions of Pasadena (the LA River route, however, is justifiably notorious, loaded with broken glass and bands of budding criminals). Contact the AAA, 2601 S Figueroa St (Mon–Fri 9am–5pm; ☎213/741-3686, ⓦwww .aaa-calif.com), or the LA office of the state Department of Transportation, known as CalTrans, 120 S Spring St (Mon–Fri 8am–5pm; ☎213/897-3656, ⓦwww.dot.ca.gov), for maps and information. The best place to **rent a bike** for the beaches is on Washington Street around Venice Pier, where numerous outlets include Spokes 'n' Stuff, 4175 Admiralty Way (☎310/306-3332) and 1700 Ocean Ave (☎310/395-4748); in summer, bike rental stands line the beach. Prices range from $10 a day for a clunker to $15 a day or more for a mountain bike. For similar cost, many beachside stores also rent **roller skates** and **rollerblades**.

Walking and hiking

Although some people are surprised to find sidewalks in LA, let alone pedestrians, **walking** is in fact the best way to see much of Downtown and districts like central Hollywood, Pasadena, Beverly Hills, Santa Monica, and Venice. You can structure your stroll by taking a **guided walking tour**, the best of which are organized by the Los Angeles Conservancy (☎213/623-CITY, ⓦ laconservancy.org), whose treks around Downtown's battered but still beating heart are full of Art Deco movie palaces, once-opulent financial monuments and architectural gems like the Bradbury Building (see p.98). Among many alternatives, it runs Downtown tours every Saturday, leaving the Biltmore Hotel on Olive Street at 10am (reservations required; $8). (See the box overleaf for details of other tour operators.) You can also take guided **hikes** through the wilds of the Santa Monica Mountains and Hollywood Hills free of charge every weekend with a variety of organizations and bureaus, including the Sierra Club (☎323/387-4287, ⓦ ww.sierraclub.org), the State Parks Department (☎818/880-0350, ⓦ www.parks.ca.gov), and the Santa Monica Mountains National Recreation Area (☎818/597-1036, ⓦ www.nps.gov/samo).

Accommodation

Since LA has 100,000-plus rooms, finding **accommodation** is easy, and, whether you seek basic budget motels or world-class resorts, the city has something for everyone. However, finding somewhere low priced and well located can sometimes be difficult, though not impossible. If you're driving, of course, you needn't worry about staying in a less than ideal location – a freeway is never far away. Otherwise you'll need to be more choosy about the district you pick, as getting across town can be a time-consuming business.

Motels and the lower-end hotels start at around $40 for a double, but many are situated in seedy or out-of-the-way areas, and often you'll gain by paying a bit more for a decent location in any of a number of other non-chain, mid-range hotels. **Bed and breakfast inns** are uncommon in LA, and tend to be quite expensive and frequently fully booked. For those on a tight budget, **hostels** are dotted all over the city, many in good locations, though at some stays are limited to a few nights. Perhaps surprisingly, there are a few **campgrounds** on the edge of the metropolitan area – along the beach north of Malibu and in the San Gabriel mountains, for example – but you'll need a car to get to them. (Hostels and campgrounds are listed at the end of this section.) **College rooms** are also sometimes available for rent during student vacation time: contact **UCLA** Interfraternity Council (☎310/825-7878) for more information.

LA is so big that if you want to see it all without constantly having to cross huge expanses, it makes sense to divide your stay between several districts. Prices – and options – vary by area. Downtown has expensively elegant and drably basic hotels; Hollywood has similar options, with motels providing even cheaper accommodation; more salubrious West LA, Santa Monica, Venice, and Malibu are predominantly mid-to-upper-range territory, with the odd hostel here and there. Among options further out, the South Bay and

Harbor Area, well connected with other parts of town, carry a good selection of low- to mid-range hotels (and a hostel) strung mostly along the Pacific Coast Highway. It's only worth staying in Orange County, thirty miles southeast of Downtown, if you're aiming for Disneyland or are traveling along the coast: hotels under $75 a night are a rarity and you must book at least a week in advance, especially if a convention is in town. Unfortunately, many of the plentiful rooms along Katella Avenue and Harbor Boulevard in Anaheim are decrepit and depressing, even though they charge up to $100 a night. A far better alternative is the handful of hostels and coastal campgrounds in easy reach.

Since there are no **booking agencies** and visitor centers don't make accommodation reservations (though they will offer information and advice), you can only book a room through a travel agent or by phoning the hotel directly. Ask if there are special weekend or midweek rates. Especially at the lower end of the price scale, hotels are cheaper if booked by the week than by the night.

The hotels are listed below by neighborhood, with specific accommodation options for gay and lesbian travelers listed on p.191. In case you're arriving on a late flight, or leaving on an early one, we've also listed a few places to stay near the airport: cheap hotels near LAX are blandly similar and generally around $40–60, but most have complimentary transportation to and from the terminals.

Airport hotels

Quality Inn 5249 W Century Blvd ☎310/645-2200 or 1-800/228-5151, ⓦwww.qualityinn.com. Featuring ten floors of comfortable, well-equipped rooms and a restaurant and bar, this motel also offers free LAX shuttles every fifteen minutes and a location a half-mile west of the 405 freeway. ❸

Renaissance Hotel 9620 Airport Blvd ☎310/337-2800, ⓦwww.renaissancehotels.com. The best of the higher-end accommodations close to LAX, along a veritable hotel row. With wood-and-marble decor, ample rooms, and luxurious suites with Jacuzzis. ❽

Travelodge LAX South 1804 E Sycamore Ave ☎310/615-1073, ⓦwww.travelodge.com. Reliable chain motel just five minutes south of LAX; convenient for the South Bay. Rates include use of the pool and free tea, coffee, and breakfast. ❸

Downtown and around

See the map on p.93 for hotel locations.

Biltmore Hotel 506 S Grand Ave at 5th St ☎213/624-1011 or 1-800/222-8888, ⓦwww.thebiltmore.com. Neoclassical 1923 architecture combined with modern luxury to make your head swim, with a health club modeled on a Roman bathhouse, cherub and angel decor, and a view overlooking Pershing Square. Significantly cheaper rates on weekends. Now part of the Millennium chain. ❽

Figueroa Hotel 939 S Figueroa St at Olympic Blvd ☎213/627-8971 or 1-800/421-9092, ⓦwww.figueroahotel.com. Mid-range hotel on the south side of Downtown, with a Jacuzzi-equipped pool and 24-hour coffee shop. ❹

Holiday Inn Downtown 750 Garland Ave at 8th St ☎213/628-5242 or 1-800/628-5240, ⓦwww.holidayinnla.com. On the western fringe of Downtown beside the Harbor Freeway, with predictable *Holiday Inn* rooms, restaurant, lounge, and laundry. ❺

Miyako Inn 328 E 1st St ☎213/617-2000, ⓦwww.miyakoinn.com. Despite the grim, concrete-box exterior, this good-value hotel features rooms with fridges, spa, and karaoke bar. ❻

New Otani Hotel 120 S Los Angeles St ☎213/629-1200 or 1-800/421-8795, ⓦwww.newotani.com. Luxury hotel mainly for business travelers, with comfortable rooms and an appealing and authentic Japanese garden and restaurant. ❼

Omni Los Angeles 251 S Olive St at 4th St ☎213/617-3300 or 1-800/327-0200, ⓦwww.omnilosangeles.com. Bunker Hill property loaded with upscale amenities, including some suites with Jacuzzis. Adjacent to MOCA and the Music Center. ❽

Park Plaza 607 S Park View St, between 6th St and Wilshire Blvd ☎213/384-5281. Facing dicey MacArthur Park, with a stunning marble floor and sumptuous lobby popular with filmmakers – but the rooms are quite ordinary. ❻

Westin Bonaventure 404 S Figueroa St, between 4th and 5th sts ☎213/624-1000 or 1-800/228-3000. Luxurious postmodern masterpiece or oversized nightmare, depending on your point of view, and recently remodeled to brighten the once-drab character of the rooms. Five glass towers, six-story lobby with a "lake." Breathtaking exterior elevator – featured in the climax of Clint Eastwood's *In the Line of Fire* – ascends to a rotating cocktail lounge. ⑧

Hollywood
See the map on p.111 for hotel locations.

Best Western Hollywood Hills 6141 Franklin Ave ☎323/464-5181, ⓦwww.bestwesterncalifornia .com. Part of the nationwide chain, with cable TV and heated pool, at the foot of the Hollywood Hills. ④

Dunes Sunset Motel 5625 Sunset Blvd ☎323/467-5171. On the dingy eastern side of Hollywood, but far enough away from the weirdness of Hollywood Boulevard to feel safe; adequate rooms and good access to Downtown. ③

Holiday Inn Hollywood 1755 N Highland Ave ☎323/462-7181 or 1-800/465-4329, ⓦwww .holiday-inn.com. Massive and fairly expensive, but perfectly placed near the Chinese Theatre and Hollywood & Highland Mall. The price becomes more reasonable with triple occupancy. ⑥

Hollywood Metropolitan Hotel 5825 Sunset Blvd ☎1-800/962-5800 or 323/962-5800, ⓦwww.metropolitanhotel.com. Sleek high-rise in central Hollywood. Good value for the area, with adequate rooms and disabled access. ⑤

Hollywood Roosevelt 7000 Hollywood Blvd, between Highland and La Brea ☎323/466-7000, ⓦwww.hollywoodroosevelt.com. The first hotel built for the movie greats, now in the Clarion chain. The rooms are plain, but the place reeks atmosphere, with a "History of Hollywood" exhibit on the second floor. Also offers Jacuzzi, pool, and fitness center. ⑥

Hollywood Towne House 6055 Sunset Blvd ☎323/462-3221. Motel-type accommodation with decayed exterior and 1920s-era phones that only connect to the front desk. The rooms themselves are clean and comfortable enough. ③

Renaissance Hollywood 1755 N Highland Blvd ☎323/856-1200, ⓦwww.renaissancehollywood .com. The hotel centerpiece of the new Hollywood & Highland mall, with upscale rooms and suites, and prime location in the heart of Tinseltown. ⑦

Saharan Motor Hotel 7212 Sunset Blvd ☎323/874-6700, ⓦwww.saharanmotel.com. Unexciting but functional, with some rooms having kitchenettes and fridges. Comparatively good value, considering its central location. ③

Sunset 8 Motel 6516 Sunset Blvd ☎323/461-2748. Though a bit of a dive, a longstanding motel favorite for its old-time pop design and dirt-cheap rates. If you see a clean room, grab it for a brief stay near Hollywood's traditional sights, including the Hollywood Athletic Club. ②

West LA and Beverly Hills
See the map on p.123 for hotel locations.

Beverly Hills Hotel 9641 Sunset Blvd ☎1-800/283-8885 or 310/276-2251, ⓦwww.beverly-hillshotel.com. Painted bold pink and green and surrounded by its own exotic gardens, this famous hotel to the stars is pretty hard to miss. Marilyn Monroe once stayed here, and one of the bungalows is decorated in her honor. ⑨

Beverly Hilton 9876 Wilshire Blvd ☎1-800/922-5432 or 310/274-7777, ⓦwww.hilton.com. Despite its high-profile chain status and excellent location near downtown Beverly Hills, an upscale hotel offering few surprises, though nice, standard amenities, and one of the few remaining *Trader Vic's* bars. ⑧

Beverly Laurel Motor Hotel 8018 Beverly Blvd ☎323/651-2441. The hotel coffee shop, *Swingers* (see p.168), attracts the most attention here, primarily as a hangout for locals and inquisitive tourists. No-frills accommodation, with very basic rooms, but a good location. ④

Bevonshire Lodge Motel 7575 Beverly Blvd ☎323/936-6154. Well situated for both West LA and Hollywood, not far from Fairfax district. All of the functionally decorated rooms come with a refrigerator, and for a few dollars more you can have a kitchenette. ③

Chateau Marmont 8221 Sunset Blvd ☎323/626-1010, ⓦwww.chateaumarmont.com. Swank French-style suites and bungalows, the one-time haunt of John and Yoko; it also saw the likes of Boris Karloff, Greta Garbo, Errol Flynn, Jean Harlow, and, tragically, John Belushi. ⑨

Claremont Hotel 1044 Tiverton Ave ☎310/208-5957. Inexpensive small hotel, with unexciting rooms but excellent location – very close to UCLA and Westwood Village. ③

Hotel Bel Air 701 Stone Canyon Rd ☎1-800/648-1097 or 310/472-1211, ⓦwww.hotelbe-lair.com. LA's nicest hotel bar none, and the only officially approved business in Bel Air, in a lushly overgrown canyon above Beverly Hills. Go for a beautiful brunch by the swan pond if you can't afford the rooms, which can reach $450 a night. ⑨

Hotel Del Flores 409 N Crescent Drive at Little Santa Monica ☎310/274-5115, ⓦwww .hoteldelflores.com. Three blocks from Rodeo Drive, this place is small, pleasant, and excellent value – shared baths bring the cost down significantly. ③–④

Le Montrose 900 Hammond St ☎310/855-1115, ⓦwww.lemontrose.com. West Hollywood hotel with Art Nouveau stylings, featuring rooftop tennis courts, pool, and Jacuzzi. Most rooms are suites with full amenities. ⑧

Le Parc 733 N West Knoll ☎1-800/578-4837 or 310/855-8888, ⓦwww.leparcsuites.com. West Hollywood apartment hotel with studios, one- and two-bedroom suites, rooftop pool and Jacuzzi with view of the hills. ⑧

Maison 140 140 S Lasky Drive ☎310/281-4000, ⓦwww.maison140.com. New, high-profile entry for swank hipsters, featuring rooms with CD players and nice appointments, plus salon, bar, fitness room, and complimentary breakfast. ⑦

The Standard 8300 Sunset Blvd ☎323/654-2800, ⓦwww.standardhotel.com. Hands down LA's best "party hotel," with a groovy social scene centered around the chic pool and quirky retro-1970s lobby. Unfortunately, the rooms – though clean and comfortable enough – are fairly spartan, hip decor notwithstanding. A new, less exciting Downtown branch is at 550 S Flower St (☎213/892-8080). Both ⑥

Santa Monica, Venice, and Malibu

See the map on p.137 for hotel locations.

Bayside Hotel 2001 Ocean Ave, Santa Monica ☎310/396-6000, ⓦwww.baysidehotel.com. Just a block from Santa Monica beach and Main Street. Bland exterior and no phones, but generally comfortable, basic rooms – some with ocean views. ④

Cadillac Hotel 8 Dudley Ave, Venice ☎310/399-8876, ⓦwww.thecadillachotel.com. Stylish Art Deco hotel on the Venice Boardwalk. Although the suites are nice, some of the lower-end rooms are spartan and have few amenities. On-site sundeck, pool, gym, and sauna. ⑤

Channel Road Inn 219 W Channel Rd, Pacific Palisades ☎310/459-1920, ⓦwww.channelroad-inn.com. Fourteen B&B rooms in a romantic getaway nestled in lower Santa Monica Canyon (northwest of the city of Santa Monica), with ocean views, a hot tub, and free bike rental. Eat free grapes and sip champagne in the sumptuous rooms, each priced according to its view. ⑦–⑨

Hotel Carmel 201 Broadway, Santa Monica ☎310/451-2469, ⓦwww.hotelcarmel.com. A

good bet for lodging near the beach, with the ocean two blocks away and the Third Street Promenade a block in the other direction. ⑥

Hotel Shangri-La 1301 Ocean Ave, Santa Monica ☎310/394-2791, ⓦwww.shangrila-hotel.com. Wonderfully restored Art Deco treasure overlooking Palisades Park and the beach, offering mostly well-appointed suites. ⑧

Inn at Venice Beach 327 Washington Blvd ☎310/821-2557 or 1-800/828-0688, ⓦwww.innatvenicebeach.com. A good, basic choice for visiting Venice Beach and the canals, with simple, tasteful rooms featuring fridges and balconies. ⑤

Loew's Santa Monica Beach Hotel 1700 Ocean Ave, Santa Monica ☎310/458-6700, ⓦwww .loewshotels.com. A deluxe, salmon-colored edifice overlooking the ocean and the Santa Monica Pier, appealing both to tourists and jet-setters. The finest rooms top $450, with lesser rooms being adequate, if a bit cramped and overpriced. ⑧

Malibu Riviera Motel 28920 PCH ☎310/457-9503. Quiet place outside town, less than a mile from the beach, with clean and basic rooms, a sundeck, and Jacuzzi. Fairly isolated from the rest of the city. ⑤

Malibu Surfer Motel 22541 PCH ☎310/456-6169, ⓦwww.malibusurfmo.qpg.com. Frightful decor, but located across from the beach and boasting a pool, king-sized beds, refrigerators, and TVs. Sufficient parking, too. ④

Santa Monica Beach Travelodge 1525 Ocean Ave ☎310/451-0761, ⓦwww.travelodge.com. Predictably clean and basic chain lodging, excellent for its beach proximity. To save a few bucks, try the less appealing units on the eastern edge of town, in a grim, colorless building, 3102 Pico Blvd (☎310/450-5766). ④

Viceroy 1819 Ocean Ave, Santa Monica ☎310/451-8711, ⓦwww.viceroysantamonica.com. The old *Pacific Shore Hotel*, remodeled into a luxury item, with great bay views and nicely appointed rooms with CD players, on-site pool, and lounge. The high-end rooms reach nearly $500. ⑧

The South Bay and Harbor Area

Barnabey's 3501 N Sepulveda Blvd, Manhattan Beach ☎310/545-8466, ⓦwww.barnabeyshotel .com. One of the finest hotels in the area, with clean and spacious rooms, whirlpool, and LAX airport transit. ⑦

Hotel Hermosa 2515 PCH, Hermosa Beach ☎310/318-6000, ⓦwww.hotelhermosa.com. Plush hotel with basic rooms starting at moderate prices (though rising up to $350 suites), and a short walk to the beach. Central South Bay location adds to the value. ④–❾

Motel 6 5665 E 7th St, Long Beach ☎562/597-1311, ⓦwww.motel6.com. Decent rooms at cheap prices; good mainly for travelers on their way south to Orange County or San Diego. ❸

Rodeway Inn 50 Atlantic Ave, Long Beach ☎562/435-8369, ⓦwww.rodewayinn.com. Inoffensive chain-motel accommodation not far from the marina and convention center. ❺

Sea Sprite Motel 1016 Strand, Hermosa Beach ☎310/376-6933, ⓦwww.seaspritemotel.com. Right next to the beach along a popular strip. Several different room options come with varying prices, including weekly rates for longer stays. ❺

Seahorse Inn 233 N Sepulveda Blvd, Manhattan Beach ☎1-800/233-8050 or 310/376-7951. Faded pastel exterior but clean and simple rooms. Further from the beach than others, but with a pool. ❸

Vagabond Inn 6226 PCH, Redondo Beach ☎310/378-8555, ⓦwww.vagabondinn.com. Inexpensive lodging in a beachside tourist zone. Cleaner than comparable motels in the area. ④

Disneyland and around

Best Western Stovall's Inn 1110 W Katella Ave, Anaheim ☎714/778-1880, ⓦwww.stovallshotels.com. Along with *Pavilions* at 1176 W Katella Ave (☎714/776-0140) and *Park Place Inn* at 1544 S Harbor Blvd (☎714/776-4800), a reliable member of the nationwide chain. ❸–❺

Desert Palm Inn and Suites 631 W Katella Ave, Anaheim ☎1-800/635-5423, ⓦwww.anaheimdesertpalm.com. Very comfortable and spacious rooms with refrigerators, microwaves, VCRs, and continental breakfast. Conventions in town make prices leap. ❺

Disneyland Hotel 1150 W Cerritos Ave, Anaheim ☎714/956-6400, ⓦdisneyland.disney.go.com/disneylandresort. The place to go for a pricey Disney-themed wedding with Mickey in attendance. Quite overpriced (theme park admission is separate), but the Disneyland monorail does stop right outside. ❽

Holiday Inn Anaheim at the Park 1221 S Harbor Blvd, Anaheim ☎714/758-0900, ⓦwww.holiday-inn.com. Safe, clean lodging not far from the Magic Kingdom. ❺

Motel 6 2920 W Chapman Ave, Anaheim ☎714/634-2441, ⓦwww.motel6.com. Unexciting chain-motel rooms, but given the surrounding options, the best bargain in the area. ❷

Red Roof Inn 1251 N Harbor Blvd, Anaheim ☎714/635-6461, ⓦwww.redroof.com. One of the more worthwhile options in town, offering rooms

with fridges and microwaves, pool, spa, and free shuttle to Disneyland, about three miles away. ❸

The Orange County Coast

Hotel Laguna 425 S Coast Hwy, Laguna Beach ☎949/494-1151, ⓦwww.hotellaguna.com. Atmospheric and comfortable, with luxurious appointments and location in the center of Laguna Beach. Price of room depends on quality of view. ❺–❽

Little Inn by the Bay 2627 Newport Blvd ☎949/673-8800, ⓦwww.littleinnbythebay.com. Eighteen nice, comfortable rooms near Newport Beach; the cheapest accommodation in the area, with in-room fridges, microwaves, and complimentary breakfast. Close to Balboa Peninsula. ❺

Mission Inn Motel 26891 Ortega Hwy, at I-5 ☎949/493-1151. Rooms at this reasonably priced place come with use of Jacuzzi and pool. Located in distant San Juan Capistrano. ④

Ocean View Motel 16196 PCH, Huntington Beach ☎562/592-2700. Family-run establishment with clean, comfortable rooms. Get a Jacuzzi in your room for an extra $15. ❸

Seacliff Motor Hotel 1661 S Coast Hwy, Laguna Beach ☎949-494-9717 or 1-866/732-1400, ⓦwww.seaclifflaguna.com. Recently renovated motel with close ocean access, heated pool, and complimentary breakfast. Rates jump if you want a room with a sea view or a balcony. ❺–❼

Seal Beach Inn and Gardens 212 Fifth St, Seal Beach ☎562/493-2416, ⓦwww.sealbeachinn.com. Although located in a drab and uneventful burg, a fine bed-and-breakfast offering nice rooms with sumptuous appointments two blocks from the sands. ❼

The San Gabriel and San Fernando valleys

The Artists Inn 1038 Magnolia St, South Pasadena ☎626/799-5668, ⓦwww.artistsinns.com. A themed bed-and-breakfast with ten different rooms and suites (some with spas) honoring various painters and styles – best of all is the Italian Suite, with an antique tub and a sun porch. ❼

Best Western Colorado Inn 2156 E Colorado Blvd, Pasadena ☎626/793-9339, ⓦwww.bestwesterncalifornia.com. Comfortable chain accommodation just north of San Marino's Huntington Museum. ❺

Ritz-Carlton Huntington Hotel 1401 S Knoll, Pasadena ☎626/568-3900, ⓦwww.ritzcarlton.com. Utterly luxurious and refurbished landmark 1906 hotel, discreetly tucked away in residential southern

Pasadena. Suites start at $400, with more basic rooms about half the price. ❽

Safari Inn 1911 W Olive St, Burbank ☎818/845-8586, ⓦwww.anabelle-safari.com. A classic mid-century motel, renovated but still loaded with pop-architecture touches (tiki and googie styles). Features a pool, fitness room, Burbank airport shuttle, and in-room fridges, with some suites also available. ❺

Sheraton Universal 333 Universal Terrace, Burbank ☎818/980-1212 or 1-800/325-3535, ⓦwww.starwood.com. With the neighboring *Universal City Hilton*, 555 Universal Terrace (☎818/506-2500, ⓦwww.hilton.com), a large and luxurious hotel on the Universal Studios lot, with health club and elegant restaurant. Both ❽

Vagabond Inn Hotel 1203 E Colorado Blvd at Michigan, Pasadena ☎626/449-3170, ⓦwww.vagabondinn.com. Friendly budget chain motel, usefully placed for exploring Pasadena. Also at 120 W Colorado St in Glendale (☎818/240-1700). Both ❹

Hostels

Banana Bungalow 2775 Cahuenga Blvd W, in Cahuenga Pass ☎323/851-1129 or 1-800/446-7835, ⓦwww.bananabungalow.com. Popular large hostel near Universal City and US-101, with free airport shuttles, city tours to Venice Beach and Magic Mountain, and a relaxed atmosphere. Outdoor pool, free parking, and as much beer as you can drink every second night for $3. Dorms $18–21, and more expensive private singles and doubles $60+.

HI-Anaheim/Fullerton 1700 N Harbor Blvd at Brea, Fullerton ☎714/738-3721, ⓦwww .hostelweb.com/losangeles/fullerton. Convenient and comfortable, five miles north of Disneyland on the site of a former dairy farm. The hostel's excellent facilities include a grass volleyball court, golf driving range, and picnic area. There are only 22 dorm beds, so reservations are a must. Check-in 4–11pm, mornings open 8am–noon. OCTA bus #43 stops outside. Members $15, others $18.

HI-LA/Santa Monica 1436 2nd St at Broadway, Santa Monica ☎310/393-9913, ⓦwww .hostelweb.com/losangeles/los_angeles. A few blocks from the beach and pier, the building was LA's Town Hall from 1887 to 1889, and retains its historic charm, with a pleasant inner courtyard, ivy-covered walls, and a skylight. Members $25, others $28; private rooms for $66 and $72 – the price includes laundry machines and huge kitchens. Smoking and drinking are prohibited. Reservations essential in summer; open 24hr.

HI-LA/South Bay 3601 S Gaffey St #613, San Pedro ☎310/831-8109, ⓦwww.hostelweb.com /losangeles/south_bay. Sixty beds in old US Army barracks, with a panoramic view of the Pacific Ocean. Ideal for seeing San Pedro, Palos Verdes, and the whole Harbor Area. Open 7am–midnight. $15 members, $18 others; private rooms $37 and $40 per person. MTA bus #446 passes close by, but it's a two-hour journey from Downtown. You can also take the SuperShuttle from LAX.

Hollywood International Hostel 6820 Hollywood Blvd ☎1-800/750-6561, ⓦwww.hollywoodhos-tels.com. One of three good-value locations in this area, this one in the heart of Hollywood, with 24hr check-in, breakfast, and shuttle from LAX or Union Station. Dorms $16, private rooms $40.

Hostel California 2221 Lincoln Blvd, Venice ☎310/305-0250. Twelve six-bed dorms with kitchens, pool table, big-screen TV, linen, and parking. Cheap shuttle bus to and from LAX. $15 members, $18 others, or $100 a week. Private rooms $34.

Huntington Beach Colonial Inn Hostel 421 8th St, Huntington Beach ☎714/536-3315, ⓦwww .huntingtonbeachhostel.com. Four blocks from the beach and mostly double rooms. Sleeping bags allowed. Open 8am–11pm. Key rental after 1pm, $1 (plus $20 deposit). Dorms $20, private rooms $22.50 per person.

Orange Drive Manor 1764 N Orange Drive, Hollywood ☎323/850-0350, ⓦorangedrivehos-tel.com. Centrally located hostel (right behind the Chinese Theater) offering tours of film studios, theme parks, and houses of the stars. $18, private rooms $36.

Orbit Hotel 7950 Melrose Ave ☎323/655-1510 or 1-877/ORBIT-US, ⓦwww.orbithotel.com. Assertively retro-1960s hotel and hostel with sleek Day-Glo furnishings and ultra-hip modern decor, offering complimentary breakfast, movie screening room, patio, café, private baths in all rooms, shut-tle tours, and $20 per-day car rental. Located just west of the most frenetic and colorful part of Melrose. Dorm rooms $19, private rooms $49.

USA Hostels – Hollywood 1624 Schrader Ave ☎323/462-3777 or 1-800/LA-HOSTEL, ⓦwww.usahostels.com. A block south of the center of Hollywood Boulevard, near major attractions and with a game room, private baths, main bar, Internet access, tours of the area, and garden patio, as well as airport and train shuttles. Shared rooms $16–19 and private rooms from $40.

Venice Beach Cotel 25 Windward Ave, Venice ☎310/399-7649, ⓦwww.venicebeachcotel.com. Located in historic, colonnaded beachside building – a "cotel" – with dorm rooms $15–18, private rooms $35–49.

LA area campgrounds

Reserve America (☏1-800/444-7275, ⊛www.reserveamerica.com) processes reservations at many of the **campgrounds** listed below and can look for an alternative if your chosen site is full. It charges a $7 fee per reservation per night up to a maximum of eight people per site, including one vehicle.

Bolsa Chica Campground ☏714/846-3460. Facing the ocean in Huntington Beach, near a wildlife sanctuary and birdwatchers' paradise. $18 for campers with a self-contained vehicle. No tent camping.

Chilao Flat on Hwy-2 twenty miles northeast of Pasadena ☏626/574-1613. The only campground in the San Gabriel Mountains reachable by car, though there are many others accessible on foot. For more details contact the Angeles National Forest Ranger Station at 701 N Santa Anita Ave, Arcadia (☏626/574-1613). $18.

Dockweiler Beach County Park 8255 Vista del Mar ☏310/305-9545. On a noisy coastal strip, almost at the western end of the LAX runways. Mainly for RVs, tent sites by reservation only. A popular urban beach, which can get a little dicey on weekends. $18–25.

Doheny State Beach Campground 25300 Dana Point Harbor Drive ☏949/496-6171 or ☏1-800/444-7275. Often packed with families, especially at weekends. Located at southern end of Orange County, not far from Dana Point Harbor. $12–24.

Leo Carrillo State Park northern Malibu ☏818/706-1310 or ☏1-800/444-7275. Pronounced "Ca-REE-oh," near one of LA's best surfing beaches, 25 miles northwest of Santa Monica on Pacific Coast Hwy, and served twice an hour in summer by MTA bus #434. $12–37.

Malibu Creek State Park 1925 Las Virgenes Rd, in the Santa Monica Mountains ☏818/706-8809 or ☏1-800/444-7275. A rustic campground in a park which can become crowded at times. Sixty sites in the shade of huge oak trees, almost all with fire pits, solar-heated showers, and flush toilets. One-time filming location for TV show *M*A*S*H*. $12–45.

San Clemente State Beach Campground 3030 Avenida del Presidente, two miles south of San Clemente ☏714/492-7146 or ☏1-800/444-7275. A prime spot for hiking, diving, and surfing, around an area that was once home to Richard Nixon's "Western White House." $12–20.

Neighborhoods and orientation

Spilling over a vast, flat basin and often lacking clear divisions between neighborhoods, LA is far from a conventional city. Traveling from one end of town to the other takes you through virtually every social extreme imaginable, from mind-boggling beachside luxury to some of the most severe inner-city poverty in the US – both partially the result of the city's explosive growth within an area of 465 square miles. With the basin bordered by desert to the east, mountains to the north, and ocean to the southwest, the millions of new arrivals who have poured in have filled in the spaces between what were once smaller, geographically isolated communities, creating a metropolis on a mammoth scale - which more resembles a chaotic third-world amalgamation than anything else in America.

If LA has any kind of urban core, however, it is **Downtown**. Located in the center of the basin, its towering office blocks of Bunker Hill punctuate an otherwise low and level skyline. With everything from avant-garde art to the abject dereliction of Skid Row, Downtown offers a taste of almost everything you'll find elsewhere around the city, compressed into an area of small, easily walkable blocks. It's a good place to get your initial bearings and is the hub of the transportation network.

Around Downtown – a serviceable label for an assortment of areas with little in common except for being adjacent to Downtown – demonstrates still more of LA's diversity: decaying Victorian relics of the turn-of-the-century hilltop suburbs, Art Deco buildings that characterize 1920s LA, arrival zones for the city's enormous population of Central American immigrants, and the sprawl of impoverished streets which makes up South Central LA.

Away from Downtown, you'll probably spend most of your time in the broad corridor that runs 25 miles west to the coast. Here are LA's best-known and most interesting districts, the first of which, **Hollywood**, has streets teeming with movie myths and legends – even if the genuine glamour is long gone. Tourists flock here, and it's also where some of LA's most eccentric artists, bohemians, and street people choose to parade themselves. Neighboring **West LA**, also called the Westside, is home to the city's newest money – shown off in the incredibly expensive shops of Beverly Hills and the lively nightspots of the Sunset Strip – and its western edge merges into **Santa Monica** and **Venice**, the quintessential Southern California of palm trees, white sands, and laid-back living. The coastline itself is the major draw, stretching north from here twenty miles to the northern edge of LA and to **Malibu**, noted for its celebrity residences and their keenly guarded privacy – and for the wildfires that have destroyed many of those residences.

South along the coast from Venice, the three cities of the **South Bay** – Manhattan Beach, Hermosa Beach, and Redondo Beach – are quieter, mostly inhabited by middle-class commuters, and a long way in spirit from the more bustling and fad-conscious portions of the city. The beaches are the sole focus of attention here - their bluffs and coves leading on to the **Harbor Area** – though despite recent facelifts and some mildly enjoyable resort areas, there's nothing to detain you in the South Bay for more than a few hours at a time.

Orange County, southeast of the Harbor Area, is mainly depressing suburban sprawl, and almost the only reason most people come here is to visit **Disneyland**, the city's biggest single tourist attraction and the mother of all theme parks. If you're not keen on seeing the self-styled "happiest place on Earth," it's best to hug the coast and continue south, along the **Orange County Coast**, whose string of individualistic, libertarian communities provides for a few days' exploration on the way to San Diego.

North of Downtown, LA has also grown on the other side of the hills that make up the northern wall of the basin to the **San Gabriel and San Fernando valleys**, which stretch east and west until LA fades into desert, mountains, and ocean. The valleys are distanced from mainstream LA life socially as well as geographically, their inhabitants the butt of most Angeleno hick jokes and constantly threatening to secede from the city. The chief reasons for venturing here include a number of worthwhile art collections and a couple of working (and tourable) film studios, as well as the most famous of LA's cemeteries.

LA's museums and aquariums

18th Street Arts Complex p.138
Air and Space Gallery p.106
Aquarium of the Pacific p.146
Avalon Casino Museum p.149
Avila Adobe museums p.94
Banning House p.146
Bergamot Station p.138
Bowers Museum of Cultural Art p.153
Cabrillo Marine Aquarium p.145
California African-American
   Museum p.106
California Heritage Museum p.139
California Science Center p.105
Chinese American Museum p.94
Craft and Folk Art Museum p.126
Drum Barracks and Civil War
   Museum p.146
Fantasy Foundation p.114
Fisher Gallery – USC p.104
Forest Lawn Museum p.163
Frederick's of Hollywood Lingerie
   Museum p.115
Gene Autry Western Heritage
   Museum p.120
George C. Page Museum p.126
Getty Center p.134
Grier-Musser Museum p.192
Griffith Observatory p.119
Heritage Square p.110
Hollywood Bowl Museum p.122
Hollywood Entertainment Museum
   p.117
Hollywood Heritage Museum p.113
Hollywood History Museum p.117
Huntington Library p.162
International Surfing Museum p.155
Japanese-American National
   Museum p.100
LA County Museum of Art p.124
LA County Museum of Art West p.124
Laguna Art Museum p.157
Long Beach Museum of Art p.124

Malibu Lagoon Museum p.172
Manhattan Beach Roundhouse
   and Aquarium p.144
Maritime Museum – San Pedro p.145
Mission San Juan Capistrano
   Museum p.157
Murphy Sculpture Garden p.134
Museum in Black p.109
Museum of Contemporary Art
   (Downtown) p.96
Museum of Contemporary Art
   (Geffen Contemporary) p.100
Museum of Contemporary Art
   (Pacific Design Center) p.130
Museum of Jurassic Technology p.127
Museum of Latin American Art p.147
Museum of Neon Art p.99
Museum of Television and Radio
   p.132
Museum of Tolerance p.133
Natural History Museum of
   LA County p.106
Norton Simon Museum p.160
Orange County Museum of Art p.156
Pacific Asia Museum p.159
Pasadena Museum of California
   Art p.159
Petersen Automotive Museum p.126
Richard Nixon Library and
   Birthplace p.153
Ronald Reagan Presidential
   Library p.158
Santa Monica Museum of Art p.138
Sherman Library and Gardens p.156
Skirball Cultural Center p.135
Southwest Museum p.110
UCLA Hammer Museum p.133
UCLA Ocean Discovery Center p.139
USC Lindhurst Galleries p.104
USLA Wight Art Gallery p.134
Wells Fargo History Museum p.97
Will Rogers Museum p.141

Downtown LA

Nowhere else do the social, economic, and ethnic divisions of LA clash quite as loudly and visibly as in the square mile (bordered by the 10, 110 and 101 freeways) that makes up **DOWNTOWN LA**. In the space of a few short blocks, adobe buildings and Mexican market stalls give way to Japanese shopping plazas and avant-garde art galleries, and you're as likely to rub shoulders with a high-flying yuppie as with a down-and-out drunk. Although it's long been the commercial focus of the city (and always the seat of local govern-

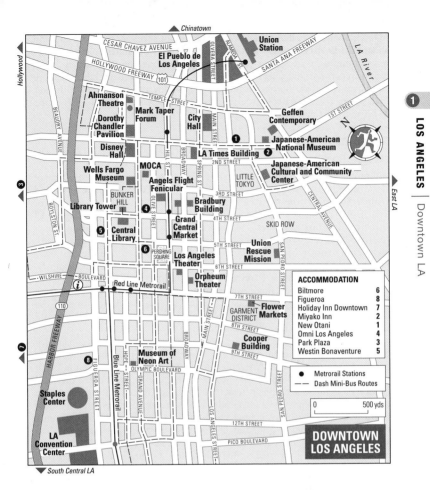

Union
Station

CESAR CHAVEZ AVENUE

El Pueblo de
Los Angeles

HOLLYWOOD FREEWAY [101]

SANTA ANA FREEWAY

LA River

OLIVERA STREET

ALAMEDA ST.

MAIN ST.

TEMPLE STREET

Ahmanson
Theatre

Mark Taper
Forum

City
Hall

Geffen
Contemporary

1ST STREET

Dorothy
Chandler
Pavilion

N

BEAUDRY AVENUE

Disney
Hall

LA Times Building ❷

Japanese-American
National Museum ❶

LOS ANGELES | Downtown LA

❶

BOYLSTON ST.

Wells Fargo
Museum

MOCA

2ND STREET

Japanese-American
Cultural and Community
Center

East LA

Angels Flight
Fenicular

SPRING ST.

LITTLE
TOKYO

CENTRAL AVENUE

❸

BUNKER
HILL

Library Tower

Bradbury
Building

3RD STREET

OLIVE STREET

❹

Grand
Central
Market

4TH STREET

SKID ROW

❺ Central
Library

HILL ST.

❻

5TH STREET

Union
Rescue
Mission

SAN PEDRO STREET

PERSHING
SQUARE

Los Angeles
Theater

6TH STREET

WILSHIRE BOULEVARD

ⓘ

Red Line Metrorail

Orpheum
Theater

7TH STREET

HARBOR FREEWAY

[110]

GARMENT
DISTRICT

Flower
Markets

MAIN STREET

8TH STREET

Cooper
Building

BROADWAY

9TH STREET

Blue Line Metrorail

❼

❽

Museum of
Neon Art

OLYMPIC BOULEVARD

GRAND AVENUE

HOPE STREET

FIGUEROA STREET

LOS ANGELES STREET

ACCOMMODATION	
Biltmore	6
Figueroa	8
Holiday Inn Downtown	7
Miyako Inn	2
New Otani	1
Omni Los Angeles	4
Park Plaza	3
Westin Bonaventure	5

● Metrorail Stations
-- Dash Mini-Bus Routes

0   500 yds

Staples
Center

12TH STREET

PICO BOULEVARD

LA
Convention
Center

**DOWNTOWN
LOS ANGELES**

ment), as businesses spread out across the basin in the postwar boom years, the
area became more dilapidated. Various revitalization initiatives in the 1980s –
spearheaded by LA's mega-bureaucracy, the Community Redevelopment
Agency (CRA) – helped to create museums, office towers, and a rash of plush
new condos for young professionals, but these have ultimately only served to
intensify the extremes, and despite the development money that flows freely
from city coffers, Downtown is unlikely to usurp the Westside as the focus of
tourism or cultural activity. Still, it remains the city's most changed – and
changing – neighborhood.

   Each part of Downtown has its own history, museums, and architecture.
Much of it can be seen on foot, starting with LA's historic and governmental heart at the **Civic Center**, crossing into the brasher and more modern
and corporate-tower-dominated **Bunker Hill**, continuing through the
chaotic streets and splendid movie theaters of **Broadway**, and finally, if you
have the nerve, skirting Skid Row (an estimated 15,000 homeless live on
Downtown's streets) and checking out the lively Garment District on the
Eastside.

Downtown can easily be seen in a day, and if your feet get tired you can hop aboard the **DASH buses** which run every five to ten minutes on six loop systems through key areas (look for the silver-signed bus stops). Parking in lots is expensive on weekdays (around $5–10 per hour), but on weekends is more affordable (a flat $3–8); street parking is a good alternative, except on Bunker Hill, where the meters cost at least $2 per hour. Downtown is the hub of the MTA networks and easily accessible by public transportation.

The Civic Center, El Pueblo de Los Angeles, and Chinatown

Although the bland municipal buildings of LA government form the focus of the **Civic Center**, the general area also includes **Chinatown** to the north and **Union Station** to the northeast. Just across US-101 from the current seat of local government, you can get a glimpse of LA's earlier frontier days at **El Pueblo de Los Angeles**, 845 N Alameda St (daily 9am–5pm; free; ☎213/628-2381, ⓦwww.ci.la.ca.us/ELP), the site of the original late-eighteenth-century Spanish settlement of Los Angeles, where the few early buildings that remain evoke a strong sense of LA's Spanish and Mexican origins. The plaza church, **La Placita**, is the city's oldest and has long served as a sanctuary for illegal Central American refugees (with immigration again becoming a potent political issue). Try and squeeze in during one of the Mariachi Masses (Sun 11.30am & 4.30pm), held completely in Spanish and accompanied by a six-piece mariachi band.

Along with its Mexican heritage, the pueblo also features the remnants of Chinese, Italian, and even French settlements. With groundbreaking finally occurring for the **Chinese American Museum** (scheduled to open in 2003; information ☎213/626-5240; ⓦwww.camla.org), which will detail the local history of Chinese settlement, society, and culture, the zone may soon have more to offer than just a few old facades and shuttered buildings. The city's first **firehouse** – later a boardinghouse and saloon - has a small but intriguing roomful of fire-fighting gear, and is now open for free viewing (Tues–Sun 10am–3pm), though the handsome, Mission-style **Pico House**, LA's most luxurious hotel when it opened in 1870, is closed. **Olvera Street**, which runs north from the plaza (daily 10am–7pm; free; ⓦwww.olvera-street.com), is a curious attempt at restoration, contrived in part as a pseudo-Mexican village market and now comprising about thirty old-looking buildings. Taken over for numerous festivals throughout the year, like the Day of the Dead on November 2, when Mexicans traditionally honor the spirits of the departed (see p.186), the street is at its best on such communal occasions.

Like other historic districts around the country, especially Virginia's Williamsburg, Olvera Street is not simply a charming vestige that just happened to thwart ruin. Rather, its re-emergence was the work of one Christine Sterling, who, with other powerful citizens and help from the city government, tore down the slum she found here in 1926 and built much of what you see today, incorporating some of the salvageable historic structures. Working for the next twenty years to organize fiestas and popularize the city's Mexican heritage, she lived in the early nineteenth-century **Avila Adobe** at 10 Olvera St – touted as the oldest structure in Los Angeles, although almost entirely rebuilt out of reinforced concrete following the 1971 Sylmar earthquake. Inside the house are two **museums** (daily 9am–5pm; free): one featuring an idealized view of pueblo-era domestic life and offering more information on Ms

Sterling; the other, across the landscaped courtyard, telling the sanitized official version of how the LA authorities connived to secure a water supply for the city (for the real story, see p.361).

Across the street, the **Sepulveda House** (Mon–Sat 10am–3pm; free; ☎213/628-1274) is a quaint 1887 Eastlake structure that offers rooms highlighting different periods in Mexican-American cultural history, shows an informative film (Mon–Sat 11am & 2pm) on the history of Los Angeles, and acts as the park's visitor center. For a more detailed look at the pueblo, there are also free **guided walking tours** (on the hour Tues–Sat 10am–1pm) from the information booth at 130 Paseo de la Plaza.

Union Station, across from Olvera Street at 800 N Alameda St, echoes LA's roots in a rather different way. It is a striking mix of monumental Art Deco and Mission Revival architecture, finished in 1939, and the site of the original Chinatown, whose residents were forced to relocate when construction on the station began. Currently, with the country's national rail system – Amtrak – crippled by budget cuts and mismanagement, the building is no longer the evocative point of arrival and departure it once was. However, the structure itself is in fine condition, with a spacious vaulted lobby, heavy wooden benches and intact Art Deco signs, surrounded by courtyards planted in informal combinations of fig trees and jacarandas. Once thronged with passengers, it now sees just a few trains each day, along with the occasional movie crew – the station famously doubled as police headquarters in the film *Blade Runner*. The nearby **Gateway Transit Center** is less elegant, but more functional as the hub of the region's bus lines.

What is now **CHINATOWN** was established by 1938 along North Broadway and North Spring Street following its residents' abrupt transplantation from the site of Union Station. It's not the bustling affair you'll find in a number of other US cities, however, and unless it's Chinese New Year, when there's a parade of dragons and firework celebrations, there's little point in turning up here except to eat in one of the restaurants. (To get a truer sense of contemporary Chinese culture, visit **Alhambra** or **Monterey Park**, both lively ethnic suburbs located just beyond LA's eastern boundary.)

South of the Santa Ana Freeway from Olvera Street, most of the **Civic Center** is a collection of plodding bureaucratic office buildings, one of which – the County Courthouse – became briefly famous during the O.J. Simpson trial. Standing out among the drab white boxes, LA's Art Deco **City Hall**, 200 N Spring St, is known to the world through LAPD badges seen in TV shows ever since *Dragnet*, and was until 1960 the city's tallest structure. The building's crown is as close as most visitors will ever get to seeing the Mausoleum at Halicarnassus, one of the seven ancient wonders of the world, which provided a curious, only-in-LA architectural inspiration. You can still get a good look at the inside of the building on its free tours, which include its 28th-story 360° observation deck (daily 10am & 11am; reserve on ☎213/485-4423, ⓦ www.lacityhall.org).

Northeast of City Hall, at 310 N Main St, the **Children's Museum** is closed at the time of writing, though it is due to reopen next to the Geffen Contemporary in 2004 (for information call ☎213/687-8801, ⓦ www.childrensmuseumla.org). Nearby, on the south side of the Civic Center plaza, the **Los Angeles Times** building offers free tours (Mon–Fri 11.15am; ☎213/237-5757, ⓦ www.latimes.com) showing how the West Coast's biggest newspaper is put together.

Bunker Hill

Until a century ago the area south of the Civic Center, **BUNKER HILL**, was LA's most elegant neighborhood, its elaborate Victorian mansions and houses connected by funicular railroad to the growing business district down below on Spring Street. As with all of Downtown, though, the population soon moved to new, outlying suburbs and many of the old homes were converted to boardinghouses, later providing the seedy film noir backdrop for detective films, notably the apocalyptic 1955 Mike Hammer movie *Kiss Me Deadly*. These structures were in turn wiped out by 1960s urban renewal and replaced with a forest of grim, anonymous high-rises.

The **Angels Flight** funicular, removed in 1969 but since restored and repainted, is a bright and colorful memory of a long-departed era. Hop aboard one of the two trains near the corner of Hill and Fourth streets and, for a mere 25¢, ascend to the top of Bunker Hill, viewing the Beaux Arts charm of older Downtown structures to the east, and be dwarfed by the office blocks of the **FINANCIAL DISTRICT**, which looms above you with austere modernity. Most of the fifty-story towers have a concourse of shops and restaurants at their base, high-style shopping malls intended to provide a synthetic street life for the brokers and traders, and about as dreary as you might expect. One of the few notable structures is the **Gas Company Tower**, 555 W 5th St, a metallic blue building whose crown symbolizes a natural gas flame on its side.

The Museum of Contemporary Art

The largest and most ambitious development in the district is the **California Plaza** on Grand Avenue, a billion-dollar complex of offices and luxury condos centering on the **Museum of Contemporary Art (MOCA)** (Tues–Sun 11am–5pm, Thurs 11am–8pm; $8, students $5, free Thurs 5–8pm; ☎213/621-2766, ❀www.moca.org), which opened at the end of 1986 in an effort to raise the cultural stature of the area, and of the whole city. Designed by showman architect Arata Isozaki as a "small village in the valley of the skyscrapers," it justifies a look for the building alone, its playful exterior a welcome splash of color among the dour skyscrapers, an array of geometric red shapes recognizable from the occasional TV commercials filmed here.

If you're more interested in the architecture than the art, you're free to wander around the rooftop terrace, courtyard café, and gift shop. A barrel-vaulted entrance pavilion on Grand Avenue opens out to an outdoor sculpture plaza, and stairs lead down from the upper plaza to the smaller courtyard, between the café and the main entrance to the galleries.

Much of the gallery is used for temporary exhibitions, and the bulk of the permanent collection is mid-twentieth-century American, particularly from the Abstract Expressionist period, including work by Franz Kline and Mark Rothko. You'll also find plenty of Pop Art, in Robert Rauschenberg's urban junk, Claes Oldenburg's papier-mâché representations of hamburgers and gaudy fast-foods, and Andy Warhol's print-ad black telephone. Don't be surprised to find a few minimalist creations, either, such as Donald Judd's mind-numbing, machine-produced metal boxes – the artistic equivalent of Downtown's steel towers.

Unfortunately, there are few singularly great pieces from the established names, and most of the compelling ideas are expressed by the paintings and sculpture of the newer stars of the art world – Alexis Smith's quirky assemblages, Martin Puryear's anthropomorphic wooden sculptures, and Lari Pittman's spooky, sexualized silhouettes. The museum is also strong on photography, and features the two-thousand-print collection of New York dealer Robert Freidhaus, exhibiting the work of Diane Arbus, Larry Clark, Robert Frank, Lee Friedlander, John Pfahl, and Gerry Winograd, as well as a few choice, and thoroughly disturbing, images by Cindy Sherman.

The theater on the lower floor of MOCA hosts some bizarre multimedia shows and performances, as well as the more standard lectures and seminars (☎213/621-2766 for details). The best time to visit MOCA is on a Thursday evening in summer, when entry is free, and concerts, usually jazz or classical and also free, are played outdoors under the red pyramids. At other times, a ticket to MOCA also entitles you to same-day entrance to the Geffen Contemporary (see p.100), the museum's renovated-warehouse exhibition space on the east side of Downtown.

Disney Hall and Our Lady of the Angels

Just north of the museum, around the stodgy music and theater establishments of the **Music Center**, 135 Grand Ave (see "Performing arts," p.183), is the long-awaited, almost-completed **Disney Hall**, First Street at Grand Avenue, based on a 1987 design by pioneering architect Frank Gehry and strikingly prescient of his later-designed but already-built Guggenheim Museum in Bilbao, Spain. Delayed for many years, the Hall is finally on track to become LA's most notable example of contemporary architecture, a 2300-seat acoustic showpiece whose titanium exterior will resemble something akin to colossal broken eggshells. The entire complex is due to open in the fall of 2003, inaugurating the upcoming season of the LA Philharmonic, which will make this venue its new home (for the latest update, check out ⓦ www.disneyhall.org).

Cater-corner to Disney Hall and newly opened in September 2002 stands LA's other widely anticipated colossus, the $200-million **Our Lady of the Angels** Catholic church, 555 W Temple St (tours Mon–Fri 1 & 3pm, Sat 11.30am & 2pm, Sun 11.30am & 2.30pm; free; ⓦ www.olacathedral.org). The centerpiece of the local archdiocese, this is a truly massive structure in its own right – eleven stories tall and capable of holding three thousand people – and solidly built of concrete. Decorated in an unfortunate shade of ochre, the church's fortress-like exterior suggests a huge parking lot or prison. Still, the interior is the undeniable highlight, featuring tapestries of saints, giant bronze doors, ultra-thin alabaster screens for diffusing light, a grand marble altar, and $30 million worth of art and furnishings laid out in an interior space longer than a football field.

South of MOCA

To the **south of MOCA**, the shallow but amusing **Wells Fargo History Museum**, 333 Grand Ave (Mon–Fri 9am–5pm; free; ☎213/253-7166), at the base of the shiny towers of the Wells Fargo Center, is worth a look if you have some time to kill. Telling the history of Wells Fargo & Co, the bank of Gold Rush California and current international giant, the museum displays among other things a two-pound nugget of gold, some mining equipment, and a simulated stagecoach journey from St Louis to San Francisco.

A block away, the shining glass tubes of the **Westin Bonaventure Hotel** (see "Accommodation," p.86) have become one of LA's most unusual landmarks. The only LA building by modernist architect John Portman, best known for Atlanta's Peachtree Plaza, the structure doubles as a shopping mall and office complex – an M.C. Escher-style labyrinth of spiraling ramps and balconies that is disorientating enough to make it necessary to consult a color-coded map every twenty yards or so. But brace yourself and step inside for a ride in the glass elevators that run up and down the outside of the building (famously showcased in Clint Eastwood's *In the Line of Fire*), giving views over much of Downtown and beyond.

From the *Bonaventure*'s rotating skyline bar you'll get a bird's-eye view of one of the city's finest buildings, the **Richard J. Riordan Central Library**, across the street at 630 W 5th St (Mon–Thurs 10am–8pm, Fri–Sat 10am–6pm, Sun 1–5pm; ☎213/228-7000, ⓦwww.lapl.org/central), restored after an arson attack many years back and recently renamed for LA's former mayor. The concrete walls and piers of the lower floors, enlivened by Lee Laurie's figurative sculptures symbolizing the "Virtues of Philosophy" and the "Arts," form a pedestal for the squat central tower, which is topped by a brilliantly colored pyramid roof. The library, built in 1926, was the last work of architect Bertram Goodhue (who also designed much of the campus of Pasadena's CalTech University), and its pared-down, angular lines set the tone for many LA buildings, most obviously City Hall. Keep in mind that not all the interior design is original to Goodhue, especially the colossal atrium added by the renovators, which seems to appear out of nowhere after you step off the escalators to the upper floors.

In exchange for planning permission and air rights, the developers of the **Library Tower** across Fifth Street – the tallest office building west of Chicago – agreed to pay some fifty million dollars toward the restoration of the library. Now owned by Wells Fargo, the cylindrical tower features Lawrence Halprin's huge **Bunker Hill Steps** at its base, supposedly modeled after the Spanish Steps in Rome. From the **Source Figure**, one of Robert Graham's creepy nude sculptures, at the top, the steps curve down Bunker Hill between a series of terraces with uneventful outdoor cafés and boutiques. If you don't feel like walking, the Steps also feature a less appealing escalator.

Broadway and Pershing Square

Though it's hard to picture now, **Broadway** once formed the core of Los Angeles's most fashionable shopping and entertainment district, brimming with movie palaces and department stores. Today it's largely taken over by the clothing and jewelry stores of a bustling Hispanic community, which operate out of the ground floors of often-empty hundred-year-old buildings, the salsa music and street culture making for one of the city's most electric environments. You can sample a vivid taste of the area amid the pickled pigs' feet, sheep's brains and other delicacies inside the indoor **Grand Central Market**, on Broadway between Third and Fourth. It's a real scrum but without doubt the best place (at least for carnivores) to enter into the spirit of things.

The **Bradbury Building** (Mon–Sat 9am–5pm; free), across the street, marks a break from the mayhem of the market, its magnificent sunlit atrium surrounded by wrought-iron balconies, and open-cage elevators alternating up and down on opposite sides of the narrow court, with elaborate open staircases at either end. The whole place is an art director's dream – not surprisingly, most of the income for this 1893 office building is generated by film shoots: *Blade Runner* and *Citizen Kane* were both filmed here. Tourists are now only permitted in the lobby, but it's worth a look for the great view up. (Los Angeles Conservancy tours often begin here; see p.84 for more information.)

Aside from the street life, the best things about Broadway are the great movie palaces of the **Theater District**, some of whose "enchanted realms" still function today, if not exactly as their original movie-studio owners intended. Two are especially noteworthy: next to the Grand Central Market, the opulent 1918

Million Dollar Theater, 307 S Broadway, its whimsical terracotta facade mixing buffalo heads with bald eagles in typical Hollywood Spanish Baroque style, was originally built by theater magnate Sid Grauman, who went on to build the Egyptian and Chinese theaters in Hollywood (see p.117). It's now a South American-style evangelical meeting hall, and entry is, of course, free to all, though the interior spaces have not been renovated for the better. The **Los Angeles Theater**, at 615 S Broadway, is even more extravagant, built in ninety days for the world premiere of Charlie Chaplin's *City Lights* in 1931, crowning what had become the largest concentration of film theaters in the world. Often considered the best movie palace in the city, and one of the finest in the country, the theater's plush lobby behind the triumphal arch facade is lined by marble columns supporting an intricate mosaic ceiling, while the 1800-seat auditorium is enveloped by trompe l'oeil murals and lighting effects. Although it's no longer open to the public for regular screenings, a June program called *Last Remaining Seats* draws huge crowds to this and the nearby **Orpheum** (842 S Broadway) and **Palace** (630 S Broadway), theaters to watch revivals of classic Hollywood films, many from the silent era. If you're in town at the time, don't miss it (tickets $18 per film; call ⓣ213/623-CITY for details).

With the advent of TV, the rise of the car, and LA's drift to the suburbs, the movie palaces lost their customers and fell into decline. An underground parking lot was built in **Pershing Square** in an attempt to bring the punters back – a task for which it failed. The redesign of the square itself, unfortunately, has turned the public park into a bleakly synthetic space only a bureaucrat could love. Inspired by the work of Mexican architect Luis Barragan, the square's bright purple campanile is its only highlight, towering as it does over charmless concrete benches and a dearth of grass and other plants. Needless to say, local street people and random lunatics are abundant.

Nevertheless, some of the buildings around the square have – albeit after years of neglect – emerged in fine form. The most prominent of these, the **Biltmore Hotel**, stands over the west side of the square, its three brick towers rising from a Renaissance Revival arcade along Olive Street. Inside, the grand old lobby that was the original main entrance has an intricately painted Spanish-beamed ceiling that you can admire over a pricey glass of wine, and if you don't mind paying a top-dollar charge, the hotel's accommodation is also outstanding (p.85). A block south, at 617 S Olive St, the Art Deco **Oviatt Building** is another sumptuous survivor. The ground floor housed LA's most elegant haberdashery, catering to dapper types such as Clark Gable and John Barrymore, and has since been converted into the pricey *Cicada* restaurant. If you can't afford the Italian food, the elevators, which open onto the street level exterior lobby, are still worth a look, featuring hand-carved oak paneling designed and executed by Parisian craftsman René Lalique. Also striking is the intricate 1928 design of the building's exterior, especially its grand sign and its looming clock above.

Four blocks to the south, at 501 W Olympic Blvd, the adulterated visage of Mona Lisa smiles at you through blue-and-yellow tubing at the **Museum of Neon Art** (Wed–Sat 11am–5pm, Sun noon–5pm; $5.00; ⓣ213/489-9918, ⓦwww.neonmona.org). Offering a small exhibition space featuring classic neon signs, more modern interpretations of the noble gas and a range of bizarre kinetic art, the museum is best for its monthly bus tours of LA's best neon sights (see p.83). Finally, three blocks to the southwest, the LA Convention Center and, particularly, the Staples Center, are sleek modern structures that offer little of interest except to conventioneers and sports fans.

The Eastside

A block east of Broadway, LA's old financial district, along Spring Street between Fourth and Seventh streets, was once at the center of the city's commerce and banking, but has since been largely depopulated and now features mainly barren Neoclassical facades and shuttered entrances. That said, a handful of nightclubs, galleries, and theaters have recently tried to inject a little authentic street life back into this former ghost town, though the prospects of their long-term success seems dicey, especially given the district's closeness to **Skid Row**. This shabby, downtrodden area around Los Angeles Street south of City Hall has a more than slightly threatening air, and as a longstanding seedy neighborhood, also has a few arty associations to match. The Doors posed here for the cover of their album, *Morrison Hotel*, and Charles Bukowski was just one luminary of the booze'n'broads school of writers who've used the bars and poolrooms as a source of inspiration.

South of Skid Row, the lively **Garment District**, with its Mexican-food wagons and cut-rate shops, offers a respite from the bleak streets and attracts an energetic multi-ethnic crowd. The **Cooper Building**, which takes up most of the Ninth Street block between Santee and Los Angeles streets, is famous for its occasional designer sample sales and houses at least fifty stores where you'll find big markdowns on outfits that might normally be out of your price range. Nearby, at the atmospheric **Flower Market**, 766 Wall St (Mon, Wed & Fri 8am–noon, Tues & Thurs 6am–11am, Sat 6am–noon; ⓦwww.laflowerdistrict .com), you can mingle with the wholesalers and buy flowers for a fraction of the high-street prices.

In the 1980s, the northern boundaries of Skid Row were pushed back by the colorful shopping precinct of **Little Tokyo** – the clearest evidence of the Pacific Rim money that accounted for most of the new construction in LA during that time, then diminished with the economic declines in both LA and Japan. For a closer look into the community, head for the **Japanese-American Cultural and Community Center**, 244 S San Pedro St (ⓦwww.jaccc.org), whose **Doizaki Gallery** (Tues–Fri noon–5pm, Sat & Sun 11am–4pm; free), shows traditional and contemporary Japanese drawing and calligraphy, along with costumes, sculptures, and other associated art forms. The center also includes the **Japan America Theater**, which regularly hosts Kabuki theater and more contemporary groups. Improbably shoehorned between the two and easy to miss, the stunning **James Irvine Garden**, with a 170-foot stream running along its sloping hillside, is a real cultural treasure. Although named after its biggest financial contributor, it really owes its existence to the efforts of two hundred Japanese-American volunteers who gave up their Sundays to carve the space out of a flat lot, turning it into the "garden of the clear stream" and making the area seem a world away from LA's outside expanse of asphalt and concrete. From the cultural center, a zigzagging pathway takes you through the Shoji screens, sushi bars, shops, and Zen rock gardens of the **Japanese Village Plaza** – really just a glorified mall – and along to the **Japanese-American National Museum** at First and Central (Tues–Sun 10am–5pm, Thurs 10am–8pm; $6; ⓦwww.janm.org), a converted Buddhist temple that now houses exhibits on everything from origami to the internment of Japanese-Americans during World War II.

Across the street from Little Tokyo is the **Geffen Contemporary**, 152 N Central Ave (same hours, prices, and website as MOCA, to which a ticket also entitles same-day entrance; see p.96) – an exhibition space in a converted police garage, designed by local maverick Frank Gehry. Initially developed as the temporary home of the Museum of Contemporary Art, the museum's success was such that it was kept on as an alternative exhibition space to its more mainstream sibling.

Around Downtown

When you leave Downtown you enter the LA sprawl, diverse environs scythed by freeways, with large distances separating their points of interest. Cumulatively, there's quite a bit worth seeing, in areas either on the perimeter of Downtown or simply beginning here and continuing for many miles south or west. The districts immediately northwest of Downtown, **Angelino Heights** and **Echo Park**, are where the upper crust of LA society lived luxuriously at the turn of the century in stylish Victorian houses (now mostly in various states of preservation), vivid indicators of the prosperity of their time, just as the nondescript drabness surrounding them now evidences the blight that later befell the area. Much the same applies to the zone around **MacArthur Park**, which contains some of the impressive commercial architecture that set the stylistic tone for the city in the 1920s, as well as some of its current, and most notorious, drug-dealing havens.

The other areas that surround Downtown are too far apart for it to make sense to try to see them consecutively; each is a ten- to forty-minute drive away from the next. Directly south of Downtown, the long succession of unimaginative low-rent housing developments is interrupted only by the nearly walled-off **USC campus**, populated by conservative, well-coddled students, and the neighboring **Exposition Park**, with acres of gardens and several museums, several of which merit going out of your way to see. Beyond here lies one of LA's most depressed areas, the vast urban bleakness of **South Central LA**. A counterpoint to the commercial vibrancy of Downtown, this district surrounds the main route (I-110) between Downtown and the Harbor Area, and it's generally a place to visit with caution or with someone who knows the area, though is safe enough in daytime around the main drags.

More appealing is the colorful **East LA**, the largest Mexican-immigrant enclave outside Mexico, and a buzzing district of markets, shops, and street-corner music that gives a tangible insight into the other, relatively unacknowledged, side of LA. (More recent arrivals from Central America often end up in the **Temple–Beaudry** barrio, located to the immediate west of Downtown.) As long as you stick to the main thoroughfares and travel during daylight, you're unlikely to encounter any trouble. It's less hectic northeast of Downtown, where, on the way to Pasadena, amid the preserved homes of **Highland Park**, the **Southwest Museum** holds a fine and extremely comprehensive collection of Native American artifacts.

Angelino Heights and Echo Park

Long before there was a Malibu or a Beverly Hills, some of the most desirable addresses in Los Angeles were in **ANGELINO HEIGHTS**, LA's first suburb, just northwest of Downtown off US-101, laid out in the flush of a property boom at the end of the 1880s on a pleasant little hilltop. Though the boom soon went bust, some of the elaborate houses that were built here, especially along **Carroll Avenue**, have survived and been restored as reminders of the optimism and energy of the city's early years. There's a dozen or so in all, and most repay a look for their catalog of late-Victorian details – wraparound verandas, turrets and pediments, set oddly against the Downtown skyline and occasionally used in ads for paint, among other things. One, with a weird Great Pyramid roof, was even used as the set for the haunted house in Michael Jackson's *Thriller* video. The neighborhood also has been decreed a "Historic Preservation Overlay Zone" – about as close as LA gets to an official designation of preservation – which is one of several such zones you can periodically tour through the LA Conservancy (☎213/623-CITY, ⓦwww.laconservancy .org).

At the foot of the hill, to the west of Angelino Heights, **ECHO PARK** is a small oasis of palm trees and lotus blossoms set around a lake. In the large white **Angelus Temple** on the northern side of the lake, the evangelist **Aimee Semple McPherson** used to preach sermons to five thousand people in the 1920s, with thousands more listening in on the radio. The first in a long line of media evangelists, "Sister Aimee" died in 1944, but the building is still used for services by her Four Square Gospel ministry, who dunk converts in the huge water tank during mass baptisms. Roman Polanski's film *Chinatown* pays homage to the park by having detective Jake Gittes follow the town water boss to clandestine meetings, spying on him in a rowboat – such as the ones you can still rent (along with paddleboats) from vendors located along Echo Park Boulevard.

MacArthur Park and around

Wilshire Boulevard leaves Downtown between Sixth and Seventh streets as the main surface route across 25 miles of Los Angeles to Santa Monica's beachside Palisades Park. It was named after another of the city's colorful, largerthan-life characters, the oil baron and entrepreneur Gaylord Wilshire, who, aside from his petroleum profits, made a fortune selling an electrical device that claimed to restore graying hair to its original color. Wilshire used his money to buy up a large plot of land west of Westlake Park, later renamed **MACARTHUR PARK**, through the center of which runs his eponymous thoroughfare, previously known as the "Old Road." When the property market collapsed in 1888, Gaylord discovered politics, ran for Congress (and lost), and later moved to England, where he made friends with George Bernard Shaw and the Fabian Socialists.

A century later, the park has fallen into disrepair and remains a venue for drug deals after dark, along with more than a few shady dealings by local cops, who were alleged in a recent police scandal to have framed and beaten suspects in the vicinity. Despite the grim background, however, the park can be agreeable at times, and the adjacent Red Line Metrorail connection has turned its scattered patches of green and seemingly idyllic lake into the closest relief from Downtown – though the ambient soundtrack frequently includes the rantings of crazed street preachers and other characters. Don't miss the overhead sign for the Westlake Theater, though, which proudly advertises a classic moviehouse that has since become a grungy swap meet, or flea market.

Much more inviting, the one functional museum of some note in the area can be found nearby at 403 S Bonnie Brae St, where the **Grier-Musser Museum** (Wed–Fri noon–4pm, Sat 11am–4pm; $6, kids $3; ⓦhome .attbi.com/~gmuseum) provides a glimpse of the luxurious furnishings and stylish architecture of the nineteenth century, when this now-decrepit neighborhood was a pleasant middle-class suburb, and the local Victorian homes featured copious Gothic turrets, gingerbread ornamentation, and Italianate windows.

Half a mile west of MacArthur Park, the **Bullocks Wilshire** department store, 3050 Wilshire Blvd, is a stunning monument to 1920s Los Angeles, the most complete and unaltered example of Zigzag Art Deco architecture in the city. Built in 1929, in what was then a beanfield in the suburbs, Bullocks was the first department store in LA built outside Downtown and the first with its main entrance at the back of the structure, adjacent to the parking lot – catering to the automobile in a way that was to become the norm in this car-obsessed city. Transportation was the spirit of the time, and throughout the building, triumphant murals and mosaics of planes and ocean liners glow with activity in a studied celebration of the modern world. The building was badly vandalized during the 1992 riots and closed for five years. It has since reopened as the law library of adjacent **Southwestern University**, but is still off limits to the general public, unless you can get someone, perhaps a student, to give you an impromptu tour.

The **Ambassador Hotel**, just past Vermont Avenue at 3400 Wilshire Blvd, is another landmark of the boulevard's golden age. From the early 1920s to the late 1940s, when the hotel was the winter home of transient Hollywood celebrities, its *Cocoanut Grove* club was a favorite LA nightspot. The large ballroom hosted some of the early Academy Award ceremonies, and was featured in the first two versions of *A Star is Born* – though the hotel's most notorious event occurred on June 5, 1968, when **Bobby Kennedy** was fatally shot in the hotel kitchen while trying to avoid the press after winning the California presidential primary. Now closed to public view, the building's demolition was held up for years as a result of a legal feud between LA's school district (LAUSD) and Donald Trump, a fight recently won by the LAUSD. As school bureaucrats debate what to do with the site, some conservation groups have put forth their own ideas, advocating the complex's re-use for academic purposes – plans that might be feasible in almost any other city, but in preservation-challenged LA seem unlikely at best. Across the street, another of LA's landmarks sits in a perversely altered state. The **Brown Derby** restaurant, once the city's prime example of programmatic architecture (or buildings shaped like objects – in this case, a hat), has now been relocated to the roof of an adjacent mini-mall, repainted, redecorated, and now all but unrecognizable.

Wilshire Boulevard continues west into the so-called "Miracle Mile" (see p.124), while two blocks south of Wilshire, between Vermont and Western, **Koreatown** is home to the largest concentration of Koreans outside Korea and five times bigger than Chinatown and Little Tokyo combined. In reality, the comparison is unfair, for Koreatown is an active residential and commercial district, not just a tourist sight, and boasts as many bars, theaters, community groups, banks, and shopping complexes as it does restaurants – which are, in any case, quite good and authentic. The more fruitful comparison would be with the vibrant enclave of **Monterey Park**, east of LA, which is the focus of regional Chinese culture just as surely as Koreatown is of Korean culture.

The USC Campus

The **USC** (University of Southern California) **CAMPUS**, a few miles south of Downtown, is an enclave of wealth in one of the city's poorer neighborhoods, South Central LA. USC, or the "University of Spoiled Children," is one of the most expensive universities in the country, its undergraduates thought of as more likely to have rich parents than fertile brains. Indeed, the stereotype is often borne out, both by their easygoing, suntanned, beach-bumming nature, and by USC being more famous for sporting prowess than academic achievement. Alumni include O.J. Simpson, who collected college football's highest honor, the Heisman Trophy, when he played for the school, and some of Richard Nixon's henchmen, like H.R. Haldeman. There have been attempts to integrate the campus population more closely with the local community, but USC continues to be something of an elitist island, right down to its own fast-food outlet, and its students are cheerfully oblivious to, or openly contemptuous of, the substantial blight around them.

Though sizeable, the campus is reasonably easy to get around. You might find it easiest to take the free 50min **walking tour** (leaving on the hour Mon–Fri 10am–3pm; ☎213/740-6605, ⓦ ww.usc.edu). Without a guide, a good place to start is in the **Doheny Library** (Mon–Thurs 8.30am–10pm, Fri 8.30am–5pm, Sat 9am–5pm, Sun 1–10pm; free), an inviting Romanesque structure where you can pick up a campus map and investigate the large stock of overseas newspapers and magazines on the second floor – though they tend to be a bit outdated and UCLA (see p.134) has a better selection. Another good place for general information is the **Student Union** building, just across from the library. Among the generally unremarkable eateries found here, a **café** under the Wolfgang Puck banner, featuring nouveau pizzas and salads, provides some respite.

Of things to see, USC's art collection is housed in the **Fisher Gallery**, 823 Exposition Blvd (Tues–Sat noon–5pm; free), though it is only open for several major international exhibitions each year, focusing on a wide range of art, from international and multicultural to avant-garde and contemporary. Elsewhere, you can see smaller shows of students' creative efforts in the **Helen Lindhurst Architecture Gallery**, in the USC School of Architecture, 850 W 37th St (Mon–Fri 9am–5pm; free), and **Helen Lindhurst Fine Arts Gallery**, inside Watt Hall (Mon–Fri 9am–4pm; free). Finally, the campus is also home to the **School of Cinema-Television**, a mainstream rival to the UCLA film school in Westwood. Ironically, **Steven Spielberg**, one of the biggest box-office directors in history, couldn't get in to USC when he applied as an aspiring director. Now, his name is hallowed here, and writ large on the wall of the large and expensive sound-mixing center he later funded. The overall effect, though, is a little underwhelming, and you'll find little reason to linger for more than a few minutes, glancing at big Hollywood names on the drab brick and concrete buildings.

Between USC and Exposition Park, sports fans may want to stop at the **Coliseum** on Hoover Boulevard. The site of the 1932 and 1984 Olympic Games has fallen on hard times lately, with the Raiders American football team long gone and possible deals to land a new franchise repeatedly failing amid corporate infighting and lack of local interest. However, USC home games are still played here (tickets $30–55; ☎213/740-GOSC, ⓦ usctrojans.ocsn.com), and the imposing grand arch on the facade and muscular, headless commemorative statues create enough interest to make the place worth a look.

Exposition Park

Across Exposition Boulevard from the campus, **EXPOSITION PARK** is, given the grim nature of the surrounding area, one of the most appreciated parks in LA, incorporating lush landscaped gardens, a sports stadium, and a number of good, or at least adequate, museums. It's large by any standard, but the park retains a sense of community – a feeling bolstered by its function as a lunchtime picnic place for school kids. After eating, their favorite spot tends to

The LA riots and Rampart police scandal

The unexpected acquittal in 1992 of five white Los Angeles police officers, charged with using excessive force after they were videotaped kicking and beating black motorist Rodney King (after pulling him over for speeding through the suburb of Pacoima), could almost have been calculated to provoke a **violent backlash** in LA's poverty-stricken ghettos. What few predicted, however, was the sheer scale of the response to the verdict, which was partly – and ironically – fueled by the almost total lack of a police presence during the first evening's bloodshed. The violence and anger far surpassed the Watts Riots of 1965 (see opposite), beginning in South Central LA with motorists being pulled from their cars and attacked, and quickly escalating into a chaos of arson, shooting, and looting that spread across the city from Long Beach to Hollywood. Downtown police headquarters were surrounded by a mixed crowd of blacks, Hispanics, and whites, chanting "No Justice, No Peace," as Governor Pete Wilson and Mayor Tom Bradley appealed for calm on live TV. Before long, the arsonists around town gave way to looters, who became the focus of the national media's attention, openly stealing stereos, appliances, and even diapers from large and small retail stores. Ultimately, it took the imposition of a four-day dusk-to-dawn curfew, and the presence on LA's streets of several thousand well-armed US National Guard troops, to restore calm – whereupon the full extent of the rioting became apparent. The worst urban violence seen in the US this century (second only to the bloody, Civil War-era New York draft riots) left 58 dead, nearly 2000 injured, and caused an estimated $1 billion worth of damage. With much of the devastation in the city's poorest areas, a relief operation of Third World dimensions was mounted to feed and clothe those most severely affected by the carnage. A second federal trial, on charges that the officers violated Mr King's civil rights, resulted in prison sentences for two of the officers.

Although ignited by a single incident, the riots were a very real indication of the **racial tensions** in a city whose controllers and affluent inhabitants have traditionally been all too ready to turn a blind eye to social problems – and it didn't help that the trial occurred in right-wing Simi Valley, best known for its large population of retired cops. Prompted by the Rodney King case, the Christopher Commission was set up to investigate racial prejudice within the LAPD. Sadly, its recommendations had all too blatantly not been implemented by the time of the **Rampart police scandal**. In 2000, the police department's paramilitary culture was once again exposed, this time in the form of elite CRASH units sent to investigate drug-related crimes around the MacArthur Park and Temple-Beaudry barrios. Accused by ex-cop-turned-informant Rafael Perez of all manner of vigilante actions – from framing suspects for drug arrests to beating innocent civilians to shooting suspects in cold blood – most of the alleged perpetrators in blue walked away from the charges, the momentum for their conviction either dissipating by a lack of social outrage or a lack of interest on the part of the local district attorney. Unfortunately, it is this very apathy, the tacit acceptance of such behavior on the part of local police, and by implication their political leaders, that has historically led to new cycles of anger and despair in the inner city, and cataclysmic riots in later decades.

be the **California Science Center** (daily 10am–5pm; free, parking $6; ⓦ www.casciencectr.org), set among a cluster of **museums** off Figueroa Street at 700 State Drive (unless otherwise stated, all daily 10am–5pm; free), a multi-million-dollar showcase for scientific education, not unlike such museums elsewhere in the US. With scores of working models and thousands of pressable buttons, some of the museum's highlights include a walk-in microscope, dizzying motion simulators, and a giant talking robot that offers simple biology instruction – for the most part, little more than lightweight, pop-science "infotainment" geared for the kids.

In the vicinity, an **IMAX Theater** (information and schedules at ☎213/744-2015) plays a range of eye-popping documentaries on a gigantic curved screen. Because of the general lack of storytelling in many of the films, one screening (most are around 30min) is usually enough to get a sense of the theater. Nearby, the recently renovated **Air and Space Gallery** is marked by a sleek jet stuck to its facade, offering a series of satellites and telescopes, a slew of airplanes and rockets, and the menacing presence of an LAPD helicopter "air ship" – to complement their constant drone in the skies above. To the south, head for the stimulating **California African–American Museum**, 600 State Drive (Tues–Sun 10am–5pm; free; ⊛www.caam.ca.gov), which has diverse, temporary exhibitions on the history and culture of black people in the Americas, as well as a good range of painting and sculpture from local and national artists.

Not far away, the **Natural History Museum of Los Angeles County** (Mon–Fri 9.30am–5pm, Sat–Sun 10am–5pm; $8; ☎213/763-3466, ⊛www.nhm.org) has much appeal as the home of the park's biggest collection, as well as its most striking building and best museum overall – an explosion of Spanish Revival architecture with echoing domes, travertine columns and a marble floor. Foremost among the exhibits is a tremendous stock of dinosaur bones and fossils, and some individually imposing skeletons (usually casts) including the crested duckbilled dinosaur, the skull of a Tyrannosaurus Rex, and the astonishing frame of a Diatryma – a huge prehistoric bird incapable of flight. Exhibits on rare sharks, the combustible native plant chaparral, and a spellbinding insect zoo – centered on a sizeable ant farm – add to the appeal, but there's a lot here beyond strictly natural history, and you should allow several hours at least for a comprehensive look around. In the fascinating pre-Columbian Hall are Mayan pyramid murals and the complete contents of a reconstructed Mexican tomb, while the Californian history sections document the early (white) settlement of the region during the Gold Rush era and after, with some amazing photos of Los Angeles in the 1920s. Topping the whole place off is the gem collection, several breathtaking roomfuls of crystals, and a enticing display of three hundred pounds of gold, safely protected from your prying fingers. On a sunny day, spare some time for walking through Exposition Park's **Rose Garden** (daily 10am–5pm; free). The flowers are at their most fragrant in April and May, when the bulk of the 45,000 annual visitors come by to admire the 16,000 rose bushes and the overall prettiness of their setting.

South Central LA

Lacking the scenic splendor of the coast, the glamour of West LA and the history of Downtown, **SOUTH CENTRAL LA** (comprised of such prominent neighborhoods as **Watts**, **Compton**, **Inglewood**, and **Crenshaw**) hardly ranks on the tourist circuit – especially since it burst onto the world's TV screens as the focal point of the April 1992 **riots** (see box). Still, it's an integral part of the city, especially in terms of size: a big, roughly circular chunk reaching from the southern edge of Downtown to the northern fringe of the Harbor Area. The population was once mostly black, but is increasingly Hispanic and Asian, interspersed here and there by elderly and working-poor whites. The dislocations occasioned by immigration have made for surprising trends and more than a little racial hostility. Watts, for example, once overwhelmingly black, now has a Hispanic majority, and many of the burned-out riot zones are no longer African-American at all, the few structures rebuilt now displaying signs written in Spanish. As a whole, South Central doesn't look so terribly run down at first sight, mostly made up of detached bungalows enjoying their own patch of palm-shaded lawn. But this picture is deceptive and doesn't conceal for long the fact that many residents are poor, get an abysmal deal at school and at work, and have very limited chances of climbing the social ladder and escaping to the more affluent parts of the city.

What will immediately strike you in South Central LA is the sheer monotony of the place: every block for twenty-odd miles looks much like the last, peppered with fast-food outlets, dingy liquor stores and abandoned factory sites, with the occasional Hispanic outdoor market to brighten the gloom. Like most commuters, you'll see almost nothing of the area by driving through on the Harbor Freeway (I-110), which is largely confined to its own isolated, walled-off channel.

Watts

The district of **WATTS**, on the eastern side of South Central, achieved notoriety as the scene of the six-day **Watts Riots** of August 1965. The arrest of a 21-year-old unemployed black man, Marquette Frye, on suspicion of drunken driving, gave rise to charges of police brutality and led to bricks, bottles and slabs of concrete being hurled at police and passing motorists during the night. The situation had calmed by the next morning, but the following evening, both young and old were on the streets, giving vent to an anger generated by years of unfair treatment by Chief William Parker's quasi-militarized LAPD – and other white-dominated institutions. Weapons were looted from stores and many buildings set alight (though few residential buildings, black-owned businesses or community institutions, such as libraries and schools, were touched); street barricades were erected, and the events took a more serious turn. By the fifth day, the insurgents were approaching Downtown, which – along with the fear spreading through white LA – led to the call-out of the National Guard: 13,000 troops arrived, set up machine-gun placements and road blocks, and imposed an 8pm-to-dawn curfew, causing the rebellion to subside.

In the aftermath of the uprising, which left 36 dead, one German reporter said of Watts, "it looks like Germany during the last months of World War II." Much of it still does – Watts is by far the ugliest part of South Central LA. The promises of investment made after 1965 never amounted to much; indeed, any forward strides made during the 1970s have long since been wiped out by wider economic decline, and eclipsed by the events of 1992. Although city politicians continue to pontificate about helping out the area, and business leaders occasionally promise to build a supermarket here or a bank there, this is still LA's economic ground zero.

Watts hit the headlines for a second time in 1975, when members of the Symbionese Liberation Army (SLA), who had kidnapped publishing heiress Patti Hearst, fought a lengthy – and televised – gun battle with police until the house they were trapped in burned to the ground. The site of the battle, at 1466 E 54th St, is now a vacant lot, though the surrounding houses are still riddled with bullet holes, visible reminders of another unpleasant chapter in local history.

Despite the district's violent and troubled history, there is one valid reason to come here, to see the internationally famous, Gaudí-esque **Watts Towers**, sometimes called the Rodia Towers, at 1765 E 107th St. Constructed from iron, stainless steel, old bedsteads, and cement, and decorated with fragments of bottles and around 70,000 crushed seashells, these striking pieces of street art were built by Simon Rodia, who had no artistic background or training at all, but labored over the towers' construction from 1921 to 1954, refusing offers of help and unable to explain either their meaning or why he was building them. Once finished, he left the area, refused to talk about the towers, and faded into obscurity. The towers managed to stave off bureaucratic hostility and structural condemnation for many decades; finally, they were declared a cultural landmark. The site is open by appointment only; call or visit the adjacent Watts Tower Arts Center, 1727 E 107th St (Tues–Sat 10am–4pm, Sun noon–4pm; free; ☏323/847-4646, ⓦ www.artscenecal.com/WattsTowers), for more information.

About five miles north, the **Dunbar Hotel**, 4225 S Central Ave, marks the first US hotel built specifically for blacks and patronized by almost every prominent African-American during the 1930s through the 1950s. Lying on a strip that once hosted many classic diners and nightclubs, the hotel is only visible in its restored lobby and facade, as it is now a home for the elderly (information through the OASIS senior center at ☏323/231-6220). It does, however, host the Central Avenue Jazz Festival in August (more details at ☏213/847-3169), which gives a hint of the area's swing and vigor in the old days.

Compton and Inglewood

Between Watts and the Harbor Area, only a few districts are of passing interest. Despite its fame as the home of many of LA's rappers – NWA, for example, sang venomously of its ills on their album *Straight Outta Compton* – not to mention of tennis phenoms Serena and Venus Williams, **COMPTON** is not a place where strangers should attempt to sniff out the local music scene. History buffs secure in their cars, however, might enjoy a stop for the free conducted tours at the **Dominguez Ranch Adobe**, 18127 S Alameda St (Tues & Wed 1–4pm, second & third Sun of each month 1–4pm; ☏310/631-5981), a restored mission that chronicles the social ascent of its founder, Juan José Dominguez – one of the soldiers who left Mexico with Padre Junípero Serra's expedition to found the California missions – whose long military service was acknowledged in 1782 by the granting of these 75,000 acres of land. As the importance of the area grew, so did the influence of Dominguez's descendants, who became powerful in local politics.

Closer to LAX, on the other side of the Harbor Freeway, **INGLEWOOD**, unenticing in itself, is home to the **Hollywood Park Racetrack**, (☏310/419-1500, ⓦ www.hollywoodpark.com), a landscaped track with lagoons and tropical vegetation, and a state-of-the-art computer-operated screen to give punters a view of the otherwise obscured back straight. Next door are the white pillars that ring **The Forum**, the 17,000-seat arena that was the former headquarters of both the LA Lakers (basketball) and the LA Kings (hockey), and is now mostly a concert venue (see "Listings" on p.196). Nearer to the 405 freeway, two gems of pop architecture are worth a look: **Randy's Donuts**, 805 Manchester Blvd, famed for its giant rooftop donut, and **Pann's**, a mile north at La Tijera and Centinela boulevards, one of the last true "Googie" coffee shops around, with a pitched roof, big neon sign, exotic plants, and wealth of primary colors. If you have a taste for more historic architecture, or are continuing on a mission tour from Dominguez Ranch, make sure to check out the **Centinela Adobe**, just south of *Pann's* at 7636 Midfield Ave (Wed & Sun 2–4pm; free), an 1834 structure loaded with period antiques and a nice array of Victorian clothing and furniture.

Crenshaw

As a general rule, it's not a good idea to venture into South Central looking for entertainment, unless you're with a local. The **CRENSHAW** district and adjacent **Leimert Park**, on its western fringe, may be an exception. Where the old center of African-American culture was once along Central Avenue, it is now here, especially with the recent tide of Hispanic immigration pushing more black residents to the western side of South Central. Crenshaw and Leimert Park feature a number of restaurants, fine book and record stores, the flagship moviehouse of Magic Johnson's theater chain, and an uneventful shopping mall. Two notable sights include the striking **Leimert Theater**, 3300 43rd Place, now a church, which features a towering oil-derrick sign with neon accents; and the **Museum in Black**, 4331 Degnan Blvd (Tues–Sat 11am–6pm; donation), exhibiting a wide range of African-American art and history, including slave-purchasing documents that date back nearly three hundred years. Beyond Crenshaw, the black upper-middle class resides in **Baldwin Hills**, a picturesque district marred by a slew of oil wells.

East LA

You can't visit LA without being made aware of the Latino influence on the city's demography and culture, whether it be through the thousands of Hispanic restaurants, the innumerable street names in Spanish, or, most obviously, through the sheer volume of Spanish spoken by people on the streets, which derives from many different dialects, from Tijuana to Oaxaca, from Guatemala to Colombia.

Of the many Hispanic neighborhoods all over LA, one of the most long-standing is **EAST LA**, which begins two miles east of Downtown, across the concrete-clad dribble of the Los Angeles River. There was a Mexican population here long before the white settlers came, and from the late nineteenth century onward millions more arrived, coming here chiefly to work on the land. As the white inhabitants gradually moved west towards the coast, the Mexicans stayed, creating a vast Spanish-speaking community that's one of the most historic in the country, as well as one of the most unfamiliar to outsiders.

Activity in East LA (commonly abbreviated to "ELA" or "East Los") tends to be outdoors in lively markets and bustling shops, where the customers are primarily Mexican-American. Non-Hispanic visitors are comparatively thin on the ground, but you are unlikely to meet any hostility on the streets during the day – though you should steer clear of the rough and very male-dominated bars and avoid the whole area after dark. **Guadalupe**, the Mexican image of the Virgin Mary, appears in mural art all over East LA, nowhere better than at the junction of Mednik and Cesar Chavez avenues. When a housing project across the street was demolished in the early 1970s, one wall, bearing a particularly remarkable image of Mary surrounded by a rich band of rainbow colors, was saved from the wrecking ball and reinstated across the street. Lined with blue tile, it now forms an unofficial shrine where worshippers place fresh flowers and candles.

Other than the street life and murals, there are few specific "sights" in East LA. The best plan is just to turn up on a Saturday afternoon – the liveliest part of the week – and stroll along **Cesar Chavez Avenue**, formerly Brooklyn Avenue, going eastward from Indiana Street and look at the wild pet shops, with free-roaming parrots and cases of boa constrictors, and at the **botanicas shops**, which cater to practitioners of Santería – a religion that is equal parts voodoo and Catholicism. Browse amid the shark's teeth, dried devil fish and plastic statuettes of Catholic saints, and buy magical herbs, ointments or candles after consulting the shopkeeper and explaining (in Spanish) what ails you. Only slightly less exotic fare can be found in **El Mercado de Los Angeles**,

3425 E 1st St, an indoor market somewhat similar to Olvera Street (see p.94) but much more authentic.

Afterwards, head through the freeway-caged LA district of **Boyle Heights**, which through the 1940s was a center for Jewish culture but has since become a solid Hispanic enclave, especially for new immigrants from Mexico and Central America. Go to the junction of **Soto** and **Cesar Chavez** where, at 5pm each afternoon, Norteños combos (upright bass, accordion, guitar, and banjo sexto) showcase their talents for free, hoping to be booked for weddings. Although this area can be relaxed and colorful during the day, it should be strongly avoided at night, when the local gangs make their presence felt.

Highland Park

North of Downtown, the **Pasadena Freeway** curves along a dry riverbed towards the foothill community whose name it bears. The freeway, LA's first, was completed in 1941 as the Arroyo Seco Parkway, as it was designed to be lined with charming greenery and flower plantings – an idea not very suitable for a place like LA. Highway engineers have since learned their lessons, but be aware that this antiquated roadway has stop signs on the on-ramps and exit ramps so short and sharp that the speed limit is 5mph.

Just off the road, two miles from Downtown, **HIGHLAND PARK** has a number of exuberantly detailed Victorian houses brought together from around the city to form **Heritage Square**. This fenced-off ten-acre park at 3800 Homer St (grounds Fri 10.30am–3.30pm, Sat & Sun 11.30am–4.30pm, tours on the hour Sat & Sun noon–3pm; $5) has been derided by some critics as an architectural "petting zoo." Although the buildings are interesting enough, the park's freeway-adjacent home is a less than ideal spot to escape into a Victorian world of buggies and gingerbread. Just beyond the next freeway exit, at 200 E Ave 43, the **Lummis House** (Fri–Sun 1–4pm; free) is the well-preserved home of Charles F. Lummis, a publicist who was at the heart of LA's nineteenth-century boom. An early champion of civil rights for Native Americans, and one who worked to save and preserve many of the missions, Lummis built his home as a cultural center of turn-of-the-century Los Angeles, where the literati of the day would meet to discuss poetry and the art and architecture of the Southwest. He built it in an ad hoc mixture of Mission and Medieval styles, naming it *El Alisal* after the many large sycamore trees that shade the gardens, and constructing the thick walls out of rounded granite boulders taken from the nearby riverbed, and the beams over the living room of old telephone poles. The solid wooden front doors are similarly built to last, reinforced with iron and weighing tons, while the plaster-and-tile interior features rustic, hand-cut timber ceilings and home-made furniture.

The Southwest Museum

Although people in LA scarcely know about it, the **SOUTHWEST MUSEUM** (Tues–Sat 10am–5pm; $6, $4 students; ⓦ www.southwestmuseum .org), which rises castle-like below Mount Washington, was Charles F. Lummis's most enduring achievement and is well worth an afternoon's visit. Half a mile north of the Lummis House (take the #81 or #83 bus from Downtown), the museum is the oldest in Los Angeles, and was founded in 1907. Its name is a bit deceptive – there are displays of Native American artifacts from all over North America, with exhibits of pre-Columbian pottery, coastal Chumash rock art, and a full-sized Plains Indian Cheyenne teepee. Its traveling exhibitions, educational programs, and theatrical events have made it an international center for indigenous American cultures. The Braun Research Library has an unmatched collection of recordings and photographs of Native Americans from the Bering Straits to Mexico, and the museum shop features Navajo rugs, kachina dolls, and turquoise jewelry, as well as an extensive selection of books and specialist publications. Nearby, the **Casa de Adobe**, administered by the museum, is a 1917 attempt to recreate a Mexican hacienda, featuring a small museum of its own that details LA history up to the nineteenth century. Currently closed for seismic retrofitting, the Casa is only open for special events (call ☏323/221-2163 for more information).

Hollywood

If a single word epitomizes the LA dream of glamour, money, and overnight success, it is **HOLLYWOOD**. Ever since American movies and their stars became international symbols of the good life, Hollywood has been a magnet to millions of tourists on celebrity-seeking pilgrimages and an equal number of hopefuls drawn by the prospect of riches and glory. Even if their real chances of success were infinitesimal, enough people were taken in by the dream to make Hollywood what it is today – a weird combination of insatiable optimism and total despair.

In reality, Hollywood was more a center of corruption and scandal than the city of dreams the studio-made legend suggests. Successful Hollywood residents actually spent little time here – leaving as soon as they could afford to for the privacy of the hills or coast. Although the area continues to be a secondary center for the film business, with technical service companies like prop shops

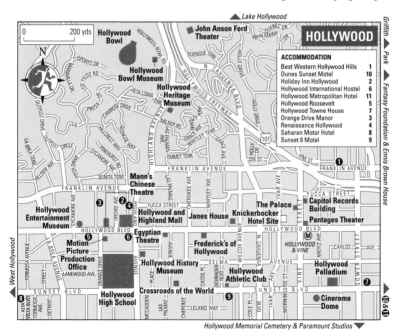

and equipment suppliers abundant, most of the big film companies relocated long ago to places like Burbank, leaving Hollywood in isolation, with prostitution, drug dealing, and seedy adult bookstores becoming the harsh reality clouding the more glamorous fantasies. Things have brightened up slightly in the last few years, however, with public and private capital financing the construction of new tourist plazas and shopping malls - places which, in their focus on the golden age of moviemaking, try to take the tarnish off the Hollywood myth once more.

Orientation

Approaching from Downtown, **East Hollywood** is the first taste of the district, an assortment of cheap housing and low-rent businesses with a few interesting sights scattered here and there, among them **Los Feliz**, which has become a trendy place to live and socialize, so much so that some pop stars have opened boutiques here. Further west, **Central Hollywood** is a compact area loaded with movie history, swamped by an eccentric street mix of social derelicts and star-struck tourists. Whether the memories have been turned into bizarre shrines, or forgotten and left to rot, you'd have to be totally uninterested in filmlore to find the place dull. Protecting Hollywood from the outside world, the rising slopes of the Santa Monica Mountains contain **Griffith Park** – several thousand acres of nature offering rugged hiking trails and busy sports and picnic grounds, which form a scenic northern edge to the area. Beyond the park, the more southerly of the slopes comprise the high ground known as the **Hollywood Hills**: exclusive homes perched on snaking driveways that are the most tangible reminders of the wealth generated in the city – and the substantial roll call of household names that has sprung from it.

East Hollywood: Silver Lake and Los Feliz

Typically unseen by most visitors, **EAST HOLLYWOOD** is mostly inhabited by Hispanic immigrants who have yet to fulfill the American dream, with the dingier parts of Sunset Boulevard – the main drag – contrasting dramatically with the chic western side of the strip. Still, even here, the perimeter neighborhoods bordering the hills are highly sought after, the streets around Beachwood Avenue have evolved into popular places to live and hang out, and upscale Mediterranean-style homes now litter the hillside.

Four blocks north of Sunset, **SILVER LAKE** was once home to some of Hollywood's first studios, since converted into restaurants and galleries, or at least warehouses and storage units. Walt Disney opened his first studio at 2719 Hyperion Ave in 1926 (now a grocery store), and the Keystone Kops were dreamed up in Mack Sennett's studio at 1712 Glendale Blvd, when the zone was known as **Edendale**, and where just a single sound studio now remains. Another faded bit of movie history can be found in the vicinity of 930 Vendome St, where a lengthy stairway was a location for Laurel and Hardy's 1932 flick *The Music Box*, in which the lads tried to haul a piano up the many steps, to humorous effect. Otherwise, there are no official "sights" in Silver Lake, except for a collection of interesting modernist houses in the hills designed by the likes of Richard Neutra and R.M. Schindler, and the district is generally known as the hip, edgy counterpart to West Hollywood: a gay-oriented spot that, with its cozy bars, quirky dance clubs, and alternative leftist bookstores, caters to a more working-class, Hispanic crowd than the whiter, more upscale, and better-known western end of Hollywood.

Although you'd never believe it these days, Hollywood started life as a **temperance colony**, created to be a sober, God-fearing alternative to raunchy Downtown LA, eight miles away by rough country road. Purchased and named by a pair of devout Methodists in 1887, and allegedly home to the country's largest Presbyterian church, the district remained autonomous until 1911, when residents were forced, in return for a regular water supply, to affiliate their city to LA as a suburb. The film industry, then gathering momentum on the East Coast, needed a place with guaranteed sunshine and a diverse assortment of natural backdrops to enable pictures to be made quickly, and most importantly, a distant spot to dodge Thomas Edison's patent trust, which tried to restrict filmmaking nationwide. Southern California, with its climate, scenery, and isolation, was the perfect spot. A few offices affiliated to Eastern film companies appeared Downtown from 1906 and the first true studios opened in nearby Silver Lake, but independent hopefuls soon discovered the cheaper rents on offer in Hollywood. Soon, the first **Hollywood studio** opened in 1911, and within three years the place was packed with filmmakers – many of them, like **Cecil B. DeMille**, who shared his barn-converted office space with a horse, destined to be the big names of the future.

The industry expanded fast, bringing riches and fame – with momentum provided by the overnight success of DeMille's The Squaw Man, filmed inside the former barn itself – and now reopened as the **Hollywood Heritage Museum**, 2100 N Highland Blvd (Sat & Sun 10am–3.30pm; $3; ☎323/874-4005, ⊚www.hollywoodheritage.org), exhibiting interesting antiques and treasures from the silent era. Yet moviemaking was far from being a financially secure business, and it wasn't until the release of D.W. Griffith's **The Birth of a Nation** in 1914 that the power of film was demonstrated. The film's racist account of the Civil War and Reconstruction (the KKK are the "heroes") caused riots outside cinemas and months of critical debate in the newspapers (Woodrow Wilson approvingly described it as "writing history with lightning"), and for the first time drew the middle classes to moviehouses – despite the exorbitant $2 ticket price. It was also the movie which first perfected the narrative style and production techniques that gradually became standard in classic Hollywood cinema – close-ups, cross-cutting, etc.

Modern Hollywood took shape from the 1920s on, when film production grew more specialized, the "star system" was perfected, and many small companies either went bust or were incorporated into one of the handful of bigger studios that came to dominate filmmaking. The **Golden Age** of the studio system was at its peak from the 1930s through the late 1940s, when a Supreme Court ruling put an end to studio monopolies owning their own exhibitors and theaters. Despite lean years from the later 1950s until the 1970s, and the onslaught of competition from television, Hollywood's enduring success is in making slick, unchallenging movies that sell – from Rhett Butler romancing Scarlett O'Hara to Yoda dueling with a light saber.

Ultimately, of course, no matter how much lip service Hollywood pays to the "independent cinema" (mainly by purchasing brash upstarts like Miramax), it's been big names, big bucks, and conservatism that have kept the town alive. With its profits gnawed into by TV and rock music, the film industry today rarely even thinks about taking artistic risks, even as it regularly takes unnecessary financial ones.

Nearby **LOS FELIZ** has fair-sized Hispanic and gay contingents, and on summer nights its bars are full of students from the local **American Film Institute** campus (Los Feliz Boulevard at Western Avenue) and would-be bohemians from the Hollywood Hills. Tim Burton's Ed Wood was partly shot, and premiered, at the architecturally impressive **Vista** movie theater, just off Hollywood Boulevard near Virgil – across from the former site of D.W. Griffith's Intolerance film set, which featured giant pillars and elephant statues, and has since been "re-created" in the Hollywood & Highland shopping mall further west (see p.116). **Hollyhock House**, on a small hill close to the junction of Vermont Avenue at 4800 Hollywood Blvd (Tues–Sun noon–3pm; $3), was the first of architect Frank Lloyd Wright's contributions to LA and was largely supervised by his student, Rudolf Schindler, later one of LA's preeminent architects. Covered with Mayan motifs and stylized, geometric renderings of the hollyhock flower, the house, completed in 1921, is an intriguingly obsessive dwelling, whose original furniture (now replaced by detailed reconstructions) continued the conceptual flow. The bizarre quality of the building was obviously too much for its oil heiress – and socialist – owner, Aline Barnsdall, who lived here only for a short time before donating both the house and the surrounding land to the city authorities for use as a cultural center, now the **Barnsdall Art Park**. Recently renovated and featuring a number of galleries devoted to the work of regional adult (and child) artists, the complex makes for a pleasant stop while you're waiting for the Hollyhock tour to begin. If you've no interest in art or architecture, the park is still worth a visit as one of the few quiet spots around here to enjoy a view of the Hollywood Hills in one direction, and Downtown and beyond in the other.

Another Wright building, the 1924 **Ennis-Brown House**, looms over Los Feliz at 2655 Glendower Ave. One of four of his local structures to feature "textile" concrete block, its ominous, pre-Columbian appearance has added atmosphere to over thirty film and TV productions, from Vincent Price's *The House on Haunted Hill* to David Lynch's *Twin Peaks*, and the house is open for 90min tours (Tues, Thurs & Sat 11am, 1pm & 3pm; $15; reserve at ☎323/660-0607, ⓦwww.ennisbrownhouse.org). Nearby, at 2495 Glendower, the **Fantasy Foundation** (Sat by appointment only; free; ☎323/MOON-FAN) boasts a truly amazing hoard of more than 300,000 items of horror, fantasy, and sci-fi memorabilia. Forrest J. Ackerman, former editor of *Famous Monsters of Filmland* magazine and winner of science fiction's first Hugo award, has filled eighteen rooms of the "Ackermansion" with such delights as the fake breasts worn by Jane Fonda in *Barbarella*, the robot from *Metropolis*, and the life masks of Boris Karloff, Bela Lugosi, and Lon Chaney. Sixty-nine years in the making, this unique collection is enhanced by the draw of the man himself: numerous personal anecdotes and bits of gossip make his one-on-one tour a must.

Central Hollywood

The few short blocks of **CENTRAL HOLLYWOOD** contain the densest concentration of faded glamour and film mythology in the world, a pervasive sense of nostalgia that makes the area deeply appealing in a way no measure of commercialism can diminish. Although you're much more likely to find a porno theater than spot a star, the decline that blighted the area from the early 1960s is slowly receding in the face of prolonged efforts by local authorities – including repaving Hollywood Boulevard with a special glass-laden tarmac that sparkles in the streetlights and inviting all manner of new malls to take root here. Nevertheless the place still gets hairy after dark away from the main tourist zones, when the effects of homelessness, drug addiction, and prostitution are more evident, and petty thieves go hunting for the odd purse or wallet.

Along Hollywood Boulevard

Following **HOLLYWOOD BOULEVARD** west, the first notable sight is the junction of **Hollywood and Vine**, a juxtaposition of street names that still tingles the spines of dedicated Hollywood-philes. During the early golden years, the rumor spread that any budding star had only to parade around this junction to be spotted by big-name film producers or directors (the major studios were in those days all concentrated nearby), who nursed coffees behind the windows of neighboring restaurants. In typical Hollywood style, the whole tale was blown wildly out of proportion, and while many real stars did pass by, it was only briefly on their way to and from work, and the crossing did nothing but earn a fabulous reputation. The only thing marking the myth today, apart from disappointed tourists, is a small plaque on the wall of a pizza joint.

The Red Line subway also stops here, so if you feel inclined to make a trip Downtown or to the San Fernando Valley, this is the spot – an underground station decorated with film reels and familiar Hollywood imagery that is one of the few artistically interesting stops in LA's mass transit network. Above ground, at 1750 N Vine St, the **Capitol Records Tower** resembles a stack of 45rpm records and serves as the music company's headquarters, its 1950s design supposedly inspired by an offhand Johnny Mercer remark. Nearby, at 6233 Hollywood Blvd, the **Pantages Theater** has a bland facade but one of the city's greatest interiors, a melange of Baroque styling that mainly highlights touring stage productions these days.

The bulky **Knickerbocker Hotel**, 1714 Ivar Ave, now a retirement center, was where the widow of legendary escapologist Harry Houdini conducted a rooftop seance in an attempt to assist her late spouse in his greatest escape of all. During the 1930s and 1940s, the hotel had a reputation for rooming some of Hollywood's more unstable characters, and a number of lesser names jumped from its high windows. At 1817 Ivar St stands the flea-bag boardinghouse where author and screenwriter **Nathanael West** lived during the 1930s, after coming west to revive his flagging financial situation – and ultimately failing. Gazing over the street's parade of extras, hustlers, and make-believe cowboys, West penned the dark satirical portrait of Hollywood, *The Day of the Locust*, the apocalyptic finale of which was inspired by Hollywood Hills wildfires in the summer of 1935 (and which includes a character with the oddly prescient name of Homer Simpson). Back on Hollywood Boulevard, at no. 6608, the purple-and-pink **Frederick's of Hollywood** is a local landmark. Opened in 1947, it has been (under-)clothing Hollywood's sex goddesses ever since, and many more mortal bodies all over the world through its mail-order outlet. Inside, the **lingerie museum** (Mon–Fri 10am–9pm, Sat 10am–7pm, Sun 11am–6pm; free) displays some of the company's corsets, bras, and panties, donated by a host of famous wearers, ranging from Liz Taylor and Lana Turner to Cher and Madonna.

A little further on, at no. 6708, the very first Hollywood premiere (*Robin Hood*, an epic swashbuckler starring Douglas Fairbanks Sr), took place in 1922 at the **Egyptian Theatre**. Financed by impresario Sid Grauman, in its heyday the Egyptian was a glorious fantasy, modestly seeking to re-create the Temple of Thebes, with usherettes dressed as Cleopatra. This great old building was damaged in the 1994 earthquake, but has since been lovingly restored by the American Cinematheque film foundation, and now plays an assortment of Hollywood classics, avant-garde flicks, and foreign films to small but appreciative crowds. Tourists, however, are encouraged to check out a short documentary, presented hourly, chronicling the rise of Hollywood as America's movie capital (Sat & Sun 2pm & 3.30pm; $7; ⓦwww.americancinematheque.com). Alternatively, you can get the grand tour of the theater itself in hour-long in-depth visits to sights like the backstage dressing rooms and projection booth, usually presented twice monthly in the middle of the month (10.30am only;

$7; call for details at ☏323/461-2020, ext 115). Much less appealing, the east-ern corners of the Hollywood and Highland intersection feature a handful of dreary tourist traps – wax museum, oddities gallery, world-record exhibit – that are worthwhile only if you're very easily amused.

Much of the pavement along this stretch of Hollywood Boulevard is marked by the brass nameplates of the **Walk of Fame** (officially beginning at Hollywood and Vine). The laying of the plates began in 1960, instigated by the local chamber of commerce, which thought that by enshrining the big names in radio, television, movies, music, and theater, it could somehow restore the boulevard's faded glamour and boost tourism. However, dubious choices are often made; the Rolling Stones, for example, took decades to gain a star, long after they were past their prime, while such questionable picks as TV's *Rugrats* cartoon characters are enshrined frequently. Selected stars have to part with several thousand dollars for the privilege of being included: among them are Marlon Brando (1717 Vine St), Marlene Dietrich (6400 Hollywood Blvd), Michael Jackson (6927 Hollywood Blvd), Elvis Presley (6777 Hollywood Blvd), and Ronald Reagan (6374 Hollywood Blvd).

West of the Egyptian Theatre, the **Hollywood & Highland** complex, on the west side of the eponymous intersection, must rank as one of LA's most frus-trating attractions. After nearly a billion dollars of public and private invest-ment, the commitment of a major hotel, boutiques, and restaurants, and the relocation of the Oscars to the specially-designed Kodak Theater on site, this towering beacon of commerce – which was supposed to revitalize Hollywood and give the district a cultural renaissance – is no better than your average suburban shopping mall. Loaded with big-name fashion chains and swank eateries, Hollywood & Highland still has the same tired feel as most any other shopping plaza, with fortress-like walls shielding consumers from the potential seediness of Hollywood Boulevard and private security keeping watch over "undesirable" elements. Even more ominous is its chosen theme: the Babylonian set from the 1916 D.W. Griffith film *Intolerance*, from which the mall borrows heavily in its super-sized columns, elephant statues, and colossal archway. Unrivaled in film history for almost fifty years, the movie was Hollywood's first real financial disaster, helping to ruin the career of its direc-tor and making the movie studios permanently wary of taking any sort of cre-ative risks.

Hollywood impressions at the Chinese Theatre

Opened in 1927 as a lavish setting for premieres of swanky new productions, the **Chinese Theatre** was for many decades *the* spot for movie first nights, and the public crowded behind the rope barriers in the thousands to watch the movie aris-tocrats arriving for the screenings. The main draw, of course, has always been the assortment of **cement handprints** and **footprints** embedded in the theater's fore-court. The idea came about when actress Norma Talmadge accidentally – though some say it was a deliberate publicity stunt – trod in wet cement while visiting the construction site with owner Sid Grauman, who had established a reputation for cre-ating garish movie palaces with gloriously vulgar designs based on exotic themes. The first formally to leave their marks were Mary Pickford and Douglas Fairbanks Sr, who ceremoniously dipped their digits when arriving for the opening of *King of Kings*, and the practice continues today. It's certainly fun to work out the actual dimensions of your favorite film stars, and to discover if your hands are smaller than Julie Andrews' or your feet are bigger than Rock Hudson's (or both).

One site that the mall has very nearly ruined already is **Mann's Chinese Theatre**, 6925 Hollywood Blvd, which has for no good reason been swallowed up by the complex, enveloped by a curving stucco wall, and expanded into a multiplex (beyond the three theaters pre-dating the mall). As for what remains of the building, it's an odd version of a classical Chinese temple, replete with dubious Chinese motifs and upturned dragontail flanks, and the lobby's Art Deco splendor and the grand chinoiserie of the auditorium make for interesting viewing. Afterward, on the street outside the theater, you can hop aboard a tour for a look at the "homes of the stars" (see p.82), along with hundreds of other sightseers.

To catch a movie in the making, cross the road to the **Motion Picture Production Office**, 7038 Hollywood Blvd, 5th Floor (Mon–Fri 8am–6pm), which issues a "shoot sheet" every weekday ($1–2), detailing exactly what's being filmed around town that day. Most film shoots hire a couple of off-duty LAPD officers for security, but not all sets are impenetrable. A few doors down, 7000 Hollywood Blvd, the **Hollywood Roosevelt** was movieland's first luxury hotel (see "Accommodation," p.86). Opened in the same year as the Chinese Theatre, it fast became the meeting place of top actors and screenwriters, its *Cinegrill* restaurant feeding and watering the likes of W.C. Fields, Ernest Hemingway, and F. Scott Fitzgerald, not to mention legions of hangers-on. In 1929 the first Oscars were presented here, beginning the long tradition of Hollywood rewarding itself in the absence of honors from elsewhere. Look inside for a view of the splashing fountains and elegantly weighty wrought-iron chandeliers of its marble-floored lobby, and for the pictorial **History of Hollywood** on the second floor. The place is thick with legend: on the staircase from the lobby to the mezzanine Bill "Bojangles" Robinson taught Shirley Temple to dance; and the ghost of Montgomery Clift (who stayed here while filming *From Here to Eternity*) apparently haunts the place, announcing his presence by blowing a bugle. Surviving lounge divas like Eartha Kitt still put on the occasional show at the Cinegrill cabaret.

Across the street, the **Hollywood Entertainment Museum**, 7021 Hollywood Blvd (Tues–Sun 11am–6pm; $8.75, students $4.50; ☎323/465-7900, ⓦwww.hollywoodmuseum.com), occupies a lower level of the crudely "futuristic" Hollywood Museum Center. While highlighted by the full set of the TV show *Cheers* and the bridge of the Enterprise from *Star Trek*, along with rotating exhibitions and various antiques and curios from Hollywood history, the museum is a rather amateurish collection of odds and ends from old TV programs and movies, largely presented without context or any apparent purpose. Unfortunately, it's also the closest thing to an actual movie museum that Hollywood has at present. Locals continue to wait for the long-delayed Max Factor Museum, nearby at 1660 Highland Blvd, to re-open as the **Hollywood History Museum**, which will exhibit on its four levels the fashion, sets, make-up, special-effects, and art design of the Golden Age of movies. To see if it's finally open, call ☎323/464-7770, or surf over to ⓦwww.Hollywoodhistorymuseum.com for more information.

Along Sunset Boulevard

Paralleling Hollywood Boulevard to the south is another famous stretch nearly as steeped in movie legend, **SUNSET BOULEVARD**, which sports both contemporary decay and countless sites for Tinseltown nostalgia. You might start your explorations at the corner of Sunset and **Gower Street**, where during the industry's formative years, unemployed movie extras would hang around here hoping for a few days' work with one of the small B-movie studios, helping the junction earn the nicknames "Gower gulch" and "poverty row."

Another remaining shard of the boulevard's old-time glory can be found at no. 6360, where the huge white **Cinerama Dome** was built in 1963 to exhibit giant three-projector films on a curved screen, and is now part of a larger retail complex of theaters, shops, and eateries. Luckily, you can still see (single-projector) blockbusters in the dome on a large, curved screen – as fun and engaging a cinematic experience as any in LA. Nearby, the delectable Spanish Revival-style building at 6525 Sunset Blvd was, from the 1920s until the 1950s, known as the **Hollywood Athletic Club**. Another of Hollywood's legendary watering holes, the likes of Charlie Chaplin, Clark Gable, and Tarzan himself (Johnny Weissmuller) lounged beside its Olympic-sized pool, while Johns Barrymore and Wayne held drinking parties in the apartment levels above. After standing empty for 25 years, the building re-opened in 1990 as a pool hall, bar, and restaurant, only to close again at the end of the decade and remain shuttered, though opening for special parties and events.

The grouping of shops at **Crossroads of the World**, 6672 Sunset Blvd, isn't much to look at these days, but when finished in 1936, was one of LA's major tourist attractions and one of the very first local malls. The central plaza supposedly resembles a ship, surrounded by shops designed with Tudor, French, Italian, and Spanish motifs – the idea being that the shops are the ports into which the shopper would sail. Oddly enough, time has been kind to this place, and considering the more recent and far brasher architecture found in the city, this has a definite, if muted, charm. However, it can be seen in its full glory in the 1997 film *LA Confidential*, which also uses the nearby *Formosa Café* (see p.178) and *Frolic Room* bar, 6245 Hollywood Blvd, as period emblems of 1950s LA swagger. Finally, nearby **Paramount Studios**, entrance at 5555 Melrose Ave, is best known for its gate – famously seen in the film *Sunset Boulevard* – though at present, tours are no longer offered, with the studio mysteriously citing "security concerns" for the suspension.

Hollywood Forever Cemetery

Not surprisingly for a town obsessed with marketing and PR, even the cemeteries – and not only the actors – are renamed to draw the crowds. Thus the former Hollywood Memorial Park has been reincarnated as **HOLLYWOOD FOREVER CEMETERY** (daily 8am–5pm; free), though the graves have luckily been kept in the same places. Close to the junction of Santa Monica Boulevard and Gower Street and overlooked by the famous water tower of the neighboring Paramount Studios, the cemetery displays myriad tombs of dead celebrities, most notably in its southeastern corner, where a cathedral mausoleum includes, at no. 1205, the resting place of **Rudolph Valentino**. In 1926 10,000 people packed the cemetery when the celebrated screen lover died aged just 31, and to this day on each anniversary of his passing (23 August), at least one "Lady in Black" will likely be found mourning – a tradition that started as a publicity stunt in 1931 (the first weeping damsel claimed to be a former paramour of Valentino's but was exposed as a hired actress) and has continued ever since. While here, spare a thought for the more contemporary screen star, Peter Finch, who died in 1977 before being awarded a Best Actor Oscar for his film *Network*. His crypt is opposite Valentino's and tourists often lean their rears unknowingly against it while photographing Rudolph's marker.

Fittingly, outside the mausoleum, the most pompous grave belongs to **Douglas Fairbanks Sr**, who, with his wife Mary Pickford (herself buried at Forest Lawn Glendale), did much to introduce social snobbery to Hollywood.

Even in death Fairbanks keeps a snooty distance from the pack, his ostentatious memorial (complete with sculptured pond) only reachable by a shrubbery-lined path from the mausoleum. If you revel in Tinseltown's post-life pretension, there are countless self-important obelisks and grandiose grave-markers throughout the park, under which LA's somebodies and nobodies finally, in death, mix. One of the cemetery's more recent arrivals was **Mel Blanc**, "the man of a thousand voices" – among them Bugs Bunny, Porky Pig, Tweety Pie, and Sylvester – whose epitaph simply reads "That's All, Folks."

Despite its morbid glamour, the cemetery also has a contemporary function. As you enter, you will notice the many tightly packed rows of glossy black headstones with Orthodox crosses and Cyrillic lettering. These mark the resting places of Russian and Armenian immigrants, who increasingly populate the graveyard just as their living counterparts populate Central and West Hollywood.

Griffith Park

Built on land donated by Gilded Age mining millionaire Griffith J. Griffith, vast **GRIFFITH PARK**, between Hollywood and the San Fernando Valley (daily 5am–10.30pm, mountain roads close at dusk; free), is a combination of gentle greenery and rugged mountain slopes that offers a welcome respite from the often mind-numbing chaos of LA. The largest municipal park in the country, it's also one of the few places where the city's many racial and social groups at least go through the motions of mixing together. Above the land-scaped flat sections, where the crowds assemble to picnic, play sports, or visit the fixed attractions, the hillsides are rough and wild, marked only by foot and bridle paths, leading into desolate but appealingly unspoiled terrain that gives great views over the LA basin and out towards the ocean. Bear in mind, though, that while the park is safe by day, its reputation for after-dark violence is well founded.

There are four **main entrances** to Griffith Park. Western Canyon Road, north of Los Feliz Boulevard, enters the park through the **Ferndell** – as the name suggests, a lush glade of ferns, from which numerous trails run deeper into the park – continuing up to the **Griffith Observatory**, 2800 E Observatory Rd, familiar from its use as a backdrop in *Rebel Without A Cause* and numerous low-budget sci-fi flicks. Although the observatory is an obvious icon of LA, and one of the city's most enjoyable spots, it is nonetheless closed for renovation until the spring of 2005, including its Hall of Science, planetarium, laserium, and massive telescope. Until then, a "satellite facility" is promised on the north side of Griffith Park, about which you can find out more, along with the overall progress of renovation, by calling ☎323/664-1191 or visiting ⓦwww.griffithobs.org.

Hiking in Griffith Park

The steeper parts of **Griffith Park**, which blend into the foothills of the Santa Monica Mountains, offers a variety of **hiking trails**. You can get maps from the **ranger station**, at 4400 Crystal Springs Rd (daily during daylight hours; ☎323/662-6573) – also the starting point for guided hikes and atmospheric evening hikes, held whenever there's a full moon. The rangers also have maps for drivers that detail the best vantage points for views over the whole of Los Angeles, not least from the highest place in the park – the summit of Mount Hollywood.

Descending from the observatory on Vermont Canyon Road (effectively the continuation of Western Canyon Road) brings you to the small **bird sanctuary**, set within a modest-sized wooded canyon. Across the road is the **Greek Theatre** (T 323/665-1927, W www.greektheatrela.com), an open-air amphitheater that seats nearly five thousand beneath its quasi-Greek columns – though if you're not going in for a show (the Greek is a venue for big-name rock, jazz, and country music concerts during the summer), you'll see just the bland exterior.

The **northern end** of the park, over the hills in the San Fernando Valley, is best reached directly by car from the Golden State Freeway, although you can take the park roads (or explore the labyrinth of hiking trails) that climb the park's hilly core. At the end of the journey, don't bother with the cramped and dismal **LA Zoo** (daily 10am–5pm; $8.25, kids $3.25; W www.lazoo.org) or the unkempt old locomotives of **Travel Town** (daily 10am–5pm; free).

The Gene Autry Western Heritage Museum

Sharing a parking lot with the zoo, the **Gene Autry Western Heritage Museum**, near the junction of the Ventura and Golden State freeways at 4700 Western Heritage Way (Tues–Sun 10am–5pm, Thurs 10am–8pm; $7.50, students $5; W www.autry-museum.org), bears the name of the "singing cowboy" who cut over six hundred discs from 1929, starred in blockbuster Hollywood Westerns during the 1930s and 1940s, became even more of a household name through his TV show in the 1950s, and died in 1999 after a very lengthy career – which included a stint as owner of baseball's California Angels franchise in Anaheim. Autry fans hoping for a shrine to the man who penned the immortal "That Silver-Haired Daddy of Mine," are in for a shock, however: the **collection** – from buckskin jackets and branding irons to Frederic Remington's sculptures of turn-of-the-century Western life and the truth about the shootout at the OK Corral – is a serious and credible attempt to explore the mindset and culture of those who participated in the colonization of the West. It also contains a nod to Hollywood, with a sizeable collection of movie artifacts, posters, and assorted memorabilia, most of it discussed in an analytical, non-jingoistic fashion.

The Hollywood Hills

Apart from offering the chance to appreciate just how flat the LA basin is, the views from the **HOLLYWOOD HILLS** feature perhaps the oddest, most opulent, selection of properties to be found anywhere. Around these canyons and slopes, which run from Hollywood itself into Benedict Canyon above Beverly Hills, mansions are so commonplace that only the half-dozen fully blown castles (at least, the Hollywood versions) really stand out.

Mulholland Drive, named after LA's most renowned hydro-engineer, runs along the crest, passing some of the most famous sites – Rudolph Valentino's extravagant **Falcon Lair** (1436 Bella Drive), Errol Flynn's **Mulholland House** (7740 Mulholland Drive), and the former home of actress Sharon Tate, where some of the Manson family killings took place. Plus, there's a number of run-of-the-mill million-dollar residences belonging to an assortment of luminaries, visionaries, former politicians, and movie moguls, some of whom have helped forge LA's reputation for ostentatious and utterly decadent living – most visibly in **Mount Olympus**, a high-kitsch real-estate tract loaded with faux palazzos, pseudo-Roman statuary, goofy marble urns, and snarling stone lions. Doubtless the most bizarre sight, though, is the **Chemosphere**, at 776 Torreyson Drive, a giant UFO house hovering above the canyon on a long

The Hollywood sign

One thing you can see from more or less anywhere in Hollywood is the **Hollywood Sign**, erected on Mount Lee to spell "Hollywoodland" in 1923 as a promotional device to sell property at the foot of the hills, and at one time decorated with enough high-wattage light bulbs to be seen as far away as the coast. The "land" part was removed in 1949, leaving the rest as a world-renowned symbol of the entertainment industry here. It has also (unjustifiably) gained a reputation as a suicide spot, ever since would-be movie star Peg Entwhistle terminated her career and life here in 1932, aged 24 – no mean feat, with the sign being as difficult to reach then as it is now. Stories that this act led to a line of failed starlets desperate to make their final exit from Tinseltown's best-known marker are untrue however – though many troubled souls may have died of exhaustion while trying to get to it. Less fatal mischief has been practiced by students of nearby Caltech, who on one occasion renamed the sign for their school. More unsavory acts of sign desecration have also occurred, most of them too juvenile and numerous to mention. Because of this history, there's no public road to the sign (Beachwood Drive comes nearest, but ends at a closed gate) and you'll incur minor cuts and bruises while scrambling to get anywhere near. In any case, infrared cameras and radar-activated zoom lenses have been installed to catch graffiti writers, and innocent tourists who can't resist a close look are also liable for a steep fine. For a much simpler look, you can check out the sign from your computer by visiting ⊛ www.hollywoodsign.org, where the letters are visible day or night.

pedestal, designed by quirky architect John Lautner. Unfortunately, most of the area's other houses are hidden away, and there's no real way to explore in depth without your own car and a knowledgeable friend to help pinpoint the sights, spread widely across every hillside. You could use one of the guided tours (see p.82), but for the most part you're better off doing your own exploring, preferably with a copy of the latest *Thomas Guide* map and, if possible, a detailed and updated guide to LA architecture.

Lake Hollywood

Hemmed in among the hills between Griffith Park and the Hollywood Freeway, **LAKE HOLLYWOOD** feels like a piece of open country in the heart of the city. The clear, calm waters, actually a reservoir intended for drought relief, are surrounded by clumps of pines in which squirrels, lizards, and a few scurrying skunks and coyotes easily outnumber humans. You can't get too near the water, as metal fences protect it from the general public, but the footpaths that encircle it are pleasant for a stroll, especially for a glimpse of the stone bear heads that decorate the reservoir's curving front wall. There's no social kudos associated with being seen trotting around the footpath – which may explain why so few Angelenos deem it worthy of their presence. Nevertheless, the lake has figured in a few Hollywood films, notably the disaster epic *Earthquake*, which showed the dam bursting and flooding the basin to devastating effect, another in a long line of LA-apocalypse movies.

You can only reach the lake by car. Although opening and closing times vary widely throughout the year, the lake **access road** is generally open from 7am until noon and 2pm until 7pm on weekdays, and 7am until 7.30pm on weekends: to get to it, go north on Cahuenga Boulevard past Franklin Avenue and turn right onto Dix Street, left into Holly Drive and climb to Deep Dell Place; from there it's a sharp left on Weidlake Drive. Follow the winding little street to the main gate.

The Hollywood Bowl

Near the Hollywood Freeway at 2301 N Highland Ave, the **HOLLYWOOD BOWL** is an open-air auditorium that opened in 1921 and has since gained more fame than it deserves. The Beatles played here in the mid-1960s, but the Bowl's principal function is as the occasional summer home of the Los Angeles Philharmonic, which gives evening concerts from July to September (information at ☎323/850-2000, ⊛www.hollywoodbowl.org). These are far less highbrow than you might imagine, many of them featuring spirited crowd-pleasers like *Victory at Sea* and the *1812 Overture*. It's long been the chic thing to eat a picnic in the grounds before making the climb to your seat, and nowadays the consumption tends to continue throughout the show, often rendering the music barely audible above the crunching of popcorn and fried chicken and the clink of empty wine bottles rolling down the steps. If that racket alone doesn't bother you, there's also the constant drone of jumbo jets flying above the Bowl on their long final descent toward LAX. Although not a choice spot for lovers of fine music, the venue can still be fun, with ticket prices starting at $1. If you're really broke, come to the Bowl during summer mornings (Tues, Thurs & Fri 9am–noon) and listen to rehearsals for free.

More about the Bowl's history can be gleaned from the video show inside the **Hollywood Bowl Museum** (June–Aug Tues–Sat 10am–8pm, Sun 4.30–7.30pm; Sept–May Tues–Sat 10am–4.30pm; free; ☎323/850-2000, ⊛www.hollywoodbowl.org) near the entrance. It's not an essential stop by any means, but is worth a visit if you have any affection for the grand old concrete structure. With a collection of musical instruments from around the world, the museum also features recordings of notable symphonic moments in the Bowl's history and architectural drawings by Lloyd Wright, Frank's son (more famous for his Wayfarer's Chapel; see p.145), who contributed a design for one of the Bowl's many shells.

West LA

LA's Westside begins immediately beyond Hollywood in **WEST LA**, which contains some of the city's most expensive, and exclusive, neighborhoods. Bordered by the Santa Monica Mountains to the north and the Santa Monica Freeway to the south, West LA, perhaps more than anywhere but the beaches, embodies the stylish images that the city projects to the outside world. Actually, the reality is often less dazzling: away from the showcase streets are the usual long, residential blocks, only marginally less drab than normal with their better tended lawns, more upscale supermarkets, cleaner gas stations, and tastier fast food.

One of the best reasons to come to West LA is the surprisingly impressive collection of the **LA County Museum of Art (LACMA)**, on the eastern perimeter of the **Fairfax District**, and forming the centerpiece of the resurgent cultural zone touted as the **Museum Mile**. West of Fairfax Avenue, and north of Beverly Boulevard, **West Hollywood** is known for its art and design, loaded with posey restaurants and boutiques, and is surprisingly small-scale, except for a giant design center at its core. **Beverly Hills**, a little way further west, is less friendly but more affluent: you may need an expense account to buy a sandwich but it's a matchless place to indulge in window-shopping on the way to the more roundly appealing **Westwood**. The main activity in this

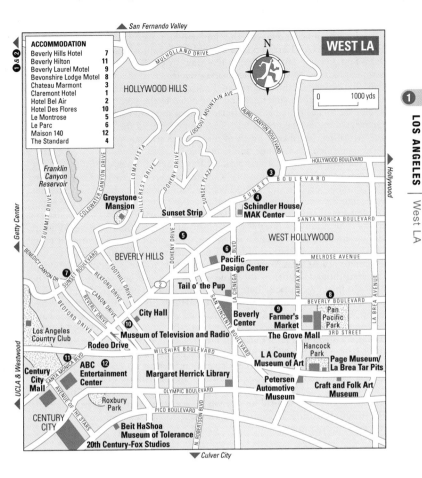

ACCOMMODATION

Beverly Hills Hotel	7
Beverly Hilton	11
Beverly Laurel Motel	9
Bevonshire Lodge Motel	8
Chateau Marmont	3
Claremont Hotel	1
Hotel Bel Air	2
Hotel Des Flores	10
Le Montrose	5
Le Parc	6
Maison 140	12
The Standard	4

low-rise, Spanish Revival, fairly pedestrianized area has always been movies –
seeing them rather than making them. The original Art Deco palaces still retain
most of their original glory, and are a short way from the **UCLA Campus**,
home to a number of galleries and museums, and altogether more engaging for
visitors than the fortress atmosphere of USC. The **Sepulveda Pass** forms the
western edge of West LA and leads the visitor to two museums that have relocated here in the last few years: the **Getty Center** and the **Skirball Cultural
Center**, both positioned high above the basin's turmoil.

Fairfax Avenue, Farmers Market, and Miracle Mile

The West LA section of **FAIRFAX AVENUE**, between Santa Monica and
Wilshire, is still the backbone of the city's Jewish culture. Apart from temples,
yeshivas, kosher butcher shops, and delicatessens, there's little actually to see
here, but by local standards it's a refreshingly vibrant neighborhood, and easily
explored on foot.

Fairfax continues down to the longstanding wooden structures of the **FARMERS MARKET**, 6333 W 3rd St (June–Sept Mon–Fri 9am–9pm, Sat 9am–8pm, Sun 10am–7pm; Oct–May Mon–Sat 9am–6.30pm, Sun 10am–5pm; free; ⓦ www.farmersmarketla.com), a rabbit warren of fast-food stalls and produce stands. Started in 1934 as a little agricultural co-op during the Depression, the market has since expanded to the point where it now sees 40,000 visitors *daily*, and has engendered a monstrous new mall next door: **The Grove**, a three-level colossus that offers branches of all the major chain stores, and which has paved over much of the market's parking lot - making parking spots that much more scarce, and expensive.

To the east on Third Street, pleasant **Pan Pacific Park** once featured the wondrous Pan Pacific Auditorium, a masterpiece of late Art Deco architecture and filming location for the Olivia Newton John kitsch classic *Xanadu*. Although the structure burned down in a 1989 fire, a hint of its breezy architectural style is still visible in the lettering and curving pylon of an adjacent sports facility. Further on, the **May Company** department store on Wilshire Boulevard, at Fairfax Avenue, was built in 1934 and has been compared to an oversized, golden perfume bottle ever since; its main contemporary function is as the site of **LACMA West**, an exhibition annex to the larger museum down the road (hours and prices the same as LACMA; see below). Originally, the May Company was placed here to signal the western entrance to the premier property development of the time, the **MIRACLE MILE**, which stretched along Wilshire eastward to La Brea Avenue and is still lined with faded Art Deco monuments. The department stores have long since closed, but an unprecedented number of museums now create an impressive "Museum Mile" in their place. Although many of the office blocks are empty, look out for the old site of **Desmond's**, a former department store at no. 5514 consisting of a Zigzag Moderne tower stepping up from a streamlined two-story pedestal and, just east of La Brea Avenue, the 1929 black-and-gold **Security Pacific Bank**. The bank gives you a small hint of what LA's greatest Art Deco structure, the **Richfield Building** Downtown, must have looked like before it was summarily destroyed in 1968.

The Museum Mile

As you will immediately tell, the **LA County Museum of Art**, 5905 Wilshire Blvd (Mon, Tues & Thurs noon–8pm, Fri noon–9pm, Sat–Sun 11am–8pm; $7, students $5; ⓦ www.lacma.org), comprises a rather ugly cluster of oversized beige-and-green blocks, which were plopped down along the Miracle Mile in 1965 and have been mostly dismissed or scorned ever since. Because of this disregard, the museum plans to close in mid-2004 and undergo a massive **demolition** and **rebuilding** under the guiding hand of renowned Dutch architect Rem Koolhaas, who has planned a showcase structure for LA's art unlike anything else in town – built on stilts and roofed over with a translucent plastic tent. The only remaining buildings left will be the Japanese Pavilion (see below) and LACMA West (see above), which will also be the only part of the museum open during the reconstruction.

Until LACMA closes, make sure to check out its wide-ranging stock of art, some of which is among the best in the world, justifying a lengthy visit. And if you arrive on a Tuesday before 1pm, check out the schedule of classic Warner Bros films playing in the **Leo S. Bing Theater**, where you can see anything from a film noir to a screwball comedy for only $3.

LACMA is enormous, and there's no way you could see it all in one trip;

you're best off either focusing on the contemporary art and traveling exhibitions in the **Anderson Building** (the concrete block on Wilshire Boulevard) or diving into the fine selection of Old Masters and world art in the **Ahmanson Building** (the concrete block on Ogden Drive). Get a **map** of the complex from the information desk in the central courtyard. Alongside many excellent collections of Southeast Asian sculpture and Middle Eastern decorative arts in the Ahmanson Building, the **Fearing Collection** consists of funeral masks and sculpted guardian figures from the ancient civilizations of pre-Columbian Mexico. Where the museum really excels, however, is in its specializations, notably the prints and drawings in the **Rifkind Center for German Expressionist Studies**, which includes a library of magazines and tracts from Weimar Germany, and the **Pavilion for Japanese Art**. Currently the only attractive building on the site, the pavilion was created by iconoclastic architect Bruce Goff to resemble the effects of traditional shoji screens, filtering varying levels and qualities of light through to the interior. Displays include painted screens and scrolls, ceramics, and lacquerware, rivaling the collection of the late Emperor Hirohito as the most extensive in the world, and viewable on a gently sloping ramp that spirals down to a small, ground-floor waterfall that trickles pleasantly amid the near-silence of the gallery.

The roof combs of the pavilion make a playful reference beyond the museum to the tusks of a model mastodon sinking slowly into the adjacent **La Brea Tar Pits**, a large pool of smelly tar ("la brea" in Spanish). Tens of thousands of years ago, such creatures tried to drink from the thin layer of water covering the tar in the pits, only to become stuck fast and preserved for modern science. Millions of bones belonging to the animals (and one set of human bones) have been found here and some of them reconstructed in the next-door **George C. Page Discovery Center** (Mon–Fri 9.30am–5pm, weekends opens at 10am; $6, students $3.50; ⓦ www.tarpits.org), where you can spot the skeletons of your favorite extinct Ice Age-era creatures, from giant ground sloths to menacing saber-toothed tigers. Tar still seeps from the ground, but most of the sticky goo oozes behind chain link fences.

On the opposite side of LACMA, at 6060 Wilshire Blvd, the **Petersen Automotive Museum** (Tues–Sun 10am–6pm, Fri 10am–9pm; $10, parking $6; ⓣ 323/930-CARS, ⓦ www.petersen.org) is the baby of media mogul Robert Petersen, with three floors paying sumptuous if superficial homage to the automobile, featuring special exhibits of movie stars' cars, customized lowriders, and vintage footage of land-speed record attempts in the desert. It fails to explain the reasons behind the collapse of LA's early public transportation system and is not critical by any means, but it does have enough mint-condition classic models to render the car-crazy delirious with joy.

The last significant museum on the Museum Mile, and also the one in the most precarious state, is the **Craft and Folk Art Museum**, 5814 Wilshire Blvd (Wed–Sun 11am–5pm; $3.50; ⓣ 323/937-4230), which has had some difficulty staying open and attracting a significant following. If you're interested in this sort of thing – handmade objects from rugs to paintings to mugs to clothing, often with a multicultural twist – it's worth a look if you're in the area. Further south, a mile from Wilshire down La Brea Avenue, **St Elmo's Village**, at 4830 St Elmo Drive (ⓣ 323/931-3409, ⓦ www.stelmovillage.org), is a more authentic folk arts project now thirty years old, the colorful murals and sculptures here growing out of efforts to foster a constructive and supportive environment for local youth. It's now also the site of the **Festival of the Art of Survival**, an annual celebration of folk and popular art and music held each Memorial Day.

①

A trip to Culver City

South of West LA and east of Venice you can find one of LA's most overlooked spots, **CULVER CITY** – one of the towns that helped give rise to the American movie industry in the 1910s. Much of this tradition is still visible at the gates of the old Triangle Pictures, 10202 Washington Blvd (now part of the off-limits Sony lot), the early studio of film pioneer and producer **Thomas Ince**, who was a major figure in the industry until he was mysteriously killed on William Randolph Hearst's yacht (an event chronicled in the recent Peter Bogdanovich film, *The Cat's Meow*). Fans of *Gone with the Wind* may recognize Ince's other former studio complex up the road at 9336 Washington Blvd – predictably, this Colonial Revival "mansion" is no more than a facade.

While you're in the area, take a look at the **Hayden Tract**, LA's premier showplace for deconstructivist architecture, lying near Hayden Avenue and National Boulevard, featuring the stunning work of avant-garde master-builder Eric Owen Moss. A few of his more striking works include Pittard Sullivan, 3535 Hayden Ave, a giant gray box with massive wooden ribs; 8522 National, at that same address, featuring a jangled-up facade with a white staircase leading to nowhere; The Box, just to the east, another gray box, this one with a riveted cubic window that looks ready to tumble down to the street below; and the huge Samitaur, 3457 S La Cienega Blvd, massive gray warehouse-like offices with gnarled, jagged points and a truly freakish sense of geometry. His most recent marvel, The Pterodactyl, unfortunately lies hidden in a private parking lot.

If movie history and weird architecture aren't enough for you, top off your trip with a visit to the always-bizarre **Museum of Jurassic Technology**, 9341 Venice Blvd (Thurs 2–8pm, Fri–Sun noon–6pm; $4; ⓦ www.mjt.org). As much an art museum as a science center, this institution has little to do with distant history or roving dinosaurs. Rather, it features a great range of oddities from the pseudo-scientific to the paranormal to the just plain creepy, including trailer-park artworks, exhibitions of folk superstitions, narrative rants by crank scientists, and displays of unearthly Amazonian insects. The ultimate effect is quite unnerving, as these vivid, eerie exhibits are shown in dark rooms without windows or sunlight. However, if you assume the museum is merely the work of a local crank, consider that its creator David Wilson was a 2001 winner of a MacArthur "Genius" Award, due largely to his enterprising work for this quirky institution.

West Hollywood

Between Fairfax Avenue and Beverly Hills, **WEST HOLLYWOOD** was for many years a separate administrative entity from the rest of Los Angeles, notorious for its after-hours vice clubs and general debauchery. Things changed in 1983, however, when the autonomous city of West Hollywood was established, partly to clean up the place and partly to represent the interests of the gay community, elderly residents, and property renters. There are still sleazy rent-boy areas around La Brea Avenue in the east, but much of the rest has smartened up considerably, from the new sculpture garden down the median of **Santa Monica Boulevard**, the district's main drag, to the flashy dance clubs and designer clothing stores in the rest of the neighborhood. In front of the **Tomkat Theater**, beneath a marquee that has proclaimed everything from *Deep Throat* to *In Thrust We Trust*, the **Porno Walk of Fame** is devoted entirely to X-rated film stars. By way of contrast, the eastern end of the boulevard has become home to a large and growing contingent of Russians, many of whom don't mesh too well with the gay scene around them.

Melrose Avenue, LA's trendiest shopping street, runs parallel to Santa Monica Boulevard four blocks south, a streetscape where neon and Art Deco abound among a rash of secondhand clothiers, exotic antique shops, avant-garde galleries, record shops, and high-attitude restaurants. Recently, though, a crush of designer boutiques has been gaining ground at the expense of the older, quirkier tenants, the result being a less iconoclastic feel to the strip and more of a homogenized, touristy atmosphere. The west end of Melrose is even more upmarket, with furniture shops and art galleries spread out around the hulking, bright blue glass mass of the **Pacific Design Center**, a design marketplace near San Vicente Boulevard, known as the "Blue Whale" for the way it dwarfs its low-rise neighbors, along with its newer counterpart, a geometric emerald monolith known as the "Green Giant." Recently, the center also added a Westside branch of the **Museum of Contemporary Art** (Tues–Sun 11am–5pm, Thurs 11am–8pm; $3; Ⓦwww.moca.org/museum/moca_pdc.php), focusing on architecture and industrial and graphic design with a sleek, modern bent, and often participating in multi-site exhibitions with the two Downtown branches (see pp.96 and 100).

The stylistic extremes of Melrose Avenue are also reflected in the area's domestic architecture. Four blocks east of La Cienega Boulevard, the 1922 **Schindler House**, 835 N King's Rd (Wed–Sun 11am–6pm, tours on the hour Sat–Sun 11.30am–2.30pm, and by appointment; $6), was for years the blueprint of California Modernist architecture, with sliding canvas panels designed to be removed in summer, exposed roof rafters, and open-plan rooms facing onto outdoor terraces – banal in replication but compelling in the original. Coming from his native Austria via Frank Lloyd Wright's studio to work on the Hollyhock House (p.114), Schindler was so pleased with the California climate that he built this house without any bedrooms, romantically planning to sleep outdoors year-round in covered sleeping baskets on the roof; he misjudged the weather, however, and soon moved inside. Now functioning as the **MAK Center for Art and Architecture**, the house plays host to a range of avant-garde music, art, film, and design exhibitions, from the work of famous modernists like John Cage and Eric Owen Moss to lesser known photographers, artists, and architects (program information at ℡323/651-1510, Ⓦwww.makcenter.com).

Four blocks west, **La Cienega Boulevard** divides West Hollywood roughly down the middle, separating the next-wave trendies on the Hollywood side from the establishment couturiers on the Beverly Hills border. La Cienega ("the swamp" in Spanish) holds a mixture of LA's best and priciest restaurants and art galleries, and passes the huge **Beverly Center** shopping mall at Beverly Boulevard – a nightmarish fortress of brown plaster that is nonetheless the city's main consumer icon. A smaller, but more appealing, structure, and one that managed to survive the wrecking ball by some adroit repositioning, is **Tail o' the Pup**, the world-famous hot-dog stand shaped like a (mostly bun) hot dog, which was moved a block away from La Cienega to 329 San Vicente Blvd to make way for a garish hotel.

Further south, on the Beverly Hills border at 333 S La Cienega, the Academy of Motion Picture Arts and Sciences' **Margaret Herrick Library** (Mon–Tues & Thurs–Fri 10am–6pm; Ⓦwww.oscars.org/mhl) is a non-circulating research library that holds a huge hoard of film memorabilia and scripts inside a Moorish-style building that was once a water-treatment plant.

WEST HOLLYWOOD AND THE MUSEUM MILE

N

0   500 yds

RESTAURANTS

Astro Burger	15
Barefoot	43
Barney's Beanery	7
Café La Boheme	17
Cajun Bistro	3
Campanile	56
Canter's Deli	34
Carlitos Gardel	14
Cava	47
Chianti Cucina	26
Chin Chin	6
Cobalt Cantina	30
Duke's	10
East India Grill	33
Eat A Pita	32
Ed Debevic's	53
El Carmen	48
El Coyote	42
Erewhon	41
Flora Kitchen	50
French Quarter	12
The Gumbo Pot	49
Hard Rock Café	39
Inaka	46
India's Clay Oven	57
Jerry's Famous Deli	38
Kate Mantilini	51
La' Brea	52
Locanda Veneta	44
L'Orangerie	21
Mark's	22
Matsuhisa	55
Mel's Diner	4
Mishima	45
Noura	28
Newsroom Café	36
Pink's Hot Dogs	25
Real Food Daily	31
Swingers	40
Tail o' the Pup	37
Tommy Tang's	27
Yukon Mining Company	18

BARS & NIGHTCLUBS

7969	13
Coconut Teaszer	2
The Conga Room	58
Doug Weston's Troubadour	29
Formosa Café	19
House of Blues	5
Key Club	8
Largo	35
Lava Lounge	1
Molly Malone's	54
The Palms	20
The Plaza	24
Rage	23
The Roxy	9
Tom Bergin's	59
The Viper Room	16
Whisky-a-Go-Go	11

For reviews of all the above places, see "Eating", "Drinking: bars, pubs and cafés" and "Nightlife" listings starting on p.166.

Sunset Strip

Above western Hollywood, bisected by La Cienega Boulevard, the roughly two-mile-long conglomeration of restaurants, plush hotels, and nightclubs on Sunset Boulevard has long been known as **SUNSET STRIP**. These establishments first began to appear during the early 1920s, along what was then a dusty dirt road serving as the main route between the Hollywood movie studios and the West LA "homes of the stars." F. Scott Fitzgerald and friends spent many leisurely afternoons over drinks here, around the swimming pool of the long-demolished *Garden of Allah* hotel; and the nearby *Ciro's* nightclub was the place to be seen in the swinging 1940s, its husk surviving today as the original *Comedy Store* (see p.188). With the rise of TV, the Strip declined, only reviving in the 1960s when a scene developed around the landmark *Whisky-a-Go-Go* club, which featured seminal psychedelic rock bands such as Love and Buffalo Springfield during the heyday of West Coast flower power, as well as the manic theatrics of Jim Morrison and The Doors. Since then, the striptease clubs and "head shops" have been phased out, and this fashionable area now rivals Beverly Hills for entertainment-industry executives per square foot. Some tourists come to the strip just to see the enormous **billboards**. The ruddy-faced and reassuring Marlboro Man is now gone, but there are many more along the strip that consistently re-invent the medium: fantastic commercial murals animated with eye-catching gimmicks, movie ads with names like Schwarzenegger in gargantuan letters, and self-promotions for only-in-LA characters like the busty blonde "Angelyne," who can often be seen looming over Tinseltown in all her Day-Glo splendor.

Greta Garbo was only one of many stars and starlets to appreciate the quirky character of the huge Norman castle that is the **Chateau Marmont** hotel, towering over the east end of Sunset Strip at no. 8221. Built in 1927 as luxury apartments, this stodgy block of white concrete has long been a Hollywood favorite for its elegant private suites and bungalows (see "Accommodation," p.86). Howard Hughes used to rent the entire penthouse so he could keep an eye on the bathing beauties around the pool below; and the hotel made the headlines in 1982 when comedian John Belushi died of a heroin overdose in the bungalow that he used as his LA home.

Beverly Hills

Probably the most famous small city in the world, **BEVERLY HILLS** has over the years sucked in more than its fair share of wealthy residents (local pawnbrokers have an Oscar and a Ferrari for sale). Predictably, it's not a particularly welcoming place outside the major tourist zones, especially if your clothes don't match the elegant attire of the residents – the pets in Beverly Hills are better dressed and groomed than some of the people elsewhere in LA. Of course, visitors are expected to stroll the designer boutiques of Rodeo Drive, if not necessarily to purchase anything. Just don't try to make off with any of the fancy merchandise: Beverly Hills has more police per capita than anywhere else in the US.

Beverly Hills divides into two distinct halves, separated by the disused train line down Santa Monica Boulevard. Below the tracks are the flatlands of comparatively modest houses on rectangular blocks, set around the flashy **Golden Triangle** business district that fills the wedge between Santa Monica and Wilshire boulevards. **Rodeo Drive** cuts through the triangle in a two-block-long, concentrated showcase of the most expensive names in international fashion. It's a dauntingly stylish area, each boutique trying to outshine the rest: none as yet charges for admission, though some require an invitation. Avoid the tourist trap of **Two Rodeo** nearby, a faux European shopping alley that is the height of pretentious kitsch. For a complete overview of the shopping scene, including Rodeo Drive and beyond, take a trip on the Beverly Hills Trolley (daily noon–5pm summer, Sat only rest of year; $5), which offers tourists a 50-minute glimpse of the town's highlights, departing hourly from the corner of Rodeo and Dayton Way. More worthwhile is the **Museum of Television and Radio**, 465 N Beverly Drive (Wed–Sun noon–5pm, Thurs until 9pm; $6, students $4; Ⓦ www.mtr.org), which features a collection of more than 75,000 TV and radio programs and is LA's first real attempt at providing a media museum of scholarly value. The city still awaits a decent film museum, however.

Above Santa Monica Boulevard is the upmarket part of residential Beverly Hills, its gently curving drives converging on the florid pink plaster **Beverly Hills Hotel**, on Sunset and Rodeo (see "Accommodation," p.86). Built in 1913 to attract wealthy settlers to what was then a town of just five hundred people, the hotel's social cachet makes its *Polo Lounge* a prime spot for movie execs to power-lunch. In the verdant canyons and foothills above Sunset, a number of palatial estates lie hidden away behind landscaped security gates. **Benedict Canyon Drive** climbs up from the hotel near many of them, including, at 1740 Green Acres Drive, Harold Lloyd's **Green Acres**, where the actor lived for forty years. With its secret passageways and large private screening room, the home survives intact, though the grounds, which contained a waterfall and a nine-hole golf course, have since been broken up into smaller lots.

The grounds of the biggest house in Beverly Hills, **Greystone Mansion**, are now maintained as a public park by the city, which uses it to disguise a massive underground reservoir. The fifty-thousand-square-foot manor was once the property of oil titan Edward Doheny, who was not only a huge figure in LA history, but was also a major player in the Teapot Dome scandal of the 1920s. It was Doheny's bribe to Interior Secretary Albert Fall for prime Wyoming real estate that got the debacle started. Although the house itself is rarely open (except for filming music videos by the likes of Meatloaf and for Democratic Party fundraisers), you can visit the sixteen-acre **Greystone Park** (daily 10am–5pm) at 905 Loma Vista Drive, which affords fine views of the LA sprawl and its attendant pollution.

Century City

The gleaming boxes of **CENTURY CITY**, just west of Beverly Hills, were erected during the 1960s on the backlot of the 20th Century-Fox film studio. The plate-glass office towers aren't at all inviting, rising sharply and inhospitably skywards from rarely used sidewalks – a typically Sixties disaster, planned at a time when pedestrian concerns were considered irrelevant. The district's main focus, as is so often the case in LA, is a large shopping mall, the **Century City Shopping Center**, 10250 Santa Monica Blvd, loaded with upscale boutiques and department stores, but still a rather grim display of 1960s corporate modernism. To the west, look through the front gates of the still-functional **20th Century-Fox** studios to catch a glimpse of the intact New York City street set used for the filming of *Hello Dolly!* – though don't bother trying to get inside the place unless your cousin's a production assistant.

Less frivolously, just east of Century City, below Beverly Hills, an inauspicious white building houses the **Simon Wiesenthal Center for Holocaust Studies** at 9786 W Pico Blvd. The US headquarters of the organization devoted to tracking down ex-Nazis, the center has an extensive library of

Holocaust-related documents, photographs, and accounts – but the main draw for visitors is the affecting **Beit HaShoa Museum of Tolerance** (April–Oct Mon–Thurs 11.30am–6pm, Fri 11.30am–5pm, Sun 11am–7.30pm; Nov–March Fri 11.30–3pm; $9, students $5.50; ⓦwww.wiesenthal.com/mot), an extraordinary interactive resource center aimed at exposing the lies of revisionist historians. The most technologically advanced institution of its kind, it uses videotaped interviews to provide LA's frankest examination of the 1992 riots and leads the visitor through re-enactments outlining the rise of Nazism to a harrowing conclusion in a replica gas chamber.

Westwood and UCLA

Just west of Beverly Hills, on the north side of Wilshire Boulevard, **WEST-WOOD**, sometimes known as Westwood Village, is one of LA's more user-friendly neighborhoods, a grouping of low-slung Spanish Revival buildings that went up in the late 1920s, along with the nearby campus of the nascent University of California at Los Angeles (UCLA). It's an area that's easily explored on foot and one very much shaped by the proximity of the university campus. Because of its ease for pedestrians, the neighborhood has limited parking; for minimum frustration, find a cheap parking lot and dump your vehicle there for a few hours while you explore. Otherwise, you'll be constantly feeding a meter or risking a sizeable parking ticket from one of the legions of aggressive meter maids.

Broxton Avenue, Westwood's main drag, is one of West LA's top spots for record stores, video-game arcades, and diners. It's also a big movie-going district, with thirty or so cinema screens within a quarter-mile radius. Much of the original Spanish design has survived the intervening years of less imaginative construction, though the ordinary businesses of the old days have been replaced by fancy boutiques and designer novelty shops. The spire at the end of the street, at 961 Broxton Ave, belongs to the 1931 **Fox Village** theater, which, together with the neon-signed **Bruin** across the street, is sometimes used by movie studios for sneak previews of films to gauge audience reaction. But no matter how crummy the Hollywood blockbusters might be, you'll not fail to be impressed by the theaters' elegant Art Deco architecture. South of the village, Westwood Boulevard has a few more cinemas, some interesting shops and a number of specialist bookstores below Wilshire Boulevard. This section of Wilshire exploded in the 1970s and 1980s with oil-rich high-rise developments, leading to a change of scale that would seem bizarre anywhere outside of LA. Modest detached houses sit next to twenty-story condo towers in which penthouses with private heliports sell for upwards of $12 million.

Inside one of the towers on the corner with Westwood Boulevard, the **UCLA Hammer Museum**, 10899 Wilshire Blvd (Tues–Sat 11am–7pm, Thurs 11am–9pm, Sun 11am–5pm; $4.50, students $3, Thurs 6–9pm free; ⓦwww.hammer.ucla.edu), comprises a sizeable art stash amassed over seven decades by the flamboyant and ultra-wealthy boss of the Occidental Petroleum Corporation, Armand Hammer. Art critic Robert Hughes called the paintings here "a mishmash of second- or third-rate works by famous names," but while the Rembrandts and Rubenses may be less than stunning, the nineteenth-century pieces like Van Gogh's intense and radiant *Hospital at Saint Remy* more than make amends. In any case, under the management of neighboring UCLA, the institution has recently shifted gears to present more contemporary, avant-garde, and multicultural exhibits.

Across Wilshire from the museum, at the end of the driveway behind the tiny

Avco cinema, at 1218 Glendon Ave, you'll find Hammer's speckled marble tomb sharing the tiny cemetery of **Westwood Memorial Park** with the likes of movie stars Peter Lorre and Natalie Wood, wildman jazz drummer Buddy Rich, and, to the left of the entrance in the far northeast corner, the lipstick-covered plaque that marks the resting place of Marilyn Monroe.

The UCLA campus

The **UCLA CAMPUS** is the dominant feature in Westwood, a group of lovely Romanesque buildings spread generously over well-landscaped grounds. It's worth a wander if you've time to kill, particularly for a couple of good exhibition spaces. The Student Union building, at the north end of Westwood Boulevard, half a mile north of Westwood, has a bowling alley, a good bookstore and a "rideboard" offering shared-expense car rides; and there's also a decent coffeehouse in Kerckhoff Hall, just behind.

Before embarking on your exploration, pick up a **map** from various information kiosks scattered around campus. Of things to see, the spacious rotunda of the **Powell Library**, on one side of the central quadrangle, was where Aldous Huxley put in long hours at the card catalogs in the late 1930s, researching his novel *After Many a Summer*, based on the life and legend of William Randolph Hearst. At the northern end of campus – fronted by the large **Franklin D. Murphy Sculpture Garden** (always open; free) which contains work by Rodin, Maillol, Moore, and various modern artists, shaded by jacaranda trees – the **Wight Art Gallery** holds a variety of top-quality visiting exhibitions (Mon–Fri 9am–5pm; free).

Just to the east, UCLA's **film school** is less industry-dominated than its counterpart at USC, and has produced offbeat film-makers like Francis Ford Coppola, Alison Anders, and Alex Cox; it also has one of the most extensive collections of old films and TV programs in the world, examples of which are shown to the public in the James Bridges Theater (tickets usually $7). Check the bulletin board in the lobby, phone ☎310/206-FILM, or visit ⓦwww.cinema.ucla.edu for the current schedule. Also worth a look is the nearby **Fowler Museum of Cultural History**, Bruin Walk at Westwood Plaza (Wed–Sun noon–5pm, Thurs noon–8pm; $5, students free; ⓦwww.fmch.ucla.edu), a prime spot to view folk art from around the world, in the form of textiles, clothing, religious icons, masks, sculptures, and other integral cultural items.

The Sepulveda Pass and the Getty Center

The gap through the Santa Monica Mountains known as the **SEPULVEDA PASS** was, like the boulevard, named for Mexican soldier Francisco Sepúlveda, who gained ownership in 1839 of the Rancho San Vicente y Santa Monica, which once encompassed the surrounding area. Now, the pass is best known for the 405 Freeway that cuts through it, but it also contains part of Sepulveda Boulevard, the longest road in the county of Los Angeles, which leads from Long Beach into the San Fernando Valley. Starting at Sunset Boulevard just northwest of UCLA, you can follow the pass as it divides several of LA's most exclusive residential zones. **Brentwood** to the west is an insular enclave best known for being the former home of O.J. Simpson and his murdered wife Nicole; to the east, **Bel Air** is a hillside community that is similarly well-heeled and boasts a particularly fine hotel, the *Bel Air* (see p.86), though little else beyond gated mansions and narrow, curving streets.

A short distance away, Getty Center Drive leads up to the monumental **GETTY CENTER** (daily 10am–6pm, Sat & Sun 10am–9pm; free, parking $5; ⓦwww.getty.edu), a gleaming complex that towers over the city as oil baron J. Paul Getty once towered over his competitors. Although reservations for parking are no longer essential on weekends, they are required on weekdays (call ☏310/440-7300). For some, arriving by cab or bus (the #561 line, which you can pick up at LAX) provides a simpler alternative.

Designed by arch-modernist Richard Meier, the center was built for around $1 billion and was a decade in the making. Originally, Meier planned for the whole museum complex to be constructed from white metallic panels – his signature style – but protests from the Brentwood neighbors below forced him to redesign part of it in travertine, in the end a good aesthetic choice for its classical appeal. Although the Getty Foundation plunked down a ten-figure sum for the Center, it still has billions in reserve and must, by law, spend hundreds of millions each year from its endowment. Thus, it plays an elephantine role on the international art scene and can freely outbid its competitors for anything it wants. If he were still around, J. Paul would have been proud.

Getty started building his massive collection in the 1930s, storing much of it in his house until the Getty Museum opened in 1974, on a bluff overlooking the Pacific Ocean. That site is now closed, but will reopen sometime in 2004 as a showcase for the foundation's antiquities (see p.141). As the collection is, not surprisingly, determined by the enthusiasms of Getty himself, there's a formidable array of ornate furniture and decorative arts, with clocks, chandeliers, tapestries, and gilt-edged commodes, designed for the French nobility from the reign of Louis XIV, filling several overwhelmingly opulent rooms. Getty was much less interested in painting – although he did scoop up a very fine stash from the Renaissance and Baroque periods, including works by Rembrandt, Rubens, and La Tour – but a large collection has been amassed since his death, featuring all the major names from the thirteenth century to the present: drawings by Raphael and Bernini, paintings of the Dutch Golden Age, and a handful of French Impressionists, to name just a few. The museum's biggest catch is probably Van Gogh's *Irises*, which was snatched up for a still-undisclosed sum. Elsewhere in the museum, there's an extensive and highly absorbing collection of photographs by Man Ray, Laszlo Moholy-Nagy, and other notables, along with a respectable assortment of sculpture from the seventeenth to the nineteenth centuries. Needless to say, given its founder's distaste for modern art – as well as, ironically, modern architecture – it's no surprise that the museum has little twentieth-century art beyond photography, the limited number of examples mostly appearing in periodic exhibitions.

From the museum, continue up the Sepulveda Pass until you come to the **Skirball Cultural Center**, 2701 N Sepulveda Blvd (Tues–Sat noon–5pm, Sun 11am–5pm; $8, students $6; ⊛www.skirball.org), which devotes its attention to the history, beliefs, and rituals of Judaism. Concentrating on the more mystical elements of the faith, the fairly absorbing center hosts a range of exhibitions and lectures designed to illuminate the American Jewish experience, offering a broad overview of Judaic and popular history and culture, from Hanukkah lamps to a Holy Ark from a German synagogue to cels from the animated Exodus film, *The Prince of Egypt*.

Santa Monica Bay

Set along an unbroken, twenty-mile strand of white beaches, and home to a diverse assortment of LA's finest stores, restaurants, and galleries, the small communities that line the **Santa Monica Bay** have none of the smog or searing heat that can make the rest of the metropolis unbearable. The entire area is well served by public transit, near enough the airport, and there's a wide array of accommodation, making the area a good base for seeing the rest of LA.

Santa Monica, lined by palm-tree-shaded bluffs above the Pacific Ocean, is the oldest, biggest, and best known of the towns. Once a wild beachfront playground and memorable location for many scenes from the underworld stories of Raymond Chandler, it's a self-consciously healthy and liberal community, which has enticed a large expatriate British community of writers and rock stars, ranging from Rod Stewart to John Lydon. In recent years, however, once-liberal policies towards homeless people have become more severe, as have rent-control laws, courtesy of a state effort to keep landlords and property owners happy. Directly south, **Venice**'s once-expansive beachfront boardwalk brings together a lively mixture of street performers, roller skaters, and casual voyeurs, while its remaining network of canals gives a hint of what the place used to look like, nearly a hundred years ago.

North from Santa Monica along the Pacific Coast Highway, **Pacific Palisades** is a gathering of hugely expensive houses clinging to the lower foothills of the nearby mountains, though really not much to see beyond some pioneering postwar architecture. A few miles inland, though, **Will Rogers State Park** was the home and now museum of one of the legends of the American West, with some rewarding hiking paths leading into the neighboring canyons. A few miles further along the coastal road, **Topanga Canyon** offers more hiking, its reputation as haven of back-to-nature hippiedom gone, but still with a surprisingly wild set of trails leading into the deep, wooded canyons and sculptured rock outcrops of the Santa Monica Mountains.

Malibu, at the top of the bay, twenty miles from Santa Monica and the northern and westernmost edge of the LA region, is a whole other world, studded with beach colony houses owned by those who are famous enough to need privacy and rich enough to afford it, despite the constant threat of hillside wildfires. However, you don't have to be a millionaire to enjoy its fine surfing beaches, or the birds, seals, and whales that seasonally migrate offshore.

Santa Monica

As little as a century ago, most of the land between **SANTA MONICA** and what was then Los Angeles was covered by beanfields and citrus groves, interrupted by the occasional outposts of Hollywood and Beverly Hills. Like so much of the state, the land was owned by Collis Huntington's Southern Pacific Railroad, which tried – and failed – to make Santa Monica into the port of Los Angeles, which was ultimately built at Wilmington, near Long Beach. The linking of the beachfront with the rest of Los Angeles by the suburban streetcar system meant the town instead grew into one of LA's premier resorts – a funfair city that was the inspiration for Raymond Chandler's anything-goes "Bay City," described in *Farewell, My Lovely*. Today, Chandler wouldn't recognize the place: changes in gaming laws and the advent of private swimming pools have led to the removal of the offshore gambling ships and many of the bathing clubs, and Santa Monica is among the city's more elegant seaside towns. It's also well known for its rent control and stringent planning and development regulations – keeping the skyline fairly low and the number of skyscrapers to a minimum – perceived infractions for which local right-wingers refer sneeringly to the city as the "People's Republic."

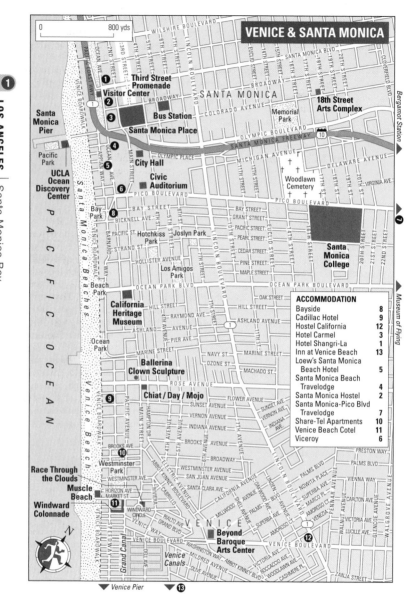

VENICE & SANTA MONICA

ACCOMMODATION	
Bayside	8
Cadillac Hotel	9
Hostel California	12
Hotel Carmel	3
Hotel Shangri-La	1
Inn at Venice Beach	13
Loew's Santa Monica Beach Hotel	5
Santa Monica Beach Travelodge	4
Santa Monica Hostel	2
Santa Monica-Pico Blvd Travelodge	7
Share-Tel Apartments	10
Venice Beach Cotel	11
Viceroy	6

Lying across Centinela Avenue from West LA, Santa Monica splits into three distinct portions. The town itself, holding a fair chunk of Santa Monica's history and its day-to-day business, is mostly inland but is more interesting closer to the coastal bluffs. Just to the west there's the pier and beach, while Main Street, running south from close to the pier towards Venice, is a style-conscious quarter, with designer restaurants and fancy shops.

The Town

Santa Monica reaches nearly three miles inland, but most of its attractions lie within a few blocks of the beach. Make your first stop the **Visitor Information Office**, 1400 Ocean Ave (daily 10am–4pm; ☎310/393-7593, ⓦwww.santamonica.com), in a kiosk just south of Santa Monica Boulevard in **Palisades Park**, the cypress-tree-lined strip that runs along the top of the bluffs and makes for striking views of the surf below. The visitor center's handy free map shows the layout of the town and the routes of the Santa Monica Big Blue Bus transit system, a useful Westside complement to the MTA network (☎310/451-5444, ⓦwww.bigbluebus.com).

Two blocks east of Ocean Boulevard, between Wilshire and Broadway, the **Third Street Promenade** is the closest LA comes to vibrant street life. A pedestrian stretch long popular with buskers and itinerant evangelists, the promenade underwent a successful refurbishment a decade ago and now attracts a lively crowd of characters. It's fun simply to hang out in the cafés, bars, and nightclubs, play a game of pool, or browse through the many secondhand and fine-art book shops – independent businesses that are becoming increasingly uncommon under the onslaught of the chain retailers who have virtually conquered the northern end of the strip between Wilshire Boulevard and Arizona Avenue. The mall is anchored at its southern end by the expensive **Santa Monica Place**, a white stucco shopping precinct that is among architect Frank Gehry's less inspired work. It has the usual assortment of upmarket chain stores and a mandatory food court, all executed in an exhausted postmodern idiom, with faded pastel colors and gloomy chain-link fencing.

Santa Monica has a number of fine **galleries** selling works by emerging local and international artists. **Bergamot Station**, a collection of former tramcar sheds at 2525 Michigan Ave, near the intersection of 26th and Cloverfield, houses a multitude of small art galleries (most open Tues–Fri 10am–6pm; ⓦwww.bergamotstation.com). Many of LA's latest generation of artists – such as Lari Pittman, Manuel Ocampo, Robert Williams, and Erika Rothenberg – have shown here, and the highlight is, of course, the **Santa Monica Museum of Art**, in Building G-1 (Tues–Sat 11am–6pm, Sun 11am–5pm; $3; ⓦwww.smmoa.org). This is a good space to see some of the most engaging and curious work on the local scene, in temporary exhibits ranging from simple paintings to complex, space-demanding installation art. Among the regular galleries, don't miss the **Gallery of Functional Art**, Building. E-3 (free; ⓦwww.galleryoffunctionalart.com), which offers an array of mechanical gizmos and eccentric furniture like cubist lamps and neon-lit chairs. The **Side Street Projects**, 1629 18th St (Wed–Sat noon–6pm; free; information at ☎310/829-0779), is another of the town's ambitious young art spaces – involving both education and exhibition – which forms a part of the **18th Street Arts Complex**, 1639 18th St (ⓦwww.18thstreet.org), a hip and modern center for various types of art, much of it experimental. The performance space Highways, 1651 18th St (☎310/315-1459, ⓦwww.highwaysperformance.org), is one such example in the complex (see p.189), showcasing edgy political and gender-based work.

Further inland, it's less easy to stumble upon Santa Monica's worthwhile sights. On the northern border, **San Vicente Boulevard**'s grassy tree-lined strip is a joggers' freeway, while south of San Vicente, the flashy eateries and boutiques of **Montana Avenue** are better for spotting B-list stars than for finding any bargains.

Santa Monica pier and beach

Despite the many attractions on top of the bluffs, the real focal point of Santa Monica life is down below, on the beach and around **SANTA MONICA PIER**, the only reminder that the city was ever anything but a quiet coastal suburb. Jutting out into the bay at the foot of Colorado Avenue, the pier is a great example of its kind, with a giant helter-skelter and a restored 1922 wooden **carousel** (Mon–Fri 9am–6pm; 50¢ a ride). However, the more recent carnival center, **Pacific Park** (Mon–Fri 11am–11pm, Sat & Sun 11am–12.30am; $16, kids $9; ⓦ www.pacpark.com), featuring a rollercoaster and various other thrill rides, is a rather overpriced attempt to lure back the suburban families – you're better off saving your money for a real theme park. Much more appealing, at the foot of the pier at 1600 Ocean Front Walk, the **UCLA Ocean Discovery Center** (summer Tues–Fri 3–6pm, Sat 11am–6pm, Sun 11am–pm; Sept–May Sat & Sun 11am-5pm; $3; ⓦ www.odc.ucla.edu) presents engaging exhibits on local marine life and gives you the chance to touch sea anemones and starfish, though its aim is mainly to educate children in oceanography.

The grand beach houses north of the pier were known as the "Gold Coast," because of the many Hollywood personalities who lived in them. The largest still standing, the **North Guest House**, 415 Palisades Beach Rd, was built as the servants' quarters of a massive 120-room house, now demolished, that William Randolph Hearst built for his mistress, actress Marion Davies. MGM boss Louis B. Mayer owned the adjacent Mediterranean-style villa, which was later rumored to be the place where the Kennedy brothers had their liaisons with Marilyn Monroe. Later re-christened as the *Sand and Sea* beach club, the old Hearst complex was closed after the 1994 Northridge earthquake, though there have been plans to redevelop the swimming pool, cabanas, and other structures for use as a public facility.

For a good look around the coastline of Santa Monica, the **bike path**, which begins at the pier, heads twenty miles south to Palos Verdes. On foot, you can wander south along the beach to Pico Boulevard and head two blocks inland to Main Street.

Main Street

The completion of the Santa Monica Freeway in 1965 brought Santa Monica's beachfront homes within a fifteen-minute drive of Downtown and isolated the bulk of the town from **MAIN STREET**, five minutes' walk from the pier. Here, the collection of novelty shops, kite stores, and classy restaurants now forms one of the most popular shopping districts on the Westside. Beyond shopping, eating, and drinking, though, there's not much to do or see. One of the few actual sights, the **California Heritage Museum**, 2612 Main St (Wed–Sun 11am–4pm; $3), is the city's effort to preserve some of its architectural past in the face of new money. Two houses were moved here to escape demolition: one hosts temporary displays on Californian cultural topics like old-time amusement parks, and has several rooms restored to variously evoke the years 1890–1930, while the other is known as the *Victorian Restaurant* and serves tea on its patio at weekends (reserve on ☎ 310/392-8537). For a more comprehensive day of consumerism, you can travel between Main Street and the Santa Monica Promenade on the **Tide Shuttle** (daily noon–10pm, Sat & Sun until midnight), ponying up a mere quarter to hit all the shopping highlights, as well as travel along the sands south of the pier.

Just north of the Heritage Museum, **Ocean Park Boulevard** was one of the main routes to the coast via the old streetcars of the Pacific Electric, and the entire beachfront between here and the Venice border – now overshadowed by massive gray condominiums – used to be the site of the largest and wildest of the amusement piers, the fantastic **Pacific Ocean Park**. "P-O-P," as it was known, had a huge rollercoaster, a giant funhouse, and a boisterous midway arcade, described by architectural historian Reyner Banham as a "fantasy in stucco and every known style of architecture and human ecology." Sadly, not a trace remains.

Venice

Immediately south of Santa Monica, **VENICE** was laid out in the marshlands of Ballona Creek in 1905 by developer Abbot Kinney as a romantic replica of the northern Italian city. Intended to attract artists from Los Angeles to sample its pseudo-European air, this twenty-mile network of canals, lined by sham palazzos and waterfront homes, never really caught on, although a later remodel into a low-grade version of Coney Island postponed its demise for a few decades. With the coming of the automobile, many of the canals were filled in, and the area, now part of the city of Los Angeles, fell into disrepair, with most of the home sites being taken over by oil wells. This grim era features in Orson Welles' 1958 film *Touch of Evil*, in which derelict Venice stars as a seedy Mexican border town.

Kinney was, however, ahead of his time. A fair bit of the original plan survives, and the bohemian atmosphere has since worked to draw in the artistic community he was aiming at, making Venice one of the coast's trendier spots. Main Street, for instance, is home to the offices of advertising firm **Chiat Day Mojo**, just south of Rose Street. Marked by Claes Oldenburg's huge pair of binoculars at the entrance, the Frank Gehry-designed offices have no assigned desks, leaving employees to roam free with laptops and mobile phones, through spartan rooms lined with original modern art. Just to the north, the frightening *Ballerina Clown*, a gargantuan sculpture by Jonathan Borofsky, looms over a nearby intersection, its stubbly clown head and lithe body making for an unforgettably disturbing combination. Elsewhere, a strong alternative arts scene centers around the **Beyond Baroque Literary Arts Center and Bookshop** in the old City Hall at 681 Venice Blvd (Tues–Fri 10am–5pm, Sat noon–5pm; ☎310/822-3006, Ⓦwww.beyondbaroque.org), which holds regular readings and workshops of poetry, prose, and drama.

Windward Avenue is the town's main artery, running from the beach into what was the Grand Circle of the canal system – where the curvaceous, rollercoaster facade of the 1987 **Race Through the Clouds** building pays tribute to the old theme park – now paved over and ringed by a number of galleries and the Venice post office, inside of which a mural depicts the early layout. Leading to the beach, the original Romanesque **arcade**, around the intersection with Pacific Avenue, is alive with health-food shops, used-record stores and roller-skate rental stands, but sadly, less of it remains with passing years. Here and there colorful and portentous giant **murals** cover the whitewashed walls of the original hotels, and of the Venice Pavilion on the beach. The few remaining **canals** are just a few blocks south, where the original quaint little bridges survive, and you can sit and watch the ducks paddle around in the still waters. It's a great place to walk around, though if you're in a car and wish to avoid the tiny, maze-like streets between the canals, there's only one way to see the area. Head north on Dell Avenue between Washington and Venice boulevards, a route that often draws a procession of slow-moving motorized gawkers.

Still, it's **Venice Beach** that draws most people to the town, and nowhere else does LA parade itself quite so openly, sensuously, and aggressively as it does along the **Venice Boardwalk**, a wide pathway also known as Ocean Front Walk. Year-round at weekends and every day in summer it's packed with jugglers, fire-eaters, Hare Krishnas, roller-skating guitar players and, of course, teeming masses of tourists. You can buy anything you might need to look like a local without ever leaving the beach: cheap sunglasses, T-shirts, personal stereos, and tennis shoes. South of Windward is **Muscle Beach**, a legendary weightlifting center where serious hunks of muscle pump serious iron, and high-flying gymnasts swing on the adjacent rings and bars. If you'd like to check the place out yourself, contact the Venice Beach Recreation Center, 1800 Ocean Front Walk, for more information (☎310/399-2775).

Incidentally, be warned that Venice Beach **at night** is a dangerous place, taken over by street gangs, drug dealers, and assorted psychos, and walking on the beach after dark is illegal in most stretches.

Pacific Palisades and Will Rogers State Historic Park

The district of **PACIFIC PALISADES**, rising on the bluffs two miles north of Santa Monica pier, is slowly but very surely falling away into the bay, most noticeably on the point above Chautauqua Boulevard and Pacific Coast Highway – otherwise known as "PCH." With each winter's rains, a little bit more of the bluffs gets washed away in mud slides, blocking traffic on PCH, and gradually shrinking the backyards of the clifftop homes. Although there are few places of interest among the suburban ranch houses, a handful of the most influential buildings of postwar LA were constructed here. The **Eames House**, for example, at 203 Chautauqua St, was fashioned out of prefabricated industrial parts in 1947 as part of the influential Case Study Program, intended to provide an instructive example of Southern California modernism to the rest of suburban America. Only the grounds and exterior are viewable, by appointment only (Mon–Fri 10am–4.30pm; free; ☎310/459-9663, ⓦ www.eamesoffice.com).

In complete contrast, a mile east along Sunset Boulevard from the top of Chautauqua is the **WILL ROGERS STATE HISTORIC PARK** (summer daily 8am–dusk; rest of year daily 8am–6pm; free, parking $6), a steep climb from the MTA bus (#2, #302, #576) stop. This was the home and ranch of the Depression-era cowboy philosopher and journalist Will Rogers, one of America's most popular figures of the time, and renowned for his down-home, common-sense thinking, and the saying that he "never met a man he didn't like." After his death in a plane crash in 1935, there was a nationwide thirty-minute silence. The overgrown ranch-style house serves as an informal **museum** (daily 10am–5pm; free), filled with cowboy gear and Native American art; and the 200-acre park has miles of foot and bridle paths, including polo grounds where matches take place during the spring and summer (Apri–Oct Sat 2–4pm, Sun 10am–noon; free). Just north of Sunset Boulevard's intersection with PCH, the **Getty Villa** sits on a picturesque bluff overlooking the ocean. Once the site of the Getty Museum (now in West LA; see p.134), the villa is closed to the public but is due to reopen as an antiquities center in 2004 (call for an update at ☎310/440-7300, or visit ⓦ www.getty.edu/museum/villa).

Topanga Canyon

Surprisingly for LA, **TOPANGA CANYON** provides an excellent natural refuge. With hillsides covered in golden poppies and wildflowers, a hundred and fifty thousand acres of these mountains and the adjacent seashore have been protected as the Santa Monica Mountains National Recreation Area, where you can still spot a variety of deer, coyotes, and even the odd mountain lion. Like LA itself, the area is not without its element of danger, especially in winter and early spring, when mudslides threaten houses and waterfalls cascade down the cliffs. Park rangers offer free guided hikes throughout the mountains most weekends (information and reservations ☎818/597-9192), and there are self-guided trails through the canyon's Topanga State Park, off Old Topanga Canyon Road at the crest of the mountains, with spectacular views out over the Pacific. If you'd like to find out more, the visitor center in neighboring Thousand Oaks, 401 W Hillcrest Drive (Mon–Fri 8am–5pm, Sat & Sun 9am–5pm; ☎805/370-2301, ⓦwww.nps.gov/samo), offers additional maps and information on hiking trails.

Beyond Topanga Canyon, the beaches and ocean-views are blocked off by mile after mile of private homes all the way to Malibu. There are a few semi-hidden beach-access points – along PCH at nos. 19900, 22700, 20300, and 24300 – but most of the rock stars and others who can afford to live here treat the sands and seas as their own. Any bit of land below the high-tide line is legally in the public domain, so try not to act like a trespasser.

Malibu

Everyone has heard of **MALIBU** – the very name conjures up images of beautiful people sunbathing on a palm-fringed beach and lazily consuming cocktails. And while the image is not so very far from the truth, you might not think so on arrival. As you enter the small town, the succession of ramshackle surf shops and fast-food stands scattered along both sides of PCH around the graceful Malibu Pier don't exactly reek of money, but the secluded estates just inland are as valuable as any in the entire US, even though many are subject to being battered by hillside wildfires that are notoriously difficult to control.

Facing south by the pier, **Surfrider Beach** was the surfing capital of the world in the 1950s and early 1960s, popularized by the many *Beach Blanket Bingo* movies filmed here, starring Annette Funicello and Frankie Avalon. It's still a big surfing spot: the waves are best in late summer, when storms off Mexico cause them to reach upwards of eight feet. Just beyond is **Malibu Lagoon State Park** (daily 9am–7pm; parking $6), a nature reserve and bird refuge; birdwatching walks around the lagoon are offered some weekends. A small **museum**, 23200 PCH (tours Wed–Sat 11am–3pm; $3), gives you the historical rundown, from the Chumash era up to the arrival of Hollywood movie stars, with special emphasis on the long-running "Rindge saga" (see below) that informs much of Malibu's modern history.

Most Malibu residents live in the estates, McMansions and small ranches that lurk in the narrow canyons on the edges of the town, together forming a well-off, insular community with a long-established dread of outsiders. Up until the 1920s all of Malibu was owned by one **May K. Rindge**, who hired armed guards and dynamited roads to keep travelers from crossing her land on their way to and from Santa Monica. Rindge fought for years to prevent the state from building the Pacific Coast Highway across her property, but lost her legal battle in the State Supreme Court, and her money in the Depression. Her son took over the ranch and quickly sold much of the land, establishing the **Malibu Colony** at the mouth of Malibu Canyon as a haven for movie stars. There's very little to see here except the garage doors of the rich and famous; if you must get a glimpse of the elite, visit the **Malibu Colony Plaza**, near the area's gated entrance, good for star-spotting and buying provisions, or the

Malibu Country Mart, 3835 Cross Creek Rd, where A- and B-listers can often be found buying veggies or sipping espressos.

Much of **Malibu Creek State Park**, at the crest of Malibu Canyon Road along Mulholland Drive, used to belong to 20th-Century Fox studios, which filmed many Tarzan pictures here and used the chaparral-covered hillsides to simulate South Korea for the TV show *M*A*S*H*. The 4000-acre park includes a large lake, some waterfalls, and nearly fifteen miles of hiking trails, making it crowded on summer weekends but fairly accessible and pleasant the rest of the time (to camp here, see "Accommodation," p.90). Nearby **Paramount Ranch**, near Mulholland Drive at 2813 Cornell Rd, is another old studio backlot, with a phony railroad crossing, cemetery, and Western movie set used for, among other things, the interminable TV drama *Dr. Quinn Medicine Woman*.

Finally, a few miles west of Cornell Road, the glory days of the **Peter Strauss Ranch** are long past, when it was known as "Lake Enchanto" in the 1930s and 1940s and boasted colorful rides and chic resort amenities. These days, little is left of the resort, but the site has become an excellent natural refuge with hiking trails and occasional exhibitions of sculpture, and classical and blues concerts (information at ☎818/597-1036).

The beaches

Five miles up the coast from Malibu Pier, **Zuma Beach** is the largest of the LA County beaches, easily connected to the San Fernando by Kanan Dume Road. Adjacent **Point Dume State Beach**, below the bluffs, is more relaxed, especially up and over the rocks at its southern tip, where **Pirate's Cove** is used by nudists. The rocks here are also a good place to look out for seals and migrating gray whales in winter, as the point above – best accessed by automobile or a longish path – juts out into the Pacific at the northern lip of Santa Monica Bay. **El Matador State Beach**, about 25 miles up the coast from Santa Monica, is about as close as you can get to the private-beach seclusion enjoyed by the stars. Thanks to its northern location and an easily missable turn off PCH, its rocky-cove sands are a recluse's dream. Another five miles along PCH, where Mulholland Drive reaches the ocean, **Leo Carrillo** ("ca-REE-oh") **State Beach Park** marks the northwestern border of LA County and the end of the MTA bus route (#434). The mile-long sandy beach is divided by Sequit Point, a small bluff that has underwater caves and a tunnel you can pass through at low tide, and is also one of LA's best campgrounds (see p.90). Five miles further on, at **Point Mugu State Park**, there are some good walks through mountain canyons, and campsites right on the beach. Point Mugu is also the site of the US Navy's Pacific Missile Test Center, which takes up most of the five miles of coast south of Ventura (see p.441).

The South Bay and harbor area

South of Venice, the charmless high-rise condos of Marina del Rey and the faded resort town of Playa del Rey offer little to interest visitors; beyond that, the coast – seen along the oceanside strip of Vista del Mar – is dominated by the perimeter of LAX, a huge oil refinery, and LA's main sewage treatment plant. South of this industrial zone, however, is an eight-mile strip of beach towns – **Manhattan Beach**, **Hermosa Beach**, and **Redondo Beach** – collectively known as the **SOUTH BAY**. These are more low-slung, quieter, more suburban, and smaller than the Westside beach communities. Along their shared beach-side bike path the joggers and roller skaters are more likely to be locals than outsiders, and all three can make a refreshing break if you like your beaches without trendy packaging. Each has a beckoning strip of white sand, and Manhattan and Hermosa are well equipped for surfing and beach sports. They're also well connected to the rest of the city – within easy reach of LAX and connected by regular buses to Downtown LA.

Visible all along this stretch of the coast, the large green peninsula of **Palos Verdes** is an upmarket residential area, while the comparatively rough-hewn working town of **San Pedro** (where you can find a good youth hostel, the area's cheapest accommodation; see p.89) is sited on the LA harbor, the busiest cargo port in the world and still growing. On the other side of the harbor, **Long Beach**, connected to Downtown by bus #60, is best known as the resting place of the *Queen Mary*, even though it's also the region's second largest city with nearly half a million people. Perhaps the most enticing place in the area is **Santa Catalina Island**, twenty miles offshore and easily reached by ferry. It's almost completely conserved wilderness, with many unique forms of plant and animal life and just one main town, **Avalon**.

Manhattan Beach, Hermosa Beach, and Redondo Beach

Accessible along the bike path from Venice, or by car along PCH, **MANHATTAN BEACH** is a likable place with a healthy well-to-do air, home mainly to white-collar workers whose middle-class stucco homes tumble towards the beach, uncluttered by high-rise hotels. There's not much to see or do away from the beach, and surfing is the major local pastime – a two-week international surf festival occurs each August – along with beach volleyball, evidenced by the profusion of nets across the sands. Visit the **Historical Center** in the post office building at 1601 Manhattan Beach Blvd (Sat & Sun noon–3pm; free) for its entertaining collection of photos and oddities from the city's earliest days. If these whet your appetite, you can purchase (for $1) a map that describes a history-oriented **walking tour**. One other thing to check out if you're in the area is the **Roundhouse and Aquarium** at the end of the city pier (Mon–Fri 3pm–dusk, Sat & Sun 10am–dusk; free), a mildly interesting spot where you can look at sharks and lobsters, and fiddle around with the helpless creatures in a tide-pool "touch tank."

HERMOSA BEACH, across Longfellow Boulevard, is lower-income than Manhattan Beach, its houses smaller and less showy, but is in many ways more enjoyable, with the hint of an authentic bohemian air in places. The center, near the foot of the pier around Hermosa and Pier avenues, is the setting for one of the South Bay's best-known nightspots, *The Lighthouse* (see p.183). While the area around the beach – known as the Strand here - is the main draw, there are enough good restaurants and shops to keep you busy as well.

Despite some decent strips of sand, and fine views of Palos Verdes' stunning greenery, **REDONDO BEACH**, south of Hermosa, is much less inviting than its relaxed neighbor. Condos and hotels line the beachfront, and the eateries around the yacht-lined King's Harbor are off limits to curious visitors.

Palos Verdes

A great green hump marking LA's southwest corner, **PALOS VERDES** offers only limited interest, but it can be enjoyable to explore the bluffs and coves along its protected coastline. **Malaga Beach**, by Torrance County Beach just south of Redondo, is a popular scuba-diving spot; **Abalone Cove**, reached from the parking lot on Berkentine Road, off Palos Verdes Drive, boasts rock and tide pools and offshore kelp beds with rock scallops, sea urchins and, of course, abalone. A couple of miles east at the end of a path off Peppertree Drive, Smugglers Cove is a renowned **nudist beach**.

While you're in the area, don't miss **Wayfarer's Chapel**, 5755 Palos Verdes Drive S (Ⓦ www.wayfarerschapel.org) designed by Frank Lloyd Wright's son, Lloyd, as a tribute to the eighteenth-century Swedish scientist and mystic Emanuel Swedenborg. The ultimate aim is for the redwood grove around the chapel to grow and weave itself into the glass-framed structure – a fusing of human handiwork with the forces of nature in a symbolic union. Unsurprisingly, the place is one of LA's top choices for weddings. A few miles further on, just before the end of Palos Verdes Drive, **Point Fermin Park** is a small tip of land poking into the ocean, where a curious little wooden lighthouse dates from 1874 (no admittance), and a whale-watching station lets you read up on the winter migrations. Bottle-nosed dolphins can often be seen during their fall departure and spring return, and there's also the less seasonally dependent thrill of spotting hang-gliders swooping down off the cliffs.

From the park, it's an easy stroll along Bluff Place and down the 29th Street stairway to Cabrillo Beach and the excellent **Cabrillo Marine Aquarium**, 3720 Stephen White Drive (Tues–Fri noon–5pm, Sat–Sun 10am–5pm; $2, parking $6.50; Ⓦ www.cabrilloaq.org), displaying a diverse collection of marine life that has been imaginatively and instructively assembled: everything from predator snails and the curious "sarcastic fringehead" to larger displays on otters, seals, and whales.

Finally, about ten miles inland on the peninsula and not really close to anything else worth seeing, the curious **South Coast Botanic Garden**, 26300 Crenshaw Blvd (daily 9am–5pm; $5), was once the site of a huge landfill stuffed with 3.5 tons of trash, but has since been covered over and turned into a charming array of themed gardens filled with cacti, ferns, bromeliads, and several different types of palm trees. The only hint of its former life is its undulating terrain: unsettling evidence of the refuse slowly shifting below the surface.

San Pedro and around

From the Cabrillo aquarium, three miles further on along Bluff Place, the scruffy harbor city of **SAN PEDRO** is in stark contrast to the affluence of Palos Verdes. It was a small fishing community until the late nineteenth century, when the construction of the LA harbor nearby brought a huge influx of labor, much of it from Portugal, Greece, and Yugoslavia. Many of these, and their descendants, never left the place, lending a striking racial mix to the town, manifest around the narrow sloping central streets in one of LA's densest groupings of ethnic groceries. Its unique character, so different in many ways from the rest of the city, has led many of its residents to push for secession, an option currently under review by other parts of town as well, from Hollywood to the San Fernando Valley.

A good chunk of the district's nautical history is revealed in the **Maritime Museum**, on the harbor's edge at the foot of Sixth Street (Tues–Sun

10am–5pm; $1; ⓦ www.lamaritimemuseum.org), a storehouse for art and artifacts from the glory days of San Pedro's fishing and whaling industries, focusing on everything from old-fashioned clipper-ship voyages to contemporary diving expeditions. Nearby, the **Bloody Thursday Monument**, on the corner of Sixth and Beacon close to the City Hall, is another reminder of the city's gritty past. Marking the 1934 strike by local waterfront workers, it commemorates the two who were killed when police and private guards opened fire. A fifteen-minute walk along the shore from the museum brings you to the overrated **Ports O' Call Village** – a dismal batch of wooden and corrugated-iron huts supposedly capturing the flavor of seaports around the world.

Between San Pedro and Long Beach (connected by LADOT bus #142) soar two tall road bridges, giving aerial views of oil wells and docks, and the vast Naval Supplies Center. Just inland, the community of **Wilmington** is the site of the Greek Revival **Banning House**, 401 E Main St (guided tours hourly Tues–Thurs 12.30–2.30pm, Sat & Sun 12.30–3.30pm; $3; ⓦ www.banning-museum.org), the opulent Victorian home of mid-nineteenth-century entrepreneur Phineas Banning, who made his fortune when the value of his land increased astronomically as the harbor was developed. Through his promotion of the rail link between the harbor and central LA he also became known as "the father of Los Angeles transportation" – no mean accolade at a time when the local transportation system was one of the best in the world. While you're in the area, make sure to visit the **Drum Barracks and Civil War Museum**, 1052 Banning Blvd (hourly tours Tues–Thurs 10am–1pm, Sat & Sun 11.30am–2.30pm; $3; ⓦ www.drumbarracks.org), the place from which Union troops used LA as a staging point for attacks in the Southwest against Confederates and, later, Indians. The sole remaining (rickety) building houses a collection of military antiques and memorabilia, such as a 34-star US flag, and assorted guns and muskets, including an early version of a machine gun.

Long Beach

Combined with San Pedro, **LONG BEACH** is home to the third-largest port in the world, and biggest outside China. Once the stomping ground of off-duty naval personnel, the city's porn shops and sleazy bars lasted until the 1980s, when a billion-dollar cash infusion into the town led – in the downtown area at least – to a spate of glossy office buildings, a convention center, sparkly new hotels, a swanky shopping mall, and a preservation campaign that has restored some of the best turn-of-the-century buildings on the coast. Inland from downtown, however, it's a different story – grim, uninviting housing developments on the perimeter of South Central LA.

Downtown Long Beach is clearly the place to spend most of your time, especially along Pine Avenue, with the best of Long Beach's rescued architecture and numerous thrift stores, antique/junk emporiums, and bookstores. Nearby, on Third Street, is the **mural** *Activities in Long Beach*, whose depiction of the local population appears to be contemporary, but was in fact painted in the 1930s under Roosevelt's New Deal. From the mural, the pedestrian Promenade leads towards the sea, passing a concrete, open-air auditorium – often the site of free art and music events – and crossing the busy Ocean Boulevard into **Shoreline Village**, a waterfront entertainment belt that used to feature carnival rides and a carousel up to the 1940s, but is now mostly a ragtag collection of shops and restaurants. You can, however, explore the intriguing, though pricey, **Aquarium of the Pacific** (daily 9am–6pm; $18.75, kids $10; ⓦ www.aquariumofpacific.org), which exhibits the aquatic flora and fauna of three distinct climates and regions from around the world, including the local Southern Pacific, Northern Pacific, and tropical zones.

Ocean Boulevard leads away from Shoreline Village down to the **Breakers Hotel**: twelve pink stories of Spanish Revival design topped by a green copper roof. A mile further on, 2300 Ocean Blvd was once owned by Fatty Arbuckle and now houses the **Long Beach Museum of Art** (Tues–Sun 11am–5pm; $5; ⓦwww.lbma.org), fringed by a sculpture garden and featuring a good collection of contemporary Southern Californian art and some experimental work in a video annex. Several blocks north of the ocean, the **Museum of Latin American Art**, 628 Alamitos Ave (Tues–Fri 11.30am–7pm, Sat 11am–7pm, Sun 11am–6pm; $5; ⓦwww.molaa.com), is LA's only museum devoted to the increasingly broad subject of Hispanic art. Showcasing artists from Mexico through South America, the collection includes big names like Diego Rivera and José Orozco as well as lesser-known newcomers using styles that range from social criticism to magical realism.

Between November and March, more than fifteen thousand whales cruise the "Whale Freeway" past Long Beach on their annual migration to and return from winter breeding and berthing grounds in Baja California. *Shoreline Village Cruises*, 429 Shoreline Village Drive (☎562/495-5884), and *Star Party Cruises*, 140 N Marina Drive (☎562/799-7000), operate good whale-watching trips for around $15.

The Queen Mary

Long Beach's most famous attraction is, of course, the mighty ocean liner **QUEEN MARY** (daily 10am–6pm; $19 guided tours, kids $15; ⓦwww.queenmary.com), acquired by the local authorities with the specific aim of bolstering tourism – which it has succeeded in doing, well beyond expectations. The *Queen Mary* lies across the bay, opposite Shoreline Village, and is accessible either by a lengthy walk or the free Long Beach Transit **shuttle** from downtown (information at ☎562/591-2301, ⓦwww.lbtransit.org). Now a luxury hotel, the ship's exhibits suggest that all who sailed on the vessel – the flagship of the Cunard Line from the 1930s until the 1960s – enjoyed the extravagantly furnished lounges and luxurious cabins, all carefully restored and kept sparkling. But a glance at the spartan third-class cabins reveals something of the real story: the tough conditions experienced by the impoverished migrants who left Europe hoping to start a new life in the USA. The red British telephone kiosks around the decks and the hammy displays in the engine room and wheelhouse – closer to *Star Trek* than anything nautical – don't help, but it's nonetheless a marvelous ship, well worth a look.

Santa Catalina Island

Though overlooked by many visitors, **SANTA CATALINA ISLAND** is an inviting mix of uncluttered beaches and wild hills twenty miles off the coast. Claimed by the Portuguese in 1542 as San Salvador, and renamed by the Spanish in 1602, it has stayed firmly outside the historical mainstream. Since 1811, when the indigenous Tongva Indians were forced to resettle on the mainland, the island has been in private ownership, and has over the years grown to be something of a resort – a process hastened by businessman William Wrigley Jr (part of the Chicago chewing-gum dynasty), who financed the Art Deco Avalon Casino, the island's major landmark, in the 1920s. Occupying mostly LA county territory, the island is a popular destination for boaters and nature lovers, and its small marina overflows with luxury yachts and cruise ships in summer. Even so, tourism has been held largely at bay: the hotels are unobtrusive among the whimsical architecture and cars are a rarity, as there's a ten-year waiting list to bring one over from the mainland. Consequently, most of the 3000 islanders walk, ride bikes, or drive electric golf carts.

Arrival and orientation

Depending on the season, a round-trip **ferry** from San Pedro or Long Beach to Catalina Island's one town, **Avalon**, costs between $30 and $40. Catalina Cruises (☎1-800/228-2546) and Catalina Express (☎562/519-1212 or 1-800/481-3470, ⓦwww.catalinaexpress.com) run several services daily. From Newport Beach (see p.156) to Avalon, the Catalina Passenger Service (☎949/673-5245) runs a daily round-trip for about $30. If you get seasick or feel extravagant, **helicopter** services to Avalon, costing $121 round-trip (plus tax), are offered by Island Express (☎310/510-2525, ⓦwww.islandexpress .com) from Long Beach and San Pedro.

Catalina Safari Shuttle Bus (☎1-800/785-8425) runs between Avalon and Two Harbors for $40 round-trip, $28 for kids. Catalina Island Company (☎1-800/343-4491) offers **tours** of the island, ranging from views of the casino ($12) to a fuller four-hour affair exploring the island's natural setting ($44.50) – the only way to see the interior of Catalina without hiking. **Golf carts**, for which you need a driver's license, and **bikes** (both banned from the rough roads outside Avalon) can be rented from stands throughout the island, including at Catalina Golf Carts (☎310/510-1600, ⓦwww.catalinagolfcarts.com). Bikes run $10–25 per day, depending on the model, while golf carts are much steeper, at $30–40 per hour only.

The waters around Catalina are rich in yellowtail, calico bass, barracuda, and sharks. Catalina Island Sportfishing, 114 Claressa St (☎310/510-2420), and Catalina Mako, 17 Cabrillo Drive (☎1-800/296-MAKO), run **charter fishing trips** for around $100–120 an hour (though you can fish for free from the pier), and snorkel and scuba gear is available for rent at *Catalina Divers Supply* (☎310/510-0330 or 1-800/353-0330, ⓦwww.catalinadiverssupply.com).

Practicalities

Be warned that the price of hotel **accommodation** in Avalon hovers upwards of $90, and most beds are booked up throughout the summer and at weekends. The most interesting **hotel** is the *Zane Grey Pueblo Hotel* (☎310/510-0966 or 1-800/446-0271, ⓦwww.zanegreyhotel.com; ❺), detailed below, but the cheapest is usually the *Atwater*, 125 Sumner Ave (☎310/510-2500 or 1-800/626-1496; ❸), or the *Catalina Bayview*, 124 Whittley Ave (☎310/510-7070; ❸). The only budget option is **camping** ($12 per person, kids $6). *Hermit Gulch* (☎310/510-8368) is the closest site to Avalon and thus the busiest. Three other sites – *Blackjack*, *Little Harbor*, and *Two Harbors* – in Catalina's interior (all bookable at ☎310/510-8368, ⓦwww.scico.com/camping) are usually roomier.

For **eating**, *Catalina Cantina*, 313 Crescent Ave (☎310/510-0100), is the best, offering tasty and affordable Mexican staples washed down with margaritas, with live music on weekends.

Avalon

AVALON can be fully explored on foot in an hour, with maps issued by the **Chamber of Commerce** at the foot of the ferry pier (☎310/510-1520, ⓦwww.visitcatalina.org). The best place to begin is at the **Avalon Casino**, a 1920s structure that still shows movies, featuring mermaid murals, gold-leaf ceiling motifs, an Art Deco ballroom, and a small **museum** (daily 10.30am–4pm, Jan–Mar closed Thurs; $1.50) displaying Native American artifacts from Catalina's past.

On the slopes above the casino, the **Zane Grey Pueblo Hotel**, 199 Chimes Tower Rd (see above), is the former home of the Western author, who visited Catalina with a film crew to shoot *The Vanishing American* and liked the place so much he never left, building for himself this pueblo-style house, complete with a beamed ceiling and thick wooden front door. Its hotel rooms are themed after his books, and the pool is shaped like an arrowhead.

The interior

If possible, venture into the **interior** of Catalina. You can take a tour (see above) if time is short; if it isn't, get a free **wilderness permit**, which allows you to hike and camp, from the Chamber of Commerce or the **Parks and Recreation office** (☏310/510-0688), both in Avalon. Mountain biking requires a $50 permit from the **Catalina Island Conservancy**, 125 Claressa Ave, Avalon (☏310/510-2595, ⓦwww.catalinaconservancy.org), or the Two Harbors campsite.

The carefully conserved wilderness of the interior holds a wide variety of native flora and fauna, including the Catalina Shrew, so rare it's only been sighted twice, and the Catalina Mouse, bigger and healthier than its mainland counterpart thanks to abundant food and lack of natural enemies. There are also buffalo, descended from a group of fourteen left behind by a Hollywood film crew and now a sizeable herd wandering about the island. One place definitely worth visiting, a mile and a half inland from town via Avalon Canyon Road, is the **Wrigley Memorial and Botanical Garden** (daily 8am–5pm; $3), administered by the Catalina Island Conservancy. Here, all manner of natural delights are displayed on nearly forty acres, with a special emphasis on native, endangered plants, such as the local varieties of manzanita, ironwood, mahogany, and the wild tomato – a poisonous member of the nightshade family. Also fascinating is chewing gum-magnate Wrigley's own cenotaph (he's buried elsewhere), a striking monument of Georgia marble, blue flagstone, and red roof-tiles.

Anaheim: Disneyland and around

In the early 1950s, illustrator and filmmaker Walt Disney conceived a theme park where his internationally famous cartoon characters – Mickey Mouse, Donald Duck, Goofy, and the rest – would come to life, animated quite literally, and his fabulously successful company would rake in even more money from them.

Disneyland opened in 1955, in anticipation of the acres of orange groves thirty miles southeast of Downtown – in **ANAHEIM** and **Orange County** – becoming the next center of population growth in Southern California. Disney was, of course, quite prescient in his guess, but since then these once-staunchly conservative suburbs have emerged as one of the US's fastest growing areas, with Hispanics and Asians increasingly populating cities like Anaheim, Garden Grove, Santa Ana, and Westminster (the latter being a key center for Vietnamese expatriates) – to the chagrin of old-time Orange

County Anglos, many of whom have left the center of the county in white flight to find more hospitable digs in Irvine, Dana Point, and San Juan Capistrano – or even further, in Phoenix and Salt Lake City.

Even though it only exists on roughly one square mile of land, Disneyland continues to dominate the Anaheim area and contribute to its commercial growth, and the boom doesn't look like it's slowing. If you're not coming to see Disneyland, you may as well give the place a miss: beyond the park, there's not much beyond tacky souvenir shops, dreary fast-food joints, and a bland convention center. But if you do come, or are staying in one of Anaheim's many hotels (see "Accommodation," p.88), the creakier rides at **Knott's Berry Farm** go some way to restoring antique notions of what amusement parks used to be like, and the **Crystal Cathedral** is an imposing reminder of the potency of the evangelical movement. If you're a sports fan, note that baseball's Anaheim Angels play at Anaheim Stadium and hockey's Mighty Ducks play at Arrowhead Pond; the latter team is owned by the town's mouse-in-chief.

Disneyland

Simply put, **DISNEYLAND**, 1313 Harbor Blvd (summer daily 8am–1am; rest of year Mon–Fri 10am–6pm, Sat 9am–midnight, Sun 9am–10pm; $45, $35 kids, parking $7; ☏714/781-4565, ⓦwww.disneyland.go.com), is world-renowned as one of the defining hallmarks of American culture, a theme-park phenomenon with the emphasis strongly on family fun. Thus while it has been known for people to cruise around Disneyland on LSD, it is not a good idea; the authorities take a dim view of anything remotely antisocial, and anyone acting out of order will be thrown out. In any case, the place is surreal enough without the need for mind-expanding drugs. Bear in mind, too, that Disneyland is not LA's only large-scale amusement park; the whirlwind rides at Magic Mountain, for example (see p.166), are always much better.

Practicalities

Disneyland is about 45 minutes by **car** from Downtown LA on the Santa Ana Freeway (I-5). By **train** from Downtown (there are ten a day), it's a thirty-minute journey to Fullerton, from where OCTD buses will drop you at Disneyland or Knott's Berry Farm. By **bus**, MTA #460 from Downtown takes about ninety minutes, and Greyhound runs thirteen buses a day and takes 45 minutes to get to Anaheim, from where it's an easy walk to the park.

As for **accommodation**, most people try to visit Disneyland just for the day and spend the night somewhere else, or at home. It's not a very appealing area, loaded with dismal trinket stores and rundown diners, and most of the hotels and motels close to Disneyland cost well in excess of $75 per night; still, the park is at its least crowded first thing after opening, so staying nearby can help avoid the crowds. If you must stay, the *HI-Anaheim/Fullerton* hostel is by far the best bet (see p.89).

A massive central kitchen produces all the **food** that's eaten in the park (you're not permitted to bring your own), unloading popcorn, hot dogs, hamburgers, and other all-American junkfood from the many stands by the ton. For anything healthier, you'll need to leave the park and travel a fair way. The "Eating" listings on p.166 suggest some of the more palatable options.

The main park

Not including the new California Adventure annex (see below), the Disneyland admission price includes all the rides, although during peak periods you might have to wait in line for hours – lines are shortest when the park opens, so choose a few top rides and get to them very early. From the front gates, **Main Street** leads through a scaled-down, camped-up replica of a turn-of-the-century Midwestern town, filled with souvenir shops, food stands, and penny arcades, toward Sleeping Beauty's Castle, a pseudo-Rhineland palace at the heart of the park that isn't much more than a giant prop. **New Orleans Square**, nearby, arguably contains the two best rides in the park: the Pirates of the Caribbean, a boat trip through underground caverns, singing along with drunken pirates, and the Haunted Mansion, a riotous "doom buggy" tour in the company of the house spooks. In **Adventureland**, the antiquated Jungle Cruise offers "tour guides" making crude puns about the fake animatronic beasts creaking amid the trees, and Tarzan's Treehouse is little more than a movie tie-in taking up the space once occupied by the Swiss Family Robinson Treehouse.

Much more appealing is the nearby **Indiana Jones Adventure**, involving an interactive archeological dig and 1930s-style newsreel leading up to the main feature – a giddy journey along 2500ft of skull-encrusted corridors in which you face fireballs, burning rubble, venomous snakes and, inevitably, a rolling-boulder finale. Less fun is **Frontierland**, the smallest and most "all-American" of the various theme lands, supposedly taking its cues from the Wild West and the tales of Mark Twain, with the less savory and more complex elements care-fully deleted or sanitized. The main attraction, Big Thunder Mountain Railroad, is a drab, slow-moving coaster, while Splash Mountain at least has the added thrill of getting drenched by a log-flume ride. **Fantasyland**, across the drawbridge from Main Street, shows off the cleverest, but also the most senti-mental, aspects of the Disney imagination: Peter Pan, a fairytale flight over London, and It's a Small World, a tour of the world's continents in which ani-mated dolls warble the same cloying song over and over again. Tots who just can't get enough saccharine can wander into **Toontown**, a cartoonish zone aimed only for the under-10 set and generally unbearable for older, thrill-seek-ing visitors.

Fantasyland eventually gives way to **Tomorrowland**, Disney's vision of the future, where the Space Mountain rollercoaster zips through the pitch-black-ness of outer space, silly scientists dabble with 3-D trickery in *Honey, I Shrunk the Audience*, and R2D2 pilots a runaway space cruiser through George Lucas's Star Tours galaxy. This fun zone has been updated somewhat in recent years, with new rides like the Jules Verne-inspired Astro Orbiter taking the place of old favorites like the torpid PeopleMover. One of the more interesting recent additions is Innoventions, which comes larded with a lot of futurist babble but is really little more than a fun opportunity to look at, and play with, the latest special effects. In addition to these attractions, **firework displays** explode every summer night at 9pm, and all manner of parades and special events cel-ebrate important occasions – such as Mickey Mouse's birthday.

The California Adventure

The latest adjunct to Disneyland, taking over a large chunk of its south park-ing lot, is the much-anticipated **CALIFORNIA ADVENTURE**, technically a separate park but wholly connected to the main one in architecture, style, and spirit – it does for California's history and culture what Epcot Center in Florida does to the rest of the world's – namely, remove all the rough edges and make it digestible for even the youngest children. Aside from its more exciting rollercoasters and slightly better food, the California Adventure is really just another "land" to visit, albeit a much more expensive one – you cannot get access to both parks with a single-day admission ticket. Instead, you'll have to shell out another $45 or plunk down $111 for a three-day pass that covers both (even kids are charged $90 for this).

Despite all the hype about the new section, it's hard to justify spending the money when most of Disneyland's classic, and memorable, attractions are on the other side of the park. That said, there are a handful of highlights if you're looking to visit both areas. **Grizzly River Run** is a fun giant-inner-tube ride, splashing around through various plunges and "caverns"; **Soarin' Over California** is a fairly exciting trip on an experimental aircraft that buzzes you through hairpin turns and steep dives; and the **Pacific Pier** zone has a slew of old-fashioned carnival rides that only faintly recall the wilder, harder-edged midways of California's past. There's also a rather tame zone devoted to Tinseltown, the **Hollywood Pictures Backlot** which, aside from a few theaters, special-effects displays, and eateries, is mainly notable for its loose borrowing of the set design from D.W. Griffith's 1916 film *Intolerance* – exotic columns, squatting elephants, and all – while failing to mention that movie's astonishing, unprecedented box-office failure. (This curious design is also used in the new Hollywood & Highland mall; see p.116.)

Knott's Berry Farm

It's hard to escape the clutches of Disneyland even when you leave: everything in the surrounding area seems to have been designed to service the needs of its visitors. However, if you're a bit fazed by the excesses of Disneyland, you might prefer the more traditional **KNOTT'S BERRY FARM**, four miles northwest off the Santa Ana Freeway at 8039 Beach Blvd (summer Mon & Sun–Thurs 9am–11pm, Fri–Sat 9am–midnight; rest of year Mon–Fri 10am–6pm, Sat 10am–10pm, Sun 10am–7pm; $40, kids $30, or $20 for entry after 4pm; ⓦwww.knotts.com). This relaxed, though still pricey, park was born during the Depression, when people began lining up for the fried-chicken dinners prepared by Mrs Knott, a local farmer's wife. To amuse the children while they waited for their food, Mr Knott reconstructed a Wild West ghost town and added amusements until the park had grown into the sprawling sideshow of rollercoasters and carnival rides that stands today. Unlike Disneyland, this park can easily be seen in one day, as long as you concentrate on the rollercoasters, which now make Knott's second only to Magic Mountain (see p.166) for number of thrill rides per acre. Although there are ostensibly six themed lands here, several of them, namely the **Ghost Town** and **Indian Trails**, consist only of mid-level carnival rides, fast-food stands, and uneven historical interpretation. **Camp Snoopy** is the Knott's equivalent of Disney's Toontown, and just as tiresome, while the so-called **Wild Water Wilderness** isn't really a theme area at all, but simply a showplace for the moderately exciting Bigfoot Rapids giant-inner-tube ride.

Simply put, you should spend most or all of your time in just two areas, **Fiesta Village** – home to Montezooma's Revenge, the original one-loop coaster, and Jaguar, a high-flying coaster that spins you around the park concourse – and especially the **Boardwalk**, which is all about thrill rides: the Boomerang, a forward-and-back coaster that can easily induce nausea; WindJammer, two racing coasters looping and dipping around each other; Supreme Scream, a delightfully terrifying freefall drop; Hammerhead, featuring huge loops; and the new Perilous Plunge, a hellish drop at a 75-degree angle that's far more exciting than any old log-flume ride. The Boardwalk, Knott's version of a carnival midway, with its death-defying rides and vomit-inducing thrills, easily puts Disney's Pacific Pier (see above), with its softer-edged, toddler-friendly attractions, to complete shame.

Knott's has recently added its own adjacent water park, **Soak City USA** (May–Sept only, hours vary but generally 10am-8pm; $23, kids $16, $13 for entry after 3pm; Ⓦwww.knotts.com/soakcity), offering 21 rides of various heights and speeds, almost all of them involving the familiar water slides – either with or without an inner tube – that can really bring out the sweltering masses on a hot summer day.

South of Disneyland

To the **south of Disneyland**, the giant **Crystal Cathedral**, just off the Santa Ana Freeway on Chapman Avenue (tours Mon–Sat 9am–3.30pm; free; Ⓦwww.crystalcathedral.org), is a Philip Johnson design of tubular space frames and plate glass walls that forms part of the vision of evangelist Robert Schuller, who, not content with owning the world's first drive-in church (next door to the cathedral), commissioned this dramatic prop to boost the ratings of his televised sermons – raising $1.5 million for the construction of the building during one Sunday service alone. His shows reach their climax with the special Christmas production, using live animals in biblical roles and people disguised as angels suspended on ropes. A more worthwhile attraction, perhaps, lies in the nearby, unappealing burg of Santa Ana, where the splendid **Bowers Museum of Cultural Art**, 2002 N Main St (Tues–Sun 10am–4pm; $12, kids $7; Ⓦwww.bowers.org), features a great range of anthropological treasures from early Asian, African, Native American, and pre-Columbian civilizations. Showcasing artifacts as diverse as ceramic Mayan icons, hand-crafted baskets from native Californians, and highly detailed Chinese funerary sculpture, the museum is an essential stop for anyone interested in civilizations outside the West. A same-day ticket also allows entry to the adjacent **Kidseum** (Sat & Sun 10am–4pm), a less invigorating look at the same subject, made easily digestible for bored youngsters.

The Richard Nixon Library and Birthplace

Mickey Mouse may be its most famous resident, but conservative Orange County's favorite son is former US president Richard Milhous Nixon, born in 1913 in what is now the freeway-caged **Yorba Linda**, about eight miles northeast of Disneyland. Here, the **RICHARD NIXON LIBRARY AND BIRTHPLACE**, 18001 Yorba Linda Blvd (Mon–Sat 10am–5pm, Sun 11am–5pm; $6, kids $2; Ⓦwww.nixonfoundation.org), is an unrelentingly hagiographic library and museum that features oversized gifts from world leaders, amusing campaign memorabilia, and a collection of obsequious letters written by and to Nixon (including one he sent to the boss of McDonald's proclaiming the fast-food chain's hamburgers to be "one of the finest food buys in America").

However, it's in the constantly running archive radio and TV recordings that the distinctive Nixon persona really shines through, from his notorious Checkers Speech (see box) to his disastrous debates with John F. Kennedy. Throughout the museum, Nixon's face leers down in Orwellian fashion from almost every wall, but only inside the **Presidential Auditorium** (at the end of the corridor packed with notes attesting to the former president's innocence in the Watergate scandal) do you get the chance to ask him a question. Many possibilities spring to mind, but the choice is limited to those already programmed into a computer. Ten or so minutes after making your selection, Nixon's gaunt features will fill the overlarge screen and provide the stock reply – though "I am not a crook" is never one of the correct answers.

Qualified as a lawyer and fresh from wartime (non-combat) service in the US Navy, **Richard Milhous Nixon** entered politics as a Republican congressman in 1946, smearing his incumbent rival as a closet Communist – a trait he would soon perfect. Shortly after arriving in Washington, Nixon joined the **House Un-American Activities Committee** (HUAC), a group of scaremongers led by the fanatical Joseph McCarthy. Through the now notorious anti-Communist "witch trials," McCarthy and Nixon wrecked the lives and careers of many Americans and, in the process, launched Nixon to national prominence, culminating in his becoming Eisenhower's vice president in 1953, aged just 39.

It almost didn't happen, though. Just before the election, the discovery of undeclared income precipitated the "fund crisis," which cast doubts over Nixon's honesty. Incredibly, his **Checkers Speech** convinced 58 million viewers of his integrity, with a broadcast to rival the worst soap opera. His performance climaxed with the statement that, regardless of the damage it may do to his career, he would not be returning the cocker spaniel dog (Checkers) given to him as a gift and now a family pet.

Eight years later, Nixon was defeated in his own bid for the nation's top job by the even younger John F. Kennedy, due largely to his embarrassment during their 1960s live TV debates, in which Nixon refused to wear make-up and, with a visible growth of beard, perspired freely under the TV lights, looking like the very embodiment of sleaze. The election loss led him into the **wilderness years.** Staying out of the public spotlight, he took several highly lucrative posts and wrote *Six Crises*, a book whose deep introspection came as a surprise – and convinced many of the author's paranoia. Seeking a power base for the next presidential campaign, Nixon contested the governorship of California in 1962. His humiliating defeat at the hands of Pat Brown (father to Jerry) did nothing to suggest that six years later he would narrowly defeat Hubert Humphrey to be **elected president** in 1968.

Nixon had attained his dream, but the country he inherited was more divided than at any time since the Civil War. The **Vietnam War** was at its height, and his large-scale illegal bombing of Cambodia earned him worldwide opprobrium. Nixon was not, however, a right-winger by modern standards. By breaking with his own party's right wing, he was able to re-establish diplomatic relations with China, begin arms reduction talks with the Soviet Union, create the Environmental Protection Agency, and reluctantly oversee the implementation of court-ordering busing to alleviate racial segregation. Nixon's actions surprised many and contributed to his winning re-election in 1972.

Despite his huge victory over George McGovern, Nixon's second term was ended prematurely by the cataclysmic **Watergate Affair.** In January 1973, seven men were tried for breaking into and bugging the headquarters of the Democratic Party in the Watergate Building in Washington, an act that was financed with money allocated to the Committee to Re-Elect the President (CREEP). Nixon may not have sanctioned the actual bugging operation, but there was ample evidence to suggest that he participated in the cover-up. Ironically, his insistence on taping all White House conversations to ease the writing of his future memoirs was to be the major stumbling block to his surviving the crisis. Facing the threat of impeachment, President Nixon **resigned** in 1974.

The full **pardon** granted to Nixon by his successor, Gerald Ford, did little to arrest a widespread disillusionment with the country's political machine, but did ensure Ford's defeat in the 1976 presidential election. Ultimately, thanks in part to Nixon, the rose-tinted faith, long held by many Americans, in the unflinching goodness of the president per se seemed irredeemably shattered. Remarkably, the years since his ignoble demise saw him quietly seek to establish elder-statesman credentials, opining on world and national affairs through books and newspaper columns. He died in 1994 and was buried at Yorba Linda.

The Orange County Coast

As Disneyland grew, so did the rest of Orange County. Besides providing tourist services, the region became a major center for light industry and home to many of the millions who poured into Southern California during the 1960s and 1970s. But it was expansion without style, and those who could afford to soon left the anonymous inland sprawl for the more colorful coast. As a result, the **ORANGE COUNTY COAST**, a string of towns from the edge of the Harbor Area to the borders of San Diego County 35 miles south, is suburbia with a shoreline: swanky condos line the sands, and the ambience is easygoing, affluent, and conservative or libertarian depending on the area.

As the names of the main towns suggest – **Huntington Beach**, **Newport Beach**, and **Laguna Beach** – there's no real reason beyond sea and sand to go there. But they do provide something of a counterpart to LA's more cosmopolitan side, and, despite the destructive brushfires of 1993 and after, form appealing stopovers on a leisurely journey south. Unlike most of LA's beach districts, the communities here don't stand shoulder-to-shoulder but are a few miles apart, in many instances divided by an ugly power station but sometimes by a piece of undeveloped coast. The one place that genuinely merits a stop is just inland at **San Juan Capistrano**, site of the best kept of all the Californian missions. Further on, there's little to see before you reach adjoining San Diego County, but the campground at **San Clemente** provides the only cheap accommodation along the southern part of the coast.

The fastest trip from LA to San Diego skips the coast by passing through Orange County on the inland San Diego Freeway, the 405. The coastal cities, though, are linked by the more appealing Pacific Coast Highway (PCH), part of Hwy-1, which you can pick up from Long Beach (or from the end of Beach Boulevard in Anaheim), though it's often busy in the summer. OCTD bus #1 rumbles along PCH roughly hourly during the day, though Greyhound connections aren't so good: San Clemente gets nine buses a day and San Juan Capistrano gets two in the early morning, but there are none to Huntington, Laguna, or Newport beaches. Amtrak connects Downtown LA (or Disneyland) to San Juan Capistrano, though you can travel all the way along the coast from LA to San Diego using local buses for about $4 – but you should allow a full day for the journey. A slightly pricier, but possibly more worthwhile, transit option is the Metrolink commuter train line (see "Public Transportation," p.80), which not only connects Downtown LA with Orange County down to San Clemente, but continues on to Oceanside in San Diego County.

Huntington Beach

HUNTINGTON BEACH is the first place of note on the Orange County Coast, the wildest of the beach communities, and one that you don't need a fortune to enjoy. It's a compact town composed of engaging, ramshackle single-story cafés and beach stores grouped around the foot of a long pier, off PCH at Main Street – also the place where the **Surfers Walk of Fame** commemorates the sport's towering figures. Otherwise, the beach is the sole focus: it was here that California surfing began, imported from Hawaii in 1907 to encourage day-trippers to visit on the Pacific Electric Railway. You can check out the **International Surfing Museum**, 411 Olive Ave (Sept–May Wed–Sun noon–5pm; June–August open daily; $2; ⓦwww.surfingmuseum .org), which features exhibits on such legendary figures as Corky Carroll and

Duke Kahanamoku, historic posters from various world surfing contests, and an array of traditional, contemporary, and far-out boards, including one shaped like a Swiss Army Knife. If all this appeals to you, see the full glory of the sport at the **Pro Surfing Championship**, a world-class event held each June. In October, the largely blonde and suntanned locals celebrate a plausible **Oktoberfest** with German food and music, and the burg is also a surprisingly good place to stay, with Orange County's cheapest beds in a **youth hostel** three blocks from the pier (see "Accommodation," p.89).

Newport Beach and Corona Del Mar

Ten miles south of Huntington, **NEWPORT BEACH** could hardly provide a greater contrast. With ten yacht clubs and ten thousand yachts, this is upmarket even by Orange County standards, an image-obsessed town that people visit to acquire a tan they can show off on the long stretches of sand or in the bars alongside. Needless to say, you'll need a pocketful of credit cards and a presentable physique to join them.

The beach is spread around a natural bay that cuts several miles inland, and although there are hardly any conventional "sights" in town, the place to hang out is on the thin **Balboa Peninsula**, along which runs the three-mile-long strand. The most youthful and boisterous section is about halfway along, around **Newport Pier** at the end of 20th Street. North of here, beachfront homes restrict access, but to the south, around the second of Newport's two piers, the **Balboa Pier** is a tourist-friendly zone that holds a marina from which you can escape to Catalina Island (see p.147), or take a boat ride on the *Pavilion Queen* (summer daily, hourly cruises 11am–dusk; rest of year daily 11am–3pm; $8) around Newport's own, much smaller, islands. Away from the peninsula, Newport Beach is home to the **Orange County Museum of Art**, 850 San Clemente Drive (Tues–Sun 11am–5pm; $5, free Tues; ⓦ www.ocma.net), a surprisingly good institution that stages engaging exhibitions of contemporary work.

Just a few miles along PCH from Newport, **CORONA DEL MAR** is a much less ostentatious place, worth a short stop for its good beach and the **Sherman Library and Gardens**, 2647 East PCH (daily 10.30am–4pm; $3; ⓦ www.slgardens.org), devoted to the horticulture of the American Southwest and raising many vivid blooms in its botanical gardens, including cacti, orchids, roses, and an array of different herbs. Between here and Laguna Beach lies an unspoiled three-mile-long coastline, protected as **Crystal Coves State Park** – perfect to explore on foot, far from the crowds.

Laguna Beach

Six miles south of Crystal Coves, nestled among the crags around a small sandy strip, **LAGUNA BEACH** developed late in the nineteenth century as a community of artists, drawn by the beauty of the location. You may need a few million dollars to live here nowadays, but still there's a relaxed and tolerant feel among the inhabitants, who range from rich industrialists to upper-middle-class gays and lesbians to holdouts from the 1960s, when Laguna became a hippie haven – Timothy Leary was known to hang out at the *Taco Bell* on PCH. The scenery is still the great attraction, and despite the upswell in population, Laguna remains relatively unspoiled with a still-flourishing arts scene in the many streetside galleries.

PCH passes right through the center of Laguna, a few steps from the small main **beach**. From the beach's north side, an elevated wooden walkway twists

Laguna's festivals

Laguna hosts a number of large summer **art festivals** over six weeks in July and August. The best-known – and most bizarre – is the **Pageant of the Masters**, in which the participants pose in front of a painted backdrop to portray a famous work of art. It might sound ridiculous, but it's actually quite impressive and takes a great deal of preparation – something reflected in the prices: $15–65 for shows that sell out months in advance. You may, however, be able to pick up cancellations on the night (shows begin at 8.30pm; ☎1-800/487-3378, 949/494-1145, or ⊛www.foapom.com for more information). The idea for the pageant was hatched during the Depression as a way to raise money for local artists, and the action takes place at the Irving Bowl, close to where Broadway meets Laguna Canyon Road, a walkable distance from the bus station. The pageant is combined with the **Festival of the Arts** (10am–11.30pm; $5; information as above) held at the same venue, showcasing the work of up to 150 local artists.

The excitement of both festivals waned in the Sixties, when a group of hippies created the alternative **Sawdust Festival**, 935 Laguna Canyon Rd (June 28–Sept 1, 10am–10pm; $6.50, season pass $12; ☎949/494-3030, ⊛www.sawdustartfestival .org), in which local artists and craftspeople set up makeshift studios to demonstrate their skills. It is now just as established but easier to get into than the other two.

around the coastline above a conserved **ecological area**, enabling you to peer down on the ocean and, when the tide's out, scamper over the rocks to observe the tidepools. From the end of the walkway, make your way by the posh beach-side homes and head down the hill back to the center. You'll pass the **Laguna Art Museum** 307 Cliff Drive (Tues–Sun 11am–5pm; $5; ⊛lagunaartmuseum .org), which has changing exhibitions from its stock of Southern Californian art from the 1900s to the present. A few miles further is less-touristy **SOUTH LAGUNA** where the wonderfully secluded Victoria and Aliso beaches are among several below the bluffs.

San Juan Capistrano

Further south, and three miles inland along the I-5 freeway, most of the small town of **SAN JUAN CAPISTRANO** is built in a Spanish Colonial style derived from the **Mission San Juan Capistrano**, Ortega Highway at Camino Capistrano in the center of town (daily 8.30am–5pm; $6; ⊛www.missionsjc .com), a short walk from the Amtrak stop. The seventh of California's missions, founded by Junípero Serra in 1776, the mission was within three years so well populated that it outgrew the original chapel. Soon after, the **Great Stone Church** was erected, the ruins of which are the first thing you see as you walk in. The huge structure had seven domes and a bell tower, but was destroyed by an earthquake soon after its 1812 completion, and the ruins themselves are now decaying rapidly, requiring up to $20 million in projected restoration. For an idea of how it might have looked, see the full-sized replica – now a church – just northwest of the mission.

The rest of the mission is in an above-average state of repair. The **chapel** is small and narrow, decorated with Indian drawings and Spanish artifacts, set off by a sixteenth-century altar from Barcelona. In a side room, the chapel of St Pereguin is a tiny room kept warm by the heat from the dozens of candles lit by miracle-seeking pilgrims who arrive here from all over the US and Mexico. Other restored buildings include the kitchen, smelter, and workshops used for dyeing, weaving, and candlemaking. There's also a rather predictable **museum** (open during mission hours; free), giving a broad history of the Spanish progress through California and displaying odds and ends from the mission's past.

The city is further noted for its **swallows**, popularly thought to return here from their winter migration on March 19. They sometimes do arrive on this day – along with large numbers of tourists – but are much more likely to show up as soon as the weather is warm enough, and when there are enough insects on the ground to provide a decent homecoming banquet.

San Clemente

Five miles south of San Juan Capistrano down I-5, **SAN CLEMENTE** is a pretty little town, its streets contoured around the hills, lending an almost Mediterranean air. Because of its proximity to one of the largest military bases in the state, **Camp Pendleton**, it's a popular weekend retreat for military personnel, and is also home to some of Orange County's better surfing beaches, especially toward the south end of town, and has a reasonable campground, too (see "Accommodation," p84). It's here, around the city's southern tip, that San Clemente had a brief glimmer of fame when President Richard Nixon convened his **Western White House** here from 1969 to 1974, regularly meeting with cronies and political allies. The 25-acre estate is located off of Avenida del Presidente and is visible from the beach – though off limits if you want a closer look.

The San Gabriel and San Fernando valleys

The northern side of LA is defined by two long, wide valleys lying beyond the hills from the central basin, starting close to one another a few miles north of Downtown and spanning outwards in opposite directions – east to the deserts around Palm Springs, west to Ventura on the Central Coast.

To the east, the **SAN GABRIEL VALLEY** was settled by farmers and cattle ranchers who set up small towns on the lands of the eighteenth-century Mission San Gabriel, foothill communities which grew into prime resort towns, luring many here around the turn of the century. **Pasadena**, the largest of the modest cities, holds many elegant period houses, as well as the fine **Norton Simon Museum**, and has lately become most notable for its "Old Pasadena" outdoor shopping mall, featuring dining, movie-going, and various cultural activities. Above Pasadena, the southern slopes of the San Gabriel Mountains are peppered with detritus from the resort days, and make great spots for hiking and rough camping, though you'll nearly always need a car to get to the trailheads. South of Pasadena, WASP-ish **San Marino** is dominated by the **Huntington Library and Gardens**, a stash of art and literature ringed by botanical gardens that itself is worth a trip to the valley.

North of Downtown LA, and spreading west, the **SAN FERNANDO VALLEY** is *the* Valley to most Angelenos: a sprawl of tract homes, mini-malls, fast-food drive-ins, and auto-parts stores that has more of a middle-American feel than anywhere else in LA and is visually similar to much of inland Orange

Earthquake City: The San Fernando Valley

The devastating 6.7 magnitude **earthquake** that shook LA on the morning of January 17, 1994, was one of the most destructive disasters in US history. Fifty-five people were killed, two hundred more suffered critical injuries, and the economic cost is estimated at $8 billion. One can only guess how much higher these totals would have been had the quake hit during the day, when the many collapsed stores would have been crowded with shoppers and the roads and freeways full of commuters.

As it was, the tremor toppled chimneys and shattered windows all over Southern California, with the worst damage concentrated at the epicenter in the San Fernando Valley community of **Northridge**, where a dozen people were killed when an apartment building collapsed. At the northern edge of the valley, the I-5/Hwy-14 interchange was destroyed, killing just one motorist but snarling traffic for at least a year; while in West LA, the Santa Monica Freeway overpass collapsed onto La Cienega Boulevard at one of LA's busiest intersections. The Northridge event followed a quake in the eastern desert around Landers a few years earlier, and just eclipsed LA's previous worst earthquake in modern times, the 6.6 magnitude temblor of February 9, 1971, which had its epicenter in Sylmar – also in the Valley.

Small earthquakes happen all the time in LA, usually doing no more than rattling supermarket shelves and making dogs howl. In the unlikely event a sizeable earthquake strikes when you're in LA, protect yourself under something sturdy, such as a heavy table or a door frame, and well away from windows or anything made of glass. In theory, all the city's new buildings are "quake-safe"; the extent of the crisis in January 1994, however, has forced the city to re-examine and reinforce buildings – though as the quake recedes in memory, the job seems to diminish in perceived importance. So when the inevitable "Big One," a quake in the 8+ range, arrives, no one knows exactly what will be left standing.

County. There are a few isolated sights, notably **Forest Lawn Cemetery** – a prime example of graveyard kitsch that's hard to imagine anywhere except in LA – but otherwise, beyond a couple of minor historical sites, it's the movies that bring people out here. Rising land values in the 1930s pushed many studios out of Hollywood and over the hills to **Burbank**, a colorless burg now overpowered by several major film and TV companies, several of which are open to the public. At the far west end, ultra-conservative **Simi Valley** is known for two things: finding four white police officers not guilty of beating black motorist Rodney King in April 1992 (see p.105), and providing a home for the **Ronald Reagan Presidential Library** (daily 10am–5pm; $5, kids free; Ⓦ www.reagan.utexas.edu), containing all the papers pertaining to the eight-year reign of the Gipper.

Pasadena

In the 1880s, wealthy East Coast tourists who came to California looking for the good life found it in **PASADENA**, ten miles north of LA, where luxury hotels were built and a funicular railway cut into the nearby San Gabriel Mountains, leading up to taverns and observatories on the mile-high crest. Many of the early, well-heeled visitors stayed on, building the rustically sprawling houses that remain, but as LA grew so Pasadena suffered, mainly from the smog which the mountains collect. The downtown area underwent a major renovation in the 1980s, with modern shopping centers being slipped in

behind 1920s facades, but the historic parts of town have not been forgotten – unusual for LA. Maps and booklets detailing self-guided tours of city architecture and history are available from the **Pasadena Visitors Bureau**, 171 S Los Robles Ave (Mon–Fri 8am–5pm, Sat 10am–4pm; ☎626/795-9311, Ⓦwww.pasadenacal.com). The town's most notable attraction, the New Year's Day **Tournament of Roses**, began in 1890 to celebrate and publicize the mild Southern California winters, and now attracts over a million visitors every year to watch its marching bands and elaborate flower-emblazoned floats (see box on p.184).

Between Fair Oaks and Euclid avenues along Colorado Boulevard, the historic shopping precinct of **Old Pasadena** draws an increasingly large number of visitors for its fine restaurants, galleries, and theaters. A block north of Colorado, a replica Chinese Imperial Palace houses the **Pacific Asia Museum**, 46 N Los Robles Ave (Wed–Sun 10am–5pm; $5, students $3; Ⓦwww.pacificasiamuseum.org), which has a wide range of objects from Japan, China, and Thailand, from ceramic artifacts to hand-woven garments to finely detailed scrolls. One particular highlight is the Courtyard Garden, with koi fish, marble statues, and trees native to the Far East. Just around the corner, at 490 E Union St, is the city's newest museum and one of its most interesting, the three-story **Pasadena Museum of California Art** (Wed–Sun 10am–5pm, Fri closes at 8pm; $6, students & kids free; Ⓦwww.pmcaonline.org), which despite its bland name offers an eye-opening focus on the many aspects of the state's art world since it became an official part of the US in 1850, in all kinds of media from painting to photography to digital art.

The Norton Simon Museum

Although not as famous, the collections of the **NORTON SIMON MUSEUM**, 411 W Colorado Blvd (Wed–Mon noon–6pm, Fri noon–9pm; $6, students $4; ❽www.nortonsimon.org), are at least as good as the LA County or Getty museums. Established and overseen by the eponymous industrialist until his death in 1993, the museum sidesteps the hype of the LA art world to concentrate on the quality of its presentation, which is now even more dramatic and aesthetically compelling after a recent renovation. You could easily spend a whole afternoon or day wandering through the spacious galleries, as well as a sculpture garden inspired by Claude Monet's own Giverny.

The core of the collection is **Western European painting** from the Renaissance to the modern era. It's a massive collection, much of it rotated, but most of the major pieces are on view constantly. Highlights include Dutch paintings of the seventeenth century – notably Rembrandt's vivacious *Titus, Portrait of a Boy* and Frans Hals' quietly aggressive *Portrait of a Man*, and Italian Renaissance work from the likes of Botticelli, Raphael, Giorgione, and Bellini. There's also a good sprinkling of French Impressionists and post-Impressionists: Monet's *Mouth of the Seine at Honfleur*, Manet's *Ragpicker*, and a Degas capturing the extended yawn of a washerwoman in *The Ironers*, plus works by Cézanne, Gauguin, and Van Gogh. Unlike the Getty, the Norton Simon also boasts a solid collection of modernist greats, from Georges Braque and Pablo Picasso to Roy Lichtenstein and Andy Warhol. As a counterpoint to the Western art, the museum has a fine collection of **Asian sculpture** and many highly polished Buddhist and Hindu figures, a mixture of the contemplative and the erotic, some inlaid with precious stones.

Arroyo Seco

The residential pocket northwest of the junction of the 134 and 210 freeways, known as **ARROYO SECO**, or "dry riverbed" in Spanish, features some of LA's best architecture and some of the Valley's most worthwhile attractions. Orange Grove Avenue leads you into the neighborhood from central Pasadena and takes you to the **Pasadena Historical Society**, 470 W Walnut St at Orange Grove Avenue (Wed–Sun noon–5pm; $6, kids free; ❽www .pasadenahistory.org), which has fine displays on Pasadena's history, but is most interesting for the on-site **Feynes Mansion** (Wed–Sun 1.30–3pm, tours hourly Thurs–Sun 1–3pm; free with admission). Decorated with its original 1905 furnishings and paintings, this elegant Beaux Arts mansion was once the home of the Finnish Consulate, and much of the folk art on display comes from Pasadena's "twin town" of Jarvenpää in Finland.

But it's the **Gamble House**, nearby at 4 Westmoreland Place (hour-long tours Thurs–Sun noon–3pm; $8, students $5; ❽www.gamblehouse.usc.edu), which brings people out here. Built in 1908, this masterpiece of Southern California Craftsman architecture helped give rise to a style you'll see replicated all over the state, at once relaxed and refined, freely combining elements from Swiss chalets and Japanese temples in a romantic, sprawling shingled house. Broad eaves shelter outdoor sleeping porches, which in turn shade terraces on the ground floor, leading out to the spacious lawn. With the same attention to detail, all the carpets, cabinetry, and lighting fixtures were designed specifically for the house and remain in excellent condition. The area around the Gamble House is filled with at least eight other **houses** by the two brothers (the firm of Greene & Greene) who designed it, including Charles Greene's own house at 368 Arroyo Terrace (closed to the public).

A quarter of a mile north of the Gamble House is a curious structure by Frank Lloyd Wright, "La Miniatura," also known as the **Millard House**, which you can glimpse through the gate opposite 585 Rosemont Ave, a small, concrete-block house supposedly designed to look like a jungle ruin. Also in the vicinity are houses by noted architects Gregory Ain, Craig Ellwood, and Richard Neutra, and the area definitely rewards driving through its hilly concourses and serene setting (preferably with a copy of David Gebhard's LA architecture guide).

Almost incongruously, the 104,000-seat **Rose Bowl** is just to the north, out of use for most of the year but home to a very popular **flea market** on the second Sunday of each month and, in the autumn, the place where the UCLA football team plays its home games (☎310/825-2101). The other kind of football was also played here in 1994, when the site hosted the World Cup Final. Finally, if you can't get enough of the Rose Parade, visit its headquarters at the **Tournament House**, 391 S Orange Grove Blvd (tours Feb–Aug 2–4pm; free; ☎626/449-4100, ⓦwww.tournamentofroses.com), due to re-open in mid-2003 after a renovation that will restore the 1914 pink Renaissance Revival mansion – once owned by William Wrigley himself – back to its original splendor.

Into the foothills
On the other side of the Foothill Freeway, **Descanso Gardens**, 1418 Descanso Drive (daily 9am–5pm; $5, kids $1; ⓦwww.descansogardens.org), in the city of La Cañada Flintridge, concentrates all the plants you might see in the mountains into 155 acres of landscaped park, especially brilliant in the spring when all the camellias, tulips, lilies, and daffodils are in bloom. From La Cañada, the winding **Angeles Crest Highway** (Hwy-2) heads up into the mountains above Pasadena, an area once dotted with resort hotels and wilderness camps. Today you can hike up any number of nearby canyons and come across the ruins of old lodges that either burned down or were washed away towards the end of the hiking era in the 1930s, when automobiles became popular.

One of the most interesting trails is a five-mile round trip following the route of the Mount Lowe Railway, once one of LA's biggest tourist attractions, from the top of Lake Avenue up to the old railway and the foundations of "**White City**" – formerly a mountaintop resort of two hotels, a zoo, and an observatory. The Crest Highway passes through the **Angeles National Forest**, capped by Mount Wilson, high enough to be the major siting spot for TV broadcast antennae, and with a small **museum** (daily 10am–4pm; $1; ⓦwww.mtwilson.edu) near the 100-inch telescope of the 1904 Mount Wilson Observatory.

The Huntington Library and Gardens
South of Pasadena, **San Marino** is a dull, upper-crust suburb with little of interest beyond the **Huntington Library, Art Collections and Botanical Gardens**, off Huntington Drive at 1151 Oxford Rd (Tues–Fri noon–4.30pm, Sat & Sun 10am–4.30pm; $10, students $7; ⓦwww.huntington.org). Part of this comprises the collections of Henry Huntington, the nephew of the childless multimillionaire Collis P. Huntington, who owned and operated the Southern Pacific Railroad – which in the nineteenth century had a virtual monopoly on transportation in California. Henry, groomed to take over the company from his uncle, was dethroned by the board of directors and took his sizeable inheritance to Los Angeles, where he bought up the existing streetcar

routes and combined them as the Pacific Electric Railway Company. The company's "Red Cars" soon became the largest network in the world, and Huntington the largest landowner in the state, buying up farmland and extending the streetcar system at a huge profit. He retired in 1910, moving to the manor he had built in San Marino, devoting himself full time to buying rare books and manuscripts, and marrying his uncle's widow Arabella and acquiring her collection of English portraits.

You can pick up a self-guided walking tour of each of the three main sections from the bookstore and information desk in the covered pavilion. The **Library**, right off the main entrance, has a two-story exhibition hall containing rare manuscripts and books, among them a Gutenberg Bible, a folio edition of Shakespeare's plays, and the **Ellesmere Chaucer**, a circa-1410 illuminated manuscript of the *Canterbury Tales*. Displays around the walls trace the history of printing and of the English language from medieval manuscripts to a King James Bible, from Milton's *Paradise Lost* and Blake's *Songs of Innocence and Experience* to first editions of Swift, Dickens, Woolf, and Joyce.

To decorate the **main house**, a grand mansion done out in Louis XIV carpets and later French tapestries, the Huntingtons traveled to England and returned laden with the finest art money could buy; most of it still hangs on the walls. Unless you're a real fan of eighteenth-century English portraiture, head through to the back extension, added when the gallery opened in 1934, which displays, as well as works by Van Dyck and Constable, the stars of the whole collection – Gainsborough's *Blue Boy* and Reynolds' *Mrs Siddons as the Tragic Muse*. More striking, perhaps, are Turner's *Grand Canal, Venice*, awash in hazy sunlight and gondolas, and Blake's *Satan Comes to the Gates of Hell*, which is quite the portrait of Old Nick, in this case battling Death with spears.

Nearby, the **Scott Gallery for American Art** displays paintings by Edward Hopper and Mary Cassatt, and a range of Wild West drawings and sculpture, though for all the art and literature, it's the grounds that make the Huntington really special. The acres of beautiful themed **gardens** surrounding the buildings include a Zen Rock Garden, complete with authentically constructed Buddhist Temple and Tea House, and a Desert Garden with the world's largest collection of desert plants, including twelve acres of cacti in an artful setting. While strolling through these botanical wonders, you might also call in on the Huntingtons themselves, buried in a neo-Palladian **mausoleum** at the northwest corner of the estate.

Foothill Boulevard

Parallel to the Foothill Freeway (I-210), **FOOTHILL BOULEVARD** was once best known as part of Route 66, formerly the main route across the US, and still the one with the most nostalgia attached to it. The freeway stole Route 66's traffic and glory, and following Foothill Boulevard out of Pasadena nowadays leads to the town of **Arcadia**, whose **State and County Arboretum**, 301 N Baldwin Ave (daily 9am–5pm; $5, students $3; ⓦ www.arboretum.org), has trees arranged according to their native continents. The site was once the 127-acre ranch of "Lucky" Baldwin, who made his millions in the Comstock silver mines in the 1870s, then settled here in 1875 and built a fanciful white Victorian palace along a palm-treed lagoon (later used in the TV show *Fantasy Island*) on the site of the 1839 Rancho Santa Anita. He also bred horses, and raced them on a neighboring track that has since grown into the **Santa Anita Racetrack** (racing Oct to early Nov & late Dec to late April, Wed–Sun, post time 12.30pm or 1pm; $4; ⓦ www.santaanita.com), one of the more glamorous racetracks in California.

Directly north of Arcadia, the city of **Sierra Madre** lies directly beneath Mount Wilson and is worth a visit if you're a hiker, as the seven-mile round-trip trail up to the summit is one of the best hikes in the range. (The trailhead is 150 yards up the private Mount Wilson Road.) Southwest of Sierra Madre stands the valley's original settlement, the church and grounds of **Mission San Gabriel Arcangel**, 428 S Mission Drive (daily 9am–4.30pm; $5; ⓦ sangabrielmission.org). Still standing at the corner of Mission and Serra in the heart of the small town of **San Gabriel**, the mission was established here in 1771 by Junípero Serra and the current building finished in 1812. Despite decades of damage by earthquakes and the elements, the church and grounds have been repaired and re-opened, their old winery, cistern, kitchens, gardens, and antique-filled rooms giving some sense of mission-era life.

Glendale and Forest Lawn Cemetery

GLENDALE, eight miles north of Downtown LA and the gateway to the San Fernando Valley, was once a fashionable suburb of LA. Now it's a nondescript bedroom community, and there are few reasons to come here. While the marvelous **Alex Theater**, 268 N Brand Blvd, is an undeniably appealing piece of green-and-yellow Art Deco with a towering pylon (and now serves as a performing arts venue), and the **Brand Library** 1601 W Mountain St, is a striking 1902 confection with white "Islamic" domes and minarets, Glendale is best known for its branch of **FOREST LAWN CEMETERY**, 1712 S Glendale Ave (daily 8am–5pm; free; ⓦ www.forestlawn.org). Immortalized with biting satire by Evelyn Waugh in *The Loved One*, it is still at the vanguard of the American way of death. Founded in 1917 by a Dr Hubert Eaton, this became the place to be seen dead, its pompous landscaping and pious artworks attracting celebrities by the dozen.

It's best to climb the hill and see the cemetery in reverse from the **Forest Lawn Museum**, whose hodgepodge of historical bric-a-brac includes coins from ancient Rome, Viking relics, medieval armor, and a mysterious sculpted Easter Island figure, discovered being used as ballast in a fishing boat in the days when the statues could still be removed from the island. How it ended up here is another mystery, but it is the only one on view in the US. Next door to the museum, the grandiose **Resurrection and Crucifixion Hall** houses the biggest piece of religious art in the world: *The Crucifixion* by Jan Styka – an oil painting nearly 200ft tall and 50ft wide – though you're only allowed to see it during the ceremonial unveiling every hour on the hour. Besides this, Eaton owned a stained-glass re-creation of Da Vinci's *Last Supper* and, wanting to complete his set of "the three greatest moments in the life of Christ," he commissioned American artist Robert Clark to produce *The Resurrection* – viewable only during unveilings every half-hour. If you'd rather not stick around for the showings of these hulking curiosities, you can always check out the scaled-down replicas just inside the entrance.

From the museum, the terrace gardens lead down past sculpted replicas of the greats of classical European art, and on to the **Freedom Mausoleum**, home to a handful of the cemetery's better-known graves. Just outside the mausoleum's doors, Errol Flynn lies in an unspectacular plot (unmarked until 1979), rumored to have been buried with six bottles of whiskey at his side, while nearby is the grave of Walt Disney, who wasn't frozen, as urban legend would have it. Inside the mausoleum itself you'll find Clara Bow, Nat King Cole, Jeanette MacDonald, and Alan Ladd all close to each other on the first floor. Downstairs are Chico Marx and his brother Gummo, the Marx Brothers' agent and business manager. To the left, heading back down the hill, the **Great Mausoleum** is chiefly noted for the tombs of Clark Gable (next to Carole Lombard, who died in a plane crash just three years after marrying him), and Jean Harlow, in a marble-lined room which cost over $25,000, paid for by fiancé William Powell.

A number of other **Forest Lawn cemeteries** continue the style of the Glendale site, to a much less spectacular degree. There's a Hollywood Hills branch in Burbank (6300 Forest Hills Drive, close to Griffith Park) which has a formidable roll call of ex-stars – Buster Keaton, Stan Laurel, Liberace, Charles Laughton, and Marvin Gaye – but little else to warrant a visit. The others, Covina Hills, Cypress Beach, and Long Beach, are best avoided.

Burbank and the studios

Although Hollywood is synonymous with the movie industry, in reality most of the big studios moved away long ago, and much of the grimy business of actually making films goes on over the hills in otherwise boring **BURBANK**, just west of Glendale. Hot, smoggy, and often downright ugly, Burbank nonetheless has a media district bustling with production activity, thanks to the great demand from overseas markets, cable TV, and broadcast networks. Disney's "wacky" animation building (involving a starry wizard's hat) is visible from the 134 freeway, while **Warner Bros**, Warner Boulevard at Hollywood Way, offers worthwhile "insider" tours of its sizeable facilities (Mon–Fri 9am–4pm; $33; reserve at ☎818/972-TOUR, ⊛www.burbank.com/warner_bros_tour). **NBC**, 3000 W Alameda St (Mon–Fri 9am–4pm; $7; ☎818/840-3537), allows 90min tours of the largest production facility in the US, and gives you the chance to be in the audience for the taping of a TV program (phone ahead for free tickets), such as Jay Leno's *Tonight Show*.

The largest of the old backlots belongs to **Universal Studios** (summer daily 8am–10pm; rest of year daily 9am–7pm; $45; ☎818/508-9600, ⊛www.universalstudioshollywood.com), which mainly uses the space for predictable thrill rides based on movies like *Backdraft*, *Jurassic Park*, and *Back to the Future*. The four-hour-long "tours" are more like a trip through an amusement park than a film studio, the first half featuring a tram ride through a make-believe set where you can experience the fading magic of the parting of the Red Sea and a collapsing bridge, the second taking place inside the corny Entertainment Center, where unemployed actors and stuntmen engage in Wild West shootouts and stunt shows based on the latest movies. You never actually get to see any filming.

Also part of the complex, the **Universal Amphitheater** hosts pop concerts in the summer; a twenty-screen multiplex has a lobby reminiscent of 1920s movie palaces; and **Universal CityWalk** is a few square blocks of neon-lit theme shops and restaurants, free to all who pay the $7 parking (redeemable at the cinemas), a place where pop bands churn out MOR covers, street performers warble slick set-pieces, and giant TV screens run ads for the latest Universal release.

The Western San Fernando Valley

On the **western end** of the San Fernando Valley, the Ventura Freeway (US-101) passes below the increasingly expensive hillside homes of **Sherman Oaks** and **Encino**, close to which **Los Encinos State Historic Park**, 16756

The LA aqueduct

Just beyond Mission San Fernando, I-5 runs past two of LA's main reservoirs, the water of which has been brought hundreds of miles through the **California Aqueduct** from the Sacramento Delta, and through the **LA Aqueduct** from the Owens Valley on the eastern slopes of the Sierra Nevada Mountains. However, the legality of the arrangements by which Los Angeles gained control of such a distant supply of water is still disputed. Agents of the city, masquerading as rich cattle-barons interested in establishing ranches in the Owens Valley, bought up most of the land along the Owens River before selling it, at great personal profit, to the City of Los Angeles. These cunning tactics provided the inspiration for Roman Polanski's 1974 movie *Chinatown*. For more on the Owens Valley, see p.337.

Moorpark St, is all that remains of the original Native American settlement and later Mexican hacienda that were here. The high-ceilinged rooms of the 1849 adobe house open out onto porches, shaded by oak trees (in Spanish, "encinos") and kept cool by the two-foot-thick walls. Damaged in the 1994 earthquake, the complex has recently been renovated, and is open to the public once more. Nearer the 405, at 6100 Woodley Ave in Van Nuys, the **Tillman Japanese Garden** (grounds Mon–Thurs & Sun noon–4pm; tours by reservation only Mon–Thurs; $3; ☎818/751-8166) is an enjoyable little spot – adorned with stone lanterns, bonsai trees, low bridges, a teahouse, and artful streams and pools – which surprisingly use reclaimed water from an adjacent treatment plant and sit in the giant flood plain of the Sepulveda Dam Recreation Area.

West of Encino, Topanga Canyon Boulevard crosses the Ventura Freeway, leading south towards Malibu (p.142) or north to **Stony Point**, a bizarre sandstone outcrop that has been used for countless Western shootouts, and is now a popular venue for LA's lycra-clad rock climbers. The area, though crossed by both Amtrak and Metrolink trains, certainly has a desolate spookiness about it, and it comes as little surprise to learn that during the late 1960s the Charles Manson "family" lived for a time at the **Spahn Ranch**, just west at 12000 Santa Susana Pass.

Mission San Fernando and Magic Mountain

At the north end of the Valley, the San Diego, Golden State, and Foothill freeways join together at I-5, the quickest route north to San Francisco. Just east of the junction, at 15151 San Fernando Mission Blvd, the church and many of the buildings of **Mission San Fernando Rey de España** (daily 9am–5pm; $5) had to be completely rebuilt following the 1971 Sylmar earthquake. It's hard to imagine now, walking through the nicely landscaped courtyards and gardens, but eighty-odd years ago, director D.W. Griffith used the then-dilapidated mission as a film site for movies such as *Our Silent Paths*, his tale of the Gold Rush. Nowadays, there's a good collection of historic pottery, furniture and saddles, and a replica of an old-time blacksmith's shop.

Another twenty miles north, Hwy-14 splits off east to the Mojave Desert, while I-5 continues north past Valencia and **Magic Mountain**, 26101 Magic Mountain Parkway (summer daily 10am–10pm; rest of year Sat & Sun only 10am–8pm; $43, kids $27, $6 parking; ⓦwww.sixflags.com/parks/magic-mountain), a three-hundred-acre complex that has some of the wildest roller-coasters and rides in the world – a hundred times more thrilling than anything at Disneyland. Among them are the appropriately named Goliath coaster, full of harrowing 85mph dips, and Déjà Vu, a high-speed gut-wrencher that twists and jerks you in several different directions at once. The adjacent waterpark, **Hurricane Harbor** (same hours; $22, kids $15, or $53 for both parks; Ⓦwww.sixflags.com/parks/hurricaneharborla), is another fun choice, providing plenty of aquatic fun if you don't mind getting splashed by throngs of giddy pre-adolescents.

Eating

Whatever you want to eat and however much you want to spend, LA's **restaurants** leave you spoiled for choice. **Budget food** is, of course, plentiful here, ranging from historic diners to street-corner coffee shops and cafés to big franchise burgers. Almost as common, and just as cheap, **Mexican food** is the closest thing you'll get to an indigenous LA cuisine. The options are almost endless for quick and cheap meals, and include free food available for the price of a drink at **happy hours**. Many of the city's **higher-end restaurants** serve superb food in consciously cultivated surroundings, driving up their prices on the back of a good review, and getting away with it because they know the place will be packed with first-timers trying to impress their chums by claiming that they've been eating there for years.

As any tourist knows, LA is littered with **celebrity-owned** outfits – like the financially troubled *Planet Hollywood* in Beverly Hills – but the food is usually so unremarkable we haven't listed them. For chowing down, celebrity-watching, or just enjoying a nice view, you're better off practically anywhere else.

Budget food: coffee shops, delis, diners, and drive-ins

Budget food is everywhere in LA, at its best in the many small and stylish **coffee shops**, **delis**, and **diners** that serve soups, omelets, sandwiches, and burgers; it's easy to eat this way constantly and never have to spend much more than $6 for a full meal. There are of course the franchise fast-food joints on every street, though the local chains of **hamburger stands** (many open 24hr) are always much better. *Fatburger*, originally at San Vicente and La Cienega on the border of Beverly Hills, has branches everywhere.

Unfortunately, the best of the 1950s **drive-ins**, such as *Tiny Naylors* in Hollywood, have been torn down. So too have some of the classic googie-style **diners** met their demise; the venerable *Ships* franchise now comprises only a boarded-up ruin in Culver City and a leftover boomerang sign near a West LA gas station.

Downtown and around

Cassell's Hamburgers 3266 W 6th St ☎213/480-8668. No-frills takeout hamburger stand that some swear by, serving up nearly two-thirds of a pound of beef per bun. Closes at 4pm.
Clifton's Cafeteria 648 S Broadway ☎213/627-

1673. Classic 1930s cafeteria, the last remaining of a chain of six, and with much bizarre decor: redwood trees, waterfall and mini-chapel. The food is traditional meat-and-potatoes American, and

LA restaurants

24-hour eats p.168	Italian/Spanish/Greek p.173
Budget food p.166	Japanese/Chinese/Thai/Korean p.174
Mexican/Latin American p.170	Indian/Sri Lankan/Middle Eastern p.176
American/California cuisine/Cajun p.172	Vegetarian/Wholefood p.176

cheap too. Open until midnight.

Grand Central Market 317 S Broadway ☎213/624-9496. Selling plenty of tacos, deli sandwiches, and Chinese food, plus even a few more exotic items, like pig ears and lamb sweetbreads. A recent renovation makes this a fun, cheap place to eat.

Langer's Deli 704 S Alvarado St ☎213/483-8050. "When in doubt, eat hot pastrami" says the sign, though you still have to choose from over twenty ways of eating what is easily LA's best pastrami sandwich. Nearby MacArthur Park Metrorail station may help you escape the dicey neighborhood.

Original Pantry 877 S Figueroa St ☎213/972-9279. There's always a queue for the hearty portions of very meaty American cooking – chops and steaks, mostly – in this 24-hr diner owned by former mayor Dick Riordan. The quirky, old-fashioned brochures are also worth a look.

Philippe the Original French Dip 1001 N Alameda St ☎213/628-3781. 1908 sawdust café that invented the eponymous sandwich, which is served loaded with turkey, ham, lamb, or beef – an amazingly good and filling treat for only $4.

Tommy's 2575 Beverly Blvd, west of Downtown ☎213/389-9060. One of the prime LA spots for big, greasy, tasty burgers – and, many would say, the best. Just watch out for the Rampart neighborhood at night: one of LA's more dangerous drug-dealing zones. 24hr.

The Yorkshire Grill 610 W 6th St ☎213/623-3362. New York-style deli with big sandwiches and friendly service for under $10. Lunchtime is crowded with yuppies and locals; get there early.

Hollywood

Astro Burger 7475 Santa Monica Blvd ☎323/874-8041. Not just burgers, but sandwiches and even veggie meals are the appeal of this lower-Hollywood diner – along with the late hours, until 3am weekdays, 4am weekends.

Hampton's 1342 N Highland Ave ☎323/469-1090. Longstanding comfort-food favorite, with hefty hamburgers served with a choice of over fifty toppings, plus an excellent salad bar.

Maurice's Snack 'n' Chat 5549 W Pico Blvd ☎323/931-3877. Everything here is cooked to

order: spoon bread or baked chicken requires a call two hours ahead, though you could just drop in for fried chicken, pork chops, grits, or salmon croquettes. Cash only.

Mel's Drive-In 8585 Sunset Blvd ☎310/854-7200. Calorie-packing milkshakes, fries and, of course, burgers make this 24hr diner an essential stop if you've got the late-night munchies.

Pink's Hot Dogs 709 N La Brea Ave ☎323/931-4223. The quintessence of chili dogs. Depending on your taste, these monster hot dogs are lifesavers or gut bombs. Open til 2am, or 3am weekends.

Roscoe's Chicken and Waffles 1514 N Gower St ☎323/466-7453. An unlikely spot for Hollywood's elite, this diner attracts all sorts for its fried chicken, greens, goopy grav, and thick waffles. Listen to the ringing pagers and cell phones as you wait in line for breakfast with movie-industry bigshots. One of four area locations.

Topz 8593 Santa Monica Blvd ☎310/659-8843. A local chain of fast-food joints that focuses, somehow, on the healthier side of eating burgers, hot dogs and french fries, with lo-cal cooking oils and lean meats on the culinary agenda. Six other locations, the closest at 7514 Melrose Ave ☎323/852-0146.

Yukon Mining Company 7328 Santa Monica Blvd ☎323/851-8833. Excellent 24-hr coffee shop with comfort food and a curious clientele – don't be surprised to see a crowd of newly arrived Russians, neighborhood pensioners, and glammed-up drag queens. Open until 2am.

West LA

The Apple Pan 10801 W Pico Blvd ☎310/475-3585. Grab a spot at the counter and enjoy freshly baked apple pie and nicely greasy hamburgers across from the imposing Westside Pavilion mall. An old-time joint that opened just after World War II.

Barney's Beanery 8447 Santa Monica Blvd ☎323/654-2287. Two hundred bottled beers and hot dogs, hamburgers, and bowls of chili served in a hip, grungy environment, which used to be a haunt of Jim Morrison. Open until 2am.

Canter's Deli 419 N Fairfax Ave ☎323/651-2030. Huge sandwiches for around $7 and excellent kosher soups served by famously aggressive waitresses in pink uniforms and running shoes. Open

24-hour eats

These places satisfy hunger at all hours. For full restaurant reviews, see the appropriate sections.

Bob's Big Boy 4211 W Riverside Drive, Burbank ☎818/843-9334 – p.170
Canter's Deli 419 N Fairfax Ave, West LA ☎323/651-2030 – p.168
Jerry's Famous Deli 8701 Beverly Blvd, West LA ☎310/289-1811 – p.168
Mel's Drive-In 8585 Sunset Blvd ☎310/854-7200 – p.167
Original Pantry 877 S Figueroa St, Downtown ☎213/972-9279 – p.167
Pacific Dining Car 1310 W 6th St, Downtown ☎213/483-6000 – p.172
Tommy's 2575 Beverly Blvd, west of Downtown ☎213/389-9060 – p.167
Yukon Mining Company 7328 Santa Monica Blvd, West Hollywood ☎323/851-8833 – p.168

24-hr. Live music on Tuesday nights in *Canter's* adjoining "Kibitz Room."

Duke's 8909 Sunset Blvd ☎310/652-3100. A favorite haunt of visiting rock stars (the *Roxy* and *Whisky-a-Go-Go* clubs are up the street), this place attracts a motley crew of night owls and bleary-eyed locals.

Ed Debevic's 134 N La Cienega Blvd ☎310/659-1952. The last four digits of the phone number give you a hint: a rollicking 1950s diner with brash singing waitresses, burgers'n'fries, and beer. A bit overpriced, aimed more at tourists than locals.

Hard Rock Café in the Beverly Center, Beverly Blvd at San Vicente ☎310/276-7605. Almost unavoidable for most visitors, highlighted by rock'n'roll decor, loud music, and fancy merchandise; the bland, greasy food is an afterthought. Also at 1000 Universal Center Drive, Universal City (☎818/622-7626) and 451 Newport Center Drive, Newport Beach (☎949/640-8844), though all the branches are about the same.

Jerry's Famous Deli 8701 Beverly Blvd ☎310/289-1811. The most engaging of the many *Jerry's* locations in LA, featuring a sizeable deli menu and open 24hr. Occasionally, celebrities stop in to nosh.

John o' Groats 10516 W Pico Blvd ☎310/204-0692. Excellent cheap breakfasts and lunches (mostly staples like bacon and eggs), but come at an off hour; the morning crowd can cause a headache.

Johnny Rockets 474 N Beverly Drive ☎310/271-2222. Chrome-and-glass, Fifties-derived hamburger joint, open until 2am at weekends. One of many in a local chain.

Kate Mantilini 9109 Wilshire Blvd ☎310/278-3699. Tasty, upscale versions of classic American diner food, served up in a stylish interior designed by edgy architectural firm Morphosis. Open until 1am weekdays, 2am weekends.

Nate 'n' Al's 414 N Beverly Drive ☎310/274-0101. The best-known deli in Beverly Hills, popular with movie people and one of the few reasonable places in the vicinity.

Swingers Beverly Laurel Motor Hotel 8020 Beverly Blvd ☎323/653-5858. Basic and cheap American food served in a strangely trendy motel environment, luring a large crowd of hipsters and poseurs, as well as a few movie-star wannabes.

Tail o' the Pup 329 N San Vicente Blvd ☎310/652-4517. Worth a visit for the roadside pop architecture alone, though the dogs and burgers are good too. Relocated here from a short distance away.

Santa Monica, Venice, and Malibu

Bicycle Shop Café 12217 Wilshire Blvd, Santa Monica ☎310/826-7831. Serves light meals, fish, and salads, and also a good place to drink. Take note of the plethora of bike decor: chains, frames, and wheels are everywhere, delighting cycle enthusiasts. Open until 2am weekends.

Café 50s 838 Lincoln Blvd, Venice ☎310/399-1955. No doubts about this place: Ritchie Valens on the jukebox, burgers on the tables.

Café Montana 1534 Montana Ave, Santa Monica ☎310/829-3990. Eclectic menu is highlighted by solid breakfasts, excellent salads, and hearty grilled fish, in an upmarket section of Santa Monica.

Crocodile Café 101 Santa Monica Blvd, Santa Monica ☎310/394-4783. Pizzas, sandwiches and burgers are the dining allure at this inexpensive nouveau fast-food spot, part of a local chain.

Norm's 1601 Lincoln Blvd, Santa Monica ☎310/450-0074. One of the last remaining classic diners, this local chain has nine other LA branches and serves $3 breakfasts and similarly cheap lunches. Great googie architecture, too.

Rae's Diner 2901 Pico Blvd, Santa Monica ☎310/828-7937. Classic 1950s diner with heavy comfort food. Its turquoise-blue facade and interior has been seen in many films, notably Quentin Tarantino's *True Romance*.

Reel Inn 18661 PCH, Malibu ☎310/456-8221. Seafood diner by the beach, with appealing prices and a good atmosphere. Also at 1220 W 3rd St, Santa Monica (☎310/395-5538).

The Sidewalk Café 1401 Ocean Front Walk, Venice ☎310/399-5547. Somewhat grim interior and only adequate food, but a prime spot for watching the daily parade of beach people, especially during the morning hours. Open until midnight on weekends.

The South Bay and Harbor Area

East Coast Bagels 5753 E PCH, Long Beach ☎562/985-0933. Located in a dreary mini-mall, but with an excellent wide selection of bagels, ranging from New York staples to California hybrids like the jalapeno-cheddar bagel stuffed with cream cheese.

Hof's Hut 4823 E 2nd St, Long Beach ☎562/439-4775. One bite of the *Hut*'s juicy Hofburger and you know you've found the real deal. Four other Long Beach locations, and five in Orange County.

Johnny Reb's 4663 N Long Beach Blvd, Long Beach ☎562/423-7327. The waft of BBQ ribs, catfish, and hushpuppies alone may draw you to this prime Southern spot, where the portions are hefty and the price is cheap.

The Local Yolk 3414 Highland Ave, Manhattan Beach ☎310/546-4407. As the name suggests, everything done with eggs, plus muffins and pancakes. Breakfast and lunch only.

Pier Bakery 100 Fisherman's Wharf #M, Redondo Beach ☎310/376-9582. A small but satisfying menu with jalapeno cheese bread and cinnamon rolls. Probably the best food in this touristy area.

Tony's Famous French Dips 701 Long Beach Blvd, Long Beach ☎562/435-6238. The name says it all, but alongside the dips is a beckoning array of soups and salads.

Disneyland and around

Angelo's 511 S State College Blvd, Anaheim

☎714/533-1401. Straight out of *Happy Days*, a drive-in complete with roller-skating car-hops, neon signs, vintage cars, and, incidentally, good burgers.

Heroes 305 N Harbor Blvd, Fullerton ☎714/738-4356. The place to come if you're starving after hitting the theme parks, a spot to knock back one of the countless beers available or chow down on items like hamburgers, beef stroganoff, or meatloaf.

Knott's Chicken Dinner Restaurant located just outside Knott's Berry Farm at 8039 Beach Blvd, Buena Park ☎714/220-5080. Serving cheap and tasty meals for over 65 years. People flocked here for delicious fried chicken dinners long before Disneyland was around, and they still do, along with a mean boysenberry pie.

Mimi's Café 18342 Imperial Hwy, Yorba Linda ☎714/996-3650. Huge servings, low prices, and a relaxing atmosphere down the street from the Nixon Library. Part of a sizeable Los Angeles and Orange County chain.

Orange County Coast

Café Zinc 350 Ocean Ave, Laguna Beach ☎949/494-2791. A popular breakfast counter offering simple soup-and-salad meals and other light fare. Good for a day on the sands.

The Cottage 308 N Coast Hwy, Laguna Beach ☎949/494-3023. Solid breakfasts, but even better lunches of seafood, chicken, and pasta make this a favorite for hungry beachgoers.

Duke's 317 PCH, Huntington Beach ☎714/374-6446. Best to stick to staples like steak and salad at this frenetic beachside favorite, which is best for its prime location near the pier.

Harbor House Café 34157 PCH, Dana Point ☎949/496-9270. Worth seeking out for its prime breakfasts, particularly the over-stuffed, gut-busting omelets – a huge slew of them, with a veritable laundry list of options.

Ruby's 1 Balboa Pier, Newport Beach ☎949/675-RUBY. The first and finest of the retro-streamline 1940s diners that have popped up all over LA – in a great location at the end of Newport's popular pier. Mostly offers the standard burgers, fries, and soda fare.

The San Gabriel and San Fernando valleys

Art's Deli 12224 Ventura Blvd, Studio City ☎818/762-1221. Long-time film-industry favorite (mainly for old-timers, not for the nubile), with a good range of hefty, scrumptious sandwiches and soups.

Benita's Frites 1000 Universal Center Drive, Universal City ☎818/505-8834. Delicious french fries served in a paper cone, and ready for your choice of multiple toppings, including mayonnaise.

Bob's Big Boy 4211 W Riverside Drive, Burbank ☎818/843-9334. The classic chain diner, fronted by the plump burger lad, and a veritable pop-architecture classic, saved from demolition through the efforts of "Googie" preservationists. 24hr.

Dr Hogly-Wogly's Tyler Texas Bar-B-Q 8136 Sepulveda Blvd, Van Nuys ☎818/780-6701. Long lines for some of the best chicken, sausages, ribs, and beans in LA, despite the depressing surroundings in the middle of nowhere.

Fair Oaks Pharmacy and Soda Fountain 1526 Mission St, South Pasadena ☎626/799-1414. A fabulously restored old-fashioned soda fountain with many old-time drinks like lime rickeys and egg creams.

Goldstein's Bagel Bakery 86 W Colorado Blvd, Pasadena ☎626/792-2435. If money's tight, feast on day-old 15¢ bagels; otherwise enjoy what some call LA's best bagels, made in a New York style. In the Old Pasadena shopping district.

Pie & Burger 913 E California Blvd, Pasadena ☎626/795-1123. Classic coffee shop, with good burgers and excellent fresh pies.

Porto's Bakery 315 N Brand Blvd, Glendale ☎818/956-5996. Popular and cheap café serving Cuban flaky pastries and sandwiches, rum-soaked cheesecakes, and muffins, danishes, croissants, torts and tarts, and cappuccino.

Rose Tree Cottage 395 E California Blvd, Pasadena ☎626/793-3337. Scones, shortbread and high tea in a country-home setting so thoroughly English that it's the West Coast HQ of the British Tourist Board.

Wolfe Burgers 46 N Lake Ave, Pasadena ☎626/792-7292. Knockout gyros, chili, tamales, and burgers.

Mexican and Latin American

LA's **Mexican** restaurants offer the city's best – and most plentiful – foodstuffs, serving tasty, healthy, and filling meals for as little as $5. Those in East LA are some of the finest, though you can find a good selection of both authentic and Americanized fare all over the city. **Caribbean** food is less visible but, when sought out, can be quite rewarding. The cuisine of the rest of **Latin America** is also increasingly popular, whether it be a mix of flavors and spices from Central American countries like Honduras and Nicaragua, a tasty blend of local seafood and native Peruvian cuisine (aka "Peruvian seafood"), or the hot, garlicky platters of Argentine beef that have found aficionados throughout the Westside.

Downtown and around

Burrito King 2109 W Sunset Blvd, Echo Park ☎213/484-9859. Excellent burritos and tasty tostadas from this small stand; open until 2am. Also nearby at 2827 Hyperion Ave, Silver Lake (☎323/663-9378).

Ciro's 705 N Evergreen Ave, East LA ☎323/267-8637. A split-level cave of a dining room, serving enormous platters of shrimp and mole specials. The flautas are the main draw, and they also offer takeout.

El Cholo 1121 S Western Ave ☎323/734-2773. One of LA's first big Mexican restaurants and still one of the best – offering a solid array of staples like enchiladas and tamales – despite the frequent presence of drunken frat-rats from nearby USC.

King Taco 942 N Broadway ☎323/266-3585. One in a chain of many such restaurants around Downtown, with many varieties of tacos – most of them quite savory.

Luminarias 3500 W Ramona Blvd, Monterey Park ☎323/268-4177. Dance to salsa and merengue between bites of seafood-heavy Mexican food. The Spanish name refers to honorary candles in brown paper bags. See "Live music," p.187.

Hollywood

Casa Carnitas 4067 Beverly Ave, south of Hollywood ☎323/667-9953. Tasty Mexican food from the Yucatán: the dishes are inspired by Cuban and Caribbean cooking – lots of fine seafood, too.

Havana on Sunset 5825 Sunset Blvd ☎323/464-1800. Like the name says, everything is Cuban at this festive eatery, from the lively music to the rich, authentic meals of soups, seafood, and garlic-heavy entrees.

Mario's Peruvian Seafood Restaurant 5786 Melrose Ave ☎323/466-4181. Delicious and authentic Peruvian fare: supremely tender squid, rich and flavorful mussels, with a hint of soy sauce in some dishes.

Mexico City 2121 N Hillhurst Ave ☎ 323/661-7227. Spinach enchiladas and other Californian versions of Mexican standards served in a decent corner of East Hollywood.

Yuca's Hut 2056 N Hillhurst Ave ☎ 323/662-1214. A small hidden jewel with good al fresco burritos.

West LA

Baja Fresh 475 N Beverly Drive ☎ 310/858-6690. Cheap, but enjoyable, Mexican food served for a hungry crowd of window shoppers and movie-industry wannabes – thus the emphasis on "healthy" eating.

Carlitos Gardel 7963 Melrose Ave ☎ 323/655-0891. Seriously rich and tasty Argentine cuisine – ie, heavy on the beef and spices, with sausages and garlic adding to the potent kick.

El Coyote 7312 Beverly Blvd ☎ 323/939-2255. An eatery known to practically every Westsider, for better or worse. Labyrinthine restaurant serving heavy Mexican food, more than you can stand. But cheap and lethal margaritas are the primary draw to the gloomy setting.

El Mexicano 1601 Sawtelle Blvd ☎ 310/473-8056. Cozy deli and adequate restaurant; the deli is like an old-fashioned general store, selling fruit, vegetables, and canned products from south of the border.

La Salsa 1154 Westwood Blvd ☎ 310/208-7083. The place to come for fresh, delicious soft tacos and burritos.

Versailles 10319 Venice Blvd ☎ 310/558-3168. Busy and noisy authentic Cuban restaurant with excellent fried plantains, paella, and black beans and rice. Also nearby at 1415 S La Cienega Blvd (☎ 310/289-0392).

Santa Monica, Venice, and Malibu

Gaucho Grill 1251 Third Street Promenade, Santa Monica ☎ 310/394-4966. One in a fine local chain of Argentine beef-houses, where the steaks come rich and garlicky, and the spices can bowl you over.

Mariasol 401 Santa Monica Pier, Santa Monica ☎ 310/917-5050. Cervezas with a view, hidden away at the end of the pier. The small rooftop deck

affords a sweeping panorama from Malibu to Venice.

Marix Tex-Mex Playa 118 Entrada Drive, Pacific Palisades ☎ 310/459-8596. Flavorful fajitas and big margaritas in this rowdy beachfront cantina. Also at 1108 N Flores St, Hollywood ☎ 323/656-8800.

The South Bay and Harbor Area

El Pollo Inka 1100 PCH, Hermosa Beach ☎ 310/372-1433. Good Peruvian-style chicken to make your mouth water. For a closer visit, try the one at 11701 Wilshire Blvd, Westwood (☎ 310/571-3334).

Pancho's 3615 Highland Ave, Manhattan Beach ☎ 310/545-6670. Big portions of old favorites like tacos and burritos, and fairly cheap for the area.

Taco Surf 211 Pine Ave, Long Beach ☎ 562-983-1337. As you might guess, fish tacos are the main draw here, though the rest of the eatery's south-of-the-border fare is also quite palatable. Also at 5316 1/2 E 2nd St in Long Beach (☎ 562/434-8646).

The San Gabriel and San Fernando valleys

Don Cuco's 3911 W Riverside Drive, Burbank ☎ 818/842-1123. Good food, mainly familiar Mexican staples, with a great Sunday brunch. One of several in a Valley chain.

El Tepayac 800 S Palm Ave, Alhambra ☎ 626/281-3366. Huge, luscious burritos and hot salsa. Also in Mid-Wilshire at 3400 W 3rd St (☎ 213/739-2239).

Izalco 10729 Burbank Blvd, North Hollywood ☎ 818/760-0396. Salvadoran cuisine presented with grace and style, from plantains and pork ribs to corn cakes and pupusas – a bit of a pleasant surprise for the area.

Merida 20 E Colorado Blvd, Pasadena ☎ 626/792-7371. Unusual Mexican restaurant in the Old Pasadena shopping strip, featuring dishes from the Yucatán; try the spicy pork, wrapped and steamed in banana leaves.

Señor Fish 618 Mission St, South Pasadena ☎ 626/403-0145. Somewhat drab-looking joint with great fish tacos and charbroiled halibut for under $10. Also at 424 E 1st St, Downtown (☎ 213/625-0566).

American, California cuisine, and Cajun

American cuisine – with its steaks, ribs, baked potatoes, and salads – has a low profile in faddish LA, although it's available almost everywhere and usually won't cost more than $10 for a comparative blow-out. More prominent –

and more expensive, at upwards of $20 – is **California cuisine**, based on local ingredients (though originating in San Francisco), more likely grilled than fried, and stylishly presented with a nod to nouvelle French cuisine. Another rage is spicy, fish-based **Cajun cooking**, still available in its authentic form and often inexpensive.

Downtown and around

Café Pinot 700 W 5th St ☎213/239-6500. Located next to the LA Public Library, this elegant restaurant offers a touch of French cooking for its nouvelle California cuisine – one of the best known in LA for that style.

Checkers Restaurant 535 S Grand Ave in the *Wyndham Checkers Hotel* ☎ 213/891-0519. One of the most elegant Downtown restaurants, serving top-rated California cuisine. If you're lucky, you can escape with a bill under $100 for two.

Engine Co. No. 28 644 S Figueroa St ☎213/624-6996. All-American grilled steaks and seafood, served in a renovated 1912 fire station. Great French fries and an excellent wine list round out this classic local eatery.

Pacific Dining Car 1310 W 6th St ☎213/483-6000. Would-be English supper club where the Downtown elite used to cut secret deals, located inside an old railroad carriage. Open 24hr for (very expensive) steaks. Breakfast is the best value.

Water Grill 544 S Grand Ave ☎213/891-0900. One of the top-notch spots for munching on California cuisine in LA, or anywhere, with the focus on seafood, prepared in all manner of colorful and ever-changing ways. Extremely pricey, though.

Hollywood

Cha Cha Cha 656 N Virgil Ave ☎323/664-7723. Offering paella, black-pepper shrimp, jerk chicken, and other Caribbean treats. Also at 762 Pacific Ave, Long Beach ☎562/436-3900.

Hollywood Canteen 1006 N Seward St ☎323/465-0961. A dark club scene with fish, steak, and clam chowder – just the right ambience to make you feel like a Tinseltown big shot. Not as pricey as similar joints in the area.

Musso & Frank Grill 6667 Hollywood Blvd ☎323/467-7788. A 1919 classic, loaded with authentic Hollywood atmosphere and history in a dark-paneled dining room. The drinks (see p.178) are better than the pricey, mostly upscale diner, food.

Off Vine 6263 Leland Way ☎323/962-1900. Dine on eclectic Cal cuisine – pecan chicken, duck sausage, and Grand Marnier soufflé – in a renovat-

ed but still funky Craftsman bungalow. Increasingly popular among the snoots.

Patina 5955 Melrose Ave ☎323/467-1108. The height of the culinary elite, this ultra-chic place delivers exquisite California cuisine, satisfying the palate while depriving the wallet. Recently underwent a massive renovation, making the entire place darker and clubbier.

Pig 'n Whistle 6714 Hollywood Blvd ☎323/463-0000. Historic 1927 eatery refurbished as a swank Cal-cuisine restaurant, with the emphasis on all things porcine, from ribs to pork roast to bacon. Although much of the old spirit and decor are the same, the prices are not: no diner has food this pricey.

Pinot Hollywood 1448 Gower St ☎323/461-8800. Upmarket American food crossed with nouvelle French, in a spacious environment with 24 types of martinis and Polish potato vodka. You may even spot a celebrity or two, lurking in the shadows.

West LA

Barefoot 8722 W 3rd St ☎310/276-6223. Good pastas, pizzas, and seafood between Beverly Hills and the Beverly Center. Considering the prime location, very affordable.

Café La Boheme 8400 Santa Monica Blvd, West Hollywood ☎323/848-2360. The dark, somewhat spooky decor is matched by the indulgent melange of Cal-cuisine flavors mixed with pan-Asian cooking, for a truly memorable experience.

Cajun Bistro 8301 Sunset Blvd, West Hollywood ☎323/656-6388. Funky, unpretentious Cajun joint on a central part of the strip that offers tasty Louisiana cooking – especially the jambalaya – without busting your wallet.

Flora Kitchen 460 S La Brea Ave ☎323/931-9900. Perhaps the city's best restaurant connected to a flower shop – in this case, the nearby Rita Flora. Apart from flowers, the key attractions here are the California cuisine-style sandwiches, made with a host of tasty, fresh ingredients.

The Gumbo Pot 6333 W 3rd St in the Farmers Market ☎323/933-0358. Delicious, dirt-cheap Cajun food in a busy setting; try the gumbo yaya (chicken, shrimp, and sausage) or the fruit-and-potato salad.

L'Orangerie 903 N La Cienega Blvd, West

Hollywood ☎310/652-9770. Nouvelle California-style French cuisine; if you haven't got the $150 it takes to sit down, enjoy the view from the bar.
McCormick and Schmick's 206 N Rodeo Drive, Beverly Hills ☎310/859-0434. Swank seafood joint for business types known for a great week-end dinner special.
Spago 176 N Cañon Drive ☎310/385-0880. Now that the original Sunset Strip branch of LA's most famous restaurant has closed, you'll have to go to this stuffier Beverly Hills location to get a taste of über-chef Wolfgang Puck's latest Cal-cuisine concoctions, among them his famous designer pizzas.

Santa Monica, Venice, and Malibu

17th Street Café 1610 Montana Ave, Santa Monica ☎310/453-2771. Seafood, pasta, and burgers at moderate prices in a chic part of town. Nicely casual, unpretentious atmosphere.
Gladstone's 4 Fish 17300 PCH ☎310/573-0212.

An inevitable tourist stop at the junction of Sunset Boulevard, known best for its prime beachfront location – not for its heavily fried and breaded seafood.
Granita 23725 W Malibu Rd ☎310/456-0488. If you can't get enough of Wolfgang Puck (see *Spago*, above), check out his Malibu entry – a heady mix of Cal-cuisine and Italian flavors. Delicious and pricey, and good for spotting a few names here and there.
Killer Shrimp 523 Washington Blvd, Marina del Rey ☎310/578-2293. When all you want is shrimp, and lots of it, this popular, somewhat drea-ry-looking spot is the place to come. For a pretty cheap price, you can happily stuff your maw with crustaceans.
Michael's 1147 3rd St, Santa Monica ☎310/451-0843. Longstanding favorite for California cuisine, served here amid modern art. This venerable establishment always attracts the crowds for its rich, tasty lobster, salmon, and veal.

Italian, Spanish, and Greek

After years of having nothing more exotic than the takeout pizza chains, LA has woken up to the delights of regional **Italian** cooking, and there is a growing number of specialist restaurants, especially around the Westside, serving excellent Italian food. Another recent phenomenon is **designer pizza**, invented at the restaurant *Spago* (see above) and topped with duck, shiitake mushrooms, and other exotic ingredients. The problem with all this? It doesn't come cheap. A pasta dish in the average Italian restaurant can cost upwards of $12, and the least elaborate designer pizza will set you back $15. **Spanish** food and tapas bars have also become popular, and pricey. In contrast, if you want **Greek** food, you'll have to look hard – restaurants are good but uncommon.

Downtown and around

California Pizza Kitchen 330 S Hope St ☎213/626-2616. Mid-priced designer pizza at this national chain. Nothing too adventurous, but centrally located on Bunker Hill.
Ciao Trattoria 815 W 7th St ☎213/624-2244. Housed in a striking Romanesque building, full of lovely historic-revival decor, a solid choice for upscale, Northern Italian dining. Somewhat pricey, but not as bad as you might think.
Cicada 617 S Olive St ☎213/488-9488. Housed in the stunning Art Deco Oviatt Building (see p.99), this Northern Italian restaurant offers fine pasta for half the price of its fish and steak entrees.

Hollywood

Chianti Cucina 7383 Melrose Ave ☎ 323/653-

8333. Old-fashioned 1930s restaurant amid Melrose chaos south of Hollywood. Try the deli-cious raviolis or go with the well-crafted chicken and lamb dishes.
Louise's Trattoria 4500 Los Feliz Blvd ☎323/667-0777. Everybody in LA knows this chain: some love it for its good mid-priced pizzas, some hate it for its overcooked, uninspired pasta. You decide.
Miceli's 1646 N Las Palmas Ave ☎323/466-3438. Hefty, old-style pizzas that come laden with gooey cheese and plenty of tomato sauce. It's hardly nouvelle cuisine, but you'll be too busy scarfing it down to notice.
Palermo 1858 N Vermont Ave ☎323/663-1178. As old as Hollywood, and with as many devoted fans, who flock here for the rich Southern Italian

pizzas, cheesy decor, and gallons of cheapish red wine. If you like huge platefuls of spaghetti in chunky red sauce, this is the place.

West LA

Ca'Brea 346 S La Brea Ave ☎323/938-2863. One of LA's best-known, and best, choices for Italian cuisine, and especially good for osso buco and risotto. Getting in is difficult, so reserve ahead and expect to pay a bundle.

Campanile 624 S La Brea Ave ☎323/938-1447. Incredible but very expensive Northern Italian food; if you can't afford a dinner, try the dessert or the best bread in Los Angeles at the adjacent *La Brea Bakery*.

Cava 8384 W 3rd St ☎323/658-8898. The Latin and Iberian dishes are quite good, but the real attraction is tasty tapas accompanied by shots of prime sherry – and, of course, the salsa music. Always a fun spot to dine.

Locanda Veneta 8638 W 3rd St ☎310/274-1893. Scrumptious ravioli, risotto, veal, and carpaccio – you can't go wrong at one of LA's pre-viously quiet culinary joys. But be prepared to wait: the word is out, and all the foodies have arrived.

Santa Monica, Venice, and Malibu

Abbot's Pizza Company 1407 Abbot Kinney Blvd, Venice ☎310/396-7334. Named after the old-time founder of the district, this home of the bagel-crust pizza allows your choice of seeds, tangy cit-rus sauce, or shiitake and wild mushroom sauce. Also at 1811 Pico Blvd, Santa Monica (☎310/314-2777).

Valentino 3115 Pico Blvd, Santa Monica ☎310/829-4313. Some call this the best Italian cuisine in the US, served up in classy surroundings with great flair. For a hefty sum, you can be the judge.

Wildflour Pizza 2807 Main St, Santa Monica ☎310/392-3300. Serving up a great thin-crust pizza, this cozy little spot often draws the crowds.

Wolfgang Puck Express 1315 3rd St, Santa Monica ☎310/576-4770. On the second floor of a food mall, watch Promenade tourists below while

munching on great pizzas and salads. One of a national chain.

The South Bay and Harbor Area

Alegria Cocina Latina 115 Pine Ave, Long Beach ☎562/436-3388. Quality tapas and gazpacho served with plenty of sangria on the patio, and to the beat of live flamenco every night, in a prime location in Downtown Long Beach.

Giovanni's Salerno Beach 195 Culver Blvd, Playa Del Rey ☎310/821-0018. Ungodly kitsch decor – Christmas lights throughout the year are a common sight – and cheap Southern Italian food, but you can walk off the heavy meal at nearby Dockweiler Beach.

L'Opera 101 Pine Ave ☎562/491-0066. Very swank Italian dining – mixed with a fair bit of California-cuisine style – in a historic old building near the center of Long Beach's Downtown activity.

Mangiamo 128 Manhattan Beach Blvd, Manhattan Beach ☎310/318-3434. Like the name says, "Let's eat!" Fairly pricey but worth it for the specialist Northern Italian seafood – and right off the beach, too.

The San Gabriel and San Fernando valleys

Café Santorini 64–70 W Union St, Pasadena ☎626/564-4200. A fine mix of Greek and Italian food – capellini, souvlaki, and risotto – with a little Armenian sausage thrown in as well. Located in a relaxed plaza and offering some patio dining.

Greek Bistro 17337 Ventura Blvd, Encino ☎818/789-2888. High-spirited spot with sizeable portions of native cooking – dolmas, kebabs, sou-vlaki, and the like – mixed with colorful, energetic dancing.

La Scala Presto 3821 W Riverside Drive, Burbank ☎818/846-6800. Fine antipasti, pizza, and pasta at this solid Italian eatery, one of several in a local chain.

Market City Caffè 33 S Fair Oaks Ave, Pasadena ☎626/568-2303. Southern Italian cuisine featur-ing a range of Mediterranean delights, along with a supreme antipasto bar.

Japanese, Chinese, Thai, and Korean

LA's most fashionable districts offer great **sushi** bars and **dim sum** restaurants, favored by foreign visitors and fast-lane yuppies alike, where you can easily eat your way through more than $30. Lower priced and less pretentious outlets tend to be Downtown, where you can get a fair-sized meal for around $12. **Thai** and **Korean** food – for which you can expect to pay around $15 per meal – are increasingly popular as well.

Downtown and around

Buffet Palace 3014 Olympic Blvd ☎213/480-8949. Korean spot with good, spicy barbecued beef.

Dong Il Jang 3455 W 8th St (☎213/383-5757). Cozy Korean restaurant where the meat is grilled at your table, with the added draw of tempura dishes and a sushi bar. Located in the middle of bustling Koreatown.

Grand Star Restaurant 934 Sun Mun Way, Chinatown ☎213/626-2285. Go late as there's video karaoke from 8pm–1am at this traditional Chinese place on Sun, Tues, and Wed. Also offers takeout.

Mandarin Deli 727 N Broadway #109 ☎213/623-6054. Very delectable and cheap noodles, pork and fish dumplings, and other hearty staples in the middle of Broadway's riot of activity. Also at 356 E2nd St (☎213/617-0231).

Mitsuru Café 117 Japanese Village Plaza, Little Tokyo ☎213/613-1028. Exotic snow cones made with *kintoki* (bean paste) or milk *kintoki* (sweet custard). Try the *imagawayaki* – adzuki beans baked in a bun. Located in a popular mall.

Mon Kee's 679 N Spring St, Chinatown ☎213/628-6717. Long-standing favorite for fresh fish and rich, hearty seafood soups.

Ocean Seafood 750 N Hill St ☎213/687-3088. Cavernous but often busy Cantonese restaurant serving inexpensive and excellent food – abalone, crab, shrimp, and duck are among many standout choices.

Pho 79 727 N Broadway #120 ☎213/625-7026. Great spot for noodles, a Vietnamese chain without too many frills, but with excellent flavors.

Hollywood

Chan Dara 1511 N Cahuenga Blvd ☎323/464-8585. Terrific Thai food, and the locals know it. Also at other LA locations: 310 N Larchmont Blvd (☎323/467-1052) and 11940 W Pico Blvd (☎310/479-4461).

Shibucho 3114 Beverly Blvd ☎213/387-8498. Seriously tasty, locally popular sushi bar just south of Silver Lake; go with someone who knows what to order, as the sole waitress doesn't speak English. Otherwise, the squid and eel are quite fine, along with the famed *toro*, an expensive but delicious tuna delicacy.

Tommy Tang's 7313 Melrose Ave ☎323/937-5733. Terrific, very chic Thai restaurant in a hot shopping zone, and the incongruous setting for Tuesday drag nights, when the male waiters can be seen "en femme."

Vim 831 S Vermont Ave ☎213/386-2338. Authentic Thai and Chinese food at low prices.

Especially good are the seafood soup and the old favorite pad thai.

West LA

Chin Chin 8618 Sunset Blvd ☎310/652-1818. Flashy but good dim sum café, a longstanding favorite and one of several around town. Open till midnight.

Chung King 11538 W Pico Blvd ☎310/477-4917. The best neighborhood Chinese restaurant in LA, serving spicy Szechuan food: don't miss out on the *bum-bum* chicken and other house specialties.

Matsuhisa 129 N La Cienega Blvd ☎310/659-9639. The biggest name in town for sushi, charging the highest prices. Essential if you're a raw-fish aficionado with a wad of cash; otherwise, you can dine two or three times at other fine, and much cheaper, Japanese restaurants.

Mishima 8474 W 3rd St ☎323/782-0181. Great miso soup and *udon* and soba noodles, at very affordable prices at this chic, popular Westside eatery.

Mori Sushi 11500 W Pico Blvd ☎323/479-3939. A quietly stylish spot that resists trendiness, but still offers up some of the city's finest sushi, often presented in spare and elegant arrangements and almost always delicious.

The Sushi House 12013 W Pico Blvd ☎310/479-1507. Reggae and sushi coalesce in a small bar with limited seating. Try the "Superman," a rainbow-colored roll of salmon, yellowtail, whitefish, and avocado.

Santa Monica, Venice, and Malibu

Chaya Venice 110 Navy St, Venice ☎310/396-1179. Elegant mix of Japanese and Mediterranean foods in an arty sushi bar, with a suitably snazzy clientele.

Chinois on Main 2709 Main St, Santa Monica ☎310/392-9025. Expensive Wolfgang Puck restaurant, mixing nouvelle French and Chinese cuisine for a ravenous crowd of yuppie diners and self-appointed food critics.

Flower of Siam 2553 Lincoln Blvd, Venice ☎310/827-0050. Some swear by this spicy but succulent, authentic Thai food, guaranteed to set your tastebuds on fire and your eyes watering.

Lighthouse Buffet 201 Arizona Ave, Santa Monica ☎310/451-2076. All-you-can-eat sushi; indulge to your heart's content for under $10 at lunchtime or $20 in the evening.

The San Gabriel and San Fernando valleys

Genmai-Sushi 4454 Van Nuys Blvd, Sherman

Oaks ☎818/986-7060. "Genmai" is Japanese for brown rice, but you can get soft-shell crabs in *ponzu* sauce, along with sushi and macrobiotic dishes.

Saladang 363 S Fair Oaks Ave, Pasadena ☎626/793-8123. Don't miss out on the pad thai, curry, and salmon at this chic spot, or the spicy noodles that would pass muster anywhere. The restaurant's new annex offers even spicier, more exotic Thai concoctions.

Sushi Nozawa 11288 Ventura Blvd, Studio City ☎818/508-7017. Traditional sushi dishes served to trendy, and somewhat masochistic, regulars, who don't mind being berated by the famously imperious chef: if you sit at the bar, he will decide what you'll eat. Period.

Indian, Sri Lankan, and Middle Eastern

Indian and **Sri Lankan** food is surging in popularity in LA – with menus embracing uniquely Californian dishes. **Middle Eastern** places in LA are few, and tend to be fairly basic. Most of the Indian and Middle Eastern restaurants in Hollywood or West LA fall into a fairly mid-range price bracket – around $10 for a full meal, less for a vegetarian Indian dish.

Hollywood

Chamika Catering 1717 N Wilcox Ave ☎323/466-8960. Inexpensive papadums, rotis (garlic and coconut stuffed pancakes) and chicken, beef, or lamb curries, marinated in special Sri Lankan sauces.

Electric Lotus 4656 Franklin Ave ☎323/953-0040. While somewhat cramped and located in a mini-mall, a fine choice for traditional staples – pakoras, vindaloo, curries, etc – at affordable prices.

India's Oven 6357 Wilshire Blvd ☎323/655-4596. Bring your own bottle to this friendly Indian restaurant, where you'll get large, delicious portions of old favorites like stuffed naans, vindaloos, and curries. Also at 11645 Wilshire Blvd (☎310/307-5522).

West LA

Clay Pit 145 S Barrington Ave ☎310/476-4700. Some of LA's best Indian food, featuring delights like lamb-stuffed keema naan and a fine tandoori chicken – all for around $15, though prices have gone up since the restaurant moved from the Wilshire area further east.

East India Grill 345 N La Brea Ave ☎323/936-8844. Southern Indian cuisine given the California treatment: impressive specialties include spinach curry, ginger chicken, curried pasta, and "parmesan naan."

Eat A Pita 465 N Fairfax Ave ☎323/651-0188. Open-air stand serving cheap, cheerful, and sizeable falafel and hummus plates, as well as tasty vegetable-juice drinks.

Koutoubia 2116 Westwood Blvd ☎310/475-0729. Good authentic Moroccan lamb, couscous, and seafood.

Moun of Tunis 7445 Sunset Blvd ☎323/874-3333. Mouthwatering Tunisian fare presented in huge, multi-course meals, heavy on the spices and rich on the exotic flavors.

Noura Cafe 8479 Melrose Ave ☎323/651-4581. Moderately priced Middle Eastern specialties. For beginners, the "taster's delight" plate – hummus, baba ganoush, tabouli, falafel, fried eggplant, zucchini, and stuffed grape leaves – is a good, filling bet.

Shamshiry 1916 Westwood Blvd ☎310/474-1410. Top Iranian restaurant in the area, offering scrumptious kebabs, pilafs, and exotic sauces.

Vegetarian and wholefood

As you might expect, LA has a great many **wholefood** and **vegetarian** restaurants, most of them on the consciousness-raised Westside. Some veggie places can be a good value ($5 or so), but watch out for the ones that flaunt themselves as a New Age experience and include music – these can be three times as much. Otherwise, for a picnic try the local *Trader Joe's* chain – which supplies imported cheeses, breads, and canned foods – or the area's **farmers markets**, loaded with organic produce and advertised in the press. (For health-food stores, see "Shopping," p.192.)

West LA

A Votre Santé 242 S Beverly Drive, Beverly Hills ☎310/860-9441. Scrambled tofu and fried vegetables are on the agenda – along with veggie and turkey burgers – at this Westside mini-chain. Open for breakfast and lunch.

Erewhon 7660 Beverly Blvd ☎323/937-0777. A good old-fashioned juice bar and deli, where you can gulp down as many wheatgrass concoctions and bee-pollen smoothies as you can stand.

Inaka Natural Foods 131 S La Brea Ave ☎323/936-9353. Located in the trendy La Brea district and featuring vegetarian and macrobiotic food with a strong Japanese theme. Live music on weekends.

Newsroom Café 120 N Robertson Blvd ☎310/652-4444. A prime spot to see B-list celebrities with A-list attitudes eating veggie burgers and drinking wheatgrass "shooters." Especially popular for lunching; also offers magazine racks (thus the name) and Internet terminals.

Real Food Daily 414 N La Cienega Blvd ☎310/289-9910. Avocado rolls, beet bisque, and salads draw a good crowd at this vegan restaurant, which also operates a branch at 514 Santa Monica Blvd, in Santa Monica (☎310/451-7544).

Santa Monica, Venice, and Malibu

Figtree's Café 429 Ocean Front Walk, Venice ☎310/392-4937. Tasty veggie food and grilled fresh fish on a sunny patio just off the Boardwalk. Health-conscious yuppies come in droves for breakfast.

Inn of the Seventh Ray 128 Old Topanga Rd, Topanga Canyon ☎310/455-1311. The ultimate New Age restaurant in a supremely New Age area, serving vegetarian and other wholefood meals in a relatively secluded environment.

Mäni's Bakery 2507 Main St, Santa Monica ☎310/396-7700. An array of veggie treats – from sugarless brownies to meatless sandwiches – may draw you to this coffeehouse and bakery for breakfast or lunch. Look hard enough and you might see a weight-obsessed celebrity darting in.

Shambala Café 607 Colorado Ave, Santa Monica ☎310/395-2160. Apart from organic chicken, the menu is meat-free, with shrimp, pasta, tofu, eggplant, and some very interesting seaweed dishes.

The South Bay and Harbor Area

Good Stuff 1300 Highland Ave, Manhattan Beach ☎310/545-4775. Healthy eating, vegetarian or otherwise, is the focus at this popular spot, with a range of filling sandwiches and fruit plates.

Papa Jon's 5006 E 2nd St, Long Beach ☎562/439-1059. Meatless Mexican entrees and garden burgers are the highlights of this quiet eatery, which also offers totally vegan meals as well as an on-site market.

The Spot 110 2nd St, Hermosa Beach ☎310/376-2355. A staggering array of veggie dishes, based on Mexican and other cuisines, and free of refined sugar or any animal products.

Drinking: bars and pubs

Social **drinking** in LA is far less popular than it is in San Francisco. Many bars are simply places to pose while waiting to meet friends, before heading off to pose again somewhere more exotic. However, it is possible to have a good time, provided you don't smoke, a practice now banned in most establishments under recent California law. You should be able to get a drink almost anywhere, and for serious, uninterrupted drinking there are bars and cocktail lounges on every other corner – just look for the neon signs.

As you'd expect, LA's bars reflect their locality: a clash of artists and financial whiz kids Downtown; serious hedonists and leather-clad rock fans in Hollywood; movie-star wannabes and self-styled producers in West LA; a batch of jukebox- and dartboard-furnished bars in Santa Monica (evidence of the British contingent in the area); and the less hip, more casual beachside bars of the South Bay. A few hard-bitten bars are open the legal maximum hours (from 6am until 2am daily), though the busiest hours are between 9pm and midnight. During **happy hour**, usually from 5–7pm, drinks are cheap and sometimes half-price, and there'll be a selection of snacks like taco dips, chips, buffalo wings, and sometimes more substantial appetizers.

Downtown and around

Akbar 4356 Sunset Blvd ☏ 323/665-6810. A curious blend of patrons – manual laborers and bohemians, gays and straights, old-timers and newbies – frequent this cozy, unpretentious watering hole.

Barragan's 1538 W Sunset Blvd ☏ 213/250-4256. Actually a Mexican restaurant with reasonably palatable food, but allegedly producing the most alcoholic margarita in LA.

Bona Vista at the *Westin Bonaventure*, 404 S Figueroa St ☏ 213/624-1000. Thirty-five floors up, this rotating cocktail lounge spins faster after a few expensive drinks, offering a fine view of the sunset.

Casey's Bar 613 S Grand Ave ☏ 213/629-2353. White floors, dark wood-paneled walls, and nightly piano music; something of a local institution.

HMS Bounty 3357 Wilshire Blvd ☏ 213/385-7275. Authentic, somewhat divey, experience. Advertising "Food and Grog," a grungy bar that's a hot spot for hipsters and grizzled old-timers – they come for the dark ambience, cheap drinks, and kitschy nautical motifs.

Redwood 316 W 2nd St ☏ 213/617-2867. Not overly flashy or eventful, but a solid Downtown choice for serious drinking, attracting a mix of office workers, newspaper hacks, and only a few outsiders.

Hollywood

Boardners 1652 N Cherokee Ave ☏ 323/462-9621. A likably unkempt neighborhood bar in the middle of Hollywood's prime tourist territory. Occasional guitar-poets provide the soundtrack.

Cat 'n' Fiddle Pub 6530 Sunset Blvd ☏ 323/468-3800. A boisterous but comfortable pub with darts, British food, and expensive English beers on tap, and live jazz on Saturdays. See also "Live music," p.186.

Deep 1707 N Vine St ☏ 323/462-1144. Prime guilty-pleasure drinking in the middle of tourist central, a watering hole/dance club with elevated floors for dirty go-go dancing and an assertively sleazy style – not true Hollywood raunch, just an incredible simulation.

The Dresden Room 1760 N Vermont Ave ☏ 323/665-4298. Wednesday night is open-mike, otherwise the husband-and-wife lounge act takes requests from the crowd of old-timers and goatee-wearing hipsters. Seen in the movie *Swingers*.

Formosa Café 7156 Santa Monica Blvd ☏ 323/850-9050. Started during Prohibition, a creaky old Hollywood institution alive with the ghosts of Bogie and Marilyn. Imbibe in the potent spirits, but stay away from the insipid food.

The Garage 4519 Santa Monica Blvd ☏ 323/662-6802. With a funky lounge and a pool room, this lively Silver Lake bar and club offers live music after 9pm – much of it punk rock and rockabilly, though with the occasional drag show thrown in for good measure.

Lava Lounge 1533 N La Brea Ave ☏ 323/876-6612. Wallow in the cheesy retro decor and slurp down a glowing cocktail to the sounds of pounding rockabilly and freewheeling surf music.

Martini Lounge 5657 Melrose Ave ☏ 323/467-4068. With two bars, pool room, and dancefloor, this is quite the bar experience, and always draws a good selection of rock performers to accompany your libations.

Musso and Frank Grill 6667 Hollywood Blvd ☏ 323/467-7788. If you haven't had a drink in this 1940s landmark bar (located in the center of the district), you haven't been to Hollywood. It also serves pricey food. See also "Eating," p.172.

Pinot Hollywood 1448 Gower St ☏ 323/461-8800. Nearly thirty types of martini and Polish potato vodka, served in airy surroundings with an upscale crowd. See "Eating," p.172.

The Powerhouse 1714 N Highland Ave ☏ 323/463-9438. Enjoyable, longstanding rockers' watering hole just off Hollywood Boulevard; few people get here much before midnight.

Tiki Ti 4427 W Sunset Blvd ☏ 323/669-9381. Tiny grass-skirted cocktail bar straight out of *Hawaii-Five-0*, packed with kitschy pseudo-Polynesian decor, on the edge of Hollywood. Powerful cocktails are around $7 a slug.

West LA

Barney's Beanery 8447 Santa Monica Blvd ☏ 310/654-2287. Well-worn poolroom/bar, stocking over 200 beers, with a solid, rock'n'roll-hedonist history. It also serves food, of sorts (see "Eating," p.168).

El Carmen 8138 W 3rd St ☏ 323/852-1552. Groovy faux dive-bar with a south-of-the-border theme, pushed to the extreme, with black-velvet pictures of Mexican wrestlers, steer horns, stuffed snakes, and much tongue-in-cheek grunge.

Molly Malone's Irish Pub 575 S Fairfax Ave ☏ 323/935-1577. Self-consciously authentic Irish bar, from the music to the shamrocks in the foaming Guinness.

Tom Bergin's 840 S Fairfax Ave ☏ 323/936-7151. Old-time drinking joint from 1936, a great place for Irish coffee (supposedly invented here), and less rough-and-ready than Molly Malone's down the road. You can spot the regulars from the pictures on the walls.

Santa Monica, Venice, and Malibu

14 Below 1348 14th St, Santa Monica ☏ 310/451-5040. At this casual bar, pool tables and a fireplace compete for your attention with rock, folk, and blues performers, who play nightly.

Oar House Saloon 2941 Main St, Santa Monica ☏ 310/396-6658. Bar on the edge of Venice, but still on the Main Street shopping strip, and popular with students who get suitably rowdy on weekend nights.

Tantra Bar 23 Windward Circle, Venice ☏ 310/452-2222. Inside the *St Mark's* club, a lively bar with dark and moody decor, salsa and jazz music, and central location not far from the boardwalk.

Ye Olde King's Head 116 Santa Monica Blvd, Santa Monica ☏ 310/451-1402. British-heavy joint with jukebox, dartboards, and signed photos of all your favorite rock dinosaurs; don't miss the steak-and-kidney pie or the fish'n'chips.

The San Gabriel and San Fernando valleys

Amazon 14649 Ventura Blvd, Sherman Oaks ☏ 818/986-7502. A wonderland of kitsch, where you can knock back potent tropical concoctions in a self-consciously fake Polynesian setting: waterfalls, ferns, and so on.

Blue Saloon 4657 Lankershim Blvd, North Hollywood ☏ 818/766-4644. A Valley bar enlivened by a wide range of live music, including rock, country, blues, and reggae. The fairly cheap drinks are also a draw.

The Colorado 2640 E Colorado Blvd ☏ 626/449-3485. A bright spot along a bleak Pasadena stretch. Salty bartenders, cheap drinks, and a couple of pool tables amid a decor based around hunting.

The John Bull Pub 958 S Fair Oaks Ave, Pasadena ☏ 626/441-4353. Although shepherd's pie and fish'n'chips are still served, along with warm English beers, this classic pub has recently had a swanky facelift – better for tourists than grizzled old-timers.

Coffeehouses

If you want something of the bar atmosphere without the alcohol, the city's many vibrant **coffeehouses** are good places to be seen, not least because they won't leave you too drunk to drive home – a crime that carries harsh penalties in California.

All-Star Theater Café 999 N Doheny Drive #604, West Hollywood ☏ 323/962-8898. Antiques store/café with a 1920s feel and overstuffed armchairs. Open 7pm–3am weekends.

Anastasia's Asylum 1028 Wilshire Blvd, Santa Monica ☏ 310/394-7113. Comfortable place with quirky décor and customers, and strong coffee and tea; also with nightly entertainment, of varying quality.

Bourgeois Pig 5931 Franklin Ave, Hollywood ☏ 323/962-6366. Hip environment and outrageously overpriced cappuccinos – you really pay for the atmosphere of mirrors, chandeliers, and loveseats.

Cobalt Café 22047 Sherman Way, Canoga Park ☏ 818/348-3789. Grungy but hip coffeehouse in the Valley, with coffee, food, and live music – along with poetry readings.

Coffee Table 2930 Rowena Ave, Los Feliz ☏ 323/644-8111. Casual, unpretentious space with affordable coffees and relaxed surroundings – a nice antidote to the *Bourgeois Pig*, further west.

Highland Grounds 742 N Highland Ave, Hollywood ☏ 323/466-1507. The posiest of LA's coffee bars, serving iced latte, pancakes, and even beer. At night it's a club, with poetry and up-and-coming bands, and even a bit of alcohol.

Hot Wired Café 11651 Riverside Drive, North Hollywood ☏ 818/753-9929. Ultra-caffeinated java in a Valley joint with a range of curious entertainment, from Monday night blues jams to comics and acoustic strummers several nights of the week.

Java Man 157 Pier Ave, Hermosa Beach ☏ 310/379-7209. Tables lit by halogen lamps, and a rotating display of work from local artists. Not far from the beach.

King's Road Espresso House 8361 Beverly Blvd, West Hollywood ☏ 323/655-9044. Sidewalk café in the center of a busy shopping strip. Popular with the hipster crowd as well as a few interloping tourists.

The Novel Café 212 Pier Ave, Santa Monica ☏ 310/396-8566. Used books and high-backed wooden chairs set the tone; good coffees, teas, and pastries, though with many self-consciously studious patrons.

Sacred Grounds 399 W 6th St, San Pedro ☏ 310/514-0800. Combination coffeehouse and club with a sizeable stage, offering open-mike night, music jams, and even some marginal comedy acts.

The World Café 2820 Main St, Santa Monica ☏ 310/392-1661. Surf the Net with other technophiles, or drag yourself away and drink in the dark café/bar. Crowded and touristy.

Nightlife: clubs and discos

Like most things in LA, **nightlife** is very style-conscious, and the city's clubs may be the wildest in the country. Ranging from posey hangouts to industrial noise cellars, even the more image-conscious joints are like singles bars, with plenty of dressing-up, sizing-up, and picking-up going on, and everybody claiming to be either a rock musician or in the movies. Nowadays, many of the more interesting and unusual clubs are transient, especially those catering to the house, ambient, and rave scene. As a result, the trendier side of the club scene is hard to pin down, and you should always check the *LA Weekly* before setting out.

Weekend nights are the busiest, but during the week things are often cheaper, though rarely any less enjoyable. Everywhere, between 11pm and midnight is the best time to turn up. Most of the cover charges range widely, depending on the night and the "club" being presented (often $5–20; call ahead). The minimum age is 21, and it's normal for ID to be checked, so bring your passport or other photo ID. You should obviously dress with some sensitivity to the club's style, but prohibitive dress codes are a rarity.

Most of the top clubs are either in Hollywood or along a ten-block stretch of West Hollywood. Beverly Hills is a lifeless yuppie desert, Downtown is home to a handful of itinerant clubs operating above and below board, and the San Fernando Valley's more rough-and-ready scene is usually confined to the weekends.

For gay and lesbian clubs and discos, see p.191.

Downtown and around

Atlas 3760 Wilshire Blvd ☎ 213/380-8400. Wednesday and weekend nights are the scene for uptempo house and hip-hop grooves, with a little reggae and R&B thrown into the mix. Stylish scene requires appropriate dress; the venue is in the classic Art Deco Wiltern complex.

The Echo 1822 Sunset Blvd ☎ 213/413-8200. Like the name says, an Echo Park scene with scrappy rap and dance DJs performing nightly, spinning a range of old- and new-school favorites.

LA Entertainment Center 333 S Boylston St, ☎ 213/989-7979. Salsa, rock, and dance on weekend nights. One of the few Downtown clubs that adds a bit of spark to a formerly dead nocturnal scene.

Mayan 1038 S Hill St ☎ 213/746-4674. Formerly a groovy pre-Columbian-styled movie palace, now hosting Latin rhythms and nonstop disco and house tunes on three dance floors. Fri and Sat only, no jeans or sneakers.

The Smell 247 S Main St ☎ 213/625-4325. Formerly the legendary *Al's Bar*, now a similar space with groovy art grunge, including strange designs, rock, and punk music, and a notoriously grim location.

Stock Exchange 618 S Spring St (☎ 213/489-3877). An attempt to broaden the Downtown club scene on a previously deserted stretch of road, spinning enough funk and disco tunes to make the yuppie crowd gyrate with abandon.

Hollywood

A.D. 836 N Highland Blvd ☎ 323/460-6668. Spooky neo-Gothic, generally bizarre club that plays host to a range of interesting club nights, most notably, the glam scene *Cherry* on Fridays.

Arena 6655 Santa Monica Blvd ☎ 323/462-0714. Work up a sweat to funk, hip-hop, and house sounds on a massive dancefloor inside a former ice factory. Gay-friendly scene, playing host to different, ever-changing club nights.

Bar Sinister 1652 N Cherokee ☎ 323/769-7070. A collection of sprightly dance beats most nights of the week, then memorably spooky Goth music and anemic-looking vampire types on Saturdays. Connected to *Boardner's* bar (see p.178).

Blue 1642 N Las Palmas ☎ 323/462-7442. Goth, industrial, and some retro-80s draw the pallid and neo-zombie contingent to this combo restaurant and club, nightly except Tuesdays and Thursdays.

Club Ghetto 5520 Santa Monica Blvd ☎ 323/966-9555. Trendy scene of the moment, with Wednesday night hip hop and dance sounds, accompanied by quasi-strip shows and drag performers.

The Conga Room 5364 Wilshire Blvd ☎ 323/938-1696. A high-profile celebrity investment results in a surprisingly appealing feast of Cuban food and

Latin music. Has expanded into an adjacent former camera shop, which is now called "La Boca del Conga Room."

The Derby 4500 Los Feliz Blvd ☎323/663-8979. Restored supper club in east side of Hollywood with gorgeous high wooden ceilings and round bar that was one of the originators of the retro-swing craze, thanks to the movie *Swingers*.

Dragonfly 6510 Santa Monica Blvd ☎323/466-6111. Unusual decor, two large dance rooms, and house and disco club nights that are continually buzzing.

Florentine Gardens 5951 Hollywood Blvd ☎323/464-0706. Stuck between the Salvation Army and a porno theater, but popular with the LA dance crowd, especially the under-21 set.

The Ruby 7070 Hollywood Blvd ☎323/467-7070. A wide range of feverish dance clubs nightly, except Mondays and Tuesdays, everything from retro-kitsch to grinding industrial to perky house and garage.

West LA

Coconut Teazer 8117 Sunset Blvd ☎323/654-4773. Poseurs, rockers, and voyeurs mix on two dancefloors. The DJs play all night so you don't have to stop dancing until 6am.

Key Club 9039 Sunset Blvd ☎310/274-5800. A hot spot in the most lively section of the strip, attracting a young, hip group for its hip-hop, funk, and house music spinning nightly.

Ultra Suede 661 N Robertson Blvd, West Hollywood ☎310/659-4551. The spot for superior retro-dancing on Wednesday and weekend nights, heavy on 1970s disco and 80s technopop. Neighboring *Factory* nightclub plays similar tunes, though with a touch of 60s pop as well.

The Viper Room 8852 Sunset Blvd ☎310/358-1880. Though owned by Johnny Depp, less posey and trendy than many clubs in the area. Notoriety comes from River Phoenix's overdose here in 1993. See also "Live music," p.183.

Santa Monica

Lush 2020 Wilshire Blvd, Santa Monica ☎310/829-1333. Retro-sounds reign supreme here, from tacky 80s power pop to hip-hugging 70s disco grind.

The Mix 2810 Main St, Santa Monica. ☎310/399-1953. Weekend dance music scene focusing on house, techno, and jungle beats.

Sugar 814 Broadway, Santa Monica ☎310/899-1989. Hard-hitting electronica, from big beat to house to techno, served up in a shiny and gorgeous glass-and-steel interior.

Temple Bar 1026 Wilshire Blvd, Santa Monica ☎310/392-1077. Popular, if chaotic, mix of different groove styles, from rap to R&B, with heavy doses of world beat thrown in as well. Always a frenetic, engaging scene.

The West End 1301 5th St, Santa Monica ☎310/394-4647. As at *Lush*, DJs spin old 1970s and 1980s favorites and bartenders serve up sugary, fern-bar cocktails.

The San Gabriel and San Fernando valleys

Bigfoot Lodge 3172 Los Feliz Blvd, Atwater Village ☎323/662-9227. Not far from Griffith Park to the east, a serious bar scene with rock, punk, and funk tunes nightly, with live bands and DJs.

CIA 11334 Burbank Blvd, North Hollywood ☎818/506-6353. Odd venue where art and music collide, with curious visual installations and a range of sounds from punk to avant-garde.

Gitana 260 E Magnolia Blvd, Burbank ☎818/846-4400. Giant dance-and-dining complex with pool tables, cigar bar and eclectic tunes on the dancefloor. Mixed crowd of tourists and locals.

The Muse 54 E Colorado Blvd ☎626/793-0608. Old Town Pasadena is the site where dance, funk, and hip-hop tunes mingle in one tri-level club with no less than eleven pool tables.

Live music

LA has a near-overwhelming choice of **live music** venues. Because new bands haven't broken through until they've won over an LA crowd, there's seldom an evening without something exciting going on. Since the nihilistic punk bands of nearly 25 years ago drew the city away from its spaced-out slacker image, LA's **rock music** scene has been second to none: there's a proto-rock star at every corner, and the guitar case is in some districts, like Hollywood, almost de rigueur. The old **punk** scene has been revitalized with up-and-coming bands, and even newfangled heavy metal can be found here and there. The influence and popularity of **hip-hop** is also prevalent, whether mixed in dance music by Westside DJs or in its more authentic form in the inner city.

There are always plenty of British and European names on tour, from major artists to independents, and an enormous number of venues. Most clubs open at 8pm or 9pm; headline bands are usually onstage between 11pm and 1am. Cover ranges widely from $5 to $30, and you should phone ahead to check set times and whether the gig is sold out. You'll need to be 21 and will likely be asked for ID. As ever, *LA Weekly* is the best source of **listings**.

Surprisingly, **country music** is fairly common, too, at least away from trendy Hollywood, and the valleys are hotbeds of bluegrass and swing. There's also **jazz**, played in a few genuinely authentic downbeat dives, though more commonly found in diluted form in upscale restaurants. Latin **salsa** music is immensely popular among LA's Hispanics, and can be found in a few Westside clubs, but particularly in the bars of East LA – generally male-oriented gathering places where visitors may well feel out of place. Finally, there's a small live **reggae** scene, occasionally featuring big names but more often sticking to the increasingly numerous local bands.

What's on and tickets

Apart from the radio stations listed below, which carry details, previews, and sometimes free tickets for forthcoming events, the best sources of **information** are the *LA Weekly* and the "Calendar" section of the Sunday *LA Times*. You can buy seats for concerts or sports events from **Ticketmaster**, which has branches in Tower Records stores, and charge-by-phone numbers (℡213/480-3232 or 714/740-2000). A quick way through the maze of LA's **theaters** is to phone **Theatre LA** (℡213/614-0556, ⓦwww.theatrela.org) and ask for the availability of discount tickets for a given show.

Radio stations

KFI 640 AM (ⓦwww.kfi640.com) Tub-thumping talk radio, mostly from a far-right perspective.

KFWB 980 AM (ⓦwww.kfwb.com) Frequent local news, plus talk shows.

KNX 1070 (ⓦwww.knx1070.com) News with half-hourly sports reports.

KXTA 1150 AM (ⓦwww.xtrasports1150.com) Sports and talk.

KLON 88.1 FM (ⓦwww.klon.org) Blues and jazz.

KPCC 89.3 FM (ⓦwww.kpcc.org) Jazz and blues concerts, plus arty talk radio. Another NPR affiliate.

KCRW 89.9 FM (ⓦwww.kcrw.org) One of the country's better NPR affiliates, with new music, transatlantic imports, and world news. Great evening music programs leaning toward trance, dub, and eclectic tunes.

KUSC 91.5 FM (ⓦwww.kusc.org) Classical, jazz, and world music.

KCBS 93.1 FM (ⓦwww.arrowfm.com) "The Arrow": classic rock tunes.

KZLA 93.9 FM (ⓦbeta.kzla.com) Popular country hits.

KLSX 97.1 FM (ⓦwww.fmtalki.com) Talk radio, shock jocks, Howard Stern.

KSSE 97.5 FM (ⓦwww.superestrella.com) Latino pop favorites and salsa.

KKBT 100.3 FM (ⓦwww.thebeatla.com) "The Beat": soul, R&B, and hip hop.

KRTH 101.1 FM (ⓦwww.kearth101.com) "K-Earth": nothing but oldies, advertised incessantly around town.

KIIS 102.7 FM (ⓦwww.kiisfm.com) Top 40 pop hits.

KBIG 104.3 FM (ⓦwww.kbig104.com) Pop and dance, with some disco sprinkled in.

KMZT 105.1 FM (ⓦwww.kmzt.com) "K-Mozart": Not surprisingly, classical music.

KPWR 106 FM (ⓦwww.power106.fm) "K-Power": Hip-hop and R&B with some Latin pop.

KROQ 106.7 FM (ⓦwww.kroq.com) Hard rock with a touch of grunge.

Major performance venues

Greek Theater 2700 N Vermont Ave, Griffith Park ☎323/665-1927, ⓦ www.greektheatrela.com. Outdoor, summer-only venue with a broad range of mainstream rock and pop acts and seating for five thousand. Parking can be a mess, so arrive early.

Hollywood Palladium 6215 Sunset Blvd, Hollywood ☎323/962-7600, ⓦ www.hollywood-palladium.com. Once a big-band dance hall, with an authentic 1940s interior, now a home to all manner of hard rock, punk, and rap outfits.

Kodak Theatre 6801 Hollywood Blvd, Hollywood ☎323/308-6363. Part of the colossal Hollywood & Highland mall, a media-ready theater partly designed to host the Oscars, which it will for many years, as well as top-name pop and rock acts.

Staples Center 865 S Figueroa St, Downtown ☎213/624-3100, ⓦ www.staplescenter.com. Big new glassy sports arena (home to the LA Lakers) with millions of municipal and corporate lucre behind it. A good showcase for Top 40 rock and pop acts.

Universal Amphitheater 100 Universal City Plaza ☎818/622-4440, ⓦ www.hob.com/venues/con-certs/universal. A big but acoustically excellent auditorium with regular rock shows. Located on the Universal Studios lot.

Wiltern Theater 3790 Wilshire Blvd, Mid-Wilshire ☎323/388-1400. A striking blue Zigzag Art Deco movie palace, now converted into a top performing space for standard pop acts as well as edgy alternative groups.

Rock venues

The Cat Club 8911 Sunset Blvd, West Hollywood ☎310/657-0888. Hard, meaty jams every night of the week, with the focus on rock, punk, and rocka-billy – no surprise since the owner's a former Stray Cat.

Doug Weston's Troubadour 9081 Santa Monica Blvd, West Hollywood ☎310/276-6168. An old 1960s mainstay. Used to be known for heavy riffs and shaggy manes, now for more alternative and acoustic line-ups.

El Rey Theatre 5515 Wilshire Blvd, Mid-Wilshire ☎323/936-4790. Although not as famous as its Sunset Strip counterparts, this rock and alternative venue is possibly the best spot to see explosive new bands and still-engaging oldsters. Also offers a variety of dance club nights.

Gabah 4658 Melrose Ave, Hollywood ☎323/664-8913. Eclectic spot serving up a mix of reggae, funk, dub, and rock – even flamenco. The dicey neighborhood leaves much to be desired; always

let the valet take charge of your car.

Largo 432 N Fairfax Ave, West LA ☎323/852-1073. Cozy cabaret with some unusual live acts, though mostly jazz, rock, and pop.

The Lighthouse 30 Pier Ave, Hermosa Beach ☎310/376-9833. Adjacent to the beach, this old favorite has a broad booking policy, which spans rock, jazz, and reggae as well as karaoke and comedy.

The Opium Den 1605 1/2 Ivar Ave, Hollywood ☎323/466-7800. A strip club turned nightclub, with an array of up-and-coming rock and punk acts taking turns on the overly small stage.

The Palace 1735 N Vine St, Hollywood ☎323/462-3000. Great old venue from 1924 that hosts a solid range of rock and alternative acts during the week, then becomes a dance club on weekend nights.

The Roxy 9009 Sunset Blvd, West LA ☎310/276-2222. The showcase of the music industry's new signings, intimate and with a great sound system, on the western – but still frenetic – end of the strip.

Spaceland 1717 Silver Lake Blvd, Silver Lake ☎213/833-2843. Excellent spot to catch up-and-coming local and national rockers and other acts.

The Viper Room 8852 Sunset Blvd, West Hollywood ☎310/358-1880. Great live acts, a famous owner, and a headline-hitting past. Expect almost any musician to show up onstage. See also "Nightlife," p.181.

Whisky-a-Go-Go 8901 Sunset Blvd, West Hollywood ☎310/652-4202. Another longstanding hot spot for LA's rising musicians; mainly hard rock.

Country and folk venues

The Blue Saloon 4657 Lankershim Blvd, North Hollywood ☎818/766-4644. An old favorite for country and rockabilly, now with a bit more eclec-tic line-up. For its libations, see "Drinking," p.179.

Crazy Jack's 4311 W Magnolia Blvd, Burbank ☎818/845-1121. Before the country music starts at 9pm, this place offers free dance lessons Tues & Thurs–Sat. Don't miss the Dixieland nights.

The Foothill Club 1922 Cherry Ave, Signal Hill ☎562/984-8349. Located near Long Beach, a glo-rious dance hall from the days when hillbilly was cool, complete with mural showing life-on-the-range. Also presents rock and pop acts.

McCabe's 3103 W Pico Blvd, Santa Monica ☎310/828-4497. LA's premier acoustic guitar shop; long the scene of some excellent and unusual folk and country shows, with the occa-sional alternative crooner thrown in as well.

January

1 Tournament of Roses in Pasadena. A parade of floral floats and marching bands along a five-mile stretch of Colorado Boulevard. (Information at ☎626/795-9311, ⊛www.tournamentofroses.com.)

mid Martin Luther King Parade and Celebration. The civil rights hero is honored with spirited activities at King Park and Baldwin Hills–Crenshaw Mall, among many other city-wide locations (☎310/314-2188).

February

early to mid Chinese New Year. Three days of dragon-float street parades, tasty food, and various cultural programs, based in Chinatown and Alhambra (☎213/617-0396).

mid Mardi Gras. Floats, parades, costumes, and plenty of singing and dancing at this Brazilian fun fest in West Hollywood (☎310/289-2525).

mid to late Queen Mary Scottish Festival. All the haggis you can stand at this two-day Long Beach celebration, along with highland dancing and bagpipes (☎562/435-3511).

end The Academy Awards. Having recently been moved up a month, the Oscars are presented at the Kodak Theater in the Hollywood & Highland mall (see p.116). Bleacher seats are available to watch the stars arrive (⊛www.oscars.org).

March

mid St Patrick's Day. Parade along Colorado Boulevard in Old Town Pasadena (☎626/796-5049). No parade but freely flowing green beer in the "Irish" bars along Fairfax Avenue.

late Spring Festival of Flowers. An explosion of color in the San Fernando Valley's Descanso Gardens (see p.161; ☎818/952-4401).

end Cowboy Poetry and Music Festival. Plenty of folk music from the Old West and accompanying cowboy poems – some excellent, some cornpone – are the highlights of this three-day Santa Clarita celebration, just north of LA (☎661/286-4078 or 1-800/305-0755).

April

early California Poppy Festival. Head out to distant Lancaster to see an amazing display of fiery blossoms (☎661/723-6077).

Saturday before Easter The Blessing of the Animals. A long-established ceremony, Mexican in origin. Locals arrive in Olvera Street to have their pets blessed, then watch the attendant parade (☎213/625-5045).

weekend nearest 13 Thai New Year. Focus of activity at North Hollywood's Wat Thai Temple (☎818/997-9657).

mid Long Beach Grand Prix. Scores of locals come out to watch the Indy cars race around Shoreline Drive (☎562/752-9524).

May

5 Cinco de Mayo. A day-long party to commemorate the Mexican victory at the Battle of Puebla. Spirited parade in Olvera Street, and several blocks Downtown blocked off for Chicano and Hispanic music performances (☎213/625-5045).

mid Venice Art Walk. Peer into the private studios of big-name and up-and-coming local artists (☎310/664-7911).

late UCLA Jazz & Reggae Festival. Spirited music, food, and activities take place on the campus (☎310/825-9912).

June

early Beach Bash. In the South Bay town of Hermosa Beach, extreme-sports athletes compete in events like skateboarding, freestyle biking, and inline skating, and everyone else plays beach volleyball. (☎310/376-0951).

early Valley Jewish Festival. The largest such event west of the Mississippi. Activities begin at Pierce College, in the San Fernando Valley district of Woodland Hills (☎818/587-3205).

second weekend Irish Fair and Music Festival. Sizeable music, food, and cultural celebration held at Woodley Park in Encino, in the San Fernando Valley (☎626/503-2511).

late Bayou Festival. Heaps of Creole food, wild parades, and plenty of high-spirited Cajun and Zydeco music at this colorful Long Beach event (☎562/427-3713).

late Gay Pride Celebration. Parade on Santa Monica Boulevard in West Hollywood. Carnival atmosphere, 250 vendors, and an all-male drag football cheerleading team (☎323/860-0701).

July

4 Independence Day. *Queen Mary* in Long Beach hosts a particularly large fireworks display, as well as colorful entertainment. Festivities also in Santa Monica and many other LA communities (☎562/435-3511).

first weekend after 4 Lotus Festival. Echo Park celebration with dragon boats, ethnic food, pan-Pacific music, and resplendent lotus blossoms all around the lake (☎213/485-5448).

early July to late August Festival of the Arts/Pageant of the Masters. Laguna Beach's eye-opening street festival, with food, music, and dancing, and people posing as paintings (see p.156).

mid Greek Festival. Food and music celebration in a Redondo Beach Orthodox Church (☎310/540-2434).

August

early Culmination of the South Bay's International Surf Festival (☎562/570-3100).

mid Nisei Week in Little Tokyo. A celebration of Japanese America, with martial arts demonstrations, karaoke, Japanese brush painting, baby shows, and performance (☎213/687-7193).

late African Marketplace and Cultural Faire. Arts and crafts displays and street performers, at Crenshaw's Rancho Cienega park (☎323/734-1164).

late Sunset Junction Street Fair. A spirited neighborhood party – always one of LA's most enjoyable fetes – along Sunset Boulevard in Silver Lake, with live music, ethnic food, and a carnivalesque atmosphere. Draws a big crowd of locals in the know (☎323/661-7771).

September

5 LA's birthday. A civic ceremony and assorted street entertainment around El Pueblo de Los Angeles to mark the founding of the original pueblo in 1781 (☎213/485-9777).

mid Koreatown Multicultural Festival. Dancing, parading, and Tae Kwon Do exhibitions (☎213/730-1495).

last two weeks Los Angeles County Fair in Pomona, in the San Gabriel Valley. The biggest county fair in the country, with livestock shows, eating contests, and fairground rides (☎909/623-3111).

late Watts Towers Day of the Drum/Jazz Festival. Two days of community spirit and free music – a wealth of African, Asian, Cuban, and Brazilian drumming – with the towers as the striking backdrop. Taking place at the same time, and in the same location, the Jazz Festival is the most longstanding such event in LA (☎213/847-4646).

late through October Oktoberfest. In the South Bay town of Torrance, plenty of hearty German food, beer, and dancing (☎310/327-4384).

October

second weekend LA Street Fair and Carnival. Free rock music, theater, and comedy on the streets of Sherman Oaks in the San Fernando Valley. At the same time as West continued

Hollywood Street Festival, a display of handmade arts and crafts (☎310/781-2020).
mid Scandinavian Festival. Folk dancing with assorted food and art. Held in Santa Monica (☎213/661-4273).
31 Halloween Parade. More West Hollywood frolicking (☎213/848-6547).

November

2 Dia de los Muertos (Day of the Dead) celebrated throughout East Los Angeles and for the tourists on Olvera Street. Mexican traditions, such as picnicking on the family burial spot, are upheld (☎213/485-9777).
Saturday after Thanksgiving Doo-dah Parade. Quintessential LA event featuring absurd or bizarre characters marching through Pasadena. Surprisingly popular (☎626/440-7379).
late Griffith Park Light Festival. Tremendous electrical spectacle along Crystal Springs Road in the park, with tunnels of light, thematic displays, and representations of familiar LA sights like the Hollywood sign. A hugely popular draw (☎213/485-8743).

December

1 Hollywood Christmas Parade. The first and best of the many Yuletide events, with a cavalcade of mind-boggling floats (☎323/469-2337).
early Belmont Shore Christmas Parade. East Long Beach is the setting for holiday floats and marching bands (☎562/434-3066).
mid Christmas Boat Parade. Marina del Rey is the site for this annual display of brightly lit watercraft (☎310/821-7614).

Rusty's Surf Ranch 256 Santa Monica Pier ☎310/393-7437. Offers not only surf music – and displays of old-time long boards – but also rock, pop, folk, and even karaoke. Always a popular spot for tourists, near the end of the pier.

Jazz and blues venues

The Baked Potato 3787 Cahuenga Blvd W, North Hollywood ☎818/980-1615. A small but near-legendary contemporary jazz spot, where many reputations have been forged. Don't come looking for bland lounge jazz/muzak – instead, expect to be surprised.
Catalina Bar & Grill 1640 N Cahuenga Blvd, Hollywood ☎323/466-2210. A Hollywood jazz institution with plenty of style and atmosphere, with filling meals and potent drinks.
Cat 'n' Fiddle Pub 6530 Sunset Blvd, Hollywood ☎323/468-3800. An English-style pub with jazz on Sundays from 7pm until 11pm; no cover. See also "Drinking," p.178.
Harvelle's 1432 4th St, Santa Monica ☎310/395-1676. Near the Third Street Promenade, a stellar blues joint for more than six decades offering different performers nightly and a popular band showcase on Tuesday nights.
House of Blues 8430 Sunset Blvd, West Hollywood ☎323/848-5100. Over-commercialized mock sugar shack, with good but pricey live acts. Very popular

with tourists (also a branch at Disneyland; ☎714/778-2583). Cover can reach $30 or more.
Jazz Bakery 3233 Helms Ave, Culver City ☎310/271-9039. More performance space than club, the brainchild of singer Ruth Price. The best local musicians play alongside big-name visitors. In an actual former bakery building.
Knitting Factory 7021 Hollywood Blvd ☎323/463-0204. West Coast branch of New York landmark club, featuring a wide range of eclectic interpretation, much of it avant-garde.
Spazio 14755 Ventura Blvd, 2nd Floor, Sherman Oaks ☎818/728-8400. Swank Italian eatery that's one of the bigger-name spots for mainstream jazz, hosting regular nightly performances.
World Stage 4434 Degnan Blvd, Leimert Park ☎323/293-2451. Bare-bones rehearsal space that attracts top-name players like drummers Billy Higgins and Max Roach. Thursday jams, Friday and Saturday gigs.

Salsa venues

Club Samba 701 Long Beach Blvd, Long Beach ☎562/435-6238. Friday night Brazilian lessons followed by dancing, Saturday night samba lessons followed by live samba, and bossa nova music on Sunday nights.
The Conga Room 5364 Wilshire Blvd ☎323/938-1696. Live Cuban, salsa, and South American

music throughout the week at this hip, lively club on the Miracle Mile. See also "Nightlife," p.180.

El Floridita 1253 N Vine St, Hollywood ☎ 323/871-8612. Decent Mexican and Cuban food complements a fine line-up of Cuban and salsa artists, who play on weekends and jam on other nights.

Luminarias 3500 Ramona Blvd, Monterey Park, East LA ☎ 323/268-4177. Hilltop restaurant (see p.170) with regular live salsa reckoned to be as good as its Mexican food.

Zabumba 10717 Venice Blvd, Culver City (310/841-6525. In a colorful building amid drab surroundings, this venue is more bossa nova Brazilian than straight salsa, but it's still great, and very lively.

Reggae venues

Club 49 49 Pine Ave, Long Beach ☎ 562/437-5326. As with other clubs and restaurants featuring the music, reggae is not the sole focus here. Instead, a range of live music and DJs enlivens the surf'n'turf meals, often including Jamaican beats, depending on the night.

Domenico's 82 N Fair Oaks Ave, Pasadena ☎ 626/449-1948. Old Pasadena Italian restaurant hosting reggae several nights a week.

Golden Sails Club Room 6285 E PCH, Long Beach ☎ 562/596-1631. Some of the best reggae bands from LA and beyond show up at this hotel on Friday and Saturday nights.

Classical music, opera, and dance

Despite its size, LA has very few outlets for **classical music**. The Los Angeles Philharmonic (☎ 213/850-2000, ⊛ www.laphil.org), the only major name in the city, performs regularly during the year, and the Los Angeles Chamber Orchestra (☎ 213/622-7001, ⊛ www.laco.org) and LA Master Chorale (☎ 1-800/787-LAMC, ⊛ www.lamc.org) appear sporadically at different venues. Otherwise, attractions are thin, and often limited to fly-by-night groups of trained musicians who perform together for a brief time at rotating venues. Watch the press, especially the *LA Times*, for details, and expect to pay from $10 to $75 for most concerts, much more for really big names.

As for **opera**, LA Opera (☎ 213/972-8001, ⊛ www.laopera.org) stages productions between September and June, as does Orange County's Opera Pacific (☎ 949/474-4488 or 1-800/34-OPERA, ⊛ www.operapacific.org), which performs grand opera and operettas, while Long Beach Opera (☎ 562/439-2580, ⊛ www.lbopera.com) is more engaging and cutting-edge. Prices range from $10 to $120. **Dance** in Los Angeles has its annual big event with the **Dance Kaleidoscope**, held over two weeks in July at the John Anson Ford Theater and organized by the Los Angeles Area Dance Alliance (☎ 323/343-5120) – a co-operative of LA dance companies that provides a central source of information. Otherwise check for performances at the **universities**, where many important names in dance have residencies.

Major venues

The Dorothy Chandler Pavilion in the Music Center, 135 N Grand Ave, Downtown ☎ 213/972-7211 or 972-7460, ⊛ www.musiccenter.org. Home to the LA Philharmonic from October until May and used by LA Opera and other top names.

The Hollywood Bowl 2301 N Highland Ave, Hollywood ☎ 323/850-2000, ⊛ www.hollywoodbowl.org. The LA Philharmonic gives open-air concerts here (July–Sept Tues–Sat evenings; see p.122 for more on the Bowl), often of the pops variety.

Japan America Theater 244 S San Pedro St, Little Tokyo ☎ 213/680-3700, ⊛ www.jaccc.org. Dance and performance works drawn from Japan and the Far East.

John Anson Ford Theater 2850 Cahuenga Blvd, Hollywood ☎ 323/461-3673, ⊛ www.lacountyarts.org/ford. Besides the summer Dance Kaleidoscope, this open-air venue also has eclectic productions by local groups.

Orange County Performing Arts Center 600 Town Center Drive, Costa Mesa ☎ 714/556-ARTS or 949/740-2000, ⊛ www.ocpac.org. Orange County home of the Pacific Symphony Orchestra and Opera Pacific, as well as touring big names in pop and jazz.

The Pacific Amphitheater 100 Fair Drive, Costa Mesa ☎ 949/740-2000 A big open-air venue: Orange County's answer to the Hollywood Bowl.

Pasadena Dance Theatre 1985 Locust St,

Pasadena ☎626/683-3459, ⊛www.pasade-nadance.org. One of the San Gabriel Valley's most prominent dance venues, hosting diverse groups throughout the year.

Royce Hall on the UCLA campus, Westwood ☎310/825-9261 or 825-2101, ⊛www.performin-garts.ucla.edu. Classical concerts, with such groups as the LA Chamber Orchestra, throughout the college year.

The Shrine Auditorium 665 W Jefferson, South

Central LA ☎213/749-5123, box office at 655 S Hill St. Huge 1926 Moorish curiosity that hosts touring pop acts, choral gospel groups, and countless award shows (but not the Oscars anymore).

UCLA Center for the Performing Arts office at 10920 Wilshire Blvd, Westwood ☎310/825-4401, ⊛www.performingarts.ucla.edu. Coordinates a wide range of touring companies, and runs an "Art of Dance" series with an experimental emphasis between September and June.

Comedy

LA has a very wide range of **comedy clubs**. While rising stars and beginners can be spotted on the "underground" open-mike scene, most of the famous and soon-to-be-famous comics, both stand-up and improv, appear at the more established clubs, most of them in Hollywood, West LA, or the valleys. These venues usually have a bar, charge a $10–15 cover, and put on two shows per evening, generally starting at 8pm and 10.30pm – the later one being more popular. The better-known places are open nightly, but are often solidly booked on Fridays and weekends.

Comedy venues

Acme Comedy Theater 135 N La Brea Ave, Hollywood ☎323/525-0202. A fancy venue with sketch and improv comedy, as well as variety shows.

Bang Theater 457 N Fairfax Ave, Hollywood ☎323/653-6886. One-person shows and long-form improvisation are the specialties at this small theater/comedy club. Cheap cover, often $5.

Comedy & Magic Club 1018 Hermosa Ave, Hermosa Beach ☎310/372-1193. Strange couplings of magic and comedy. Jay Leno sometimes tests material here. Tickets can run $10–25.

Comedy Sportz 5919 Franklin Ave, Hollywood ☎323/856-4796. As you might guess, comedy competitions arranged like sports contests, with plenty of feedback from the audience and all kinds of high-spirited theatrics.

The Comedy Store 8433 W Sunset Blvd, West LA ☎323/656-6225. LA's comedy showcase and popular enough to be spread over three rooms – which means there's usually space, even at weekends. Run by Pauly Shore's mom.

Groundlings Theater 7307 Melrose Ave, West LA ☎323/934-9700. Another pioneering improvisational venue where only the gifted survive.

Ha Ha Café 5010 Lankershim Blvd, North

Hollywood ☎818/508-4995. Amateur and even a few professional comedians face off for your amusement on Thursday nights, at this combination comedy club and café space.

HBO Workspace 733 N Seward St, Hollywood ☎323/993-6099. If you're in the mood for free experimental comedy, this is the place. HBO runs it as a proving ground for risky acts.

The Ice House 24 N Mentor Ave, Pasadena ☎626/577-1894. The comedy mainstay of the Valley, very established and fairly safe; often amusing, with the occasional big name. Two-drink minimum.

The Improvisation 8162 Melrose Ave, West LA ☎323/651-2583. Longstanding brick-walled joint known for hosting some of the best acts working in the area. One of LA's top comedy spots – so book ahead.

LA Connection 13442 Ventura Blvd, Sherman Oaks ☎818/784-1868. Cozy space for sketch comedy, group antics, and individual jokesters. Seldom less than memorable.

The Laugh Factory 8001 Sunset Blvd, West Hollywood ☎323/656-1336. Stand-ups of varying standards and reputations, with the odd big name. Features a variable open-mike night.

Theater

From huge Broadway shows to small avant-garde productions, LA has a very active **theater** scene. While the bigger venues host a predictable array of retread musicals and classics with an all-star cast of celebrities, there are over a hundred "Equity waiver" theaters with fewer than a hundred seats, enabling non-Equity-cardholders to perform, and a vast network of fringe writers, actors, and directors. Many good alternative theaters have sprung up in Hollywood west of Cahuenga Boulevard, revolving around **The Complex**, a group of six small theaters at 6470–6 Santa Monica Blvd. Tickets are less expensive than you might expect: a big show will cost you at least $30 (matinees are cheaper), smaller shows around $10 to $25. Always book ahead.

Fringe theaters

Cast-At-The-Circle 800 N El Centro Ave, Hollywood ☎ 323/466-0944. Small Hollywood theater hosting a variety of smaller productions and edgy one-man and -woman shows.

Highways 1651 18th St, Santa Monica ☎ 310/453-3711. Located in the 18th Street Arts Complex, an adventurous performance space that offers a range of topical drama and politically charged productions.

Lee Strasberg Creative Center 7936 Santa Monica Blvd, West Hollywood ☎ 323/650-7777. Although method acting is plentiful here – as well as a few stars in the crowd – all types of plays and styles are performed.

Odyssey Theater Ensemble 2055 S Sepulveda Blvd, West LA ☎ 310/477-2055. Well-respected Westside theater company with a modernist bent.

Open Fist Theater 1625 N La Brea Ave, Hollywood ☎ 323/882-6912. A small arts group presenting edgy and alternative works with a limited cast of spirited unknowns, though sometimes with larger names dropping in.

Powerhouse Theater 3116 2nd St, Santa Monica ☎ 310/396-3680. Cozy venue, worth visiting for the adventurous and risk-taking experimental shows.

Major theaters

Alex Theater 216 N Brand Blvd, Glendale ☎ 1-800/872-8997. Gloriously restored movie palace bedecked with green-and-yellow decor and neon spire, hosting a fine range of musical theater, dance, comedy, and film.

Coronet Theater 366 N La Cienega Blvd, West Hollywood ☎ 310/657-7377. Solid Westside choice that's home to the LA Public Theater – whose productions include the odd famous name – and the Youth Academy of Dramatic Arts.

Geffen Playhouse 10886 Le Conte Ave, Westwood ☎ 310/208-5454. One of the smaller of the major theaters, sometimes with one-person shows, but often packing the house, thanks to solid Hollywood connections.

Mark Taper Forum 135 N Grand Ave, Downtown ☎ 213/972-0700. Theater in the three-quarter round, mostly known for its conservatism and adherence to the mainstream repertoire. Located in the Music Center complex.

Pantages Theater 6233 Hollywood Blvd, Hollywood ☎ 323/468-1770. Quite the stunner: an exquisite, atmospheric Art Deco theater, in the heart of historic Hollywood, hosting major touring Broadway productions.

South Coast Repertory 655 Town Center Drive, Costa Mesa ☎ 714/708-5555. Orange County's major entry for institutional theater, with well-executed takes on canonical dramatic works, and recently refurbished.

Film

Major feature **films** are often released in LA months (or years) before they play anywhere else, and a huge number of cinemas show both the new releases and the classics – with fewer screens showing independent and foreign movies. Depending on where you go and what you see, a ticket will be from $5 to $8.50.

For **mainstream cinema**, Westwood has a high concentration of moviehouses, as does the Santa Monica Promenade. Of the multi-screen facilities, the Universal City 18, at Universal Studios (☎818/508-0588), is a plush complex that includes a pair of pseudo-Parisian cafés, and the AMC Century 14, 10250 Santa Monica Blvd (☎310/553-8900), despite being in a shopping mall, has big screens and good sound. For all their screens, though, only six or seven films are typically shown in the multiple theaters. Another, more enterprisingly programmed, venue is the Goldwyn Cinemas (☎310/475-0202) in the Westside Pavilion mall in West LA, which has four small screens featuring arty independent films.

For **cheap** and **free films**, the places to hit are the Bing Theater at the LA County Art Museum, 5905 Wilshire Blvd (☎323/857-6010), which has afternoon screenings of Warner Bros classics and charges just $3; UCLA's James Bridges Theater is another excellent choice for foreign, art, and revival cinema (☎310/206-FILM). Otherwise, the best places to find **art-house** and **cult films** are the New Beverly Cinema, 7165 Beverly Blvd (☎323/938-4038), especially strong on imaginative double bills, and the Nuart Theater, 11272 Santa Monica Blvd (☎310/478-6379), which runs rarely seen classics, documentaries, and foreign-language films, and sometimes Oscar contenders for a mere week at the end of December. The three small screens of the Los Feliz Theater, 1822 N Vermont Ave (☎323/664-2169), show international and low-budget American independent movies; while the nearby Vista Theatre, 4473 Sunset Blvd (☎323/660-6639), is a small, nicely remodeled gem that's good for both art-house fare and Hollywood schlock.

If you're looking for a golden-age-of-film **atmosphere**, you'll need either to take in an action double bill in one of the historic Downtown movie palaces (described on p.98), where the delirious furnishings may captivate your attention longer than the double bills, or visit one of the Hollywood landmarks. The Chinese Theatre, 6925 Hollywood Blvd (☎323/464-8186; see p.117), with its large screen, six-track stereo sound, and wild chinoiserie interior, shows relentlessly mainstream films, and has recently and unfortunately been incorporated into a giant shopping mall. If this doesn't appeal, you can always indulge in the Cinerama Dome's giant curved screen, 6360 Sunset Blvd (☎323/466-3401; see p.118), newly restored and part of a new entertainment complex called ArcLight. Also spellbinding are the art-friendly Egyptian, 6712 Hollywood Blvd (☎323/466-FILM; see p.115), Disney's animation- and musical-oriented El Capitan, 6834 Hollywood Blvd (☎323/467-7674), and South Pasadena's foreign and classics venue The Rialto, 1023 Fair Oaks Ave (☎626/799-9567).

Finally, if you have even the slightest interest in films from the golden age of Charlie Chaplin and Buster Keaton, make sure to visit the Silent Movie Theater, 611 N Fairfax Ave (☎323/655-2510), offering an enjoyable mix of comedies and adventure flicks – Douglas Fairbanks swashbucklers and the like – along with darker fare like Fritz Lang's *Metropolis* and even the occasional talkie.

Gay and lesbian LA

Although nowhere near as big as San Francisco's, LA's **gay and lesbian scene** is well established. The best-known area is the city of **West Hollywood**, which is synonymous with the (affluent, white) gay lifestyle, not just in LA but all over

California. The section of West Hollywood on Santa Monica Boulevard east of Doheny Drive has restaurants, shops, and bars primarily aimed at gay men. Another established community is **Silver Lake**, home to the bars and restaurants on Hyperion and Sunset boulevards, and with much more of a vibrant ethnic and working-class mix.

Gay couples will find themselves readily accepted at just about any LA **hotel**, but there are a few that cater especially to gay travelers and can also be useful sources of information on the local scene. This is also true of a number of gay-friendly restaurants. For up-to-date gay-oriented publications, see "Information" on p.78.

Gay resources

AIDS Project Los Angeles 1313 Vine St, Hollywood ☎ 323/993-1600, ⊛ www.apla.org. Sponsors fundraisers throughout the year and a well-attended annual walkathon.

A Different Light 8853 Santa Monica Blvd, West Hollywood ☎ 310/854-6601, ⊛ www.adlbooks .com. The city's best-known gay and lesbian book-shop, with art shows, readings, music events, and comfortable chairs for lounging.

Gay and Lesbian Community Services Center 1625 N Schrader Blvd, Hollywood ☎ 323/993-7400, ⊛ www.laglc.org. Counseling, health-testing and information. Publishes *The Center News*, a bimonthly magazine.

Gay Community Yellow Pages 1604 Vista Del Mar Ave, Hollywood ☎ 323/469-4454. Gay busi-nesses, publications, services, and gathering places listed yearly; available all over LA.

Gay hotels

Coral Sand Hotel 1730 N Western Ave, Hollywood ☎ 323/467-5141, ⊛ www.coralsands-la.com. Cruisy spot exclusively geared towards gay men. All rooms face the inner courtyard pool. ❹

Holloway Motel 8465 Santa Monica Blvd, West Hollywood ☎ 323/654-2454, ⊛ www .hollowaymotel.com. Typical clean roadside motel, if rather dreary looking. Comes with complimenta-ry breakfast. ❺

Hollywood Metropolitan 5825 Sunset Blvd ☎ 323/962-5800, ⊛ www.metropolitanhotel.com. Spanish-style hotel with a mix of small, comfort-able rooms and larger suites, featuring the *Havana on Sunset* restaurant on site (see p.171). Just off US-101. ❹

Ramada 8585 Santa Monica Blvd, West Hollywood ☎ 1-800/845-8585 or 310/652-6400, ⊛ www.the-gayhotel.com. The self-styled "Gay Hotel," a mod-ern place with clean and comfortable rooms, in the center of the community. ❺

San Vicente Inn 854 N San Vicente Blvd, West Hollywood ☎ 310/854-6915, ⊛ www.gayresort .com. Small and comfortable bed-and-breakfast located just north of Santa Monica Boulevard. ❺

Gay and lesbian restaurants

Cobalt Cantina 616 N Robertson Blvd ☎ 310/659-8691. Stylish spot for rich California cuisine, with a nod to Mexican cooking.

French Quarter 7985 Santa Monica Blvd, West Hollywood ☎ 310/654-0898. Inside the *French Market Place*, a New Orleans theme restaurant with food that's more tasty than it is authentic.

Mark's 861 N La Cienega Blvd, West Hollywood ☎ 310/652-5252. High-end establishment serving California cuisine.

Yukon Mining Company 7328 Santa Monica Blvd ☎ 323/851-8833. Slightly seedy but fun 24hr joint with a wide mix of customers, gay and straight. Widely known in the scene for its colorful clientele.

Gay and lesbian bars and clubs

7969 7969 Santa Monica Blvd, West Hollywood ☎ 323/654-0280. Legendary club back in business after closing due to fire, and offering high-energy dance tunes on weekend and Tuesday nights.

Arena 6655 Santa Monica Blvd, Hollywood ☎ 323/462-0714. Many clubs under one roof, large dance floors throbbing to funk, house, and hi-NRG grooves, and sometimes with live bands and mind-blowing drag shows. See also "Nightlife," p.180.

Jewel's Catch One 4067 W Pico Blvd, Mid-City ☎ 323/734-8849. Sweaty barn catering to a mixed crowd – gay and straight, male and female – all on two wild dancefloors.

The Palms 8572 Santa Monica Blvd, West Hollywood ☎ 310/652-6188. Mostly house and dance nights at West Hollywood's most established lesbian bar.

The Plaza 739 N La Brea Ave, Hollywood ☎ 323/939-0703. Nondescript little joint hosts funky, mind-blowing drag shows to a multi-ethnic, mostly gay crowd.

Queen Mary 12449 Ventura Blvd, Studio City ☎ 818/506-5619. Older drag club, much more established than the *Plaza*, and a bit more staid.

Rage 8911 Santa Monica Blvd, West Hollywood

☎310/652-7055. Very flashy gay men's club playing the latest hi-NRG and house. Also with drag comedy. Drinks are fairly cheap.
Rudolpho's 2500 Riverside Drive, Silver Lake ☎323/669-1226. Every second Saturday of the month, it's time to "dress up, drag down" to Dragstrip 66 night at this Mexican restaurant. Other nights are reserved for salsa, rockabilly, and dance music.

Women's LA

LA has a fairly organized network of services for **women**, with many resource centers, bookstores, publications, and clubs. Women travelers are unlikely to encounter any problems which aren't applicable to all the West Coast (for more on which see Basics, p.64), but the resources here are much more developed.

There are many good sources of information on the local women's movement. *LA Woman*, Los Angeles's largest women's magazine, profiling local personalities and providing a calendar of events, is available from most newsstands and bookstores – notably the Sisterhood Bookstore, 1351 Westwood Blvd (☎310/477-7300), a West LA landmark south of Westwood, selling books, music, cards, jewelry, and literature of the women's movement. The *Women's Yellow Pages* (☎310/398-5761, ⓦwww.wypwrs.com), another good resource, is a yearly listing of over 1400 women-owned businesses and services.

Shopping

Shopping in LA is an art. The level of disposable income in the wealthy parts of the city is astronomical, and touring the more outrageous stores can be a great insight into LA life – revealing who's got the money and what they're capable of wasting it on. Whether you want to buy a new light bulb or pair of socks, lay waste to a wad or simply be a voyeur in the orgy of acquisition, there are big **department stores**, **huge malls** – where most of the serious shopping goes on – and **Rodeo Drive**, two blocks of the world's most exclusive shopping. The trendiest boutiques line **Melrose Avenue**, between La Brea and Fairfax avenues, **Old Town Pasadena** boasts a few more upmarket chains, while the few blocks above Prospect on Vermont Avenue in **Los Feliz** are home to some of the underground's groovier shops.

The city also has a good assortment of specialist stores, with extensive selections of **books** and **records**, as well as **food** stores, from corner delis and supermarkets to fancy cake stores and gourmet markets. You'll also find several stores selling perfect LA souvenirs, like the **LA County Coroner Gift Shop** at 1104 N Mission Rd (☎213/343-0760), which sells everything from skeleton-decorated beach towels and T-shirts to toe-tag key chains – all typical LA merchandise.

Department stores and malls

Each of LA's neighborhoods has a collection of ordinary **stores** and **mini-malls**. You'll find the best sources of cheap toiletries and staples at places such as Walmart and Target. A step up from these in price and quality, though still good for general shopping, are **department stores**, which are often included within massive **malls** and resemble self-contained city suburbs, around which Angelenos do the bulk of their serious buying.

Rodeo Drive

The black hole for expense accounts is **Rodeo Drive** in Beverly Hills, a solid line of exclusive stores that includes Ralph Lauren, 444 N (☎310/281-7200), catering to well-heeled WASPS who fancy themselves as English gentry. Besides thousand-dollar suits and monogrammed Wellingtons, there are exquisitely carved walking sticks and mounted game heads, and a huge assortment of wooden dogs, bronze dogs, and paintings of dogs. At the foot of Rodeo Drive are LA's premier department stores, including Barney's, 9570 Wilshire Blvd (☎310/276-4400), and Neiman-Marcus, 9700 Wilshire Blvd (☎310/550-5900), who sell everything from $5 Swiss truffles to his'n'hers leopard skins. Nearby, **Two Rodeo**, the area's mock-European tourist trap, competes for buyers' attention in a much cruder and less appealing fashion.

The malls

Beverly Center 8500 Beverly Blvd, West Hollywood ☎310/854-0070. Seven acres of boutiques, Macy's and Bloomingdale's, a multiplex cinema, and a *Hard Rock Café*, all in one complex that resembles a giant brown concrete bunker – trimmed in hideous green and purple.

Century City Marketplace 10250 Santa Monica Blvd, Century City ☎310/553-5300. Outdoor mall with a hundred upscale shops. The place to come to see stars do their shopping, and to catch a first-run movie in the fine cineplex AMC Century 14.

Del Amo Fashion Square Hawthorne Blvd at Carson St, Torrance ☎310/542-8525. The South Bay's own supermall, one of LA's largest, with five major anchor stores and a wealth of mid-level retailers and suburban shoppers.

The Grove 6301 W 3rd St, Mid-Wilshire ☎323/571-8830. A giant, open-air megastructure in the vicinity of the Farmers Market; the latest variant of LA mall design, with all the usual chain retailers and restaurants, movie theaters, and a somewhat more stylish design than the typical "dumb-box" construction found elsewhere.

Hollywood & Highland at the same intersection in Hollywood ☎323/960-2331. Another new mega-mall, with a design inspired by an ancient silent film set, but offering the same old corporate boutiques and trendy shops.

Santa Monica Place Broadway at 2nd St, Santa Monica ☎310/394-5451. Three tiers of shops and an outdated postmodern design.

Third Street Promenade between Broadway and Wilshire Blvd, Santa Monica. One of the most popular shopping precincts in LA, and all the more enjoyable for being outdoors. Chain stores reign supreme north of Arizona Avenue, less so elsewhere.

Westside Pavilion Pico Blvd at Westwood Blvd, West LA ☎310/474-6255. Giant shopping complex centered on the Nordstrom department store, which provides regular customers with a personal "shopper." Three stories and two wings of mostly chain stores.

Food and drink

Since eating out in LA is so common, you may never have to shop for **food** at all. But if you're preparing a picnic, or want to indulge in a spot of home cooking, there are plenty of places to stock up. **Delis**, many open round the clock, are found in many areas; **supermarkets** are almost as common, some open 24 hours, or at least until 10pm – Pavilions, Ralphs, and Trader Joe's are the names to look out for. There are also **ethnic groceries** and **markets** and more expensive **gourmet markets** and **stores**, not to mention a bizarre collection of one-off outlets for all kinds of food oddities. To buy **drinks** you need go no further than the nearest supermarket – Trader Joe's is the cheapest and best.

Pastries and cakes

Cobbler Factory 33 N Catalina Ave, Pasadena ☎626/449-2152. Bakery in Old Pasadena selling a range of scrumptious, fruity cobblers from $5–35, depending on how huge you want them.

Diamond Bakery 335 N Fairfax Ave, West LA ☎323/655-0534. Great old Jewish bakery with legendary pumpernickel bread and a mouth-watering array of cookies and other sweets.

Hansen Cakes 193 S Beverly Drive, Beverly Hills ☎310/273-3759. Local institution with a collection of nicely decorated, and very tasty, cakes.

La Brea Bakery 624 S La Brea Ave, West LA ☎ 323/939-6813. Perhaps LA's best bakery, selling everything from cheap sourdough rolls to thick, heavy breads made with olives, cherries, and cheese. Connected to the equally appealing *Campanile* restaurant (see p.174).

Mousse Fantasy 2130 Sawtelle Blvd #110, West LA ☎ 310/479-6665. Japanese version of a French patisserie, though in a crowded strip mall. The green tea mousse cake is a taste of heaven.

Mrs Field's Cookies 907 Westwood Blvd, Westwood ☎ 310/208-0096. Chewy, sweet cookies, made to a "secret recipe" that has plenty of devoted fans – nationwide branches include nine others in LA.

Delis and groceries

Bay Cities Italian Deli 1517 Lincoln Blvd, Santa Monica ☎310/395-8279. A gigantic store with piles of fresh pasta, spices, meats, sauces, and many French and Middle Eastern imports.

The Cheese Store 419 N Beverly Drive, Beverly Hills ☎ 310/278-2855. Over four hundred types of cheese from all over the world, including every kind produced in the US. Typically high prices to match.

Claro's Italian Market 1095 E Main St, Tustin ☎ 714/832-3081. A compact but well-stocked haven of Italian wines, chocolate, crackers, and own-brand frozen meals. Worth the drive out to distant Orange County.

Gastronom 7859 Santa Monica Blvd ☎ 323/654-9456. Despite the unappealing name, a prime spot for stocking up on Russian foodstuffs, with smoked fish and caviar as some of the highlights.

Full o' Life 2515 W Magnolia Blvd, Burbank ☎ 818/845-8343. This mother of all health-food stores dates back to 1959, offering an organic market, deli, dairy, restaurant, and book department, with nutritionists and a naturopath on the premises daily.

La Canasta in El Mercado 1736 W 6th St, Westlake ☎ 213/484-6159. A good assortment of authentic Mexican and Central American food: chilis, *chayotes*, and tasty desserts.

Say Cheese 2800 Hyperion Ave, Silver Lake ☎ 323/665-0545. A distinctive array of French and other international cheeses, priced moderately to steeply. The delicious sandwiches may be your best bet.

Standard Sweets and Snacks 18600 Pioneer Blvd, Artesia ☎ 562/860-6364. Good Indian finger-food joint selling vegetarian *dosas* (pancakes) and appealing sweets.

Wild Oats Community Market 3476 S Centinela Ave, West LA ☎ 310/636-1800. An excellent organic wine store and deli that also offers flavorful fruit drinks at its smoothie bar.

Books

LA is home to a great variety of **bookstores**, from chain dealers like Barnes and Noble and Borders to the more appealing **specialist** and **secondhand bookstores**, worthy of several hours' browsing along miles of dusty shelves.

Specialist bookstores

A Different Light 8853 Santa Monica Blvd, West Hollywood ☎ 310/854-6601. The city's best-known gay and lesbian bookstore, with monthly art shows, readings, and musical events. See also "Gay and lesbian LA," p.191.

Koma Books 548 S Spring St, Downtown ☎ 323/239-0030. Mayhem, true crime, zines, and paranoid conspiracy rants: the extremes of information in print. A small shop with a large mail-order base.

Bodhi Tree 8585 Melrose Ave, West Hollywood ☎ 310/659-1733. New Age, occult, and all things spiritually trendy. Cozy space abounds with enlightened regulars, in a very chic part of town.

Book Soup 8818 W Sunset Blvd, West Hollywood ☎ 310/659-3110. Great selection, right on Sunset Strip, open daily until midnight. Narrow, winding aisles stuffed pell-mell with books. Celebs are sometimes known to come in, attempting to look studious.

Either/Or 950 Aviation Blvd, Hermosa Beach ☎ 310/374-2060. A voluminous fiction selection and a wide variety of New Age tomes, with free publications littering the floor. Open till 11pm.

Hennessey and Ingalls 1254 Third Street Promenade, Santa Monica ☎ 310/458-9074. An impressive range of art and architecture books makes this bookstore the best in LA in its field, though quite expensive.

Larry Edmunds Book Shop 6644 Hollywood Blvd, Hollywood ☎ 323/463-3273. Stacks of books, many of them out of print, on every aspect of film and theater, with movie stills and posters.

Midnight Special 1318 Third Street Promenade, Santa Monica ☎ 310/393-2923. A large general bookstore, with eccentrically filled shelves and a broad focus on lefty politics and social sciences. Always attracts a good crowd of regulars and tourist interlopers.

Norton Simon Museum Bookstore 411 W Colorado Blvd, Pasadena ☎626/449-6840. Prices in this museum-attached store are lower than in any other major art bookstore in LA, and the stock is superb – often with sizeable volumes on artists in the museum's collection.

Samuel French Theatre & Film Bookshop 7623 Sunset Blvd, West Hollywood ☎323/876-0570. Small store loaded with books on acting, movies, and the performing arts. Always a popular spot, especially for writers and actors.

Sisterhood Bookstore 1351 Westwood Blvd, West LA ☎310/477-7300. Westside landmark with music, cards, books, and literature pertaining to the national and international women's movement. See also "Women's LA," p.192.

Vroman's 695 E Colorado Blvd, Pasadena ☎626/449-5320. One of the Valley's major retailers, offering a good selection with a café. Although there are no real bargains, other, smaller used-book stores can be found within a few blocks.

Secondhand books

Acres of Books 240 Long Beach Blvd, Long Beach ☎562/437-6980. Worth a trip down the Blue Line Metrorail just to wallow in LA's largest, and most disorganized, secondhand collection.

Atlantis Book Shop 144 S San Fernando Blvd ☎818/845-6467. History, fiction, and politics are some of the specialties, but especially the paranormal, extraterrestrial, and mythological – as the name indicates.

Brand Book Shop 231 N Brand Blvd, Glendale ☎818/507-5943. Valley used-book seller with a broad range of liberal arts titles and particular strengths in entertainment, history, and politics.

Cosmopolitan Book Shop 7017 Melrose Ave ☎323/938-7119. The cozier Westside equivalent to *Acres of Books*, a dealer loaded with thousands of titles stacked high on oversized bookcases, on a variety of subjects but especially strong on film and media.

Wilshire Books 3018 Wilshire Blvd, Santa Monica ☎310/828-3115. The best used bookstore in LA for its size, which is quite small and cramped. Still, a solid collection of art, politics, religion, music, science, and other books, all well-organized.

Music

Record stores are even more plentiful than bookstores in LA. Although the number of stores selling LPs has dropped, the plunge has stopped for the moment, thanks to the demand of die-hard fans and new-school DJs scratching vinyl for dance and hip-hop grooves. Most of the stores below carry used LPs, CDs, and cassettes.

A-1 Record Finders 5639 Melrose Ave ☎213/732-6737. One of the top spots on the West Coast for tracking down old vinyl records, featuring rows of LPs from many different eras and countless genres, whether an obscure 1960s garage-rock band or a legendary blues singer of the 1940s.

Aron's Records 1150 N Highland Ave, Hollywood ☎323/469-4700. Secondhand discs – all styles, all prices, huge stock. Getting help can be a problem; the place is often packed.

Heavy Rotation 12354 Ventura Blvd, Studio City ☎818/769-8882. Cheap prices for used CDs, laserdiscs, cassettes, and video games, as well as an interesting selection of promotional records scattered throughout the stock.

Moby Disc 28 E Colorado Blvd, Pasadena ☎626/449-9975. Solid secondhand and deletion stocklist of all genres.

Penny Lane 12 W Colorado Blvd, Pasadena ☎626/564-0161. New and used records at cheap prices; this store features listening stations from which you can sample up to a hundred discs. Also in LA at 7563 Melrose Ave (☎323/651-3000) and 10914 Kinross Ave (☎310/208-5611).

Poo-Bah Records 1101 E Walnut Ave, Pasadena ☎626/449-3359. American and imported New Wave, plus other genres.

Record Surplus 11609 W Pico Blvd, West LA ☎310/478-4217. Massive LP collection of surf music, ancient rock'n'roll, 60s soundtracks and unintentionally hilarious spoken-word recordings.

Rhino Records 1720 Westwood Blvd, West LA ☎310/474-8685. The biggest selection of international independent releases, stocked with rock, punk, funk, and everything else, not to mention the countless records put out by Rhino Records itself.

Vinyl Fetish 7305 Melrose Ave, West Hollywood ☎323/935-1300. Besides the punk and post-punk sounds, a good place to discover what's new on the LA music scene.

Listings

Airport information Burbank/Glendale/Pasadena ⊕818/840-8847, ⊛www.burbankairport.com; John Wayne/Orange County ⊕949/252-5006, ⊛www.ocair.com; LAX ⊕310/646-5252, ⊛www.los-angeles-lax.com; Long Beach ⊕562/570-2600, ⊛www.lgb.org; Ontario ⊕909/937-2700, ⊛www.lawa.org/ont/ontframe

Automobile Club of Southern California 2601 S Figueroa St, South Central LA ⊕213/741-3686, ⊛www.aaa-calif.com. For maps, guides, and other motoring information.

Beach information Coastal weather conditions for Malibu ⊕310/457-9701, Santa Monica 310/578-0478, South Bay ⊕310/379-8471.

Coast Guard Search and Rescue Los Angeles/Long Beach ⊕562/980-4444, Orange County/Newport Beach ⊕949/834-3800

Consulates UK, 11766 Wilshire Blvd #1200, West LA (⊕310/481-0031); Canada, 550 S Hope St, 9th Floor, Downtown (⊕213/346-2700); Australia, 1900 Century Plaza Towers, 2049 Century Park East, Century City (⊕323/229-4800); New Zealand, 12400 Wilshire Blvd #1150, Westwood (⊕310/207-1605)

Currency exchange Outside of banking hours, daily at LAX 6am–11pm (⊕310/649-1939).

Dental treatment The cheapest place is USC School of Dentistry, 925 W 34th St (⊕1-888/USC-DENT, ⊛www.usc.edu/hsc/dental/patient_care) on the USC Campus, costing $50–200. Turn up and be prepared to wait all day. You can also get emergency treatment at the LA Dental Society, 3660 Wilshire Blvd #1152 (⊕213/380-7669, ⊛www.ladentalsociety.com).

Directory inquiries Local ⊕411 (this is a free call at pay phones); long distance 1, then area code, then 555-1212.

Emergencies ⊕911. For less urgent needs: fire ⊕323/890-4194; civil defense and disaster services ⊕213/974-1120; police ⊕213/625-3311; poison control center ⊕1-800/777-6476; food poisoning reports ⊕213/240-7821; earthquake tips ⊕818/787-3737.

Hospitals The following have 24hr emergency departments: Cedars-Sinai Medical Center, 8700 Beverly Blvd, Beverly Hills (⊕310/855-6517 or 423-8780, ⊛www.csmc.edu); Good Samaritan Hospital, 1225 Wilshire Blvd, Downtown (⊕213/977-2121, ⊛www.goodsam.org); UCLA Medical Center, 10833 Le Conte Ave, Westwood (⊕310/825-9111, ⊛www.healthcare.ucla.edu).

International newspapers The USC and UCLA campuses have libraries holding overseas newspapers. Day-old English and European papers are on sale at Universal News Agency, 1645 N Las Palmas Ave (daily 7am–midnight), and World Book and News, 1652 N Cahuenga Blvd (24hr), both in Hollywood.

Left luggage At Greyhound stations and LAX for around $1 a day ($2.50 for larger lockers).

Mexican Tourist Office and Consulate 2401 W 6th St, 5th floor, Downtown (⊕1-800/44-MEXICO or 213/351-2069, ⊛www.visitmexico.com). Call for general information or pick up a tourist card – necessary if you're crossing the border. Mon–Fri 9am–5pm.

Pharmacies 24hr pharmacy at Kaiser's West LA hospital, 6041 Cadillac Ave (⊕323/857-2151, ⊛www.kaiserpermanente.org) and at Horton & Converse, 11600 Wilshire Blvd, West LA (⊕310/478-0801).

Post office The main Downtown post office is at 760 N Main St (⊕213/617-4405), north of Union Station. Zip Code is 90012; pick up letters Mon–Fri 8am–3pm; hours are Mon–Fri 8am–7pm, Sat 8am–4pm.

Smog LA's air quality can often be very poor and, especially in the valleys in late summer, sometimes quite dangerous. An air-quality index is published daily; if the air is really bad, warnings are issued on TV, radio, and in newspapers. For more information contact the South Coast Air Quality Management District (⊕1-800/CUT-SMOG, ⊛www.aqmd.gov).

Sports Baseball: the LA Dodgers (⊕323/224-1-HIT, ⊛www.dodgers.com) play at Dodger Stadium near Downtown, seats $6–21; the American League champion Anaheim Angels (⊕1-888/796-4256 or 714/663-9000, ⊛www.angelsbaseball .com) at Anaheim Stadium in Orange County, seats $7–26. Basketball: the Staples Center Downtown hosts the NBA champion LA Lakers (⊕213/480-3232, ⊛www.lakers.com), seats $22–165+, and the less successful LA Clippers (⊕213/742-7430, ⊛www.clippers.com), seats $10–120, as well as hockey's LA Kings (⊕1-888/KINGS-LA, ⊛www.lakings.com), seats $20–100. LA's other hockey team, the Mighty Ducks, plays in Orange County at Anaheim's Arrowhead Pond (⊕714/704-2500, ⊛www.mightyducks.com), seats $15–175. Football: Los Angeles currently has no professional football teams, but Pasadena's 102,000-capacity Rose Bowl (⊕626/577-3100, ⊛www.rose-bowlstadium.com) is used for the annual New Year's Day Rose Bowl football game and is the home field for UCLA's football team (☎310/UCLA-WIN, ⓦuclabruins.ocsn.com), tickets $12–35.

Traffic Check radio news channels for updates on which freeways are suffering from congestion; if a highway section is particularly immobile, a "SigAlert" will be issued, meaning "avoid at all costs." Radio stations emphasizing traffic reports include KNX 1070 AM and KFWB 980 AM; also try ⓦwww.sigalert.com on the Internet.

Travel details

Amtrak trains

Los Angeles to: Anaheim (10 daily; 45min); Fullerton (for Disneyland) (10 daily; 35min); Las Vegas (1 daily; 10hr 30min); Oxnard (5 daily; 1hr 37min); Palm Springs (2 daily; 2hr 40min); Sacramento (1 daily; 14hr); San Bernardino (1 daily; 2hr); San Diego (10 daily; 2hr 50min); San Francisco (3 daily; 9–12hr, with required bus connections); San Juan Capistrano (10 daily; 1hr 17min); Santa Barbara (5 daily; 2hr 45min); Tucson (2 daily; 10hr); Ventura (4 daily; 1hr 50min).

Greyhound buses

Los Angeles to: Las Vegas (20 daily; 5–7hr); Palm Springs (10 daily; 3–4hr); Phoenix (12 daily; 7–9hr); Portland (7 daily; 23hr); Salt Lake City (3 daily; 16hr); San Diego (30 daily; 3hr); San Francisco (17 daily; 8–12hr); Seattle (7 daily; 27hr); Tijuana, Mexico (16 daily; 3hr 30min); Tucson (10 daily; 10–12hr).

San Diego and around

CHAPTER 2   # Highlights

❋ **Balboa Park** The museum centerpiece of San
Diego, a 1400-acre green
space loaded with histo-
ry, science, and art, and
crowned with the city's
popular zoo. See p.215

❋ **Old Town State Historic
Park** Stroll among these
twenty-five preserved
structures from mid-nine-
teenth century San Diego,
and take in the adjacent
re-creation of an eight-
eenth-century Mexican
street market. See p.219

❋ **Mission Basilica San
Diego de Alcalà** This
complex features
medieval stalls, a muse-
um with Native American
craftworks, and the
state's oldest cemetery.
See p.221

❋ **Villa Montezuma** A
bizarre explosion of
Victorian architecture in
a classic 1887 home, the
villa is loaded with stylized decor – and has a
reputation for being
haunted. See p.221

❋ **Mission Beach** The
most free-spirited and
hedonistic of the city's
surfing beaches, with
acres of bronzed flesh
and bikini babes, chaotic
bars, and even carnival
rides. See p.225

❋ **Tijuana** This Mexican
border town is a long-
time favorite for its easy
access from San Diego,
the numerous bargains
in its bazaars, and its
shopping alleys. See
p.243

San Diego and around

Lacking much of the urban chaos, freewheeling lifestyles, extremes of wealth and poverty, and social vitality of its neighboring megalopolis to the north, **San Diego** and its surrounding county represent the acceptable, conservative face of Southern California. Surpassed long ago by Los Angeles in the race to become the essential city of Southern California, San Diego was for some time considered an insignificant blot between Los Angeles and Mexico, home only to right-wing pensioners and cloistered suburbanites. That perception may slowly be changing, however, as visitors come to appreciate the city's gracefully curving bay, appealing oceanside vistas, clutch of fine museums, and big-name tourist attractions that rival anything in LA.

Outside San Diego County's eponymous urban center, you can find a host of compelling destinations. The **North County** includes the small, enticing coastal communities from the northern edge of San Diego itself to the Camp Pendleton marine base, as well as the inland vineyards and avocado groves that reach east into wilder mountain country. Beyond the tiny and insular beach towns, some of which have barely changed since the Gold Rush, several deep forests and state parks are ideal for exploring via hiking trails and obscure backroads.

South of San Diego, there's little until you reach Mexico, where **Tijuana**, just 25 miles south, serves as a fine base for visiting **Baja California**. While it may be far from the most charming destination in Mexico, Tijuana nonetheless maintains a certain low-key, if somewhat seedy, allure for thousands of day-tripping Californians every weekend. Moreover, with most of the border formalities waived for anyone traveling less than twenty miles or so into Mexico, quick visits to the party-heavy beach burgs of Rosarito and Ensenada are also a tempting draw.

Of course, there's also heavy traffic in the other direction, as countless Mexicans stream into Southern California, above and below official radar. Many are hotel and restaurant workers, but first- and especially second-generation immigrants are gradually becoming integrated into less menial levels of the workforce. However, unlike in LA, where Latino newcomers are beginning to flex their political muscle, those of San Diego County are largely ghettoized, still viewed by the white gentry as welfare-cheating detriments to society, rather than essential boosters of the local economy.

San Diego

Baking in the sun, its humidity tempered by ocean breezes, **SAN DIEGO** is an ideal holiday resort for hordes of tourists, most of whom arrive for its terrific beaches, major attractions like the San Diego Zoo and SeaWorld, and excellent museums in Balboa Park. More enterprising visitors may also wish to explore the city's historic Downtown, surprisingly restored and preserved in this developer-friendly community.

The traditional image of San Diegans as conformist, affluent, and Republican is true to a large extent – San Diego has as much in common with Salt Lake City or Phoenix as it does with Los Angeles or San Francisco. Yet it's also an amiable and easy-going place, where increasing numbers of liberal and libertarian young students and professionals are slowly diminishing the dull smugness and orthodoxy for which the city was long notorious. The presence of three college campuses – SDSU, UCSD, and USD – has also helped the city lose some of its rigid and reactionary character.

Some history

The first European to land on Californian soil, Portuguese adventurer and Spanish agent Juan Rodríguez Cabrillo, put ashore at Point Loma, ten miles from the center of today's San Diego, in 1542. White settlement didn't begin until two centuries later, however, with the building in 1769 of a Catholic mission – the first in California – and a military garrison on a site overlooking San Diego Bay. Later conflict between land-holding *Californios* and the fresh waves of settlers from the east led to America's capture of San Diego in 1847, an event contemporaneous with the Mexican/American War. However, the city missed out on the new mail route to the West and was plagued by a series of droughts through the 1860s, causing many bankruptcies and economic problems. Although the transcontinental Santa Fe Railroad link was short-lived – repeated flooding forced the terminus to be moved north to Los Angeles, permanently depriving San Diego of direct rail service to the East – its establishment resulted in an economic boom through the 1880s. In 1915, the first of two international expositions in Balboa Park, which were to establish San Diego's nationwide reputation, occurred.

In part because of its lack of direct railway access to the East Coast, the city has long been overshadowed by Los Angeles in trade and economic significance, though it has used its strategic seaside location to become a military stronghold. During World War II, the US Navy took advantage of the city's many sheltered bays and made San Diego its Pacific Command Center – a function it retains. Although the military continues to play a large role in the local economy, in recent years its importance has been overshadowed by tourism.

Perhaps more than anything else, then, it is San Diego's reputation as an ocean-oriented "resort city" that provides much of its modern relevance. Although it has a formidable population of 1.2 million people, making it the seventh-largest city in the US, for most visitors it's synonymous only with getting a sparkling bronze tan, yachting around the bay, surfing a killer break, and hanging out at the zoo.

Arrival and information

Drivers will find it simple to reach the city center from any of three interstate highways: I-5, the main link from Los Angeles and the rest of California, passes through the northern parts of the central city; from the east, I-8 runs through Hotel Circle before terminating in Ocean Beach; and I-15, coming from inland San Diego County and Arizona, cuts through the city's eastern suburbs. The road system in San Diego suffers from poor planning, however, and often if you miss a freeway exit, you may be in for a long, frustrating detour; specific directions are essential. **Parking lots** are scattered around

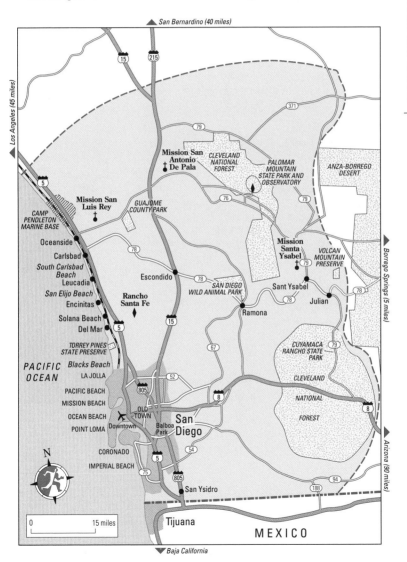

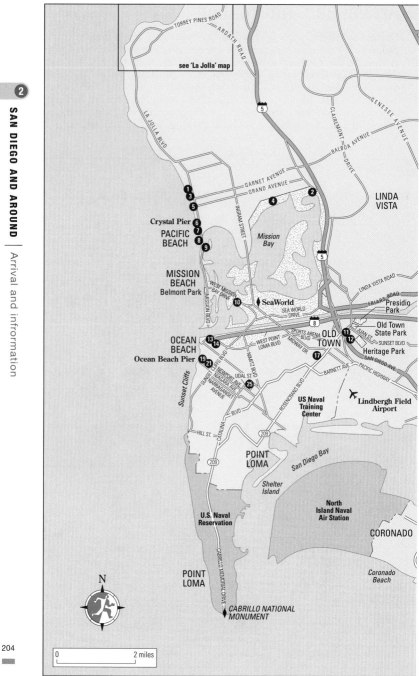

TORREY PINES ROAD
ARDATH ROAD

see 'La Jolla' map

5

LA JOLLA BLVD

GENESEE AVENUE

CLAIRMONT AVENUE

BALBOA AVENUE

GARNET AVENUE
GRAND AVENUE

LINDA
VISTA

INGRAM STREET

Crystal Pier

PACIFIC
BEACH

Mission
Bay

5

MISSION
BEACH
Belmont Park

WEST MISSION BAY DRIVE

MISSION BLVD

SeaWorld

LINDA VISTA ROAD

FRIARS ROAD

Presidio
Park

SEA WORLD
DRIVE

8

SPORTS ARENA BLVD

OCEAN
BEACH

Ocean Beach Pier

SUNSET CLIFFS BLVD

NIMITZ BLVD

WEST POINT
LOMA BLVD

MIDWAY DR

OLD
TOWN

JUAN ST

Old Town
State Park

SUNSET BLVD

Heritage Park

SAN DIEGO AVE

NEWPORT AVE
NIAGARA AVE
NARRAGANSETT
AVENUE

UDAL ST

BARNETT AVE

PACIFIC HIGHWAY

ROSECRANS BLVD

CATALINA BLVD

HILL ST.

209

US Naval
Training
Center

Lindbergh Field
Airport

Sunset Cliffs

POINT
LOMA

209

San Diego Bay

Shelter
Island

U.S. Naval
Reservation

North
Island Naval
Air Station

CORONADO

POINT
LOMA

CABRILLO MEMORIAL DRIVE

CABRILLO NATIONAL
MONUMENT

Coronado
Beach

N

0   2 miles

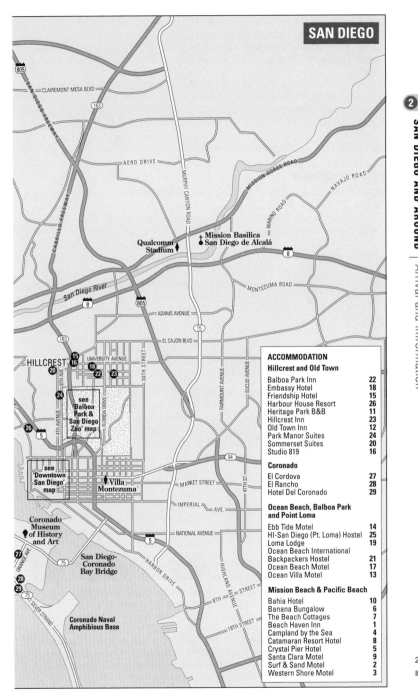

SAN DIEGO

ACCOMMODATION

Hillcrest and Old Town

Balboa Park Inn	22
Embassy Hotel	18
Friendship Hotel	15
Harbour House Resort	26
Heritage Park B&B	11
Hillcrest Inn	23
Old Town Inn	12
Park Manor Suites	24
Sommerset Suites	20
Studio 819	16

Coronado

El Cordova	27
El Rancho	28
Hotel Del Coronado	29

Ocean Beach, Balboa Park and Point Loma

Ebb Tide Motel	14
HI-San Diego (Pt. Loma) Hostel	25
Loma Lodge	19
Ocean Beach International Backpackers Hostel	21
Ocean Beach Motel	17
Ocean Villa Motel	13

Mission Beach & Pacific Beach

Bahia Hotel	10
Banana Bungalow	6
The Beach Cottages	7
Beach Haven Inn	1
Campland by the Sea	4
Catamaran Resort Hotel	8
Crystal Pier Hotel	5
Santa Clara Motel	9
Surf & Sand Motel	2
Western Shore Motel	3

Downtown, and there's plenty of metered parking – free overnight, but not allowed on evenings reserved for street cleaning.

All forms of **public transportation** drop you in the heart of Downtown San Diego. **Trains** use the Santa Fe Railroad Depot, close to the western end of Broadway, while the Greyhound **bus** terminal is more central at Broadway and First Avenue. Lindbergh Field **airport** is only two miles from Downtown; it has two terminals, East and West, connected to Downtown by bus #2 ($1.50), the service starting around 6am and finishing just after midnight. Given the short distance, **taxis** to Downtown aren't expensive, and quite a few hotels – even some of the budget ones – offer guests a free **airport limo** service. The main **car rental** firms all have desks at the airport (see "Listings" on p.235).

Information

A good first stop in the city is the **International Visitor Information Center**, 11 Horton Plaza, Downtown at F Street and First Avenue (Mon–Sat 8.30am–5pm, June–Aug also Sun 11am–5pm; ☎619/236-1212, ⓦwww.sandiego.org, Ⓔsdinfo@sandiego.org), which has maps, the useful *Official Visitors Guide*, as well as other publications covering city arts and golf courses. Another useful source is the HI-AYH office inside the hostel foyer at 521 Market St (daily 7am–midnight; ☎619/525-1531, ⓦwww.sandiegohostels.com). For eating and entertainment information, the free, weekly *San Diego Reader* and *Metropolitan* can both be found in many shops, bars, and clubs; the "Night and Day" section of Thursday's *San Diego Union-Tribune* (35¢) is also useful.

City transportation

Despite its size, **getting around** San Diego without a car is slow but not terribly difficult, whether you use buses, the tram-like trolley, or a rented bike. Traveling can be harder at night, with most routes closing down around 11pm or midnight. The transportation system won't break anyone's budget, especially with longer-term tickets and passes reducing costs over a few days or weeks. **Taxis** are also an option: the average fare is $2 for the first mile and $1.50 for each mile thereafter.

Buses

Of the three major companies operating **buses** in the San Diego area, by far the most prominent is San Diego Transit Corporation, or SDTC (☎619/233-3004 or 1-800/266-6883), which offers a typical one-way fare of $2, or up to $3.50 for the most distant routes; transfers are free, and the exact fare is required when

---

Reduced-rate tickets and passes

If you intend to use public transportation a lot, buy the **Day Tripper Transit Pass**, which lasts one-to-four consecutive days ($5, $8, $10, and $12, respectively) and is valid on any San Diego Transit bus, as well as the trolley and the San Diego Bay ferry (which sails between Broadway Pier Downtown and Coronado; $2 each way, $2.50 including bicycles – see p.222 for more details). If you're around for a few weeks and using buses regularly, get a **Monthly Pass**, giving unlimited rides throughout one calendar month for $54, or the half-price, two-week version which goes on sale midway through each month (pass information at ☎1-800/COMMUTE, ⓦwww.sdcommute.com).

The following buses connect **Downtown San Diego** with the surrounding area:

Balboa Park #1, #3, #3A, #7 #7A, #7B, #25	Imperial Beach #901, #933, #934
	La Jolla #30, #34, #34A
Coronado #19, #901, #902, #903, #904	Mission Beach #34, #34A
East San Diego #1, #7, #7B, #15,	Ocean Beach #923
#15A, #70, #115	Old Town #5, #5A, #34, #34A
Hillcrest #1, #3, #11, #16 #25	Pacific Beach #30, #34, #34A

boarding (dollar bills are accepted). Service is reliable and frequent, particularly Downtown, which is known on route maps and timetables as "Center City." Other major operators include North County Transit District (fares $1.50; ℡1-800/COMMUTE, Ⓦwww.gonctd.com) and County Transit System (fares $2; ℡619/874-4001).

If you have any queries about San Diego's local buses, call **The Transit Store**, at First and Broadway (Mon–Sat 8.30am–5.30pm; ℡619/234-1060), for detailed timetables, the free *Regional Transit Guide*, and information on the Day Tripper Transit Pass and monthly passes. If you know your point of departure and destination, you can get automated bus information by phoning ℡619/685-4900.

The Trolley

Complementing city bus lines is the **San Diego Trolley**, often called the "Tijuana Trolley" because it travels sixteen miles from the Santa Fe Depot (departures from C Street) to the US–Mexico border in San Ysidro – a 45-minute trip. Fares are $1.25–2.50, depending on how long you stay on. One-way tickets should be bought from the machines at trolley stops, which also offer round-trip tickets; occasionally an inspector may request proof of payment. Apart from being a cheap way to reach Mexico, the trolley is a valuable link to the southern San Diego communities of National City, Chula Vista, and Palm City. From the transfer station at Imperial and 12th, the trolley's Euclid Avenue line makes much of southeastern San Diego easily accessible, and it also runs to Old Town San Diego, where a transit center links the trolley to ten bus lines as well as with the North County Coaster. Trolleys leave every fifteen minutes during the day; the last service back from San Ysidro leaves at 1am (hourly through Saturday night), so an evening of south-of-the-border revelry and a return to San Diego the same night is quite possible. The trolley service resumes its normal hours on Sunday morning at 5am, from Central Station in Old Town's Central Transit Station.

Not to be confused with the San Diego Trolley, the **Old Town Trolley Tour** is a two-hour narrated trip around San Diego's most popular spots, including Downtown, Balboa Park, the San Diego Zoo, Old Town, and Coronado, aboard an open-sided motor-driven carriage. A single ticket (available daily 9am–4pm, summer until 5pm; $24, kids $12) lasts all day and you can board and reboard the trolley at any of its stops. If you're short of time, the tour is a simple way to cover a lot of ground quickly, and the driver's commentary is corny but reasonably informative. Leaflets detailing the route are found in hotel lobbies and at tourist information offices (℡619/298-8687, Ⓦwww.trolleytours.com).

The Coaster

North County San Diego is linked to Downtown via a simple light-rail system called **The Coaster**, which includes eight stops from Oceanside through Carlsbad, Encinitas, Solana Beach, Sorrento Valley, and Old Town, ending up at the Santa Fe Railroad Depot. On weekday mornings, six trains run southbound, with the same number returning northbound for the late-afternoon and early-evening commute, while four trains make the trip on Saturdays. Fares range from $3.50 to $4.75 one way, $1.50 to $2.25 for seniors, and $95 to $130 for a monthly pass (information ☎1-800/COASTER). The Coaster also provides a good alternative way of reaching Los Angeles, with transfers at Oceanside onto the Metrolink commuter rail system (see "Public transportation" in Los Angeles, p.80), which links San Diego County all the way to Downtown LA and even up to Oxnard in Ventura County.

Cycling

San Diego is a good city for **cycling**, with many miles of bike paths as well as some fine park and coastal rides. **Rental shops** are easy to find, especially around bike-friendly areas, and some outlets also rent out skateboards, rollerblades and surfboards (prices for all start around $5 per hour, $12 per day; and $25–35 per day for surfboards). Reliable outlets include Bicycle Barn, 746 Emerald St, Pacific Beach (☎858/581-3665); Rent-a-Bike, 523 Island St, Downtown (☎619/232-4700); Hamel's Action Sport Center, 704 Ventura Place, Mission Beach (☎858/488-50500); and Cheap Rentals, 3685 Mission Blvd, Mission Beach (☎858/488-9070). You can carry bikes on the San Diego Bay ferry for an extra 50¢, and on several city bus routes for no added charge. Board at any bus stop displaying a bike sign and tack your machine securely to the back of the bus. The Transit Store (☎619/234-1060) provides information on bicycle commuting, and distributes free passes that allow you to take your bike on the trolley.

Accommodation

Accommodation is readily available in San Diego, with abundant hotels and motels, and a decent selection of hostels and B&Bs – only travelers with tents are likely to feel restricted, with just a few inconveniently located and comparatively expensive **campgrounds** from which to choose.

Downtown offers the best base if you're without a car and features two hostels and a batch of surprisingly inexpensive hotels in renovated buildings. Prices are marginally more expensive at the many beach motels, though Ocean Beach and Pacific Beach have hostels, too. Another group of motels can be found around Old Town (useful if you're driving or just staying for a night while seeing the immediate area), and some of the cheapest motels line the approach roads to the city.

Bed and breakfasts are increasingly popular, especially in Hillcrest. Contact the Downtown visitor center (see p.206), or send $3.95 for the *Bed & Breakfast Directory for San Diego*, PO Box 3292, San Diego, CA 92163 (☎619/297-3130, ⓦwww.sandiegobandb.com).

If you're arriving in summer, when prices increase and availability is limited, it's wise to **book in advance**. The International Visitor Center Downtown has numerous accommodation leaflets (many of which carry discount vouchers) and will phone hotels, motels, or hostels on your behalf at no charge.

Gay travelers are unlikely to encounter hostility in San Diego, and several hotels and bed and breakfasts are particularly noted for their friendliness (see "Gay and lesbian San Diego," p.234).

Downtown

See the map on p.212 for locations.

Corinthian Suites 1840 Fourth Ave ☎619/236-1600, ℻619/231-4734. Gay-friendly hotel with clean rooms, cable TV, refrigerators, and microwaves, in a great location two blocks from Balboa Park. ❸

Golden West Hotel 720 Fourth Ave ☎619/233-7596. Certifiably seedy old favorite dating from 1913. Great historic lobby, central location in the Gaslamp District, and rock-bottom rates balanced by murky rooms and creepy clientele. Ask to see your room first. ❶

Horton Grand 311 Island Ave at Third Ave ☎619/544-1886 or 1-800/542-1886, ⓦwww.hortongrand.com. Classy, modernized amalgam of two century-old hotels, with fireplaces in most of the 108 rooms, staff dressed in Victorian-era costumes, on-site restaurant, and piano bar. ❻

J Street Inn 222 J St between Third and Fourth aves ☎619/696-6922. Located near the Gaslamp District, Greyhound terminal, and the waterfront, this little gem has in-room microwaves, refrigerators, and cable TV. ❹

La Pensione 1700 India St ☎619/236-8000. Great value small hotel in a quiet area within walking distance of the city center. The rooms, around a central court, are small but tastefully decorated and equipped with microwave, fridge, cable TV, and on-site laundry. ❸

Maryland Hotel 630 F St ☎619/239-9243. Amenable, restored hotel, if somewhat lacking in frills, in a good Downtown location with available long-term rates. Restaurant and laundry access on site. ❸

The U.S. Grant 326 Broadway between Third and Fourth aves ☎619/232-3121 or 1-800/237-5029, ⓦwww.usgranthotel.com. Directly across from Horton Plaza, Downtown's poshest address since 1910, with Neoclassical design, countless chandeliers, marble floors, and cozy but elegant rooms. ❼

Villager Lodge 600 G St at Seventh Ave ☎619/238-4100, ⓦwww.villagerlodge.com. Fairly unexciting but serviceable hotel, with cable TV, microwaves, wet bars, and fridges in each room. ❺

Wyndham Emerald Plaza 400 Broadway ☎619/239-4500, ⓦwww.wyndham.com/emeraldplaza. Upscale, high-rise lodging geared for business travelers, with spacious rooms, pool, spa, and exercise facilities. ❽

Hillcrest, Balboa Park, and Old Town

See the map on p.204 for locations. For Hillcrest, see also "Gay and lesbian San Diego," p.234.

Balboa Park Inn 3402 Park Blvd, Hillcrest ☎619/298-0823, ⓦwww.balboaparkinn.com. Elegant, gay-oriented B&B within walking distance of Balboa Park and the museums. The 26 themed suites (with Parisian, Impressionist, and Tarzan motifs, to name a few) have coffee makers and mini-fridges. ❺

Embassy Hotel 3645 Park Blvd, Balboa Park ☎619/296-3141. Basic accommodation close to Balboa Park and with all the usual amenities – restaurant, some kitchenettes, and free in-room movies and local phone calls – for low rates. ❷

Heritage Park B&B 2470 Heritage Park Row, Old Town ☎619/299-6832 or 1-800/995-2470, ⓦwww.heritageparkinn.com. A restored Queen Anne mansion in Heritage Park, chock-full of Victorian trappings. Breakfast and afternoon tea are included, and classic movies are shown nightly. ❻

Old Town Inn 4444 Pacific Hwy, Old Town ☎1-800/643-3025, ⓦwww.oldtown-inn.com. Convenient location within a few strides of the Old Town's liveliest areas, offering complimentary breakfast and clean, simple rooms. ❹

Sommerset Suites 606 Washington St, Hillcrest ☎619/692-5200 or 1-800/962-9665, ⓦwww.sommersetsuites.com. Eighty well-equipped suites with kitchenettes, offering pool, spa, central location, and complimentary breakfast. ❻

Studio 819 819 University Ave, Hillcrest ☎619/542-0819, ⓦwww.studio819.com. Standard but safe budget accommodation in the heart of Hillcrest. Primarily a residential hotel, though it offers a microwave, kitchenette, and fridge in each room. ❷

Coronado and Ocean Beach

See the map on p.204 for locations.

Ebb Tide Motel 5082 W Point Loma Blvd, Ocean Beach ☎619/224-9339. Modest-sized motel that's handy for the beach and features clean, adequate rooms with kitchenettes and cable TV. ❸

El Cordova 1351 Orange Ave, Coronado ☎619/435-4131 or 1-800/229-2032 , ⓦwww.elcordovahotel.com. The best deal in Coronado, but no secret, so you'll need to reserve at least six months ahead. Lovely rooms in Hacienda-style buildings built in 1902, and arranged around lovely gardens. There's the obligatory pool, and some rooms have kitchenettes. ⑥

El Rancho 370 Orange Ave, Coronado ☎619/435-2251, ⓦwww.geocities.com/ranchomot. Small but attractive motel with pleasant decor, and one of the cheapest deals on this side of the water. Rooms come equipped with microwaves and fridges, and some even have Jacuzzis. ④

Hotel del Coronado 1500 Orange Ave, Coronado ☎619/522-8000 or 1-800/468-3533, ⓦwww.hoteldel.com. The luxurious place that put Coronado on the map and is still the area's major tourist sight (see p.223) – especially after a recent $55 million restoration. ⑧

Loma Lodge 3202 Rosecrans St, Ocean Beach ☎619/222-0511 or 1-800/266-0511, ⓦwww.lomalodge.com. Among the best values in the district, a decent motel with an agreeable pool and complimentary breakfast; good for exploring the peninsula, though not close to the beach. ③

Ocean Beach Motel 5080 Newport Ave, Ocean Beach ☎619/223-7191. Small, drab motel right across the street from the beach. Not too pretty, but some rooms have ocean views and kitchenettes, and you can't beat the location. ③

Ocean Villa Motel 5142 W Point Loma Blvd, Ocean Beach ☎619/224-3481 or 1-800/759-0012. Usefully placed for visiting the sands; the ocean-view rooms feature kitchenettes, fridges, and microwaves; there's also a pool. ③

Mission Beach and Pacific Beach
See the map on p.204 for locations.

Bahia Resort Hotel 998 W Mission Bay Drive, Mission Beach ☎858/488-0551 or 1-800/576-4229, ⓦwww.bahiahotel.com. Sprawling resort offering a restaurant, pool, hot tub, tennis courts, and very close proximity to the beach. ⑦

Beach Cottages 4255 Ocean Blvd, Mission Beach ☎858/483-7440, ⓦwww.beachcottages.com. Beside the beach, three blocks south of the pier, this relaxing spot offers a range of accommodation, from cottages to motel rooms to apartments. Most units have kitchenettes, all have fridges. ④-⑦

Beach Haven Inn 4740 Mission Blvd, Pacific Beach ☎858/272-3812 or 1-800/831-6323, ⓦwww.beachhaveninn.com. Comfortable, tastefully decorated rooms around a heated pool; continental breakfast included. One of the nicest places to unwind at the beach. ⑥

Catamaran Resort Hotel 3999 Mission Blvd, Pacific Beach ☎1-800/422-8386,

ⓦwww.catamaranresort.com. A range of upscale units, from entry-level garden-view rooms to swank bayside suites; also with on-site restaurant, bar, water sports, spa, Jacuzzi, and volleyball courts. ⑦-⑨

Crystal Pier Hotel 4500 Ocean Blvd, Pacific Beach ☎858/483-6983 or 1-800/748-5894, ⓦwww.crystalpier.com. Quaint, deluxe cottages situated on the pier. All units are suites with private decks and most have kitchenettes. Very pricey, but you stay literally on the water. ⑧

Santa Clara Motel 839 Santa Clara Place, Mission Beach ☎858/488-1193. Adequate, no-frills rooms with kitchenettes. An easy walk from the sands and a good half-mile north of Belmont Park. ③

Surf & Sand Motel 4666 Mission Blvd, Pacific Beach ☎858/483-7420. Clean and cozy motel near the beach, with pool, cable TV, and mini-fridges or kitchenettes. ⑥

Western Shore Motel 4345 Mission Bay Drive, Mission Beach ☎858/273-1121. A very standard but clean motel approximately two miles from the water. ③

La Jolla
See the map on p.227 for locations.

The Grand Colonial 910 Prospect St ☎858/454-2181 or 1-800/826-1278, ⓦwww.thegrandcolonial.com. A Twenties landmark in the heart of La Jolla and a short walk from the cove. Cozy but elegant rooms and some larger suites, with excellent package deals – especially in winter. ⑦-⑨

Hotel Parisi 1111 Prospect St ☎1-877/4-PARISI, ⓦwww.hotelparisi.com. Top-notch boutique hotel with a New Age twist, offering "feng shui" design and rooms with balconies, CD and VCR players, and some ocean views. If all this luxury still doesn't relax you, call the hotel's resident shrink for advice. ⑨

La Jolla Bed & Breakfast 7753 Draper Ave ☎858/456-2066 or 1-800/582-2466, ⓦwww.innlajolla.com. Designed in 1913 by early-modernist Irving Gill, a collection of fifteen themed rooms – topped by the Irving Gill Penthouse – with tranquil gardens, great service, and nice proximity to the beach and art museum. ⑦

La Jolla Cove Suites 1155 Coast Blvd ☎858/459-2621 or 1-888/LA-JOLLA, ⓦwww.lajollacove.com. Kitchen-equipped rooms and suites right by the sea – some of the rooms have sprawling oceanfront balconies. Also with on-site Jacuzzi, pool and complimentary breakfast. ⑦

La Valencia Hotel 1132 Prospect St ☎858/454-0771 or 1-800/451-0772. Radiant pink favorite of Hollywood celebs in the 1920s. Today a less glamorous spot, but no less plush, with beautiful decor, nice sea views, pool, spa, and fitness center. ⑧

Prospect Park Inn 1110 Prospect St ☎858/454-0133 or 1-800/433-1609, ⓦwww.prospectparkinn.com. Charming European-style lodge, well priced for the area, with ocean views, fridges, balconies, complimentary breakfast, and afternoon tea on the sundeck. The inn offers studios and a nice range of rooms. ⑦

Hostels

Banana Bungalow 707 Reed Ave, Pacific Beach ☎858/273-3060 or 1-800/5-HOSTEL, ⓦwww.bananabungalow.com. Although the rooms are small and drab, the beachside location, volleyball, cookouts, and lively atmosphere make it worthwhile. Free buffet breakfasts, keg nights, and a communal kitchen are included. Six-person dorms run $18. Turn off Mission Boulevard at no. 4250, or take bus #34.

Grand Pacific Hostel 726 Fifth Ave between F and G sts, Downtown ☎619/232-3100 or 1-800/438-8622, ⓦwww.usahostels.com/sandiego/s-index. Well-placed hostel on the edge of the Gaslamp District. Beds in six- to eight-bed rooms with sheets and continental breakfast for $19; doubles available for $46. Free bike use, organized

tours to Tijuana, and a discount shuttle to LA make this one of the best city hostels.

HI-Point Loma Hostel 3790 Udall St, Ocean Beach ☎619/223-4778 or 1-800/909-4776, ⓦwww.hostelweb.com/sandiego. Well-run and friendly, though without the party atmosphere prevailing in other hostels. Located a few miles from the beach and six miles from Downtown (via bus #35), the hostel features a large kitchen, a patio, and a common room. Eight-bed (or smaller) dorms $15–$18, private rooms for three or more, $20 per person.

HI-San Diego Downtown Hostel 521 Market St at Fifth, Downtown ☎619/525-1530 or 1-800/909-4776, ⓦwww.hostelweb.com/sandiego. Centrally located, especially good for the Gaslamp District and Horton Plaza. $18 for HI members, $21 for others, and private doubles from $40. Free coffee and bagels. No curfew.

Ocean Beach International Backpackers Hostel 4961 Newport Ave, Ocean Beach ☎619/223-7873 or 1-800/339-7263, ⓦmembers.aol.com/OBlhostel/hostel. Lively spot a block from the beach, offering barbecues, bike and surfboard rentals, and nightly movies. Space in a four-bed dorm $16, double rooms $18, all with sheets, showers, and continental breakfast.

Campgrounds

Of the city's half-dozen **campgrounds**, only two accept tents. The best-placed of these is *Campland on the Bay*, 2211 Pacific Beach Drive (☎858/581-4200 or 1-800/4-BAYFUN, ⓦwww.campland.com), where a basic site starts at $40, though more elaborate "Super Sites" can run $90–173. *Campland* boasts a number of pools and hot tubs, as well as a marina, activity rentals, and a general store; it is linked to Downtown by bus #30. For a more serene alternative, San Elijo Beach State Park, Rte 21 south of Cardiff-by-the-Sea, offers sites from $17–$25. Call ☎1-800/444-7275 for reservations.

The City

With the urban core and suburban sprawl of many other American metropolises, San Diego manages to retain a relaxed atmosphere and slow pace that make it ideal for casual visitors and beachside sun worshippers.

The city divides into several easily defined sections, the most prominent of which is, of course, **Downtown**, where anonymous high-rise bank buildings and hotel complexes stand beside older, more modest structures from San Diego's earlier boom days, notably in the **Gaslamp District**, home to a number of worthwhile cafés and bars. Along with being the hub of the public transit system, Downtown offers most of the city's premier nightlife, and has much of its inexpensive accommodation.

A few miles northeast, the well-maintained parkland of sizeable **Balboa Park** contains many of the city's major museums and the ever-popular San Diego

Zoo, and is perfectly suited for strolls and picnics through acres of carefully tended gardens and natural greenery. Just to the northwest of Downtown, **Old Town San Diego** was the spot where the first white settlement developed near the site of the original San Diego Mission, an area now featuring an array of modern shops and theme restaurants evoking the style of Old Mexico. Although the sense of history here strains credibility, it's still worth seeing, at least for a brief visit, and is easily accessible via a convenient trolley stop. Other districts near Downtown don't have any official "sights," but can be interesting as well. **East San Diego** offers a large college campus that livens up what is an otherwise featureless sprawl, while **Hillcrest**'s eclectic mix of yuppies, gays, bohemians, and artists makes it one of the city's best areas for dining and nightlife.

If you're mainly interested in total relaxation, simple beach-bumming or mild amusement, the **beach towns** and the aquatic diversions of the **SeaWorld** theme park, both within easy reach of Downtown, are good for a half-day trip – or longer.

Downtown San Diego

Vibrant and colorful, **DOWNTOWN**, roughly bordered by the curve of the San Diego Bay and I-5 freeway, is the inevitable nexus of San Diego and the best place to start a tour of the city. Begun in the late 1970s, various preservation and restoration projects have improved many of the area's older buildings (notably in the restaurant district of Little Italy; see "Eating," p.228), resulting in several blocks of stylishly renovated turn-of-the-century architecture, while

the more recent corporate towers showcase the city's growing economic dependence on the Pacific Rim. Although Downtown is largely safe by day, at night it can be unwelcoming, with the financial zone becoming a high-rise dead zone. After-dark activities are therefore best confined to the popular and well-policed Gaslamp District.

Along Broadway

Creating an excellent first impression of San Diego for travelers arriving by train, the **Santa Fe Railroad Depot**'s tall Moorish archways were built to welcome visitors to the 1915 Panama–California International Exposition in Balboa Park. The depot's old historic-revival architecture provides a dramatic contrast to the postmodern contours of the neighboring **American Plaza**, an array of high-rise offices and glass-roofed public areas built during San Diego's international finance-fueled boom of the mid-1980s. The plaza encompasses the main terminal of the San Diego Trolley, as well as the Downtown branch of the **Museum of Contemporary Art**, or MCA San Diego, 1001 Kettner Blvd (11am–5pm; closed Wed; free; ⓦ www.mcasandiego.org), which frequently stages compelling temporary shows, and has a permanent collection focusing on American minimalism, Pop Art, and the Latino art of Southern California and Mexico. (The museum also has a La Jolla branch; see p.226.)

American Plaza marks the western end of **BROADWAY**, which slices through the center of Downtown and is most lively between Fourth and Fifth avenues, where the pedestrian traffic is a mix of shoppers, sailors, yuppies, homeless people, and tourists. Many visitors linger around the fountains on the square outside **Horton Plaza**, between First and Fourth avenues south of Broadway (Mon–Fri 10am–9pm, Sat 10am–8pm, Sun 11am–7pm, Summer and holidays Mon–Sat 10am–9pm, Sun 11am–7pm; ⓦ www.westfield.com/us/centres/california/hortonplaza), a giant mall of 137 stores and San Diego's de facto city center. Completed in 1985 at a cost of $140 million, Horton Plaza's quick success caused local real estate prices to soar and condo development to surge – and ensured that the city remained fertile terrain for mall-building for decades to come. For better or worse, the complex's whimsical, colorful postmodern style, loaded with quasi-Art Deco and southwestern motifs, heavily influenced the architecture of the city and of Southern California as well. Inevitably a colossal tourist draw, the plaza has no roof, which makes it ideal for the region's sunny climate. The open-air food court lies on the top level, and features all the usual fast-food suspects, though its main appeal is people-watching, especially on Saturdays when the suburban mall rats are ubiquitous. All the typical American department stores and chain stores are represented, though the 21-foot-tall **Jessop Clock**, on level one, is the real – perhaps the only – highlight, an intriguing antique from the California State Fair of 1907.

Further along, Broadway is less appealing until you reach a handful of the secondhand bookstores (such as Wahrenbrock's Book House, 726 Broadway) and the **Central Library**, 820 E St (Mon–Thurs 10am–9pm, Fri & Sat 9.30am–5.30pm, Sun 1–5pm; ⓦ www.ci.san-diego.ca.us/public-library), which has book sales on Friday and Saturday and an extensive reference section, where you can pore over California magazines and newspapers. Tucked away on an upper floor, the **Wangenheim Room** (Mon, Wed & Fri 1.30–4.30pm or by appointment; ☏ 619/236-5807) holds the fascinating collection of turn-of-the-century patrician Julius Wangenheim. The collection includes Babylonian cuneiform tablets, palm-leaf books from India, silk scrolls from China, and many more global curios documenting the history of the written word.

A bit less important, but still an interesting diversion, the **Firehouse Museum**, six blocks north of Broadway at 1572 Columbia St (Thurs & Fri 10am–2pm, Sat & Sun 10am–4pm; $2; ☎619/232-FIRE, ⓦwww.sdfirehousemuseum.org), is situated in San Diego's oldest firehouse and displays firefighting equipment, paraphernalia, and uniforms, with photographs vividly recalling some of San Diego's most horrific conflagrations, and the horses and firefighters who had to control them.

The Gaslamp District

South of Broadway, the **GASLAMP DISTRICT** occupies a sixteen-block area running south to K Street, bordered by Fourth and Seventh avenues. The core of San Diego when it was still a frontier town, the district – known then as **Stingaree** after the stingray found in San Diego Bay – was rife with prostitution, opium dens, and street violence until its revitalization in the late 1970s, when it started to mutate into the tourist-oriented zone it is today.

The remaining flophouses and dive bars make a dramatic contrast with the nearby yuppie-centric cafés, antique stores, and art galleries – all under the glow of ersatz "gaslamps" powered by electricity. The focus of San Diego nightlife, especially on Fridays and Saturdays, the district's relatively high police profile is designed to keep the area clean and safe, and to keep the tourists coming. While a bit artificial and overdone in places, the Gaslamp District is still intriguing to explore, not least for the scores of late nineteenth-century buildings in various stages of renovation. They're best discovered – and the area's general history gleaned – during the two-hour **walking tour** (Sat 11am; $8, includes admission to the William Heath Davis House; ☎619/233-4692) that begins from the small cobbled square at the corner of Fourth and Island avenues.

The square is within the grounds of the **William Heath Davis House**, 410 Island Ave (Tues–Sun 11am–3pm; ☎619/233-4692; $3), whose owner founded "New Town" San Diego and built his saltbox-styled home here in 1850, believing that a waterfront location would stimulate growth (the fledgling city had previously been located a few miles inland and to the north – the site of Old Town San Diego; see p.219). Although Davis was initially wrong and had to leave the city in short order, eventually dying penniless, the more influential Alonzo Horton did manage to fulfill some of his goals for waterfront growth in later years. Copious with photographs, each room of the house commemorates a different period, making the house a worthwhile stop if you're in the neighborhood.

Even without the walking tour, there are a few other interesting sights in the area, including the **Horton Grand Hotel**, opposite the William Heath Davis House, created in the mid-1980s by cobbling together two older hotels, the **Grand Horton** and the **Brooklyn Kahle Saddlery** – where Wyatt Earp lived for seven years in the early twentieth century. Dating back to the 1880s, the hotels were carefully dismantled and moved about four blocks from their original sites. In the lobby of the *Horton Grand*, the small **Chinese Museum** (☎619/544-1886; free) is a reminder of the once-thriving Chinatown area, where railroad laborers and their families lived. If you fancy staying at the hotel, see "Accommodation" on p.209.

The Embarcadero, Seaport Village, and around

The once shabby streets south of the Gaslamp District are now occupied by expensive condominiums, providing a fitting setting for the San Diego Convention Center, a $165-million complex that opened in 1989 and is mainly notable for its sail-like roof resembling the yachts in the nearby **marina**. In the same area, the pathway of the **EMBARCADERO** runs a mile or so along San Diego Bay, curling around to the western end of Downtown.

Although the path is favored by local strollers, joggers, and kite-flyers, most tourists get no farther than **SEAPORT VILLAGE**, a predictable collection of souvenir shops and restaurants, often with free clown and puppet shows for the kids. Beyond this, the Embarcadero leads to a trio of vintage ships at the **Maritime Museum**, 1492 Harbor Drive (daily 9am–9pm, closes at 8pm in winter; $6; ☎619/234-9153, ⓦwww.sdmaritime.com), highlighted by the **Star of India**, built in 1863 and now the world's oldest iron sailing ship still afloat. However, the adjacent *Berkeley*, which served for sixty years as a San Francisco Bay ferry, and the *Medea*, a small steam-powered yacht with no special displays, are of lesser appeal.

Architecture enthusiasts may enjoy the nearby **San Diego County Administration Center**, 1600 Pacific Hwy (Mon–Fri 8am–5pm; free; ☎858/694-3900), one of the more distinctive public buildings in California: a rich mix of Spanish Colonial and Beaux Arts styles, decorated with gold and azure tiles. From Harbor Drive you can walk right through the building's foyer to its main entrance, on the way viewing the eye-catching *Guardian of Water* statue and three interior murals.

Balboa Park and the San Diego Zoo

Although the fourteen hundred sumptuous acres of **BALBOA PARK** feature one of the largest collections of museums in the US, the park's real charm is its verdant landscape of trees, gardens, promenades, and Spanish Colonial buildings – and of course, the ever-popular **SAN DIEGO ZOO**. A desolate stretch of cacti, rattlesnakes, and lizards until 1898, the park began to take shape when one Kate Sessions began cultivating nurseries and planting trees in lieu of rent. The first buildings were erected for the 1915 Panama–California International Exposition, held to celebrate the opening of the Canal, and memories of its success lingered well into the Depression, until in 1935 another building program occurred for the California–Pacific International Exposition.

Along El Prado

Most of the major museums flank **EL PRADO**, the park's pedestrian-oriented east–west axis, which encompasses the charming Plaza de Panama at the heart of the park, where you'll find the **Timkin Museum of Art** (Tues–Sat 10am–4.30pm, Sun 1.30–4.30pm; Sept closed; free; ⓦgort.ucsd.edu/sj/timken). While there are a sufficient number of interesting paintings to make the stifling, formal atmosphere and evangelical zeal of the attendants worth enduring, most of the works – from the early Renaissance to the Impressionist era – are fairly minor, including those of Rembrandt and El Greco. More appealing is the museum's stirring collection of Russian religious icons.

Adjacent to the Timkin Museum, on the north side of the Plaza, the **San Diego Museum of Art** (Tues–Sun 10am–6pm, Thurs 10am–9pm; $8, kids $3; ⓦwww.sdmart.org) has few individually striking items in its permanent collection, but is the main venue for any big shows that come through town. There's a solid stock of European paintings from the Renaissance to the nineteenth century, highlighted by Hals and Rembrandt, matched by a fairly uninspiring American selection and a few bright rooms filled with modern works, especially by California artists. The biggest surprises are found amid the exquisitely crafted pieces in the Asian section, mainly from China and Japan but with smaller works from India and Korea. The Interactive Multimedia Art Gallery

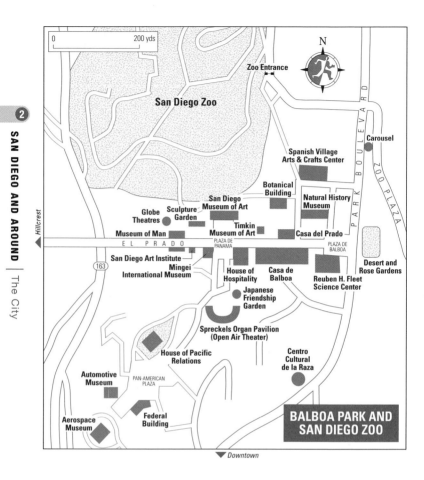

Map: Balboa Park and San Diego Zoo showing locations including Zoo Entrance, San Diego Zoo, Carousel, Spanish Village Arts & Crafts Center, Botanical Building, Natural History Museum, San Diego Museum of Art, Globe Theatres, Sculpture Garden, Timkin Museum of Art, Casa del Prado, Museum of Man, El Prado, Plaza de Panama, Plaza de Balboa, San Diego Art Institute, Mingei International Museum, House of Hospitality, Casa de Balboa, Desert and Rose Gardens, Reuben H. Fleet Science Center, Japanese Friendship Garden, Spreckels Organ Pavilion (Open Air Theater), House of Pacific Relations, Centro Cultural de la Raza, Automotive Museum, Pan-American Plaza, Federal Building, Aerospace Museum

BALBOA PARK AND SAN DIEGO ZOO

Downtown

Explorer (IMAGE) lets you browse the collection and take home copies of your favorite pieces, while the outside **Sculpture Court and Garden** offers free exploration at any time, with a number of important works by artists like Henry Moore and Alexander Calder. There's also a pleasant, though pricey, restaurant nearby.

Just across El Prado, the **Mingei International Museum** (Tues–Sun 10am–4pm; $5; ⓦwww.mingei.org) has a rotating collection of folk art, featuring everything from weather vanes and carousels to furniture made from bottle caps. None of the exhibits is permanent, though previous exhibitions have focused on a wide range of items, including African, pre-Columbian, and Romanian art, as well as home-made toys and garments from around the world. Next door, the **San Diego Art Institute** (Tues–Sat 10am–4pm, Sun noon–4pm; $3; ⓦwww.sandiego-art.org) is a sporadically interesting venue for the works of its members, while in the institute's David Fleet Young Artists' Gallery, work by students at various San Diego area schools is on display.

The contents of the **Museum of Man** (daily 10am–4.30pm; $6; ⓦwww.museumofman.org), which straddles El Prado, veer from the banal to the engaging to the bizarre, including demonstrations of tortilla-making and Mexican loom weaving, replicas of huge Mayan stones, interesting Native American artifacts, and various Egyptian relics. Also containing an eclectic selection, the **Casa de Balboa**, built for the 1915 Exposition, houses four museums, three of which are definitely worth a look: the **Museum of Photographic Arts** (daily 10am–5pm, Thurs 10am–9pm; $6; ⓦwww.mopa.org), offers a fine permanent collection dating back to the daguerreotype and includes the work of Matthew Brady, Alfred Stieglitz, Paul Strand, and other big names; the **San Diego Historical Society Museum** (Tues–Sun 10am–4.30pm; $5; ⓦwww .sandiegohistory.org), virtually next door, charts the booms that have elevated San Diego from uninviting scrubland into the seventh-largest city in the US within 150 years; and the **Model Railroad Museum** (Tues–Fri 11am–4pm, Sat & Sun 11am–5pm; $4; ⓦwww.sdmodelrailroadm.com), the most curious of all, displays tiny, elaborately conceived replicas of cityscapes, deserts, and mountains, as well as the industrious little trains that chug their way through them – a must for all aficionados of miniature railways.

Closer to the Park Boulevard end of El Prado, the **Reuben H. Fleet Science Center** (Mon, Tues & Thurs 9.30am–5pm, Wed 9.30am–6pm, Sun 9.30am–7pm, Fri & Sat 9.30am–8pm; Science Center $6.75, Science Center and theater or simulator $11, all three $15; ⓦwww.rhfleet.org) is one of the more recently added features of Balboa Park, an assortment of child-oriented exhibits of varying interest, focusing on the glitzier aspects of contemporary science. Predictably, the most impressive sensations are provided by the **Space Theater**s' dome-shaped tilting screen and 152 loudspeakers, which showcase stomach-churning trips into volcanoes, over waterfalls, and through outer space. Although the complex's high-tech motion simulator has dubious scientific value, it does make for an entertaining amusement-park ride.

Near the Science Center, on the west side of the Plaza de Balboa, the compelling **Natural History Museum** (daily 9.30am–4.30pm; $7; ⓦwww.sdnhm.org) features a great collection of fossils, a curious array of stuffed creatures, hands-on displays of minerals, and entertaining exhibits on dinosaurs and crocodiles. The approach may not be too scholarly, but is well-suited to the casual visitor with only a sketchy knowledge of paleontology. A short walk behind the Natural History building, the **Spanish Village Arts**

Balboa Park Museums: Practicalities

Ideally, you should come to Balboa Park on Tuesdays, when free admission is offered for several rotating museums, usually two to four depending on the Tuesday; don't come on Mondays, when the bigger collections are closed. None of the museums is essential viewing, but at least three – the Museum of Man, the Museum of Photographic Arts, and the San Diego Museum of Art – can keep you engrossed for a few hours. The cheapest way to see them is to buy the $30 **Balboa Park Passport**, which allows admission to the park's thirteen museums and is valid for a week, although you can visit each museum once only. This passport, along with a $55 variant that includes the San Diego Zoo, is available at all the museums and at the **visitor center** (daily 9am–4pm; ☎619/239-0512, ⓦwww.balboapark.org), located in the **House of Hospitality** on the Prado. This is the best place to find information about each individual museum, and to buy the useful Balboa Park map and guide for $1.

The park, within easy reach of Downtown on **buses** #7, #16, or #25, is large but fairly easy to navigate on foot – if you tire, the free **Balboa Park tram** runs frequently between the main museum groupings and the parking lots.

△ Balboa Park, San Diego

and Crafts Center (daily 11am–4pm; free; ⓦwww.spanishvillageart.com)
dates from the 1935 Expo and, of course, was designed in the style of a Spanish
village. Some three hundred craftspeople now display their work in forty different studios and galleries, and you can watch them hard at work, practicing
their skills at painting, sculpture, photography, pottery, and glass-working. It's
fun to look over the various artworks, though the price tags attached to them
can be rather daunting.

The rest of the park

The fifteen-minute walk to the Aerospace Museum, the major collection away
from El Prado, takes you past several spots of varying interest. There's a **puppet theater** (Wed–Fri shows at 10am & 11.30am, Sat & Sun at 11am, 1pm &
2.30pm; $2, kids $1.50; ☎619/685-5045), in the Pacific Palisades building; the
Spreckels Organ Pavilion (free Sunday concerts, 2–3pm), home to the
world's largest pipe organ; and the series of cottages comprising the **House of
Pacific Relations** (Sun noon–5pm; free), an international collection of kitsch
that evokes a cut-rate version of Epcot Center – enjoy the proffered tea, coffee, and cakes, but don't expect any multicultural education.

More compelling is the **Aerospace Museum**, at the southern end of Pan
American Plaza (daily 10am–5.30pm; $8; ⓦwww.aerospacemuseum.org),
which not only offers an interesting history of aviation – loaded with 69 planes
like the Spitfire, Hellcat, and the mysterious spy plane *Blackbird* – but also presents *Star Station One*, a hands-on demonstration imparting knowledge about
the International Space Station. There's also a replica of the *Spirit of St Louis* in
the entrance hall. Next to the Aerospace Museum, the **Automotive Museum**
(daily 10am–4pm; $7, kids $3; ⓦwww.sdautomuseum.org) continues the technological theme, with a host of classic cars and motorcycles, including a 1948
Tucker Torpedo – one of only fifty left.

Visiting all the museums in Balboa Park could well leave you too jaded even
to notice the unassuming round building on the edge of the area, beside Park
Boulevard. This, the **Centro Cultural de la Raza** (Thurs–Sun noon–5pm;

free; Ⓦwww.centroraza.com), mounts interesting temporary exhibits on Native American and Hispanic life in an atmosphere altogether less stuffy than the showpiece museums of the park, focusing on murals, folk art, literature, dance, and theater.

The San Diego Zoo

The **San Diego Zoo** (daily mid-June to early Sept 7am–10pm; daily early Sept to mid-June 9am–4pm; $19.50, kids $11.75; Ⓦwww.sandiegozoo.org), immediately north of the main museums, is one of the city's biggest and best-known attractions. As zoos go, it's undoubtedly one of the world's finest, with more than four thousand animals from eight hundred different species, among them very rare Chinese pheasants, Mhorr gazelles, and a freakish two-headed corn snake – as well as some pioneering techniques for keeping them in captivity: animals are restrained in "psychological cages," with moats or ridges rather than bars. It's an enormous place, and you can easily spend a full day here; take a bus tour early on to get a general idea of the layout, or survey the scene on the vertiginous Skyfari overhead tramway. Bear in mind, though, that many of the creatures get sleepy in the midday heat and retire behind bushes to take a nap. Moreover, the much-hyped pair of visiting Chinese **pandas** (resident at the zoo until 2008) spend a lot of time sleeping or being prodded by biologists in the park's Giant Panda Research Station, where the creatures recently became parents to Hua Mei, a very rare example of a panda born in the Western Hemisphere. Aside from this facility, there's also a children's zoo in the park, with walk-through bird cages and an animal nursery.

Regular **admission** only covers entry to the main zoo and the children's zoo; to add a 35-minute bus tour and a round-trip ticket on Skyfari, you'll need the $32 Deluxe Ticket Package. A $46.80 ticket also admits you to the San Diego Wild Animal Park (near Escondido; see p.241) within a five-day period.

Old Town

In 1769, Spanish settlers chose what's now **Presidio Hill** as the site of the first of California's missions. After their military service, as the soldiers began to leave the mission and the presidio, or fortress, they settled at the foot of the hill. This settlement was the birthplace of San Diego, later to be administered by Mexican officials and afterwards by early migrants from the eastern US. The area was preserved in 1968 as **Old Town State Historic Park** (locally referred to as "Old Town") and commemorates San Diego from the 1820s through the 1870s. Featuring 25 structures, some of them original **adobe dwellings**, the district's period atmosphere is somewhat diminished by the inevitable souvenir shops. Still, while it's undoubtedly touristy, it's also a good place to get a sense of the city's Hispanic roots away from its modern high-rises.

To get to Old Town, take bus #5 or #34 or the trolley from Downtown; by car, take I-5 and exit on Old Town Avenue, following the signs. Alternatively, from I-8 turn off onto Taylor Street and left onto Juan Street; signs should prevent any confusion. Most things in the park which aren't historical – the shops and restaurants – open around 10am and close at 10pm (though a number of the restaurants are open until midnight or later), but the best time to be around is during the afternoon, when you can learn something about the general history of the area and enter the more interesting of the adobe structures (including several that are otherwise kept locked) with an excellent **free walking tour**, leaving at 2pm from outside the Seeley Stables, just off the central plaza. You can get details on this, and other aspects of the park, from the **visitor cen-**

ter (daily 10am–5pm; ☎619/220-5422), located inside the Robinson-Rose House, where you can pick up a fine walking-tour book.

Exploring Old Town

Many of the historic structures in the park are thoughtfully preserved and display many of their original furnishings, giving a good indication of early San Diego life. Most of the houses are open daily from 10am to 4pm or 5pm and offer free admission. One of the more significant structures is the **Casa de Estudillo** on Mason Street, built by the commander of the **presidio**, José Mariá de Estudillo, in 1827. The chapel in this poshest of the original adobes served as the setting for the wedding in Helen Hunt Jackson's overblown, though influential, romance about early California, *Ramona*. When the house was bought in 1910 by sugar baron J.D. Spreckels, he advertised it as "Ramona's Marriage Place." Next door, the **Casa de Bandini** was the home of the politician and writer Juan Bandini and acted as the social center of San Diego during the mid-nineteenth century. After California became part of the United States, the house became the **Cosmopolitan Hotel**, considered among the finest in the state, its many elegant period appointments still visible in the dining room. Of somewhat less appeal are the **San Diego Union Building**, where the city's newspaper began in 1868, and the **Seeley Stables**, stuffed with Old West memorabilia.

An idealized recreation of an eighteenth-century Mexican street market, **Bazaar del Mundo**, abuts the state park. Though rife with tacky gift shops, it's enjoyable enough on a Sunday afternoon, when there's free music and folk dancing in its tree-shaded courtyard. It's also a fair place to **eat**: stands serve fresh tortillas, and the two sit-down Mexican restaurants are decent enough if you can grab an outside seat.

Just beyond the park gates on San Diego Avenue, the **Thomas Whaley Museum** (daily 10am–5pm; closed Tues in winter; $5) was the first brick building in California. Once the home of Thomas Whaley, a New York entrepreneur who came to California during the Gold Rush, it displays furniture and photos from his time, as well as a reconstruction of a courtroom from 1869, when the building housed the county courthouse. Many people come, however, because of the house's supposed current occupants – the place has been officially stamped by the US Department of Commerce as haunted, possibly by one of the occupants of the neighboring **El Campo Santo Cemetery**. Once the site of public executions (Antonio Garra, leader of an 1851 uprising by the San Luis Rey Indians, was forced to dig his own grave here before he was killed), the inscriptions on the cemetery's tombs read like a *Who's Who* of late nineteenth-century San Diego, though the cemetery (Spanish for "holy field") is most renowned for being haunted by the ghost of "Yankee Jim" Robinson, hanged in 1852 by a local kangaroo court for the crime of stealing a rowboat.

Modest though it is, the cemetery makes a somewhat more interesting stop than **Heritage Park**, just north on Juan Street, where several Victorian buildings have been gathered from around the city and preserved, instead of summarily destroyed in a manic burst of urban renewal. They're now shops and offices and, in one case, a bed and breakfast (the *Heritage Park B&B*; see "Accommodation" p.209). The view of the harbor from the park is worth the climb, as is the walk along Conde Street, which lets you peer into the atmospheric, sculpture-filled interior of the **Old Adobe Chapel**, dating from the 1850s and used as a place of worship until 1917.

Presidio Hill: Serra Museum and the San Diego Mission

The Spanish Colonial building that now sits atop Presidio Hill is only a rough approximation of the original 1769 mission – moved in 1774 – but contains the intriguing **Junípero Serra Museum**, 2727 Presidio Drive (Fri–Sun 10am–4.30pm; $5; ☏619/297-3258), which includes a collection of Spanish furniture dating back to the sixteenth century, along with various weapons, diaries, and historical documents pertaining to the man who led the Spanish colonization of California. The museum additionally offers an acerbic commentary on the yeoman struggles of a few devoted historians to preserve anything of San Diego's Spanish past against the wishes of dollar-crazed developers. The **Mormon Battalion Visitor Center**, nearby at 2510 Juan St (daily 9am–9pm; free), lets you relive, via artifacts, paintings, and multimedia presentations, the 2000-mile saga of the Mormon Battalion March during the Mexican-American War – the longest US military infantry march in history.

Outside the Serra Museum, the **Serra Cross** serves as a modern marker on the site of the original mission. To find the actual mission, you'll need to travel six miles north to 10818 San Diego Mission Rd, where the **Mission Basilica San Diego de Alcalá** (daily 9am–5pm; $3 donation suggested; ⓦwww.missionsandiego.com) was relocated to be closer to a water source and fertile soil and further from conflict with Native Americans – which still didn't prevent Padre Luis Jayme, California's first Christian martyr, from being clubbed to death there in 1775. The present building (take bus #43 from Downtown), the fifth to be constructed on this site, is still a working parish church, offering confession, weddings, baptisms, and daily masses at 7am and 5pm. Walk through the dark and echoey church – the fourteenth-century stalls and altar were imported from Spain – to the **garden**, where two small crosses mark the graves of Native American neophytes, making this California's oldest cemetery. A small **museum** holds a collection of Native craft objects and historical articles from the mission, including the crucifix held by Junípero Serra at his death in 1834. Despite claims that the missionary campaign was one of kidnapping, forced baptisms, and the treatment of natives as virtual slaves, Serra was beatified in 1998 during a Vatican ceremony.

East San Diego and Hillcrest

Scruffy **EAST SAN DIEGO** is largely suburban sprawl, only really of interest if you want to venture into its western fringes as far as 1925 K St, the site of **Villa Montezuma** (Fri–Sun 10am–4.30pm; also open Thurs in Dec; $5; ☏619/239-2211), doubtless one of the more unusual entries on the National Register of Historic Places. Ignored by most visitors to San Diego, possibly due to its location, the villa is a florid show of Victoriana, with a rich variety of onion domes and all manner of loopy eccentricities. Known to some as the "haunted house," a nickname that seems entirely reasonable, it was built for Jesse Shepard – English-born but noted in the US as a composer, pianist, author, and all-round aesthete – and financed by a group of culturally aspiring San Diegans in 1887. The glorious stock of furniture remains, as do many ornaments and oddments and the dramatic stained-glass windows. It's a place that well reflects Shepard's introspective nature and interest in spiritualism, both of which must have been entirely out of step with brash San Diego through the boom years, or even today. To get to the villa without a car, either make the long walk (about 45min) from Downtown, take bus #3, #5, or #16, each stopping within about five blocks, or use the trolley, transferring to the Euclid Avenue line and getting off near 20th Street.

North of Downtown and on the northwest edge of Balboa Park, **HILL-CREST** is an increasingly lively and artsy area, thanks to the wealthy liberals who've moved into the district in recent years. Although it doesn't challenge Haight-Ashbury in San Francisco or Silver Lake in LA for urban vitality, it does manage to retain a certain bohemian air, acting as the center of the city's **gay community** and the home of a handful of gay-oriented hotels (see "Gay and lesbian San Diego," p.234). The streets around University and Fifth, easily reached from Downtown on bus #3 or #11, hold a selection of interesting cafés and restaurants (see "Eating," p.229), book and music shops, and an appealing collection of Victorian homes.

The beaches

Although San Diego features a fine array of museums, historic sites, and animal parks, many visitors skip those sights altogether to spend a few days on the city's renowned **beaches**. In most cases, they lack seclusion and any sense of privacy, but they are fine for sunbathing and swimming, and opportunities abound for getting with the mythical spirit of Southern California by trying out rollerblades, boogieboards, and surfboards.

Directly south of Downtown across the bay, **Coronado** is a plush, well-heeled settlement, best known as the site of a large naval base. Traditionally, Coronado's visitors have been wealthy health enthusiasts, here for its sea breezes, palm trees, and famous (and famously expensive) hotel. Just beyond, and much less upscale, **Imperial Beach**'s chief draw is simply the peace of a rarely crowded stretch of sand, and, if you have an equestrian bent, its nearby horse-riding trails.

Across the bay to the north, the rugged **Point Loma Peninsula** marks the entrance to San Diego Bay, with trees along its spine and a craggy shoreline often marked by explorable tide pools – though offering little opportunity for sunbathing. **Ocean Beach**, further north at the end of the I-8 freeway, was once known to be extremely lively, though is now tempered by a neighboring exclusive community with little taste for debauchery. These days, much of Ocean Beach's former vitality has moved to **Mission Beach**, eight miles northwest of Downtown, and the adjoining, and slightly more salubrious, **Pacific Beach** – "PB" – linked by an exuberant beachside walkway. Both beaches encompass a peninsula that provides the western edge of **Mission Bay**, known best as the site of the colossal tourist draw of **SeaWorld**, several miles inland. To see the area at its most chic and upscale, travel a few miles further north up the coast to stunning **La Jolla**, whose coastline of perfect caves and coves is matched by short, litter-free streets lined with small coffee bars, art galleries, and a stylish modern art museum.

Coronado

Across San Diego Bay from Downtown, the bulbous isthmus of **CORONADO** is a well-scrubbed resort community with a major naval station at its western end. Although it has an interesting New England air, with an assortment of cozy, "saltbox" houses, Coronado is of limited interest, save for a historic hotel and the long, thin beach – a natural breakwater for the bay – that runs south. The simplest way to get here is on the **San Diego Bay ferry** ($2 each way, $2.50 with bikes), which leaves Broadway Pier daily on the hour between 9am and 9pm, and until 10pm Fridays and Saturdays, returning on the half hour. Tickets are available on the pier at **San Diego Harbor Excursion**, 1050 N Harbor Drive (℡619/234-4111, ⊛www.sdhe.com). From the ferry landing on First Street, shuttle bus #904 (half-hourly 9.30am–5.30pm; $1) runs the mile up Coronado's main street, Orange Avenue, to the *Hotel del Coronado*. Alternatively use bus #901 (or #19, though this only goes as far as the naval station) from Downtown. By road, you cross the **Coronado Bridge** (southbound drivers without passengers have to pay a $1 toll), its struts decorated with enormous murals depicting daily Hispanic life, best seen from the community park beneath the bridge in the district of Barrio Logan.

The town of Coronado grew up around the **Hotel del Coronado**, at 1500 Orange Ave, a Victorian whirl of turrets and towers erected as a health resort in 1888. Using Chinese laborers who worked round-the-clock shifts, the hotel was built to appeal to well-heeled enthusiasts of healthy living, as well as rich hypochondriacs. If you're in the neighborhood, the place is certainly worth a look, its expansive grounds still something of an elite playground, if you can see past all the gawking tourists. Through the lobby and courtyard, a small basement **museum** (free) details the history of the "Del," including its most notable – or notorious – moment, when Edward VIII (then Prince of Wales) met Coronado housewife Wallis Warfield Simpson here in 1920, which eventually led to their marriage and his abdication from the British throne. Also not to be missed is the tablecloth signed by Marilyn Monroe and the rest of the cast who filmed Billy Wilder's *Some Like It Hot* here in 1958, when it doubled as a ritzy Miami Beach resort. Outside, past the tennis courts occasionally graced by world champions, are the sands upon which much of the movie's action takes place, including Monroe's memorable flirtation with Tony Curtis as he pretends to be a yachting playboy with a Cary Grant accent. A guided, hour-long **historical** tour (Mon–Sat 11am & 1pm, Sun 3pm; $15) wends its way around the hotel, beginning in the lobby.

A less grandiose place to explore Coronado's past is the **Coronado Museum of History and Art**, 1100 Orange Ave (Mon–Sat 10am–4pm, Sun noon–4pm; $4; ℡619/435-7242, ⊛www.coronadohistory.org), which offers displays chronicling the town's early pioneers and first naval aviators, as well as its history of yachting, architecture, and ferries. Adjacent to the museum, the **Coronado Visitor Center**, 1047 B Ave (Mon–Fri 9am–5pm, Sat & Sun 11am–2pm; ℡619/437-8788 or 1-800/622-8300, ⊛www.coronadovisitors.com), offers much useful information on the area.

Imperial Beach

South of the Hotel del Coronado (bus #901), follow Silver Strand Boulevard and you'll find plenty of good spots to stretch out and relax – though no food and drink facilities – foremost among them **Silver Strand State Beach** (daily 8am–dusk; $5 per vehicle), where you can rollerblade or bike in a pleasant atmosphere. There are camping facilities, but for RVs only. At the end of Silver Strand Boulevard, less engaging **IMPERIAL BEACH** contrasts unfavorably with more upscale Coronado, but it does have an enjoyable and fairly quiet beach, and one of the nation's largest sandcastle-building competitions in July, and is disturbed only by the buzzing helicopters of the naval air station. Nearby **Border Field State Park** (℡619/575-3613), noted mainly for its horse trails, is not too far from the Mexican border and reached by car along Tijuana Street from San Ysidro.

To return directly to San Diego from Imperial Beach, take bus #934 to the trolley and head north through dreary Chula Vista and National City.

Ocean Beach and Point Loma

Once ruled by a drug-running chapter of the Hell's Angels, **OCEAN BEACH**, six miles northwest of Downtown and accessible from there via bus #35, is now one of the more highly sought addresses in San Diego. Vacant plots with sea views regularly change hands for half a million dollars, and the single-story adobe dwellings that were home to several generations of Portuguese fishing families as recently as a decade ago have virtually disappeared – the few that remain look like dinky outhouses beside the garish yuppie McMansions. The new money is less on display at the main beach, half a mile south by the pier. **Newport Street**, where most young backpackers spend their time, features rows of cheap snackbars, T-shirt stalls, surf and skate rental shops, and some of the best secondhand music stores around. There is often good surf, and the beach itself can be quite fun – especially on weekends, when the local party scene really gets cranking.

South from the pier, and some of the best beaches, rise the dramatic **Sunset Cliffs**, not surprisingly a prime spot for twilight vistas. The cliffs, however, are notoriously unstable and more than a few people have tumbled over the edge following an afternoon of excess on the beach.

Beyond here, the hilly green peninsula of **POINT LOMA** is mostly owned by the US Navy, which keeps it attractive and unspoiled, though inaccessible in many places. To get here from Downtown, take the trolley to Old Town and pick up bus #26. After a long, tedious ride beyond the naval base to the point's southern extremity, the **Cabrillo National Monument** (daily 9am–5.15pm, closes at 6.15pm in summer; seven-day pass $5 per vehicle, $2 per pedestrian or cyclist; ⓦwww.nps.gov/cabr) occupies the spot where captain Juan Rodríguez Cabrillo and his crew became the first Europeans to land in California in 1542, though they quickly reboarded their vessel and sailed away. The monument's startling views, across San Diego Bay to the Downtown skyline and along the coast to Mexico, easily repay the journey here. After enjoying the view, there's ample opportunity for discovering the marine life in the numerous tide pools around the shoreline, reached on a clearly marked **nature walk** beginning close to the monument.

Also nearby, a visitor center (daily 9am–5:15pm; free with monument admission) contains information on the history and wildlife of the point, and lies near the **Old Point Loma Lighthouse** (daily 9am–5pm; free with monument admission), which offers historical tours which lead you past replica Victorian furnishings and equipment from the 1880s. As it was, the structure's main purpose was ultimately unfulfilled: soon after it was built, it was discovered that its beacon would be obscured by fog, and another lighthouse was erected at a lower elevation.

Facing the Pacific, a sheltered viewing station on the southwest-facing cliffs of the lighthouse makes it easy to see the November-to-March **whale migration**, when scores of gray whales pass by on their journey between the Arctic Ocean and their breeding waters off Baja California. High-powered telescopes and a tape-recorded lecture make the viewing station a good choice during the migration season.

Mission Bay and SeaWorld

Heading northwest from Downtown toward the coast, you pass through a drab, cheerless zone surrounding the Sports Arena – frequented by sailors for its topless bars and by unfussy tourists for its low-priced, spartan hotels – before reaching **MISSION BAY**, whose mud flats quickly become landscaped lagoons and grassy flatlands crowded with watersports fanatics. From Ocean Beach, a few miles away, Mission Bay is accessible by crossing the San Diego River on Sunset Cliffs Boulevard.

The source of Mission Bay's popularity is, of course, the formidable amusement park **SEAWORLD** (daily mid-June to Labor Day 9am–dusk, rest of the year 10am–dusk; $42.95, children $32.95, parking $7; ⓦ www.seaworld.com), the San Diego branch of an entertainment colossus that stretches from San Antonio to Orlando, which you can reach by taking SeaWorld Drive off I-5, or bus #9 from Downtown. Although the entrance fee is steep, and adding refreshments or souvenirs can nearly cause bankruptcy, SeaWorld is San Diego's most popular tourist attraction for its undeniable kid-friendly appeal. But for adults, experiencing the region's sea life by whale watching and snorkeling off the coast may be much more rewarding, and a lot cheaper. The park's entry price dictates that you allow an entire day to make it worthwhile, or tack on four more dollars for a two-day pass.

Highly regimented, SeaWorld has a large number of exhibits and timetabled events, including the killer-whale performances that make up Shamu Adventure (where you shouldn't sit in the first fourteen rows unless you're prepared to be soaked by belly flops from a high-flying orca); the Manatee Rescue, a giant freshwater "river" showcasing the gentle plant-eating mammals; the Wild Arctic, a simulated habitat featuring walruses, beluga whales, and polar bears; and the Shark Encounter, where all manner of sharks circle menacingly around visitors walking through a submerged viewing tunnel. Some of the park's newer attractions, however, have unfortunately devolved into the sort of standard-issue amusement-park fare that includes the likes of giant inner-tube rides, motion simulators, and aerial "skyrides," though if you've come here for this sort of diversion, you're better off just sticking to Disneyland.

Mission Beach and Pacific Beach

The best places to see – and be seen – in San Diego are clearly **MISSION BEACH**, the peninsula that separates Mission Bay from the Pacific Ocean, and its seamless northern extension, **PACIFIC BEACH**. If you aren't up for bronzing on the sands, you can always nurse a beer at one of the many beachfront bars while observing the toasty sands overrun with scantily clad babes and surfboard-clutching dudes. Or you could rollerblade or bike down **Ocean Front Walk**, the concrete boardwalk running the length of both beaches, and the fastest way to get about when summer traffic is bumper-to-bumper on Mission Boulevard.

Although your first impression may suggest otherwise, local city authorities have made repeated efforts to curb the anarchic hedonism and drunken debauchery long associated with this classic slice of Southern California beachlife, including approving the revitalization of the once-derelict **Belmont Park**, near the southern end of Ocean Front Walk at 3146 Mission Blvd (Mon–Thurs 11am–10pm, Fri–Sun 11am–11pm; rides $2–4; ⓦ www.belmontpark .com). The two main attractions, both from 1925, are the Giant Dipper rollercoaster, one of the few of its era still around, and the Plunge, once the largest saltwater plunge in the world, and the setting for famous celluloid swimmers Johnny Weismuller and Esther Williams. These days, the two main draws are also supplemented by an assortment of lesser carnival rides, a collection of swimwear stores, a pricey fitness center, and countless seaside snack joints. Luckily, while the funfair has encouraged more families to use the area, it hasn't diminished the beach's freewheeling character.

By following Mission Boulevard north, you cross from the spirited chaos of

Mission Beach into the sedate quarters of Pacific Beach, where expensive oceanside homes with tidy lawns suggest haute-bourgeois refinement, though there's still plenty to enjoy. A serviceable beach, for one, around Crystal Pier is a decent spot for a suntan, while Garnet Avenue, running inland from the pier, is lined by funky eating places and nightspots. Adept surfers are no strangers to Pacific Beach, either – a mile north of the pier, **Tourmaline City Surf Park**, regularly pounded by heavy waves, is reserved exclusively for the sport.

La Jolla and around

"A nice place – for old people and their parents," wrote Raymond Chandler of **LA JOLLA** (pronounced "La Hoya") in the 1950s, though that didn't stop him from moving here (his former house is at 6005 Camino de la Costa) and setting much of his final novel *Playback* in the town, renaming it "Esmeralda." Since Philip Marlowe concluded his last case, La Jolla has been infused with new money and fresh vitality, and its opulence is now less stuffy and more welcoming. The main section, around Prospect Street and Girard Avenue, has spotless sidewalks flanked by crisply trimmed grass, and the many upscale art galleries sit alongside chic cafés and swank boutiques.

Though it's fairly expensive, it's worth coming at least to savor the town's unique (if clearly contrived) elegance, which includes the ornate pink **La Valencia Hotel**, 1132 Prospect St, frequented by Hollywood's elite in the 1930s and 40s (see "Accommodation," p.210). On a quieter section of the same thoroughfare, the La Jolla site of the **Museum of Contemporary Art**, 700 Prospect St (Mon, Tues, Fri–Sun 11am–5pm, Thurs 11am–8pm; $4, free first Sun & third Tues of the month; Ⓦwww.mcasandiego.org), has a huge – and regularly changing – stock of paintings and sculptures from 1955 onwards. Minimalism, Pop Art, and regional California work are in evidence, bolstered by a strong range of temporary shows, and there are fabulous views of the Pacific surf crashing against the rocks immediately below the building's huge windows. The museum also has exhibition space Downtown; see p.213.

The building housing the museum was once the home of Ellen Scripps, a prominent local philanthropist whose seemingly endless reserves of wealth were injected into La Jolla through the first half of the century. She commissioned early-modernist architect Irving Gill (who built several distinctive buildings in La Jolla, as well as Los Angeles) to design her house, and today the Scripps name is still almost everywhere, notably in the small, neat, and tasteful **Ellen Scripps Browning Park**, on the seaward side of the museum. Where the park meets the coast is the start of **La Jolla Cove**, much of it an ecological reserve, with an underwater park whose clear waters make it perfect for snorkeling (if you can ever find a parking space nearby).

Architecture fans inspired by the work of Gill will not want to miss a chance to tour the local citadel of high modernism, and one of the premier modern structures in the US, the **Salk Institute for Biological Studies**, 10010 N Torrey Pines Rd (daily 8.30am–5pm; tours daily 11am & noon; information at Ⓣ858/453-4100 ext 1200, Ⓦwww.salk.edu), not only a respected institution for molecular biology and genetics, but also a considerably influential design by American architect Louis I. Kahn. A collection of austere geometric concrete blocks and walls, the complex features stark vistas that look out over the Pacific Ocean and a strange, almost Neoclassical serenity that's both welcome and unexpected. Although the site should be strictly avoided by fans of Victorian mansions and postmodern mall architecture, it nonetheless will appeal to anyone with a taste for Le Corbusier or any icon of the mid-twentieth-century International Style.

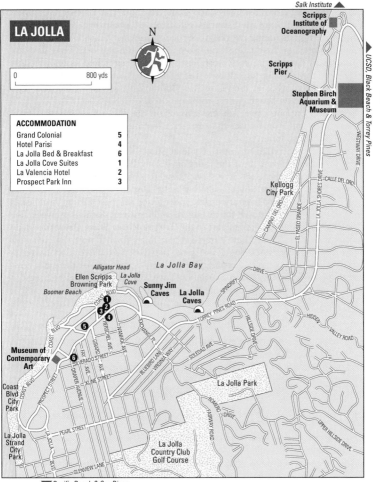

LA JOLLA

N

0 ——————— 800 yds

Salk Institute ▲

Scripps
Institute of
Oceanography

Scripps
Pier

Stephen Birch
Aquarium &
Museum

UCSD, Black Beach & Torrey Pines

WESTWAY DRIVE

Kellogg
City Park

CALLE DEL ORO

LA JOLLA SHORES DRIVE

CAMINO DEL ORO

EL PASEO GRANDE

ACCOMMODATION

Grand Colonial	5
Hotel Parisi	4
La Jolla Bed & Breakfast	6
La Jolla Cove Suites	1
La Valencia Hotel	2
Prospect Park Inn	3

Alligator Head   *La Jolla Bay*

Ellen Scripps   *La Jolla*
Browning Park   *Cove*   **Sunny Jim**
Boomer Beach   **Caves**   **La Jolla**
                                Caves

DRIVE

SPINDRIFT

TORREY PINES ROAD

HILLSIDE DRIVE

HIDDEN VALLEY ROAD

COAST BLVD

**Museum of
Contemporary
Art**

HERSCHEL AVE.

IVANHOE AVE.

GIRARD AVE.

SILVERADO STREET

FAY AVE.

DRAPER AVENUE

EXCHANGE PL.

BLUEBIRD LANE

VIRGINIA WAY

SOLEDAD AVE.

KLINE STREET

La Jolla Park

ROMERO DRIVE

Coast
Blvd
City
Park

PROSPECT STREET

COAST BLVD

FAIRWAY ROAD

La Jolla
Strand
City
Park

LA JOLLA BLVD

PEARL STREET

GLENVIEW LANE

La Jolla
Country Club
Golf Course

DRAPER DRIVE

UPPER HILLSIDE DRIVE

▼ *Pacific Beach & San Diego*

North along the coast

North of the cove, upmarket residential neighborhoods stretch from the cliff tops to the main route, Torrey Pines Road. Following this thoroughfare and then La Jolla Shores Drive, which soon branches left, several uneventful miles precede the **Stephen Birch Aquarium and Museum** (daily 9am–5pm; $9.50, kids $6, parking $3; ⓦ aquarium.ucsd.edu), part of the Scripps Institute of Oceanography, which provides entertaining up-close views of captive marine life, informative displays on the earth's ecology, and exhibits detailing the marine exploration work carried out by the Institute – a much more edifying experience than anything at SeaWorld, and a lot cheaper, too.

On a hillside setting above the museum and also reached from Torrey Pines Road, the **University of California at San Diego (UCSD)** campus is a huge, dull affair, only meriting a visit if you enjoy trekking around to locate the

227

various specially commissioned works scattered about the 1200-acre grounds. These pieces constitute the **Stuart Collection of Sculpture** (@stuartcollection.ucsd.edu), including works by Bruce Nauman, William Wegman, and Jenny Holzer. The first acquisition, from 1983, is still the best: Niki de Saint Phalle's **Sun God**, a chunky, colorful bird whose outstretched wings welcome visitors to the parking lot opposite Peterson Hall. To find the rest, pick up a leaflet from the office in the Visual Arts Building or one of the campus's two visitor information booths (more information at ☎858/534-2117).

Without a car, you can reach the campus on bus #34 or express #30 from Downtown, which terminate their routes a few miles away at the University Towne Square shopping mall.

As it leaves the UCSD campus, La Jolla Shores Drive meets North Torrey Pines Road. A mile north of the junction, Torrey Pines Scenic Drive, branching left, provides the only access (via a steep path) to **Torrey Pines City Beach Park** – almost always called **Blacks Beach** – the region's premier clothing-optional, gay-friendly beach and one of the best surfing beaches in Southern California, known for its huge barreling waves during big swells. The beach lies within the southern part of the **Torrey Pines State Preserve** (daily 8am–sunset; parking $4), best entered a few miles further north, which preserves the country's rarest species of pine, the Torrey Pine – one of two surviving stands. Thanks to salty conditions and stiff ocean breezes, the pines contort their ten-foot frames into a variety of tortured, twisted shapes best viewed at close quarters from the half-mile **Guy Fleming Trail**, a 2/3 mile loop that starts near the beachside parking lot. The small **museum and interpretive center** (daily 9am–5pm; free) will tell you all about Torrey Pines, especially if your visit coincides with a guided nature tour (Sat & Sun 11.30am & 1.30pm). The less scenic and short **beach trail** leads from the interpretive center down to Flat Rock and a popular beach, great for sunbathing and picnics. Bear in mind that there is no picnicking allowed on the cliffs above the beach. Beyond the preserve you're into the North County community of Del Mar (see p.236).

Eating

San Diego typically offers good **food** at reasonable prices, everything from old-time coffee shops to stylish ethnic restaurants. Unsurprisingly, Mexican food is much in evidence, especially in **Old Town**, while the **Gaslamp District** has the greatest concentration of hip restaurants and bars, which are especially lively on weekend nights. Ascendant **Little Italy**, on the northern fringes of Downtown, has a few decent choices but is still too small to challenge the bohemian allure of **Hillcrest**, the most appealing area to simply hang out and eat.

Downtown and Little Italy

Alambres 756 5th Ave, Downtown ☎619/233-2838. Affordable Mexican food in a casual atmosphere, popular for its Speed Lunch – served within ten minutes or it's free – and its eponymous Alambres, fat tortillas stuffed to order.

Anthony's Star of the Sea 1360 Harbor Drive, Downtown ☎619/232-7408. Expensive Franco-California-style preparations of fresh seafood, justly famed for its freshness and variety. Terrace dining available on the waterfront.

Bella Luna 748 5th Ave, Downtown ☎619/239-3222. A romantic, moon-themed bistro with an artsy feel, serving up wonderful, mid-priced dishes from different regions of Italy, with hefty servings of pasta and succulent calamari.

Café 222 222 Island Ave at 2nd, Downtown ☎619/236-9902. Hip café serving some of the city's best breakfasts and lunches, with inventive twists on traditional sandwiches and burgers (including vegetarian), at reasonable prices. Open 7am–1:45pm; no credit cards.

Caffè Italia 1704 India St, Little Italy ☎619/234-6767. Sandwiches, salads, and great desserts served in a sleek modern interior or out on the sidewalk. Don't miss the Belgian-waffle bar on Sundays.

Candelas 416 3rd Ave, Downtown ☎619/702-4455. A Gaslamp District restaurant offering swank, pricey Mexican fare with inventive combinations of seafood and meat dishes – the California cuisine influence is deliciously apparent.

The Cheese Shop 627 4th Ave, Downtown ☎619/232-2303. Scrumptious deli sandwiches stuffed with different savory meats, with the roast beef a solid pick among many good choices. Also offers filling breakfasts.

Croce's Restaurant & Jazz Bar 802 5th Ave, Downtown ☎619/233-4355. Pricey but excellent range of pastas, desserts, and salads in the Gaslamp District. The Sunday jazz brunch is not to be missed. See also "Nightlife," p.232.

Dobson's 956 Broadway Circle, Downtown ☎619/231-6771. An upscale restaurant in an old two-tier building, loaded with business types in power-ties. The cuisine is continental at its best, with puff pastries adding some zing to the otherwise familiar fare. Accompany the meal with a bottle from the excellent wine list.

Filippi's Pizza Grotto 1747 India St, Little Italy ☎619/232-5094. Thick, chewy pizzas and a handful of pasta dishes served in a small room at the back of an Italian grocery. No-nonsense atmosphere, a good spot for devouring old favorites.

Fio's Cucina Italiana 801 5th Ave, Downtown ☎619/234-3467. Very classy, fairly expensive Italian place serving the likes of lobster ravioli and *osso buco*. Invent a special occasion to sample the primo seafood and pasta.

Galaxy Grill 522 Horton Plaza, Downtown ☎619/234-7211. A Fifties-style diner that's one of the bearable choices amid a throng of fast-food joints and chain diners in this popular shopping mall. Munch a tasty burger with the other hungry shoppers.

Grand Central Café 500 Broadway, Downtown ☎619/234-2233. Loaded with train decor, this cozy café serves inexpensive, gut-busting fare, mostly fat sandwiches and lip-smacking burgers. Breakfast only on Sunday.

Olé Madrid Café 755 5th Ave, Downtown ☎619/557-0146. Enjoyable mid-priced Spanish restaurant with a smiling yuppie crowd and flamenco dancers at midweek. After dinner on weekends, it turns into a popular funk and dance venue – see "Nightlife," p.233. Closed Mondays.

Sammy's 770 4th Ave, outside of Horton Plaza, Downtown ☎619/230-8888. Affordable California cuisine in a Mediterranean atmosphere. Pasta, salads, seafood, and chicken are the staples, but the

eclectic pizzas and "messy sundaes" are the real reasons to come. One in a local chain of eateries.

Taka 555 5th Ave, Downtown ☎619/338-0555. Good mid-priced sushi and hot and cold appetizers in a modern atmosphere stuffed to the gills with hipsters.

Hillcrest and Old Town

Berta's 3928 Twiggs St, Old Town ☎619/295-2343. One of the best-kept secrets in town. A far cry from the area's many touristy Mexican restaurants, offering low-priced, authentic cooking from all over Latin America, with a range of hot and spicy concoctions to make you pound the table for more.

Café Pacifica 2414 San Diego Ave, Old Town ☎619/291-6666. A bit pricey but worthwhile for its winning mix of California cuisine and seafood. The wine list is renowned.

Casa de Bandini 2600 Calhoun St, Old Town ☎619/297-8211. The crowds come in thick, ravenous packs to sample this restaurant's delicious combo plates, potent margaritas, and appealing (or annoying) mariachi musicians. Chow down on the festive patio, and you're in the catbird seat.

Chilango's Mexico City Grill 142 University Ave, Hillcrest ☎619/294-8646. Gourmet Mexican food for under $10 is served in this tiny storefront locale that is packed to the rafters in the evenings. Try the savory south-of-the-border favorites presented in traditional styles without any cheese or bean overkill.

City Delicatessen 535 University Ave, Hillcrest ☎619/295-2747. Huge New York-style deli menu with belt-loosening portions to match and late hours (until 2am on weekends) make this the stop for the seriously ravenous.

Crest Café 425 Robinson Ave, Hillcrest ☎619/295-2510. Don't let the dumpy exterior fool you – this is solid, tasty American fare presented on the cheap. The salads, burgers, and pancakes will make your stomach happy, as will the delicious home-made desserts. Open 7am–midnight.

The Good Egg 7947 Balboa Ave, Hillcrest ☎858/565-4244. Until 9am, as much coffee as you can drink for 5¢, as long as you buy a breakfast – sample the gigantic, mouthwatering pancakes. On the northern edge of Hillcrest.

Ichiban 1449 University Ave, Hillcrest ☎619/299-7203. Seriously scrumptious Japanese cuisine, featuring a range of good rolls and sushi, in an unpretentious and popular restaurant. The combination platters are extremely well-priced.

La Piñata 2836 Juan St, Old Town ☎619/297-1631. Affordably priced Mexican food with hefty portions of old-fashioned, fattening fare. Pitchers of margaritas will give you a potent jolt to go with your enchilada combo plates.

Old Town Mexican Café y Cantina 2489 San

229

Diego Ave ☎619/297-4330. Lively and informal Mexican diner where the crowds expect to queue up before dining; only at breakfast are you unlikely to have to wait for a table.

Old Town Thai Restaurant 2540 Congress St ☎619/291-6720. A block away from most of the Old Town restaurants, serving an extensive array of standard Thai favorites, inexpensive lunches and vegetarian dishes. Closed Mondays.

Pizza Nova 3955 5th Ave, Hillcrest ☎619/296-6682. Trendy California-style pizzas with a range of savory toppings. Part of a local chain with good, palatable fare and a sizeable contingent of locals and tourists.

Taste of Thai 527 University Ave, Hillcrest ☎619/291-7525. Terrific Thai staples for reasonable prices in the center of Hillcrest; expect a wait on weekends.

The Vegetarian Zone 2949 5th Ave, Hillcrest ☎619/298-7302. A delectable selection of eclectic vegetarian offerings with a global twist, including unexpected influences from Greek and East Asian cuisines. No meat, and no smoking.

Coronado, Ocean Beach, and Point Loma

Chez Loma 1132 Loma Ave, Coronado ☎619/435-0661. Intensely aromatic and delicious selection of French cuisine, especially strong on old-line favorites, though with nouvelle influences as well. As with most Franco fare, predictably pricey.

Humphrey's by the Bay 2241 Shelter Island Drive, Point Loma ☎619/224-3577. Eclectic California cuisine, heavy on inventive seafood platters, but especially good for eye-catching bayside views, groovy weekend live music, and DJs who spin mostly funk, dance, jazz, and rock.

Kensington Coffee Company 1106 1st St, Coronado ☎619/437-8506. Aromatic coffees, imported teas, and pastries that make for a tasty snack close to the landing stage.

Mexican Village Restaurant 120 Orange Ave, Coronado ☎619/435-1822. Longstanding Mexican diner of ballroom dimensions, patronized as much for its lip-smacking margaritas and high-stepping music as for its cheap and serviceable food.

Miguel's Cocina 1351 Orange Ave, Coronado ☎619/437-4237. Savory fish tacos, lobster burritos, and a full range of other choices make this Mexican eatery worth seeking out.

Old Venice Italian Restaurant 2910 Canon Ave, Point Loma ☎619/222-5888. Upscale and hip atmosphere at moderately priced café and bar. Great for pizza, pasta, seafood, and salads – no real surprises here, just hearty favorites.

Point Loma Seafoods 2805 Emerson St ☎619/223-1109. Fast, inexpensive counter serving up San Diego's freshest fish in a basket, along with a mean crabcake sandwich that makes the locals cheer. Justly popular joint is packed on weekends; don't even try to find an adjacent parking spot.

Ranchos Cocina 1830-H Sunset Cliffs Blvd, Ocean Beach ☎619/226-7619. A healthy, moderately priced eatery with tasty dishes like *mahi-mahi* tacos or eggplant burritos – many offerings a combination of Mexican, Texan, Spanish, and even Aztec styles. Try the daily seafood and veggie specials.

Stretch's 943 Orange Ave, Coronado ☎935/435-8886. Reasonably priced American cuisine; healthy meals made with fresh natural ingredients.

Theo's 4953 Newport Ave, Ocean Beach ☎619/225-9404. Hearty subs and pizza at cheap prices. A popular choice with the locals.

The Venetian 3663 Voltaire St, Ocean Beach ☎619/223-8197. Excellently priced pizzas and pasta, mostly Italian staples with big portions and affordable prices.

Mission Beach and Pacific Beach

The Eggery, Etc. 4130 Mission Blvd, Mission Beach ☎858/274-3122. A coffee shop with imagination, serving breakfast – omelets, pancakes, and other favorites – until 2pm. Be prepared to wait on weekends.

Kono's 704 Garnet Ave, Pacific Beach ☎858/483-1669. A solid choice for breakfast or lunch on the boardwalk, with inexpensive, sizeable portions of eggs, potatoes, toast, and sandwiches, and especially plump burgers and burritos. Beware the long line of hungry surfers.

Luigi's Italian Restaurant 3210 Mission Blvd, Mission Beach ☎858/488-2818. Sup on cheap and enormous pizzas while you take part in the rowdy beachside atmosphere, screaming at one of the sports games on competing TV sets.

Mission Café 3795 Mission Blvd, Mission Beach ☎858/488-9060. A wide range of eclectic choices, from French toast and tamales with eggs to tortillas with spicy seasonings to "roll-ups" stuffed with meat and pasta. Beer, specialty coffees, shakes, and smoothies all on tap.

Palenque 1653 Garnet Ave, Pacific Beach ☎858/272-7816. Family-run restaurant with affordable dishes from various states of Mexico, with a front deck for dining on warm summer evenings.

Zanzibar Coffee Company 976 Garnet Ave, Pacific Beach ☎858/272-4762. A great place to chill out, especially on the back patio, with inexpensive snacks, pizzas, sandwiches, coffees, and desserts. As a major plus, breakfast is served all day.

La Jolla

Brockton Villa 1235 Coast Blvd ☎858/454-

7393. Superior American and California cuisine, featuring a nice range of rotating entrees, typically involving seafood, stews, and pasta. Also features solid, somewhat familiar choices for breakfast.

Cody's American Place 8030 Girard Ave ☏858/459-0040. Innovative, mid-priced California cuisine with an exotic Eurasian flair; especially notable are the seafood and pasta dishes and scrumptious burgers. Sit on the patio and catch a glimpse of La Jolla Cove.

George's at the Cove 1250 Prospect St ☏858/454-4244. Although the downstairs level of this swank eatery offers delightful Cal-cuisine, the

rooftop terrace has the unbeatable ocean views and somewhat cheaper fare.

Living Room Coffeehouse 1010 Prospect St ☏858/458-1187. One in a chain of local coffee joints, with great sandwiches, soups, quiches, and pastries with fresh ingredients, in an antique-laden living room.

Sushi on the Rock 7734-A Girard Ave ☏858/456-1138. Tempting array of inexpensive sushi combination plates, many of them quite colorful and experimental in throwing in different pan-Asian flavors and styles, and served to a soundtrack of rock and reggae.

Drinking: bars and coffeehouses

Most of San Diego's neighborhoods have a good range of **bars** and **coffee-houses**. While the Gaslamp Quarter is a good place to get dressed up for cock-tails, the beach communities south of La Jolla offer a more rowdy atmosphere, with plenty of beer and loud music, as well as early-evening happy hours to ease the pain of sunburn. Pacific Beach has the best selection of coffeehouses, most of them sporting a relaxed, bohemian atmosphere.

Bars

Karl Strauss Brewery & Grill 1157 Columbia St at B, Downtown ☏619/234-2739. Discerning beer hunters may enjoy ales and lagers brewed here on the premises, or just quaff from a sampler tray, while the menu offers a solid assortment of hefty favorites like ribs and sausages.

Kensington Club 4079 Adams Ave, Kensington District, north of Hillcrest ☏619/284-2848. Great joint for beer, wine, and cocktails, but also for wide-ranging live music selections from thumping-dance DJs to head-banging rockers to more sedate ambient groovers. High on the hip-and-cool meter.

Live Wire 2103 El Cajon Blvd, just east of Hillcrest ☏619/291-7450. With a wide range of imported beers, pinball, pool, and funky sub-bohemian decor, a fine choice for music and boozing, espe-cially with occasional DJ nights and power-chord performances from local rockers.

O'Hungry's 2547 San Diego Ave, Old Town ☏619/298-0133. Tall, dark beers and a boister-ous, sing-a-long crowd. For the Irish at heart.

Onyx Room 852 5th Ave, Gaslamp District ☏619/235-6699. Groovy underground bar with lush decor and comfortable seating, where you can listen to torch songs, knock back a few cocktails, and hit the back room for live jazz and dance tunes.

Red Fox Room 2223 El Cajon Blvd, just east of Hillcrest ☏619/297-1313. Makes a popular tan-dem nightcrawl with *Live Wire*, a block away. This old-style piano bar with good steaks draws nostal-gia buffs of all ages.

Coffeehouses

Café Crema 1001 Garnet Ave, Pacific Beach ☏858/273-3558. Wake yourself up here before going to the bars, or sober up afterwards, with one of their large coffees. Features sidewalk seating, late hours (till 4am on weekends), and on-site Internet access.

Café Lulu 419 F St, Downtown ☏619/238-0114. Hipster joint with eye-catching, mildly freakish decor, as well as a good selection of coffees and late-night food orders until 2am.

Claire de Lune 2906 University Ave, Hillcrest ☏619/688-9845. The prototypical coffeehouse atmosphere, with steaming java, teas, and sand-wiches, plenty of comfortable seating and enter-tainment that ranges from acoustic to spoken-word to avant-garde.

Gelato Vero Caffe 3753 India St, at the southern foot of Hillcrest ☏619/295-9269. Enjoy good espresso and gelato while getting clued in to local events by staff and regulars.

Upstart Crow 835 W Harbor Drive, Downtown ☏619/232-4855. In Seaport Village, a coffee bar fused with a bookstore, making for a lively cross-section of customers – and a surfeit of reading material.

Zanzibar 976 Garnet Ave, Pacific Beach ☏858/272-4762. Relatively serene retreat from the brash bars along this strip. Coffees, teas, sand-wiches, and muffins served until 2am, or 4am at weekends.

Nightlife: live music, clubs, and theater

San Diego's **nightlife** is fairly typical for a major city by the sea: while money is lavished on edifying pursuits such as theater and opera, the crowds flock to the see-and-be-seen beachside discos and boozy live-music venues. For full listings, pick up the free *San Diego Reader* (Ⓦwww.sdreader.com), buy the Thursday edition of the *San Diego Union-Tribune* (Ⓦwww.signonsandiego.com), or seek out the youth-lifestyle-oriented *Slamm/San Diego CityBeat* (Ⓦwww.sdcitybeat.com) at some of the places listed below. **Cover charges** at live-music venues range from $3 to $12, unless someone big is playing.

Live music venues

4th and B 345 B St, Downtown ☏619/231-4343. Hard-thumping dance club with two rooms and a hormone-fueled crowd of young bump 'n' grind enthusiasts. Despite the odor of testosterone, a high-spirited and funky place to shake your ass.

Belly Up Tavern 143 S Cedros Ave, Solana Beach ☏858/481-9022. Mid-sized concert hall that plays host to an eclectic range of live music – past acts include John Lee Hooker, the Fugees, and Black Uhuru.

Blind Melons 710 Garnet Ave, Pacific Beach ☏858/483-7844. Live rock, blues, and reggae bands play nightly to a crowd of beach and college hipsters in a spot right by the pier.

Brick by Brick 1130 Buenos Ave, Mission Bay ☏619/675-5483. Aggressively hip lounge that attracts nationally known alternative, blues, and hard rock acts.

Buffalo Joe's 600 5th Ave, Gaslamp District ☏619/236-1616. Very popular, almost unavoid-

able nightspot loaded with tourists and some locals, with a broad selection of live tunes, from aggressive rockers to snappy funk to tribal dance-beats to horn-rimmed nerd pop.

Casbah 2501 Kettner Blvd, Downtown ☏619/232-4355. Grungy joint that nevertheless hosts a solid, varying roster of blues, funk, reggae, rock, and indie bands. Local popularity contrasts with cramped environs.

Croce's Top Hat 802 5th Ave, Downtown ☏619/233-4355. Classy jazz in the backroom of a pricey restaurant (see "Eating," p.229), with a jazz brunch on Sundays.

Dick's Last Resort 345 4th Ave, Gaslamp District ☏619/231-9100. Old-fashioned seafood and chicken joint serving up gut-busting portions of meat to go with the fat, meaty sounds of nightly rockers with just the right snarl.

Humphrey's by the Bay 2241 Shelter Island Drive, Point Loma ☏619/523-1010. Live funk, soul , and R&B, along with weekly disco nights and live jazz on

Major venues

Any big name in contemporary music visiting San Diego is likely to appear at one of the following big-name **venues**:

Coors Amphitheatre 2050 Entertainment Circle, Chula Vista ☏935/671-3600

Open Air Theatre 5500 Campanile Drive, San Diego State University ☏619/594-6947 or 619/220-TIXS

Qualcomm Stadium 9449 Friars Rd,

Mission Valley ☏619/641-3100 or 619/283-4494

San Diego Convention Center 111 W Harbor Drive, Downtown ☏619/525-5000

San Diego Sports Arena 3500 Sports Arena Blvd, Mission Bay ☏619/224-4171 or 619/220-TIXS

Depending on availability, **half-price tickets** for theater and classical music events for that evening can be purchased (for cash only) at Arts Tix, 28 Horton Plaza at Broadway Circle (Tues–Thurs 11am–6pm, Fri & Sat 10am–6pm, Sun 10am–5pm; ☏619/497-5000, Ⓦwww.sandiegoperforms.com). Full-price advance sales are also available (credit cards accepted), and on Saturday, half-price tickets are issued for Sunday performances.

Otherwise, tickets for all major shows can be purchased from the venue directly or through Ticketmaster (☏619/220-TIXS). The **SRH Info Hotline** (☏619/973-9269) has a select list of alternative events.

Sundays, make this restaurant a local favorite for music, as well as food (see "Eating," p.230).

Patrick's II 428 F St, Gaslamp District ☎619/233-3077. Fun, no-frills Irish bar with nice range of R&B, rock, jazz, and especially blues.

Winston's Beach Club 1921 Bacon St, Ocean Beach ☎619/222-6822. A former bowling alley with rock bands most nights, along with reggae and an occasional 60s band to go with the 60s decor. Close to the pier.

Clubs and discos

Bitter End 770 5th Ave, Downtown ☎619/338-9300. Two-story venue, complete with dancefloor, martini bar, and private lounge, for the sophisticated poseur.

Blue Tattoo 835 5th Ave, Downtown ☎619/238-7191. Whether you want to indulge in a little foam dancing or just get nasty with the funk, this is the place to come. There's often a long line at this prime dance venue, as well as a strict dress code, so leave your sneakers and jeans behind.

Cafe Sevilla 555 4th Ave, Downtown ☎619/233-5979. Traditional Spanish cuisine upstairs, hip Latin American-flavored club downstairs, with flamenco, house, and funk grooves to whet your musical appetite.

Olé Madrid Café 751 5th St, Downtown ☎619/557-0146. Spanish restaurant that becomes a very popular funk and dance club at night. Arrive before 11pm if you want to get in (see "Eating," p.229).

The Room 909 Prospect St, La Jolla ☎858/459-5010. One of the few jumping joints in staid La Jolla, a mildly hip bar and dance club where yuppie locals arrive to kick up their designer heels.

Rosary Room 947 E St, Downtown ☎619/702-7160. With swank decor loaded with religious iconography and off-kilter designs, a good spot to indulge in scene-watching while grooving to dance DJs and knocking back an eclectic assortment of beer and wine.

Thrusters Lounge 4633 Mission Blvd, Pacific Beach ☎858/483-6334. Cozy bar and club where the dance beats come hard and heavy on weekends, and jazz and rock make occasional appearances the rest of the week.

Theater

There's a thriving **theater** scene in San Diego, with several mid-sized venues and many smaller fringe venues putting on quality shows. Tickets are over $40 for a major production, $12–$20 for a night on the fringe; the *San Diego Reader* carries full listings. The main **venues** are the Lyceum Stage Theatre, 79 Horton Plaza (☎619/235-8025, ⓦwww.sandiegorep.com); the three Elizabethan-style Globe theaters in the Simon Edison Complex for the Performing Arts in Balboa Park, 1363 Old Globe Way (☎619/239-2255, ⓦwww.theglobetheatres .org); the Civic Theatre, Downtown at 202 C St (☎619/570-1100, ⓦwww .sdccc.org/Civic); and the La Jolla Playhouse at the Mandell Weiss Center on the UCSD campus at 2910 La Jolla Village Circle (☎858/551-1010, ⓦwww .lajollaplayhouse.com). The alternative theatrics at Sushi Performance and Visual Art, 320 11th Ave, Downtown (☎619/235-8466, ⓦwww.sushiart.org), are sometimes pretentious but rarely boring.

Comedy

The **comedy** club scene in San Diego can barely be called a scene, with most jokes cracked (periodically) at venues like the Civic Theatre Downtown (see above) or at the restaurant and club *Humphrey's by the Bay*, in Point Loma (☎619/523-1010). If you want to catch some of the acts bound for the more glamorous venues in LA or New York, try the *Comedy Store South*, 916 Pearl St, La Jolla (☎858/454-9176).

Film

San Diego has many **cinemas**, most of them offering standard-issue Hollywood blockbusters. Scan the newspapers for full listings; admission is usually $5–8. For more adventurous programs – foreign-language films, monochrome classics, or cult favorites – look for the afternoon screenings (Mon–Sat) at the San Diego Public Library, 820 E St, Downtown. After dark, The Ken, 4061 Adams Ave (☎619/283-5909), in the Kensington area, is the most popular venue for art and revival films, changing its offerings almost every evening. The Guild (☎619/295-2000), Park (☎619/294-9264), and Hillcrest (☎619/299-2100) cinemas, all in Hillcrest, and the La Jolla Village Cinema (☎858/453-7831), can be relied on to feature solid arthouse fare. For an entirely different experience, the IMAX films at the Reuben H. Fleet Science Center (☎619/238-1233; see p.217) offer the kids an eye-popping selection of nature films and special-effects reels on a giant curved screen.

Classical music and opera

Recently infused with a multimillion-dollar private grant, the **San Diego Symphony** is finally back on its feet after escaping from bankruptcy, and performs both at the Copley Symphony Hall, Downtown at 750 B St (☎619/231-0938), and at Escondido's California Center for the Arts, 340 N Escondido Blvd (☎760/839-4138). Other upscale options include the jazz, classical, and chamber music series held at the Museum of Contemporary Art's Sherwood Auditorium, 700 Prospect St in La Jolla (☎858/454-3541), as well as the **San Diego Opera**, based at the Civic Theatre, Downtown (☎619/570-1100), which frequently boasts top international guest performers during its January-through-April season.

Gay and lesbian San Diego

Publicly centered on Hillcrest, San Diego's **gay and lesbian** culture can be easily accessed through a number of publications and resource centers, and a network of gay bars and clubs. Also, several hotels and bed and breakfast inns are noted for their friendliness towards gay and lesbian travelers – several being all but exclusively gay. For sun-worshippers, the place to go is **Blacks Beach** (see p.228) north of La Jolla.

Publications and resource centers

The primary source of gay and lesbian news, views, and upcoming events is the free weekly *Gay & Lesbian Times*, distributed through gay bars and clubs, many of the city's coffeebars, and most gay-run businesses. Also useful is the newsy, free *Update* with its Etcetera insert full of personals, classifieds, and a "What's On" bulletin board. The LA-based *Edge* is available as well. You can learn more by contacting the **Lesbian and Gay Men's Community Center**, 3916 Normal St, Hillcrest (☎619/692-2077, ⊛thecentersd.org), which has served the community for thirty years in several different locations.

Accommodation

Balboa Park Inn 3402 Park Blvd, Hillcrest ☎619/298-0823 or 1-800/938-8181, ⊛www.balboaparkinn.com. Elegant B&B in a Spanish Colonial building, within walking distance of Balboa Park and its museums and popular with gay, lesbian, and straight guests. Some rooms have kitchenettes and there's a Jacuzzi. ❺

Friendship Hotel 3942 8th Ave, Hillcrest ☎619/298-9898. One of the least expensive hotels in the area, but still offers clean rooms with TVs and refrigerators. Predominantly gay and lesbian. ❸

Harbor House Resort 642 W Hawthorn St, north of Downtown ☎619/338-9966, ⊛www.harborhouseresort.com. Serviceable rooms include refrig-

erators, ceiling fans, and some with harbor views. Also with complimentary breakfast, Jacuzzis, and sauna. ❺

Hillcrest Inn 3754 5th Ave, Hillcrest ☎619/293-7078 or 1-800/258-2280, ⊛www.bryx.com/hillcrestinn. Gay-oriented hotel in the heart of Hillcrest. The fairly basic, mostly non-smoking rooms all have baths, refrigerators, and microwaves. A bit drab but still friendly. ❸

Park Manor Suites 525 Spruce St, near Balboa Park ☎619/291-0999 or 1-800/874-2649, ⊛www.parkmanorsuites.com. The tasteful rooms – all with kitchens and nice, large sitting areas – are not quite as swank as the lobby of this residential-style inn would suggest, but then neither are the affordable prices. Continental breakfast is included. **⑤**

Bars and clubs

Bourbon Street 4612 Park Blvd, University Heights ☎619/291-0173. A chic gay crowd gathers nightly around the piano bar at this elegant New Orleans-style club north of Hillcrest, also featuring weekly karaoke and bingo.

Brass Rail 3796 5th Ave, Hillcrest ☎619/298-2233. High-energy dancing every night at this long-standing neighborhood hangout, with male go-go dancers on the weekends and periodic drag shows.

Caliph 3102 5th Ave, Downtown ☎619/298-9495. Piano bar with live music and kitschy, faux-Arabian decor, aimed mainly at an older male clientele.

Chee-Chee Club 929 Broadway, Downtown ☎619/234-4404. Old-time gay bar with casual atmosphere, rumpled crowd of regulars, and much less attitude than at some of the Hillcrest dance clubs.

The Flame 3780 Park Blvd, Hillcrest ☎619/295-4163. The city's premier lesbian club, open for dancing, pool, and occasional live acts from early evening to early morning. Tuesday is a no-holds-barred "Boys Night."

Flicks 1017 University Ave, Hillcrest ☎619/297-2056. Popular drinking joint that plays music videos on four large screens and offers pinball and pool as well.

Number One Fifth Avenue 3845 5th Ave, Hillcrest ☎619/299-1911. Casual neighborhood bar with a pleasant patio. DJs play requests some nights, mainly Fifties through Seventies.

Rich's 1051 University Ave, Hillcrest ☎619/295-2195. Originally mainly a gay club, *Rich's* now attracts numerous straights for the heavy dance grooves on weekends and "Hedonism" night on Thursday, when the hat check even accepts T-shirts and jeans. Cover charge most nights.

Listings

American Express Two main branches are Downtown at 258 Broadway (☎619/234-4455) and 1020 Prospect St in La Jolla (☎858/459-4161); both are open Mon–Fri 9am–5pm. Also at 7610 Hazard Center Drive in Mission Valley (Mon–Fri 9.30am–6pm, Sat 10am–3pm; ☎619/297-8101)

Amtrak recorded schedule information ☎619/239-9021 or 1-800/USA-RAIL

Beach and surf conditions ☎619/221-8884

Car rental Alamo, 2942 Kettner Blvd (☎619/297-0311); Avis, 3885 N Harbor Drive (☎619/231-7162 or 1-800/331-1212); Budget, 1904 Hotel Circle N (☎619/574-6975 or 1-800/283-4382); Hertz, 333 W Harbor Drive (☎619/236-9771 or 1-800/654-3131); Rent-a-Wreck, 3740 Fifth Ave (☎619/223-3300); Thrifty, 1409 Hotel Circle N (☎619/429-5000); Bargain Auto, 3860 Rosecrans St (☎619/299-0009)

Crime Victims Crisis Hotline ☎619/688-9200

Disabled assistance Accessible San Diego, 1010 2nd Ave, Suite 1630, San Diego 92101 (Mon–Fri 9am–4pm; ☎858/279-0704, ⓦwww.accessandiego.org); Access Center of San Diego, 1295 University Ave, Suite 10, San Diego 92013 (☎619/293-3500, TDD/293-7757, ⓦwww.accesscentersd.org)

Emergencies dial 911

Flea market The huge Kobey's Swap Meet takes place at the San Diego Sports Arena, 3500 Sports Arena Blvd (Thurs–Sun 7am–3pm; 50¢ admission Fri, $1 weekends; ⓦwww.kobeyswap.com)

Hospitals For non-urgent treatment, the cheapest place is the Beach Area Family Health Center, 3705

Mission Blvd, Mission Beach (☎858/488-0644).

Internet The Central Library, 820 E St, has free access. Or try Web-friendly coffee houses like *Café Crema*, 1001 Garnet Ave, Pacific Beach ☎858/273-3558

Left luggage At the Greyhound terminal ($2 for 6hr, $4 for 24hr) and, for ticketed travelers, at the Santa Fe Depot ($1.50 for 24hr).

Pharmacy 24-hour pharmacy at Sharp Cabrillo Hospital, 3457 Kenyon St, between Downtown and Ocean Beach (☎619/221-3400, ⓦwww.sharp.com)

Post offices The Downtown post office is at 815 E St (Mon–Fri 8.30am–5pm; ☎619/232-8612), but for poste restante (general delivery) use the main office at 2535 Midway Drive, between Downtown and Mission Beach (Mon 7am–5pm, Tues–Fri 8am–5pm, Sat 8am–4pm; zip code 92138; ☎619/758-7101 or 1-800/275-8777)

Rape Crisis Center/Hotline 4508 Mission Bay Drive (☎619/233-3088)

Sports Baseball's San Diego Padres (☎619/283-4494) play in the same place as football's Chargers (☎619/525-8282), Qualcomm Stadium in Mission Valley. Tickets available at the stadium box office

Traveler's Aid At the airport (daily 9am–10pm; ☎619/231-7361) and at Santa Fe Railroad Depot Downtown (☎619/234-5191)

Western Union 132 Washington St (☎619/291-8561), among other city locations (information at ☎1-800/325-6000, ⓦwww.westernunion.com).

Around San Diego

Largely north of the city, **San Diego County** runs from small bedroom communities to more rugged undeveloped country, where camping out and following forest and desert trails provide surprisingly appealing options for an area so close to a metropolis.

To the south, the Mexican border city of **Tijuana** isn't overly attractive, although it does offer many good buying opportunities for commodities ranging from souvenirs to prescription drugs, and is very easy to access by car or by the trolley.

Transportation around the region is straightforward. By car, I-5 skirts along the coast and I-15 runs a little deeper inland, while I-8 heads east from San Diego towards the southern part of the Anza-Borrego Desert (see p.283). East of I-15, throughout the scattered rural communities, the main options involve a network of smaller, less improved roads. Public transit is no problem between San Diego and the North County coast, with the San Diego Coaster running from Downtown San Diego up to Oceanside, along with frequent Greyhound buses and Amtrak trains between LA and San Diego. And while there are numerous ways to get to the Mexican border going south, travelers heading inland on public transportation will find only a skeletal bus service available.

The North County coast

The towns of the **North County coast** stretch forty miles north from San Diego to the Camp Pendleton marine base, which divides the county from the outskirts of Los Angeles. As they get farther from the city and closer to military installations, the communities generally become more working class and less bourgeois, but generally attract a mix of business commuters, beach bums, and crewcut-sporting tough guys. The main attraction is, of course, the coast itself: miles of excellent beaches with great opportunities for swimming and surfing.

Del Mar and Solana Beach

On the northern edge of the city of San Diego, the tall bluff that contains Torrey Pines State Preserve (see p.228) marks the southern boundary of **DEL MAR**, a town known mainly for its **Del Mar Racetrack**, which stages races between late July and early September (☎858/755-1141, ⓦ www.dmtc.com), and for its **San Diego County fairgrounds**. Held for three weeks just before the racing season begins, the **Del Mar Fair** (☎858/755-1161, ⓦ www.delmarfair.com) is an old-fashioned event with barbecues and livestock shows, though it's mixed with a fair amount of contemporary arts and music events. Otherwise, Del Mar is mainly a place to eat and shop well – at a price. Additionally, the train station is a short walk from an inviting beach.

SOLANA BEACH, the next town north from Del Mar, makes a better place for an overnight stop. Standard-issue motels line the coastal road, and there's even some decent nightlife – the *Belly Up Tavern*, 143 S Cedros Ave (☎858/481-9022), one of the major mid-sized music venues in the area (see "Nightlife" p.232 for details) – and some striking oceanside views from Solana

Beach County Park. If you're driving, take a quick detour inland along Hwy-8, passing the rolling Fairbanks Ranch (built by the film star Douglas Fairbanks Jr), to Rancho Santa Fe, a small but wealthy community with a distinctive Spanish architectural flavor from the 1920s and 1930s. It got a great deal of unwelcome attention in 1997 as home to the Heaven's Gate cult, which committed mass suicide upon the appearance of the Hale-Bopp comet.

Encinitas and Leucadia

The major flower-growing center of **ENCINITAS** is at its best during the spring, when its blooms of floral color are most radiant. It's no surprise that an Indian guru chose the town as the headquarters of the Self-Realization Fellowship, near Sea Cliff Roadside Park, a popular surfing beach dubbed "Swami's" by the locals. The fellowship's serene **Meditation Gardens**, around the corner at 215 K St (Tues–Sun 9am–5pm; free; ☎760/753-1811, ⓦwww.yogananda-srf.org), are open to all, and nearby are the similarly relaxing **Quail Botanical Gardens**, 230 Quail Gardens Drive (daily 9am–5pm; $5; ☎760/436-3036, ⓦwww.qbgardens.com). For more local information, call at the **visitor center**, 138 Encinitas Blvd (Mon–Fri 9am–5pm, Sat & Sun 10am–2pm; ☎760/753-6041, ⓦwww.encinitaschamber.org).

Encinitas and the adjoining community of **LEUCADIA**, three miles to the north, offer reasonably priced **accommodation**, such as the *Moonlight Beach Motel*, 233 2nd St, Encinitas (☎760/753-0623 or 1-800/323-1259; ❷–❸), nicely located for beach access with kitchenettes in all rooms. Otherwise, there's the landscaped **campground** at San Elijo Beach State Park ($18; ☎1-800/444-7275, ⓦwww.reserveamerica.com), near **Cardiff-by-the-Sea** just to the south, whose name – the whim of its founder's British wife, which also explains the presence of Manchester and Birmingham avenues – is its only interesting feature.

Carlsbad

Surfers constitute the major visitors to **South Carlsbad State Beach** (with a busy cliff-top campground for RVs only; $12, day parking $4; ☎760/438-3143 or ☎1-800/444-7275, ⓦwww.reserveamerica.com), which marks the edge of **CARLSBAD**, a coastal community with a great deal of cutesy, pseudo-Teutonic architecture. During the early 1880s, water from a local spring was deemed to have the same invigorating qualities as the waters of Karlsbad, a spa town in Bohemia (now part of the Czech Republic). Carlsbad thus acquired its name and reputation as a health resort, ably promoted by pioneer-turned-entrepreneur John Frazier, whose bronze image overlooks the (now dry) original springs. The springs are close to the junction of Carlsbad Boulevard (the coastal road) and Carlsbad Village Drive; along the latter, inside the train station, the **visitor center** (Mon–Fri 9am–5pm, Sat 10am–4pm, Sun 10am–3pm; ☎760/434-6093 or 1-800/227-5722, ⓦwww.carlsbad.org) offers a look at the town's interesting history.

The most popular attraction in Carlsbad these days is **Legoland California** (1 Lego Drive, exit Cannon Road off of I-5; $40, kids $34, parking $8; ☎760/918-5346, ⓦwww.legoland.com), where kids are encouraged to climb on larger-than-life Lego bricks, make their way through colorful mazes, operate miniature cars and boats, and view assorted world monuments built on a miniscule scale. The park is surrounded by golf courses, resorts, and a discount shopping center.

Other than the campground, the best **accommodation** is at the *Ocean Palms Beach Resort*, 2950 Ocean St (℡760/729-2493; ❹), overlooking the water but with its own pool and rooms with kitchenettes. Two good places to **eat** are *Pollos Maria*, 3055 Harding St (℡760/729-4858), for fast, tasty Mexican food, and *The Armenian Café*, 3126 Carlsbad Blvd (℡760/720-2233), where the menu is a marriage of American and Middle Eastern dishes, all presented at very affordable prices; open for breakfast, lunch, and dinner.

Oceanside, Mission San Luis Rey, and around

The most northerly town on the coast of San Diego County, **OCEANSIDE**, about five miles north of Carlsbad, is dominated by the huge **Camp Pendleton** marine base, though its Downtown is charming and its beaches are beautiful. For those without a car, it's also a major transportation center (Amtrak, Greyhound, the San Diego Coaster, local buses, and Metrolink trains to LA all pass through) and the easiest place from which to reach Mission San Luis Rey.

If you find yourself **staying** here, the *Beechwood Motel*, 210 Surfrider St (℡760/722-3866; ❷), is one of several decent and cheap motels in town. For **eating**, the *Hill Street Coffee House*, 524 S Coast Hwy (℡760/966-0985), is a rare good choice amid acres of fast-food joints, an old Victorian home offering great coffee, cakes, sandwiches, and salads, and live music on Saturday nights. The town's prime attractions include the lagoon-centered **Buena Vista Audubon Nature Center**, 2202 S Coast Hwy (Tues–Sat 10am–4pm, Sun 1–4pm; free; ℡760/439-BIRD, ⓦwww.bvaudubon.org), especially good for birdwatching and relaxing walks, and the **California Surf Museum**, 223 N Coast Hwy (Mon, Thurs–Sun 10am-4pm; free; ℡760/721-6876, ⓦwww.surf-museum.org), with displays on some of the top local surfers and boards that tackled the most wicked breaks.

Four miles inland from Oceanside along Hwy-76 and accessible on local bus #313, **MISSION SAN LUIS REY**, 4050 Mission Ave (daily 9am–4.30pm; $4; ⓦwww.sanluisrey.org), founded in 1798 by Padre Laséun, the largest of the California missions and once the center for three thousand Native American converts. Franciscan monks still inhabit the mission – even though it was repeatedly abandoned in the nineteenth century due to war and administrative struggles – and there's a **museum** and a serene candle-lit **chapel**. Even if you don't go inside, look around the foundations of the guards' barracks immediately outside the main building, and across the road, the remains of the mission's ornate **sunken gardens** (daily 9am–4.30pm; free), once *lavanderías*, where the mission's inhabitants did their washing.

Beyond the mission, any remaining hints of local history are fast being subsumed by a tidal wave of new property developments in the unexceptional community of **San Luis Rey**. For more interesting surroundings, push on another four miles to **Guajome County Park** (9.30am to an hour before dusk; $3 per vehicle, camping $16), whose centerpiece is a twenty-room adobe ranch (guided tours 11am & 2pm Sat & Sun; $2) erected in the mid-eighteenth century for the newly married Cave Couts and Ysidora Bandini, socialites who turned the place into a major hotspot. Among the many celebrities entertained here were Ulysses S. Wright and Helen Hunt Jackson, who, according to legend, based the title character of *Ramona*, her sentimental tale of Indian life during the mission era, on Ysidora's maid. After Couts' death in 1874, Ysidora fought to maintain the upkeep of the place but over the years it became dilapidated, until it was finally bought and restored by the county authorities.

Hwy-76 continues inland to Mission San Antonio de Pala and Palomar Observatory (both described below). Along the coast beyond Oceanside, the US military keeps its territory relatively undeveloped, creating a vivid impression of how stark the land was before commercialization took hold. When maneuvers aren't in progress, it's possible to pitch a tent in the lower parts of the camp area, close to the uncluttered **beach**. The northern part of the camp, around the San Onofre Nuclear Plant, is popular with surfers, thanks to its slow-rolling longboard waves, and very unpopular with environmentalists, who have been trying for decades to get the plant – built near a tectonic fault – shut down for good.

The North County inland

Unlike the coastal strip, **North County inland** has no sizeable towns and is mostly given over to farming, its terrain featuring dense forests, deep valleys, and mile-high mountain ranges. Besides a few reminders of the ancient indigenous cultures, remnants from the mission era, and a few tiny settlements – some of which may consume an hour or two of your time – it's best to make for the area's state parks and enjoy some leisurely countryside walks, or venture further east to the dramatic Anza-Borrego Desert (see p.283).

Escondido

About forty miles north of San Diego on I-15, and accessible via bus #20 from Downtown (connecting with bus #382 or #384), the little burg of **ESCONDIDO** is definitely worth a look for its **Heritage Walk** in Grape Day Park, offering a glimpse of several restored Victorian buildings (Thurs–Sat 1–4pm; free) and a 1925 railroad car with an elaborate scale model of the train that once linked Escondido to Oceanside. For more information, check out the **museum** devoted to the walk, 321 N Broadway (Thurs–Sat 1–4pm; free; ☎760/743-8267). Nearby, the **California Center for the Arts**, 340 N Escondido Blvd (Tues–Sat 10am–5pm, Sun noon–5pm; $5; ⓦwww.artcenter.org), features a surprisingly good contemporary art museum, featuring a range of traditional media as well as avant-garde video-art exhibitions, and two theaters that are the focus of a variety of music and dance performances. Next door, the comprehensive **visitors center**, 360 N Escondido Blvd (Mon–Fri 8.30am–5pm, Sat 10am–3pm; ☎760/745-4741 or 1-800/848-3336, ⓦwww.sandiegonorth.com), provides information for the entire north San Diego County area.

Five miles south of the Escondido town center and set in stunning scenery, the **Orfila Winery**, 13455 San Pasqual Valley Rd (daily 10am–6pm; ⓦwww.orfila.com), offers tastings of wines produced by a former Napa Valley vintner; while six miles north of town, the **Deer Park Winery and Auto Museum**, 29013 Champagne Blvd (daily 10am–5pm; ⓦwww.deerparkwinery.com), shows off a sizeable collection of vintage neon signs and classic cars – including a Model A Ford, Cadillac, and Crosley – to anyone who turns up to sample the product of its vines.

Not far from the winery lies Escondido's most renowned – or depressing – attraction, the **Lawrence Welk Resort**, a thousand-acre vacation complex of golf courses, guest villas, and the Welk Dinner Theater, eight miles north of the town off I-15 (no public transit) at 8860 Lawrence Welk Drive (☎760/749-3000 or 1-800/932-9355, ⓦwww.welkresort.com). Rising from accordion-playing unknown to musical juggernaut, TV bandleader Welk was the inventor of something known as "champagne music" – really little more than waltzes and polkas with a touch of sanitized swing. Displayed around the lobby of the theater, the Welk hagiography is both fascinating and disturbing, and is in any case much less filling than the cheap lunch buffet laid out in the nearby restaurant.

North from Escondido

Hwy-S6 leads fifteen miles north from Escondido to **Mission San Antonio de Pala** (Tues–Sun 6am–6pm; $2; ☎760/742-3317), close to the junction with Hwy-76 from Oceanside. Built as an outpost of Mission San Luis Rey in 1816, the mission lay in ruins until the Cupa Indians were ousted from their tribal home at the turn of the twentieth century (to make room for the building of Warner Hot Springs) and moved to this site, where the mission was revived to serve as their church. Although the current buildings are infrequently used replicas of the originals, they do offer an eerie atmosphere, with an evocative cemetery, lovely gardens, and a single-room **museum**, which contains artifacts created by the Pala tribe and dating back to the days of the original mission. There's also a small no-frills **campground** opposite the mission.

Continuing east, Hwy-76 runs into **Cleveland National Forest** (☎760/788-0250, ⊕www.r5.fs.fed.us/cleveland), home to a good number of state and federal **campgrounds**. The enormous forest stretches south from here almost to the Mexican border, although less-hearty backpackers tend to prefer the **Palomar Mountain State Park** (☎760/742-3462), on Hwy-S7, for its cooler, higher altitude (some parts rise above 5000ft) and fairly easy hiking trails. You can camp at the Doane Valley campground (☎1-800/444-7275, ⊕www.reserveamerica.com) and pick up supplies from the well-stocked Palomar Mountain General Store at the junction of routes S6 and S7.

Capable of seeing a billion light years into the cosmos, the two-hundred-inch Hale telescope of Cal Tech's **Palomar Observatory** on Hwy-S6 (daily 9am–4pm; free; ⊕www.astro.caltech.edu/palomarpublic) is something of a legend in astronomy circles. As a visitor, it's not possible to view the distant galaxies directly, though you can look in on the observatory's impressive collection of deep-space photographs taken with the powerful lens.

The North East Rural Bus System

The only bus service through the sparsely populated northeastern section of the county is the reliable but infrequent **North East Rural Bus System** (☎760/767-4287; calls answered daily 7am–noon and 2pm–5pm) that links San Diego with Escondido, Ramona, Santa Ysabel, Julian, and the Anza-Borrego Desert (see p.283) and runs daily.

The departure point in San Diego is the Grossmont Center near El Cajon, roughly ten miles east of Downtown (accessed via city bus #15). Make sure to phone at least a day in advance to check schedules – especially if you want to be picked up from Cuyamaca State Park. Board the buses either at marked stops or, where there are none, simply flag the vehicle down. A consolation for the scarcity of buses are the low **fares**: just $2.50 from San Diego to Julian, for example. Bicycles are carried free of charge but, again, you must reserve in advance.

East from Escondido

Ten miles east of Escondido on Hwy-78 (bus #307; Mon–Sat) and thirty miles north of San Diego (bus #878 or #879 from the Grossmont Center; Tues–Sat), the San Diego Zoo-affiliated **San Diego Wild Animal Park**, 15500 San Pasqual Valley Rd (daily 9am–4pm, summer closes at 8pm; $26.50, kids $19.50, combined ticket with San Diego Zoo $46.80, parking $6; Ⓦ www.sandiegozoo .org/wap), is the major tourist attraction in the area. A 2100-acre enclosure aimed mostly at kids, it features a sizeable aviary loaded with tropical birds, a mock African bush and Kilimanjaro hiking trail, elephant rides, and various films and exhibitions. The steep admission fee includes a fifty-minute ride on the Wgasa Bush Line Monorail, which skirts through the outer reaches of the park, where the animals – including lions, tigers, cheetahs, deer, and monkeys – roam about for your amusement.

In contrast to the crowded coast, the population – and the compelling vistas – becomes increasingly sparse as you press further east along Hwy-78 into a region that's difficult to access without personal transportation (see box above). If you're coming this way by car directly from San Diego, use Hwy-67 and join Hwy-78 at Ramona, eighteen miles from Escondido, and continue east for six-teen miles to **Santa Ysabel**. While unexceptional, this tiny crossroads is enlivened by **Dudley's Bakery**, 30218 Hwy-78, just before the junction with Hwy-79 (Wed–Sun 8am–5pm; Ⓣ760/225-3348, Ⓦ www.dudleysbakery.com), famous for its home-baked breads and pastries – the date, nut, and raisin loaf for one – at giveaway prices and the small **Mission Santa Ysabel**, a mile and a half north of town on Hwy-79 (Ⓣ760/765-0810; daily 7am–dusk; $1), a 1924 replacement of an 1818 original structure. Sitting in moody isolation, the mission has a small chapel and, around the side, a one-room **museum** (same hours; $1) detailing the history of the site. Outside is an Indian burial ground, and the church continues to serve several local Native American communities.

Julian

Surrounded by pines, seven miles southeast of Santa Ysabel on Hwy-78A, the hamlet of **JULIAN** was amazingly once the second-biggest town in the San Diego area, thanks to an 1869 gold discovery here. Since then, the local popu-lation has stayed constant at around 1500, its citizens earning more from har-vesting apples than from mining precious metals, and the town's formidable cider and apple pies often draw thousands of weekend visitors. Moreover, at an elevation of 4000ft, in the foothills that divide the coastal terrain from the desert, this sometimes chilly town provides a temperate base from which to make forays into the Anza-Borrego Desert (see p.283), less than ten miles to the east.

With its quaint buildings and carefully nurtured rustic charm, Julian is imme-diately appealing, but a short stroll reveals little of consequence away from the charming shops and restaurants on Main Street. For **accommodation**, the Chamber of Commerce, 2129 Main St (daily 10am–4pm; Ⓣ760/765-1857, Ⓦ www.julianca.com), has details of the town's many appealing **B&Bs**. Among these, the *Julian Gold Rush Hotel*, 2032 Main St (Ⓣ760/765-0201 or 1-800/734-5854, Ⓦ www.julianhotel.com; ❺), is the oldest functioning hotel in the state, opened in 1897 by a freed slave; rates include afternoon tea and a full breakfast. The *Julian Lodge*, 2720 C St (Ⓣ760/765-1420 or 1-800/542-1420, Ⓦ www.julianlodge.com; ❺), is only a replica of a historic hotel, but has a simi-lar country atmosphere, offering a buffet-style continental breakfast. A less expensive option is to **camp** in the Cuyamaca Rancho State Park (see box).

Hikes in the Cuyamaca Mountains

As a compelling option for **hiking** in the east-county area, the trails in the **Cuyamaca Mountains** (☎760/765-0755, ⊛www.cuyamaca.statepark.org) seldom fall below 4500ft. Outside the summer months snow is always a possibility, and even in summer, nights are cool and thunderstorms common.

Cuyamaca Peak Trail (6 miles; 4hr; 1600ft ascent). Following the vehicle-free, paved Cuyamaca Peak Fire Road, the most rewarding of the park's trails: a steep climb from the Paso Picacho campsite (reserve at ☎1-800/444-7275; $12) to a 6512ft summit, giving sweeping views east to the desert and west to the Pacific Ocean.

Harvey Moore Trail (12 miles; 7–8hr; 1000ft ascent). A well-signposted loop trail that is relatively flat and winds through several ecological zones – prairie, oak woodland, meadowland, and chaparral – all perfect territory for a cowboy such as Harvey Moore, the park's first superintendent in the 1930s. Starts a mile south of the park headquarters.

Middle Peak (6 miles; 4hr; 1000ft ascent). There are several routes to Middle Peak, all easier than the Cuyamaca Peak Trail. The most direct is Sugar Pine Trail, named after the tall pines that bear the world's longest cones. The trail starts at the Boy Scout camp, ten miles south of Julian, where the road turns sharply east at the end of the dammed Cuyamaca Lake.

Eating options include the *Julian Café*, 2112 Main St (☎760/765-2712), for the best atmosphere and meals, including the ubiquitous apple pie; *Bailey Woodpit Barbecue*, 2307 Main St (☎760/765-3757), featuring fine grilled meat served fall-off-the-bone tender; and the *Julian Pie Company*, 2225 Main St (☎760/765-2449, ⊛www.julianpie.com), a must for its succulent desserts.

If you find yourself with a few spare hours in Julian, take a look at the Gold Rush-era mining equipment and Victorian furnishings inside the **Julian Pioneer Museum**, 2811 Washington St (April–Nov daily 10am–4pm; Dec–March Sat & Sun 10am–4pm; $1), or wander half a mile up to the end of C Street and see the **Eagle Peak Mining Company** (daily 10am–3pm, weather permitting; $7), where hour-long tours of the old gold mine give a sense of the subterranean perils faced by the town's early settlers. North of Julian on Farmer Road, the **Volcan Mountain Wilderness Preserve** (open 24 hrs; free; ☎760/765-2300, ⊛www.volcanmt.org) also makes for an interesting visit, whether on self-guided hikes or monthly guided tours, with short trails passing through orchards, oak groves, and manzanitas, leading to an excellent viewpoint of the area.

Cuyamaca Rancho State Park

You could easily spend several enjoyable hours among the oaks, willows, sycamores, and Ponderosa and Jeffrey pines that fill **CUYAMACA RANCHO STATE PARK** (unrestricted entry), starting nine miles south of Julian and nine miles east of I-8 along Hwy-79. Even if you stay for days, you won't see everything. From lush sub-alpine meadows to stark mountain peaks, the park spans more than 25,000 acres, much of it designated wilderness area and only crisscrossed by a hundred miles of hiking trails (see box), many of them hugging the 5000-foot contour.

Pick up information and maps from the **park headquarters** (Mon–Fri 8am–5pm; ☎760/765-0755, ⊛www.cuyamaca.statepark.org), sixteen miles south of Julian, beside Hwy-79 in the heart of the park. At the same location, check on the park's **campgrounds** strung along Hwy-79 ($12–18;

☎1-800/444-7275, ⊛www.reserveamerica.com), chiefly **Paso Picacho**, twelve miles south of Julian, and **Green Valley**, five miles further south. These sites ($5 day-use, $12 overnight) are the only **accommodation** available unless you're prepared to hike into the $3 backcountry sites: Arroyo Seco, a mile and a half northwest of Green Valley, and Granite Spring, almost five miles east. There are also **cabins** available ($15–30).

For a historical backdrop to the striking scenery, drop into the excellent **museum** (Mon–Fri 10am–4pm, Sat & Sun 10am–2pm; free; ☎760/765-0755) in the park headquarters, which details how the local Kumeyaay natives resisted Spanish attempts to cut down the area's forests, strongly countered the arrival of settlers from the eastern US, and were one of the last groups forced onto reservations. For more on the indigenous peoples, take a stroll along the nature trails at Paso Picacho and at the park headquarters.

Tijuana and northern Baja California

TIJUANA has the odd distinction of being both one of the least culturally interesting areas in Mexico, and one of the most visited cities in the world – a place where twenty million people annually cross the border, most of them Californians and tourists on day-long shopping excursions seeking to spend money on blankets, pottery, cigarettes, tequila, dentistry, car repair, and even pharmaceutical drugs (see box p.246). Since everything is lower-priced in Tijuana than in the US (though more expensive than in the rest of Mexico), all of it is hawked with enthusiasm.

What's most dramatic about Tijuana (properly pronounced "tee-WAH-na") for first-time arrivals is the abrupt realization of the vast economic gulf separating the two countries. Crossing the **frontera**, or border, takes you past beggars crouched in corners and children scuffling for loose change thrown by tourists. It's both a depressing and revealing experience, yet for regular visitors, it's a shock that soon fades. Tijuana is, in fact, one of the wealthiest Mexican cities, thanks to the influx of well-heeled residents from Mexico City and the large number of international manufacturing companies who operate **maquiladoras** (factories) here to get a cheaper workforce.

Whatever its faults, Tijuana is, if nothing else, quite unique, and you could hardly find a more intriguing day-trip from San Diego. However, it's not typical Mexico, and if you want a proper taste of the country you'd do well to hurry on through. Things are much safer these days than decades ago when Tijuana lived up to its rough border-town image. Then, prostitution was rife and the streets extremely creepy after dark; these days the red-light area is limited to the easily avoided blocks around the junction of Avenida Artícula and Mutualismo. And while there's always a random incident of drunken frat-boys getting beaten and robbed after attending a grungy local strip club, visitors with less of a taste for debauchery will find little danger in most parts of town.

Currency in Tijuana

Dollars are accepted as readily as pesos everywhere in Tijuana, but although you can **change money** at any of the banks along Avenida Revolución or at the **casas de cambio** on both sides of the border, it's only worth doing so if you're traveling further into Mexico. That said, you'll get marginally better prices if you do pay in pesos. Bánamex and the *casas de cambio* will also change travelers' checks.

Getting there

Getting to Tijuana from San Diego could hardly be easier. The San Diego Trolley (see p.207) ends its route close to the elevated concrete walkway which leads over the border, as does bus #932 from the Santa Fe Depot in Downtown San Diego. Mexicoach operates a bus service from the US side of the border to Avenida Revolución in Tijuana (daily departures every 15min, 9am–9pm; $2 round-trip; ☎619/232-5049). Though traffic and insurance problems make public transportation a better option, if you do decide to drive, make sure you invest in auto **insurance**, which you can procure for a nominal fee in San Ysidro (see box p.248).

Crossing into Mexico, **border formalities** are minimal: simply walk through a turnstile and you're there. Customs and immigration checks are only carried out twenty miles or so inside the country, so you only need to be carrying a Mexican Tourist Card if you're continuing on from Tijuana. These are available free from any Mexican consulate in the US – the one in San Diego is

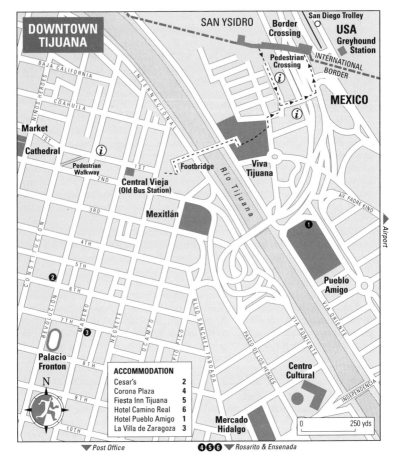

DOWNTOWN TIJUANA

SAN YSIDRO · Border Crossing · San Diego Trolley · USA · Greyhound Station · Pedestrian Crossing · INTERNATIONAL BORDER · MEXICO

BAJA CALIFORNIA · NIÑOS HEROES · COAHUILA · INTERNACIONAL

Market
Cathedral
Pedestrian Walkway · Footbridge · Viva Tijuana
Central Vieja (Old Bus Station) · Rio Tijuana
Mexitlán · AV PADRE KINO

Palacio Fronton
N

Pueblo Amigo · VIA ORIENTE

BLVD SANCHEZ TABOADA · PASEO DE LOS HEROES · VIA PONIENTE

Centro Cultural · INDEPENDENCIA

ACCOMMODATION

Cesar's	2
Corona Plaza	4
Fiesta Inn Tijuana	5
Hotel Camino Real	6
Hotel Pueblo Amigo	1
La Villa de Zaragoza	3

Mercado Hidalgo

0 — 250 yds

▼ Post Office   ❹❺❻ ▼ Rosarito & Ensenada

Airport

Downtown at 1549 India St (Mon–Fri 8am–1pm; ℡619/231-8414) – and also at the Mexican customs office just inside the Tijuana side of the border. When returning to the US, however, the formalities are very stringent (see Basics, p.20), and even if you've just traveled down for the day, you'll need to satisfy the usual entry requirements.

Accommodation

If you do want to sample Tijuana's discos into the small hours and stay overnight, the **accommodation** options are fairly good, if basic. You'll spend much less here for a **hotel** room than you would north of the border, and many passable lodgings can be found close to the central streets.

Cesar's Avenida Revolución 1079 ℡011526/685-1606. Straightforward rooms with an on-site cafeteria and pharmacy. ❸
Corona Plaza Agua Caliente 1426 ℡011526/681-8131. Serviceable choice with plain rooms and restaurant, bar, spa, and pool. ❹
Fiesta Inn Tijuana Paseo de los Héroes 18818 ℡1-888/848-2928, ⓦwww.fiestainn.com. Located close to the border, with a good selection of rooms and suites, offering amenities like computer hook-ups, satellite TV, spa, and pool facilities. ❺
Hotel Camino Real Paseo de los Heroes 10305 ℡011526/633-4001 or 1-800/7-CAMINO, ⓦwww.tjcamino.com. A very nice choice with plush rooms and two restaurants and bars. ❺
Hotel Pueblo Amigo Via Oriente 9211 ℡1-800/386-6985, ⓦwww.hotelpuebloamigo.com. Simple, tasteful rooms and suites, with on-site restaurant and bar, in a central location between the border and Zona Rio. ❻
La Villa de Zaragoza Avenida Madero 1120, between Calles 7 and 8 ℡011526/685-1837. A good bargain, with clean rooms, a/c, and cable TV, in a fairly central location. ❸

The Town

The main streets and shopping areas are a few blocks from the border in **Downtown**, where the major thoroughfare is **Avenida Revolución**, lined with street vendors and people trying to hustle you into the various shopping emporia. Stroll up and down for a while to get the mood and then retire to one of the plentiful bars and watch the tourists knocking back sizeable margaritas (the bigger bars charge $2.50 for a large one, $2 for a tequila, and about $1.50 for a beer). At night, the action mostly consists of inebriated American and Mexican youths gyrating in flashy discos and rowdy rock'n'roll bars – not hard to find around the main streets.

As a break from shopping or drinking, visit the **Centro Cultural**, or CECUT, poised like a huge golf ball amid high-rise office towers on the corner of Paseo de los Héroes y Mina and Avenida Independencia, in the Rio Tijuana area. The museum's permanent and rotating exhibits (daily 9am–8pm; 20 pesos or $2; ℡011526/684-1111, ⓦwww.cecut.org.mx) give strong accounts of Mexico's history and culture; films in the Omnimax Theate ($3.50, including museum admission) focus on Mexican landscapes and cityscapes. Nearby, on Independencia at Avenida Taboada, is the **Mercado Hidalgo**, the city market, featuring everything from produce to piñatas.

Other attractions include **Mexitlán**, Avenida Ocampo between calles 2 and 3 (Wed–Sun 9am–5pm; $3), a miniature Mexican theme park with models of famous Mexican buildings and pyramids; the moderately interesting **tequila museum**, at Festival Plaza Resort on Benito Juarez at Rosarito (daily 4pm–midnight, Fri–Sun noon–midnight; free), where you can sample over 130 different types of the renowned agave distillate; and lively matches of **jai alai** – a Basque game similar to handball – at the Moorish-style Palacio Fronton on Avenida Revolución at Calle 8 (Tues–Sat 8pm; $5).

Legal drug-buying in Tijuana

Increasingly, one of the top tourist draws in Tijuana – attracting an estimated third of all visitors – is the allure of cheap **pharmaceutical drugs**, available at Mexican pharmacies for a fraction of the cost of their obscenely overpriced US equivalents. Not surprisingly, this has opened up a whole new cottage industry, for local pharmacists (especially on Avenida Revolución), many of whom will gladly supply visitors with a sizeable quantity of different drugs – from Allegra to Zoloft – without a prescription from an American doctor (according to US law, you're allowed a three-month supply for personal use). While this has resulted in countless myths of busloads of seniors hauling back crateloads of Viagra without any difficulty, the reality is a bit more complicated. For one, if you're headed to Tijuana on a (legal) drug-buying mission, you'll still need to find a reputable **pharmacy** that won't sell you a cheap knock-off of a brand-name prescription, or worse, one that does nothing or actively harms you. You can do the research on your own before you leave, or take your health in your own hands by relying on a Mexican cabbie to take you to one he recommends. Keep in mind, though, that there have been countless accusations of shady deals between cab drivers, or organized-crime syndicates, and certain pharmacies, and just because a particular pharmacist is well known does not mean he or she is reputable. Another problem is the difficulty of returning to the US with a hefty stack of pharmaceuticals in tow. Unless you're coming back with a considerable amount of prescription drugs, it's unlikely you'll end up in jail, though you could be detained by a US Customs agent and asked all manner of probing, hostile questions and subjected to prison threats and other official browbeating. To save the trouble, you can always follow the official rules and bring back no more than a three-month supply; while anything more is out-of-bounds, most of the border guards' attention will doubtless be focused on looking for cocaine in your trunk, rather than Xanax in your shaving kit.

Eating and nightlife

As you'd expect, most of the **eating** options in Tijuana are confined to cheaper, lower-end eateries, many of them little more than street vendors selling standard Mexican fare like tacos or burritos, while a few more upscale restaurants cater to tourists looking for a more "refined" meal in Tijuana. The best choices include spots like *Café La Especial*, Avenida Revolución 718 (☎011526/685-6654), a high-spirited joint aimed at tourists, but offering rich, satisfying staples for cheap prices; and *La Fonda Roberto*, 2800 Cuauhtemoc Blvd (☎011526/686-4687), a longstanding favorite for its exotic combinations of ingredients and inventive menu including cactus salad and pumpkin *quesadillas* – also for inexpensive prices.

Apart from consuming the local cuisine, many people come to Tijuana to experience the **nightlife**. *Como Que No*, Avenida Sanchez Taboada 95 (☎011526/684-2791), is a fairly sophisticated venue, where clubgoers dress to impress. *Baby Rock*, Diego Rivera 1482, Zona Rio (☎011526/634-2404), is a very lively spot aimed at a younger crowd; while the always enticing *Rodeo Santa Fe*, on Avenida Paseo Tijuana in Pueblo Amigo Plaza, Zona Rio (☎011526/682-4967), is a wild "rodeo" staged indoors with Tex-Mex and Latino music, a mechanical bull, lots of cowboy gear, and, if you need a break from the cowpoke scene, a frenetic upstairs disco. Whatever the venue, keep in mind that most clubs in Tijuana enforce a no-sandals, no–jeans dress code.

Further into Mexico

As for traveling **further into Mexico**, the northwest of the country has fewer cultural attractions than the mainland, and many people head straight for Mexico City and the regions to the south. A closer option is the peninsula of **Baja California**, which has miles of fairly pristine coast and a few moderately sized cities. The only sensible destinations within easy reach of Tijuana are **Rosarito**, a south-of-the-border party beach, and the sizeable town of **Ensenada**. (For details, pick up the *Rough Guide to Mexico*, available in San Diego from Le Travel Store, 745 4th Ave, ☎619/544-0005.)

Rosarito

Forty-five minutes south of Tijuana, on buses from Central Vieja bus terminal at First and Madero, the old coastal road reaches the sea at **ROSARITO**, which boasts one of the best-looking beaches around, although the water is often polluted. While during the week it's much more relaxing here than in Tijuana, on weekends the town has a pervasive frat-house atmosphere. Surfers are drawn here from across the border for the fine waves at beaches like **Calafia**, at Km 35.5, and **Popotla**, at Km 33. You can rent gear at Tony's Surf Shop, Blvd Juarez 312, and the area is also popular with golfers, who frequent the Real del Mar Golf Club (☎011526/631-3401).

As for **accommodation**, the town's landmark is the historic *Rosarito Beach Hotel* (☎011526/612-0144, ⓦwww.rosaritohtl.com; ❺–❼), to which Hollywood's Prohibition refugees fled for a little of the hard stuff in the Thirties. These days, it offers elegant suites and apartments and blander, merely adequate rooms for a wide range of prices. For a cheaper option, try *Brisas del Mar* at Blvd Juarez 22 (☎011526/612-2547; ❷), just across the boulevard from the ocean, offering a pool and decent rooms with TV and air conditioning – some with hot tubs as well. For dining, there's no shortage of reasonable taco stands and inexpensive **restaurants**, many specializing in seafood. The weekend bonhomie is particularly frenzied at the beach-volleyball bar *Papas and Beer*, Boulevard Juarez near the Rosarito Beach Hotel, while at *El Patio*, Boulevard Juarez in the Festival Plaza (☎011526/612-2950), you can indulge in an upmarket taste of authentic Mexican food, featuring dishes like shrimp crepes served in a pleasant, modern atmosphere.

Ensenada

Venturing to **ENSENADA**, two hours south from Tijuana's Central Vieja, brings a hint of the real Mexico, though somewhat obscured by periodic waves of tourists. Cruise ships from San Diego dock here, and on weekends the bars are packed with American party animals, making Ensenada a favorite choice for *norteños* looking to find the closest interesting town beyond Tijuana. On Avenida Mateos, you'll find the majority of the bars, restaurants, souvenir shops, and places organizing **fishing excursions**. At the *Bodegas de Santo Tomás* winery, Miramar 666 between Calle 6 and Calle 7 (tours Mon–Sat 11am, 1pm & 3pm, Sun 11am & 1pm; $1; ☎011526/178-3333), most of the vintages can't compare even to the generic offerings from north of the border – although the restaurant in the winery is considered one of the best in Baja. Across the street, *La Esquina de Bodegas* is a pleasant café/gallery and wine-shop annex. The other famous local attraction is **La Bufadora**, a natural blowhole six miles south of Ensenada, which occasionally spouts up to eighty feet, though thirty is more common. Buses leave roughly hourly from the Tres Cabezas park on the coast road at the bottom of Avenida Riveroll.

Getting to and around Northern Baja

Getting through customs presents no problems for a quick trip to **northern Baja**: visitors to Tijuana, Rosarito, and Ensenada staying for up to 72 hours need only their passports and are not required to obtain tourist cards. **Vehicle permits** are not required in Baja, but most US rental agencies don't allow their vehicles into Mexico, so you'll need to approach companies such as California Baja Rent-a-Car (☎619/470-RENT or 1-888/470-RENT, ⊛www.cabaja.com), which rents cars for use throughout Baja. With your own vehicle ensure you get **Mexican insurance**, easily obtainable from numerous companies whose fliers are all over San Ysidro: try Instant Mexico Insurance Services, 233 Via de San Ysidro (☎619/428-4714 or 1-800/345-4701, ⊛www.instant-mex-auto-insur.com). Ultimately, it's probably easier to take the bus.

The pick of the **accommodation** (book at weekends) is the *San Nicolas*, Mateos at Guadalupe (☎011526/176-1901; ❺), which features a range of nice rooms, pool, Jacuzzi, fishing, whale-watching trips, and sports betting. As a good budget alternative, the *Hotel del Valle*, Avenida Riveroll 367, (☎011526/178-2224; ❶–❷), offers clean rooms with fans, TVs, and phones. Be sure to ask for a rate discount. For **eating**, *Hussongs Cantina*, Ruiz 113 – famous throughout Southern California – has managed to maintain its rambunctious reputation as a loud party spot on weekends. Soak up the beer with fish tacos from the **fish market** by the harbor, or the straightforward Mexican dishes at *El Charro*, Mateos 475.

Travel details

Trains

San Diego to: Anaheim (10 daily; 2hr); Los Angeles Downtown (11 daily; 2hr 45min to 3 hr 20min); Oceanside (11 daily; 45min to 1hr); San Juan Capistrano (11 daily; 1hr 15min to 2hr); Santa Barbara (6 daily; 5hr 30min to 6hr 30min); Solana Beach (11 daily; 40 min). For more information on the "Pacific Surfliner" route, call Amtrak (☎1-800/872-7245, ⊛www.amtrak.com).

US Buses

San Diego Downtown to: Anaheim (10 daily; 2hr 30min); Long Beach (8 daily; 2hr 30min); Los Angeles Downtown (30 daily; 2hr 30 min to 3hr); Oceanside (14 daily; 50min); San Clemente (7 daily; 1hr 30min); Santa Barbara (8 daily; 5hr to 6hr 30min). For more information, call Greyhound (☎1-800/231-2222; ⊛www.greyhound.com).
San Diego, Grossmont Center to: Cuyamaca (6 monthly; 2hr 30min – reservations only); Julian (1 daily; 2hr); Escondido (1 daily; 1hr 30min); Ramona (1 daily; 1hr); Santa Ysabel (1 daily; 1hr 30min). For more information, call the Northeast Rural Bus System (☎760/767-4287, ⊛www.co.san-diego.ca.us/cts/rural).

International buses

San Diego to: Tijuana (9am–9pm; 48 daily; 50min). Call Mexicoach for further details (☎619/232-5049, ⊛www.mexicoach.com).

3

The deserts, Las Vegas, and the Grand Canyon

CHAPTER 3 # Highlights

✳ **Palm Springs Celebrity Tour** This highly entertaining bus tour shepherds you past the homes of Palm Springs' rich and famous. See p.263

✳ **Palm Springs Aerial Tramway** Take a break from the scorching desert and ride the cable car up to the crisp pine forests and enjoy their stupendous panoramic views. See p.265

✳ **Joshua Tree National Park** The celebrated national park is resplendent with its unique freaky trees, gorgeous granite boulders, and coyotes that howl in the warm night air. See p.276

✳ **Historic Route 66** Trace a short stretch of the renowned Mother Road in search of classic Americana, such as *Roy's* gas station and café in Amboy. See p.294

✳ **The Liberace Museum** No visit to Las Vegas is complete without visiting this kitschy museum, devoted to the outrageous career – and clothes – of Liberace. See p.308

✳ **The Havasupai Reservation** Swim in the turquoise waterfalls of this reservation, one of the hidden jewels of the Grand Canyon. See p.319

3

The deserts, Las Vegas, and the Grand Canyon

The deserts of Southern California represent only a fraction of the half a million square miles of North American desert that stretch away eastward into another four states and cross the border into Mexico in the south. Contrary to the monotonous landscape you might expect, California's deserts are a varied and ever-changing kaleidoscope, dotted with everything from harsh settlements to posh resorts. The one thing you can rely on is that, for a large part of the year, they will be uniformly hot and dry. In fact, during the hottest summer months temperatures in the deserts can reach such dangerous heights that you'd be well advised to give them a miss altogether. And don't count on rain to cool things off – desert rainfall is highly irregular and a whole year's average of three or four inches may fall in a single storm.

Most of the 25 million acres that make up the desert are protected in state and national parks, but not all are entirely unspoiled. Three million acres are used by the US Government as military bases for training and weapons testing, and when explosions aren't shaking up the desert's fragile ecosystem, the region's many fans flock here to do their own damage, many on off-road vehicles.

In spite of this, most of the desert remains a wilderness, and with a little foresight could be the undisputed highlight of your trip. Occupying a quarter of the state, California's desert divides into two distinct regions: the **Colorado** or **Low Desert** in the south, stretching down to the Mexican border and east into Arizona, where it's an extension of the Sonoran Desert, and the **Mojave** or **High Desert**, which covers the south-central part of the state. The Low Desert is the most easily reached from LA, with the extravagantly wealthy **Palm Springs** serving as a gateway – though it's the kind of town where it helps to have a bankroll for optimum enjoyment. The hiking trails and wondrous rocks of the **Joshua Tree National Park** are the big attraction for

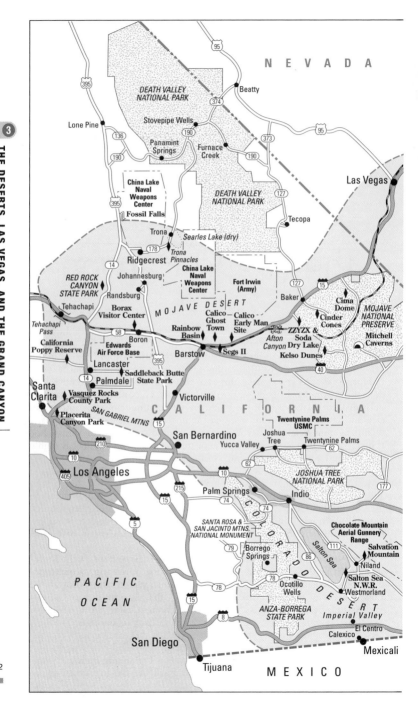

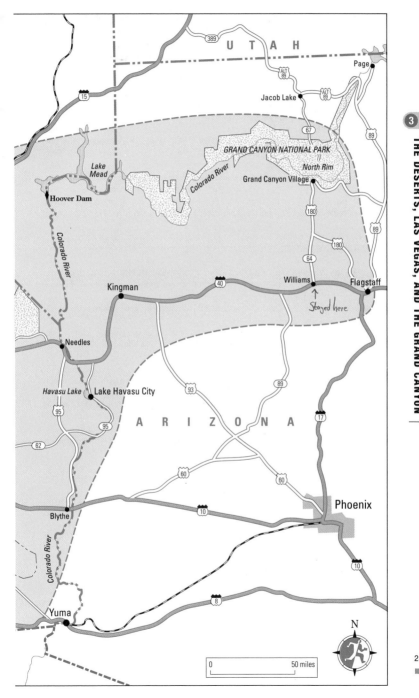

Desert survival

To survive the rigors of the desert, you have to be cool in more ways than one. Don't let adventure get the better of you and go charging off into the wilderness without heeding the warnings. The desert is rarely conquered by a pioneering spirit alone, and every year people die here. **Hikers** are particularly vulnerable, especially those who venture beyond the designated areas of the national parks, but **drivers** should also take considerable precautions whatever their destination. On the highways, filling your water jugs and gas tank should be all the preparation you need, but anything more adventurous requires planning. Above all, think. Tell somebody where you are going and your expected time of return. Carry an extra two days' **food and water** and never go anywhere without a **map**. Only the well prepared can enjoy the desert with any sense of security.

Bear in mind too that while the desert may be a danger to man, man is also a danger to the desert. Smog from Los Angeles drifts quickly eastward, and you may notice patches of it obscuring the panoramic view of the desert. Use common sense: remove nothing from the land except your trash, and leave only footprints behind.

Climate and water

First and most obviously you're up against a pretty formidable **climate**. This varies from region to region, but the basic safety procedures remain the same: not only are you doing battle with incredible heat, but at high elevations at night you should be prepared for below-freezing temperatures too. Try to time your travels to avoid the deserts between May and September, when daytime temperatures frequently exceed 120°F.

Outside of the summer months, the daytime temperatures are more manageable, ranging between the mid-sixties and low nineties. At any time of year, you'll stay coolest and best protected wearing loose, full-length clothing, plus a wide-brimmed hat, sunglasses, and copious amounts of sunscreen.

You can never drink enough **liquid** in the desert: the body loses up to a gallon each day and even when you're not thirsty you are continually dehydrating and should keep drinking. Before setting off on any expedition, whether on foot or in a car, two gallons of water per person should be prepared; one is an absolute minimum, and don't save it for the walk back, drink it as you need it. Waiting for thirst, dizziness, nausea, or other signs of dehydration before doing anything can be dangerous. If you notice any of these symptoms, or feel weak and have stopped sweating, it's time to get to the doctor. If you must booze during the day, compensate heavily with pints of water between each drink. Any activity in this heat can be exhausting so you also need to **eat** well, packing in the carbohydrates.

In summer, **camping** ventures of more than one night are all but impossible as you end up having to carry more water than is comfortable. In the valleys, you may also have to contend with **flash floods**, which can appear from nowhere: an innocent-looking dark cloud can turn a dry wash into a raging river. Never camp in a dry wash and don't attempt to cross flooded areas until the water has receded.

Roads: on wheels and on foot

Roads and **highways** across much of the desert are not maintained, and in an area where it's often a challenge to make it across existing dirt roads, trailblazing your own path through the desert is insanity. Of course you'll be tempted – if you must, rent a dune buggy or four-wheel-drive and tear about one of the off-road driving areas specifically designated for this purpose.

Even sticking to the main highways, you stand a good chance of getting an **over-**

heated engine. If your car's temperature needle rises alarmingly – most likely when negotiating steep gradients – turn the air conditioning off and the heater on full-blast to cool the engine quickly. If this fails and the engine blows, stop with the car facing into the wind and the engine running, pour water over the radiator grille, and top up the water reservoir. In an **emergency**, never leave the car: you'll be harder to find wandering around alone. Also consider taking along a windshield reflector to keep the car cool when parked, an **emergency pack** with flares, a first-aid and **snakebite kit** (see below), matches and a compass, a shovel, extra gas, and even a tire pump.

When **hiking**, try and cover most of your ground in the early morning: the midday heat is too debilitating, and you shouldn't even think about it when the mercury goes over 90°F. Almost all parks will require you to register with them – this is very wise, especially for those who are hiking alone. If you get lost, find some shade and wait. So long as you've registered, the rangers will eventually come and fetch you.

Desert wildlife

Most people's biggest fear of the desert is of encountering **poisonous creatures**. If you do, you'll be far better served by strong boots and long trousers than sport sandals and shorts. Not only do they offer some protection in case of attack, but firm footfalls send vibrations through the ground giving ample warning of your approach. Walk heavily and you're unlikely to see anything you don't want to.

Of all the **snakes** in the California desert, only the rattlesnake is poisonous. You might not be able to tell a rattler from any other kind of snake, so if in doubt, assume it is one. When it's hot, snakes lurk in shaded areas under bushes, around wood debris, old mining shafts, and piles of rocks. When it's cooler, they sun themselves out in the open, but they won't be expecting you and if disturbed may attack. While **black widow spiders** and **scorpions** are non-aggressive, they are extremely venomous and easily disturbed. A bite from any of the above is initially like a sharp pin-prick, but within hours the pain becomes severe, usually accompanied by swelling and acute nausea. Forget any misconceptions you may harbor about sucking the poison out – it doesn't work and even tends to hasten the spread of venom. The best way of inhibiting the diffusion is to wrap the whole limb firmly, but not in a tourniquet, then contact a ranger or doctor as soon as possible. Do all you can to keep calm – a slower pulse rate limits the spread of the venom. Keep in mind that even if a snake does bite you, about fifty percent of the time it's a dry – or non-venomous – strike. While snakes don't want to waste their venom on something too large to eat, it's a wise precaution to carry a **snakebite kit**, available for a couple of dollars from most sports and camping stores.

Tarantulas are not at all dangerous. A leg span of up to seven inches means they're pretty easy to spot, but if you're unlucky and get bitten, don't panic – cleansing with antiseptic is usually sufficient treatment once you've gotten over the initial pain.

Most **cacti** present few problems, but you should keep an eye out for the eight-foot **cholla** (pronounced "choya"), or jumping cholla as some are called, because of the way segments seem to jump off and attach themselves to you if you brush past. Don't use your hands to get them off, you'll just spear all your fingers; instead, use a stick or comb to flick off the largest piece and remove the remaining spines with tweezers. The large pancake pads of prickly pear cactus are also worth avoiding: as well as the larger spines they have thousands of tiny, hair-like stickers that are almost impossible to remove. You should expect a day of painful irritation before they begin to wear away. For more on the delights of desert flora and fauna, see Contexts, p.806.

△ Joshua Tree National Park

serious desert people, bridging the divide between Low and High Desert in a vast silent area of craggy trees. In contrast, the **Imperial Valley** to the south – agricultural land, though you could pass through without realizing anyone lived there – and the **Salton Sea** beyond, are undiluted Low Desert. There's no reason to visit them except that they lead into the vast expanse of the **Anza-Borrego Desert**, the largest state park in the country, boasting multifarious varieties of vegetation and geological quirks that can, with a little effort, be as rewarding as the better-known deserts to the north.

Interstate 10 crosses the Low Desert from east to west and carries a considerable flow of traffic. This includes packs of bikers heading out for a long weekend ride and some hijinks in the popular gambling resorts, like **Lake Havasu City**, that dot the stunning **Colorado River** region on the California–Arizona border. I-15 cuts north from I-40 at **Barstow**, often a first stop for those heading into the High Desert, where the **Mojave National Preserve** makes a worthwhile natural detour en route to the unnatural neon oasis of **Las Vegas**, just across the border in Nevada, where gambling is legal. Once you've got that far, a day's drive east (or a thirty-minute flight) takes you to the magnificent **Grand Canyon** in Arizona. Afterwards you can loop back into California by way of Death Valley, part of the desert region covered in Chapter Four (see p.325).

Desert practicalities

Public transportation in the desert is poor to nonexistent: Los Angeles connects easily with the major points – Palm Springs, Barstow, Las Vegas – and the Anza-Borrego is marginally accessible from San Diego, but upon arrival you're stuck without your own vehicle. If you do have a car, it will need to be in good working order – don't rely on the Thunderbird you picked up in LA for $500 to get you through the worst of the desert. Three major interstate highways cross the desert from east to west. I-15 cuts directly through the middle of the Mojave on its way from Los Angeles to Las Vegas, joined at Barstow by I-40, which then heads eastwards to the Grand Canyon. I-10 takes you from LA through the Palm Springs and Joshua Tree area, heading into Arizona.

Some fast, empty secondary roads can get you safely to all but the most remote areas of the desert, but be wary of using the lower-grade roads in between, which are likely to be unmaintained and are often only passable by four-wheel-drive. Other than in the Palm Springs area, **motels** in the California deserts are low in price, and you can generally budget for under $40 per night. However, even if cost is no object, you'll get a greatly heightened sense of the desert experience by spending some time **camping** out.

The Low Desert

Despite the **Low Desert**'s hundreds of miles of beauty and empty highways, most visitors to the region have no intention of getting away from it all. They're heading for where it's at – **Palm Springs**, a few square miles overrun with the famous, the star-struck, the aging, and the aspirational. It is said, not completely in jest, that the average age and average temperature of Palm Springs are about the same – a steady 88. This is a town that fines homeowners who don't maintain their property to what local officials deem to be a suitable standard. However, you'll find it hard to avoid as Palm Springs is the first stopping point east from LA on I-10, and hub of a resort area – the **Coachella Valley** – that stretches out for miles around, along Hwy-111. The valley's farming communities have the distinction of forming part of the most productive irrigated agricultural center in the world, growing dates, oranges, lemons, and grapefruit in vast quantities, though sadly they're steadily giving way to the condos and golf courses that comprise Palm Springs' ever-growing industry.

Fortunately you don't have to travel impossible distances to see the desert at its natural best. **Joshua Tree**, one of the most startling of California's national parks, lies less than one hour's drive east of Palm Springs, three from LA. A day-trip would give you a taste, but you really need a couple of days to get to grips with Joshua Tree's sublime landscape, taking in the sunsets and the howl of coyotes at twilight. East of the park, towards the Colorado River and Nevada, and south towards the Mexican border, the desert is arid and uncomfortable, with only the highly saline **Salton Sea** to break the monotony. A drive in this direction is rewarded, however, by the **Anza–Borrego Desert**, southwest of Joshua Tree, whose starkly beautiful vistas are punctuated by several oases and unusual vegetation.

Palm Springs and the Coachella Valley

With its manicured golf courses, condominium complexes, and some seven hundred millionaires in residence, **PALM SPRINGS** does not conform to any typical image of the desert. Purpose-built for luxury and leisure, it tends to attract conspicuous consumers and comfort seekers rather than the scruffier desert rats and low-rent retirees of less geographically desirable areas. But though it may seem harder to find the natural attractions and reasonably priced essentials among the glitz, they do exist.

Palm Springs and the adjacent resort towns of the **Coachella Valley** – Cathedral City, Desert Hot Springs, Rancho Mirage, Palm Desert, Indio, Indian Wells, and La Quinta – sit in the lushest agricultural area of the Colorado Desert, with the massive bulk of the San Jacinto Mountains and neighboring ranges looming over its low-level buildings, casting an instantaneous and welcome shadow over the area in the late afternoon. Since Hollywood stars were spotted enjoying a bit of mineral rejuvenation out here in the 1930s, Palm Springs has taken on a celebrity status all its own, a symbol

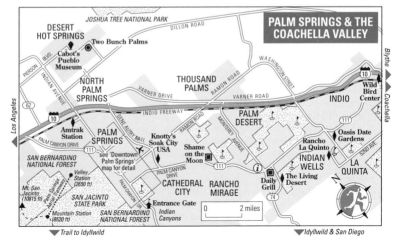

of good LA living away from the amorphous, smoggy city. In recent years it has also become a major **gay** resort (see box, below), with many exclusively gay – and generally expensive – hotels, bars, and restaurants.

For years, high-school kids arrived in the thousands, too, for the drunken revelry of Spring Break (around the end of March and beginning of April). Local antipathy finally persuaded the city council, under the leadership of the late Sonny Bono, to ban the annual invasion in 1993, and the inebriated youth promptly decamped east to Lake Havasu City (see p.298). The alcoholically inclined still flock to the area, but not to get drunk – the **Betty Ford Center**, smack in the middle of the valley at Rancho Mirage, draws a star-studded patient list to its booze- and drug-free environment, attempting to undo a lifetime's behavioral disorders during a $16,000 month-long stay.

The town's setting is superb, surrounded by the beautiful Indian Canyons with the snowcapped **San Jacinto Mountains** behind. Meteorologists have noted changes in the humidity of the desert climate around the town, which they attribute to the moisture absorbed from the hundreds of swimming pools – the consummate condo accoutrement, and the only place you're likely to want to be during the day if you come in the hotter months. When scarce water supplies aren't being used to fill the pools or nourish the nearby orchards, each of the Coachella Valley's hundred-plus **golf courses** receives around a million gallons daily to maintain their rolling green fairways.

Palm Springs wasn't always like this. Before the wealthy settlers moved in, it was the domain of the **Cahuilla**, who lived and hunted around the San Jacinto Mountains, to escape the heat of the desert floor. They still own much of the town, and via an odd checkerboard system of land allotment, every other square mile of Palm Springs is theirs and forms part of the **Agua Caliente**

Gay Palm Springs

Palm Springs now claims to have overtaken Key West as America's largest **gay resort**, the local gay press estimating that around forty percent of the town's residents are gay. You'll see rainbow flags and decals all over the place but nowhere more so than along Arenas Road, near South Indian Canyon Drive, which has become something of a gay hangout. Elsewhere businesses catering to a broader clientele are often gay run and there's a general sense that the gay and straight communities coexist happily. The local tourist machine puts out a specialist version of its free semi-annual brochure, the *Palm Springs Gay Visitor's Guide*, though you'll get a better insight into the community from the bi-weekly *The Bottom Line* ($5; Ⓦwww.psbottomline.com), or the free *Desert Post Weekly* (Ⓦwww.desertpostweekly .com), which has listings and discussions of current issues.

The single biggest draw is Easter weekend, when twenty thousand gay men flock here for the **White Party**, four days of hedonism throughout downtown Palm Springs. **Lesbians** get their turn a couple of weeks earlier during the Kraft-Nabisco women's golf tournament, held at the Dinah Shore tournament course.

Such is the power of the pink dollar in Palm Springs that virtually all hotels here are gay-friendly, though the Warm Sands district, half a mile southwest of downtown, contains around 35 exclusively **gay hotels**, most of them hedonistic fun palaces. Check the town's website Ⓦwww.palm-springs.org for suggestions, or try *Terrazzo*, 1600 E Palm Canyon Drive (☏1-866/837-7996, Ⓦwww.terrazzo-ps.com; ❼), or *Warm Sands Villas*, 555 Warms Sands Drive (☏760/323-3005 or 1-800/357-5695, Ⓦwww.warmsandsvillas.com; ❺). Women will prefer *Bee Charmer Inn*, 1600 E Palm Canyon Drive (☏760/778-5883 or 1-888/321-5699, Ⓦwww.beecharmer.com; ❻).

Indian Reservation – a Spanish name which means "hot water," referring to the ancient mineral springs on which the town rests. The land was allocated to the tribe in the 1890s, but exact zoning was never settled until the 1940s, by which time the development of hotels and leisure complexes was well under way. The Cahuilla, finding their land built upon, were left with no option but to charge rent, a system that has made them the second richest of the native tribes in America – and the money continues to pour in, thanks in part to revenue from their new **spa** and the **casinos** of Coachella Valley.

Arrival

Palm Springs lies 110 miles east of Los Angeles along the Hwy-111 turnoff from I-10. Arriving by **car**, you drive into town on North Palm Canyon Drive (Hwy-111), the main thoroughfare. Coming by **bus**, you'll arrive at the Greyhound terminus at 311 North Indian Canyon Drive, linked with LA (7 daily; 3hr) and Phoenix (3 daily, 5hr). You're unlikely to arrive by **train** as thrice-weekly services – from Los Angeles and Tucson, Arizona – all arrive in the middle of the night at a desolate platform three miles north of Palm Springs at North Indian Avenue, just south of I-10.

Alaska, American, Northwest, United, and a handful of regional carriers, **fly** into Palm Springs International Airport, 3400 E Tahquitz-McCallum Way (℡760/318-3800), where you can catch bus #21 into town. Tickets are often expensive, and if you're flying to California it is usually cheaper to fly into Los Angeles and rent a car from there.

Information

The very helpful Palm Springs **visitor center**, 2781 N Palm Canyon Drive (daily 9am–5pm; ℡760/778-8418 or 1-800/347-7746, ⓦwww.palm-springs .org), can offer accommodation deals as well as booking over the Internet. They also have an exhaustive selection of brochures including the Spring/Summer or Fall/Winter version of the *Palm Springs Visitor's Guide*, and the *Palm Springs Gay Visitor's Guide*, which is virtually the same but with more gay-oriented info. Ask too for local maps, including one that details the homes of the famous ($5), and another (also $5) guiding you past homes exemplifying the mid-century Palm Springs Modern style of architecture (see p.263). Though long ignored, homes designed by Richard Neutra, Robert Frey, and their contemporaries are now highly sought.

The windmills of Palm Springs

After trawling through the dull eastern suburbs of Los Angeles, I-10 throws you a surprise at the San Gorgonio Pass just before Palm Springs. Over four thousand **wind turbines** dot the valley, their glinting steel arms sending shimmering patterns across the desert floor. This is the largest concentration of windmills in the country, generating enough electricity to service a small city, and the conditions are perfect. The sun beating down on the desert creates a low-pressure zone that sucks air up from the cooler coastal valleys, funneling it through the San Gorgonio Pass, the only break between two 10,000-foot-plus ranges of mountains. Strong winds often howl for days in spring and early summer, reaching an average speed of between fourteen and twenty miles per hour. At the time of writing, tours of the windmills had been suspended, but if you are interested in learning more it may be worth checking with the visitor center to see if anything has started up.

Getting around

Downtown Palm Springs is only a few blocks long and wide and is manageable on foot, though for **getting around** the rest of the Coachella Valley, it is possible with the SunBus (℡1-800/347-9628, ⓦwww.sunline.org), which operates daily from 6am to 8pm (until 11pm on some routes) and charges $1 to get around town, plus an extra 25¢ for two transfers (good for two hours after purchase); a day pass costs $3. While the system is extensive and services fairly frequent, it is never a quick way to get about and you may prefer a **taxi**; call City Cab (℡760/416-2594).

To get the absolute best out of Palm Springs and the surrounding towns though, you should think about **car rental**. All the majors are at the airport, but there are usually cheaper deals with Aztec Rent-A-Car, 477 S Palm Canyon Drive (℡760/325-2294), and Foxy Wheels, 440 S El Cielo Rd (℡760/321-1234), both with cars for as little as $30 per day.

If you're not planning to stray too far, **rent a bike** from Bighorn Bicycles, 302 N Palm Canyon Drive (℡760/325-3367), who charge $22–27 for half a day, and $29–35 for a full day depending on the model.

Accommodation

Palm Springs was designed for the rich, and big luxury **resorts** are abundant here. If you want to take a shot at seeing how the other half lives, consider visiting in summer when temperatures rise and prices drop dramatically. Many of the bigger hotels slash their prices by up to seventy percent, and even the smaller concerns give twenty to thirty percent off. The visitor center (see opposite) also offers special deals. If you couldn't care less about cachet, *Motel 6* and other **low-priced chains** are still represented.

The north end of town along Hwy-111 holds the most affordable places, in the main perfectly acceptable and all with pools. **Bed and breakfast** inns are becoming more common, and with double-room rates at around $80 per night, they are a good bargain when you add up comfort, hospitality, and a nice breakfast. If you're traveling in a group, it may work out cheaper to rent an **apartment**: many of the homes in Palm Springs are used only for a brief spell and are let out for the rest of the year. Again summer is the best time to look, but there is generally a good supply throughout the year. The Coachella Valley's daily paper, the *Desert Sun* (ⓦwww.thedeseertsun.com), has rental information in its classified pages, and many rental agencies operate around town – the visitor center will be able to point you to the more affordable ones. **Camping** is not really a viable option, unless you have an RV; the only campground accommodating tents is **Lake Cahuilla** (see below); otherwise, tent-carriers will have a better time exploring Joshua Tree or Anza-Borrego.

Listed below are some of the more reasonable and/or interesting options, with summer rates quoted; in the popular October to April period, when you should also book in advance, you can expect the rates to be hiked up by a price bracket – or two or three. Also keep in mind that weekend prices are also a price bracket or two higher than weeknights. Always ask for a discount wherever you stay; the visitor center may also be helpful in this matter. Some historical quirk of snobbery on the part of the city council dictates that accommodation can't be referred to as a motel, though some of the places listed obviously are.

Hotels, motels, and B&Bs

Casa Cody 175 S Cahuilla Rd ⓣ760/320-9346 or 1-800/231-2639, ⓦpalmsprings.com/hotels/casacody. Built in the 1920s by glamorous Hollywood pioneer Harriet Cody, this historic B&B offers tastefully furnished Southwestern-style rooms, a shady garden, great pool, and wonderful breakfasts in a good location two blocks from downtown. Large kitchen suites also available. Rooms ❷, suites ❺

Desert Lodge 1177 S Palm Canyon Drive ⓣ760/325-1356 or 1-800/385-6343, ⓦwww.desertlodge.com. Spacious motel-style place with free continental breakfast and in-room movies. ❸

Ingleside Inn 200 W Ramon Rd ⓣ760/325-0046 or 1-800/772-6655, ⓦwww.inglesideinn.com. Expensive, but with enough real class to have attracted such guests as Garbo, Dalí, and Brando over the years. Built on a private estate downtown, each room has a personal steam bath and individual whirlpool. The inn's *Melvyn's Restaurant* still lures the glitterati. Rooms ❺, suites ❽

Lake Cahuilla Ave 58, La Quinta ⓣ760/564-4712 or 1-800/234-PARK. Large campground for tents and RVs located by a 135-acre stocked lake located roughly fifteen miles east of Palm Springs. There are showers, a dump station for RVs, a summer-only swimming pool, and provision for horses. RVs $16, tents $12.

Motel 6 660 S Palm Canyon Drive ⓣ760/327-4200, ⓦwww.motel6.com. The most central of the budget motels, with a good pool. ❷

Palm Court Inn 1983 N Palm Canyon Drive ⓣ760/416-2333 or 1-800/667-7918, ⓦwww.palmsprings.com/hotels/palmcourtinn. On four nicely landscaped acres, so it doesn't feel like a faceless motel. There's a Jacuzzi as well as two pools and a fitness center, and continental breakfast is included in the room rate. ❷

Park Inn & Suites 2000 N Palm Canyon Drive ⓣ760/320-0555 or 1-800/732-7755, ⓦwww.palmsprings.com/parkinn. Comfortable hotel with a beautiful outdoor pool – a must in the desert – plus continental breakfast. ❹

Quality Inn 1269 E Palm Canyon Drive ⓣ760/323-2775 or 1-800/472-4339, ⓦwww.qualityinn.com. Modern motel with spacious grounds, including a nice pool, kids wading pool, and restaurant. ❸

Rodeway Inn 1277 S Palm Canyon Drive ⓣ760/325-5574 or 1-877/424-6423. One of the budget options in town with clean, pleasant rooms, cable TV, and a pool. ❷

Vagabond Inn 1699 S Palm Canyon Drive ⓣ760/325-7211 or 1-800/522-1555, ⓦwww.vagabondinn.com. Well-run three-story motel with free continental breakfast and weekday newspaper, a good pool, coffee makers in each room, and refrigerators available. ❷

Villa Royale Inn 1620 S Indian Trail ⓣ760/327-2314 or 1-800/245-2314, ⓦwww.villaroyale.com. Beautiful inn with individually designed and exquisitely furnished rooms and suites, most with Jacuzzi, situated around a pool. In the winter season meals and drinks are served from the bougainvillea-draped restaurant. Rooms ❺, villas ❼

The Willows 412 W Tahquitz Canyon ⓣ760/320-0771 or 1-800/966-9597, ⓦwww.thewillows-palmsprings.com. The former estate of a US Secretary of State, whose friends – among them Clark Gable, Carole Lombard, and Albert Einstein – holed up here during the 1930s. Opulently decorated rooms, gorgeous lush grounds, a stunning San Jacinto Mountain backdrop, sumptuous breakfasts, and an ideal downtown location make this worth the splurge. ❽

Palm Springs

Much of your time in the Coachella Valley is going to be spent in **Palm Springs**, home to the majority of the recognized sights. It is a sprawling place but is focused in a fairly concentrated core.

Downtown Palm Springs stretches for about half a mile along Palm Canyon Drive, a wide, bright, and modern strip full of boutiques and restaurants that's engulfed the town's original Spanish-village-style structures. Despite the celebrity stars embedded in the sidewalk, the cooling misters around the better restaurants, and the neat rows of fan palms along Palm Canyon Drive, Palm Springs is looking decidedly downmarket. Only one block back from the main drag empty lots, broken asphalt, and low-rent shops clearly signal that the better shops and galleries (and their aspiring clientele) have moved east to Palm Desert and the other Coachella Valley towns. That said, Palm Springs is the only place with a strollable center and has the greatest concentration of eating places. The departure of spring-breakers and civic regeneration efforts have seen a partial revival of its fortunes, though it is a far cry from the glitz you might be expecting with schlocky T-shirt emporia and bookstores devoted exclusively to Hollywood stars jockeying for position with retail art galleries, not all of them good.

Palm Springs isn't all rampant consumerism. It is worth spending time in the Palm Springs Desert Museum, and admiring the architecture of Little Tuscany (also known as the Heritage District and "the tennis club district"), just west of North Palm Canyon Drive, where some of the finest small hotels congregate. Further afield, cactus fans should spend an hour at Moorten Botanical Garden, while plane buffs are better served at the Palm Springs Air Museum.

You'll soon want to explore further, best done by spending half a day riding the **Palm Springs Aerial Tramway** into the San Jacinto Mountains and strolling the easy trails, then returning to explore the palm-filled **Indian Canyons**.

Downtown Palm Springs

Strolling down South Palm Canyon Drive, you may well miss the **Village Green Heritage Center** at no. 221, a small brick plaza around a fountain and surrounded by a handful of buildings including the 1884 McCallum Adobe and "Miss Cornelia's Little House" made of railroad ties. In any case, time is better spent seeking out the attractive **Palm Springs Desert Museum**, 101 Museum Drive (Tues–Sat 10am–5pm, Sun noon–5pm; $7.50, first Fri of the month free; ☎760/325-0189, ⓦwww.psmuseum.org), a part-art, part-natural history collection that's especially strong on Native American and Southwestern art. Its holdings are so large that, despite the enormous exhibition space, only a small part can be shown at any given time. The only permanent display is the late actor William Holden's collection of Asian and African

| Palm Springs and the Coachella Valley

Celebrity and architectural tours

Knowing that they're in the thick of a megastar refugee camp, few can resist the opportunity to see the homes and country clubs of the international elite on a **celebrity tour**. As tacky as they are, these tours have some voyeuristic appeal, allowing you to spy on places like Bob Hope's enormous house, and the star-studded area known as **Little Tuscany** – Palm Spring's prettiest quarter, where the famous keep their weekend homes. The best part of the tour is not the houses, but the fascinating trivia about the lives of those who live (or, most often, lived) in them. Palm Springs Celebrity Tours, 4751 E Palm Canyon Drive (☎760/770-2700, ⓔcelebritytours@cs.com), conducts one-hour jaunts for $17 and, for the dedicated, longer excursions around the country clubs and the Sinatra estate (where Frank used to bring Ava Gardner) for $23. Of course, if you've got a car, you can do it yourself with a $5 map of the stars' homes from the visitor center (see p.260), but you'll miss the sharp anecdotal commentary that makes it such fun.

The recent surge in interest in the mid-twentieth-century Modernist style of architecture has raised the profile of its chief exponents, such as Richard Neutra and R.M. Schindler, who both worked in and around Palm Springs. This has brought Palm Springs renewed cachet, something you can learn about either with a self-drive map ($5) from the visitor center or by joining PS Modern Tours (☎760/318-6118, ⓔpsmoderntours@aol.com), who offer a ninety-minute morning jaunt ($40) and a longer afternoon tour ($55) for true fans.

CENTRAL PALM SPRINGS

0   1 mile

N

ACCOMMODATION

Bee Charmer Inn	11
Casa Cody	4
Desert Lodge	7
Ingleside Inn	5
Motel 6	6
Palm Court Inn	1
Park Inn & Suites	2
Quality Inn	12
Rodeway Inn	8
Vagabond Inn	9
Villa Royale	10
The Willows	3

RESTAURANTS

Las Casuelas	D
Native Foods Café	E
Peabody's	C
Le Peep	F
Thai Smile	A
Le Vallavris	B

art. The natural science exhibits focus on the variety of animal and plant life in the desert, proving that it's not all sandstorms and rattlesnakes.

Downtown's most anarchic piece of landscape gardening can be seen at **Moorten Botanical Garden**, 1701 S Palm Canyon Drive (Mon, Tues & Thurs–Sat 9am–4.30pm, Sun 10am–4pm; $2.50; ☎760/327-6555), a bizarre and somewhat shambolic cornucopia of every desert plant and cactus, lumped together in no particular order, but interesting for those who won't be venturing beyond town to see them in their natural habitat.

Out by the airport, the **Palm Springs Air Museum**, 745 N Gene Autry Trail (daily 10am–5pm; $8; ⓦwww.palmspringsairmuseum.org), contains an impressive collection of World War II European and US fighters and bombers, along with associated material on the campaigns they flew in and on the men who flew them.

Palm Springs Aerial Tramway and Mount San Jacinto State Park

When the desert heat becomes simply too much to bear, you can travel through five climatic zones from the arid desert floor to (sometimes) snow-covered alpine hiking trails on top of Mount San Jacinto by riding the **PALM SPRINGS AERIAL TRAMWAY** (Mon–Fri 10am–8pm, Sat & Sun 8am–8pm; last car down 9.45pm; $20.80, $27.80 with dinner, downhill journey only $11; ⓣ760/325-1391 or 1-888/515-TRAM, ⓦwww.pstramway.com), located on Tramway Drive, four miles southwest of Hwy-111 on the northern edge of Palm Springs. Every thirty minutes a large cable car sets off up the rocky Chino Canyon bound for the Mountain Station almost six thousand feet above at 8516ft. Each car is fitted with a rotating floor that makes two full revolutions on the twelve-minute journey giving breathtaking 360-degree views only outdone by those from the top, some 75 miles all the way to the Salton Sea. There's a welcome drop of around 30°F from the temperature in the valley, so bring something to keep warm, or hide indoors at the buffet-style restaurant, bar, obligatory gift shop, or watch a decent 23-minute video on the tramway's construction. Outside there are viewing decks, and access to a couple of forested **short trails**: the three-quarter-mile Discovery Trail loop and the mile-and-a-half Desert View Trail with views down onto the Coachella Valley way below. From November 15 through April 15, snow conditions permitting, the **Adventure Center** (Mon–Fri 10.30am–4pm, Sat & Sun 9am–4pm; same contacts as Tramway office) offers cross-country **skiing** ($18 a day), **snowshoeing** ($15 a day), and **snowtubing** ($8 an hour) high above the desert floor.

To stray further into the surrounding wilderness of the 13,000-acre **MOUNT SAN JACINTO STATE PARK**, you'll need a permit from the State Park Visitor Center (Mon–Fri 1–5pm, Sat & Sun 9am–5pm) in the Mountain Station. This gives prepared hikers the freedom to hike up to the nearby summit of the 10,834-foot Mount San Jacinto (six miles each way), down to Idyllwild (ten miles each way), or along a number of other forest trails. See the Idyllwild account on p.272 for more details of the forest.

Exploring the canyons

Hard-core desert enthusiasts visit Palm Springs for the **hiking** and **riding** opportunities in the canyons which incise the San Jacinto Mountains immediately west of Palm Springs.

The best known and most accessible of the canyons are Palm Canyon, Andreas Canyon, and Murray Canyon, known jointly as **Indian Canyons** (daily 8am–5pm though sometimes closed summer weekdays, call to check; $6; ⓣ760/325-3400 or 1-800/790-3398) on part of the Agua Caliente Indian Reservation that lies to the south of downtown. Centuries ago, ancestors of the Cahuilla tribe settled in the canyons and developed extensive communities,

Palm Springs and the Coachella Valley

made possible by the good water supply and animal stock. Crops of melons, squash, beans, and corn were grown, animals hunted, and plants and seeds gathered for food and medicines. Evidence of this remains, and despite the near extinction of some breeds, mountain sheep and wild ponies still roam the remoter areas. To reach the best of them, follow South Palm Canyon Drive about three miles south to the clearly signposted entrance, from where paved roads run to the entrance of the canyons.

Probably the most popular is **Palm Canyon**, which is, not surprisingly, choked with palms – some three thousand over seven miles – beside a seasonal stream along which runs the easy 1.5-mile Palm Canyon Trail. A one-mile loop visits the best of **Andreas Canyon**, noted for its rock formations and more popular than **Murray Canyon**, which is more difficult to reach but rewards those prepared to hike two miles with a twelve-foot waterfall.

A tiny trading post at Palm Canyon sells hiking maps, refreshments, and assorted native crafts. To indulge in real Wild West fantasy you should see things on **horseback**. Smoke Tree Stables, 2500 Toledo Ave (℡760/327-1372), offers scheduled one- and two-hour riding tours of the canyons at $30 per hour – well worth it, especially if you go early morning (tours start from 8am) to escape the midday heat. Longer rides are available by advance arrangement.

After years of hippie colonization and subsequent abandonment, the local tribe have recently re-opened **Tahquitz Canyon**, now accessible only on a two-hour tour ($12.50, ℡760/416-7044 Ⓦwww.tahquitzcanyon.com) which climbs high into the palmless canyon.

Sections of the canyons and surrounding land are set aside for the specific lunacy of **trailblazing** in jeeps and four-wheel-drives. For a taste, contact OffRoad Rentals, 59511 Hwy-111, about four miles north of the Palm Springs tram (℡760/325-0376, Ⓦwww.offroadrentals.com), who offer a range of guided quad bike and dune buggy tours (from $35), as well as rentals for those with appropriate skills. Alternatively try Desert Adventures, 67555 E Palm Canyon Drive, Cathedral City (℡1-888/440-JEEP or 760/324-JEEP, Ⓦwww.red-jeep.com), who offer excellent guided jeep adventures in the Santa Rosa Mountains from $80. One of the most popular tours takes you across the desert floor and two thousand feet up through bighorn sheep preserves, spectacular cliffs; and steep-walled canyons. It's a bit expensive, but brilliant fun for the fearless.

Activities

The desert sun will soon send you in search of a pool. In many cases you won't have to walk more than fifty feet from your room to the hotel pool, but these can be small and crowded and you may prefer the **Olympic-sized pool** at the Palm Springs Swim Center, Sunrise Way at Ramon Road (Mon, Wed, Fri 11am–5pm, all other days 11am–3pm; open later in July & Aug; $3.25; ℡760/323-8278).

Lots more water gets used up at the 22-acre **Knott's Soak City USA**, 1500 Gene Autry Trail (March–Nov Mon–Fri 10am–5pm, Sat & Sun 9am–6pm; $21.95, kids $14.95; ℡760/327-0499, Ⓦwww.knotts.com/soakcity), where you can surf on its one-acre wavepool and mess around on its thirteen waterslides. Next door, **Uprising** (all year daily; ℡760/320-6630 or 1-888/CLIMBON, Ⓦwww.uprising.com) focuses on getting kids and their parents **rock climbing** on their substantial outdoor (but shaded) artificial rocks, though rock climbers in training are welcome too. Beginners can either climb with an instructor in attendance ($30 an hour) or a pair of you can take a lesson in ropework and belay each other for as much of the day as you want ($39). They also have private guides for getting out on real rock ($200 a day for one person, $270 for two).

For a substantially more relaxing experience, visit one of Palm Springs' day spas, particularly the elaborate Spa Resort Casino, 100 N Indian Canyon Drive (daily 8am–7pm; ☎1-888/293-0180, ⓦwww.sparesortcasino.com), based around the **mineral spring** that the Cahuilla discovered on the desert floor over a century ago. Here, the basic "Taking of the Waters" ($30) gives you a sauna, spa, steam, eucalyptus rooms, and as much time in the swimming pool and fitness center as you desire; though you're encouraged to spend a lot more on massages (from $65), assorted skin and body care treatments (from $25), and of course at the on-site casino. A dozen more spas are listed in the *Palm Springs Visitor's Guide*.

The other Coachella Valley towns

Palm Springs may have the name, but it is the other towns of the Coachella Valley that now have the bulk of the swanky resorts, big-name shops, and elegant expense-account restaurants. On initial acquaintance, it is hard to tell one town from another as they form an amorphous twenty-mile sprawl broken only by around a hundred golf courses. Not all the boundaries between them are clearly marked, and on their main drags they tend to share faceless low-slung architecture – but differences become evident to those who have time to explore.

Hwy-111 runs the length of the valley through, or close to, most of the main points of interest, but if you've got a specific destination in mind and want to avoid endless stop lights, consider the faster **I-10** which runs parallel about four miles to the north.

Cathedral City and Rancho Mirage

Adjacent to Palm Springs, about five miles east along Hwy-111, **CATHEDRAL CITY** ("Cat City") is named for soaring rock formations, now, sadly, obscured by development. You may well come here to dine or tap into the **gay scene** that's second only to the one in Palm Springs, but during the day there's not a lot to see except for an **IMAX theater**, 68510 East Palm Canyon Drive (☎760/324-7333, ⓦwww.desertimax.com). For more information, head for the **visitor center**, 68845 Perez Rd #6 (Mon–Fri 8am–5pm; ☎760/328-1213).

Next in line, the generally staid **RANCHO MIRAGE** tends to attract dignitaries – and high-profile substance abusers. Home to former President Gerald Ford and his wife, it's also host to the latter's upscale drunk tank, the **Betty Ford Center**.

Palm Desert, Indian Wells, and La Quinta

PALM DESERT, directly east along Hwy-111, is the safest place to witness the animal life that flourishes despite the inhospitable climate. Here, the ever-expanding **Living Desert**, 47900 Portola Ave (daily Sept to mid-June 9am–5pm; mid-June to Aug 8am–1.30pm; $8.50; ☎760/346-5694, ⓦwww.livingdesert.org), is the area's only essential sight, now encompassing over 200 acres of land, all irrigated, manicured, and divided into sections representing different desert regions around the world. Stroll among the cacti of the Mojave or the Chihuahua gardens, through a garden specially designed to attract butterflies, or into a palm oasis. North American desert animals – coyotes, foxes, bighorn sheep, snakes, and mountain lions – have now been supplemented by sections devoted to African species, such as wild dogs, gazelles, zebras, cheetahs, and warthogs. There are shady *palapas* and cooling "mist stations" everywhere, but it is still best to arrive as the gates open for cool and fragrant morning air, particularly if you fancy the wilderness trail system, which penetrates the hill country behind the zoo. If you can't stand to walk around in the heat, take one of the frequent fifty-minute, narrated **tram tours** ($5).

You can glimpse a different species of local creature nearby on **El Paseo**. The Rodeo Drive of the desert, this mile-long strip of fashionable stores and galleries loops south off Hwy-111 and is one of the very few places in the whole Coachella Valley where you might leave your car and stroll.

Come November, the non-indigenous but increasingly populous species *homo golfus* turns out en masse for the nation's only **golf cart parade** (☎760/346-6111, ⊛www.golfcartparade.com), with decorated buggies proceeding along El Paseo.

For more on local events and sights, call at the **Palm Desert Visitor Center**, 72990 Hwy-111 at Hwy-74 (Mon–Fri 9am–5pm, Sat & Sun 9am–4pm; ☎760-/568-1414 or 1-800/873-2428, ⊛www.palm-desert.org); for wilderness information, drive three miles south along Hwy-74 to the **Santa Rosa and San Jacinto Mountains National Monument Visitor Center** (generally Fri–Mon 9am–4pm).

The adjoining city of **INDIAN WELLS** has the largest per capita income in the US, as well as the largest concentration of the Coachella Valley's grand **resorts**. It's known for its four-day New Year **Jazz Festival**, its high profile **tennis tournaments**, and its prestigious Desert Town Hall **lecture series** (⊛www.deserttownhall.org), four or five talks that run into spring. Recent speakers include Newt Gingrich, Margaret Thatcher, John Major, and Jean-Michel Cousteau.

Next heading east comes **LA QUINTA**, named for the Valley's first exclusive resort – *Rancho La Quinta* – built in 1927 and thriving during the Depression, when Hollywood's escapist popularity rose as the country's income fell. Director Frank Capra wrote the script for multiple-Academy Award winner *It Happened One Night* at the resort in 1934 and considered the place so lucky he kept coming back, bringing the likes of Greta Garbo in his wake. It's still so posh that it's not marked on the main road (take Washington Street south to Eisenhower to find it). The Santa Rosa Mountain backdrop is stunning, and the rich no longer get very duded up, so you won't feel out of place if you come for a drink at the piano lounge.

Indio

In stark contrast is neighboring **INDIO**, a low-key town whose agricultural roots show in its many date and citrus outlets (take 50th Avenue east from behind *Rancho La Quinta* to get here and you'll pass so many date groves you'll think you're in Saudi Arabia – in fact, the town of Mecca is not far away). Back on Hwy-111, stop in at the **Shields Date Gardens**, no. 59111 (daily 9am–5.30pm; free; ☎760/399-5665, ⊛www.oasisdate.com), built in 1924 but renovated in the 1950s, for a date crystal shake ($3) at the original soda fountain. Wander out to see the date palms (all with ladders attached for harvesting the dates), and don't miss the kitschy free film, *The Romance and Sex Life of the Date*, with its cheesy commentary partly recorded in the 1950s by Floyd Shields, who set the place up. The town's huge February **Date Festival** draws people from as far as LA to its wonderfully goofy camel and ostrich races.

More serious animal lovers might want to stop in at the **Wild Bird Center**, 46-500 Van Buren St (10am–5pm daily; donations; ☎760/347-2647), where injured owls, hawks, and other desert avians are cared for and, if feasible, released back into the wild.

Desert Hot Springs

Isolated on the north side of I-10, the city of **DESERT HOT SPRINGS**, twelve miles north of Palm Springs, was chosen in a national competition as having the best-tasting water in the country. The underground wells for which the town is named supply water for the multitude of swimming pools as well as for drinking. A good jumping-off point for visiting Joshua Tree, it's somewhat more casual than the other communities. One exception to this is **Two Bunch Palms** (☎1-800/472-4334, Ⓦwww.twobunchpalms.com; ❼–❽), a luxury resort nestled in between trailer parks and a favorite of celebrities from Los Angeles. Normal people are also welcome if they can pay the price – spa treatments run about $90 per hour. However, spending your days soaking in the hot-springs pool with a book and a cocktail, with intermittent breaks for mud baths and massages, is not a bad way to pass the time.

You might also want to call at **Cabot's Pueblo Museum**, 67616 E Desert View Ave (Sat & Sun 9am–4pm; donations; ☎760/329-7610, Ⓦwww .cabotsmuseum.org), in a rustic Hopi-style structure built by Cabot Yerxa over a twenty-year period.

Eating

Palm Springs restaurants run the gamut, from super posh to fast-food, with some reasonable ethnic options in between. If you come in the offseason, the desert sun may squelch your appetite sufficiently that you go without eating most of the day and find yourself ravenous at dusk. Although most of the more famous **restaurants** in Palm Springs and Cat City are ultra-expensive, more reasonable options can be found with a little effort. Dedicated diners might also want to sample what's on offer in the rest of the Coachella Valley; our recommendations only scrape the surface of the huge selection that's out there.

For the really budget-conscious, supermarket shopping is the best bet: try Von's in the Palm Springs shopping mall, which is open from early morning until around 11pm for basics.

Palm Springs and Cathedral City restaurants

Atlas 210 S Palm Canyon Drive, Palm Springs ☎760/325-8839. Modern and very stylish restaurant right on the strip, with outdoor seating and an eclectic range of well-prepared dishes such as marinated swordfish steak, lobster ravioli, or nectarine chicken curry: mains mostly $17–25.

Las Casuelas Terraza 222 S Palm Canyon Drive, Palm Springs ☎760/323-1003. *Las Casuelas* opened its original establishment in 1958 (still going strong at 368 N Palm Canyon Drive), but you can't beat this Spanish-Colonial-

style sister restaurant with a bustling atmosphere, stacks of mist-cooled outdoor seating centered on a palm-roofed bar, and usually some live entertainment. The food suffers from north-of-the-border blanding but is still good and not too pricey.

Cedar Creek Inn 1555 S Palm Canyon Drive, Palm Springs ☎760/325-7300. Casual midrange American dining with all sorts of under-$20 meal-plus-wine specials offered at less fashionable dining times such as late afternoons and midweek evenings. Everyone should find something from the huge range of pastas, steaks, seafood, and sandwiches.

El Gallito 68820 Grove St, Cathedral City ℡760/328-7794. A busy Mexican cantina that has the best food for miles and lines to prove it – get there around 6pm to avoid the crowds.

John Henry's 1785 Tahquitz Canyon Way at Sunrise Way, Palm Springs ℡760/327-7667. Large portions of eclectic American fare, from rack of lamb to imaginative fish dishes, perfectly served and at half the price you'd expect. Dinner is around $20; reserve after 2pm. Closed Sundays and June–Sept.

Le Vallauris 385 W Tahquitz Canyon Way, Palm Springs ℡ 760/325-5059 or 1-888/525-5852. Palm Springs' best restaurant does not exactly hide its light under a bushel, describing itself as "*the* restaurant where the Stars entertain their friends"; you are indeed likely to run into one or two once-renowned artistes. Even if star-gazing is not your style, the contemporary California-Mediterranean cuisine is excellent, the service impeccable, and the setting gorgeous. Expect to pay at least $80 each. Reservations essential.

Mykonos 139 E Andreas Rd, Palm Springs ℡760/322-0223. A family-run Greek place just off Palm Canyon Drive, with friendly service, large portions of excellent, unpretentious food, and low prices.

Native Foods Café 1775 E Palm Canyon Drive in the Smoke Tree Village Mall, Palm Springs ℡760/416-0070. This totally vegan café puts a creative twist on traditional vegetarian fare. An eclectic menu, including tacos, pizzas, salads, and a variety of veggie burgers, and excellent prices make this a worthwhile spot. The Jamaican jerk "steak" salad is highly recommended as is the Save the Chicken burger.

Red Tomato 68784 E Palm Canyon Drive, Cathedral City ℡760/328-7518. Patio and indoor dining on terrific thick-crust pizza, especially the garlicky "white" pies, plus Balkan-style lamb dishes, from 4pm nightly.

Thai Smile 651 N Palm Canyon Drive, Palm Springs ℡760/320-5503. Few points for decor or ambience but great, authentic Thai green curries and the occasional Szechuan dish for around $10; takeouts available.

Village Pride Coffeehouse and Juice Bar 214 E Arenas Rd, Palm Springs ℡760/323-9120. This large, comfortable, and relaxed queer coffee bar offers an alternative to the bar scene and doubles as an info center. Occasional karaoke and open mike nights.

The Wilde Goose 67938 E Palm Canyon Drive, Cathedral City ℡760/328-5775. An antique-crammed award-winning restaurant serving great food – particularly strong on steaks, seafood, and game including duck and elk – for around $40 per head.

The rest of the Coachella Valley

Agua Caliente Casino Bob Hope Drive and Ramon Road near I-10 ℡760/202-2600. All-you-can-eat buffet deals costing $10–15 are available here during the day and for as little as $7 from 11pm to 10am.

Blame it on Midnight 777 E Tahquitz Canyon ℡760/323-1200. Predominantly gay bar and grill with some sort of show most nights.

Daily Grill 73061 El Paseo, Palm Desert ℡760/779-9911. A bustling, elegant coffee shop-style restaurant with large portions at reasonable prices. The chicken pot pie is a favorite along with excellent steaks, fish, salads, and lemonade.

Shame on the Moon 69950 Frank Sinatra Drive at Hwy-111, Rancho Mirage ℡760/324-5515. Long-standing bistro with California cuisine and an intimate bar, attracting a loyal gay crowd.

Wheel-Inn Eat 16 miles west on I-10 at the Cabazon exit (marked by two 50ft concrete dinosaurs built in the 1960s and 1970s). Humble, 24-hour desert truck stop with a burly clientele and enormous portions – so unpretentious you'd think they'd never heard of Palm Springs. One of the dinosaurs houses a wonderfully kitschy gift shop.

Nightlife, bars, and clubs

The scattered nature of the Coachella Valley and the predominance of staid, moneyed residents does little to promote a thriving **nightlife**. Unless you're a member of one of the exclusive country clubs, or disco-crazy, you'll have to work to find much at all (let along anything raucous) though you might stop in at one of the resort **piano lounges**, where, if you shell out for an over-priced drink, you can sometimes catch surprisingly good jazz.

The Palm Springs visitor center (see p.260) has details of **what's on** around town, and stocks the seasonal **Palm Springs Visitor's Guide** and the gay bi-monthly *The Bottom Line*. Pick up the *Desert Guide*, a local publication, to find out the current nightlife situation. Unless you hear of something that warrants the journey you're best staying around Palm Springs, where nightlife tends to the retro side, or nearby Cathedral City which has some hipper options, especially for the gay crowd.

Palm Springs' main drag is especially crowded on Thursday evenings (Oct–May 6–10pm; June–Sept 7–10pm), when the surprisingly funky **VillageFest street fair** along North Palm Canyon Drive draws equal numbers of tourists and young locals to booths selling everything from fresh baked bread to tacky souvenirs, plus there's a kids' play zone.

For **theater**, the historic Plaza Theatre, 128 S Palm Canyon Drive, hosts the long-running **Fabulous Palm Springs Follies** (Nov–May nightly; from $37; ☏760/327-0225), which draws the older set in droves. The **Annenberg Theater** (☏760/325-4490), inside the Palm Springs Desert Museum, has a seasonal program of shows, films, and classical concerts.

If you're around in January, don't miss out on the **Palm Springs International Film Festival**, which brings more nightlife to the city than the rest of the year combined. And in late March, the **La Quinta Arts Festival** serves up fine art and entertainment.

Bars and cafés

Agua Bar & Grill Spa Resort Casino, 100 N Indian Canyon Drive ☏760/778-1515. Festive, upscale piano bar that attracts an older crowd.

Atlas (see above). Cutting-edge dance from around 10pm most nights. $10 cover.

Blue Guitar 120 S Palm Canyon Drive ☏760/327-1549. Mainly a blues and old school R&B bar, often with no cover, though could be up to $10 when someone special is playing.

Peabody's Café, Bar and Coffee 134 S Palm Canyon Drive ☏760/322-1877. An eclectic crowd of patrons here to enjoy live jazz, poetry readings, and extensive coffee selections.

Zeldaz Dance and Beachclub 169 N Indian Canyon Drive ☏760/325-2375. Pick-up joint for teeny-boppers.

Listings

Bank Bank of America, 588 S Palm Canyon Drive ☏760/340-1867

Bookstore Barnes & Noble, corner Hwy-111 & Fred Waring Drive, Palm Desert

Cinema Courtyard 10, 777 Tahquitz Canyon Way ☏760/322-3456

Hospital Desert Hospital, 1150 N Indian Canyon Drive ☏760/323-6511

Internet access The Palm Springs Public Library (see below) offers free Internet access. Alternatives include *Peabody's Coffee Shop*, 134 S Palm Canyon Dr (☏760/322-1877), and Log-On, in the Smoke Tree Village mall at 1775 E Palm Canyon Drive (closed Sun)

Left luggage at Greyhound station, 311 N Indian Canyon Drive

Library Palm Springs Public Library, 300 S Sunrise Way (Mon & Tues 9am–8pm, Wed & Thurs 9am–5.30pm, Fri 10am–5pm, Sat 9am–5.30pm; ☏760/322-8294, ⊛www.ci.palm-springs.co.us /library

Pharmacy Rite Aid Drug Store, 366 S Palm Canyon Drive

Police ☏760/323-8116 in Palm Springs; ☏760/321-0111 in Cathedral City

Post office 333 E Amado Rd (Mon–Fri 8.30am–5pm; ☏1-800/275-8777). Zip code 92262

Travel agency Canyon Travel, 300 E Arenas Rd ☏760/320-1932, ⊛www.canyontravelps.com. Mostly handles gay travel but is the only place close to downtown.

Around Palm Springs

As the largest desert community by far, the Coachella Valley towns, and Palm Springs in particular, make obvious bases for exploring the surrounding regions where urban comforts are often in short supply. They can, however, be found in **Idyllwild**, a small mountain resort set among the pines high above Palm Springs that's well set up for weekend retreats from LA. The real desert starts to the north, where the **Morongo Basin** provides access to Joshua Tree National Park via the small roadside communities of **Yucca Valley**, **Joshua Tree**, and **Twentynine Palms**.

Idyllwild

Five thousand feet up on the slopes of Mount San Jacinto, **IDYLLWILD** is the perfect antidote to the in-your-face success of Palm Springs, fifty miles away. Pine-fresh, cool, and snow-covered in winter, this small alpine town of about two thousand inhabitants has only a few chalet-style restaurants and hotels, but it's a great place to slow up the cash drain inevitably incurred on a visit to Palm Springs. It is accessible by heading twenty miles west along I-10 to Banning, then taking the exit for Hwy-243, which sweeps you up the mountain on a good but sharply curving road.

The place is always busy at weekends when city escapees flood the town, but there's a more relaxed pace midweek. At any time, there's considerable temptation to get active on the magnificent trails of the **Mount San Jacinto State Park**, either up towards Mount San Jacinto itself, or up to **Suicide Rock** and **Tahquitz**, two distinctive peaks which rise a couple of thousand feet above the town. Many of the local trails don't enter any designated wilderness and require no permits: ones worth tying include the gentle meander along beautiful **Strawberry Creek** to a more strenuous trek along **Deer Springs Trail** (six miles round-trip; 3–4hr; 1700ft ascent) to the stunning Suicide Rock. Overnight hiking and day-hikes along the popular and moderately difficult **Devil's Slide** to the top station of the Aerial Tramway (see p.265) do require a permit, available from the Forest Service's **Idyllwild Ranger Station**, 54270 Pine Crest Ave (daily 8am–4.30pm; ☎909/659-2117), which has stacks of information about hiking and camping in the area. Trail access is made more complex by the need to purchase an **Adventure Pass** ($5 per day, $30 a year; ⓦwww.fsaadventurepass.com), which allows you to park at trailheads and can be obtained at sporting goods stores and the ranger station.

Practicalities

Places to stay are well scattered along the roads that fan out from Idyllwild's central shopping area. The cheapest rooms are the little red-and-white chalets of the recently renovated *Atipahato Lodge*, 25525 Hwy-243, half a mile north of the ranger station (☎909/659-2201 or 1-888/400-0071, ⓦwww.atipahato .com; luxury cabins ➐, standard cabins ➌), where tasteful rooms have forest-view balconies and kitchenettes. Also good is the woodsy *The Fireside Inn*, 54540 N Circle Drive, about half a mile east (☎909/659-2966 or 1-877/797-3473, ⓦwww.thefireside-inn.com; ➌), with cozy wood-paneled rooms, kitchens, and fireplaces; and for real luxury there's the B&B-style *Strawberry Creek Inn*, 26370 Hwy-243 (☎909/659-3202 or 1-800/262-8969, ⓦwww .strawberrycreekinn.com; ➒), a few hundred yards south. Otherwise, you can stay in the inn's chalets and log cabins, most of which cost from $60–$125 and usually sleep four or more people. You can set up **camp** anywhere over two hundred feet away from trails and streams, or in designated Yellow Post Sites (Adventure Pass needed) with fire rings but no water. There are also drive-in campgrounds run by the Forest Service (☎1-800/444-7275) and the county park (☎1-800/234-PARK) at a cost of $8–$14 per night.

Plenty of decent **restaurants** vie for your custom, including the *Goodtimes Pub & Grill*, right in the center of town with steaks, barbecue ribs, and even fish and chips, all for around $9. On a sunny day sit out on the deck and dine at the *Bread Basket*, 54710 N Circle Drive (☎909/659-3506; closed Wed & Thurs evenings), a couple of miles from the center but worth the effort for French-toast made with apple-nut loaf ($6), mushroom stroganoff ($10), or battered halibut ($10), all washed down with microbrews or espresso coffee.

There's **Internet access** at the library, 5485 Pinecrest Ave (☎909/659-2300), which has very sporadic opening hours.

The Morongo Basin

Driving from Palm Springs (or Los Angeles) to Joshua Tree National Park, the easiest access is through the **MORONGO BASIN**, a vast tract of high desert, almost a thousand square miles of which is taken up by the Marine Corps Air Ground Combat Center, the world's largest marine base, located just north of Twentynine Palms. Mostly useful as a supply and accommodation base, the Morongo Basin does have a couple of points of minor interest, principally the wildlife haven of the **Big Morongo Canyon Preserve**, the Western charms of **Pioneertown**, and the oddball **Desert Christ Park**.

While visiting the park itself using **public transportation** is not really an option, Morongo Basin Transit Authority (☎1-800/794-6282, ⓦwww.mbtabus.com) runs a regular bus service (2 daily) between Palm Springs and the towns of Joshua Tree ($7 one-way, $11 round-trip) and Twentynine Palms ($10 one-way, $15 round-trip), but not into the park itself.

Yucca Valley

Heading north off I-10 along Twentynine Palms Highway (Hwy-62), the first point of interest is **Big Morongo Canyon Preserve**, 11055 East Drive (7.30am–sunset; donation suggested; ⓦwww.bigmmorongo.org), a wildlife refuge based around the cottonwoods and willows of a large oasis, which represents one of the largest bodies of natural surface water for miles around. Consequently, it is a big hit with both wildlife and keen birders, who might hope to spot vermilion and brown-crested flycatchers, Bell's vireo, summer tanager, and a whole lot more – the preserve host keeps a list of current sightings. The numerous boardwalks and trails meandering through the area can easily absorb a relaxing hour or two.

The Morongo Basin's largest settlement is **YUCCA VALLEY**, nine miles east, a typically unappealing string of malls running for a few miles beside Hwy-62. Between grabbing a feed or finding a place to stay (for both see p.274), you might call at the **Hi-Desert Nature Museum**, 57116 Hwy-62 (Tues–Sun 10–5pm; free; ☎619/369-7212), which holds a largely poor collection of paintings and tacky souvenirs, but also some commendable catches of snakes, scorpions, and a pine cone from the world's oldest living tree.

There are greater rewards following Pioneertown Drive, which runs north off Hwy-62. After half a mile, turn right onto Sunnyslope Drive and continue half a mile to the **Desert Christ Park** (dawn–dusk; free), which has 37 of local sculptor Antone Martin's massive fifteen-foot white concrete figures, erected in the 1950s and depicting tales from the Bible – a fittingly bizarre addition to the region. Return to Pioneertown Drive and continue 3.5 miles north to **Pioneertown**, an Old West town created in the 1940s for the filming of movies and TV serials – a nice bit of synthetic cowboy country when the real thing gets too much. It is nowhere near as unpleasant as it might sound, has a few places to stay, eat, and drink, and a bowling alley little changed since it was built.

For **tourist information** visit Yucca Valley's brand new California Welcome Center, 56711 Twentynine Palms Hwy (daily 9am–6pm; ☎760/365-5464, ⓦwww.yucca-valley.org), and you can surf the Net at the **library** (Mon, Wed & Fri 10am–6pm, Tues & Thurs noon–8pm, Sat 9am–5pm; ☎760/228-5455) next to the Hi-Desert Nature Museum. For **accommodation** try the *Desert*

View Motel, 57471 Primrose Drive (☎760/365-2886; ❷), which has a pool and some units with kitchen facilities, or *Pioneertown Motel* at Pioneertown (☎760/365-4879, ⓦwww.pionertown.com; weekends ❸, weeknights ❷), where each room has a slightly different character. There's good **food** and a great atmosphere at *Pappy & Harriet's*, also at Pioneertown (☎760/365-5956), a Tex-Mex and mesquite barbecue, where there's a blues or reggae on Thursdays, house band on Friday and Saturday nights, and open mic on Sundays. On the main road through Yucca Valley there's reliable espresso and snacks at the *Water Canyon Coffee Co*, 55844 Twentynine Palms Hwy.

Joshua Tree

Six miles east of Yucca Valley, the town of **JOSHUA TREE** centers on the intersection of Twentynine Palms Highway and Park Boulevard, which runs south to the national park's West Entrance. There's not much to it, but several decent places to stay and eat make it perhaps the best base for the park if you're not camping. The cheapest **place to stay** is the pool-equipped *High Desert Motel*, 61310 Twentynine Palms Hwy (☎760/366-1978 or 1-888/367-3898; ❷), but you might prefer the bed-and-breakfast-style *Joshua Tree Inn* (☎760/366-1188 or 1-800/366-1444, ⓦwww.joshuatreeinn.com; ❹), virtually opposite at 61259 Twentynine Palms Hwy, where comfortable rooms are set around a pool, and the convivial hosts contribute to a very relaxing atmosphere. Also consider *Spin and Margie's Desert Hideaway*, PO Box 1092, Joshua Tree (☎760/366-9124, ⓦwww.spinandmargiesdeserthideaway.com; ❺), with luxurious rooms vibrantly decorated in a desert style.

Safe at Home – Gram Parsons in Joshua Tree

A relatively minor star in his lifetime, **Gram Parsons**, the wild country outlaw of early Seventies rock, has since become one of the era's icons. His musical influence spreads wide, from ageing rockers like his old friend Keith Richards to Evan Dando, Beck, and the new breed of alt-country misfits, but his fame owes as much to his drug- and booze-fuelled life and the bizarre circumstances surrounding his death, aged 27 – a story embellished over the years by myth, fabrication, and gossip.

Joshua Tree was Gram's escape from the LA music pressure cooker, and photos show him hanging out with Richards in pharmaceutically altered states, communing with nature and scanning the night sky for UFOs. On his final visit, Gram and three friends spent September 18, 1973 consuming as much heroin, morphine, marijuana, and Jack Daniels as possible, Gram finally ODing that night in Room 8 at the *Joshua Tree Inn*.

Parsons' stepfather stood to benefit from Gram's estate if he could get the body back to Louisiana for burial. However, Gram and his friend and tour manager, Phil Kaufman, had already agreed "the survivor would take the other guy's body out to Joshua Tree, have a few drinks and burn it." Three days after Gram's death, Kaufman persuaded an airline employee to release Gram's casket, drove out to Joshua Tree, doused his body in gasoline, and executed the wishes of his deceased friend.

Fans come to stay in Room 8 at the *Joshua Tree Inn* (where you can inscribe your thoughts in a little black book and add your guitar pick to the collection), but the principal **point of pilgrimage** is a makeshift fans' shrine where his body was cremated. From the Cap Rock parking lot at the start of the Key's View Road, follow a well-defined but unmarked trail around the west side of the rock to a point close to the road intersection. Here, a rock alcove is plastered with devotional graffiti and a small concrete plinth is daubed "Gram – Safe at Home."

Several good **places to eat** huddle within a block or so of each other along Twentynine Palms Highway at its junction with Park Boulevard. Try *Crossroads Café and Tavern*, no. 61715 (☎760/366-5414), for good breakfasts, burgers, espresso, shakes, and microbrews; *Royal Siam*, no. 61599 (☎760/366-2923) for good low-cost Thai and an $8 buffet every Saturday and Sunday from 4.30–8pm (closed Tues); or *Tommy Paul's Beatnik Café*, no. 61597 (closed Mon & Tues in summer; ☎760/366-2090), a hip coffeehouse with good food and drink and live music most weekends.

Climbers and hikers needing to buy or rent gear should stop by Nomad Ventures, 61795 Twentynine Palms Hwy (☎760/366-4684), or nip across the road to Coyote Corner, 6535 Park Blvd (☎760/366-9683), where you can fill up your water jugs before heading into the park or have a **shower** (coin-operated, from $1.50) after several days of dust and sand.

The **library**, by the crossroads at 6465 Park Blvd (Mon–Fri 10am–6pm; ☎760/366-8615), has free **Internet access**.

Twentynine Palms

Fifteen miles east of the town of Joshua Tree and just two minutes' drive from the park's north entrance, the small highway-side desert town of **TWENTY-NINE PALMS** (locally known as "two-nine") is a pleasant enough little place despite the occasional artillery booms from the nearby marine base. The climate has been considered perfect for convalescents ever since physicians sent World War I poison-gas victims here for treatment of their respiratory illnesses; development of health spas and real estate offices has been considerable. The town is now billing itself as an "Oasis of Murals"; you can get a map of these interesting hyperrealistic historical artworks – there's one of the Dirty Sock Camp (named for a method used by miners to filter out gold).

The town runs for almost five miles along the highway and is divided into two sections separated by a small hill. The only sights to speak of are the national park's **Oasis Visitor Center** (see p.278) on the eastern edge of town, and the nearby **Old Schoolhouse Museum**, 6760 National Park Drive (Oct–May Wed–Sun 1–4pm; June–Aug Sat & Sun 1–4pm; donation suggested; ☎760/367-2366), containing items of local interest and a re-creation of an old schoolroom.

Pick up **information** at the Twentynine Palms Chamber of Commerce, 6455 Mesquite Ave (Mon–Fri 9am–5pm, plus June–Aug Sat 9am–1pm; ☎760/367-3445, ⓦwww.29palms.com). The best place in town to **stay** is the *Twentynine Palms Inn*, 73950 Inn Ave off National Park Drive (☎760/367-3505, ⓦwww.29palmsinn.com; winter weekends ❻, summer midweek ❸), where an array of cozy adobe bungalows and wood-frame cabins are set around attractively arid grounds and gardens, while a central pool area contains a restaurant and bar. Owned by the same large family since 1928, the inn was built on the Oasis of Mara, the only privately owned oasis in the High Desert, and (like the rest of the town) has several fault lines – including the Pinto Mountain Fault – running beneath it.

Among the cheaper options nearby are the large *Motel 6*, 71487 Twentynine Palms Hwy (☎760/367-2833; ❷), and the *El Rancho Dolores Motel*, along the same road at no. 73352 (☎760/367-3528; ❶). Both have perfectly acceptable pools and good rooms, but are nowhere near as much fun as the *Twentynine Palms Inn*.

There's low-cost **dining** at *Ramona's* (☎760/367-1929), a good Mexican at 72115 Twentynine Palms Hwy, but the best place to **eat** is the *Twentynine Palms Inn*, with excellent $12–15 meals including soup and salad. Campers in need of

a clean-up should head along to Jerry's Gym, 73782 Two Mile Rd at Adobe Rd
(☎760/361-8010) which has as-long-as-you-like **showers** with towels for $4.

Joshua Tree National Park

In a unique transitional area where the High Mojave meets the lower Colorado
desert, 800,000 acres of freaky trees, their branches ragged and gnarled, flourish in an otherwise sparsely vegetated landscape, making **JOSHUA TREE
NATIONAL PARK** one of the most unusual and fascinating of California's
national parks. In recognition of the uniqueness of the area and the need for
its preservation, the national park system took the land under its jurisdiction as
a national monument in 1936 and has vigilantly maintained its beauty ever
since. If you're staying in Palm Springs, there's no excuse not to visit; if you've
further to come, make the effort anyway.

The startling Joshua trees (see box, below), are only found in the northwestern quarter of the park, where they form a perfect counterpoint to surreal clusters of monzogranite boulders, great rock piles pushed up from the earth by
the movements of the Pinto Mountain Fault, running directly below. Often as
high as a hundred feet or more, their edges are rounded and smooth from
thousands of years of flash floods and winds, but there are enough nodules, fissures, and irregularities to make this superb **rock climbing** territory.

In all, it's a mystical, even unearthly, landscape, best appreciated at sunrise or
sunset, when the whole desert floor is bathed in red light. At noon, it can feel
like an alien and threatening furnace, with temperatures often reaching 125°F
in summer, though dropping to a more bearable 70°F in winter. If you're visiting between May and October, you must stick to the higher elevations to

The Joshua tree

Unique to the Mojave Desert, the **Joshua tree** (*Yucca brevifolia*) is one of its oldest
residents, with large examples probably over three hundred years old (the lack of
growth rings makes their age difficult to determine). The Joshua tree isn't, in fact, a
tree at all, but a type of yucca (itself a type of agave) and therefore a giant member
of the lily family.

Awkward-looking and ungainly, it got its unusual name from Mormons who traveled through the region in the 1850s and imagined the craggy branches to be the
arms of Joshua leading them to the Promised Land. Of course, Native Americans
had been familiar with Joshua trees for millennia, weaving the tough leaves into baskets and sandals, and eating the roasted seeds and flower buds. The trees became
equally useful for homesteaders who arrived in the wake of the Mormons – the lack
of better wood forced them to press the trunks of Joshua trees into use for fences
and building material.

Joshua trees only grow at altitudes over two thousand feet and prefer extreme arid-
ity and a bed of course sand and fine silt. By storing water in their spongy trunks, they
can grow up to three inches a year, ultimately reaching heights of forty feet or more.
To conserve energy, they only bloom when conditions are right, waiting for a crisp winter freeze, timely rains, and the pollinating attentions of the yucca moth before erupt-
ing in a springtime display of creamy white-green flowers, which cluster on long stalks
at the tips of the branches. Successful young saplings start life as a single shoot, but
eventually a terminal bud dies or is injured and the plant splits to form two branches,
which in turn divide over time, producing the Joshua trees' distinctive shapes.

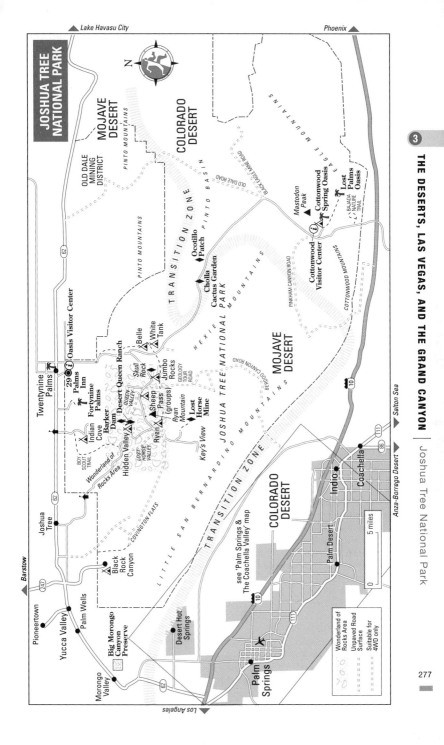

enjoy Joshua Tree with any semblance of comfort. In the Low Desert part of the park, the Joshua trees thin out and the temperature rises as you descend below three thousand feet.

Some history

"Joshua Tree" may be a familiar name today, thanks largely to U2's 1987 album of that name, but previously it was almost unknown. Unlike the vast bulk of the state, nobody, save a few Native Americans, prospectors, and cowboys, has had the chance to spoil it. Despite receiving less than four inches of annual rainfall, the area is surprisingly lush, and although craggy trees and rockpiles are what define Joshua Tree today, it was grass that attracted the first significant pioneers. Early cattlemen, having heard rumors of good pastures from the forty-niners who hurried through on their way to the Sierra Nevada gold fields, discovered that the natural corrals made perfect sites for rustlers to brand their illegitimate herds before moving them out to the coast for sale. Ambushes and gunfights were common in the area. Seeking refuge in the mountains, rustlers discovered by chance small traces of gold and sparked vigorous mining operations that continued until the 1940s. In recognition of the uniqueness of the area, and the need for its preservation, the national park system took the land under its jurisdiction as a national monument in 1936 and has vigilantly maintained its beauty ever since. The park lost some of the original area to mining interests in the 1950s, but that was more than compensated for in 1994, when it was promoted to a national park, with the addition of 234,000 acres.

Park practicalities

Less than an hour's drive northeast from Palm Springs, Joshua Tree National Park (always open; $10 per vehicle for 7 days, $5 per cyclist or hiker; ⓦwww.nps.gov/jotr) is best approached through the Morongo Basin (see p.273) along Hwy-62, which branches off I-10. Besides camping (see p.279), there is neither lodging nor anywhere to eat or buy supplies within the park, so the Morongo Basin towns of Yucca Valley, Joshua Tree, and Twentynine Palms are the main bases from which to explore. These are also the closest places served by public transportation, so visiting the park without your own wheels is not really an option: at best, you're looking at a ten-mile desert walk to get to anything of interest.

You can enter the park via the west entrance at the town of **Joshua Tree**, or the north entrance at **Twentynine Palms**, where you'll also find the **Oasis Visitor Center** (daily 8am–5pm; ☎760/367-5500). Alternatively, if you're coming from the south, there is an entrance and the **Cottonwood Visitor Center** (generally daily 8am–4pm; ☎760/367-5500), seven miles north of I-10. It's worth stopping at one of the visitor centers to collect the free national park **map** and *Joshua Tree Guide*, which are fine for most purposes, though hikers will want a more **detailed map**, the best being Trails Illustrated's *Joshua Tree National Park* map ($10).

Park staff are also at work running free, campground-based **ranger programs** (mid-Oct to mid-Dec, mid-Feb to May), which might include campfire talks, discovery walks, and geology hikes: check at visitor centers for the current schedule.

Cyclists are restricted to roads open to motor vehicles, so don't expect genuine off-road action. That said, there is an increasing number of bikeable and challenging dirt roads – Geology Tour Road, Covington Flats Road, Pinkham Canyon Road, and more – all listed in the *Joshua Tree Guide*. There is no bike rental anywhere near the park.

Joshua Tree National Park has nine **campgrounds**, all concentrated in the north-west except for one at Cottonwood by the southern entrance. All have wooden tables, places for fires (bring your own wood), and pit toilets, but only two (*Black Rock Canyon* and *Cottonwood*) have water supplies and flush toilets. These both cost $10, as does the easily highway-accessible *Indian Cove*, but all the rest are free. You can reserve sites at Black Rock and Indian Cove by phoning ☏1-800/365-2267; the rest are on a first-come–first-served basis with no facility for reservations, unless you're traveling with a group. The lack of showers and electrical and sewage hook-ups at any of the sites keeps the majority of RVers at bay, but in the popular winter months the place fills up quickly, especially at weekends.

Each campground has its merits, but for relative solitude and a great, central location, the *Belle* and *White Tank* sites are perfect, while climbers mostly stay at *Hidden Valley*. Most campgrounds are at around 4200ft, though the enormous *Jumbo Rocks* site is higher, at 4400ft, and is therefore a little cooler, while for the winter months, you may prefer the lower altitude of *Cottonwood* (3000ft) in the south. *Black Rock Canyon* and *Indian Cove* cannot be reached from within the park – if you've already entered, you have to retrace your steps to the entrances on Hwy-62. Each campsite is good for up to six people and two vehicles. Note that **water** is only available at the *Black Rock* and *Indian Cove* campgrounds, the Oasis Visitor Center, the Indian Cove Ranger Station, and the West Entrance. **Winter** nights can be very cold, and campers here between November and March should come with warm jackets and sleeping bags or head for the lower (and warmer) *Cottonwood* campground.

Over eighty percent of the park is designated wilderness where **backcountry camping** is permitted provided you register before you head out. Twelve backcountry boards are dotted through the park at the start of most trails. Here you can self-register, leave your vehicle, and study the regulations that include prohibition of camping within a mile of a road, five hundred feet of a trail, and 440 yards of a water source.

If you fancy **rock climbing** on some of the wonderful formations and don't already have the skills or equipment, book a course with one of the rock climbing schools that operate here. Both Joshua Tree Rock Climbing School (☏760/366-4745 or 1-800/890-4745, 🌐www.joshuatreerockclimbing.com), which is based in the town of Joshua Tree, and the LA-based Vertical Adventures (☏949/854-6250 or 1-800/514-8785) offer one-day basic courses for around $90 and a range of improvers' weekends for around $165–185.

Exploring the park

The best way to enjoy the park is to be selective. As with any desert area, you'll find the heat punishing and an ambitious schedule impossible in the hotter months. Casual observers will find a day-trip plenty, camping out for a couple of nights is a highlight that shouldn't be missed, and experienced hikers may want to take advantage of the park's excellent if strenuous trails. Rock climbers sometimes base themselves here for weeks. The rangers and staff at the visitor centers will be able to recommend the most enjoyable itineraries, tailored to your requirements and abilities. Pick up a *Climber Ethics* leaflet from the visitor centers, and remember never to venture anywhere without a detailed **map** (see opposite).

Many of the roads are unmarked, hard to negotiate, and restricted to four-wheel-drive use. If a road is marked as such, don't even think about taking a normal car – you'll soon come to a grinding halt, and it could be quite a few panic-stricken hours before anybody finds you. Of course, maps are even more essential if you are planning to explore the park's **hiking trails** (see box opposite).

Starting in the north of the park, granite boulders tower around the **Indian Cove** camping area, and a trail from the eastern branch of the campground road leads to **Rattlesnake Canyon** – its streams and waterfalls (depending on rainfall) breaking an otherwise eerie silence among the monoliths. The **Fortynine Palms Oasis** to the east can only be visited on foot (see opposite).

Moving south into the main section of the park, you drive through the **Wonderland of Rocks** area comprising giant, rounded granite boulders that draw **rock climbers** from all over the world. The various clusters flank the road for about ten miles giving plenty of opportunity to stop for a little bouldering or, for those suitably equipped and skilled, to try more adventurous routes. Well-signposted nature trails lead one mile to **Hidden Valley**, where cattle rustlers used to hide out, and to the rain-fed **Barker Dam**, one mile to the east. The latter is Joshua Tree's crucial water supply, built around the turn of the century by cattlemen (and rustlers) to prevent the poor beasts from expiring halfway across the park. The route back from the dam passes a number of petroglyphs.

Access to the nearby **Desert Queen Ranch** is restricted to those on the informative and entertaining ranger-led **guided walking tour** (Oct–May daily 10am & 1pm; June–Sept Sat & Sun 8am & 6pm; $5; reservations necessary March & April; ☏760/367-5555), which begins at the entrance to the ranch and takes around ninety minutes. The ranch was once home to tough desert rat and indefatigable miner Bill Keys who lived here (with his family) from 1910 until his death (aged 89) in 1969 – long after less hardy men had abandoned the arid wasteland. He was briefly famous in 1943, when he was locked away for shooting one of his neighbors over a right-of-way argument, only to be paroled by the mystery writer Erle Stanley Gardner. Keys and family made a spartan but surprisingly comfortable living from growing vegetables, mining, ranching, and working as a farrier and general trader for just about everything a desert dweller could desire. The tour visits their ramshackle home, orchard site, workshop, and even a schoolhouse that operated for seven years from 1935.

Keys is further remembered at **Keys View**, eight miles south, a 5185-foot-high vista offering the best views in the whole park. On a good day, you can see as far as the Salton Sea and beyond into Mexico – a brilliant desert panorama of badlands and mountains.

The west–east road through the park then passes the start of the Ryan Mountain hike (see box) and the turn off for Geology Tour Road, which leads down through the best of Joshua Tree's **rock formations**. A little further on, the *Jumbo Rocks* campground is the start of a hiking loop (1.7 miles) through boulders and desert washes to **Skull Rock**, which can also be easily seen from the road immediately east of the campground.

Continuing east, *White Tank* campground is worth a short stop to wander along a short trail through huge granite domes to a photogenic **rock arch**; the trail starts by site 9.

Almost at the transition zone between the Colorado and Mojave deserts and on the fringes of the Pinto Basin, the **Cholla Cactus Garden** is a quarter-mile loop through an astonishing concentration of the "jumping" **cholla** cactus (see box on p.255), as well as creosote bushes, jojoba, and several other cactus species. Come at dusk or dawn for the best chance of seeing the mainly nocturnal desert wood rat. Nearby, the near-barren desert at **Ocotillo Patch** comes stuffed with freakish spindly ocotillo plants, at their best when blooming scarlet in spring.

To get a real feel for the majesty of the desert, you'll need to leave the main roads behind and hike, or at least follow one of the short (and mostly wheelchair-accessible) **nature trails** which have been set up throughout the park to help interpret something of desert ecology and plant life.

The more strenuous **hikes** outlined below are generally safe but be sure to **stick to the trails**: Joshua Tree is full of abandoned gold mines and although the rangers are fencing them as quickly as possible, they don't have the funds to take care of all of them.

Most of the listed trails are in the slightly cooler and higher Mojave Desert, but even on the easier trails allow around an hour per mile: there's very little shade and you'll tire quickly. There's tougher stuff on the eastern side of the park around **Pinto Basin**, though this is purely territory for experienced groups of hikers well armed with maps and water supplies. If you're thinking of heading out on anything more ambitious than the hikes described here be sure to discuss your plans with a ranger; and anyone planning to stay out overnight in the wilderness must **register** at one of the trailhead backcountry boards.

Nature trails

These are listed northwest to southeast through the park.

Bajada (400-yard loop). The plantlife of a naturally sloping drainage is explored half a mile north of the South Entrance.

Cholla Cactus Garden (400-yard loop). A beautiful stroll among these superbly photogenic cacti.

Oasis of Mara (800-yard loop). A series of explanatory panels around a significant fan-palm oasis right by the Oasis Visitor Center.

Some hikes

These are listed northwest to southeast through the park.

Fortynine Palms Oasis (3 miles; 2hr). Moderately strenuous, this leaves the badly signposted Canyon Road six miles west of the visitor center at Twentynine Palms. A barren rocky trail leads to this densely clustered and partly fire-blackened oasis which, since it was named, seems to have flourished on the seepage down the canyon. There's not enough water to swim in, nor are you allowed to camp (the oasis is officially closed 8pm–7am), but a late afternoon or evening visit presents the best wildlife rewards.

Lost Horse Mine (4 miles; 3hr). Starting a mile east of Keys View Road, this moderately difficult trail climbs 450ft to the mine, which, in the 1890s, made an average of $20,000 a week. The hike takes you through abandoned mining sites, with building foundations and equipment still intact, to the top of Lost Horse Mountain.

Ryan Mountain (3 miles; 2hr). Some of the best views in the park are from the top of Ryan Mountain (5461ft), seven hundred strenuous feet above the desert floor. Start at the parking area near the *Sheep Pass* campground and follow the trail past the Indian Cave, which contains bedrock mortars once used by the Cahuilla and Serrano.

Mastodon Peak (3 miles; 2hr). Another peak climb, less strenuous than Ryan Mountain but with great views, especially south to the Salton Sea. Start from the *Cottonwood* campground.

Lost Palms Oasis (8 miles; 5hr). This moderate trail, starting from the *Cottonwood* campground, leads across desert washes, past palo verde, cottonwood, and ironwood trees to the largest stand of palms in the park. The trail offers possible scrambling side-trips to Victory Palms and Munsen Canyon. There's little surface water, but often enough to lure bighorn sheep.

The Imperial Valley and Salton Sea

The patch of the Colorado desert **south** of Joshua Tree and Palm Springs is one of the least friendly of all the Californian desert regions and its foreboding aspect discourages exploration. It's best not to come between June and September, when intense heat makes journeys uncomfortable and services are greatly reduced.

Sandwiched between Hwy-111 and Hwy-86, which branch off I-10 soon after Palm Springs and the Coachella Valley, the area from the **Salton Sea** down to the furnace-like migrant-worker towns of the agricultural **Imperial Valley** lies in the two-thousand-square-mile Salton Basin: aside from a small spot in Death Valley, the largest area of dry land below sea level in the western hemisphere. Hwy-86, for what it's worth, was California's most notorious two-lane highway, with a staggering record of deaths and accidents, though it's now been widened into four lanes. There's not a lot to come here for unless you're heading for the Anza-Borrego Desert or the Mexican border.

Created accidentally in 1905 (see box, below), the Salton Sea and its shores were once extremely toney, attracting the likes of Frank Sinatra and Dean Martin to its yacht clubs; in its 1940s heyday, the sea was actually a bigger tourist draw than Yosemite National Park. A series of mid-1970s storms caused the sea to rise and swallow shoreline developments, but more serious damage to tourism was due to the fact that the Salton Sea, with no natural outlet (it is 235 feet below sea level), has over the years become grossly polluted – plagued by agricultural runoff and toxic wastes carried in by two rivers from Mexico – and excessively saline. Fish carry a consumption warning, and people rarely swim and waterski here these days.

Still, the Salton Sea remains an important wintering area for shore birds and waterfowl. Brown pelicans come by in summer, and terns and cormorants nest here. The best place to see them is the **Sonny Bono Salton Sea National Wildlife Refuge** (daily dawn–dusk; free; Ⓦ pacific.fws.gov/salton) at the sea's southern tip. By the informative **visitor center** (Mon–Fri 7am–3.30pm and some weekends; ☎760/393-3052) there's a viewing platform, or you can take the Rock Hill Trail for a closer look, a twenty-minute walk to the water's edge. To get to the refuge, take the poorly signposted backroads off Hwy-111 south of **Niland** or off Hwy-86 at **Westmorland**; both run past fields of alfalfa, cantaloupe, tomatoes, and other crops – proof that just about anything will grow in this fertile land provided it is suitably irrigated.

If you've come this far it's worth turning east off Niland's Main Street and traveling three miles to see **Salvation Mountain**, a fantastic work of large-scale

---

The accidental sea

At 35 miles long by up to 15 miles wide, the **Salton Sea** is California's largest lake, but one which didn't exist a century ago. Over the millennia, the shallow Salton Basin has filled with floodwaters that spilled over from the Colorado River some fifty miles to the east, but each time the lake has dried up. When European Americans started pushing into the West, they recognized that the Salton Basin and the surrounding Imperial Valley could be made super-fertile by channeling water from the Colorado. In 1901, a development company did just that, but river silt soon blocked the channel and in 1905 almost the entire flow from the Colorado River was pouring into the Salton Basin. The deluge wasn't stanched for almost two years, by which time it had formed the Salton Sea – a huge freshwater lake up to fifty feet deep.

religious folk art incorporating, for example, an abandoned motorboat, to represent Noah's Ark. It stands at the entrance to **Slab City**, a huge settlement of squatters that swells in size in winter when Canadian RVers come down for warmth – and free city water.

The only other reasons you might stop are to **camp** (primitive $7, equipped sites $13, hook-ups $19) in the Salton Sea State Recreation Area, which encompasses a handful of lakeside sites along a fourteen-mile stretch of the eastern side of the Salton Sea from Bombay Beach to Mecca Beach. Agricultural work brings thousands of Mexicans north of the border, and the restaurants generally cater to them: practice your Spanish.

The Anza-Borrego Desert

Southwest of the Salton Sea, the **ANZA-BORREGO DESERT** is the largest state park in the country outside Alaska, covering 600,000 acres and, in contrast to the Imperial Valley, offering a diverse variety of plant and animal life as well as a legend-strewn history spanning Native American tribes, the first white trailfinders, and Gold Rush times. It takes its double-barreled name from Juan Baptista de Anza, a Spanish explorer who crossed the region in 1774, and the Spanish for the native bighorn sheep, **borrego cimarron**, which eats the brittlebrush and agave found here. Some of Anza-Borrego can be covered by car (confidence on gravel roads is handy), although you'll need four-wheel-drive for the more obscure – and most interesting – routes, and there are over five hundred miles of hiking trails where vehicles are not permitted at all.

During the fiercely hot summer months, the place is best left to the lizards, although most campgrounds stay open all year. The desert **blooming season**, between March and May, is popular, when scarlet ocotillo, orange poppies, white lilies, purple verbena, and other intensely colorful wildflowers are a memorable – and fragrant – sight. As well as taking the usual desert precautions (see box on p.254), you should read the comments in Basics on p.54 – this is mountain lion territory.

Though accessible from the Salton Sea along Hwy-178 or Hwy-S22, the Anza-Borrego is usually approached from San Diego, through Julian (see p.241). Approaching from Julian you'll hit the park at Scissors Crossing with most of the developed facilities to the north and much of the more interesting historical debris to the south.

Northern Anza-Borrego

Northwest of Scissors Crossing, Hwy-S2 meets Hwy-S22, which descends tortuously through fields of popcorn-shaped rock formations to **Borrego Springs**, the park's lone sizeable settlement. Here you'll find the park's visitor center (see p.286) and the main *Borrego Palm Canyon* campground, which marks the start of the **Borrego Palm Canyon Trail** (3 miles; 2hr; 350ft ascent), one of the most popular paths in the park. It follows a detailed nature trail to one of the largest oases left in the US, with a quarter-mile of stream flanked by around a thousand densely packed California fan palms (sometimes known as Washingtonia palms from their Latin name *Washingtonia filifera*) – the only palms native to the western United States.

Six miles east of Borrego Springs along S22, there's a memorial marker to Peg Leg Smith, an infamous local spinner of yarns from Gold Rush days who is further celebrated by a festival of tall tales – the **Peg Leg Liars Contest** –

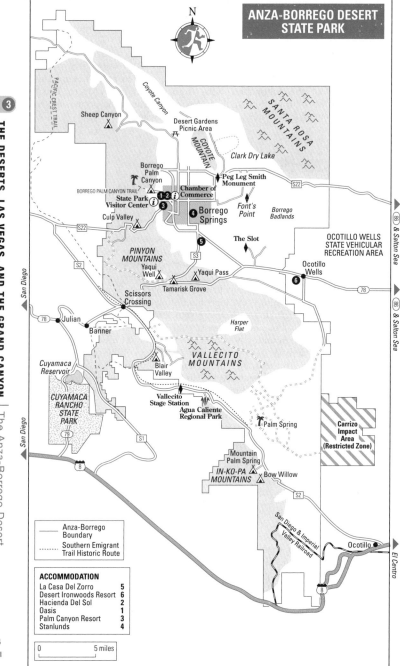

ANZA-BORREGO DESERT STATE PARK

N

Sheep Canyon

Coyote Canyon

SANTA ROSA MOUNTAINS

Desert Gardens Picnic Area

COYOTE MOUNTAIN

Clark Dry Lake

PACIFIC CREST TRAIL

Borrego Palm Canyon

Peg Leg Smith Monument

S22

BORREGO PALM CANYON TRAIL

State Park Visitor Center

Chamber of Commerce

Font's Point

Borrego Badlands

Culp Valley

Borrego Springs

S2

S22

PINYON MOUNTAINS

S3

The Slot

OCOTILLO WELLS STATE VEHICULAR RECREATION AREA

Yaqui Well

Yaqui Pass

Ocotillo Wells

Tamarisk Grove

78

Scissors Crossing

78 Julian

Banner

Harper Flat

Cuyamaca Reservoir

Blair Valley

VALLECITO MOUNTAINS

CUYAMACA RANCHO STATE PARK

Vallecito Stage Station

Agua Caliente Regional Park

Carrizo Impact Area (Restricted Zone)

79

S1

Palm Spring

8

Mountain Palm Spring

IN-KO-PA MOUNTAINS

Bow Willow

S2

San Diego & Imperial Valley Railroad

Ocotillo

El Centro

8

San Diego

San Diego

86 & Salton Sea

86 & Salton Sea

—— Anza-Borrego Boundary

······ Southern Emigrant Trail Historic Route

ACCOMMODATION

La Casa Del Zorro	**5**
Desert Ironwoods Resort	**6**
Hacienda Del Sol	**2**
Oasis	**1**
Palm Canyon Resort	**3**
Stanlunds	**4**

0   5 miles

which takes place at this spot on the first Saturday in April. Anybody can get up before the judges and fib their hearts out, the most outrageous stories earning a modest prize. Roughly four miles further on, a fairly tough dirt road (check with the visitor center for conditions) leads to **Font's Point** and a view over the **Borrego Badlands** – a long sweeping plain devoid of vegetation whose strange, stark charms are oddly inspiring. Sunset is the best time to appreciate fully the layered alluvial banding.

If you want to be outside but shaded from the sun's fierce rays, make for **The Slot**, a narrow fifty-foot-deep canyon carved from the soft rock by infrequent flooding. You can walk down into the canyon then follow it downstream for five minutes to a quarter-mile-long section where it is only just wide enough for one person to squeeze through. To get there, travel 1.5 miles east from the junction of Borrego Springs Road and Hwy-78, then follow the very sandy Buttes Pass Road for 1.8 miles keeping left at the only junction. The road is usually passable for ordinary cars but if you have any doubts about your or your vehicle's abilities, turn back.

Southern Anza-Borrego

At Scissors Crossing, Hwy-78 from Julian intersects Hwy-S2 which heads towards the park's southeast corner following the line of the old **Butterfield Stage Route**, which began service in 1857 and was the first regular line of communication between the eastern states and the newly settled West. Along the way you pass through **Blair Valley**, with its primitive campground, to **Box Canyon**, where the Mormon Battalion of 1847, following what is now known as the **Southern Emigrant Trail Historic Route**, forced a passage along the desert wash. It isn't especially spectacular, but makes for some safe desert walking, never more than a couple of hundred yards from the road. Nine miles further on, the **Vallecito Stage Station** (Sept–May 9am–sunset; June–Aug closed) is an old adobe stage rest stop that gives a good indication of the comforts – or lack of them – of early desert travel. The building is in the grounds of a county-run **campground** ($12), which requires you to pay a day-use fee of $2 per vehicle to see it.

A further three miles south, the **Agua Caliente Regional Park** (Sept–May daily 9.30am–5pm; $5 per vehicle) contains a couple of naturally fed pools, one large outdoor affair kept at its natural 96°F, and one smaller indoor pool kept at a more modest temperature and fitted with water jets. Most visitors stay at the **campground** (tents $14, hookups $18; reservations ☎858/565-3600), which surrounds the pools and gives you longer access for evening soaking.

To the south lies the least-visited portion of Anza-Borrego, good for isolated exploration and undisturbed views around Imperial Valley, where there's a vivid and spectacular clash as gray rock rises from the edges of the red desert floor, and a primitive **campground** close to the small oasis at *Mountain Palm Spring*.

Practicalities

Anza-Borrego State Park is served by **public transportation**: from San Diego, the North East Rural Bus System (☎760/767-4287; see p.240) makes a single daily trip to Borrego Springs (not Sun or Mon), arriving late in the afternoon. There's not much happening in Borrego Springs, but it's one of the most pleasant of all the desert towns, self-contained and remarkably uncommercialized. If you're camping out, it's the place to gather (expensive) supplies – but don't expect any big supermarket chains here – or to use the **Chamber of Commerce**, 786 Palm Canyon Drive (June–Sept Mon–Fri 10am–4pm;

Oct–May Mon–Sat 10am-4pm; ☎760/767-5555 or 1-800/559-5524, ⓦ www
.borregosprings.org), for details of motels and restaurants. Though the
Chamber of Commerce doesn't like to mention it, the town of Borrego
Springs is three miles southwest of the most seismically active area in the western hemisphere, Clark Dry Lake, where some ten thousand earthquakes a year
are registered. For information on this phenomenon, as well as on desert hiking, camping, and flora and fauna, head two miles west to the excellent State
Park **visitor center**, 200 Palm Canyon Drive (June–Sept Sat, Sun & holidays
9am–5pm; Oct–May daily 9am–5pm; ☎760/767-5311, ⓦ www.anzabor-
rego.statepark.org), which is so well landscaped into the desert floor you barely notice it as you approach. Here you can also pick up an informative free
newspaper, which contains a detailed map of the park. Outside, the all-access
half-mile Visitor Center Loop allows you to weave across the desert identify-
ing the flora. When the visitor center is closed, the administration office adjacent (Mon–Fri 9am–5pm) fills in.

If you're not feeling adventurous enough to camp (see box below), try one
of the handful of fairly pricey **motels** in Borrego Springs. Among the cheaper ones are *Oasis*, at 366 W Palm Drive (☎760/767-5409; ❹), *Hacienda del Sol*,
610 Palm Drive (☎760/767-5442; ❹), and *Stanlunds Resort Inn & Suites*
(☎760/767-5501; ❹), three-quarters of a mile south along Borrego Springs
Road, all sporting some rooms with kitchenettes. The new *Borrego Springs
Resort*, 1112 Tilting T Drive (☎760/767-5700 or 1-888/826-7734,
ⓕ760/767-5710, ⓦ www.borregospringsresort.com; ❺), is modern and well
equipped, and if you really want to live it up, *La Casa del Zorro*, 3845 Yaqui Pass
Rd (☎760/767-5323 or 1-800/824-1884, ⓦ www.lacasadelzorro.com; ❽), is a
beautiful hotel in a date-palm oasis with a hefty price tag which increases at
weekends.

Camping in Anza-Borrego

Anza-Borrego Desert State Park manages two developed and nine primitive campgrounds, but this is one of the few parks that allows **open camping**, giving you the
freedom to pitch a tent pretty much anywhere without a permit, although it's advisable to let someone know your plans. The few provisos are that you don't drive off-
road, don't camp near water holes, camp away from developed campgrounds, light
fires only in fire rings or metal containers, collect no firewood, and leave the place
as you found it, or cleaner.

The largest site, and the only one with RV hook-ups, is the *Borrego Palm Canyon*
campground a mile from the visitor center (hook-ups $16, tents $10). *Tamarisk
Grove*, thirteen miles south on Hwy-S3 ($10), is the only other developed site. Both
charge $2 per vehicle for day use of the facilities, which include water supply and
coin-op **showers**. Both also organize **guided hikes** and have regular discussion and
activity evenings led by a volunteer naturalist. Places can be reserved through
ReserveAmerica on ☎1-800/444-7275 (essential for holidays and weekends, and in
the March–May blooming season). The other primitive campgrounds fill on a first-
come-first-served basis; those in the backcountry always have space. All are accessible by road vehicles and are free, except for *Bow Willow*, which charges $7 and is
the only one with drinking water. Most sites are below 1500ft which is fine in winter,
but in the hotter months you might try *Culp Valley*, eight miles southwest of Borrego
Springs, at a blissfully cool 3400ft. In addition there's a commercial campground at
the Agua Caliente Regional Park (see p.285).

Most of the town's commercial activity goes on either in The Center or The Mall, opposite each other on Palm Drive. At the back of the Mall you can eat good diner **meals** at *Kendall's Café* (℡760/767-3491), while the Center has *Pablito's of the Desert* (℡760/767-5753; closed Mon & Tues), good for Mexican and margaritas. More upscale and far more interesting is the *Krazy Coyote Saloon & Grill*, 2220 Hoberg Rd (℡760/767-7788), the local favorite with a good bar, tasty American/Continental fare and a terrific desert setting. There's **Internet access** at the library by the Mall (closed Sun & Mon).

Just outside the eastern park boundary, **Ocotillo Wells** has basic facilities and the attractively located *Desert Ironwoods Resort*, 4875 Hwy-78 (℡760/767-5670; ④).

Recreational opportunities in the park are strictly controlled to preserve the fragile ecosystem. The main exception to this rule is the **Ocotillo Wells State Vehicular Recreational Area**, a region to the east of the park mapped out for dune buggies and the like. Owners drive like demons in a maelstrom of tossed sand and engine noise; if you're tempted to join them, call Recreation Headquarters (daily 8am–4pm; ℡760/767-5391) for information.

Elsewhere, **mountain biking** is permitted only on paved and dirt roads; the hiking trails are off limits. Bikes can be rented for around $30 per day from Carrizo Bikes, 648 Palm Canyon Drive (℡760/767-3872). If you'd rather have a larger saddle, try **desert horse trekking** with Smoketree Arabian Horse Rental (℡760/767-5850, ⓦsmoketree.micronpcweb.com), who offers one-hour ($55) and two-hour ($95) rides, even in summer when they start at 7am.

The High Desert

Desolate, silent and virtually lifeless, the **MOJAVE DESERT**, mythic badland of the West, has no equal when it comes to hardship. Called the High Desert because it averages a height of around two thousand feet above sea level, the Mojave is very dry and for the most part deadly flat, dotted here and there with the shaggy form of a Joshua tree and an occasional abandoned miner's shed. For most, it's the barrier between LA and Las Vegas, an obstacle to get over before they reach either city; and, short on attractions as it is, you may want to follow their example. However, you should linger a little just to see – and smell – what a desert is really like: a vast, impersonal, extreme environment, sharp with its own peculiar fragrance, and alive in spring with acres of fiery orange poppies – the state flower of California – and other brightly colored wildflowers.

You will have relatively little company. If LA is the home of the sports car, the Mojave is the land of huge dust-covered trucks, carrying goods across the state to Nevada. Other signs of life include the grim military subculture marooned on huge weapons-testing sites. There is also a hard-core group of desert fans: backdrop for the legion of road movies spawned by the underground film culture in the late 1960s and early 1970s, the Mojave is a favorite with bikers and neo-hippies drawn by the barren panorama of sand dunes and mountain ranges. Members of the California Sierra Club and other savvy in-state nature lovers light out for the less barren beauties of the Mojave National Preserve. But otherwise visitors are thin on the ground, and, for most of the year, you can rely on being in sparse company.

I-15 cuts through the heart of the Mojave, dividing it into two distinct regions. To the north lies the desolate **Western Mojave**, as well as **Death Valley** (covered in Chapter Four), and to the south lie Barstow and the **Mojave National Preserve**. **Barstow**, the lackluster capital of the Mojave, is redeemed only by its location halfway between LA and **Las Vegas** on I-15, which makes it both a potential stopover between the two points and a good base for the surrounding attractions, explorable by dune buggy, on horseback or even on foot.

If Barstow isn't exactly alluring, the huge **Mojave National Preserve**, which lies just south of the road to Las Vegas, is. Here you can see spectacular sand dunes, striking rock formations, and a huge variety of plant life, including large concentrations of Joshua trees. Much of the preserve rises to about 4000 feet, so it also offers respite from the harshest of the area's heat. South and east of here, close to the Nevada and Arizona borders, the desert is at its most demanding, largely empty, inhospitable, and potentially miserable, and the only reason you might find yourself in the region is if you're driving through on the way to the **Grand Canyon**.

The Western Mojave

The **western expanse** of the Mojave Desert spreads out on the north side of the San Gabriel Mountains, fifty miles from Los Angeles via Hwy-14. It is a barren plain that drivers have to cross in order to reach the alpine peaks of the eastern Sierra Nevada mountains or Death Valley, at the Mojave's northern edge. The few towns that have grown up in this stretch of desert over the past couple of decades are populated in the main by two sorts of people: retired couples who value the dry, clean air, and aerospace workers employed in one of the many military bases or aircraft factories. **Lancaster**, near Edwards Air Force Base, is the largest town and one of the few places to pick up supplies; **Mojave**, thirty miles north, is a main desert crossroads that caters mainly to drive-by tourists. **Tehachapi**, twenty miles west and a few thousand feet higher, offers a cool retreat. Hwy-14 joins up with US-395 another forty miles north, just west of the huge naval air base at **China Lake** and the faceless town of **Ridgecrest**, a good jumping-off point for some interesting attractions.

Lancaster and the Antelope Valley

From the north end of LA's San Fernando Valley, Hwy-14 cuts off from I-5 and heads east around the foothills of the San Gabriel Mountains, passing the site of California's earliest gold discovery in 1842, now preserved within the **Placerita Canyon Park** nature reserve (daily 9am–5pm; free). Ten miles further on stands the massive sandstone outcrop of the 745-acre **Vasquez Rocks County Park** (daily 8am–sunset; $3 per vehicle), once a hiding place for frontier bandits and bank robbers, and later used by Hollywood movie studios as the backdrop for a variety of TV shows and films including *The Flintstones*. Beyond here, Hwy-138 cuts off east, heading up to the ski resorts and lakes along the crest of the San Gabriel Mountains, while Hwy-14 cuts north across the sparsely settled flatlands of the Mojave Desert.

The biggest places for miles are the twin towns of **LANCASTER** and

PALMDALE, two soulless side-by-side communities of retirees and RV parks whose economy is wholly based on designing, building, and testing airplanes, from B-1 bombers for the military to the *Voyager*, which made the first non-stop flight around the globe in 1987. The free **Blackbird Airpark**, on 25th Street East at Avenue P in Palmdale, three miles east of Hwy-14 along Avenue P, can be recognized by the two sinister-looking black planes standing by the roadside. These are in fact the fastest and highest-flying planes ever created. The A-12 was designed in the 1950s as prototype for the SR-71 – the *Blackbird* – a reconnaissance plane that could reach 2100 miles per hour at 85,000ft. Unless you strike one of the infrequent "open cockpit" days, all you can do is circle the planes admiring the sleek lines and astonishing statistics. There are several other impressive aircraft in the park, and more are being added all the time.

If you're not a military buff, there's little to draw you into Lancaster except the need of a bed or supplies. The **Chamber of Commerce**, at 544 Lancaster Blvd (Mon–Fri 9am–5pm; ☎661/948-4518), has information on **accommodation** – at motels such as *Motel 6* (☎661/948-0435; ❷) at 43540 W 17th St, just off Hwy-14, or the more salubrious *Desert Inn*, 44219 Sierra Hwy (☎805/948 8401, ⓦwww.desert-inn.com; ❹).

To learn more of the desert sights, call at the **Mojave Desert State Parks visitor center**, 43779 15th St West (Mon–Sat 10am–4pm; ☎661/942-0662, ⓦwww.calparksmojave.com), handily sited in a mall near the Avenue K exit off Hwy-14. This is the main contact point for the surrounding sights such as the **Antelope Valley California Poppy Reserve** (daily sunrise–sunset; in poppy season $2, otherwise free), fifteen miles west of Hwy-14 on Lancaster Road. You can come to stroll the easy desert trails at any time of year, but the main reason to come is to witness the place blanketed in the bright orange of California's state flower, the Golden Poppy. It is a temperamental and unpredictable plant but given enough rain it usually blooms between mid-March and late April; for details, call the visitor center or consult the Theodore Payne Foundation for Wildflowers and Native Plants (☎818/768-3533, ⓦwww.theodorepayne.org). During the blooming season you can also visit the excellent **interpretive center** (seasonal: Mon–Fri 9am–4pm, Sat & Sun 9am–5pm), which has displays of desert flora and fauna. The building itself is proof that passive-solar underground architecture works: built into the side of a hill, it keeps cool naturally and is powered entirely by an adjacent windmill generator.

Saddleback Butte State Park, seventeen miles east of Lancaster at the junction of Avenue J and 170th Street (daily dawn–dusk; $2), centers on a smallish hill whose slopes are home to a splendid collection of Joshua trees. It's also a likely spot to catch a glimpse of the desert tortoise, for whom the park provides a refuge from the motorcyclists and dune buggy enthusiasts who tear around the region. There's a half-mile nature trail and a simple **campground** ($8), which is mostly under-used but is popular for star-gazing on summer weekends. Three miles southwest, the **Antelope Valley Indian Museum** on Avenue M (mid-Sept–June 1 Sat & Sun 11am–4pm; $3), housed in a mock Swiss chalet painted with Native American motifs, contains an extensive collection of ethnographic material from all over the state.

Mojave, Tehachapi, and Red Rock Canyon

MOJAVE, strung out along the highway thirty miles north of Lancaster, is a major junction on the interstate train network, though it's used solely by freight trains. The town itself – largely a mile-long highway strip of gas stations, $40-a-night motels and franchised fast-food restaurants, open around the clock

– is a good place to fill up on food and gas before continuing north into the Owens Valley or Death Valley.

The desert and dry lake beds east of Mojave make up **Edwards Air Force Base**, the US military testing ground for experimental, high-speed and high-altitude aircraft (such as the *Blackbird*; see above), which incorporates NASA's Dryden Flight Research Center, and backup space shuttle landing site. You used to be able to take a ninety-minute tour complete with a short film (a jingoistic cross between *The Right Stuff* and *Top Gun*) and a look at hangars full of unique airplanes, including the missile-like X-15, but in the aftermath of September 11 these have been suspended. To see if they've had a recent change of heart, contact their public affairs department (☎661/277-3510, ⓦ www.edwards.af.mil).

Tehachapi

About twenty miles west from Mojave, Hwy-58 rises to the rolling hillsides of **TEHACHAPI**, an apple-growing center that, at an elevation of around 4000 feet, offers a nice respite from the Mojave's heat. In addition to its pretty setting, the town has a couple of minor claims to fame. Some 5100 **wind generators** – both familiar three-bladed windmills and more unusual egg-beater-style Darreius turbines – make the Tehachapi Wind Resource Area, ranked along Cameron Ridge to the east, one of the world's most productive renewable energy stations. They're very visible from Hwy-58, but there are few places to stop so you may prefer to follow Oak Creek Road, a backroad to Tehachapi from the center of Mojave.

Train enthusiasts, meanwhile, cross states to see groaning Santa Fe diesels hauling their mile-long string of boxcars around the **Tehachapi Loop**, eight miles west of town. Built in the 1870s as the only means of scaling the steep slopes of the region, the tracks cleave to the rockface, doubling back on themselves to make a complete 360° loop. It is an impressive sight seeing a train (anything over 85 boxcars long) twisting around a mountain, its front end 77ft above its tail. You can't see it properly from Hwy-58, so follow the signs three miles from the Keene exit to a roadside plaque commemorating the loop's engineers.

For **information** about these and other local attractions, ranging from pick-your-own-fruit orchards and antiques shops to ostrich farms, stop in at the **Chamber of Commerce**, 209 E Tehachapi Blvd (Mon–Fri 9am-5pm, Sat & Sun 9am–4pm; ☎661/822-4180), right by the train tracks in the older section of town.

Nearby you'll find **accommodation** at the *Santa Fe Motel*, 120 W Tehachapi Blvd (☎661/822-3184, ⓕ822-7905; ❶), and the *Best Western Mountain Inn*, 416 W Tehachapi Blvd (☎661/822-5591; ❸). Eight miles southwest of town off Highline Road, there's **camping** (☎661/868-7000; $8) at a refreshing range 5500 to 7000 feet in the *Tehachapi Mountain Park*. Popular local **restaurants** include the daytime-only *Apple Shed*, 333 E Tehachapi Blvd (☎661/823-8333), good for country-style breakfasts or apple-pie breaks, and *Domingo's*, 20416 Valley Blvd (☎661/822-7611), a family-owned Mexican and seafood place in the newer section of town a mile or so west.

North of Mojave along Hwy-14

Following Hwy-14 northeast from Mojave the desert is virtually uninhabited, the landscape marked only by the bald ridges of the foothills of the Sierra Nevada Mountains that rise to the west, though you might see the odd ghostly sign of the prospectors who once roamed the region in search of gold and less precious minerals. Twenty-four miles north of Mojave, Hwy-14 passes through **Red Rock Canyon**, a brilliantly colored rocky badlands of wonderfully eroded formations.

The highway passes right through the center of the most impressive section, though if you walk just a hundred yards from the road you're more likely to see an eagle or coyote than another visitor. Better still, call at the **Red Rock Canyon State Park** (always open; $2), where the **visitor center** (open spring & fall Fri 1–9pm, Sat 9am–7pm, Sun 9am–5pm; closed summer and winter; ☎661/942-0662) can point you to a number of short trails and runs a weekend ranger program of nature walks and campfire talks, ranging from Native American visits to movie filming in the area. The adjacent *Ricardo* **campground** ($10) is fairly primitive but beautifully sited amid Joshua trees and colorful rocks.

Around 25 miles north of Red Rock Canyon, Hwy-14 meets US-395 which heads north to the Owens Valley and the western entrance to Death Valley, regions covered in depth in Chapter Four. A further twenty miles north of the junction, Cinder Rock Road leads east to **Fossil Falls**, another rather unearthly formation some 27 miles northwest of Ridgecrest. Relatively recent volcanic eruptions (about 20,000 years ago) drove lava through one of this region's dry river channels, creating what looks like a petrified cataract. Some remaining petroglyphs as well as various small artifacts and polished indentations in the rocks, used for grinding grain, attest to widespread human habitation in this area.

Boron, the Rand Mining District, and Ridgecrest

The busy Hwy-58 runs east from Mojave skirting the northern side of the Edwards Air Force Base for thirty miles to a signed exit for the **Borax Visitor Center** (daily 9am–5pm; $2 per vehicle; ⊛www.borax.com/borax6), a modern complex on a hill overlooking a vast open-cast borax mine – the largest mine in California – and processing plant. Borax is sodium borate, a crystalline mineral which was originally used as a flux to improve the working properties of gold and silver, but more recently has found applications in everything from washing detergents to heat-resistant glass and fiberglass. The center is primarily a promotional tool for the Borax company, which owns the site, but call in if only to see the seventeen-minute video (complete with a 1960s snip of Ronald Reagan advertising hand cleaner), which finishes with curtains opening on a great view into the mile-wide, 650-foot deep pit.

There's more of the history of boron extraction and the role of the twenty mule teams which hauled paired ten-ton wagons of borax out of Death Valley and elsewhere at the **Boron Twenty Mule Team Museum**, 26962 20 Mule Team Rd (daily 10am–4pm; donation), in the town of **BORON** three miles further east. The museum also has coverage of movies filmed here – parts of *Erin Brockovich* for one – and has a video about the Solar Energy Generating Station (SEGS), which spreads across the desert six miles at the junction of Hwy-58 and US-395. This vast array of shiny panels produces around 30 megawatts of electricity and is part of five such installations across the Mojave Desert.

The Rand Mining District

Following US-395 north of Boron there's no reason to stop in the first thirty miles until you reach the **RAND MINING DISTRICT**, a close cluster of three virtually deserted towns, whose lifeblood is provided by the Yellow Aster and Baltic gold mines, the last to be commercially worked in California. **Red Mountain** and **Johannesburg** are a couple of miles apart on US-395, but the real interest lies a mile to the west on a loop road between the two towns. Here you'll find **Randsburg**, a near ghost town of scruffy-looking shacks surrounded by the detritus of ancient mines. But there's a certain Wild West charm to its hundred-yard-long main street with its two bars, dozen shops, and the **Desert Museum**, 161 Butte Ave (Sat & Sun 10am–5pm; free), which has displays on the glory days of the 1890s, when upwards of three thousand people lived in the town, mining gold, silver, and tungsten out of the arid, rocky hills. The nearby **General Store** is a fascinating slice of history with its embossed tin ceiling, 1904 soda fountain (the super-thick chocolate shakes are locally celebrated), and a small restaurant surrounded by shelves of groceries and mining supplies. It is open daily (unlike the rest of the town, which pretty much shuts down during the week), and is a good source of local **information** (☎760/374-2418).

You are free to wander off and explore the local hills and old mine workings, but land-use conflict between off-roaders and the Bureau of Land Management, which is seeking to protect desert tortoise habitat, means you should ask locally about areas which may be closed.

You can **stay** in Randsburg at the *Cottage Hotel*, 130 Butte Ave (☎760/374-2285, ⓦwww.randsburg.com; ❹), and **eat** both at the general store and at the *Opera House Café*, also on Butte Avenue.

In neighboring **Johannesburg**, the simple but welcoming *Death Valley Hostel*, 301 Hwy 395 (☎760/374-2323), has forty beds ($15) and one private room (❶).

Ridgecrest

Twenty miles north of Randsburg, Hwy-178 cuts east towards Death Valley, reaching the sprawling desert community of **RIDGECREST**, dominated by the huge China Lake Naval Weapons Center. Jet fighters scream past overhead, taking target practice on land that's chock-full of ancient **petroglyphs**. Though access to the sites is strictly controlled, you can get some idea of the native culture of the Mojave Desert by visiting the **Maturango Museum**, on the corner of China Lake Boulevard and East Las Flores Avenue (daily 10am–5pm; ($2); ☎760/375-6900, ⓦwww.maturango.org), which as well as acting as regional **visitor center** (free), has exhibits on both the natural and cultural history of the region, including examples of the rock-cut figures. To get out and see the figures and designs in their natural surroundings, you may be able to join a half-day volunteer-led **tour** (spring and fall only; $25), though the most concentrated collections of petroglyphs are on the base and in the security-conscious aftermath of September 11 these are currently off limits. For the latest information call the museum or check its website, and be prepared to reserve a place well in advance.

Visitors interested in high-tech weaponry and the navy's role in the area can visit the **US Naval Museum of Armaments and Technology** (Mon–Fri 10am–4pm; free; ☎760/939-3140) on the China Lake base, though currently only US citizens are allowed to enter the base, and even for Americans security clearance is quite a rigmarole (though this will presumably be relaxed in time).

It is perhaps more rewarding to stray four miles east of town to the Bureau of Land Management's **Wild Horse and Burro corrals**, where sometimes over a thousand animals are kept while waiting for adoption. Even if you're not prepared to take one home, you can call in (Mon–Fri 7.30am–4pm; free;

@www.wildhorseandburro.blm.gov); to ensure an enthusiastic reception, bring along some apples or carrots.

Trona Pinnacles and Searles Valley

Hwy-178 runs northeast from Randsburg past the burro corrals and out into the dry and desolate **Searles Valley**, which offers a back road into Death Valley with access to Telescope Peak (see p.337). Some sixteen miles northeast of Randsburg, a five-mile dirt road (passable except after rain) leads to the **Trona Pinnacles National Natural Landmark** (unrestricted access; free) where over five hundred tufa spires stretch up to 140ft. They were considered extra-terrestrial enough-looking to form a backdrop for parts of *Star Trek V* and can be viewed best on the half-mile nature trail. The park's campground was washed out during an El Niño storm, but you are free to **camp** anyway: there are vault toilets but you'll have to bring water. There are basic supplies six miles north on Hwy-178 at the industrial and substantially run-down borax-pro-cessing town of **Trona**.

Victorville, Barstow, and around

The long desert drive from LA to Las Vegas takes you along I-15, part of which follows the original line of Route 66. You'll see little of the old road – or any-thing else of great interest – from the freeway, so you should definitely consid-er taking time out to explore a few minor attractions. **Victorville** warrants a brief detour to marvel at the cowboy kitsch of the Roy Rogers-Dale Evans Museum and the highwayside Americana in the Route 66 Museum. **Barstow** is better for what lies nearby, particularly the colored rocks of Rainbow Basin and the faux ghost town of Calico. Further east there are early human remains at the **Calico Dig**, and the etymological curiosity that is **Zzyzx**.

Victorville

I-15 heads north from San Bernardino slicing between the San Gabriel and San Bernardino mountains to reach the Mojave Desert. The first town of any size is **VICTORVILLE**, some eighty miles northeast of LA, where the **Roy Rogers-Dale Evans Museum**, 15650 Seneca Rd (daily 9am–5pm; $8; ☎760/243-4548, @www.royrogers.com), is located in a faux wooden fort sur-rounded by a vast parking lot next to the freeway: take the Roy Rogers exit and drive down Civic Street. The museum may well be moving out of state in the near future (so call in advance if you're making a special journey), but for the moment remains a huge repository of the Hollywood cowboy couple's memorabilia. Amongst the photos, magazine covers, ornately decorated saddles, and massed tooled cowboy boots, you'll find a pair of Roy and Dale inlaid mother-of-pearl guitars and a diorama featuring the stuffed forms of Trigger and Buttermilk, the horses they rode in many of their films. Also dedicated to American myth, the small **California Route 66 Museum**, 16825 D St at Fifth Street (Mon; Thurs–Sun 10am–4pm; free; ☎760/951-0436), has devo-tional displays relating to the westernmost strip of the Mother Road (see box). Relics from an old roadside attraction called "Hulaville" are the museum's most interesting feature, but there are various old-time videos and a stack of nostal-gic merchandise.

Route 66 in California

The advent of the interstates in the 1950s tolled the death knell of what John Steinbeck called The Mother Road in *Grapes of Wrath*. Route 66 was the umbilical cord between Chicago and Los Angeles, conceived in the 1920s when existing roads were stitched together to form a single 2400-mile route across eight states. It was just one of many such migration routes but is the one that most captured the public imagination – not least through Nat King Cole's 1946 hit *(Get your kicks on) Route 66* – and became America's most famous highway. As freeways obliterated the old road and franchise hotels and restaurants populated their flanks, the old diners and mom-and-pop motels gradually disappeared, further enhancing its iconic status.

Large sections of the old route disappeared long ago, but it was the realization that some of the last vestiges were about to disappear that kickstarted a revival. Sections of the original route have since sprouted Route 66 signs, though these were promptly liberated by fans and you now tend to see "Historic Route 66" painted onto the asphalt. After considerable lobbying by Route 66 associations, Bill Clinton passed a National Preservation Bill benefiting the Route 66 Corridor in 1999, and the tourist machine now promotes the old road vigorously. Some 320 miles of the original route ran through California, and Kingman, Barstow, and San Bernardino all get a mention in the famous song, but the best-preserved section is in the Mojave Desert east of Barstow. Fans will want to visit the small **museums** in Victorville (see p.293) and Barstow (see below), or even try to track down the *Wigwam Motel* in San Bernardino, a classic piece of Americana, but for most it is enough to drive the desert section that loops south off I-40 from Ludlow to Essex. One essential stop is *Roy's* gas station and café at Amboy, a place that seems familiar from dozens of road-trip movies and car commercials.

For more information, check out websites such as ⓦ www.national66.com and ⓦ www.historic66.com.

Barstow and around

Almost thirty miles northeast of Victorville along the thundering, seemingly endless I-15, **BARSTOW** looms up out of the desert, providing a welcome opportunity to get out of the car. Though capital of the Mojave and the crossroads of three major thoroughfares (I-40 and Hwy-58 also run through here), it's a small town, consisting of just one main road lined with a selection of motels and restaurants that make an overnight stop possible. This main street was once part of the famed **Route 66** (see box, above), so fans of neon will enjoy some classic examples, and two nearby **outlet malls** attract area bargain hunters. There, however, the town's appeal ends. For many months of the year, the relentless sun manages to keep people in their air-conditioned homes for a good part of the day; in summer, Barstow can seem more like a ghost town.

Historical interest focuses on the grand 1911 Casa del Desierto (the "House of the Desert"), built as a train station with associated restaurant and lodging. Trains still stop here and the building remains striking but is largely empty and has a forlorn air despite containing a couple of small museums. The **Western American Railroad Museum** (Fri–Sun 10am–4pm; donation suggested; ☎760/256-9276, ⓦ www.barstowrailmuseum.org), is dedicated to preserving the history of southwest railroading, while the **Route 66 "Mother Road" Museum**, 681 N 1st Ave (Fri–Sun 11am–4pm; free; ⓦ www.barstow66muse-um.itgo.com), is full of highway Americana. For those with less specialized interests, there's the **Mojave River Valley Museum**, 270 E Virginia Way (daily 11am–4pm; free; ⓦ admenu.com/mvm), containing material on the history and natural history of the area with a sizeable archeological collection including material from the Calico Dig (see p.296).

Getting out of town, your first stop should be **Rainbow Basin** (unrestricted access), eight miles north along Fort Irwin Road. A rock formation which, after thirty million years of wind erosion, has been exposed as a myriad of almost electric colors, it features plenty of fossilized animal and insect remains. Most visitors will probably be content to weave the car through the tricky four-mile loop road around the canyon and marvel at the prettiness of it all. You can camp here (see "Practicalities" opposite) at minimally equipped sites.

Two designated **off-road recreational areas** lie south of Barstow: **Rasor** and **Stoddard Valley**. If you didn't bring your own dune buggy, you're out of luck – there's nowhere to rent them in Barstow – but you can always travel out to the dunes and get friendly with someone there. Camping is permitted in much of Stoddard Valley, a pretty area of rolling hills but one that's dotted with abandoned mineshafts. Watch where you lay your backpack down.

Heading eight miles east on I-40, just past Dagget, the original Department of Energy's Solar One Power Plant has been replaced by the **SEGS II Solar Power Plant**, which, marked by a hundred-acre field of mirrors, is a surreal example of how California is putting its deserts to use. Anyone who has seen the film *Bagdad Café* will remember the light reflections the mirrors give off for miles around.

Practicalities

The **California Welcome Center** (daily 9am–8pm; ☎1-888/422-7786), four miles west of Barstow in the Tanger Outlet Mall off I-15 at the Lenwood Road exit, has a good selection of maps of the surrounding area, lodging and restaurant guides, and various flyers on local attractions. There's also the **Chamber of Commerce**, 409 E Fredricks St (Mon–Fri 9am–5pm; ☎760/256-8617, ⓔbacc@barstowchamber.com), right in town.

If you're arriving by **bus** or **train**, you'll be dropped at the combined Greyhound and Amtrak station in the Casa del Desierto (see opposite), on First Street. Over the tracks, Main Street is the best place to look for **motels**, generally only distinguished by the condition of the neon sign outside. Cruise up and down until you find the best deal, but among those you might try are *Days Inn*, 1590 Coolwater Lane (☎760/256-1737; ❷), or for a little more comfort, the corporate-style *Ramada Inn*, 1511 E Main St (☎760/256-5673; ❹). You can **camp** eight miles north of Barstow in the simple *Owl Canyon* campground ($6) at Rainbow Basin (see above), or if you need more facilities, at **Calico**, a re-created ghost town (see below) with shaded canyons where you can pitch a tent for $18, hook up campers for $22 per night, or stay in one of the cabins (❶).

Food in Barstow, though far from exotic, is plentiful and cheap. Restaurants sit snugly between the many hotels on Main Street and are usually of the rib-and-steak variety – *Idle Spurs Steak House*, 290 Old Hwy-58, is tops in that mode. However, you can get good authentic Mexican food at *Rosita's*, 540 W Main St, or the more Americanized and extremely good Mexican at *Carlos & Toto's*, 901 W Main. Evening **entertainment** comes in the form of a few grubby bars frequented by bike gangs, the least threatening of which is *Katz*, 127 W Main St at First, open from 6am to 2am.

East of Barstow: along I-15

Most people who stop in Barstow are not here to enjoy the desert, but to visit the contrived **Calico Ghost Town** (daily 9am–5pm; $6, admission free with camping; ☎1-800/TOCALICO, ⓦwww.calicotown.com), seven miles northeast along

I-15 then three miles north. In the late nineteenth century, Calico produced millions of dollars' worth of silver and borax and supported a population of almost four thousand. Attractively set in the color-streaked Calico Hills, but subject to the extreme heat of the Mojave, the town was quickly deserted when the silver ran out. It's since been rather cynically – and insensitively – restored, with souvenir shops and hot-dog stands, and a main thoroughfare lined with ersatz saloons, an old school house, a vaudeville playhouse, and shops kitted out in period styles. However, should you so desire, there are miles of mining shafts and tunnels open to crawl around in – until claustrophobia forces you up for air.

Various festivals brighten up Calico, the best of which is May's **Spring Festival**, featuring the World Tobacco Spitting Championships. Huge beast-like men gather to chew the wad and direct streams of saliva and tobacco juice at an iron post, cheered on by rowdy crowds who take their sport seriously and their drink in large quantities. There is also a chili cook-off, music, and a he-man triathlon.

Primitive males are also featured at the **Calico Early Man Site** (visit by guided tour only Wed 1.30pm & 3.30pm, Thurs–Sun 9.30am, 11.30am, 1.30pm & 3.30pm; $2.50, minimum of two people; Ⓦwww.ca.blm.gov/barstow), at the Minneola Road exit off I-15, six miles northeast of the Calico exit then 2.5 miles north. More popularly known as the "Calico Dig," it has become one of the most important archeological sites in North America since it was excavated in 1964 by Louis Leakey. Some of the old tools and primitive shelter found here have been dated at around 20,000 years old, controversially establishing mankind's presence here several thousand years earlier than was previously thought: debate rages on.

After driving 23 miles further east of the site, take the Afton Road turnoff from I-15 to get to **Afton Canyon**, dubbed the "Grand Canyon of the Mojave." At a couple of hundred feet deep it's far less impressive than the Arizona original, but it's only three miles off I-15 and is striking nevertheless, with multicolored strata formed by erosion from an extinct lake. The lake may be gone, but Afton Canyon is one of the three places where the Mojave River flows above ground throughout the year, making this a marshy mecca for almost two hundred types of birds and desert creatures. There's camping here on a first-come-first-served basis ($10).

Back on I-15 there's little of interest in the next twenty miles until the junction with Zzyzx Road. This leads just over four miles south to the western edge of the preserve and the oasis of **Zzyzx** at the base of rocky hills and on the edge of the usually arid Soda Dry Lake. From 1905 to 1940, the site was on the Tonopah & Tidewater railroad, and when the company decamped, the charismatic quack, preacher, and LA radio personality Curtis "Doc" Springer set up a mineral springs resort. He renamed the spot Zzyzx, correctly surmising that the odd name would draw custom. Unfortunately, he never actually owned the land, and in 1974 he was evicted and the resort closed. Some dilapidated buildings continue to rot away, but most have been transformed into California State University's Soda Springs Desert Studies Center. If there are no happy-to-be-distracted researchers around, you can just stroll around the artificial palm-fringed lake on what is effectively a nature trail, and search for evidence of the area's colorful history.

From the Zzyzx Road junction on I-15 it is six miles to Baker.

③

Baker and the Eastern Mojave

There's not much to **BAKER** – essentially a strip of fairly expensive gas stations and fast-food joints plus a couple of decent motels and restaurants – but it is a handy spot for refueling both body and rig, and as a base for exploring some of California's remoter corners. Death Valley lies immediately north, and it is in honor of the town's proximity to the country's hottest place that Baker has the **world's tallest functioning thermometer**, rising as high as 134 feet to commemorate the highest temperature ever recorded in the US – 134°F in 1913. Baker is also a springboard for the Mojave National Preserve, for which you can pick up information at the **Mojave National Preserve Desert Information Center** (daily 9am–5pm; ☎760/733-4040), at the base of the thermometer.

One man's small empire along Baker Boulevard near the thermometer contains most of the best places to stay and eat. For **lodging**, try the *Bun Boy Motel* (☎760/733-4363; ❸) or the *Wills Fargo Motel* (☎760/733-4477; ❷), which has a pool and slightly more character to its rooms. The supplies at the town's **general store** aren't cheap, but this is your last chance to stock up. (If you buy a lottery ticket here, you may never have to worry about such matters again – the place has produced the most jackpot winners in the state of California.) Standing out from the fast-food joints, the great value *Mad Greek* (☎760/733-4354), serving a huge and eclectic range of cuisines from Greek and Middle Eastern such as gyros, kebabs, and falafel, to burgers, sandwiches, Mexican dishes, and delicious fresh strawberry shakes.

Mojave National Preserve

In 1994, 1.4 million acres of undeveloped country wedged between I-15 and I-40 were set aside as the **MOJAVE NATIONAL PRESERVE** (🌐www.nps.gov/moja), a perfect spot to take a break from the freeway and maybe camp out a night or two to prepare for the excesses of Las Vegas seventy miles ahead. It is a little higher than much of the desert hereabouts, making it a little cooler in summer but also subject to winter snows.

Immediately west of Baker, Kelbaker Road shoots past a series of dramatic black-red **cinder cones**, created relatively recently (a thousand years ago), before reaching the graceful Mission Revival-style **Kelso Depot**, built in 1924 for workers on the Union Pacific Railroad. Closed in 1985, the building is in the process of being restored as a visitor center for the preserve, possibly by mid-2003. Visible to the south of the depot are the spectacular **Kelso Dunes**, a golden five-mile stretch of sand reaching up as high as seven hundred feet. The faint booming sound you might hear is caused by dry sand cascading down the steep upper slopes.

Turn northeast at Kelso to get to the small town of **Cima** (there's a little store here, but no gas) and the adjacent **Cima Dome**, a perfectly formed batholith rising some 1500ft above the desert floor. Cloaked in Joshua trees, parts of it can be visited on foot. To the southeast, along Black Canyon Road, you'll see a turnoff for the *Mid Hills* **campground** (open all year; $12; 5600ft) beautifully sited in piñon-juniper woodland; from here a moderately difficult eight-mile trail winds through Wild Horse Canyon and ends up at the park's other developed campground, *Hole-in-the-Wall* (open all year; $12; 4400ft). Named by Bob Hollimon, a member of the Butch Cassidy gang, because it reminded him of his former hideout in Wyoming, Hole-in-the-Wall sits in at an elevation of 4500 feet among striking volcanic rock formations. If you've driven here and don't want to take a long hike, an interpreted nature trail leads from the seasonal **visitor center**. In the offseason, you'll still find someone at the visitor center for the 5900-acre **Providence Mountain State Recreation Area**, a further ten miles south, then six miles west. Vegetation here changes from scrubby bushes at lower desert elevations to the piñon pines that grow along rocky Fountain Peak (6996ft) and Edgar Peak (7171ft). Some people come to camp at the small campground (six spaces only; $8), but most are here to tour **Mitchell Caverns** (early Sept–late May Mon–Fri 1.30pm, Sat & Sun 10am & 1.30pm; $3; ☎760/928-2586), which were used by the Chemehuevi Indians for almost five hundred years. There's one brief claustrophobia-inducing part, but otherwise this ninety-minute walk through stalactites and stalagmites and rarer limestone formations is superb.

The Colorado River area

Lined with rich vegetation, the **Colorado River** comes as a welcome respite after the barren environment of the eastern portion of the Colorado Desert. The strength of the river, over a thousand miles long, has by this southern stage of its course been sapped by a succession of dams (though even in the Grand Canyon there are whitewater rapids), until here it proceeds towards the Gulf of California in a stately flow, marking the border between California and Arizona.

If you're not heading east to the Grand Canyon itself – or if you're looking for an overnight stop en route, the stretch between Needles, the small border town on I-40, and Blythe a hundred miles south where I-10 meets Hwy-95 – and especially **Lake Havasu City** in between the two – is marginally the most interesting area. Most of the small waterfront settlements that dot its course are dependent on watersports, though some, such as **Laughlin** in Nevada, right on the border with California and Arizona, have taken advantage of Arizona's restrictions on gambling and turned themselves into mini-Vegases. Many enjoy considerable popularity with packs of bikers who make a weekend of driving across the desert, spending all their money on gambling and drink, and then riding back again.

Lake Havasu City

Ten miles east of the California state line on I-40, a twenty-mile detour south on Hwy-95 brings you to the most incongruous sight of the Southwestern deserts. At **LAKE HAVASU CITY**, the old gray stones of **London Bridge** reach out across the stagnant waters of the dammed Colorado River.

Californian chainsaw manufacturer **Robert P. McCulloch** moved his factory to this unlikely spot – occupied by a disused military airstrip – in 1964, so he could try out his new sideline in outboard motors on the waters of Lake Havasu. Three years later, he heard Johnny Carson mention that London Bridge was up for sale; in the words of the nursery rhyme, it really was falling down, unable to cope with the newfangled automobiles. McCulloch bought it for $2,460,000, and painstakingly shipped ten thousand numbered blocks of granite across the Atlantic. Lacking anything for the bridge to span, he dug a channel that turned a riverbank promontory into the island of **Pittsburg Point**. Despite the jibes that McCulloch thought he was buying picturesque Tower Bridge – the turreted one that opens in the middle – instead of merely the latest in a long line of London Bridges, dating only from 1831, his investment paid off handsomely. The bridge now ranks second among Arizona's tourist attractions, after the Grand Canyon, and Lake Havasu City has become a major vacation resort and retirement center, with a population of thirty thousand.

That said, it's not often you see anything quite as **boring** in Arizona as London Bridge. Lake Havasu City is one of those places with an undeniable attraction for the parched urbanites of cities such as Phoenix, who flock to fish on the lake or charge up and down in motorboats and on jet skis, but it holds minimal appeal for travelers from further afield. Be warned that between March and June, it's almost permanently filled with students on **Spring Break**, drinking and partying around the clock.

Only when you cross the bridge onto the island and then look back, do you appreciate how large Lake Havasu City has grown, sprawling up the gentle slope away from the river. Most of those broad hillside streets are lined with condo blocks and minor malls; the only place tourists bother to visit is the **English Village**, a mock-Tudor shopping mall, which also holds a handful of riverview restaurants, at the base of the bridge. Out on the island, if you head south from the bridge past the *Island Inn Resort*, you'll soon come to **London Bridge Beach**. The "beach" is more grit than sand, and few people swim from it. With its bizarre fringe of date palms, however, and its panorama of weird desert buttes and the Chemehuevi Mountains, it does at least linger in the memory.

Practicalities

A **visitor center** at 420 English Village can tell you anything you want to know about Lake Havasu (daily 10am–4pm; ☎928/453-3444, ⓦwww.golakehavasu .com). Several operators offer short **river cruises** from the quayside of the English Village, charging around $13 for an hour-long trip focusing on the bridge, or $25 for a two-hour excursion to see rock formations upriver, and **jet ski** rentals are also widely available at around $40 per hour.

Lake Havasu City has a good 25 or so **motels**, though relatively few are immediately obvious from Hwy-95. They range from the perfectly adequate *Havasu Motel*, 2035 Acoma Blvd (☎928/855-2311; ❷), by way of the fancier, all-suite *Ramada at Lake Havasu*, 271 S Lake Havasu Ave (☎1-800/528-5169 or 928/855-5169; ❸), to the extravagant riverfront *London Bridge Resort*, 1477 Queen's Bay Rd (☎1-800/624-7939 or 928/855-0888; winter ❹, summer ❼), where the lobby is all but filled by a gilt replica stagecoach.

For a night out, the districts at either end of London Bridge are your best bet. The *City of London Arms* (☎928/855-8782) is a lively **pub** in the English Village on the mainland, while *Shugrue's* (☎928/453-1400), across the bridge in the Island Fashion Mall, serves good fresh fish – even sushi – as well as salads and pasta.

Las Vegas

Little emphasis is placed on the gambling clubs and divorce facilities – though they are attractions to many visitors – and much is being done to build up the cultural attractions. No cheap and easily parodied slogans have been adopted to publicize the city, no attempt has been made to introduce pseudo-romantic architectural themes or to give artificial glamor or gaiety. Las Vegas is itself – natural and therefore very appealing to people with a wide variety of interests.

WPA Guidebook to Nevada, 1940

Shimmering from the desert haze of Nevada like a latter-day El Dorado, **LAS VEGAS** is one of the most dynamic, spectacular cities on earth. At the start of the twentieth century, it didn't even exist; now it's home to over one million people, with enough newcomers arriving all the time for the city to need a new school every month. Boasting fourteen of the world's twenty largest hotels, it's a monument to architectural exuberance, whose flamboyant, no-expense-spared **casinos** lure in thirty-seven million tourists each year.

Las Vegas has been stockpiling superlatives since the 1950s, but never rests on its laurels for a moment. First-time visitors tend to expect the city to be a repository of **kitsch**, but the casino owners are far too canny to be sentimental about the old days. Yes, there are a few Elvis impersonators around, but what characterizes the city far more is its endless quest for **novelty**. Long before they lose their sparkle, yesterday's showpieces are blasted into rubble, to make way for ever more extravagant replacements. A few years ago, when the fashion was for fantasy, Arthurian castles and Egyptian pyramids mushroomed along the legendary Strip; now Vegas demands nothing less than entire cities, and has already acquired pocket versions of New York, Paris, Monte Carlo, and Venice.

While Las Vegas has certainly cleaned up its act since the early days of Mob domination, there's little truth in the notion that it's become a **family** destination. In fact, for kids, it's not a patch on Orlando. Only five percent of visitors bring children, and the crowds that cluster around the exploding volcanoes and pirate battles along the Strip remain almost exclusively adult. Neither is Vegas as consistently **cheap** as it used to be. It's still possible to find inexpensive rooms and cut-price buffets, but the casino owners have finally discovered that high-rollers happy to lose hundreds of dollars per night don't mind paying premium prices to eat at top-quality restaurants, and the latest developments budget on room rates of more like $300 than $30 per night.

Your first hours in Las Vegas are like entering another world, where the religion is luck, the language is money, and time is measured by the revolutions of a roulette wheel. Once you're acclimated, the whole spectacle can be absolutely exhilarating, assuming you haven't pinned your hopes – and your savings – on the pursuit of a fortune. Las Vegas is an unmissable destination, but one that palls for most visitors after a couple of (hectic) days.

If you've come solely to gamble, there's not much to say beyond the fact that all the casinos are free and open 24 hours per day, with acres of floor space packed with ways to lose money: **million–dollar slots**, **video poker**, **blackjack**, **craps**, and much much more. The casinos love it if you try to play a system; with the odds stacked against you, your best hope of a large win is to bet your entire stake on one single play and then stop, win or lose.

Some history

Las Vegas has one of the shortest histories of any city in the world. The only US city founded in the twentieth century to boast over a million inhabitants, it's also perhaps the only one that has consistently prioritized the need to attract visitors over the quality of life of its own residents.

The name *Las Vegas* – Spanish for "the meadows" – originally applied to natural springs that from 1829 onwards replenished travelers on the Old Spanish Trail. For the rest of the nineteenth century, the Paiute Indians shared the region with Mormon ranchers, and the valley had a population of just thirty in 1900. Things changed in 1905, with the completion of the now-defunct rail link between Salt Lake City and Los Angeles. Las Vegas itself was founded on May 15 that year, when the railroads auctioned off lots around what's now Fremont Street.

Getting married in Las Vegas

Perhaps the second most popular reason to visit Las Vegas, after making your fortune, is to **get married**. Over a hundred thousand weddings are performed here each year, many so informal that bride and groom just wind down the window of their car during the ceremony, and a Vegas wedding has become a byword for tongue-in-cheek chic. What's surprising is that most marriages are deeply formal affairs. Both the casinos and a horde of independent wedding chapels compete to offer elaborate ceremonies with all the traditional trimmings, from white gowns and black limousines, to garters and boutonnieres.

You don't have to be a local resident or take a blood test to get wed here. Assuming you're both at least eighteen years old, carrying picture ID, and not already married, simply turn up at the Clark County Marriage License Bureau, downtown at 200 S 3rd St (Mon–Thurs 8am–midnight, continuously from Fri 8am to Sun midnight; ☎702/455-4415, ⓦwww.co.clark.nv.us/clerk/marriage-information.ht), and buy a marriage license for $50 cash.

Wedding chapels claim to charge as little as $50 for basic ceremonies, but at that sort of rate even the minister is an "extra," costing an additional $40. Reckon on paying at least $100 for the bare minimum, which is liable to be as romantic a process as checking in at a hotel and to take about as long. The full deluxe service ranges up to around $600. Novelty options include plighting your troth amid the pirates aboard *HMS Britannia* outside *Treasure Island* (☎702/894-7700); on the deck of the *USS Enterprise* at the Hilton (☎702/697-8750); floating on a gondola in the *Venetian*'s Grand Canal (☎702/414-4253); or cavorting in medieval costume at *Excalibur* (☎702/597-7278).

Chapels

Candlelight Wedding Chapel 2855 Las Vegas Blvd S ☎702/735-4179 or 1-800/962-1818, ⓦwww.candlelightchapel.com. Busy little chapel across from *Circus Circus*, where you get a carnation bouquet with the $179 wedding package, or a garter with the $499 option.

Graceland Wedding Chapel 619 S Las Vegas Blvd ☎702/474-6655 or 1-800/824-5732, ⓦwww.gracelandchapel.com. Home of the King – an Elvis impersonator will act as best man, give the bride away, or serenade you, but unfortunately he can't perform the service.

Little Church of the West 4617 Las Vegas Blvd S ☎702/739-7971 or 1-800/821-2452. Once part of the *Last Frontier* casino, this fifty-year-old chapel is on the National Register of Historic Places and has moved progressively down the Strip to its current site, south of *Mandalay Bay*. Among the more peaceful and quiet places to exchange your Vegas vows – if that's really what you want.

Little White Chapel 1301 S Las Vegas Blvd ☎702/382-5943 or 1-800/545-8111, ⓦwww.alittlewhitechapel.com. Where Bruce Willis and Demi Moore married each other, and Michael Jordan and Joan Collins married other people. Open all day every day, with ceremonies in the roofed-over driveway (or "Tunnel of Love") for those in a major hurry.

Ironically, Nevada was the first state to outlaw gambling, in 1909, but it became legal once more in 1931, and the workers who built nearby Hoover Dam flocked to Vegas to bet away their pay-packets. Hotel-casinos such as the daringly large 65-room *El Rancho* began to appear in the early 1940s, but the Midwest Mafia were the first to appreciate the potential for profit. Mobster Bugsy Siegel raised $7 million to open the *Flamingo* on the Strip in December 1946; early losses forced him to close within a month, and although he swiftly managed to re-open, his erstwhile partners were dissatisfied enough to have him murdered in LA in June.

By the 1950s, Las Vegas was booming. The military had arrived – mushroom clouds from desert **A-bomb tests** were visible from the city, and visitors would drive out with picnics to get a better view – and so too had big guns like **Frank Sinatra**, who debuted at the *Desert Inn* in 1951, and **Liberace**, who received $50,000 to open the *Riviera* in 1955. As the stars gravitated towards the Vegas honeypot, nightclubs across America went out of business, and the city became the nation's undisputed live-entertainment capital.

The beginning of the end for Mob rule in Vegas came in 1966, after reclusive tycoon **Howard Hughes** moved into the *Desert Inn*. When the owners tired of his non-gambling ways, he simply bought the hotel, and his clean-cut image encouraged other entrepreneurs to follow suit. **Elvis** arrived a little later; the young rock'n'roller had bombed at the *New Frontier* in 1956, but started a triumphant five-year stint as a karate-kicking lounge lizard at the *International* (now the *Las Vegas Hilton*) in 1969.

Endless federal swoops and stings drove the Mob out of sight by the 1980s, in time for Vegas to re-invent itself on a surge of junk-bond megadollars. The success of Steve Wynn's *Mirage* in enticing a new generation of visitors from 1989 onwards spawned a host of imitators. *Excalibur* and the *MGM Grand* were followed first by *Luxor* and *New York–New York* and then, as the millennium approached, by the opulent quartet of *Bellagio*, *Mandalay Bay*, the *Venetian*, and *Paris*. The 21st century, however, started with a bunch of shocks. Unsuccessful investments elsewhere forced Steve Wynn to sell *Bellagio* and the *Mirage* to the MGM group; the new *Aladdin* swiftly went bankrupt; and the tragedy of September 11, 2001, hit the Las Vegas economy hard.

And yet, once again, Las Vegas has bounced back, with the *Venetian* after an uncertain start going from strength to strength as the flagship for all that the city does best, and Wynn himself announcing his biggest casino yet, *Le Rêve* – named for a Picasso painting – on the site of the old *Desert Inn*. City boosters point out that only fifteen percent of Americans have so far seen Vegas and they're confidently expecting the rest to turn up any day now.

Arrival, information, and getting around

Las Vegas's busy **McCarran International Airport** (℡702/261-5211, ⓦ www.mccarran.com) is a mile east of the southern end of the Strip, and four miles from downtown. Some hotels run free shuttle buses, while Bell Trans (℡702/380-7990, ⓦ www.bell-trans.com) run **minibuses** from the airport to the Strip ($4) and downtown ($5.25); a **cab** to the Strip costs from $10 for the southern end up to $20 further north. Greyhound's long-distance **buses** use a terminal at 200 S Main St downtown, but Amtrak **trains** no longer serve Las Vegas.

If you plan to see more of Vegas than the Strip, a **car** is invaluable, though **public transport** does exist. CAT buses (℡702/228-7433, ⓦ www.catride.com) serve the whole city; #301 and #302 connect the Strip to downtown ($2). The

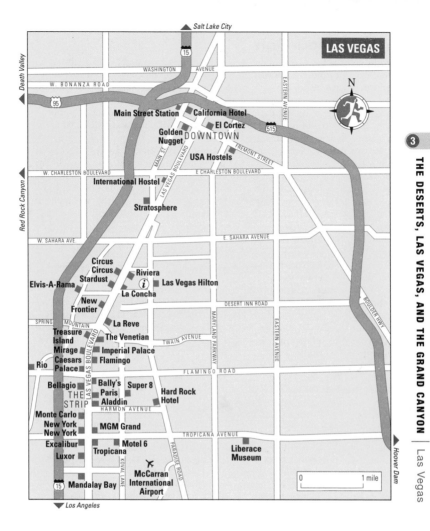

Las Vegas Strip Trolley (☎702/382-1404) plies the Strip between *Mandalay Bay* and the *Stratosphere*, for a flat fare of $1.50, while the similar **Downtown Trolley** (☎702/229-0624) loops between the *Stratosphere* and downtown for 50¢. Several Strip casinos are also connected by free **monorail systems**, but these don't link up with each other, and most require you to walk through the full length of the casinos in order to use them.

Any number of free sheets and magazines provide local **information**. There are also **visitor centers** at 3150 Paradise Rd (daily 8am–5pm; ☎702/892-7575 or 1-800/332-5333, ⓦwww.vegasfreedom.com), half a mile east of the Strip at the vast Convention Center, and at 711 E Desert Inn Rd (Mon–Fri 8am–5pm; ☎702/735-1616, ⓦwww.lvchamber.com), though neither is easy to reach on foot, or stocks anything particularly useful.

Accommodation

Although Las Vegas has well over 125,000 motel and hotel rooms (almost all hitched to casinos), it's always best to book accommodation ahead. Whatever you may have heard, the casinos no longer offer incredibly cheap deals; with occupancy rates averaging ninety percent year-round, they don't need to. True, serious gamblers can get their accommodation free, but to count as "serious" you'd have to commit yourself to gambling several thousand dollars, which is a strange definition of "free."

Room rates are entirely dictated by supply and demand. Even if you stay in the same room for several days, you'll be charged a different rate for each day, depending not only on the day of the week but also which conventions or events may be happening in town, as well as the general level of business. The one sure-fire way to get a cut-price room is to **visit during the week** rather than the weekend. Rates everywhere rise enormously on Friday or Saturday; expect to pay perhaps $30 to $50 extra per night in a lower-end property, such as *Circus Circus* or the *Stratosphere*, and about $100 extra in the big-name casinos, like *Caesars Palace* or the *Venetian*. On top of that, many hotels won't accept Saturday arrivals. **Room taxes** add an additional eleven percent downtown, nine percent elsewhere.

The **Las Vegas Convention & Visitors Authority** offers a reservations service on ☎1-800/332-5334. It's also worth trying both general **online reservations** websites such as ⓦwww.expedia.com and ⓦwww.travelocity-com, and local reservation specialists like Las Vegas Hotels (☎1-877/897-4420, ⓦwww.vegashotel.com) and Las Vegas Rooms (☎1-866/846-3888, ⓦwww.lasvegasrooms.com).

The Strip

Aladdin Resort and Casino 3667 Las Vegas Blvd S ☎702/785-5555, ⓦwww.aladdincasino.com. More manageable than most of its giant neighbors, with each of its 2600 rooms within easy reach of an elevator. If short on Arabian Nights themes, the rooms are spacious, and dining and shopping are first class. Sun–Thurs ❹, Fri & Sat ❼

Bellagio Resort & Casino 3600 Las Vegas Blvd S ☎702/693-7111 or 1-888/987-6667, ⓦwww .bellagiolasvegas.com. The very top end of the Vegas spectrum. Extremely luxurious rooms, superb pool complex, and the best restaurants in town (see p.310). Sun–Thurs ❼, Fri & Sat ❽

Caesars Palace 3570 Las Vegas Blvd S ☎702/731-7110 or 1-800/634-6661, ⓦwww.caesars.com. *Caesars'* older rooms still burst with pseudo-Roman splendor, while those in the newer tower are more conventionally elegant. Paying $10 extra can get you a suite with a four-poster bed. Sun–Thurs ❺, Fri & Sat ❽

Circus Circus Hotel/Casino 2880 Las Vegas Blvd S ☎702/734-0410 or 1-800/444-2472, ⓦwww.circuscircus.com. Still the best option for families: kids love the theme park and circus acts, adults love the low rates. Rooms in the motel-like Manor section at the back are pretty grim; pay a little more to stay in one of the towers instead.

Sun–Thurs ❷, Fri & Sat ❹

La Concha 2955 Las Vegas Blvd S ☎702/735-1255 or 1-800/331-2431. Space Age edifice that's one of the Strip's last characterful old motels. Behind its arched entrance lie three hundred ordinary rooms and a couple of swimming pools. Sun–Thurs ❷, Fri & Sat ❸

Luxor Las Vegas 3900 Las Vegas Blvd S ☎702/262-4000 or 1-800/288-1000, ⓦwww.luxor.com. Vast smoked-glass pyramid, in which all the two thousand extra-large rooms face outwards, with tremendous views. Unlike the extra two thousand rooms in the newer tower next door, however, most have showers not baths. Sun–Thurs ❸, Fri & Sat ❺

Mandalay Bay Resort & Casino 3950 Las Vegas Blvd S ☎702/632-7777 or 1-888/632-7000, ⓦwww.mandalaybay.com. This upscale, young-adult playground is a long way from the central Strip, but all its luxurious rooms have both baths and walk-in showers, and there's a spectacular wave pool. Sun–Thurs ❺, Fri & Sat ❼

The MGM Grand Hotel/Casino 3799 Las Vegas Blvd S ☎702/891-7777 or 1-800/929-1111, ⓦwww.mgmgrand.com. Waiting for any kind of service, especially check-in, at the world's largest hotel – 5005 rooms and counting – can be horrendous, but you get a great standard of accommodation for the price. Sun–Thurs ❸, Fri & Sat ❺

New York–New York Hotel & Casino 3790 Las Vegas Blvd S ☎702/740-6050 or 1-800/693-6763, ⓦwww.nynyhotelcasino.com. Thanks to sheer attention to detail, the most exuberantly enjoyable casino on the Strip. The rooms are very nice, if a bit small, and filled with Art Deco flourishes. Sun–Thurs ❹, Fri & Sat ❻

Paris–Las Vegas Casino-Resort 3655 Las Vegas Blvd S ☎702/946-7000 or 1-888/266-5687, ⓦwww.parislasvegas.com. If not the absolute pinnacle of luxury, rooms and services at the flamboyant *Paris* are still pretty good, and for location, views, and ambience it more than holds its own. Sun–Thurs ❺, Fri & Sat ❼

The Stratosphere Hotel & Casino 2000 Las Vegas Blvd S ☎702/380-7777 or 1-800/998-6937, ⓦwww.stratlv.com. Despite its unfashionable location at the far north end of the Strip, the *Stratosphere* survives thanks to low rates and a steady flow of budget tour groups. No accommodation in the tower, so don't expect amazing views, just large, plain but good-value rooms. Sun–Thurs ❷, Fri & Sat ❹

The Venetian 3355 Las Vegas Blvd S ☎702/414-1000 or 1-888/283-6423, ⓦwww.venetian.com. The Strip's best-value luxury hotel. Even the standard rooms are split-level suites, offering gorgeous antique-style canopied beds, plus roomy living areas, marble bathrooms, and a mind-blowing array of shops and restaurants at hand (see p.310). Sun–Thurs ❼, Fri & Sat ❽

Downtown and off-Strip Accommodation

California Hotel & Casino 12 Ogden Ave at First St ☎702/385-1222 or 1-800/634-6255, ⓦwww.thecal.com. Most of the guests in this mid-range downtown casino are Hawaiian, and Hawaiian food and drink dominate the bars and restaurants. The actual rooms are plain but adequate. Sun–Thurs ❷, Fri & Sat ❸

El Cortez Hotel & Casino 600 E Fremont St ☎702/385-5200 or 1-800/634-6703, ⓦwww.elcortez.net. Veteran downtown casino, where the cut-price rooms in the main building are better than the dismal gaming area might suggest. The mini-suites in the new tower are good value at $44, while the bargain-basement accommodation

in *Ogden House* across the street costs just $18 for a private room with bathroom. ❶

Hard Rock Hotel & Casino 4475 Paradise Rd ☎702/693-5000 or 1-800/473-7625, ⓦwww.hardrockhotel.com. Over a mile east of the Strip, "the world's only rock'n'roll casino" can't match Las Vegas's giants for size or splendor. Instead it's relatively intimate and even chic, with above-average rooms, high-class restaurants, a fabulous pool, and the odd big-name rock gig. Sun–Thurs ❺, Fri & Sat ❼

Las Vegas USA Hostels 1322 E Fremont St ☎702/385-1150 or 1-800/550-8958, ⓦwww.usahostels.com. Former *Howard Johnson* motel, in a slightly forbidding neighborhood ten blocks east of downtown, that's much the better of the city's two independent hostels, with dorm beds from $13 and private doubles from $38. Rates include free breakfast, cheap dinners are also available, and there's a heated swimming pool. The friendly staff arrange national-park and city tours, including a weekly clubbing night. ❶/❷

Las Vegas International Hostel 1208 Las Vegas Blvd S ☎702/385-9955. Bare-bones private hostel in a dilapidated former motel, in an insalubrious area on the fringes of downtown. Dorm beds cost $14, rooms with shared bath little over $20, with $2 discounts for students and hosteling association members. ❶

Main Street Station 200 N Main St at Ogden ☎702/387-1896 or 1-800/465-0711, ⓦwww.mainstreetcasino.com. Downtown's best-value option, two blocks from Fremont Street, with four hundred large guest rooms plus a brewpub and good restaurants. Ask for a room on the south side, not right next to the freeway. Sun–Thurs ❷, Fri & Sat ❸

Rio Suite Hotel & Casino 3700 W Flamingo Rd ☎702/252-7777 or 1-877/784-5737, ⓦwww.playrio.com. Though west of the interstate, the *Rio* makes a serious attempt to rival the Strip giants. The restaurants, bars, and buffets are all excellent, the pool is great, and the rooms are large and luxurious. However, the prices are not cheap, and the Strip stands half a mile away, along a highway no one would dream of walking. Sun–Thurs ❻, Fri & Sat ❼

The City

Though the Las Vegas sprawl measures fifteen miles wide by fifteen miles long, most tourists stick to the six-mile stretch of **Las Vegas Boulevard** that includes the **downtown** area, slightly southeast of the intersection of I-15 and US-95, and the **Strip**, home to the major casinos. In between lie two somewhat seedy miles of gas stations, fast-food drive-ins, and wedding chapels, while the rest of town is largely residential, and need barely concern you at all.

The Strip

For its razor-edge finesse in harnessing sheer excess to the serious business of making money, there's no place like the **LAS VEGAS STRIP**. It's hard to imagine that Las Vegas was once an ordinary city, and Las Vegas Boulevard a dusty thoroughfare scattered with edge-of-town motels. After six decades of capitalism run riot, with every new casino-hotel setting out to surpass its neighbors, the Strip is locked into a hyperactive craving for thrills and glamour, forever discarding its latest toy in its frenzy for the next jackpot.

The southern Strip

As the Strip pushes deeper into the desert, the newest casinos rise at its southern end, not far west of the airport. The procession north kicks off with the gilt tower of 1999's Burmese-themed **Mandalay Bay**. Financed through profits from *Luxor* and *Excalibur*, *Mandalay Bay* is more upmarket than either, and its excellent restaurants and the *House of Blues* keep it lively at night. During the day, all it has to offer sightseers is the **Shark Reef** aquarium (daily 10am–11pm; $14, under-12s $10), where crocodiles, jellyfish and, of course, sharks lurk in a steamy, half-submerged temple complex, and the so-called "coral" is actually multicolored plastic.

Next door stands the 36-story smoked-glass pyramid of **Luxor**. From the palm-fringed avenue of sphinxes guarding the entrance, to the reconstruction of Tutankhamun's tomb inside, the whole building plays endless variations upon the Egyptian theme of archeology, and it ranks as a real must-see. In Las Vegas's closest approximation to Disneyland, three simulator rides and 3-D movies combine to relate a confusing saga of derring-do that's overpriced at $24.

Luxor's architect, Veldon Simpson, had previously designed **Excalibur**, immediately north. A less-sophisticated mock-up of a medieval castle, complete with drawbridge, crenellated towers, and a basement stuffed with sideshows for the kids, it's usually packed out with low-budget tour groups. Its brief reign as the world's largest hotel, from 1990 to 1993, ended when the five-thousand-room **MGM Grand** – another Simpson creation – opened across the street. Turnover here is so phenomenal that when crowds after the Holyfield–Tyson debacle in 1997 mistook popping champagne corks for gunfire, forcing the tables to close down for two hours, losses were estimated in millions of dollars. Its **Lion Habitat** is a walk-through zoo where lions lounge around another ruined temple (daily 11am–11pm, free; $20 to have your photo taken with a lion cub).

The northwest corner of the intersection of Las Vegas Boulevard and Tropicana Avenue – reputedly the busiest traffic junction in the US – is occupied by an exuberant re-creation of the Big Apple, **New York–New York**. Twelve skyscrapers, fronted by the Statue of Liberty, form the skyline of this miniature Manhattan built, like the original, in response to space limitations. Perhaps mercifully, the copycat skyline does not include those of the World Trade Center, so although the facade became an obvious site for memorials in the wake of September 11, 2001, it hasn't acquired any extra symbolic significance. Unusually, the interior is every bit as carefully realized, with a lovely rendition of Central Park at dusk. In one respect, it even surpasses New York; for $10 you can swoop around the whole thing at 65mph on the hair-raising Manhattan Express **rollercoaster**.

The central Strip

North of the *MGM Grand*, the $1.4-billion **Aladdin** opened in 2000 as the first mega-casino of the new millennium. Beset by funding difficulties, it was tipped into bankruptcy by the terrorist attacks of September 2001; the Middle-Eastern theme didn't exactly help. Nonetheless, the *Aladdin* remains open, and ironically the factors that held it back financially – that you can explore its gigantic **Desert Passage** shopping mall, go to concerts at its 7000-seat auditorium, and get to and from your hotel room without ever crossing the casino floor – mean that it's actually quite a nice place.

Next door, **Paris** was the 1999 handiwork of the same team that created *New York–New York*. With a half-size Eiffel Tower straddling the Arc de Triomphe and the Opera, it all feels a little compressed, but once again the attention to detail is a joy, and there's a fine assortment of top-notch French restaurants. Elevators soar through its roof and up to the summit of the Eiffel Tower, for stunning views (daily 10am–midnight; $9).

The Eiffel Tower was cheekily positioned to enjoy a perfect prospect of **Bellagio**, opposite, *Mirage*-owner Steve Wynn's 1998 attempt to build the best hotel in world history. *Bellagio's* main block, a stately curve of blue and cream pastels, stands aloof from the Strip behind an eight-acre artificial lake, in which hundreds of fountains erupt every half-hour in water-ballets, with booming music and colored lights. Inside, its proudest boasts are the **Via Bellagio**, a mall of glamorous designer boutiques, and the opulent **Conservatory** (admission free), where the flowerbeds beneath a Belle Epoque canopy of copper-framed glass are replanted every six weeks.

Across Flamingo Road from *Bellagio* – via the intersection where rapper Tupac Shakur was gunned down in 1996 – **Caesars Palace** still encapsulates Las Vegas at its best. Beyond a vast labyrinth of slots and green baize, peopled by strutting Roman centurions and Cleopatra-cropped waitresses, lies the extraordinary **Forum** mall, with its blue-domed ceiling endlessly cycling from dawn to dusk, and its ornate fountains where animatronic statues come to life at regular intervals.

Nighttime crowds jostle for space on the sidewalk outside the glittering **Mirage**, beyond *Caesars*, to watch a half-hearted volcano erupt every fifteen minutes, spewing water and fire into the lagoon below. Next door, a pirate galleon and a British frigate do noisy battle outside **Treasure Island** (every ninety minutes after dark; free). Around the back, at 3401 Industrial Rd, you can admire (if not step on) the King's very own blue suede shoes at **Elvis-A-Rama** (daily 10am–7pm; $15). As well as a stunning array of Elvis memorabilia, the museum puts on hourly impersonator shows, included in the admission price.

Across the Strip, the facade of another 1999 newcomer, the **Venetian**, includes facsimiles of six major Venice buildings, as well as the Rialto Bridge and the Bridge of Sighs. The main emphasis within is on the **Grand Canal Shoppes**, reached via a stairwell topped by vivid frescoes. The ludicrous **Grand Canal** itself, complete with gondolas and singing gondoliers ($12.50 a ride), is quintessential Las Vegas, and as such utterly irresistible – it's *upstairs*, for goodness' sake.

In 2001, the *Venetian* opened two distinct, ultra-modern **art museums**. The **Guggenheim Hermitage** (daily 9am–8.30pm; $15, under-13s $7) provides much-needed funds for St Petersburg's State Hermitage Museum in return for displaying its finest treasures on changing rotation. Exhibitions so far have concentrated on Impressionism and Cubism, with Monet, Picasso, and Van Gogh well represented. Further back on the ground floor, the much larger **Guggenheim Las Vegas** (daily 9am–11pm; $15, under-13s $7) is a more dramatic and versatile space, intended to display sculpture, architecture, and mixed-media presentations as well as painting. The *Venetian* also holds the first, ridiculously expensive, US outpost of **Madame Tussaud's** waxwork museum.

This calls itself the **Celebrity Encounter** (Mon–Thurs & Sun 11am–7pm, Fri & Sat 11am–10pm; $14, under-13s $10.75), because visitors can pose with, touch, caress, and mock effigies such as Siegfried and Roy, Liberace, Tom Jones, and Frank Sinatra.

The northern Strip
The family-oriented **Circus Circus**, another mile north, uses live circus acts to pull in the punters – a trapeze artist here, a fire-eater there – and also has an indoor theme park, the **Adventuredome** (Mon–Thurs 11am–6pm, Fri 11am–midnight, Sat & Sun 10am–midnight), where you pay separately for each rollercoaster or river-ride. If you really want to cool off, you'd do better to head on to the flumes and chutes of Vegas's one water park, **Wet'n'Wild**, 2601 S Las Vegas Blvd (summer daily 10am–8pm; $27).

Half a mile east of *Circus Circus* at 3000 Paradise Rd, the **Las Vegas Hilton** is home to the expensive **Star Trek Experience** (daily 11am–11pm; $25). If you're lucky enough to arrive when the lines are short, it's still worth lingering over the glossy display panels that recount such historical highlights as World War III in 2053 and the birth of Spock in 2230. The whole thing culminates when you're caught up in a dramatic plot to prevent Jean-Luc Picard ever being born and sent on a mildly vomitous motion-simulator ride through deep space.

Half a mile towards downtown from *Circus Circus* stands the 1149-foot-tall **Stratosphere**, whose outdoor deck and indoor viewing chamber near the summit offer amazing panoramas ($5). Two utterly demented thrill rides can take you even closer to heaven; the world's highest rollercoaster ($5) swirls around the outside, while the ludicrous Big Shot ($8) shunts you to the very top of an additional 160-foot spire, from which you free-fall back down again.

Downtown and the Liberace Museum
As the Strip has gone from strength to strength, **downtown** Las Vegas, the city's original core, has by comparison been neglected. Long known as "Glitter Gulch," it consists of a few compact blocks of lower-key casinos, though Fremont Street, its principal thoroughfare, has been roofed with an open-air mesh to create the **Fremont Street Experience**. This "Celestial Vault" is studded with over two million colored light bulbs, choreographed by computer in dazzling nightly displays (hourly, 8pm–midnight; free), but there's a long way to go before the district as a whole can compete with the Strip once again.

All Las Vegas's handful of museums are eminently missable, with one unarguable exception: the **Liberace Museum**, two miles east of the Strip at 1775 E Tropicana Ave (Mon–Sat 10am–5pm, Sun 1–5pm; $7; ⓦwww.liberace.org). Popularly remembered as a beaming buffoon who knocked out torpid toe-tappers, Liberace, who died in 1987, started out playing piano in the rough bars of Milwaukee during the 1940s. His story is recalled by a yellowing collection of cuttings and family photos, along with electric candelabra, bejeweled quail eggs with inlaid pianos, rhinestone-covered fur coats, glittering cars, and more.

Lake Mead and the Hoover Dam
LAKE MEAD, the vast reservoir created by the construction of the Hoover Dam in 1935, makes a bizarre spectacle thirty miles southeast of the city, its blue waters a vivid counterpoint to the surrounding desert. Even if you don't need details of how to sail, scuba dive, water ski, or fish from the marinas along the five-hundred-mile shoreline, call in at the Alan Bible visitor center (daily 8.30am–4.30pm; ⓣ702/293-8990, ⓦwww.nps.gove/lame), four miles northeast of Boulder City on US-93, to enjoy a sweeping prospect of the whole thing.

Eight miles further southeast, beyond the rocky ridges of the Black Mountains, US-93 reaches the **HOOVER DAM** itself. Designed to block the Colorado River and provide low-cost electricity for the cities of the Southwest, it's among the tallest dams ever built (760ft high), and used enough concrete to build a two-lane highway from the West Coast to New York. Thanks to September 11, 2001, the dam no longer offers extensive behind-the-scenes tours, but you can still ride an elevator to the turbine room at the bottom. Regular half-hour guided tours leave from the **Hoover Dam Visitor Center** on the Nevada side of the river (daily 8.30am–5.45pm; $10, $5 parking; ℡702/293-1824).

Eating

As recently as the early 1990s, Las Vegas's **restaurant** scene was governed by the notion that visitors were not prepared to pay for gourmet food. All the casinos laid on pile-'em-high buffets and 24-hour coffee shops, but the only quality restaurants were upscale Italian places far from the Strip. Now the situation has reversed, as the major casinos lure culinary superstars to open Vegas outlets, and many tourists come specifically to eat at some of the best restaurants in the United States, without having to reserve a table months in advance or pay sky-high prices. Which is not to say that fine dining comes cheap, just that most of the big-name restaurants are less expensive, and less snooty, than back home.

The restaurant choice on the Strip in particular is overwhelming, and you'll almost certainly find a good one to suit your tastes and budget in your own hotel. For that reason, the places reviewed here tend towards the higher end of the spectrum; they're the ones it's worth making a special effort to reach.

Almost every casino still features an all-you-can-eat **buffet**, open to guests and non-guests alike. Even at the worst, you're bound to find something you can keep down, while at its best, the traditional buffet experience is like being granted unrestricted access to the food court in an upmarket mall; you'll get good fast food, but not great cooking. The best such buffets tend to be neither on the Strip nor downtown, but in casinos like the *Rio* and the *Stations* chain that depend on locals as well as tourists. By contrast, those at the largest Strip casinos like *Excalibur* and the *MGM Grand* are often poor. A new development, however, has been for high-end casinos like *Bellagio* and *Paris* to raise buffet prices to a level that makes it possible to provide true gourmet feasts.

Restaurants

America *New York–New York*, 3790 Las Vegas Blvd S ℡702/740-6451. Cavernous diner, featuring a vast 3-D "map" of the United States. Each menu item supposedly comes from some specific part of the country, with entrees including Texan barbecue ribs for $13 and New York pizzas for $7–9. At any hour of day or night, there really is something for everyone. Daily 24 hours.

Border Grill *Mandalay Bay*, 3950 Las Vegas Blvd S ℡702/632-7403. At the Strip's finest Mexican restaurant, lunch offerings include sandwiches, like a portabello torta ($11), and a chicken Caesar salad ($12); dinner is more expensive, with a roasted half-chicken mole at $17.50 and a 16oz gaucho steak at $28. In summer, tables spread across a large patio. Mon–Thurs & Sun 11.30am–10pm, Fri & Sat 11.30am–11pm.

Commander's Palace *Desert Passage, Aladdin*, 3663 Las Vegas Blvd S ℡702/892-8272. New Orleans' renowned haute Creole restaurant – repeatedly voted the best restaurant in the US – is formal but friendly, though the prices can come as a shock. Classic appetizers like shrimp remoulade ($9.50) and oysters Rockefeller ($8.50); entrees such as pecan-crusted Gulf fish ($27.50) or veal chop Tchoupitoulas ($39); and bananas Foster for dessert ($7). Daily 11.30am–2pm & 6–11pm.

Fat Burger 3765 Las Vegas Blvd S ℡702/736-4733. There's no more to this gleaming, all-American burger joint than meets the eye; just walk or drive in from the Strip at any time and get a perfect burger, fries, and a shake. Daily 24 hours.

Il Fornaio *New York–New York*, 3790 Las Vegas Blvd S ℡702/650-6500. Rural-Italian restaurant that's the nicest place to enjoy *New York–New York*. Pizzas for $12, or full meals like mixed antipasto ($9.50) followed by seafood linguini

($19) or rotisserie chicken ($16). The delicious olive breads, pastries, and coffees are also sold in a separate deli nearby. Mon–Thurs & Sun 7am–10pm, Fri & Sat 7am–midnight.

Mon Ami Gabi *Paris*, 3655 Las Vegas Blvd S ☎702/944-4224. The only casino-restaurant to offer open-air seating right on the Strip, with the feel of a French pavement bistro. At lunch, try the glorious onion soup ($6.50); mussels as an appetiser ($11) or entrée ($20); or thin-cut steak *frites* ($19–21). Dinner features more expensive steak cuts and fish entrees. Mon–Thurs & Sun 11.30am–3.30pm & 5–11pm, Fri & Sat 11.30am–3.30pm & 5pm–midnight.

Mr Lucky's 24/7 *Hard Rock Hotel*, 4455 Paradise Rd ☎702/693-5000. Very stylish 24-hour coffee shop, with open kitchen and faux-fur booths, where the food is well above average too. As well as the usual breakfast items, it serves burgers, sandwiches, pizzas, and pasta dishes for $6–10, a 12-oz steak for $15, and milkshakes or microbrews for $4. Daily 24 hours.

Olives *Bellagio*, 3600 Las Vegas Blvd S ☎702/693-8181. *Bellagio*'s best-value gourmet restaurant, facing the Eiffel Tower across the lake, where the largely Mediterranean menu is uniformly fresh and quaint. It's a great lunch spot, with $10–13 appetizers like crispy fried oysters on jumbo ham hocks; $10 pizzas (or "individual ovenbaked flatbreads"); and specials such as barbecued yellow-fin tuna ($18.50). Dinner entrees are pricier, at $28–40. Daily 11am–2.30pm & 5–11.30pm.

Wolfgang Puck Café *MGM Grand*, 3799 Las Vegas Blvd S ☎702/895-9653. Brightly tiled designer-diner-cum-café, where the large breakfast menu includes well-priced benedicts and omelets, and three eggs for $6. Later on, $10 or so buys one of Puck's signature postmodern pizzas, pad thai noodles or meatloaf go for $13–17, and coriander-crusted ahi costs $20. No reservations. Daily 11am–11pm.

Zefferino Grand Canal Shoppes, *The Venetian*, 3355 Las Vegas Blvd S ☎702/414-3500. Very romantic, yet utterly playful high-class Italian restaurant, with ornate balconies overlooking the Grand Canal. Dinner entrees can be pricey, with a basic ravioli at $25 and fish soup at $45, but the

$20 three-course set lunch, served daily except Sundays, is exceptional value. Mon–Sat 11.30am–1am, Sun 10am–2.30pm & 5–11pm.

Buffets

The Buffet *Bellagio*, 3600 Las Vegas Blvd S ☎702/791-7111. Far and away Las Vegas's best buffet; the sheer range is extraordinary. For breakfast ($12), as well as bagels, pastries, and eggs, there's salmon smoked or baked, fruit fresh or in salads, and omelets cooked to order. Lunch offerings ($15) can include sushi, cold cuts, dim sum, and seared quail, plus fresh-baked focaccia and tasty fruit tarts. At dinner, costing $25 Mon–Thurs & Sun and $32 including champagne Fri & Sat, the stakes are raised again with lobster claws, fresh oysters, and venison.

Feast Around The World *Sunset Station*, 1301 W Sunset Rd ☎702/547-7777. All the *Stations* of local casinos offer similarly appealing buffets at unbeatable prices, with a wide range of international cuisines; breakfast is $5, lunch $7, and dinner $9. Thursday is Hawaiian night, Friday and Saturday are steak and wine, and T-bone, respectively.

Garden Court Buffet *Main Street Station*, 200 N Main St ☎702/387-1896. Everything is clean and spruce, if not wildly exciting, at downtown's best-value buffet. Dishes range from fried chicken and corn, to tortillas and fajitas, or pork chow mein and oyster tofu. Breakfast varies $5–7, lunch $7–9, and dinner $10–12.

Le Village Buffet *Paris*, 3655 Las Vegas Blvd S ☎702/967-7000. *Paris*'s buffet showcases only delicious French dishes. The seafood is superb, whether it's the scallops, shrimp, and crab in Sunday's brunch or the Dover sole and rich *bouillabaisse* midweek; roast chicken comes fricasseed, as *coq au vin*, or with mustard; vegetables are super-fresh; and there's a full cheese board. Breakfast is $11, lunch $15, and dinner $22.

Todai Seafood Buffet Desert Passage, *Aladdin*, 3663 Las Vegas Blvd S ☎702/892-0021. Magnificent all-you-can-eat Japanese spreads, with unlimited sushi and sashimi plus hot entrees, noodles, and barbecued and teriyaki meats. Lunch Mon–Fri $15, Sat & Sun $17; dinner Mon–Thurs & Sun $26, Fri & Sat $28.

Bars and clubs

As the perfect fuel to turn a dithering gawker into a diehard gambler, alcohol is very easy to come by in Las Vegas. If you want a drink in a casino, just wait for a tray-toting waitress to come and find you. All the casinos do have actual **bars** as well, and the old-fashioned Las Vegas **lounge** has also returned in force. Las Vegas has also come of age as a **clubbing** capital; the success of nightclubs at hipper casinos like the *Hard Rock* and *Mandalay Bay* has prompted their rivals to follow suit, often with spectacular results. If you fancy sampling a few, **Club-A-Go-Go** run escorted tours of three top-name clubs, including party bus and instant VIP admission (Wed, Thurs & Fri; $40; ☎1-800/258-2218 or ⊕www.clubagogo.com).

As for **live music**, check newspapers like the free *City Life* (⊕www.lvcitylife .com) and the *Las Vegas Review Journal* (⊕www.lvrj.com) to see who's appearing when you're in town, or call the casinos directly.

The Beach 365 Convention Center Drive ☎702/731-1925, ⊕www.beachlv.com. Round-the-clock multiroom dance club that's a permanent Spring Break, attracting a very young crowd to the massive dancefloor downstairs and sports bar upstairs. Daily 24 hrs. Cover (men only) usually $10.

Club Utopia 3765 Las Vegas Blvd S ☎702/392-7979, ⊕www.clubutopia.net. Pioneering Strip dance club, where the three dance rooms delight young locals with an emphasis on trance and techno. Wed–Sat 10pm–10am. $10.

Gipsy 4605 Paradise Rd ☎702/731-1919. High-profile gay dance club, where apart from the free cruise nights on Wednesdays, there's normally live entertainment to justify the $5 cover charge, with go-go boys Friday and Saturday, and beer busts most nights. The elaborate lost-city decor attracts young ingenues and local celebs. Daily except Mon 10pm–5am.

House of Blues *Mandalay Bay*, 3950 Las Vegas Blvd S ☎702/632-7600. The Strip's premier live-music venue, the voodoo-tinged, folk-art-decorated *House of Blues* has a definite but not exclusive emphasis toward blues, R&B, and the like. Prices range from $25 up to $100.

Studio 54 *MGM Grand*, 3799 Las Vegas Blvd S ☎702/891-7254. Three-story, four-dancefloor re-creation of New York's legendary *Studio 54*. The music varies little from night to night, rarely straying from house and other forms of electronica. Tues–Sat 10pm–5am. Men Tues–Thurs $10, Fri & Sat $20.

Triple Seven Brewpub *Main Street Station*, 200 N Main St ☎702/386-4442. Roomy, high-ceilinged downtown brewpub with poor service but great beers and tasty food. Daily 11am–7am.

Venus Lounge *The Venetian*, 3265 Las Vegas Blvd S ☎702/414-4870. Gloriously kitsch retro-lounge, right by the Strip, with plush couches, live music at weekends, and go-go dancers in giant martini glasses, plus a lovingly re-created tiki bar, *Taboo Cove*. Wed–Sun 5pm–5am. Cover weekends only, up to $20.

Entertainment

There was a time when Las Vegas represented the pinnacle of any show-business career. In the early 1960s, when Frank Sinatra's Rat Pack were shooting the original *Ocean's 11* during the day then singing the night away at the *Sands*, the city could claim to be the capital of the international entertainment industry. It was even hip. Now, however, although the money is still there, the world has moved on. As the great names of the past fade from view, the tendency instead is to rely on lavish stunts and special effects. Incidentally, this book went to press before the opening of the new four-thousand-seater **Colosseum** at *Caesars Palace*, where Celine Dion is due to perform five shows per week for three years, with ticket prices ranging from $90 up to $150.

Blue Man Group *Luxor*, 3900 Las Vegas Blvd S ☎702/262-4400. Enter a strange and unfamiliar world, in which three bald, blue performance artists sell out a 1250-seat theater inside a giant pyramid every night of the week. Don't expect stars, or a plot, or even words; instead you get synchronized eating of breakfast cereal and live endoscopies on audience members, plus deafening, exhilarating drumming and stunning special effects. Mon, Wed–Fri & Sun 7pm & 10pm; Tues 7pm; Sat 4pm, 7pm & 10pm. $79–90.

Lance Burton *The Monte Carlo*, 3770 Las Vegas Blvd S ☎702/730-7160. Las Vegas's best family show. Master magician Lance Burton kicks off with impressive stunts involving playing cards, handkerchiefs, and doves, then moves on to large-scale illusions like the disappearance of an airplane and a narrow escape from hanging. Tues–Sat 7pm & 10pm. $55 & $60.

Legends in Concert *The Imperial Palace*, 3535 Las Vegas Blvd S ☎702/794-3261. Celebrity-tribute show, with a changing roster that ranges from Tina Turner to Tim McGraw. The slick Four Tops are unbeatable, and a tongue-in-cheek Elvis clowning through *Viva Las Vegas* makes a fitting finale. Daily except Sun 7.30pm & 10.30pm. $35, including two drinks; ages 12 and under $19.50.

Mystère *Treasure Island*, 3300 Las Vegas Blvd S

☎1-800/392-1999. The Cirque du Soleil's original Las Vegas show is such a visual feast that it barely matters whether you see its dreamscape symbolism as profound or meaningless. Above all, it's a showcase of fabulous circus skills, with tumblers, acrobats, trapeze artists, pole climbers, clowns, and strong men, but no animals apart from fantastic costumed apparitions. Wed–Sun 7.30pm & 10.30pm. $88, ages 12 and under $35.

O *Bellagio*, 3600 Las Vegas Blvd S ☎702/693-7722. Las Vegas's most expensive show; a remarkable testament to what's possible when the budget is barely an issue. Any part of the stage at any time may be submerged to any depth. One moment a performer walks across a particular spot, the next someone dives headfirst into it. From the synchronized swimmers onwards, the Cirque du Soleil display their magnificent skills to maximum advantage. Highlights include a colossal trapeze frame, draped like a pirate ship, and flying footmen in swirls of velvet drapery. Mon, Tues & Fri–Sun 7.30 & 10.30pm. $93.50–121.

Siegfried and Roy *The Mirage*, 3400 Las Vegas Blvd S ☎702/792-7777. Austrian magicians Siegfried and Roy, the highest-paid entertainers in Vegas history, put on an impressive display, causing elephants and even dragons to vanish, and teleporting themselves across the arena. However, while you may not know how it's done, they're basically technicians operating industrial machinery; only when their beloved white lions and tigers show up do they finally perk up enough to take a cloying, self-congratulatory bow. Mon, Tues & Sun 7.30pm, Fri & Sat 7.30pm & 11pm. $105.50, including drinks.

The Grand Canyon

The **GRAND CANYON OF THE COLORADO** in Arizona, three hundred long and featureless driving miles from Las Vegas, is one of those sights that you really have to see once in your life. Once you've ventured east of the California state line, it would be a real shame to exclude it from your itinerary.

Although almost five million people visit **Grand Canyon National Park** every year, the canyon itself remains beyond the grasp of the human imagination. No photograph, no set of statistics, can prepare you for such vastness. At more than one mile deep, it's an inconceivable abyss; at from four to eighteen miles wide, it's an endless expanse of bewildering shapes and colors, glaring desert brightness and impenetrable shadow, stark promontories, and soaring never-to-be-climbed sandstone pinnacles.

Somehow it's so impassive, so remote – you could never call it a disappointment, but at the same time many visitors are left feeling peculiarly flat; in a sense, none of the available activities can quite live up to that first stunning sight of the chasm. The **overlooks** along the rim all offer views that shift and change unceasingly from dawn to dusk; you can **hike** down into the depths on foot or by mule, hover above in a **helicopter**, or **raft** through the whitewater rapids of the river itself; you can spend a night at **Phantom Ranch** on the Canyon floor, or swim in the waterfalls of the idyllic **Havasupai Reservation**; and yet that distance always remains – the Grand Canyon stands apart.

The vast majority of visitors come to the **South Rim**, described in full on the next few pages – it's the most accessible part of the Canyon, there are far more facilities (mainly at **Grand Canyon Village**), and it's open year-round. There's another lodge and campground at the **North Rim**, which by virtue of its isolation can be a whole lot more evocative (for accommodation reservations, see p.315), but at one thousand feet higher this is usually closed by snow from mid-October until May. An even less eventful drive from Las Vegas will get you there, via St George in southern Utah. Few people visit both rims; to get from one to the other demands either a two-day hike down one side of the Canyon and up the other, or a 215-mile drive by road. Until the 1920s, the average visitor would stay for two or three weeks; these days, it's more like two or

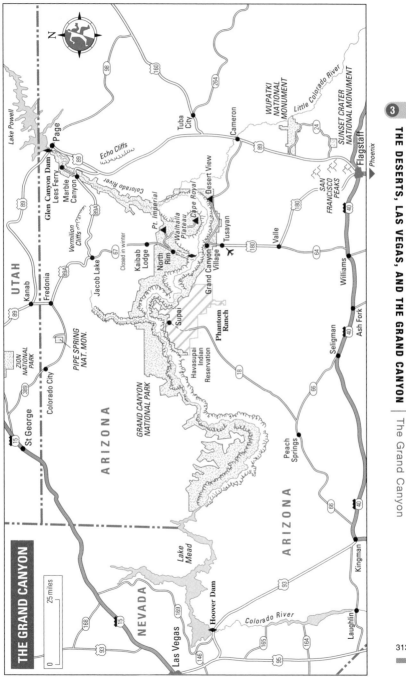

THE GRAND CANYON

0   25 miles

N

three hours – of which forty minutes are spent actually looking at the Canyon.

Finally, there's a definite risk that on the day you come the Grand Canyon will be invisible beneath a layer of fog; many people blame the 250 tons of sulphurous emissions pumped out every day by the Navajo Generating Station, seventy miles upriver at Page. Admission to the park, valid for seven days on either rim, costs $20 per vehicle, or $10 per pedestrian or cyclist.

Canyon practicalities

Most visitors enter from the south and base themselves – even if they're there just to do a quick hit of a few scenic overlooks – around the South Rim; that's where most trails begin from, as well as where the relatively few lodges and eating establishments are located.

Arrival

The most usual **approach** to the South Rim of the Grand Canyon is by road, turning north off I-40 at **Williams** to drive the last 56 miles on Hwy-64, or detouring further east via the larger town of **Flagstaff** and then following Hwy-180 past the San Francisco Mountains. The two roads join twenty miles before the Canyon, at Valle. Most of this stretch is through thick ponderosa pine forests, so the ride up from Williams on the restored **steam trains** of the Grand Canyon Railway is not especially scenic, even if the crew keep you entertained with Western-style antics (departs Williams daily 10am; $55 round-trip, with higher fares for more luxurious carriages; ☎928/773-1976 or 1-800/843-8724, ⓦ www.thetrain.com). Passengers who arrive on Flagstaff's two daily **Amtrak** trains can reach Grand Canyon Village on the Open Road Tours and Transportation buses ($20; ☎928/226-8060 or 1-800/766-7117, ⓦ www.openroadtours.com); one leaves Flagstaff at 8.30am, calls at Williams at 9 am, and arrives at the Canyon's Maswik Transportation Center at 10.15am, the other leaves Flagstaff at 3pm and Williams at 3.30pm, reaching the Canyon at 4.45pm. Return services leave Maswik at 11.45am and 5.45pm, arriving at Williams at 1pm and 7pm respectively, and Flagstaff at 1.30pm and 7.30pm.

The small airport at Tusayan – six miles from the South Rim, and used primarily by "flight-seeing" tour companies (see p.318) – also welcomes scheduled services, especially from Las Vegas, with operators such as Scenic Airlines (☎702/638-3300 or 1-800/634-6801, ⓦ www.scenic.com) and Air Vegas (☎928/638-9351, 702/736-3599 or 1-800/255-7474, ⓦ www.airvegas.com).

Transport

You arrive at a time when, to put it charitably, the park is in a state of flux. So far, a proposed new transportation scheme, under which private vehicles would be banned from the Canyon area, with visitors ferried around instead on a **light-rail** network, has been only minimally implemented, and it's looking as if it never will be. All that's happened so far is the construction of the large new open-air **Canyon View Information Plaza**, located well short of the Grand Canyon Village center near Mather Point (daily: May to mid-Oct 8am–6pm; mid-Oct to April 8am–5pm; ⓦ www.nps.gov/grca). It looks great, but as, ludicrously, there's no parking available, it's done nothing to relieve traffic congestion.

For the foreseeable future, **Grand Canyon Village** remains accessible to private vehicles, as is the road **east** from the village to **Desert View**. Both the road **west** from the village to **Hermit's Rest**, however, and the short access road to **Yaki Point** – the first overlook east of Mather Point, and the trailhead for the popular **South Kaibab Trail** – are only open to private vehicles during the months of December, January, and February. The park runs three free **shuttle bus** routes: the ponderous **Village Route**, which loops laboriously between Grand Canyon Village and the information plaza; the **Kaibab Trail Route** between the plaza and Yaki Point; and the eight-mile **Hermit's Rest Route**, which heads west to eight Canyon overlooks.

Accommodation

All the **lodges** in the village charge similar prices, with no budget accommodation alternative. To see the Canyon, it makes little difference where in the village you stay; very few rooms in the "rim-edge" properties offer much of a view, though the older properties, the *El Tovar Hotel* (❻) and the *Bright Angel* (❹), are much more attractive in their own right than the motel-like *Thunderbird* and *Kachina* lodges (both ❻). Both *Maswik Lodge* (cabins and rooms ❹) and *Yavapai Lodge* (❻) are ten minutes' walk from the rim.

Camping facilities (and a laundry) are available at the year-round **Mather campground and RV park**, south of the main road through Grand Canyon Village. Sites for up to two vehicles and six people cost $15 per night between April and November, when reservations, which are strongly recommended, can be made up to five months in advance through Biospherics (℡1-800/365-2267 or 301/722-1257 from outside the US, ⊛reservations.nps.gov). No reservations are accepted between December and March, when sites are first-come-first-served, and the fee drops to $10 per night. The adjacent **Trailer Village** consists exclusively of RV sites with hook-ups, costing $24 per site per night for two people, plus $2 extra for each additional adult (reservations ℡303/297-2757, ⊛www.grandcanyonlodges.com). The summer-only *Desert View* campground, 26 miles east, is first-come-first-served, costs $10, and has no hook-ups. It's also possible to camp inside the Canyon itself, if you first obtain a permit from the Backcountry Reservations Office near *Maswik Lodge* (daily 8am–noon & 1–5pm; ℡928/638-7875; permits $10 + $5 per person per night).

If all the park accommodation is full, the nearest alternative is the underwhelming service village of **Tusayan**, just over a mile south of the park entrance. *Seven Mile Lodge* (℡928/638-2291; ❸) offers the least expensive rooms; the new *Grand Hotel* (℡928/638-3333; ⊛www.gcanyon.com; ❺) is more stylish. The most popular of the commercial campgrounds outside the park – with families, at least – is *Flintstone's Bedrock City* (mid-March to Oct; ℡928/635-2600; $12–16), 22 miles south at the junction of Hwy-64 and Hwy-180, which has its own prehistoric theme park.

All in-park **accommodation reservations** – for the lodges on both the South and the North rims, as well as for Phantom Ranch and RV camping – are handled by Xanterra Parks & Resorts, PO Box 699, Grand Canyon, AZ 86023 (same-day ℡928/638-2631, advance ℡303/297-2757 or 1-888/297-2757, ⊛www.grand-canyonlodges.com). The best rooms are often booked as much as a year in advance, and your chances of turning up without a reservation and finding a place in summer are minimal.

THE DESERTS, LAS VEGAS, AND THE GRAND CANYON | The Grand Canyon

Eating

Thanks to the Canyon's remoteness and lack of water, **food** prices tend to be well above average; if you're on a tight budget, bring your own. However, *Yavapai* and *Maswik* lodges have reasonable basic cafeterias, open until 10pm. *Bright Angel Lodge* has its own restaurant, as well as the *Arizona Steakhouse*, both also open until 10pm, and both costing $15–30. At *El Tovar* (reservations on ☏928/638-2631 ext 6432), where the dining room looks right out over the Canyon, the sumptuous menu is enormously expensive. Breakfast is the most affordable meal; lunch and dinner can easily cost upwards of $40. In Tusayan, *We Cook Pizza & Pasta* (☏928/638-2278) is good but pricey.

Grand Canyon Village

GRAND CANYON VILLAGE is not a very stimulating place to spend any time. However, in the absence of significantly cheaper accommodation within fifty miles (for example, in Tusayan at the park entrance), there's little option but to stay here. The centerpiece is the magnificent terrace in front of **Bright Angel Lodge** (usually the liveliest spot in town) and the black-beamed 1905 **El Tovar Hotel**, which gives many visitors their only look at the Canyon – though the Colorado itself is too deep in the Inner Gorge to be seen from here. Further back are more lodges and gift shops, and employee housing, with the post office, the general store, and the campground about a mile east through the woods.

Geology and history of the Canyon

Layer upon layer of different rocks, readily distinguished by color and each with its own fossil record, recede down into the Grand Canyon and back through time, until the strata at the riverbed, which are among the oldest exposed rocks on earth. And yet the Canyon's **formation** remains a mystery. Satellite photos show that the Colorado actually runs through the heart of an enormous hill (what the Indians called the Kaibab, "the mountain with no peak"); experts cannot agree on how this could happen. Studies show that the Canyon still deepens, at the slow rate of 50ft per million years. Its fantastic sandstone and limestone formations were not literally carved by the river, however; they're the result of erosion by wind and extreme cycles of heat and cold. These features were named – **Brahma Temple**, **Vishnu Temple**, and so on – by Clarence Dutton, a student of comparative religion who wrote the first Geological Survey report on the Canyon in 1881.

It may look forbidding, but the Grand Canyon is not a dead place. All sorts of desert **wildlife** survive here – sheep and rabbits, eagles and vultures, mountain lions and, of course, spiders, scorpions, and snakes. The **human** presence has never been on any great scale, but signs have been found of habitation as early as 2000 BC, and the **Ancestral Puebloans** were certainly here later on. A party of **Spaniards** passed through in 1540 – less than twenty years after Cortés conquered the Aztecs – searching for cities of gold, and one Father Garcés spent some time with the Havasupai in 1776. It was **John Wesley Powell**'s expeditions along the fearsome and uncharted waters of the Colorado in 1869 and 1871–72 that truly brought the Canyon to public attention. A few abortive attempts were made to mine different areas, but facilities for tourism were swiftly realized to be a far more lucrative investment. With the exception of the Indian reservations, the Grand Canyon is now run exclusively for the benefit of visitors; although even as recently as 1963 there were proposals to dam the Colorado and flood 150 miles of the Canyon, and the Glen Canyon dam has seriously affected the ecology downstream.

Along the South Rim

It's possible to **walk** along the South Rim for several miles in either direction from the village, the first few of them on railed, concrete pathways. The most obvious short excursions are to see the sun rise and set. At or near the village, the giant wall that reaches out in the west overshadows much of the evening view. If, however, you walk right out to **Hopi Point** at its end, looking down as you go onto the Bright Angel Trail as it winds across the Tonto Plateau, you may well see a magical sunset, with the Colorado – 350ft wide at this point – visible way below.

The best place within walking distance to watch the dawn is **Mather Point**, close to the visitor center. Nearby, if you can tear your eyes away from its panoramic bay windows, the **Yavapai Observation Station** (daily: hours vary from 8am–8pm in summer down to 8am–5pm in winter; free) has illuminating displays on how the Canyon may have been formed.

Further dramatic views are available along the **East Rim Drive** – although unless you take an excursion you'll need your own vehicle to see them. **Desert View**, 23 miles out from the village, is at 7500ft the highest point on the South Rim. Visible to the east are the vast flatlands of the Navajo Nation; to the northeast, Vermillion and Echo Cliffs, and the gray bulk of Navajo Mountain ninety miles away; to the west, the gigantic peaks of the Vishnu and Buddha temples. Through the plains comes the narrow gorge of the Little Colorado; somewhere in the depths, before it meets the Colorado itself, is the *sipapu*, the hole through which the Hopi believe that men first entered this, the Third World. The odd-looking construction on the very lip of the Canyon is **Desert View Watchtower**, designed by Mary Colter in 1932 in a conglomeration of Native American styles (though a steel frame props it all up) and decorated with Hopi pictographs. It contains a gift shop, as does the general store a few yards away. Groups of tarantulas are often seen in the evenings at Desert View, scuttling back into the warmth of the Canyon for the night.

Into the Canyon

Hiking any of the trails that descend into the Grand Canyon offers something more than just another view of the same thing. Instead you pass through a sequence of utterly different landscapes, each with its own distinct climate, wildlife, and topography. However, while the Canyon can offer a wonderful wilderness experience, it's essential to remember that it can be a hostile and very unforgiving environment, gruelling even for expert hikers.

The South Rim is 7000 feet above sea level, an altitude that for most people is fatiguing in itself. Furthermore, all hikes start with a long, steep descent – which can come as a shock to the knees – and unless you camp overnight you'll have to climb all the way back up again when you're hotter and wearier. If you're day-hiking, the golden rule is to keep track of how much time you spend hiking down and allow twice that much to get back up again. Average summer temperatures inside the Canyon exceed 100°F; to hike for eight hours in that sort of heat, you have to drink an incredible thirty pints of water. Always carry at least a quart per person, and much more if there are no water sources along your chosen trail. You must have food as well, as drinking large quantities without also eating can cause water intoxication.

There's only space here to detail the most popular trail, the **Bright Angel**. Many of the others, such as the **Hermit**, date from the days prior to 1928, when the obstreperous Ralph Cameron controlled access to the Bright Angel and many other rim-edge sites by means of spurious mining claims and the

Grand Canyon tours

As well as managing the park lodges, Xanterra (see p.315) operates guided **bus tours** along the South Rim, including the four-hour **Desert View Tour** to the east, timed to coincide with sunset at Desert View ($27.50); the two-hour **Hermit's Rest Tour** to the west ($15.50); and shorter **Sunrise** and **Sunset** tours ($12). It's also responsible for the famous **mule rides** down the Bright Angel Trail from Grand Canyon Village, for which reservations are accepted up to a year in advance. Riders must be at least four feet seven inches tall (1.38 meters), speak fluent English, and weigh not more than 200 pounds (91kg). All rides set off early in the morning, with one-day, seven-hour round-trips as far as Plateau Point costing $120.76. Overnight trips to **Phantom Ranch**, where you spend the rest of the day beside the river and sleep in two-person cabins, cost $338.07 for one person and $604.87 for two. **Two-night** rides, available between mid-November and March only, are $461.80 and $781.06 respectively. Reservations for both buses and mules are handled by the "transportation desk" in each lodge, or call ☎928/638-2631.

Airplane tours cost from around $75 for 30min ($45 child) up to as long as you like for as much as you've got. Operators include Air Grand Canyon (☎928/638-2686 or 1-800/247-4726, ⌨www.airgrandcanyon.com) and Grand Canyon Airlines (☎928/638-2359 or 1-866/235-9422, ⌨www.grandcanyonairlines.com). **Helicopter tours**, from $100 for 30min, are offered by AirStar Helicopters (☎928/638-2622 or 1-800/962-3869, ⌨www.airstar.com) and Papillon Helicopters (☎928/638-2419 or 1-800/528-2418, ⌨www.papillon.com), who also operate $442 day-trips to the Havasupai Reservation. All are based in Tusayan, at or near the airport.

Fred Harvey company had to find other ways to get its customers down to the Colorado. These other trails tend to be overgrown now, or partially blocked by landslides; check before setting out.

Bright Angel Trail

The **BRIGHT ANGEL TRAIL**, followed on foot or mule by thousands of visitors each year, starts from the wooden shack in the village that was once a photographic studio. It takes 9.6 miles to switchback down to **Phantom Ranch** beside the river, but park rangers have a simple message for all would-be hikers: don't try to hike down and back in a single day. It might not look far on the map, but it's harder than running a marathon. The longest feasible day-hike is to go instead as far as **Plateau Point** on the edge of the arid Tonto Plateau, an overlook above the Inner Gorge, from which it is not possible to descend any further – a twelve-mile round-trip that will probably take you at least eight hours. In summer, water can be obtained along the way.

The first section of the trail was laid out by miners a century ago, along an old Havasupai route, and has two short tunnels in its first mile. After another mile, the **wildlife** starts to increase (deer, rodents, and the ubiquitous ravens), and there are a few **pictographs** which have been all but obscured by graffiti.

At the lush **Indian Gardens** almost five miles down, where you'll find a ranger station and campground with water, the trails split, to Plateau Point or down to the river via the Devil's Corkscrew. The latter route leads through sand dunes scattered with cacti and down beside **Garden** Creek to the Colorado, which you then follow for more than a mile to get to Phantom Ranch.

Phantom Ranch

It's a real thrill to spend a night at the very bottom of the Canyon, at the 1922 **PHANTOM RANCH**. The cabins are reserved exclusively for mule riders (see box above), while beds in the four ten-bunk **dorms** ($28) are usually reserved way in advance, through Xanterra (see p.315), but it's worth checking for cancellations at the *Bright Angel Lodge* transportation desk as soon as you reach the South Rim. Do not hike down without a reservation, and even if you do have one, reconfirm it the day before you set off. All supplies reach Phantom Ranch the same way you do (an all-day hike on foot or mule), so **meals** are expensive, a minimum of $17 for breakfast and $20 for dinner.

The Havasupai Reservation

The **HAVASUPAI RESERVATION** really is another world. A 1930s anthropologist called it "the only spot in the United States where native culture has remained in anything like its pristine condition"; things have changed a little since then, but the sheer magic of its turquoise waterfalls and canyon scenery make this a very special place. Traditionally, the Havasupai would spend summer on the Canyon's floor and winter on the plateau above. However, when the reservation was created in 1882, they were only granted land at the bottom of the Canyon, and not until 1975 did the concession of another 251,000 acres up above make it possible for them to resume their ancient lifestyle.

Havasu Canyon is a side canyon of the Grand Canyon, about 35 miles west of Grand Canyon Village as the raven flies, but almost two hundred miles by road. Turn off the interstate at Seligman or Kingman, onto AZ-66, which curves north between the two, stock up with food, water, and gas, and then turn on to Arrowhead Hwy-18. Plans to build a road – or even a tramway – down into Havasu Canyon have always been rejected, in part because much of the income of the five or six hundred Havasupai comes from guiding visitors on foot, mule, or horseback. Instead, the road ends at Hualapai Hilltop, from where an eight-mile trail zigzags down a bluff and leads through the stunning waterless Hualapai Canyon to the village of **SUPAI**. Riding down costs $70 one-way, $120 for a round-trip, while hiking is free; all visitors, however, pay a $20 entry fee on arrival at Supai.

Beyond Supai the trail becomes more difficult, but leads to a succession of spectacular waterfalls, including Havasu Falls, one of the best for swimming, and Mooney Falls, named after an unfortunate prospector who dangled here for three days in the 1890s, at the end of a snagged rope, before falling to his death.

A **campground** (☎928/448-2141), charging $10 per night, stretches between Havasu and Mooney Falls, and Supai itself holds the motel-like *Havasupai Lodge* (☎928/448-2111; ❹), along with a café, a general store, and the only post office in the US still to receive its mail by pack train. Only visitors who have made definite advance arrangements at either the campground or lodge should set off from the trailhead; note also that from time to time Supai is hit by freak floods, which can result in the temporary closure of both.

Flagstaff

Northern Arizona's most attractive and characterful town, **FLAGSTAFF**, occupies a superbly dramatic location beneath the San Francisco Peaks, halfway between New Mexico and California. Straddling the I-40 and I-17 interstates, it's a major waystation for tourists en route to the Grand Canyon, just eighty miles northwest, but it's also a worthwhile destination in its own right.

Downtown, where barely a building rises more than three stories, oozes Wild West charm. Its main thoroughfare, Santa Fe Avenue, used to be **Route 66**, while before that it was the pioneer trail west. A stroll around its central few blocks is gloriously evocative of the past, though these days the diners and saloons are interspersed with outfitter stores and coffee bars, and the local cowboys and Indians share the sidewalks with students from Northern Arizona University.

The exceptional **Museum of Northern Arizona** (daily 9am–5pm; $5; ⓦwww.musnaz.org), three miles northwest on Hwy-180 (and not on a local bus route), provides a good introduction to Arizona's Native American cultures, past and present, as well as background on the formation of the Grand Canyon.

Practicalities

Two Amtrak trains still pull in each day – the 5.15am to Albuquerque and the 9.26pm to Los Angeles – at the wooden stationhouse right in the heart of town, adjoining the helpful visitor center at 101 W Santa Fe Ave (Mon–Sat 7am–6pm, Sun 7am–5pm; ☎928/774-9541 or 1-800/842-7293, ⓦwww .flagstaffarizona.org). Open Road Tours and Transportation run twice-daily **bus services** via Williams to the Grand Canyon (daily 8.30am & 3pm; $20; ☎928/226-8060 or 1-800/766-7117; ⓦwww.openroadtours.com), while Greyhound, 399 S Malpais Lane (☎928/774-4573 or 1-800/231-2222), connects with Las Vegas, LA, San Diego, and San Francisco.

Two good central **hostels**, south of the tracks and run by the same management, offer dorm beds for around $16 and private rooms for more like $30. Both the *DuBeau International Hostel*, 19 W Phoenix Ave (☎928/773-1656 or 1-800/398-7112; ❶), and the *Grand Canyon International Hostel*, 19 S San Francisco St (☎928/779-9421 or 1-888/442-2696, ⓦwww.grandcanyonhostel .com; ❶), run excursions up to the Grand Canyon. The *Monte Vista*, 100 N San Francisco St (☎928/779-6971 or 1-800/545-3068, ⓦwww.hotelmontevista .com; ❸–❺), is a pleasant little hotel where the assorted restored rooms, with and without attached bathrooms, are named for celebrity guests from Bob Hope to Michael Stipe. Chain motels abound just off the interstate further east, with the smart, good-value *Super 8 West*, 602 W Route 66 (☎928/774-4581; ❷), closer at hand, less than a mile southwest of downtown. The best campground is three miles south on US-89A, at *Fort Tuthill County Park* (☎928/774-5139).

As for **food**, *Macy's European Coffee House & Bakery*, south of the tracks at 14 S Beaver St (☎928/774-2243), offers good breakfasts and substantial vegetarian dishes later on, while *Pasto*, downtown at 19 E Aspen Ave (☎928/779-1937), serves well-priced Italian dinners. The *Mad Italian* at no. 101 S San Francisco St (☎928/779-1820) is a highly sociable bar with several pool tables, while the *Museum Club*, 3404 E Route 66 (☎928/526-9434), is a real oddity: a 1930s log-cabin taxidermy museum that somehow transmogrified into a classic Route 66 roadhouse, saloon, and country music venue, and became a second home to hordes of dancing cowboys.

For **Internet access**, head to *Biff's Bagels & Internet Café*, 1 S Beaver St (☎928/226-0424; Mon–Sat 7am–3pm, Sun 8am–2pm; ⓦwww.biffsbagels.com).

Travel details

Trains

LA to: Barstow (1 daily & 1 Amtrak Thruway daily; 3hr); Flagstaff (1 daily; 10hr); Las Vegas (1 daily; 5hr 20min); Palm Springs (4 weekly; 2hr 20min).

Buses

All buses are Greyhound unless otherwise stated. **Grand Canyon to:** Flagstaff (2 Open Road Tours daily; 2hr).

Las Vegas to: Barstow (10 daily & 2 Amtrak Thruway daily; 3hr); Flagstaff (2 daily; 5hr).
LA to: Barstow (14 daily; 3hr); Las Vegas (16 daily & 2 Amtrak Thruway; 4hr/6hr); Palm Springs (12 daily; 3hr).
Palm Springs to: Bakersfield (9 daily and 1 Amtrak Thruway daily; 5hr 45min); Joshua Tree (1 Morongo Basin Transit Authority daily; 55 min).
San Diego to: Borrego Springs (1 Northeast Rural Bus System daily; 2hr 50min).

Death Valley and the Eastern High Sierra

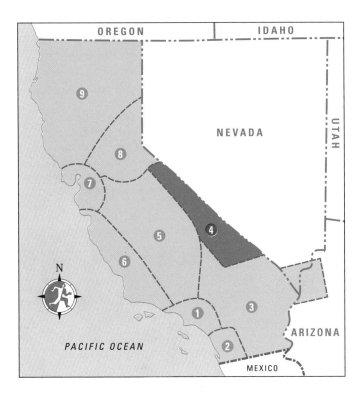

CHAPTER 4

Highlights

* **Rhyolite** This striking ghost town on the fringes of Death Valley is filled with buildings from its Gold Rush days as well as a wonderful collection of fiberglass sculptures. See p.329

* **Mono Lake** Take a canoe or kayaking trip amid the lakeside tufa towers, which create an otherworldly – and highly photogenic – landscape. See p.360

* **Bristlecone Pine Forest** The gnarled and wizened forms of the world's oldest living things – some nearly five millennia old – are on display in this forest. See p.344

* **Furnace Creek Inn** This 1920s adobe hotel is the perfect – in fact the only – place to experience Death Valley in luxury. See p.330

* **Mount Whitney** Take the strenuous hike to the highest point in the continental US and enjoy the luxurious view of the neighboring High Sierra peaks. See p.341

* **Whoa Nellie Deli** A casual restaurant at a gas station at the junction of US-395 and Hwy-120 East, the *Whoa Nellie* has justly gained a reputation for great food and a lively atmosphere. See p.362

Death Valley and the Eastern High Sierra

T
he far eastern edge of California, rising up from the Mojave Desert and cleaving to the border with Nevada, is a long narrow strip as scenically dramatic as anywhere else in the state, veering from blistering desert to ski country, much of it in the lee of the mighty Sierra Nevada mountains. It's a region devoid of interstates, scarcely populated, and, but for the scant reminders of gold-hungry pioneers, developed in only the most tentative way.

At the region's base, technically forming the Mojave's northern reach but more usually visited along with the Owens Valley, is **Death Valley**. With the highest average summer temperatures on earth and so remote that it's almost a region unto itself, this vast national park is a distillation of the classic desert landscape: an arid, otherworldly terrain of brilliantly colored, bizarrely eroded rocks, mountains, and sand dunes, a hundred miles from the nearest town.

Heading north, the towering **eastern** peaks of the Sierra Nevada drop abruptly to the largely desert – and deserted – landscape of the Owens Valley far below. Seen from the eastern side, the mountains are perfectly described by their Spanish name, **Sierra Nevada**, which literally translates as "snowcapped saw." Virtually the entire range is preserved as wilderness, and hikers and mountaineers can get to higher altitudes quicker here than almost anywhere else in California: well-maintained roads lead to trailheads at over eight thousand feet, providing swift access to spires, glaciers, and clear mountain lakes. **Mount Whitney**, the highest point in the continental US, marks the southernmost point of the chain, which continues north for an uninterrupted 150 miles to the backcountry of Yosemite National Park.

At the foot of Mount Whitney, the five-mile-wide **Owens Valley** starts, hemmed in to the east by the **White Mountains**, nearly as high but drier and less hospitable than the High Sierra, and home to the ancient, gnarled **bristlecone pines**. In between the two mountain ranges, US-395 runs the length of the Valley, which has few signs of settlement at all beyond the sporadic roadside towns and the larger **Bishop**.

An hour's drive further north, **Mammoth Lakes** is the Eastern Sierra's busiest resort, thick with skiers in winter, and with fishers and mountain bikers in summer. Finally, at the point where many turn west for Yosemite, bizarre rock formations rise from the placid blue waters of ancient **Mono Lake**, set in

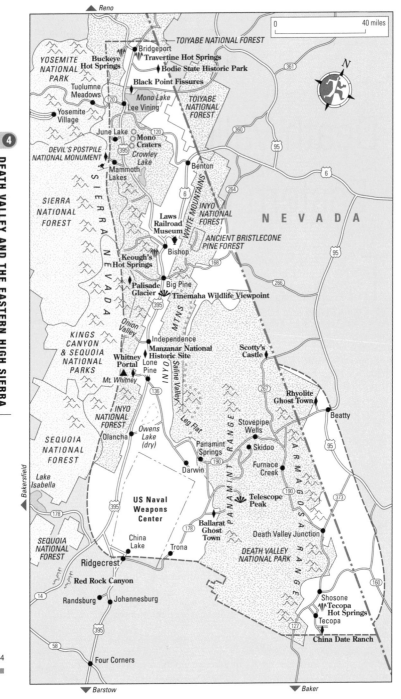

▲ *Reno*

0   40 miles

N

TOIYABE NATIONAL FOREST

Bridgeport
Travertine Hot Springs
Buckeye
Hot Springs
Bodie State Historic Park

YOSEMITE
NATIONAL
PARK

Black Point Fissures

Tuolumne
Meadows

Mono Lake

120

Lee Vining

TOIYABE
NATIONAL
FOREST

Yosemite
Village

361

360

June Lake
120
Mono
Craters
95

DEVIL'S POSTPILE
NATIONAL MONUMENT

395

Crowley
Lake

Mammoth
Lakes

Benton

6

264

SIERRA
NATIONAL
FOREST

S
I
E
R
R
A

WHITE MOUNTAINS

INYO
NATIONAL
FOREST

N E V A D A

Laws
Railroad
Museum

ANCIENT BRISTLECONE
PINE FOREST

Bishop

95

N
E
V
A
D
A

Keough's
Hot Springs

168

Palisade
Glacier

Big Pine

395

Tinemaha Wildlife Viewpoint

266

Onion
Valley

KINGS
CANYON
& SEQUOIA
NATIONAL
PARKS

Independence

Manzanar National
Historic Site

Lone
Pine

Scotty's
Castle

Whitney
Portal

Mt. Whitney

I
N
Y
O

Saline Valley

267

Rhyolite
Ghost Town

136

Beatty

INYO
NATIONAL
FOREST

Leg Flat

Stovepipe
Wells

95

Olancha

Owens
Lake
(dry)

SEQUOIA
NATIONAL
FOREST

Panamint
Springs

Skidoo

Furnace
Creek

190

P
A
N
A
M
I
N
T

A
M
A
R
G
O
S
A

R
A
N
G
E

Darwin

190

373

Lake
Isabella

178

US Naval
Weapons
Center

Telescope
Peak

R
A
N
G
E

SEQUOIA
NATIONAL
FOREST

China
Lake

Ballarat
Ghost
Town

395

178

Trona

Death Valley Junction

DEATH VALLEY
NATIONAL PARK

160

Ridgecrest

Red Rock Canyon

Randsburg   Johannesburg

14

Shosone
Tecopa
Hot Springs
Tecopa

127

China Date Ranch

395

58

Four Corners

▼ *Barstow*   ▼ *Baker*

◄ *Bakersfield*

a dramatic desert basin of volcanoes and steaming hot pools. Beyond, and far enough out of most people's way to deter the crowds, lies the wonderful ghost town of **Bodie**, which preserves a palpable sense of gold-town life eight thousand feet up in a parched, windswept valley.

Getting around

Getting around the region is best done by car, primarily using **US-395** – the lifeline of the Owens Valley and pretty much the only access to the area from within California. Once north of Mojave, where Hwy-58 branches west to Bakersfield, no road crosses the Sierra Nevada until Hwy-120, a spur over the 10,000-foot Tioga Pass into Yosemite. To the east Hwy-190 cuts through the Panamint Range into Death Valley.

Neither Amtrak nor Greyhound run any services in the region and the only long-distance **public transportation** is the bus service run by Carson Ridgecrest Eastern Sierra Transit or CREST (☎760/872-1901 or 1-800/922-1930); which runs along the Owens Valley linking Ridgecrest (see p.292) and Carson City (see p.701), both of which have onward connections. Buses generally have bike racks or space onboard.

In addition there are a number of small companies running minibuses up to mountain trailheads, but these are more like taxi services and have no regular schedule.

Death Valley National Park

Initially **DEATH VALLEY** seems an inhuman environment: burning hot, apparently lifeless and almost entirely without shade, much less water. If you just drive through in half a day, it can appear barren and monotonous, but longer acquaintance reveals multiple layers of interest. Death Valley itself is just the central portion (but very much the focal point) of the much larger **DEATH VALLEY NATIONAL PARK**, which extends a hundred miles from north to south and is almost as wide in some parts. Grand vistas sweep down from the sub-alpine slopes of the eleven-thousand-foot **Telescope Peak** to **Badwater**, the lowest point in the western hemisphere at 282 feet below sea level; sharply silhouetted hills are folded and eroded into deeply shadowed crevices, their exotic mineral content turning million-year-old mud flats into rainbows of sunlit phosphorescence; and stark hills harbor the bleached ruins of mining enterprises that briefly flourished against all odds.

It seems impossible that the landscape could support any kind of life, yet it is home to a great variety of living creatures, from snakes and giant eagles to tiny fish and bighorn sheep. What little vegetation there is can be fascinating both for its adaptation to the rigors of the environment and the almost sculptural effect it has on the landscape.

Throughout the summer, the **air temperature** in Death Valley averages 112°F – with a recorded high of 134°F – and there are frequent periods when it tops 120°F daily. At such times, the ground can reach near boiling point, so it's best to stay away, leaving the place to car manufacturers who have been bringing their latest models out here for extreme testing ever since Dodge paved the way in 1913.

For advice on **desert survival**, see the box on p.254.

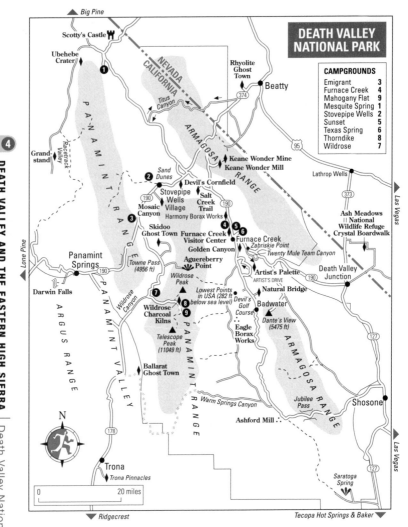

DEATH VALLEY
NATIONAL PARK

CAMPGROUNDS

Emigrant	3
Furnace Creek	4
Mahogany Flat	9
Mesquite Spring	1
Stovepipe Wells	2
Sunset	5
Texas Spring	6
Thorndike	8
Wildrose	7

Unless you're a real glutton for sweaty, potentially fatal punishment, it's better to come during the spring, especially March and early April, when wildflowers may be in bloom (though many years they refuse to play ball) and daytime temperatures average a manageable 83°F, dropping to the mid-fifties at
night. Any time between October and May, it's generally mild and dry, with
occasional rainfall on the surrounding mountains causing flash floods through
otherwise bone-dry gullies and washes.

Throughout the park, roads and services are sparse, mostly concentrated in
the central north–south valley, after which the park is named. Hwy-190 runs
the length of the valley linking **Furnace Creek** and **Stovepipe Wells**, the
park's two main outposts for provisions and accommodation. Forays from these

bases give access to extensive **sand dunes**, intriguing **ghost towns**, cool high country camping in the **Panamint Range**, and the incongruous mansion that is **Scotty's Castle**.

Geology and history
The sculpted rock layers exposed in Death Valley, tinted by oxidized traces of various **mineral deposits**, comprise a nearly complete record of the earth's past, from 500-million-year-old mountains to relatively young **fossils**, and deposits left on the valley floors by the Ice Age lakes, which covered most of the park's low-lying areas. There's also dramatic evidence of volcanic activity, as at the massive **Ubehebe Crater** on the north side of the park.

Humans have lived in and around Death Valley for thousands of years, beginning about ten thousand years ago, when the Valley was still filled by a massive lake; the climate was then quite mild and wildlife was more abundant than it is today. Later, wandering tribes of desert **Shoshone** wintered near perennial freshwater springs in the warm valley, spending the long, hot summers at cooler, higher elevations in the surrounding mountains; there is still a small, inhabited Timbisha Shoshone village near the *Furnace Creek Ranch* (see p.330), and you can listen to their Timbisha Free Radio on 91.1FM (Mon–Fri 8am–4pm, Sat & Sun noon–8pm).

The first non-natives passed through in 1849, looking for a shortcut to the Gold Rush towns on the other side of the Sierra Nevada; they ran out of food and water but most managed to survive, though the death of one of their number encouraged a survivor to dub the place Death Valley. For the next 75 years, the only people willing to brave the hardships of the desert were miners, who searched for and found deposits of gold, silver, and copper.

The most successful mining endeavors were centered on **borates**, a harsh alkaline used in detergent soaps (and, eventually, in a variety of industries – everything from cosmetics to nuclear reactors). In the late nineteenth century, borate miners developed twenty-mule-team wagons to haul the borate ore across the deserts to the railroad line at Mojave. In the 1920s, the first tourist facilities were developed, and in 1927 the *Furnace Creek Inn* was built on the site of the former Furnace Creek mining camp. Six years later, the two million acres of Death Valley and its environs were purchased by the US government, to be preserved as a national monument. In 1994, as part of the **California Desert Protection Act**, Congress accorded it national park status and added a further 1.3 million acres to its area, making Death Valley the largest national park in the country outside Alaska.

Getting to Death Valley
Death Valley is a long way from anywhere, with **Las Vegas** (see p.300) being the nearest city, over 130 miles away. There's **no scheduled public transportation** into the park, and though **Beatty**, forty miles north of Furnace Creek in Nevada, does have a bus service, it is of little use for getting to Death Valley unless you have a bicycle. The following are the main routes into the park; be sure to top up your **gas** tank before you head into the park as it is expensive here.

From the south: Tecopa Hot Springs and Shoshone
Hwy-127 branches off I-15 at Baker (see p.297 – the last stop for supplies on the southern route into Death Valley – and cuts across fifty miles of desolate Mojave landscape into the Armagosa Valley before reaching any civilization. A

couple of miles east of Hwy-127, two dilapidated settlements of scrappy trailer homes make unexpectedly decent places to stop off.

TECOPA HOT SPRINGS has become a popular winter retreat, thanks to its natural **hot springs** (always open except Mon & Fri 7am–noon; free), bequeathed in perpetuity by a local chief provided they remain gratis. Separate male and female clothing-free bathhouses are ugly and subject to a long list of largely commonsense rules, but relaxing nonetheless.

While in the area, drive seven miles southeast to **China Ranch Date Farm**, China Ranch Road (daily 9am–5pm; ☎760/852-4415, ⓦwww.chinaranch .com), where you are free to wander among the mostly-young groves, follow a shady streamside nature trail, explore wider along the Old Spanish Trail (a pack route between old mission stations which ran nearby), then repair to the cactus garden for a refreshing date shake and, of course, buy some dates. Many people **stay** across the road from the hot springs at the bleak campground (tents $10, hook-up $14), though the hostel in nearby **Tecopa**, and the *Ranch House Inn*, by the China Ranch Date Farm, are both better bets (see p.332 for both).

The hamlet of **SHOSHONE**, eight miles north of Tecopa Hot Springs, wouldn't really rate a mention but for a decent motel (see p.332) within striking distance of the park, and *C'est Si Bon* (closed Tues & Wed), the best café for miles around, located in a former railroad building now tastefully decorated with artworks and photos. Apart from good espresso and Internet access, the café sells Thai iced tea, smoothies, granola and yogurt breakfasts, cheese platters, crepes, home-made cakes, and more.

While here, it is worth spending a few minutes at the small **museum** and Death Valley **Chamber of Commerce** (daily 8am–4pm; ☎760/852-4524, ⓦwww.deathvalleychamber.org) and ask them to direct you to **Doublin Gulch**, a series of hand-hewn cave homes once used by miners, and so named because early in the twentieth century the area was so popular it kept "doublin" in size. The last resident moved out in 1986.

The route into Death Valley continues north through Death Valley Junction (see below).

From the southeast: Ash Meadows and Death Valley Junction

For the most direct and interesting route from Las Vegas, take US-95 or Las Vegas Boulevard south to Blue Diamond Route (Hwy-160 west), which leads past the scenic **Red Rock Canyon Recreation Area** to the town of **Pahrump**; the Smith's supermarket there is a good spot to load up on supplies. Just past the town, turn left at Bella Vista Road, which is signposted for the **ASH MEADOWS NATIONAL WILDLIFE REFUGE** (daily sunrise–sunset), a desert oasis which contains the US's greatest concentration of endemic species – some 24 plants and animals found nowhere else in the world. Head for the Crystal Spring Boardwalk Trail, which runs a third of a mile to a spring, where rare desert pupfish dwell.

Beyond the turnoff for the refuge is the tiny and virtually abandoned settlement of **DEATH VALLEY JUNCTION**. It offers no fuel or supplies, but its *Amargosa Hotel* (see p.332) houses the **Amargosa Opera House**, the creation of Marta Becket, a New York dancer and artist who settled here in the late 1960s. The inside of the theater is painted with trompe l'oeil balconies peopled by sixteenth-century Spanish nobles and revellers. Ballet-pantomimes, in which Ms Becket takes almost all the parts herself, are staged here through the winter (Oct, Dec & Jan Sat only, Nov & Feb–early May Mon & Sat; $15; ☎760/852-4441) with performances starting at 7.45pm.

From Death Valley Junction it is an easy thirty-mile drive to Furnace Creek, passing Zabriskie Point and the junction for Dante's View (see p.334 for both) along the way.

From the northwest: Rhyolite and Beatty

An alternative route into Death Valley from Las Vegas runs past the Nellis Air Force Base and the old US nuclear weapons testing range beside US-95 to **BEATTY**, where there's a small chamber of commerce, at 119 Main St (Tues–Sat 9am–5pm; ☎775/553-2424), a couple of **places to stay** including an HI hostel (see p.332), and a couple of casinos with 24hr restaurants.

Don't pass up the opportunity to visit the appealing ghost town of **RHYO-LITE**, up a side road three miles west of Beatty. Rhyolite was a gold-mining town whose mines were prematurely closed in 1912, after just six boom years. Mismanagement and a lack of technological know-how were largely to blame, and the working Bullfrog Mine just outside the town attests to the area's continuing mineral wealth. By then the town had spread over the hillside (made of the rock that gave the town its name) and had its own train station. The station is still the dominant structure, but the remains of other buildings, including a jail, schoolhouse, and bank, still stand, as does Tom Kelly's **bottle house** built of some fifty thousand beer and spirit bottles in 1906. A more recent attraction is the roadside Goldwell Open Air Museum, a distinctly off-beam **sculpture garden** (unrestricted access) complete with structures built from car parts and an arresting series of white fiberglass figures arranged in imitation of *The Last Supper*. It is mostly the work of Belgian artist Albert Szulalski, who died in 2000 after completing the huge metal miner and similarly proportioned penguin that greet you as you enter town.

From Rhyolite, you'll coast down into the park on Hwy-374, watching Death Valley unfold from above. You'll also have the chance to explore the one-way **Titus Canyon** road, which winds past several crumbling lead mines on its way to Scotty's Castle (p.335). High-clearance or four-wheel-drive vehicles are recommended.

From the southwest: the Panamint Range and Ballarat

Probably the least used access road to Death Valley is from the southwest, leading from Ridgecrest past the Trona Pinnacles (see p.293) and the industrial borax town of **Trona** and into the park. This allows the quickest access into the more mountainous backcountry of the national park on the western slopes of the **PANAMINT RANGE**.

Twenty miles north of Trona, a signposted road heads three miles east to the scant, eroded adobe ruins of the former gold-mining town of **BALLARAT**. Four-wheel-drive roads head further into the hills, where one fairly popular destination is Barker Ranch in Goler Wash where Charles Manson and his "family" holed up after the notorious Tate-LaBianca murders in 1969.

Almost ten miles north of the Ballarat junction the highway splits: left to Panamint Springs on a good road, or right along the winding **Emigrant Canyon Road** towards Telescope Peak (see p.337) in the park itself.

From the west: Owens Lake and Darwin

From the west, two routes (Hwy-138 and Hwy-190) spur off Hwy-395 towards Death Valley. They run either side of the dry bed of what, until the 1920s, used to be **OWENS LAKE**, which for a time in the nineteenth century saw steamships carrying bullion bars. The water that would naturally flow into the lake has been diverted to Los Angeles via the aqueduct that parallels US-395, leaving a pan of toxic alkali dust. Schemes are now under way to control this by planting native vegetation and reintroducing some water to the ecosystem.

Almost thirty miles east of Hwy-395, and just before the Death Valley National Park boundary, a seven-mile paved side road leads to **DARWIN**, another virtual ghost town that once had a population of over forty thousand and is now just about hanging on with fifty residents and a small post office. Only tumbledown wooden ruins remain of the town which was built in the 1870s by prospectors searching for seams of silver, inspired by tales of an Indian who repaired an explorer's rifle by fashioning a gunsight out of solid silver.

Park entrance and information

Entrance to the park is $10 per vehicle, or $5 if you are walking or cycling. For that, you get unrestricted entry for seven days, an excellent map, and a copy of the Death Valley National Park newspaper with up-to-date details on campgrounds and visitor services.

Most visitor facilities are concentrated in two settlements, each comprising little more than a gas station, motel, a restaurant or two, and a grocery store. The busiest of the two, **Furnace Creek**, is right in the center of the Valley and has an excellent **visitor center** (daily 8am–6pm; ☏760/786-3220, Ⓦ www.nps.gov/deva) with a small but interesting **museum** (same hours; free) and a twelve-minute orientational slide program. **Stovepipe Wells**, 25 miles to the northwest, is slightly smaller. More information is available from the **ranger stations** close to the park boundaries. The main ones are on the west side at *Wildrose* campground on Hwy-178 and on the northern edge of the park at Scotty's Castle. There are **no banks** in the park but Furnace Creek and Stovepipe Wells both have ATMs.

Accommodation

To get the full impact of a desert visit, you really need to **camp** out. For most of the year you don't even need a tent – it isn't going to rain – though a sleeping bag is a good idea. Camping is also much the cheapest way to stay in Death Valley: all the campgrounds are operated by the National Park Service and most cost $10 a night, while sites without a water supply are free. If camping isn't an option you are limited to fairly expensive **hotels** and **motels** inside the park, or lower-cost possibilities on the fringes. Reservations should be made as early as possible, especially during peak holiday periods. The following listings cover all the rooms in the park and the settlements nearby, but also see Lone Pine (p.339) for accommodation slightly further afield.

Inside the park

Furnace Creek Inn Furnace Creek ☏760/786-2345 or 1-800/236-7916, Ⓦ www.furnacecreekresort.com. A beautifully situated hotel built of adobe in the 1920s amid date palms and tended lawns, this is the place to stay if you're in the Valley with money to burn. Rooms are modern but tastefully done, many with great views across the Valley of the Panamint Range. Best of all, you can spend the day in the pool, which has bar service in the more fashionable cooler months, when prices are hiked by fifty percent. ❼

Furnace Creek Ranch Furnace Creek ☏760/786-2345 or 1-800/236-7916, Ⓦ www.furnacecreekresort.com. Functional, family-oriented, and cheaper than the *Furnace Creek Inn*, but with little atmosphere and no sense of being in a desert. The comfortable but ordinary motel rooms are rather overpriced. They also offer showers to non-guests for $2. ❺

Panamint Springs Resort Panamint Springs
☎775/482-7680, ⊛www.deathvalley.com. Simple
but decent motel (though without a pool) 35 miles
west of Stovepipe Wells with a restaurant and bar
where you can sit and lunch on the shady terrace
or sip a beer in the warm night air. The adjacent
campground has $12 tent sites, $25 RV hook-ups,
and $3 non-guest showers. ❸

Stovepipe Wells Motel Stovepipe Wells
☎760/786-2387, ⊛www.xanterra.com. The best-
priced option inside the park, offering comfortable
rooms, a mineral-water pool, a restaurant with
buffet meals, and a bar. ❸

△ Bristlecone pines in the White Mountains

Camping in Death Valley

Most National Park sites cannot be reserved and stays are limited to thirty days (so that people don't move in for the winter). Take note of the **altitude** listed for each, as this gives an idea of the temperatures you might expect.

The **main sites** are at *Furnace Creek* (mid-Oct to mid-April $16, mid-April to mid-Oct $10, reservable up to five months in advance in winter months; ☏1-800/365-2267; 196ft) which fills up very early on winter weekends; at the enormous *Sunset* (Oct–April; $10; 196ft), which is virtually an RV parking lot; and the designated "quiet" *Texas Spring* (Oct-April; $12; sea level), both close to *Furnace Creek*; and at *Stovepipe Wells* (Oct–April; $10; sea level) – though the smaller and relatively shady site at *Mesquite Spring* (all year; $10;1800ft), near Scotty's Castle on the north side of the park, is much more pleasant. There is one **free site** with water, the tent-only *Emigrant* (all year; 2100ft), eight miles west of Stovepipe Wells. This is on the way to the only place with guaranteed shade, the canyons on the forested slopes of Telescope Peak, on the western edge of the park. Here there are three free sites, *Wildrose* (all year, water available April–Nov; 4100ft), *Thorndike* (open March–Nov; 7400ft), and *Mahogany Flat* (March–Nov; 8200ft), just off the mostly paved Wildrose Road. The upper two are usually only accessible in high clearance or four-wheel-drive vehicles. Fires are allowed in all sites except *Sunset* and *Emigrant*, but designated fireplaces must be used and no collecting of firewood is allowed. There's also a commercial campground at Panamint Springs (see p.330).

Free **backcountry camping** is allowed in most areas of the park provided you keep two miles away from any roads (paved or otherwise) and two hundred yards from water sources. No permits are required, but voluntary backcountry **registration** is strongly recommended.

On the fringes

Amargosa Hotel Death Valley Junction ☏760/852-4441, ☏760/852-4138, ☏armagosa@kay-net.com. Pleasantly run-down adobe hotel built by the Pacific Coast Borax Company in 1924. It has no TVs or phones, but boasts an attached opera house (see above). Ask to see a few of local artist Mart's hand-painted rooms before choosing, as they vary enormously – there's a trompe l'oeil wardrobe in the Jezebel room and cherubs in the Baroque. ❷

HI-Desertaire Hostel 2000 Old Spanish Trail, Tecopa ☏760/852-4580, ☏little-egypt30@hotmail.com. A relaxed hostel an hour south of Furnace Creek. There are only ten beds ($12) and one family room (❶), but you can sleep outside in the warm desert air in a wooden tower with commanding views of the surrounding desert. Book the first night by phone or in writing: PO Box 306, Tecopa, CA 92389.

Happy Burro Hostel 100 Main St, Beatty ☏775/553-9130, ☏happyburrro@pahrump.com. HI hostel centrally located in Beatty, but the dorms are a little cramped and lacking in atmosphere. One double available. Members $15, nonmembers $18. ❶

Phoenix Inn 350 First St, Beatty ☏775/553-2250 or 1-800/845-7401, ☏info@phnxinn.com. On a quiet side street, and one of the few Beatty motels not in or attached to a casino. ❷

Ranch House Inn Tecopa ☏760/852-4358. Attractive and welcoming B&B in a 1920s cottage on the China Ranch Date Farm (see p.328). It's imaginatively decorated, peaceful, and includes a full breakfast served on the screened porch. Dinner is also available ($13) and you can BYO wine. ❺

Shoshone Inn Shoshone ☏760/852-4224. Recently remodeled motel an hour south of Furnace Creek on Hwy-127 with access to local warm springs, and Tecopa Hot Springs eight miles south. ❸

Shoshone RV Park Shoshone ☏760/852-4524. Shady RV park and campground with sites from $10 and access to the local warm springs.

Exploring Death Valley

You can get an unforgettable feel for Death Valley just by passing through, and you could quite easily see almost everything in a day. If you have the time, though, aim to spend at least a night here, if possible camped out somewhere far from the main centers of activity. Even if you've got your own car, the best way to experience the huge, empty spaces and the unique landforms of Death Valley is to leave the roads (and virtually all other visitors) behind and wander off – taking care to remember the way back. Sunrise and sunset are the best times to experience the color that's bleached out by the midday sun, and they're also the most likely times for seeing the **wildlife**, mostly lizards, snakes, and small rodents, which hide out through the heat of the day.

Most of the park's recognized sights lie south of Furnace Creek **along the Badwater road** where colorful rocks line Artist's Drive and a small pond marks the lowest point in the western hemisphere. The hills immediately to the east offer a couple of great viewpoints – **Dante's View** and **Zabriskie Point** – but the bulk of visitors head swiftly north past the **Keane Wonder Mine** to the ever popular **Scotty's Castle**. It is out on a limb, so leave time to explore **Ubehebe Crater** and **Racetrack Valley** while you're up here. On Death Valley's western flank rises the **Telescope Peak**, a much cooler place to go hiking or exploring the **Wildrose Charcoal Kilns**.

Along the Badwater road

Many of the park's most unusual sights are located south of Furnace Creek along the road to Badwater, which forks off Hwy-190 by the *Furnace Creek Inn*. A good first stop, two miles along, is **Golden Canyon**. Periodic rainstorms over the centuries have washed a fifty-foot-deep slot-shaped gully through the clay and silt here, revealing golden-hued walls that are particularly vibrant in the early evening. A three-quarter-mile-long interpretive trail winds into the U-shaped upper canyon, and a loop hike (see box on p.336) continues from there.

Five miles further on, signs point to **Artist's Drive**, a twisting one-way loop road, perhaps best left until the drive back, especially if this means catching the afternoon sun on the **Artist's Palette**, an evocatively eroded hillside covered in an intensely colored mosaic of reds, golds, blacks, and greens.

A couple of miles further south, a dirt road heading west leads a mile to the **Devil's Golf Course**, a weird field of salt pinnacles and hummocks protruding a couple of feet from the desert floor. Capillary action draws saline solutions from below the surface where alternate layers of salt and alluvial deposits from

---

Park activities

Besides hiking and sightseeing, Death Valley offers ample opportunities for **mountain biking**. Only roads open to road vehicles are accessible to cyclists (hiking trails are off limits), but this still leaves plenty to go at for those who bring their wheels along: there are no rentals available. The map provided with your entry ticket shows the major four-wheel-drive routes: Echo Canyon into the Funeral Mountains and the Inyo Mine, Cottonwood Canyon from Stovepipe Wells, and the Warm Springs Canyon/Butte Valley road in the south of the park are all worthwhile. Topographical maps are available at Furnace Creek visitor center.

Horseback riding (Nov to mid-May; ☎760/786-3339) is offered at the Furnace Creek Ranch for $25 an hour, and when the phase of the moon is right, $35 for an hour-long evening ride.

After a day in the desert, swimming in a tepid pool is an ideal way to enjoy a balmy evening. Guests have priority in the pools at the *Furnace Creek Ranch* and the *Stovepipe Wells Motel*, but at quiet times they are open to the public ($2). **Golfers** can even play a round at the verdant palm-fringed 18-hole course at Furnace Creek (mid-May to mid-Oct $30, mid-Oct to mid-May $55; ☎760/786-2345).

Badwater Ultramarathon

Driving through Death Valley in late July can seem like madness even in an air-conditioned vehicle, but an international field of almost a hundred masochists now choose this time of year to run the grueling **Badwater Ultramarathon** (Ⓦ www.bad-waterultra.com), one of the most demanding, extreme, and prestigious in the world. Searing heat and draining dehydration are constant threats on this 135-mile road race which kicks off at Badwater 282 feet below sea level and, after a total elevation of around 14,000, finishes at the 8360ft Whitney Portal, the trailhead for ascents of Mount Whitney.

One Al Arnold was the first to run the course in 1977, but the race didn't actually get under way until 1988 and has been run every year since, with most competitors in the invitation-only field managing to finish. The current men's record, set by the Russian Anatoli Kruglikov, is 25 hours and 9 minutes; while in the 2002 event, American Pam Reed knocked almost two hours off the women's record (and beat all the men in the field) to record a time of 27 hours 57 minutes.

ancient lakes have been laid down over the millennia. As the occasional rainfall evaporates, the salt accretes to form a landscape as little like a golf course as you could imagine.

It is another four miles south to **Badwater**, an unpalatable but non-poisonous thirty-foot-wide pool of water, loaded with chloride and sulphates, that's also the only home of the endangered, soft-bodied Death Valley snail. Notice how much hotter it feels in the humid air beside the water. From the pool, two rather uninteresting hikes, both around four miles long, lead across the hot, flat valley floor to the two **lowest points in the western hemisphere**, both at 282ft below sea level. Neither are marked and there's little satisfaction in being just two feet lower than you were at the roadside.

Zabriskie Point and Dante's View

The badlands around **ZABRISKIE POINT**, overlooking Badwater and the Artist's Palette, four miles south of Furnace Creek off Hwy-190, were the inspiration for Antonioni's eponymous 1970 movie. The point's sculpted spires of banded rock are less interesting than **DANTE'S VIEW**, a further 21 miles south off Hwy-190 and then ten miles on a very steep (and very hot) road. At a point almost six thousand feet above the blinding white saltpan of Badwater, the valley floor does indeed look infernal. The view is best during the early morning, when the pink and gold Panamint Mountains across the Valley are highlighted by the rising sun.

North from Furnace Creek

In the township of Furnace Creek, you could spend a few minutes in the **Borax Museum** (daily 10am–4pm; free), which rather ploddingly tells the story of the mineral and its excavation, but you are better advised to head two miles north to the old **Harmony Borax Works** (unrestricted entry) where a quarter-mile interpretive trail tells of the mine and processing plant.

Twelve miles to the north, the **Keane Wonder Mine** and **Keane Wonder Mill** (unrestricted entry to both) were indeed wonderful during their heyday between 1904, when the mine was discovered by Jack Keane, and 1916. Gold and silver worth $1.1 million was extracted at the mountainside mine and worked at in the valley-floor mill, where it was carried down a three-quarter-mile-long aerial tramway which is still more or less intact. From the parking lot by the remains of the mill, a very steep path climbs alongside the thirteen tramway towers to the lowest of the mineshafts. It is only a mile but seems a lot more in the noonday heat. Don't be tempted to seek shelter in the adits and shafts leading off the path; all are dangerous and most unfenced.

Just east of Stovepipe Wells and north of Hwy-190, the most extensive of the Valley's **sand dunes** spread out, some fifteen rippled and contoured square miles of ever-changing dunes, some as much as a hundred feet high. Most people are happy to photograph them from the road (best in late afternoon), but while there are no formal trails, it is easy enough to pick a route out to the nearest of the dunes (about half a mile away) or even to the top of the highest dune (3–4 miles round-trip).

On the opposite side of Hwy-190 stands the **Devil's Cornfield**, an expanse of tufted arrowweed grasses perched on mounds that make them look like corn shocks. Stovepipe Wells is a good place to take a break with views of the dunes, and is handy for trips to **Mosaic Canyon** (see "Hikes" box, p.336).

Scotty's Castle

On the northern edge of the park (45 miles from the visitor center) and thus well out of the way of most of the rest of the tourist attractions, **SCOTTY'S CASTLE** (tours depart daily 9am–5pm; $8) is nevertheless the most popular single stop in the park; hordes of overheated tourists wait in long lines for the chance to wander through the surreal attraction of this unfinished but still luxurious mansion. Executed in extravagant Spanish Revival style, the castle was built during the 1920s as the desert retreat of wealthy Chicago insurance broker Albert Johnson. He was seldom there, so local cowboy, prospector, and publicity hound, "Death Valley" Scotty, who managed the construction, claimed the house was his own and financed by his hidden gold mine – a fantasy Johnson was happy to indulge. The $2 million house features intricately carved wooden ceilings, waterfalls in the living room, and, most entertaining of all, a remote-controlled player piano. In winter, it is best to arrive as the doors open to avoid long waits for the fifty-minute-long **tours** of the opulently furnished house, left pretty much as it was when Johnson died in 1948. Scotty himself lived here until 1954 and is buried on the hill just behind the house: a good place to wander while waiting for your tour.

Ubehebe Crater, Racetrack Valley, and the Eureka Sand Dunes

Eight miles southwest of Scotty's Castle – though it might as well be five hundred miles for all the people who venture here – gapes the half-mile-wide **UBEHEBE CRATER**, the rust-colored result of a massive volcanic explosion some three thousand years ago; a half-mile south sits its thousand-year-old younger brother, **Little Hebe**. Beyond the craters the road (high clearance vehicles recommended) continues south for another 27 dusty miles to **RACETRACK VALLEY**, a two-and-a-half-mile-long mud flat across which giant boulders seem slowly to be racing, leaving faint trails in their wake. Scientists believe that the boulders are pushed along the sometimes icy surface by very high winds; sit and watch (but don't hold your breath). Park two miles south of the **Grandstand**, then walk half a mile southeast for the best view of the rocks and their tracks.

The expansion of Death Valley when it became a national park claimed several features formerly outside its boundaries. The **EUREKA SAND DUNES**, forty miles northwest of Scotty's Castle, are the most exciting. Far more extensive than those around Stovepipe Wells, these stand up to seven hundred feet above the surrounding land, making them the highest dunes in California and

Anything more than a short stroll in the desert heat can become an ordeal. This is less true when hiking the Telescope Peak and Wildrose Peak trails in the Panamint Range, but you still need to carry all your **water** with you and will want a wide-brimmed hat. Always register your intended route at the visitor center or any of the ranger stations and for anything a little more adventurous than the walks listed here, get yourself a **topographic map** from the visitor center. All listed distances and times are for the round-trip.

Golden Canyon to Zabriskie Point (5 miles; 3hr; 500ft ascent). On an unmaintained, moderately strenuous trail to Zabriskie Point. Done in reverse, it is all downhill.

Gower Gulch Loop (4 miles; 2–3hr; 200ft ascent). Worthwhile loop walk starting at Golden Canyon and following the interpretive trail to marker #10. Then follow a trail down Gower Gulch back to the start. A leaflet is available from the visitor center.

Mosaic Canyon (1 mile; 30min; 100ft ascent). A rough three-mile access road just west of Stovepipe Wells leads to the trailhead for a relatively easy hike through this narrow canyon full of water-polished marble and mosaic-patterned canyon walls. Beyond this most heavily trafficked section, the canyon carries on for another mile and a half, with some scrambling at the upper end.

Telescope Peak (14 miles; 8hr; 3000ft ascent). The easy-to-follow but moderately strenuous trail climbs from the trailhead by *Mahogany Flat* campground, skirting a pair of 10,000-foot peaks, through bristlecone pines to the summit and its grand panorama of Death Valley and across to Mount Whitney and the eastern face of the Sierra Nevada mountains. Sign the summit register while you admire the view. There's no water en route except for snowmelt (often well into June), which should be treated. Crampons and ice axes may be required in harsh winters, and at all times you should self-register in the book a short way along the trail.

Wildrose Peak (8 miles; 5hr; 2000ft ascent). If winter conditions or your own level of fitness rule out Telescope Peak, this hike makes a perfect, easier alternative. Start by the Charcoal Kilns on Wildrose Canyon Road and wind up through piñon pines and juniper to a stunning summit panorama.

a dramatic place to witness sunrise or sunset. While here, keep your eyes open for the Eureka Dunes grass and evening primrose, both indigenous to the area and federally protected.

Aguereberry Point, Wildrose Charcoal Kilns, and Telescope Peak

To escape the heat and dust of the desert floor, head south from Stovepipe Wells into the **Panamint Range** along Emigrant Canyon Road. Ten miles up the canyon, a nine-mile dirt track turns off to the east toward the very meager remains of **Skidoo Ghost Town**, a 1915 gold-mining camp of seven hundred people that was watered by snowmelt from Telescope Peak, 23 miles away, and kept informed by telegraph from Rhyolite. There's very little to see, so a better side trip is to **AGUEREBERRY POINT**, a wonderful viewpoint looking six thousand feet down into Death Valley, and reached along a six-mile dirt road off Emigrant Canyon Road.

Yet further south the *Wildrose* campground (see p.332) marks the start of a steep five-mile road up Wildrose Canyon to the **WILDROSE CHARCOAL KILNS**. This series of ten massive, beehive-shaped stone kilns some 25 feet high was used in the 1880s to make charcoal for use in the smelters of local silver mines. The road then deteriorates (high-clearance recommended) and climbs through juniper and pine forests past the free *Thorndike* campground to its end at *Mahogany Flat*, where there's another free campground and the trail-head for the strenuous hike up **TELESCOPE PEAK**, which at 11,049ft is the highest – and coolest – point in the park (see box opposite). From the summit you can see both the highest (Mount Whitney) and the lowest (near Badwater) points in the continental United States.

Darwin Falls, Lee Flat, and Saline Valley

A mile west of Panamint Springs along Hwy-190, a two-mile dirt road leads south to a trailhead from where a mile-long creekside trail up a small canyon leads to the thirty-foot, spring-fed **DARWIN FALLS**. It is hardly dramatic, but does feed a welcome and shady cottonwood oasis, though because it sup-plies Panamint Springs with water, swimming here is not allowed.

You might not expect to see Joshua trees in Death Valley, but **LEE FLAT**, a dozen miles west of Panamint Springs, has a whole forest of them on its high-er slopes. At this point most visitors continue west towards Hwy-395 (see p.325), but adventurous drivers with sturdy vehicles might fancy exploring the northwestern corner of the park. A dirt road leads north past more Joshua trees at Lower Lee Flat, then continues on a very rough and unsigned fifty-mile trek out to **SALINE VALLEY** – obtain the best map you can and ask for local advice about road conditions. Old mine workings and the remains of a dilap-idated salt tramway can be seen along the way, but the highlights are the gen-erally clothing-free **hot springs** at Saline Warm Spring and Palm Hot Spring. Be prepared to camp out at the free, primitive site nearby. After a dip it is pos-sible to continue north to meet US-395 at Big Pine.

Eating and drinking

There's not a great variety of **eating places** in Death Valley – you're limited to the hotel dining rooms and restaurants at Furnace Creek and Stovepipe Wells, all of which are somewhat overpriced. The Furnace Creek Ranch is the only place with any choice, housing both the *Fortyniner Café*, a diner-cum-coffee shop, and the *Wrangler Buffet and Steakhouse*. For gourmet dining, make for the *Inn Dining Room* at the *Furnace Creek Inn* (for dinner reservations ☏760/786-2345; no shorts in the cooler months), where the likes of tortilla lime soup ($6), rattlesnake empañada ($13), and pepper steak ($25) are served up in a room almost unchanged since the 1920s. Beatty, with restaurants attached to all-night casinos, offers a number of inexpensive diners, though it's quite a long drive back to the park after dark.

To quench a **thirst** after a day in the sun, do as the few locals do and head to the *Corkscrew Saloon*, also at Furnace Creek Ranch and open until 1am; or head up to the *Furnace Creek Inn* for cocktails on the terrace. Expensive **gro-cery stores** with a limited supply are located at Furnace Creek and at Stovepipe Wells.

The Owens Valley

Rising out of the northern reaches of the Mojave Desert, the Sierra Nevada mountains announce themselves with a bang two hundred miles north of Los Angeles at **Mount Whitney**, the highest point on a silver-gray knifelike ridge of pinnacles that forms a nearly sheer eleven-thousand-foot wall of granite. It provides a wonderful backdrop to the **OWENS VALLEY**, a hot, dry, and

After coming through the Mojave or Death Valley, it seems hard to imagine that many of the passes across the Sierra Nevada can remain closed well into June. The authorities try to open **Tioga Pass** (into Yosemite), just below Mono Lake, by Memorial Day (at the end of May), but harsh winters sometimes leave it closed until late June or even early July. Passes to the north of here, **Hwy-108** and **Hwy-4**, tend to open a couple of weeks earlier, in mid-May. All three close again with the first heavy snowfall, perhaps around late October or early November. **Hwy-88**, yet further north, stays open all year. For information on the state of the highways call CalTrans at ☎ 1-800/427-7623 (see box on p.30).

Eastern Sierra **trailheads** are equally affected by snow, with most only accessible from May until early November. Even in June and early July the trails leading from the trailheads can be impassable without ice axe and crampons.

numinously thrilling stretch of desolate semi-desert landscape running from **Lone Pine** north beyond **Bishop**.

The small towns along its length don't really amount to much, and if you're intent on visiting California's more cultural sights, you could easily drive through in half a day. However, for scenic beauty and access to a range of outdoor activities the Owens Valley is hard to beat. Twisting mountain roads rise quickly from the hot valley floor to cool ten-thousand-foot-high trailheads ideal for **hiking** among Sierra lakes and forests or setting out for the summit of Mount Whitney or any of hundreds of other peaks.

The Owens Valley comes billed as the deepest valley in the US and with its floor averaging 4000ft and the mountains either side topping out above 14,000ft that seems completely believable. Its eastern wall is formed by the contiguous **Inyo Mountains** and **White Mountains**; rounded and weathered in comparison with the Sierra and less dramatic, though with their own beauty, especially around the wonderful **Ancient Bristlecone Pine Forest** which contains the world's oldest trees.

US-395 runs the length of the Owens Valley, a vital lifeline through a region that is almost entirely unpopulated outside of the few small towns, though a few solitary souls live in old sheds and caravans off the many dirt roads and tracks that cross the floor of the Valley. Naturally a semi-desert with only around five inches of rain a year, the region relies on Sierra snowmelt which once made the area a prime spot for growing apples and pears. But since 1913, its plentiful natural water supply has been drained away to fill the swimming pools of Los Angeles.

Lone Pine, Mount Whitney, and around

LONE PINE isn't much more than a single-street rural town strung with motels, gas stations, and restaurants, but it is lent a more vibrant air by being at the crossroads of desert and mountains. Any night of the week, there'll be desert rats mixing with Mount Whitney wilderness hikers and tourists recovering from the rigors of Death Valley. It also makes a good base and supply post for exploring the area, particularly if you're not prepared to camp out.

Part of what really makes it special is the unparalleled access it provides to the 14,497-foot summit of **MOUNT WHITNEY** – the highest point in the US outside Alaska. The view of the sharply pointed High Sierra peaks which dominate the town – captured by photographer Ansel Adams in a much-reproduced shot of the full moon suspended above stark cliffs – is fantastic.

Arrival and information

CREST **buses** stop outside Statham Hall, not far from the **Chamber of Commerce**, 126 S Main St (Mon–Fri 8am–4pm; ☎760/876-4444 or 1-877/253-8981, ⓦwww.lone-pine.com), which is fine for local information. For details of hiking, camping, high pass conditions in the whole of eastern California – including the High Sierra, Owens Valley, White Mountains, and Death Valley – you're better off visiting the excellent **Eastern Sierra Interagency Visitor Center** (daily 8am–4.50pm; ☎760/876-6222, ⓦwww.r5.fs.fed.us/inyo), a mile south of town on US-395 at the junction of Hwy-136, the Death Valley road. Most of the region is protected within the massive **Inyo National Forest**, and if you're planning to spend any amount of time in the area, pick up the very helpful **map** ($6), which covers everything between Mount Whitney and Yosemite National Park, including all hiking routes and campgrounds. Interestingly, this is the only map that makes clear the extent of the City of Los Angeles's holdings in the Owens Valley – basically the entire Valley floor, bought in the early years of the twentieth century to slake the thirst of the expanding city (see "The Battle for Mono Lake" box on p.361). Wilderness permits are issued at the **Mount Whitney Ranger Station**, 640 S Main St (daily: June–Oct 8am–5pm; Nov–May 8am–4.30pm; ☎760/876-6200).

In summer, the **swimming pool** at the high school on Muir Street south of town is open daily ($2); after a week in the mountains, you can get cleaned up at Kirk's Sierra Barber Shop, 104 N Main St, where you can take a **hot shower** for $4.

Accommodation

If you're looking for a **motel**, try the *Dow Villa Motel/Historic Dow Hotel*, 310 S Main St (☎760/876-5521 or 1-800/824-9317, ⓦwww.dowvillamotel.com; ❶–❺), the older section built in 1923 to house movie industry visitors (John Wayne always requested Room 20). There's an impressive range of accommodation, from basic bathless rooms in the hotel (❶), rooms with bath (❷), and plush motel units (❹–❺), some with VCR and whirlpool. The *Best Western Frontier Motel*, 1008 S Main St (☎760/876-5571 or 1-800/231-4071; ❸), offers a heated pool, basic continental breakfast, and some rooms with mountain views; the *Alabama Hills Inn*, 1920 S Main St (☎760/876-8700 or 1-800/800-6468, ⓦwww.alabamahillsinn.com; ❸), features large modern rooms and pool.

There are also plenty of **campgrounds** nearby, all off Whitney Portal Road, which heads west from town at the lights. The closest is the *Portage Joe* campground ($6; 3800ft) on Tuttle Creek Road, though you can save a few dollars by driving a couple of miles further to the *Tuttle Creek* campground (free; no water; 4000ft) on Horseshoe Meadow Road. At the Mount Whitney trailhead, twelve miles west of Lone Pine lie a couple more sites: the family-oriented *Whitney Portal* (late-May to mid-Oct; $12; 8000ft; ☎1-877/444-6777), and the hikers' *Whitney Portal Trailhead* (late-May to mid-Oct; $6; 8300ft; maximum one-night stay).

Eating

Lone Pine's range of **restaurants** isn't great, but the *Mt Whitney Restaurant*, 227 S Main St (☎760/876-5751), backs up its claim to serve "the best burgers in town" with over half a dozen types of patties – bean, ostrich, venison, veggie – on which to build your creation; *Pizza Factory*, 301 S Main St (☎760/876-4707), produces pretty decent pizza; and *Pepe's*, 104b N Main St (☎760/876-4768; closed Tues), serves basic but filling Mexican. There's **Internet access** and good coffee at *The Espresso Parlor*, 123 N Main St.

Alabama Hills

Between Lone Pine and the Sierra Nevada stand the **ALABAMA HILLS**, a rugged expanse of brown, tan, orange, and black granite and some metamorphic rock that's been sculpted into bizarre shapes by 160 million years of erosive winds and rains. Some of the oddest formations are linked by the **Picture Rocks Circle**, a paved road that loops around from Whitney Portal Road, passing rocks apparently shaped like bullfrogs, walruses, and baboons; it takes a degree of imagination and precise positioning to pick them all out, but it is an attractive drive nonetheless, especially at sunset. A map (free from the visitor centers) details the best spots and marks the sites used as backdrops for many early Westerns, including the 1939 epic *Gunga Din*.

There's also plenty of scope for exploration, either mountain biking along the dirt roads and narrow trails (the loose sand is firmest in fall after the first rains), or hiking and scrambling among the rocks. Dusk is particularly pleasant with the scent of sagebrush in the air. As a focus for your wanderings there are a couple of fairly unspectacular but photogenic natural rock arches to see. The visitor centers have rough explanatory maps, but the best is off Movie Road, just west of Lone Pine, where a ten-minute walk should find you at this eight-foot span.

In celebration of its movie heritage, the town now hosts the **Lone Pine Film Festival** (Ⓦ www.lonepinefilmfestival.org), held over Columbus Day weekend (the second weekend in October), showing only films made in the area. There are also plans for a movie museum at the corner of US-395 and Hopalong Cassidy Lane, though this may take some time to come to fruition.

Whitney Portal

Ten miles west of the Alabama Hills lies **Whitney Portal** (usually accessible May to early Nov), the eight-thousand-foot-high trailhead for hiking up Mount Whitney. Even if a full-on slog to the summit is furthest from your mind, you might appreciate a refreshing break from the valley frazzle in the cool shade of the pines and hemlocks. What's more there's a small café and general store for when you need fortifying between strolls around the trout-stocked pond, along the cascading stream, or up the Mount Whitney Trail to Lone Pine Lake (five miles round-trip; no permit required).

Manzanar War Relocation Center

Just west of US-395, twelve miles north of Lone Pine, on the former site of the most productive of the Owens Valley apple and pear orchards, stand the concrete foundations of the **MANZANAR WAR RELOCATION CENTER** (daytime access only; free; ℡760/878-2194, Ⓦ www.nps.gov/manz), where more than ten thousand Americans of Japanese descent were corralled during World War II. Considering them a threat to national security, the US government uprooted whole families and confiscated all their property; they were released at the end of the war, though claims for compensation were only settled in 1988, when the government agreed to pay damages amounting to millions of dollars and, finally, offered an official apology. Ringed by barbed wire, the one-square-mile camp was filled with row upon row of wooden barracks but, as part of an agreement with the landowner, everything was razed when the camp was closed in late 1945. Now only a couple of pagoda-like sentry posts, an auditorium, and a small cemetery remain among the sagebrush and scraggy cottonwoods. As the bronze plaque on the guardhouse says: "May the injustices and humiliation suffered here as a result of hysteria, racism and economic exploitation never emerge again." This was a sentiment shared by

Climbing up to the 14,497-foot **summit** of Mount Whitney is a real challenge: it's a very strenuous, 22-mile round-trip, made especially difficult by the lack of oxygen in the rarefied air of what is the highest point in the 48 contiguous states (see advice on Acute Mountain Sickness in Basics, p.55). Vigorous hikers starting before dawn from the 8365-foot trailhead can be up and back before dark, but a couple of days spent acclimatizing up here is advisable, and the whole experience is enhanced by camping out at least one night along the route. The trail gains over a mile in elevation, cutting up past alpine lakes to boulder-strewn Trail Crest Pass – the southern end of the 211-mile John Muir Trail that heads north to Yosemite. From the pass it climbs along the clifftops, finally reaching the rounded hump of the summit itself, where a **stone cabin** serves as an emergency shelter – though not one you'd choose to be in during a lightning storm. Water is available along the first half of the route but must be filtered or treated.

Ambitious hikers with some experience of scrambling or technical rock climbing might like to tackle the **"Mountaineers' Route,"** which follows the North Fork of Lone Pine Creek, taking a more direct and much steeper (though no quicker) route to the summit past the base of the numerous rock climbs on the mountain's east face. Ropes aren't generally needed, but a head for heights is. Ask for directions and current advice at the ranger station and at the Whitney Portal store.

The **Inyo National Forest** also manages permits for various other sections of the 78,000-acre wilderness area detailed in this chapter. Except for the Whitney Trail, day-use permits are not required in the Inyo wilderness area, but a permit ($5) is needed if you want to spend the night; inquire at the Eastern Sierra Interagency Visitor Center (see below) for the ranger station nearest the region you'd like to hike. Out of season (Nov–April), self-issue permits are available at the various trailheads.

Obtaining permits

Such is the popularity of Whitney, that from May to October **overnight hikers** must obtain a permit ($15 reservation fee) through the Whitney Zone **lottery**, which takes place in February. Dates in July, August, and September (the only time the trail is completely free of snow) fill up fast, so May (when you may need an ice axe), June, and October (when there may be some snow on the ground) are better bets. Day hikers also require a permit but a different quota is used and it may be easier to get a place, though you should seriously consider your ability and fitness.

Apply for an overnight or day-use **wilderness permit** by phone, fax, or mail through Inyo National Forest Wilderness Permit Office, 873 N Main St, Bishop, CA 93514 (T760/873-2483, F760/-873-2484, Wwww.r5.fs.fed.us/inyo), making sure it is postmarked or dated in February. Application forms can be downloaded from the website. If you're not that organized (or miss out) your best shot is to hope for a cancellation. Starting from May 1 you can apply for any spaces at least two days before your planned ascent; check availability on the website. Free **last minute permits** can be obtained from the Mount Whitney Ranger Station (see above) a day in advance of your planned ascent at 11am: avoid weekends when demand is highest. Overnight hikers are also required to pack their food in a **bear-resistant food canister** which can be rented from the ranger station ($5 per trip) and local sporting goods stores.

Once armed with a permit, hikers should drive to Whitney Portal or catch the shuttle bus service; Inyo Trailhead Transportation (T760/876-0035) is the current concessionaire but that frequently changes. Day hikers will want to **camp** at the first-come-first-served *Whitney Portal Trailhead* campground ($6) ready for an early start. Overnight hikers have more leisure and can plan to hike to one of two designated campgrounds (both first-come-first-served and free): *Outpost Camp* at 3.8 miles and *Trail Camp* at 6.2 miles.

many at the time, and photographer **Ansel Adams** (see box, p.426) spent several weeks here in 1943 depicting the prisoners as industrious and loyal Americans. Some of the former internees return each year, on the last Saturday in April, in a kind of pilgrimage. They often leave mementos on a kind of cenotaph in the cemetery, which is inscribed with Japanese characters meaning "soul-consoling tower."

Manzanar has recently been taken over by the National Park Service which has staff on site to help interpret the limited remains. You can take an **Auto Tour** around the camp (pick up a leaflet by the gate) and there are seasonal **walking tours** (mid-June to Sept Thurs–Sun; free), for which you'll need to meet at the main entrance. Currently there are thirty-minute tours at 8.15am and 11am, and a ninety-minute version at 9am. The auditorium is now being restored and turned into an interpretive centre and museum and is due for completion sometime late in 2003.

Independence and around

Six miles north of Manzanar, the sleepy town of **INDEPENDENCE** takes its heroic name not from any great libertarian tradition but from a Civil War fort that was founded north of the town on the Fourth of July, 1862. Every year on that day, there's a parade down Main Street (US-395) followed by a mass barbecue and fireworks show in **Dehy Park**, along tree-shaded Independence Creek on the north side of town. The park is marked by a large steam locomotive, which once ran from here to Nevada on narrow gauge tracks and is now being gussied up again.

The main reason to stop is to visit the **Eastern California Museum** at 155 N Grant St (daily except Tues 10am–4pm; donation; ℡760/878-0364), three blocks west of the porticoed County Courthouse, which contains an evocative and affecting exhibit about Manzanar, detailing the experiences of many of the young children who were held there. In the absence of any remaining barracks at the site, the museum has reconstructed part of a family-sized unit, and also holds an extensive collection of evocative photos of camp life (not always on show) taken by Toyo Miyatake, who was interned at Manzanar and managed to smuggle in a lens and film holders.

The museum also has displays on the region's history, from native Paiute basketry to old mining and farming equipment, and on the natural environment of the Owens Valley, including the **California bighorn sheep**, a protected species which inhabits the mountains to the west of Independence. Nimble creatures that roam around the steep, rocky slopes and sport massive, curling horns, they now number only around a hundred and fifty, and efforts to establish new populations are thwarted by appreciative mountain lions who promptly eat them.

Outside the museum, there's a reconstructed pioneer village made up of old buildings from all over the Owens Valley that have been brought together and restored, and a fledgling Native Plant Garden along Independence Creek.

Practicalities

If you're in the anti-camping camp, Independence offers a few **places to stay** indoors. Try the inexpensive *Independence Courthouse Motel* at 157 N Edwards St (℡760/878-2732 or 1-800/801-0703; economy ❶, queen ❷), or the *Winnedumah Hotel*, 211 N Edwards St (℡760/878-2040, ⓦwww.winnedumah .com; B&B ❸, hostel rooms ❶, dorms $18), once a film-star haven that has retained its 1920s atmosphere, especially in the comfy lounge, which comes decorated with native crafts. The hotel doubles as an HI-AYH **hostel** with fairly basic facilities and the option of a continental breakfast ($4), which is otherwise included. There are also rooms at *Wilder House*, 325 Dusty Lane, off US-395, two miles north (☎1-888/313-0151 or 760/878-2119, ⓦwww.wilderhouse.com; ❹), with three suites, heated pool, hot tub, and German-style dinners and breakfasts. There's also the *Independence Creek* campground ($6) three miles west of town on Onion Valley Road.

For **food** stop by *Mair's Market*, or make for *Rock 'n' Rhino*, 123 N Edwards St (☎760/878 0052), easily the liveliest place in town and with a surprising urban air for somewhere so rural. Call in for espresso coffee and a deli sandwich or full meals of gourmet pizza, or hang out in the garden sipping microbrews and wine into the night. The *Pines Café*, across the street, has simpler diner fare.

Around Independence

West from Independence, the minor Onion Valley Road twists up the mountains to **Onion Valley**, fifteen miles away. Once there, you'll find the Onion Valley **campground** (June–Sept; $11; ☎1-877/444-6777) and a trailhead for **hiking** across the Sierra Nevada into Kings Canyon National Park, a sixteen-mile journey over Kearsage Pass to Cedar Grove (see p.402). This is the easiest and shortest route across the Sierra and you can get the required **wilderness permit** from the Inyo National Forest Wilderness Reservation Service (see box on p.345) or, offseason, at the trailhead.

On the opposite side of the Owens Valley, a small blip on the Inyo Mountains ridgeline turns out to be a seventy-foot-high granite monolith known as **Winnedumah**. Sacred to the local Paiute, it is apparently the body of a brave who was turned to stone when an enemy warrior yelled "Winnedumah," or "stand right where you are." He awaits release by the Great Spirit. An exhausting full-day boulder-hopping hike will get you to the rock: pick up instructions from the Eastern California Museum (see opposite).

Ten miles north of Independence is the actual start of the **LA Aqueduct**, though the waters that flow into it have been channeled through a long pipe from around Mono Lake. Follow any of the dirt tracks that head east from US-395 and you can't fail to spot the traces of the railroads built to haul in the material needed to construct the great ditch – which Space Shuttle astronauts claim to have seen while orbiting the globe.

Twenty miles north of Independence, the **Tinemaha Wildlife Viewpoint** warrants a brief pause to see if you can spot any of the five-hundred-strong herd of **tule elk**, now-protected California natives which were nearly wiped out by the end of the nineteenth century. A few dozen were relocated here from the San Joaquin Valley in 1914, and they seem to be thriving.

Big Pine and around

The town of **BIG PINE** is slightly larger than Independence, 28 miles south, but it doesn't have much more in the way of services. It does, however, act as a gateway to three of the most impressive natural phenomena in California: the **Palisade Glacier** in the Sierra Nevada to the west of town; the ancient Bristlecone Pine Forest in the barren **White Mountains** to the east; and the northern reaches of Death Valley, in particular the Eureka Sand Dunes (see p.335) and the hot springs of the Saline Valley (see p.337).

Just off US-395 some eight miles north of Big Pine, there's a worthwhile diversion to **Keough's Hot Springs**, Keough's Hot Springs Road (daily except Tues 11am–7pm; $7; ☎760/872-4670), a mineral-water-fed swimming pool and hot soaking pool that was once the social center of the region and is being progressively restored. A couple of hundred yards before the springs' entrance a dirt road cuts north to some natural hot springs where locals have created a couple of clothing-optional bathing pools.

Practicalities

Information about all these can be gleaned from the **visitor center**, 126 S Main St (daily 8am–4.30pm; ☏760/938-2114, ⊛www.bigpine.com). There are a couple of good value **motels** along US-395 - the *Big Pine Motel*, 370 S Main St (☏760/938-2282; ➊), and the slightly nicer *Starlight Motel*, 511 S Main St (☏760/938-2011, ℻938-2525; ➋), which has HBO and a little patio. There is also the *Glacier View* **campground** (tents $14, hook-up $17) half a mile north of town at the junction of Hwy-168, and several more camping spots up Glacier Lodge Road (see below). Good diner **food** is available at the *Country Kitchen*, 181 S Main St, almost opposite the visitor center.

The White Mountains

Rising to the east of Big Pine, the intimidating **WHITE MOUNTAINS** are effectively an alpine desert: bald, dry, and little-visited, yet almost as high as the Sierra. The range is made up of some of the oldest, fossil-filled rock in California and geologically has more in common with the Great Basin to the east than the spiky Sierra, which came into being several hundred million years later. It looks like it too: the scrubby, undulating high country appears more Scottish than Californian. The mountains are accessible only by car (or bike) via Hwy-168. Be sure to fill up on gas and **drinking water**, both of which are unavailable east of US-395.

The gnarled trees that are the prime reason for coming here stand on the lower slopes in the ancient **Bristlecone Pine Forest**, but snow renders them inaccessible for all but three or four months in the summer. **Schulman Grove** ($2 per person or $5 per car) is the most accessible collection, some 23 miles from Big Pine along a paved road that twists up from Hwy-168. The grove is split up into two self-guided nature trails. One, the mile-long Discovery Trail, passes by a number of splendid examples; the other, longer Methuselah Trail loops around past the oldest tree, the 4700-year-old Methuselah, though you'll have to guess which of the trees it is since it is unmarked due to fears of vandalism. Both trails start at the **visitor center** (late May–Aug Wed–Sun 10am–4pm; Sept and Oct Sat & Sun 10am–4pm; ☏760/873-2500) which explains the importance of the grove's namesake, Dr Edmund Schulman. An early practitioner of dendrochronology, he revealed the extreme age of these trees in the mid-1950s and applied the knowledge gained from core samples of the trees to correct a puzzling error in early carbon-dating techniques. It turned out that artifacts from the Balkans, previously thought of as stylistic variations on Middle Eastern wares, were in fact a thousand years older, so changing our perception of history. If you want to know more, show up at one of the free ranger talks scheduled frequently through July and August, plus there is usually a ranger-led walk on Saturdays.

Patriarch Grove, twelve miles further on, along a dusty dirt road that gives spectacular views of the Sierra Nevada to the west and the Great Basin ranges of the deserts to the east, contains the Patriarch Tree, the largest of the bristlecone pines. Four miles beyond here, a research station (closed to the public) studies the physiology of high-altitude plant and animal life, which is in many ways similar to that of the arctic regions. From here you can **hike to the summit of White Mountain** (15 miles round-trip; 6–8 hr; 2500ft ascent), the highest point in the range, and at 14,246 feet the third highest in California,

Bristlecone pines

Great Basin **bristlecone pines** (*pinus longaeva*) are the oldest known living things on earth. Some of them have been alive for over 4500 years (1500 years more than any sequoia), earning them a place in the *Guinness Book of Records*. The oldest examples cling to thin alkaline soils (predominantly dolomite) between 10,000 and 11,000 feet, where the low precipitation keeps the growing season to only 45 days a year. But such conditions, which limit the trees' girth expansion to an inch every hundred years, promotes the dense resin-rich and rot-resistant wood that lasts for millennia. Battered and beaten by the harsh environment into bizarrely beautiful shapes and forms, they look like nothing so much as twenty-foot lumps of drift-wood. The most photogenic examples comprise mostly **dead wood**, the live section often sustained by a thin ribbon of bark. Even when dead, the wind-scoured trunks and twisted limbs hang on without decaying for upwards of another thousand-odd years, slowly being eroded by wind-driven ice and sand.

Bristlecones thrive at lower altitudes and richer soils than those in the White Mountains, growing tall and wide. But they seldom live as long as specimens subjected to the harsher conditions and, in fact, they're hardly recognizable as bristlecone pines, only the five-needle bundles and the egg-shaped, barbed cone which lends the tree its name giving the game away.

For more information, consult the Inyo Forest website at ⓦwww.r5.fs.fed.us/inyo or better still the excellent ⓦwww.sonic.net/bristlecone.

though local boosters like to claim that recent satellite measurements suggest it may just top Whitney in the altitude stakes. A gate prevents unauthorized vehicles from getting to the research station, though all-terrain **mountain bikes** are permitted to continue. In fact, the canyons running down from the ridge between the bristlecone groves are tailor-made for thrill-seekers, who race down the steep washes at incredibly high speeds.

There is **camping** available, but no water; the only campground is 8600ft up at *Grandview* (May–Oct; free), two miles south of Schulman Grove. Backcountry camping is not permitted in the ancient Bristlecone Pine Forest, but is allowed in the surrounding forest provided you have a campfire permit for your stove. The ranger station in Bishop can provide this and tell you which springs and small creeks (if any) are flowing.

The Palisade Glacier

The **PALISADE GLACIER** is the southernmost glacier in the US and the largest in California. It sits at the foot of the impressive Palisade Crest, center of one of the greatest concentrations of enjoyable alpine climbing in the Eastern Sierra: Norman Clyde Peak in the south is named after California's most prolific early mountaineer; the immense bulk of Temple Crag offers a range of routes unparalleled outside of Yosemite Valley; and, to the north, Thunderbolt Peak and Mount Agassiz are highlights of the Inconsolable Range. The Palisade Glacier itself is an excellent introduction to snow and ice climbing.

Hikers not suitably equipped for (or skilled at) technical climbing can still get a sense of this wondrous area by hiking from the trailhead at Big Pine Canyon, ten miles west of Big Pine at the end of Glacier Lodge Road; follow Crocker Street in Big Pine. July, August, and September are the best (snow-free) months for hiking, best done along the trail to **First Lake** (9 miles round-trip; 5–7hr; 2300ft ascent). From here there is a network of shorter trails to six more lakes and one to the **base of the Palisade Glacier** (18 miles round-trip from the parking lot; 10–12hr; 4600ft ascent). Backcountry campers must obtain a **permit** (see box on p.341).

At the trailhead, you'll find three **campgrounds** (late April–Oct; $13) – Sage Flat, Upper Sage Flat, and Big Pine Creek – all above 7000ft and with water and toilets; and the free *First Falls* walk-in site at 8200ft, a mile beyond the trailhead. *Glacier Lodge* (℡760/938-2837, ⓦwww.jewelofthesierra.com; ❹), right at the end of the road, is a slightly more luxurious option, with cabins, RV parking ($15–18), overnight parking for hikers ($3), a limited general store, and showers ($4).

Bishop

BISHOP, fifteen miles north of Big Pine, rivals Mammoth Lakes as the **outdoor pursuits** capital of the Eastern Sierra. It may not have downhill skiing on its doorstep but its proximity to the wilderness makes it an excellent base from which to explore the surrounding mountains; if you want to try cross-country skiing, fly-fishing, and especially rock climbing, there's no better place to be, with some of the world's best mountaineers offering their services through lessons and guided trips. With an urban population of 3500 and several thousand more in outlying districts, it is the largest town in the Owens Valley, yet maintains a laid-back ambience which makes it worth hanging around to enjoy. There's even a real town center, though the pleasure of strolling through it is mitigated by eighteen-wheelers thundering through.

Arrival and information

Almost everything of interest lies along Main Street (US-395) where you'll find the CREST **bus stop** at 201 S Warren St (℡760/872-1901) and the main **visitor center**, 690 N Main St (Mon–Fri 9am–5pm, Sat & Sun 10am–4pm; ℡760/873-8405 or 1-888/395-3952, ⓦwww.bishopvisitor.com), which hands out a comprehensive town visitor guide. For specific information on **hiking** and **camping** in the area, contact the **White Mountain Ranger Station**, 798 N Main St (June–Sept daily 8am–5pm; Oct–May Mon–Fri 8am–4.30pm; ℡760/873-2500), which also issues the first-come-first-served wilderness permits.

Accommodation

There's a reasonable range of **accommodation** for which booking in advance is advised on summer weekends (especially during **festivals**; see "Listings" below). There are campgrounds in town (see below), and plenty of Inyo National Forest sites all around.

Best Western Creekside Inn 725 N Main St ℡760/872-3044 or 1-800/273-3550. Modern upscale hotel in the center of town offering large rooms (some with kitchenette), complimentary breakfast, and an outdoor pool. ❻

Brown's Town Campground Schober Lane, off US-395, a mile south of town ℡760/873-8522. Large Old West-themed RV and tent campground with a pool, kids' play area, and other facilities, and costing $14 for tents and up to $19 for full hook-up.

Chalfant House 213 Academy St ℡760/872-1790 or 1-800/641-2996, ⓦwww.chalfanthouse.com. Antique-filled Victorian-era B&B just off the 200 block of North Main Street. Rooms all have private bath, ceiling fans, and a/c, and there's full

gourmet breakfast. ❺

El Rancho Motel 274 W Lagoon St ℡760/872-9251 or 1-888/872-9251. Well-maintained budget motel on the south side of town with cable TV, ceiling fans, and some rooms with kitchenette. Popular with fishers, so book well in advance for weekends. ❸

Thunderbird Motel 190 W Pine St ℡760/873-4215, ⓕ760/873-6870. Basic motel just off Main Street with continental breakfast included. ❷

Joseph House Inn 376 W Yaney St ℡760-872-3389, ⓦwww.395.com/josephhouse. Upscale B&B in three acres of gardens with nicely decorated rooms, full gourmet breakfast, and cheese and crackers on arrival. Two-night minimum at weekends. ❼

The Town

Specific sights in town are few, though anyone interested in gorgeous images of the Sierra, Owens Valley and beyond should pay a visit to **Mountain Light Gallery**, 106 S Main St at Line Street (Mon–Thurs 9am–6pm, Fri–Sun 10am–9pm; free; ☎760/873-7700, ⓦ www.mountainlight.com), where you can see works by Galen Rowell, one of the world's foremost landscape photojournalists until his untimely death in a plane crash in 2002. Also a talented rock climber and mountaineer, Rowell photographed the region for over thirty years and extended his oeuvre to Patagonia, the Himalayas, northern Canada, Alaska, Antarctica, and elsewhere. You'll have to part with well over $500 to obtain one of the large-scale framed photos that line the walls, but it is well worth half an hour's browsing.

You should also drive a mile or so west to the **Paiute-Shoshone Indian Cultural Museum**, 2301 W Line St (Mon–Fri 9am–5pm, Sat & Sun 9am–4pm; $4; ☎760/873-9478), run by local natives who mostly live on a reservation on the edge of town, similar to those found outside each of the Valley settlements. Here, they put on displays of basketry and weaving, food gathering and processing, and of traditional ways of building; they also run a good bookstore. Their ancestors once roamed the area and left their mark all over the Owens Valley in the form of petroglyphs, the best examples of which are found a few miles outside town (see p.349).

Outdoor activities

Outdoor enthusiasts congregate in Bishop, their rigs laden with tents, sleeping bags, mountain bikes, rock-climbing gear, fishing tackle, crampons, and ice axes.

All year round there is somewhere to **rock climb**: in winter the sport climbs of the Owens River Gorge (see p.349) see a good deal of traffic, as do bouldering areas such as the nearby Happy Boulders and the Buttermilk Boulders (see below). As the daytime temperature pushes a hundred, climbers decamp to the High Sierra peaks, particularly Rock Creek, about twenty miles north of Bishop, and Tuolumne in Yosemite (see p.427). For more information, visit Wilson's Eastside Sports, 224 N Main St (☎760/873-7520, ⓦ www.eastsidesports.com), an excellent mountaineering and sporting goods supply shop with gear rental and a climbers' notice board.

Much more of the money that flows into Bishop comes from the brigades of fishing enthusiasts, who spend their summer vacations angling for rainbow trout placed in the streams and lakes by the state government. When the high country lakes and streams are still frozen or inaccessible there's still good fishing around Bishop, though the main trout season generally runs from late April to late October. As a taster of things to come, the Blake Jones Trout Derby takes place in mid-March at the Pleasant Valley Reservoir, six miles north along US-395; then there's a huge assembly of fisherfolk on the last Saturday in April around **Crowley Lake**, an artificial reservoir built to hold water diverted from Mono Lake, thirty miles north of town.

Eating and drinking

With a huge 24-hour Vons store at 1190 N Main St, and a number of good cafés and diners, Bishop is a good place to feast after a few days in the hills and to buy **food** and **supplies** for the next leg.

Amigo's Mexican Restaurant 285 N Main St ☎760/872-2189. Mainstream Mexican with a good range of Tex-Mex staples at good prices.
Erick Schat's Bakkery 736 N Main St

☎760/873-7156. Huge and bustling pseudo-Dutch bakery which has been making their "Original Sheepherder Bread" since early in the twentieth century. There are dozens of other varieties – multigrain, sourdough, etc – and tables for tucking into their sandwiches ($8) and cakes. **Jack's Restaurant and Bakery** 437 N Main St. Well-regarded diner that bakes its own bread, used in their extensive range of burgers and sandwiches. Leave space for a plate of their locally famous waffles or a slice of fruit pie. Open from 6am for breakfast.

Kava Coffeehouse 206 N Main St ☎760/872-1010. Hip, central café serving some of Bishop's best coffee and muffins plus tasty breakfasts from 7am and sandwiches, melts, and quiche (all around $7) later on. There's also fast Internet access, an open mic night every second Wednesday, and chess on Tuesday evenings.

Whiskey Creek 524 N Main St ☎760/873-7174. Among Bishop's more upscale restaurants with a sunny deck and an attached bar (where you can also eat) serving Whiskey Creek microbrews. Maybe start with lime-, garlic-, and tequila-glazed tiger prawns ($9) and follow with ribs or halibut ($17) and a deep-dish boysenberry pie ($5).

Listings

Climbing and hiking guides For expert instruction or guided rock climbing, alpine climbing, and ski mountaineering contact: John Fischer Mountain Guide (☎760/873-5037, pescador@qnet.com); Nidever Mountain Guides (760/648-8274, ⓦ www.themountainguide.com); Sierra Mountain Center, 174 W Line St (☎760/873-8526, ⓦ www.sierramountaincenter.com); Sierra Mountain Guides (☎760/872-3811, Ⓕ872-3811, ⓦ www.cosleyhouston.com); or Sierra Mountaineering International, 235 N Main St (☎760/872-4929, ⓦ www.sierramountaineering.com).

Festivals Bishop comes alive over Memorial Day weekend for Mule Days (☎760/872-4263, ⓦ www.muledays.org), with a huge parade, mule-drawn chariot racing, a county hoe down, arts and crafts fair and much more. The Tri-County Fair over Labor Day weekend includes a Wild West Rodeo.

Library 210 Academy St (☎760/873-5115) has speedy **Internet access** and is open Mon–Thurs 10am–8pm, Fri 10am–6pm, Sat 10am–1pm.

Medical treatment Northern Inyo Hospital, 150 Pioneer Lane (☎760/873-5811) has 24hr emergency and intensive care.

Movies Bishop Twin Theatre, 237 N Main St, shows the latest Hollywood offerings.

Post Office 595 W Line St (☎760/873-3526). For general delivery use zip code 93514.

Showers and laundry Hikers and backcountry campers in need of a shower can get one at South Lake at *Bishop Creek Lodge* (see below). In Bishop there are showers at the Bishop City Pool, 688 N Main St (late May–early Sept Mon–Sat 7am–8pm), and showers and laundry at the Wash Tub, 236 Warren St (daily 7am–9pm).

Around Bishop and north towards Mammoth

You may well stay and eat in Bishop, but the main attractions lie outside town, either west along South Lake Road, which runs to a Sierra trailhead, north onto the so-called volcanic tablelands to see native petroglyphs, north towards the Owens River Gorge.

If you don't have your own vehicle, you can still access the surrounding area using Kountry Korners (☎760/872-4411 or 1-877/656-0756) and Inyo Trailhead Transportation (☎760/876-0035), which effectively operate as trailhead taxi services and charge according to distance and numbers.

West along Hwy-168

Hwy-168 runs west from Bishop past the Paiute-Shoshone Indian Cultural Center and climbs some fifteen miles through aspens and cottonwoods to a cluster of alpine lakes and 10,000-foot trailheads.

Roughly six miles west of Bishop a small dirt Buttermilk Road runs northwest into an arid land of lumpy hills and large golden granite rocks known as the **Buttermilk Boulders**. Year-round, rock climbers travel the state to pit themselves against an almost limitless selection of low-lying boulder problems in a beautiful location. Visit Wilson's Eastside Sports (see above) for details and guidebooks.

Hwy-168 ends at the dammed **Lake Sabrina**, where there's a restaurant that sells fishing tackle and rents boats. Nearby, **South Lake**, also nineteen miles from Bishop, is flanked by *Bishop Creek Lodge* (☏760/873-4484, ⓦwww .bishopcreekresorts.com; ❺), with a general store, fishing shop, boat rentals, cabins, and $2 public showers. A number of **hiking routes** set off up into the High Sierra wilderness from trailheads at these lakes. The trail from South Lake over Bishop Pass heads into Dusy Basin, where you can see the effects of centuries of glaciation in the bowl-like cirques and giant "erratic" boulders left by receding glaciers. Another path follows the northern fork of Bishop Creek under the rusty cliffs of the Paiute Crags, before climbing over Paiute Pass into the Desolation Lakes area of the John Muir Wilderness. There are a number of **campgrounds** between 7500 and 9000 feet up – almost all with water and costing $14 a night. The shady *Sabrina* site, right by the lake of the same name, is perhaps the best.

Laws and the Red Rock Canyon petroglyphs

On the northern edge of Bishop, US-395 divides from US-6, which runs north and east into Nevada. Four miles along US-6 is the **Laws Railroad Museum** (daily 10am–4pm; donation; ⓦwww.thesierraweb.com/bishop /laws), a handful of relocated old buildings and a slender black train known as the "Slim Princess" arranged in the restored old town of **LAWS**. From 1883 to 1959 this was an important way station on the narrow-gauge Carson and Colorado Railroad, which ran along the eastern side of the Owens Valley from Carson City to the northern shores of Owens Lake, just south of Lone Pine.

Northwest of Laws a stark desert plateau harbors the **Red Rock Canyon Petroglyphs**, where ancient native peoples have carved mysterious designs – spirals, geometric forms, even spacey figures – onto the rocks. Many beautiful examples exist, but several have been vandalized (and even stolen) over the years, so to help protect them the Bureau of Lands Management, in conjunction with the native owners, require visitors to sign in at the BLM, Suite E, 785 N Main St in Bishop (Mon–Fri 8.30am–4pm; ☏760/872-4881). There are no permits, fees, or gates to open, but they'll give you a map that pinpoints three petroglyph concentrations, the most interesting being Red Rock Canyon.

North along US-395

Around ten miles north of Bishop, US-395 starts climbing the **Sherwin Grade**, twelve miles of steady climbing which brings you from 4000 feet to the 6500-foot **Mono Basin**. As you climb the grade, Power Plant Road heads off on the right to the precipitously steep **Owens River Gorge**, another excellent rock-climbing spot in an area which until recently was completely dry. Since 1994, the Los Angeles Department of Water and Power has been forced to allow water to flow down the gorge and the flora and fauna are slowly returning along with trout fishers and hikers.

Mammoth Lakes and around

MAMMOTH LAKES, forty miles north of Bishop, and the associated skiing, snowboarding, and mountain biking hot spot of **Mammoth Mountain**, jointly make up the Eastern Sierra's biggest resort, and one that is only challenged in California by those around Lake Tahoe. During the winter months, masses of weekend skiers speed through the Owens Valley on their way to some of the state's premiere pistes, which rise above this pine-shrouded town. It is for this and the summer fishing that Mammoth is traditionally known, although the town is now increasingly hyped for its accessible mountain-biking terrain and a number of on- and off-road bike races.

Despite its popularity with LA weekenders, Mammoth has always been a fairly low-key resort, but that is rapidly changing as corporate resort owner, Intrawest, gears up to propel Mammoth into the ranks of the winter sports mega-resorts like those at Vail in the Rockies, and Whistler/Blackcomb in Canada. Intrawest is now the majority owner of the ski operation and large chunks of Mammoth real estate, and is pushing ahead with what they like to call the "**Mammoth Renaissance**." Already there's a new Village at Mammoth on Minaret Road, full of swanky stores and linked to the mountain by the new Village Gondola. Lots of new lodging has been built along with Mammoth's second golf course, and Intrawest is lobbying hard for a much expanded airport, which may soon see flights from San Jose, LAX, and may later receive American Airlines flights from Dallas and Chicago.

Residents are torn between enthusiasm for the new opportunities presented and nostalgia for the way things used to be, but for the moment Mammoth remains unbeatable for outdoor activities and is scenically as dramatic as just about anywhere in the Sierra. You may find the testosterone overload oppressive and the town overpriced, but it is easy to escape to the hills during the day and return each evening to good food, lively bars, and even a couple of movie theaters.

Arrival and information

Hwy-203 runs three miles west from US-395 into the town of Mammoth Lakes, from where it continues six miles to the base station for Mammoth Mountain, then ascends the San Joaquin Ridge and drops down to the Devil's Postpile National Monument.

Year-round **CREST buses** (see p.325) stop three times a week in the McDonald's parking lot on Hwy-203. There's also a seasonal **YARTS service** to Tuolumne Meadows and Yosemite Valley (July & Aug daily; June & Sept Sat & Sun only; Ⓦ www.yarts.com) which departs from *Mammoth Mountain Inn* at 7am and returns that evening. In the ski season, get around on the five-route **Mammoth Shuttle** which goes everywhere you'll want to. During the warmer months, **rent a bike** (see "Listings," p.358), and make use of the summer **shuttle** which plies a route between the main ski lodge and Devil's Postpile National Monument, some fifteen miles west of town.

The best source of practical information for the area is the combined US Forest Service and Mammoth Lakes **visitor center** (daily 8am–5pm; Ⓣ 760/924-5501, Ⓦ www.visitmammoth.com) on the main highway half a mile east of the town center.

Accommodation

About every second building in Mammoth is a condo, but there are numerous other **accommodation** opportunities (including a hostel), so beds are at a premium only during ski-season weekends. Winter prices are highest, summer rates (quoted here, and still fairly high) come next, and in between some relative bargains can be found. If you fancy staying in a **condo** try contacting Mammoth Mountain Reservations (Ⓣ 760/934-5000 or 1-800/462-5577, Ⓦ www.mammothres.com).

There is also mile upon mile of backcountry (see "Hiking" box, p.355) in which to pitch a tent, and plenty of family sites with campers almost

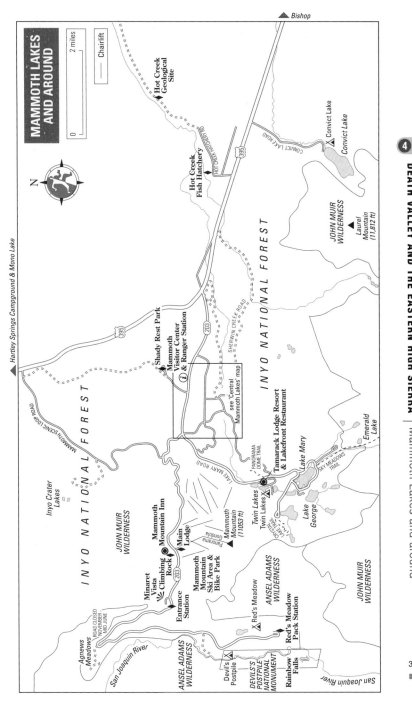

MAMMOTH LAKES
AND AROUND

Chairlift

0   2 miles

▲ *Bishop*

N

▲ *Hartley Springs Campground & Mono Lake*

Hot Creek
Geological
Site

Hot Creek
Fish Hatchery

395

HOT CREEK HATCHERY RD

CONVICT LAKE ROAD

Convict Lake
✕ Convict Lake

JOHN MUIR
WILDERNESS

Laurel
Mountain
(11,812 ft)

INYO NATIONAL FOREST

MAMMOTH SCENIC LOOP ROAD

Inyo Crater
Lakes

JOHN MUIR
WILDERNESS

Minaret
Vista ⛰ Climbing
Rock

Mammoth
Mountain Inn
● Main
Lodge

203

Shady Rest Park
Mammoth
Visitor Center
ⓘ & Ranger Station

395

203

SHERWIN CREEK ROAD

see 'Central
Mammoth Lakes map'

Tamarack Lodge Resort
& Lakefront Restaurant

INYO NATIONAL FOREST

PANORAMA
DOME TRAIL

LAKE MARY ROAD

Lake Mary

Emerald
Lake

SKY MEADOWS TRAIL

Panorama Gondola

Mammoth
Mountain
(11053 ft) ▲

Twin Lakes
Twin Lakes ✕

Lake George

CRYSTAL LAKE TRAIL

Mammoth
Mountain Ski Area &
Bike Park

Entrance
Station

ROAD CLOSED
NOVEMBER -
MID JUNE

Agnews
Meadows

San Joaquin River

ANSEL ADAMS
WILDERNESS

ANSEL ADAMS
WILDERNESS

✕ Red's Meadow

Red's Meadow
Pack Station

JOHN MUIR
WILDERNESS

✕ Devil's
Postpile

DEVIL'S
POSTPILE
NATIONAL
MONUMENT

Rainbow
Falls

San Joaquin River

4

DEATH VALLEY AND THE EASTERN HIGH SIERRA | Mammoth Lakes and around

Mammoth Lakes and around

351

overwhelmed by choice. There are some twenty **campgrounds** within a ten-mile radius of town; the two main concentrations being around Twin Lakes and along the Devil's Postpile–Red's Meadow road. Almost all come with water, cost $13–15, and are let on a first-come-first-served basis. The Inyo National Forest Mammoth Lakes visitor guide (available free from the visitor center) has full details along with rules for free dispersed camping on national forest lands around about.

Motels, B&Bs, and condos

Cinnamon Bear Inn 113 Center St ☏ 760/934-2873 or 1-800/845-2873, ⓦ www.cinnamon-bearinn.com. Reasonably priced, 22-room B&B inn close to downtown with comfortable rooms, all with TV and phone (and some with VCR), use of hot tub, wine-and-nibbles happy hour on arrival, and a full breakfast. Midweek ❹, weekends ❺

Davison Street Guest House Hostel 19 Davison St ☏ 760/924-2188, ⓔ davison@mammoth-guest.com, ⓦ www.mammoth-guest.com. Wooden A-frame chalet with mountain views, and about the closest thing to a hostel that Mammoth has. There's a spacious lounge, good communal cooking facilities, four-bed rooms (summer $50, winter weekdays $58, winter weekends $68), and dorm bunks ($18, $22, $28). ❶–❸

Mammoth Country Inn 75 Joaquin Rd ☏ 760/934-2710 or 1-866/934-2710, ⓦ www.mammothcountryinn.com. Welcoming and good-value B&B in a quiet neighborhood with seven recently renovated and tastefully themed rooms, all with private baths and some with Jacuzzis. There's wine and hors d'oeuvres on arrival, and full and delicious breakfasts. Weekend ❺, midweek ❹

Mammoth Mountain Inn 1 Minaret Rd ☏ 760/934-2581 or 1-800/626-6684, ⓦ www.mammothmountain.com. The place to stay if you need to be right at the foot of the ski tows and adjacent to the bike park. Its run-of-the-mill hotel rooms are a touch sterile, but you'll be well looked after and there are bars and restaurants on site. Some rooms come with microwave and fridge, while condos are fully fixtured. Winter rates are one price code higher. Rooms ❺–❻, condos ❼

Mammoth Mountain RV Park Hwy-203 ☏ 760/934-3822, ⓦ www.gocampingamerica.com. Year-round fully featured RV park right in town opposite the visitor center, with indoor spas, kids' play areas, tent sites ($18), and a range of full hook-up sites ($25–30).

Shilo Inn 2963 Main St ☏ 760/934-4500 or 1-800/222-2244, ⓦ www.shiloinns.com. Comfortable seventy-room motel in the heart of Mammoth Lakes, with gym, indoor pool, spa,

sauna, cable TV, coffeemakers, and complimentary breakfast. ❺–❻

Sierra Nevada Rodeway Inn 164 Old Mammoth Rd ☏ 760/934-2515 or 1-800/824-5132, ⓦ www.mammothsnri.com. At the budget end of Mammoth motels but still with large comfy rooms, pool, spa, and sauna, and on-site restaurant. Weekends ❺, midweek ❹

Snowcreek Resort Old Mammoth Rd, by the golf course ☏ 760/934-4445 or 1-800/545-4499, ⓦ www.snowcreek.com. Well-appointed condos with a two-night minimum stay, substantial spring and fall discounts, and use of the pool, spa, and tennis club. Especially good value for groups. ❻

Swiss Chalet Lodge 3776 Viewpoint Rd ☏ 760/934-2403 or 1-800/937-9477, ⓦ www.mammoth-swisschalet.com. Plain rooms with TV and phone in an aging but recently remodelled place that's one of the few low-cost establishments in Mammoth with mountain views, especially from the upper floor. Also a good sauna, a large indoor hot tub with views, and a reception desk full of cuckoo clocks. Weekends ❹, midweek ❸

Tamarack Lodge & Resort Lake Mary Rd ☏ 760/934-2442 or 1-800/626-6684, ⓦ www.tamaracklodge.com. Lodge rooms (❹–❼) or rustic cabins (❻–❾) with fully-equipped kitchens, beautifully situated beside Twin Lake right on the edge of a cross-country ski area. ❹–❾

Camping and RVs

Convict Lake (late-April to Oct; $15; 7600ft). Wooded, lakeside National Forest campground just west of US-395 around four miles south of the Mammoth turnoff, with the longest opening season in the area. Showers are available at the nearby *Convict Lake Resort* (☏ 760/934-3800, ⓦ www.convictlake.com; $1 for two minutes).

Devil's Postpile (mid-June to mid-Oct; $15; 7600ft). National Park Service campground half a mile from the rocks themselves along the Devil's Postpile–Red's Meadow road, and a good base for hikes to Rainbow Falls or along the John Muir Trail.

Hartley Springs (June–Oct; free; 8200ft). Just one of several primitive waterless campgrounds in

the area, this one located 1.5 miles west of US-395 along Glass Flow Road around eleven miles north of the Mammoth turnoff.
New Shady Rest (mid-May to Oct; $13; 7800ft). Large and busy campground close to town, where several sites can be reserved on ☏1-877/444-6777.
Red's Meadow (mid-June to mid-Oct; $15; 7600ft). National Forest campground along the Devil's Postpile–Red's Meadow road and within easy hiking distance of Devil's Postpile, Rainbow Falls, and a nice nature trail around Sotcher Lake. It also comes with a natural hot spring bathhouse open to all (donations appreciated).
Twin Lakes (mid-May–Oct; $14; 8600ft). The longest-opening of five near-identical sites in this area of glacially scooped lake beds, a mile southwest of Mammoth Lakes township. Lakeside setting among the pines and plenty of hiking trails nearby.

Mammoth Mountain: biking, hiking, and other activities

Mammoth is all about getting into the outdoors. Aside from eating, drinking and mooching around the sports shops and factory clothing outlets, you'll find little reason to spend much time in town, though anyone interested in Mammoth's gold mining and timber milling origins may fancy a visit to the small **Mammoth Museum**, 5489 Sherwin Creek Rd (mid-June–Sept 9.30am-4.30pm; free), located in a 1920s log cabin.

There's much more fun to be had four miles west of the center up on the slopes of the dormant volcano that is **Mammoth Mountain**, where the **Panorama Gondola** (late June–Sept daily 9am–6pm; $16 round-trip) will whisk you to the top of Mammoth Mountain in eight minutes, for fine mountain views all around.

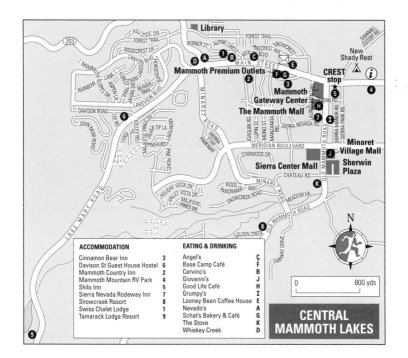

ACCOMMODATION

Cinnamon Bear Inn	3
Davison St Guest House Hostel	6
Mammoth Country Inn	2
Mammoth Mountain RV Park	4
Shilo Inn	5
Sierra Nevada Rodeway Inn	7
Snowcreek Resort	8
Swiss Chalet Lodge	1
Tamarack Lodge Resort	9

EATING & DRINKING

Angel's	C
Base Camp Café	F
Cervino's	B
Giovanni's	J
Good Life Café	H
Grumpy's	I
Looney Bean Coffee House	E
Nevado's	A
Schat's Bakery & Café	G
The Stove	K
Whiskey Creek	D

CENTRAL MAMMOTH LAKES

N

0   800 yds

If you'd rather work up a sweat there are a number of ways to do just that: mountain biking, hiking (see both below), plus stacks of people willing to get you mobile: **ballooning**, **kayaking**, and **rock climbing** are all covered in "Listings" on p.358, and **horseback riding** is discussed in the box on p.357.

Mountain biking

Once the ski runs have freed themselves of the winter snows, the slopes transform into the 3500-acre **Mammoth Mountain Bike Park** (late June–Sept daily 9am–6pm; ☎760/934-0706, ⓦwww.mammothmountain.com) with over eighty miles of groomed singletrack trails. Chairlifts quickly give you and your bike and altitude boost, allowing you to hurtle down the twisting sandy trails, brushing pines and negotiating small jumps and tree roots. The emphasis here is definitely on going downhill, and when you're transported to the rarefied eleven-thousand-foot air at the top of the chairlift you very quickly appreciate the logic of this. The bike park produces a color map of the mountain showing the lifts and trails in three grades of difficulty, and indicates X-Zones where they've created enhanced freeriding terrain for the more aggressive riders. Beginners often take the **Downtown** run into Mammoth (from where a bike shuttle bus returns you to the bike park), while those with a little more skill or ambition might opt for the **Beach Cruiser**, which carves its way down the western side of the mountain from near the summit. Experts and those with a death wish can tackle the **Kamikaze**, scene of the ultimate downhill race which has traditionally formed the centerpiece of the annual World Cup racing weekend (usually around the middle of July), at which competitors hit speeds of sixty miles per hour.

The basic **park use fee** ($10) gives you access to the trails, and you can rent bikes for $36 a day. In addition there's a complex selection of deals such as the Park Pass (one day $29, two days $53), which gives all-day access to the Panorama Gondola to the summit and the bike shuttle from town. Gondola and bike rental combos include a half-day package ($49) giving four hours' bike rental and two gondola rides, and a full-day unlimited deal ($62).

If you don't fancy forking out for use of the bike park, or just prefer some-thing a little gentler, there is plenty more **trail riding** around the resort, made comfortable by mid-summer temperatures reliably in the seventies. Several bike stores around town will point you in the right direction and rent bikes (see below) which can also be taken to the bike park. Likely candidates include: the relatively gentle Shady Rest Park, close to central Mammoth; the Lakes Basin area near *Tamarack Resort*; and Inyo and Mono craters. The visitor center offers free trail maps and a brochure on route descriptions and trail ethics.

Hiking

Interwoven among the bike trails on Mammoth Mountain are a couple of **hik-ing paths** which top out at the summit. The views are stupendous but, in com-mon with many volcanoes, the hiking isn't the best and you're better off riding the gondola to the summit (see above) and saving your legs for hikes elsewhere.

Listed in the box below are some of the best of the **short hikes** around Mammoth. No permits are required for these, though you'll need to obtain a free **wilderness permit** if you want to spend the night in the Ansel Adams or John Muir wilderness areas to the south and west. On all trailheads into the wilderness there is an overnight quota season from May to October when numbers of overnight hikers setting off from each trailhead is limited. Call the Wilderness Reservations Office in Bishop (☎760/873-2483, ⓕ873-2484, ⓦwww.r5.fs.fed.us/inyo) up to six months and at least two days in advance. There is a $5 reservation fee.

Crystal Lake (3.5 miles round-trip; 2hr; 650ft ascent). From the Lake George trail-head the path skirts high above Lake George revealing increasingly dramatic views as you climb towards Crystal Lake, hunkered below Crystal Crag. Fit hikers can tack on the Mammoth Crest Trail (a further 2.5 miles round-trip; 2–3hr; 1000ft ascent).

Panorama Dome Trail (1 mile round-trip; 30min; 100ft ascent). Great views over the town and the Owens Valley reward this short sylvan trail from Twin Lakes on Lake Mary Road (see town map p.351).

Sky Meadows (4 miles; 1.5–2hr; 1200ft ascent). Delightful hike along the wildflower-flanked Coldwater Creek past Emerald Lake to Sky Meadow at the foot of the strik-ing Blue Crag. Starts at the southern end of Lake Mary.

Devil's Postpile to Rainbow Falls (5 miles; 2hr; 300ft ascent). Moderate hike that combines the two key features of the Devil's Postpile National Monument. Start from the *Devil's Postpile* campground and stroll to the monument itself, then continue to the top of Rainbow Falls.

Fishing

There is no Mammoth Lake, but the town of Mammoth Lakes makes a great base for hooking brook, rainbow, and brown trout in the dozens of lakes all about. During the main summer season many anglers head for Mary Lake, the largest hereabouts, where you can rent boats and spend the day hooking fish in beautiful surroundings. You won't be alone, but with a little imagination it is easy enough to find a peaceful spot. Pick up information from one of the many fishing shops in town, such as Kittredge Sports, 3218 Main St (☎760/934-7566, ⓦwww.kittredgesports.com), which has a board outside giving the lat-est on the region's fishing spots along with fly and spinner advice.

The artificial **Crowley Lake** (see p.347) is also a popular spot and is just twelve miles south along US-395. For **river fishing**, the San Joaquin, over the hill near the Devil's Postpile, is a winner for those in search of trout.

Along Minaret Road: Devil's Postpile National Monument

From the ski area, the narrow and winding **Minaret Road** (typically open mid-June to Oct) climbs briefly to a nine-thousand-foot pass in the San Joaquin Ridge, then plummets into the headwaters of the Middle Fork of the San Joaquin River, ending some eight miles beyond at the Red's Meadow pack sta-tion. This is the only road access into the evocatively named **DEVIL'S POST-PILE NATIONAL MONUMENT** (day-pass $5, three-day pass $10, National Park and Golden Eagle passes not accepted), which centers on a collection of slender, blue-gray basalt columns ranged like hundreds of pencils stood on end. Some are as tall as sixty feet, others are twisted and warped; while vulnerable sections are shorter where the brittle rock has cracked and the upper sections have fallen forward to form a talus slope of shattered rubble. It was formed as lava from Mammoth Mountain cooled and fractured into multi-sided forms, a phenomenon best appreciated by skirting round to the top of the columns. The Postpile itself is a half-mile stroll from the *Devil's Postpile* campground where there is a small **visitor center** (mid-June to Oct daily; hours vary), from where rangers guide daily walks and lead evening campfire programs.

The second highlight of the National Monument is **Rainbow Falls**, where the Middle Fork of the San Joaquin River plunges 101 feet into a deep pool,

Winter and spring in Mammoth

With one of the longest Californian seasons (from early November often until well into June), three thousand vertical feet of skiing, and more than its fair share of dreamy deep powder, **Mammoth Mountain** (daily 8.30am–4pm; ℡1-800/626-6684, lift and snow conditions ℡1-888/766-9778, ⓦwww.mammothmountain.com) ranks as one of California's premier ski mountains. It is well balanced, too, with roughly equal areas of beginner, intermediate, and expert terrain plus snow parks and halfpipes designed with snowboarders in mind. Add to that a cat's-cradle of intersecting gondolas and chairlifts – seemingly being added to each year and now numbering thirty – bundles of snow-making equipment, and a whole resort of bars and restaurants designed with après-ski in mind, and you can hardly go wrong. As if this weren't enough, your lift ticket is also valid at June Lake (see p.359), a few miles north.

Pick up **lift tickets** ($57 weekdays, $60 weekends) from the Main Lodge on Minaret Road, where you can also rent **equipment** ($24 for basic skis, boots, and poles; $30 for snowboard and boots), and book **lessons** ($32 per half-day).

Off the mountain there are stacks of **cross-country skiing** trails; *Tamarack Lodge Resort* (see "Accommodation," above) offers ski packages, including instruction, tours, and rentals, and charges $18 a day for access to the trails.

If you prefer a motorized approach to the white stuff, you can rent gear and clothing from DJ's Snowmobile Adventures (℡760/935-4480, ⓦwww.snowmobilemammoth.com) who have one-hour (single $55, double $72), two-hour ($85/115), and half-day ($167/245) rentals. Beyond that, there's **ice skating**, **bobsled riding**, and even shooting down the bobsled course on a giant inner tube.

the spray refracting to earn its name, especially at midday. It is two miles away through Red's Meadow, reached on a pleasant hike (see box, opposite).

Throughout the summer, Minaret Road is closed throughout the day and you must access Devil's Postpile by **shuttle bus** (daily 7am–7pm; free with National Monument entry), which leaves every thirty minutes from the Mammoth Mountain Main Lodge Gondola Building. Campers are allowed vehicular access at all times, and in the early morning and late evening others can drive along Minaret Road; drive over before 7am and you can come back whenever you wish. During the day, the furthest you can drive without taking the shuttle bus is **Minaret Vista**, a parking lot high on the San Joaquin Ridge with wonderful views of the **Minaret Peaks**, a spiky volcanic ridge just south of pointed Mount Ritter – one of the Sierra's most enticing high peaks.

Eating, drinking, and nightlife

Mammoth offers by far the widest selection – and some of the best examples – of **restaurants**, **cafés**, and **bars** (some with live **music**) on this side of the Sierra. That may be reason enough to stick around for a while, but if you've got used to the relative austerity elsewhere in the mountains, the drain on your finances may come as something of a shock. If you're just after replenishing your cooler, pick up **groceries** at Vons, in the Minaret Village mall, and healthy goodies at Sierra Sundance Earth Foods in The Mammoth Mall.

Angel's Main St at Sierra Blvd ℡760/934-7427. The menu has a Southwestern kick at this broadly appealing and family-friendly restaurant. The *Angel's* salad ($4) and jalapeño corn fritters ($6) are very good and there is a decent selection of burgers ($8–9) and $10 mains such as spinach

and mushroom lasagna, and chicken pot pie, all washed down with Mammoth Brewing Company microbrews.

Base Camp Café Main St ℡760/934-3900. Great low-cost café usually bustling with the outdoors and active set here for the hearty breakfasts

($4–7), tasty soups and sandwiches, bargain daily specials, organic espresso coffees, and micro-brews. Also open for dinner until 8pm.

Cervino's 3752 Viewpoint Rd ℡760/934-4734. Excellent northern Italian fine dining; try portobello mushrooms stuffed with goat's cheese and pecans ($10) followed by veal served with prosciutto in a sage-butter sauce ($23).

Giovanni's Minaret Village Mall, Old Mammoth Rd (℡760/934-7563. The favorite local stop for low-cost dining; three out of ten for decor and ambience but very good pasta and pizza, and great lunchtime deals.

Good Life Café The Mammoth Mall ℡760/934-1734. Doesn't cater to vegetarians and vegans as well as they'd like you to believe, but probably the best around with veggie burritos, good salads, and vegetable wraps as well as plenty of burgers and egg dishes at modest prices, all served inside or on the sunny deck.

Grumpy's 361 Old Mammoth Rd ℡760/934-8587. Sports bar with pool table, video games, and a good grill serving the likes of the half-pound Grumpy Melt with ortega chilis and grilled onions, and a fine halibut and chips.

Lakefront Restaurant Tamarack Lodge ℡760/934-3534. Superb lake views accompany dishes from a menu with French-California leanings, which might include cognac-flambéed quail

salad ($11), walnut-crusted chicken breast ($21), and a sumptuous selection of desserts and ports.

Looney Bean Coffee House Main St ℡760/934-1345. The most vibrant of Mammoth's coffee bars with good coffee, muffins, and the like, served up to dedicated regulars either inside (where there's Internet access and a stack of magazines) or out on the terrace. Stays open late in the ski season.

Nevados Main St and Minaret Rd ℡760/934-4466. Another favorite with the foodies with an eclectic menu from crisp *nori*-wrapped shrimp with *wasabi* to hazelnutcrust rack of lamb and a $35 prix fixe deal for an appetizer, main, and dessert.

Schat's Bakery & Café 3305 Main St ℡760/934-6055. Easily the best range of baked goods in town, either to take out or eat in with a coffee.

The Stove 644 Old Mammoth Rd ℡760/934-2821. Long-standing Mammoth favorite, serving egg, waffle and pancake breakfasts, sandwiches and full meals later on – all in massive portions.

Whiskey Creek Main St and Minaret Rd ℡760/934-2555. Traditional American dining in one of the town's better restaurants, noted for its seafood, Sierra Ranch salad, and meatloaf. It's also one of the livelier bars in town, serving its own Mammoth Brewing Company beers and often putting on bands, especially at weekends.

④

DEATH VALLEY AND THE EASTERN HIGH SIERRA | Mammoth Lakes and around

Sierra pack trips

Want to explore the High Sierra but don't fancy carrying all your food and camping gear? Help is at hand in the form of **pack stations** which offer **horseback trips** ranging from a single night to seven-, ten-, or even twenty-day trips over the Sierra Crest and into Yosemite or Kings Canyon national parks. Cheapest are custom **spot trips**, where you and your gear are taken to a suitable campsite then picked up at some pre-arranged time. Rates depend on numbers and distance traveled, but taking a group of four to a destination 4–6 hours away, you might expect to pay $350–550 each round-trip. Multi-night **trail rides** with a guide usually work to a schedule advertised in advance and are likely to cost around $130–160 a day. For these you'll generally be teaming up with others. Most outfitters also rent stock for carrying gear and will even use horses to drop off gear for you at a specified location.

Below we've listed a few popular packers from south to north up the Owens Valley:

Sequoia Kings Pack Trains ℡760/387-2797 or 1-800/962-0775, ℗www.sequoiak-ingspacktrains.com. Independence-based packers serving King's Canyon National Park and Mount Whitney.

Rainbow Pack Outfitters ℡760/873-8877. Located near South Lake, west of Bishop with great rides into Dusy Basin and LeConte Canyon on the Middle Fork of the Kings River.

Red's Meadow ℡760/934-2345 or 1-800/292-7758, ℗www.reds-meadow.com. Right by Devil's Postpile (see p.355), and four miles north at Agnew Meadow.

Mammoth Lakes Pack Outfit ℡1-888/475-8748, ℗www.mammothpack.com. Mammoth-based, working a slightly different area to the Red's Meadow crowd.

Listings

Ballooning Mammoth Balloon Adventures (☎760/937-UPUP, ⊛www.mammothballoonadventures.com) offer sunrise flights year-round for $165 with passengers encouraged to help inflate and deflate the balloon.

Banks Several around town (all with ATMs) including the Bank of America, corner of Main Street and Old Mammoth Road.

Bookstores Booky Joint in the Minaret Village Mall (☎760/934-3240) has the best all-round selection; Book Warehouse, 3399 Main St (☎760/924-3551), is stacked with remaindered books of all sorts at bargain prices.

Cinemas First-run Hollywood fare at the Plaza Theatre in the Sherwin Plaza Mall and Minaret Cinema in the Minaret Village Mall (both ☎760/934-3131).

Festivals During the annual Jazz Jubilee, held over four days around the second weekend in July (details on ☎760/934-2478, ⊛www.mammothjazz.org), bars, restaurants, and impromptu venues around town pack out with predominantly trad-jazz types. There's also the more blues-oriented Bluesapalooza (☎760/934-0606), held over the first weekend in August.

Internet access The library (see below) has free surfing machines, and email charged at $1 per ten minutes; *Looney Bean Coffee House* charges slightly more.

Kayaking Caldera Kayaks (☎760/935-4942, ⊛www.calderakayak.com) are based ten miles south of Mammoth at Crowley Lake Marina, run guided kayak trips on Mono and Crowley lakes ($65), and rent out gear (singles $40–45 a day, doubles $50–55).

Laundry Mill City Laundry, corner of Main Street and Old Mammoth Road. Also coin-op machines at *Mammoth Mountain Inn* (7am–10pm).

Library The public library is located at 960 Forest Trail (Mon–Fri 10am–7pm, Sat 9am–5.30pm) and has **Internet access**.

Mountain biking Footloose Sports, corner of Main Street and Old Mammoth Road (☎760/934-2400, ⊛www.footloosesports.com), rent front and full suspension bikes ($10/hr, $32–36/day), plus the latest demo models ($10/48) and organize weekly group rides; Mammoth Sporting Goods, Sierra Center Mall (☎760/934-3239, ⊛www.mammothsportinggoods.com), offer slightly better rates for a similar range of machines and also run group rides (currently Wed 5.30pm and Sat 9am).

Photographic supplies Speed of Light Photo & Video, 1 Minaret Village Mall ☎760/934-8415.

Rock and alpine climbing Mammoth Zip & Climb (☎760/934-2571) run family-oriented sessions on a 32-foot artificial **climbing rock** (late June–Sept daily 10am–6pm; $14 an hour, $28 per day, shoes $3) in front of the *Mammoth Mountain Inn*. To get out on the real stuff, contact Mammoth Mountaineering School (☎760/924-9100 or 1-800/239-7942, ⊛www.mammothweb.com/recreation/mountaineering), who run rock classes at all grades from $80 and are based at Sandy's Ski & Sports on Main Street; or Southern Yosemite Mountain Guides (☎1-800/231-4575, ⊛www.symg.com) who offer a rock and alpine guiding service at $330 a day for up to six people. The Bishop-based guide services (see p.348) also run trips in the Mammoth area.

Showers In Mammoth township try Twin Lakes Store (daily 7am–8pm; $2; ☎760/934-7295) or *Mammoth Mountain Inn* (see "Accommodation"; daily 7am–10pm; $5 with towel). In the Devil's Postpile area, head for the natural hot spring bathhouse at the Red's Meadow campground (donations appreciated).

Around Mammoth

Mammoth makes a good base for exploring a little of the **surrounding area**, even as far as Mono Lake and Bodie Ghost Town (see p.362). Closer to hand, there's warm bathing at Hot Creek and a mass of fine alpine scenery around the June Lake Loop.

Hot Creek Geological Site

Just east of US-395 is one of the more easily accessible examples of the region's volcanic activity in the hot springs that bubble up at the **Hot Creek Geological Site** (daily dawn–dusk; free), on Hot Creek Hatchery Road three miles south of the exit for Mammoth Lakes. Jets of boiling water mix with the otherwise chilly, snowmelt water to form pools ranging from tepid to scalding; you have to search to find a happy medium, and it's a bit of a challenge since the flows are ever-changing. Note, too, that the US Forest Service discourages bathing, because of the risk of burns and the sometimes high chemical content – not that anyone takes much notice. Paths and wooden steps lead down to the most likely spots, but wear shoes – as well as bathing suits, which are required – as there may be broken glass underfoot. For more on the region's hot springs, see box below.

June Lake Loop

The relatively crowded slopes of Mammoth Mountain sends some skiers and summer visitors a few miles further north to the relative solitude of **June Lake** and its neighbors, Grant, Silver, and Gull lakes. Reached by way of the sixteen-mile **June Lake Loop** road, which branches off US-395 fifteen miles north of the Mammoth exit, this region of high-altitude lakes is one of the most striking in these parts, and offers Mammoth's attractions on a more manageable scale.

The small township of **June Lake**, two miles off US-395, is the most alpine-looking of any Sierra community and a place where imitation Swiss chalets don't look entirely out of place. There's a reasonable range of roofed accommodation here (ⓦwww.junelake.com), but the region is primarily a place for **camping**, easily done at one of several $12 Forest Service campgrounds scattered beside the various lakes, including the relatively busy *June Lake* and *Oh! Ridge* locations (both reservable on ☎1-877/444-6777), and the more serene first-come-first-served *Grant Lake*, nine miles further on, where there is boat and fishing tackle rental.

Vulcanism and hot springs in the Eastern Sierra

One of the pleasures of any extended visit to the Owens Valley is soaking your bones in one of the numerous **hot springs**. None is well signposted, and most are primarily used by locals who are welcoming enough if you are respectful. Most springs are tucked away miles down some rutted dirt road and often comprise little more than a ring of rocks or a hollowed-out tub into which people have diverted the waters to create pools of differing temperatures. Most are **clothing-optional**, but you'll stand out as a tourist if you don't strip off. We've mentioned several springs in the text – those in the Saline Valley (p.337), Keough's Hot Springs (p.343), Travertine Hot Springs, and Buckeye Hot Springs (both p.363) – but aficionados will want to get hold of *Hot Springs of the Eastern Sierra* by George Williams III, which has full descriptions and detailed directions.

The springs are all the result of groundwater being heated by magma, which rises close to the surface in these parts. In fact Mammoth Mountain stands on the edge of a geologically volatile region known as the **Long Valley Caldera**. A vast oval some eighteen miles by twelve, the Caldera was formed 760,000 years ago when a massive eruption spread ash as far away as Nebraska. Vulcanism has continued with the creation of Mammoth Mountain around 50,000 years ago, the Mono Craters and, most recently, **Paoha Island** in Mono Lake only 300 years back.

In the last couple of decades, scientists have been alerted to ongoing activity manifest in swarms of earthquakes and measurable ground swelling which normally precedes eruptions. One cluster of earthquakes in 1989 is thought to have triggered the release of carbon dioxide from an underground gas reservoir, and since 1994 this gas seeping up through the soil has killed 120 trees near Horseshoe Lake.

An eruption is not likely in the near future, but the United States Geological Survey continues to monitor the region extensively for ground temperature changes, land deformation, and frequency and amplitude of quakes. For more, visit the relevant section of the USGS website ⓦlvo.wr.usgs.gov.

Mono Lake

The blue expanse of **MONO LAKE** sits in the middle of a volcanic desert tableland, its sixty square miles reflecting the statuesque, snowcapped mass of the eastern Sierra Nevada. At over a million years old, it's an ancient lake with two large volcanic islands – the light-colored **Paoha** and the black **Negit** – surrounded by salty, alkaline water. It resembles nothing more than a science-fiction landscape, with great towers and spires formed by mineral deposits ringing the shores; hot springs surround the lake, and all around the basin are signs of lava flows and volcanic activity, especially in the cones of the Mono Craters, just to the south.

The lake's most distinctive feature, the strange, sandcastle-like **tufa** formations, were increasingly exposed from the early 1940s to the mid-1990s as the City of Los Angeles drained away the waters that flow into the lake (see box opposite). The towers of tufa were formed underwater, where calcium-bearing freshwater springs well up through the carbonate-rich lake water; the calcium and carbonate combine and sink to the bottom as limestone, slowly growing into the weird formations you can see today. Before striking out for a close look at the lake and its tufa, call in at the excellent **Mono Basin Scenic Area Visitor Center**, a mile north of Lee Vining beside US-395 (daily May–Oct 9am–5.30pm; Nov–April generally weekends only 9am–4pm; ☎760/873-208, ⓦwww.r5.fs.fed.us/inyo). Exhibits and a good short film detail the lake's geology, and rangers give talks on various aspects of its ecology; the center organizes ninety-minute **guided walks** (July to early Sept daily 10am, 1pm & 6pm) around the tufa formations.

The Mono Lake Committee (see opposite) runs regular hour-long **canoe trips** (mid-June to mid-Sept Sat & Sun 8am, 9.30am & 11am; $17; reservations recommended ☎760/647-6595), which give a closer look at what the lake has to offer. Otherwise, you can go by kayak with Crowley Lake-based Caldera Kayaks (☎760/935-4942, ⓦwww.calderakayak.com), who run natural history tours on Mono Lake ($65) and rent kayaks for $40 a day (doubles $50). Both trips require advance reservations as far in advance as you can manage.

Under your own steam, visit **South Tufa** ($3; valid one week), one of the best places to look at the tufa spires, five miles east of US-395 via Hwy-120. Nearby is **Navy Beach** (free), where there are more (though less spectacular) spires, and the opportunity to float in water at least twice as buoyant as (and a thousand times more alkaline than) sea water. Adjacent to the south shore of the lake stands **Panum Crater**, a 700-year-old volcano riddled with deep fissures and fifty-foot towers of lava, visited on **Plug Trail** and **Rim Trail**, two short and fairly easy trails. This is the most recent of the **Mono Craters**, a series of volcanic cones that stretch twelve miles south from here towards Crowley Lake. This constitutes the youngest mountain range in North America, entirely formed over the last forty thousand years.

On the north shore of the lake, three miles along US-395, a side road leads to **Mono County Park**, where a guided boardwalk trail leads down to the lakefront and the best examples of mushroom-shaped tufa towers. A further five miles along this (mostly washboard gravel) side road is the trailhead for the **Black Point Fissures**, the result of a massive underwater eruption of molten lava some thirteen thousand years ago. As the lava cooled and contracted, cracks and fissures formed on the top, some only a few feet wide but as much as fifty feet deep. You can explore their depths, but pick up a directions sheet from the Visitor Center and be prepared for hot, dry, sandy conditions.

Mono Lake is one of the oldest on the continent and has survived several ice ages and all the volcanic activity that the area can throw at it, but the lake's biggest threat has been the City of Los Angeles, which owns the riparian rights to Mono Lake's catchment.

From 1892 to 1904, the small but rapidly growing city of Los Angeles experienced a twelve-year drought and started looking to the Owens River as a reliable source of water that could be easily channeled to the city. Under the auspices of the Los Angeles Department of Water and Power, the city bought up almost the entire Owens Valley, then diverted the river and its tributaries into a 223-mile gravity-fed aqueduct to take this water to LA. Farms and orchards in the once-productive Owens Valley were rendered useless without water, and Owens Lake near Lone Pine was left to dry up entirely.

The aqueduct was completed in 1931 – but by this time LA needed even more water. Consequently, in 1941, LA diverted four of the five streams that fed Mono Lake through an eleven-mile tunnel into its Owens Valley Aqueduct. This was an engineering marvel, dug through the volcanically active Mono Craters, but it has been overshadowed by the legal battle surrounding the depletion of the lake itself, long one of the biggest **environmental controversies** raging in California.

Over the next fifty years, the **water level** in Mono Lake dropped over forty feet, a disaster not only because of the lake's unique beauty, but also because Mono Lake is the primary nesting ground for **California gulls** and a critical resting point for thousands of migratory eared **grebes** and **phalaropes**. The lake was down to roughly half its natural size, and as the levels dropped, the islands in the middle of the lake where the gulls lay their eggs became peninsulas, and the colonies fell prey to coyotes and other mainland predators. Also, as less fresh water reached the lake, the landlocked water became increasingly saline, threatening the unique local ecosystem. About all that will thrive in the harsh conditions are brine shrimp and alkali flies, both essential food sources for the birdlife. Humans are not immune to the harmful effects – winds blowing across the salt pans left behind by the receding lake create clouds containing selenium and arsenic, both contributors to lung disease.

Seemingly oblivious to the plight of the lake, the City of Los Angeles built a second aqueduct in 1970 and the water level dropped even faster, sometimes falling eighteen inches in a single year. Prompted by scientific reports of an impending ecological disaster, a small group of activists set up the **Mono Lake Committee** (@ www.monolake.org) in 1978, fighting for the preservation of this unique ecosystem partly through publicity campaigns – "Save Mono Lake" bumper stickers were once de rigueur for concerned citizens – and partly through the courts. Though the California Supreme Court declared in 1983 that Mono Lake must be saved, it wasn't until 1994 that emergency action was taken. A target water height of 6377ft above sea level (later raised to 6392ft) was grudgingly agreed to make Negit Island once again safe for nesting birds. Streams dry for decades are now flowing again, and warm springs formerly located by lakeside interpretive trails are now submerged. The target level – 18 feet higher than its recorded minimum, but still 25 feet below its pre-diversion level – won't be reached for at least another ten years, by which time the agreement is up for re-negotiation, something that concentrates the ongoing efforts of the Mono Lake Committee.

Lee Vining

Within easy walking distance of Mono Lake, the appealing small town of **LEE VINING** offers the usual range of visitor services along either side of US-395, but not a great deal more. The town's **Mono Lake Committee Information**

Center (daily: July & Aug 9am–10pm; rest of year 9am–5pm; ☎760/647-6595, ⓦwww.leevining.com) is partly the showcase for the committee's battle for Mono Lake, featuring an excellent thirty-minute video presentation, but also has helpful staff, many books on the Eastern Sierra, and a tasteful gift shop.

There are several **motels** all close together along US-395 including the well-presented *Murphey's* (☎760/647-6316 or 1-800/334-6316, ⓦwww.murpheysyosemite.com; ❸), with a large hot tub and some units with kitchens, and the slightly cheaper but inferior *El Mono Motel* (☎760/647-6310; ❸). The *Mono Vista RV Park* (☎760/647-6401) caters to RVs ($22–27) and tents ($15), and has showers for non-guests ($2 for 5min; daily 9am–6pm); and there are a number of $7 forest service **campgrounds** along Lee Vining Creek off Tioga Pass Road, Hwy-120 (see p.352).

The best **dining** around these parts is at *Whoa Nellie Deli* (☎760/647-1088) in the unlikely setting of the Mobil gas station at the junction of US-395 and Hwy-120 East. There's always a lively atmosphere, and they dish up great tortilla soup, jambalaya ($8), fish tacos ($9), burgers and steaks, along with espresso coffees, microbrews, and margaritas. There's also the diner-style *Nicely's Restaurant* (☎760/647-6477) on US-395, a great Fifties vinyl palace that opens at 6am; and the *Mono Inn Restaurant* (☎760/647-6581; closed Tues and Nov–April; ⓦwww.anseladams.com), almost five miles north along US-395, owned by Ansel Adams' granddaughter, which serves up lovingly prepared meals on the patio or inside, both with a superb lake view. There's a strong south-of-the-border strain, with mains ($20–25) such as medallions of lamb with tomatillo mint sauce eaten with home-made jalapeño bread.

If you're heading through Lee Vining on the way to **Yosemite National Park**, it is worth considering using the town as an affordable base for exploring the Tuolumne Meadows area, around twenty miles distant. Yosemite Valley is about two hours' drive from Lee Vining and therefore too far away to use this as a base.

Bodie Ghost Town and around

In the 1880s, the gold-mining town of **BODIE**, eighteen miles north of Lee Vining then thirteen miles (three of them dirt) east of US-395, boasted three breweries, some sixty saloons and dance halls, and a population of nearly ten thousand. It also had a well-earned reputation as the raunchiest and most lawless mining camp in the West. Contemporary accounts describe a town that ended each day with a shootout on Main Street, while church bells, rung once for every year of a murdered man's life, that seemed never to stop sounding. The town boomed for less than ten years, starting in 1877, when a fairly poor existing mine collapsed, exposing an enormously rich vein. Within four years this was the second largest town in the state after San Francisco, even supporting its own Chinatown. By 1885, gold and silver currently valued at around $1.2 billion had been extracted, but a drop in the gold price made mining largely unprofitable. The town gradually declined and eventually closed down for good in 1942 after the second of two disastrous fires virtually destroyed the town.

What remains has been turned into the **Bodie State Historic Park** (daily: June to mid-Sept 8am–7pm; March–May & mid-Sept to Oct 8am–5pm; Nov–Feb 8am–4pm; $1; ☎760/647-6445, ⓦceres.ca.gov/sierradsp/bodie), where lack of theme-park tampering gives the place an authentically eerie atmosphere absent from other US ghost towns. Bodie is almost 8400 feet above sea level and, although the park is open throughout the year, snow often prevents vehicular access between December and April; call for road conditions. If you can get in during that time, bundle up: Bodie is often cited on the national weather report as having the lowest temperature in the US. And any time, remember to bring all you need: there are no services at the site.

A good self-guided tour booklet ($1) leads you around many of the 150-odd wooden buildings – about six percent of the original town – surviving in a state of arrested decay around the intact town center. Some buildings have been re-roofed and others supported in some way, but it is by and large a faithful preservation: even the dirty dishes are much as they were in the 1940s, little damaged by sixty years of weathering. The **Miner's Union Building** on Main Street was the center of the town's social life; founded in 1877, the union was one of the first in California, organized by workers at the Standard and Midnight mines. The building now houses a small **museum** (June–Aug daily 9am–6pm; May & Sept daily 9am–5pm; free), which paints a graphic picture of mining life. Various **tours** depart from here in the summer, particularly on weekends, though schedules are flexible and you should call ahead if you have specific interests. The history talk is free, but there's also a fifty-minute tour of the **Standard Consolidated Stamp Mill** ($5) otherwise off limits, and one along a ridge ($5) which offers some of the best views of Bodie. Other highlights of the town include the **Methodist church** with its intact pipe organ, the **general store** with its beautiful pressed-steel ceiling, and the **saloon**.

Bridgeport

Seven miles north of the Bodie road junction along US-395 is tiny **BRIDGE-PORT**, an isolated village in the middle of a mountain-girt plain that provided the new start in life for fugitive Robert Mitchum in the film noir masterpiece *Out of the Past*. The gas station he owned in the film is long gone, though the place is otherwise little changed; a pretty high-country ranching community typically full of **fishermen** through the summer. If you want to join their ranks, head to Ken's Sporting Goods, 258 Main St (℡760/9332-7707), for local information and all the tackle you could desire. Ask also about the local hot springs, which are one of the most popular ways to wind down after a day wrestling trout: **Travertine Hot Springs** are handily placed a couple of miles south of town, while **Buckeye Hot Springs**, roughly fifteen miles west of Bridgeport, are widely regarded as some of the best in the Owens Valley but are hard to find. Otherwise it is only worth stopping here to stroll Bridgeport's small and time-warped Main Street past the dainty white 1880 **County Courthouse**, and to visit the small local history **museum** (daily late May–Sept 10am–4pm; $1.50), behind the town park in a restored old schoolhouse.

With the lure of the springs, you may want to stay overnight, and **accommodation** ranges from a beautifully furnished B&B, *The Cain House*, 340 Main St (℡760/932-7040 or 1-800/433-2246, ⓦwww.cainhouse.com; closed Nov–May; ❺), through decent motels such as the *Silver Maple Inn*, 310 Main St (℡760/932-7383, ⓦwww.silvermapleinn.com; closed Nov–May; ❹), to the decidedly decrepit *Victoria House* across the street (℡760/932-7020; closed Nov–May; ❶), a building which, like several in Bridgeport, is said to have been transported here from Bodie. The *Best Western Ruby Inn*, 333 Main St (℡760/932-7241; ❹), is one of the only lodgings that stays open year round.

For **eating**, there are good breakfasts and lunches at *Hays Street Café*, 21 Hays St, on the southern approach to town; reasonably priced grills, sandwiches, and specialty pizzas at *Rhino's Bar & Grill*, 226 Main St (℡760/932-7345); and top-rated fine dining at *1881*, 362 Main St (℡760/932-1918; June–Oct daily, rest of year Thurs–Sun), where swordfish in ginger and scallion butter ($24) might be followed by vanilla *crème brûlée* ($5.50). A drive six miles south along US-395 is rewarded by reliably excellent dining at *Virginia Creek Settlement* (℡760/932-7780; closed Mon), renowned in the region for its fresh and tasty steaks (from $18), pasta dishes ($10–12), and pizzas (from $10) – particularly the excellent gorgonzola.

From Bridgeport, US-395 continues north into Nevada, through the capital Carson City and the gambling city of Reno, both described fully in Chapter Eight.

Travel details

Neither Greyhound buses nor Amtrak trains run any services within this chapter. The only long-distance bus services are the CREST bus along the Owens Valley (see p.325) and the YARTS service from Mammoth Lakes to Yosemite (see p.350).

Buses

Bishop to: Big Pine (3 weekly; 15min); Bridgeport (3 weekly; 2hr); Carson City (3 weekly; 3hr 45min); Independence (3 weekly; 45min); Lee Vining (3 weekly; 1hr 25min); Lone Pine (3 weekly; 1hr 10min); Mammoth Lakes (3 weekly; 50min); Ridgecrest (3 weekly; 2hr 30min).

Carson City to: Bishop (3 weekly; 3hr 45min); Bridgeport (3 weekly; 1hr 50min); Lee Vining (3 weekly; 2hr 20min); Mammoth Lakes (3 weekly; 3hr).

Mammoth Lakes to: Bishop (3 weekly; 50min); Lee Vining (3–5 weekly; 30min); Tuolumne Meadows (summer 2–7 weekly; 1hr); Yosemite Valley (summer 2–7 weekly; 3hr).

Ridgecrest to: Big Pine (3 weekly; 2hr); Bishop (3 weekly; 2hr 20min); Independence (3 weekly; 1hr 35min); Lone Pine (3 weekly; 1hr 20min).

The San Joaquin Valley and the Western High Sierra

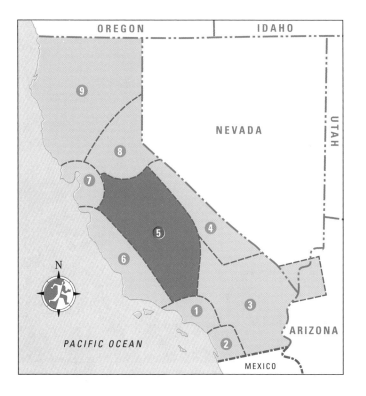

CHAPTER 5

Highlights

✳ **Buck Owens' Crystal Palace** Visit this honky-tonk, the country music showcase for the legendary Bakersfield Sound, and take in a show and the museum display. See p.372

✳ **Kern River** Some of California's finest and most accessible white-water rafting is available on this river, which emanates from the lofty slopes of Mount Whitney. See p.373

✳ **A&W Root Beer Drive-In** If you are passing through Modesto, be sure to stop at this classic 1950s diner known for its roller-skating waitresses. See p.386

✳ **Giant Forest** The densest collection of the world's largest trees, the mighty sequoias, can be found in this section of Sequoia National Park, accessible by a myriad of trails. See p.396

✳ **Hike Half Dome** Follow the wonderful Mist Trail to the summit of Yosemite's most famous peak, which forms the sheerest cliff in North America. See p.428

✳ **Ahwahnee Hotel** Stay at Yosemite's finest lodging tastefully appointed with Native American motifs, or – if you'd rather save your money – simply take tea in the hotel's Great Lounge. See p.419

The San Joaquin Valley and the Western High Sierra

The vast interior of California – stretching three hundred miles from the edges of the Mojave Desert in the south right up to the Gold Country and Northern California – comprises the wide floor of the agricultural **San Joaquin Valley**, flanked on the east by the massive Sierra Nevada mountains. It's a region that contains unparalleled beauty, yet the ninety percent of Californians who live on the coast are barely aware of the area, encountering it only while driving between LA and San Francisco on the admittedly tedious I-5, and consider it the height of hicksville.

The San Joaquin Valley is radically different from anywhere else in the state. During the 1940s, this arid land was made super-fertile by a massive program of aqueduct building, using water flowing from the mountains to irrigate the area. The valley, as flat as a pancake, now almost totally comprises farmland, periodically enlivened by scattered cities that offer a taste of ordinary Californian life away from the glitz of LA and San Francisco. More than anywhere else in the state, the abundance of low-paying agricultural jobs has encouraged decades of immigration from south of the border, and there are now towns in the San Joaquin Valley where Spanish is the first language and **taquerias** outnumber burger joints ten to one. Fertile land and cheap labor has brought relative wealth to large numbers of San Joaquin Valley residents who have responded by becoming increasingly mobile. This, and town planning, which dictates that everyone must drive everywhere, has led to a dense photochemical haze – trapped by mountains on both flanks – that is often so thick the pristine peaks once visible throughout the year are now seldom seen.

If coastal Californians pass through the San Joaquin Valley, it is to reach the **national parks** that cover the foothills and upper reaches of the Sierra Nevada mountains. From the valley, a gentle ascent through rolling, grassy foothills takes you into dense forests of huge pine and fir trees, interspersed with tranquil lakes and cut by deep rocky canyons. The most impressive sections are protected within three national parks. **Sequoia** is home to the last few stands of huge prehistoric trees, giant sequoias that form the centerpiece of a rich natural landscape. **Kings Canyon** shares a common border with Sequoia – together they make up one huge park – and presents a similar, slightly wilder array of Sierra wonders. **Yosemite**, with its towering walls of silvery granite artfully sculpted by Ice Age glaciers, is the most famous of the parks and one of the absolute must-sees in California. While only a few narrow, twisting roads penetrate the hundred miles of wilderness in between these three parks, the entire region is crisscrossed by hiking trails leading up into the pristine alpine backcountry of the **Western High Sierra**, which contains the glistening summits of some of the highest mountains in the country.

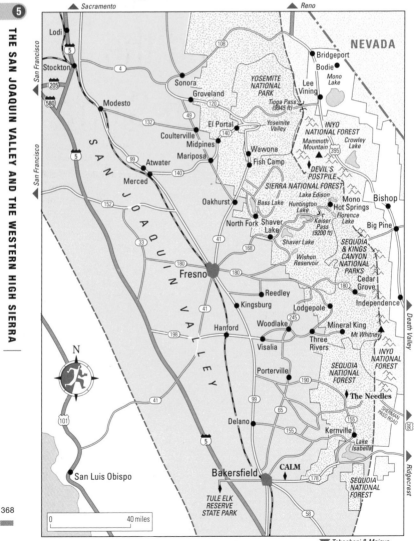

Drivers who aren't particularly interested in exploring the wilds can simply barrel through on I-5, an arrow-straight interstate through the western edge of the San Joaquin Valley that's the quickest route between LA and San Francisco. Four daily **trains** and frequent Greyhound **buses** run through the valley, stopping at the larger cities and towns along Hwy-99 – Merced being the most useful with its bus connections to Yosemite. Otherwise, getting to the mountains is all but impossible without your own vehicle, though with a bit of advance planning, you might be able to join one of the many camping trips organized by the Sierra Club, the California-based environmentalist group (see p.56).

The San Joaquin Valley

The **SAN JOAQUIN VALLEY** grows more fruit and vegetables than any other agricultural region of its size in the world – a fact that touches the lives, in one way or another, of every one of its inhabitants. The area is much more conservative and Midwestern in feel than the rest of California, but even if the nightlife begins and ends with the local ice cream parlor, it can all be refreshingly small-scale and enjoyable after visiting the big cities of the coast. Admittedly, none of the towns have the energy to detain you long, and, between the settlements, the drab hundred-mile vistas of almond groves and vineyards can be sheer torture. The weather, too, can be a challenge – summers in the San Joaquin are frequently scorching and winters experience the cold and thick Tule fog, so aim to visit in spring or fall, particularly March when the fruit trees are in full bloom.

Bakersfield, the first town you come to across the rocky peaks north of Los Angeles, is hardly the most prepossessing destination, but in recent years its **country music** scene has burgeoned into the best in the state. And, surprisingly enough, there are few better places on this side of the Atlantic to sample **Basque cuisine**. Bakersfield also offers a museum recording the beginnings of the local population, and the chance to sample some of the state's finest **whitewater rafting** on the nearby Kern River. Further on lies **Visalia**, a likeable community, and the well-restored turn-of-the-century town of **Hanford**.

In many ways the region's linchpin, **Fresno** is the closest thing to a bustling urban center the valley has – and it's just about impossible to avoid. Though economically thriving, it's frequently voted the least desirable place to live in the US, and on arrival it's easy to see why. Its redeeming features, such as they are, take a bit of time to discover, though you shouldn't pass up the opportunity to visit the bizarre labyrinth of **Forestiere Underground Gardens**.

Beyond Fresno, in the northern reaches of the valley, lie sedate **Merced** and slightly more boisterous **Modesto**, the inspiration for George Lucas's movie *American Graffiti*. At the top end of the valley, **Stockton** is scenically improved by the delta that connects the city to the sea, but is otherwise a place of few pleasures, though you may pass through on your way from San Francisco to the Gold Country or the national parks.

Bakersfield and around

An unappealing vision behind a forest of oil derricks, **BAKERSFIELD**'s flat and featureless look does nothing to suggest that this is one of the nation's liveliest country music communities, with a batch of venues where locally and nationally rated musicians will blow your socks off. It also has the country's largest community of Basque descent, making it *the* place to taste Basque cuisine, at its best in one of the specialist restaurants run by descendants of sheepherders who migrated to the San Joaquin Valley in the early twentieth century. Speed freaks will find entertainment in Bakersfield's assorted motorsports, all a far cry from the town's beginnings in 1851 when Colonel Thomas Baker made his field available as a stagecoach rest stop.

Country music and Basque cuisine aside, there's not much reason to visit, though in the last few years the moribund downtown area has seen something of a renaissance, with half a dozen new bars opening up, and on the outskirts of town a progressive small **zoo** warrants a visit.

If the hills are calling out to you, it's only an hour's drive east to **Lake Isabella**, a reservoir in the Sierra foothills that's well geared to family camping and watersports. Without your own equipment, you're better off making for **Kernville**, a few miles up the Kern River, which provides the venue for a full range of springtime **whitewater rafting**.

Arrival, information, and accommodation

Bakersfield is an important public transportation hub and the downtown area – half a dozen blocks each way from the junction of 19th and J streets – is

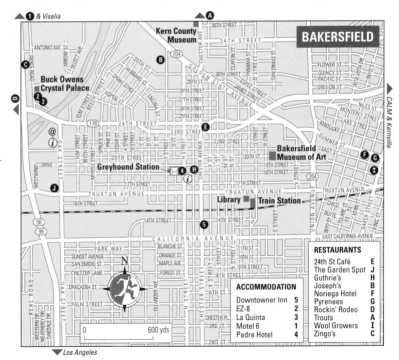

home to both the **Amtrak station**, 601 Truxton Ave, the southern terminus of Amtrak's San Joaquin route from San Francisco (connections to LA via Thruway bus), and the **bus station**, 1820 18th St. Traveling by Greyhound you may need to change routes here – although overnight stops are rarely necessary. The best source of information is the **Kern County Board of Trade**, 2101 Oak St (Mon–Fri 8am–5pm; ☎661/861-2367 or 1-800/500-5376, ⓦwww.visitkern.com), which conveniently has free **Internet access**, though only a single machine. The **Bakersfield Chamber of Commerce**, 1725 Eye St (Mon 9am–5pm, Tues–Fri 8am–5pm; ☎661/327-4421, ⒻF327-8751), is slightly less useful but handier to downtown.

Bakersfield is dotted with clusters of cheap **motels**, though there is little else. Two handily placed a short stagger from *Buck Owens' Crystal Palace* are the *EZ-8*, 2604 Buck Owens Blvd (☎661/322-1901, ⒻF323-9013; ❶), and the adjacent, and considerably smarter *La Quinta*, 3232 Riverside Drive (☎661/325-7400 or 1-800/531-5900; ❹); both have pools. A couple of miles north around the Olive Drive exit, off Hwy-99, you get fractionally better value for money at the pool-equipped *Motel 6*, 5241 Olive Tree Court (☎661/392-9700; ❶). The best bet in the center of town is the *Downtowner Inn*, 1301 Chester Ave (☎661/327-7122, ⒻF327-8350; ❷). **Campers** should head fifteen miles east to the shores of Lake Ming at the *Kern River County Park* (mid-Oct to mid-March $10, mid-March to mid-Oct $18), where there are grassy and reasonably shaded sites but no hook-ups.

The Town

The town owes its existence to the fertile soil around the Kern River – once the longest river in the state but now dammed to form Lake Isabella – and to the discovery of local oil and gas deposits. To learn more of these fortuitous finds, visit the **Kern County Museum**, a mile north of downtown at 3801 Chester Ave (Mon–Fri 8am–5pm, Sat 10am–5pm, Sun noon–5pm; $6; ⓦwww.kcmuseum.org), which documents the town's petrochemical roots through the new exhibit due to open in the summer of 2003. Bakersfield's development is further illustrated through an impressive collection of over fifty (mostly) restored rail wagons and buildings, many of them dating from the late nineteenth or early twentieth century. Also on the grounds, the hands-on science exhibits of the **Lori Brock Children's Discovery Center** provide an excuse to get the kids out of the heat of the day.

For something a little more highbrow, visit the **Bakersfield Museum of Art**, 1930 R St (Tues–Fri 10am–4pm, Sat & Sun noon–4pm; $5; ⓦwww.bmoa.org), which usually has interesting touring exhibits, along with its own collection, which includes works by Georgia O' Keeffe and Diego Rivera.

Wildlife fans will have to stray a little further out, where the greatest interest is at the **California Living Museum (CALM)**, 10500 Alfred Harrell Way (Tues–Sun 9am–5pm; $4.50; ⓦwww.calmzoo.org), some twelve miles east of town off the road to Kernville. It is effectively a small zoo, but one focusing solely on Californian native species and only those animals that have been injured and cannot be returned to the wild. Stroll around the landscaped grounds past the golden and bald eagles, pause to admire the black bears and bobcats, then repair to the reptile house with its array of snakes and lizards. The animals tend to hide from the heat of the day, so come early or aim for the first Saturday of the month from June to September when the place stays open until 8pm.

Tule elk enthusiasts might want to drive half an hour west to the **Tule Elk Reserve State Park**, Morris Road (daily 8am–sunset; free), where around

The main reason to dally for more than a few hours in Bakersfield is to hear **country music** – on any weekend the town's numerous honky-tonks reverberate to the sounds of the best country musicians in the US, many of them local residents.

The roots of Bakersfield's country music scene are with the dust bowl Okies who arrived in the San Joaquin Valley during the Depression, bringing their hillbilly instruments and campfire songs with them. This rustic entertainment quickly broadened into more contemporary styles, developed in the bars and clubs that began to appear in the town, where future legends such as Merle Haggard and Buck Owens (who now owns the local country radio stations, KUZZ 107.9 FM and KCWR 107.1 FM) cut their teeth. A failed attempt to turn Bakersfield into "Nashville West" during the 1960s, and bring the major country music record labels here from their traditional base, has left the town eager to promote the distinctive **"Bakersfield Sound"**: a far less slick and commercial affair than its Tennessee counterpart. You can gain an inkling of the Bakersfield Sound from the 1988 hit *Streets of Bakersfield*, a duet by Buck Owens and Dwight Yoakam, but you really need to get out and listen to some live music.

Venues

To find out **what's on**, read the Friday Entertainment section of the *Bakersfield Californian* (ⓦ www.bakersfield.com), check the flyers at the tourist offices mentioned above, or phone one of the venues we've listed. Fridays and Saturdays are the liveliest nights, although there's often something to enjoy during the week, even if it's only the free **country dancing lessons** offered several nights a week at *Rockin' Rodeo* (see below). There's never a cover charge for someone spinning platters, and seldom one for live sets, usually entailing one band playing for four or five hours from around 8pm and taking a fifteen-minute break every hour – though big names might demand $5 a head. Stetson hats and Nudie shirts are the sartorial order of the day, and audiences span generations.

Most venues are hotel lounges or restaurant backrooms, though there are a couple which don't fit the mold: one not to be missed is *Trouts*, 805 N Chester Ave (☎ 661/399-6700), a country music bar a couple of miles north of downtown that's been in business for over forty years. Closer to town, the ersatz-Western *Buck Owens' Crystal Palace*, 2800 Buck Owens Blvd (☎ 661/328-7560), represents the latest addition to the master's ever-expanding empire: a cabaret-style set-up (entry $6, $8, or $10 for the best tables) with burgers and grills available while local and touring bands perform midweek (Tues–Thurs) and Buck (now into his seventies) does a turn on Friday and Saturday nights at 7pm, playing numbers from his own back catalogue, classic country tunes, and beyond. Write your request on a napkin and he may play it. If you can't make Buck's set, it is broadcast live on KCWR 107.1 FM. Cases around the walls make up a small **museum** (daily except Fri 11am–4pm and visible during any show; free) of knickknacks Buck has picked up over the years – promo photos, Buck Rogers bolo tie clasps, platinum records, red-white-and-blue guitars, and a glittering display of rhinestone jackets. The other hotspot to add to your itinerary is the younger and more clubby *Rockin' Rodeo*, 3745 Rosedale Hwy (☎ 661/323-6617), with a New Country/Rock DJ every night and a Texas-style oval dancefloor.

thirty of these beasts can be seen from a viewing platform, best at 3pm when they are fed nearby. Large herds used to roam these lands, but hunting and loss of habitat forced them to the brink of extinction early in the twentieth century; only projects like this and a major relocation to the Owens Valley (see p.337) have saved them. To get there, follow Stockdale Highway west for twenty miles, then just after crossing I-5, follow the signs a mile or so south on Morris Road.

Appropriately for an oil town, Bakersfield is a speed freak's paradise, with all manner of car racing and even drag boat racing on the Kern River's Lake Ming some fifteen miles east of town. There's drag racing at the Famoso Raceway (Ⓦwww.famosoraceway.com), twenty miles north of town, NASCAR at Mesa Marin Raceway (mid-March–Oct; Ⓦwww.mesamarin.com), ten miles east of town on Hwy-178, and all manner of racing around a high banked oval at the Bakersfield Speedway (Ⓦwww.bakersfieldspeedway.com), eight miles north. Tickets can usually be bought at the gate.

Eating, drinking, and nightlife

Don't pass Bakersfield without **eating** Basque food. The most authentic experience is at the turn-of-the-century *Noriega Hotel*, 525 Summer St (Ⓣ661/322-8419), where louvered shutters and ceiling fans cool diners communally sat at long tables and served an all-you-can-eat set menu of soup, salad, beans, pasta, a meat dish, and cheese to finish, along with jug wine to wash it all down. There are three sittings ($10 breakfast from 7–9am, $11 lunch at noon sharp, and $17 dinner at 7pm), and reservations are recommended for dinner which will include the Basque specialty of pickled tongue. There's similar fare at *Pyrenees*, 601 Sumner St (Ⓣ661/323-0053), where dining hours are more flexible, and at *Wool Growers*, 620 E 19th St (Ⓣ661/327-9584), where there's an *à la carte* menu.

If Basque doesn't appeal, the diner-style *24th Street Café*, 1415 24th St, does top-rate breakfasts; *Joseph's*, hidden back off the road at 3013 F St (Ⓣ661/322-7710), serves a huge, very impressive calzone to a band of dedicated regulars; while *The Garden Spot*, 3320 Truxton Ave, makes healthy eating a pleasure with an all-you-can-eat salad bar buffet for around $8. To stay in tune with Bakersfield's country-music persona, eat at *Zingo's*, 3201 Buck Owens Blvd, a 24-hr truck stop whose frilly-aproned waitresses deliver plates of diner staples; or try the extensive Sunday brunch at the *Buck Owens' Crystal Palace* (9.30am–2pm; $17).

Nightlife now extends beyond slide-guitar and torch songs with a number of places downtown offering local rock bands several nights a week, usually with no cover charge. Stroll 19th Street and see what turns up, but you'll probably end up at *Guthrie's Alley Cat*, 1525 Wall St, tucked down an alley parallel to 18th and 19th streets.

Lake Isabella, Kernville, and the Kern River

After a night spent in Bakersfield's smoky honky-tonks, you might like to clear your head by driving forty-five miles east to the mile-wide **LAKE ISABELLA**, typically alive with windsurfers, jet skiers, and anglers. Mountain biking and rock climbing are also popular activities here, and the place is heaving in the summer. Information on activities and rental outlets are available from the lakeside **visitor center** (mid-May to Oct daily 8am–5pm; Nov to mid–May Mon–Fri 8am–4.30pm; Ⓣ760/379-5646, Ⓕ379-8597); half a mile north of Hwy-178 along Hwy-155. Developed though barely shaded **campsites** ring the dry, sagebrush lakeside, almost all costing $16 a pitch: there are always first-come-first-served sites or you can reserve at least a week in advance with ReserveUSA (Ⓣ1-877/444-6777, Ⓦwww.reserveusa.com). If the frenetic lake activity doesn't suit, backtrack to the riverside *Hobo* campground ($14) on Old Fern Canyon Road, parallel to Hwy-178.

Lake Isabella is fed by the **Kern River**, which churns down from the slopes of Mount Whitney and spills into the lake at the small, appealing town of

Kern River adventures

Three main sections of the Kern River are regularly rafted: the **Lower Kern**, downstream of Lake Isabella (generally June–Aug); the **Upper Kern**, immediately upstream of Kernville (early May–June); and **The Forks**, fifteen miles upstream of Kernville (early May–June).

By far the most popular section is the Upper Kern, the site for the **Lickety-Split** rafting trip – one for families and first-timers, with some long, bouncy rapids. This one-hour excursion (including the bus ride to the put-in) costs around $22, and with over half a dozen operators running trips throughout the day, there is little need to book ahead. Other trips run less frequently, and you should reserve in advance, though you've got a better chance mid-week when crowds are thinner and prices a few dollars lower. The pick of these are the day-trips on the Upper Kern, which run close to the $130 mark ($140 at weekends), the two-day Lower Kern trip ($290, weekends $340), and the three-day backcountry trips on The Forks which range around $650–800. Wetsuits (essential early in the season and for the longer trips) are extra. Within this basic framework there are any number of permutations: check with Chuck Richards' Whitewater, 11200 Kernville Rd (☎760/379-4444 or 1-800/624-5950, ⊛www.chuckrichards.com), or Whitewater Voyages (☎1-800/400-7238, ⊛www.whitewatervoyages.com).

As you'd expect, kayaking is also big here, and Sierra South, 11300 Kernville Rd (☎760/376-3745 or 1-800/457-2082, ⊛www.sierrasouth.com), supplement their rafting operation with one of southern California's top **kayaking** schools, offering Eskimo rolling sessions, instruction at all levels, and guided multi-day river trips, all generally costing around $150 a day. They also offer full-day beginner **rock climbing** lessons ($110) on the nearby Kernville Slab, as do Mountain & River Adventures, 11113 Kernville Rd (☎760/376-6553 or 1-800/861-6553, ℗376-1267, ⊛www.mtnriver.com), who stretch up to intermediate grades and have their own outdoor climbing wall three miles north along Sierra Way.

If you have the equipment for private rafting or kayaking expeditions, you'll still need to grab a free **permit** from any of the area's Forest Service offices.

KERNVILLE on its northern shore. It is a peaceful retiree-dominated place, but come on a summer weekend, or anytime in July and August, and it is full of adrenaline junkies blasting mountain bikes along the local trails or negotiating the rapids in all manner of aquatic paraphernalia. Most people come to ride the Kern, which ranks as one of the steepest navigable rivers in the United States, dropping over 12,000ft along 150 miles, and producing some of the world's most exhilarating whitewater opportunities. The tougher stuff is generally left to the experts, but during the season, which usually runs from May until early August (longer if there has been a heavy winter), commercial rafting operators vie for custom (see box). If you've got time to kill while friends raft, delve into the Native, gold mining, and lumbering history in the **Kern Valley Museum**, 49 Big Blue Rd (Thurs–Sun 10am–4pm; free), or take a look at their video library of movies filmed in the area.

Kernville is big enough to have a bank, ATM, post office, and supermarket, but only campers will find ultra-cheap **accommodation**. Central motels start at around $60, the best value being *The Kernville Inn*, 11042 Kernville Rd (☎760/376-2206 or 1-877/393-7900, ℗376-3735; rooms ❸, with kitchen ❹–❺), right in the center and with a pool and comfortable rooms, some with kitchens. Up the scale, there's the *Kern River Inn B&B*, 119 Kern River Drive (☎760/376-6750 or 1-800/986-4382, ⊛www.kernriverinn.com; ❺), and the luxurious *Whispering Pines Lodge*, 13745 Sierra Way (☎760/376-3733 or 1-877/241-4100,

@www.kernvalley.com/whisperingpines; rooms ❻, suites ❼), a mile north of town, with a nice pool, balconies overlooking the river, and a delicious breakfast served on the terrace. *Falling Waters River Resort*, three miles north of town at 15729 Sierra Way (☎760/376 2242 or 1-888/376-2242, @www.chuck-richards.com; rooms ❷, cottages ❺), has decent budget motel rooms and plusher self-catering cottages marred by overenthusiastic decor. Tent **campers** can stay in the various RV parks around town, but are better off in the string of riverside campgrounds to the north (see below).

There are several **restaurants** around town including the reliable and authentic *That's Italian*, 9 Big Blue Rd (☎760/376-6020; closed Mon & week-day lunches), by the central park, and the *Pizza Barn*, 11401 Kernville Rd (☎760/376-1856), which churns out decent product in a bar with big-screen sports. Espresso coffee is good at the *Big Blue Bear* gift shop, opposite *That's Italian*, and if you don't mind driving fifteen miles north, there's great steak at *McNally's*, Sierra Way (☎760/376-2430).

If you can't find all this yourself, consult the central **Chamber of Commerce**, 11447 Kernville Rd (Mon–Sat 10am–3pm; ☎760/376-2629, @www.kernvillechamber.org); for information on the wooded country to the north call in at the **Sequoia Forest Ranger Station**, 105 Whitney Rd (mid-May to Oct daily 8am–5pm; Nov to mid–May Mon–Fri 8am–4.30pm; ☎760/376-3781, ℻376-3795), next to the museum.

Giant Sequoia National Monument and the Sequoia National Forest

Wedged between Lake Isabella and the Sequoia National Park lies the **SEQUOIA NATIONAL FOREST**, a vast canopy of pine trees punctuated by massive, glacier-polished domes and gleaming granite spires. Much of it is untouched wilderness that's barely less stunning than the national parks to the north, and in recognition of this a large section of this was re-designated the **GIANT SEQUIOA NATIONAL MONUMENT** (unrestricted access) as one of Bill Clinton's final gestures before leaving office. Naturally, it is packed with giant sequoias (in 38 small groves), and, as it is far less visited than the national parks, it is perfect if you're seeking total solitude; hiking trails run vir-tually everywhere. Backcountry camping only requires a free permit for your stove or fire, available from the Sequoia Forest ranger stations that are dotted around the perimeter of the forest and which also have details of the scores of drive-in campsites which stud the forest – some free, others up to $14 a pitch.

There's **no public transportation** through here; the roads are in good shape though, if subject to **snow closure** in winter (mid-Nov to mid-May). The best access is along Sierra Way from Lake Isabella, which passes through Kernville and follows the Upper Kern River past numerous shaded, waterside, $14 camp-sites (reserve for summer weekends on ☎1-877/444-6777) to Johnsondale Bridge, twenty miles north of Kernville. From the bridge, hikers can follow the **River Trail** upstream passing the numerous rapids of The Forks section of the Kern, great for spotting rafters and kayakers on weekend afternoons and even for camping at one of several free walk-in sites along the river; the first is about ten minutes' hike.

The road splits at Johnsondale Bridge. The eastern branch follows the Sherman Pass Road which cuts through the Golden Trout Wilderness to Hwy-395 and the Owens Valley, passing numerous free "dispersed" **camp-grounds**: essentially just designated sites with no toilets or piped water. Sticking with Sierra Way, you turn west and start climbing to tiny Johnsondale

– just a seasonal store and restaurant – where a trail access road cuts 23 miles north to the Jerkey Meadow trailhead. Along the Jerkey Meadow road there are great views of The Needles, and abundant dispersed **camping**, best at Camping Area 4, four miles along, where the stream has sculpted a lovely series of **bathing pools** and smooth rocks for sunning yourself. The *Lower Peppermint* campground ($12), a few miles further along, has toilets and water.

Continuing along Sierra Way it is seven miles to a road junction where you join the twisting and narrow **Western Divide Highway** (Hwy-190) which, after a couple of miles, passes the **Trail of a Hundred Giants** ($3 per vehicle), an easy, shaded interpretive trail around the second most southerly stand of giant trees. Among more sequoias across the road is the *Redwood* campground ($14).

Continuing north, you catch glimpses of magnificent Sierra vistas as the road climbs above the 7000-foot mark, but for the best views it is worth pressing on five miles to the 7200-foot exfoliated scalp of **Dome Rock**, just half a mile off the highway, or **The Needles**, a further three miles on. This series of tall pinnacles – the Magician, the Wizard, and the Warlock, among others – present some of America's most demanding crack climbs, and can be visited on the moderate, undulating hiking and biking **Needles Lookout Trail** (5 miles round-trip; 2hrs), which starts three miles off the highway up a dirt road. The final switchback leads to a fire-lookout station (open June–Oct Wed–Sun 9am–6pm), precariously perched atop a rock pinnacle with supreme views over the Kern Valley and across to Mount Whitney. Nearby **accommodation** extends to the *Quaking Aspen* campsite (mid-May to mid-Nov; $14) half a mile to the north of the Needles, the woodsy *Mountain Top B&B*, half a mile to the south (℡559/542-2639 or 1-888/867-4784, ℠www.mountaintopbnb.com; ❺), and the adjacent *Ponderosa Lodge* (℡559/542-2579; ❹), with pleasant motel rooms, a restaurant, bar, grocery store, and expensive gas. The Western Divide Highway then executes endless twists and turns forty miles down to the valley town of Porterville, where you can turn right for Sequoia and Kings Canyon national parks or continue straight to rejoin Hwy-99.

Visalia

As you leave Bakersfield heading north towards Fresno on Hwy-99, the oil wells fade into full-blown agricultural territory. Only a couple of towns warrant much of your time, the first and largest being **VISALIA**, seventy miles north of Bakersfield and just east of Hwy-99 on Hwy-198. Owing to a large oak forest that offered both shade and timber for home-building, Visalia was the first place in the San Joaquin Valley to be settled. Although the forest is gone, large numbers of oaks and sycamores are still planted around the city and local people put an extraordinary amount of care into the upkeep of parks and gardens. In short, it's a pretty place, with a compact and leafy town center that invites evening strolls down to the local restaurant in the relative cool of the evening.

Central Visalia is best seen on foot: self-guided walking tours of the grand old houses in its older parts can be obtained free from the **Chamber of Commerce** (see below). Further out, **Mooney Grove Park**, three miles down South Mooney Boulevard (nominally $5 per vehicle, though often free midweek), contains the **Tulare County Museum** (mid-May to mid-Sept daily except Tues 10am–4pm; $2; ℡209/733-6616), which has good Yokuts basketry and a collection of buildings and agricultural equipment brought here from around the region. It is marked by a huge slice of a giant sequoia.

Close to the park's south entrance, and visible from South Mooney Boulevard, you'll find a bronze replica of the *End of the Trail* statue, which was made for the 1915 Panama–Pacific International Exposition in San Francisco and was intended to mark the closing of the western frontier. It portrays the defeat of Native Americans at the hands of advancing white settlers and is intentionally gloomy. The statue became well known throughout the West, and still inspires a host of copies; the original was situated here for fifty years before being given to the National Cowboy Heritage Center in Oklahoma City.

To get a sense of what the Visalia area was like before the city's founding, drive seven miles east along Hwy-198 and half a mile north along Road 182 to the **Kaweah Oaks Preserve**, over three hundred acres of oak and sycamore woodland threaded by easy trails, though a little too close to the highway to be genuinely peaceful.

Practicalities

Greyhound buses, and Orange Belt Stages from Hanford, arrive at the **bus station** at 1927 E Mineral King Ave, inconveniently distant from either downtown or the **Chamber of Commerce** at 720 W Mineral King Ave (Mon–Fri 8.30am–5pm; ☎559/734-5876, ⓦwww.visaliachamber.org). There's free **Internet access** at the Tulare County Library, 200 W Oak Ave (☎559/733-6954).

As the closest substantial town to the southern entrance of the Sequoia National Park – less than an hour's drive away along Hwy-198 – Visalia makes a comfortable base for exploring this raw wilderness. The most sumptuous **accommodation** is at the pool- and spa-equipped *Ben Maddox House B&B*, 601 N Encina St (☎559/739-0721 or 1-800/401-9800, ⓦwww.benmaddox.com; ❺), a large redwood house built in 1876 for Ben Maddox, the man who brought hydroelectricity to the San Joaquin Valley. An adjacent house has additional rooms with self-catering facilities. South Mooney Boulevard has the densest concentration of **motels**: *Mooney Motel* at no. 2120 (☎559/733-2666; ❷) has a small pool and simple, recently renovated rooms, or you might prefer the slightly plusher *Econolodge*, no. 1400 (☎559/732-6641 or 1-800/242-4261; ❸), or *Lamp Liter Inn*, 3300 W Mineral King Ave (☎559/732-4511 or 1-800/662-6692, ⓕ732-1840; ❹), which has a very nice pool and a sports bar and grill restaurant on site.

Visalia also has some of the best places to **eat** for miles around: try *Merle's*, 604 S Mooney Blvd, a Fifties-style drive-in diner with semi-circular vinyl booths and a reputation for its chocolate mudslide sundae. Alternatively, wander around downtown and choose from *Café 225*, 225 W Main St (☎559/733-2967), a modern bistro-style place with an eclectic menu that features artichoke fritters ($6), baked red snapper ($14), prosciutto and roasted garlic pizza ($9); *Java Jungle*, 208 W Main St (☎559/732-5282), for good coffee and occasional acoustic bands; and *Brewbakers*, 219 E Main St (☎559/627-2739), which serves its own microbrews with bar meals. Upscale diners are catered for at the *Vintage Press*, 216 N Willis St (☎559/733-3033), where you might ease down wild mushrooms sautéed in cognac followed by red snapper with toasted almonds and capers, a dessert and coffee, for around $50 a head, much more if you explore the vast and wonderful wine list.

Hanford

HANFORD, twenty miles west of Visalia on Hwy-198, was named after James Hanford, a paymaster on the Southern Pacific Railroad who became popular with his employees when he took to paying them in gold. The town formed part of a spur on the railroad and remains a major stopover on the route between Los Angeles and San Francisco. Today it exhibits a calm and restful air – if you're seeking anything more active you'll be disappointed.

Hanford's visitor center (see overleaf) can give you a map of the center of town detailing the now spotless and spruced-up buildings around Courthouse Square, once the core of local life at the beginning of the twentieth century. The honey-colored **Courthouse** (Mon–Sat 10am–6pm, Sun 10am–5pm; free) retains many of its Neoclassical features – not least a magnificent staircase – and has, more recently, been occupied by shops and galleries. As you'd expect, the old Hanford jail, rather pretentiously modeled on the Paris Bastille, is only a ball-and-chain's throw away. It was used until 1968 and is now restored as a restaurant (*The Bastille*; see overleaf), although you can wander through to see the old cells – now and again used for secluded dining.

Much less ostentatiously, rows of two-story porched dwellings, four blocks east of the square, mark the district that was home to most of the eight hundred or so Chinese families who came to Hanford to work on the railroad. At the center of the community was the **Taoist Temple** on China Alley (open for groups of 6–20 only and by appointment; more details from the visitor center or call ☎559/582-4508). Built in 1893, the temple served a social as well as a spiritual function, providing free lodging to work-seeking Chinese immigrants, and was used as a Chinese school during the early 1920s. Everything inside is original, from the teak burl figurines to the marble chairs, and it's a shame that entry is so restricted. You can, however, take a look at another institution of Hanford's Chinese community: the **Imperial Dynasty Restaurant**, two doors on from the temple, still run by the family who opened it fifty years ago. The interior is simple and modest, but the fame of the cooking – oddly French and Italian, not Chinese – has spread far and wide and prices have risen as a result.

Mildly absorbing oddments from Hanford's past are gathered at the **Hanford Carnegie Museum**, 109 E Eighth St (Tues–Fri noon–3pm, Sat noon–4pm; $1; ☎559/584-1367), filling part of the interior of the town's elegant 1905 library – one of many small-town libraries financed by altruistic millionaire industrialist Andrew Carnegie.

For something more diverting, head six miles south of town to the **Ruth & Sherman Lee Institute for Japanese Art**, 15770 Tenth Ave (Sept–May Tues–Sat 1–5pm, closed July & Aug; free; ⊛www.shermanleeinstitute.org), incongruously located on the walnut orchard of local cattle rancher Bill Clark. With the guidance of friends and mentors Ruth and Sherman Lee, Clark has been amassing Japanese scrolls, folding screens, lacquerware, and sculpture since the 1970s and even designed the institute's Japanese-inspired building and his adjacent house and garden. Slip off your shoes and admire the dragon-in-clouds temple ceiling before entering the main room where you can sit on tatami mats to view the works up close. Only a small portion of the collection is on show at one time but there are always outstanding pieces, some dating back to the tenth century and many from the Edo Period (1615–1868). In particular, look out for two superb thirteenth-century sculptural pieces: the *Bodhisattva of the Wish-granting Jewel* and the *Daiitoko Myoo* – the institute's signature piece – with its multi-limbed figure astride a kneeling ox.

Practicalities

Orange Belt Stages (☎1-800/266-7433) provide twice-daily **bus** links to Visalia and the Greyhound station at Goshen Junction, near Visalia (for connections to Los Angeles and San Francisco), and also run a service across to San Luis Obispo on the coast. The town's **visitor center** (Mon–Fri 9am–5pm; ☎559/582-5024, ⓦwww.visithanford.com) is conveniently located inside the handsomely restored Amtrak depot at 200 Santa Fe Ave. Free **Internet access** is available at the library at 401 Douty St.

If you decide to **stay** in Hanford your choice is limited to the Victorian-styled *Irwin Street Inn*, 522 N Irwin (☎559/583-8000, ⓦwww.irwinstreetinn .com; rooms ❹, suites ❻), and a couple of motels, the cheapest and most central being the *Downtown Motel*, 101 N Redington (☎559/582-9036; ❷). For **eating**, the most atmospheric place is *The Bastille*, 113 Court St, a fine steakhouse also serving mountainous lean burgers and sandwiches until late, followed by *Art Works*, 120 W Sixth St, a good espresso café doing a great range of smoothies, showcasing local art, and sometimes putting on live music. During the day, don't miss the rich creaminess of the made-on-the-premises ice cream at *Superior Dairy*, 325 N Douty St, just across from *The Bastille*.

Fresno

Almost classic in its ugliness, **FRESNO**, with its population of 400,000, is the largest city between LA and San Francisco, and an increasingly Hispanic one. It is very much the hub of business in the San Joaquin Valley, though in some

ways feels little more than an overgrown farming town. For many years, Fresno seemed to miss out on the restoration programs that improved similar communities elsewhere in California, but recently the business heart has been rejuvenated. Witness the stridently modern buildings like the delta-winged steel-and-glass form of the **Fresno City Hall** close to the Amtrak station, and the new stadium for Fresno's Triple A baseball team, the Grizzlies, right downtown.

Still, there's an odd mix of civic pride and urban decay, the latter fuelling Fresno's status as one of the US's crime hot spots: Fresno's residents once looked down their noses at Bakersfield, but the position is now largely reversed. For all that, Fresno does have its good points, and you might even want to spend a night here to take in the fascinating Forestiere Underground Gardens in the northern suburbs and something of the nightlife in the vibrant Tower District.

If you're in the region in late February and early March you might also consider following at least part of the 62-mile **Blossom Trail** (free map from the visitor center; see below), which weaves among fruit orchards, citrus groves, and the vineyards which make Fresno the world's raisin capital.

Arrival, information, and accommodation

The **bus** and **train** terminals are downtown – Greyhound at 1033 H St and Amtrak at Tulare and Q – both an easy walk from the **visitor center**, on the corner of Fresno and O streets (June–Aug Mon–Fri 9am–5pm, Sat 10am–3pm; Sept–May Mon–Fri 10am–4pm, Sat 11am–3pm; ☎559/237-0988, ⓦwww.fresnocvb.org), located in a distinctive, conical-roofed water tower that dates back to 1894. Here you can check details on everything in and around the city including the nearby Fresno County Library, 2420 Mariposa St (☎559/488-3195), where there is free **Internet access**.

Downtown is just about small enough to walk around if you don't mind the heat, but non-drivers will want to make use of the Fresno Area Express ($1, exact change; ☎559/498-1122), if only to reach Forestiere Underground Gardens. Route #20, picked up downtown on Van Ness (every 30–60min) comes within a mile, and you can transfer to the #9 for the last stretch. Routes #26 and #28 travel between Van Ness and the Tower District.

If you decide to **stay**, you'll appreciate the low prices at numerous **motels**, all with pools, clustered together near the junction of Olive Avenue (the Tower District's main drag) and Hwy-99. Some charge rock-bottom rates for rooms that are well below par, so the best deals here are the *Welcome Inn*, 777 N Parkway Drive (☎559/237-2175; ❶), and *Motel 6*, 1240 N Crystal Ave (☎559/237-0855, ⓕ497-5869; ❷). For smarter rooms, a better pool and an exercise room, splash out on the *Best Western Parkside Inn*, 1415 W Olive Ave (☎559/237-2086 or 1-800/442-2284; ❸). **Downtown**, there's the budget *Super 8*, 2127 Inyo St at L Street (☎559/268-0621, ⓕ233-9300; ❷), which has a pool, and the more upscale *La Quinta Inn*, 2926 Tulare Street (☎559/442-1110 or 1-800/531-5900; ❹).

The Town and around

To get the best of Fresno, you'll have to leave the center, and if time is short, the place to start is Forestiere Underground Gardens, a fascinating warren of rooms hewn out of the hardpan to protect one man and his crops from the heat. The Kearney Mansion also warrants an hour of your time before you return to the lesser attractions of downtown.

△ The majestic sequoias

Forestiere Underground Gardens and Kearney Mansion

The one place which turns Fresno into a destination in its own right is **Forestiere Underground Gardens**, 5021 W Shaw Ave (late May–early Sept Wed–Sun tours at 10am, noon & 2pm; late March–late May & early Sept–mid-Nov Sat & Sun tours at 10am, noon & 2pm; $7; ☎209/271-0734), seven miles northwest of the center, a block east of the Shaw Avenue exit off Hwy-99. A subterranean labyrinth of over fifty rooms, the gardens were constructed by Sicilian émigré and former Boston and New York subway tunneler Baldasare Forestiere, who came to Fresno in 1905. In a fanatical attempt to stay cool and protect his crops, Forestiere put his digging know-how to work, building underground living quarters and skylit orchards with just a shovel and wheelbarrow. He gradually improved techniques for maximizing his yield but wasn't above playful twists like a glass-bottomed underground aquarium and a subterranean bathtub fed by water heated in the midday sun. He died in 1946, his forty years of work producing a vast earth honeycomb, part of which was destroyed by the construction of Hwy-99 next door, while another section awaits restoration. Wandering around the remainder of what he achieved is a fascinating way to pass an hour out of the heat of the day, enlivened by the tour guide's homespun anecdotes.

With more time to spare, head seven miles west from downtown along Kearney Boulevard, a long, straight, palm-lined avenue that was once the private driveway through the huge Kearney Park ($3 per car; free with Mansion entry) to the **Kearney Mansion** (Fri–Sun tours at 1pm, 2pm & 3pm; $4). It was built for M. Theo Kearney, an English-born turn-of-the-century agricultural pioneer and raisin mogul, who maintained it in the opulent French Renaissance style to which he seemed addicted. He had even grander plans to grace Fresno with a French chateau, the mind-boggling designs for which are displayed here. Regarded locally as something of a mystery man, Kearney apparently led a busy social life on both sides of the Atlantic, which may explain why he died during an ocean crossing following a heart attack.

Downtown Fresno

Once you've seen Forestiere Underground Gardens and the Kearney Mansion, you've really seen the best of the town. Downtown sights are limited to a quintet of minor museums, all worthy of half an hour of your time, if only to get out of the searing heat. The **Meux Home Museum**, corner of Tulare and R streets (guided tours Fri–Sun noon–3.30pm; $5; ☎559/233-8007, Ⓦwww.meux.mus.ca.us), is Fresno's only surviving late-nineteenth-century house, built for what was then the staggering sum of $12,000. This was the home of a doctor who arrived from the Deep South, bringing with him the novelty of a two-story house and a plethora of trendy Victorian features. What isn't original is the convincing reconstruction, and the turrets, arches, and octagonal master bedroom help make the place stylish and absorbing – quite out of sync with the Fresno that has sprawled up around it.

Each of the three museums clustered a dozen blocks to the west helps illustrate the historic and continuing importance of immigration to Fresno – now a predominantly Hispanic city. The **Metropolitan Museum**, 1555 Van Ness Ave (Tues–Sun 11am–5pm; $7, free Thurs 5–8pm; ☎559/441-1444, Ⓦwww.fresnomet.org), mainly hosts temporary exhibitions but has a small collection of jigsaw puzzles dating back a century and a half, and a delightful display of over two hundred mostly nineteenth-century Chinese snuffboxes arranged thematically – flowers, deities, mythological creatures, and so on.

Fresno's most famous son, the novelist and scriptwriter **William Saroyan**, gets hagiographic treatment in the museum despite his early desire to leave Fresno and never come back. He did keep coming back, however, creating a fictional identity for Fresno in his writing and died here in 1981 at the age of 72. He is best known for his Pulitzer Prize–winning *The Time of Your Life*, and *The Human Comedy*, which he also wrote and adapted for the screen, earning himself an Academy Award. He refused to pick up his award after a tiff with Louis B. Mayer, but the Oscar is on display along with his Underwood typewriter and panels with telling quotes from his life. Along the street, **Arte Américas**, 1630 Van Ness Ave (Tues–Sat noon–5pm; $2, free Thurs 5–8pm; ☎559/266-2623, ⓦwww.arteamericas.org), has several galleries exploring mostly Hispanic-American visual and performing arts along with Mexican and Central and South American contributions. Fresno's black history is told at the **African American Historical and Cultural Museum**, 1857 Fulton St (Mon–Fri 9am–4pm; $4; ☎559/268-7102), though the hundreds of portraits and assorted newspaper clippings are unlikely to divert you long from the often impressive temporary exhibits and the African statuary for sale in the museum store.

A couple of miles north of downtown, the **Fresno Art Museum**, 2233 N First St at Clinton, in Radio Park (Tues–Fri 10am–5pm, Sat & Sun noon–5pm; $4, Tues free; ☎559/441-4221, ⓦwww.fresnoartmuseum.com), has a changing roster of high quality modern art that is usually worth browsing, plus an attractive sculpture garden and rooms devoted to pre-Columbian Mexican art spanning Mesoamerican styles from 2500 years ago until the arrival of the Spanish in the early sixteenth century. There's also a relatively minor but beautiful 1926 Diego Rivera canvas, *El Dia de las Flores, Xochimilco*, along with an explanation of how it came to be here.

The Tower District

In a town with a tradition of almond-growing and cattle-rustling, Fresno's **Tower District**, three miles north of downtown, comes as a pleasant surprise. Proximity to the City College campus made the area something of a hippy hangout during the Sixties; today it has a well-scrubbed liberal feel, plus several blocks of antique shops and bookstores, ethnic restaurants and coffeehouses to fill a few hours of idle browsing.

On the Tower District's western edge at the end of Olive Avenue, the tree-filled **Roeding Park** (Feb–Oct $1 per car, Nov–Jan free) boasts the **Chaffee Zoological Gardens** (daily 9am–5pm; $6), a couple of amusement parks and a lake. This is where Fresnoites come to convince themselves that the city is a nice place to live, and when strolling here on a day that's not totally baking you could almost believe them.

Eating and drinking

To pick up fresh, good **food**, head for the **farmers market** at Fulton and San Joaquin (Tues, Thurs & Sat 7am–2pm), and downtown check out the *Kern St Coffee Company*, 2134 Kern St, for good java. Otherwise, the Tower District, centered on the Tower Theatre at the junction of Olive and Wishon avenues, is very much the place to eat and drink. You'll get decent diner food along with locally famed chicken (and fruit) pies at bargain prices at *Grandmarie's Chicken Pie Shop* (☎559/237-5042), 861 E Olive Ave; and good-value lunches and dinners, plus excellent home-brewed beers, at the *Butterfield Brewing Company Bar & Grill*, 777 E Olive Ave (☎559/264-5521). The *Daily Planet*, 1211 N Wishon

Ave (☎559/266-4259), serves a fixed-price four-course dinner (usually under $20) in Art Deco surroundings, and for seafood that's surprisingly good this far from the coast, head to the moderately priced *Tower Bay Fish Co*, 737 E Olive Ave (☎559/442-3474). For something special, visit the dinner-only *Veni Vidi Vici*, 1116 N Fulton St (☎559/266-5510; closed Mon), for the likes of *calamari* and rock shrimp salad ($10) followed by five-spice pork chop with red Thai curry glaze ($25).

To find out what's going on, check out ⦿www.towerdistrictnews.com, which lists **upcoming events** and gigs, including ones at the 250-seat *Roger Rocka's Dinner Theater*, 1226 N Wishon (☎559/266-9494, ⦿www.tower2000.com; closed Mon & Tues), where Broadway-style shows are preceded either by a sumptuous buffet (Wed, Thurs & Sun matinee; $32.50 all up), or a fine dining meal (Fri & Sat; $35).

Northern San Joaquin Valley

The towns of the northern San Joaquin Valley largely follow the pattern of those strung along Hwy-99 further south. Founded on agriculture, all had the hearts ripped out of them by suburban sprawl in the latter half of the twentieth century, leaving only winos, crazies, and a lot of poor Mexican immigrants. But in recent years the town centers have rebounded. There's enough of their old downtown streets left to evoke something out of an Edward Hopper painting, but the smartened-up cityscapes are all increasingly pleasant places to stroll, the ubiquitous taquerias now joined by java joints.

None of the three main towns warrant more than a few hours' exploration. You may spend the night in **Merced**, especially if **Yosemite-bound**; **Modesto** offers a couple of interesting sites and vestiges of the 1950s, and **Stockton** has a certain down-at-heel charm.

Merced

The best thing about sluggish **MERCED**, fifty miles north of Fresno, is its courthouse, a gem of a building in the main square that's maintained as the **County Courthouse Museum** (Wed–Sun 1–4pm; free). This striking Italian Renaissance-style structure, with columns, elaborately sculptured window frames, and a cupola topped by a statue of the Goddess of Justice (minus her customary blindfold), was raised in 1875, dominating the town then as it does now. Impressively restored in period style, the courtroom retained a legal function until 1951, while the equally sumptuous offices were vacated in the 1970s, leaving the place to serve as storage space for local memorabilia – most exotic among which is a Taoist shrine, found by chance in the back room of a Chinese restaurant.

Six miles north of Merced, close to the dormitory community of **Atwater** – and signposted off Hwy-99 – lies the **Castle Air Museum** (daily: June–Sept 9am–5pm; Oct–May 10am–4pm; $6; ⦿www.elite.net/castle-air). Forty-odd military aircraft – mostly bulky bombers with a few fighters thrown in, including the world's fastest plane, the SR-71 – are scattered outdoors, while inside there's a static B52 simulator, assorted military paraphernalia, and a collection of some 120 model planes crafted by one enthusiast from redwood. Route #8 of Merced's transit system, "The Bus" (Mon–Sat only; ☎1-800/384-3111), runs out here every hour or so for $1 each way.

Practicalities

Neither of these sights are much of a reason to visit Merced, though the convenient **bus links to Yosemite** are. Greyhounds from Bakersfield, Sacramento, and San Francisco stop downtown at the **Transpo Center** on W 16th St at N Street, where you'll find **Merced California Welcome Center**, 710 W 16th St (June–Aug Mon–Fri 8am–7pm, Sat & Sun 8am–3.30pm; Sept–May Mon–Fri 8am–5pm Sat & Sun 11am–3pm; ℡209/384-2791, ⓦwww .yosemite-gateway.org), which covers the region, and the **Chamber of Commerce**, 690 W 16th St (Mon–Fri 8.30am–5pm; ℡209/384-3333 or 1-800/446-5353, ⓦwww.merced-chamber.com), which is good for specifically local information. The **Amtrak station** is somewhat isolated at 24th and K streets, about ten blocks away on the opposite side of the town center: follow K Street off W 16th Street. Train and bus stations are both stops for the three or four daily **YARTS buses** (℡1-877/989-2787, ⓦwww.yarts.com) to Yosemite: see p.411 for more on getting to Yosemite.

If you are relying on public transportation, by far the best **place to stay** is the reservations-only *HI-Merced Home Hostel* (℡209/725-0407, ⓔmerced-hostel@juno.com; $16). Check-in hours and access hours are limited (7–9am & 5–10pm) but this is a small price to pay for a ride to and from the stations, an enthusiastic welcome, as much information as you can handle and a free dessert every evening. It is a great place to hook up with Yosemite-bound travelers, who might wish to team up and rent a car from Aide Rent A Car, 1530 W 16th St (℡209-722-8084), which usually has vehicles from as little as $35 a day.

Drivers in need of a motel should take the Mariposa/Yosemite exit from Hwy-99 which leaves you right by two good places to stay: the *Holiday Inn Express*, 730 Motel Drive (℡209/383-0333; ❹), and the bargain *Happy Inn*, 740 Motel Drive (℡209/722-6291; ❶), both with pool and continental breakfast. Closer to the Transpo Center, try the extremely cheap *Slumber Motel*, 1315 W 16th St (℡209/722-5783; ❶), with a small pool and cable TV.

For **something to eat**, you'll find authentic Mexican at *La Nina's*, 1327 18th St at T (closed Mon), some ten blocks from the bus station. For a broad range of ethnic and American dishes at very reasonable prices, try the popular *Paul's Place*, 2991 G St at Alexander – try the Portuguese linguisa sausage omelet. Downtown, *Wired* at 450 W 18th St does good espresso and muffins and has fast **Internet access**.

Modesto and around

Forty miles north of Merced along Hwy-99 you reach **MODESTO**, a town which got its unusual name after prominent San Francisco banker William Ralston was too modest to accept the new town being named after him. Much later, it was the childhood home of movie director George Lucas, and became the inspiration (though not the location) for his movie *American Graffiti*, the classic portrayal of growing up in small-town America during the late 1950s. The movie contains a number of references to local people, particularly the teachers who rubbed Lucas the wrong way in his formative years. Sadly, local ordinances (enacted in 1992 after several years of bad behavior) have put an end to the fine art of **cruising**, though in recent years The Car Show (middle weekend in June) has stepped in with dozens of classic cars from all over the state and beyond dusted off and cruised through the city. About the only other reminder of those heady days is the **Lucas Plaza Statue**, a rather token duck-tail, bobbysox, and '57 Chevy affair at the corner of J Street and McHenry Avenue. A more evocative celebration of the era is the **A&W Root Beer Drive-In**, 1404 G St, which has roller-skating waitresses serving root beer floats ordered from illuminated car-side menus. Despite the ban, you'll still see the better-kept cruising rigs parked here on Friday and Saturday nights until 10pm.

It may seem hard to believe, but as a fairly typical valley town, Modesto does have a history stretching back beyond the Fifties. Its (comparatively) distant past is encapsulated by the shabbily grand **Modesto Arch** – erected in 1912 over Ninth and I to attract attention to the city's expanding economy. The slogan "Water, Wealth, Contentment, Health" clearly lays out the priorities of the city fathers in a time where the need for irrigation was paramount.

More imposingly, the Victorian **McHenry Mansion** at 406 15th St (Mon–Thurs & Sun 1–4pm, Fri noon–3pm; free) is jam-packed with fixtures, fittings, and the personal features of a family whose fate was linked with Modesto's for years. Robert McHenry was a successful wheat rancher in the mid-nineteenth century who did much to bring about a general uplift in the agricultural well-being of the area. Surprisingly, his luxurious dwelling was still being rented out as apartments, at quite low rates, as recently as the early 1970s.

A block from the mansion, a fine Victorian building originally financed by the McHenry family as the fledgling city's library now operates as the **McHenry Museum**, 1402 I St (Tues–Sun noon–4pm; free), which sports mock-ups of a doctor's office, blacksmith's shop, dentist's surgery, and gathering of cattle brands, revealing something of bygone days, although lacking the period atmosphere of the mansion. Adjoining the museum, the **Central California Art League Gallery** (Tues–Sat 10am–4pm; free) displays a show of regional painting and sculpture that should consume no more than a few minutes.

For many visitors the area's chief attraction has been the gustatory pleasures of a visit to the **Hershey's Chocolate Factory**, 120 S Sierra Ave, thirteen miles east in Oakdale. The free weekday tours have been suspended since September 11, but may start up again, and disappointed chocaholics could always call at the gift shop (Mon–Sat 9am–5pm; ☎209/848-8126).

Practicalities

There's not much reason to stop and spend the night in Modesto – if you're looking for a place to stop before diving into Yosemite for a day-trip, Merced is the better bet. However, if you decide to stay, you can find out more about the town and pick up maps at Modesto's **visitor center**, 1114 J St (Mon–Fri 8.30am–5pm; ☎209/571-6480 or 1-800/266-4282, ⓦwww.visitmodesto.com).

Greyhound **buses** stop downtown at the Modesto Transportation Center at J Street and Ninth handy for **accommodation** such as the huge, upscale *Doubletree Hotel*, 1150 9th St (☎209/526-6000; ❺), which includes a pool, sauna, and exercise room, though slightly less handy than the *Chalet Motel*, 115 Downey St (☎209/529-4370, Ⓕ579-9545; ❸), a mile away at the junction with J Street, which also has a pool. There's also bed and breakfast at *Vineyard View B&B*, 2839 Michigan Ave (☎209/523-9009; ❹).

You'll find downtown liberally supplied with decent **places to eat**. *J Street Café*, 1030 J St (closed Sun), is a relaxing spot for good espresso, muffins, and sandwiches; *India Oven*, 1022 11th St, has good value all-you-can-eat lunch and dinner buffets ($6 & $10); and *DeVa*, 1202 J St, is an affordable café and coffeehouse that serves meals throughout the day. Beer drinkers should seek out *St Stan's Brewery, Pub and Restaurant*, 821 L St (☎209/524-2337), where you've a choice of a dozen draught beers to wash down a burger or more substantial meal.

Stockton and around

The immediately striking thing about **STOCKTON**, perched at the far northern limit of the San Joaquin Valley some thirty miles north of Modesto, is the sight of ocean-going freighters so far inland. The San Joaquin and Sacramento rivers converge here, creating a vast delta with thousands of inlets and bays, and a sixty-mile deep-water canal (built in the early 1930s) enables vessels to carry the produce of the valley's farms past San Francisco and directly out to sea. But the geography that aided commerce also saddled Stockton with the image of being a grim place to live and a tough city to work in. During the Gold Rush it was a supply stop on the route to the mines, and it became a gigantic flophouse for broken and dispirited ex-miners who gave up their dreams of fortune and returned here to toil on the waterfront. Though valiant efforts have been made to shed this reputation and beautify the less attractive quarters, it's still primarily a hard-working, sleeves-rolled-up city.

A smattering of buildings downtown evoke the early decades of the twentieth century, thanks to which Stockton is often in demand as a film set. John Huston's downbeat boxing picture, *Fat City*, for example, was shot here.

Marginally more appealing are the blocks bordered by Harding Way and Park Street, and El Dorado and California streets, a short way north of the center. This area has been preserved as the **Magnolia Historical District**, with sixteen intriguing specimens of domestic architecture spanning seven decades from the 1860s. To find them all, pick up the free leaflet from the **San Joaquin CVB**, downtown at 46 W Fremont St (Mon–Fri 9am–5pm; ☎209/943-1987 or 1-800/350-1987, ⓦwww.visitstockton.org).

Roughly a mile west of the Magnolia District, in Victory Park, Stockton gathers totems of its past in the varied and large stock of the **Haggin Museum**, 1201 N Pershing Ave (Tues–Sun 1.30–5pm; $5; ☎209/940-6300, ⓦwww.hagginmuseum.org). Not surprisingly, much is given over to agriculture, including the city's finest moment: the invention by local farmers of a caterpillar tread to enable tractors to travel over muddy ground, adapted by the British for use on tanks and standard use since for the military everywhere. In tremendous contrast, the museum also contains a batch of nineteenth-century French paintings, including works by Renoir and Gauguin, as well as Bouguereau's monumental *Nymphs Bathing*.

Practicalities

Stockton's **Greyhound station** is at 121 S Center St. **Amtrak** has two stops: downtown at 735 S San Joaquin St, and half a mile east at the corner of Aurora and Sacramento streets.

Even traveling by public transportation doesn't mean you have to stay overnight in Stockton; connections both onwards to San Francisco and south down the valley are plentiful – but it can be worth stopping here to **eat**, ethnic restaurants being in good supply. For Chinese there's *On Lock Sam*, 333 S Sutter St (☎209/466-4561), run by the same family since 1898, or *Dave Wong's*, 5602 N Pershing Ave. Downtown, try the stuffed sandwiches at the *Fox Café*, in the foyer of the restored Fox Theater at 220 Main St, and *Yasoo Yani*, 326 E Main St (☎209/464-3108), where Nick's Greek salad is more than a meal. There's more choice along the so-called **Miracle Mile**, a stretch of Pacific Avenue starting around a mile north of downtown – follow Madison from the CVB. Here, among the bookshops, espresso bars, and restaurants, you'll find the Mexican-Southwestern *Fernando's Santa Fe Café*, 2311 Pacific Ave (closed Sun), which turns out tasty fajitas for $13. Afterwards, stroll across the road for a microbrew to the *Valley Brewing Company*, 157 W Adams St. For entertainment, you may catch stars of yesteryear at the Fox Theater, downtown.

If you're forced to stay over, there's a **campground** eight miles south of Stockton–*Dos Reis Park* (☎209/953-8800), just off I-5 – or you can stay in the city in one of the plentiful mid-range chain **hotels** and budget **motels**, mostly near the Waterloo Road exit off Hwy-99. Downtown, try the *Stockton Travelers Motel*, 631 N Center St (☎209/466-8554; ❷), or if this seems a little unsavory, go for the *Days Inn*, 33 N Center St (☎209/948-6151, ☏948-1220; ❹), close to the Greyhound station.

Micke Grove Park and Lodi

If Stockton begins to pall, or it's simply too nice a day to spend in a city, venture ten miles north to the Armstrong Road exit off Hwy-99 for the pastoral relief – at least outside weekends and holidays – of the **Micke Grove Park** (daily 8am–dusk; parking $4 at weekends, $2 midweek), an oak grove which holds a Rose Garden, a Japanese Garden, and a zoo. It also features the **San Joaquin Historical Museum** (Wed–Sun 1–4.45pm; $2), recording the evolution of the local agricultural industry and, more revealingly, the social history that accompanied it. Don't miss the Stockton clamshell dredge bucket, a tool used in the reclamation of the delta and restored and displayed like a major work of art.

Just three miles north of the park sits **LODI**, a small country town immortalized in song by Creedence Clearwater Revival ("Oh Lord, stuck in Lodi again"). Undoubtedly, it was no place to get stuck then, but in the last decade its downtown – centered on its ceremonial Mission Revival-style Lodi Arch – has been rejuvenated with brick paving, trees, and a liberal lick of paint. After an absence of thirty years, Amtrak trains once again call at the smart station, downtown on Sacramento Street, though departures are too infrequent to encourage getting off. Still, it is now a pleasant place to wander around aided by a map from the **Chamber of Commerce**, 35 S School St (Mon–Fri 8.30am–4.30pm; ☎209/367-7840, ⓦwww.lodichamber.com).

Lodi is best known for its **wineries**, mostly located in an area centered on the **Lodi Wine & Visitor Center**, 2545 W Turner Rd, 3 miles northwest of town (daily 10am–5pm; ⓦwww.lodiwine.com), where you can taste three flights of three wines ($3 per flight), one flight always concentrating on the region's famed red Zinfandel. They'll furnish you with a map of local boutique vineyards, most of whom offer free tastings.

Sequoia and Kings Canyon national parks

Separate parks but jointly run and with a long common border, the **SEQUOIA AND KINGS CANYON NATIONAL PARKS** contain an immense variety of geology, flora, and fauna. **Sequoia National Park**, as you might expect from its name, contains the thickest concentration – and the biggest individual specimens – of giant sequoia trees to be found anywhere. These ancient trees tend to outshine (and certainly outgrow) the other features of the park – an assortment of meadows, peaks, canyons, and caves. Notwithstanding a few notable exceptions, **Kings Canyon National Park** doesn't have the big trees but compensates with a gaping canyon gored out of the rock by the Kings River, which cascades in torrents down from the High Sierra during the snow-melt period. There's less of a packaged tourism feel here than in Yosemite: the few established sights (principally the big trees) are near the main roads and concentrate the crowds, leaving the vast majority of the landscape untrammeled and unspoiled, but well within reach for willing hikers. Through it all runs the **Generals Highway**, actually a fairly slow and winding paved road which links two of the biggest sequoias hereabouts, the General Sherman Tree and the General Grant Tree.

To the north of the parks lies the even more vast and almost equally spectacular **Sierra National Forest** (now also designated as part of the Giant Sequoia National Monument), which is bound by fewer of the national-park-style restrictions on hunting and the use of motorized playthings. Consequently there is a greater potential for disturbance, though this is counteracted by the sheer immensity of the region.

The **best time to come** is in late summer and fall, when the days are still warm, the nights are getting chilly at altitude, the roads remain free of snow, and most visitors have left. Bear in mind that although most roads are kept open through the winter, snow blocks Hwy-180 into Kings Canyon and the road into Mineral King (see "Winter in the parks" box on p.391). May and June can also be good, especially in Kings Canyon where snowmelt swells the Kings River dramatically and the canyonside yuccas are in bloom.

Some history

The land now encompassed by the Sequoia and Kings Canyon national parks was once the domain of **Yokuts sub-tribes** – the Monache, Potwisha, and Kaweah peoples – who made summer forays into the high country from their permanent settlements in the lowlands, especially along the Marble Fork of the Kaweah River. The first real European contact came with the 1849 California **Gold Rush**, when prospectors penetrated the area in search of pasture and a direct route through the mountains. Word of abundant lumber soon got out and loggers came to stake their claims in the lowlands. The high country was widely ignored until, in 1858, local natives led Hale Tharp, a cattleman from Three Rivers, up to the sequoias around Moro Rock. Tharp spent the next thirty summers up there in his log home where he was occasionally visited by John Muir, who wrote about the area and brought it to the attention of the

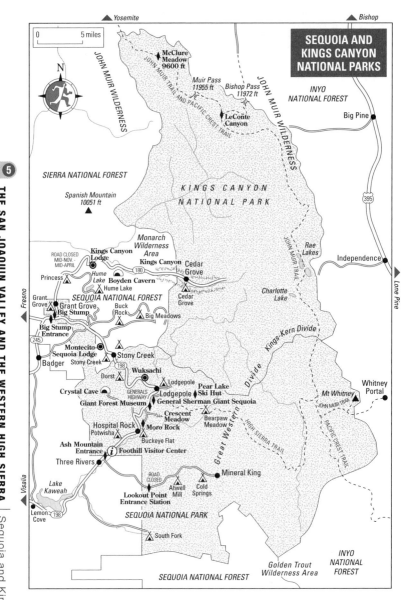

general public and the loggers. Before long, narrow-gauge railways and log flumes littered the area, mainly for clearing fir and pine rather than the sequoias, which tended to shatter when felled. Nonetheless, Visalia conservationist George Stewart campaigned in Washington for some degree of **preservation** for the big trees and, in 1890, four square miles around Grant Grove

The high country of both parks is covered in a blanket of **snow**, usually from November until April or May, and while this limits a great deal of sightseeing and walking, it also opens up opportunities for some superb cross-country skiing. With chains, **access** is seldom much of a problem. Both main roads into the parks – Hwy-198 to Giant Forest and Hwy-180 to Grant Grove – are kept open all year, except for extraordinary circumstances when they are still cleared quickly. The Generals Highway is usually open as far north as Lodgepole and as far south as the *Montecito-Sequoia Lodge*, but the stretch in between is often cleared only when no further snowfalls are expected: it's best then to choose one section of the parks as a base. The Cedar Grove section of Kings Canyon is off limits to cars from mid-November to mid-April, but Grant Grove stays open all year. Facilities are restricted and camping is only available at snow-free lowland sites.

The big winter activities up here are **cross-country skiing** and **snowshoeing**. The northern highway gives access to two places at the hub of miles of marked trails: the Grant Grove Ski Touring Center at Grant Grove (Nov–April; call KCPS on ☏559/335-5500), where there's ski and snowshoe rental, guided naturalist snowshoe walks at weekends, restaurants, and accommodation; and the *Montecito-Sequoia Lodge* (see "Accommodation," below), a resort with its own groomed trails, also open to visitors for around $18 a day. Nearby, the mile-long Big Meadows Nordic Ski Trail is perfect beginner's terrain. To the south, the Wolverton Ski Touring Center, just over two miles south of Lodgepole (Nov–April; call DPNS on ☏559/565-3301), has excellent day-use facilities along with rentals, lessons, and a retail shop. Unless you're a super-hardy camper, you'll need to return to Three Rivers for somewhere to stay.

Experienced skiers and snowshoers might want to spend the night 9200 feet up at the ten-berth **Pear Lake Ski Hut** (mid-Dec to April; $20 per person), beautifully sited at the end of a steep six-mile trail from Wolverton Meadow: contact the Sequoia Natural History Association (☏559/565-3759, ⓦwww.sequoiahistory.org) for reservations.

became Sequoia National Park, the country's second national park after Yellowstone. In 1940 this was incorporated into the newly formed Kings Canyon National Park.

Arrival and information

Although easy to reach by **car** – a fifty-mile drive along the tortuous Hwy-198 from Visalia or a slightly longer but faster journey from Fresno on Hwy-180 – Sequoia and Kings Canyon are not served by public transportation. RVs longer than 22 feet and anything with a trailer shouldn't consider tackling Hwy-198. Visitors should prepare by stocking up with **cash** and **gas** before entering the parks, though some of both is available (see "Listings," p.402).

The parks are always open: **park entry** costs $10 per car, or $5 per hiker or biker and is valid for seven days. This will be collected at the entrance stations, where you'll be given an excellent map and a copy of the free quarterly newspaper with the latest listings of ranger programs, **guided hikes**, and other interpretive activities, as well as general information on the parks.

For information, consult the parks' **website** (ⓦwww.nps.gov/seki), or call at one of the four **visitor centers**: the park headquarters at **Foothills**, a mile north of the southern (Hwy-198) entrance to the park (daily: June–Aug 8am–5pm; Sept–May 8am–4.30pm); and others at Lodgepole, Grant Grove Village, and Cedar Grove Village (see the relevant accounts for details). There is also a useful **ranger station** at Mineral King. For details of hikes and camp-sites in the surrounding Sequoia National Forest, visit the **Hume Lake Ranger District Office**, 35860 Hwy-180 at Clingan's Junction, 17 miles west of the Big Stump entrance (Mon–Sat 8am–4.30pm; ℡559/338-2251, Ⓦwww.r5.fs.fed.us/sequoia).

There is also a comprehensive 24-hour recorded information line (℡559/565-3341), with details on camping, lodging, road conditions, and the facility to order information by mail.

Accommodation

Inside the parks, all facilities, including accommodation, are managed by one of two concessionaires: Kings Canyon Park Services (KCPS ℡559/335-5500 or 1-866/522-6986, Ⓦwww.sequoia-kingscanyon.com), who operate in Cedar Grove and Grant Grove; and Delaware North Parks Services (DNPS ℡559/565-4070 or 1-888/252-5757, Ⓦwww.visitsequoia.com), who cover Lodgepole and Wuksachi. In recent years, the opening of two new lodges to replace those removed from Giant Forest (see below), has raised the standard of **accommodation**, shifting away from rustic towards greater luxury, though simple cabins are still available. You can occasionally pick up cancellations on the day, but space is at a premium during the summer when booking a couple of months in advance is advisable. Rates quoted are for summer season, but huge savings can be had outside peak times, especially at the pricier places.

Heavy demand and the relatively high price of accommodation forces many to stay **outside the parks**, in the motels and B&Bs lining the approach roads a few miles from the entrances. The best selection is in the south at Three Rivers, where booking ahead is advised at weekends through the summer and holidays.

Under the first two headings below, all available roofed accommodation has been included, with just a selection of the best places to stay listed under the final two headings. For **camping**, see the box opposite.

In the parks

Bearpaw High Sierra Camp mid-June to mid-Sept; call DNPS. Soft beds, fluffy towels, hot showers, and hearty meals served up in magnificent wilderness are the trump cards for this cluster of wooden-floored permanent tents (sleeping a total of twelve) on the High Sierra Trail, 11 miles' walk east of Giant Forest Village: just follow the High Sierra Trail from Crescent Meadow. There's no electricity, everything is helicoptered in for the season, and all meals are included in the price tag. Bookings are accepted from January 2 when most weekends and holidays are taken, though you've a reasonable chance of an on-spec place on weeknights in June and September. $155 per person.

Cedar Grove May–Oct; call KCPS. Cozy lodge with private bathroom and air conditioning, right by the Kings River and in the same block as the restaurant and shops. ❺

Grant Grove and John Muir Lodge all year; call KCPS. The widest selection of ways of sleeping under a roof, most options accommodating up to

four people. The most basic are the canvas-roofed cabins (❷), which are too cold for winter use, rising through the more solid rustic cabins (❸) with cooking stove, to comfortable standard cabins (❺) with baths, and the swanky new *John Muir Lodge* (rooms ❻, suites ❽) with very comfortable hotel rooms. **Wuksachi Lodge** all year; call DNPS. Directly competing with the *John Muir Lodge* for the best rooms in the park, the *Wuksachi* consists of several blocks of rooms (ask for mountain views on the upper floor) widely scattered in the woods around an elegant central lounge and restaurant area. Rooms ❼, suites ❽

In Sequoia National Forest

Kings Canyon Lodge mid-April to mid-Nov; ℡559/335-2405. Small lodge located midway between Grant Grove and Cedar Grove offering woodsy cabins with private bathroom (❹) along with pleasant rooms (❹), some sleeping four with private bathroom (❺). Burgers, sandwiches, and breakfasts are served in the lively bar with pool table. ❹–❺

Except during public holidays, there is always plenty of **camping space** in the parks and the surrounding National Forest. All sites operate on a first-come-first-served basis except for *Lodgepole* and *Dorst,* which can be reserved through the National Park Reservation System (NPRS: ℡1-800/365-2267, ⨍301/722-1174, ⓦwww .reservations.nps.gov), and *Princess* and *Hume Lake,* which are reserved through the Forest Service (℡1-877/444-6777, ⓦwww.reserveusa.com). RV drivers won't find any hook-ups, but there are dump stations at *Potwisha, Lodgepole,* and *Dorst.* Collecting "dead and down" firewood is permitted in both the National Park and National Forest, but for cooking you really want to bring along a portable stove. For **backcountry** camping, see the "Hiking" box on p.400. There are public **showers** at several locations (see "Listings," p.403).

Campsites are listed south to north, and the night-time temperatures you can expect are indicated by the site's altitude. **Fees** are sometimes reduced or waived outside the main summer season and when piped water is disconnected, especially in winter.

South Fork (all year; $8; 3600ft). Trailer-free site a twisting thirteen miles east of Lake Kaweah on the very southwestern tip of the park. River water available.

Cold Springs Mineral King (late May–Oct; $8; 7500ft). Excellent shaded riverside site 25 miles west of Hwy-198, with some very quiet walk-in sites. River water available.

Atwell Mill Mineral King (late May–Oct; $8; 6650ft). Slightly less appealing than *Cold Springs,* but still quiet and pleasant, and five miles closer to the highway. Some tent-only sites. Water available.

Potwisha (all year; $14; 2100ft). Smallish, RV-dominated site close to Hwy-198 three miles northeast of the park's southern entrance and beside the Marble Fork of the Kaweah River. Water available.

Buckeye Flat (all year; $14; 2800ft). Peaceful, trailer-free site six miles east of Hwy-198, close to the park's southern entrance and beside the Middle Fork of the Kaweah River. Water available.

Lodgepole (all year; $16; 6700ft). Largest and busiest of the sites, four miles north of Giant Forest Village and close to the highway. Reserve through NPRS in the high season, when there are pay showers, a camp store, water, and flush toilets.

Dorst (late May–early Sept; $16; 6800ft). Another large site, eight miles north of Lodgepole, with flush toilets and water during the season. Reserve through NPRS in summer.

Buck Rock (late May–Oct; free; 7500ft). Excellent and under-utilized National Forest site three miles west of the highway, midway between Lodgepole and Grant Grove Village. No water.

Big Meadows (late May–Oct; free; 7600ft). Similar site to *Buck Rock,* a mile further west among exfoliated granite domes. No water.

Princess (late May–Sept; $14; 5900ft). National Forest campground with water and toilets, handily sited on the way into Kings Canyon. Reserve through Forest Service.

Hume Lake (mid-May to Oct; $16; 5200ft). Reservable National Forest site with water, toilets, and lake swimming for the brave.

Sunset, **Azalea,** and **Crystal Spring**, Grant Grove Village. (*Azalea* year round, others as needed; $14; 6500ft). Comparable large sites all within a few hundred yards of the Grant Grove visitor center.

Sheep Creek, **Sentinel**, **Canyon View**, and **Moraine** Cedar Grove Village (early May to Oct; $14; 4600ft). A series of all-but-contiguous forest sites around the Cedar Grove visitor center. *Canyon View* is tents-only.

Montecito-Sequoia Lodge ☎1-800/227-9900, reservations ☎650/967-8612 or 1-800/227-9900, ⓦwww.mslodge.com. On the Generals Highway (Hwy-198) between Grant Grove Village and Giant Forest Village, this large but low-key family vacation camp is tastefully set next to an artificial lake with all manner of activity programs: canoeing, tennis, swimming, and volleyball in summer; and snow-shoeing, skating, and cross-country skiing in winter (see box, opposite). It is booked solid from mid-June to early Sept (except, curiously, Saturday nights), but at other times you can almost always stay in rustic cabins (❻) or lodge rooms with private bath (❼). Packages booked through the reservation number include breakfast and dinner, and cost from $69 per person.

Stony Creek Generals Highway; late May to Oct; call KCPS. Plain, comfortable motel-style rooms with showers in a block with a good restaurant and a grocery store. ❻

Along Hwy-198: Lemon Cove and Three Rivers

Buckeye Tree Lodge 46000 Hwy-198, Three Rivers ☎559/561-5900, ⓦwww.buckeyetree. com. Small but comfortable modern rooms with TV, video, private bathrooms, and verandahs overlooking the foaming river, plus a five-berth cottage (❼), all located right by the park entrance and equipped with a nice pool. ❺

Gateway Lodge 45978 Hwy-198, Three Rivers ☎559/561-4133, ⓦwww.gateway-sequoia.com. Spartan but perfectly functional motel-style rooms and a large house sleeping six with self-catering

facilities ($250). It is located right by the park entrance and beside the Kaweah River. Midweek ❺, weekends ❻

Plantation B&B 33038 Hwy-198, Lemon Cove ☎559/597-2555 or 1-800/240-1466, ⓦwww. theplantation.net. Luxurious B&B with comfortable en-suite rooms (some with balconies) and truly delicious breakfasts, located on a citrus orchard 17 miles from the park entrance. Rooms follow a *Gone with the Wind* theme to the extent that the Belle Watling room comes bordello-hued with a mirrored bedstead. Outside there's a heated pool, hot tub, and an acre of ageing orange trees and youthful palms that's ideal for relaxing. Rooms ❻, suites ❼

Sierra Lodge 43175 Hwy-198, Three Rivers ☎559/561-3681 or 1-800/367-8879, ⓦwww.sierra-lodge.com. An older-style but spacious and clean lodge with modernized rooms with bathrooms, many with decks, plus suites, some of which have cooking facilities. All have use of a pool and Internet access. Rooms ❹, suites ❺

Three Rivers Motel & RV Park 43365 Hwy-198 ☎559/561-4413. RV-only site with a few aging and very basic cabins (some with kitchens) at the lowest prices for miles around. ❸

Along Hwy-180

Sierra Inn Motel 37692 Hwy-180, Dunlap ☎559/ 338-2144, ⒻF338-0789. Small and functional motel rooms with TV and air conditioning, located 14 miles west of the Big Stump entrance and next to a sandwiches-and-steaks restaurant and bar. ❸

Eating

There are **food** markets and fairly basic cafeterias at Lodgepole (the most extensive), Stony Creek, and Cedar Grove Village, though none of them are spectacular and prices will be higher than places outside the park, such as Three Rivers. Much the same applies to restaurants, with Three Rivers offering the best local selection at reasonable prices. In the restaurants inside the parks, diner fare prevails, with the exception of the restaurant at *Wuksachi*.

In the parks and surrounding national forest

Grant Grove Restaurant Grant Grove. Basic diner fare – burgers, sandwiches, and breakfasts – plus fish, chicken, and steak dinners for $12–17. There's also an espresso cart out on the umbrella-shaded terrace.

Lodgepole Deli Lodgepole. The best of the parks' budget eating places with respectable low-cost breakfasts, sandwiches, and pizza.

Montecito-Sequoia Lodge Resort which also serves nutritious buffet meals to non-residents.

Hearty breakfasts (8–9.30am; $9), lunches (noon–1.30pm; $9), and dinners (6–7.30pm; $16) are all served communally at large tables, and there's a bar operating until 9pm.

Stony Creek Generals Highway (late May to Oct; call KCPS). A kind of upscale diner with decent burgers, pasta, steaks, desserts, espresso, and modest prices.

Wuksachi Lodge Dining Room Wuksachi. The finest dining in the twin parks, with the likes of Baja chicken sandwiches ($8), steaks ($24), and herb-crusted pork tenderloin ($21), plus a full buffet

Sequoia and Kings Canyon

5

breakfast for $9, all served in a modern baronial-style room. The bar is open daily until 11pm; reserve for dinner with DNPS.

Three Rivers

Gateway Restaurant 45978 Hwy-198. Superbly set restaurant with a sunny deck overlooking the Kaweah River. Burgers, sandwiches, and pasta dishes go for $8–10, meat and fish mains for around $15–20.

We Three Bakery 43368 Hwy-198. A good and friendly stop for breakfast, especially for the freshly baked cakes and pastries. Open Wed–Sun 7.30am–3pm.

Sequoia National Park

The two main centers in **SEQUOIA NATIONAL PARK** are **Giant Forest** and **Lodgepole** – the starting points for most of the hiking trails. To the south there's also the more isolated Mineral King area. While trees are seldom scarce – patches where the giant sequoias can't grow are thickly swathed with pine and fir – the scenery varies throughout the park: sometimes subtly, sometimes abruptly. Everywhere paths lead through deep forests and around meadows; longer treks rise above the tree line to reveal the barren peaks and superb sights of the High Sierra.

The history of the park is laced with political intrigue. In the 1880s, the Giant Forest area was bought by the Co-operative Land Purchase and Colonization Association, a group of individuals known as the **Kaweah Colony** that had the idea of forming a workers' colony here. They began what became the four-year task of building a road from the San Joaquin Valley up to Giant Forest, intending to start commercial logging of the huge trees there. Owing to legal technicalities, however, their rights to the area were disputed, and in 1890 a bill (probably instigated by a combination of agricultural and railroad interests) was passed by the Senate which effected the preservation of all sequoia groves. The colony lost everything and received no compensation for the road, which remained in use for thirty years – although decades later the ex-leader of the colony acknowledged that the eventual outcome was of far greater benefit to society as a whole than his own scheme would have been.

Three Rivers, Kaweah, and Mineral King

Approaching the park from the south, you pass through **THREE RIVERS**, a lowland community strung out for seven miles along Hwy-198 and providing the greatest concentration of accommodation and places to eat anywhere near the parks. As you approach the center of town, a sign directs you three miles west to what remains of the Kaweah Colony, essentially just the **Kaweah Post Office**, which is the smallest still operating in California. What is little more than a shed still has the original brass-and-glass private boxes, and even outside normal opening times the tiny lobby acts as the local secondhand book exchange.

A couple of miles north of Three Rivers, the century-old, twisting Mineral King Road branches 25 miles east into the southern section of the park to **MINERAL KING**, sitting in a scalloped bowl at 7800ft surrounded by snowy peaks and glacial lakes. This is the only part of the high country accessible by car and makes a superb hiking base when you can reach it – essentially late-May to mid-October, or a little longer if the snows hold off. Eager prospectors built the thoroughfare hoping the area would yield silver. It didn't, the mines were abandoned, and the region was left in peace until the mid-1960s when Disney threatened to build a huge ski resort here, only to be defeated by the conservation lobby, which campaigned for the region's inclusion in the Sequoia National Park, something finally achieved in 1978. Now there's just a couple of basic campgrounds and near-complete tranquility. Having negotiated the seven-hundred-odd twists and turns from the highway, you can relax by the river before hiking up over steep Sawtooth Pass and into the alpine bowls of the glaciated basins beyond. There's also a gentler introduction to the flora and fauna of Mineral King by way of a short **nature trail** from the Cold Springs campground.

Pick up practical information and wilderness permits from the **ranger station** (late May–Sept daily 7am–3.30pm; ☎559/565-3768) opposite the *Cold Springs* campground. Permits are required until late September and are in great demand, especially in July and August. Reservations can be made in advance from March 1, and some permits are offered on a first-come-first-served basis. The *Silver City Mountain Resort* (☎559/561-3223, ⓦwww.silvercityresort.com; deluxe chalets ❽, comfy cabins ❻, rustic cabins ❹) is near the *Atwell* campground and is the only place you'll find food; it has limited provisions and a café/restaurant.

Giant Forest

Entering the park on **Hwy-180 from Visalia**, you pass **Hospital Rock**, easily spotted by the side of the road and decorated with rock drawings and grain-grinding holes from an ancient Monache settlement. The rock got its name from a trapper who accidentally shot himself in the leg and was treated by the local tribe – who are further remembered by a small outdoor exhibition telling something of their evolution and culture. The road opposite leads to the small and appealing *Buckeye Flat* campground.

From Hospital Rock, the road soon becomes the **Generals Highway** and twists rapidly uphill into the densely forested section of the park, the aptly labeled **Giant Forest**. A major tourist draw, with the greatest accessible concentration of giant sequoias, Giant Forest contained a small village until 1998, but concerns over the health of the sequoias prompted the Park Service to raze the settlement. Almost three hundred hotel and restaurant structures built virtually on top of the sequoias' root systems have been removed, intrusive paths have been re-routed, and the whole area is in the process of being restored and re-seeded. The former shop, restaurant, and gas station have been transformed into the **Giant Forest Museum** (daily 9am–4.30pm; free), which admirably illustrates the life and times of the giant sequoias. Outside, the fire-damaged Sentinel Tree is barricaded off to allow seedlings a chance to get established.

Various short hikes fan out from here through the trees, including the **Beetle Rock Trail** (5min round-trip), which affords a view down to the San Joaquin Valley, and the **Big Trees Trail** (0.6 mile loop; 30min), which follows a well formed boardwalk along the perimeter of Round Meadow.

Along Crescent Meadow Road

A spur off the main highway, **CRESCENT MEADOW ROAD** provides easy access to a host of photo opportunities. The first attraction is the **Auto Log**, a fallen trunk originally chiseled flat enough for motorists to nose up onto it, though this practice has now been stopped. Beyond here, a side loop leads to the dramatic **Moro Rock**, a granite monolith streaking wildly upward from the green hillside. Views from its remarkably level top can stretch 150 miles across the San Joaquin Valley and, in the other direction, to the towering Sierra. Thanks to a concrete staircase, it's a comparatively easy climb to the

The life of the giant sequoia

Call it what you will, the sierra redwood, *sequoiadendron giganteum*, or just big tree, the **giant sequoia** is the earth's most massive living thing. Some of these arboreal monsters weigh in at a whopping one thousand tons, courtesy of a thick trunk that barely tapers from base to crown. They're also among the oldest trees found anywhere, many reaching two, or even three, thousand years of age.

Sequoias are only found in a few dozen isolated groups on the western slopes of California's Sierra Nevada and grow naturally between 5000 and 8500 feet in a band from just south of Sequoia National Park to just north of Yosemite National Park. Specimens planted all over the world during the nineteenth century seem to thrive but haven't yet reached the enormous dimensions seen here.

The cinnamon-colored bark of young sequoias is easily confused with that of the incense cedar, but as they age, there's no mistaking the thick spongy outer layer that protects the sapwood from the fires that periodically sweep through the forests. Fire is, in fact, a critical element in the propagation of sequoias; the hen-egg-sized female cones pack hundreds of seeds but require intense heat to open them. Few seeds ever sprout as they need perfect conditions, usually where old tree has fallen and left a hole in the canopy allowing plenty of light to fall on rich mineral soil.

Young trees are conical, but as they mature the lower branches drop off to leave a top-heavy crown. A shallow, wide root system keeps them upright, but eventually heavy snowfall or high winds topple aging trees. With its protective bark and tannin-rich timber, a giant sequoia may lie where it fell for hundreds of years. John Muir discovered one still largely intact with a 380-year-old silver fir growing out of the depression it had created.

summit (which is also reputed to make a good platform for feeling vibrations of distant earthquakes), although at nearly 7000ft the altitude can be a strain.

Back on the road, you pass under the **Tunnel Log**: a tree that fell across the road in 1937 and has since had a vehicle-sized hole cut through its lower half. Further on, **Crescent Meadow** is, like other grassy fields in the area, more accurately a marsh, and too wet for the sequoias that form an impressive boundary around. Looking across the meadow gives the best opportunity to appreciate the changing shape of the ageing sequoia. The trail circling its perimeter (1.5 miles; 1hr; mainly flat) leads to **Log Meadow**, to which a farmer, Hale Tharp, searching for a summer grazing ground for his sheep, was led by local Native Americans in 1856. He became one of the first white men to see the giant sequoias, and the first to actually live in one – a hollowed-out specimen which still exists, remembered as **Tharp's Log**. Peer inside to appreciate the hewn-out shelves. From here the loop presses on to the still living **Chimney Tree**, its center completely burnt out so that the sky is visible from its hollow base. Hardy backpackers can pick up the John Muir Trail here and hike the 74 miles to Mount Whitney (the tallest mountain in the continental US; see p.338).

The big trees and Crystal Cave

North of Crescent Meadow Road, the Generals Highway enters the thickest section of Giant Forest and the biggest sequoia of them all (reachable on foot by various connecting trails). The three-thousand-year-old **General Sherman Tree** is 275ft high, has a base diameter of 36ft, and was, for a time, renamed the Karl Marx Tree by the Kaweah Colony. While it's certainly a thrill to be face-to-bark with what is widely held to be the largest living thing on earth, its extraordinary dimensions are hard to grasp in the midst of all the almost equally monstrous sequoias around – not to mention the other tremendous batch that can be seen on the **Congress Trail** (2 miles; 1–2hr; negligible ascent), which starts from the general Sherman Tree itself.

When you've had your fill of the magnificent trees, consider a trip nine miles from Giant Forest along a minor road to **Crystal Cave** (45min guided tours mid-May–Sept daily 11am–4pm; $8) which has a mildly diverting batch of stalagmites and stalactites. The early morning tours are not usually full, and whatever time you go, remember to take a jacket. Those with a deeper interest in the cave's origins and features should join the two-hour **Discovery Tour** (mid-June–Aug daily 4pm; $15). Tickets for both trips can only be purchased at the Lodgepole and Foothill visitor centers at least a couple of hours beforehand.

North of Giant Forest, the Generals Highway passes the short spur road to **Wolverton**, site of a pack station (see "Listings," p.402) and an important trailhead for some serious hikes (see box, p.400).

Lodgepole and around

Whatever your plans, you should stop at **LODGEPOLE VILLAGE** – a couple of miles north of Wolverton – for the geological displays, film shows, and general information at the **visitor center** (June–Aug daily 8am–6pm; May & Sept daily 9am–5pm; Oct–April Fri–Mon 9am–4.30pm; ☎559/565-3782). With its grocery store, burger bar, showers, laundromat, and campground, Lodgepole is very much at the center of Sequoia's visitor activities, and its situation at one end of the Tokopah Valley, a glacially formed canyon (not unlike the much larger Yosemite Valley), makes it an ideal starting point to explore a number of hiking trails (see box, overleaf). Foremost among them is the **Tokopah Valley Trail** – leading from Lodgepole through the valley to the base of Tokopah Falls, beneath **The Watchtower**, a 1600-foot cliff. The top of The Watchtower and its great view of the valley are accessible by way of the **Lakes Trail**, or try the sharpest ascent of all the Lodgepole hikes, the **Alta Peak and Alta Meadows Trail**, which rises four thousand feet over seven miles.

Beyond Lodgepole the Generals Highway turns west and runs four miles to **Wuksachi**, with a fancy modern lodge and restaurant, partly designed to replace Giant Forest Village. The road soon swings north again and passes into the Sequoia National Forest – where there is accommodation and food to be had at both **Stony Creek** and the *Montecito-Sequoia Lodge*, and free camping at a couple of primitive sites – before striking into the Kings Canyon National Park.

Kings Canyon National Park

KINGS CANYON NATIONAL PARK is wilder and less visited than Sequoia, with just two small settlements containing the park's main visitor facilities: Grant Grove lies close to the Big Stump entrance, and Cedar Grove huddles in the bottom of the canyon some 25 miles to the east at the start of most of the marked hikes. The one real road (closed in winter; usually mid-Nov to mid-April) links the two, spectacularly skirting the colossal canyon. Away from these two places, you're on your own. The vast untamed park has a maze of canyons and a sprinkling of isolated lakes – the perfect environment for careful self-guided exploration.

Grant Grove, the Big Stump Area, and Hume Lake

Confusingly, **GRANT GROVE** is an enclave of Kings Canyon National Park within the Sequoia National Forest, but unless you're planning a major backcountry hike across the parks' boundaries you'll have to pass through here before reaching Kings Canyon proper. Grant Grove has the largest concentration of visitor facilities in the Kings Canyon National Park, with accommodation, post office, restaurant, small supermarket, showers, and a useful **visitor center** (daily: June–Aug 8am–6pm; May & Sept daily 8am–5pm; Oct–April 9am–4.30pm; ☎559/565-4307) with all the background information you'll need.

This concentrated stand of sequoias, sugar pines, incense cedar, black oak, and mountain dogwood is named after the **General Grant Tree** which, along with the **Robert E. Lee Tree** (also here), rivals the General Sherman for bulk. A half-mile trail (guides $1) wends its way among these and other giants, calling in at the **Fallen Monarch**, which you can walk through, and the **Gamlin Cabin**, where Israel and Thomas Gamlin lived while exploiting their timber claim until 1878. The massive stump of one of the trees' scalps remains after a slice was shipped to the 1876 Centennial Exhibition in Philadelphia – an attempt to convince cynical easterners that such enormous trees really existed.

Two miles south of Grant Grove, the **BIG STUMP AREA** unsurprisingly gets its name from the gargantuan stumps that litter the place – remnants from early logging of sequoias carried out during the 1880s. A mile-long trail (almost meaningless without the free leaflet from the Grant Grove visitor center) leads through this scene of devastation to the **Mark Twain Stump**, the headstone of another monster killed to impress: a sliver of this one resides in the American Museum of Natural History and another was sent to London's British Museum. Look too for the meager foundations of the sawmill and pine boughs laid on the ground to break the fall of their larger kin.

Hume Lake and around

About eight miles north of Grant Grove, a minor road spurs off three miles to **HUME LAKE**, actually a reservoir built in 1908 to provide water for logging flumes, and now forming the heart of an underpopulated area of the Sequoia National Forest. It's a delightful spot to swim or launch your canoe, is handily placed for the local hiking trails, and makes a good place to **spend a night** beside the lake at the comparatively large *Hume Lake* **campground** (see p.393). At the head of the lake, the facilities of the *Hume Lake Christian Camp* provide expensive gas, groceries, a post office, and a coffee shop.

Kings Canyon Highway

For most, Hume Lake doesn't even warrant a diversion from the northern park's main attraction, **Kings Canyon**, which some measurements make the deepest canyon in the US, at some 7900ft. Whatever the facts, its wall sections of granite and gleaming blue marble, and the white pockmarks of spectacularly blooming yucca plants (May and early June in particular) are visually outstanding: this is especially true from Junction View as Hwy-180 winds its way down to the riverside. A vast area of the wilderness beyond is drained by the South Fork of the Kings River, a raging torrent during the springtime snowmelt spate, and perilous for wading at any time: people have been swept away even when paddling close to the bank in a seemingly placid section.

Hiking in Sequoia and Kings Canyon

The **trails** in Kings Canyon and Sequoia see far less traffic than those in Yosemite, but can still get busy in high summer. There are no restrictions on day-walks, but a quota system (operational late May–late Sept) applies if you are planning to camp in the backcountry. Numbers are limited, but around a quarter of the places are offered on a first-come-first-served basis and, provided you are fairly flexible, you should be able to land something by turning up at the ranger station nearest your proposed trailhead early in the afternoon on the day before you wish to start. **Wilderness permits** are free, but advance reservations cost $10 (per group per entry into the wilderness) and can be obtained by mailing or faxing Wilderness Permit Reservations, Sequoia & Kings Canyon National Park, HCR89 Box 60,Three Rivers, CA 93271 (℻ 559/565-4239), stating entry and exit dates, desired route with an alternative, number of people, and estimated camping spots. Reservations are accepted after March 1 and at least three weeks before your start date, and outside the quota period, permits can be self-issued at trailheads: only Visa and MasterCard are accepted. More details are available on the park website and in the free *Backcountry Basics* newspaper available in the park. The visitor centers also sell localized hiking maps ($2 each) and more detailed topographical maps.

Remember that this is **bear country**: read the box on p.413. Bear canisters can be rented ($3 per trip and $75 deposit) at Mineral King, Foothills, Lodgepole, Grant Grove, and Cedar Grove; and bought ($75) at the Lodgepole store.

From Mineral King, Sequoia

Eagle Lake Trail (7 miles round-trip; 4-6hr; 2200ft ascent). Starting from the parking area a mile beyond the ranger station, this trail starts gently but gets tougher towards Eagle Lake. Highlights include the Eagle Sink Hole (where the river vanishes) and some fantastic views.

Groundhog Meadow Trail (2 miles round-trip; 1–2hr; 900ft ascent). A short but demanding trail which switchbacks up to Groundhog Meadow, from where there's a great view of Sawtooth Ridge. Starts a quarter of a mile back from the road beyond the ranger station.

Mosquito Lakes No. 1 Trail (7 miles round-trip; 4–5hr; 1150ft ascent). Follows the first half of the Eagle Lake Trail, then branches left to the lowest of the Mosquito Lakes at 9000ft.

Mosquito Lakes No. 5 Trail (10 miles round-trip; 6–8hr; 2300ft ascent). As above plus a bit, bringing you to the uppermost lake at over 10,000ft. Stupendous views.

Paradise Peak via Paradise Ridge Trail (9 miles round-trip; 9hr; 2800ft ascent). Superb walk starting opposite the *Atwell Mill* campground and climbing steeply to Paradise Ridge, which affords views of Moro Rock. From there it is a fairly flat stroll to the 9300-foot Paradise Peak.

From Giant Forest, Wolverton, and Lodgepole, Sequoia

Alta Peak and Alta Meadows Trail (14 miles round-trip; 8–10hr; 4000ft ascent). Strenuous but rewarding trail rising four thousand feet over seven miles. The trail

You approach the canyon through a section of the Sequoia National Forest with two rewarding excursions. The first is a short drive to the **Chicago Stump**, yet another epitaph to a felled giant, this one carted in numbered sections to Chicago in 1895 where it was reassembled for the World's Columbian Exposition. A more alluring diversion leads past another sequoia graveyard, **Stump Meadow**, to a trailhead for the **Boole Tree**, the world's fattest sequoia and one that towers above the forest where all other sequoias were felled.

starts at the Wolverton trailhead and splits after three miles: there's an easy, level walk to Alta Meadow and its fine views of the surrounding peaks (and a four-mile trail to the desolate Moose Lake), or the daunting near-vertical hike to the stunning Alta Peak.

Little Baldy Trail (3.5 miles round-trip; 2–3hr; 700ft ascent). Starting from Little Baldy Saddle, six miles north of Lodgepole, this loop trail leads to the rocky summit of Little Baldy.

Tokopah Trail (3 miles round-trip; 2–3hr; 200ft ascent). Easy valley walk beside the Marble Fork of the Kaweah River and leading to impressive granite cliffs and the Tokopah Falls, which cascades into a cool pool, perfect for a bracing dip. Starts at the eastern end of the Lodgepole campground.

The Watchtower and Lakes Trail (13 miles round-trip; 6–8hr; 2300ft ascent). A popular if fatiguing trail leading up from the Wolverton trailhead to The Watchtower (3–5hr round-trip), an exposed tower of granite overlooking Tokapah Falls far below. From there the path leads past three lakes in increasingly gorgeous and stark glacial cirques. The two furthest lakes, Emerald Lake (9200ft) and Pear Lake (9500ft), have campgrounds which, for the really adventurous (and experienced), make good starting points for self-guided trekking into the mountains.

From Kings Canyon

Cedar Grove Overlook Trail (5 miles round-trip; 3–4hr; 1200ft ascent). Starting half a mile north of Cedar Grove Village on Pack Station Road, this switchback trail rises through forest and chaparral to a viewpoint overlooking Kings Canyon.

Don Cecil Trail to Lookout Peak (13 miles round-trip; 7–9hr; 4000ft ascent). Starting 400 yards east of Cedar Grove Village, a strenuous trail that largely follows the pre-highway road route. After two miles you reach the shady glen of Sheep Creek Cascade before pressing on up the canyon to the wonderfully panoramic summit.

Hotel Creek-Lewis Creek Loop Trail (8 miles round-trip; 5hr; 1200ft ascent). Follows the first two miles of the Cedar Grove Overlook Trail, before branching downhill and returning to Cedar Grove through some extensively fire-damaged forest.

Mist Falls Trail (8 miles round-trip; 3–5hr; 600ft ascent). An easy sandy trail starts from Road's End, eventually climbing steeply past numerous thundering cataracts to Mist Falls, one of the largest waterfalls in the twin parks.

Rae Lakes Loop (4–5 days round-trip). One of the best of the multi-day hikes in these parts following the Kings River up past Mist Falls and beyond, through Paradise Valley and Castle Domes Meadow to Woods Creek Crossing, where it meets the John Muir Trail. It follows this for eight miles, passing Rae Lakes before returning to Kings Canyon along Bubbs Creek and the South Fork of the Kings River. Trail maps ($4.50) are available from the Lodgepole visitor center.

Despite this and some fine examples of fire scarring, it is seldom visited, perhaps on account of its position on a 2.5-mile loop trail: take the gentler left-hand trail and you'll be there in around half an hour.

Near the foot of the canyon, the road passes the less diverting of the region's two show caves, the **Boyden Cavern** (daily: June–Aug 10am–5pm; late April–May & Sept–early Nov 11am–4pm, 45min tours on the hour; $9), whose interior has a number of bizarre formations grown out of the forty-thousand-year-old rock, their impact intensified by the stillness and cool inside. The cave stays at a constant 55°F, causing the numerous small animals who tumble in through the hole in the roof to enter instant hibernation.

Cedar Grove

Once properly into the national park, the canyon sheds its V-shape and gains a floor, where the settlement of **Cedar Grove** sprawls among incense cedars. With a lodge, a food store and snack bar, several campgrounds, and, across the river, a **ranger station** (June–Aug daily 9am–5pm; May, Sept & Oct hours reduced; ℡559/565-3793), this is as close to a built-up area as the park gets.

Three miles east are the **Roaring River Falls** which, when in spate, undoubtedly merit their name. Apart from the obvious appeal of the scenery, the main things to see around here are the **flowers** – leopard lilies, shooting stars, violets, Indian paintbrush, lupines, and others – and a variety of birdlife. The longer hikes through the creeks, many of them seven or eight miles long (see box on p.400), are fairly stiff challenges and you should carry drinking water. An easy alternative is to potter along the **nature trail** (1.5 miles; 1–2hr; flat) around the edge of **Zumwalt Meadow**, a beckoning green carpet a mile beyond the falls and a short walk from the road, beneath the forbidding gray walls of Grand Sentinel and North Dome mountains. The meadow boasts a collection of big-leaf maple, cat's-tails, and creek dogwood, and there's often a chance of an eyeful of animal life.

Just a mile further, Kings Canyon Road comes to an end at **Copper Creek**, from where a network of hiking trails penetrates the multitude of canyons and peaks that constitute the Kings River Sierra. Almost all are best enjoyed armed with a tent and some provisions. To obtain **wilderness permits** in this area, call at the Road's End Wilderness Permit Station (June to mid-Sept daily 7am–4pm; rest of Sept Fri & Sat 7am–2pm) at the end of Hwy-180. The less ambitious only need to venture a hundred yards riverward to **Muir Rock**, to see where John Muir (see box on p.411) conducted early meetings of the Sierra Club. On the way back down the valley, cut right just before the road crosses the Kings River and follow the unmarked **River Road** (westbound only) along the north side of the river back to Cedar Grove.

Listings

Banks There are no banks in either park, but credit cards and travelers' checks are widely accepted. Grant Grove and Lodgepole have ATMs, though they are sometimes out of cash.

Cycling Bikes are not permitted off trails, limiting you to park roads, many of which are very steep and with limited space for passing. A better bet is the network of trails in the surrounding national forest.

Gas There is no gas available in the parks, so drivers should fill up with cheap gas in Visalia or Fresno, or slightly pricier stuff at Three Rivers. In desperation, you can get expensive gas at the *Hume Lake Christian Camp* (see opposite) or at *Kings Canyon Lodge* on Hwy-180, which claims to have the oldest gravity-fed pumps in the country, dating back to the 1920s.

Horseback riding Stables and pack stations exist in five locations through the national parks and surrounding forest mostly open from mid- or late May to early September: Mineral King (℡559/561-3039), Wolverton (℡559/565-3039), Grant Grove (℡559/565-3464), Big Meadows (℡559/565-3404), and Cedar Grove (℡559/565-3464). All offer anything from an hour or two in the saddle (roughly $40 for two hours) to multi-day back-country excursions.

Internet access No public facilities in the parks. The closest is Three Rivers Library, 42052 Eggers Drive (Mon 10am–1pm & 2–6pm, Tues noon–5pm & 6–8pm, Thurs 10am–1pm & 2–6pm), five miles south of the park entrance.

Laundry Lodgepole (daily 9am–5pm) and Cedar Grove Village (daily 8am–8pm) both have coin-operated laundries.

Post offices Both post offices accept General Delivery mail: at Lodgepole (Mon–Fri 8.30am–4pm) write to c/o General Delivery, Sequoia National Park, CA 93262; and at Grant Grove (Mon 9.30am–3pm, Tues–Thurs 9.30am–1pm, Fri 9.30am–4.30pm) write to Kings Canyon National Park, CA 93633.

Phones Public phones in the two parks don't accept coins; make sure you have some kind of phonecard.

Rafting From late April to the end of June, Kaweah Whitewater Adventures, 42323 Hwy-198, Three Rivers (℡ 559/561-1000 or 1-800/229-8658, ✆ www.kaweahwhitewater.com), run a series of rafting trips on the Kaweah River between Three Rivers and Lake Kaweah. Trips range from a relatively gentle two hours ($50) to serious Class IV and V full-day trips for $130.

Roads For road conditions call ℡ 559/565-3341.

Showers There are coin-op showers at Lodgepole (summer daily 8am–1pm & 3–8pm; min $2), Stony Creek (mid-May to mid-Sept daily 10am–noon & 2–6pm; $4), Grant Grove Village (summer daily 1am–4pm), and Cedar Grove Village (summer daily 9am–5pm).

The Sierra National Forest

Consuming the entire gaping tract of land between Kings Canyon and Yosemite, the **SIERRA NATIONAL FOREST** boasts some of the California interior's most beautiful mountain scenery, though it is less well known – and less visited – than either of its national park neighbors. A federally run area that lacks the environmental protection given to the parks, many of the rivers here have been dammed and much of the forest developed into resort areas that are better for fishing and boating than hiking. San Joaquin Valley residents stream up here at weekends through the summer. That said, there are far fewer people and any number of remote corners to explore, not least the rugged, unspoilt terrain of the vast **John Muir Wilderness**, and the neighboring **Ansel Adams Wilderness**, which contain some of the starkest peaks and lushest alpine meadows of the High Sierra. If you want to discover complete solitude and hike and camp in isolation, this is the place to do it – the sheer challenge of the environment can make the national parks look like holiday camps. But don't try any lone exploration without thorough planning aided by accurate maps, and don't expect buses to pick you up if you're tired. Public transportation is virtually nonexistent. We haven't highlighted any walks in this area: there are hundreds of them and any of the **ranger stations** can suggest suitable hikes, supply free permits (necessary for any overnight hikes into most of the forest), and sell you the detailed *Sierra National Forest Map* ($6.50), useful even if you are driving.

The paltry network of roads effectively divides the forest into three main areas: the more southerly **Pineridge District**, accessible by way of Hwy-168; the **Bass Lake and Mariposa districts**, just off Hwy-41 between Fresno and Yosemite; and the **Sierra Vista National Scenic Byway**, which reaches out into the Sierra to the southeast of Yosemite. Call ℡ 559/855-5360 for road information.

The Pineridge District and the John Muir Wilderness

A forty-mile drive from Fresno along Hwy-168 through a parched and knobbly landscape dotted with blue, live, and scrub oak soon brings you to the best place for adventurous hiking, the **PINERIDGE DISTRICT**. Around **Kaiser Pass**, which scrapes 9200ft, you'll find isolated alpine landscapes, served by decent

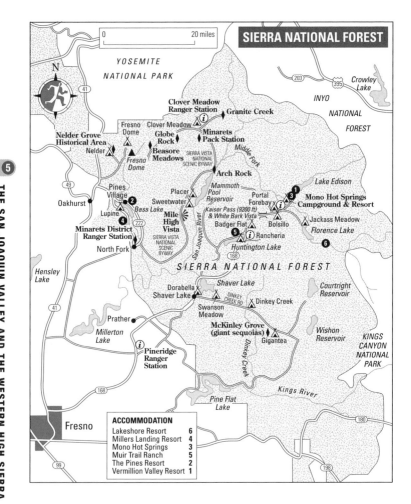

SIERRA NATIONAL FOREST

0   20 miles

YOSEMITE
NATIONAL PARK

Crowley
Lake

INYO

NATIONAL
FOREST

Clover Meadow
Ranger Station   Granite Creek

Fresno   Clover Meadow
Dome   Minarets
Globe   Pack Station
Nelder Grove   Rock
Historical Area
Nelder   Beasore   SIERRA VISTA
Fresno   Meadows   NATIONAL
Dome   SCENIC BYWAY   Arch Rock

Lake Edison

Pines   Placer   Mammoth
Village   Pool   Portal   Mono Hot Springs
Reservoir   Forebay   Campground & Resort
Oakhurst   Sweetwater
Bass Lake   Kaiser Pass (9200 ft)
Lupine   Mile   & White Bark Vista
High   Badger Flat   Bolsillo   Jackass Meadow
Minarets District   Vista
Ranger Station   SIERRA VISTA   Rancheria   Florence Lake
NATIONAL
SCENIC   Huntington Lake
North Fork   BYWAY

Hensley   SIERRA NATIONAL FOREST
Lake

Shaver Lake   Courtright
Dorabella   Reservoir
Shaver Lake   DINKEY   Dinkey Creek
CREEK RD
Swanson
Prather   Meadow
McKinley Grove
Millerton   (giant sequoias)   Wishon
Lake   Gigantea   Reservoir   KINGS
Pineridge   CANYON
Ranger   NATIONAL
Station   PARK

Kings River

Pine Flat
Lake

Fresno

ACCOMMODATION	
Lakeshore Resort	6
Millers Landing Resort	4
Mono Hot Springs	3
Muir Trail Ranch	5
The Pines Resort	2
Vermillion Valley Resort	1

campgrounds, a couple of minor resorts, and even some hot springs. The western section of the district is dominated by the weekend boating and fishing play-
grounds of Huntington and Shaver lakes, while the east, up and over Kaiser Pass
and around three hours' drive from Fresno, is big-time hiking territory.

The region is swamped by **reservoirs** – Edison, Florence, Mammoth Pool,
Redinger, and others – built as part of the "Big Creek" project which, more
than anything else, made the San Joaquin the agricultural heart of California.
With only modest hyperbole, the Sierra meltwater in these parts is touted as
"the hardest-working water in the world."

Many campgrounds in the Sierra National Forest can be booked between Memorial
Day and Labor Day through **ReserveUSA** (☎1-877/444-6777, ⓦwww.reserveusa.
com) for $10 per booking.

Hwy-168 – aka **The Sierra Heritage National Scenic Byway** – penetrates seventy miles into the forest among the snow-capped peaks of the **JOHN MUIR WILDERNESS**. It's a drive of at least four hours, even in good weather - and this is an area prone to bad weather and road closure, although you can always get to the lakes. The best-placed source of information is the **Pineridge Ranger Station** (daily 8am–4.30pm; ☎559/855-5360), located along Hwy-168 at Prather, five miles west of the forest entrance.

Shaver and Huntington lakes

From the ranger station, the good and fast Hwy-168 climbs rapidly over eighteen miles from undulating foothills studded with oaks to **SHAVER LAKE**, a mile-high community scattered among the pines, where Dinkey Creek Road (see below) cuts deep into the forests to the south. If you fancy an afternoon dodging the jet skiers out on the lake, drop in at Shaver Lake Watersports (☎559/841-8222), on the highway in Shaver, to rent windsurfers, canoes, and double kayaks (all $45 a day). Otherwise, there's little reason to stop except for groceries, gas, and meals at one of the half-dozen restaurants, notably the inconspicuous but ever popular *Village Restaurant and Bakery*, Hwy-168. Non-campers may choose to **stay** at one of several lodges and cabins, all of which charge around twenty percent more at weekends. Try the fully self-contained lodging at *Knotty Pine Vacation Cabins*, 41851 Hwy-168 (☎559/841-6526; ❹), or more rustic cabins three miles east at *Shaver Lake Lodge*, 44185 Hwy-168 (☎559/811-3326; ❸–❺), where the cheaper units come without bedding, though the plush ones have queen-sized beds and a kitchenette. The *Lodge* serves burger-and-fries-type **meals** in the bar or on the sunny deck overlooking Shaver Lake. There are a couple of decent **campsites** hereabouts: *Dorabella*, near the lake on Dorabella Road (mid-May to mid-Sept; reservable; $16), which has water; and *Swanson Meadow*, three miles east on Dinkey Creek Road ($12) beside some gorgeous meadows.

Beyond Shaver Lake, Hwy-168 heads twenty miles east to **HUNTINGTON LAKE**, climbing the 7500-foot Tamarack Ridge that effectively separates the lake from the San Joaquin Valley. This lake is more isolated than its neighbor over the hill, but is almost equally popular; again watersports and angling are the pastimes of choice.

Just before the lake, the *Rancheria* campground (open all year; reservable; $16) marks the turnoff to **Rancheria Falls**. A side road, east off Hwy-168, leads a mile to a trailhead from where the mile-long **Rancheria Falls Trail** (350ft ascent) heads off through broadleaf woods to the 150-foot falls. A mile beyond the turnoff, Hwy-168 reaches the lake by the **Eastwood Visitor Center** (late May–early Sept daily except Tues & Wed 8am–5pm; ☎559/893-6811), where the Kaiser Pass Road splits east over Kaiser Pass (see below). Continuing west around Huntington Lake you soon hit the 1920s *Lakeshore Resort* (☎559/893-3193, ⓦwww.lakeshoreresort.com; rooms ❹, suites ❺), with rustic knotty pine **cabins** sleeping four. There's a great **restaurant**, a lively bar, a gas station, post office, and general store all a few yards from the lake. From here on, the lakeshore is almost entirely taken up by $16 campsites. If you crave solitude, head to the lake's western end, where a winding forty-mile, partly-gravel road skirts the whole of the Kaiser Wilderness, passing a couple of free, primitive campgrounds, before rejoining Kaiser Pass Road on the east side. It's a trek, but once you're here you'll feel a million miles from anywhere.

Beyond Kaiser Pass: Mono Hot Springs and around

Beyond the Eastwood Visitor Center (see above), you're into the wild country, climbing Kaiser Pass on a rapidly deteriorating road up to 9200 feet, passing the *Badger Flat* campground (free; no water) along the way. Eight miles from Eastwood, a mile-long side road (passable in a high clearance vehicle) leads to **White Bark Vista**, one of the best mountain views in these parts. Over the pass is a vast basin, draining the south fork of the San Joaquin River. The lumpy single-lane road drops past the beautifully situated *Portal Forebay* campground ($12; lake water), and the **High Sierra Ranger Station** (late May–early Sept Thurs–Mon 8am–4.30pm; ☎559/877-7173) heralds a fork from where two very narrow and winding seven-mile roads split: north to Lake Edison, its approach marred by a huge earth dam, and west to Florence Lake.

    MONO HOT SPRINGS, two miles north of the junction on the road to Lake Edison, is the best thing about the region and a great place to relax and clean up after hikes. For the full hot springs experience, head for the *Mono Hot Springs Resort* (mid-May to mid-Oct; ☎559/325-1710, ⓦwww.monohot-springs.com; rustic cabins ❷, modern cabins ❹). Located on the banks of the San Joaquin River, the *Resort* is a modest affair with individual mineral baths ($4), showers ($3), and massages for $35 per half-hour. Outside, there's a chlorinated spa filled with spring water, costing $4 for an all-day pass. Accommodation at the resort ranges from simple cabins with communal ablutions and no linen, to much more commodious affairs with toilets and kitchen. Rates are thirty percent higher at weekends, when reservations are essential. The resort also has a small restaurant, a limited general store, the *Mono Hot Springs* campground (early June to late Sept; reservable; $14), and a post office used for mail and food pick-ups by hikers on the nearby John Muir and Pacific Crest trails. Better still, across the river there's a five-foot-deep concrete **bathing tank** (unrestricted access) that's perfect for soaking your bones while stargazing. This is just one of many pools on this side of the river; ask around.

    Beyond Mono Hot Springs, the road continues past several more campgrounds amid wonderful scenery to **Lake Edison** and the *Vermillion Valley Resort* (☎559/259-4000, ⓦwww.edisonlake.com; tent cabins ❷, motel units ❹), mainly geared towards boaters and anglers but also useful for folk heading out into the John Muir Wilderness. Save yourself a dull seven-mile hike by taking the small **ferry** (June–Sept twice daily; $15 round-trip) across the lake.

    Florence Lake is more immediately appealing than Lake Edison: there's a greater sense of being hemmed in by mountains, and it is reached through an unearthly landscape of wrinkled granite shattered over the centuries by contorted junipers. There's a small store, the *Jackass Meadow* campground (late May–Sept; reservable; $14), located unnervingly below the dam, and another **ferry** across the lake (late May to late Sept; 5 daily; $8 each way). This ferry trip opens up multi-day hikes along the John Muir and Pacific Crest trails, and to the northern end of Kings Canyon National Park. If you can't face being totally self-sufficient, you can sometimes stay at the *Muir Trail Ranch* (from mid-June to Sept; ☎209/966-3195, ⓦwww.muirtrailranch.com), a cabin and tent retreat with hot pools and horses located in magical scenery four miles beyond the far end of Florence Lake. When not taken over by groups, it is open for short stays (usually the first three weeks in June and the last week in Sept) at $115 a night for room, breakfast, sack lunch, and dinner, but not including horses, charged at $50 a day. Access is by the cross-lake ferry, and then you either hike or arrange to be met with a horse.

Dinkey Creek Road and McKinley Grove

The region to the southeast of Shaver Lake is accessible along **DINKEY CREEK ROAD,** which threads its way through thirty miles of thick forests and around lush meadows to the Wishon Reservoir. It is altogether less alpine than the regions farther east, but no less impressive and a good deal warmer. Deep in the forest almost twenty miles southeast of Shaver Lake lies **MCKIN-LEY GROVE**, a stand of giant sequoias that is somewhat less impressive than others in the Sierra, though it is always an honor to be among these giants. The adjacent *Gigantea* campground ($14) is free outside the main summer season. Beyond lies Wishon Reservoir from where tracks penetrate the Woodchuck and Red River Basin portions of the John Muir Wilderness.

Bass Lake

The northern reaches of the Sierra National Forest are most easily reached from **Oakhurst** (see "Approaching Yosemite", on p.411), the center of the Mariposa District and just seven miles west of much the biggest tourist attraction in the area – the pine-fringed **BASS LAKE**. A stamping ground of Hell's Angels in the 1960s – the leather and licentiousness memorably described in Hunter S. Thompson's *Hell's Angels* – Bass Lake is nowadays a family resort, crowded with boaters and anglers in summer, but a good spot to rest for a day or two. For detailed campground and hiking information, consult the Minarets District Ranger Station (see below).

Road 222 runs right around the lake, though not always within sight of it. At the main settlement, **Pines Village**, you can buy groceries, eat moderately well, and **spend the night** at *The Pines Resort* (☎559/642-3121 or 1-800/350-7463, ⊛www.basslake.com; ❼) in luxurious two-story chalets with kitchens or even more palatial lakeside suites. By the southwestern tip of the lake, *Miller's Landing Resort*, 37976 Rd 222 (☎559/642-3633 or 1-866/6574386, ⊛www.millerslanding; ❷–❼), offers cabins without bathrooms right up to fancy chalets and suites. *Miller's Landing* is also the best place to rent aquatic equipment – **canoes** and **fishing boats** are $25 and $75 a day respectively, while **jet skis** cost $75 an hour – and they have public showers and laundry.

The western side of Bass Lake is slung with $16-a-night family **campgrounds**, most oriented towards long stays beside your camper. In summer, book well in advance (see box), though no-shows are sometimes available at the California Land Management Office, 39900 Rd 222, on the southwest side of the lake (late May to early Sept Mon–Fri 8am–8pm, Sat & Sun 8am–9pm; ☎559/642-3212). For tent campers, the best site is *Lupine* ($16), just north of Miller's Landing.

Sierra Vista National Scenic Byway

If Bass Lake is too commercial and overcrowded for you, the antidote starts immediately to the north. The **SIERRA VISTA NATIONAL SCENIC BYWAY** makes a ninety-mile circuit east of Hwy-41, topping out at the Clover Meadow Station (7000ft), which is the trailhead for much of the magnificent **Ansel Adams Wilderness**. Apart from a lot of trailheads and campgrounds, there's not a great deal to it, though the views are fantastic and people are scarce. A straight circuit (snow-free July–Oct at best) takes five hours, and is especially slow going on the rough dirt roads of the north side. Stock up on supplies before you start: there are a couple of stores and gas stations dotted along its length but they're not cheap and the range is limited. Accommodation on the circuit is largely limited to campgrounds, all (except two free sites) costing $11–13.

The best source of information on the circuit is the **Minarets District Ranger Station** (Mon–Fri 8am–4.30pm; ☎559/877-2218) in the hamlet of North Fork at the southern end of Bass Lake, where you can pick up a **map** – important, as there are numerous confusing forestry roads and few signposts.

The south side

Before setting out from North Fork, check out the **Sierra Mono Indian Museum** (Tues–Sat 9.30am–3.30pm; $3), with some good examples of local Native American basketry and beadwork, as well as a lot of stuffed animals in glass cases. Once on your way, there's little to stop for on the first 25 miles until **Mile High Vista**, which reveals endless views of muscle-bound mountain ranges and bursting granite domes stretching back to Mammoth Mountain (see p.353). A little further on, an eight-mile side road cuts south to the dammed **Mammoth Pool**, where anglers boat on the lake and smoke their catch at one of the four **campgrounds**. The quietest of them are *Sweetwater* ($11; 3800ft) and *Placer* ($11; 4100ft), away from the pool but by streams.

Back on the Scenic Byway, you'll pass the rather disappointing **Arch Rock**, where the earth under a slab of granite has been undermined to leave a kind of bridge, and continue climbing to a small ranger outpost (late June–Sept daily 8am–noon & 1–5pm; ☏559/877-2218), and the Minarets Pack Station (mid-June to Sept; ☏559/868-3405, ⓦwww.highsierrapackers.org/min; ❶). Apart from a general store and reasonable meals, the station offers simple lodging and horseback trips from $55 a day. It's a great base for wilderness trips, many of which start by the **Clover Meadow Ranger Station**, a couple of miles up a spur road (June–Oct daily 9am–5pm; permits available). Nearby are two free and wonderfully sited campgrounds, *Clover Meadow* and *Granite Creek*, both at 7000 feet, the former with potable water.

The north side

The Minarets Pack Station marks the start of the descent from the backcountry and the end of the asphalt; for the next few miles you're on rough dirt, generally passable in ordinary passenger vehicles when clear of snow. The hulking form of **Globe Rock** heralds the return to asphalt, which runs down to **Beasore Meadow**, where the summer-only Jones Store has supplied groceries, gas, and meals for the best part of a century, and offers showers to hikers. A short distance further on you reach Cold Springs Meadow, the junction with Sky Ranch Road (follow it left to continue the loop) and a spur to the wonderful *Fresno Dome* campground ($11; no water; 6400ft), a great base for a moderately strenuous walk to the top of the exfoliated granite namesake.

The Scenic Byway then passes several $11 campsites, most without running water, en route to the **Nelder Grove Historical Area** (unrestricted entry), a couple of miles north along a dirt road. Over a hundred giant sequoias are scattered through the forest here, though the overall impression is of devastation evidenced by the number of enormous stumps among the second-growth sugar pine, white fir, and cedar. The mile-long "Shadow of the Giants" interpretive walk explains the logging activities which took place here in the 1880s and early 1890s and, with its low visitor count, offers a more serene communion with these majestic trees than in any of the national parks. A second interpretive trail leads from the attractive but often mosquito-ridden *Nelder Grove* campground (free; 5500ft; stream water) to **Bull Buck Tree**, once a serious contender for the world's largest tree. From here it is only seven twisting miles back to Hwy-41, reached at a point around four miles north of Oakhurst.

Yosemite National Park

No temple made with hands can compare with the Yosemite. Every rock in its
walls seems to glow with life. Some lean back in majestic repose; others,
absolutely sheer or nearly so for thousands of feet, advance beyond their
companions in thoughtful attitudes, giving welcome to storms and calms alike,
seemingly aware, yet heedless, of everything going on about them.

John Muir, *The Yosemite*

More gushing adjectives have been thrown at **YOSEMITE NATIONAL
PARK** than at any other part of California. But however excessive the hyperbole may seem, once you enter the park and turn the corner that reveals
Yosemite Valley – only a small part of the park but the one at which most of the
verbiage is aimed – you realize it's actually an understatement. For many,
Yosemite Valley is, very simply, the single most dramatic piece of geology to
be found anywhere in the world. Just seven miles long and one mile across at
its widest point, it's walled by near-vertical, three-thousand-foot-high cliffs
whose sides are streaked by cascading waterfalls and whose tops, a variety of
domes and pinnacles, form a jagged silhouette against the sky. At ground level,
too, the sights can be staggeringly impressive. Grassy meadows are framed by
oak, cedar, maple, and fir trees, with a variety of wild flowers and wildlife – deer,
coyotes, and even black bears are not uncommon. As if that wasn't enough, in
the southern reaches of the park near **Wawona**, sequoias grow almost as densely and to as vast dimensions as those in the Sequoia National Park.

Understandably, tourists are even more common. Each year Yosemite has to
cope with almost four million visitors, and if you're looking for a little peace
it's advisable to avoid the Yosemite Valley and Wawona on weekends and holidays. That said, the whole park is diverse and massive enough to endure the
crowds: you can visit at any time of year, even in winter when the waterfalls
turn to ice and the trails are blocked by snow, and out of high summer even
the valley itself resists getting crammed. Further-flung reaches of the park,
especially around the crisp alpine **Tuolumne** (pronounced Too-ol-uh-me)
Meadows, and the completely wild backcountry accessible beyond them, are
much less busy all year round – nature in just about the most peaceful and ele-
mental setting you could imagine. Everywhere you go, it is, of course, essential
to be careful not to cause ecological damage or upset the wildlife population.

Yosemite has had more than its fair share of negative press in the past few
years. There have been BASE jumping deaths and a series of brutal murders,
though *Outside* magazine claims that the chances of being killed in an
American national park are around two million to one, about the same as
drowning in your own bath. Yosemite Valley has also experienced severe flooding and rockfall close to visitor accommodation, two major considerations in
the drafting of the **Yosemite Valley Plan**, which aims to improve safety and
enhance the park's appeal for visitors. Due to be implemented over the next
ten to fifteen years, the plan calls for constructing buildings away from hazardous areas, removing some valley roads to allow meadow restoration, extending the valley shuttle bus system and, most contentious of all, reducing day-use
parking in the valley and requiring visitors to bus in from outlying parking lots.
Small modifications are already under way, but you can still drive into Yosemite
Valley, a situation unlikely to change for many years, if ever.

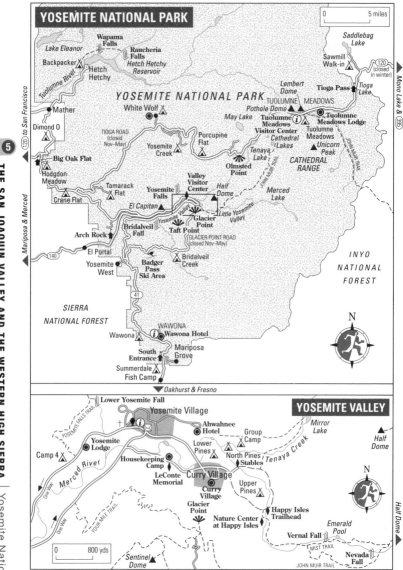

Some history

Yosemite Valley was created over thousands of years by glaciers gouging through and enlarging the canyon of the Merced River; the ice scraped away much of the softer portions of granite but only scarred the harder sections, which became the present cliffs. As the glaciers melted a lake formed, filling the valley, and eventually silting up to create the present valley floor.

John Muir was one of nature's most eloquent advocates, a champion of all things wild who spent ten years living in Yosemite Valley in the 1870s, and the rest of his life campaigning for its preservation. Born in Scotland in 1838, he grew up in Wisconsin, became a mechanical inventor, and embarked on his first journey at the age of 27, noting in his diary, "All drawbacks overcome ... joyful and free... I chose to become a tramp."

After walking a thousand miles to Florida with little more than a volume of Keats' poems and a plant press for company, he wound up in California in 1868 and asked for "anywhere that is wild." Working in Yosemite Valley as a sheep herder, mill worker, and hotel clerk, he spent every waking moment exploring the mountains and waterfalls, traveling light, and usually going to sleep hungry under the stars.

He dubbed the Sierra Nevada the "Range of Light," and spent years developing his theory of how glaciers shaped the range. His articles gradually won him academic acceptance, and the general public was soon devouring his journal-based books, such as *My First Summer in the Sierra* and *The Yosemite*, which became classics.

Muir was desperate to protect his beloved landscape from the depredations of sheep grazing, timber cutting, and homesteading, and through magazine articles and influential contacts goaded Congress into creating Yosemite National Park in 1890. Two years later, he set up the **Sierra Club**, an organization whose motto "take only photographs; leave only footprints" has become a model for like-minded groups around the world. Despite his successes, in 1913 Muir failed to save the Hetch Hetchy Valley from being dammed (see p.427), a blow that hastened his death a year later.

The publicity actually aided the formation of the present National Park Service in 1916, which promised – and has since provided – greater protection. Muir's name crops up throughout California as a memorial to this inspirational figure, not least in the 212-mile John Muir Trail which twists through his favorite scenery from Yosemite Valley south to Mount Whitney.

The Awahneechee people occupied the area quite peaceably for some 4000 years until the mid-nineteenth century, when the increasingly threatening presence of white Gold Rush settlers in the San Joaquin Valley led the tribes here to launch raiding parties against the nearest encampments. In 1851, Major James Savage led a force, the Mariposa Battalion, in pursuit of the Native Americans, trailing them into the foothills and beyond, and becoming the first white men to set foot in Yosemite Valley. It wasn't long before the two groups clashed properly, and the original population was moved out to white settlements to make way for farmers, foresters, and, soon after, tourists (the first group of sightseers arriving in 1855). Moves were quickly afoot to conserve the natural beauty of the area: in 1864 Yosemite Valley and the Mariposa Grove were preserved as the Yosemite Land Grant, the nation's first region specifically set aside to protect the wilderness. In 1890 it became America's third national park, thanks in great part to the campaigning work of Scottish naturalist John Muir (see box above).

Approaching Yosemite

Getting to Yosemite by car is straightforward, though on summer weekends parking can be a problem. Three roads enter the park from the west: Hwy-41 from Fresno, Hwy-140 from Merced, and Hwy-120 from Stockton and the San Francisco Bay area. All are generally kept open throughout the year as far as the valley, though in extreme circumstances Hwy-140 is the first to close. The only road into the eastern side of the park is Hwy-120, the 10,000-foot Tioga Road, which branches off US-395 close to Lee Vining – though this is usually closed from late October to early June and in bad weather. **Gas** (see "Listings" p. 433) is not available in Yosemite Valley, and though Crane Flat, some fifteen miles away has 24-hour pumps, it is expensive; fill up before heading into Yosemite.

In an effort to encourage visitors to arrive by **public transportation**, the Park Service and local authorities have introduced the YARTS bus system (☎209/388-9589 or 1-877/989-2787, ⓦwww.yarts.com), which runs a useful service along Hwy-140 from Merced (see p.384), which in turn has Amtrak and Greyhound connections. There are four or five departures daily picking up at both the Merced Transpo Center and the Amtrak station and arriving (after brief stops en route at all towns and significant accommodation) in the valley almost three hours later: **timetables** are available on the YARTS website and from visitor centers in the area. **Tickets** can be bought on board, and the round-trip **fare** (which includes the park entrance fee) to Yosemite from Merced is $20, from Mariposa and Midpines $10, and from El Portal just $7. YARTS also runs a limited summer service from Mammoth Lakes (see p.349), and Lee Vining, over Tioga Pass and through Tuolumne Meadows to Yosemite Valley.

Generally speaking, anything called a **sightseeing tour** that begins outside the park will involve you in an unsatisfying race through the valley. Alternatives which don't fit this pattern include San Francisco-based tours in converted "communal" buses run by **Green Tortoise** (☎415/956-7500 or 1-800/867-8647, ⓦwww.greentortoise.com). These are geared towards active, outdoorsy types who enjoy camping out and pitching in. Their **weekend trip** (mid–April to mid–Sept; departs 9pm Fri returns 7am Mon; $99, plus $31 food fund) heads to the valley and the Mariposa Grove; a slightly more expensive **three-day trip** (June–Oct) also allows half a day in Tuolumne Meadows and time around nearby Mono Lake as well as some hot springs. **Incredible Adventures** (☎415/642-7378 or 1-800/777-8464, ⓦwww.incadventures.com) offer enjoyable minibus tours from San Francisco. The **one-day trip** ($93) includes a quick jaunt around the main Yosemite Valley sights and three hours to explore and hike. The more satisfying **two-day** ($150) and **three-day camping-based tour** ($200) includes high-country hiking around Tuolumne and visiting the sequoias.

The hinterland towns

The heavy demand for accommodation within the park drives many to consider staying in one of the small, mostly former gold-mining towns along the main access roads. These are increasingly gearing themselves to park-bound tourists and do a reasonable job offering both lodging and food (for both of which see the following pages), though they are a poor substitute for actually staying in the park.

Approaching from the east: Lee Vining

From sometime around late May or early June until late October you can approach Yosemite from the east over the ten-thousand-foot Tioga Pass from US-395 and the town of **LEE VINING** (see p.361). You are almost two hours' drive from the Yosemite Valley heartland, but this area provides unparalleled access to the Tuolumne Meadows high country. Unless you want to stay in Lee Vining, or at *Tuolumne Meadows Lodge* (see p.419), your best bet is to **camp** just outside the park at the *Sawmill Walk-in* campground or the campgrounds in Lee Vining Canyon (see p.422 for all).

Approaching from the west: Groveland, Coulterville, Mariposa

Better bets for bases outside of the park are the western towns, particularly tiny **GROVELAND**, forty miles from the valley on Hwy-120, which retains verandahed wooden sidewalks and exudes a liberal air. South of here, and slightly off the main routes into the park, lies **COULTERVILLE**, the entirety of its diminutive heart listed as a State Historical Site. Most of the buildings and covered boardwalks date back to the mid-nineteenth century when this was on the main stage route into Yosemite. Travelers often stayed at **George Coulter's Hotel**, now transformed into a small local **museum** (Feb–April Sat & Sun 10am–4pm; May–Dec Wed–Sun 10am–4pm; donations suggested), while others – John Muir and Theodore Roosevelt among them – stayed across the road at *Hotel Jeffrey* (see "Accommodation" on p.420). Built in 1854, it remains the centerpiece of the town, and after a few minutes following the self-guided tour around the old town you should definitely repair to the long wooden bar of the hotel's *Magnolia Saloon*. Horse tack and mining paraphernalia hang from the ceiling, old aquatints and prints cover the walls, and there might even be someone bashing away at the honky-tonk piano in the corner.

Further south, Hwy-140 runs through the bustling Gold Rush town of **MARIPOSA**, 45 miles from the valley, which, in the **Mariposa Country Courthouse**, corner of Jones and 10th streets (free tours by arrangement ℡209/966-3685), boasts the oldest law enforcement establishment west of the Mississippi still in continuous use. Built without nails, the lumber was rough-cut from a nearby stand of white pine, and you can still see the saw marks on the hand-planed spectator benches. The town's heritage is further celebrated at the **Museum and History Center**, corner of Jesse and 12th streets (March–Oct daily 10am–4.30pm; Feb, Nov & Dec daily 10am–4pm; Jan closed; donations suggested; ℡209/966-2924), mildly diverting for its mock-up of a Gold Rush-era store and the large-scale mining paraphernalia scattered outside. In truth, you're better off at the **California State Mining and Mineral Museum**, two miles south on Hwy-49 (May–Sept daily 10am–6pm;

Smarter than the average bear

You may never encounter a **bear** anywhere else in California, but spend a couple of days in Yosemite Valley and you may well see one, probably breaking into a car or roaming the campgrounds looking for a free meal. Banging pots and yelling - from a safe distance, of course - will probably drive them off, but dependence on human food leads to several bears being shot each year. Safe food storage is now mandatory in the park and, as they say, "a fed bear is a dead bear," so do them and yourself a favor by keeping all food and fragrant items - deodorant, sunscreen, toothpaste, etc - either inside your room or in the metal bear boxes located in campgrounds and parking lots. Bring a padlock if you're concerned about your things being stolen.

It is important to remember that tents do not deter bears, nor do cars. Yosemite bears have learned to recognize coolers, bags of groceries, food wrappers, and even empty soda cans inside vehicles, and once on the scent, all the bear needs to do is pop a window by leaning on it or peel back a door with one paw.

You can report bear-related problems to the Bear Management Team on ℡209/372-0473.

Oct–April daily except Tues 10am–4pm; $1; ☎209/742-7625), which revels in the glory days of the mid-nineteenth century with realistic reconstructions of a mine and stamp mill plus a vault where, among the assorted treasures, lies the largest existing nugget ever uncovered in California, a thirteen-pound chunk valued at over $1 million. There's a very helpful **visitor center** in Mariposa at 5158 Hwy-140 (mid-May to mid-Sept Mon–Sat 7am–8pm, Sun 8am–5pm; mid-Sept to mid-May Mon–Sat 8am–5pm, Sun closed; ☎209/966-7081 or 1-800/208-2434, ⓌWww.mariposa.org), with all you need to know about Yosemite and around. Free **Internet access** is available at the library, beside the courthouse at Jones and 10th (Tues–Fri 9.30am–4.30pm or later, Sat 10am–4.30pm).

Further east along Hwy-140, on the way to Yosemite, the small towns of **Midpines** and **El Portal** also offer affordable lodging outside of the park (see "Accommodation" on p.420).

Approaching from the south: Oakhurst and Fish Camp

Yosemite visitors arriving from the south will come through **OAKHURST**, fifteen miles south of the southern park entrance, a booming sprawl of malls and sky-high signs for chain hotels and fast-food joints. Nonetheless, it makes a handy base for the southern section of the park and, with your own transport, day-trips into Yosemite Valley, fifty miles away, are quite feasible. The relocated buildings of the **Fresno Flats Historical Park**, almost a mile from the center on Road 427 (unrestricted access) won't detain you for long, though you should make use of the **Yosemite Sierra Visitors Bureau**, 40367 Hwy-41 (Mon–Sat 9am–5pm, Sun 9am–1pm; ☎559/683-4636, ⓌWww.go2yosemite.net), which stocks armloads of information on Yosemite.

Winter in Yosemite

From December to April, those prepared to cope with blocked roads – the Tioga Pass is always closed in winter – and below-freezing temperatures are amply rewarded at Yosemite; thick snow, frozen waterfalls, and far fewer people make for almost unimaginable beauty and silence. **Accommodation** is cheaper at these times too (check the website for special deals), and much easier to obtain, though weekends can still get pretty full. Many low-country **campgrounds** are open, and restrictions on backcountry camping are eased – you'll want a good sleeping bag and tent.

Much of Yosemite is fabulous **skiing** territory. Lessons, equipment rental, tows, and 25 miles of groomed cross-country trails are available at the **Badger Pass Ski Area** (ⓌWww.badgerpass.com) on the road to Glacier Point, accessible via a shuttle from the valley. All-day lift tickets cost $31, daily equipment rental will set you back $22 for downhill, $16 for cross-country, and $30 for snowboards. Lessons start from $28. If you want someone to take you out on Badger Pass's groomed trails, contact the Yosemite Cross Country Ski School (☎209/372-8444), who run all manner of beginners, improvers, and Telemark and skating lessons, and lead overnight ski tours. In Yosemite Valley there's **ice skating** at the open-air Curry Village rink (normally $6.50, plus $3 skate rental).

Be aware if driving into the park that **tire chains** are recommended from November to April and can be rented in towns approaching the park. Inside the park, they are only available for sale.

Useful contacts and websites

National Park Reservation Service (NPRS) PO Box 1600, Cumberland, MD 21502 ☏301/722-1257 or 1-800/436-7275, ⓦreservations.nps.org. Advance campground reservations by mail, website, or phone (7am–7pm PST).

Yosemite Concession Services (YCS) 5410 East Home, Fresno, CA 93727. Lodging reservations ☏559/252/4848, tour reservations ☏209/372-1240, Badger Pass ski conditions ☏209/372-1000, ⓦwww.yosemitepark.com. YCS runs virtually all park lodging, restaurants, tours, activities, and shuttle buses. Reservations can be made up to a year and a day in advance, Mon–Fri 7am–7pm, Sat & Sun 8am–5pm.

Yosemite National Park ☏209/372-0200, ⓦwww.nps.gov/yose. Detailed website and recorded info covering everything about the park including weather and road conditions.

Wilderness Permits and Information Wilderness Permits, PO Box 545, Yosemite, CA 95389 ☏209/372-0740, ⓦwww.nps.gov/yose/wilderness. Park Service contact for obtaining wilderness permits for overnight stays in the backcountry.

The tiny huddle of hotels which makes up **FISH CAMP** lies ten miles north of Oakhurst, handy for Wawona, the Mariposa Grove, and something to keep the kids quiet – *The Logger*, 56001 Hwy-41 (March–Oct daily; $12.50; ☏559/683-7273, ⓦwww.ymsprr.com), an oil-burning train that plies a two-mile track into the forest from where hewn timber was once carted. In the height of summer, several trains run each day giving you the option of spending some time at the picnic area in the woods at the far end.

Arrival, information, and park transport

Yosemite is always open: **park entry** costs $20 per vehicle including passengers, $10 for each cyclist and hiker, and is valid for seven days. Pay at the ranger stations when you enter, or if they're closed, at the visitor center in the valley, or when you leave. To encourage use of public transportation, bus passengers are currently exempt entry fees.

On arrival at any of the park entrances, you'll be given an excellent map of the park, the pertinent and comprehensive, half-yearly *Yosemite Guide*, along with the weekly *Yosemite Today* listings insert which covers current events and the extensive range of (mostly free) ranger programs. If you have more specific inquiries, try the park's most useful **visitor center** at **Yosemite Village** (daily mid-June to mid-Sept 8am–6pm; mid-Sept to mid-June 8.30am–5pm; ☏209/372-0265), where you can pick up information and maps, including a topographic map ($9) essential for any adventurous hikes. There are other visitor centers at **Tuolumne Meadows** (mid-June to Sept 9am–5pm, later in July & Aug; ☏209/372-0263), at the **Big Oak Flat** entrance (May–Sept daily 9am–6pm; Oct & Nov Thurs–Mon 9am–5pm; ☏209/379-1899), and **Wawona** (daily mid-May to mid-Sept 8.30am–4.30pm; ☏209/375-9501). For **free** hiking permits and all the route planning help you could ask for, pop next door to the **Wilderness Center** (mid-June to Aug daily 7am–6pm; Sept to late Oct daily 8am–5pm; ☏209/372-0745): wilderness permits are self-issued once the Wilderness Center closes.

Useful **phone numbers** and **websites** are covered in the box (see above), and all manner of other services are included in the "Listings" section (see p.434).

THE SAN JOAQUIN VALLEY AND THE WESTERN HIGH SIERRA | Yosemite National Park

Rock climbing

Rock climbers the world over flock to Yosemite, drawn by the challenge of inching up three-thousand-foot walls of sheer granite that soar skyward under the California sun. Quite simply, the valley is seen as the pinnacle of climbing aspirations, with acres of superb, clean rock, easily accessible world-class routes, and reliable summer weather drawing a vibrant climbing community bubbling over with campfire tales.

The best place to marvel at climbers' antics is **El Cap Meadows**, always dotted with tourists craning their necks and training binoculars on the biggest slab of granite of them all, **El Capitan**. The apparently featureless face hides hairline crack systems a thousand feet long, seemingly insurmountable overhangs and gargantuan towers topped off with narrow ledges only given any sense of scale by the flea-like figures of climbers. If you can't spot them, look for their haul sacks; or come out here after dark, when the light from head torches and the faint, distant chatter give the game away.

The routes are highly convoluted, but the most famous, **The Nose** route of El Capitan, lies straight ahead, tracing a line up the prow of the cliff and passing the relative luxury of El Cap Towers. This twenty-foot by six-foot patio, over 1500 feet above the valley floor, is used as a bivvy spot by climbers who typically spend three to five nights on the route. "In-a-day" attempts usually involve 24 hours of continuous climbing, though the current record stands at an astounding three hours and twenty-four minutes. The renowned **North American Wall** route lies to the right passing directly through a massive stain on the rock, which looks remarkably like a map of North America.

Bathooks and bugaboos

Many of the most celebrated routes in Yosemite are what's known as "Big Wall" routes, tackled by **aid climbing**, where bits of metal are hammered into cracks and hauled on to achieve upward movement. The demands of ever harder climbs have pushed the development of an extensive armory that's totally baffling to the uninitiated: bathooks, birdbeaks, bongs, bugaboos, circleheads, fifi hooks, a funkness device, lost arrows, and RURPs are all employed either to grapple a ledge or wedge into cracks of different sizes. The scale of Yosemite's walls is such that few cracks can be followed from bottom to top and to get from one crack to another, climbers employ death-defying **pendulums**, and repeatedly sweep across the face gaining momentum until they can lunge out at a tiny flake or fingertip hold. All this "nailing" and swinging takes time and most Big Wallers are forced to spend nights slung in a kind of lightweight camp bed known as a **portaledge**. Food, gallons of water, sleeping bags, warm clothing, and wet-weather gear must all be lugged up in haul sacks, along with a boombox and a rack of CDs deviously strapped and arranged so they can't be dropped – after all, it can get a bit tedious hammering away up there for hours on end. As Yosemite veteran John Long writes: "Climbing a wall can be a monumental pain in the ass. No one could pay you enough to do it. A thousand dollars would be too little by far. But you wouldn't sell the least of the memories for ten times that sum."

Some history

Yosemite has long captured the imagination of climbers but technical rock climbing didn't kick off here until 1933, when four Bay Area climbers reached what is now known as the Lunch Ledge, 1000 feet up Washington Column – the tower opposite Half Dome. With the aid of heavy steel **pitons** for driving into cracks, and equally weighty **carabiners** for attaching the ropes to the pitons, climbers began to knock off climbs such as the fifteen-pitch **Royal Arches** route, which weaves its way up the ledges and slabs behind the *Ahwahnee Hotel*.

After World War II, demobbed climbers employed newly developed, tough nylon ropes and lightweight safety equipment to push standards to new levels, and pipe dreams became realistic propositions. An early conquest, in 1947, was **Lost Arrow Spire**, which rises to the right of Yosemite Falls and is easy to spot in the early morning and late afternoon light when the spire casts a shadow on the wall nearby. This was the first route intentionally approached as a multi-day ascent, much of the groundwork being laid by Swiss-born blacksmith **John Salathé**. He was at the cutting edge of climbing, putting up technically demanding aid routes through the late 1940s and early 1950s, and even fashioning his own tougher carbon-steel pitons from the axles of a Model A Ford.

For the next twenty years Salathé's mantle was assumed by classical purist **Royal Robbins** and **Warren Harding**, who was prepared to bang in a piton just about anywhere if it would help him get up something new. Little love was lost between them but when Robbins' team first scaled the face of **Half Dome** in 1957, Harding was on the summit to congratulate them. It was a magnificent effort and ranked as the hardest climb in North America at the time. Yosemite became an international forcing ground for aid climbing, and Americans were suddenly matching, and even surpassing, the achievements of previously dominant Europeans.

Now even the mighty El Cap seemed possible. **The Nose** was the most obvious line but refused to submit for seventeen months, even after Warren Harding used four massive pitons fashioned from stove legs scavenged from the Berkeley city dump and drove them into what are still known as the Stoveleg Cracks. Harding and two colleagues finally topped out in 1958 after a single thirteen-day push, the culmination of 47 days' work on the route.

With these critical ascents completed, climbers' aspirations broadened and the 1960s became the **Golden Age** of climbing in the Yosemite Valley, when it drew a motley collection of dropouts and misfits, many ranking among the world's finest climbers. Almost all the major walls and hundreds of minor routes were completed at this time. Purists at the top of their sport became disenchanted with the artificiality of aid ascents and began to "free" pitches: not hauling up on all the hardware, but using it only for protection in case of a fall. The culmination of years of cutting-edge climbing, and months of route-specific training was Lynn Hill's ground-breaking free ascent of The Nose in 1993, praised and admired by all, if ruefully by some in Yosemite's traditionally macho climbing community.

Practicalities

The **best months** for climbing in the Yosemite Valley are April, May, September, and October. In summer, the climbs on the domes around Tuolumne Meadows are cooler and usually considered a better bet. Some areas, notably the southeast face of El Capitan, are occasionally off limits to protect the nesting sites of peregrine falcons. Whatever type of climbing you do, follow the guidelines for **"minimum impact climbing"** – never chip holds or add bolts to existing routes, and remove all litter, including human waste.

Everyone stays at the bohemian **Camp 4**, near Yosemite Lodge, a trampled, dusty, and noisy site often entirely taken over by climbers. It is relatively cheap, with a great sense of camaraderie, and an excellent **bulletin board** for teaming up with climbing partners, selling gear, organizing a ride, or just meeting friends. Normally, you can only stay for seven nights at a stretch, but after the middle of September you're allowed to settle in for a month.

For a more organized introduction to the climber's craft or to brush up on a few skills, engage the services of the Yosemite Mountaineering School, which is based at Tuolumne Meadows in summer (June–Aug; ☎209/372-8435) and in Yosemite Valley for the rest of the year (☎209/372-8344). Experts run daily courses ranging

continued overleaf

continued....

from the one-day beginners' classes ($70–90) through various intermediate classes to private full-day guided climbs (one person $220, two people $155 each).

Rock-climbing **gear** is available from the Mountain Shop in Tuolumne Meadows (summer only), and the well-stocked and competitively priced Mountain Shop in Curry Village (daily 8am–6pm).

The essential **guidebooks** to local climbs are Don Reid's *Yosemite: Free Climbs* and *Yosemite: Big Walls*, published by Falcon Guides, and Chris McNamara's *Supertopos*, which are available in bookstores and downloadable at ⓦ www.super-topos.com. To catch something of the spirit of the scene, read *Camp 4: Recollections of a Yosemite Rockclimber* (The Mountaineers) by Yosemite veteran Steve Roper, and *The Vertical World of Yosemite* (Wilderness Press), a collection of inspiring stories on the valley, both available in the Ansel Adams Gallery. You can also glean something of what it is all about by checking out the small but interesting rock-climbing **exhibition** in the Winter Club Room in the *Ahwahnee Hotel*.

Park transport

The three roads from the San Joaquin Valley end up at **Yosemite Valley**, roughly in the center of the park's 1200 square miles, and home to its most dramatic scenery. At the southern edge of the park, Hwy-41 passes the **Mariposa Grove** and **Wawona**; from here it's 27 miles further to the valley. **Tuolumne Meadows** is in the high country, sixty-odd miles northeast of the valley, close to the Tioga Pass entrance (Hwy-120) on the eastern side of the park.

While having your own vehicle is a boon for exploring the wider park, traffic congestion spoils everyone's fun on the valley floor, and if you're driving in just for the day, leave your vehicle in the day-use parking lots at Yosemite and Curry villages. You can then use the free and frequent **shuttle buses** which operate on the valley floor, running anticlockwise on a loop that passes through, or close to, all the main points of interest, trailheads, and accommodation areas. In high season, they run roughly every twenty minutes between 7am and 10pm to most sections of the valley, with slightly reduced hours at other times.

Although bicycles are not allowed off paved surfaces, **cycling** is an excellent way to get around the valley with twelve miles of dedicated bike paths along the valley floor. Yosemite Lodge and Curry Village (April–Nov only) both rent city bikes for $5.50 per hour or $21 per day.

For straying further afield use the hikers' buses which call at roadside trailheads on the way to Tuolumne Meadows and Glacier Point, and double as round-trip narrated tours for those on a tighter schedule. The **Tuolumne Meadows Hikers' Bus** (mid-June to early Sept; $14.50 one way, $23 round-trip) makes the two-and-a-half-hour run to Tuolumne Meadows, leaving hotels around Yosemite Valley around 8.20am and departing Tuolumne at 2.35pm giving just over three hours at the Meadows. The **Glacier Point Hikers' Bus** (June–Oct; $15 each way) runs up to Glacier Point three times a day, where it stays for around an hour.

Failing that, there are always **guided tours** (☎209/372-1240), which range from the rather dull two-hour valley floor spin, costing $20.50, to the all-day Mariposa and Glacier Point Grand Tour (June–Oct) at $55; all bookable through accommodation reception areas.

Accommodation

Once in the park, **accommodation** can be a problem; it's almost essential to book well in advance and anything other than camping can be expensive. Even canvas tents cost what you would pay for a reasonable motel elsewhere. All accommodation in the national park – the majority of it right in the valley – is operated by **Yosemite Concession Services** (see "Useful contacts and websites" box, p.415) and should be booked a few weeks ahead; longer for holiday weekends. Places generally reduce their charges in winter, though weekend prices remain close to high-season levels. One solution to the problem is to stay just outside the park (see "Approaching Yosemite" on p.411) and commute into it daily.

If you are really well organized you might also want to consider the High Sierra Camp Vacations (see "Listings," p.434).

In the valley

Ahwahnee Hotel a short distance from Yosemite Village at shuttle stop 3 (call YCS). Undoubtedly the finest place to stay in Yosemite, with rooms decorated in the hotel's Native American motif. Usually booked months in advance despite room rates starting close to $400, but worth visiting to view the wonderfully grand public areas, or for a drink or a meal. ❼

Curry Village a mile from Yosemite Village at shuttle stops 14 and 20 (call YCS). A large area dotted mostly with canvas tent cabins each fitted with four beds on a wooden plinth. There are also cramped solid-walled cabins and spacious motel-style rooms and some attractive cottages. Cottages ❺, rooms ❺, cabins with bath ❺, cabins without bath ❹, tent cabins ❸

Housekeeping Camp half a mile from Yosemite Village at shuttle stop 13 (call YCS). Ranks of simple concrete-walled plastic-roofed cabins with beds on sleeping platforms and the use of a fire grate and picnic table. April to late Oct only. ❸

Yosemite Lodge half a mile west of Yosemite Village at shuttle stop 8 (call YCS). Sprawling middle-market accommodation popular with tour groups, its proximity to half-decent restaurants, grocery stores, and a pool making it perhaps the most convenient accommodation in the valley. Rooms are motel-style, all with private bath and phone but no TV or a/c. ❻

The rest of the park

Tuolumne Meadows Lodge Tuolumne Meadows (call YCS). A large cluster of canvas tent cabins each with four beds and a wood-burning stove, but no electricity, located at nearly 9000ft and perfect for the first or last night of a long hiking trip. Only available mid-June to mid-Sept. Meals served. ❸

Wawona Hotel Wawona (call YCS; front desk ☎209/375-6556). An elegant New England-style hotel, parts of which date from 1879, with marvelous public areas, distinctive wooden verandahs dotted with white wicker chairs, and grounds which include a pool, tennis courts, and a nine-hole golf course. Rooms all lack phone, TV, and a/c, but have been gracefully restored with old-style furniture, Victoria patterned wallpaper, and ceiling fans – though those in the main lodge are fairly small and lack bathrooms. Rooms with bath ❼, without bath ❺

White Wolf Lodge about halfway from the valley to Tuolumne Meadows (call YCS). Spacious four-berth tent cabins with wood-burning stove and candles perfectly sited for day-hikes to Lukens and Harden Lakes, and the Grand Canyon of the Tuolumne River. Late June–early Sept only. ❹

Yosemite Falls B&B 7210 Yosemite Park Way, Yosemite West ☎209/375-1414, ⊛www.yosemitefalls.com. Extravagant B&B where rooms all have private bath, satellite TV, VCR, and a complimentary bottle of bubbly. Spend the evening around the bar's pool table, then fortify yourself for another day's sightseeing with a huge breakfast. Located in a small enclave fourteen miles from Yosemite Valley, just outside the national park but only accessible from Wawona Road. ❼

Yosemite Peregrine 7509 Henness Circle, Yosemite West ☎209/372-8517 or 1-800/396-3639, ⊛www.yosemitewest.com/peregrin. Well-appointed B&B a few blocks from the *Yosemite Falls B&B*, tastefully decorated in Southwestern or woodsy themes, and with a hot tub. Home-cooked breakfast is served on the deck if the weather cooperates. The adjacent *Falcon's Nest* (same contact details) has a couple of more budget-oriented rooms and a two-night minimum (❺). ❻

Hwy-120: Groveland and Coulterville

The following are listed by increasing distance from Yosemite.

Yosemite Lakes 31191 Hwy-120, five miles from the Big Oak Flat entrance ☎209/962-0100 or

419

1-800/533-1001, ℱ 209/962-0106. Reasonable family-oriented resort that benefits from being close to the park. Tent sites are well spaced ($22; full hook-up $30), there are rustic share-bath bunkhouse cabins (❷), and conical canvas-walled yurts – with polished wood floors, a deck, cooking facilities, shower and toilet – which sleep four in considerable comfort. ❻

Yosemite Westgate Buck Meadows Lodge
7633 Hwy-120, 15 miles from the Big Oak Flat entrance ℡ 209/962-5281 or 1-800/253-9673, ⓦ www.insight.com. The closest standard motel to the park on Hwy-120 is comfortable and has all the expected facilities including cable TV, phone, pool, and spa. There's a decent diner next door and two kids under twelve stay free with two adults; rates drop dramatically in winter. ❻

Groveland Motel & Indian Village 18933 Hwy-120, Groveland, 25 miles from the Big Oak Flat entrance ℡ 209/962-7865 or 1-888/849-3529, ⓦ www.grovelandmotel.com. Some fairly basic a/c cabins with cable TV (❹), an assortment of mobile homes, mostly with small kitchens (❹), and a three-bedroom house that sleeps six (❼) scattered around wooded grounds, plus concrete-floored teepees (❶) each with a double bed.

Hotel Charlotte 18959 Hwy-120, Groveland, 25 miles from the Big Oak Flat entrance ℡ 209/962-6455 or 1-800/961-7799. Basic but full of character, this warm and no-nonsense eleven-room hotel dates back to 1921. Rooms are mostly small and without phone or TV, and some share beautiful old-fashioned bathrooms. Rates include a good continental breakfast, and there's a common TV room. ❹

Groveland Hotel 18767 Hwy-120, Groveland, 25 miles from the Big Oak Flat Entrance ℡ 209/962-4000 or 1-800/273-3314, ⓦ www.groveland.com. Gorgeous mining-era hotel with luxurious individually styled antique-filled rooms, mostly with deep baths. Suites (❽) feature spa tubs and real fires. ❻

Hotel Jeffrey junction of Hwy-49 & Hwy-132, Coulterville, 30 miles from the Big Oak Flat entrance ℡ 209/878-3471 or 1-800/464-3471, ⓦ www.yosemitegold.com/jefferyhotel. Classic Gold Rush-era hotel used by original Yosemite sightseers as well as John Muir and Theodore Roosevelt. Rooms are mostly old-fashioned and smallish, but there are also some two- and three-room suites. All have access to a communal lounge and sunny deck. Suites ❻, en-suite rooms ❺, rooms ❹

Hwy-140: Mariposa, Midpines, and El Portal

The following are listed by increasing distance from Yosemite.

Yosemite View Lodge 11136 Hwy-140, El Portal, two miles west of the Arch Rock entrance ℡ 209/379-2681 or 1-888/742-4371, ⓦ www.yosemite-motels.com. Vast and luxurious – though slightly soulless – complex beside the tumbling Merced River, hard against the park boundary. The modern rooms all have a/c, phone, cable TV, but you pay a premium to get river view, fireplace, in-room spa, and kitchenette. Often booked out but try for no-shows. Premium rooms ❼, basic rooms ❻

Yosemite Redbud Lodge Hwy-140, 11 miles west of the Arch Rock entrance ℡ 209/379-2301. Eight rooms, all with a/c, fridge, barbecue, fresh fruit, muffins, tea and coffee, plus a good deal of character. Suites have fireplaces, kitchenette, and a small deck overlooking the river, and they'll even loan you a lunch cooler for your day in the park. Suites ❺, rooms ❹

Yosemite Bug Hostel & Lodge 6979 Hwy-140, Midpines, 23 miles west of the Arch Rock entrance. ℡ 209/966 6666, ⓦ www.yosemitebug.com. Set in twenty acres of woodland, this low-cost to mid-range lodge, HI-AYH hostel and campground is the handiest budget lodging near Yosemite. Self-catering facilities exist for those staying in dorms, but there's also the excellent licensed *Recovery Bistro* (see p.432) on site. Comfortable mixed and single-sex dorms ($13, non-members $16) are supplemented by tent cabins (❶), shared-bath private rooms (❷), and very comfortable and distinctively decorated en-suite rooms with decks but no phone or TV (❺). Pitching your own tent costs $17 per site. There's Internet access, a lounge with books and games, access to a good summer swimming hole, and mountain-bike rental ($15 a day, guests $12), and a *YARTS* bus stop outside. Reservations essential May–Oct. ❶–❺

EC Yosemite Motel 5180 Jones St, Mariposa, 35 miles from the Arch Rock entrance ℡ 209/742-6800, ℱ 742-6719. Pleasant and good-value motel with some new large a/c rooms mostly with two beds; all rooms have shower/tub combos and cable TV. There's a heated pool and spa, and rates may drop to as little as $55 a night in winter. ❹

Sierra View Motel 4993 7th St, Mariposa, 35 miles from the Arch Rock entrance ℡ 209/966-5793 or 1-800/627-8439, ℱ 209/742-5669. Peaceful, welcoming, and good-value budget motel just off Mariposa's main drag, offering continental breakfast with smallish rooms and larger suites, all equipped with a/c. ❸

Highland House B&B 3125 Wild Dove Lane, Mariposa, 35 miles from the Arch Rock entrance ℡ 209/966-3737 or 1-888/477-5089, ⓦ www.highlandhousebandb.com. Tucked away amid ponderosa pines and incense cedars over six miles off Hwy-140, it is worth the effort to reach this superb and tranquil B&B. It's three elegantly furnished rooms all have private bathroom with tub and shower, and the suite (⑥) has a four-poster bed, fireplace, and VCR. The breakfasts are gorgeous, and the common area even comes with a pool table. ⑤

Sierra House B&B 4981 Indian Peak Rd, Mariposa, 40 miles from the Arch Rock entrance ☎1-800/496-3515 or ☎/℉209/966-3515, ⓦwww.sierrahousebnb.com. Welcoming rural B&B right beside Hwy-49, four miles southeast of Mariposa, where the three rooms all have private facilities, though you'll need to go for the Middle East Room (⑤) to get a clawfoot bath. A full breakfast is served and you can plan your day in the lounge or out on the sunny porch. ④

Hwy-41: Oakhurst and Fish Camp

The following are listed by increasing distance from Yosemite.

Owl's Nest Lodging 1235 Hwy-41, Fish Camp ☎559/683-3484, ⓦwww.owlsnestlodging.com. Perhaps the best deal on the southern side of the park, with large guest rooms for two (④) and self-contained chalets (⑥) that sleep up to six. Nicely decorated, friendly, and right by a stream. Closed Nov–March. ④–⑥

White Chief Mountain Lodge 7776 White Chief Mountain Rd, Fish Camp ☎559/683-5444, ⓔwhitechiefmtnlodge@sierratel.com. Located just 300 yards off Hwy-41, the *White Chief* offers basic but clean motel units (③) and nicer cabins for up

to four (⑥), along with a very good on-site restaurant (see p.433). Closed Nov–March. ④

Narrow Gauge Inn 48571 Hwy-41, Fish Camp ☎559/683-7720 or 1-888/644-9050, ⓦwww.narrowgaugeinn.com. Attractive lodge with a wide selection of rooms, many with a balcony and views over the forest, and a fine on-site restaurant (see p.433). All rooms come with phone, TV, and continental breakfast, and the inn has a pool and spa. Closed Jan–March. ⑥

Sierra Sky Ranch 50552 Rd 632, 12 miles from South Entrance ☎559/683-8040, ⓦwww.sierra-tel.com/skyranch. Converted former ranch with broad verandahs, an outdoor pool, a huge rustic lounge/restaurant/bar, and a range of rooms, all quite different: ask to see a few. ④–⑥

Snowline Lodge 42150 Hwy-41, 3 miles north of Oakhurst ☎ & ℉559/683-5854. Slightly run-down motel offering small cabins with bathrooms and TV, plus an outdoor pool. ③

Hounds Tooth Inn 42071 Hwy-41, 3 miles north of Oakhurst ☎559/642-6600 or 1-888/642-6610, ⓦwww.houndstoothinn.com. Modern B&B with a dozen individually-decorated rooms, most with either a fireplace or spa bath and all air conditioned. Complimentary wine served each evening, and the buffet breakfasts are delicious. ⑤

The Homestead 41110 Rd 600, 2.5 miles off Hwy-49 in Ahwahnee, near Oakhurst ☎559/683-0495, ⓦwww.homesteadcottages.com. Just a handful of very attractive and beautifully outfitted adobe cottages – a/c, TV, gas grill – each with full self-catering facilities, comfortable lounge area, and a nice deck. Two-night minimum stay at weekends. ⑦

Camping

As with any national park, **camping** is the best way to really feel part of your surroundings, though this is perhaps less true in Yosemite Valley, where the campgrounds are large and crowded. In summer it is almost essential to book beforehand (see "Useful contacts" box, p.415): reservations open in one-month chunks, four months in advance, so to book for the month beginning July 15 you can, and should, call from March 15. Otherwise you'll need to show up at the Curry Village Reservations Office very early in the morning and hope for cancellations. Other than the *Camp 4*, all valley sites cost $18 and none have **showers** or **laundry** facilities (see "Listings," p.434). Camping in the valley is restricted to a month in any calendar year but between May and mid-September a week is the maximum stay. Camping outside recognized sites in the valley is strictly forbidden.

In addition to the main campgrounds there are **backpacker campgrounds** in Yosemite Valley, Tuolumne Meadows, and Hetch Hetchy, designed for hikers about to start (or just finishing) a wilderness trip and costing $5 per night – you must have a wilderness permit to use these.

Finally, with enough time you really should get out to one of several primitive campgrounds in the backcountry. Designed specifically for hikers, these have fire rings and some form of water source, which must be treated. To use them, or to camp elsewhere in the backcountry, you must get a **free wilderness permit** (see "Hiking" box, p.428) – as ever, you must camp a mile from any road, four miles from a populated area, and at least a hundred yards from water sources and trails. Remember to carry a stove and fuel as indiscriminate use of trees could jeopardize future freedom to camp in the backcountry. Camping on the summit of Half Dome is not permitted.

In the valley

Camp 4 Walk-in (all year; $5 per person; 4000ft). First-come-first-served campground west of and away from the other valley sites, popular with rock climbers. It is a fairly bohemian place with six-person sites just a few yards from a dusty parking lot. It is often full by 9am, especially in spring and fall, so join the line early.

North Pines, Upper Pines, Lower Pines (March–Oct, Upper Pines all year; $18; 4000ft). Largely indistinguishable, pine-shrouded sites, all with toilets, water, and fire rings. Popular with RV users. Reservations essential.

Outside the valley

Bridalveil Creek (July–early Sept; $12; 7200ft). High country first-come-first-served campground off Glacier Point Road with good access to wilderness trails.

Crane Flat (June–Sept; $18; 6200ft). Northwest of the valley, at the start of Hwy-120 and close to a stand of sequoias. Reservations required.

Hodgdon Meadow (all year; $18; 4900ft). Relatively quiet campground right on the park's western boundary just off Hwy-120. Take Old Big Oak Flat Road for half a mile. Reservations required May–Sept, first-come-first-served ($12) at other times.

Porcupine Flat (July–early Sept; $8; 8100ft). Attractive and small first-come-first-served campground near the road to Tuolumne Meadows, nearly forty miles from the valley. Stream water.

Tamarack Flat (June–Sept; $8; 6300ft). Small campground two miles off the Hwy-120 Tioga Road, 23 miles from the valley and with only limited RV access. Stream water.

Tuolumne Meadows (July–Sept; $18; 8600ft). Large and popular streamside campground beside a sub-alpine meadow that is effectively three campgrounds in one. Half the sites are available by advance reservation, half by same-day reservation, and a further 25 sites ($5 per person) are available for backpackers with wilderness permits. There are flush toilets, piped water, and showers ($3) nearby at the *Tuolumne Lodge*.

Wawona (all year; $18; 4000ft). The only site in the southern sector of the park, approximately a mile north of the *Wawona Hotel*. Some walk-in sites are reserved for car-free campers. Reservations required May–Sept; rest of year $12.

White Wolf (July–early Sept; $12; 8000ft). First-come-first-served tent and RV site a mile north of Hwy-120 midway between the valley and Tuolumne Meadows.

Yosemite Creek (July–early Sept; $8; 7600ft). First-come-first-served tent-only site ideal for escaping the crowds, though it can fill up very quickly in the summer. Inconveniently sited five miles off Hwy-120, but almost equidistant between the valley and Tuolumne Meadows. Stream water.

Outside the park

Dimond O Evergreen Road, off Hwy-120 West (April–Nov; $13; 4400ft). National Forest campground one mile west of the Big Oak Flat entrance, with tent and RV sites, piped water and pit toilets.

Lee Vining Creek off Hwy-120 East (late April–Oct; $7; 7800ft). A series of almost identical streamside National Forest campgrounds along Poole Power Plant Road, 9 miles west of the Tioga Pass entrance.

Sawmill Walk-in Mile 1.5 Saddlebag Lake Road, 3.7 miles east of the Tioga Pass entrance (June to mid-Oct; $7; 9800ft). Primitive walk-in campground around four hundred yards from its parking lot, superbly sited amid jagged peaks that feel a world away from the glaciated domes around Tuolumne.

Summerdale Hwy-41 (May–Oct; $14; 5000ft). National Forest campground 1.5 miles south of the park's South entrance and handy for both Wawona and the Mariposa Grove.

Yosemite Valley

Even the most evocative photography can only hint at the pleasure to be found in simply gazing at **YOSEMITE VALLEY**. From massive hunks of granite rising five thousand feet up from the four-thousand-foot valley floor to the subtle colorings of wild flowers, the variations in the valley can be both enormous and discreet. Aside from just looking, there are many easy walks around the lush fields to waterfalls and lakes, and much tougher treks up the enormous cliffs (see box, p.417).

The valley's defining features are its enormous cliffs and thundering waterfalls; in fact nowhere else in the world is there such an array of cascades concentrated in such a small area, though a mild winter can cause many of these falls to dry up as early as July.

If there is any drawback, it's that this part of Yosemite is the busiest, and you're rarely far from other visitors or the park's commercial trappings, notably in **Yosemite Village** and **Curry Village**, the two main concentrations of shops and restaurants. Most of the crowds can be easily left behind by taking any path which contains much of a slope, but a couple of days exploring the valley leaves you more than ready to press on to the park's less populated regions.

The big cliffs

However you approach the valley, your view will be partially blocked by **El Capitan**, a vast monolith jutting forward from the adjacent cliffs and looming 3593ft above the valley floor. One of the largest pieces of exposed granite in the world, "The Captain" is a full 320 acres of gray-tan granite seemingly devoid of vegetation and almost vertical. El Cap's enormous size isn't really apparent until you join the slack-jawed tourists craning their necks and training binoculars and cameras on rock climbers on the face. Eventually you'll pick out flea-sized specks inching up what appears to be a flawless wall, though closer inspection reveals a pattern of flakes, fissures, and small ledges. The most accessible sequence of these comprises what is probably the most famous rock-climbing route in the world, **The Nose** (see box, p.417).

Impressive though El Capitan is, for most people it is the arching **Half Dome** that instantly grabs their attention. A stunning sight topping out at 8842 feet, it rises almost 5000 feet above the valley floor, with its two-thousand-foot northwest face only seven degrees off the vertical, making it the **sheerest cliff in North America**. Though impressive from the valley, the best views of Half Dome are from Glacier Point (see p.430) especially around sunset.

Ambitious day-hikers (see p.428) wanting to get up close and personal can make it to the shallow saddle of the dome's thirteen-acre summit, tackling the final 400 feet by way of a steep steel-cable staircase hooked on to the rock's curving back. Once at the almost flat summit, the brave (or foolish) can inch out towards the edge of the projecting lip for a vertiginous look straight down the near-vertical face. While the cables remain all year, the cable supports and wooden slats only stay in place from late May to mid–October, making a winter ascent very difficult (though not impossible). Keep clear of the summit if there are any signs of impending storms; lightning strikes during almost every thunderstorm, which can occur at any time of year.

The major waterfalls

At 2425 feet, **Yosemite Falls** is widely claimed to be the fifth highest waterfall in the world, and the highest in North America. It is a somewhat spurious assertion, since it is actually two falls separated by 675 feet of churning rapids and chutes known as **Middle Cascade**. Nonetheless, the 1430-foot **Upper Yosemite Fall** and the 320-foot **Lower Yosemite Fall** are magnificent, especially in May and early June when runoff from melting snow turns them into a foaming torrent. The flow typically dries up by mid-August, leaving a dark stain of algae and lichen to mark the spot. A flat, quarter-mile, asphalt trail (from shuttle bus stop 6) leads along an avenue of incense cedars and ponderosa pines that frame Upper Yosemite Fall, which appears to be stacked directly above Lower Yosemite Fall, creating a perfect photo op.

Perhaps the most sensual waterfall in the park is the 620-foot **Bridalveil Fall**, a slender ribbon at the valley's western end, which in Ahwahneechee goes by the name of *Pohono* or "spirit of the puffing wind." While Bridalveil seldom completely dries up, it is best seen from April to June when winds blow the cascade outward up to twenty feet away from its base, drawing the spray out into a delicate lacy veil. The quarter-mile trail from the parking lot is four miles west of the village and not accessible by shuttle bus.

Two of the park's most striking falls are guaranteed to still be active year-round, but are sequestered away from the road up the Merced River Canyon, near Happy Isles (see opposite). It is a relatively easy walk to get a glimpse of the distant 317-foot **Vernal Fall**, a curtain of water about eighty feet wide that casts bright rainbows as you walk along the wonderful Mist Trail (see box, p.428). It requires much more commitment to hike steeply upstream as far as the 594-foot **Nevada Fall**, but it is worth the effort for a close look at this sweeping cascade that drops for half its height then fans out onto the apron below.

Yosemite Village

Very much the heart of the valley, **YOSEMITE VILLAGE** is not really a cohesive "village" at all, but a settlement of scattered low buildings where mule deer wander freely. You'll find yourself returning time and again to visit shops, restaurants, banking facilities, Internet access, the post office (see "Listings" on p.434 for the last three), and one of the park's **main visitor centers** (see p.415 for hours). Here, you can watch a couple of free short films: the dull orientational *One Day in Yosemite* (runs continuously) and the new 23-minute *Spirit of Yosemite* (every 30min), which has great footage of Yosemite through the seasons. For more great images of the park walk a few steps east to the **Ansel Adams Gallery**, which is full of fine-art prints, posters, and postcards.

Immediately west of the visitor center a hefty nine-foot **slice of a giant sequoia** trunk marks the **Yosemite Museum** (daily: June-Aug 8am-5.30pm; Sept-May 9am-4.30pm; free), which contains a small selection of artifacts focusing on Native American heritage, specifically the local Ahwahneechee and the neighboring Mono Lake Paiute, with whom they traded and inter-married. One of the few crafts to flourish after contact with whites was **basketwork**: fine examples on display include a superbly detailed 1930s Mono Lake Paiute basket almost three feet in diameter, and its even larger Miwok/Paiute equivalent, painstakingly created by famed basket maker Lucy Telles. Basket-making demonstrations are given by Ahwahneechee practitioners throughout the day.

A couple of **feather-trimmed dance capes** warrant a look, as does the buckskin dress worn by natives in the 1920s and 1930s during tourist demonstrations of basket weaving and dance. Though completely alien to the Miwok tradition, the Plains-style buckskin clothing and feather headdresses fulfilled the expectations of the whites who came to watch.

Outside, a self-guided trail weaves around the **Indian Village of Ahwahneechee** (always open; free) with its cluster of reconstructed Indian buildings.

Fifty yards west of the museum, the **Yosemite Pioneer Cemetery** (always open; free) holds just three dozen graves of early white settlers. Among the simple headstones are the graves of early orchardist **James Lamon**, and park guardian **Galen Clark**, both marked with century-old sequoias.

By contrast, and worth a quick look even if you don't intend to stay or eat there, is the **Ahwahnee Hotel**, a short signposted walk or shuttle bus ride from Yosemite Village. It was built in grand style in 1927 from local rock, and is decorated with Native American motifs and some wonderful rugs and carpets. It was intended to blend into its surroundings and attract the richer type of tourist, and still does both fairly effortlessly – pop in for a few minutes to sink into the deep sofas, view the collection of paintings of Yosemite's early days, or browse the rock climbing and skiing exhibitions in the Winter Club Room off the Great Hall.

Curry Village and the eastern valley

At some point, almost everyone finds themselves at the eastern end of the valley which has the densest concentration of accommodation: all the main campgrounds are here along with the permanent cabins of *Housekeeping Camp* and the tent cabin complex of **CURRY VILLAGE**. This is a direct descendant of **Camp Curry**, which was started in 1899 by David and Jeannie Curry, who were keen to share their adopted home in the valley and charged just $12 a week for a "good bed, and a clean napkin every meal." It is now a rambling area of tent cabins and wooden chalets centered on a small complex of restaurants, shops, pay showers, a post office, and an outdoor amphitheater hosting ranger programs and evening shows. There's also a winter ice rink, bike rental, and a kiosk that rents rafts for use on the nearby Merced River.

The western end of Curry Village is marked by the **LeConte Memorial Lodge** (April-Sept Wed-Sun 10am-4pm; free; shuttle stop 12), a small rough-hewn granite-block structure where the **Sierra Club** maintains displays on its history, runs a conservation library, and has a fascinating relief map of the valley dating back to around 1885. The Lodge itself was built by the Sierra Club in 1903 to commemorate the eminent geologist and early supporter of John Muir, **Joseph LeConte** (1823-1901), and as the Sierra Club's Yosemite headquarters, it was managed for a couple of summers in the early 1920s by **Ansel Adams**, who was happy to do anything if it meant he could spend more time in the valley. Their evening programs (usually Fri–Sun; free) are a little more highbrow than those elsewhere in the park and might include a slide show or talk by some luminary; check *Yosemite Today* for details.

Shuttle buses head east from Curry Village to the **Nature Center at Happy Isles** (early May to mid-Sept daily 10am-noon & 1–4pm; free; shuttle stop 16), containing a most **family-friendly** set of displays on flora and fauna plus a hands-on exhibit allowing you to feel how hunks of rough granite get weathered down to sand, and an exhibit on a year in the life of a bear. At the rear of the Nature Center, be sure to check out the **rockfall exhibit** where a number of explanatory panels highlight the pulverized rock and flattened trees that resulted from the 1996 rockfall.

Perhaps one of the most rewarding of the easy trails leads from shuttle stop 17 around the edge of the valley floor to **Mirror Lake** (2 miles; 1hr; 100ft ascent). This compellingly calm lake (typically dry in late summer) lies beneath the great bulk of Half Dome, the rising cliff reflected on the lake's surface, and is best seen in the early morning, before too many others arrive. Most visitors to Mirror Lake follow the traffic-free paved road from the shuttle stop, but several easily found diversions steer you clear of the asphalt and the crowds.

Few photographers have stamped their vision as unforgettably as **Ansel Adams** has done with Yosemite Valley. While he worked all over the American West, Yosemite was Adams' home and the site of his most celebrated works, icons of American landscape photography such as 1944's *Clearing Winter Storm* and *Jeffrey Pine*; *Sentinel Dome* from the following year; and *Moon and Half Dome* from 1960.

Born in 1902 into a moderately wealthy San Francisco family, Adams was given his first camera – a Box Brownie – when he was fourteen, on his first trip to Yosemite. Though classically trained as a concert pianist, he claimed that he knew his "destiny" on that first visit to Yosemite, and soon turned his attentions to the mountains, returning every year and taking up a job as custodian of the Sierra Club headquarters.

He first made a mark in 1927 with *Monolith, The Face of Half Dome*, his first successful **visualization**: Adams believed that, before pressing the shutter, the photographer should have a clear idea of the final image and think through the entire photographic process, considering how lenses, filters, exposure, development, and printing need to be used to achieve that visualization. This approach may seem obvious today, but compared to the hit-and-miss methods of the time, it was little short of revolutionary. Visualization was made easier by applying the **zone system** of exposure calculation, which, though not new, was codified and promoted by Adams as the basis for his teaching. This blend of art and science divides the range of possible tones into ten zones from velvet black (I) through middle gray (V) to pure white (X), and allows precise tone control, something Adams felt was the key to full expression through photography.

As Adams fine-tuned his artistic theories through the 1930s, the idea of photography as fine art was still considered novel, and Adams spent much of his time lobbying for more respect for his craft. Adams was therefore delighted when, in 1940, he was made vice-chairman of the newly established **Department of Photography** at the Museum of Modern Art (MoMA) in New York City. Even so, there was still very little money in photography, and Adams continued to take commercial assignments, including shooting menu photos for Yosemite's *Ahwahnee Hotel*. Commercial and personal work through the 1940s and 1950s earned Adams a wider audience. While still demanding the highest standard of reproduction, the artist had tempered his perfectionism, and allowed his work to appear on postcards, calendars, and posters. By now, he was virtually a household name, and for the first time in his life he began making money to match his status as the grand old man of Western photography. His final triumph came in 1979, when MoMA put on the huge "Yosemite and the Range of Light" exhibition. That same year, he was asked to make an official portrait of President Jimmy Carter – the first time a photographer had been assigned an official presidential portrait – and was subsequently awarded the nation's highest civilian honor, the Medal of Freedom.

Throughout his life, Adams had another great passion, one that he pursued with the same fervor as photography: **conservation**. Back in 1932, the artist had a direct hand in creating Kings Canyon National Park. Two years later, he became a director of the **Sierra Club**, a position he held until 1971, overseeing several successful environmental campaigns. He never quit campaigning for the cause of conservation, and, after an interview in which he suggested he'd like to drown Ronald Reagan in his own martini, agreed to meet the president to promote the environmental cause.

Adams died on April 22, 1984, aged 82, and has become even more honored. The mountain that had been widely known as Mount Ansel Adams since 1933 now bears that name officially, and a huge chunk of the High Sierra south of Yosemite National Park is known as the Ansel Adams Wilderness.

Northern Yosemite

From the valley, Big Oak Flat Road climbs rapidly to Crane Flat, where there's a store and the closest gas station to the valley. From here Hwy-120 runs west to the Big Oak Flat entrance and **Hetch Hetchy**, once a scenic rival for Yosemite Valley, though now partially filled with a water supply for San Francisco.

East of Crane Flat, **Tioga Road** (also Hwy-120) climbs through dense forests into the Yosemite high country around Tenaya Lake, Tuolumne Meadows, and Tioga Pass – open grasslands pocked by polished granite domes and with a southern horizon delineated by the sawtooth crest of the **Cathedral Range**.

Hetch Hetchy

John Muir's passion for Yosemite Valley was matched, if not exceeded, by his desire to preserve the beauty of **HETCH HETCHY**, eighteen miles north of the valley, and close to the Oak Flat entrance. Once a near replica of Yosemite Valley with grassy, oak-filled meadows and soaring granite walls, it is now largely under the dammed waters of the slender Hetch Hetchy reservoir. When it came under threat from power-and water-supply interests in San Francisco in 1901, Muir battled for twelve years, instigating the first environmental letter-writing campaign to Congress. Eventually, in 1913, the cause was lost to a federal bill which paved the way for the Tuolumne River to be blocked by the **O'Shaughnessey Dam**. Hetch Hetchy is no longer a match for its southern kin, but the view of granite domes and waterfalls from the path which crosses the dam gives some sense of what it must have been like. It is barely worth the trip though, unless you plan on using the backpacker campground (wilderness permit required) as a base for trekking through the little-visited northern reaches of the park. A short and mostly flat alternative crosses the dam, passes through a short tunnel, and follows the north bank of the reservoir to **Wapama Falls** (five miles round-trip) and on to **Rancheria Falls** (a further four miles each way); both are at their best in May and June but are dry by August.

Tioga Road and Tuolumne Meadows

From Crane Flat, the eastbound **TIOGA ROAD** soon passes a parking lot from where there's a mile-long walking trail to the **Tuolumne Grove** of giant sequoias, which is nowhere near as spectacular as the Mariposa Grove (see below), but more convenient.

The road then climbs steadily through deep pine forests past the *White Wolf* and *Porcupine* campgrounds rising above 8000 feet just before **Olmsted Point**, which is up there with Glacier Point as one of the finest views on Yosemite's roads, looking down Tenaya Creek towards Half Dome. In the late 1950s, when the Tioga Road was being upgraded, Ansel Adams fruitlessly fought against its re-routing past here and along the gorgeous shores of **Tenaya Lake** to Tuolumne.

The alpine area around **TUOLUMNE MEADOWS** (literally "meadow in the sky") has an atmosphere quite different from the valley, 55 miles (about a ninety-minute drive) away. Here, at 8600ft, it is much more open; you almost seem to be level with the tops of the surrounding snow-covered mountains and the air always has a fresh, crisp bite. That said, there can still be good-sized blasts of carbon monoxide at peak times in the vicinity of the campground and *Tuolumne Lodge* (see p.419) – the only accommodation base in the area.

There are no restriction on **day hiking** in Yosemite, so for all the following hikes you need only equip yourselves properly – map, raingear, food, etc – get to the trailhead and set off. Unless otherwise noted, the following distances and times are for a round-trip.

Day-hikes from Yosemite Valley

Mist Trail to the top of Vernal Fall (3 miles; 2-3hr; 1000ft ascent). If you only do one hike in Yosemite, this should be it, especially during the spring snowmelt when Vernal Fall is often framed by a rainbow, and hikers get drenched in spray; bring a raincoat or plan to get wet. Start at shuttle stop 16 and head uphill crossing a footbridge with great views of Vernal Fall. Then follow the Mist Trail along a narrow path which, though hardly dangerous, demands sure footing and a head for heights. At the top of the fall, either retrace your steps to the trailhead, or return via the John Muir Trail.

Half Dome (17 miles; 9–12hr; 4800ft ascent). This is one of the valley's finest and most arduous walks, initially following the Mist Trail (see above) and continuing around the back of Half Dome. The final 400ft ascent is over the huge, smooth, humped back aided by a pair of steel cables and wooden steps which are partly removed in winter (mid-Nov to late May) to discourage ascent: there's usually a pile of free-use gloves at the base of the cables to protect tender hands. Once at the summit, anyone concerned about their outdoor credibility will want to edge out to the very lip of the abyss and peer down the sheer 2000ft northwest face. If you plan a one-day assault, you'll need to start at the crack of dawn.

Four-mile Trail to Glacier Point (10 miles; 5-6hr; 3200ft ascent). The steep asphalt path from the valley floor to Glacier Point doesn't give much of a sense of being in the wilderness, but the magnificent views make this one of the valley's more popular day walks. Generally open mid-May to Oct.

Upper Yosemite Fall (7 miles; 4hr; 2700ft ascent). This perennially popular, energy-sapping hike climbs steeply to the north rim of the valley with great views of Upper Yosemite Fall for much of the way, and the opportunity to sit virtually on the edge of the fall and gaze down at the Lilliputian activity below in Yosemite Village. Its northern aspect keeps the trail open longer than most (April–Dec) but is best done during the spring snowmelt: start before 7am to avoid the worst of the midday heat. Start just by the *Camp 4* campground (shuttle stop 7).

Day hikes from Tuolumne Meadows

Soda Springs and Parsons Lodge (4-mile loop; 2hr; negligible ascent). An easy meander around some of Tuolumne Meadows' best and most accessible features: especially good in the late June and July wildflower season. Cross the meadow from a trailhead 300 yards east of the visitor center to reach the *Soda Springs and Parsons Lodge*, then follow a broad trail to the base of Lembert Dome; then either walk back along Tioga Road or use the shuttle bus.

Its location almost five thousand feet higher than Yosemite Valley makes Tuolumne Meadows a better starting point for **hiking** into the surrounding High Sierra wilderness, though you can expect to still find snow on the trails in June and into July. We've covered a number of hikes in the area s(see box above).

The meadows themselves are the largest in all of the Sierra: twelve miles long, between a quarter and half a mile wide, and threaded by the meandering Tuolumne River. Snow usually lingers here until the end of June, forcing the

Lembert Dome (3.7-mile loop; 2–3hr; 850ft ascent). This hike up the Meadows' most prominent feature offers expansive views from the summit and examples of glacially polished rock and "erratic" boulders left behind by retreating glaciers. Start at the parking lot at the dome's base and follow signs for Dog Lake, then head right to ascend via the bare rock of the dome's northeast corner. Descend, then turn right to complete a loop around the dome.

Cathedral Lakes (8 miles; 4–6hr; 1000ft ascent). A candidate for the best Tuolumne day-hike, this route follows several miles of the John Muir Trail as far as a pair of gorgeous tarns in open alpine country with long views to a serrated skyline. Hike from the trailhead just west of the Tuolumne Meadows visitor center, gradually getting improved views of the twin spires of Cathedral Peak. Near its base are Upper Cathedral Lake (where there is excellent camping) and Lower Cathedral Lake, a divine spot lodged in a cirque now partly filled with lush meadows and split by a ridge of hard rock polished smooth by ancient glaciers.

Overnight hiking

Camping out overnight opens up the majority of Yosemite's eight hundred miles of backcountry trails. Choosing from the enormous range of trails is almost impossible, though some of the most popular are those which run between Yosemite Valley and Tuolumne Meadows, a two-day hike for anyone with reasonable fitness. Further suggestions are outlined in the dedicated *Rough Guide to Yosemite*.

To camp out overnight you need a **wilderness permit** which is available free of charge from ranger stations – at Wawona, Big Oak Flat, Hetch Hetchy, and Tuolumne – and the Wilderness Center in Yosemite Village (daily: mid-June to Aug 7am–6pm; April to mid-June & Sept to late Oct 8am–5pm; closed in winter). Numbers are limited by a quota system, but with a little flexibility you'll often find you can get a permit the day before you wish to start your hike. Large groups, people with tight schedules, and anyone hiking at busy times should **reserve in advance** ($5 per person) from 24 weeks to two days ahead of your trip. Book either by phone (℡209/372-0740), via the website (⊛www.nps.gov/yose/wilderness), or by writing to Wilderness Permits, PO Box 545, Yosemite, CA 95389 and stating your name, address, daytime phone number, the number in your party, method of travel (foot, ski, horse, etc), start and finish dates, entry and exit trailheads, and main destination. Suggesting alternate dates and trailheads are a good idea too. Checks should be made payable to the Yosemite Association and credit card bookings should include the number and expiry date. Don't despair if you have trouble landing the trail you want: paths are so numerous that you may start at a less popular trailhead but end up doing largely the same hike. From November to April when demand is lowest, permits are self-issued at trailheads. When obtaining your permit you'll be instructed in **backcountry etiquette** (see below), especially water purification and waste disposal, and be encouraged to rent a **bear-resistant food canister** (obligatory if camping above 9600 feet). **Camping gear** can be rented quite reasonably from Yosemite Mountaineering School (see p.417).

wildflowers to contend with a short growing season. They respond with a glorious burst of color in July, a wonderful time for a wander.

The distinctive glaciated granite form of **Lembert Dome** squats at the eastern end of the meadows gazing across the grasslands towards its western twin, **Pothole Dome**, which makes for a great sunset destination. The mountain scenery is particularly striking to the south, where the **Cathedral Range** offers a horizon of slender spires and knife-blade ridges. Look out for the appropriately-named **Unicorn Peak**, and **Cathedral Peak**, textbook example of a glaciated "Matterhorn," where glaciers have carved away the rock on all sides leaving a sharp pointed summit.

Some of the best views are from the naturally carbonated **Soda Springs** (see "Hiking" box, p.428), described in 1863 as "pungent and delightful to the taste." And so it is, though the Park Service discourages drinking it.

Tuolumne Meadows Hikers' Bus (mid-June to early Sept; $14.50 one-way, $23 round-trip) runs up here once a day from Yosemite Valley stopping at trailheads along the journey, and at various points around Tuolumne Meadows including the **visitor center** (see p.415). There's also a **free shuttle** service linking Tuolumne to Olmsted Point, just west of Tenaya Lake (July to early Sept 7am–6pm).

Southern Yosemite

Lying south of Yosemite Valley, **SOUTHERN YOSEMITE**'s broad swathe of sharply peaked mountains extends from the foothills in the west twenty miles to the Sierra crest in the east. In summer, visitors congregate at **Wawona**, where the hotel and campground provide most services, or at the nearby **Mariposa Grove**, the most impressive of the park's stands of giant sequoias. Roughly midway between Yosemite Valley and Wawona, Glacier Point Road carves its way to the park's **viewpoint** par excellence at **Glacier Point**, right on the rim of Yosemite Valley and on a level with the face of Half Dome.

Glacier Point, Sentinel Dome, and Taft Point

The most spectacular views of Yosemite Valley are from **GLACIER POINT**, the top of a 3200-foot almost sheer cliff, 32 miles by road (usually open mid-May to late Oct) from Yosemite Valley. The valley floor lies directly beneath the viewing point, and there are tremendous views across to Half Dome (easy from here to see how it got its name) and to the distant snow-capped summits of the High Sierra. It's possible to get there on foot using the very steep Four-Mile Trail (see the box on p.428), though you may prefer to use the **Glacier Point Hikers' Bus** (June–Oct 2 daily; $15 each way) to get here from the valley then hike down.

The road to Glacier Point passes the **Badger Pass ski area** (generally open mid-Dec to early April; ☏209/372-8430, ⊛www.badgerpass.com), which has a few short tows and a ski school which runs excellent **cross-country ski** trips eleven miles to Glacier Point. You'll also pass a number of signposted trailheads for easy and longer hikes. One of the best is to the 8122-foot summit of **SENTINEL DOME** (two miles round-trip), a gleaming granite scalp topped by a gnarled and much photographed skeleton of a Jeffrey pine, which still bore cones until the mid-1970s, when a drought finally killed it off. From the Sentinel Dome parking lot, a second dusty, undulating trail leads west to **TAFT POINT** (2 miles round-trip), which trades Glacier Point's Half Dome vista for a view across the valley to the top of El Capitan and Yosemite Falls. Far fewer people follow this trail, perhaps because of the vertiginous drops all around, only protected by the flimsiest of barriers in one spot. Here, the granite edges have been deeply incised to form what is known as the **Taft Point Fissures**.

Wawona and the Mariposa Grove

There's a decidedly relaxed pace at **WAWONA**, 27 miles (or an hour's drive) south of Yosemite Village on Hwy-41. Most people spend their time here strolling the grounds of the landmark *Wawona Hotel* (see p.419), surrounded by a nine-hole golf course where $24 will get you a full eighteen-hole round (plus $10 for club rental, if needed), on the Sierra's oldest course. There are also tennis courts ($2 per hour). Close by is the **Pioneer Yosemite History Center**, a collection of buildings culled from the early times of white habitation, which can be visited on a self-guided walking tour (free). The jail, homesteads, covered bridge and the like are good for a scoot around, and through the summer months (particularly weekends) the buildings are open and interpreted by attendant rangers. Once away from the main road, the area makes a quiet spot for a picnic.

The Mariposa Grove, three miles east of Hwy-41 on a small road which cuts off just past the park's southern entrance, is the biggest and best of Yosemite's groves of giant sequoia trees. To get to the towering growths, walk the two-and-a-half-mile loop trail from the parking lot at the end of the road, or take the narrated **Big Trees Tram Tour** around the grove (May–Oct 9am–5.30pm; $11), which follows a paved road to the major sights. There is also a free shuttle to the parking area from Wawona.

Trails around the sequoia groves call first at the **Fallen Monarch**, familiar from the 1899 photo, widely reproduced on postcards, in which cavalry officers and their horses stand atop the prostrate tree. The most renowned of the grouping, well marked along the route, is the **Grizzly Giant**, thought to be 2700 years old and with a lower branch thicker than the trunk of any non-sequoia in the grove. Other highlights include the **Wawona Tunnel Tree** through which people drove their cars until it fell in 1969, the similarly bored **California Tunnel Tree**, which you can walk through, and all manner of trees which have grown together, split apart, been struck by lightning, or are simply staggeringly large. It's also worth dropping into the **Mariposa Grove Museum** (daily 9am–4pm; free), towards the top end of the trail, which has modest displays and photos of the mighty trees. For more on the life of the sequoia, see the box on p.397.

Eating, drinking, and entertainment

With a couple of notable exceptions, **eating** in Yosemite is more a function than a pleasure. Food, whether in restaurants or in the grocery stores around Yosemite Village (where there's a well-stocked supermarket), Curry Village, Wawona, and Tuolumne Meadows, is much more expensive inside the park than out. **Outside the park**, the choice is considerably better, with plenty of good restaurants and a smattering of bars in the gateway towns of Groveland, Mariposa, and Oakhurst.

The park's restaurants serve beer and wine, plus there's a lively **bar** at *Yosemite Lodge*, a swankier affair at the *Ahwahnee Hotel*, and a lounge with occasional piano entertainment at the *Wawona Hotel*.

To help visitors interpret Yosemite, the Park Service and related organizations run a number of **ranger programs** – nature hikes, photo walks, talks about bears, etc – most of which are free. In addition there is **evening entertainment** in the form of ranger-led campfire talks at most of the campgrounds, occasional star-gazing sessions, natural history slide shows, and music shows. The *Yosemite Today* newspaper carries a full catalog of events, along with listings of the *Yosemite Theater* program ($7), which presents two ninety-minute one-man shows featuring the talents of actor Lee Stetson, who has been impersonating John Muir since 1982.

In the valley

Ahwahnee Bar *Ahwahnee Hotel* (noon–11pm).
Intimate piano bar perfect for indulging in a "wine
flight" with four half-glasses for $17, a "bourbon
flight" of four small shots for $18, or something
from their selection of Armagnacs, ports, classic
martinis ($8.50), and other cocktails. There's also
light food such as a chicken salad ($10), an
antipasto plate ($20), and a daily dessert.

Ahwahnee Dining Room *Ahwahnee Hotel*
☎209/372-1489. One of the most beautiful
restaurants in the US, built in baronial style with
34-foot-high ceilings of exposed beams, rustic iron
chandeliers, and floor-to-ceiling leaded windows.
The food is by far the best in Yosemite, and dinner
might consist of a salmon terrine or an endive and
watercress salad ($11) followed by seared ahi
tuna with shoyu butter and *wasabi* ($28). Dishes
are simpler earlier in the day with items like a
three-egg frittata ($13) or an apple crepe ($14) for
breakfast, then a portobello mushroom and sun-
dried tomato roll ($11) or a smoked duck Caesar
salad ($14.50) for lunch. The Sunday brunch ($32)
is particularly stupendous. Casual dress is permitted during the day, but formal wear is expected for
dinner (sports coats are available free of charge).

Curry Village Pavilion *Curry Village.* Lively cafeteria serving great value all-you-can-eat breakfasts ($10) with plenty of fresh fruit, juices, eggs,
bacon, hash browns, waffles, yoghurt, and the like.
Dinner ($12) suffers a little from over-cooked
vegetables and sloppy preparation, but you can
still fill up on salads, build-your-own tacos, chicken-fried steak, simple pasta dishes, cakes, and
sodas. Alcoholic drinks are not available.

Degnan's Café, Deli & Loft *Yosemite Village.*
Three eating spots in one building. There's a daytime café serving reasonable espressos and specialty teas plus a selection of danishes, cinnamon
rolls (both around $2), and lunchtime wraps ($3–6)
served inside or out; a takeout deli with bowls of
soup ($2.50–3.25) and chili ($4–5), and massive
sandwiches, burritos, and salads at under $6; and
a gourmet pizza restaurant ($14–18 for medium;
$17–22 for a large).

Pizza Patio and Terrace Bar *Curry Village.* Very
much the place to repair on balmy evenings after a
hard day in the hills. Fight for an outdoor table
while you wait for a pretty decent build-your-own
pizza (from $12 for twelve slices), and maybe a
pint of good draft beer ($4) or a margarita ($4.50).

Yosemite Lodge Food Court *Yosemite Lodge.*
Bright and cheerful self-serve café/restaurant serving a full range of cold and cooked breakfasts
($4–7), muffins, danishes, and coffee (but no
espresso), plus lunches and dinners that range from

a grilled chicken sandwich ($5) or tuna salad ($5) to
pasta and meatballs ($9) or chicken, vegetables and
rice ($8). There is some outdoor seating.

The rest of the park

Tuolumne Meadows Grill *Tuolumne Meadows.*
Basically a burger joint, also serving small and
pricey breakfasts and sandwich lunches.

Tuolumne Meadows Lodge ☎209/372-8413.
Family-style breakfasts ($5–10) and burgers,
steak, chicken, and fish dinners ($10–17) served
in a large tent beside the Tuolumne River.

Wawona Hotel Dining Room Semi-formal dining
off white linen tablecloths, though the food is neither very expensive nor particularly special. Still,
you can lunch on the likes of chicken alfredo, ratatouille or a club sandwich ($8), then dress smart
for dinner, such as pan fried trout ($16) and a
raspberry nut cake ($4). There's also a wonderful
Sunday brunch buffet (Easter–Thanksgiving
7.30am–1.30pm; $16.95) and a Saturday
Barbecue (late May to early Sept 5–7pm).

White Wolf Lodge just off Hwy-120 ☎209/252-
4848. Large portions of good-value American food
in rustic surroundings for $13–17. Breakfast and
dinner only.

Hwy-120: Groveland

Cocina Michoacana 13955 Hwy-120, Groveland.
Authentic and low-priced Mexican spot; six bucks
will get you a great breakfast of scrambled eggs
with strips of steak, and later they serve a full
range of favorites including great fajitas ($16–18
for two) and melt-in-the-mouth breaded shrimps.

Iron Door 18761 Main St, Groveland. With its grill
and soda fountain, the *Iron Door* is a fine place to
eat, with a locally famous garlic soup, fine New
York steak ($18), buffalo and black bean burgers,
and a host of other dishes all beautifully prepared
and presented. But what makes it special is the
atmospheric bar, reliably claimed to be the oldest
saloon in California. It comes with pool table and
all manner of paraphernalia on the walls plus a
live band most weekends.

Victorian Room *Groveland Hotel*, 18767 Hwy-120
☎209/962-4000. The best restaurant in town with
a seasonally changing menu and nightly chef's specials that might run to crab cakes with cilantro and
caper sauce, and honey-glazed baby back pork ribs.
Expect to pay $40–50 for three courses including a
glass or two from their extensive wine list.

Hwy-140: Mariposa,
Midpines, and El Portal

Café at the Bug *Yosemite Bug Hostel & Lodge*,
Midpines. Superb value licensed café with quality
food at a good price. Wholesome breakfasts

5

($4–6), packed lunches ($5.50), and dinners ($7–13) are served to all comers. If you don't mind the slightly frenetic hostel atmosphere, it's definitely worth the drive out for the likes of slow roasted Cajun pork or baked trout filet with butter pecan sauce. Good microbrews on tap as well.

Charles Street Dinner House 5043 Hwy-140, Mariposa ☏ 209/966-2366. Mariposa's premiere fine-dining establishment. Discerning diners might kick off with a Portobello ravioli parmesan ($12) and follow with a scallop and abalone blend served with toasted almonds and lemon butter ($13), though the wise will leave space for the mocha ice-cream pie ($5). There's a full wine list, and all dishes are cooked to order, so set the evening aside. Closed Mon, Tues & Jan.

High Country Café Hwy-140 & Hwy-49. Daytime health-food café with sandwiches ($5) along with salads, enchiladas, and carrot cake. There's also a health-food store next door offering good bread, organic fruit, and goodies in bulk bins that are perfect for trail mix. Closed Sun.

Meadows Ranch Café 5024 Hwy-140, Mariposa. An 1896 former general store that's now an excellent family restaurant with attached juice bar, espresso café, and bar. Regulars arrive early for tasty baked goods or a hearty breakfast ($5–8), and return throughout the day for sandwiches, burgers, pasta dishes, and Mexican staples, mostly under $10.

Hwy-41: Oakhurst and Fish Camp

Kyoto Kafe 40423 Hwy-41. Good cheap home-style Japanese food served in spartan surroundings until around 8pm. Try the yakitori chicken or the *yaki soba* (both $7), washed down with *sake* or beer.

The Narrow Gauge Inn 48571 Hwy-41, Fish Camp ☏ 559/683-6446. Fine dining in an Old World setting with candlelight, a warming fire, and everything carefully prepared. Start by dipping sourdough into a rich fondue and continue with charbroiled swordfish or filet mignon. Expect to pay $40 each, more with wine. Closed Jan–March.

Mountain House junction of Hwy-41 & Bass Lake Road, 3 miles north of Oakhurst. The best of the local diner-style restaurants with burgers, sandwiches, and pasta dishes, along with a locally renowned New York steak ($17) and charbroiled trout ($12).

Three Sisters Café 39993 Hwy-41 near junction with Hwy-49. Make an effort to fit in with the very limited opening hours at this small restaurant where breakfast might consist of chicken-fried pork cutlet with eggs ($7) or eggs forestiere, with wild mushroom sauce ($8). For dinner there's usually an eclectic specials list ranging from lamb scaloppini to Navajo buffalo stew, all well worth the $15 price tag. Only open Wed–Sun 8am–1.15pm and Thurs–Sun 5–7.15pm.

Yosemite Coffee and Roasting Company 40879 Hwy-41, a mile north of Oakhurst. Relaxed java joint with mismatched chairs and newspapers, ideal for breakfast burritos, toothsome muffins, sandwiches, cakes, and good espresso at modest prices.

Listings

Banks The Bank of America in Yosemite Village is open daily from 8am to 4pm and operates a 24hr ATM. There are more ATMs at Yosemite Village, *Yosemite Lodge*, *Curry Village*, Wawona, and El Portal (all charge a transaction fee of $2 on US accounts), but there is no provision for foreign currency exchange.

Bike rental Bikes are only allowed on the valley's flat, paved roads and bikeways so the basic single-speed bikes ($5.5/hr, $21/day) available at *Yosemite Lodge* (all year) and *Curry Village* (summer only) are quite adequate.

Books The Yosemite Village Visitor Center has a good selection of Yosemite-related books and maps; the Ansel Adams Gallery specializes in photography and nature publications; and the Mountain Shop at *Curry Village* stocks climbing guides.

Campfires Summertime air-quality restrictions exist limiting campfires to 5pm to 10pm from May to mid-October. For ecological reasons, firewood must not be gathered in the valley or above 9600 feet, but is available for sale at stores throughout the park.

Camping equipment Camping gear can be rented from the Yosemite Mountaineering School at Curry Village – expect to pay $10 for a sleeping bag and $8 for a pack, and comparable rates for tents, bear canisters, snowshoes, etc – and bought from the Village Sport Shop in Yosemite Village, or better from the Mountain Shop in *Curry Village*. The store in Tuolumne Meadows also stocks camping equipment, climbing gear, and lightweight food.

Gas Available at good prices in Oakhurst, moderate prices in Mariposa and Groveland and expensively in the park, year-round at Wawona and Crane Flat, and seasonally at Tuolumne Meadows. The valley has no gas.

Guided trips The Yosemite Mountaineering School (☎ 209/372-8344, ⊛ www.yosemitemountaineeringschool.com) runs guided backpacking, rock climbing, and alpine trips from around $125 each per day for groups of four or more.

Horseback riding Saddle trips accommodating riders of all standards are run from stables in Yosemite Valley (April–Oct; ☎ 209/372-8348), Tuolumne Meadows (early June–Sept; ☎ 209/372-8427), and Wawona (May–Sept; ☎ 209/375-6502): scenic rides cost $40 for two hours, $80 for the day. There are also multi-day High Sierra Saddle Trips starting at $620 for four days.

High Sierra camp vacations Visitors organized enough to enter a lottery (mid-Oct to Nov) can apply for July to September stays in a series of five dormitory-style tent cabin complexes – complete with proper beds, hot showers, and meals cooked for you – dotted around the Yosemite high country. Most combine them in a circuit, either the seven-day guided hike with one rest day, the six-day mule-back saddle trip, or the four-day saddle trip. Prices are around $110 a night per person and include a delicious breakfast and dinner. *Merced Lake*, the largest of the camps, sometimes has spare short-notice spaces for those willing to hike the thirteen miles from Yosemite Valley or the fifteen miles from Tuolumne Meadows. Obtain a lottery application form either by calling ☎ 559/253-5674 (Mon–Fri 8am–4.30pm) or downloading one from the accommodation section of the ⊛ www.yosemitepark.com website.

Internet access Limited facilities at the Yosemite Village Public Library (see below) and at the libraries and copy centers in the hinterland towns.

Laundry There's a coin-op affair at *Housekeeping Camp* (8am–8pm).

Library A public research library (Tues–Fri 8am–noon & 1–5pm) is situated upstairs from the museum entrance in Yosemite Village and contains all manner of Yosemite, backcountry, and climbing information, including recent magazines and daily papers. There is also a public library which opens for three or four hours a day (Mon 11am–2pm, Tues 10am–2pm, Wed 11am–3pm, Thurs 3–6pm) and is located close to the Yosemite Village visitor center in a building signed "Girls Club."

Lost property ☎ 209/372-4357 for items lost at hotels and restaurants; ☎ 209/379-1001 for stuff lost elsewhere.

Medical assistance Yosemite Medical Clinic, between Yosemite Village and the *Ahwahnee Hotel* (☎ 209/372-4637) has 24-hour emergency care, drop-in and urgent care (daily 8am–7pm), and accepts appointments (Mon–Fri 8am–5pm, Sat

9am–noon). Dental treatment (☎ 209/372-4200) is also available.

Photography The Ansel Adams Gallery in Yosemite Village stocks slide, professional, and ordinary print film at reasonable prices, and run free two-hour guided photography walks. There are also year-round photography walks run by the park concessionaire in Yosemite Valley, and summer-only versions at Glacier Point, Wawona, and Tuolumne Meadows. Check *Yosemite Today* for all times.

Post office Located in Yosemite Village (Mon–Fri 8.30am–5pm, Sat 10am–noon) and accepting general delivery (aka poste restante). Also year-round services at *Yosemite Lodge* (Mon–Thurs 11.30am–2.45pm, Fri 11.30am–4.30pm) and Wawona (Mon–Fri 9am–5pm, Sat 9am–1pm), and summer-only service at Curry Village (Mon–Fri 11.30am–2.30pm) and Tuolumne Meadows (Mon–Fri 9am–5pm, Sat 9am–1pm). The park's zip code is 95389.

Rafting Inside the park itself, *Curry Village* rents guideless six-berth rafts ($13.50 per person; minimum 2; June and July only) allowing you to float gently along the placid and relatively gentle section of the Merced River – the cost includes a return bus ride. Outside the park, from April to June, far more rugged (Class III–IV) one-day stretches are run in the traditional guided fashion by Mariah Wilderness Expeditions (☎ 1-800/462-7424, ⊛ www.mariahwe.com), Ahwahnee Whitewater (☎ 1-800/359-9790, ⊛ www. ahwahnee.com), Whitewater Voyages (☎ 1-800/ 400-RAFT, ⊛ www.whitewatervoyages.com) and others, all charging around $115–140 midweek and $140–155 at weekends.

Recycling Glass, aluminum, newspapers, and plastic are recycled at Yosemite Village, and beverage containers may be returned for a small deposit at all retail outlets.

RVs Campers can use all the main campgrounds, but there are no hook-ups in Yosemite. Dump stations are in Yosemite Valley, Wawona, and Tuolumne Meadows (summer only).

Showers In Yosemite Valley at *Curry Village* (24 hours; $2) where outside the peak summer season there is often nobody to either provide a towel or take your money. Outside the valley the only public showers are at *Tuolumne Lodge* (see "Accommodation", p.419; $3).

Swimming There are pools in the valley at *Yosemite Lodge* and *Curry Village* (both free to hotel guests and $2 for others), the *Wawona Hotel* and *Ahwahnee Hotel* both have pools for guests, and there numerous small river beaches throughout the valley and at Wawona.

5

Travel details

Trains

The **San Joaquin** service runs four times daily between Bakersfield and Emeryville, near Oakland, from where Amtrak Thruway buses run into San Francisco. Amtrak Thruway bus connections from San Diego, Orange County, Santa Barbara, Palm Springs, and Los Angeles link with the train at Bakersfield.

Bakersfield to: Fresno (1hr 45min); Hanford (1hr 15min); Merced (2hr 45min); Emeryville (6hr); Stockton (4hr).

Buses

Buses are either Greyhound, Amtrak Thruway, or Orange Belt Stages (☎1-800/266-7433), which often use Amtrak stations as hubs for their network.

Bakersfield to: Merced (13 daily; 4–5hr).
Fresno to: Merced (10 daily; 1hr 10min); Modesto (12 daily; 2hr); Stockton (8 daily; 3hr).
Hanford to: San Luis Obispo (1 daily; 3hr).

Los Angeles to: Bakersfield (16 daily; 2hr 30min–3hr); Fresno (17 daily; 4–6hr); Merced (10 daily; 6–7hr); Modesto (11 daily; 6–8hr); Stockton (12 daily; 6hr 30min–8hr 30min); Visalia (6 daily; 4–5hr).
Merced to: Los Angeles (11 daily; 6–7hr); Modesto (10 daily; 1hr); Sacramento (7 daily; 3hr); San Francisco (6–7 daily; 4–5hr); Yosemite (3–5 daily; 2hr 45min).
San Francisco to: Bakersfield (7 daily; 7hr 30min); Fresno (8 daily; 5–6hr); Merced (6–7 daily; 4–5hr); Modesto (4 daily; 3–4hr); Stockton (4 daily; 2hr 30min–3hr 30min); Visalia (3 daily; 7–9hr).
Stockton to: Lodi (5 daily; 30min); Merced (8 daily; 2hr); Sacramento (12 daily; 1hr).
Visalia to: Hanford (2 daily; 1hr 30min).

Flights

Fresno to: Los Angeles (hourly or better; 1hr 10min); San Francisco (7 daily; 45min).

6

The Central Coast

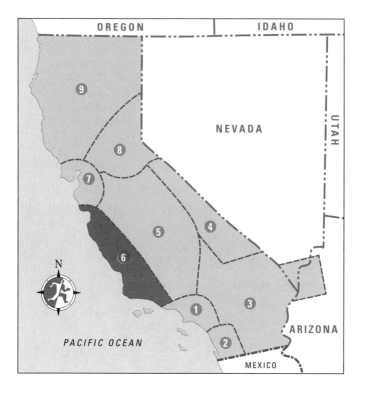

CHAPTER 6

Highlights

* **Mission San Antonio**
The best conserved of all the missions, and an evocative place to imagine the past. See p.467

* **Hearst Castle**
Unquestionably, one of the most intriguing sights in America: a multi-million-dollar – and still unfinished – memorial to William Randolph Hearst. See p.463

* **Hiking to the waterfalls around Big Sur** The raw, eye-popping coast is very popular, but it's well worth taking a trek into the interior to see some of the natural waterfalls in the national parks. See p.471

* **The John Steinbeck Center in Salinas** This spectacular new museum unearths the real man behind the stories. See p.469

* **The Monterey Aquarium** A world-class museum in a small Californian town – the new *Jellies* exhibit is freakish, stylish, and informative. See p.483

* **Santa Cruz boardwalk** A classic Californian seaside boardwalk, filled with old rides and an amusement arcade – irresistible, cheesy fun. See p.495

6

The Central Coast

The four hundred miles of coastline in between LA and San Francisco is arguably one of the most beautiful oceanside stretches of land anywhere in the world. From sandy beaches to rocky cliffs and from rural charm to upscale sophistication, the allure of the **CENTRAL COAST** is wide in range. Sparsely populated outside a few medium-sized towns, much of the area is barely disturbed by modern life. Indeed, first-time visitors may be surprised to find just how much of the region survives in its natural state, despite nestling snugly between two of America's largest and richest cities. The mountain ranges that separate the shore from the farmlands of the inland valleys are for the most part pristine wilderness, sometimes covered in thick forests of tall and slender redwood trees, while, in winter especially, fast-flowing rivers and streams course down valleys to the sea. All along the shore, sea otters and seals play in the waves, and endangered gray whales pass close by on their annual migration from Alaska to Mexico.

Big Sur, where the brooding Santa Lucia Mountains rise steeply out of the thundering Pacific surf, is the heart of the region, and **Point Lobos**, at its northern tip, is the best place to experience this untouched environment at its most dramatic. Nature aside, though, the Central Coast also marks the gradual transition from Southern to Northern California. The two largest towns here, **Santa Barbara** and **Santa Cruz**, are poles apart: Santa Barbara, a hundred miles north of Los Angeles, is a conservative, wealthy resort; in Santa Cruz, 75 miles south of San Francisco, long hair and tie-dyes are very much the order of the day. What the two towns have in common is miles of broad, clean **beaches**, with chilly waters but excellent surf, and a branch of the University of California energizing the local nightlife. In between, the small town of **San Luis Obispo** provides a languorous contrast to them both, and is a feasible base for the Central Coast's biggest tourist attraction, **Hearst Castle**, the opulent hilltop palace of publishing magnate William Randolph "Citizen Kane" Hearst.

The Central Coast also contains the bulk and the best of the late eighteenth-century Spanish colonial **missions** – the first European settlements on the West Coast, set up to convert the natives to Christianity while co-opting their labor. Almost all of the towns that exist here today grew up around the adobe walls and red-tiled roofs of these Catholic colonies, strung out along the Pacific. Each was deliberately situated a long day's walk from the next and typically composed of a church and a cloistered monastery, enclosed within thick walls to prevent attack by native tribes. **Monterey**, a hundred miles south of San Francisco, was the capital of California under Spain, and later Mexico, and today retains more of its early nineteenth-century architecture than any other

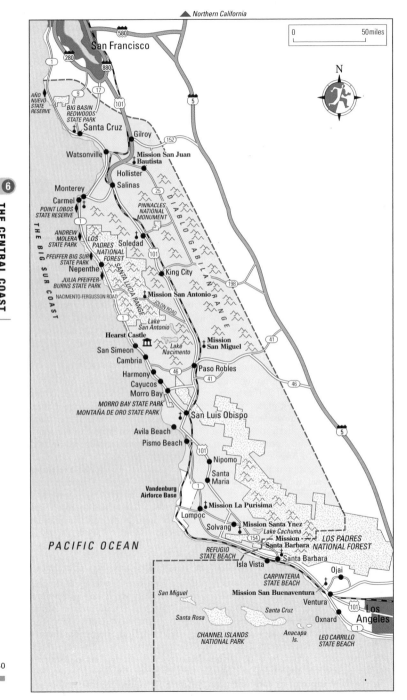

0   50 miles

N

San Francisco

580

280

880

1

9

17

101

5

AÑO
NUEVO
STATE
RESERVE

BIG BASIN
REDWOODS
STATE PARK

Santa Cruz   Gilroy

152

Watsonville   **Mission San Juan
                      Bautista**

Hollister

Monterey   Salinas

Carmel   25

POINT LOBOS
STATE RESERVE

PINNACLES
NATIONAL
MONUMENT

ANDREW
MOLERA
STATE PARK   LOS
                    PADRES   Soledad
PFEIFFER BIG SUR   NATIONAL
STATE PARK   FOREST

Nepenthe   101

JULIA PFEIFFER-   **King City**
BURNS STATE PARK

NACIMENTO-FERGUSSON ROAD   198

                    JOLON ROAD   **Mission San Antonio**

                    Lake
                    San Antonio

Hearst Castle   Lake
                          Nacimiento   41

San Simeon   **Mission
                                    San Miguel**
Cambria

Harmony   46   **Paso Robles**

Cayucos   41   46

Morro Bay

MORRO BAY STATE PARK
MONTAÑA DE ORO STATE PARK

San Luis Obispo

Avila Beach   5

Pismo Beach

101   Nipomo

Santa
Maria

**Vandenburg
Airforce Base**

Mission La Purisima

Lompoc   **Mission Santa Ynez**

          Solvang   Lake Cachuma
                    154   **Mission
PACIFIC OCEAN   Santa Barbara**   LOS PADRES
                                                    NATIONAL FOREST
          REFUGIO
          STATE BEACH   Santa Barbara

Isla Vista   Ojai

          CARPINTERIA
          STATE BEACH

San Miguel   **Mission San Buenaventura**

                                        Ventura   101   LOS
          Santa Cruz   Angeles
Santa Rosa   Oxnard   1

          CHANNEL ISLANDS   Anacapa
          NATIONAL PARK   Is.   LEO CARRILLO
                                        STATE BEACH

THE BIG SUR COAST

SANTA LUCIA RANGE

DIABLO GABILAN RANGE

city in the state; it's also a good base for one of the most beautiful of the missions, which stands three miles south in the uppercrust seaside resort of **Carmel**.

Practicalities

Getting around the Central Coast is easy by Californian standards: some of the best views in the state can be had from Amtrak's Coast Starlight train, which runs right along the coast up to San Luis Obispo before cutting inland north to San Francisco. Greyhound buses stop at most of the towns, particularly those along the main highway, US-101 – though the best route, if you've got a car, is the smaller Hwy-1, which follows the coast all the way but takes twice as long. Places to stay are relatively easy to find, at least outside summer weekends when otherwise quiet towns and beaches are packed solid with vacationing families. Opportunities for camping are plentiful, too, in a string of state parks, beaches, and forests.

Ventura and Ojai

The valleys of suburban Los Angeles meet the Pacific Coast at **VENTURA**, a longstanding farming and fishing community that's slowly being submerged beneath fast-food joints and mini-malls, many spilling over from the larger industrial city of **Oxnard** to the south (useful mainly for its Metrolink train connections to downtown LA; see p.80). Ventura offers a few good reasons to stop if you're in the area, including buying fresh strawberries and other seasonal produce from the many roadside stalls, and catching a boat out to the offshore Channel Islands (see below) from the harbor four miles southwest of town. Perhaps the most compelling sight in town, though, is just north of the US-101 and Hwy-1 intersection, where the restored **Mission San Buenaventura**, 211 E Main St (Mon–Fri 10am–5pm, Sat 9am–5pm, Sun 10am–4pm; $1 donation; ☎805/643-4318, ⓦwww.anacapa.net/~mission), was raised in 1782 as the ninth of the 21 California missions and the last founded by Father Junípero Serra. Although it's been repeatedly damaged by neglect or earthquakes and then restored – not always for the better – it still retains a quaint parochial charm that makes it a worthwhile stop for passers-by or more intrepid "mission tourists." Also on Main Street are two small but engaging museums: the **Albinger Archaeological Museum**, at no. 113 (Wed–Sun 10am–2pm, summer 10am–4pm; free; ☎805/648-5823), has exhibits explaining 3500 years of local history, from ancient Native American cultures to the mission era – highlighted by parts of that structure's original foundation. Across the street, the **Ventura County Museum of History and Art**, 100 E Main St (Tues–Sun 10am–5pm; $4; ⓦwww.vcmha.org), takes up where the former leaves off, with exhibits on local pioneer families and antique agricultural machinery.

Amtrak trains pull in near Harbor Boulevard and Figueroa Street, three blocks from the Greyhound stop at Thomson Boulevard and Palm Street. The **visitor center**, 89 California St, Suite C (Mon–Fri 8.30am–5pm, Sat 9am–5pm, Sun 10am–4pm; ☎805/648-2075 or 1-800/333-2989, ⓦwww.ventura-usa.com), can help with accommodation and has local bus maps. As Ventura is a base for visiting the Channel Islands, there is a **Channel Islands National Park visitor center** (daily 8.30am–5pm; ☎805/658-5730, www.nps.gov/chis) next to the ferry landing in Ventura Harbor, which has well-presented displays on the geology and the native plant and animal life of the islands, including seals, sea lions, pelican rookeries, and giant kelp forests. It also has current information on arranging trips, and an **observation tower** from which, on fine days, you can view the islands.

Nestled in the hills above Ventura, the small town of **OJAI** (pronounced "O-hi") is a wealthy resort community frequented by weekend jet-setters from LA, shown in the many exclusive health spas and tennis clubs that dot the surrounding countryside. It's also headquarters of the Krishnamurti Society, which spreads the word of the theosophist who lived and lectured here during the 1920s, considering the Ojai Valley "a vessel of comprehension, intelligence and truth." The **Krishnamurti Library**, several miles northeast of town at 1130 McAndrew Rd (Wed 1–9pm, Thurs–Sun 1–5pm; ☎805/646-4948, ⓦwww.kfa.org), details his liberal, nondenominational ideas on spirituality, along with a new **retreat** ($45, $75 per couple) centered in a classic ranch house, where you can get into the holistic spirit by taking nature walks in a shaded glade and reading up on the master's teachings. In town, the **Ojai Valley Museum**, 130 W Ojai Ave (Wed–Fri 1–4pm, Sat–Sun 10am–4pm; donation; ☎805/640-1390), housed in a former Mission Revival church built in 1919, has ambitious exhibits on history, agriculture, and art, highlighted by a Chumash garden that recalls the local peoples that predated the arrival of American settlers. Given its location in a historic chapel, the **visitor center** next door (Mon–Fri 9am–4.30pm, Sat & Sun 10am–4pm; ☎805/646-8126, ⓦwww.the-ojai.org) is the best place for information on the town's historical attractions and numerous old-fashioned B&Bs. On a country farm ten minutes from downtown, the friendly *Farm Hostel* (☎805/646-0311, ⓦwww.hostel-handbook.com/farmhostel), offers free pickup from the Greyhound and Amtrak stations in Ventura and dorm beds for $12, but you must have an international air-travel ticket or current visa to stay there. On the opposite end of the price scale, the cushy *Ojai Valley Inn & Spa* (☎805/646-5511 or 1-800/422-6524, ⓦwww.ojairesort.com; ❽), on Country Club Road, is a luxurious spa and hotel complex aimed at golfers, but if you'd prefer to rough it, near Ojai is the massive **Los Padres National Forest**, with some good hiking and several decent campgrounds (reservations: ☎1-800/280-2267); the area ranger station, 1190 E Ojai Ave (daily 8.30am–4pm; ☎805/646-4348), provides information and maps.

The Channel Islands National Park

Stretching north from Santa Catalina Island off the coast of Los Angeles, a chain of fascinating desert islands has been preserved as **CHANNEL ISLANDS NATIONAL PARK**, offering excellent hiking trails and close-up views of sea lions, as well as fishing and scuba- and skin-diving through the many caves, coves, and shipwrecks in the crystal-clear Pacific waters. All five of the main islands are accessible, though the closest, Anacapa, some fourteen miles south of Ventura, sees the most eco-tourist traffic. Perhaps the best time of all to visit the islands is between February and April, when you have the opportunity of **whale watching.**

Tiny **Anacapa** is actually two islets: **West Anacapa** is largely a refuge for nesting brown pelicans and is closed to the public – with the exception of **Frenchy's Cove**, a pristine beach and good base for scuba or snorkeling expeditions – while **East Anacapa** has a small visitor center and a mile-and-a-half-long nature trail. There are no beaches here, but swimming in the cove where the boats dock is allowed. West of Anacapa, **Santa Cruz** is the largest and highest of the islands, and **Santa Rosa**, with its grasslands, is less rugged but still has its share of steep ravines. Hiking inland requires a permit (☎805/658-5711, ⓦwww.nps.gov/chis/for information) and divers can explore the two exposed wrecks on either side of the island. The most distant island – windswept **San Miguel**, fifty miles offshore – is thought to be the burial place of sixteenth-century Spanish explorer Juan Cabrillo. No grave has been found, but a monument has been erected at Cuyler Harbor on the eastern end. Seasoned hikers may also wish to make the rugged cross-island trip to Point Bennett to spy on the plentiful wildlife.

South of the main group lies **Santa Barbara Island**, named by Sebastian Vizcaíno, who dropped by on St Barbara's Day, December 4, in 1602. The island's appeal these days is largely ornithological, as kestrels, larks, and meadowlarks can all be seen on land gradually recovering its native flora after years of destruction by now extinct rabbits.

If you're considering visiting the Channel Islands, the best introduction to their unique geology, flora, and fauna can be found in Ventura at the park's **visitors center**, 1901 Spinnaker Drive (daily 8.30am–5pm; free; ☎805/658-5730), which also offers models, films, and telescopes to view the islands at a distance.

Practicalities

The Nature Conservancy acquired ninety percent of the islands in 1988 as part of its effort to protect environmentally significant lands and has made them accessible to the public on **day-trip tours** – the only way to visit the park by boat, through operators that run from Ventura Harbor. Anacapa is served by several tours run by Island Packers, 1867 Spinnaker Drive, three miles west of US-101 and a mile south of town (☎805/642-7688 for 24hr recorded information, ☎805/642-1393 for reservations 9am–5pm, ⓦwww.islandpackers.com). Trips include all-day trips ($37), half-day cruises without landings ($24), two-day camping excursions ($48), and whale-watching excursions which last about three hours and start at $25. The fifteen-mile trip takes ninety minutes each way, and there's a free, very basic **campground** a half-mile walk from the landing cove on East Anacapa. Bring plenty of food and especially water, as none is available on the boat or on the island. Permits are required for camping. Boats don't run every day and often fill up, so call several days ahead.

The other islands are more difficult to visit, but Island Packers runs boats, less frequently, to them all. Day-trips to the western end of Santa Cruz (3hr each way) are $42, overnight excursions to the eastern end are $54; visits to Santa Rosa (5hr one-way; $62 for the day, $80 including camping) are often combined with a camping stop on San Miguel ($90), while Santa Barbara day-trips are $49 and $75 for camping. Truth Aquatics, 301 W Cabrillo Blvd (☎805/962-1127 or 805/963-3564, ⓦwww.truthaquatics.com), has alternative itineraries to all the islands on smaller vessels at higher prices, including two-day hiking, diving, and kayaking excursions. An alternative way to reach Santa Rosa is to **fly** with Channel Islands Aviation (☎805/987-1301, ⓦwww.flycia.com), which runs day-trips and weekend excursions ($106 & $162, respectively) from Camarillo Airport off Hwy-101, twenty miles south of Ventura. Santa Cruz is also the venue for kayak trips from Ventura and Santa Barbara (see p.449).

Santa Barbara

The six-lane 101 freeway that whips through the coastal hills above Ventura slows to a more leisurely pace a hundred miles north of Los Angeles at **SANTA BARBARA**, a seaside resort colony that for years has been known as the "home of the newly wed and the nearly dead." Despite the vast modern El Paseo Nuevo shopping mall in the center of town and a growing selection of budget hotels and fast-food joints on the outskirts, Santa Barbara has managed to preserve the homogeneity of its charming architecture. Beautifully situated on the gently sloping hills above the Pacific, the town's low-rise Spanish Colonial Revival buildings feature red-tiled roofs and white stucco walls, a

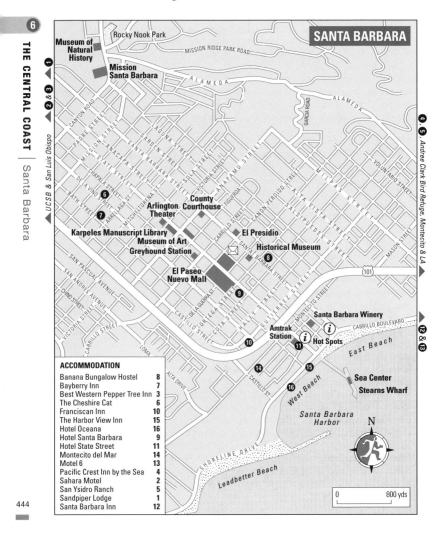

SANTA BARBARA

ACCOMMODATION

Banana Bungalow Hostel	8
Bayberry Inn	7
Best Western Pepper Tree Inn	3
The Cheshire Cat	6
Franciscan Inn	10
The Harbor View Inn	15
Hotel Oceana	16
Hotel Santa Barbara	9
Hotel State Street	11
Montecito del Mar	14
Motel 6	13
Pacific Crest Inn by the Sea	4
Sahara Motel	2
San Ysidro Ranch	5
Sandpiper Lodge	1
Santa Barbara Inn	12

THE CENTRAL COAST | Santa Barbara

lovely background to the golden, palm-lined beaches below, winding along a gently curving bay.

Once home to Ronald Reagan, and a weekend escape for much of the old money of Los Angeles, Santa Barbara has both a traditional conservative side, as well as a more freewheeling libertarian character among the younger set. Still, it's a fairly provincial place; local culture is confined predominantly to playing volleyball, surfing, cycling, sipping coffee, or cruising in expensive convertibles along the shore. After an essential visit to the mission, a quiet lunch, and a leisurely walk along the pier, it shouldn't take much longer than half a day to get a sense of the place and move on.

Arrival, information, and transportation

Getting to Santa Barbara is easy. Greyhound **buses** arrive from LA and San Francisco every few hours, stopping downtown at 34 W Carrillo St, while Amtrak **trains** stop at the old Southern Pacific station at 209 State St, a block west of US-101. Santa Barbara **airport** (☎805/683-4011), eight miles from the town center (near the University of California at Santa Barbara) at 515 Marxmiller Drive in Goleta, has a limited and very expensive scheduled service to other Californian cities.

For more information on Santa Barbara, or for help with finding a place to stay, contact the **Visitor Information Office** on East Beach at 1 Santa Barbara St (Mon–Sat 9am–5pm, Sun 10am–5pm; ☎805/965-3021, Ⓦwww.santabarbara.com). For information on **hiking** in the general area, the US Forest Service office at 6144 Calle Real (☎805/683-6711, Ⓦwww. r5.fs.fed.us/lospadres) in Goleta, near the University of California at Santa Barbara, can steer you toward the many good trails accessible from downtown.

Getting around Santa Barbara mainly involves walking, though there's the quarter-a-ride **State Street shuttle** that loops between downtown and the beach on a ten-minute schedule, and along the waterfront to Montecito every thirty minutes (daily 10.15am–6pm; ☎805/683-3702). Other areas are covered by Santa Barbara Metropolitan Transit District **buses** (also at ☎805/683-3702, Ⓦwww.sbmtd.gov). If you want to **rent a car**, the best value is U-Save Auto Rental, 510 Anacapa St (☎805/963-3499, Ⓦwww.usavesantabarbara.com), which rents late-model cars for as little as $22 a day including 150 daily free miles. Major operators Budget (☎805/963-6651) and Hertz (☎805/967-0411) have offices at the airport.

Accommodation

Home to some of the West Coast's most deluxe resorts – often romantic hideaways for celebrities – Santa Barbara is among the most expensive places to **stay**, with rooms averaging over $120 a night. However, there is a **hostel**, and with a bit of advance planning, finding somewhere reasonable shouldn't take too big a bite out of your budget – especially if you are willing to stay in one of the junkier chain **motels** along the western stretch of State Street. The least expensive as well as most of the more moderate places are usually booked throughout the summer, but if you get stuck, enlist the assistance of *Hot Spots*, a 24-hour hotel reservation center and espresso bar at 36 State St (☎805/564-1637 or 1-800/793-7666, Ⓦwww.hotspotsusa.com), which offers information and specials on lodging. Also, while there are no **campgrounds** in Santa Barbara proper, there are several spots along the coast to the north, including El Capitan State Beach and Refugio State Beach (both at ☎805/968-1033 or

1–800/444-7275; $12–20), and to the south, including the Carpinteria State Beach (☎805/684-2811 or 1–800/444-7275; $12-18); both sites are accessible through ⓦwww.reserveamerica.com. In the mountains of the Santa Ynez Valley, there are a number of other options, including sites around Lake Cachuma (☎805/688-4658; $16–21).

Banana Bungalow Hostel 210 E Ortega St ☎805/963-0154 or 1-800/3-HOSTEL, ⓦwww.bananabungalow.com. Catering to raucous backpackers, with a party atmosphere prevailing, caused as much by the 2.30am curfew as by the occasional keg parties. ❶

Bayberry Inn 111 W Valerio St ☎805/569-3398, ⓦwww.bayberryinnsantabarbara.com. Lovely little spot offering eight comfortable B&B rooms themed around various berries, and with canopy beds and tasteful period furnishings. ❼

Best Western Pepper Tree Inn 3850 State St ☎805/687-5511 or 1-800/338-0030, ⓦwww.bestwestern.com. A bit away from the city center, a comfortable spot that offers slightly better rates than most accommodation of the same type along the beach. ❻

The Cheshire Cat 36 W Valerio St ☎805/569-1610, ⓦwww.cheshirecat.com. Tastefully decorated B&B with hot tub, bikes for guests' use, and Alice in Wonderland theme. Complimentary wine on arrival and breakfast under a palm tree. Ten minutes' walk from the main restaurant zone. ❻

Franciscan Inn 109 Bath St ☎805/963-8845, ⓦwww.franciscaninn.com. Comfortable, quiet and very clean motel just a block from the beach, with a pool, spa, and complimentary breakfast. ❺

Harbor View Inn 28 W Cabrillo Blvd ☎805/963-0780 or 1-800/755-0222, ⓦwww. harborviewinnsb com. One of the more appealing luxury hotels around, offering on-site restaurant and bar, pool and Jacuzzis, and elegant rooms with oceanfront views and refrigerators. ❽

Hotel Oceana 202 W Cabrillo Blvd ☎1-800/965-9776, ⓦwww.hoteloceana.com. Appealing new entry in the high-end bracket, a Mission-style resort with splendid architecture, elegant rooms loaded with amenities, spa, fitness center, and oceanside views. ❼

Hotel Santa Barbara 533 State St ☎805/957-9300 or 1-888/259-7700, ⓦwww.hotelsantabarbara.com.

Surprisingly good rates for comfortable, well-decorated rooms, complimentary breakfast, and a prime downtown location. ❻

Hotel State Street 121 State St ☎805/966-6586. Near the wharf and beach in a colorful old Mission-style building, though it is subject to some noise from the nearby railway and only offers communal bathrooms. Reasonable rates include breakfast. ❷

Montecito del Mar 316 W Montecito St ☎1-888/464-1690, ⓦwww.santabarbarahotel316 .com. One of the city's best deals, a Spanish Revival inn with a wide range of accommodations, offering well-appointed entry-level rooms, three spas, complimentary breakfast, and excellent location three blocks from the sands. ❹

Pacific Crest Inn 433 Corona Del Mar ☎805/966-3103. Affordable (though unexciting) basic lodging, but a good alternative to the more pricey neighbors along the beach. ❹

Sahara Motel 2800 State St ☎805/687-2500. As basic as it gets, but also as cheap as it gets in Santa Barbara. ❷

San Ysidro Ranch 900 San Ysidro Lane ☎805/969-5046 or 1-800/368-6788, ⓦwww.sanysidroranch.com. Gorgeous, ultra-posh resort with private cottages in lovely gardens (Jackie and JFK spent their honeymoon here), in the hills a ten-minute drive south of town. ❾

Sandpiper Lodge 3525 State St ☎1-800/687-5326. Comfortable, motel-type lodging in uptown part of the city, with basic and clean rooms, pool, spa, and complimentary breakfast. ❸

Santa Barbara Inn 901 E Cabrillo Blvd ☎805/966-2285 or 1-800/231-0431, ⓦwww.santabarbarainn.com. Upscale oceanfront rooms with large pool, lovely views, and splendid amenities. Though luxurious – especially with the swank *Citronelle* restaurant (see p.450) – still has the odd look of a fancy motel. ❾

The Town

The mission-era feel of Santa Barbara is no accident. After a devastating **earthquake** in 1925, the city authorities decided to rebuild virtually the entire town as an apocryphal Spanish Colonial village – even the massive "historic" El Paseo shopping mall is covered in pseudo-whitewashed adobe plaster – with quaint arcades linking shops, offices, and restaurants. It's surprisingly successful, and the square-mile town center, squeezed between the south-facing beaches

△ A sea lion on the Pacific Coast

and the foothills of the Santa Ynez Mountains, attracts one of the region's liveliest street scenes. The main drag, **State Street**, is home to an assortment of diners, bookstores, coffee bars, and nightclubs catering as much to the needs of locals – among them twenty thousand UCSB students – as to visitors.

The town's few genuine mission-era structures are preserved as **El Presidio de Santa Barbara** (daily 10.30am–4.30pm; $4; ⓦ www.sbthp.org), in the center of which are the barracks of the old fortress **El Cuartel**, standing two blocks east of State Street at 123 Canon Perdido St. The second-oldest building in California, the 1782 barracks now house historical exhibits and a scale model of the small Spanish colony. A block away at 136 E De la Guerra St, the **Santa Barbara Historical Museum** (Tues–Sat 10am–5pm, Sun noon–5pm; $3; ⓣ 805/966-1601, ⓦ www.santabarbaramuseum.com) presents other aspects of the city's past, from Ice Age geology to artifacts from native settlements to photographs of more recent times.

On the corner of State and Anapamu streets, at 1130 State St, the **Santa Barbara Museum of Art** (Tues–Thurs & Sat 11am–5pm, Fri 11am–9pm, Sun noon–5pm; $6; ⓦ www.sbmuseart.org) is of greater interest. A refreshingly accessible small museum, it features some fine classical Greek and Egyptian statuary, a fairly decent array of American paintings, a smattering of French Impressionists, and an Asian collection of some note. Just east of here, at 1100 Anacapa St, the still-functional **County Courthouse** (Mon–Fri 8am–5pm, Sat & Sun 10am–5pm; free) is a first-rate piece of Spanish Revival architecture, an idiosyncratic variation on the mission theme that is widely known as one of the finest public buildings in the US. Take a break in the sunken gardens, explore the quirky staircases, or climb the seventy-foot-high **clock tower** for a nice view out over the town. Two blocks up State Street, at no. 1317, the landmark 1930s **Arlington Theater** (ⓣ 805/963-4408) is an intact and functional movie palace and performance arts venue – home to the Santa Barbara Symphony (ⓣ 805/898-9526, ⓦ www.thesymphony.org) – with a trompe l'oeil interior that simulates a Mexican village plaza. Nearby, at 21 Anapamu St, the beautifully decorated **Karpeles Manuscript Library** (daily 10am–4pm; free; ⓣ 805/962-5322, ⓦ www.rain.org/~karpeles) is the surprising home to a diverse array of original documents such as the Constitution of the Confederate States of America and the original manuscripts of many famous writers, scientists, composers, and politicians – among them Mark Twain, Thomas Edison, John Locke, and Jorge Luis Borges. Falling slightly out of the town's center, not far from Highway 101, the **Santa Barbara Winery**, 202 Anacapa St at Yanonali Street (10am–5pm; ⓣ 805/963-3646, ⓦ www.sbwinery.com), is worth a detour to see one of the oldest commercial wineries in the county.

The beaches and around

Half a mile down State Street from the town center, Cabrillo Boulevard runs along the south-facing shore, a long, clean strip stretching from the yacht and fishing harbor beyond palm-lined **West Beach** to the volleyball courts and golden sands of **East Beach**, which hosts an outdoor arts and crafts market every Sunday, displaying both the inspired and kitschy work of local artists. At the foot of State Street, take a stroll among the pelicans on **Stearns Wharf**, the oldest wooden pier in the state, built in 1872. It was nearly destroyed in November 1998, when a third of it was engulfed in flames, but restoration efforts have brought the structure back to its former glory. Postcards of the flaming pier remain popular at the tourist shops which line the wharf, along with seafood restaurants, ice-cream stands, and the **Sea Center** (closed until

2003), an annex of the Museum of Natural History (see below), which offers a standard selection of whale bones and tot-friendly tide pools.

Just west of the pier, athletes keep in shape in the fifty-meter **Los Baños del Mar swimming pool**, an open-air, year-round facility ($2.50; ☏805/966-6110); **windsurfers** can be rented from beachfront stalls, and **kayaks** are available from Paddle Sports, 100 State St (☏805/899-4925, ⓦwww.paddlesportsofsantabarbara.com), and Aqua Sports, 111 Verona Ave (☏805/968-7231), starting at $20 for two hours and $40 for a full day. These are just two of several companies that conduct lessons and run all-inclusive paddling and snorkeling trips out to Santa Cruz Island (about $150). Wheel Fun Rentals, 22 State St (☏805/966-6733, ⓦwww.wheelfunrentals.com), and Cycles 4 Rent Inc., 101 State St (☏805/966-3804, ⓦwww.cycles4rent.com), offer **bicycles** for around $17–34 a day, and provide a map of Santa Barbara's extensive system of bike paths. The longest and most satisfying path leads west along the bluffs all the way to Isla Vista and UCSB, and passes a mile or so back from the rarely crowded, creekside **Arroyo Burro Beach** (locally known as "Hendry's"), four miles west of the wharf at the end of Las Positas Road. Alternatively, head along the beachfront bike path two miles east past the small-but-worthwhile **Santa Barbara Zoo**, 500 Ninos Drive (daily 10am–5pm; $8; ☏805/962-6310, ⓦwww.santabarbarazoo.org) – notable for its sharks, stingrays, and turtles, plus a handful of monkeys – and cycle around the Andree Clark Bird Refuge (unrestricted access) just beyond, an enclosed saltwater marsh where you can see a variety of seabirds, including egrets, herons, and cormorants.

The Mission and around

The one sight that does even more than the beaches to put Santa Barbara on the map is the mission from which it takes its name. In the hills above the town at 2201 Laguna St, **Mission Santa Barbara** (daily 9am–5pm; $4; ⓦwww.sbmission.org) is known as the "Queen of the Missions." Its colorful twin-towered facade – facing out over a perfectly manicured garden towards the sea – combines Romanesque and Spanish Mission styles, giving it a heavy, imposing character lacking in some of the prettier missions in the chain. The present structure, built to replace a series of three adobe churches that had been destroyed by earthquakes, was finished and dedicated in 1820. In 1925, another earthquake damaged the mission, and the ensuing restoration costs totaled nearly $400,000. Today, a small **museum** displays historical artifacts from the mission archives, and the cemetery contains remains of some 4000 Native Americans, many of whom helped build the original complex, which included a notable system of aqueducts, waterworks, a grist mill, a pottery kiln, and two reservoirs. The inside, much like the rest of Santa Barbara, is something of a disappointment as there's nothing particularly grand about the decor. To get to the mission, take the SBMTD bus, or walk or ride the half-mile from State Street up Mission Street and Mission Canyon.

Just beyond the mission at 2559 Puerta del Sol Rd, the **Museum of Natural History** (daily 10am–5pm; $7; ⓦwww.sbnature.org) has intriguing and informative displays on the plants and animals of Southern California. It can be viewed after walking through an entrance constructed out of the skeleton of a blue whale. Across the road from the museum, **Rocky Nook Park** is a great place to picnic or wander among the trees.

Eating

Not surprisingly for a resort town, Santa Barbara has a number of very good and very expensive **restaurants**, but it also has many more affordable options that offer a range of cuisines. Since it's right on the Pacific, you'll find a lot of seafood and sushi; Mexican places are also numerous and of a very high standard. Smoothies – blended fruit-and-yoghurt milkshakes – are everywhere, a welcome snack on a hot summer day.

Andrias Harborside Restaurant 214 State St ☎805/966-3000. Enjoy good, mid-range meals throughout the day, along with Happy Hour, in a lively atmosphere at a new location – closer to the train station than the harbor.

Chad's 625 Chapala St ☎805/568-1876. A popular local favorite, serving modern American cuisine in the intimate atmosphere of a historic Victorian home at relatively modest prices, considering the quality.

Citronelle 901 E Cabrillo Blvd, in the *Santa Barbara Inn* ☎805/963-4717. Stylish big-name restaurant you've read about in all the food-fashion mags, with a range of delicious entrees like the lamb shank and porcupine shrimp, sweeping coastal views, and unsurprisingly exorbitant prices.

Edomasa 2710 De la Vina ☎805/687-0210. Affordable, cozy sushi joint with a fairly decent menu and nice presentation. Frequented more by locals than tourist interlopers.

El Paseo 10 El Paseo ☎805/962–6050. Upscale Mexican restaurant serving mainly the familiar staples, though in a historic home with a colorful fountain courtyard.

Esau's Coffee Shop 403 State St ☎805/965-4416. Ancient-looking café serving Santa Barbara's most popular greasy-spoon breakfasts, namely the omelets. Open until 1pm daily; additional hours for the drinking crowd from 9pm–3am on Fri and Sat only.

Joe's Café 536 State St ☎805/966-4638. Long-established bar and grill. A great place to stop off for a burger and a beer, more or less midway between the beach and the downtown museums.

La Tolteca Restaurant 600 N Milpas St ☎805/899-4857. Fine Mexican food in a casual atmosphere, serving authentic cuisine for lunch and dinner.

Mousse Odile 18 E Cota St ☎805/962-5393. A local favorite for French cuisine with a California flair, focusing on pasta, steak, and seafood entrées. Pricey but intimate.

Natural Café 508 State St ☎805/962-9494. Scrumptious, cheap veggie meals in a prime spot for people watching.

Palazzio Trattoria Italiana 1026 State St ☎805/564-1985. One of the better Italian restaurants in town, with sizeable portions, moderate prices, and one mean *tiramisu*.

Paradise Café 702 Anacapa St ☎805/962-4416. Stylish, slightly upmarket 1940s-era indoor/outdoor grill, with good steaks and fresh seafood.

Pascucci 729 State St ☎805/963-8123. Somewhat snooty but worth it for cheap and delicious pastas, gourmet pizzas, and panini served in a small, elegant dining room or outside among the shoppers.

Pierre Lafond 516 State St ☎805/962-1455. The best place in town for a home-cooked continental breakfast, café-style.

Sushi-Teri 1013 Bath St ☎805/963-1250. One in a chain of four local sushi joints, with impressively cheap prices and solid Asian cuisine, offering hefty chicken bowls, mouth-watering rolls, and a nice selection of fish platters.

Your Place 22 N Milpas St ☎805/966-5151. Affordable, top-shelf Thai food, and the locals know it. Especially good for the mei krob and pad thai staples.

Waterfront Grill 113 Harbor Way ☎805/564-1200. Specializing in seafood and views. Downstairs is casual fine dining. Escape the higher prices by heading upstairs to the *Endless Summer Bar and Café*, and enjoy the surfing-inspired decor.

Drinking and nightlife

There are quite a few **cafés**, **bars**, and **clubs** along the length of State Street, especially in the downtown area; for the most up-to-date **nightlife** listings, check out a copy of the free weekly *Santa Barbara Independent*, available at area bookstores, record stores, and convenience marts.

Coffee Bean & Tea Leaf 811-A State St ☎805/966-2442. A good place to watch the locals parade back and forth on the strip.

Fathom 423 State St ☎805/730-0022. Ostensibly a frenetic gay disco, making it all the more popular with trendy straights and venturesome tourists.

Hot Spots Espresso Bar 36 State St ☎805/963-4233. A block from the beach, this cozy spot is open 24hr for java, pastries, and munchies. It also offers one of the city's better information services.

Madhouse Martini Lounge 434 State St ☎805/962-5516. Mellow spot that cashes in on the retro-cocktail craze with a fine assortment of exotic cocktails, along with the requisite stiff martinis.

Santa Barbara Brewing Company 501 State St ☎805/730-1040. Serviceable American fare – burgers, seafood, and such – with microbrewed beers and live music on weekends.
Sojourner Cafe 134 E Cañon Perdido ☎805/965-7922. Coffee, beer, wine, and a range of vegetarian food in a friendly bohemian setting, with live music some nights.
Wine Cask Intermezzo 813 Anacapa St ☎805/966-9463. Darkly elegant spot with primo

vino and tasty desserts, especially good for after-hours romancing, when smart locals plop down on one of the comfortable couches or luxuriate by the fireplace.
Zelo 630 State St ☎805/966-5792. One of Santa Barbara's more fashionable bars and restaurants, which evolves into a dance club as the night wears on, offering alternative dance, Latin, retro, and other eclectic fare throughout the week. Closed Mon.

On from Santa Barbara

Continuing north from Santa Barbara you can either cut inland through the wine region of the Santa Ynez Valley (see below) or continue along the coast where you'll pass **Goletta Beach** – popular with families – as well as the characterless town of **Isla Vista**, which borders the forty-year-old campus of the **University of California at Santa Barbara**. Isla Vista Beach has some good tidepools and, at the west end, a popular surfing area at **Coal Oil Point** ("Devereux" to locals); the estuary nearby has been preserved as a botanical study center and nature refuge, where birdwatchers will find much of interest.

All along this part of the coast **the beaches** face almost due south, so the surf is very lively, and in winter the sun both rises and sets over the Pacific. About twenty miles out from Santa Barbara, **El Capitan State Beach** is a popular surfing beach, while **Refugio State Beach**, another three miles along, is one of the prettiest in California, with palm trees dotting the sands at the mouth of a small creek, giving the area a tropical feel. Inland on Refugio Road, up the canyon high in the hills, stands Rancho El Cielo, the one-time Western White House of retired President Ronald Reagan. Ten miles west, **Gaviota State Beach** is not as pretty, but there's a fishing pier and a large wooden railway viaduct that bridges the mouth of the canyon. All the state beaches have **campgrounds**, and reservations can be made through ParkNet (☎1-800/444-7275; $12).

Just beyond Gaviota, the highways split, US-101 heading inland and the more spectacular Hwy-1 branching off nearer the coast. Half a mile off the highway, but a world away from the speeding traffic, is the small **Las Cruces hot spring** (daylight hours; parking $2), a pool of 95°F mineral water set in a shady, peaceful ravine. To get there, take the turnoff for Hwy-1, but stay on the east side of the freeway and double back onto a small road a quarter of a mile to the parking lot at the end. Walk half a mile or so up the trail until you smell the sulfur.

The Santa Ynez Valley

An alternative to the coastal route out of Santa Barbara is to take Hwy-154 up and over the very steep **San Marcos Pass** through the **Santa Ynez Valley**, a pleasant route through a prime wine-growing region that's popular with leather-clad bikers and masochistic cyclists.

Three miles out of Santa Barbara, the walls of the **Chumash Painted Cave**, on the narrow Painted Caves Road, are daubed with pre-conquest Native American art. You can't actually enter the sandstone cave as it has been closed off to protect against vandalism. But peering through the bars will give you a good look at the colorful paintings inside.

Several miles further, beyond the San Marcos Pass, Paradise Road follows the Santa Ynez River up to **Red Rocks**, an excellent swimming area amidst the stony outcrops. **Lake Cachuma**, six miles further along Hwy-154, is a popular recreation area with a large **campground** ($16; ☎805/686-5054, ⓦwww.sbparks.org/docs/cachuma); it's not actually a lake but a massive reservoir that holds the over-stretched water supply for Santa Barbara.

Beyond the lake, Hwy-246 cuts off to Solvang, while Hwy-154 continues on through the vineyards around **Los Olivos**, where wineries like Fess Parker, Firestone, and Bridlewood are clustered. The Santa Barbara County Vintners' Association (☎805/688-0881 or 1-800/218-0881, ⓦwww.sbcountywines.com) publishes a handy wine-touring map to the area which includes each winery's address and hours.

⑥ Solvang and around

It is difficult to imagine anyone falling for the sham windmills and plastic storks that fill the saccharine-sweet town of **SOLVANG**, but people come by the busloads to see the community, which was established in 1911 by expat Danish teachers from the Midwest looking for a place to found a Danish folk school. Nowadays, the town, three miles off US-101 on Hwy-246, lives on tourism, and locals dress in "traditional" costume to entertain visitors. There are **visitors information** stands around the little town run by the local CVB (daily 10am–4pm; ☎805/688-6144 or 1-800/GO-SOLVANG, ⓦwww.solvangusa.com), but the only things that make the town worth a stop are the fresh coffee and pastries sold in one of the many Danish bakeries in town.

While Solvang may mean "Sunny Fields" in Danish, life wasn't so bright for the thousands of Native Americans buried in the cemetery at the **Mission Santa Ines**, 1706 Mission St (June–Sept daily 9am–7pm; Oct–May daily 9.30am–5.30pm; $3; ☎805/688-4815, ⓦwww.missionsantaines.org), hidden away behind the rows of gingerbread buildings on the eastern edge of town. A century before the Danes tried to make the place look like home, the Spanish were here doing the same, and in 1804 they erected the nineteenth Spanish mission in their chain here. Though the structure has undergone numerous restorations, the buildings are original, and the trompe l'oeil green-marble trim on the church's interior walls is one of the best surviving examples of mission-era decorative art. There is also one of the better mission museums, displaying period furnishings and church documents, including a set of plaques thanking the Franciscan fathers for improving the lives of the native Chumash.

If you'd like to see for yourself how the natives fared, head over to **Santa Ynez**, three miles east of Solvang, where the **Chumash Casino** (24 hours; ☎1-800/728-9997, ⓦwww.chumashcasino.com) has been trying its best to suck in whatever money tourists haven't blown on Danish pastries. In recent years, there have been attempts by California lawmakers to make slot machines, even on Native American lands, illegal: they haven't succeeded thus far, so you can still shake hands with the one-armed bandit all you like. Passing through the town proper, it's hard to imagine a town that serves as a sharper contrast to prosperous Solvang, or what another blow to the local economy would do.

If the whole spectacle makes you weary of humanity, you can always escape to the **Nojoqui** (pronounced No-ho-kee) **Falls County Park** (daily 8am–sunset; ☎805/688-4217), six miles from Solvang off US-101, where a gentle ten-minute walk brings you to a 75-foot waterfall. The route to the park is gorgeous, winding along Alisal Road under thick garlands of Spanish moss that dangle from a canopy of oak trees.

Lompoc

Hwy-1 splits off US-101 near Gaviota on a marvelous route through the inland valleys of the Santa Ynez Mountains. **LOMPOC** (pronounced Lom-*poke*), the only town for miles, calls itself the "flower seed-growing capital of the world" and claims to produce as much as three-quarters of the flower seeds sold on earth. In summer, you'll see a thick carpet of color over the gently rolling landscape of the surrounding countryside. For a leaflet detailing where particular species have been planted this season, contact the **Lompoc Valley Chamber of Commerce**, 111 South I St (Mon–Fri 9am–5pm; ☎805/736-4567 or 1-800/240-0999, ⓦwww.lompocshopping.com), where you can also find out about the folksy **murals** which, in recent years, have sprung up to beautify an otherwise faceless downtown.

Lompoc Museum, 200 South H St (Tues–Fri 1–5pm, Sat & Sun 1–4pm; $1; ☎805/736-3888), is strong on Chumash and other Native American artifacts. It also has material on the town's **original mission site**, the scant remains of which can be found three blocks to the south on F Street off Locust Avenue.

Lompoc is also the home of **Vandenberg Air Force Base**, sprawled along the western side of town, where various new missiles and guidance systems get put through their paces over the Pacific Ocean. Their vapor trails are visible for miles, particularly at sunset, though the only way to see any of it up close is by the Amtrak Coast Starlight train (see p.441), which runs along the coast. The route was **Jack Kerouac**'s favorite rail journey – he worked for a while as a brakeman on the train and subsequently used the "Midnight Ghost" for a free ride between LA and the Bay Area. Aerospace enthusiasts who plan at least a week ahead can visit the air base on four-hour **tours** (Wed 10am–2pm; free; reservations required; ☎805/606-3595, ⓦwww.vandenberg.af.mil) that visit launch pads and a missile silo.

The **beaches** along this section of coast are secluded, undeveloped, and nearly inaccessible much of the year, either because of bad weather or impending missile launches. **Jalama Beach** (daily 8am–sunset; $5; ☎805/736-6316 or 805/736-3504, ⓦwww.spbarks.com/docs/jalama) at the end of Jalama Road, twisting fourteen miles off Hwy-1, spreads beneath coastal bluffs where you can camp overnight ($15). If you're only planning on stopping by during the day, head to the large sand dunes of **Ocean Beach** (free), a broad strand at the mouth of the Santa Ynez River ten miles west of Lompoc, the nesting grounds of many sea birds.

La Purisima Mission State Park

Four miles east of Lompoc and signposted off Hwy-246, **La Purisima Mission State Park** (daily 9am–5pm; $2 per family vehicle, up to nine people; ☎805/733-3713, ⓦwww.lapurisimamission.org) is the most complete and authentic reconstruction of any of the 21 Spanish missions in California and one of the best places to get an idea of what life might have been like in these early colonial settlements. La Mission la Purísima Concepción de Maria Santisima, as it's called, was founded in 1787 on a site three miles north of here, and by 1804 had converted around 1500 Chumash, five hundred of whom died in a smallpox epidemic over the next two years. In 1812, an earthquake destroyed all the buildings, and the fathers decided to move to the present site. This was the only mission in the chain to be built in a linear fashion rather than in the defensive quadrangle style, used both to confine Native Americans and to keep them out – an especially important detail as the number of able-bodied residents had been slashed by the epidemic. The complex did not last long, however, after the missions were secularized in 1834; like all the rest, it was soon abandoned and gradually fell into disrepair.

The buildings that stand here today were rebuilt on the ruins of the mission as part of a Depression-era project for the unemployed. From 1933 to 1940 over two hundred men lived and worked on the site, studying the remaining ruins and rebuilding the church and outbuildings using period tools and methods. Workers made adobe bricks from straw and mud, shaped roof timbers with handtools, and even took the colors of their paints from native plants.

The focus of the mission is a narrow church, furnished as it would have been in the 1820s; nearby, at the entrance, small but engaging displays of documents and artifacts from the mission era and photographs of the reconstruction are housed in the old wagon house that serves as a **museum** and gift shop. On summer weekends you might catch a "living history day," when volunteers dress up as padres and natives and hold a traditional Mass, along with craft demonstrations that are evocative, if hokey, fun. Call ℡805/733-1303 or check Ⓦwww.lapurisimamission.org for more information.

Pismo Beach and Avila Beach

Most of the land along the Santa Maria River, 75 miles north of Santa Barbara, is given over to farming, and both Hwy-1 and US-101 pass through a number of agriculture-based towns and villages. **Santa Maria** is the largest and most developed, though it's hardly worth stopping except to refuel or for a peek at the historic planes on display at the **Museum of Flight**, 3015 Airpark Drive (Fri–Sun 10am–4pm; free; ℡805/922-8758, Ⓦwww.smmof.org). Other towns seem hardly to have changed since the 1930s, when thousands of Okies, as they were known, fled to the region from the dust bowl of the Midwest – an era portrayed in John Steinbeck's novel and John Ford's movie, *The Grapes of Wrath* (see p.469 for the National Steinbeck Center in Salinas). Twenty-five miles north of Lompoc, Hwy-1 passes through the center of **Guadalupe**, a small farming village where Spanish signs and advertisements far outnumber those in English, and ramshackle saloons, cafés, and vegetable stalls line the dusty streets. Along the coast, just several miles west, lies the **Guadalupe/Nipomo Dunes Preserve** (daily 8am–sunset; free; ℡805/343-2455, Ⓦwww.dunescenter.org), where you can look for whales out at sea or climb the 500ft sand dunes. The highest on the California coast, the dunes surround wetlands that are an essential habitat for endangered sea birds.

Pismo Beach

The dunes stretch ten miles up the coast, reaching as far as two miles inland and ending just south of the boisterous town of **PISMO BEACH**, where the two highways merge. The southern portion of the dunes, three miles south of the town, is open to off-road vehicle enthusiasts, who excite themselves flying up and over the sandpiles of the **Pismo Dunes State Vehicle Recreation Area** in dune buggies and four-wheel-drives, motoring along the beach to reach them. Recently, the State Coastal Commission voted to allow even greater vehicle access to California's only drive-on beach, bringing some four million dollars in tourist revenue to the area. Thankfully, the northern portion of the dunes inland is protected as a **nature reserve**.

North of the nature reserve, between the town and the dune buggy area, a number of beachfront **campgrounds** line Hwy-1; mostly RV-packed, they all charge around $20 a site. The **Pismo Beach State Park** has hot showers and beach camping for $12 (call ParkNet ☎1-800/444-7275), and is a good place to see the black-and-orange Monarch butterflies that winter in the eucalyptus trees here from October to February and leave before the summer crowds. However, the once-plentiful **Pismo clams** that gave the town its name (from the local Indian word *pismu*, or "blobs of tar" that the shells resemble) have been so depleted that any you might dig up nowadays are probably under the four-and-a-half-inch legal minimum size.

Most of the town's commercial activity happens at the junction where Pomeroy Avenue crosses Hwy-1. If you have no interest in dunes or watersports, you're in the wrong place, as the dozens of surf shops around you will attest. You can, however, walk out on the gigantic pier for views back to town over the heads of surfers riding the waves.

Practicalities

The **Chamber of Commerce**, 581 Dolliver St (Mon–Sat 9am–5pm, Sun 10am–4pm; ☎805/773-4382, ⓦwww.pismochamber.com), will help with accommodation, and there are a number of affordable **motels**, including the *Sea Gypsy*, 1020 Cypress St (☎805/773-1801 or 1-800/592-5923, ⓦwww.seagypsymotel.com; ❶), and the *Ocean Palms*, 390 Ocean View Ave (☎1-805/773-4669; ❸). For something right on the beach, try the *Edgewater*, 280 Wadsworth Ave (☎805/773-4811 or 1-800/634-5858, ⓦwww.edgewater-inn.com; ❹), which has a heated pool, hot tubs, and some rooms with kitchens. If you have a little more to spend, *The Best Western Shorecliff Lodge*, 2555 Price St (☎805/773-4671, ⓦwww.shorecliff.com; ❺), is dramatically situated, with a cliff-hugging swimming pool, gazebo, and excellent views.

For **dining** options, people have been known to drive to Pismo Beach just to sample the clam chowder at the fun but touristy *Splash Café*, 197 Pomeroy Ave (☎805/773-4653). For fancier dining, try *Giuseppe's*, an old-world Italian restaurant with hearty, simple food, 891 Price St (☎805/773-2870). The only **public transportation** is Greyhound, which stops downtown five times a day in each direction.

Avila Beach

North of Pismo Beach the coastline becomes more rugged, with caves and tidepools below ever-eroding bluffs, and sea lions in the many coves. The three-mile-long strand in front of the summer resort town of **AVILA BEACH**, the last outpost of Southern California beach life, is finally recovering from a devastating ecological disaster brought on by a spill from the nearby Unocal Refinery. The ambitious clean-up and reconstruction project that began soon after the spill has helped restore much of the area to its pre-disaster status.

The area has a high concentration of burger stands and one good budget **motel**, the *Inn at Avila Beach*, 256 Front St (☎805/595-2300, ⓦwww.avilabeachca.com; ❹). On the road into town, *Sycamore Mineral Springs*, at 1215 Avila Rd (☎805/595-7302 or 1-800/234-5831, ⓦwww.sycamoresprings.com; ❻–❼), boasts rooms with their own private mineral baths. The *Olde Port Inn* (☎805/595-2515), dramatically situated out on Port San Luis, is *the* spot to **eat** in Avila and has magnificent views.

On the beach, you'll find teenagers on the loose from their families cruising the boardwalk, while anyone old enough takes refuge in the loud, local **bars**. The party atmosphere continues all summer long, and no one seems to mind the presence of the **Diablo Canyon Nuclear Plant**, which straddles an earthquake fault six miles up the coast (for what it's worth, three long bursts of a loud siren indicate catastrophe). The scenic route north from here to San Luis Obispo, **See Canyon Road**, cuts off north a mile from US-101, climbing gradually up the narrow, overgrown canyon between sharply profiled volcanic cones, with great views out over the Pacific.

San Luis Obispo

SAN LUIS OBISPO is almost exactly halfway between LA and San Francisco and a main stopoff for both Amtrak and Greyhound. It's an underappreciated gem: primarily an agricultural town, the influx of students from adjacent Cal Poly have perked up the town's nightlife considerably and it's a pleasant place to dawdle and browse. The town center boasts interesting architecture, from turreted Victorian residences along **Buchon Street** to the south of the town

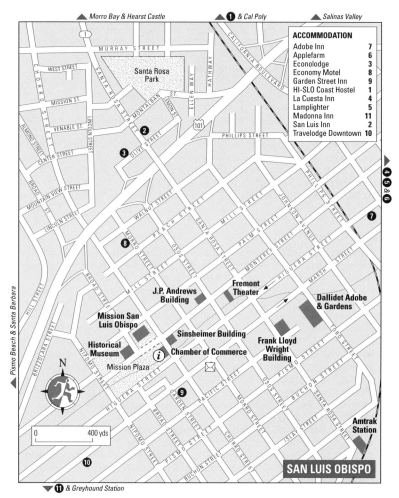

ACCOMMODATION

Adobe Inn	7
Applefarm	6
Econolodge	3
Economy Motel	8
Garden Street Inn	9
HI-SLO Coast Hostel	1
La Cuesta Inn	4
Lamplighter	5
Madonna Inn	11
San Luis Inn	2
Travelodge Downtown	10

center to the Art Deco Fremont Theater on Monterey Street. There are a number of good places to eat, a couple of pubs and nightclubs, and – outside summer holiday weekends – affordable accommodation. All these factors make it a smart base from which to explore Hearst Castle, too (see below).

Arrival and information

The Greyhound terminal is at 150 South St, half a mile down Higuera Street from the center of town near US-101, and there are regular **bus connections** with both LA and San Francisco. Amtrak trains and Thruway buses stop several times each day in each direction at the end of Santa Rosa Street, half a mile south of the business district. You can pick up a free walking-tour map highlighting much of the town's best architecture from the **Chamber of Commerce** at 1039 Chorro St (Mon & Sun 10am–5pm, Tues & Wed 8am–5pm, Thurs & Fri 8am–8pm, Sat 10am–8pm; ☏805/781-2777, ⓦwww.slochamber.org), which will also help with finding accommodation. The **Visitors and Conference Bureau** at 1037 Mill St (Mon–Fri 8am–5pm; ☏1-800/634-1414 and 805/541-8000, ⓦwww.sanluisobispocounty.com or ⓦwww.visitslo.com) may also come in handy. To find out what's on and where, check out the free weekly *New Times* (ⓦwww.newtimeslo.com) or check out the "Ticket" supplement every Friday to the local *San Luis Obispo Tribune* (50¢).

Accommodation

Monterey Street was the site of the world's first (and long gone) **motel** – the *Motel Inn* (see box, overleaf). Rates in its modern counterparts are generally low. The best **camping** nearby is south of town beyond Pismo Beach, or north off Hwy-1 in Morro Bay.

Apple Farm Inn 2015 Monterey St ☏805/544-2040 or 1-800/374-3705, ⓦwww.applefarm.com. Charming inn with homely Victoriana furnishings including canopy beds, excellent, B&B-style breakfasts, and an affable staff. Rates are lower in the Court building than the Inn proper. ④–⑥

Econolodge 950 Olive St ☏805/544-8886, ⓦwww.econolodge.com. Part of a national chain, this branch offers a good standard of accommodation at a great price. ④

Economy Motel 652 Morro St ☏805/543-7024. A particularly good value among the budget choices for its consistent low prices and clean rooms. ①

Garden Street Inn Bed & Breakfast 1212 Garden St ☏805/545-9802, ⓦwww.gardenstreetinn.com. Very central B&B in a restored 1880s house with comfortable rooms (some with TV, all with phone). There is complimentary wine on arrival and gourmet cooked breakfasts. ⑥–⑦

HI-San Luis Obispo Coast Hostel 1292 Foothill Blvd ☏805/544-4678. A 20min walk from the center following Santa Rosa Street north, this comfortable hostel has dorm beds at $14 for members, $17 for others. Office open 7.30–10am, 4.30–10pm. ①

La Cuesta Inn 2074 Monterey St ☏805/543-2777 or 1-800/543-2777, ⓦwww.lacuestainn.

com. As popular with businesspeople as vacationers, with spacious modern rooms and a good-sized swimming pool and spa. ③–④

Lamplighter Inn & Suites 1604 Monterey St ☏805/547-7777, ⓦ www.lamplighterinn.com. Older but comfortable motel with a pool. Popular with families. ③–④

Madonna Inn 100 Madonna Rd ☏805/543-3000 or 1-800/543-9666, ⓦwww.madonnainn.com. Local landmark (see below) set in over 2000 acres, but the very standard "theme" rooms in this shocking kitsch monstrosity are a big disappointment at such inflated rates, especially after touring the imposingly pink, chalet-style lobby. More last days of Elvis in Vegas than the hip-swiveling hound-dog. ⑥–⑧ rooms, ⑨ suites.

San Luis Inn 404 Santa Rosa St ☏805/544-0881, ⓦwww.sanluisinn.com Clean, standard rooms, free continental breakfasts, and a heated pool. ②

Travelodge Downtown 345 Marsh St ☏805/543-6443 or 1-800/458-8848. Simple motel but excellent value and location. There is another chain location at 1825 Monterey St (☏805/543-5110). ②

The Town

San Luis is eminently walkable, with a compact core centered in the late eighteenth-century **Mission San Luis Obispo de Tolosa**, 751 Palm St at Chorro (daily: May–Sept 9am–5pm; Oct–April 9am–4pm; $2; ☎805/543-6850, ⓦwww.oldmissionslo.org). A fairly plain and unremarkable church, it was the fifth structure in the mission trail and the prototype for the now ubiquitous red-tiled roof – developed as a replacement for the original, flammable thatch, which caught fire here in 1776 during attack by Native Americans. Between the mission and the tourist office, **Mission Plaza**'s terraces step down along San Luis Creek, along which footpaths meander, criss-crossed by bridges every hundred feet and overlooked by a number of stores and outdoor restaurants on the south bank. Downstream, across a small park, the **San Luis Obispo County Historical Museum**, 696 Monterey St (Wed–Sun 10am–4pm; free; ☎805/543-0638), holds a low-key collection of local artifacts tending toward the domestic and housed in a richly detailed 1904 Carnegie Library building. The main drag, **Higuera Street** (pronounced "Hi-Geara"), a block south of Mission Plaza, springs to life every Thursday afternoon and evening for the **Farmer's Market**, when the street is closed to cars and filled with vegetable stalls, mobile barbecues, and street-corner musicians. All of San Luis (and a fair smattering of tourists) comes out to sample the foods and entertainment of this weekly county fair.

Though a number of commercial buildings of minor architectural note are detailed on the Chamber of Commerce's **self-guided walking tour**, the only one not to be missed is the doctor's surgery designed by Frank Lloyd Wright at Santa Rosa and Pacific streets, although there's no admittance except for patients. Close by, at the end of Pacific Street, stands the **Dallidet Adobe and Gardens**, at no. 1185 (June–Aug Sun 1–4pm, otherwise by appointment;

The world's first mo-tel

The *Milestone Motel* opened in San Luis Obispo in December 1925, designed to take advantage of mushrooming car ownership among Americans after World War I. Initially, enthusiastic Model T drivers had used automobile "campgrounds" for overnight stays, pitching tents alongside their cars. Since San Luis Obispo is almost exactly halfway between San Francisco and Los Angeles, it became an especially popular place to stop. Savvy architect Arthur Heineman, who'd recently overseen the development of a series of residential bungalows, recognized the potential of adapting the bungalow concept for the travel industry, combining the convenience of a campground with the comfort and respectability (and higher prices) of a hotel.

Heineman and his brother Alfred opened the first motel in the auto nexus of San Luis Obispo but envisaged a chain stretching from San Diego to Seattle, each one-day's journey from the next, much like the first European settlements along the Camino Real – hence the Mission-style architecture of the existing *Milestone* building. Unfortunately, only one motel was built, and Heineman didn't even manage to copyright the word he'd formed as a contraction of "motor" and "hotel." It entered the dictionary in 1950, long after hundreds of copycats had sprung up across America.

The *Milestone*, then known as the *Motel Inn*, closed in the early 1990s, and fell into ten years of disrepair until its new owners launched an ambitious restoration plan a couple of years ago, which included linking it with the nearby *Apple Farm Inn*. Work is progressing slowly, and there's no firm date for its reopening – for up-to-date information, call *Apple Farm* at ☎805/544-2040 or 1-800/374-3705.

donation suggested; ☎805/543-6762), one of the county's oldest buildings, which was constructed by a disillusioned French forty-niner who, eluded by a fortune in the Mother Lode, ended up living in town. It's set among manicured grounds with two redwoods that are more than 125 feet tall.

If you have neither the time nor the inclination to sample the small-town charms of San Luis, at least stop to look at the now famous **Madonna Inn** (see "Accommodation" above). Featured in the cult classic film *Aria*, the *Inn* has rooms decorated in a variety of themes from fairy-tale princesses to Stone Age cavemen; its signature shocking pink has even been registered as an official color in the PMS printing system. A very different sort of place is the **Shakespeare Press Museum** on the Cal Poly campus (Mon–Fri by appointment; free; ☎805/756-2495, ⓦwww.grc.calpoly.edu) – nothing to do with the Bard, but a great collection of old printing presses and lead typefaces collected mainly from the frontier newspapers of California's Gold Rush towns.

Eating

Higuera Street is the place to head to **eat**, especially during the Thursday afternoon Farmer's Market, when barbecues and food stalls set up amidst the jostling crowds.

Apple Farm Restaurant 2015 Monterey St ☎805/544-6100. In the four-star *Apple Farm Inn*, this casual, family-style restaurant serves up traditional American dishes (try the chicken and dumplings) and is a surprisingly good value.

Benvenuti Ristorante 457 Marsh St ☎805/541-5393. Slightly upscale Italian food in an almost painfully cute restored Victorian house. Good wine list and lots of patio seating.

Big Sky Café 1121 Broad St ☎805/545-5401. An airy, modern place with an emphasis on Cajun and Creole food. $7 dishes and an assortment of coffees.

Blazing Blenders 1108 Broad St ☎805/546-8122. A small, studenty juice bar, with limited seating, massive fish tank, and meal-sized smoothies ($3.50).

Buona Tavola 1037 Monterey St ☎805/545-8000. Small and stylish bistro with good range of moderately priced northern Italian food and wine.

Café Roma 1020 Railroad Ave ☎805/541-6800. Extremely popular family-owned Italian restaurant with excellent pasta dishes served in a romantic setting for around $10.

F. McLintock's 686 Higuera St ☎805/541-0686. Mainstream bar restaurant that's always reassuringly busy: standard burgers, pasta, and sandwiches in

an Old West atmosphere for around $8 each.

Linn's S.L.O. Bin 1141 Chorro St ☎805/546-8444. Casual restaurant featuring a large variety of salads, soups, and sandwiches.

Oasis 675 Higuera St ☎805/543-1155. Unexpectedly delicious Middle Eastern cuisine in a souk-like setting: try the chicken delight with sweet potatoes and raisins. Excellent-value set lunches.

Royal Thai 777 Foothill Blvd in Foothill Plaza ☎805/544-9777. Extensive Thai menu – stick with chicken and beef to keep costs down. The lunch express menu is hearty, quick, and cheap.

Taj Palace 795 Foothill Blvd ☎805/543-0722. The city's one Indian choice is slightly pricier than what you might find in a city with more competition, but good.

Tortilla Flats 1051 Nipomo St ☎805/544-7575. Raucous, neon-lit Mexican restaurant, better known for copious margaritas than great food, but with free happy hour nachos and dancing from 9pm.

Z Pie 1060 Osos St ☎805/544-9743. Eccentric and tasty modern takes on the pot pie, with fillings including steak and cabernet or shrimp and roasted garlic, all for around $5. Filling and fun.

Bars and nightlife

San Luis Obispo's sizeable student population keeps **nightlife** edgier than you might expect for a small Californian town. Stop by the superb Boo Boo Records, 978 Monterey St (☎805/541-0657), one of the true holdouts in the tradition of great, independent record stores; their stock of music is vast, and you can also pick up CDs by, and tickets for, local bands. Reliable venues include the Performing Arts Center at Cal Poly (℡805/756-2787) and the Avila Beach Resort in nearby Avila Beach (℡805/786-2570)

You'll also find a couple of popular **bars** and **cafés** on and just off Higuera, around the Mission Plaza area. The café *Linnaea's*, 1110 Garden Street (℡805/541-5888, ⓦwww.linnaeas.com), serves good espresso and offers live music on Friday and Saturday nights, as well as an open mike night for budding rock stars each Wednesday. Otherwise, stop by *SLO Brewing Company*, 1119 Garden St (℡805/543-1943, ⓦwww.slobrew.com), which also hosts regular music and live performances.

Morro Bay and the coast to Cambria

North of San Luis Obispo the highways diverge again, US-101 – favored by trains and buses – speeds up through the Salinas Valley (see p.466), while Hwy-1 takes the more scenic route along the coast. The first dozen miles of Hwy-1 follow the line of a ridgeback string of hills, a series of plugs from extinct volcanoes, the most prominent of which have been dubbed the **Seven Sisters**. Two more continue the chain; the last is invisible under the sea, while the eighth is the **Morro Rock** in the sea close to the coast; according to local lore, it was named by the sixteenth-century explorer Juan Cabrillo, who thought it looked like the Moorish turbans in southern Spain. Nowadays, it's off limits to the public in order to protect the nesting areas of the endangered peregrine falcons; in any case it's most impressive from a distance, dominating the fine harbor at **MORRO BAY**, where the local fishing boats unload their catches to sell in the many fish markets along the waterfront.

This easy-paced resort town is accessible from San Luis Obispo via CCAT **buses** #7, 12, and 8 (twelve departures daily; $1, day-pass $3; ℡805/541-CCAT, ⓦwww.slorta.org), though apart from the many seafood restaurants the only places worth coming here for are spread around the bay, miles from public transportation. You get one of the best views of the rock and surrounding coastline from the top of **Cerro Alto**, a 2620-foot volcanic cone with good hiking and camping, eight miles east of Morro Bay off Hwy-41.

Closer in, on a point above the bay a mile south of town at the end of Main Street, but providing a good view of Morro Rock, there's the **Museum of Natural History** (closed for remodelling until late 2003, call for hours; $2; ℡805/772-2694, ⓦwww.mbspmuseum.org). When it reopens, it will be a state-of-the-art interactive ecology museum, although it's definitely pitched more to curious kids than adults. Otherwise, the **campground** across the street in **Morro Bay State Park** (reserve through ParkNet ℡1-800/444-7275) costs $12 a night and has hot showers. Across the bay, the thin sandy peninsula that protects the harbor is hard to reach except by boat – it's entirely undeveloped and about the only place where you stand a chance of finding any Pismo clams. You can rent **kayaks**, which cost about $8 per hour, from the likes of Kayak Horizons, 551 Embarcadero (℡805/772-6444, ⓦkayakhoriz @thegrid.net), or hike the two miles out there from Los Osos Valley Road.

Montaña de Oro State Park (daily dawn–dusk; free; ℡805/528-0513, ⓦwww.parks.ca.gov), four miles south at the end of Los Osos Valley Road, is much more primitive than Morro Bay State Park, and has some excellent tidepools as well as a good beach at Spooner's Cove. The windswept promontory stands solidly against the crashing sea, offering excellent hiking along the shore and through the sagebrush and eucalyptus trees of the upland hillsides, which in spring are covered in golden poppies.

There are $10 **campgrounds** in the park (call ParkNet ☎1-800/444-7275), and numerous reasonably priced **motels** in town, including a *Motel 6*, 298 Atascadero Rd (☎805/772-5641 or 1-800/4MOTEL6; ❷), close to the beach, and the cozier *El Morro Masterpiece Motel*, 1206 Main St (☎805/772-5633, Ⓦwww.masterpiecemotels.com; ❸). For **eating** try *Hofbrau Der Albatross*, 901 Embarcadero (☎805/772-2411), a deluxe burger joint with bratwurst on the menu; *Lolo's*, 2848 Main St (☎805/772-5686), for Mexican cuisine; and *The Coffee Pot Restaurant*, 1001 Front St (☎805/772-3176), for hearty breakfasts and lunches. The **Chamber of Commerce** is at 880 Main St (Mon–Fri

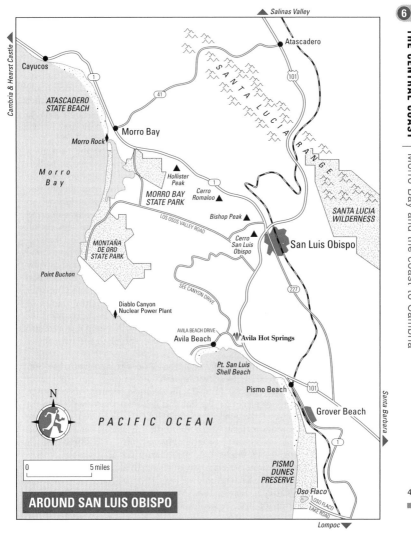

AROUND SAN LUIS OBISPO

8.30am–5pm, Sat 10am–4pm; ☎805/772-4467 or 1-800/231-0592, ⓦwww
.morrobay.org).

The next town north is **Cayucos**, four miles along Hwy-1, originally a small
port built by Englishman James Cass in the 1870s, and now a sleepy place
ranged along sandy beaches with a nice pier: it's a pleasant enough pit-stop on
a journey along the coast. *The Cypress Tree Inn*, 125 S Ocean Ave (☎805/995-
3917, ⓦwww.clia.com/cypresstreemotel-cayucos; ❶), is just one block from
the beach. For coffee, muffins, and pastries, you can't beat *Kelley's*, 155 N
Ocean Ave (☎805/995-2980). Surprisingly, the town also has some of the
area's best **nightlife** in *Ye Olde Cayucos Tavern and Card Room*, 130 N Ocean St
(☎805/995-3209), in the heart of the two-block-long ramshackle center, with
live bands on weekends and late-night poker games. The **Chamber of
Commerce** is at 767 Main St (Sept–April daily 9am–4pm; May–Aug daily
9am–5pm; ☎805/927-3624, ⓦwww.cambriachamber.org).

Cambria

About six miles to the north, you could drive right past **Harmony** without
even noticing it. This tiny hamlet has a population of 18, yet manages to operate several gift shops and offer wine tastings at Harmony Cellars (daily
10am–5pm; ☎805/927-1625). **CAMBRIA**, a few miles further, is a rather
twee, self-conscious town, glutted with pricey amenities thanks in part to
everything it's done to cash in on its proximity to San Simeon and Hearst
Castle, seven miles north. Hidden away in a wooded valley half a mile off Hwy-
1, Cambria was an established town serving the local ranchers and fishermen
long before Hearst Castle became the region's prime tourist attraction. Still, it
manages to keep its growing pains to a minimum, perhaps because its residents
have enacted ordinances that make view-blocking development illegal. The
older section of town, known as Main Village, is half a mile east of Hwy-1 on
Main Street, while the newer part with most of the cheaper hotels is referred
to as East Village. It's a comfortable enough place to stretch your legs or kill
some time till your scheduled tour at the castle begins, and holds one acknowledged oddity: **Nit Wit Ridge**, 881 Hillcrest Drive (tours daily by appointment; $10; ☎805/927-2690, ⓦwww.nitwit.com). This weird, whimsical folly
was the brainchild of one Art Beal, who came to Cambria from San Francisco
in the 1920s and bought a plot of land where, over a fifty-year period, he built
a Baroque castle out of trash. Recycling old toilet seats as picture frames or
water pipes as handrails, this eccentric misfit's glorious folly lay abandoned for
ten years after his death in 1989. Now, though, it's gradually being restored, and
a tour of the labyrinthine house is an offbeat counterpoint to the luxuries of
Hearst Castle.

The **Chamber of Commerce**, 767 Main St (Mon–Fri 9am–5pm, Sat–Sun
10am–4pm; ☎805/927-3624, ⓦwww.cambriachamber.org), can help with
accommodation. Back across Hwy-1, picturesque, seafront Moonstone
Beach Drive has plenty of places to stay, but you'll pay for the views. The most
reasonable rates are at *Castle Inn*, at no. 6620 (☎805/927-8605; ❹). More
affordable, though less dramatically situated are the *Cambria Palms Motel*, 2662
Main St (☎805/927-4485; ❶), or the *Bluebird Inn* at 1880 Main St
(☎805/927-4634 or 1-800/552-5434; ❶). **Camping** is available at San
Simeon State Park (☎805/927-0235), two miles north along the coast, where
sites with showers cost $14, $7 without.

You'll find good **food** at *Linn's*, 2277 Main St (☎805/927-0371), which
serves a good selection of brunch staples along with salads and sandwiches;

Robin's, 4095 Burton Drive (☎805/927-5007), which serves internationally influenced California meals at reasonable prices; and the *Sow's Ear*, 2248 Main St (☎805/927-4865), which attracts locals and visitors alike with giant American dinners heavy on seafood and meat. The *West End Bar & Grille*, 774 Main St (☎805/927-5521), is a friendly neighborhood pub with a large selection of beers, good meals, and live music.

Hearst Castle and San Simeon

Forty-five miles northwest of San Luis Obispo, **HEARST CASTLE** sits on a hilltop overlooking rolling ranchlands and the Pacific Ocean. Far and away the biggest single attraction for miles, the former holiday home of publishing magnate **William Randolph Hearst** is one of the most opulent and extravagant houses in the world. Its interior combines walls, floors, and ceilings torn from European churches and castles with Gothic fireplaces and Moorish tiles. Nearly every room is bursting with Greek vases and medieval tapestries, and even the many pools are lined with works of art. Ironically, the same financial power and lust for collecting that allowed Hearst to hoard these artifacts to himself have made them viewable to more people than ever would have seen them had they stayed in their respective lands. The castle, once only a weekend retreat for the most famous politicians and movie stars of the 1920s and 1930s – Hearst's highly selective range of guests included Winston Churchill, Charlie Chaplin, and Charles Lindbergh – now brings in more than a million visitors a year.

The Castle

Hearst Castle, which Hearst himself referred to as "the ranch" (the official name is now "Hearst San Simeon State Historic Monument"), is the extravagant palace one would expect from the man whose domination of the national media inspired Orson Welles's classic film *Citizen Kane*. The structure is actually more of a complex of buildings than a "castle." Three guesthouses circle the hundred-room main **Casa Grande**, in which Hearst himself held court. What may come as a surprise is the harmony with which the many diverse art treasures that Hearst collected were brought together by architect Julia Morgan, who designed each room and building in the spirit of the masterpieces destined to be housed inside (and received only $80,000 for her efforts). After the death of Hearst's mother in 1919, construction began on the southern edge of the inherited 250,000-acre ranch that became Hearst's own private free-roaming zoo with lions, tigers, zebras, and bears. The work was never truly completed: rooms would often be torn out as soon as they were finished in order to accommodate more acquired treasure. The main facade, a twin-towered copy of a Mudejar cathedral, stands at the top of steps that curve up from an expansive **swimming pool** (one of the most photographed in the world), which is filled with pure spring water and lined by a Greek colonnade and marble statues. Indoors there is another pool, lined with blue Venetian glass and gold tiles, with soft lights reflecting in the water's steamy surface.

Highlights inside the castle include the **Refectory**, lined with choir stalls from Spanish and Italian churches, and the **Gothic Suite**, where Hearst conducted his daily business in Middle Age splendor. The **private cinema** shouldn't be missed either – inside, Hearst saw first cuts of leading Hollywood films of the day before they were released to the general public. Outside the Castle proper there are several other major buildings, including the seventeen Neptune Pool dressing rooms, still hung with period swimwear and sports equipment; the Casa del Mar, an elaborate guesthouse with a largely Eastern theme; and the Casa del Monte, a smaller guesthouse with fully-furnished rooms overlooking the Santa Lucia Mountains. The estate's extensive Italian- and Spanish-influenced gardens, terraces, and walkways require a full tour in themselves as they feature hundreds of species of rare and imported flowers, bushes, and trees.

Castle practicalities

To see Hearst Castle, you must take one of the guided **tours** (June–Aug daily 8am–4pm; Sept–May daily 8am–3.20pm; $10–14; ☎916/414-8400 ext 4100 or 1-800/444-4445, ⓦwww.hearst-castle.org). The Experience Tour ($14), which includes a lush, slushy film on the building's construction plus an introductory spin around the guesthouse and the main rooms of the Casa Grande, is best for the first visit – to guarantee a spot on the tour, make a **reservation**. If you're coming back, or are simply fascinated enough to stay for the whole day, there are three other tours ($10 each): Tour Two takes in the upper floors of the main house, including Hearst's library and bedroom suite, which occupies an entire

William Randolph Hearst, the real life of Citizen Kane

It would be quite easy to portray **William Randolph Hearst** (or "W.R.") as a power-mad monster, but in retrospect he seems more like a very rich, over-indulged little boy. Born in 1863, the only son of a multi-millionaire mining engineer, he was avidly devoted to his mother, Phoebe Apperson Hearst, one of California's most sincere and generous philanthropists, a founder of the University of California and the Traveler's Aid society.

Hearst learned his trade in New York City working for the inventor of inflammatory "Yellow Journalism," Joseph Pulitzer, who had four rules for how to sell newspapers: emphasize the sensational; elaborate on the facts; manufacture the news; and use games and contests. When he published his own newspaper, Hearst took this advice to heart, his *Morning Journal* fanning the flames of American imperialism to ignite the Spanish-American War of 1898. As he told his correspondents in Cuba: "You provide the pictures, and I'll provide the war." Hearst eventually controlled an empire that, at its peak during the 1930s, sold 25 percent of the newspapers in the entire country, including two other New York papers, the *Washington Times*, and the *Detroit News* – as well as *Cosmopolitan* and *Good Housekeeping* magazines. In California , Hearst's power was even more pronounced, with his San Francisco and Los Angeles papers controlling over sixty percent of the total market.

Somewhat surprisingly, considering his warmongering and extreme nationalism, Hearst was fairly middle-of-the-road politically, a lifelong Democrat who served two terms in the House of Representatives but failed in bids to be elected mayor of New York and president of the US. Besides his many newspapers, Hearst owned eleven radio stations and two movie studios, in which he made his mistress Marion Davies a star. Although Hearst was married, his estranged wife disliked Hearst Castle, so Marion was queen-consort there. Her relationship with Hearst endured despite constant accusations of gold-digging and swirling rumors around a mysterious death onboard Hearst's boat (allegedly, Hearst murdered the man who was Davies' lover, and covered it up, a story recently featured in the movie *The Cat's Meow*). When the Depression hit, Hearst was forced to sell off most of his holdings but remained a wealthy man; he continued to exert power and influence until his death aged 88 at Marion Davies' ranch in 1951.

floor; Tour Three concentrates primarily on the Casa del Monte guesthouse; Tour Four (spring & summer only) is of the grounds, gardens, and wine cellar. From April through October, docents in period dress take visitors on evening tours of the castle ($20), speaking of Hearst in the present tense. These romantic tours end at the lamplit Neptune Pool, where guides tell stories of the legends who frolicked with each other there after dark. For more information on the tours, call the recorded information line at ☎805/927-2020 or 1-800/444-4445.

All tours take about two hours, and leave from the parking lot and visitor center on Hwy-1, where you also buy tickets. While waiting for the tour bus, find out more about Hearst and his castle from the excellent **museum** (daily 9am–5pm; free) in the rear half of the visitor center, beyond the point where you board the buses.

Finally, try and visit the castle first thing in the morning, when coastal fogs often hide the castle from the world below. After a long bus ride from the visitor center to the top of the steep hill on which the mansion rests, you poke through the clouds into sunlight, as if entering Heaven. The cherubic white statues seem to lift off the icy blue pool along with the last misty vapors of the morning.

San Simeon and north

The boarded-up pier of **SAN SIMEON**, an all-but-abandoned harbor town along the coast just north of Hearst Castle, is where all of Hearst's treasures were unloaded, as were the many tons of concrete and steel that went into the building of the house. Before the Hearsts bought up the land, San Simeon was a whaling and shipping port, of which all that remains is a one-room schoolhouse and the 1852 Sebastian's Store, a combination post office, café, and souvenir shop. The beach south of the pier is protected by San Simeon Point, which hooks out into the Pacific, making it safe for swimming. Along the highway three miles south there's a concentrated blot of gas stations, fast-food restaurants, and **motels**, mostly overpriced with the exception of a few along Castillo Drive, such as the *Motel 6 Premiere*, no. 9070 (☎805/927-8691 or 1-800/4-MOTEL6, ⓦwww.motel6.com; ❷) and the *Inns of California-San Simeon*, no. 9280 (☎805/927-8659 or 1-800/556-0400, ⓦwww.innsofcal.com; ❷), both with heated pools and rates that tend to double on weekends in summer. There's **camping** four miles south along the beach at San Simeon State Park (see p.462).

North of Hearst Castle the **coastline** is mostly rolling grasslands and cattle ranches, still owned and run by the Hearst family, with few buildings on the distant hills. About three miles past San Simeon, a small strip of sand provides a resting point for a large colony of seals in the fall and early winter; trails – officially off limits to the public, though easily negotiated by the brave and healthy – lead past a gate near the car park down to the beach, where you can watch the huge piles of blubber cuddle one another and frolic in the waves. Beyond here the highway seems to drop off in mid-air, marking the southern edge of Big Sur (see p.471), one of the most dramatic stretches of coastline in America.

The Salinas Valley and Steinbeck Country

If you're in a hurry, US-101 through the **Salinas Valley** takes four hours to cover the 220 miles between San Luis Obispo and San Francisco, compared to the full day it takes to drive the more scenic coast along Hwy-1 through Big

Sur. In any case, as both Greyhound and Amtrak take the inland route, you may not have the choice; Amtrak's Thruways service barrels through the area, while Greyhound's local buses stop at all the small rural towns. The four-lane freeway closely follows the path of El Camino Real, the trail that linked the 21 Spanish **missions** through the miles of farmland along the Salinas River that are some of the most fertile in the nation and earned it the nickname of the "Salad Bowl of the World," thanks to the millions of lettuces produced here each summer.

This region is also popularly known as **Steinbeck Country** for having nurtured the imagination of Nobel Prize-winning writer John Steinbeck, whose naturalistic stories and novels, including the epic *East of Eden*, were set in and around the valley.

The Salinas Valley

North of San Luis Obispo over the steep Cuesta Pass, US-101 drops down into the **SALINAS VALLEY** and, before long, **Atascadero**: a small town laid out to a curiously grand plan in 1914 that centers on its Palladian City Hall, 6500 Palma Ave, a huge red-brick edifice whose domed rotunda now houses a small **museum** (Mon–Sat 1–4pm; free; ℡805/466-8341) describing the area's history. A few miles north, **Templeton** has a strip of historic Wild West buildings along Main Street, among them the town's museum and information center in the **Albert Horstman House** (Fri–Sun 1–4pm; free; ℡805/434-0807). Down the block at no. 424, chocolate is a science at Herrmann's Chocolate Lab (Mon–Thurs 11.30am–7pm, Fri–Sat 11.30am–8pm, Sun 11.30 am–6.30pm; ℡805/434-3007, ⓦwww.hermannschocolatelab.com), which sells chocolate-dipped everything and can custom shape chocolate with some advance notice.

Paso Robles (pronounced "Robe-ulls"), a few more miles north, is a thriving little town surrounded by horse ranches, nut farms, and a number of **wineries** that are among the finest in the state. The Paso Robles Vintners and Growers (℡805/239-8463, ⓦwww.pasowine.com) publish a free map to their wine country, which can also be picked up at the town's Chamber of Commerce, 1225 Park St (Mon–Fri 8.30am–5pm, Sat 10am–4pm; ℡805/238-0506 or 1-800/406-4040, ⓦwww.pasorobleschamber.com). The pick of the many vineyards include three situated just east of town on Hwy-46: Eberle (daily 10am–6pm; ℡805/238-9607, ⓦwww.eberlewinery.com), Meridian (daily 10am–5pm; ℡805/237-6000, ⓦwww.meridianvineyards.com), and the lively Tobin James Cellars (daily 10am–6pm; ℡805/239-2204, ⓦwww.tobin-james.com). In town, there are a number of **accommodations** of much better value than anything you'll find closer to Hearst's former abode. The *Holiday Inn Express Hotel*, at 2455 Riverside Ave (℡805/238-6500 or 1-800/465-4329, ⓦwww.holidayinnpaso.com; ❺), is a reasonable mid-range option; for more luxury, stay at the *Paso Robles Inn*, 1103 Spring St (℡805/238-2660 or 1-800/676-1713, ⓦwww.pasoroblesinn.com; ❺), which has rooms with two-person tubs on the balconies, with water fed from local hot springs.

In the center of town, just off the town square, excellent **restaurants** include *El Oasis*, 1704 Spring St (℡805/239-7606), serving budget-priced, cooked-to -order Mexican food in an old shack, and the *Park Grill* at 1510 Park St (℡805/239-3721), with everything from burgers and pizza to pastas and salads. Ten miles east of town, past the junction of Hwy-41 near Cholame, pay your respects at the stainless-steel monument near the site where **James Dean** crashed in a silver Porsche Speedster on September 30, 1955.

Even if you're racing up US-101, it's only a thirty-minute break from your journey for an essential peek at one of the least visited yet the most intact and authentic of California's Spanish missions, **Mission San Miguel Arcangel**, 801 Mission St (daily 9.30am–4.30pm; free; ☎805/469-3256), just off the freeway in the small town of **San Miguel**. Founded in 1797 as the sixteenth mission in the chain, the current building dates from 1816 and is the only mission to have suffered the revisionist tendencies of a restoration. It was actually used for a while as a saloon and dance hall, though the chapel was left pretty much unscathed, with colorful painted decoration and a marvelous sunburst reredos, complete with a striking *Eye of God*, all painted by Native Americans. The other buildings are interesting too, in their rough imprecision, with irregularly arched openings and unplastered walls forming a courtyard around a cactus garden. The *Western States Inn*, right off Hwy-101 at 1099 K St (☎805/467-3674; ❸), is the only hotel in town and has surprisingly comfortable rooms.

There's a second mission, accessible only by car, twenty miles west of US-101 along the Jolon Road (G-18), which splits off the highway twelve miles north of San Miguel near the town of Jolon. The **Mission San Antonio de Padua** (summer daily 8am–6pm; winter daily 8am–5pm; $1; ☎831/385-4478, ⓦwww.missionsanantoniopadua.com) is a rarely visited restoration of the 1771 original settlement. Less sanitized than some of the other California missions, it gives a very good idea of what life might have been like for the missionaries and their converts. Third to be founded, this mission was among the most prosperous of the entire chain, and around the extensive grounds, in a wide valley of oak trees and tall grasses, a number of scattered exhibits describe the work that went on in the long-abandoned vineyard, tannery, and gristmill. There's a monastic peace to Mission San Antonio these days, and the brown-robed Franciscan friars who live here are rarely disturbed, despite being eerily situated inside Hunter Liggett Army Base. Indeed, the only sign of the military is at the gates of the base, five miles east of the mission, where you'll have to show your passport or some other form of ID. The large house across the valley from the mission used to belong to Hearst, who sold it and most of the land between here and Hearst Castle to the government in 1940 to help clear a $120-million debt. Today, the *Hacienda Guest Lodge* (☎831/386-2900, ⓦwww.usawines.com/hacienda; ❶ without bath, ❷ with bath), as it's now called, offers basic, if rather monastic, **accommodation**.

Nearby **Jolon** has a market and gas station, and the washed-out ruins of an 1840s stagecoach stop at the *Old Dutton Hotel*. **Lake San Antonio** (daily 24 hrs, visitors center open Mon–Fri 8am–4pm; $6 per vehicle; ☎805/472-2311 or 1-888/588-2267, ⓦwww.co.monterey.ca.us/parks), five miles southeast, has swimming, first-come-first-served **camping** ($18–22) and showers along the west shore, as does the Nacimiento Reservoir further south. There are normally more campsites along the Nacimiento–Fergusson Road, which leads west from Jolon on a tortuous but picturesque journey over the mountains to Big Sur (see p.471); in 1999, 80,000 acres of the **Ventana Wilderness** burned in a tragic fire – started by a particularly violent lightning storm – that took months to be contained. Though things are nearly back to normal, it's not uncommon for natural disasters to befall this area and visitors should call ahead for the latest updates before planning any excursions in the area. The **US Forest Service office**, off the freeway at 406 S Mildred Ave (Mon–Fri 8am–4.30pm; ☎831/385-5434, ⓦwww.r5.fs.fed.us/lospadres), handles questions about the area and issues backpacking permits for the **Santa Lucia Mountains**, which divide the Salinas Valley from the Big Sur coast.

The Jolon Road loops back to US-101 at **King City**: "the most metropolitan cow town in the West," as it likes to be known. On the town's western edge, just off US-101, San Lorenzo Park is the site of the **Agricultural and Rural**

Life Museum (daily 10am–4pm; free, parking weekdays $3, weekends $5; ☎831/385-8020), a collection of old barns, farmhouses, and a one-room schoolhouse, all gathered here from various sites in Monterey County. The park also has a campground along the Salinas River.

The Pinnacles National Monument and around

From King City, you have a choice of approaches to the bizarre rock formations of the **Pinnacles National Monument**. Either follow G-13 and Hwy-25 to the eastern entrance and the visitor center (park daily 7.30am–8pm, visitor center daily 8am–4.30pm; $5 per vehicle, good for seven days; ☎831/389-4485, ⓦwww.nps.gov/pinn), or continue up Hwy-101 to Soledad (see below) and turn onto Hwy-146 to the more spectacular western side. Contrary to what appears on some maps, no road goes right through the monument, but the place is small and it is quite possible to hike from one side to the other and back in a day.

This region of startling volcanic spires, brilliant reds and golds against the blue sky, is best visited in the spring, when the air is still cool and the chaparral hillsides are lushly sprinkled with wildflowers, in particular the orange California poppy and deep-lilac owl's clover. Its many **trails** include a popular two-mile loop around the high peaks on the **Juniper Canyon Trail**, and the two-mile **Balconies Trail** to the multicolored, 600-foot face of the Balconies outcrop – good for rock climbing (register at the visitor center and use only brown chalk when climbing) – and a nearby series of talus **caves** (take a flashlight) formed by huge boulders that have become wedged between the walls of the narrow canyons. These dark caves were popular with bandits who would hide out here after robbing stagecoaches. Rangers at both the east and west entrances can set you up with information and permits if you're interested in trying out some of the more advanced trails or if you'd like to do **climbing**, **top-roping** or **bouldering**. The trails are exposed so avoid hiking in the middle of the day in summer, and remember to carry plenty of water. There are several private and state-run **campgrounds** on either side of the park, the largest of which is the swimming pool-equipped *Pinnacles Campground Inc.* (reservations office open Tues–Thurs 4–6pm, Fri 4–9pm, Sat–Sun 9am–5pm; $7 per person; ☎831/389-4462, ⓦwww.pinncamp.com) – reservations are essential in summer.

Soledad, Mission Soledad, and Paraiso Hot Springs

The nearest town to the Pinnacles is **SOLEDAD**, a quiet farming community twelve miles west of the western entrance, best known as the site of the Soledad State Penitentiary – a grim building looming alongside US-101 two miles north of town where black militant "Soledad Brother" George Jackson was imprisoned for many years. The town itself has a definite Mexican flavor, its *panaderias* selling cakes and fresh tortillas – a good place to stock up on food and drink for a trip to the monument. But the main reason to stop is **Mission Nuestra Señora de la Soledad** (daily 10am–4pm; free; ☎831/678-2586), three miles west of US-101 on the south side of town. The thirteenth mission in the chain lay neglected for over a hundred years until it was little more than a pile of mud. Never a great success (perhaps because of its full name, which translates as the "most sorrowful mystery of the solitude"), the mission suffered through a history of epidemics, floods, and crop failures. Parts have been dutifully restored and now contain a museum on mission life, but the ruins adjacent to the rebuilt church are the most evocative section.

More hedonistically, you could head out to **Paraiso Hot Springs**, 34358 Paraiso Springs Rd (daily 8am–5pm; ☎831/678-2882), seven miles further west, high above Soledad in the foothills of the Santa Lucia Mountains. A palm-treed oasis looking out across the Salinas Valley to the Gabilan Mountains and the Pinnacles National Monument, the natural hot springs were popular with the local Native Americans for their healing properties, and have been operated as a commercial venture since 1895. The series of outdoor pools costs $25 a day to enter (there's an additional $5 charge to use the 106°F indoor bath), and you can camp here overnight for $5 more; there are also various cabins starting at $88.40 for double occupancy.

Salinas and around

The second-largest city between LA and San Francisco, and the seat of Monterey County, **SALINAS**, twenty miles north of Soledad and Paraiso, is a sprawling agricultural town of 120,000 people. It's best known as the birthplace of **John Steinbeck**, and for the **California Rodeo** (tickets $11–18; ☎1-800/549-4989, ⓦwww.carodeo.com), held during the third week in July and the biggest in the state. These attractions aside, you may well find yourself here anyway – Salinas is a main stop for Greyhound buses and the Coast Starlight train, and makes an inexpensive base for exploring the perhaps more obvious attractions of the **Monterey Peninsula**, twenty miles away over the Santa Lucia Mountains, with the MST bus #21 making the 55-minute trip every hour from the Transit Center on Salinas Street.

Salinas and the agricultural valley to the south are often bracketed together as Steinbeck Country. The writer John Steinbeck was born and raised in Salinas, but left the town in his mid-twenties to live in Monterey and later in New York City. His childhood home at 132 Central Ave (daily 11.30am–2pm; ☎831/424-2735) has been turned into an English-style tearoom called the *Steinbeck House* – there isn't much to see, so this is only a stop for diehard Steinbeck fans. The gigantic new **National Steinbeck Center**, 1 Main St (daily10am–5pm; $9.95; ☎831/796-3833, ⓦwww.steinbeck.org), on the other

---

The novels of John Steinbeck

John Steinbeck's novels and stories are as valuable and interesting for their historical content as for their narratives. **The Grapes of Wrath**, his best-known work, was made into a film starring Henry Fonda while still at the top of the bestseller lists, having captured the popular imagination for its portrayal of the miseries of the Joad family on their migration to California from the dust bowl. *Cannery Row* followed in 1945, a nostalgic portrait of the Monterey fisheries, which ironically went into steep decline the year the book was published. Steinbeck spent the next four years writing *East of Eden*, an allegorical retelling of the biblical story of Cain and Abel against the landscape of the Salinas Valley; in this book, which he saw as his masterpiece, Steinbeck expresses many of the values that underlie the rest of his work. Much of Steinbeck's writing is concerned with the dignity of labor, and with the inequalities of an economic system that "allows children to go hungry in the midst of rotting plenty." Although he was circumspect about his own political stance, when *The Grapes of Wrath* became a bestseller in 1939 there was a violent backlash against Steinbeck in Salinas for what were seen as his Communist sympathies. Later, he was so wounded at the outcry over his worthiness of the Nobel Prize for Literature in 1962 that he never wrote another word. He died in New York City in 1968; today his ashes are buried in Salinas in the **Garden of Memories Cemetery**, 768 Abbott St.

hand, is an excellent introduction, taking you on a sprightly, interactive journey through his life and work. A fifteen-minute biographical film shown in a constant loop at the museum's entrance is an informative and lively introduction to Steinbeck, and sets the tone for the rest of the museum. If you know very little of the author, then you will find the exhibits throughout engaging enough and might even be inspired to purchase a novel or two from the center's large supply. However, if you're already well versed in Steinbeck and his oeuvre, your time will be better spent using the center's informative map to cruise by all the actual places in the surrounding area that were influential in the writer's life.

Today, as much as in Steinbeck's day, Salinas is a hotbed of labor disputes, with the gap between the low-paid manual laborers who pick the produce and the wealthy owners of agribusiness empires who run the giant farms still unbridged. In the 1960s and early 1970s, the United Farm Workers union, under the leadership of Cesar Chavez and Dolores Huerta, had great success in organizing and demanding better pay and working conditions for the almost exclusively Latino workforce, most notably masterminding a very effective boycott of the valley's main product, lettuce. But workers are once again under siege, with wages less than half of what they were two decades ago amidst increasing worries about the dangers of exposure to pesticides and agricultural chemicals.

At the end of West Laurel Drive, a mile west of US-101, the **Boronda Adobe** is worth a visit only if you have an afternoon to spare. Located in the middle of a beautiful drive through rich farmland, the simple, Old California-style building has been virtually unaltered since its construction in 1848, and rests alongside other historic structures that have been brought to the site as part of an expanding regional history center.

Between Salinas and the Monterey Peninsula, twenty miles distant via Hwy-68, are a couple of other places of divergent interest. **Spreckels**, five miles southwest, is a small factory town built in 1898 for employees of the Spreckels sugar factory, at the time the largest in the world: the small, torchlike wooden objects on the gable ends of the many workers' cottages are supposed to represent sugar beets. Parts of the movie *East of Eden* were filmed here, including the famous scene when James Dean – playing Cal – hurls blocks of ice down a chute to get his father's attention.

Practicalities

Hourly Greyhound buses between LA and San Francisco stop in the center of town at 19 W Gabilan St near Salinas Street, while Amtrak trains leave once a day in each direction, two blocks away at 40 Railroad Ave. For a handy **place to stay**, try the *Traveler's Hotel* at 16 E Gabilan St (☎831/758-1198; ❷), which is more convenient than pleasant; frankly, if you're driving, choose from the many $45-a-night motels along Main Street on either side of US-101. For help with finding a place to stay, and for a free map and guide to the places that Steinbeck wrote about, contact the **Chamber of Commerce** at 119 E Alisal St (Mon 9am–5pm, Tues–Fri 8.30am–5pm; ☎831/424-7611, ⓦwww.salinaschamber.com). There are quite a few good Mexican **restaurants** around the city, the best, oldest, and most central being *Rosita's Armory Café*, 231 Salinas St (☎831/424-7039), open daily from 9am until midnight for fine food and stiff margaritas.

6

The Big Sur Coast

BIG SUR is the nebulous name used to describe the ninety miles of rocky cliffs and crashing seas along the Californian coast, just south of the Monterey Peninsula. It's not an official designation, and there are no marked boundaries: instead, you'll know you're in Big Sur when the estuaries and beaches of the Central Coast have been replaced by craggy rock faces and distant redwood groves. Named by the Spanish *El Pais Grande del Sur* (the "big country to the south" of their colony at Monterey), it's still a wild and undeveloped region that's breathtakingly unspoilt given its proximity to San Francisco and other cities.

Before Hwy-1 was completed in 1937, the few inhabitants of Big Sur had to be almost entirely self-sufficient, farming, raising cattle, and trapping sea otters for their furs. The only connections with the rest of the world were by infrequent steamship to Monterey, or by a nearly impassable trail over the mountains to the Salinas Valley. Despite the better transport links, the area's growing more remote as each year passes, with fewer people living here today than a hundred years ago; most of the land is still owned by a handful of families, many of whom are descendants of Big Sur's original pioneers. Locals have banded together to protect the land from obtrusive development and to fight government plans to allow offshore oil drilling, and their ornery determination seems to be paying off.

The Big Sur Coast is also the protected habitat of the **sea otter**, and **gray whales** pass by close to the shore on their annual winter migration. Visit in April or May to see the vibrant **wildflowers** and lilac-colored ceanothus bushes, though the sun shines longest, without the morning coastal fog, in early autumn through until November. Hardly anyone braves the turbulent winters, when violent storms drop most of the eighty inches of rain that fall each year in the region, often taking sections of the highway with it into the sea. Summer weekends, however, see the roads and campgrounds packed to overflowing and the wildness of the area is dampened by the hundreds of people you'll see.

Resist the temptation to try and see Big Sur in a single day: the best way to enjoy its isolation and beauty is slowly. Leave the car behind as often as you can and wander through parks and wilderness preserves, where a ten-minute walk takes you from any sign of the rest of the world.

Arrival, information, and getting around

The only public transportation through Big Sur is the summer-only (May–Oct) MST bus #22 from Monterey (see p.480), which runs as far south as Nepenthe, four times a day in each direction. Whether coming from San Francisco to the north or San Luis Obispo to the south, it's always a good idea to stop by the local tourism offices at either end of the long coastal road to check on the current weather and driving conditions.

There is no Big Sur Village as such, and facilities like gas stations and grocery stores are surprisingly scarce – expect those you do find to be premium priced, so it's best to fill your gas tank and go shopping before you hit the deserted coastline. Pick up a copy of the free *El Sur Grande* newspaper (ⓦ www.bigsurcalifornia.org) as soon as you can, since its comprehensive listings are an invaluable resource: you can find it at park information offices and some stores along the route. Otherwise, call the **Chamber of Commerce** (Mon, Wed, Fri 9am–1pm; ☏831/667-2100, ⓦ www.bigsurcalifornia.org) or stop by the Pfeiffer Big Sur State Park headquarters (☏831/667-2315).

While the narrow Hwy-1 is a perennial favorite with cyclists despite its pre-cipitous curves, most visitors will need a car to travel through the area, follow-ing the dramatic coast road as it winds a tortuous, exhilarating route through bedrock cliffs five hundred feet above the Pacific Ocean. The three main inhab-ited areas are at Big Sur's northern end, close to the **Pfeiffer Big Sur State Park**: around the post office two miles south of the park; at Fernwood, a mile north past the main entrance; and at The Village, a further mile and a half north. It's the northern end of Big Sur around Hwy-1 that's both developed and most interesting for first-time visitors. Pfeiffer Big Sur State Park is a fantastic base for exploring: you can swim among giant boulders, hike up redwood canyons to a waterfall, or sunbathe on a fine sandy beach. If you're feeling more intrepid, venture into the **Ventana Wilderness** or the **Santa Lucia Mountains**, although note that both have recently suffered great damage due to wildfires.

There's no official notation for addresses in Big Sur, so we've used the distance from major landmarks as an approximate guide for listings along Hwy-1.

Accommodation

In keeping with Big Sur's backwoodsy qualities, most of the available **accom-modation** is in rustic (but rarely inexpensive) mountain lodges, and the very few rooms on offer are full most nights throughout the summer, especially on weekends. Mid-range accommodation is limited to a few cabins and motels, usually adjoining a privately operated campground or right along the highway, and not really ideal for getting the total Big Sur experience.

Lodges and cabins

Big Sur Campgrounds and Cabins a mile north of Pfeiffer Big Sur State Park on Hwy-1 ☎831/667-2322. Campground with the best of the cabins: wooden tent affairs sleeping up to three for $40 and fancier places from $65. ⑤
Big Sur Lodge in Pfeiffer Big Sur State Park ☎ 831/667-3100 or 1-800/424-4787, ⊛www .bigsurlodge.com. These plushly furnished rooms have porches and enormous sit-down showers but no phones, TVs, alarm clocks, or radios; the park entrance fee's included in the rate. There's also a pricey café onsite (around $25 per entrée). ⑤
Big Sur River Inn Resort two and a half miles north of Pfeiffer Big Sur State Park on Hwy-1 ☎831/667-2700 or 1-800/548-3610. Woodsy lodge with a handful of very nice (if pricey) rooms

overlooking the river, and more basic motel-style rooms across Hwy-1. ④
Deetjen's Big Sur Inn on Hwy-1 seven miles north of Julia Pfeiffer Burns State Park ☎831/667-2377. Built by Norwegian immigrant "Grandpa" Deetjen, this compound is now a non-profit organization, offering lodging in ski-lodge-style log cabins, with fireplaces, rocking chairs, and old-fashioned leaded windows. ④ shared bath, ⑤ private
Glen Oaks Motel just over a mile north of Pfeiffer Big Sur State Park on Hwy-1 ☎831/667-2105. Simple rooms, friendly staff, and one of the best bargains in the area. There's a separate cottage that can make a smart option for groups of 4. No credit cards. ④, cottage ⑥

Southern Big Sur

The southern coastline of Big Sur is the region at its most gentle – not unlike Portugal's Algarve, with sandy beaches hidden away below eroding yellow-ochre cliffs. The landscape grows more extreme the further north you go. Twenty miles north of Hearst Castle, a steep trail leads down along Salmon Creek to a coastal waterfall, while the chaparral-covered hills above were booming during the 1880s with the gold mines of the **Los Burros Mining District**.

Another ten miles north, the cliffs get steeper and the road more perilous around the vista point at **Willow Creek**, where you can watch the surfers and

Camping in Big Sur

Public campgrounds are dotted all along **the Big Sur Coast**, in addition to a few less-developed ones in the **Santa Lucia Mountains** above, where you can also see deer, bobcats, and (rarely) mountain lions. Sites along the coast are popular year-round, and all, unless otherwise stated, are available for around $16 a night on a first-come-first-served basis, so get there early in the day to ensure a space. Reservations are, however, taken at the **State Park** sites (call ParkNet ☎1-800/444-7275): most cost $12, other than *Andrew Molera*, which is a bargain at $1 per site. For further **information** on camping in Big Sur, phone the park directly (☎831/667-2315). The following campgrounds are listed south to north.

Plaskett Creek ☎877/444-6677 or 805/434-1996. Thirty miles north of Hearst Castle and a mile south of Pacific Valley. Across the highway from the ocean with some hiker/biker sites. $16

Kirk Creek ☎805/434-1996. Three miles north of Pacific Valley and more exposed, but right on the ocean and with hiker/biker sites. $16

Limekiln State Park ☎831/667-2403. Two miles south of Lucia, with hot showers, general store, and developed trail to the limekilns. $12

Julia Pfeiffer Burns State Park ☎831/667-2315. This has two campgrounds, beautifully situated overlooking the Pacific at the end of the Overlook Trail. There's no water, the toilets are primitive, and the area is often windy and chilly even in summer. $12

Pfeiffer Big Sur State Park This is the main campground in the area, with spacious and well-shaded sites, many among the redwoods. Hot showers, a well-stocked store, a laundrette, and some (officially) biker-only sites. $12

Andrew Molera State Park The only walk-in site around. A vast ten-acre meadow, half a mile from the beach, with water and latrines. First-come-first-served basis, so show up early. Camping payment waives day-use fee. $1

There are also four commercially operated **campgrounds** in the Big Sur Valley: *Ventana* (☎831/667-2712; $24 per site), *Fernwood* (☎831/667-2422; $24), *Riverside* (☎831/667-2414, ◍www.riversidecampground.com; $28), and *Big Sur* (☎831/667-2322; $26). All charge about $24 a night for two people, offer deluxe facilities, and accept reservations; they also rent out **cabins** (see "Accommodation" below). By Californian standards, all are fairly crowded, and all but *Riverside* mix tents with RVs.

the sea otters playing in the waves. **Jade Cove**, a mile north, takes its name from the translucent California jade stones that are sometimes found here, mainly by scuba divers offshore. The rocky cove is a ten-minute walk from the highway, along a brambly trail marked by a wooden stile in the cattle fence: the close-up views of the crashing waves reinforce the awesome power of the sea.

Just beyond the Plaskett Creek **campground**, half a mile to the north, **Sand Dollar Beach** is a good place to enjoy the surf or watch for **hang-gliders**, launched from sites in the mountains off the one-lane Plaskett Ridge Road. This steep road is good fun on a mountain bike, and passes by a number of free, basic campgrounds along the ridge, ending at the paved Nacimiento–Fergusson Road. Check at the **Pacific Valley ranger station** (irregular hours; ☎805/927-4211) for up-to-date information on backcountry camping, since some areas may be closed in summer during the peak of the fire season. The station also handles the 25 permits a day allowed to people wanting to hang-glide, ten of which are given out on a first-come-first-served basis on the day. **Pacific Valley Center**, a mile north, has an expensive gas station, a grocery store, and a good coffee shop, open from 8am until dark.

Kirk Creek to Julia Pfeiffer Burns State Park

The coastal **campground** at **KIRK CREEK** (see p.473) sits at the foot of the Nacimiento–Fergusson Road, which twists over the Santa Lucia Mountains to the Salinas Valley. The road passes the excellent Mission San Antonio de Padua (see p.467), but it would be a shame to break the continuity of the drive up the coast, and in any case the views are better coming over the hills in the other direction. Two miles north of here, **Limekiln Creek** is named after the hundred-year-old kilns that survive in good condition along the creek behind the privately owned **campground**. In the 1880s local limestone was burned in these kilns to extract lime powder for use as cement, then carried on a complex aerial tramway to be loaded onto ships at Rockland Landing. The ships that carried the lime to Monterey brought in most of the supplies to this isolated area.

Esalen, ten miles further north, is named after the local Native Americans, the first tribe in California to be made extinct. Before they were wiped out, they frequented the healing waters of the natural **hot spring** here, at the top of a cliff two hundred feet above the raging Pacific surf – now owned and operated by the Esalen Institute (information ☎831/667-3000, reservations ☎831/667-3005, ⒲www.esalen.org). Since the 1960s, when all sorts of people came to Big Sur to smoke dope and get back to nature, Esalen has been at the forefront of the "New Age" human potential movement. Today's devotees tend to arrive in BMWs on Friday nights for the expensive, reservation-only massage treatments, yoga workshops, and seminars on "potentialities and values of human existence" – if you want to join them, make sure to reserve a place well in advance.

JULIA PFEIFFER BURNS STATE PARK (daily dawn–dusk; free; ☎831/667-2315, ⒲www.parks.ca.gov), three miles north of Esalen along McWay Creek, has some of the best day-hikes in the Big Sur area: a ten-minute walk from the parking area leads under the highway along the edge of the cliff to an overlook of McWay Falls, which crash onto a beach below Saddle Rock. A less-traveled path leads down from Hwy-1 two miles north of the waterfall (at milepost 37.85) through a two-hundred-foot-long tunnel to the wave-washed remains of a small wharf at **Partington Cove**, one of the few places in Big Sur where you can get to the sea.

Nepenthe and Pfeiffer Beach

Just before you reach **NEPENTHE** (see below), you'll pass the Henry Miller Library across Hwy-1 (daily 11am–6pm, closed Tues; free; ☎831/667-2574, ⒲www.henrymiller.org). Miller's own home, further south on the Big Sur Coast, is now a private residence, but this house was owned by his old friend Emil White, and stands as a ramshackle bookshop-cum-monument to the work of the author who lived in the area on and off until the 1960s. There's little Millerabilia, but the secluded front lawn is a pleasant and cheap place to grab a coffee. It's with Nepenthe that Big Sur's commercial development starts in earnest: it's little more than a complex of restaurants and stores named after the mythical drug that induces forgetfulness. It stands atop the hilltop site where star-crossed lovers Orson Welles and Rita Hayworth once shared a cabin. The terribly overpriced restaurants here have been emptying the pockets of reflective visitors in search of upscale romance since the 1960s, though *Café Kevah* (see "Eating and drinking," below), on a slightly lower terrace in the same building, is more affordable and has better views (although a coffee still costs $4). Downstairs there's an outdoor sculpture gallery and a decent bookstore, including a wide selection of works by Miller.

Two miles north along Hwy-1, the unmarked Sycamore Canyon Road leads a mile west to Big Sur's best beach, **PFEIFFER BEACH** (open until dusk), a sometimes windy, white-sand stretch dominated by a charismatic hump of rock whose color varies from brown to red to orange in the changing light. Park where you can at the end of the road and walk through an archway of cypress trees along the lagoon to the sands. Note that the beach has been undergoing major renovations and, at time of writing, has remained closed for more than a year with no scheduled reopening date – call ☏831/667-2315 for up-to-date information.

The Big Sur River Valley

Two miles north of Pfeiffer Beach, Hwy-1 drops down behind a coastal ridge into the valley of the Big Sur River, where most of the accommodation and eating options are located. The first stop should be the Big Sur Ranger Station (summer daily 8am–6pm; winter daily 8am–4.30pm; ☏831/667-2315), which handles the camping permits for the Ventana Wilderness in the mountains above and is the center for information on all the other parks in the area. A popular hike leads steeply up from the Pine Ridge trailhead behind the station, ten miles into the mountains to **Sykes Hot Springs** (unrestricted entry), just downstream from the free campground at *Sykes Camp* along the Big Sur River. This is an overnight expedition, at least five hours' walk each way; don't forget to pick up a fire permit, if you plan to cook.

Plumb in the middle of the valley, the **Pfeiffer Big Sur State Park** (daily dawn–dusk; $3 per vehicle; ☏831/667-2315, ⓦwww.parks.ca.gov) is one of the most beautiful and enjoyable parks in California, with miles of hiking trails and excellent swimming along the Big Sur River. In late spring and summer, the river has deep swimming holes among the large boulders in the bottom of the narrow steep-walled gorge, and the water is clean and clear. Nude sun-bathing is tolerated (except on national holidays, when the park tends to be overrun with swarms of screaming children) and, since it's sheltered a mile or so inland, the weather is warmer and sunnier than elsewhere along the coast. This is also the main **campground** ($24) in the Big Sur region.

The most popular hiking trail in the park leads to the sixty-foot **Pfeiffer Falls**, half a mile up a narrow canyon shaded by redwood trees, from a trailhead opposite the entrance. The thoroughly functional bridges over the river have an understated grace, as does the nearby amphitheater – built by the Civilian Conservation Corps during the Depression – where rangers give excellent campfire talks and slide shows about Big Sur during the summer season.

Eating and drinking

Most of the places to **eat and drink** in Big Sur are attached to the inns and resorts listed on p.472. Many of these are fairly basic burger-and-beer bars right along the highway, but there are a few special ones worth searching out, some for their good food and others for their views of the Pacific. Because of its isolation, prices anywhere in Big Sur are around 25 percent higher than you'd pay in town.

Big Sur River Inn Resort at the north end of The Village ☏831/667-2700. The slightly upscale restaurant features a creative range of sautéed and grilled seafood starters and hearty main dishes served in a spacious, redwood-log dining room. In summer, you can linger over lunch and cocktails on the sunny terrace or in the riverside garden; in winter, the fireplace attracts locals and visitors alike. Live entertainment on the weekend.

Café Kevah Nepenthe ☏831/667-2344. Tasty, if slightly overpriced, organic concoctions served up café-style on a sunny, outdoor terrace; some of the best views around, but stick to the snacks. March–Dec 9am–4pm.

Deetjen's Big Sur Inn on Hwy-1 seven miles north of Julia Pfeiffer Burns State Park ☎831/667-2378. Excellent, unhurried breakfasts ($8) and a variety of top-quality fish and vegetarian dinners ($13–25) in a snug, redwood-paneled room.

Fernwood Hwy-1 a mile north of Pfeiffer Big Sur State Park ☎831/667-2422. For burgers or fish-and-chips, this budget diner is the place. There's a small grocery store/deli in the same building if you want to pick up supplies for a picnic.

Glen Oaks Restaurant Hwy-1 in The Village ☎831/667-2264. Gourmet California cuisine – mostly fresh fish and pasta dishes $12–16, with some vegetarian options – in a cozy, flower-filled cottage.

Nepenthe Nepenthe ☎831/667-2345. Next to the *Café Kevah*, this overpriced steak-and-seafood place has raging fires, an amazing view, and a James Bond-ish après-ski atmosphere.

North to Monterey

Though it's rarely visited, **Andrew Molera State Park** (daily dawn–dusk; parking $2; ☎831/667-2315, ⓦwww.parks.ca.gov), five miles north of Pfeiffer Big Sur State Park, is the largest park in Big Sur with two and a half miles of rocky oceanfront reached by a mile-long trail. It occupies the site of what was the El Sur Ranch. This was one of the earliest and most successful Big Sur cattle ranches, initially run in the early nineteenth century by Juan Bautista Alvarado, who became California governor in 1836; later, it was overseen by English sea captain Roger Cooper, whose cabin is preserved here. Although the cabin itself isn't open to the public, you can reach the site on some of the fifteen miles of hiking trails also used for guided two-hour **horseback rides** from the stables ($25–59 weather permitting; ☎831/625-5486 or 1-800/942-5486, ⓦwww.molerahorsebacktours.com). There is also walk-in **camping** (see box above).

From the north end of the park the Old Coast Road takes off inland from Hwy-1 up over the steep hills, affording panoramic views out over miles of coastline. The part-paved, roughly ten-mile road winds over wide-open ranch lands and through deep, slender canyons until it rejoins the main highway at **Bixby Creek Bridge**, fifteen miles south of Carmel. When constructed in 1932, this was the longest single-span concrete bridge in the world, and it is the most impressive (and photogenic) engineering feat of the Coast Road project, a local construction program sponsored by the WPA during the Depression.

A mile and a half north, beyond the **Point Sur Light Station** (weather permitting tours Sat 10am & 2pm, Sun 10am, additional tours July–Aug Wed 10am & 2pm, Thurs 10am; $5; ☎831/625-4419, ⓦwww.pointsur.org), a paved road turns off up **Palo Colorado Canyon**, past a number of houses and the remains of an old lumber mill obscured behind the redwood trees, finishing up eventually at *Bottcher's Gap* campground on the edge of the Ventana Wilderness. On the coast at the foot of the road, the derelict buildings at **Notley's Landing** were once part of a bustling port community. The northernmost stop on the wild Big Sur Coast is at the wildflower-crammed **Garrapata State Park** (daily dawn–dusk; free; ☎831/624-4909, ⓦwww.parks.ca.gov), three miles south of Point Lobos and the Monterey Peninsula. A mile-long trail leads from Hwy-1 out to the tip of **Soberanes Point**, about ten miles south of Carmel – a good place to watch for sea otters and gray whales.

The Monterey Peninsula

The dramatic headlands of the **MONTEREY PENINSULA** mark the northern edge of the spectacular Big Sur Coast, a rocky promontory where gnarled cypress trees amplify the collision between the cliffs and the thundering sea. The manicured towns of the Peninsula thrive now thanks to the regular flow of tourists, but still retain individual characters. **Carmel-by-the-Sea** is by far the toniest: it's secluded, unshowy and a little sniffy, though the election of Clint Eastwood as mayor a few years ago showed its starstruck side: Oscar-winner or not, you'll need a cool million or so to snap up a home here. To the west, **Pebble Beach** is a small village, similar to Carmel in its self-conscious refinement, while at the tip of the peninsula, with spectacular views out across the ocean, stands **Pacific Grove**, known for its butterflies and Victorian architecture, a pleasant if rather sleepy place. The most convenient and practical base on the Peninsula is **Monterey** itself: the largest town, it was the capital of California under the Spanish and the Mexicans, and retains many old adobe houses and places of genuine historic appeal. The local population is a little younger on average than in the other towns, and this also means Monterey has the liveliest nightlife and restaurant scene.

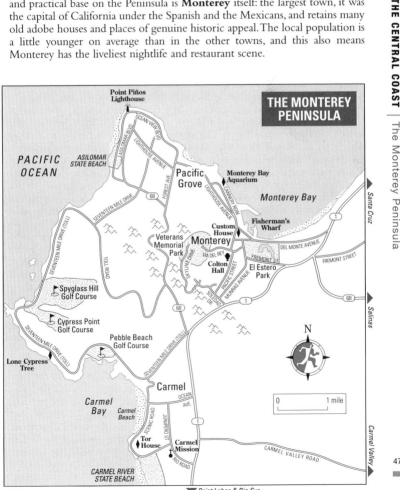

Arrival, information, and getting around

The Monterey Peninsula juts out into the Pacific to form the Monterey Bay, a hundred miles south of San Francisco; coastal Hwy-1 cuts across its neck, and Hwy-68 links up with US-101 at Salinas, twenty miles east. Greyhound **buses** (three daily in each direction between LA and San Francisco) stop at the Exxon station, 1042 Del Monte Ave, along the Monterey waterfront. Amtrak trains stop in Salinas, connecting with local bus #21 for the 55-minute trip (every hour) to Monterey.

Monterey's **visitor center**, 401 Camino El Estero at Franklin Street (April–Oct Mon–Sat 9am–6pm, Sun 9am–5pm; Nov–March Mon–Sat 9am–5pm, Sun 10am–4pm; ☎831/649-1770 or 1-888/221-1010, ⊛www.montereyinfo .org), has free parking, lots of advertiser-based brochures, and hotlines to local hotels; there's a smaller satellite office at the Maritime Museum (see below). Both it and the less busy Chamber of Commerce **tourist office** at 380 Alvarado St (Mon–Fri 8.30am–5pm) can help with accommodation. The **Monterey County Visitors Center**, 137 Crossroads Blvd, in the shopping center on the outskirts of Carmel (daily 9.30am–6pm; ☎888/221-1010) has extensive information on the entire peninsula and will help with hotel reservations. The **Pacific Grove Chamber of Commerce** (Mon–Fri 9am–5pm, Sat 11am–3pm; ☎831/373-3304 or 1-800/656-6650, ⊛www.pacificgrove .org), across from the Natural History Museum at Forest and Central, has walking-tour maps of Pacific Grove's historic buildings and can help find a room in the many local bed-and-breakfast inns. In Carmel Valley, call the Chamber of Commerce (☎831/659-4000 or 1-888/659-4228) for local information, notably on the raft of wineries. The best guides to **what's on** in the area are the widely available freebies *Go!*, *The Coast Weekly* (⊛www.coastweekly.com), and *Peninsula*, all with listings of movies, music, and art galleries.

Getting around is surprisingly easy. Monterey-Salinas Transit (MST) buses (☎831/424-7695) run between 7am and 6pm (11pm on some routes), radiating out from Transit Plaza in the historic core of Monterey, and covering the entire region from Nepenthe on the Big Sur Coast north to Watsonville near Santa Cruz and inland to the agricultural heartland of the Salinas Valley. The region is divided into four zones: the peninsula, Salinas, Big Sur, and the north coast, and fares are $1.75 per zone. Passes are available on board, costing $3.50 for an all-day, single-zone pass, and $7 for an all-routes, all-zones day-pass. The most useful routes are buses #4 and #5, which link Monterey with Carmel; #21, which runs between Monterey and Salinas; and #1, which runs along Lighthouse Avenue out to Pacific Grove; there's also the WAVE shuttle bus which runs every ten minutes from downtown to the Monterey Bay Aquarium on Cannery Row, and from Cannery Row to Pacific Grove, costing $1.25 but free June–Aug (☎831/899-2555). The only way to get to the Big Sur Coast on public transportation is on bus #22, which leaves four times a day, in summer only.

Another option is to **rent a bike**: in Monterey, try Adventures by the Sea, 201 Alvarado Mall ($6 per hour or $30 for two days; ☎831/372-1807, ⊛www.adventuresbythesea.com), outside the Maritime Museum, or Bay Bikes, 640 Wave St on Cannery Row ($10 for 2 hrs, $4 each additional hour or $22 per day; ☎831/659-5824, ⊛www.montereybaybikes.com;). For more leisurely riding, Monterey Mopeds at 1250 Del Monte north of the Wharf (☎831/373-2696, ⊛www.electrictransport.com) rents mopeds for $20 per hour and $75 per day.

Accommodation

What Santa Barbara is to Southern California, the Monterey Peninsula is to the north, meaning the area is among the most exclusive and expensive resort areas in California, with **hotel** and **bed-and-breakfast** room rates averaging $120 a night. This may tempt you to stay elsewhere – in Santa Cruz, or in agricultural Salinas – and come here on day-trips; the other budget option is to avail yourself of one of the many motels along North Fremont Street (also a good place for cheap eats) or Munras Avenue, about one mile from the center.

The only **camping** within walking distance is in Veteran's Memorial Park (☎831/646-3865), site of Steinbeck's fictional Tortilla Flat, at the top of Jefferson Street in the hills above town. It's only $3 a night if you're on foot or bike, or $15 per car, and is operated on a first-come–first-served basis.

Motels and hostels

Bide-a-Wee Motel 221 Asilomar Blvd, Pacific Grove ☎831/372-2330. Nicely spruced-up rooms with modern, homely furnishings including fridge and microwave. Rates more than double at weekends. ❸

Borg's Ocean Front Motel 635 Ocean View Blvd, Pacific Grove ☎831/375-2406. Good value for basic rooms, some with great views from Lovers' Point: be aware that the oceanfront rooms are almost double the others in cost. ❸ without view, ❺ with view

Carmel River Inn Rio Road at Hwy-1, Carmel ☎831/624-1575 or 1-800/882-8142, ⓦwww.carmelriverinn.com. Clean, pleasant, and functional motel that was the model for Brian Moore's novel *The Great Victorian Collection*. Right on the banks of the Carmel River, near the beach and Carmel Mission. ❺

Cypress Gardens Resort Inn 1150 Munras Ave, Monterey ☎831/373-2761 or 1-877/922-1150, ⓦwww.cypressgardensinn.com. One of the better Munras motels, with a leafy garden and a large pool. ❸

Econolodge 2042 Fremont St, Monterey ☎831/372-5851. Comfortable, standard rooms with free local calls and continental breakfasts. ❷

El Dorado Inn 900 Munras Ave, Monterey ☎831/373-2921 or 1-800/722-1836. Cheap, basic accommodation at budget rates in a motel-style, two-story building. ❷

HI-Monterey 778 Hawthorne St, Monterey ☎831/649-0375, ⓦwww.montereyhostel.org. Standard hostel in downtown Monterey near Cannery Row, with dorm beds costing $20 members, $23 non-members. There's a three-day maximum stay and an 11pm curfew. ❶

Lovers Point Inn 625 Ocean View Blvd, Pacific Grove ☎831/373-4771. Rooms here are fine, though bland; the exterior makes up for the interior's ordinary decor, though – from kitsch oddities

like heart-shaped numbers on each room door to the salmon-and-turquoise color scheme. ❺

Montero Lodge 1240 Munras Ave, Monterey ☎831/375-6002. More basic accommodation at budget rates, though prices can double on popular weekends. ❷

Pacific Grove Motel Lighthouse Ave at Grove Acre, Pacific Grove ☎831/372-3218 or 1-800/525-3373. Simple, small motel in marvelous setting, 100 yards from the sea. Rates rise in summer and at weekends. ❶

Hotels and inns

Carmel Resort Inn Carpenter and 2nd Ave, Carmel ☎831/624-3113 or 1-800/454-3700. One of the least expensive properties in Carmel; cottage rooms have fireplaces. ❸

Del Monte Beach 1110 Del Monte Ave, Monterey ☎831/649-4410. A bargain B&B close to the center of Monterey. All the usual trappings for half the normal cost. ❸

Green Gables Inn 104 5th St, Pacific Grove ☎831/375-2095 or 1-800/722-1774, ⓦwww.foursisters.com. Plush doubles in one of the prettiest houses in a town of fine homes, on the waterfront just a few blocks from the Monterey Bay Aquarium. ❺

Homestead 8th St and Dolores, Carmel ☎831/624-4119. This centrally placed B&B, with rooms and cottages in attractive gardens, has just undergone a major renovation, and rates have risen accordingly: it's still one of the better deals in town, though. ❹

Horizon Inn 3rd St and Junípero, Carmel ☎831/624-5327 or 1-800/350-7723, ⓦwww.horizoninncarmel.com. Comfy bed-and-breakfast place with a pool. ❻

Mariposa Inn 1386 Munras Ave, Monterey ☎831/6491414 or 1-800/824-2295. The best deal in town, offering cozy rooms with fireplaces and full amenities at reasonable rates. ❹

Monterey Hilton 1000 Aguajito Rd, Monterey ☎831/373-6141 or 1-800/HILTONS, ⓦ www.hilton.com. Plush hotel on the outskirts of town, set around a rambling garden, with extensive amenities, including swimming pool and ample parking. ❹

Pacific Grove Inn 581 Pine Ave at Forest, Pacific Grove ☎831/375-2825 or 1-800/732-2825, ⓦ www.pacificgrove-inn.com. Thoughtfully modernized 1904 mansion with 17 spacious rooms, five blocks from the shore. ❺

Rosedale Inn 775 Asilomar Blvd, Pacific Grove ☎831/655-1000 or 1-800 /822-5606, ⓦ www.rosedaleinn.com. These log cabin-style rooms are refreshingly modern, with ceiling fans and pine furniture, as well as fireplaces and Jacuzzi baths; what makes the real difference is the affable, easy-going staff. ❻

Seven Gables Inn 555 Ocean View Blvd, Pacific Grove ☎831/372-4341, ⓦ www.7gables-grand-view.com. You'll enter this restored Victorian house through the gloriously overdone Rococo parlor, dripping with gold fixtures; then continue to the plumply furnished mini-suites. Afternoon snacks are a meal in themselves and breakfast is enormous. The same management also runs the equally sumptuous *Grandview Inn* nearby (☎831/372-4341; $175–290). ❼–❾

Monterey

The town of **MONTEREY** rests in a quiet niche along the bay formed by the forested Monterey Peninsula, proudly proclaiming itself the most historic city in California, a boast which, for once, may be true. Its compact town center features some of the best vernacular **buildings** of California's Spanish and Mexican colonial past, most of which stand unassumingly within a few blocks of the tourist-thronged waterfront. The single best stop – and one of the unmissable highlights of the region – is the **Monterey Bay Aquarium**, a mile west of town at the end of Cannery Row.

Monterey was named by the Spanish merchant and explorer Vizcaíno, who landed in 1602 to find an abundant supply of fresh water and wild game after a seven-month voyage from Mexico. Despite Vizcaíno's enthusiasm for the site, the area was not colonized until 1770, when the second mission in the chain – the headquarters of the whole operation – was built in Monterey before being moved to its permanent site in Carmel. Under the Spanish, the Presidio de Monterey was also the military headquarters for the whole of Alta California, and thereafter Monterey continued to be the leading administrative and commercial center of a territory that extended east to the Rocky Mountains and north to Canada, but had a total population, excluding Native Americans, of less than seven thousand.

American interest in Monterey was purely commercial until 1842, when an American naval commodore received a false report that the US and Mexico were at war, and that the English were poised to take California. Commodore Catesby Jones anchored at Monterey and demanded the peaceful surrender of the port, and two days later, the American flag was raised. The armed but cordial US occupation lasted only until Jones examined the official documents closely and realized he'd got it all wrong (and his exuberance cost him his job). When the Mexican–American War began in earnest in 1846, the United States took possession of Monterey without resistance. The discovery of gold in the Sierra Nevada foothills soon focused attention upon San Francisco, and Monterey became something of a backwater, hardly affected by the waves of immigration which followed.

The Waterfront and Old Monterey

More than half a century ago, when Monterey first tried to pass itself off to wealthy visitors from San Francisco and beyond as an upscale resort, there was a great deal of doubt whether or not the demand would ever match the supply. Today, those worries have been put neatly to bed along with the visiting

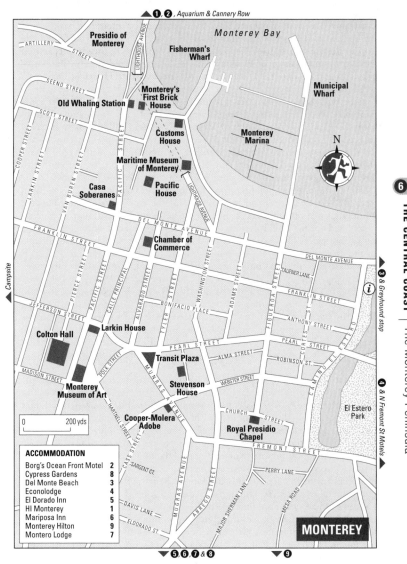

▲ ❶, ❷, Aquarium & Cannery Row

Monterey Bay

Presidio of
Monterey

ARTILLERY STREET

Fisherman's
Wharf

LIGHTHOUSE AVENUE

SEENO STREET

Monterey's
First Brick
House

Old Whaling Station

Municipal
Wharf

SCOTT STREET

Customs
House

Monterey
Marina

COOPER STREET

LARKIN STREET

VAN BUREN STREET

Maritime Museum
of Monterey

N

Casa
Soberanes

PACIFIC

Pacific
House

LIGHTHOUSE AVENUE

FRANKLIN STREET

DEL MONTE AVENUE

Chamber of
Commerce

DEL MONTE AVENUE

PIERCE STREET

PACIFIC STREET

CALLE PRINCIPAL

ALVARADO STREET

WASHINGTON STREET

ADAMS STREET

TAUFNER LANE

FIGUEROA STREET

FRANKLIN STREET

CORTES STREET

CAMINO EL ESTERO

JEFFERSON STREET

BONIFACIO PLACE

TYLER STREET

ANTHONY STREET

◀ Campsite

▶ ❸ & Greyhound stop

ⓘ

Larkin House

Colton Hall

PEARL STREET

PEARL STREET

ALMA STREET

ROBINSON ST.

MADISON STREET

POLK STREET

Transit Plaza

MUNRAS AVENUE

Stevenson
House

WEBSTER STREET

Monterey
Museum of Art

HARTNELL STREET

Cooper-Molera
Adobe

CHURCH STREET

El Estero
Park

Royal Presidio
Chapel

FREMONT STREET

SARGENT CT.

CASS STREET

MUGRAS AVENUE

ABREGO STREET

PERRY LANE

MESA ROAD

0   200 yds

DAVIS LANE

ELDORADO ST.

MAJOR SHERMAN LANE

MONTEREY

ACCOMMODATION

Borg's Ocean Front Motel	2
Cypress Gardens	8
Del Monte Beach	3
Econolodge	4
El Dorado Inn	5
HI Monterey	1
Mariposa Inn	6
Monterey Hilton	9
Montero Lodge	7

▼ ❺, ❻, ❼ & ❽   ▼ ❾

▶ ❹ & N Fremont St Motels ▶

6

THE CENTRAL COAST | The Monterey Peninsula

mass that stays here nightly, and tourism is now Monterey's main livelihood. A good deal of the trade is concentrated along the waterfront around the tacky **Fisherman's Wharf**, where the catch-of-the-day is more likely to be families from San Jose than the formerly abundant sardines. Most of the commercial fishermen moved out long ago, leaving the old wharves and canneries as relics of a once-prosperous industry; fat sea lions float by under the piers.

The most prominent building near the wharf, at the foot of Pacific Street, is the modern **Maritime Museum of Monterey** (daily 11am–5pm; $5; ☎831/372-2608, ⓦwww.mntmh.org) with well-displayed but essentially

481

mundane collections of ships in glass cases enlivened by interesting background on the town's defunct sardine industry. If none of this appeals, you should still pop in for the free, fourteen-minute film on Monterey history in preparation for a stroll on the **Path of History**. This loosely organized, roughly mile-and-a-half-long trail connects 37 sites in the **Monterey State Historic Park** scattered throughout the quarter-mile square of the modern city. The path is marked with small yellow discs at regular intervals on the sidewalk, and a companion booklet ($3) giving detailed information on each site is available from most local tourist offices. Many of Monterey's historic buildings have survived in pristine condition: if you want to see inside, the best option is to join one of the ninety-minute guided **walking tours** of the Path of History (Mon–Thurs 10am & 2pm, Fri–Sun 10am, 11am & 2pm; $5; ☏831/649-7118, ⓦ www.mbay.net/~mshp/), which leave from the Maritime Museum.

Among the essential buildings to visit, the **Pacific House** (daily 10am–5pm; free; ☏831/649-2907) is on the east side of the plaza outside the Maritime Museum; since its construction in 1847, it has been a courthouse, a rooming house, and a dance hall. It is now the best of the local **museums**, with displays on Monterey history and a fair collection of Native American artifacts. While in the area, wander by the **Customs House** (daily 10am–4pm; free). This is the oldest governmental building on the West Coast, portions of which were built by Spain in 1814, Mexico in 1827, and the US in 1846. The balconied building has been restored and now displays 150-year-old crates of confiscated coffee and liquor in a small museum inside. A block west, outside the **Old Whaling Station**, don't miss the battered, diamond-shaped paving stones made by enterprising locals from whalebone vertebrae, which have lasted surprisingly well. Next door stands Monterey's **First Brick House** (daily 10am–4pm; free), which was built in 1847 and has a small display on the area's buildings.

But the best place to get a feel for life in Old Monterey is at the **Larkin House** (45min tours twice daily Mon–Thurs, three times daily Fri–Sun, call to confirm; free; ☏831/649-7118, ⓦ www.mbay.net/~mshp/), on Jefferson Street a block south of Alvarado, home of the first and only American Consul to California and successful entrepreneur, Thomas Larkin. New England-born Larkin, the wealthy owner of a general store and a redwood lumber business, was one of the most important and influential figures in early California. He was actively involved in efforts to attract American settlers to California and lobbied the Californians to turn towards the United States and away from the erratic government of Mexico. Through his designs for his own house, and the Customs House near Fisherman's Wharf, Larkin is credited with developing the now-familiar Monterey style of architecture, combining local adobe walls and the balconies of Southern plantation homes with a puritan Yankee's taste in ornament. The house, the first two-story adobe in California, is filled with many millions of dollars' worth of antiques and is surrounded by gorgeous gardens.

As unhappy with the American military government as he had been with the Mexicans, Larkin helped to organize the Constitutional Convention that convened in Monterey in 1849 to draft the terms by which California could be admitted to the US as the 31st state – which happened in 1850. The meetings were held in the grand white stone building just down the street from his house, the then newly completed **Colton Hall**, built by William Colton, the first American *alcalde* (mayor-judge) of Monterey. It's now an engaging **museum** (April–Oct daily 10am–12pm, 1–5pm; Nov–March daily 10am–12pm, 1–4pm; free; ☏831/646-5640), furnished as it was during the convention, with quill pens on the tables and an early map of the West Coast, which was used to draw up the boundaries of the nascent state. The **Monterey Museum of Art** at 559 Pacific St (Wed–Sat 11am–5pm, Sun 1pm–4pm; $5, free third Thurs and first Sun each month; ☎831/372-5477, ⓦwww.montereyart.org), presents a strong case for its much-touted title of "best small-town museum in the US." The museum's four galleries – featuring a rotating collection of mostly local art as well as temporary exhibits – are housed in a two-room adobe surrounded by splendid rose and rhododendron gardens and surrounded in turn by stone walls inlaid with painted tiles.

Stevenson House, at 530 Houston St (closed for refurbishment, call ☎831/649-1770 or 1-888/221-1010 for further information), is an old rooming house filled with Robert Louis Stevenson memorabilia. The writer collected much of it on his travels round the South Sea Islands, and his family bequeathed the ephemera to the museum after his death: at the moment, the place is going through a major refit, and there's no confirmed date for its reopening. Two blocks east, on Church Street at the top of Figueroa, stands the oldest building in Monterey, the **Royal Presidio Chapel** (daily 8.30am–6pm; free). This small and much-restored Spanish colonial church was built in 1795 as part of a mission founded here by Junípero Serra in 1770, the rest of which was soon removed to a better site along the Carmel River. In the rear garden is a fragment of the ancient oak tree under which explorer Vizcaíno said Mass back in 1602.

There are two other notable historic buildings in Monterey: the first is the **Cooper-Molera Adobe**, 525 Polk St (June–Aug daily 10am–5pm; Sept–May daily 10am–4pm; free; ☎831/649-7109, ⓦwww.mbay.net/~mshp/), which illustrates architecturally the evolution of Monterey. This housing complex was built by New England sea captain John Rogers Cooper, who settled locally and married a Mexican woman. On this site there are in fact two houses. The first is a squat, old-fashioned Mexican-style house, known as the Diaz adobe, with simple, whitewashed walls, no closets, and thick adobe bricks to serve as primitive air conditioning. The second is a more formal, fashionable home that Cooper himself constructed in the early 1850s and follows an East Coast design, with a double parlor, decorative printed wallpaper, and fitted carpeting.

A few blocks north, at the corner of Pacific and Del Monte, stands **Casa Soberanes** (June–Aug daily 10am–5pm; Sept–May daily 10am–4pm; free; ☎831/649-7118, ⓦwww.mbay.net/~mshp). This is a classic California-style adobe building built in the 1830s, with its floating balconies supported only by heavy floor beams, red tiling, and symmetrical doors and windows. The interior of the house has been somewhat modernized, but the low ceilings and boxy rooms of its original construction have been preserved.

Cannery Row and the Monterey Bay Aquarium

A waterfront **bike path** runs from the wharf along the disused railroad two miles out to Pacific Grove, following the one-time Ocean View Avenue, renamed **CANNERY ROW** after John Steinbeck's evocative portrait of the rough-and-ready men and women who worked in and around the thirty-odd fish canneries here. During World War II, Monterey was the sardine capital of the Western world, catching and canning some 200,000 tons of the fish each year. However, overfishing meant that by 1945 the fish were more or less all gone, and the canneries were abandoned, falling into disrepair until the 1970s, when they were rebuilt, redecorated, and converted into shopping malls and flashy restaurants, many with names adopted from Steinbeck's tales.

Ride, walk, or take the WAVE shuttle from Fisherman's Wharf to visit the engaging **MONTEREY BAY AQUARIUM**, a mile west of town at the end

The Gold Rush of 1849 bypassed Monterey for San Francisco, leaving the community little more than a somnolent Mexican fishing village – which was pretty much how the town looked when a 29-year-old, feverishly ill Scotsman arrived by stagecoach, flat broke and desperately in love with a married woman. **Robert Louis Stevenson** came to Monterey in the fall of 1879 for fresh air and looking for Fanny Osbourne, whom he had met while traveling in France two years before. He stayed here for three months, writing occasional articles for the local newspaper and telling stories in exchange for his meals at Jules Simoneau's restaurant behind what is now the **Stevenson House**, halfway between the Larkin House and the Royal Presidio Chapel (see p.483). It's said that he started *Treasure Island* here and used Point Lobos (see p.487) as inspiration for Spyglass Hill.

Stevenson witnessed Monterey (no longer politically important but not yet a tourist attraction) in transition, something he wrote about in his essay *The Old and New Pacific Capitals*. He foresaw that the lifestyle that had endured since the Mexican era was no match for the "Yankee craft" of the "millionaire vulgarians of the Big Bonanza," such as Charles Crocker, whose lavish *Hotel Del Monte* which opened a year later (the site is now the Naval Postgraduate School, east of downtown), turned the sleepy town into a seaside resort of international renown almost overnight.

of Cannery Row (daily 10am–6pm, last ticket 5.30pm; $17.95, $3 audio tour; ☎831/648-4888 or 1-800/756-3737, ⓦwww.montereybayaquarium.org). Reservations at Monterey's single most popular attraction are essential in any season. Built upon the foundations of an old sardine cannery and housed in modernist buildings that blend a sense of adventure with pleasant promenades along the Bay, the aquarium is one of the largest, most stunning displays of underwater life in the world. The showstopper here is the brand new *Jellies: Living Art* exhibition, a trippy Star Trek-inspired chance to see outlandishly odd jellyfish up close; this hypnotically stunning experience takes you through a series of black rooms, each illuminated by the jellyfishes' throbbing, glassy bodies. Aside from this, there's the gigantic Outer Bay display, outlining the ecosystem of the deep waters just beyond the bay; a highlight is the enormous swimming tank, featuring butt-ugly sunfish, lazy hammerhead sharks, and foul-tempered tuna. Upstairs, there's the kid-friendly Splash Zone plus petting pools; the museum also opens directly onto the bay, so you can wander out and peer into wild tidepools after wandering round the captive tanks. Try not to miss the sea otters at feeding time (usually 10.30am, 1.30pm & 3.30pm); the playful critters were hunted nearly to extinction for their fur – said, with some one million hairs per square inch, to be the softest in the world. Otherwise, stop off at the 335,000-gallon Kelp Forest for a fish feeding frenzy (11.30am, 4pm).

Pacific Grove

PACIFIC GROVE – or "Butterfly Town USA," as it likes to call itself – stands curiously apart from the rest of the Peninsula, less known but more impressively situated than its two famous neighbors. The town began as a campground and Methodist retreat in 1875, a summertime tent city for revivalist Christians in which strong drink, naked flesh, and reading the Sunday papers were firmly prohibited. The Methodists have long since gone, but otherwise the town is little changed. Its quiet streets, lined by pine trees and grand old Victorian wooden houses, are enlivened each year by hundreds of thousands of golden **monarch butterflies**, which come here each winter from all over the western US and Canada to escape the cold and have become the town's main tourist attraction. In fact, the migration of these little orange-and-black butterflies is so important to the local economy that they're protected by local law; there's a $1000 fine for molesting a monarch.

Downtown Pacific Grove centers upon the intersection of Forest Street and Lighthouse Avenue, two miles northwest of central Monterey. Two blocks north, at 667 Lighthouse Ave, the **Bookworks** bookstore and café (Sun–Thurs 9am–10pm, Fri & Sat 9am–11pm; ℡831/372-2242), is the place to pick up more detailed guides to the local area, or just stop for a cup of coffee and a pastry. A block down Forest Street, on the corner of Central Avenue, the **Pacific Grove Museum of Natural History** (Tues–Sun 10am–5pm; free; ℡831-648-5716, ⓦ www.pgmuseum.org) has an interesting collection of local wildlife, including lots of butterflies, over four hundred stuffed birds, a relief model of the undersea topography, and exhibits on the ways of life of the native Costanoan and Salinan peoples. Across the park, the **Chautauqua Hall** was for a time in the 1880s the focus of town life as the West Coast headquarters of the instructional and populist Chautauqua Movement, a left-leaning, traveling university that reached thousands of Americans long before there was any accessible form of higher education. Nowadays, the plain white building is used as a dance hall, with a three-piece band playing favorites from the Thirties and Forties every Saturday night, and square dancing on Thursday.

About the only reminder of the fundamentalist camp meetings are the intricately detailed, tiny wooden **cottages**, along 16th and 17th streets, which date from the revival days; in some cases wooden boards were simply nailed over the frames of canvas tents to make them habitable year-round. Down Central Avenue at 12th Street, at the top of a small wooded park overlooking the ocean, stands the deep-red Gothic wooden church of **Saint Mary's By-The-Sea**, Pacific Grove's first substantial church, built in 1887, with a simple interior of redwood beams polished to a shimmering glow, and an authentic signed Tiffany stained-glass window, nearest the altar on the left.

Ocean View Boulevard, which runs between the church and the ocean, circles along the coast around the town, passing the headland of **Lovers Point** – originally called Lovers of Jesus Point – where preachers used to hold sunrise services. Surrounded in early summer by the colorful red and purple blankets of blooming ice plants, it's one of the peninsula's best **beaches**, where you can lounge around and swim from the intimate, protected strand – if you're lucky enough to have arrived on one of the rare fog-free days in summer – or rent a glass-bottomed boat and explore the sheltered cove. Ocean View Boulevard runs another mile along the coast out to the tip of the peninsula, where the 150-year-old **Point Piños Lighthouse** (Thurs–Sun 1–4pm; free; ℡831/648-5716, ⓦ www.pgmuseum.org) is the oldest continuously operating lighthouse on the California coast.

Around Pacific Grove, there are two worthwhile detours. One follows the coastal road as it changes from Ocean View Boulevard to Sunset Drive, leading on to **Asilomar State Beach**, a wild stretch with dramatic surf, too dangerous for swimming, though the rocky shore provides homes for all sorts of tidepool life. The second tracks the **Butterfly Trees** on Ridge Road, a quarter of a mile inland along Lighthouse Avenue: this is where you should be able to spot giant brown clumps of monarchs discretely congregating high up in the treetops during season (Nov–early March). The quickest way out of town is to follow Hwy-68 from the end of Sunset Drive inland over the hills: it joins Hwy-1 just north of Carmel. But if you've time, the **Seventeen Mile Drive** (daily dawn–dusk; $8 per car; ℡831/649-8500) is a privately owned, scenic toll road which loops from Pacific Grove along the coast south to Carmel and back again; on the way, it swoops past the golf courses and country clubs of Pebble Beach. Don't miss the trussed-up figure of the **Lone Cypress** halfway along the route, as it's the subject of many a postcard; there are enough beautiful vistas of the rugged coastline to make it almost worth braving the hordes who pack the roads on holiday weekends.

Carmel

Set on gently rising headlands above a sculpted rocky shore, **CARMEL** is confined to a few neat rows of quaint shops and miniature homes running along either side of Ocean Avenue towards the largely untouched coastline. Besides all the rampant cuteness, Carmel's only real crime is its ridiculously inflated price scale.

The town's reputation as a rich resort belies its origins: there was nothing much here until the San Francisco earthquake and fire of 1906 led a number of artists and writers from the city to take refuge in the area, forming a bohemian colony on the wild and uninhabited slopes that soon became notorious throughout the state. The figurehead of the group was the poet George Sterling, and part-time members included Jack London, Mary Austin, and the young Sinclair Lewis. But it was a short-lived alliance, and by the 1920s the group had broken up, and an influx of wealthy San Franciscans had put Carmel well on its way to becoming the exclusive corner it is today.

Today, more than a decade after the retirement of headline-grabbing Clint Eastwood as mayor, Carmel seems the epitome of parochial snobbishness. Local laws, enacted to preserve the gingerbread charm of the town, prohibit parking meters, street addresses, and postal deliveries (all mail is picked up in person from the post office), and franchise businesses are banned outright within the city limits.

Carmel's center, fifteen minutes south of Monterey on MST bus #4 or #5, doesn't have much to recommend it. Indeed, it is largely designer-shopping territory: Carmel Plaza Mall at Ocean Avenue and Mission Street holds branches of Saks Fifth Avenue and Louis Vuitton, and there are a number of tacky, overpriced art **galleries** along Dolores Street (there's even a clothing store for pampered lap dogs on Ocean Avenue). The Weston Gallery on Sixth Street between Dolores and Lincoln (Tues–Sun 10.30am–5.30pm; ☎831/624-4453) is worth a look, however, hosting regular shows of the best contemporary photographers and featuring a permanent display of works by Fox Talbot, Ansel Adams, and Edward Weston – who lived in Carmel for most of his life. To get the lowdown on the other galleries, check out the free, widely available *Carmel Gallery Guide*.

The town's best feature, however, is the largely untouched nearby coastline, among the most beautiful in California. **Carmel Beach** is a tranquil cove of emerald blue water bordered by soft white sand and cypress-covered cliffs; the tides are deceptively strong and dangerous, so be careful if you chance a swim. A mile south from Carmel Beach along Carmel Bay, **Tor House** was, when built in 1919, the only building on a then treeless headland. The poet Robinson Jeffers (whose very long, starkly tragic narrative poems were far more popular in his time than they are today) built the small cottage and adjacent tower by hand, out of granite boulders he carried up from the cove below. There are hourly guided tours of the house and gardens (Fri & Sat 10am–3pm; $7; ⓦ www.torhouse.org); to make a reservation in advance call ☎831/624-1813 (Mon–Thurs 10am–3pm), or for same-day bookings call ☎831/624-1840 (Fri–Sat 10am–4pm). The tours overload visitors with an obsequious account of the now-forgotten writer's life and work, but the house itself is pleasant enough. Note that the entrance is at 26304 Ocean View Ave, one block back from the clifftop; note, too, that's there's little parking, since this is a residential neighborhood.

Another quarter of a mile along Scenic Road, around the tip of Carmel Point, you'll find the idyllic, mile-long **Carmel River State Beach** (T831/624-4909). It's less visited than the city beach, and includes a bird sanctuary on a freshwater lagoon that offers safe and sometimes warm swimming. Again, if you brave the waves, beware of the strong tides and currents, especially at the south end of the beach, where the sand falls away at a very steep angle, causing big and potentially hazardous surf.

Carmel Mission

Half a mile or so up the Carmel River from the beach, also reachable by following Junípero Avenue from downtown, **Carmel Mission Basilica** (Sept–May Mon–Sat 9.30am–4.15pm, Sun 10.30am–4.15pm; longer hours June–Aug, call for details; $2; T831/624-3600, Wwww.carmelmission.org) – San Carlos Borromeo de Carmelo – was founded in 1770 by Junípero Serra as the second of the California missions and the headquarters of the chain. Father Serra never got to see the finished church – he died before its completion and is buried under the floor in front of the altar. Finally completed by Father Lasuen in 1797, the sandstone church has undergone one of the most painstakingly authentic restorations in the entire mission chain, a process well detailed in one of the three excellent **museums** in the mission compound. By 1937, when the reconstruction began, the mission had lain derelict for more than eighty years and was little more than its foundations and a few feet of wall; but today the whimsically ornate structure stands firmly as the most romantic mission in the chain. The dainty building has a dark side too: three thousand local Native Americans are buried in the adjacent **cemetery**.

Point Lobos State Reserve

Two miles south of the mission along Hwy-1, accessible in summer on MST bus #22, the **POINT LOBOS STATE RESERVE** (summer daily 9am–7pm, last entry 6.30pm; winter daily 9am–5pm, last entry 4.30pm; $4 parking; T831/624-4909, Wwww.parks.ca.gov) has plenty of natural justifications to support its claim of being "the greatest meeting of land and water in the world." There are over 250 bird and animal species along the **hiking trails** in the area, and the sea here is one of the richest underwater habitats in California. Because the point juts so far out into the ocean, there are some of the earth's best undisturbed views of the ocean: craggy granite pinnacles, landforms that inspired Robert Louis Stevenson's *Treasure Island*, reach out of jagged blue coves. Sea lions and otters frolic in the crashing surf, just below the many vantage points along the park's coastal trail. Gray whales are often seen offshore – sometimes as close as a hundred yards away – migrating south in January and returning with young calves in April and early May. The park, named after the *lobos marinos* – the noisy, barking sea lions that group on the rocks off the reserve's tip – protects some of the few remaining Monterey cypress trees on its knife-edged headland, despite being buffeted by relentless winds.

Except for a small parking lot, the reserve is closed to cars, so lines sometimes form along the highway to wait for a parking space. A worthwhile guide and map is included in the admission fee.

Carmel Valley

About fifteen miles inland, east along route G16, lies **Carmel Valley Village**, where the weather is warmer and more predictable than the coast: that's one of the reasons this country hamlet can bill itself as the epicenter of the Monterey County's wine country, a cluster of vineyards encompassing an area as far afield as King City to the south on Hwy-101. In the **CARMEL VALLEY** that surrounds the village, you'll find a number of vineyards in a quiet pastoral setting – a big breath of relief after crowded, coastal Carmel: most are known for their red wines, since the searing summer heat (up to 105°F) suits hardier varietals better. The Monterey County Vintners and Growers Association (☎831/375-9400) publishes a map to the area, and the **Chamber of Commerce** (Mon–Fri 11am–5pm, Sat 11am–3pm; ☎831/659-4000 or 1-888/659-4228, ⓦwww.carmelvalleychamber.com) lures visitors from Carmel with a new local map – available from most any visitors' center in Monterey County – crammed with shopping and dining possibilities. One of the most pleasant wineries for tastings is Joullian, 2 Village Drive (daily 11am–5pm; ☎831/659-8100, ⓦwww.joullian.com), where the friendly, knowledgeable staff will be happy to talk at length about the region's history and current winemaking strengths.

Eating

There are many excellent **eating places** all over the Peninsula, and though prices tend to float near resort prices, the competition for tourist dollars insures quality. For a full list of the hundreds of eating options in the area, check out a copy of the free, weekly, and widely available *Go!* or *Coast Weekly*. If you're on anything like a tight budget, the best eats are on the north side of Monterey along North Fremont Street, on and around Lighthouse Avenue (just south of Cannery Row), and in the shopping malls along Hwy-1 south of Carmel.

Restaurants

Bytes 403 Calle Principal, Monterey ☎831/372-2987. There's no reason to wait till after lunch to check your email here. Full computer services and a full espresso bar as well as a selection of relatively affordable sandwiches.

Carmel Bakery Ocean Ave between Lincoln & Dolores, Carmel ☎831/626-8885. Refreshing low-key café on the main drag serving old-fashioned gooey cakes and coffee to browsing locals.

Fishwife at Asilomar Beach, 1996 Sunset Drive at Asilomar, Pacific Grove ☎831/375-7107. Long-standing local favorite, serving great food at reasonable prices in cozy, unpretentious surroundings. Try the king prawns sautéed in red peppers and lime juice with rice and steamed vegetables for $15.

India's Clay Oven 150 Del Monte Ave, 2nd floor, Monterey ☎831/373-2529. If you're overcome by the sudden desire for papadums and saag paneer, you now know where to go for slightly upscale versions of the same – the best local Indian option. Expensive.

La Boheme Dolores St between Ocean and 7th sts, Carmel ☎831/624-7500. A worthwhile splurge, Carmel-style, this French-inspired bistro offers a single, multi-course menu fixe that changes daily for $25–30 plus wine and service. Charming if a little chintzy.

Little Napoli Dolores St between Ocean and 7th sts, Carmel ☎831/626-6335. One of the town's many excellent mid-range Italian restaurants, this tiny eatery serves oversized portions of fresh pasta with original sauces in an atmosphere with all the romantic charm you'd expect from a Carmel address.

Massaro and Santos 32 Cannery Row #H-1, Coast Guard Pier, Monterey ☎831/649-6700. Dine here for views out across the bay and meaty, fish-crammed stews like bouillabaise, not to mention dozens of daily specials – entrées are round $15 but save room for the gooey, gorgeous desserts.

Old Monterey Café 489 Alvarado St, Monterey ☎831/646-1021. Reasonable more-than-you-can-eat breakfasts, with great omelets and buckwheat pancakes, plus tasty sandwiches; breakfast and lunch only.

Paolina's San Carlos between Ocean & 7th sts, Carmel ☎831/624-5599) Fresh home-made pastas in a casual courtyard setting at half the price of other Carmel dining.

Papa Chano's Taqueria 462 Alvarado St, Monterey ☎831/646-9587. One of the few bargain eateries in town, this fast-food-style taqueria nevertheless serves juicy, authentic Mexican specialties – the *chorizo* (spicy sausage) is particularly tender.

Pasta Mia Trattoria 481 Lighthouse Ave, Pacific Grove ☎831/375-7709. Family-owned restaurant offering tasty home-made pastas, grilled seafood, and veal in a rustic, homely setting. The pasta entrées run for about $12.

Patisserie Boissière Mission St between Ocean & 7th, Carmel ☎831/624-5008. With savory quiches, salads, and even Coquille Saint Jacques on the menu, this mid-range restaurant also serves the pastries you'd expect from the name and prepares picnic lunches with advance notice.

Pepper's Mexicali Café 170 Forest Ave, Pacific Grove ☎831/373-6892. Gigantic plates of Mexican food for around $10 per person, piled high with fresh, local produce: less healthful than it sounds but guaranteed to fill even the biggest stomach.

Porta Bella Ocean Ave between Lincoln and Monte Verde, Carmel ☎831/624-4395. Upscale, flower-filled bistro, serving fancy French food in a pleasant setting, with crisp white tablecloths and a charming garden tucked away beneath a vine-filled trellis at the back. Watch the local ladies who lunch, lunch.

Robata Grill & Sake Bar 3658 The Barnyard, Carmel ☎831/624-2643. Local favorite for sushi and tempura in a warm, wood-paneled setting. Not cheap, but tasty and unpretentious for its locale.

Sardine Factory 701 Wave St, Monterey ☎831/373-3775. California seafood cuisine served in French château splendor at less-than-expected prices, although it's still pretty wallet walloping.

Schooners in the *Monterey Plaza Hotel*, 400 Cannery Row, Monterey ☎831/372-2628. Colorful upscale California bistro in a historic hotel with views over the bay. Try a grilled, local Castroville artichoke, served with herbed mayonnaise.

Stokes Adobe 500 Hartnell St, Monterey ☎831/373-1110. Built in 1833, the historic former home is now an elegant restaurant serving Mediterranean cuisine with a Californian flare.

Tuck Box Tearoom Dolores St between Ocean and 7th, Carmel ☎831/624-6365. Breakfast, lunch, and afternoon tea in half-timbered mock-Tudor Old England cottage; costly, kitschy, and fun.

Cafés, bars, and nightlife

The Peninsula has always been better known as a sleepy, romantic getaway than as a hub of hip nightlife. However, the best selection of bars is in Monterey, and the local **Jazz Festival** in mid-September (☎1–800/307-3378) is the oldest continuous festival in the world, drawing crowds from afar. Check out the widely available *Go!* or *Coast Weekly* for the most current listings.

Bay Books 316 Alvarado St, Monterey ☎831/375-1855. Sip coffee until 10pm (11pm at weekends) while browsing in one of Monterey's better bookshops.

Bookworks 667 Lighthouse Ave, Monterey ☎831/372-2242. Café frequented by locals, featuring live music and light lunch fare at reasonable prices, although it's not open very late, usually closing around 8pm.

Britannia Arms Pub & Restaurant 444 Alvarado St, Monterey ☎831/656-9543. ⓦwww.britanni-aarms.com. This authentic-feeling British pub is oddly incongruous in the heart of Monterey; it's filled with a largely local, laid-back crowd and serves greasily tasty traditional pub grub.

Club Octane 321d Alvarado St, Monterey ☎831/646-9244, ⓦ www.cluboctane.com. Lively downtown club with three dancefloors and a youngish, collegiate crowd – more fun than hip. Closed Tues & Wed.

Lighthouse Bar & Grill 281 Lighthouse Ave, Monterey ☎831/373-4488, ⓦ www.lighthouse-barandgrill281.com. Rather dilapidated gay bar with a low-key, pub atmosphere, pool tables, and an older crowd.

Lallapalooza 474 Alvarado St, Monterey ☎831/645-9036.Martini bar with poppy, olive-themed art on the walls, a small sidewalk terrace and stylish oval bar – the dressiest place to drink in town. There's a reasonable restaurant attached, too.

The Mucky Duck 479 Alvarado St, Monterey ☎831/655-3031. The menu at this friendly and popular Tudor-style bar/restaurant features British food with a California flair. Occasional live music; DJ dancing on back patio.

North from Monterey

The landscape around the **Monterey Bay**, between the peninsula and the beach town of Santa Cruz, 45 miles north, is almost entirely given over to agriculture. **Castroville**, ten miles north along Hwy-1, has two claims to fame, one more glamorous than the other. Today, surrounded by farmland, it produces more than 85 percent of the nation's artichokes (try them deep-fried in one of the local cafés); more than fifty years ago in 1947, the first woman to be crowned Artichoke Queen was one Norma Jean Baker, later known as Marilyn Monroe. The wide **Pajaro Valley**, five miles further north, is covered with apple orchards, blossoming white in the spring. The marshlands that ring the bay at the mouths of the Salinas and Pajaro rivers are habitats for many of California's endangered species of coastal wildlife and migratory birds. **Moss Landing** is an excellent place to stop for seafood – try dramatically situated *Phil's Fish Market*, 7600 Sandholt Rd (T831/633-2152), where you can pick from the catch of the day then fish a bottle of white wine for yourself from the cooler. At the nearby **Elkhorn Slough Estuarine Sanctuary** (Wed–Sun 9am–5pm, free guided tours Sat & Sun 10am, 1pm; $2.50; T831/728-2822, Wwww.elkhornslough.org) you may spot a falcon or an eagle among the 250 species of birds that call it home. Guided nature boat tours can be booked through Elkhorn Slough Safari on the harbor (T831/633-5555). The beaches along the bay to Santa Cruz are often windy and not very exciting, though they're lined by sand dunes into which you can disappear for hours on end.

Sunset State Beach, fifteen miles south of Santa Cruz, has **campgrounds** (book through ParkNet T1-800/444-7275; information only T831/763-7062; $12) along a seven-mile strand. Four miles inland, east of Hwy-1, the earthquake-devastated town of **Watsonville** was more or less the epicenter of the October 1989 Loma Prieta tremor that rattled San Francisco. Its once-quaint downtown of ornate Victorian houses and 1930s brick structures was virtually flattened, and more recently the area economy has been hard hit by closure of its Green Giant vegetable-packing plant, once one of the largest in the country. Like many American cities, the place is saturated with fast-food restaurants and outlet malls and there isn't a lot of interest for travelers, but Watsonville is still the main transfer point between the Monterey and Santa Cruz **bus** systems, so you may well have to pass through.

San Juan Bautista and Gilroy

Inland from the Monterey Bay area, on US-101 between Salinas and San Francisco, tiny **SAN JUAN BAUTISTA** is an old Mexican town that, but for a modest scattering of craft shops, has hardly changed since it was bypassed by the railroad in 1876. The early nineteenth-century **Mission San Juan Bautista** (daily 9.30am–4.45pm; $2; T831/623-4528, Wwww.oldmission-sjb .org), largest of the Californian mission churches–and still the parish church of San Juan Bautista–stands on the north side of the town's central plaza, its original bells still ringing out from the bell tower. The arcaded monastery wing that stretches out to the left of the church contains relics and historical exhibits, including a vast collection of ceremonial robes. If it all looks a bit familiar, you may have seen it before – the climactic stairway chase scene in Alfred Hitchcock's *Vertigo* was filmed here. Note that the **San Andreas Fault** runs just a few yards in front of the church.

The town that grew up around the mission was once the largest in central California and has been preserved as a **state park** (daily 10am–4.30pm; $1; T831/623-4881) with exhibits around the evocative central square interpreting the restored buildings. On the west side of the plaza, the two-story, balconied adobe Plaza Hotel was a popular stopping place on the stagecoach route between San Francisco and Los Angeles; next door, the 1840 **Castro–Breen Adobe**, administrative headquarters of Mexican California, later belonged to the Breen family – survivors of the ill-fated Donner party (see p.696) – who made a small fortune in the Gold Rush.

Across from the mission, the large **Plaza Hall** was built to serve as the seat of the emergent county government, but when the county seat was awarded instead to Hollister – a small farming community eight miles east, and scene of a motorcycle gang's rampage that inspired the movie *The Wild One* – the building was turned into a dancehall and saloon. The adjacent stables display a range of old stagecoaches and wagons, and explain how to decipher an array of cattle brands, from "lazy H" to "rockin' double B."

The commercial center of San Juan Bautista, a block south of the plaza, lines Third Street in a row of evocatively decaying facades. If you're hungry, the best of the half-dozen **places to eat** is the unfussy *Mission Café* at 300 3rd St, on the corner of Mariposa (☎831/623-2635), which serves breakfast and lunch and is especially notable for its friendly staff; for dinner, try *Joan & Peter's German Restaurant*, 322 3rd St (☎831/623-4521), with its hearty specials of *bratwurst* and *wurstteller* for around \$10. For **information** contact the Chamber of Commerce, 402a 3rd St (Mon–Fri 10am–4pm; ☎831/623-2454, ⓦwww.san-juan-bautista.ca.us).

A bit further north, you'll know you've come to **GILROY** by the smell, for this farming community is best known for its garlic. For information on the annual summer Garlic Festival, which features everything from vampire-chasing garlands to garlic ice cream (not nearly as bad as it sounds), contact the Gilroy Visitors Bureau, 7780 Monterey St (Mon–Fri 9am–5pm, Sat 10am–3pm; ☎408/842-6436, ⓦwww.gilroyvisitor.org).

Santa Cruz

Seventy-five miles south of San Francisco, the unassuming and edgy community of **SANTA CRUZ** is a hard place to pin down. In many ways it's the quintessential Californian coastal town with miles of beaches for sunning and surfing, thousands of acres of mountaintop forests for hiking, and a lively historic boardwalk amusement park – complete with a wild wooden rollercoaster – for strolling. But there's another side to Santa Cruz: the town has grown unwieldy (and more expensive) over the last couple of decades, fuelled largely by its role as a dormitory suburb for San Jose and Silicon Valley. It's also home to a great number of homeless people who've spilled over from San Francisco and neighboring communities to benefit from the town's numerous liberal resources, joining with its hippie past to bring out the crustier side of local life. Some of Santa Cruz's suburbs have a redneck feel more akin to the Central Valley than the laid-back languid coast; all this means that you rarely get an impression of a resort totally at ease with itself. The underlying conflicts are one of the many reasons why the town is so slow to change and makes an intriguingly schizophrenic place to visit.

The town's enduring reputation as a holdout from the 1960s is only fitting since this is where it all began. Ken Kesey and his Merry Pranksters turned the local youth on to the wonders of LSD years before it defined a generation, a mission recorded by Tom Wolfe in *The Electric Koolaid Acid Test*. The area is still considered among the most politically and socially progressive in California – one reason that Santa Cruz has become known, in recent years, as a lesbian mecca (see below). The town is also surprisingly untouristy: no hotels spoil the miles of wave-beaten coastline – in fact, most of the surrounding land is used for growing fruit and vegetables, and roadside stalls are more likely to be selling apples or sprouts than postcards and souvenirs. Places to stay are for once good value and easy to find, and the town sports a range of bookstores and coffeehouses, as well as some lively bars and nightclubs where the music varies from hard-core surf-punk to longtime local Neil Young and friends.

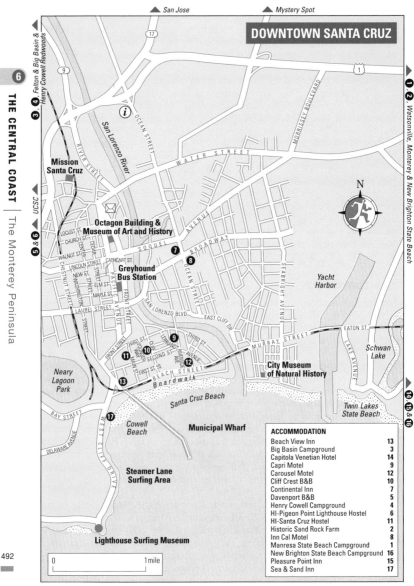

DOWNTOWN SANTA CRUZ

San Jose

Mystery Spot

Felton & Big Basin & Henry Cowell Redwoods

Watsonville, Monterey & New Brighton State Beach

UCSC

Mission Santa Cruz

San Lorenzo River

OCEAN STREET

RIVER STREET

WATER STREET

MORRISSEY BOULEVARD

N

Octagon Building & Museum of Art and History

LOCUST ST

CHURCH ST

WALNUT ST

CEDAR

CHURCH CENTER

CATHCART ST

PACIFIC AVENUE

SOQUEL AVENUE

BROADWAY

OCEAN STREET

SEABRIGHT AVENUE

Yacht Harbor

LINCOLN STREET

NEW ST

WASHINGTON

ELM ST

MAPLE ST

CHESTNUT STREET

Greyhound Bus Station

FRONT STREET

SAN LORENZO BLVD

EAST CLIFF DR

LAUREL STREET

THIRD ST

THIRD ST

LEIBRANDT AVENUE

RIVERSIDE AVE

MURRAY STREET

EATON ST

LAKE AVENUE

Schwan Lake

Neary Lagoon Park

FRONT STREET

MAIN ST

WATER ST

SECOND ST

FIRST ST

BEACH STREET

Boardwalk

City Museum of Natural History

Santa Cruz Beach

BAY STREET

Twin Lakes State Beach

DELAWARE AVENUE

WEST CLIFF DRIVE

Cowell Beach

Municipal Wharf

Steamer Lane Surfing Area

Lighthouse Surfing Museum

ACCOMMODATION	
Beach View Inn	13
Big Basin Campground	3
Capitola Venetian Hotel	14
Capri Motel	9
Carousel Motel	12
Cliff Crest B&B	10
Continental Inn	7
Davenport B&B	5
Henry Cowell Campground	4
HI-Pigeon Point Lighthouse Hostel	6
HI-Santa Cruz Hostel	11
Historic Sand Rock Farm	2
Inn Cal Motel	8
Manresa State Beach Campground	1
New Brighton State Beach Campground	16
Pleasure Point Inn	15
Sea & Sand Inn	17

0   1 mile

Arrival, information, and city transportation

By **car**, Santa Cruz is on Hwy-1, 45 miles north of Monterey; Hwy-17 runs over the mountains, 33 miles from San Jose and US-101. **Greyhound buses** (☎831/423-1800) stop five times a day in each direction at 425 Front St in the center of town, with connecting services to all the major cities in the state. Amtrak Thruway buses connect the town with San Jose four times daily; there's also a weekly Green Tortoise. Coming from the Monterey Peninsula, local MST and SCMTD buses link up in Watsonville.

The **Santa Cruz Conference and Visitors Center** at 1211 Ocean St (Mon–Sat 9am–5pm, Sun 10am–4pm; ☎831/425-1234 or 1-800/833-3494, ⊛www.santacruz.org) has lots of handy information on places to stay, and sells a detailed map of the entire county for $1.50. To find out what's on in the area, check out the free magazine rack at the **Bookshop Santa Cruz**, 1520 Pacific Ave (☎831/423-0900), where you'll find generally useful weeklies like *Good Times* and the *Santa Cruz Metro*; another option is to pick up a copy of the local newspaper, *The Santa Cruz Sentinel*.

Santa Cruz has an excellent **public transportation system**, based around the Metro Center wedged between Front Street and Pacific Avenue, and operated by the Santa Cruz Metropolitan Transit District or SCMTD (information Mon–Fri 8am–5pm; ☎831/425-8600, ⊛www.scmtd.com), which publishes *Headways*, a free bilingual guide to getting around the area. The basic fare is $1 and an all-day pass costs $3. Some of the most useful routes are #1, which runs up the hill to UCSC; #71 to Watsonville; #67 along the eastern beaches; and #3 to the western beaches. Route #35, which runs up Hwy-9 into the mountains to Big Basin Redwoods State Park, is equipped with bike racks.

Though there are buses to most of the beaches, you might find it easier to get around by **bicycle** – in fact, Santa Cruz is a bike-crazy town. Options for rental (all around $25 per day) include Another Bike Shop, 2361 Mission St (☎831/427-2232), Dave's Recycled Bikes, 822 Pacific Ave (closed Mon; ☎831/423-1169), or Electric Sierra Cycles, 302 Pacific Ave (☎831/425-1593 or 1-877/372-8773). The waterfront Go-Skate, 601 Beach St (☎831/425-8578), is the place to go for renting **skates** and **surfboards**. You can get ocean-going **kayaks** for $20 for 2 hours or $35 a day from Venture Quest on the wharf and at 125 Beach St (daily 10am–6pm; ☎831/427-2267, ⊛www.kayaksantacruz.com), and Santa Cruz Boat Rentals, 15 Municipal Wharf (☎831/426-4690, ⊛www.santacruzboatrentals.com), rent skiffs and fishing equipment along with bait and tackle.

Accommodation

Compared to most California beach resorts, **accommodation** in Santa Cruz is inexpensive and easy to come by, especially during the week or outside of summer: most of the establishments we've listed offer good-value weekly rates and there's a clump of inexpensive motels along Ocean Street. **Camping** opportunities in and around Santa Cruz are abundant and varied, from beaches to forests and points in between; **reservations** for all state park campgrounds are handled through ParkNet (☎1-800/444-7275).

Hotels, motels, and B&Bs

Beach View Inn 50 Front St ☎831/426-3575, ⊛www.beach-viewinn.com. Clean budget motel near the boardwalk. ❸

Carousel Motel 110 Riverside Ave ☎831/425- 7090 or 1-800/214-7400. Recently remodelled offseason bargain with clean, simple rooms, right next to the boardwalk; free continental breakfast. Rates double in summer. ❷

Capitola Venetian Hotel 1500 Wharf Rd, Capitola

831/476-6471 or 1-800/332-2780. Quirky, age-ing beachfront hotel just across the bridge from Capitola's lively esplanade. All rooms have kitchens, some are two-bedroom suites; rates increase at weekends when there's a two-night minimum. Weekly rental begins at $325.

Capri Motel 337 Riverside Ave ☎831/426-4611. The cheapest of a dozen or so budget motels near the beach and the boardwalk. ❶

Cliff Crest B&B Inn 407 Cliff St ☎831/427-2609, ⓦwww.cliffcrestinn.com. Plushly furnished 1887 Queen Anne-style Victorian home with only five guest rooms, set in lovely gardens at the top of Beach Hill. It's within walking distance of the boardwalk and rates include a full breakfast served in the conservatory and afternoon sherry. ❼

Continental Inn 414 Ocean St ☎831/429-1221, ⓦwww.continentalinn.net. Top value for an off-the-bottom-rung motel. Comfortable if basic rooms and an easy walk to everything. ❸

Davenport Bed and Breakfast Inn 31 Davenport Ave, Davenport ☎831/423-1160 or 1-800/870-1817, ⓦwww.swanton.com/BnB. This is the only accommodation in Davenport, and it's a funky inn, with slightly run-down ethnic decor, rooms filled with brightly colored throws and mirrored pillows. ❺

Historic Sand Rock Farm 6901 Freedom Blvd, Aptos ☎831/688-8005, ⓦwww.sandrockfarm .com. Owned by a local chef, this five-room guesthouse has been lovingly restored and filled with Arts & Crafts antiques. A secluded bolthole away from the beach. ❻

Inn Cal Motel 370 Ocean St ☎831/458-9220 or 1-800/550-0055 . Across the river from the center of town, with clean, no-frills double rooms. A winter bargain and very popular (hence pricier) in summer. ❸

Pleasure Point Inn 2-3665 E Cliff Drive ☎408/291-0299, ⓦwww.pleasurepointinn.com. A well-designed, hip B&B with clifftop views, a roof sundeck, and hot tub: rooms have built-in stereos, Jacuzzi baths, and all amenities. Highly recommended for those allergic to chintz. ❼

Sea and Sand Inn 201 West Cliff Drive ☎831/427-3400. This small, upscale motel is well situated on the wharf, with great views over the bay and subdued decor. Complimentary breakfast. ❺

Hostels

HI-Pigeon Point Lighthouse Hostel Pescadero ☎650/879-0633. Located some 25 miles north of town, near Año Nuevo State Park, but well worth the effort for a chance to bunk down in the old lighthouse keeper's quarters right on the point. Dorm beds $13–15 per person, plus $3 for non-HI members; more expensive private doubles, and there's an excellent hot tub ($6 per half-hour) hanging out over the thundering surf. Office open 7.30–10am, 5.30–10pm. ❶

HI-Santa Cruz Hostel 321 Main St ☎831/423-8304, ⓦwww.hi-santacruz.org. Well-situated hostel in a set of 1870s cottages just a couple of blocks from the beach. The atmosphere is informal but the place is closed during the day and is often booked up in advance. Members $17–20; office open 7–10pm for reservations. ❶

Campgrounds

Big Basin Redwoods State Park 21600 Big Basin Way on Hwy-236, Boulder Creek ☎831/338-8860 or 1-800/444-7275. High up in the hills; sites with showers for $12, and numerous backcountry sites for hikers and mountain bikers. ❶

Henry Cowell Redwoods State Park 101 N Big Trees Park Rd, Felton ☎831/335-4598 or 1-800/444-7275. In the hills above town and UC Santa Cruz, in a redwood grove along the San Lorenzo River. Bus #35 serves the park, and sites cost $12 a night. ❶

Manresa State Beach Campground 205 Manresa Rd, La Selva Beach ☎831/761-1795 or 1-800/444-7275 Isolated, tent-only site by a forested ravine that runs into the sand. Sites with showers $12. ❶

New Brighton State Beach 1500 Park Ave, Capitola (☎831/464-6330 or 1-800/444-7275). Three miles south of Santa Cruz on the edge of the beachfront village of Capitola, set on bluffs above a lengthy strand. Sites cost $12 a night, including hot showers. ❶

The Town

Santa Cruz provides a sharp contrast to the upscale resort sophistication of Monterey Peninsula across the bay. This sleepy community of 45,000 residents, along with 10,000 students, is spread out at the foot of thickly wooded mountains along a clean, sandy shore. There's not a lot to see in the town, almost all of which is within a ten-minute walk of the beach, apart from the many blocks of Victorian wooden houses.

The sluggish San Lorenzo River wraps around the town center, two blocks east of **Pacific Garden Mall**, a landscaped, prettified, and pedestrianized stretch of Pacific Avenue that is Santa Cruz's main street, lined with bookstores, record and beachwear shops, and cafés. Disheveled hippies, trapped forever in their favorite decade, wander ceaselessly along the mall's length, brushing shoulders with wealthy shoppers who dodge occasionally into clothing and furniture stores. The homeless and the practically homeless cluster around park benches in the area, playing instruments, distributing literature, or simply dozing off.

One place that survived the massive 1989 earthquake which damaged a large portion of the town is the ornate brick-and-stone **Octagon Building**, 118 Cooper St, at the north end of Pacific Avenue. Completed in 1882 as the Santa Cruz Hall of Records, it now houses the museum store along with an exhibit or two from the adjacent **Museum of Art and History** at 705 Front St (Tues–Wed, Fri–Sun 11am–5pm, Thurs 11pm–7pm; $4; ☎831/429-1964, ⓦwww.santacruzmah.org), which has a sprightly display on the region's checkered history. Several blocks away, past the clocktower fountain on Pacific and up the hill at 126 High St, fragments dating from the region's earlier Spanish colonial days are shown off in a restored army barracks, next to a scaled-down replica of **Mission Santa Cruz** (daily 9am–5pm; free; ☎831/426-5686, ⓦwww.geocities.com/athens/aegean/715/). The original adobe church, the sixteenth in the mission chain, was destroyed by an earthquake in 1857; the half-scale replica that stands on its site today was built in the twentieth century and is dwarfed by a large Gothic Revival church next door.

Between the town center and the beach, **Beach Hill** rises at the foot of Pacific Avenue, its slopes lined with some of Santa Cruz's finest turn-of-the-century homes, such as the striking Queen Anne-style house at 417 Cliff St, and the slightly odd structure around the corner at 912 3rd St, constructed out of the remains of a shipwreck.

The boardwalk and around

Standing out at the foot of the low-rise town in a slightly run-down neighborhood, the **Santa Cruz Boardwalk**, 40 Beach St (June–Aug daily 11am–10pm; fall and spring weekends only, call for hours; closed Dec; $1.80–3.60 per ride, unlimited rides $23.95; ☎831/426-7433 or 831/423-5590, ⓦwww.beachboardwalk.com), stretches half a mile along the sands, one of the last surviving beachfront amusement parks on the West Coast. Packed solid on weekends with teenagers on the prowl, most of the time it's a friendly funfair where barefoot hippies mix with mushroom farmers and their families. First opened in 1907 as a gambling casino, the elegant *Coconut Grove* at the west end has recently undergone a $10 million restoration, and the grand ballroom now hosts 1940s swing bands and salsa and R&B combos, offering a change of pace from the raucous string of bumper cars, shooting galleries, log flume rides, and Ferris wheels that line up beside the wide beach, filled in with every sort of arcade game and test of skill. The star attraction is the 80-year-old **Giant Dipper**, a wild wooden rollercoaster that's been ridden by more than 45 million people and is listed on the National Register of Historic Places; it often doubles for a Coney Island attraction in the movies.

Half a mile west of the boardwalk, the hundred-year-old wooden **Municipal Pier** juts out into the bay, crammed with fresh-fish shops, burger joints, and seafood restaurants, at the end of which people fish for crabs. You don't need a license and can rent tackle from one of the many bait shops. Just east of the boardwalk, across the river, the small **Santa Cruz City Museum of Natural**

History, 1305 East Cliff Drive (Tues–Sun 10am–5pm; $2; ☏831/420-6115, Ⓦwww.santacruzmuseums.org), marked by a concrete whale, has concise displays describing local animals and sea creatures and a brief description of the local Native American culture.

The beaches

The **beach** closest to town, along the boardwalk, is wide and sandy, with lots of volleyball courts and water that is warm enough for swimming in summer. Not surprisingly, it can get crowded, rowdy, and dirty, so for a bit more peace and quiet, or to catch the largest waves, simply follow the coastline east or west of town to one of the smaller beaches hidden away at the foot of the cliffs: most are undeveloped and easily accessible.

From the City Museum, **East Cliff Drive** winds along the top of the bluffs, past many coves and estuaries. The nearest of the two coastal lagoons that border the volleyball courts of **Twin Lakes State Beach** half a mile east at Seventh Avenue (☏831/429-2850), was dredged and converted into a marina in the 1960s. The other, **Schwann Lake**, is still intact, its marshy wetlands serving as a refuge for sea birds and migrating waterfowl. Twin Lakes is often warmer than the surrounding area, thanks to its proximity to Schwann Lagoon; beyond here, you'll come to **Lincoln Beach** and good tidepools at **Corcoran Lagoon**, a half-mile on.

East Cliff Drive continues past popular surfing spots off rocky **Pleasure Point**, to the small beachfront resort of **Capitola**. The town, three miles east of central Santa Cruz, began as a fishing village, living off the many giant tuna that populated the Monterey Bay, but soon became popular as a holiday spot, with its own railway line. The large wooden trestle of the now-disused railroad still dominates what is now a moneyed town, rising over the soft and peaceful sands of **Hooper Beach**, west of the small fishing pier. Capitola is especially attractive in late summer, when the hundreds of begonias – the town's main produce – are in bloom; at any time of year, the town is a relaxing escape from the rowdier Santa Cruz crowd. The **Chamber of Commerce**, 716G Capitola Ave (Mon–Fri 10am–4pm; ☏831/475-6522, Ⓦwww.capitolachamber.com), has all the usual information.

A bit further east you'll come upon **Aptos** – originally named Awatos, meaning "where the waters meet," by Native Americans. It's the most conservative settlement in the area and was devastated in 1989 by the earthquake whose epicenter was close by in the forest of Nisene Marks. Otherwise, it's best known for the shortest parade on earth every Fourth of July and the remains of the *Palo Alto*, an experimental concrete ship which dropped anchor in 1919 to become a long-defunct restaurant and dancehall. The **Chamber of Commerce**, at 7605A Old Dominion Court (Mon–Fri 9am–5pm, Sat 10am–5pm, Sun 10am–4pm; ☏831/688-1467, Ⓦwww.aptoschamber.com), has plenty of information and can help with accommodation reservations.

The beaches west of the Santa Cruz Boardwalk, along **West Cliff Drive**, see some of the biggest waves in California, not least at **Steamer Lane**, off the tip of Lighthouse Point beyond the Municipal Pier. Cowell Beach, just north of the municipal pier, is the best place to give surfing a try; Club Ed (☏831/459-9283), in the parking lot, will rent boards and assist with lessons. Otherwise, plenty of surfers also gather just off Pleasure Point Beach (☏831/454-7956). The ghosts of surfers past are animated at the **Surfing Museum** (Thurs–Mon noon–4pm; donation suggested; ☏831/420-6289, Ⓦwww.cruzio.com/~scva /surf), housed in the old lighthouse on the point, which holds surfboards ranging from twelve-foot redwood planks used by the early pioneers to modern, high-tech, multi-finned cutters. A clifftop bicycle path runs two miles out from here to **Natural Bridges State Park** (8am–dusk; $6 per car; ☎831/423 - 4609), where waves have cut holes through the coastal cliffs, forming delicate arches in the remaining stone; three of the four bridges after which the park was named have since collapsed, leaving large stacks of stone sticking out of the surf. The park is also famous – like Pacific Grove further south – for its annual gathering of monarch butterflies, thousands of whom return each winter.

Above Santa Cruz: UCSC and the mountains

The **University of California at Santa Cruz**, on the hills above the town (served by SCMTD bus #1), is very much a product of the 1960s: students don't take exams or get grades, and the academic program stresses individual exploration of topics rather than rote learning. Architecturally, too, it's deliberately different. Its 2000-acre park-like campus is divided into small, autonomous colleges, where deer stroll among the redwood trees overlooking Monterey Bay – a decentralized plan drawn up under the then-governor Ronald Reagan, which cynics claim was intended as much to diffuse protests as to provide a peaceful backdrop for study. You can judge for yourself by taking one of the guided tours that start from the **visitor center** at the foot of campus (☎831/459-0111). If you don't have time to visit the entire campus, at least stop by the **UCSC Arboretum** (daily 9am–5pm; free; ☎831/427-2998, ⓦwww2.ucsc.edu/arboretum), world famous for its experimental cultivation techniques and its collections of plants from New Zealand, South Africa, Australia, and South America, all landscaped as they would be in their original habitats.

On the south side of the San Lorenzo River, three miles up Branciforte Drive from the center of town, there's a point within the woods where normal laws of gravity no longer apply. Here, trees grow at odd angles, balls roll uphill, and bright yellow stickers appear on the bumpers of cars that pass too close to the **Mystery Spot** (frequent 40min tours; June–Aug daily 9am–7pm; Sept–May 9am–4.20pm; $5; ☎831/423-8897, ⓦwww.mysteryspot.com). Many explanations are offered – including extraterrestrial interference – but most of the disorientation is caused by perspective tricks used in the exhibits spread out around the forest to magically attract tourist dollars.

High up in the mountains that separate Santa Cruz from Silicon Valley and the San Francisco Bay Area, SCMTD bus #35 runs to the village of **Felton**, six miles north of Santa Cruz on Hwy-9, where the hundred-year-old **Roaring Camp and Big Trees Narrow Gauge Railroad** (summer daily 11am–3pm; rest of year departures on most weekdays at 11am, Sat & Sun at 10.30am, 11am, 12.15pm, 2pm, 2.30pm; parking $5, steam train ride $15.50, beach train ride $17; ☎831/335-4484, ⓦwww.roaringcamp.com), steams on a six-mile loop amongst the massive trees that cover the slopes of the **Henry Cowell Redwoods State Park** (dawn–dusk; $6 per car; ☎831/335-4598) along the San Lorenzo River gorge. From the same station the 1920s-era **Santa Cruz Big Trees and Pacific Railway Company** (see above) powers down to the boardwalk and back (or you can board there and ride up) in around two and a half hours. **Felton Covered Bridge**, out on the same road a mile east of town is also worth a look, if you've got a car; it spans the river between heavily wooded slopes.

Buses continue further up the mountains to the **Big Basin Redwoods State Park** ($5 per vehicle; ☎831/338-8860), an hour's ride from Santa Cruz, where acres of three-hundred-foot-tall redwood trees cover some 25 square miles of untouched wilderness, with excellent hiking and camping. A popular

"Skyline-to-the-Sea" backpacking **trail** steps down through cool, moist canyons ten miles to the coast – fifteen miles north of Santa Cruz and less than ten from the former whaling town of **Davenport** – at **Waddell Creek Beach**, a favorite spot for watching world-class windsurfers negotiate the waves. From here, SCMTD bus #40 (twice daily) can take you back to town.

Eating

Restaurants in and around Santa Cruz are surprisingly diverse: from vegetarian cafés and all-American burger-and-beer bars to elegant dining options including a number of good seafood establishments on the wharf. The Wednesday afternoon **Farmers Market** downtown, popular with local hippies, is a good place to pick up fresh produce.

Bittersweet Bistro 787 Rio Del Mar Blvd, Rio Del Mar ☎831/662-9799. Delicately prepared gourmet fish and pasta dishes for $15–20. Don't miss the beautifully presented desserts. A few miles east of Santa Cruz along Hwy-1, but worth the trip.
Café Cruz 2621 41st Ave, Soquel ☎831/476-3801. Tasty, reasonably priced Italian food in a Tuscan-inspired courtyard setting, inauspiciously located across from K-Mart. Delicious smoked chicken specials.
Charlie Hong Kong's 1141 Soquel Ave ☎831/426-5664. Small, pagoda-like hut with limited outdoor seating serving tasty, mostly vegetarian noodle dishes for under $5.
Ciao Bella 9127 Hwy-9, Ben Lomond ☎831/336-9221. A shrine to everything outlandish, this bar/restaurant a few miles from downtown is known more for its campily outrageous atmosphere than for its food. Great fun, even so, especially when the leather short-sporting owner is holding court. Reservations essential.
Clouds Downtown 110 Church St ☎831/429-2000. Well-seasoned meats and Cal-Italian dishes in a pleasantly upbeat environment. The stuffed portobello mushrooms are especially good. Entrées go for $10–20.
Costa Brava 1222 Pacific Ave ☎831/425-7871. Innovative Latin American food with Italian and Californian influences. Exceptional atmosphere and portions for the price. There's another location at 505 Seabright Ave ☎831/423-8190.
The Crepe Place 1134 Soquel Ave ☎831/429-6994. Thirty-year local institution that serves bargain stuffed crepes with savory and sweet fillings – try the Crepe Gatsby. The flower-filled, tumbleweed back garden is a groovy place to lounge on a warm summer evening. Highly recommended.
Crow's Nest Santa Cruz Yacht Harbor, 2218 East Cliff Drive ☎831/476-4560. The modern American, fish-dominated menu here's tasty, if a little overpriced, but the real reason to come is for the spectacular views across the bay: eat dinner

early and catch a fiery sunset. There's also a standard pub-style bar upstairs.
Davenport Restaurant and Cash Store in the *Davenport Inn*, 31 Davenport Ave, Davenport ☎831/426-4122. Rustic atmosphere in a peaceful coastal inn with undisturbed views of the coast and notoriously decadent cinnamon rolls.
Gabriella Wine Shop 1016 Cedar St ☎831/457-1217. Snack on light, flavor-packed panini and a glass of wine at this café, or gorge yourself on fresh Cal-Italian food in a rustic setting at the nearby restaurant (no. 910; ☎831/457-1677) owned by the same team. The tiny secluded patio is a first-date dream.
El Palomar 1336 Pacific Ave ☎831/425-7575. Don't be put off by the location (on the ground floor of a historic building that was once a resort hotel and now houses government-subsidized apartments). This mid-range Mexican serves standard dishes, most with a fishy twist, for between $11–15 per entrée.
Santa Cruz Coffee Roasting Co 1330 Pacific Ave ☎831/459-0100. Just the place to start the day, with an excellent range of coffees, by the bean or by the cup.
Shadowbrook 1750 Wharf Rd, Capitola ☎831/475-1511. Very romantic, very upscale steak and seafood place, stepping down along the banks of a creek.
Taqueria Vallarta 1101-A Pacific Ave ☎831/471-2655. It looks like a fast-food joint, but the food is cooked to order and authentic, and they even serve rice and tangy tamarind drinks. Don't be shy to ask for plenty of tortilla chips with your order – the self-service salsa bar has a delicious range to try.
Walnut Avenue Café 106 Walnut Ave ☎831/457-2307.This diner is a hearty local favorite serving massive, cheap breakfasts, and lunches, only a block from Pacific Avenue Mall.
Zoccoli's Deli 1534 Pacific Ave at Water St ☎831/423-1711. Old Italian deli serving up hearty food, including a minestrone that's a meal in itself:

find it by the wafting smells of garlic and basil that snake down the sidewalk from its outdoor café. Mon–Sat 10am–6pm, longer hours in summer. **Zoccoli's Pasta House** 431 Front Ave ☎831/423-1717. Same owners as the deli of the same name, this restaurant serves giant mid-range pasta dinners in a casual setting.

Bars and nightlife

Santa Cruz has the Central Coast's rowdiest **nightlife**, ranging from coffee-houses to bars and nightclubs where the music varies from surf-thrash to reggae to the rowdy rock of local resident Neil Young – sometimes all on the same dancefloor. Residents may wear tie-dye, but that doesn't mean they're not capable of breaking into fistfights. For hanging out, your best bet is the range of espresso bars and coffeehouses lining Pacific Avenue; otherwise, we've listed a range of nightlife options – check with *Good Times* for the latest listings. The Rio Theatre, 1205 Soquel Ave (☎831/423-8209, ⓦwww.riotheatre.com), is an arthouse **cinema** that shows first-run foreign and indie films as well as hosting eclectic concerts: don't miss the building itself, which is a postwar masterpiece.

99 Bottles of Beer 110 Walnut Ave ☎831/459-9999. This airy pub-style bar offers more than 40 beers on tap: the crowd's friendly and more mainstream than in many other local drinking holes.
Asti 715 Pacific Ave ☎831/423-7337. Divey, old-timers' cocktail lounge that now attracts a sizeable crowd of postmodern arty types who enjoy its retro grittiness.
Caffè Pergolesi 418a Cedar St ☎831/426-1775. Fun, friendly coffeehouse in an old wooden house with a garden. Open until around midnight.
The Catalyst 1011 Pacific Ave ☎831/423-1336. The main venue for big-name touring artists and up-and-coming locals, this medium-sized club has something happening nearly every night. Usually 21 and over only; cover varies.
Henfling's Firehouse Taven 9450 Hwy-9, Ben Lomond ☎831/336-8811. Softcore biker bar with good live blues and classic rock most nights.
Lulu Carpenter's 1545 Pacific Ave ☎831/429-9804. Stylish yet cozy café, serving gooey cakes, coffees and drinks, open from 6.30am until midnight. Housed in one of the few downtown buildings to survive the 1989 earthquake, it has a bar/lounge vibe, an open courtyard out back, and is lively most evenings.
Kuumbwa Jazz Center 320 Cedar St ☎831/427-2227. The Santa Cruz showcase for traditional and modern jazz, in a friendly and intimate garden setting tucked back in a small alley. Mondays are usually the big-name nights, as performers like Chick Corea stop off on their way to San Francisco. Cover ranges from $1–15.
Red Room 1003 Cedar St ☎831/426-2994. Hip spot for cocktails and conversation.

Gay and Lesbian Santa Cruz

Santa Cruz is gaining ground fast as one of the country's hippest lesbian hang-outs, and there's also a sizeable local gay population. For information, stop by the well-connected LGBT Diversity Center, 177 Walnut Ave (☎831/425-5422, ⓦwww.diversitycenter.org), or check in at Herland, 1014 Cedar St (☎831/429-6636, ⓦherland@cruzio.com), a lesbian/feminist store selling books and CDs that also has a large message board for events. Otherwise, grab one of the monthly free **newspapers** – either *La Gazette* for girls or *Manifesto*, which has listings for boys too. Most local **accommodation** is gay-friendly, although the *Compassionflower Inn*, 216 Laurel St (☎831/466-0420, ⓦwww.compassionflowerinn.com; ⑥), in a gorgeously restored Victorian mansion is especially lovely; it's a self-proclaimed "Bed, Bud & Breakfast" that allows those with doctors' approval to light up on the premises. As for **nightlife**, there are two main options: *Blue Lagoon*, 923 Pacific Ave (☎831/423-7117), for boys, where good DJs spin techno and hip hop on weekends and *Club Dakota*, 1209 Pacific Ave (☎831/454-9030, ⓦwww.dakota.com), for girls and a few guys, which is open Mon–Fri 4pm–2am, Sat–Sun 2pm–2am (21 and over, and bring

ID). Further afield, the camp disco extravaganza at *Franco's Norma Jean Club*, 10639 Merritt St in Castroville (℗831/633-2090), named in honor of Marilyn Monroe, also attracts gay locals and visitors from around the area.

The coast north to San Francisco

The **Año Nuevo State Reserve**, New Year's Creek Road (8am–sunset; parking $5; ℗650/879-0227), twenty-five miles north of Santa Cruz, was named by the explorer Vizcaíno, who sailed past on New Year's Day 1603. It's a beautiful spot to visit at any time of year, and in winter you shouldn't miss the chance to see one of nature's most bizarre spectacles – the mating rituals of the Northern Elephant Seal. These massive, ungainly creatures, fifteen feet long and weighing up to three tons, gather on the rocks and sand dunes to fight for a mate. The male's distinctive, pendulous nostrils aid him in his noisy honking, which is how he attracts the females; their blubbery forms are capable of diving deeper than any other mammal, to depths of over 4500ft. Obligatory three-hour **tours** (℗650/879-2025 for information; $4) are organized during the breeding season (Dec 15–Mar 31); throughout the year you're likely to see at least a few, dozing in the sands. See "Contexts'" p.808, for more on the elephant seal's mating habits, and on other coastal creatures.

Five miles north of Año Nuevo, Gazos Creek Road heads inland three miles to **Butano State Park** (8am–sunset; $2 per car; ℗650/879-2040), which has five square miles of redwood trees, views out over the Pacific, and **camping** amongst the redwoods for $12 (reserve through ParkNet ℗1-800/444-7275). Another two miles north along Hwy-1, and fifty miles south of the Golden Gate Bridge, the beginning of the San Francisco Peninsula is marked by the **Pigeon Point Lighthouse** and the adjacent **hostel** (see p.494), where you can spend the night in the old lighthouse keeper's quarters and relax in a hot tub, cantilevered out over the rocks. Pigeon Point took its name from the clipper ship, *Carrier Pigeon*, that broke up on the rocks off the point, one of many shipwrecks that led to the construction of the lighthouse in the late nineteenth century.

The cargo of one of these wrecked ships inspired residents of the nearby fishing village of **Pescadero**, a mile inland on Pescadero Road, literally to "paint the town," using the hundreds of pots of white paint that were washed up on the shore. The two streets of the small village are still lined with white wooden buildings, and the descendants of the Portuguese whalers who founded the town keep up another tradition, celebrating the **Festival of the Holy Ghost** every year, six weeks after Easter, with a lively and highly ritualized parade. Pescadero is also well known as one of the better places to **eat** on the entire coast, with the excellent *Duarte's* restaurant, 202 Stage Rd (℗650/879-0464), and, at the other end of the price scale, *Los Amigos*, a celebrated fast-food Mexican restaurant in the gas station on the corner.

Half Moon Bay is really the next place of note north along the coast, and is covered in the San Francisco and the Bay Area chapter on p.625.

Travel details

LA to: Amtrak's Coast Starlight leaves at 9.30am for Oakland (1 daily; 10hr 45min; a shuttle bus connects to San Francisco); Salinas (1 daily; 8hr 15min); San Jose (1 daily; 9hr 50min); San Luis Obispo (3 daily; 5hr 20min); Santa Barbara (1 daily; 2hr 30min); and continues on through Sacramento, Chico, Redding, through Oregon to Seattle.

One train a day leaves Oakland at 9.30am on the return route.

All buses are Greyhound unless otherwise stated.

LA to: Salinas (8 daily; 8hr); San Francisco (19 daily; 8–12hr; also one Green Tortoise per week in each direction along the coast); San Luis Obispo (7 daily; 4hr 45min); Santa Barbara (11 daily; 3hr 10min); Santa Cruz (6 daily; 10hr 30min).

Oakland to: Santa Cruz (4 daily; 2 hr).

San Francisco to: LA (19 daily; 8–12hr); Monterey (6 daily; 4hr); Sacramento (21 daily; 2hr 20min); Salinas (10 daily; 2hr 45min); San Luis Obispo (6 daily; 6hr); Santa Barbara (6 daily; 7hr); Santa Cruz (4 daily; 2hr 40min); San Jose (16 daily; 1hr 30min).

San Jose to: Santa Cruz (4 daily; 1hr).

6

THE CENTRAL COAST | Travel details

San Francisco and the Bay Area

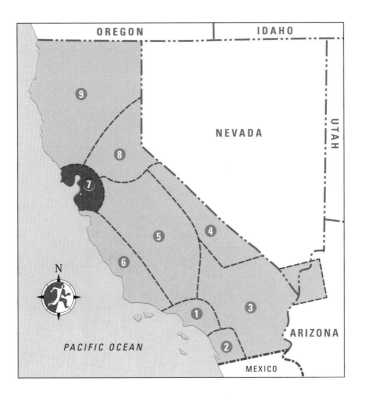

CHAPTER 7

Highlights

* **Jackson Square** Time-travel back to see how San Francisco looked before the devastating fire and earthquake of 1906. See p.528

* **Valencia Street** Check out the hipster artery of the Mission, where Anglo and Latino cultures collide. See p.546

* **Tien Hou temple, Chinatown** Festooned with gold and red lanterns, cloudy with heady incense, this temple is a precious relic of old Chinatown. See p.530

* **Cable cars** Famous for a good reason, these glorious old trams offer both irresistible photo opportunities and a leisurely way to avoid climbing downtown San Francisco's heftiest hills. See p.526

* **Telegraph Avenue, Berkeley** This lively strip gives you the chance to check out a dazzling array of politically subversive stalls, book and music stores, and cafés. See p.603

* **Whale watching, Point Reyes** The lighthouse at the westernmost point of the Point Reyes National Seashore is a great spot to spot migrating gray whales. See p.642

San Francisco and the Bay Area

O ne of the prettiest and most liberal cities in the US – it certainly has had more platitudes heaped upon it than any other – **SAN FRAN-CISCO** is in serious danger of being clichéd to death. In the last twenty-five years, though, the city has undergone a steady transition from the iconoclasm that made it famous to become a swanky, high-end town with a palpable air of widespread affluence. One by one, the central neighborhoods have been smartened up, with poorer families edged out into the suburbs, leaving only a couple of areas that could still be considered transitional. Ironically, some of the groups who began on the margins, like the gay and lesbian community, are now wealthy and influential, even a little conservative.

For all the change, however, San Francisco remains an outdoorsy, surprisingly small city whose people pride themselves on being the cultured counterparts to their cousins in LA, as if it were the last bastion of civilization on the lunatic fringe of America. A steadfast rivalry exists between the two cities: San Franciscans like to think of themselves as less obsessed with money, less riddled with status than those in the south – a rare kind of inverted snobbery, which Angelenos sniffily dismiss and which you'll come across almost immediately. But San Francisco has its own element of narcissism, rooted in the sheer physical aspect of the place. Downtown streets lean upwards on impossible gradients to reveal stunning views of the city, the Bay, and beyond. It has a romantic weather pattern, blanket fogs roll in unexpectedly to envelop the city in mist, adding a surreal quality to an already unique appearance.

This is not, however, the California of monotonous blue skies – the temperatures rarely exceed the seventies, and even during summer they can drop much lower, when consistent and heavy fogs muscle in on the city and the area as a whole. Autumn is the best time to visit, as warm temperatures and cloudless skies fill the days of September and October.

San Francisco proper occupies just 48 hilly square miles at the tip of a slender peninsula, almost perfectly centered on the California coast. But its metropolitan area sprawls out far beyond these narrow confines, east and north across to the far sides of the Bay, and south back down the coastal strip. This is the **BAY AREA**, one of the most rapidly growing regions in the US: less than 750,000 people live in the actual city, but there are seven million in the Bay

Area as a whole. It's something of a mixed bag. In the East Bay, across one of the two great bridges that connect San Francisco with its hinterland, are industrial **Oakland** and the radical locus of **Berkeley**; while to the south lies the gloating new wealth of **the Peninsula**, which has earned the tag of "Silicon Valley" thanks to its multi-billion-dollar computer industries, wiping out the agriculture which still predominated as recently as twenty-five years ago. Across

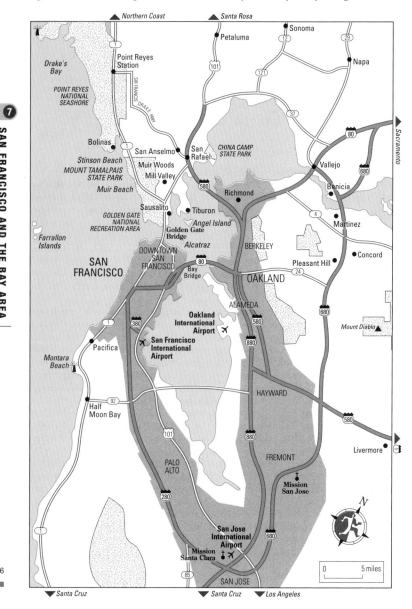

the Golden Gate Bridge to the north, **Marin County** is the Bay Area's wealth-iest suburb, its woody, leafy landscape and rugged coastline a bucolic – though in places very chic – harbinger of the delights of California's earthy northern coast. Specific practical information on the different Bay Area locales is given within the various regional accounts, which begin on p.587.

San Francisco

A compact and highly approachable place of some four dozen or so hills by the Bay, San Francisco is one of the few US cities in which you can survive com-fortably without a car. Indeed, given how expensive and time-consuming park-ing can be – not to mention how agreeable its year-round climate – walking is the ideal daytime mode for taking in the city's world-renowned museums, stately Victorian homes, sophisticated and historic neighborhoods, and stirring hilltop vistas. After dark, San Francisco is quite safe for visitors exercising rea-sonable caution, affording an eclectic array of international cuisine as well as a vibrant nightlife for gays and straights.

Some history

The original inhabitants of San Francisco were **Ohlone Indians**, who lived in some 35 villages spread out around the Bay. In 1776, **Mission Dolores**, the sixth in the chain of Spanish Catholic missions that ran the length of California, was established and harsh mission life, combined with the spread of European diseases, killed off the natives within a few generations. Mexicans took over from the Spanish in the early 1820s, but their hold was tenuous, and the area finally came under American rule after the **Bear Flag Revolt** of 1846, which took place a few miles north in Sonoma. The bloodless coup was supported by local land-owning *alcaldes* (a hybrid of judge and mayor), who recognized the potential of huge profits. The coup brought US Marines, sail-ing on the *USS Portsmouth*, into the San Francisco Bay that year, prompting one soldier, John Fremont, to christen its spectacular entrance the "**Golden Gate.**" The Marines docked their boat at the tiny town plaza founded in 1835 by British sailor William Richardson and renamed it **Portsmouth Square**, raising an American flag and claiming the city for the United States. The fol-lowing year, the hamlet known as Yerba Buena was rechristened San Francisco, honoring the dying wish of Father Junípero Serra, the Franciscan founder of Mission Dolores.

Just over ten years later, in 1848, San Francisco's population exploded when pioneer Sam Brannan bounded across Portsmouth Square waving bottles of gold dust he claimed came from the Sierra foothills and ignited the **Gold Rush**. Within a year, fifty thousand pioneers had arrived from all over the country as well as overseas, especially China, turning San Francisco from a muddy village and wasteland of dunes into a thriving supply center and tran-sit town. By the time the **transcontinental railroad** was completed in 1869, San Francisco was a lawless, rowdy boomtown of bordellos and drinking dens, something the monied elite – who hit it big on the much more dependable

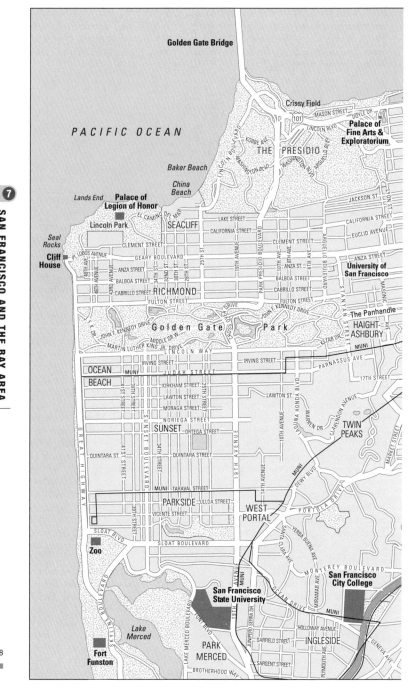

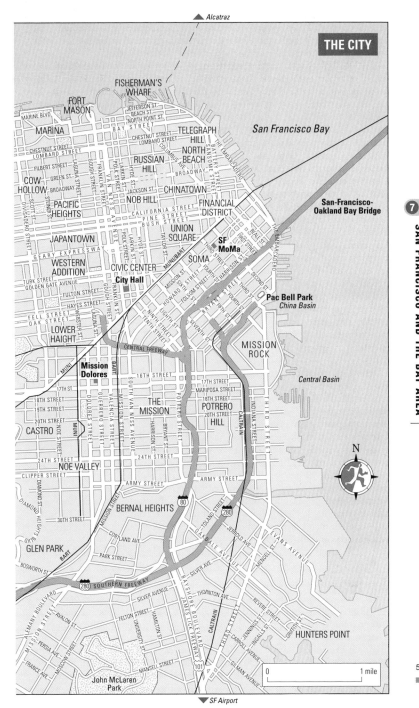

Alcatraz

THE CITY

San Francisco Bay

FISHERMAN'S WHARF

FORT MASON

MARINE BLVD

JEFFERSON ST.
BEACH ST.
NORTH POINT ST.
BAY STREET

MARINA

CHESTNUT STREET
LOMBARD STREET

CHESTNUT STREET
LOMBARD STREET

TELEGRAPH HILL

FILBERT STREET

GREEN ST.

NORTH BEACH

RUSSIAN HILL

COLUMBUS AVENUE

BROADWAY

San-Francisco-
Oakland Bay Bridge

COW HOLLOW

BROADWAY

PACIFIC HEIGHTS

SCOTT ST.
STEINER ST.
DIVISADERO STREET

JACKSON ST.

CHINATOWN

NOB HILL

CALIFORNIA STREET

PINE STREET

BUSH STREET

FINANCIAL DISTRICT

San-Francisco-
Oakland Bay Bridge

JAPANTOWN

GEARY EXPRESSWAY

UNION SQUARE

SF MoMa

WESTERN ADDITION

TURK STREET
GOLDEN GATE AVENUE

CIVIC CENTER

SOMA

City Hall

FULTON STREET

HAYES STREET

HOWARD ST
FOLSOM ST.

LOWER HAIGHT

FELL STREET
OAK STREET

Pac Bell Park
China Basin

CENTRAL FREEWAY

Mission Dolores

16TH STREET

MISSION ROCK

Central Basin

17TH STREET
MARIPOSA STREET
18TH STREET

18TH STREET
19TH STREET
20TH STREET

THE MISSION

POTRERO HILL

20TH STREET

CASTRO

24TH STREET

24TH STREET

NOE VALLEY

CLIPPER STREET

ARMY STREET

ARMY STREET

DIAMOND HEIGHTS BLVD

30TH STREET

BERNAL HEIGHTS

GLEN PARK

CORTLAND AVE.

PARK STREET

OAKDALE AVENUE

EVANS AVENUE

BOSWORTH ST.

280 SOUTHERN FREEWAY

SILVER AVE.

JERROLD AVE.

MENDELL

ALEMANY BOULEVARD

AVALON ST.

SILVER AVENUE

THORNTON AVE.

REVERE STREET

PERSIA AVE.
MOSCOW STREET

UNIVERSITY STREET

FELTON STREET
HAMILTON ST.

BAYSHORE BOULEVARD

JAMES LICK FREEWAY

HUNTERS POINT

FRANCE AVE.

MANSELL STREET

GILMAN AVENUE

John McLaren Park

0   1 mile

SF Airport

N

SAN FRANCISCO AND THE BAY AREA

7

509

silver Comstock Lode – worked hard to mend, constructing wide boulevards, parks, a cable car system, and elaborate Victorian redwood mansions, the latter replacing the whores as San Francisco's famed "Painted Ladies."

In 1906, however, a massive **earthquake**, followed by three days of fire, wiped out most of the town. Rebuilding began immediately, resulting in a city more magnificent than before, drawing anew writers, artists, and free spirits. In the decades that followed, writers like Dashiell Hammett and Jack London lived and worked here, as did Diego Rivera and other WPA-sponsored artists. During the Great Depression of the 1930s, San Francisco's position as the nexus of trade with Asia, coupled with its engineering projects – including both the Golden Gate and Bay bridges – lessened the agonies of the Depression for its residents. While the strict anti-immigration laws against the Chinese and the deportation of its Japanese citizens during World War II remains in memory, people here prefer to canonize the exploits of the Beat Generation in North Beach and Cow Hollow during the Fifties and the message of the Hippies during 1967's "Summer of Love" in the Haight-Ashbury district.

The city also prides itself on being the **gay capital** of the world: one of the most prominent local Democratic politicians is openly gay former stand-up comedian Tom Ammiano, who at time of writing is rumored as the potential next mayor of the city. San Francisco basks in its reputation as a liberal oasis and a model of tolerance – there's nowhere you won't see gay couples walking proudly hand in hand, for instance. But it also struggles with a certain smugness thank to its self-consciously open-minded attitude: the local mantra seems to be "live and let live" rather than "live with and let live," and different groups are tribally separated along lines of race, gender, and sexuality.

Despite its boldface fame as the hub of counterculture, San Francisco has always meant business and wealth, evinced today by a walk through the skyscraper-filled Financial District. Exquisite restaurants, new art museums, "shopping-entertainment" in designer malls, and the further gentrification of neighborhoods point to a **second Gold Rush**. San Francisco was the cradle of Internet mania, another example of the city's eye for the main chance – for a while many locals worried that one day they'd live in "SanFrancisco.com," a bedroom community of bistros for Silicon Valley. Tenancy rates throughout the city hovered at 99 percent full and housing prices rocketed: the once shabby South of Market area was bursting with Internet start-ups, at least until the Internet bubble itself burst and most went bust. Now, the city's reclaiming a calmer sense of self, although it's troubled more and more by a growing homeless population and local bureaucratic inefficiency that prevents much progress being made on their behalf.

Arrival

All international and most domestic flights arrive at **San Francisco International Airport** (SFO), located about fifteen miles south of the city. There are several ways of getting into town from here, each of which is clearly signed from the baggage reclaim areas. The least expensive is to take a San Mateo County Transit (SamTrans) **bus**, which leave every half-hour from the upper level of the airport; the #KX express ($3) takes around 25 minutes to reach the Transbay Terminal downtown, while the slower #292 ($1.10) stops frequently and takes nearly an hour. On the #KX, you're allowed only one carry-on bag; on the #292, you can bring as much as you want provided you can carry it onto the bus yourself. The SFO Airporter bus ($10) makes pick-ups outside each baggage claim area every fifteen minutes and travels to both Union Square and the Financial District. The Supershuttle, American Airporter Shuttle, and Yellow Airport Shuttle **minibuses** depart every five minutes from the upper level of the circular road and take passengers to any city-center destination for around $12 a head. Be ruthless – competition for these and the several other companies running shuttle services is fierce and lines nonexistent. **Taxis** from the airport cost $25–30 (plus tip) for any down-town location, more for East Bay and Marin County – definitely worth it if you're in a group or too tired to care. If you're planning to drive, the usual **car rental** agencies operate free shuttle buses to their depots, leaving every fifteen minutes from the upper level. A shuttle **train**, now under construction, will speed up the process once completed. Driving from SFO, head north on grit-ty US-101 or northwest on prettier I-280 for the 20–30-minute drive down-town.

Several domestic airlines fly into **Oakland International Airport** (OAK; see p.589 for details), across the Bay. As close to downtown San Francisco as SFO, OAK is efficiently connected with the city by the $2 AirBART shuttle bus, which drops you at the Coliseum BART station. Get on BART and San Francisco's downtown stops are fifteen minutes away ($2.75). The third region-al airport, **San Jose International** (SJO), also serves the Bay Area, but should only be considered if you plan to begin your stay in Silicon Valley. Fares in and out of SJO are comparable to the airports north and public transportation to the city is inconvenient.

Buses, trains, and driving

All of San Francisco's **Greyhound** services use the Transbay Terminal at 425 Mission St, near the Embarcadero BART station in the South of Market (SoMa) district. Green Tortoise buses stop behind the Transbay Terminal on First and Natoma. Amtrak **trains** stop across the Bay in Oakland, from where free shuttle buses run across the Bay Bridge to the Transbay Terminal, or you can take BART. A more efficient route is to get off the train at Richmond, where a transfer to the nearby BART can get you into San Francisco more quickly. Although technically closer to San Francisco, don't get off at the stop before Oakland, Emeryville, as consistent public transportation to the city doesn't exist (though you can hail a cab here).

From the east, the main route **by car** into San Francisco is I-80, which runs via Sacramento all the way from Chicago. I-5, fifty miles east of San Francisco, serves as the main north–south route, connecting Los Angeles with Seattle. From I-5, I-580 takes you to the Bay Area. US-101 also runs the length of California from north to south, but if you have time and a tolerance of wind-ing roads, take Hwy-1, the Pacific Coast Highway, which traces the edge of California.

Information

The **San Francisco Visitor Information Center**, on the lower level of Hallidie Plaza at the end of the cable car line on Market Street (Mon–Fri 9am–5pm, Sat–Sun 9am–3pm, winter hours vary; ☎415/283-0177 or recorded information line ☎415/283-0177, ⓦwww.sfvisitor.org), has free maps of the city and the Bay Area, oodles of pamphlets on hotels and restaurants, and can help with lodging and travel plans. Its free *San Francisco Book* and *Visitors Planning Guide* provide detailed, if somewhat selective, information about accommodation, entertainment, exhibitions, and stores. The center also sells the **City Pass** ($33.25; ⓦwww.citypass.net), a half-price ticket valid for entry to the Exploratorium, California Palace of the Legion of Honor, Steinhart Aquarium and Academy of Sciences, M.H. de Young Museum, the Museum of Modern Art, and passage on a Blue and Gold Fleet San Francisco Bay cruise – all that, plus a free week's pass on MUNI transit (see below).

The city's several **newspapers** are indispensable sources of information. Two dailies have competed for decades – the morning *Chronicle* (ⓦwww.sfgate.com; 50¢) and afternoon *Examiner* (25¢). There's been turbulence in recent years after the *Examiner* was threatened with closure: it's now under new owners but many locals sniff at its now tabloid sensibility and muckraking news operation. Both papers have extensive arts and food reporting: check the Ex Files in the weekend *Examiner*, and Sunday edition's *Datebook* (also known as the "Pink Pages") contains previews and reviews for the coming week. The city's alternative press picks up the slack the more conservative dailies leave behind, resulting in two fine free weekly papers, *The Bay Guardian* (ⓦwww.sfbg.com) and *SF Weekly* (ⓦwww.sfweekly.com), available from racks around town. Both offer more in-depth features on local life and better music and club listings than the dailies. More detailed information on the East Bay can be found in its daily, the *Oakland Tribune*, and alternative free weekly, the East Bay Express, as well as in UC-Berkeley's two free daily student newspapers. Down south, look to the *San Jose Mercury News*, the thick daily that focuses on the Peninsula. **Online**, check out ⓦwww.sfstation.com for the best of the many websites that cover the Bay Area.

City transportation

San Francisco is a rare American city where you don't need a car to see everything. In fact, given the chronic shortage of parking downtown, horrible traffic, and zealous meter maids, going without one makes more sense. The **public transportation** system, MUNI, though much maligned by locals for its unpredictable schedule, covers every neighborhood inexpensively via a system of cable cars, buses, and trolleys. **Cycling** is a good option, though you'll need stout legs to tackle those hills. **Walking** the compact metropolis is still the best bet, with each turn revealing surprises.

MUNI

The city's public transportation is run by the San Francisco Municipal Railway, or **MUNI** (☎415/673-6864, ⓦwww.sfmuni.com). A comprehensive network of buses, trolley buses, and cable cars run up and over the city's hills, while the underground trains become streetcars when they emerge from the downtown metro system to split off and serve the suburbs. On buses and trains the flat fare (correct change only) is $1; with each ticket you buy, ask for a free transfer – good for another two rides on a train or bus in any direction within ninety minutes to two hours of purchase. Note that cable cars cost $2 one way, and do not accept transfers. The best option if you're in town for a while is to buy a MUNI passport pass, available if one-day, three-day, and seven-day denominations ($6, $10, $15). It's valid for unlimited travel on the MUNI system and BART stations (see below) within the city limits. A fast pass costs $35 for a full calendar month and also offers unlimited travel within the city limits. MUNI trains run throughout the night on a limited service, except those on the M-Ocean View line, which stop around 1am. Most buses run all night, but services are greatly reduced after midnight. For more information, pick up the handy MUNI map ($2) from the Visitor Information Center or bookstores.

Main MUNI routes

Useful bus routes

#5	From the Transbay Terminal, west alongside Haight-Ashbury and Golden Gate Park to the ocean.
#7	From the Ferry Terminal (Market Street) to the end of Haight Street and to Golden Gate Park.
#15	From Third Street (SoMa) to Pier 39, Fisherman's Wharf, via the Financial District and North Beach.
#20	(Golden Gate Transit) From Civic Center to the Golden Gate Bridge.
#22	From the Marina up Pacific Heights and north on Fillmore.
#28 & #29	From the Marina through the Presidio, north through Golden Gate Park, the Richmond, and Sunset.
#30	From the CalTrain depot on Third Street, north to Ghirardelli Square, via Chinatown and North Beach, and out to Chestnut Street in the Marina district.
#38	From Geary Street via Civic Center, west to the ocean along Geary Boulevard through Japantown and the Richmond, ending at Cliff House.

MUNI train lines

MUNI F-Market Line	Restored vintage trolleys from around the world run downtown from the Transbay Terminal up Market Street and into the heart of the Castro. The new extension along the refurbished Embarcadero to Fisherman's Wharf is one of MUNI's most popular routes.
MUNI J-Church Line	From downtown to Mission and the edge of the Castro.
MUNI K-Ingleside Line	From downtown through the Castro to Balboa Park.
MUNI L-Taraval Line	From downtown west through the Sunset to the zoo and Ocean Beach.
MUNI M-Ocean View	From downtown west by the Stonestown Galleria shopping center and San Francisco State University.
MUNI N-Judah Line	From the Caltrain station, past the new baseball stadium, along South Beach to downtown west through the Inner Sunset to Ocean Beach.

Cable car routes

Powell-Hyde	From Powell Street/Market along Hyde through Russian Hill to Fisherman's Wharf.
Powell-Mason	From Powell Street/Market along Mason via Chinatown and North Beach to Fisherman's Wharf.
California Street	From the foot of California Street at Robert Frost Plaza in the Financial District through Nob Hill to Polk Street.

BART and other train services

Along Market Street downtown, MUNI shares station concourses with **BART** (Bay Area Rapid Transit; ☏415/989-2278, ⊛www.bart.gov), which is the fastest way to get to the East Bay – including downtown Oakland and Berkeley – and outer suburbs east and south of San Francisco. Tickets aren't cheap ($1.10–$4.70), but the trains feature four routes that follow a fixed schedule, usually arriving every ten minutes. Trains run from 4am weekdays, 6am Saturdays, 8am Sundays until midnight, and tickets can be purchased on the station concourse; save your ticket after entering the station, as it is also needed when exiting the train. Free schedules are available at BART stations.

The CalTrain commuter railway (depot at Fourth and Townsend, South of Market) links San Francisco south to San Jose; call ☏1-800/660-4287 or log onto ⊛www.caltrain.com for schedules and fares.

Driving: taxis and cars

Taxis ply the streets and, while you can flag them down (especially downtown), finding one can be difficult. The granting of more taxi licenses is a contentious issue in San Francisco, with many arguing that the streets are clogged enough. Phoning around, try Veterans (☏415/552-1300) or Yellow Cab (☏415/626-2345). Fares (within the city) begin with a fee of $1.70 to start the meter and $1.80 per mile thereafter, plus the customary fifteen-percent tip.

The only reason to **rent a car** in San Francisco is if you want to explore the Bay Area, the Wine Country, or the landscape north or south along the coast. Driving in town, pay attention to San Francisco's attempts to control downtown traffic: the posted speed limit is 30mph, speeding through a yellow light is illegal, and pedestrians waiting in a crosswalk have the right-of-way. In addition, it's almost impossible to make a left turn anywhere in town, meaning you'll have to get used to looping the block, making three rights instead of one left. Cheap, available parking is even rarer than a left-turn signal, but it's worth playing by the rules: police issue multiple tickets for illegally parked vehicles and won't hesitate to tow your car if it's violating any posted laws. Downtown, plenty of garages exist, most advertising rates beginning at $2.50 per fifteen minutes. Take care to observe the San Francisco law of curbing wheels – turn wheels into the curb if the car points downhill and away from the curb if it points up; violators are subject to a $20 ticket. Bridge tolls are collected only when entering San Francisco by car: the Golden Gate Bridge toll costs $3, while the Bay Bridge runs $2.

Cycling, scootering, and skating

Cycling is a great way to experience San Francisco. Golden Gate Park, the Marina and Presidio, and Ocean Beach all have great, paved trails and some off-road routes. And throughout the city, marked bike routes – with lanes – direct riders to all major points of interest, but note that officials picked the routes for their lack of car traffic, not for the easiest ride. Blazing Saddles, which rents bicycles, has several locations (☏415/202-8888, ⊛www.blazingsaddlessanfrancisco.com or ⊛www.bikethebridge.com) – two of the most convenient are 1095 Columbus Avenue at Francisco, North Beach and Pier 41. Rental for bikes is $7 an hour, $28 a day In addition to renting bikes at rates comparable to the above, Bike & Roll, 722 Columbus Ave at Lombard, North Beach (☏415/771-TREK, ⊛www.adventurebicycle.com), also rents tandem bikes ($45 a day). For a tranquil trek through undeveloped nature, head north over the Golden Gate Bridge (the western side is reserved solely for bikes) to either Angel Island (see p.640) or into the Marin Headlands for a series of off-road trails along cliffs, ocean, and into valleys (see p.635).

San Francisco's roads and pathways aren't rollerblade-ready, but there are a few good **places to skate** around the Marina and, to a lesser extent, in Golden Gate Park. On Sunday, most of Golden Gate Park's roads are closed to autos, bringing out hordes of bladers. Skaters also use the flat sidewalk along Ocean Beach, and the good trails around Lake Merced, although both are away from the action of downtown. San Francisco's many plazas are more welcoming to **skateboarding**, even if local law conspires to ban thrashers from city limits. Skates on Haight, 1818 Haight St at Stanyan, Haight-Ashbury (℡415/752-8375, Ⓦwww.skatesonhaight.com), rents both boards and blades for $6 an hour.

Organized tours

One way to orient yourself is an **organized tour**. Gray Line Tours (℡415/558-9400, Ⓦwww.graylinesanfrancisco.com), for example, take three-and-a-half fairly tedious hours to tour the city for around $37 a head. Likewise, San Francisco Sightseeing (℡415/434-TOUR, Ⓦwww.sanfranciscosightseeing.com) zip you around to all the major must-sees in the city for $37, with deals that combine city stops with Muir Woods, Alcatraz, or even Monterey, the Wine Country, or Yosemite in a day. Considerably more exciting is the El Camión Mexicano, the Mexican Bus Tour (call for itineraries and reservations; ℡415/546-3747, Ⓦwww.mexicanbus.com) through the Mission district, which takes in local Mexican restaurants and salsa clubs for drinking and dancing for $38.

For breathtaking views of the Bay, take a chilly 75-minute Bay cruise with the Blue & Gold Fleet (℡415/705-5555, Ⓦwww.blueandgoldfleet.com) from Pier 39 and Pier 41 – though be warned that everything may be shrouded in fog, making the price less than worth it. If you want to take a loop out under the Golden Gate Bridge and back, several independent boat operators troll for your business along Fisherman's Wharf ($10). Expensive aerial tours of the city and Bay Area in light aircraft are available from several operators, such as San Francisco Helicopter Tours (℡650/635-4500 or 1-800/400-2404, Ⓦwww.sfhelicoptertours.com), which offers a variety of spectacular flights over the Bay Area beginning at $110 per passenger for a twenty-minute flight.

Accommodation

Full-time residents of San Francisco complain constantly about skyrocketing rents, and it's no different for the visitor. Expect accommodation to cost around $100 per night in a reasonable hotel or motel, slightly less out of season. We've listed some smart bargains below (some as cheap as $50 a night offseason) but if you want to snag one of these cheaper rooms, it's essential to call around and book ahead. You'll also normally find significantly better rates in rooms that share baths. In all cases, bear in mind that all quoted room rates are subject to a **fourteen percent room tax**.

The **Visitor Information Center** (℡1-888/782-9673, Ⓦwww.sfvisitor.org) can provide the latest accommodation options; and **San Francisco Reservations** (Mon–Fri 6am–11pm, Sat–Sun 8am–11pm; ℡510/628-4450 or 1-800/677-1500, Ⓦwww.hotelres.com) will find you a room from around $100 a double.

For **B&Bs**, the city's fastest-growing source of accommodation, contact a specialist agency such as Bed and Breakfast California (☎408/867-9662, ⓦwww.bbintl.com) or Bed and Breakfast San Francisco (Mon–Fri 9am–5.30pm; ☎415/899-0060, ⓦwww.bbsf.com). If funds are tight, look into one of the many excellent **hostels** (listed below), where beds start at around $22. Specifically gay and lesbian accommodation is listed on p.576; there are some mixed gay-straight places, too, which we've included in the listings below.

Downtown and Chinatown

See map on p.524

Allison 417 Stockton St at Sutter, Chinatown
☎415/986-8737 or 1-800/628-6456. Shockingly good-value prime location hotel, one of the best options for budget travel anywhere in the city with rooms that are big, bright, and spotless. There are

family suites that sleep four, with rates heavily negotiable offseason, plus a few rooms with shared bath that are even cheaper. ❶ (shared bath), ❸ (private bath)

Baldwin Hotel 321 Grant Ave at Bush, Chinatown ☎415/781-2220 or 1-800/6-BALDWIN, ⓦwww.baldwinhotel.com. Surprisingly quiet, given

---

7

Walking tours

A great way to get to know the quieter, historical side of San Francisco is to take a **walking tour**. The better ones keep group size small and are run by natives who truly love their subject matter and jobs. Some, like those sponsored by the library, are free. Reservations are recommended for all walks. The Visitor Information Center can give you a full list of available walks – every neighborhood has at least one – but among those you should consider are:

City Guides (☎415/557-4266, ⓦwww.walking-tours.com/cityguides). A terrific free series sponsored by the library covering every San Francisco neighborhood, as well as themed walks on topics ranging from the Gold Rush to the Beat Generation. Schedule varies – call for details.
Cruisin' the Castro (☎415/550-8110, ⓦwww.webcastro.com/castrotour). The Grand Dame of San Francisco walks, Ms. Trevor Hailey, leads you through her beloved neighborhood and explains how and why San Francisco became the gay capital of the world. Tour includes the story of the rise and murder of Harvey Milk, the city's first openly gay politician, as well as other tales from this beautiful neighborhood continually under threat from developers. Highly recommended. $40 per person, including brunch.
Haight-Ashbury Flower Power Walking Tour (Tues & Sat 9.30am; ☎415/863-1621, ⓦwww.hippiegourmet.com). Learn about the Human Be-in, Grateful Dead, Summer of Love and also the Haight's distant past as a Victorian resort destination. $15 per person.

Mangia! North Beach (Sat 10am; ☎415/415/397-8530, ℮gaw@sbcglobal.net) Culinary tour of North Beach's Italian nooks, run by larger-than-life local food writer Grace-Ann Walden. $50 including lunch.
Mission Mural Walk (Sat & Sun 11am, 1.30pm ☎415/285-2287, ⓦwww.precitaeyes.org). Two-hour presentation by mural artists leads around the Mission district's outdoor paintings. Includes a slide presentation on the history and process of mural art. $12 per person; call for schedule of walks.
Victorian Home Walk (daily 11am; ☎415/252-9485, ⓦwww.victorian-walk.com). Leisurely tour through Pacific Heights and Cow Hollow where you'll learn to tell the difference between a Queen Anne, Italianate, and Stick-Style Vic. $20 per person for a two-hour tour. Meet by the clock in the lobby of the *Westin St Francis Hotel*.
Wok Wiz Tours (daily 10am; ☎415/981-8989, ⓦwww.wokwiz.com). A walk through Chinatown run by chef-writer Shirley Fong-Torres and her team. Plenty of anecdotes but a little thin on historical information. $28 per person, $40 per person including lunch.

its hub location in the heart of Chinatown, the *Baldwin*'s rooms are oatmeal and taupe, outfitted in neutral colors with simple furnishings and ceiling fans. Rooms are rented weekly offseason so negotiate hard if you're staying fewer than seven nights. ❾ per week / ❹ per night

Clift 495 Geary St at Taylor, Theater District ☎415/775-4700 or 1-800/658-5492, ⓦwww .ianschragerhotels.com. Ian Schrager and Philippe Starck's latest masterpiece is the converted *Clift Hotel*. The rooms are vaguely oriental and vintage Starck, with quirky touches like the Louis XIV-style chairs with mirrors on the seat and back, and sleigh beds – pity the bathrooms are so small. ❼

Commodore International 825 Sutter St at Jones, Theater District ☎415/923-6800 or 1-800/338-6848, ⓦwww.thecommodorehotel.com. Each room is named after a different area attraction (such as the Haas-Lilienthal house or Mission murals), which is then glossed on a plaque by the door. They are decorated in warm, earthy colors offset by shiny steel Neo-Deco fixtures. If you're traveling in a group of four or more, ask about the funky, airy Panoramic Suite where rates start at only $200. ❹

Gates Hotel 140 Ellis St at Powell, Union Square ☎415/956-4186. The large, salmon-pink rooms here are spartan and a little frayed, but clean. The rock-bottom rates for its Union Square location make up for the lack of luxuries. ❷

Grant Hotel 753 Bush St at Mason, Chinatown ☎415/421-7540 or 1-800/522-0979, ⓦwww.granthotel.citysearch.com. Good value for its location, this hotel has small but clean rooms, overpowered a little by the relentlessly maroon carpets. Basic but convenient. ❷

Hotel Astoria 510 Bush St at Grant, Chinatown ☎415/434-8889 or 1-800/666-6696, ⓦwww.astoria-sf.com. Located right next to the arch at the entrance to Chinatown, the *Hotel Astoria*'s decor is friskier than many other budget hotels, with TV and full in-room amenities; continental breakfast is included in the rate and there's discounted parking nearby ($20/24 hrs). ❸

Monaco 501 Geary St at Taylor, Union Square ☎415/292-0100 or 1-800/214-4220, ⓦwww.monaco-sf.com. One of the newer, quirky boutique hotels in town, housed in a historic Beaux Arts building. There are canopied beds in each room, and the rest of the decor's equally riotous, colorful, and a little over the top. Ask about the complimentary goldfish. ❽

Sir Francis Drake 450 Powell St at Sutter, Union Square ☎415/392-7755 or 1-800/227-5480, ⓦwww.sirfrancisdrake.com. The lobby here's a hallucinogenic evocation of all things heraldic: it's

crammed with faux British memorabilia, chandeliers, and drippingly ornate gold plasterwork. Thankfully, the rooms are calmer, with a gentle apple-green color scheme and full facilities. The hotel's known for the bar *Harry Denton's Starlight Room* on the 21st floor. ❼

Triton 342 Grant Ave at Bush, Chinatown ☎415/394-0500 or 1-888/364-2622, ⓦwww.hotel-tritonsf.com. Trippy, eccentric hotel that offers modern amenities like a 24hr gym and in-room fax, as well as weirder services like nightly Tarot card readings and an eco-floor of environmentally sensitive rooms. The rooms themselves are stylish but gaudy, painted in rich clashing colors and plenty of gold. ❼

Westin St Francis 335 Powell St at Sutter, Union Square ☎415/397-7000 or 1-800/WESTIN1, ⓦwww.westin.com. This completely renovated landmark hotel has a sumptuous lobby, four restaurants and lounges, a fitness center, and a spa. Yet aside from the views across downtown, the rooms are disappointingly plain. Worth entering the lobby to see the famous clock, ornate ceiling, painting of Queen Elizabeth amidst American celebs, and the steps where President Gerald Ford almost met his end from a would-be assassin's bullet. ❽

North Beach and Nob Hill
See map on p.524 for locations.

Boheme 444 Columbus Ave at Vallejo, North Beach ☎415/433-9111, ⓦwww.hotelboheme .com. Smack in the middle of Beat heartland, this small, 15-room hotel has tiny but dramatic rooms, with canopied beds and Art Deco-ish bathrooms, all done in rich, dark colors. Columbus Avenue can be noisy, so if you're a light sleeper, ask for a room at the back. ❼

Mark Hopkins InterContinental One Nob Hill, 999 California St at Mason, Nob Hill ☎415/392-3434, ⓦwww.interconti.com. Grand, castle-like hotel that was once the chic choice of writers and movie stars: it's more corporate these days in both clientele and design, thanks to a massive recent renovation. All rooms are identical, but rates rise as the floors do. The *Top of the Mark* rooftop bar is popular with tourists. ❾

Sam Wong Hotel 615 Broadway at Grant, North Beach ☎415/362-2999, ⓦwww.swhotelsf.com. Well-located hotel on the boundary between Chinatown and Little Italy. The decor in the large rooms is modern Asian with carved armoires and headboards and bright yellow bedspreads. ❺

San Remo 2237 Mason St at Chestnut, North Beach ☎415/776-8688 or 1-800/352-7366, ⓦwww.sanremohotel.com Quirky option close to

Fisherman's Wharf. Rooms in this warren-like converted house are cozy and chintzy: all share spotless bathrooms and a few have sinks. Bear in mind that there are no phones or TVs in the bedrooms and no elevator. ❷

Washington Square Inn 1660 Stockton St at Union, North Beach ☎415/981-4220 or 1-800/388-0220, ⓦ www.washingtonsquareinn.citysearch.com. This B&B-style hotel overlooking Washington Square has large, airy rooms, decorated in modern shades of taupe and cream, and friendly, amenable staff. ❻

The northern waterfront and Pacific Heights
See map on p.524 for locations.
Bel Aire Travelodge 3201 Steiner St at Greenwich, Cow Hollow ☎415/921-5162 or 1-800/280-3242. Don't confuse this sprightly, good-value *Travelodge* with the grotty property across the road: rooms here are recently refurbished, if a little dark, but the friendly owners make up for it. ❸

Cow Hollow Motor Inn 2190 Lombard St at Steiner, Cow Hollow ☎415/921-5800, ⓦ www.cowhollowmotorinn.com. Swiss chalet-style inn, with plentiful parking and charmingly retro common areas. The rooms, though, are utterly modern, recently refurbished and enormous. ❹

Del Sol 3100 Webster St at Lombard, Cow Hollow ☎415/921-5520 or 1-877/433-5765, ⓦ www.jdvhospitality.com. Funky, offbeat updated motor lodge with a tropical theme, plus a swimming pool. The color scheme combines zesty walls with chunky mosaics and palm trees wrapped in fairy lights: the best place for budget cool in the city. ❺

Laurel Inn 444 Presidio Ave at California, Laurel Heights ☎415/567-8467 or 1-800/552-8735, ⓦ www.thelaurelinn.com. This Laurel Heights hotel is steps from Sacramento Street's antique shops and near the bustling Fillmore strip of cafés and stores. All rooms come with a VCR and CD player; the decor's a stylish update of 1950s Americana, with muted graphic prints and simple fixtures. ❻

Surf Motel 2265 Lombard St at Pierce, Cow Hollow ☎415/922-1950. This old school motel has two tiers of bright, simple rooms that are sparklingly clean. Ask for a room at the back, since the busy Lombard Street thoroughfare roars past the main entrance. ❸

Van Ness Motel 2850 Van Ness Ave at Chestnut, Polk Gulch ☎415/776-3220 or 1-800/422-0372, ⓦ www.vannessmotel.citysearch.com. Standard, bland motel with largeish rooms, notable more for its location than the hotel itself, within walking distance of Fort Mason. It's also convenient for the Polk Street drag. ❸

SoMa, the Tenderloin, and the Civic Center
See map on p.524 for locations.
Carriage Inn 140 7th St at Mission, SoMa ☎415/552-8600. Enormous, elegant rooms with sofas and working fireplaces. There's free room service breakfast each morning and shuttle to Union Square: the only downside is its location, on a slightly sketchy block of SoMa. ❻

Four Seasons 757 Market St at 3rd, SoMa ☎415/633-3000, ⓦ www.fourseasons.com. Sparkling new hotel on Market Street with spectacular views across the city: its plush rooms are the ultimate indulgence, from the soft, luxurious comforters to the stand-alone two-person shower stocked with Bulgari beauty products. There's an enormous onsite health club with a pool and vast gym that's free to hotel guests. *The* place to stay if you win the lottery or someone else is paying. ❾

Hotel Griffon 155 Steuart St at Mission, SoMa ☎415/495-2100 or 1-800/321-2201, ⓦ www.hotelgriffon.com. Secluded hotel close to the waterfront: rooms are elegant and understated, with exposed brick walls, window seats, CD player, and refrigerator. ❽

The Mosser 54 4th St at Market, SoMa ☎415/986-4400, ⓦ www.victorianhotel.com. This hotel is a recent funky conversion fusing Victorian touches like ornamental molding with mod leather sofas. The chocolate-and-olive rooms may be tiny but each is artfully crammed with amenities including multi-disc CD players. Highly recommended – one of the best values in town, especially for its central location. ❹

Palace Hotel 2 New Montgomery St at Market, SoMa ☎415/512-1111, ⓦ www.sfpalace.com. Hushed, opulent landmark building, known for its fabulous, historic *Garden Court* tearoom: the grand lobby and corridors are mismatched with rooms that are small for the sky-high prices, decorated in lush golds and greens like an English country house. Stay here for snob value rather than good value. ❾

The Phoenix 601 Eddy St at Larkin, Tenderloin ☎415/776-1380 or 1-800/248-9466, ⓦ www.sftrips.com. This raucous retro motel conversion is a favorite with up-and-coming bands when they're in town. There's a small pool, and the 44 rooms are eclectically decorated in tropical colors with changing local artwork on the walls – ask for the "Tour Manager Room," which has a fridge, fax, and microwave. The adjacent *Backflip* bar keeps the party going into the early hours. ❺

The Renoir 45 McAllister St at 7th, Civic Center ☎415/626-5200 or 1-800/576-3388, ⓦwww.renoirhotel.com. This wedge-shaped building is a historic landmark. The superior rooms cost $20 more than standard – worth the extra if you can snag one of the oddly shaped large rooms at the building's apex. Especially popular during Gay Pride for its Market Street views along the parade route. ❺

The Mission and the Castro

See map on p.547 for locations.
Beck's Motor Lodge 2222 Market St at Sanchez, Castro ☎415/621-8212 or 1-800/227-4360. This is one of only two accommodation options in the area that isn't a B&B. The clientele's more mixed than you'd expect from its location, and the soft, bluish rooms are plusher than the gaudy yellow motel exterior might suggest. If you're a light sleeper, ask for a room well away from the road, as it can be noisy. ❺
Dolores Park Inn 3641 17th St at Dolores, Mission ☎415/621-0482, ⓦwww.doloresparkinnbnb.com. Housed in an artfully restored Italianate Victorian, this sumptuous B&B offers only four rooms, one of which has an en-suite bath. They're all large, though, and crammed with a Baroque assortment of ornate European antiques; the owner even keeps a photo book of past guests. Its seclusion close to the park is a major plus. ❻
Travelodge Central 1707 Market at Valencia, Mission ☎415/621-6775 or 1-800/578-7878. Very basic motel-style lodging, but couldn't be more conveniently located – the free onsite parking makes up for the slightly worn, floral motel rooms. ❹
Twin Peaks Hotel 2160 Market St at Dolores, Castro ☎415/863-2909. This hotel's basic and very spartan: the small, simply furnished rooms have vanities and large TVs, but almost all share bathrooms. A bit like a brusque boarding house, but the prices make up for the lack of amenities. ❷ (shared), ❸ (private bath)
Village House 4080 18th St at Castro, Castro ☎415/864-0994 or 1-800/900-5686, ⓦwww.24henry.com. Oddly, given its location, this newish B&B is mixed gay-straight and popular with visiting parents. The rooms are grand and a little gaudy, with primary colored walls and plenty of closet space. For camp Eastern extravagance, ask for room #2; or take a trip back to the 1980s in room #4. ❹

Haight-Ashbury and west of Civic Center

See map on p.551 for locations.
Archbishop's Mansion 1000 Fulton St at Steiner, Fillmore ☎415/563-7872 or 1-800/543-5820, ⓦwww.thearchbishopmansion.com. The last word in camp elegance, this B&B stands on the corner of Alamo Square and is crammed with $1m worth of antiques, including the very chandelier that featured in the ballroom of *Gone with the Wind* and Noel Coward's baby grand piano. Built to house an archbishop, it's also served as a school for wayward Catholic boys; now it caters to wayward boys of a different kind, attracting plenty of gay travelers. ❼
Best Western Miyako 1800 Sutter St at Buchanan, Japantown ☎415/921-4000 or 1-800/528-1234, ⓦwww.bestwestern.com/miyakoinn. Recently renovated, this standard corporate hotel is one of the few options in Japantown and around that isn't a B&B. Nothing special, but there can be great price deals off-season. ❻
The Carl 198 Carl St at Stanyan, Haight-Ashbury ☎415/661-5679 or 1-888/661-5679, ⓦwww.citysearch.com/sfo/carlhotel. Plainer than many of the surrounding B&Bs, this hotel is a bargain for its Golden Gate Park location. Small but florally pretty rooms, with microwaves and fridges; the six with shared bath are especially well-priced. ❹ (private), ❸ (shared)
Château Tivoli 1057 Steiner St at Fulton, Fillmore ☎415/776-5462 or 1-800/228-1647, ⓦwww.chateautivoli.com. Rooms in this lavishly furnished Victorian mansion are named after artists like Isadora Duncan and Mark Twain: there's history everywhere, whether in the building itself (built for an early local lumber baron) or the furniture (one of the beds was owned by Charles de Gaulle). Grand, and very serious, but a luxurious alternative to many of the cozy B&Bs elsewhere. ❻ (shared bath), ❼ (private)
Hayes Valley Inn 417 Gough St at Hayes, Hayes Valley ☎415/431-9131 or 1-800/930-7999. Homely, apple-green rooms in a secluded location: furnishings are minimal, and baths are shared, but the friendly, well-stocked kitchen/breakfast room is a major plus. ❸
Queen Anne 1590 Sutter St at Octavia, Fillmore ☎415/441-2828 or 1-800/227-3970, ⓦwww.queenanne.com. Gloriously excessive restored Victorian, that began as a girls' school before becoming a bordello. Each room is stuffed with gold-accented Rococo furniture and bunches of silk flowers: the parlor (where afternoon sherry is served) is over-filled with museum-quality period

furniture. Miss Mary Lake, former principal of the school, is said to still make periodic, supernatural appearances in Room 410. ⑥

The Red Victorian Bed, Breakfast and Art 1665 Haight St at Cole, Haight-Ashbury ☎415/864-1978, ⓦwww.redvic.com. Quirky B&B and Peace Center, owned by Sami Sunchild and decorated with her ethnic arts. Rooms vary from simple to opulent: the best feature is the shared bathrooms, including a goldfish-filled toilet cistern. Breakfast's a lavish but highly communal affair, so be prepared to chat with your neighbors while you eat. ④

Stanyan Park Hotel 750 Stanyan St at Waller, Haight-Ashbury ☎415/751-1000, ⓦwww.stanyanpark.com. Overlooking Golden Gate Park, this small hotel has 35 sumptuous rooms that are oddly incongruous in its counter-culture neighborhood, busily decorated in country florals with heavy drapes and junior four-poster beds. Continental breakfast and an ample, cookie-filled afternoon tea are included. ⑥

The Richmond and the Sunset

Ocean Park Motel 2690 46th Ave at Wawona, Ocean Beach ☎415/566-7020. A fair way from downtown (25min by MUNI), this is nonetheless a great Art Deco motel (San Francisco's first) and an outstanding example of Streamline Moderne architecture. It's convenient for the beach and the zoo, plus there's a kids' play area and an outdoor hot tub and Jacuzzi for adults. ④

Oceanview Motel 4340 Judah St at LaPlaya, Ocean Beach ☎415/661-2300, ⓦwww.oceanviewmotel.citysearch.com. No-frills lodging out in the Sunset district. ③

Hostels

Green Tortoise 494 Broadway at Montgomery, North Beach ☎415/834-1000 or 1-800/867-8647. This laid-back hostel is the choicest option if money's tight: there's room for 130 people in dorm beds and double rooms (with shared bath). Both options include free Internet access, use of the small onsite sauna, and complimentary breakfast. There's no curfew, and the front desk is staffed 24 hours: there's a ten-night maximum stay. $19 dorms, $48 rooms.

HI-San Francisco City Center 685 Ellis St at Larkin, Tenderloin ☎415/474-5721, ⓦwww.norcalhostels.org. Recent conversion from the old *Atherton Hotel*, this is a spiffy new hostel; its 272 beds are divided into four-person dorms, each with en-suite bath. There's no curfew, and overall it's friendly, funky, and California cool: good for meeting other travelers, since there are plenty of activities laid on (nightly movies, communal pancake breakfast); its only downside is the location in a sketchier part of the Tenderloin. $22 members, $25 non-members; private rooms $66 members, $69 non members.

HI-San Francisco Fort Mason Building 240, Fort Mason ☎415/771-7277, ⓦwww.hiayh.org or ⓦwww.norcalhostels.org. On the waterfront between the Golden Gate Bridge and Fisherman's Wharf, this is a choice option for the outdoorsy traveler, a standard hostel housed in a historic former Civil War barracks. Be aware that although public transport connects the hostel with the main sights, it's a little out of the way on the federal complex at Fort Mason. The upside of its federal land location is that it can't require a membership fee so it's even cheaper than hostels elsewhere. $22.50.

HI-San Francisco Union Square 312 Mason St at Geary, Union Square ☎415/788-5604. With almost 300 beds, this downtown hostel still fills up quickly in peak season: four-person dorms are spotless, sharing bathroom facilities between eight people. The private rooms are pricier and sleep two people. Open 24 hours, there's a kitchen with microwave and vending machines, a funky little reading room and Internet access ($1 for 10 min). Dorms $22 members, $25 non-members; private rooms $60 members, $66 non-members.

Interclub/Globe Hostel 10 Hallam Place, SoMa ☎415/431-0540. Lively South of Market hostel with young clientele and 33 rooms, split between dorms and private rooms. There's free coffee and, best of all, no curfew. $16 per person; doubles $40.

Pacific Tradewinds Guesthouse 680 Sacramento St at Kearny, Chinatown ☎415/433-7970 or (May–Oct only) 1-800/486-7975, ⓦwww.hostels.com/pt. The best budget option in the center of town, this small hostel offers free, high-speed Internet access, a clean kitchen, plus a large, communal dining table that's an easy way to get to know fellow travelers. It's certainly an international hub – house rules are posted in almost forty languages, including Afrikaans and Catalan. There are only 38 beds so book ahead in high season. $20 per person.

San Francisco International Guest House 2976 23rd St at Treat, Mission ☎415/641-1411. This out of the way hostel is known to be popular with European travelers; given its somewhat sketchy location, it can feel rather isolated. There are dorms as well as a few private rooms, starting at $15 per person daily, with a 5-day minimum stay, less if you stay a month. Reservations aren't accepted and when you arrive, ring the bell for 2976 as there's no official sign. **YMCA Central Branch** 220 Golden Gate Ave at Leavenworth, Tenderloin ☎415/885-0460, ⓦwww.centralymcasf.org. Rooms may be simple, but this is one of the best deals in the city center: $12 overnight parking, free breakfast, free use of YMCA fitness center, Internet access at a nominal fee, and onsite laundry. There are private rooms as well as a few dorms (12 beds for men, 8 for women in summer) so book ahead. Be aware of the YMCA's location in a grimy part of the Tenderloin. $25.95 including tax (dorm), $73.56 including tax (private bath).

The City

The first thing that strikes visitors to San Francisco is that it is a city of hills and distinct neighborhoods. Here, as a general rule, geographical elevation is a stout indicator of wealth – the higher you live, the better off you are. Commercial square-footage is surprisingly small and mostly confined to the downtown area, and the rest of the city is made up of primarily residential neighborhoods with street-level shopping districts, easily explored on foot. Armed with a good map and strong legs, you could plough through much of the city in a couple of days, but frankly the best way to get to know San Francisco is to dawdle, unbound by itineraries. The most interesting districts merit – at the very least – half a day each of just hanging out.

The forty-odd hills that rise above the town usually serve as geographic barriers between neighborhoods. The flattest stretch of land, created by landfill and bulldozing, at the top right-hand corner of the Peninsula, bordered by I-80 to the south, US-101 to the west, and the water, comprises **downtown**. The city center is bisected by the wide, diagonal thoroughfare of **Market Street**, which is the main reference point for your wanderings. Lined with stores and office buildings, Market Street begins at the water's edge of the **Embarcadero** and runs southwest along the corporate high-rises of the **Financial District**; the cable car and shopping quarter of **Union Square**; beside the scruffy **Tenderloin** district and chic Hayes Valley; and reaches the primarily gay district of the **Castro**. It then spirals around **Twin Peaks**, the most prominent of San Francisco's heights.

South and east of Market Street stands **SoMa**, which used to be one of the city center's few industrial enclaves, until the artsy, nightclubbing crowd discovered it. It was at the heart of the dot-com boom when Internet start-ups paid sky-high rents to stake their claim in SoMa's warehouses and lofts. Commercial development poured in, from Sony's laughable **Metreon** mall to the glorious waterfalls at **Yerba Buena Gardens** and the new **San Francisco Museum of Modern Art**. SoMa has suffered after the Internet industry collapsed, and many of its sparkling new office buildings now lie empty, vacated by vanished companies. SoMa's waterfront, long-neglected **South Beach** has been re-zoned for housing and businesses, and is anchored by **Pac Bell Ballpark**, the waterfront stadium built for baseball's San Francisco Giants.

South of SoMa sits San Francisco's largest, and one of its most interesting, neighborhoods, the **Mission**. Built around Mission Dolores and, thanks to fog-blocking hills, almost always sunny, the largely Hispanic Mission district offers enough food, cinema, nightclubs, and shops to fill a separate vacation – or at least a day off the well-trodden tourist path around downtown.

North and west of Market Street, the land rises dramatically, and with it, property values, as evinced by the stunning mansions atop the province of robber barons: **Nob Hill**. Beside the posh residential quarter, a short cable car ride or walk away, rests clustered **Chinatown**, a thriving neighborhood of apartments, restaurants, temples, and stores built around **Portsmouth Square**, the spiritual heart of San Francisco. The land east of the square, towards the Bay, used to be entirely water before hundreds of sailors heading for the Gold Rush abandoned their ships, resulting in an unnatural extension of the waterfront. The beached boats rapidly piled up along the shore of Portsmouth Square, until merchants began using the dry-docked vessels as hotels, bars, and shops. Now it's filled by the towering Transamerica Pyramid, which shadows the **Jackson Square** historical neighborhood of restored redbrick businesses. The diagonal artery **Columbus Avenue**, which separates Portsmouth from Jackson squares, is the spine of the Italian enclave of **North Beach**, much loved by Beat writers and espresso drinkers. North Beach extends to the northernmost tip of the city, the tourist-trap waterfront known as **Fisherman's Wharf**, but not before passing the peaks of **Russian Hill**, home to the famously curvy Lombard Street, and **Telegraph Hill**, perch of the celebrated Coit Tower.

New paved trails along the northern water's edge lead west towards the **Golden Gate Bridge**, but not before passing the expansive green parkland of **Fort Mason** and through the ritzy **Marina** district, home to the Palace of Fine Arts and some of the city's best shopping. High above, the mansions and Victorians of **Pacific Heights** snuggle up against neighborhood cafés and designer boutiques, along with spectacular views of the bridges and Bay. The Heights slope down to the south to workaday **Japantown** and suburban **Western Addition** districts. Directly west of here, you'll come to **Haight-Ashbury**, once San Francisco's Victorian resort quarter before hippies and flower children took over. Today it's a rag-tag collection of used-clothing stores and hippies squeezing as much money as they can out of their fading past.

The western and southern sides of San Francisco are where most of the city's residents live, and – much to their dismay – the area is experiencing skyrocketing rents. **Geary Boulevard**, the main east–west passage, begins in the Financial District and ends at the Pacific Ocean in the **Richmond** district. Geary's lined with some of the city's best Asian and Russian restaurants, while a block north, the Clement Street area is known as "New Chinatown" for its collection of Chinese groceries, hot-pot restaurants, and dumpling cafeterias. The Richmond is hugged by nature on three of its sides: the beaches, the Golden Gate Bridge, and **Presidio** to the north; Land's End and Ocean Beach to the west; and the expansive Golden Gate Park to the south. On the other side of Golden Gate Park, the **Sunset** district stretches on in suburban sameness south, though the district's Ninth Avenue and Irving Street strip of restaurants is the city's most famous collection of boutique eateries.

Union Square

UNION SQUARE is the focus of downtown San Francisco. The sixteen-block area's filled with stores, hotels, and flocks of tourists, while the plaza itself, on the block north of Geary between Powell and Stockton streets, recently underwent a grueling and lengthy refit that transformed its hitherto rather shabby appearance. In the center of the square, the 97-foot-tall Corinthian column commemorates Admiral Dewey's success in the Spanish–American War: the voluptuous female figure on top of the monument was modeled on **Alma de Bretteville Spreckels,** who founded the California Palace of the Legion of Honor art museum (see p.555). Though the site takes its name from its role as gathering place for pro-Unionist speechmakers on the eve of the Civil War, these days it's remembered more for the attempted assassination of President Gerald Ford outside the bordering *Westin St Francis hotel* in 1975. The opulent hotel also featured prominently in many of Dashiell Hammett's detective stories, including *The Maltese Falcon* – in fact, during the 1920s he worked there as a Pinkerton detective, investigating the notorious rape and murder case against silent film star Fatty Arbuckle.

The southern side of the plaza is dominated by a gigantic **Macy's** department store, but if you're looking for more interesting, albeit pricier, browsing, head east to **Maiden Lane**. Before the 1906 earthquake and fire, it was known as Morton Street, one of San Francisco's lowest-class red-light districts. An average of around ten homicides a month occurred here, and prostitutes used to lean out low-hung windows of "cribs" that bore signs that read "Men taken in and done for." Other than shopping, though, there's one major sight: the only **Frank Lloyd Wright-designed building** in San Francisco, at no. 140. From the outside, it's a squat orange-brick building, oddly lacking in Wright's usual obsession with horizontal lines; the interior, though, is extraordinary, a swooping, sweeping, curved ramp that links the floors and is a clear ancestor of the famed Guggenheim in New York. The building's now occupied by the Xanadu ethnic art gallery – if it's open, feel free to wander inside, but don't expect a warm welcome from the gallery's staff. For detailed information on the shops in the area, see p.580, "Shopping."

Around the corner, at the intersection of Kearney and Market, lies **Lotta's Fountain**, one of the city's most beloved landmarks. Restored and repainted in 1999, Lotta's Fountain served as the legendary message center after the 1906 earthquake, where distraught locals gathered to hear the latest damage reports. Named in honor of actress Lotta Crabtree, the fountain enjoyed its greatest moment when world-renowned opera diva Luisa Tetrazinni sang a free Christmas Eve performance atop it in 1910.

If you're heading back up to the waterfront, **cable cars** run beside Union Square along Powell Street but are usually too packed to board at the **Hallidie Plaza** terminus. There are three line-dodging tips for cable car riders. First, come late in the day – by 7pm or so, the line should be much shorter; second, if you're here during peak hours, head a block north along Powell Street since drivers usually leave a bit of extra room on board at the start of the journey. Finally, if the Powell Street lines are just too busy, the California Street line (terminus at California and Market streets) crawling up Nob Hill is less popular and normally line-free.

Theater District

The area between tourist-heavy Union Square and the grubby Tenderloin is known as the **THEATER DISTRICT**, although most of the playhouses lack the grandeur of many old theaters. Despite its proximity to the tourist hub of the city, this neighborhood is a convenient bolthole from the crowds and a secluded place to stay in the center of the city. The district's anchored by the American Conservatory Theater's **Geary Theater**, 415 Geary St (☎415/742-2228). The company usually performs major plays five nights a week – for details, see below.

The blocks of Post and Sutter streets, which cut through this area, are home to some of downtown's least visible landmarks: some fourteen **private clubs** hidden behind discreet facades. Money isn't the only criteria for membership to these highly esteemed institutions, though being *somebody* usually is. Most notorious is the **Bohemian Club**, at 624 Taylor St, whose Bohemian Grove

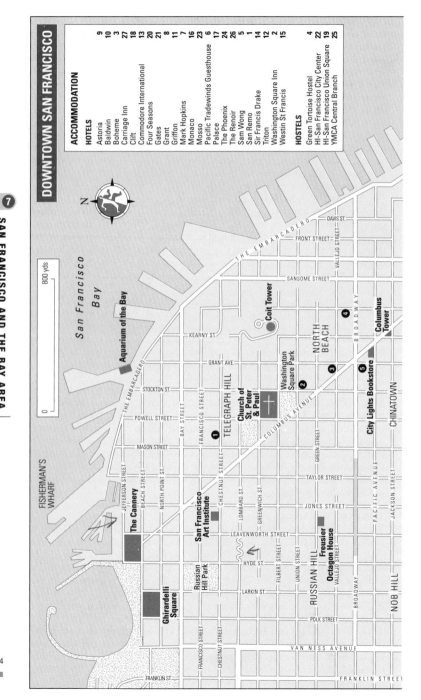

DOWNTOWN SAN FRANCISCO

ACCOMMODATION

HOTELS

Astoria	9
Baldwin	10
Boheme	3
Carriage Inn	27
Clift	18
Commodore International	13
Four Seasons	20
Gates	21
Grant	8
Griffon	11
Mark Hopkins	7
Monaco	16
Mosso	23
Pacific Tradewinds Guesthouse	6
Palace	17
The Phoenix	24
The Renoir	26
Sam Wong	5
San Remo	1
Sir Francis Drake	14
Triton	12
Washington Square Inn	2
Westin St Francis	15

HOSTELS

Green Tortoise Hostel	4
HI-San Francisco City Center	22
HI-San Francisco Union Square	19
YMCA Central Branch	25

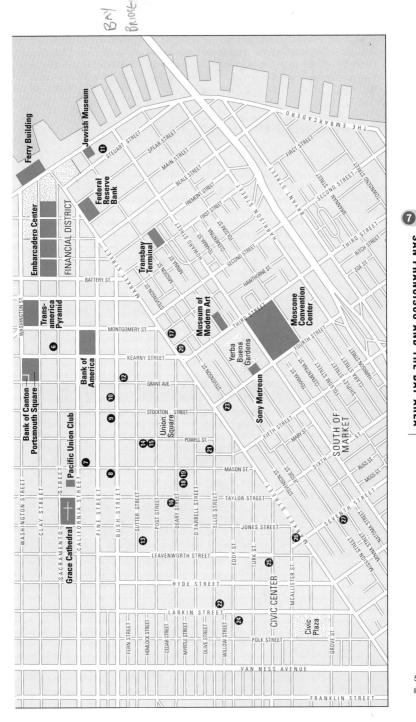

BAY BRIDGE

Ferry Building

Jewish Museum

THE EMBARCADERO

STEUART STREET

SPEAR STREET

MAIN STREET

BEALE STREET

FIRST STREET

SECOND STREET

THIRD STREET

TOWNSEND STREET

Embarcadero Center

Federal Reserve Bank

FINANCIAL DISTRICT

FREMONT STREET

FIRST STREET

MARKET STREET

HOWARD STREET

FOLSOM STREET

HARRISON STREET

BRYANT STREET

BRANNAN STREET

THIRD STREET

RITCH ST.

ZOE ST.

❶ **11**

Transbay Terminal

MISSION ST

MINNA ST

NATOMA ST

TEHAMA ST

CLEMENTINA ST

SECOND STREET

HAWTHORNE ST.

Moscone Convention Center

BATTERY ST.

Trans-america Pyramid

WASHINGTON ST

STEVENSON ST

MONTGOMERY ST.

Museum of Modern Art

THIRD STREET

Yerba Buena Gardens

FOURTH STREET

❻ **6**

KEARNY STREET

❶ **17**

❷ **20**

Bank of America

Bank of Canton Portsmouth Square

Pacific Union Club

❶ **12**

GRANT AVE.

STEVENSON ST

Sony Metreon

MISSION STREET

TEHAMA ST

CLEMENTINA ST

FIFTH STREET

MARY ST.

SHIPLEY STREET

CLARA STREET

HARRISON STREET

SOUTH OF MARKET

RUSS ST.

MOSS ST.

❶ **10**

STOCKTON STREET

❾ **9**

❷ **23**

Union Square

❼ **7**

❶ **14**
❶ **15**

POWELL ST.

❷ **21**

❽ **8**

MASON ST.

❶ **18** ❶ **19**

SIXTH STREET

SEVENTH STREET

MINNA STREET

NATOMA STREET

MARKET STREET

Grace Cathedral

CLAY STREET

WASHINGTON STREET

SACRAMENTO STREET

CALIFORNIA STREET

PINE STREET

BUSH STREET

SUTTER STREET

POST STREET

TAYLOR STREET

JONES STREET

❶ **16**

GEARY STREET

O'FARRELL STREET

ELLIS STREET

❶ **13**

LEAVENWORTH STREET

EDDY ST.

TURK ST.

❷ **26**

❷ **27**

JESSIE ST

STEVENSON ST

MCALLISTER ST.

HYDE STREET

❷ **25**

CIVIC CENTER

LARKIN STREET

❷ **22**

❷ **24**

Civic Plaza

FERN STREET

HEMLOCK STREET

CEDAR STREET

MYRTLE STREET

OLIVE STREET

WILLOW STREET

POLK STREET

GROVE ST.

VAN NESS AVENUE

FRANKLIN STREET

retreat at the Russian River (see p.734) is where ex-presidents and corporate giants assemble for Masonic rituals and schoolboy larks; the San Francisco chapter is housed in a Lewis Hobart Moderne-style building. Organized in 1872 as a breakfast club for newspapermen, it evolved into a businessmen's club with an artsy slant, numbering Ambrose Bierce, Jack London, Bret Harte, and Frank Norris among its members.

The Financial District

From Hallidie Plaza to the waterfront, Market Street traces the southern edge of the **FINANCIAL DISTRICT**, San Francisco's business hub clogged with banks, including the famous **Bank of America**, founded here by Italian immigrant A.P. Giannini in 1901. As with most central business districts, this isn't a place that hums at the weekends: to see it at its liveliest, wander through on a weekday lunchtime.

At the western end of the Financial District stands the **Wells Fargo History Museum**, in the Wells Fargo Bank, 420 Montgomery St (Mon–Fri 9am–5pm; free; ☎415/396-2619, ⓦwww.wellsfargo.com), a pleasant but toothless exhibition space. The glowing accounts of the bank's contributions to the Old West tarnish are unintentionally humorous, and include a wall of 150 employee luminaries although the display of old letters upstairs is more intriguing.

Another notable Financial District museum further east on the edge of Chinatown is the tiny **Pacific Heritage Museum**, 608 Commercial St (Tues–Sat 10am–4pm; free; ☎415/399-1124, ⓦwww.citysearch.com/sfo/pacificheritage). The rolling exhibits of Asian art are fine, but the real draw is the structure itself – a late-nineteenth-century US Subtreasury building, now neatly incorporated into a modern skyscraper.

The cable cars

San Francisco's **cable cars** first appeared in 1873, the brainchild of Andrew Hallidie, an enterprising engineer with an eye for the main chance. Scots-born Hallidie is said to have been inspired to find an alternative to horse-drawn carriages when he saw a team of horses badly injured while trying to pull a dray up a steep hill in the rain. More than equine welfare was under threat – his father had patented a strong wire rope that had been extensively used in the mines of eastern California but, as the Gold Rush there slowed, Hallidie needed a new application for his family's signature product and a privately owned transit system like the cable cars was the ideal solution.

The cable-car **pulley system** was dubbed "Hallidie's Folly" by doubtful locals, but doubters were soon proved wrong as high sections of San Francisco like Nob Hill suddenly became accessible, and businesses and homes were constructed along cable-car routes. At their peak, just before the 1906 earthquake, more than six hundred cable cars traveled on eight lines and 112 miles of track throughout the city, traveling a maximum 9.5 mph.

Unfortunately, though, the cable system was vulnerable to the onset of the automobile thanks to the devastation after the earthquake, when large chunks of the tracks were wrecked. However, when it was rumored in 1947 that the ailing system would be phased out altogether, a local activist organized a citizens' committee to save them. The protests worked, and seventeen years later the cars were put on the National Register of Historic Places and the remaining seventeen miles (now down to ten) was saved. Now there are 44 cars in use – each unique – and around 23 miles of moving cable underground. Since the mid-1980s, MUNI has been rebuilding the cars by hand: the process has taken far longer than the ten years originally estimated, requiring as much as 3000 hours and $275,000 per car.

The Embarcadero

At the northeastern edge of the Financial District, the thin, long waterfront district known as **THE EMBARCADERO** is centered on the **Ferry Building**. Once cut off from the rest of San Francisco by the double-decker Embarcadero Freeway – damaged in the 1989 earthquake and torn down in 1991 – this structure, at the foot of Market Street, was modeled on the cathedral tower in Seville, Spain. Before the bridges were built in the 1930s, it was the arrival point for fifty thousand cross-Bay daily commuters, and a few ferries still dock here. The area in front of the Ferry Building is the site of the much-loved **Ferry Plaza Farmers' Market** (year-round Sat 8.30am–1.30pm; also April–Nov Tues 10.30am–2.30pm), a good place for local produce. San Francisco foodies make pilgrimages here to sample snacks from the city's pricey restaurants, which often set up temporary stalls among the fruit and vegetables.

Nearby **Justin Herman Plaza** was named in honor of the pasha of urban renewal who tore down acres of historic buildings in the Western Addition in the 1960s. It's perhaps fitting that it should be home to one of the ugliest modernist sights in the city, the **Vaillancourt Fountain**, a tangled mass of concrete tubing clearly inspired by air-conditioning ducts. It's famous as the site of an impromptu concert by right-on rockers U2 in the late 1980s, when Bono left his artistic mark on the structure by spray-painting "Rock and Roll Stops the Traffic." Unfortunately, the concert itself also stopped soon afterwards, supposedly when he misinterpreted a sign hanging from a nearby window that read "SF loves U2," believing that "SF" stood for Sinn Fein. The five-mile **waterfront**, which stretches north and south from the foot of Market Street, was teeming during the first half of the twentieth century with ships loading and unloading cargo. The area experienced something of a slump after World War II, but recent development, including the building of a new MUNI station and the extension of the cable-car lines, has brought San Franciscans back here to jog, bike, and skate.

Inland from the waterfront, the area's dominated by the four massive modern skyscrapers known as the **Embarcadero Center**. It's filled with stores, restaurants, and, oddly, dozens of doctors, all geared to filling the lunch times of the thousands of local office workers; there's little to detain a visitor other than a couple of fine hotels (see p.516, "Accommodation"). Building One is the only one you might feel compelled to enter, crowned by the Sky Deck (daily noon–9pm; $5; ⓣ415/772-0550, ⓦwww.embarcaderocenter.com), from which you can observe the cityscape from the 41st floor.

Two blocks west, at the corner of Washington and Montgomery streets, stands San Francisco's tallest building, the **Transamerica Pyramid**, 600 Montgomery St (ⓣ415/983-4100, ⓦwww.tapyramid.com), a glossy, controversial landmark designed by LA-based architect William Pereira in 1972. Nicknamed "Pereira's Prick" thanks to its phallic shape, it's so tall and thin it looks more like a squared-off rocket than a pyramid. The building does have four triangular sides, rising from a square city block to a lofty point high above; it's fully earthquake-proof and was unscathed by the earthquake of 1989, although there's no longer public access to the viewing platform on the 27th floor. Rudyard Kipling, Robert Louis Stevenson, Mark Twain, and William Randolph Hearst all rented office space in the building that once stood at the corner of Montgomery and Washington streets and regularly hung around the famous *Bank Exchange* bar within. Legend also has it that Dr Sun Yat-Sen – whose statue is in Chinatown, three blocks away – wrote the Chinese constitution and orchestrated the successful overthrow of the Manchu dynasty from his second-floor office here.

Jackson Square historic district

Confusingly, there's no plaza in **JACKSON SQUARE**. The area bordered by Washington, Columbus, Sansome, and Pacific streets wasn't known by that name until the 1960s, when interior designers who'd recently opened showrooms here decided on a suitably artsy yet old-fashioned tag to replace the notorious **Barbary Coast**, the district of San Francisco where vice flourished during the nineteenth century. The constant stream of sailors provided an endless supply of customers looking for illicit entertainment, and the area was nicknamed "Baghdad by the Bay" for its unsavory reputation as a nexus for shanghai'ing: hapless young males were given Mickey Finns and, unconscious, taken aboard sailing ships into involuntary servitude. Though buildings here remarkably survived the 1906 disaster, the rowdy, raunchy businesses were hugely affected as nearby poor, residential areas were leveled. The double whammy of fire and fury (chiefly, the relentless campaigning from William Randolph Hearst's *Examiner* newspaper against the district) soon put an end to most illicit fun here.

Remains of San Francisco's earliest days can be seen today in the restored red-brick buildings of Jackson Square's **historic district,** bordered by Washington, Columbus, Sansome, and Pacific streets. Standing on **Jackson Street** is the one place in the city where you can hope to imagine what early San Francisco looked like. Here you'll find the only cluster of downtown buildings that escaped the great fire of 1906 unharmed. The **Hotaling Building** (pronounced hote-UH-ling), at nos. 451–455, was a distillery that was saved by a savvy manager at the height of the fire. Afterward, local wags came up with the doggerel: "If as they say God spanked the town for being so over frisky, why did he burn the churches down and spare Hotaling's whiskey?"

Montgomery Street, on the district's western flank, has retained much of its historic character, and several of the buildings have interesting histories. **No. 732** was the home of San Francisco's first literary magazine, the *Golden Era*, founded in the 1850s; it helped launch the careers of Bret Harte and Mark Twain. Later, John Steinbeck and William Saroyan later spent many a night drinking in the vanished *Black Cat Café* down the street. In the middle of the block, **nos. 722–728** (the Belli and Genella buildings) have been stripped of their original stucco and done up in overwrought Victorian mode. The building was at one time a theater, but has also been a Turkish bath, a tobacco warehouse, and an auction room. The building was bought by the flamboyant San Francisco lawyer Melvin Belli, but his widow's plans to turn the site into a museum have come to nothing. Today, the building has fallen into disuse, hidden from view by shuttered windows, encroaching ivy, and gnarled tree branches, and has a sadly ruined feel.

As the district merges with North Beach and Chinatown, at the intersection of Jackson Street and Columbus Avenue stands the distinctive green-copper siding of the **Columbus Tower**, 906 Kearney St. It's now owned by director and San Francisco native Francis Ford Coppola and his office, with doubtless spectacular views, is in the rounded tower that gives the building its name. Unfortunately, it's not open to the public.

Portsmouth Square

One block south of Columbus Tower, **PORTSMOUTH SQUARE** was San Francisco's original city center and the first port of entry. Today, it's hard to imagine the city springing up from this once dusty patch of land nestled between Nob, Telegraph, and Rincon hills, but it was here that Englishman

William Richardson received permission from Mexican rulers to begin a trading post on the coast of the Bay. John Montgomery came ashore in 1846 to claim the hamlet for the United States, raising a flag whose location is marked by the Stars and Stripes that flies in the square today. A small settlement was built on the edges of the square, but it was Sam Brannan's 1848 cry of "Gold!" here (see p.507) that sent property prices and development skyrocketing to levels from which they still haven't returned.

There are four points of interest in Portsmouth Square aside from the American flag. The first is a monument to writer **Robert Louis Stevenson**, featuring a replica of the galleon *Hispaniola* from his novel, *Treasure Island*: Stevenson spent much time observing the locals in Portsmouth Square during his brief sojourn in San Francisco and the Monterey Peninsula in the late 1870s. The plaque nearby honors **California's first public school**, built here in 1848; while the third monument is a tribute to cable-car poobah **Andrew Hallidie**, whose first line ran on Clay Street down the steps. The most recent addition to the square recognizes its role in the modern Chinatown: Thomas Marsh's bronze *Goddess of Democracy*, erected in memory of the 1989 Tian'anmen Square protests. Whatever the time of day, the square is filled with elderly Chinese practising *t'ai chi*, playing chess, or watching their grandchildren climb the new playground equipment. **Portsmouth Square** now marks the beginning of Chinatown.

Chinatown

CHINATOWN's twenty-four square blocks smack in the middle of San Francisco make up the second-largest (after New York City) Chinese community outside Asia. Its roots lie in the migration of Chinese laborers to the city after the completion of the transcontinental railroad, and the arrival of Chinese sailors keen to benefit from the Gold Rush. San Francisco is still known in China as "Old Gold Mountain," its storied moniker from the nineteenth century. The city didn't extend much of a welcome to Chinese immigrants: they were met by a tide of vicious racial attacks and the 1882 Chinese Exclusion Act that banned new immigration, a law that resulted in thousands of single Chinese men being forbidden from both dating local women and bringing wives from China. A rip-roaring prostitution and gambling quarter developed, controlled by gangs known as tongs. With the loosening of immigration rules due to China's partnership with the US during World War II, and decades of hard work by its residents, Chinatown has grown into a self-made success.

Many visitors assume that the neighborhood remains autonomous – cut off from San Francisco by language and cultural barriers. But Chinatown's residents are as American as the rest of the city's citizens, and the district has one of its highest voter turnouts come election day. Nowadays the population of Chinatown, descendants of Cantonese- and Fujianese-speaking southern mainlanders, as well as Taiwanese, have been joined by Mandarin-speaking northerners, Vietnamese, Koreans, Thais, and Laotians, turning the area into **Asiatown**. By day the area bustles with activity, by night it's a blaze of neon. Overcrowding is compounded by a brisk tourist trade – sadly, however, Chinatown boasts some of the tackiest stores and facades in the city, more like shopping in a bad part of Hong Kong than in Beijing. Indeed, Chinese tourists are often disappointed in the neighborhood's disorder and pandering to tourists – for a truer sense of everyday Chinese life in San Francisco, you're better off heading to the Richmond district (see p.554).

One major improvement to Chinatown – an attempt to keep tourists coming – is the new nightmarket which happens under the stars every Saturday night from 6pm to 11pm in Portsmouth Square, spring through autumn. Free performances of classical opera and traditional music are surrounded by stalls pitching everything from fresh honey to leather jackets.

The best way to approach Chinatown is through the dramatic **Chinatown Gate**, on the southern end of Grant Avenue at Bush. Facing south, per *feng shui* precepts, it's a large dragon-clad arch, with a four-character inscription that reads *Xia tian wei gong* or "The reason to exist is to serve the public good," given by the People's Republic of China to the city in 1969. It's hard to see how that idea is carried out on the blocks ahead: Grant's sidewalks are paved with plastic Buddhas, cloisonné "health balls", noisemakers, and chirping mechanical crickets that assault the ear and eye from every doorway. One of the oldest thoroughfares in the city, Grant Avenue – originally called Dupont Street – was a wicked ensemble of opium dens, bordellos, and gambling huts policed, if not terrorized, by tong hatchet men. After the 1906 fire, though, the city decided to rename it in honor of president and Civil War hero Ulysses S. Grant and so in the process excise the seedy excesses for which it had been famous. Note the two pagoda-topped buildings on the corner of Grant and California streets, the Sing Fat and Sing Chong, important because they were the first to be constructed after the 1906 fire, signaling Chinese resolve to remain on the much-coveted land.

A few blocks west, running parallel to Grant Avenue, **Stockton Street** is refreshingly undertouristed, the commercial artery of the area for locals, packed with grocery stores and dim sum shops, as well as herbalists and fishmongers. Between Stockton Street and Grant Avenue, narrow Waverly Place also runs north–south and holds three opulent but skillfully hidden temples: **Jeng Sen** on the second floor of no. 146, **Norras** at no. 109, and **Tien Hou** (pronounced TEE-en How) on the fourth floor of no. 125. This last is especially impressive, a Taoist temple dedicated to the Goddess of Heaven, with an ornate interior with splashes of gold and vermilion, and a ceiling dripping with tassels and red lanterns. All three temples are still in use and open to visitors (daily 10am–5pm): note the pyramids of oranges, considered lucky because the Cantonese pronunciation of orange sounds similar to the word for wealth. Although the temples don't charge admission, it's respectful to leave a donation and not use cameras or camcorders inside.

Detour east along Washington Street from Grant Avenue to find the eye-catching **Bank of Canton** building, no. 743, a small red pagoda-like structure built in 1909 for the Chinese American Telephone Exchange: note how the roof curves out and then back on itself, since evil spirits travel in a straight line. It stands on the original site of the offices of Sam Brannan's *California Star* newspaper, which carried the news of the earliest ore discoveries back to the East Coast in 1848 and so played a major role in creating the Gold Rush. Visitors interested in Buddhism should head to Buddha's Universal Church at no. 720, where America's largest Zen sect gives free tours on the second and fourth Sunday of each month, the only time it's open to the public. This five-story building was painstakingly built by the sect's members from an exotic collection of polished woods, adorned everywhere by the mosaic images of Buddha.

North Beach

Bordering Chinatown at the junction of Grant Avenue and Broadway, and Fisherman's Wharf to the south, **NORTH BEACH** has always been a gateway for immigrants. Italian immigration to San Francisco was ignited, unsurprisingly, by the Gold Rush, although it gained momentum at the end of the nineteenth century, when this area began to develop the characteristics – delis, wine bars, salami grocers – of a true "Little Italy." The freewheeling European flavor here, coupled with a robust nightlife and wide availability of housing, attracted rebel writers like Lawrence Ferlinghetti, Allen Ginsberg, and Jack Kerouac in the 1950s, making North Beach the nexus of the **Beat movement** (see box).

The main drag of North Beach is **Columbus Avenue**, proudly tagged as Little Italy by the flags painted on each lamppost, and now one of San Francisco's liveliest nighttime drags. At its southern end at the crossroads of **Columbus and Broadway**, you'll find the former site of many old bars and

The Beats in North Beach

Beat literature didn't begin in San Francisco, but emerged a decade earlier in New York, where bohemian Jack Kerouac had joined with the Ivy League-educated Allen Ginsberg, as well as William Burroughs, to bemoan the conservative political climate there. The group quickly grew frustrated with New York and moved out West, most of them settling in North Beach and securing jobs at the docks to help longshoremen unload the fishing boats. The first rumblings of interest in the movement were signaled by the opening, in 1953, of the first bookstore in America dedicated solely to paperbacks: Lawrence Ferlinghetti's City Lights Bookstore (see overleaf) drew attention to the area as the latest literary capital of California.

But it wasn't until the publication four years later of Ginsberg's pornographic protest poem *Howl* – originally written simply for his own pleasure rather than for printing – that mainstream America took notice. Police moved in on City Lights to prevent the sale of the book, inadvertently catapulting the Beats to a national notoriety – assisted by press hysteria over their hedonistic antics, including heavy drinking and an immense fondness for pot – that matched what fame was based on the literary merits of their work. Ginsberg's case went all the way to the Supreme Court, which eventually ruled that so long as a work has "redeeming social value" it could not be considered pornographic. Within six months, Jack Kerouac's *On the Road*, inspired by his friend Neal Cassady's benzedrine monologues and several cross-country trips, had shot to the top of the bestseller lists, cementing the Beats' fame. It's said that the word Beatnik was coined by legendary local newspaper columnist Herb Caen, who noted that the writers were as far out as the recently launched Soviet rocket, Sputnik, and so jokily christened them Beatniks. Soon, North Beach was synonymous across America with a wild and subversive lifestyle, an image that soon drove away the original artsy intelligentsia, many of whom ended up in Haight-Ashbury. Instead heat-seeking libertines swamped the area, accompanied by tourists on "Beatnik Tours," who were promised sidewalks clogged with black-bereted, goateed trendsetters banging bongos. (The more enterprising fringes of bohemia responded in kind with "The Squaresville Tour" of the Financial District, dressed in Bermuda shorts and carrying plaques that read "Hi, Squares.") It wasn't long before the Italians who'd once dominated North Beach moved back in and reclaimed it from the dwindling Beat movement.

Almost singlehandedly, Ferlinghetti has kept the Beat legend alive in North Beach. He successfully petitioned City Hall for streets to be renamed as a tribute to the famous figures who have graced the neighborhood; indeed, the small alley that runs down the side of the City Lights store has been called "Jack Kerouac Lane." Enamored of the way Paris honors its writers with street names, Ferlinghetti also campaigned for the inclusion of local non-Beat writers and artists. Accordingly, San Francisco now has streets bearing the names of many authors, including Mark Twain, Jack London, and Dashiell Hammett.

comedy clubs from the 1950s, where politically conscious comedians like Mort Sahl and Lenny Bruce performed. Many of the venues are now porno stores, which took over spaces here during the death throes of the Beat movement. It's ironic, given San Francisco's penchant for political correctness, that one of the city's legacies is the topless waitress phenomenon: at the *Condor Club* in 1964, Carol "44 inches" Doda slipped out of her top one night and into the history books. The club's now reincarnated as the (fully clothed) *Condor Sports Bar* at 300 Columbus Ave. However, the current owners have preserved the celebrated set of neon nipples that once glowed above the door in an onsite museum, as well as photos and clippings from the *Condor Club's* heyday: one of the choicest stories is the sad tale of a randy bouncer and waitress, who climbed on top of the club's rising piano together. In the throes of passion, they accidentally hit the lever, sending the piano up to the ceiling: the man was crushed to death, but he cushioned the woman beneath him and she survived. The only other notable sex joint, *The Lusty Lady*, 1033 Kearney St at Columbus (℡415/391-3991), is a female-owned-and-operated strip club with unionized workers, successful enough to be opening satellite branches around the country.

Opposite stands **City Lights Bookstore**, 261 Columbus Ave at Broadway (Mon–Thurs & Sun 10am–11.30pm, Fri–Sat 10am–12.30am; ℡415/362-8193, Ⓦwww.citylights.com). This was the heart of Beat North Beach and struggles on as an independent bookstore, despite the encroachment of big-name chains and a surfeit of surly, Beat-inspired staff. The place is still owned by Ferlinghetti, who's now in his eighties: aside from its kooky section dividers – books filed under "Anarchism" and "Muckraking," for instance – the best reason to come here is the upstairs poetry room, where you'll find everything from $1 mini-books and poster-size poems from Beatnik legends to various collections and anthologies.

The area grows more Italian as you head north along Columbus Avenue: from Vallejo Street to the waterfront, expect plenty of cafés, delis, and restaurants selling strong coffee and salamis. One exception is the section of **Grant Avenue** north of Vallejo, where you'll find one of the best emerging shopping streets in the city, lined with clothing stores and divey cafés. It's also the site of San Francisco's oldest bar, *The Saloon* at no. 1232 (℡415/989-7666) – a rare North Beach survivor of the 1906 fire, now little more than a hole in the wall.

The soul of North Beach is **Washington Square Park**, a grassy plaza that plays host to dozens of older, local Chinese each morning, clumped in groups across the lawn to practice *t'ai chi*. Delightfully loopy local legend Lillie Coit's not-so-subtle fascination with firefighters (see opposite) can be seen on the Columbus side in the form of a big, bronze macho monument with men holding hoses. On the north side of the park, the white lacy spires of the **Church of St Peter and Paul** look like a pair of fairytale castles rising beneath the shadow of Telegraph Hill's Coit Tower: unfortunately, the interior's an unremarkable nineteenth-century confection with little to recommend it. In 1954, local baseball phenom Joe DiMaggio and Marilyn Monroe had their wedding pictures taken here (though the actual marriage took place earlier at City Hall since both were divorced).

Telegraph Hill

Dominated by Coit Tower, **TELEGRAPH HILL** is a quiet cluster of hill-hugging homes. The most direct path up the hill is Filbert Street, but be aware that the gradient east of Grant Avenue is very steep. The ten-minute walk's pleasant enough, though, past clapboard houses and flowery gardens on a terraced sidewalk – don't hurry and keep turning round to catch the breathtaking views. Since there are few parking spots at the tower, non-walkers are better holding out for the (infallibly infrequent) MUNI bus #39 to the top. Once you reach the summit, it's easy to see why it was used as a signal tower for ships entering the Golden Gate. A watchman on the hill would identify the boat's origin and name by the flags flying on the mast, and relay the information via telegraph to the docks along Fisherman's Wharf. A plaque in front of a statue honoring Christopher Columbus in **Pioneer Park**, which lies at the foot of the tower, marks the watchman's spot.

The park, which was donated to the city by private citizens in 1875, contains the best viewpoint in all of Telegraph Hill, **Coit Tower** (daily 10am–6pm; $3.75; ☎415/362-0808). Built with money bequeathed by Lillie Coit in 1929 as a tribute to the city's firemen, the tower is an attractive component of the city's skyline, and rewards those who trudge uphill with sweeping views from its observation deck. Legend has it that as a young girl, Lillie answered the cries of "Help!" and helped the Knickerbocker Engine Company No. 5 of the Volunteer Fire Department tow their engine up Telegraph Hill. Grateful firefighters made her their mascot, and even after she married wealthy Easterner Howard Coit in 1868, Lillie continued attending firemen's balls and playing poker over cigars with "her" men of Company No. 5. Local stories abound of her character and exploits, including scenes of dashing away from society balls and chasing clanging fire engines. Upon her death, she left behind $125,000 "to be expended in an appropriate manner for the purpose of adding to the beauty of the city, which I have always loved." The result is the 212-foot pillar that looks alarmingly like a firehose nozzle. Coit's rumored liaisons with firemen add fuel to the speculation that the tower was actually her parting memorial to another part of a fireman's equipment.

While waiting to ascend to the top, take some time to admire the frescoes at the interior's base. They were an early project overseen by the Public Works of Art Authority, a predecessor of the WPA that employed artists to decorate public and government buildings during the Depression. Those chosen for this project were students of the famous Mexican artist, **Diego Rivera**, who was both artistically and politically influenced by Russian Communism. As in his work, the figures are typically muscular and somber, emphasizing the glory of labor, although there's a wide variation in style and quality between panels, despite their thematic cohesion. You can take a free tour of the murals Tuesdays and Thursdays at 10.15am and Saturday at 11am.

The best way down Telegraph Hill is on the eastern side, where the Greenwich Steps cling to the hill at a 45-degree angle, one of several walkways and pedestrian streets. Another, equally lovely walkway is the **Filbert Steps**, dropping down even more steeply before plateauing at Montgomery Street in a leafy garden surrounded by simple cottages. These single-story houses were built in the 1850s by Gold Rush immigrants, who needed quick, temporary homes while they found their fortunes. At the foot of Telegraph Hill, between Battery Street and the Embarcadero stands **Levi Strauss Plaza** (daily 8am–4pm; free; ☎415/501-3295), headquarters of blue-jean inventors Levi Strauss & Co. (hence the "SF" on the pocket rivets). It's a grim, unappealing place, constructed entirely out of red brick, with looming buildings and little life on the terraces. A lackluster exhibition on blue-jean history fills the lobby, notable mostly for its pristine examples of Levi's candy-colored, satin cowboy shirts from the 1950s.

Russian Hill

West of North Beach, elegant **RUSSIAN HILL**, named for six unknown Russian sailors who died on an expedition here in the early 1800s and were buried on its southeastern tip, has the odd point of interest. The modest high-rises that you see at the top of the hill were fiercely contested when they were first built in the 1920s, prompting many of San Francisco's stringent zoning laws. Most people, though, come here for the white-knuckle drive down Lombard Street, a terracotta-tiled waterchute for cars. Its tight, narrow curves swoop down one block, and there's a 5mph speed limit here – not that you'll be able to drive much faster given the usual lines to enjoy the drive. Wealthy owners of the manicured houses along its edges have petitioned numerous times to close the road, but given how often this cutesy block is featured in San Francisco publicity shots – not to mention the city's supine bureaucracy – they're unlikely to succeed. The best time to enjoy it is early morning or, better still, late at night when the city lights twinkle below and the tourists have gone.

It's easy to get your bearings in the neighborhood, as the cable-car tracks along **Hyde Street** neatly divide the district in two. Two blocks east down the hill, the low-rise Mission-style building of the **San Francisco Art Institute**, at 800 Chestnut St (daily 9am–8pm, Tues–Sat 10am–5pm; free; ☎415/771-7020, ⓦ www.sfai.edu), clings to the side of a steep street. It's easy to miss this place, which is in fact the oldest art school in the West (past students include Jerry Garcia and Lawrence Ferlinghetti; Ansel Adams started its photography department). Unfortunately, many of its galleries are often closed, since it's still a working school. The one unmissable sight is the **Diego Rivera Gallery**, with an outstanding mural called *The Making of a Fresco Showing the Building of a City* executed by the painter in 1931 at the height of his fame.

Nob Hill

The posh hotels and Masonic institutions of **NOB HILL**, south of Russian Hill and west of Chinatown, exemplify San Francisco's old wealth: it was here that the four men who transformed California through railroads all built their houses (see box below). Once you've made the stiff climb up (or taken the California line cable car), there are very few real sights as such, apart from the astounding views over the city and beyond. Indeed, the streets are oddly deserted, and despite its dense population, there's a definite sense of isolation and privacy that exists in few other parts of the city.

Originally called California Street Hill, the 376-foot-high hill used to be scrubland occupied by sheep. The invention of the cable car made it accessible to Gold Rush millionaires, and the area became known as Nob Hill (from "nabob" a Moghul prince, or "snob," or "knob" as in rounded hill) after **The Big Four** – Leland Stanford, Collis P. Huntington, Mark Hopkins, and Charles Crocker – came to the area to construct the Central Pacific Railroad, and built their mansions here.

Ostentatious designs created out of Marin headlands redwood were the fashion: unfortunately, after the earthquake and fire of 1906, every one of the mansions on Nob Hill had burned to the ground, with a single exception. James C. Flood had bucked local fashions and instead emulated the brownstone style popular on New York's Fifth Avenue: the stone weathered the fire, as did the burnt-out shell of the as-yet-uncompleted *Fairmont Hotel*. Flood's mansion, constructed in 1886 at the cost of a cool $1 million, is now the private **Pacific**

Union Club, a retreat for the rich, closed to the public. Across California Street, you'll find another jaw-dropping view and even more startling prices at San Francisco's most famous vista-bar, *The Top of the Mark*, in the grand, castle-like **Mark Hopkins Hotel** (supposedly, where Tony Bennett found his inspiration for *I Left My Heart in San Francisco).*

Overlooking Huntington Park is one of the biggest hunks of sham-Gothic architecture in the US, **Grace Cathedral**, 1100 California St (Mon–Fri & Sun 7am–6pm, Sat 8am–6pm; free tours Mon–Fri 1–3pm, Sat 11.30am–1.30pm, Sun 12.30–2pm; ☎415/749-6300, ⓦwww.gracecathedral.org). Although this pale copy of Notre Dame in Paris was begun after the 1906 fire on land donated by the wealthy Crocker family, it took until the early 1960s to finish – and it suffers from a hodgepodge of styles as a result. The cathedral gives an impression of unloved hugeness, despite florid touches like the faithful replicas of Ghiberti's Renaissance doors from the Florence Baptistry adorning the main entrance. Utterly out of place, they're included simply because they were available: during construction, the first commercial copies of the fifteenth-century masterpiece were produced, and the supervising architect snapped them up. Inside, check out the AIDS Interfaith Chapel to the right of the main entrance with a bronze altar designed by the late pop artist Keith Haring.

Fisherman's Wharf

San Francisco doesn't go dramatically out of its way to court and fleece the tourist, but with **FISHERMAN'S WHARF** it makes a rare exception. This is the one place in town guaranteed to produce shudders of embarrassment from most locals and, even for visitors with kids, there are better places (like Golden Gate Park; see p.553) to dawdle for an afternoon. Despite its tacky reputation, though, the wharf is massively popular: a creative use of statistics allows the area to proclaim itself the most visited attraction in the entire country. If you want

---

San Francisco's steepest streets

Though no street can match Lombard for its fabled curves, the wait to go down them may force you to consider another itinerary if pressed for time. The city's second-twistiest street lies coiled in the outer Potrero Hill neighborhood, on Vermont Street between McKinley and 22nd streets: it has five full and two half-turns (compared with Lombard's eight), and its location keeps traffic flowing. Another San Francisco thrill that'll test the brakes of your car is to take a ride down any of the city's steepest streets. Since most locals prefer not to brave the steeper streets – even if that forces them to make an elaborate detour – you won't normally have to wait to freewheel down one of the following. We've included the hill's neighborhood to help find it on a map.

	degree
1) Filbert between Leavenworth and Hyde, Russian Hill	31.5
2) 22nd Street between Church and Vicksburg, Castro/Noe Valley	31.5
3) Jones between Union and Filbert, Russian Hill	29.0
4) Duboce between Buena Vista and Alpine, Lower Haight	27.9
5) Jones between Green and Union, Russian Hill	26.0
6) Webster between Vallejo and Broadway, Pacific Heights	26.0
7) Duboce between Alpine and Divisadero, Lower Haight	25.0
8) Jones between Pine and California, Nob Hill	24.8
9) Fillmore between Vallejo and Broadway, Pacific Heights	24.0

to enjoy the waterfront, a better option is a stroll through the parks in the Marina; but if you're determined to see the wharf, avoid weekends and try to get there as early as possible before the crowds descend.

Hard as it might be to believe now, Fisherman's Wharf was once a serious fishing port. The few fishermen that can afford the exorbitant mooring charges these days are usually finished by early morning and are gone before visitors arrive. You can still find some decent seafood here at some of the better restaurants (see reviews, p.560, "Eating"), but worthwhile sights or remnants of the fishing trade are few and far between. The most endearing sight at the wharf is a large colony of boisterous sea lions (no feeding allowed) that have taken over a number of floating platforms at sea level between piers 39 and 41. To see more aquatic life, check out Aquarium of the Bay at Pier 39 (summer daily 9am–8pm; rest of year Mon–Fri 10am–6pm, Sat–Sun 10am–7pm; $12.95, $6.50 kids; ☎1-888/732-3483, ⊛www.aquariumofthebay.com). Here, you'll get spectacular close-up views of fish and crustaceans that surround you as you trundle slowly along a 400ft acrylic viewing tunnel – it's just a pity about the throbbing muzak. It isn't a patch on the Monterey Aquarium, though (see p.483), so if you have time, you're better off heading down the coast instead of spending money here. Close by at Pier 45 is the new home of the eccentric Musée Méchanique (Mon–Fri 11am–7pm, Sat–Sun 10am–8pm; ☎415/386-1170, ⊛www.citysearch.museemechanique.com) which was originally housed in a creaky old building out by Cliff House (see p.555). It's an appealing collection of historic arcade games; if you want to play, bring plenty of quarters. The games range from retro classics like a 1980s Pac Man to a freakish, gap-toothed clown who'll cackle forever in return for 25¢.

Where once the wharf focused on catching fish, now it is unsuspecting tourist dollars it's after – there are dozens of tacky souvenir shops as well as bland malls. One of the more appealing is **Ghirardelli Square**, 900 N Point St at Larkin (☎415/775-5500, ⊛www.ghirardellisq.com): originally a woollen mill, it was purchased by Domenico Ghirardelli to house his expanding chocolate empire. Ghirardelli was a gold prospecter-turned-grocer who in 1865 discovered the Broma process, which sweats butter out of raw cocoa, and made a fortune. There are a few pricey shops here, and some fine restaurants, although there's no manufacturing onsite now (Ghirardelli's has moved across the Bay to cheaper premises in Oakland).

Bay cruises depart from piers 39, 41, and 431/2 several times a day. Provided the fogs aren't too heavy (which, even in summer, is often an issue), they give good city views.

Alcatraz

The rocky little islet of **ALCATRAZ**, rising out of San Francisco Bay north of Fisherman's Wharf, was originally home to nothing more than the odd pelican. In the late nineteenth century, the island became a military fortress, and in 1934 it was converted into one of America's most **dreaded high-security prisons**. Surrounded by freezing, impassable water, Alcatraz was an ideal place for a jail: this is where many of America's brand-name criminals like Al Capone and Machine Gun Kelly were held. Although conditions were softened as time passed – look for the radio jacks installed in each cell in the 1950s – a stay in one of the tiny, lonely rooms must have been psychologically grueling, especially given the islet's proximity to the glittering lights of San Francisco. Escape, of course, was impossible, thanks to the violent currents that churn constantly in the icy Bay: in all, nine men managed to get off "The Rock," but no one managed to swim to freedom.

Note that The Rock's curious name is part corruption, part mistake. An early explorer christened one island in the Bay *Isla de Alcatraces* (Island of Pelicans) in honor of the hundreds of birds who lived on it; however, the island he was referring to is not the one we now know as Alcatraz. The pelicans' old home is currently called Yerba Buena Island because a clumsy English sea captain got confused when mapping the Bay in 1826. He assumed (wrongly) that the rock he saw covered with guano must be the birds' home; so he marked that in mangled Spanglish as Alcatraz, then assigned the name Yerba Buena to the other penguin-dotted islet.

These days the island's only function is as a tourist attraction, and at least 750,000 visitors each year take the excellent hour-long, self-guided audio **tours** ($4) of the abandoned prison. These include some sharp anecdotal commentary as well as campy re-enactments of prison life featuring improvised voices of characters like Capone and Kelly. Skip the dull twelve-minute introductory film at the dock – you're far better joining one of the lively, free ranger talks on a variety of themes, which run five times daily (check the schedule when you arrive or call ☏415/705-5555, Ⓦwww.nps.gov/alcatraz). Blue and Gold Fleet runs enormous **boats** to Alcatraz, leaving from Pier 41 (frequent departures from 9.30am, last boat back at 4.30pm, 6.30pm in summer, also evening cruises, times and prices vary; $13.25 including audio tour, $9.25 without; information ☏415/773-1188, advance booking ☏415/705-5555, Ⓦwww.blueandgoldfleet.com). Advance reservations are essential: expect a two-week wait in peak season. In summer, the company also runs a day-tour that combines a visit to Alcatraz with a stop at Angel Island ($35.25).

Fort Mason, the Marina, Cow Hollow, and Pacific Heights

A little way west of the wharf, beyond Ghirardelli Square, the **Golden Gate National Recreation Area** was established in 1972 to protect much-needed central park space for the city, and now encompasses almost seventy square miles of waterfront property, from the beaches to the south right up to the cliffs of Marin County across the Golden Gate Bridge. Closest to the wharf, the **Aquatic Park** complex of buildings groups around the foot of Hyde Street, at its center the "bathhouse" – a bold, Art Deco piece of architecture now home to the **Maritime Museum**, 900 Beach St (daily 10am–5pm; free; ☏415/556-3002, Ⓦwww.maritime.org). Check out also the trippy **mural** in the main room, painted by Hilaire Hiller in 1939 and symbolizing the lost continent of Atlantis in 37 individual panels, although few of the other exhibits hold much interest. The rest of the complex includes a maritime library and a forgettable collection of ocean-going memorabilia. At the adjacent **Hyde Street Pier** (daily 9am–5.30pm; $6; ☏415/561-7100), the museum has restored a number of old wooden ships that are worth clamoring around on to get a sense of the boats that voyagers like Richard Henry Dana entrusted with their lives. The best is the square-rigger *Balclutha*, built in 1886 and the sole survivor of the great sailing ships that journeyed around Cape Horn in the 1800s. Of course, being that it's now in California, the boat also had a second career in the movies, playing bit parts in 1930s films like *Mutiny on the Bounty*.

Fort Mason

Half a mile west along the waterfront, **Fort Mason** sits behind a lovely open park giving great views of the Golden Gate Bridge. The area can be reached by walking along the Golden Gate Promenade, a stretch of pavement popular

Native American Alcatraz

For all its usefulness as a jail, the island turned out to be a fiscal disaster, and, after years of operating at massive costs, it finally closed in 1963. The remaining prisoners were distributed among decidedly less horrific detention centers, and the island remained abandoned until 1969, when a group of Native Americans staged an occupation as part of a peaceful attempt to claim the island for their people – citing treaties which designated all federal land not in use as automatically reverting to their ownership. The government, using all the bureaucratic trickery it could muster, finally ousted the floundering movement in 1971 by claiming the operative lighthouse on the Rock qualified it as active. The occupation may have seemed a failure, but in marking the 25th anniversary of the event, participant Fortunate Eagle noted that it acted as a huge bargaining chip for American Indians, citing President Nixon's return of contested lands back to Native American tribes as a victory made possible by the precedent action.

with joggers and in-line skaters. Originally a Civil War defense installation, now turned over to public use, the old buildings of Fort Mason are occupied by around fifty non-profit groups including theaters, galleries, and museums, plus a youth hostel (see p.520).

The centerpiece of the complex's museums is the **Museum of Craft and Folk Art** (Tues–Fri & Sun 11am–5pm, Sat 10am–5pm; $3, free Sat 10am–noon; ☏415/775-0991, ⓦwww.mocfa.org), which features up to ten different exhibitions each year, including both local and international work. Of the other museums here, the two best are in the large waterfront Building C at the heart of the complex: the **Museo Italo-Americano** (Wed–Sun noon–5pm; $3; ☏415/673-2200, ⓦwww.museoitaloamericano.org), with displays relating to the culture and history of the Italian community in the US; the **African-American Historical and Cultural Society** (Wed–Sun noon–5pm; $2), meanwhile, commemorates local black leaders and historical figures. The best time to visit is on the first Wednesday of every month, when every museum is not only free, but open until 7pm.

San Francisco's most theatrical piece of architecture lies a few hundred yards further west at Marina Boulevard and Baker Street. **The Palace of Fine Arts**, 3301 Lyon St (☏415/563-6504, ⓦwww.palaceoffinearts.org), is not the museum its name suggests, but a huge, freely interpreted classical ruin by Bernard Maybeck. It was erected for the Panama Pacific International Exhibition in 1915 and, when all the other buildings were torn down, the palace was saved simply because locals thought it too beautiful to destroy. Unfortunately, since it was built of wood, plaster, and burlap, it crumbled with dignity until the late 1950s when a wealthy resident put up money for the structure to be recast in reinforced concrete. To a modern eye, the palace is a mournfully sentimental piece of Victoriana, complete with weeping figures on the colonnade by sculptor Ulric Ellerhusen, said to represent the melancholy of life without art.

Next door, the **Exploratorium** is the best kids' museum in San Francisco (June–Aug Tues, Thurs–Sun 10am–6pm, Wed 10am–9pm; Sept–May Tues, Thurs–Sun, 10am–5pm, Wed 10am–9pm; $10, free first Wed of the month; information ☏415/563-7337, Tactile Dome reservations ☏415/561-0362, ⓦwww.exploratorium.edu). It crams in more than 650 hands-on exhibits, including the famous *Tactile Dome*, a total sensory-deprivation dome, explored on hands and knees, which is not for the claustrophobic (reservations essential). Plan to visit as early as possible since it can get very busy later in the day, especially during school holidays. From here, the waterfront stretches west through the Presidio National Park and the quirky Presidio pet cemetery on Crissy Field Avenue, to Fort Point, the Golden Gate Bridge, and the beach area close to Golden Gate Park (see p.553).

The Marina
The area around the Palace of Fine Arts, the **MARINA** district, is one of the city's greenest districts, enjoying a prime waterfront location and lots of open space. Homogeneously young, white, professional, and straight, it prompts derision from artier locals, who pinpoint the Marina, with its swanky yacht clubs and jogger-laden paths, as the local yuppie mother lode. Ironically, though it was built specifically to celebrate the rebirth of the city after the massive earthquake of 1906, the Marina was the worst casualty of the earthquake in 1989 – tremors tore through fragile landfill and a good number of homes collapsed into smoldering heaps. The neighborhood's commercial center runs along Chestnut Street between Broderick and Fillmore, and most of the amenities are geared to swinging singles. The local watering holes are known as "high intensity breeder bars" and there's a massive branch of Safeway, the heterosexual answer to the frenzied gay cruising that takes place in the Market Street outpost near the Castro. In fact, so prevalent is the pickup scene that the Marina location has even been dubbed, without a trace of irony, "The Body Shop."

Cow Hollow
Originally a small valley of pastures and dairies in the post-Gold Rush years, **COW HOLLOW** languished until the 1950s, when problems with open sewage and complaints from neighbors up on prestigious Pacific Heights about the smell of the cows allowed enterprising merchants to transform the area. The gorgeous old Victorian houses have since been refitted, especially around Filbert and Green streets, and the stretch of Union between Van Ness and Divisadero now holds one of the city's densest concentrations of boutiques and cafés. This street is alive with neighborhood shoppers and the very lack of tourist sights is what keeps it appealing.

The one sight that's worth seeking out is the oddball **Octagon House Museum** on the corner of Union and Gough streets (second Sun, second and fourth Thurs of each month noon–3pm; closed Jan; donation suggested; ☏415/441-7512). It's worth a peek if you happen to be there during its very limited hours of operation, thanks in part to its knowledgeable and enthusiastic docents. Built in 1861, when it was believed increased exposure to sunlight benefited one's health, the house remains in excellent, and sunny, condition. A time capsule stashed under the stairs by its first owner was discovered during recent renovations, and is a captivating glimpse of late-nineteenth-century local life including a letter, a newspaper, and photographs of his family. Next door, leafy **Allyne Park** is named after the sisters who donated the land for both the house and garden: it feels more like someone's backyard than a public space, but its redwood trees and comfy benches are an idyllic place to rest.

Pacific Heights
Perched on steep hills between Cow Hollow and Japantown, wealthy **PACIFIC HEIGHTS** is home to some of the city's most monumental Victorian piles and stone mansions – a millionaires' ghetto, beautifully poised around two windswept parks. The lavishly proportioned mansions that teeter precipitously atop these hills today are the chosen domains of stockbrokers, business magnates, and the odd best-selling novelist, like Danielle Steel (see below), who lives in one of the largest houses in the city.

The neighborhood is neatly divided by Fillmore Street: to the west are the large dwellings that earned the neighborhood its reputation; to the east, swanky Art Deco apartment buildings that do little to damage it. West of Fillmore Street, lower Pacific Heights is centered on restful **Alta Plaza Park**, at Clay and Steiner streets, where local dog walkers earn their keep by exercising pampered pooches. East of Fillmore, facing the cypress-dotted peak of **Lafayette Park** are several noteworthy mansions: the squat brownstone at 2150 Washington St at Laguna is known as the **Phelan Mansion** and was built by former mayor James Phelan. He's famous both as an anti-Asian protectionist and the senator who pushed to bring a poet laureateship to California. Not far away, stands the **Spreckels Mansion**, 2080 Washington St at Octavia: this gaudily decadent white-stone palace was constructed for sugar magnate Adolph Spreckels and his wayward wife, Alma, a former nude model who posed for the statue at the center of Union Square (see p.522). Auguste Rodin's first US patron, Alma donated her spectacular collection of his work to the California Palace of the Legion of Honor, a museum she built (see p.555). The home she and Adolph shared is now owned by romance pulpist Danielle Steel, who pumped a not-so-small fortune into the structure's restoration and upkeep. Neither of these houses is open to the public – for admission to Pacific Heights mansion, you'll have to head two blocks east to the ornate **Haas-Lilienthal House** at 2007 Franklin St at Washington (compulsory 1-hour tours leave every 20–30mins, Wed noon–3pm, Sun 11am–4pm; $5; ☎415/441-3004, ⓦwww.sfheritage.org). This double-size Queen Anne Victorian was built for his growing family by a wealthy merchant, William Haas. It's a grand symbol of old wealth, with intricate wooden towers outside, and Tiffany art-glass and stenciled leather paneling inside.

SoMa, the Tenderloin, and the Civic Center

While parts of San Francisco can almost seem to be an urban utopia, the adjoining districts of the **Tenderloin** and the **Civic Center** reveal harsher realities. Particularly in the Tenderloin, the homeless and disaffected are very much in evidence – the flipside of California's low-tax prosperity is alive and unwell – and their constant presence in front of City Hall is an ironic reminder of governmental failures. Thus far, sporadic attempts to improve the areas have been at best well-meaning hit-and-misses or, at worst, patently cosmetic gestures bound to fail. On the other hand, **SoMa** took an unimaginable upswing in recent years, thanks in part to Internet start-up companies attracted to the district's low rents. Since the dot-com crash, though, the techies have cleared out and the neighborhood has reclaimed its gritty appearance. Much of the district booms every night with the muffled reverberations of underground dance clubs, but nearer to downtown, **Yerba Buena,** a new museum and entertainment complex, draws daytime visitors, as does the new baseball stadium along the waterfront to the east.

South of Market

SOMA, the distinctly urban district **So**uth of **Ma**rket Street, stretches diagonally from the Mission in the southwest to the waterfront in the northeast. While the western sections have always been a working-class community, it's ironic, given the area's grubby recent history, that the waterfront **Rincon Hill** – not to mention the South Park district – were home to the first of the city's banking elite. By the 1870s, they were drawn away to Nob Hill by the newly invented cable car and within thirty years, South of Market had been turned over to industrial development and warehouses. The poorer community that remained was largely driven out by fires following the 1906 earthquake, and Rincon Hill was eventually cleared in 1930 to make way for the new Bay Bridge. By the 1990s factories and warehouses were relentlessly converted to offices for the fledgling Internet industry, instantly creating a bustling, lively neighborhood filled with young people. Sadly, when the Internet excesses crashed, so did SoMa, and the acres of empty office spaces are testament to its renewed struggle for economic prosperity. Despite the Web boom and bust, there are still parts of SoMa that are downright dangerous: the most notorious is Sixth Street (where you're quite likely to see drug deals go down in broad daylight). Stay accordingly alert and keep valuables hidden.

Along the Bay, an array of new upscale condominium complexes have sprung up in the nascent **South Beach** district, aided by public works aimed at improving transportation and beautifying a waterfront long hidden in the shadows of the thankfully departed freeway. A block inland from the waterfront is the **Rincon Center** at 101 Spear St and Mission. Originally a US Post Office, it was constructed in 1939, and the building is a fine example of Depression Moderne architecture, with its smooth, imposing lines, outer simplicity, and ornamented interior. The lobby of the old post office is lavishly decorated with murals about California history, the largest commission ever by the WPA, painted by Russian expat artist Anton Refregier in 1941. It became a yuppified shopping center in the 1980s and still has a few good lunch spots.

Unfortunately, the area of SoMa around Second Street was especially doomed by the dot-com bust, and many of the companies that energized the local real estate market are gone, leaving nothing but chic office furniture and "For Rent" signs in their wake. There are two appealing attractions, though, that make a detour here worthwhile: firstly, the **California Historical Society**, at 678 Mission St at Second Street (Tues–Sat 11am–5pm; $3, free first Tues of month; ☎415/357-1848, ⓦwww.californiahistoricalsociety.org). A tiny, offbeat gem, it showcases ephemera from the state's history, including maps and photographs, and is especially strong on the cultural and political fallout from early Spanish settlement. Opposite stands another appealing but overlooked attraction: the **Cartoon Art Museum**, 655 Mission St at New Montgomery (Tues–Sun 11am–5pm; $5, donation suggested first Tues of the month; T415/227-8669, W www.cartoonart.org). In its enormous slab concrete gallery space, the museum curates rotating exhibits of cells and drawings, usually a sprightly mix of high concept "art-oons" by the likes of French illustrator Möebius and populist strips like *Peanuts*.

Until it was finally, socially fumigated a decade or so ago, Third Street symbolized San Francisco's urban issues: a crime-ridden strip minutes from the tourist trail along Market Street. The new wave of development, centered on Yerba Buena Gardens, is an indication of how seriously San Francisco has tried to spiff up the neighborhood. **Yerba Buena Gardens** has inviting lawns that are often packed with office workers on warm weekday lunchtimes: don't miss the fifty-foot granite waterfall memorial to Martin Luther King Jr, inscribed with extracts from his speeches, which stretches along its eastern edge. On the terrace above the waterfall, a Sister Cities garden features flora from each of the thirteen cities worldwide that are twinned with San Francisco: look for camellias from Shanghai and cyclamen from Haifa, among others.

New attractions radiate from the gardens on each side: to the east stands the **Yerba Buena Center for the Arts**, 701 Mission St at Third (Tues–Wed, Sat–Sun 11am–6pm, Thurs–Fri 11am–8pm; $6, free first Tues of the month; T415/978-2787, W www.yerbabuenaarts.org). The center was initially conceived as a forum for community art projects but has recently expanded its repertoire, hosting international touring exhibitions and performances in its two main spaces. The small second-floor screening room shows works by local experimental filmmakers, as well as themed programs of cult and underground films – call or check the center's website for the latest schedules. Opposite the Center for the Arts is the area's – perhaps the city's – marquee museum: the **SF Museum of Modern Art** at 151 3rd St (Mon, Tues & Fri 11am–6pm, Thurs 11am–9pm, closed Wed; $9, $4.50 Thurs 6–9pm, free first Tues of the month; T415/357-4000, W www.sfmoma.org), an attraction so adored that it risks suffocating under the weight of superlatives piled on it since its construction in 1995. Certainly, it's a striking structure. Designed by Swiss architect Mario Botta at a reported cost of $62 million, SFMoMA vies to be the West Coast's premier exhibition space. It hosts touring shows from New York and Europe while struggling to assemble a collection worthy of its housing. Frankly, for now at least, the traveling exhibits are more impressive than the patchy permanent work: head to the upper floors for temporary exhibits and make sure to stop by the fine outdoor sculpture garden on the fourth floor. The best permanent holdings are of the **California school**, with works by Richard Diebenkorn as well as the husband-and-wife team of Frida Kahlo and Diego Rivera, plus a notable collection of **abstract expressionist** works by Mark Rothko, Jackson Pollock, and Robert Rauschenberg. Whatever the quality of work within, the building steals the show and is itself worth visiting: a huge central skylight floods the space with light, while the upper galleries are connected by a vertigo-inducing metal catwalk made up of tiny slats that challenges the definition of "adventurous" art.

Next to the glorious gardens stands one of the least appealing sights in the city: the **Sony Metreon,** 101 4th St at Mission (daily 10am–10pm; T415/369-6000, W www.metreon.com). If Sony made food, you could buy it here: as it is, you'll have to settle for a *Starbucks* coffee while wandering through this enormous, 3-D advert for the electronics giant. Thanks to its blatant and relentless shill on behalf of the company's products, as a mall, the Metreon's empty and rather dull: the one upside, according to locals, is that there's now a large cinema within convenient reach of downtown, as well as an **IMAX** theater (check Ⓦ www.metreon.com for schedule and prices).

Walking further down the entirely unscenic Third Street might not seem to promise much, but hidden down a short alley next to a gas station is the surprising sanctuary of **South Park**, a picturesque European-style common. The park was the nexus of SoMa's multimedia community and locals have been able to gauge the health of the ailing industry by the diminishing numbers of office workers eating lunches in the park. Its shops and cafés are pricey, but it's still an extremely pleasant place to get a meal or lounge for the afternoon. Along with Jackson Square (see p.528), this is also one of the only spots in the city that truly feels like a window into another time – it's not hard to imagine horse-drawn carriages leisurely passing the park's slender oval.

The name may not be pretty, but Pac Bell Park, the San Francisco Giants' new stadium south of South Park, is undoubtedly a major improvement over their much-maligned old home at Candlestick Park. Prone to gusts of brutally cold wind, the "Stick" (as it was semi-affectionately known) was everything you didn't want in a baseball stadium, making an afternoon at the ballgame feel like leisure time in a meat locker. The new stadium, in one of the sunniest parts of town, has an outfield that opens onto the Bay and a short rightfield fence specifically designed to allow superstar Barry Bonds to hit home runs more easily. If you want to see the stadium but not the team, twice-hourly tours leave Lefty O'Doul Plaza between 10am and 2pm on off-days. Tickets cost $10 – more than the price of a cheap seat – and sadly you don't get to see the giant Coke bottle in the outfield salute Giant home runs (Ⓣ 415/972-2000, Ⓦ www.sfgiants.com).

Farther southeast, the strip of **Folsom Street** centered on Eleventh Street isn't much to look at during the day, but comes alive at night. Longtime home to the city's leather community, the area now hosts a range of bars, clubs, and restaurants serving every subculture under the stars. Eleventh Street is the kernel of activity and an obvious destination for a night out, provided you don't mind waiting in a line or two. If you happen to be here during daytime hours, wander back east to 214 6th St at the corner of Mission to look at **Defenestration**, a Quixotic piece of public art by local artist Brian Goggin, involving furniture that has been bolted to the outside of an abandoned building. Just don't linger too long – it's one of the nastier corners in town.

The Tenderloin

The **TENDERLOIN**, sandwiched between Civic Center and Union Square on the north side of Market Street, is one of the poorest, most dangerous places in San Francisco, just minutes from its tourist center. This small, uninviting area – no more than four blocks by five – remains a blight on the heart of the city though you should be safe as long as you keep your wits about you and don't mind vagrants asking you for money. Exercise extra caution at night, and the vicinity of Taylor Street, particularly around Turk and Eddy, is best avoided altogether.

The area's oddball name has never been definitively explained. One tale is that nineteenth-century police were rewarded with choice cuts of steak for serving a particularly perilous tour of duty here. A less flattering version is that, thanks to the constant bribes they collected from the gambling houses and brothels, those same policemen were able to dine in the city's finest restaurants. Yet others say that the name is based on the district's shank shape or even its notoriety for flesh-flashing brothels: whatever the answer, it's always been the seediest part of town and the heart of San Francisco's vigorous sex industry.

Recent waves of Pakistani and South Asian immigrants have begun transforming the neighborhood, establishing numerous spots for a cheap bowl of curry or Vietnamese *pho* soup. If you're not too busy hurrying to your destination, there are a few sights worth seeing tucked into the neighborhood's dark corners, the best of which is the **Glide Memorial Church** at 330 Ellis St at Taylor (☎415/674-6000, ⓦwww.glide.org). The church provides a wide range of social services for the neighborhood's downtrodden but it's best known for its rollicking Sunday service, where you might be seated between Sharon Stone and a local drag queen dressed like her. If you're not stopping by on a Sunday, step inside to see the AIDS Memorial Chapel – the altarpiece triptych was the last work artist Keith Haring completed before his death from the disease.

At the western limits of the Tenderloin, on Polk Street, between O'Farrell and California, lies **Polk Gulch**, a congregating point for the city's transgender community, and a hub for the flesh trade. This area inherited many of the displaced residents and merchants who fled Haight-Ashbury in the early 1970s: it's now best known for the several historically famous gay bars that line the street, not to mention the young hustlers and prostitutes. The intersection of O'Farrell and Polk is home to a neighborhood landmark of sorts, the strip club known as **Mitchell Brother's O' Farrell Theater** (11.30am–2am; ☎415/776-6686). The Mitchell boys achieved considerable notoriety in the 1970s when they persuaded a young Ivory Soap model named Marilyn Chambers to star in their porno film *Behind the Green Door*, which they debuted at the Cannes Film Festival. While the pair slowly slipped back into obscurity over the ensuing decades, they made a tragic return to tabloid fame when Jim Mitchell shot and killed his brother Artie in 1991.

The Civic Center

To the immediate southwest of the grubby Tenderloin stands San Francisco's grandest architectural gesture: the complex of Beaux Arts buildings known as the **CIVIC CENTER**. This cluster was the brainchild of brilliant urban planner Daniel Burnham: even before 1906, he planned to level San Francisco and build boulevard-like traffic arteries fanning out like spokes across the city, extensive subways, and a grand civic plaza. Unfortunately, after the earthquake, the city was choked in bureaucracy, and his plan was heavily diluted until only the civic plaza was approved. Even then, it wasn't finished until several years after his death. Despite Burnham's beliefs that grand architectural answers would silence social questions, the Civic Center today is simply the Tenderloin with better buildings.

Most people arrive at the Civic Center MUNI and BART station at the corner of Market and Leavenworth streets and are immediately disgorged into the **United Nations Plaza**, built to commemorate the founding of the UN here in 1945 – look for the UN Charter etched on a black stone shard. It's filled with fountains and homeless people: not somewhere to dawdle, other than on Wednesdays and Sundays when, from dawn to dusk, the square's transformed into a **Farmers Market,** a convenient place to pick up a cheap lunch.

The first building you'll see is the **San Francisco Public Library**, 100 Larkin St at Grove (Mon & Sat 10am–6pm, Tues–Thurs 9am–8pm, Fri noon–6pm, Sun noon–5pm; ☎415/557-4400, ⓦwww.sfpl.lib.ca.us), which moved into its current location in 1996 from its original site, now the Asian Art Museum (see below). This move was controversial since the sleek new headquarters – which included a large, light-filled central atrium and plenty of space for lounging readers – didn't incorporate much space for books, and portions of the library's holdings have repeatedly been sold off in order to squeeze everything into the new stacks. It contains the James C. Hormel Gay and Lesbian Center (named in honor of the gay activist and meat magnate), the first of its kind in the nation, topped by a dome with a mural depicting leading figures in gay rights and literary movements.

Next door stands the **Asian Art Museum**, 200 Larkin St at McAllister (Tues, Wed, Fri–Sun 10am–5pm, Thurs 10am–9pm; $10; ☎415/379-8800, Ⓦwww.asianart.org), freshly relocated from its original, earthquake-crippled quarters next to the M.H. de Young Museum in Golden Gate Park (see p. 553). It displays one of the largest collections of Asian art in the Western world, with more than ten thousand paintings, sculptures, ceramics, and textiles from all over Asia – one of its best-known treasures is the oldest known Chinese Buddha image, dating back to 338 AD.

The central plaza in front of these buildings is usually filled with a combination of political protesters and the homeless. Grand **City Hall** stands on the other side of the plaza (Mon–Fri 8am–8pm, Sat & Sun noon–4pm; ☎415/554-4799, Ⓦwww.ci.sf.ca.us/cityhall). After the first city hall was destroyed in 1906, a contest with a prize of $25,000 was announced for local architectural firms to design a new building. The winning design was by Bakewell and Brown, former students of the Ecole des Beaux Arts in Paris, who wanted to create a structure inspired by the haughty, gilded dome of Les Invalides there. City Hall cost an astonishing $3.5m to build, and includes more than ten acres of marble, shipped in from Vermont, New Hampshire, and Italy. It was here in 1978 that conservative ex-Supervisor Dan White got past security and assassinated Mayor George Moscone and gay City Supervisor Harvey Milk; later, when White was found guilty of manslaughter (not murder), it was the scene of violent demonstrations as protesters set fire to police vehicles and stormed the doors of the building (see box on p.549). The best way to see the interior of the building is on one of the frequent, free tours (Mon–Fri 10am, noon, 2pm, Sat & Sun 12.30pm) – sign up at the Docent Tour Kiosk on the Van Ness Avenue side of the main building.

Directly behind City Hall on Van Ness Avenue are San Francisco's cultural mainstays, most elegant of which is the **War Memorial Opera House**, where the United Nations Charter was signed in 1945. Today, it's home to the San Francisco Opera and Ballet, and its understated grandeur is a sharp contrast to the giant modernist fishbowl of the **Louise M. Davies Symphony Hall** one block down. Built in 1980, at a cost of almost $35 million, the hall has some fans in the progressive architecture camp, though the general consensus is that it's an aberration of the otherwise tastefully harmonious scheme of the Civic Center. Both buildings enjoy a healthy patronage, and San Francisco's hidden elite gather here regularly: unfortunately, few performances are subsidized, so don't expect budget ticket prices. (For full details of ballet and opera schedules, see p.573, "Performing Arts & Film").

The Mission

San Franciscans often speak of the **MISSION** today as a "neighborhood in transition," but the phrase could easily be applied to much of the district's 200-year history. After California's annexation, the area became home to succeeding waves of immigrants: first Scandinavians, followed by a significant Irish influx, and then a sizeable Latin American settlement. Once heavily Hispanic, this tangled melting pot is growing trendier and less Spanish thanks to hip bars and restaurants, notably along Valencia Street, that jostle for space with old taquerias and grocery stores; rising rents have engendered a certain amount of ill will toward newcomers. Still, at various points in its history the Mission has been one of the city's richest neighborhoods and one of its poorest, making this latest transformation but one in a long line of facelifts. What doesn't change is the Mission's gloriously sunny skies: the mass of Twin Peaks acts as a giant windbreak and even when the rest of the city is cold and foggy, the Mission is bright and (relatively) warm. Be aware that there's often gang activity on Mission Street between Fourteenth and Nineteenth streets and it's best not to wander around map in hand whatever the time of day.

The area gets its name from the oldest building in the city, the **Misión San Francisco de Asis**, more commonly known as **Mission Dolores**, 3321 16th St at Dolores, (daily 9am–4pm; $1; ☎415/621-8203, ⓦwww.graphicmode.com/missiondolores). Its moniker dates back to the first European camp here, for the Spanish arrived on the Friday before Palm Sunday – the Friday of Sorrows – and finding an ample freshwater supply, decided to pitch their tents here, naming the site *Laguna de los Dolores*. The first mass celebrated at Mission Dolores on June 29, 1776 marks the official founding of the city, though the community was then known as Yerba Buena. The evolution of San Francisco is reflected in the mission's architecture: the original building, dating from 1782, is squat and relatively spare, while the more prominent basilica next door, built in 1913, is a riot of ornate design. Aside from periodic tour bus herds, the building can be quite serene, with a stained-glass-lit interior offering a pleasant opportunity to gaze into the city's long-erased past. The backyard cemetery (made famous in Hitchcock's *Vertigo*) holds the graves of the mission's founders, as well as hundreds of "converted" Native Americans. Far removed from the plastic gimmickry of Fisherman's Wharf, this is one of the city's best historical icons, and is well worth a visit.

A short walk from the mission down the stately, palm-tree-lined Dolores Street, arguably the most attractive stretch of asphalt in the city, brings you to the sunbather-covered slope of Dolores Park. Though during the week much of the park is little more than a glorified dog run, on weekends the southwest corner transforms into "Dolores Beach," where members of the Castro gay community come to bronze their gym-toned muscles. Aside from the mission itself, the other best known local landmark is much more recent: the **Women's Building**, 3543 18th St at Guerrero (Mon 9am–8pm, Tues–Thurs 9am–10pm, Fri 9am–8pm, Sat 10am–noon; ☎415/431-1180, ⓦwww.womensbuilding.org). The building is tattooed with an enormous, sprawling mural, known by the horrifically self-conscious name of *Maestrapeace*. Big but awkward, it was designed by seven female designers and executed by a team of 100 muralists: on one side, there's an enormous mother-goddess figure, while on the other, there's a gigantic portrait of Rigoberta Menchú, the Guatemalan woman who won the Nobel Peace Prize in 1992.

Heading east into the heart of the neighborhood, you'll hit **Valencia Street**, one of the best shopping and dining strips in the city, packed with upscale boutiques sitting next to thrift stores and taquerias alongside chic new restaurants. Browsing down this strip between Sixteenth and Twenty-fourth streets is one of the delights of San Francisco. At its northern end is the original **Levi's factory building**, 250 Valencia St, a huge lemon-yellow structure set back from the road. While the pants Levi's makes today bear only a remote resemblance to the original item, invented during the Gold Rush, the jeans have outlasted countless trends, though recently the company's finances have been so rocky that it's laid off a significant portion of its local staff. After the sole guide who led groups around the building retired in 2000, there are unfortunately no longer tours of the building's interior.

If Valencia Street is the hipster heart of the Mission, then **Mission Street** is the commercial hub of the **Latino community**: it's lined with five-and-dime shops selling a virtually identical stock of kitschy religious items, along with dozens of taquerias. It's mostly untouched by the gentrification that has bled into the northern edge of the district: there are a few groovy bars here, but this strip still primarily caters to the needs of local Latin families. The 200-odd

**THE MISSION &
THE CASTRO**

◀ Twin Peaks

Levi Strauss
Building

Mission
Dolores

Castro
Theater

THE
CASTRO

Dolores
Park

Women's Building

THE
MISSION

NOE VALLEY

Bernal Heights Park

ACCOMMODATION

24 Henry	1
Beck's Motor Lodge	3
Dolores Park Inn	5
Inn on Castro	4
San Francisco International Guest House	6
Twin Peaks Hotel	2

0   600 yds

murals you'll see everywhere underscore a strong sense of community pride and Hispanic heritage. The greatest concentration of work can be found on **Balmy Alley**, an unassuming back way between Treat and Harrison streets, where's there barely an inch of wall unadorned. The murals here are painted on wooden fences, rather than stucco walls, and consequently are regularly refreshed and replaced. The project began during a small community organizing event in 1973, but the tiny street has become the spiritual center of a burgeoning Latino arts movement that has grown out of both the US civil rights struggle and pro-democracy movements in South America. Frankly, many of the murals are more heartfelt than either skilled or beautiful; it's worth stopping by for a peek, although the heavy-handed political imagery can be wearing. For a tour of the artwork, call the **Precita Eyes Mural Arts Center**, 2981 24th St at Harrison (Mon–Fri 10am–5pm, Sat 10am–4pm, Sun noon–4pm; $12; ☎415/285-2287, ⓦwww.precitaeyes.org), which has sponsored most of the paintings since its founding in 1971.

The Castro and Twin Peaks

The next area west of the Mission district, the **CASTRO** was formerly a wild frontier, though it's settled down considerably in recent years, mellowing into middle age. Gentrified by the city's gay community during the 1970s as a primarily residential community, the Castro was part of the bacchanalian atmosphere that prevailed in San Francisco's gay culture during that decade. The assassination of gay City Supervisor Harvey Milk in 1978 (see box), which sparked the most intense rioting in the city's history, and the onset of the AIDS epidemic motivated many in the community to focus their energy on political organizing instead of the wild life. As a result the community now finds itself increasingly wealthy and politically influential – adopting the self-consciously enlightened demeanor of what is probably the world's most prominent gay community. But with this comfort has come a certain conservatism, and while activists argue that residents must still lead the fight on human rights issues such as AIDS funding and legal recognition of gay couples, many in the area seem increasingly concerned about more immediate quality-of-life issues such as chain stores and rising rents. For an insider's view, Trevor Hailey's "Cruisin' the Castro" walking tour (see p.516) is just about unbeatable.

Oddly enough, for a neighborhood bursting with energy, there's not an awful lot to do in the Castro and the best way to while away an afternoon or evening here is to wander around. The heart of the Castro is filled with stores, restaurants, and bars all flying the rainbow flag and it's usually packed with people whatever the time of day: it's especially throbbing on a Sunday afternoon, crammed with men strolling, cruising, and sipping a coffee on the sidewalk. If you're lucky, you might spot one of the **Sisters of Perpetual Indulgence**, volunteers who dress as white-faced nuns to promote safe-sex and HIV awareness in a camp parody of Catholic pageantry. If the crowds of people are too much, head for the neighborhood's side streets, scrupulously manicured and lined with neat rows of brightly painted Victorians – a world away from the stores and bars crammed along the Castro. With its lovely Art Deco neon sign rising high above the street, the **Castro Theater**, 429 Castro St, is a landmark that shines brightly in a neighborhood where people, not places, are the star attractions. Screening a well-curated schedule of classic film revivals and unusual premieres, the unofficial "Castro Cathedral" manages to find quality cinema that's more than a match for the theater's ambience. The ornate balconies, wall-mounted busts of heroic figures, and massive ceiling ornament would provide ample visual stimulation, even without a film showing on the gigantic screen. Come early for an extra treat: before each evening screening a Wurlitzer organ rises from the stage for a pre-showtime serenade. The musical medley always draws to a close with "San Francisco," as the crowd merrily claps along.

After leaving the Castro, make an effort to go to **TWIN PEAKS**, about a mile and a half along Market from the Harvey Milk Plaza. (Travel west until you hit Twin Peaks Boulevard; the #37 Corbett bus will take you to Park Ridge.) The highest point in the city, Twin Peaks gives a 360-degree view of the Peninsula. Real estate prices in the city are gauged in part by the quality of the views, so it's no surprise that the curving streets that wind around the slopes of Twin Peaks hold some of the city's most outrageously unaffordable homes. During the day, busloads of tourists arrive to point their cameras, and during the summer crowds often build up waiting for the fog to lift. It's better to go at night, picking out landmarks from either side of the shimmering artery of Market Street. If you want to avoid the crowds, Tank Hill, a small promontory just beneath Twin Peaks – where you'll need a map to find your way through the maze of small streets – is a nice option, though sometimes sketchy after dusk.

You might also consider a quick visit to Noe Valley. Despite being just a couple of blocks from both the Castro and Mission, the quiet bedroom community feels worlds apart, thanks to some very steep hills that help keep the area isolated. The neighborhood's heart is 24th Street, where baby strollers often seem to outnumber cars. Frankly, there's not much to do once here besides sipping cappuccinos or shopping for cardigans.

The assassination of Harvey Milk

In 1977, eight years after New York's Stonewall riots brought gay political activism into the spotlight, Castro camera-shop owner Harvey Milk won election as the city's first openly gay supervisor (or councilor), and quickly became one of the most prominent gay officials in the country. Milk was a celebrated figure for the city's gay community, nicknamed the "Mayor of Castro Street," so it came as a horrifying shock when, in 1978, former Supervisor Dan White walked into City Hall and shot both Milk and Mayor George Moscone dead. White was an ex-cop who had resigned from the board, claiming he couldn't live on the small salary. In fact, he was angered that the liberal policies of Moscone and Milk didn't accord with his conservative views: a staunch Catholic, White saw himself as a spokesman for San Francisco's many blue-collar Irish families and, as an ex-policeman, saw himself as the defender of the family values he believed gay rights were damaging. At his trial, White claimed that harmful additives in his fast food-laden diet had driven him temporarily insane – a plea which came to be known as the "Twinkie defense" (Twinkies being synthetic-cream cakes) – and was sentenced to five years' imprisonment for manslaughter. The gay community exploded when the news of White's light sentence was announced and the "White Night" riots that followed were among the most violent San Francisco has ever witnessed, as protesters stormed City Hall, turning over and burning police cars as they went. White was released from prison in 1985 and moved to Los Angeles, where he committed suicide shortly after. In a happier coda, current City Supervisor Tom Ammiano, a former stand-up comedian, who has said that he found the courage to come out publicly as gay through Milk's activism, is now one of the most powerful political figures in the city.

Haight-Ashbury, the Western Addition, and Japantown

Two miles west of downtown San Francisco, the **HAIGHT-ASHBURY** neighborhood lent its name to an entire era, giving it a fame on which it has traded mercilessly ever since. Originally part of the Western Addition, it was unofficially carved off following the widespread publication of a picture of the Grateful Dead, posing at the sign for the intersection of Haight and Ashbury streets – where now, with breathtaking irony, there's a branch of the Gap. For all its fame, 'The Haight' proper is tiny, spanning no more than eight blocks of attractive Edwardian and Victorian buildings. Despite some locals' nostalgia, it's changed dramatically since it emerged in the 1960s as the focus of the countercultural scene. Haight-Ashbury in the 21st century is theme-park boho, crammed with shops offering hippie-themed souvenirs or trendy boutiques selling designer clothes. Look hard enough, though, and you can still unearth the embers of its radical past: a handful of stores selling leftist literature and vintage clothing, cafés filled with dawdling intellectuals, and a few surviving hippies.

Roughly divided into half by **Divisadero Street**, the Haight consists of the Upper and Lower Haight districts, with the **Upper Haight** stretching west to the park and the **Lower Haight** running east up to Buchanan Street. Though less famous, the Lower Haight is currently the more vibrant neighborhood. Long an African-American neighborhood, the Lower Haight has been transformed over the past decade by youthful immigrants from Britain into the center of the city's rave culture. DJ shops line Haight Street between Webster and Divisadero, while bars blatantly capitalize on Old World nostalgia (even for the food). Though the Mission has stolen much of the Lower Haight's trend-hopping spotlight, the neighborhood remains very much torn between its older and newer identities – a conflicted identity that has led to some tensions. It's best to exercise caution at night, particularly in the vicinity of Webster Street.

In much the same way that the Lower Haight tends to be overshadowed by its flashier neighbor up the hill, longtime resident **Kenneth Rexroth** (1905–1982) has largely been overshadowed by the writers he inspired. As a poet, novelist, and translator of Chinese literature, Rexroth lived a wildly adventurous life that was an inspiration for Kerouac and crew. While not open to the public, you can take a walk past Rexroth's old apartment at 250 Scott St, a place where several of the early Beats crashed upon first arriving in San Francisco.

Continuing uphill toward the heart of the Haight will bring you to **Buena Vista Park**, a mountainous forest of Monterey pines and California redwoods. Used by dog walkers in the daylight hours, come nightfall the park plays host to much sex-in-the-shrubbery; walk here accompanied by day and not at all at night, unless you're male and looking for some action. Things get livelier as you move west, with the street crowded by an increasing number of musicians, panhandlers and hardcore hippie burnouts. Two blocks west, the **Grateful Dead House**, 710 Ashbury at Haight, was once ground zero for the counter culture. A 1967 drug bust only added to the band's myth, which survived countless tours and a rotating cast of keyboard players. Even the 1995 death of guitarist Jerry Garcia has done little to quell fans' devotion.

To the north of Haight Street, the **Panhandle** is a rivulet of greenery that runs like a tributary into Golden Gate Park. Though the grass is noticeably scraggly these days, it was once a ritzy thoroughfare catering to horse-drawn carriages and the lovely houses speak of wealthier times.

The Western Addition

Spreading north and east of here, the **WESTERN ADDITION** is one of the central city's few predominantly black neighborhoods and almost relentlessly poor – dangerous in parts and certainly not tourist territory. The nadir for the neighborhood was in the 1960s, when the dual forces of urban renewal and blunderheaded civic planner **Justin Herman** – honored with a public park along the Embarcadero (see p.527) – led to the demolishing of blocks of precious Victorian housing. They were replaced with acres of monolithic concrete apartment blocks, leaving few vestiges of the Western Addition's history or character. The exception that proves the rule is a small area surrounding **Alamo Square Park**, at Hayes and Scott – just uphill from the Lower Haight. A staple of every tour bus company in town, the park's southeast slope is home to small flocks of amateur photographers eager to snap a picture of "the Painted Ladies." These six Victorian houses, originally built in 1894, and colorfully and attractively restored, have been a postcard staple for years. Even if you've forgotten your camera, it's still worth the steep climb up here for the brilliant **views** across the city – on a clear day you can see over the city and across the Bay all the way to the hills of North Berkeley.

ACCOMMODATION			
Archbishop's Mansion	4	Hayes Valley Inn	5
Best Western Miyako	1	Queen Anne	2
The Carl	8	Red Victorian	6
Château Tivoli	3	Stanyan Park Hotel	7

It's worthwhile detouring downhill east from here to reach **Hayes Valley**, reborn when the freeway that once overshadowed it was demolished after the 1989 earthquake. The heart of the neighborhood is **Hayes Street** between Franklin and Octavia streets, although the district is swelling daily as new shops open. Hayes Valley is more racially integrated than many older neighborhoods, and the chichi boutiques sit alongside earthy remnants – like *Powell's Place* (see p.564, "Eating") – of the area's past. It's one of the best places to wander aimlessly and browse, and Hayes Street is lined with shady trees and sidewalk cafés, not to mention some of the funkiest galleries, homeware, and clothing stores around.

Japantown

The determinedly thorough can continue north on a dismal strip of Fillmore Street to reach **JAPANTOWN**, something of a misnomer for what is basically a shopping mall with an eastern flavor – the Japan Center – around which

Hippies

The first hippies were an offshoot of the Beats, many of whom had moved out of their increasingly expensive North Beach homes to take advantage of the low rents and large spaces in the Victorian houses of the Haight. The post-Beat bohemia that subsequently began to develop here in the early 1960s was initially a small affair, involving drug use and the embrace of Eastern religion and philosophy, together with a marked anti-American political stance and a desire for world peace. Where Beat philosophy had emphasized self-indulgence, the hippies, on the face of it at least, attempted to be more embracing, focusing on self-coined concepts such as "universal truth" and "cosmic awareness." Naturally it took a few big names to get the ball rolling, and characters like Ken Kesey and his Merry Pranksters soon set a precedent of wild living, challenging authority, and dropping (as they saw it) out of the established norms of society. Drugs were particularly important, and seen as an integral – and positive – part of the movement. LSD especially, the affects of which were just being discovered and which at the time was not actually illegal, was claimed as an avant-garde art form. It was pumped out in private laboratories and distributed by Timothy Leary and his network of supporters with a prescription ("Turn on, tune in, drop out") that galvanized a generation into inactivity. An important group in the Haight at the time was The Diggers, who, famed for their parties and antics, truly believed LSD could be used to increase creativity.

Before long, life in the Haight began to take on a theatrical quality: Pop Art found mass appeal, light shows became legion, dress flamboyant, and the Grateful Dead, Jefferson Airplane, and Janis Joplin made names for themselves. Backed by the business weight of promoter Bill Graham, the psychedelic music scene became a genuine force nationwide, and it wasn't long before kids from all over America started turning up in Haight-Ashbury for the free food, free drugs, and free love. Money became a dirty word, the hip became "heads," and the rest of the world were "straights."

Other illustrious tenants of the Haight in the Sixties included Kenneth Rexroth, who hosted a popular radio show and wrote for the *San Francisco Examiner*. Hunter S. Thompson, too, spent time here researching and writing his book *Hell's Angels*, and was notorious for inviting Angels round to his apartment on Parnassus Street for noisy, long, and occasionally dangerous drinking and drug-taking sessions.

Things inevitably turned sour towards the end of the decade, but during the heady days of the massive "be-in" in Golden Gate Park in 1966 and the so-called Summer of Love the following year, this busy little intersection became home to no less than 75,000 transitory pilgrims who saw it as the mecca of alternative culture.

only a small percentage of San Francisco's Japanese-Americans actually live. Its one notable sight here is the 100-foot **Peace Pagoda**, standing in the central plaza like a stack of poured concrete space-age mushrooms. Nearby are the **Kabuki Hot Springs**, 1750 Geary St at Fillmore (daily 10am–9.45pm; $15 weekdays before 5pm, $18 weekends and weekday evenings; ☎415/922-6000, ⊛www.kabukisprings.com), recently refurbished and funked up, but retaining at least some of the original spa's eccentricity. If you're in the area, jump over a few blocks to where Geary Street meets Gough and look at the elaborately modern **St Mary's Cathedral**, affectionately mocked by locals for its bizarre resemblance to a washing-machine agitator (earning it the nickname "Our Lady of the Maytag"). Inside, it's a surprisingly pleasant and open space, where the pulpit seems more like an afterthought than the seat of holy authority.

Golden Gate Park

Unlike most American cities, San Francisco is not short on green space, and **GOLDEN GATE PARK** is its largest, simultaneously full of the bustle of urban living and hidden natural environments offering welcome respite to city residents. The park was designed in 1871 by Park Commissioner William Hall in the style of Frederick Law Olmsted (who created Central Park in New York). Spreading three miles or so west from the Haight as far as the Pacific shore, it was constructed – on what was then an area of wild sand dunes buffeted by the spray of the nearby ocean – with the help of a dyke to protect the western side from the sea. Even so, the landscape still undergoes a natural transition as it approaches the ocean and, in contrast to the relatively placid Bay, the strong winds blowing through the Park and gusting up streets in the surrounding neighborhoods are a constant reminder of the sea's more turbulent temperament. It's generally best to visit in late morning or early afternoon – even on seemingly sunny days, a chilly fog often rolls in before dusk. Although the original planners intended to keep the park free of buildings, that proved impossible and its eastern half is now dotted with city sights like the California Academy of Sciences. Most of them date from the 1894 World's Fair, the first held in California, which was designed as a recession-busting sideshow by local newspaperman M.H. de Young. It was so successful that de Young was honored with a permanent museum in his name (see below).

Exploration of the whole place could take days of footwork. Among its more obvious attractions, there's a Japanese Tea Garden, a horticultural museum (modeled on the Palm House at Kew Gardens in London), a Shakespeare Garden with every flower or plant mentioned in the writer's plays, not to mention the usual contingent of serious joggers, cyclists, and in-line skaters.

Of the park's numerous museums, the **California Academy of Sciences** (winter daily 10am–5pm; summer daily 9am–6pm; $8.50, free first Wed of each month; ☎415/750-7145, ⊛www.calacademy.org) is a perfect place to amuse restless children and should even intrigue jaded adults. It's a joyous, eye-popping survey of natural history that includes a thirty-foot skeleton of a 140 million-year-old dinosaur, depictions of the solar system, and a colony of twenty black-footed penguins. The show-stealer, though, is the **Steinhart Aquarium** (daily 10am–5pm; included with Academy admission). This fun museum is crammed with information and up-close encounters with animals, whether the pond turtles and American alligators in the swamp environment, or the spookily illuminated electric fishes. Opposite, the **M.H. de Young Museum** (☎415/863-3330, ⊛www.thinker.org) is currently closed while its cramped, antiquated quarters are leveled and replaced by a new futuristic design that will provide the museum twice the exhibition space in a smaller structure, as well as a viewing platform across the Golden Gate Park; it's scheduled to open in 2005. In the meantime, the museum's holdings have partially been transferred to its sister site, the California Palace of the Legion of Honor (see opposite).

Slightly west of the museums is the usually crowded **Japanese Tea Garden** (daily 9am–5.30pm; $2.50). Built in 1894 for the California Midwinter Exposition, the garden was beautifully landscaped by the Hagiwara family, who were also responsible for the invention of the fortune cookie during the Pan-Pacific Exposition of 1915 (despite the prevalent belief that fortune cookies are Chinese). The Hagiwaras looked after the garden until World War II, when along with other Japanese-Americans they were sent to internment camps. A massive bronze Buddha dominates the garden, and bridges, footpaths, pools filled with shiny oversized carp, plus bonsai and cherry trees lend the place a peaceful feel – as long as you can ignore the busloads of tourists that pour in regularly throughout the day. The best way to enjoy the garden is to get there around 9am when it first opens and have a breakfast of tea and fortune cookies in the teahouse.

Perhaps the most unusual thing about Golden Gate Park is its small herd of bison, roaming around the **Buffalo Paddock** off JFK Drive near Thirty-eighth Avenue; you can get closest to these noble giants in their feeding area at the far west end. Moving towards the edge of the park at Ocean Beach, passing a tulip garden and two crumbling windmills donated by the Queen of Holland, you'll come to the **Beach Chalet** (daily 8am–midnight; free). This two-story, white-pillared building was designed by Willis Polk; housing a series of 1930s frescoes depicting the growth of San Francisco as a city and the creation of Golden Gate Park, it also holds a small visitors' center that provides information about the park's numerous guided walking tours. Upstairs there's a lively brewery/restaurant, great for late weekend brunches.

Sunset, Richmond, and the beaches

Golden Gate Park is hugged by the large, residential neighborhoods of **RICHMOND** to the north and **SUNSET** to the south. As late as the 1940s, much of what comprises these two districts was still mile after mile of sand dunes, stretching to the ocean. And while residents of the city's more intensely urban eastern half might turn up their noses and say that, in terms of liveliness, not much has changed in the half-century since, the truth is that both neighborhoods – the multi-ethnic Richmond in particular – offer some rewarding oases of activity. More than the tourist-saturated downtown neighborhoods, this area is a window into the less seen side of San Francisco: a comfortable, though occasionally lethargic, blend of cultures. Numerous good, cheap restaurants, serving food from around the world, and the California Palace of the Legion of Honor's remote cultural outpost will reward those who stop here en route to the breathtaking (but often fog-bound) coastline at the city's edge.

Partly due to the weather and partly due to the coldness of the ocean water, beach culture doesn't exist in San Francisco the way it does in Southern California, and people here tend to watch the surf rather than ride it. Powerful currents and crashing waves dissuade all but the most fearless swimmers, and as a result the city's beaches remain blissfully uncrowded. Stretching south a mile from the Golden Gate Bridge, **Baker Beach** is San Francisco's prettiest and most popular, drawing a mixed crowd of fishermen and nude sunbathers, and giving some great views of the soaring red bridge. It's also easy to reach:

stairways drop down from Lincoln Avenue, and MUNI bus #29 stops at the main parking lot every thirty minutes. A half-mile further southwest at the foot of the ritzy Sea Cliff district, **China Beach** is more protected and better for swimming, and also offers free showers and changing rooms. Rising to the west from the beaches, paths curl south around the Peninsula to **Land's End**: it takes about thirty minutes to get round the cliffs, tricky to negotiate but worth it for the brilliant views of the ocean. A small beach in a rocky cove beneath the cliffside walk is a favorite spot for gay sunbathers.

The stately **California Palace of the Legion of Honor** (Tues–Sun 9.30am–5pm; $8, free Tuesday, $2 reduction with valid MUNI transfer; ☎415/750-3600 for switchboard, 415/863-3330 for recorded information, ⓦwww.thinker.org) is one of the best museums in San Francisco. The building itself is no less staggering than its setting, built in 1920 by Alma de Bretteville Spreckels (see p.522), with a cast of Rodin's *The Thinker* set dramatically on a pedestal in the center of the museum's front courtyard.

The museum's Rodin holdings are breathtaking in their depth and range, although there are more bronzes than marble sculptures: with over 80 pieces, it's one of the best collections of its kind in the world and the Rodin rooms alone make this museum unmissable. Sadly, the magnificent museum is somewhat let down by its lackluster collection of Old Masters – many of the artworks, including those by Giambologna, Cellini, and Cranach, are "attributed to" or "the workshop of," rather than *bona fide* masterpieces. However, while the de Young museum is closed (see above), its fine art collection has been transplanted here featuring magnificent work by El Greco, Gainsborough, and David. The museum's most easily reached by taking the #38 bus from Geary Boulevard and transferring to the #18 at the Lincoln Park Golf Course.

Rounding the Peninsula, a rather bigger stop for the tour buses is **Cliff House**, 1090 Point Lobos Rd (Mon–Thurs 9am–1.30pm, Fri–Sun 8.30am–1.30pm; ☎415/386-3300, ⓦwww.cliffhouse.com), precipitously balanced on the western tip of the Peninsula above the head of Ocean Beach. There's a visitor center here (daily 10am–5pm), with information on the surrounding area and an exhibit on the original Cliff House built by Prussian immigrant Adolph Sutro in the late nineteenth-century as an exclusive resort for the leisured classes, which burned down long ago. On the lower landing is a rare **Camera Obscura** (11am–sunset, weather permitting; $2; ☎415/750-0415). Using a rotating mirror – and a trick of light – the camera allows entrants to see a panoramic view of the surrounding area. Unfortunately, the camera is mostly surrounded by water, making the view less interesting than the presentation.

Down by the water you'll find the remains of other bygone amusements – the **Sutro Baths**. This collection of opulent recreational pools, gardens, and elegant sculptures, all covered with 100,000 feet of stained glass, was sadly destroyed by fire in the 1960s. From here you can explore the ramparts and tunnels of the fortified coastline – a bit frightening at night, when the surf really starts crashing, but there's a certain romance too, and on a rare warm evening it becomes one of the city's favorite making-out spots.

Stretching to the city's southern border, buffeted by sea breezes and fog, the thin strip of **Ocean Beach** seems to constantly be on the brink of either being washed out to shore or blown into locals' backyards. Aside from a small community of particularly hearty surfers (most notably country-rock crooner Chris Isaak), the beach is the almost exclusive territory of joggers and dog walkers.

The Golden Gate Bridge

The orange towers of the **GOLDEN GATE BRIDGE** – arguably the most photographed bridge in the world – are visible from almost every point of elevation in San Francisco. As much an architectural as an engineering feat, the Golden Gate was begun in January 1933 and took only 52 months to build, opening in May 1937. Overseen by Chicago-born Joseph Strauss, the final design was in fact the brainchild of his local-born assistant, Irving Morrow. The first massive suspension bridge in the world, with a span of 4200ft, it ranked until 1959 as the world's longest. Connecting the Peninsula's northwesterly point to Marin County and Northern California, the bridge rendered the hitherto essential ferry crossing redundant, and was designed to stand winds of up to a hundred miles an hour. Handsome on a clear day, the bridge takes on an eerie quality when the thick white fogs pour in and hide it almost completely. Note that its ruddy color was originally intended as a temporary undercoat before the grey topcoat was applied, but locals liked it so much, the bridge has stayed orange ever since – and it takes more than 5000 gallons of paint annually to keep it that way.

You can either drive, bike, or walk across. The toll for southbound cars is $3, although biking is more thrilling since you teeter along under the bridge's towers. Note that cyclists headed south across the bridge are always routed along the east side, while northbound cyclists must take the west side Monday to Friday, and the east side on weekends. The half-hour walk across, though, really gives you time to take in its enormous size and absorb the views of the city behind you and the headlands of Northern California straight ahead. Pause at the midway point and consider the seven or so suicides a month who choose this spot, 260ft up, as their jumping-off spot. Monitors of such events speculate that victims always face the city before they leap – perhaps because the western walkway is closed to pedestrians. In 1995, when the suicide toll from the bridge had reached almost 1000, police kept the figures quiet to avoid a rush of would-be suicides going for the dubious distinction of being the thousandth person to leap.

Standing beneath the bridge is almost as memorable as traveling over it. **The Fort Point National Historic Site** (Fri & Sat 10am–5pm; free; ☎415/556-1693, ⊛www.nps.gov/fopo), a brick fortress built to guard the Bay in the 1850s on the initial landing place of the city's first Spanish settlers, gives a good sense of the place as the westernmost outpost of the nation. Formerly part of the Presidio Army Base (now a National Park), it was to have been demolished to make way for the bridge above, but the redesign of the southern approach – note the additional arch which spans overhead – left it intact. It's a dramatic site reachable via Marine Drive in the Presidio, the surf pounding away beneath the great span of the bridge high above – a view made famous by Kim Novak's suicide attempt in Alfred Hitchcock's *Vertigo*.

Eating

Only Paris has more restaurants per capita than San Francisco, and while the hype around the city is relentless, it's in its restaurants where that hype is unquestionably deserved. With so much agricultural land nearby it's not surprising that this is a foodie city and San Franciscans are ingredient snobs. Menus will regularly boast that **steak** comes from the Niman Ranch or that it serves only Hoffman chicken. San Francisco's obsession with restaurants dates back to the Gold Rush days, when the city was overrun with single men staying in boardinghouses, who had to find somewhere to eat every evening. Dozens of diners sprung up in response, and the city's been restaurant-crazy ever since.

For budget eating, the **dim sum** houses of Chinatown and the **Mexican** places of the Mission are not only cheap, but some of the best food in town. There are, inevitably, dozens of **Italian** restaurants in North Beach (though quality varies wildly); **French** food is a perennial favorite, at least with the power-broking crowd, although nouvelle cuisine is finally beginning to loosen its grip on San Franciscan menus. **California cuisine** nowadays has grown away from its minimalist roots, but still features the freshest food, beautifully presented. **Japanese** food is massively popular as are an increasing number of **Thai**, **Korean**, and **Indonesian** eateries. Not surprisingly, health-conscious San Francisco also has a wide range of **vegetarian** and **wholefood** restaurants, and it's rare to find anywhere that doesn't have at least one meat-free item on the menu. It's also very worthwhile to plan on one splurge meal while in town – the high price you'll pay for a world-class meal here is still far below the big-city average.

Be warned: San Francisco closes up early and you'll be struggling to find places that will serve you much after 10 or 11pm, unless they're of the 24-hour diner variety. And thanks to recent statewide legislation you now cannot smoke in any restaurant in the city.

We've divided San Francisco's restaurant scene into two sections: the first, "**Cafés and light meals**", lists cheap places to grab a light meal. The second, "**Restaurants**", is divided by neighborhood and offers a range of eateries from budget to deluxe across a wide variety of cuisines. We've also provided a run-down of some of the better round-the-clock places to eat.

Cafés and light meals

Betty's Café 167 11th St at Howard, SoMa ⊕415/431-2525. Known for its hearty $2.65 breakfast specials, including choice of meat, eggs, hash browns, and toast. No frills, but who'd expect them at prices like these.

Big Sherm's 250 Fillmore St at Waller, Haight-Ashbury ⊕415/864-1850. Avocado-lovers' heaven, serving more than thirty sandwiches all on that single theme. Try avocado with spinach, artichoke, cucumber, and pea sprouts (#31) or carrots, cucumber, and red onion (#24).

Boogaloo's 3296 22nd St at Valencia, Mission ⊕415/824-3211. Breakfast's the big draw here: black beans and *chorizo* (spicy sausage) feature heavily on the Latinized versions of American diner classics, costing $5–7 per dish. The decor's basic, but perked up with bright orange and yellow tables. Open 8am–3.30pm.

Boudin Sourdough Bakery & Cafe 156 Jefferson St at Mason, Fisherman's Wharf ⊕415/928-1849. The sourdough bread at this chain is the best around, made from a 150-year-old recipe and yeast that's descended from the first batch.

Brother in Laws Bar-B-Q 705 Divisadero St at Grove, Western Addition ⊕415/931-7427. The service and atmosphere here are dreadful, but it still packs people in thanks to delicious, crunchy short-end ribs and smokey brisket – just get them to go.

Café Flore 2298 Noe St at Market, Castro ⊕415/621-8579. Wedged into the triangle at the corner of Market and Noe streets, this café has a sunny, plant-filled courtyard that's a great place to grab a coffee and a gooey cake; be aware that it can be very cruisey, especially during the early evening.

Café Francisco 2161 Powell St at North Point, Fishermans' Wharf ⊕415/397-2602. Cheap neighborhood café that's great for a lazy breakfast lounging with the newspapers or a quiet lunchtime sandwich only blocks from the wharf.

Caffe Trieste 601 Vallejo St at Grant, North Beach ⊕415/392-6739. Small, crowded Italian coffeehouse. Its real attraction is the Saturday afternoon amateur opera hour, when old Italian ladies from the neighborhood come to gossip over a coffee and listen to charmingly off-key live singers.

San Francisco restaurants

Cafés and light meals	p.557
Downtown and Chinatown	p.559
North Beach and Nob Hill	p.560
The northern waterfront and Pacific Heights	p.560
SoMa, the Tenderloin and Civic Center	p.562
The Mission, the Castro, and south	p.563
Haight-Ashbury and west of Civic Center	p.564
The Richmond and the Sunset	p.565

Citizen Cake 399 Grove St at Franklin, Hayes Valley/Civic Center ☎415/861-2228. Stylish, pricey café/bakery with a soft jazz soundtrack serving delectable, delicate pastries: its signature cake, unsurprisingly also a nod to Orson Welles, is the "Rosebud," a rose-scented crème brûlée tart.

Cool Beans 4342 California St at 6th Ave, Richmond ☎415/750-1955. Neighborhood spot where the locals go to meet and greet over a game of backgammon or chess.

Einstein's Cafe 1336 9th Ave at Cabrillo, Richmond ☎415/665-4840. This café serves big, cheap sandwiches, and proceeds from all sales go to fund a not-for-profit organization that works with troubled youth.

El Farolito 2779 Mission St at 24th, Mission ☎415/824-7877. A scruffy local institution, this 24-hour taqueria is pretty basic but the food is outstanding and cheap. Try a *quesadilla suiza* (creamy swiss with chicken) and don't miss the delicious, tangy green salsa.

Escape from New York 1737 Haight St at Shrader, Haight-Ashbury ☎415/668-5577. Low-key pizzeria selling both whole pies and warmed-to-order slices with traditional toppings as well as California-style pesto or tomato-artichoke.

Frjtz 579 Hayes St at Laguna, Hayes Valley ☎415/864-7654. Trendy, tiny *friterie*, serving cones of crunchy Belgian-style fries with dips like tabasco-chive ketchup or spicy yoghurt peanut. The overstuffed sofa in the tiny window is a great place to hunker down and listen to live DJs playing at the decks next to the main counter.

Liguria Bakery 1700 Stockton St at Filbert, North Beach ☎415/421-3786. Marvelous old-world Italian bakery overlooking Washington Square Park, with deliciously fresh *focaccia* – the raisin's delicious if rather inauthentic. Get there early, as it simply closes when sold out.

Louie's Dim Sum 1236 Stockton St at Broadway, Chinatown ☎415/989-8380. The glistening, pearly dumplings are ranged in vast metal trays in front of you, and although variety's limited, they're all delicious and cheap ($1 for two).

Mama's 1701 Stockton St at Washington Square, North Beach ☎415/362-6421. There are cheery bright yellow tablecloths and sunny staff at this homely diner: try the crab benedict or one of the gooey, cakey French toast specials. Expect gargantuan lines at the weekend, whatever the time, so bring a book. Open Tues–Sun 8am–3pm.

Mario's Bohemian Cigar Store 566 Columbus Ave at Union, North Beach ☎415/362-0536. The "bohemian" in the name is dead-on even if there are no cigars now. Try one of the chunky, cheap house-made *focaccia* sandwiches or a pungent, fresh shot of espresso.

Mee Mee Bakery 1328 Stockton St at Broadway, Chinatown ☎415/362-3204. Little-known Chinatown gem that sells delicate almondy treats as well as a variety (Biblical, Adult) of fortune cookies starting at $2 per pound.

Mitchell's 688 San Jose Ave at 29th, Mission ☎415/648-2300. In a fairly desolate southern corner of the neighborhood is the perfect spot for an after-dinner treat. *Mitchell's* serves home-made ice cream in an array of exotic tropical flavors – try the *buko* (baby coconut), avocado, or sweet bean.

Mocca 175 Maiden Lane, Union Square ☎415/956-1188. This small café spills out onto this pedestrianized shopping street while the garlicky Italian food wafts an aroma along the block. Although the sandwiches (starting around $7) aren't cheap, they're crammed with tangy, flavor-packed Mediterranean meats and pickles.

Panchita's 3115 22nd St at Capp, Mission ☎415/821-6660. A local chainlet of Salvadorean-Mexican fusion cafés: the *pupusa* (chunky corn tortilla, grilled and stuffed with a variety of fillings) is a delicious budget snack for around $1.50.

Panelli's 1419 Stockton St at Columbus Ave, North Beach ☎415/421-2541. Old-school Italian sandwich shop in the heart of North Beach, serving meaty, enormous sandwiches for around $7 each.

Patisserie 1890 Fillmore St at Pine, Pacific Heights ☎415/923-0711. Gourmet French bakery, run by two expats, who make flaky, buttery croissants and glistening fruit tarts as well as delicious sandwiches (the gorgonzola, walnut, and pear is superb).

Pat's Café 2701 Leavenworth St at Columbus, Fisherman's Wharf ℡ 415/776-8735. Bright and basic with simple formica and a short menu of burgers and sandwiches, starting at $6.

Pizzetta 211 211 23rd Ave at California, Richmond ℡ 415/379-9880. You can rely on inventive and unusual pizza here: there's a different menu each week, offering whatever's fresh and seasonal as a pizza topping (although you'll usually find eggs on at least one option).

Rosamunde Sausage Grille 545 Haight St at Fillmore, Lower Haight ℡ 415/437-6851. Tiny storefront grill with a few stools at the bar, just serving grilled sausages on a sesame roll. Choose from a cherry-laced chicken sausage to the light flavors of a shrimp, scallop, and snapper sausage.

Saigon Sandwiches 560 Larkin St at Ellis, Tenderloin℡ 415/474-5698. Hole-in-the wall store selling outstanding made-to-order Vietnamese sandwiches for $2/each: choose between BBQ chicken, BBQ pork, and meatballs, then add lashings of fresh greens and tongue-curling hot pickles. Highly recommended.

Sears Fine Food 439 Powell St at Post, Union Square ℡ 415/986-1160. A classic breakfast joint with a hearty old-fashioned ambience: try the plate of 18 tiny Swedish pancakes or for groups of six or more, the Ranch Breakfast of pancakes, eggs, bacon, and the works. Try the big plate of tiny pancakes. Open daily 6.30am–2.30pm.

Swan Oyster Depot 1517 Polk at California, Polk Gulch ℡ 415/673-1101. No frills – and officially, no full meals – at this cheap seafood counter. Grab a stool and hang onto it (it gets crowded and competitive here) and suck down some cheap shellfish and seafood.

Restaurants

Downtown and Chinatown

Chef Jia's 925 Kearny St at Columbus, Chinatown ℡ 415/398-1626. Just a couple of doors down from the *House of Nanking*, they serve quick, tasty, and cheap specialties that, if not quite equal to the offerings of its famous neighbor, are a decent substitute when the line at *Nanking* gets too long.

Cosmopolitan Café 121 Spear St Unit B-8, in the Rincon Center, Financial District ℡ 415/543-4001. This modern American bistro is an appealing choice for dinner in a deserted area. The standard modern American food ($18–22 per entrée) is spruced up with great condiments like sweet, chunky house made ketchup, not to mention friendly, efficient service.

Farallon 450 Post St at Powell, Union Square ℡ 415/956-6969. Seafood's prepared and served with great fanfare in this Union Square notable: it's a pity that the jellyfish-inspired decor with its dangling luminescent mobiles is so offputting. The champagne-steamed clams are light and tender, while mackerel tartare and tuna carpaccio are oddly delicious, flavor-packed appetizers.

Late-night eating

Bagdad Café 2295 Market St at 16th, Castro ℡ 415/621-4434. The best price 24-hr option in the neighborhood.

Bruno's 2389 Mission St at 20th, Mission ℡ 415/648-7701. Jazz lounge serving modern American food until 2am.

Caffè Greco 423 Columbus Ave at Vallejo, North Beach ℡ 415/397-6261. Coffee and light meals at this old-fashioned Italian snack bar.

El Farolito 2779 Mission St at 24th, Mission ℡ 415/824-7877. Twenty-four-hour *taqueria* often mentioned as one of the best in the city – spartan seating, bright lighting, but great eating.

La Rondalla 901 Valencia St at 20th, Mission ℡ 415/647-7474. Christmas-themed (yes, really) Mexican restaurant serving a full menu until 2am.

Mario's Bohemian Cigar Store 566 Columbus Ave at Union, North Beach ℡ 415/362-0536. Sandwiches and light meals.

Yuet Lee 1300 Stockton St at Broadway, Chinatown ℡ 415/982-6020. Terrific Chinese seafood until 3am; daily except Tuesday.

House of Nanking 919 Kearny at Jackson, Chinatown ☎415/421-1429. This tiny spot has become a legend: expect a long but rapidly moving line, curt service, and a fabulous, underpriced meal. Those in the know let the waiters do the ordering for them.

Kokkari Estiatorio 200 Jackson St at Front, Financial District ☎415/981-0983. By far, the best Greek restaurant in town. Though the decor is purely Northern California, the cuisine is classic Greek, relying on staples such as lamb and eggplant, served both separately and cooked together as moussaka.

Le Colonial 20 Cosmo Place at Taylor, Union Square ☎415/931-3600. Lush, Franco-Vietnamese eatery, with a 1920s-themed dining room decked out with tile floors, palm fronds, and ceiling fans. The inventive, eclectic food comes in large portions, family style – try the sea bass wrapped in banana leaf.

Plouf 40 Belden Lane at Bush, Chinatown ☎415/986-6491. French seafood bistro, usually packed out with a yuppie crowd: the atmosphere's airy and the food is rustic and southern, with most entrees costing $12–16. *Plouf*, incidentally, is the French answer to "Splash!"

R&G Lounge 631 Kearny St at Clay, Chinatown ☎415/982-7877. This enormous Hong Kong–style restaurant is popular with both Chinese and Westerners. Dishes come family style, and there's a heavy bias towards seafood; if you plan 24 hours ahead, though, you can order the house special, a whole chicken hollowed out, stuffed with rice and deep fried.

Sam Woh 813 Washington St at Grant, Chinatown ☎415/982-0596. Popular late-night spot where Kerouac, Ginsberg, and others used to hold court – just don't expect smiley service. Walk through the kitchen and up the cramped stairs to reach the dining room.

North Beach and Nob Hill

Café Jacqueline 1454 Grant Ave at Green, North Beach ☎415/981-5565. A romantic, candlelit gourmet experience, this restaurant serves only chef-owner Jacqueline Margulis's signature soufflés, both savory and sweet (crab and chocolate are top picks). Since every dish is made to order, don't plan a quick bite here.

Enrico's 504 Broadway at Kearny, North Beach ☎415/982-6223. The fine, streetside patio here (a good option for smokers) and plenty of tables means that you'll rarely have to wait. The Cal-Italian food is tasty, if a little overfussy: stick with simpler dishes for a delicious meal. $17–23 entree

Harris' Restaurant 2100 Van Ness at Pacific, Pacific Heights ☎415/673-1888. Clubby and proudly old-fashioned, *Harris'* is one of the premier

steakhouses in the city: the staff is warm and welcoming (if a little over-assiduous at times), as is the decor, heavy on padded chairs and comfy booths. There's every cut of beef imaginable – from a $35 filet to a $65 Kobe ribeye – and all are buttery sweet and tender.

The Helmand 430 Broadway at Kearny, North Beach ☎415/362-0641. The decor here is simple and unassuming – unlike the food, which is unforgettable. The menu's filled with tangy and spicy Afghani staples: try the *kaddo borwani* (caramelized pumpkin) or the grilled beef tenderloin. Highly recommended.

Mc2 470 Pacific Ave at Montgomery, Jackson Square ☎415/956-0666. The modern American menu here is available in small and large plates, so you can order family style or by person: it's well-priced and packed with fresh French ingredients like rabbit, duck, and sweetbreads.

L'Osteria del Forno 519 Columbus Ave at Green, North Beach ☎415/982-1124. Tiny, authentic North Italian eatery on the main drag of Little Italy that's a glorious refuge from the nearby tourist traps. The menu's small, and driven by whatever's freshest at the market: *focaccine* sandwiches on springy, fluffy Italian bread are only $6. Try one of the bean salads.

Sushi Groove 1916 Hyde St at Union, Russian Hill ☎415/440-1905. Groovy, throbbing modern sushi restaurant that serves inventive and original *maki* rolls as well as a sprinkling of Pan-Asian fusion dishes (delicious sake martinis, too). The two downsides are the sloppy service and its tiny size, which usually means you'll have to wait for a table. The SoMa branch is bigger but hard to find since there's no sign, but just as hip and often hosts local DJs. Branch at *Sushi Groove South*, 1516 Folsom St at 11th, SoMa ☎415/503-1950.

Tommaso's 1042 Kearny St at Broadway, North Beach ☎415/398-9696. Flamboyant Mayor Willie Brown is said to love the thin crust pizzas served in the cavelike dining room here: if you want to try pasta, the seven-layer lasagne is cheesy, gooey, and delicious.

Trattoria Contadina 1800 Mason St at Union, North Beach ☎415/982-5728. This trattoria is tiny and family-owned, and still caters primarily to the local Italian community: the food's outstanding if traditional, like rigatoni with eggplant and smoked mozzarella.

The northern waterfront and Pacific Heights

Ana Mandara 891 Beach St at Polk, Fisherman's Wharf ☎415/771-6800. Yes, it's co-owned by washed up Eighties stars Don Johnson and

△ The Transamerica Pyramid

Cheech Marin, but the modern Vietnamese and Thai menu is delicious (though pricey). If you're on a tighter budget, go for drinks and appetizers in the beautiful, bamboo-decorated lounge area and listen to the fine live jazz.

Baker Street Bistro 2953 Baker St at Lombard, Cow Hollow ☎415/931-1475. Cramped but charming café with a few outdoor tables: the slightly older, neighborhood crowd enjoys simple food served by French staff. Wines are well-priced and the $14.50 *prix fixe* dinner is a bargain.

Betelnut 2026 Union St at Buchanan, Cow Hollow ☎415/929-8855. Sceney local hangout, known for its offbeat Asian menu served in smaller portions in a hybrid of the dim sum and tapas tradition. Not cheap (around $8–10 per plate) but exotic main courses such as lychee tea-smoked quail, as well as salads and dumplings, not to mention delicious green beans, are well worth sampling.

Bistro Yoffi 2231 Chestnut St at Pierce, Marina ☎415/885-5133. Chef Sarah Lewington serves eclectic modern American dishes at this charming bistro, that's refreshingly quirky given its location, packed with potted ferns and mismatched chairs. There's a great garden out back.

Ella's 500 Presidio Ave at California, Pacific Heights ☎415/441-5669. Perhaps the most famous breakfast wait in town, so put on some comfortable shoes before braving the line that forms outside for scrumptious Californian interpretations of American classics, like the mandarin pancakes with mango syrup.

Gary Danko 800 North Point at Hyde, Fisherman's Wharf ☎415/749-2060. Don't let the location put you off – this understated eatery regularly vies for the title of best restaurant in this foodie city. Granted, it's performance food, served with a self-conscious flourish, but it's utterly splurgeworthy.

Greens Fort Mason Center, Building A, Marina ☎415/771-6222. The queen of San Francisco's vegetarian restaurants, thanks to a picturesque setting on a pier at Fort Mason Center that offers spectacular views of the Bay.

The Meetinghouse 1701 Octavia St at Bush, Pacific Heights ☎415/922-6733. Once an apothecary, this restaurant is housed in a converted old Victorian house and serves old-fashioned home cooking. Classics like grilled porkchops are updated with a side of red-onion grits. It's famed for its meltingly soft biscuits and you can now buy the dough to take home with you.

Neecha 2100 Sutter St at Steiner, Pacific Heights ☎415/922-9419. Good, cheap Thai option, given its location: the pad thai is especially succulent and nutty.

Sociale 3665 Sacramento St at Locust, Laurel Heights ☎415/921-3200. This intimate Italian bistro, nestled in a small courtyard at the end of a tiny alleyway, is worth seeking out for the warm atmosphere and friendly staff, not to mention the food, which is mostly light, Cal-Italian – the mozzarella-crammed deep fried olives are worth splurging for.

SoMa, the Tenderloin, and the Civic Center

Acme Chop House 24 Willie Mays Plaza at King and 3rd, SoMa ☎415/644-0240. Vegetarian Hell, this resoundingly old-style restaurant is another brainchild of local chef wunderkind, Traci Des Jardins (see *Jardiniere*, below). This place is enormous and usually packed with businessmen chowing down on chunky, choice cuts of steak – try the filet or the butcher steak.

Asia SF 201 9th St at Howard, SoMa ☎415/255-2742. Glorious gender illusion bar/restaurant – don't you dare call them drag queens – where the waitresses perform cheeky, campy burlesque on the bar throughout the evening. The sake martinis are delicious and deadly, while the Cal-Pacific food (sushi rolls and funky salads) is inventive.

Bacar Restaurant and Wine Salon 448 Brannan St at 4th, SoMa ☎415/904-4100. This enormous three-level restaurant was white hot when it opened, crammed with thrusting dot-commers. The menu, primarily Modern American, changes seasonally and there's a live, three-piece house band most nights. The loungey downstairs bar is groovier, filled with overstuffed chairs where you can linger over appetizers and sample one of the 100+ wines served by the glass.

Café Monk 564 4th St at Brannan, SoMa ☎415/777-1331. Careful, Cal-Ital cuisine served in chic surroundings: there's a refectory-style table if you want to chat with fellow diners, and the walls are covered with portraits of famous monks – from Thelonious to Meredith. Ask for a booth in the balcony.

Fringale 570 4th St at Brannan, SoMa ☎415/543-0573. Delightful, low-key charmer on a quiet SoMa block. The service is as exceptional as the food, predominantly French but with Basque touches like serrano ham. The decor is simple and romantic – just the place to feed your date one of the sumptuous after-dinner truffles. Highly recommended.

Jardinière 300 Grove St at Franklin, Civic Center ☎415/861-5555. Run by big-name chef Traci Des Jardins, this boxy brick space caters to a pre-theater crowd with valet parking and plenty of pizzazz. A splurge, but you'll get what you pay for; there's an emphasis on indulgence from beginning (foie gras) to end (aged cheese platter). Try the gnocchi with oxtail sauce.

Lulu 816 Folsom St at 4th, SoMa ☎415/495-5775. Famed Californian restaurant with a rustic, rather cramped dining room: the shared, family-style dishes are hit and miss, although the pearl-sized *gnocchi* are meltingly fluffy; the spectacular wine list – many by the glass – is also impressive.

Momo's 760 2nd St at King, SoMa ☎415/227-8660. Mainstream sports bar, minutes from the stadium, with a surprisingly swish and upscale restaurant. Appetizers like roasted asparagus and *wasabi*-glazed tuna tartare are pungent and flavor-ful, while clever entrées include asparagus risotto with a hint of scallops and a fruity pork loin with dried-cherry reduction.

The Ramp 855 China Basin St at Illinois, China Basin ☎415/621-2378. American restaurant right on the water at the southern tip of SoMa. The crowd and the place are both super casual and there's a refreshingly diverse selection of people. The best time to come is for brunch or breakfast on the patio overlooking the water – the corned-beef hash is outstanding.

Shalimar 532 Jones St at Geary, Tenderloin ☎415/928-0333. This hole-in-the-wall serves delicious, cheap Pakistani food, all of it made to order before your eyes in the *kulcha* oven: the chicken tikka is fantastic value at only $3.50 for an enormous portion. There are a few tables if you want to linger. The same team also owns the newer, more upscale *Shalimar Garden* nearby, 417 O'Farrell St at Jones ☎415/447-4041.

Sushi Rock 1608 Polk St at Sacramento, Polk Gulch ☎415/345-1690. Reliable sushi restaurant in Polk Gulch, large enough that you should always be able to snag a table whatever the time of day. There's free seaweed salad and miso soup in front of you as soon as you've sat down; stick with the sushi as some *maki* rolls are rather bland.

Tu Lan 8 6th St at Market, SoMa/Tenderloin ☎415/626-0927. A legend ever since Julia Child first sampled the Vietnamese cooking in this cramped, dingy space on one of the seediest blocks in town. Should you sit at the sticky count-er, you'll be nearly singed by the flames from the stove. Nevertheless, the food is consistently fresh, authentic, and flavorful – just don't look up at the grubby ceiling!

The Mission, the Castro, and south

Baobab 3388 19th St, Mission ☎415/643-3558. Covering a lot of bases: all-American egg and French toast breakfasts in the morning; Senegalese food, such as fried bananas and fish

stew in the evening, and a popular bar later at night. Branch at 2323 Mission St at 19th, Castro ☎415/826-9287.

Blue 2337 Market St at Castro, Castro ☎415/863-2583. Small, retro diner restaurant that's decked out in industrial chromes and blacks, but serves deliciously simple comfort food like chicken pot pie and chili, to the early hours. Thanks to a restrictive liquor licence, *Blue* also serves inventive, original martinis and cocktails with a sake base and even a selection of root beers.

Chow 215 Church St at Market, Castro ☎415/552-2469. Unfussy comfort food, like bar-gain pastas and wood-fired pizzas, some with an Asian twist. Spaghetti and meatballs is great value for $6 and most dishes cost no more than $10. No reservations accepted, and the wait can be long. There's a branch called *Park Chow* in the Sunset (see p.565)

El Trébol 3324 24th St at Mission, Mission ☎415/285-6298. Run by a husband-and-wife team, this café serves excellent versions of Nicaraguan standards like *churrasco* (grilled beef) and *chancho con yucca* (fried pork), in haphazard atmosphere washed with Latin music. The mouth-puckering *tamarindo* drink is an experience; just don't plan on enjoying the menu to its full if you're dieting.

Emmy's Spaghetti Shack 18 Virginia St at Mission, Bernal Heights ☎415/206-2086. This uberfunky café is filled day and night with local hipsters who give it a laid-back unpretentious vibe and the chunky, tasty food makes it even more appealing: try the house meatballs and spaghetti for around $8.

Foreign Cinema 2534 Mission St at 21st, Mission ☎415/648-7600. Originally, this upscale Cal-French restaurant was a gimmicky hybrid of bistro and drive-in, with movies projected onto the large outdoor wall and speakers on each table. That's quickly fallen away to allow diners to focus on the food, including an excellent oyster/raw bar selec-tion and grilled Meyer Ranch steak. The *Laszlo* martini bar is on the same site.

Hot n' Hunky 4039 18th St at Castro, Castro ☎415/621-6365. This pink and chrome diner is a rather forlorn institution, with fading photographs of Marilyn Monroe on the walls; the food's spright-lier than the atmosphere, with juicy burgers for around $4.

Home 2100 Market St at Church, Castro ☎415/503-0333. Formerly the upscale eatery *John-Frank*, this became *Home* when John and Frank split up. The menu's now designed to offer the things that a chef cooks at home for his friends – primarily comfort food like *moules frites* – around $10–12 per entrée. It's popular with a mixed crowd of guppies and yuppies, and there's a groovy patio bar with DJs at the weekend.

Luna Park 694 Valencia St at 18th, Mission ☏415/553-8584. Outstanding new restaurant, with a groovy local vibe no matter what day of the week. It's decked out like a lush bordello with deep red walls and ornamental chandeliers, and menus come in little black books. Most of the entrées, like a tuna salad *niçoise* or *moules frites*, hover around $14. Don't miss the offbeat but excellent goat cheese fondue with grilled bread and sliced apples as an appetizer or the excellent cocktails.

Miss Millie's 4123 24th St at Church, Noe Valley ☏415/282-5598. A weekend brunch institution, thanks to fresh home-baked goods and deliciously light French toast. Expect a wait of close to an hour and be prepared to have your conversation interrupted by the dozens of yuppie babies around you; snag a table on the patio if you can.

Moki's Sushi and Pacific Grill 830 Cortland Ave at Gates, Bernal Heights ☏415/970-9336. Japanese food with a liberal dash of Hawaiian favorites, heavy on fruit and seafood. There's seating in the main room and at the sushi bar, where you can also order sashimi and *maki* rolls, but the choicest tables are on the tiny, hidden patio out back.

Roosevelt Tamale Parlor 2817 24th St at Bryant, Mission ☏415/550-9213. Just one of their massive and delectable tamales – steamed corn and meat served inside corn husks – can easily serve two people. The guacamole is heavenly.

San Miguel 3520 20th St, Mission ☏415/826-0173. Enjoy the marimba music among the tropical decor at this Guatemalan restaurant, while you munch on crunchy tostadas.

Slanted Door 584 Valencia St at 17th, Mission ☏415/861-8032. This cavernous, understated restaurant has plenty of buzz and so fills up quickly: book ahead or eat early. There are green velvet banquettes and artfully framed posters on the walls, giving a Pan-Asian minimalist impression. The menu, which changes daily, is light, French-Vietnamese; there are several deliciously fragrant chicken dishes, and the tea list is impressive and eclectic. Recommended.

Suriya Thai 1432 Valencia St at 25th, Mission ☏415/824-6655. You'll feel like you're in Bangkok at this tiny restaurant, which is crammed with antiques and palms. The flamboyant food rarely disappoints – try the emerald noodles, the pumpkin curry, or the deep-fried green papaya wedges in shredded coconut butter.

Ti Couz 3108 16th St at Valencia, Mission ☏415/252-7373. Friendly, hip, and gracious, this creperie was one of the pioneers of the newly groovy Mission scene on Valencia. It still holds its place as one of the best cheaper restaurants around, serving buckwheat savory pancakes for $6 or so and lighter, fluffier dessert crepes.

Haight-Ashbury, and west of Civic Center

Absinthe 398 Hayes St at Gough, Hayes Valley ☏415/551-1590. Brasserie-cum-bistro, with two separate dining areas, both serving robust French food in an authentic, if trendy, atmosphere. The bar's a good option round here for drinks, since it's open until 2am and serves smallish snacks for $6 or so per plate.

Cha Cha Cha 1801 Haight St at Clayton, Haight-Ashbury ☏415/386-5758. Abundantly flavorful Cuban-style tapas served in a Caribbean setting – the delicious fried shrimp comes in huge portions and the sangria is excellent. Sit at the bar if you can, since the wait for a table can be endless.

Chez Nous 1911 Fillmore St at Pine, Fillmore ☏415/441-8044. This pan-Mediterranean tapas bar draws huge crowds to Fillmore – hence the usual long wait and loud noise inside. It's worth it, though, since the menu's fresh and wide-ranging and offers dishes in both large and tapas sizes: the lamb chops and spinach gnocchi are both excellent.

EOS 901 Cole St at Carl, Cole Valley ☏415/566-3063. Visually spectacular East-West fusion cooking, including ginger Caesar salad and lemon grass risotto, as well as sumptuous desserts, plus an extensive wine bar. This is one of the neighborhood's favorite hangouts; not cheap, but worth it.

Maki Japan Center, 1825 Post St at Webster, Japantown ☏415/921-5125. One of the many tasty, tiny places in the Japan Center, this restaurant specializes in *wappan meshi*, a wood steamer filled with vegetables, meat, and rice: notable for its warm, friendly owner.

Mifune Japan Center, 1737 Post St at Fillmore, Japantown ☏415/922-0337. Everything at this noodle house on the bridge of the Japan Center is just the right temperature – the beer's ice cold, and the tangy noodles piping hot. It's more elegant than its neighbors, with a large array of soup toppings and a small selection of sushi.

On the Bridge Japan Center, 1581 Webster St at Post, Japantown ☏415/922-7765. Smallish cafeteria serving *yoshoko*, or westernized Japanese food, such as spaghetti with *kim chi* (pickled cabbage).

Powell's Place 511 Hayes St at Octavia, Hayes

Valley ☎415/863-1404. Southern-fried chicken is the house specialty, but there are daily Southern specials like chicken-fried steak. Every dinner is served with two sides, like grits or greens, as well as a couple of crumbly corn muffins. This is an authentic, laid-back café that's a survivor of pre-gentrification Hayes Valley. Highly recommended.

Stelline 330 Gough St at Hayes, Hayes Valley ☎415/626-4292. Red-checkered tablecloths, a handwritten and photocopied menu plus affable, chatty staff make this a cheap, easy place to grab a pasta lunch: it's the kid sister of *Caffè delle Stelle* down the street.

Suppenküche 601 Hayes St at Laguna, Hayes Valley ☎415/252-9289. Here, you can pair traditional beer-garden fare, such as spaetzel, sausages, and sauerkraut, with a good selection of lagers and lemony wheat beers. There's a beer-shall atmosphere, complete with bare walls, stark pine chairs, and tables.

Thep Phanom 400 Waller St at Fillmore, Lower Haight ☎415/431-2526. One of the best Thai restaurants in the city, catering to both hippie holdouts and yuppies: the curries are fragrant, pungent, and cheap, and the spinach with peanut sauce is sweet and sharp. Try the Three's Company seafood medley in coconut sauce.

Zona Rosa 1797 Haight St at Shrader, Haight-Ashbury ☎415/668-7717. By no means an "authentic" burrito – they use too many vegetables for that – but with a good and flavorful selection of *mole* and *verde* sauce-smothered fillings.

Zuni 1658 Market St at Gough, Hayes Valley ☎415/552-2522. Once nouveau and now a staple, *Zuni* features the most famous Caesar salad in town – made with home-cured anchovies – and an equally legendary *focaccia* hamburger – rustic Californian in style. The decor's heavy on brick and glass, and the restaurant's light and airy: most entrees are in the $18–22 range.

The Richmond and the Sunset

Aziza 5800 Geary Blvd at 22nd, Richmond ☎415/752-2222. Classy Moroccan eatery with opulent decor and fun touches, including a pewter ewer and basin that's passed around so you can wash your hands, plus live belly dancing Thursday to Sunday. Try the $35 tasters' menu, which has packed Middle Eastern specialties like *hummus*

and *babba ghanoush* or the tagines of rabbit spiced with paprika.

Brother's 4128 Geary Blvd at 6th, Richmond ☎415/387-3991. The oldest among a burgeoning row of Korean barbecue houses along Geary, and one of the few with the name written in English outside (making it the easiest to find), *Brother's* specializes in family-sized feasts of grilled, marinated meats.

Chapeau! 1408 Clement St at 15th, Richmond ☎415/750-9787. Downtown-quality French food at foggy Richmond prices, packed with locals enjoying a relaxed provincial atmosphere.

Fountain Court 354 Clement St at 5th Ave, Richmond ☎415/668-1100. Unusual Chinese restaurant serving authentic Shanghainese food – less familiar than Cantonese staples, perhaps, but just as delicious. Try the Shanghai dumplings or lion's-head soup.

House 1269 9th Ave at Irving, Sunset ☎415/682-3898. East-West fusion cuisine – like a Caesar salad with wok-fried scallops or garlic soy chicken wings – served in quirky, funhouse decor. Branch at 1230 Grant Ave at Columbus, North Beach ☎415/986-8612.

Park Chow 1240 9th Ave at Lincoln, Sunset ☎415/665-9912. The sequel to popular *Chow* near the Castro. Solid, consistent renditions of pizzas, pastas, and the like, perfect for a post-park lunch.

PJ's Oyster Bed 737 Irving at 9th, Sunset ☎415/566-7775. From Tuesday to Thursday this rowdy, unpretentious restaurant offers spicy, tangy Cajun dishes like blackened catfish and alligator fillets. On weekends, it broadens the menu to offer fish specials like a delicious, meaty Peruvian stew, with prawns, scallops, and mussels in a chili cream sauce. Watch out for the free Jello vodka shots the owner periodically passes around.

Q 225 Clement St at 3rd, Richmond ☎415/752-2298. There's over-the-top decor – like a table with a tree growing through it – and outlandish portions of funky comfort food (think fish tacos and mac'n'cheese) at this hip outpost.

Thanh Long 4101 Judah St at 46th Ave, Sunset ☎415/665-1146. The original restaurant by the owners of the (over) hyped *Crustacean* in Polk Gulch, this serves upscale French-Vietnamese food in a low-key atmosphere. Try the catfish claypot or one of the soft-shell crab dishes.

Drinking

While famous for its restaurants, San Francisco has a huge number of **drinking** establishments, ranging from comfortably scruffy jukebox joints to the chic watering holes of social climbers. Though spread fairly evenly over the city, happening bars are particularly numerous in North Beach and the Mission, where they line up one after the other. Some of the more colorful (and seedy) are to be found in the Tenderloin and the Haight, while yuppie cruising zones populate the Marina and slick lounges speckle downtown and have begun to spread into SoMa. According to new California law, there is **no smoking** allowed in any bar unless its sole employees are the owners, though the debate still rages and enforcement has been spotty.

The city is also dotted with excellent **cafés** serving first-rate coffees, teas, and soft drinks in addition to beer and wine. More social than utilitarian, people hang out in these generally lively venues to pass time as much as refresh themselves. Other non-drinkers looking for social alternatives to bars are opting for the old English tradition of afternoon tea. So far it has only taken root in the big hotels, but neighborhood cafés are catching on fast.

Unsurprisingly, the city has many specifically **gay bars** (see p.577), most plentifully in the Castro, Polk Street, and the Mission – although few bars are at all threatening for either gay men or lesbians, or women on their own.

Downtown and Chinatown

The Bubble Lounge 714 Montgomery St at Columbus, Financial District ☎415/434-4204. Champagne bar that attracts a young, label-touting crowd – surprisingly, the prices here are very reasonable.

Cathay House 718 California St at Grant, Chinatown ☎415/982-3388. Don't be put off by the diners in the window – sitting smack in the middle of a run-of-the-mill restaurant is an inviting circular bar, centered on a large Buddha.

Li Po's Bar 916 Grant Ave at Jackson, Chinatown ☎415/982-0072. Named after the Chinese poet, *Li Po's* is a little grotty, although that's part of its charm: it's one of the few places to drink in Chinatown.

The London Wine Bar 415 Sansome St at Sacramento, Financial District ☎415/788-4811. Claiming to be America's first wine bar, this clubby place has a worn mahogany bar and cozy paneled booths, and caters to an older crowd.

Maxfield's *Palace Hotel*, 2 New Montgomery St at Market, SoMa ☎415/392-8600. Named after the artist Maxfield Parrish, whose famous mural of the Pied Piper decorates the bar, this mahogany-paneled room is a secluded, elegant place for a martini.

Red Room *Commodore International Hotel*, 827 Sutter St at Jones, Theater District ☎415/346-7666. This trendy, sexy bar is – as its name implies – completely red: walls, furniture, glasses, and even many of the drinks. The crowd's young and mixed gay-straight, but it can be crowded at weekends.

The Redwood Room *Clift Hotel*, 495 Geary St at

Taylor, Theater District ☎415/775-4700. This club-by, landmark bar was made over by Starck & Schrager, who added lightboxes on the wall displaying paintings that shift and fade. It's fun and hip – just don't choke on the drink prices.

North Beach, Nob Hill, and the northern waterfront

Balboa Café 3199 Fillmore St at Greenwich, Marina ☎415/921-3944. This dark wood bar with its high ceilings and excellent wine list attracts plenty of prowling Marina singles.

The Crow Bar 401 Broadway at Montgomery, North Beach ☎415/788-2769. This hole-in-the-wall is an appealing escape on a club-saturated strip, with a pool table out back and an unpretentious crowd.

Gino and Carlo 548 Green St at Grant, North Beach ☎415/421-0896. This is the classic drunken pressman's bar, filled with regulars and old school locals all day. Visitors wanting to stop by to play pinball or pool won't feel unwelcome.

Hawaii West 729 Vallejo St at Stockton, North Beach ☎415/362-3220. This bar boasts a cursing parrot, a drag-queen owner, and a pool table you don't have to wait in line for. If you're lucky, the owner will serenade the crowd with some karaoke.

Matrix-Fillmore 3138 Fillmore St at Greenwich, Marina ☎415/563-4180. Inspired by the original *Matrix* that opened on the same spot in 1965 and hosted big-name rock acts, this bar couldn't be more different now. It's glamorous and a little posey, with a Marina crowd sipping wine by the

glass and dancing to mainstream house and disco.
Pier 23 Pier 23, Telegraph Hill ☎415/362-5125.
Sit out on the bayside deck under the heatlamps
and enjoy cocktails to the sound of a live band, not
to mention a gorgeous view of the Bay Bridge.
Rosewood 732 Broadway at Powell, North Beach
☎415/951-4886. Deliberately hidden bolthole,
that doesn't even have a sign outside. The interi-
or's retro groovy, and complemented by great
loungecore DJs: the downside is the pricey drinks
and the out-of-towners who pour in at weekends.
San Francisco Brewing Company 155
Columbus Ave at Pacific, North Beach ☎415/434-
3344. Probably the most touristy of the various
microbrewpubs around town, with a bland crowd
of non-locals and big shining tanks of beer. Great
happy hour deals from 4–6pm.
Spec's Adler Museum Café 12 Saroyan Place at
Columbus, North Beach ☎415/421-4112. Friendly,
dive bar in the heart of North Beach, packed with
an older, eccentric local crowd. It's known for its
chatty barstaff who'll often serve up cheese and
crackers to regulars.
Tonga Room *Fairmont Hotel*, 950 Mason St at
California, Nob Hill ☎415/772-5278. This basement Tiki lounge has grass huts and a floating
band at night, not to mention an indoor rainstorm
every fifteen minutes. Come for happy hour when
there's a terrific all-you-can-eat $6 buffet, as long
as you buy a (pricey) drink.
Tunnel Top 601 Bush St at Stockton, Union
Square☎415/986-8900 This funky bar is hidden
behind a seedy storefront on top of the Stockton
Street tunnel. Inside is arty-industrial – check out
the chandelier festooned with empty wine bottles
– and there are movies projected on the walls.
One of few tobacco-friendly places downtown.

SoMa, the Civic Center, and the Tenderloin

Backflip *Phoenix Hotel*, 601 Eddy St at Larkin,
Tenderloin ☎415/771-FLIP. A little bit of LA in the
north as aspiring models and rockers lounge by
the poolside bar, pretending it's 80 degrees outside.
Bigfoot Lodge 1750 Polk St at Washington, Polk
Gulch ☎415/440-2355. San Francisco outpost of
a campy bar from LA, themed as a 1950s ski
lodge. Expect plenty of faux wood, hunting tro-
phies, antlers – as well as an enormous papier
mâché statue of Bigfoot himself.
Bobby's Owl Tree 601 Post St at Taylor,
Tenderloin ☎415/776-9344. A true local oddity,
this bar is crammed with owls – from clocks to
statues to paintings – without a trace of hip irony.
For that reason alone, it's worth a visit for a freaky,
off-kilter experience.
Butter 354 11th St at Folsom, SoMa ☎415/863-
5964. Stylized "white trash" bar and diner featuring imitation trailer-park decor, like a bar covered
with shingles. The serving window to one side
serves only microwaveable junk food. Hip, fun, and
ironic, if a little less supercool than it once was.
Edinburgh Castle 950 Geary St at Polk, Tenderloin
☎415/885-4074. Just your average Scottish bar,
filled with heraldic Highland memorabilia, although
it's actually run by Koreans. The room upstairs regularly hosts comedy and live music.
Gordon Biersch Brewery 2 Harrison St at
Embarcadero, SoMa ☎415/243-8246. Bayfront outpost of the successful Peninsula microbrewery
housed in a converted Hills Brothers coffee warehouse with a lovely view of the bridge, good bar
food, and some of the best beers in San Francisco.

San Francisco beers

While the surrounding countryside may be devoted to winemaking, the city of San
Francisco is renowned for its beer, specifically its **microbreweries**: the best-known
local product is so-called **steam** beer, a hybrid lager-bitter. It was invented when
early local brewers, finding the ice needed for lager production too expensive,
instead fermented their yeast at room temperature like an ale: the result was a beer
with the lower ABV of lager but the hearty flavor of bitter. (The precise origin of the
odd name, unfortunately, has never been established). To find out more head over
to the Anchor Steam Brewery, 1705 Mariposa St at Carolina, Potrero Hill (☎415/863-
8350, ⓦwww.anchorbrewing.com) for a **tour**, though the product is universally available at bars and stores. Otherwise, the pick of the local microbrewpubs are:

Gordon Biersch Brewery, SoMa	above
San Francisco Brewing Company, North Beach	above
Thirsty Bear Brewing Company, SoMa	overleaf

POW! 101 6th St at Mission, SoMa ☎ 415/278-0940. A hipster bar in an unlikely part of SoMa with an *anime* theme and graffiti art on the walls. It's on one of the nastiest corners in town, so take a cab if you can.

The Ramp 855 China Basin St at Illinois, China Basin ☎ 415/621-2378. Way out on the old docks, this is well worth the half-mile trek from downtown to sit out on the patio and sip beers overlooking the abandoned piers and new boatyards.

Thirsty Bear Brewing Company 661 Howard St at 2nd, SoMa ☎ 415/974-0905. A combination brewpub and tapas bar, packed in the evenings with local office workers.

The Mission, the Castro, and south

The Beauty Bar 2299 Mission St at 19th, Mission ☎ 415/285-0323. Campy and tongue-in-cheek, this San Francisco import of New York's *Beauty Bar* is outfitted like a 1950s hair salon. Sip on a cocktail while enjoying a manicure, but come during the week if you want to avoid the crowds.

Blondie's Bar & No Grill 540 Valencia St at 16th, Mission ☎ 415/864-2419. Always packed, this fun bar with a good-sized patio serves huge cocktails and often hosts live music: as a bonus, the newly opened Wetspot back room is also smoker-friendly.

Dalva 3121 16th St at Valencia, Mission ☎ 415/252-7740. *Dalva's* divey and dark, and though the wafer-thin space is easy to miss, that doesn't stop a diverse, artsy crowd from packing in to lean against one of the narrow tables.

Doc's Clock 2575 Mission St at 21st, Mission ☎ 415/824-3627. The crowd at this women-run bar is artsy and alternative. The Deco-style bar is easy to spot, thanks to the hot-pink neon sign blazing out front.

The Lone Palm 3394 22nd St at Guerrero, Mission ☎ 415/648-0109. Like a forgotten Vegas review bar from the 1950s, this dim, candlelit cocktail lounge is a secret gem. The namesake palm is actually metal and there's a TV above the bar playing classic American movies.

Lucky 13 2140 Market St at Church, Castro ☎ 415/487-1313. A primarily hetero, divey rocker bar on the border between the Castro and the Lower Haight, filled with frat boys playing pool and listening to the Sex Pistols on the jukebox.

Luna Park 694 Valencia St at 17th, Mission ☎ 415/553-8584. The smallish bar at the front of this outstanding new restaurant has a groovy local vibe but the inventive cocktails are the real draw: try an appletini, made from Granny Smith-infused vodka.

Odeon Bar 3223 Mission St at Valencia, Bernal

Heights ☎ 415/550-6994, ⓦ www.odeonbar.com. Creepy, intriguing dive bar, run by wacky performance artist "Chicken John": the bar's stage often hosts bizarre performers and the general vibe is bohemian and eccentric.

La Rondalla 901 Valencia St at 20th, Mission ☎ 415/647-7474. It's always Christmas (literally) at this festive Mexican dive, as it's decorated year-round with an orgy of tinsel and trinkets. There's a live mariachi band most nights.

Tip Top Inn 3001 Mission St at 26th, Outer Mission ☎ 415/824-6486. Catering primarily to punky locals, this bar has a pool table and cheap drinks, although expect a cover on weekend evenings, when rock acts perform in the small back room.

Zodiac 718 14th St at Market, Castro ☎ 415/626-7827, ⓦ zodiacclub.citysearch.com. Designed by the same team as the *Red Room* (see p.566), this astrology-themed lounge has dark blue walls and purple drapes, and a friendly crowd. There are, of course, twelve fun cocktails, one for each sign – think Red Bull for Taureans – but skip the average food.

Haight-Ashbury and west of Civic Center

An Bodhran 688 Haight St at Pierce, Lower Haight ☎ 415/431-4724. Not quite on a par with the *Mad Dog* up the block, but occasional live Irish folk music makes this a popular spot. (Incidentally, it's pronounced "an bau-rawn").

Mad Dog in the Fog 530 Haight St at Fillmore, Lower Haight ☎ 415/626-7279. Aptly named by the two lads from Birmingham, England, who own the joint, this is one of the Lower Haight's most loyally patronized bars, with darts, English beer, copies of the *Sun* tabloid, and a typical pub menu that includes bangers'n'mash and ploughman's lunch.

Martin Macks 1568 Haight St at Clayton, Haight-Ashbury ☎ 415/864-0124. This neighborhood pub is popular for its simple, tasty food, but you can still grab a pint of Guinness by the bar – if you can squeeze past the crowds that usually pack in by lunchtime.

Noc Noc 557 Haight St at Steiner, Lower Haight ☎ 415/861-5811. Decor straight out of an Orwellian sci-fi film, with static-filled televisions in every corner. The bar doesn't have a license to sell hard alcohol, so all cocktails are made from sake: it's supergroovy, extra dark, and worth the trip.

Persian Aub Zam Zam 1663 Haight St at Clayton, Haight-Ashbury ☎ 415/861-2545. There's a retro jazz jukebox at this Casbah-style cocktail lounge. It was once famed for its ornery owner,

Bruno, who would arbitrarily kick out customers, usually when they ordered a drink other than his signature gin martini. After his recent death, regulars purchased the place and tried to retain the vibe.

Golden Gate Park, the beaches, and outlying areas

The Abbey 4100 Geary Blvd at 6th, Richmond ☎415/221-7767. Quintessentially Irish, this sports bar is friendly and upscale, often hosting live Irish folk music when there aren't any important games on TV.

Pig & Whistle Pub 2801 Geary Blvd at Wood, Richmond ☎415/885-4779. Thoroughly British pub, serving a good selection of English and California microbrews, with a pool table and dartboards, and excellent pub food.

Trad'r Sam's 6150 Geary Blvd at 26th, Richmond ☎415/221-0773. Open since 1939, this is a classic tiki bar, complete with flaming bowls of exotically named cocktails: it's groovier and less student-dominated during the week.

Yancy's Saloon 734 Irving St at 8th, Sunset ☎415/665-6551. Mellow, plant-festooned collegiate bar with free darts and cheap drinks.

Nightlife

Compared to Los Angeles, where you need money and attitude in equal amounts, San Francisco's **nightlife** demands little of either. This is no 24-hour city, and the approach to socializing is often surprisingly low-key, with little of the pandering to fads and fashions that goes on elsewhere. The casualness is contagious, and manifests in a **club scene** that, far as it is from the cutting edge of hip, is encouragingly inexpensive compared to other cities. Thirty to forty dollars can buy you a decent night out, including cover charges and a few drinks, and maybe even a taxi home. The live music scene is similarly economical – and, frankly, what the city does best. San Franciscans may be relatively unconcerned with fashion, but there are some excellent rock, jazz, and folk venues all over town, many entertaining you for no more than the price of a drink. Be sure to always bring **a picture ID** with you to get past the bouncers.

San Francisco has a great reputation for **opera and classical music**; its orchestra and opera company are among the most highly regarded in the country. **Theater** is accessible and much less costly than elsewhere, with discount tickets available, but most of the mainstream downtown venues – barring a couple of exceptions – are mediocre, forever staging Broadway reruns, and you'd do better to take some time to explore the infinitely more interesting fringe circuit.

Cabaret and **comedy** are also lively, and **film**, too, is almost as big an obsession as eating in San Francisco; you may well be surprised by the sheer number of movie theaters – repertory and current release – that flourish in this city.

Clubbing

Still trading on a reputation for hedonism earned decades ago, San Francisco's **nightclubs** in fact trail light years behind those of other large American cities. That said, the compensations are manifold – it is rare to encounter high cover charges, ridiculously priced drinks, feverish posing or long lines, though a few of the cavernous dance clubs in SoMa do have lines on weekends. Instead you'll find a diverse range of small to medium-sized, affordable clubs in which leather-clad goths rub shoulders with the bearded and beaded, alongside a number of gay hangouts (listed on p.579) still rocking to the sounds of high-energy funk and Motown. You'll find the occasional DJ hangout, which plays

Apart from the flyers posted up around town, the *Sunday Chronicle*'s "Pink Pages" supplement is about the best source of listings and what's-on information; you might also check the free weeklies *San Francisco Bay Guardian*, *SF Weekly*, and a host of other more specific publications listed below under the relevant sections.

The best sources for **buying tickets** to the following venues are Ticketmaster (☎415/421-TIXS, ⊛www.ticketmaster.com), which has outlets across the city in Rite Aid drugstores and Tower Records, or Tickets.com (☎415/776-1999, ⊛www.tickets.com), which recently absorbed the local Bay Area Seating Service (BASS). No matter what, expect to pay a fee in addition to the ticket price. Theater tickets are also on sale at the TIX Bay Area ticket booth on Union Square; see "Theater" on p.573 for details.

two-step and drum'n'bass but what San Francisco does best is all the old favorites – songs you know the words to; clubbing is more of a party than a pose in this city. The greatest concentration of clubs is in **SoMa**, especially the area around Eleventh Street and Folsom, though the **Mission** is similarly well provided with bars and small live-music venues – not to mention a couple of outrageous drag bars – of almost exclusively Latino origin. There are a few places in North Beach too, so just pick a neighborhood and explore.

Unlike most other cities, where the action never gets going until after midnight, many San Francisco clubs have to **close at 2am during the week**, so you can usually be sure of finding things well under way by 11.30pm. At weekends, most places stay open until 3 or 4am. Very few venues operate any kind of dress code or restrictive admission policy, and only on very busy nights are you likely to have to wait. Unfortunately, most live music and dancing opportunities are restricted to those 21-and-over, forcing underage revellers to be more creative when it comes to late-night entertainment.

Clubs

26 Mix 3024 Mission St at 26th, Mission ☎415/826-7378, ⊛www.26mix.com. Low-key Mission spot to catch top DJs, a self-proclaimed "Sound Bar" that's halfway between a large bar and smallish club. $3–5.

330 Ritch St 330 Ritch St at Townsend, SoMa ☎415/541-9574. The only constant at this small, out-of-the-way club is its location: different nights attract wildly varied crowds, but it's best known for the Thursday Popscene party, ground zero for Modish Britpoppers in San Francisco. $5–15.

1015 Folsom 1015 Folsom St at 6th, SoMa ☎415/431-1200. Multi-level superclub, popular across-the-board for late-night dancing: the music's largely house and garage, and expect marquee names like Sasha and Digweed on the main floor. $10–15.

Cat Club 1190 Folsom St at 8th, SoMa ☎415/431-3332. Predominantly lesbian club often mixing live entertainment with dancing: this is a serious late-night spot, so don't plan on arriving before the early hours. $5–10.

The Cellar 685 Sutter St at Taylor, Theater District ☎415/441-5678. Brash, kitschy bar/club decorated with dozens of mirrors: there are slouchy booths where you can lounge and enjoy the music if you'd rather not dance.

DNA Lounge 375 11th St at Harrison, SoMa ☎415/626-1409. Changes its music style nightly, but draws the same young hipsters, a mixed gay-straight crowd. Downstairs is a large dancefloor, while the mezzanine is a comfy, sofa-packed lounge where you can chill. $15–20.

Hush Hush 496 14th St at Guerrero, Mission ☎415/241-9944. A great place to hang out or dance, this hidden bar has no sign outside; inside, there's a slightly older crowd, playing pool or dancing to nu-disco and classic 1970s funk, Wedesday to Saturday.

Justice League 628 Divisadero St at Hayes, Western Addition ☎415/289-2038. This club attracts big-name DJs, primarily for hip-hop and electronica nights: it's a groovy place to dance, thanks to the graffiti artists' murals on the walls. $12–15.

Liquid 2925 16th St at Capp, Mission ☎415/431-8889. You could walk right on by without noticing it, but this tiny, fun club is a rare place for serious dancing in the Mission's otherwise loungey bar district. It's a friendly, mixed gay-straight place, that's known for its liberal attitudes toward pot smoking on the premises. $5–10.

Skylark Bar 3089 16th St at Valencia, Mission ☎415/621-9294. Club-bar hybrid, with low lighting and plenty of booths, marred slightly by its yuppified clientele: in the week, it's more geared to drinking, while at weekends it's a full-scale dance-hall.

Sno-drift 1830 3rd St at 16th, China Basin ☎415/431-4766. Alpine ski lodge-themed club, designed by the team behind the *Red Room* (see

p.566) and the *Zodiac* lounge (p.568). Almost everything here is igloo-white, including an enormous padded vinyl bar. The restaurant attached serves pricey food: if you eat there, though, you'll be excused the cover charge. Music varies, but is mainly house. $15.

Space 550 550 Barneveld Ave at Oakdale, Hunter's Point ☎415/289-2001. This enormous warehouse club is known for its trancey, industrial dance programming: although it's a long way out, in an iffy part of town, serious clubbers will think it's worth the trek. $5–15.

Live music: rock, jazz, blues, and folk

San Francisco's music scene reflects the character of the city as a whole: laid back and not a little nostalgic. The options for catching live music are wide and the scene is consistently progressive, characterized by the frequent emergence of good young bands. San Francisco has never recaptured its crucial Sixties role, though in recent years the city has helped launch acid jazz (beat-heavy jazz that's become *de rigueur* dinner-party music across the country), a classic swing revival, and the East Bay pop-punk sound.

Bands are extremely easy to catch. Many restaurants offer live music, so you can eat, drink, and dance all at once and often with no cover charge; ordinary neighborhood bars regularly host groups, often for free, and there are any number of good and inexpensive small venues spread out across the city. Few fall into any particular camp, with most varying their bill throughout the week, and it can be hard to specify which of them cater to a certain music style.

What follows is a pretty comprehensive list of established venues, but be sure to check the weeklies or the local websites Ⓦwww.sfstation.com or Ⓦwww.bayarea.citysearch.com. Between the lot you should be able to find exhaustive listings of events in the city and Bay Area as a whole.

The large performance venues

Although San Francisco has a couple of major-league concert halls, bear in mind that some of the Bay Area's best large-scale venues, where the big names tend to play, are actually across the Bay in Oakland and Berkeley. See the relevant listings later in this chapter.

Bimbo's 365 Club 1025 Columbus at Chestnut, North Beach ☎415/474-0365, Ⓦwww.bimbos365 .com. Don't let the strange name put you off: the savvy booker here schedules underground European acts, kitschy tribute bands, and big-name rock acts in equal proportion – check for the latest listings. $20 and up.

The Fillmore Auditorium 1805 Geary St at Fillmore, Japantown ☎415/346-6000, Ⓦwww .thefillmore.com. A local landmark, the Fillmore was at the heart of the 1960s counterculture, master-minded by the legendary Bill Graham. It reopened in 1994 after several years' hiatus and is home now to rock and alt-rock touring acts. Cover varies.

The Great American Music Hall 859 O'Farrell St at Polk, Tenderloin ☎415/885-0750, Ⓦwww.

musichallsf.com. Starting out as a bordello in the 1900s, the Music Hall's fortunes soon went into decline. It was resuscitated in the 1970s and now the gorgeous venue plays host to a wide variety of rock, country, and world music acts. $10–20.

The Warfield 982 Market St at 6th, SoMa ☎415/775-7722, Ⓦwww.thefillmore.com/ warfield.asp. Smaller than its sister venue the Fillmore, with seating, and so better suited to more intimate shows. $25 and up.

Rock, blues, folk, and country

Biscuits and Blues 401 Mason St at Geary, Union Square ☎415/292-2583, Ⓦwww.biscuitandblue .citysearch.com Certainly a tourist trap, but this is still one of the best spots in town to catch classic New Orleans jazz and delta blues, accompanied by delicious, if overpriced, soul food. Show times vary. $5–15.

Boom Boom Room 1601 Fillmore St at Geary, Japantown ☏415/673-8000, ⊛www .boomboomblues.com Gritty venue in the Fillmore close to the Japan Center, that was owned by the late bluesman John Lee Hooker until he died in 2001: the dark low-rise building plays host to a fine selection of touring blues and funk artists. $5–12.

Bottom of the Hill 1233 17th St at Missouri, Mission ☏415/621-4455, ⊛www.bottomofthehill .com. The best place in town to catch up-and-coming or determinedly obscure rock acts. Frequently packed for shows, there's a small patio out back to catch a breath of fresh air or, on Sundays, have a bite of barbecue. $5–10.

Hotel Utah Saloon 500 4th St at Bryant, SoMa ☏415/421-8308, ⊛www.thehotelutahsaloon.com. Singer-songwriters take the stage at this small South of Market bar, dating back to 1908. $5–10.

Last Day Saloon 406 Clement St at 5th, Richmond ☏415/387-6343, ⊛www.lastdaysa-loon.com. A must-see for live music in the otherwise sleepy Richmond district, popular with nearby students. The line-up varies, with over-dependence on jangly pop and hippie rock, but it's always worth checking out. $5–10.

Lost and Found Saloon 1353 Grant Ave at Columbus, North Beach ☏415/675-5996. This neighborhood watering hole, once a Beatnik stronghold, now hosts live music on weekends, and the program's geared toward whatever will get the crowd on the dancefloor. $5–10.

The Make-Out Room 3225 22nd at Mission, Mission ☏415/647-2888, ⊛www.makeoutroom .com Run by the same team behind the *Latin American Club*, this small dark space is primarily a place to drink at the enormous mahogany bar, but there are regular performances by local indie bands on Sundays and Mondays. $6–10.

Tongue & Groove 2513 Van Ness Ave at Union, Cow Hollow ☏415/928-0404, ⊛www .tongueandgroovesf.com. This large venue has two spaces: the front is dominated by a stage, while the back room is loungier and more geared to drinking. The booker here is an A&R rep for Madonna's Maverick Record label so expect smart, edgy bands and unusual performers. $8–10.

Paradise Lounge 308 11th St at Folsom, SoMa ☏415/621-1912. Three stages vie for your attention at this enormous cornerstone of the 11th Street club district. If rock, punk, and country

aren't your thing, duck upstairs to play pool by the bar. $5–10.

Slim's 333 11th St at Folsom, SoMa ☏415/522-0333, ⊛www.slims-sf.com. Owned by local Boz Skaggs, what was once a blues bar is now a prime venue to catch an array of punk, alternative, and world music, played mostly by local bands. $12–17.

Jazz and Latin

Black Cat 501 Broadway at Kearny, North Beach ☏415/981-2233. A reincarnation of the famed 1960s nightspot is today an upscale supper club serenading a rather more straight-laced clientele with poetry readings or swing and acid jazz performances. $5; closed Sunday.

Blue Lamp 561 Geary St at Jones, Tenderloin ☏415/430-2160, ⊛www.bluelamp.com. Rather unfriendly looking hole-in-the-wall offers live blues, funk, and jam rock just a short walk from the hotel district. No cover.

Bruno's 2389 Mission St at 20th, Mission ☏415/648-7701, ⊛www.brunoslive.com. Like something from a Scorsese movie, this retro restaurant has an intimate live venue attached, filled with 1960s-style white-vinyl furniture surrounding a tiny stage. The music's a mixture of jazz and nu-school R&B: if you eat in the (rather average) restaurant, there's no cover charge. $5–7; closed Monday.

Café du Nord 2170 Market St at Sanchez, Castro ☏415/861-5016, ⊛www.cafedunord.com. Primarily a jazz club, this subterranean club (formerly a speakeasy) is a great place to enjoy cocktails: the varied booking provides constant surprises. $3–8.

Elbo Room 647 Valencia St at 17th, Mission ☏415/552-7788, ⊛www.elbo.com. The birthplace of acid jazz, a popular local variant that emphasizes a danceable groove over complex improvisation. Also hosts world-music performers. $4–7.

The Plough and Stars 116 Clement St at 2nd, Richmond ☏415/751-1122. The Irish expat community crams into this terrific pub for hearty pints of Guinness and live music six nights a week at 8.30pm. No cover.

The Ramp 855 China Basin at Illinois, China Basin ☏415/621-2378. A bayside restaurant serving up live salsa on summer Sunday afternoons: it closes at 10pm weeknights, 8.30pm weekends.

Red Devil Lounge 1695 Polk St at Clay, Polk Gulch ☏415/921-1695, ⊛www.reddevillounge .com. Competing with the *Elbo Room* for fans of acid jazz and funk, this neo-Goth lounge is kitschly decorated with gargoyles. The music, though, is

7

mainstream cool and it's a reliable option if you want to dance. $5–10.

Roccapulco 3140 Mission St at Cesar Chavez, Outer Mission ☎415/648-6611, ☻www.roccapulco.citysearch.com. Catering to the Mission's Latino population, this large club books salsa and Tejano music, including performers rarely heard in the US and big names like Celia Cruz. Wednesdays there

are salsa lessons, Thursdays are Latino hip-hop nights, while the live acts dominate Fridays and Saturdays. $8–15.

The Up & Down Club 1151 Folsom St at 7th, SoMa ☎415/626-2388. A mix of live and DJ-spun danceable grooves – there's usually jazz downstairs. It's co-owned by yoga-loving supermodel Christy Turlington. $5.

Classical music, opera, and dance

San Francisco has an excellent reputation for the **performing** arts – there are five major symphonies based in the Bay Area, for example. It's also the only city on the West Coast to have its own professional **opera** and **ballet** companies – even if some observers sniff that quantity doesn't always guarantee quality. During the summer months, look out for the free concerts in Stern Grove (at Nineteenth Avenue and Sloat Boulevard), where the symphony orchestra, opera, and ballet give open-air performances for ten successive Sundays (starting in June).

Concert halls

San Francisco Symphony Louise M. Davies Symphony Hall, 201 Van Ness Ave at Hayes, Civic Center ☎415/864-6000, ☻www.sfsymphony.org. The permanent home of the San Francisco Symphony Orchestra, which offers a year-round season of classical music and sometimes performances by other, often offbeat musical and touring groups. Established in 1909 as a small musical group, the orchestra rose to international prominence in the 1950s when it started touring and recording. Although not quite on a par with the New York Philharmonic or Chicago Symphony, the tenure of conductor Michael Tilson Thomas has catapulted it into the top half-dozen US orchestras. Prices obviously depend on the performance, but are marginally lower than either the opera or ballet, with the least expensive seats going for around $20 and bargain standby tickets available 2 hours before performances.

San Francisco Ballet War Memorial Opera House, 301 Van Ness Ave at Grove, Civic Center ☎415/864-3330, ☻www.sfballet.org. The city's ballet company, the oldest and third largest in the US, puts on an ambitious annual program

(Feb–May) of both classical and contemporary dance, and a Christmas production of *Nutcracker*. Founded in 1933, the ballet was the first American company to stage full-length productions of *Swan Lake* and *Nutcracker*. Tickets range upward from $30.

San Francisco Opera War Memorial Opera House, 301 Van Ness Ave at Grove, Civic Center ☎415/864-3330, ☻www.sfopera.org. The Opera House, designed by architect Arthur Brown Jr, the creator of City Hall and Coit Tower, makes a very opulent venue for the San Francisco Opera Association, which has been performing here since the building opened in 1932. Still probably the strongest of San Francisco's cultural trio, the Opera Association has a main season that runs from the beginning of September through the end of January, and its opening night is one of the principal social events on the West Coast. In addition, there is also a summer season during June and July. Tickets cost upwards of $20 – for which you do at least get supertitles. Standing room begins at a bargain $15, and 250 tickets are available (one per person) at 10.30am on the day of performance.

Theater

The majority of the city's **theaters** congregate downtown around the Theater District. Most aren't especially innovative (although a handful of more inventive fringe places are scattered in other parts of town, notably SoMa), but tickets are reasonably cheap – up to $30 a seat – and there's usually good availability. Check out the *Sunday Chronicle*'s "Pink Pages" to read up on the latest productions around town.

Most tickets can be purchased either through the individual theater's box offices or by calling **BASS** (☎415/478-2277). For last-minute bargains try the

Tix Bay Area booth inside Union Square garage, between Stockton and Powell streets (Tues–Thurs 11am–6pm, Fri & Sat 11am–7pm; ☎415/433-7827).

Downtown

American Conservatory Theater (ACT) Geary Theater, 415 Geary St at Taylor, Theater District ☎415/742-2228, ⊛www.act-sfbay.org. San Francisco's flagship theater company, the Tony Award-winning ACT puts on eight major plays each season. The city's best serious theater venue often has rush tickets available ninety minutes before the show.

Golden Gate Theater 1 Taylor St at Golden Gate Avenue and Market Street, Tenderloin ☎415/551-2000, ⊛www.bestofbroadway-sf.com. Originally constructed during the 1920s and recently restored to its former splendor, the Golden Gate's marble flooring, rococo ceilings and gilt trimmings make it one of San Francisco's most elegant theaters. It's a pity that the programs don't live up to the surroundings – generally a mainstream diet of Broadway musicals.

Lorraine Hansberry Theater 620 Sutter St at Mason ☎ 415/474-8800. The impressive mainstay of African-American theater in San Francisco. Traditional theater as well as contemporary political pieces and jazz/blues musical revues.

Orpheum Theater 11192 Market St at 8th, Tenderloin ☎ 415/551-2000, ⊛www .bestofbroadway-sf.com. Arguably the top local space, in terms of seating capacity and glitz, hosting big-name Broadway productions.

Stage Door Theater 420 Mason St ☎415/788-9453. Attractive, medium-sized turn-of-the-century theater, run by the American Conservatory Theater group.

Theatre on the Square 450 Post St at Powell, Union Square ☎415/433-9500, ⊛www.theatreon-thesquare.com. Converted Gothic theater with drama, musicals, comedy, and mainstream theater pieces.

Elsewhere

Beach Blanket Babylon *Club Fugazi*, 678 Green St at Powell, North Beach ☎415/421-4222. A local institution, this revue, based loosely on the story of Little Red Riding Hood, combines the silliness of a small-town pageant with the over-the-top tackiness of a Vegas revue. Camp and tacky, yes, but great fun. Tickets start at $25.

Intersection for the Arts 446 Valencia St at 16th, Mission ☎415/626-3311. Well-meaning, community-based group that tackles interesting productions in inadequate facilities.

Magic Theatre Fort Mason Center, Building D, Fort Mason ☎415/441-8822, ⊛www.magictheatre.org. The busiest and largest company after the ACT, and probably the most exciting, the Magic Theater specializes in the works of contemporary playwrights and emerging new talent; Sam Shepard traditionally premieres his work here.

New Conservatory Theater Center 25 Van Ness Ave at Market, Civic Center ☎415/861-8972, ⊛www.nctscf.org. This mid-size theater is known for its Pride season of gay-themed plays, as well as performances of musicals in concert. Tickets start at $20.

Theater Artaud 450 Florida St at Mariposa, Mission ☎415/621-7797, ⊛www.theaterartaud .org. Modern theater in a converted warehouse offering dance and theater performances, many less obscure than the theater's artsy name might imply.

Theater Rhinoceros 2926 16th St at S Van Ness, Mission ☎415/861-5079, ⊛www.therhino.org. The city's prime gay-oriented theater space actually has two spaces, hosting everything from raunchy revues to issues-based dramas.

Comedy

Comedians have always found a welcoming audience in San Francisco – after all, local political bigwig Tom Ammiano started out as a stand-up performer. Few of the comedians are likely to be familiar: as with any cabaret you take your chances, and whether you consider a particular club to be good will depend on who happens to be playing the week you go. You can expect to pay roughly the same kind of cover in most of the clubs ($7–15), and two-drink minimums are common. There are usually two shows per night, the first kicking off around 8pm and a late show starting at around 11pm. For bargains, check the press for "Open Mike" nights when unknowns and members of the audience get up and have a go; there's rarely a cover charge for these evenings and, even if the acts are diabolical, it can be a fun night out.

Comedy venues

Cobb's Comedy Club The Cannery, 2801 Leavenworth St at Beach, Fisherman's Wharf ☎415/928-4320. Pricey and usually full of tourists, but the standard of the acts is fairly consistent. Worth a look if everything else is booked up.

The Marsh 1062 Valencia at 21st, Mission ☎415/641-0235, ⓦwww.themarsh.org.

Successful alternative space hosting solo shows, many with a political bent.

The Punch Line 444 Battery St at Washington, Jackson Square ☎415/397-7573. Frontrunner of the city's "polished" cabaret venues, this place has an intimate, smoky feel that's ideal for downing expensive cocktails and laughing your head off. The club usually hosts the bigger names in the world of stand-up and is always packed.

Film

San Franciscans attend more **movies** than residents of any other city in America and there's a staggering assortment of current-release and repertory film houses, with programs that range from the latest general-release films to Hollywood classics, iconoclastic Sixties pieces, and a selection of foreign and art films. For screening times and locations of current-run films, call ☎415/777–FILM.

Cinemas

AMC Kabuki 8 Japan Center, 1881 Post St at Fillmore, Japantown ☎415/922-4AMC. Part of the Japan Center complex, this multiplex screens a mixture of indie and big-budget titles. Validated parking at the underground parking lot.

Artists' Television Access (ATA) 992 Valencia St at 21st, Mission ☎415/824-3890, ⓦwww.atasite .org. Nonprofit media center that puts on the city's most challenging barrage of film, video, and performance art, often with a political or psychosexual bent; or sometimes just trashy entertainment. Screenings Thurs–Sat.

The Castro Theater 429 Castro St at Market, Castro ☎415/621-6120. San Francisco's most beautiful movie house, offering a steady stream of reruns, art films, Hollywood classics, and (best of all) a Wurlitzer organ played between films by a man who rises up from below the stage.

Landmark's Embarcadero Cinema 1 Embarcadero Center at Sansome, Financial District ☎415/352-0810. A good choice for American, international, and some art films. Five screens, two with digital sound; free parking on weekends and evenings with valida-

tion, or just take the BART.

Four Star 2200 Clement St at 23rd, Richmond ☎415/666-3488, ⓦwww.hkinsf.com. Way out in the fog belt, but worth a visit for the interesting mix of Asian, international, and American culture films; two screens.

Landmark's Lumière 1572 California St at Polk, Polk Gulch ☎415/352-0810. Another opulent Spanish Revival art house, a bit run down but often with an interesting program of obscure art films as well as a select choice of current-release films.

The Red Vic 1727 Haight St at Cole, Haight-Ashbury ☎415/668-3994, ⓦwww.redvic-moviehouse.com. Friendly collective, housed in a room full of ancient couches where you can put your feet up and munch on organic popcorn.

The Roxie 3117 16th St at Valencia, Mission ☎415/863-1087, ⓦwww.roxie.com. An adventurous rep house and film distributor, the Roxie is one of the few theaters in the country willing to take a risk on documentaries and little-known foreign directors. Usually the risk pays off.

Film festivals

The San Francisco Film Festival, specializing in political and short films you wouldn't normally see, is held at the Kabuki eight-screen cinema, the Castro Theater, and the Pacific Film Archive in Berkeley (see p.602), at the end of April and first week or so of May. Tickets sell extremely fast and you'll need to book well in advance for all but the most obscure movies. If you know you're going to be in town, call ☎415/931-FILM or buy tickets on the Web at ⓦwww.sfiff.org. Just as popular is the Lesbian, Gay, and Transgender Film Festival, held in June at the Castro and other theaters. Call ☎415/703-8663 or check ⓦwww.frameline.org for program and ticket information.

Gay and lesbian San Francisco

San Francisco's reputation as a city of **gay celebration** is not new – in fact it may be a bit outdated. Though still considered by many to be the gay capital of the world, the gay community here has made a definite move from the outrageous to the mainstream, a measure of its political success. The exuberant energy that went into the posturing and parading of the 1970s has taken on a much more sober, down-to-business attitude, and these days you'll find more political activists organizing conferences than drag queens throwing parties. Nowadays San Franciscans appreciate and recognize the huge economic and cultural impact of gays on the city, and to be an openly gay politician or businessperson is not as much of an issue to locals as it would be anywhere else in the United States, making it easy to forget things were not always this way.

Socially, San Francisco's gay scene has also mellowed, though in what is an increasingly conservative climate in the city generally, gay parties, parades, and street fairs still swing better than most. Like any well-organized section of society, the gay scene definitely has its social season – see the events listing below for highlights. **Lesbian culture** flowered in the 1980s, but today, though women's club nights do exist, the scene is more in evidence in bookstores than bars. Many dykes have claimed Oakland for their own, though Bernal Heights and some areas of the Mission continue to be girl-friendly.

Details of gay accommodation, bars, and clubs appear below; mention of gay bookstores and theater and film venues are under the relevant headings throughout this chapter.

Gay and lesbian accommodation

Choose any hotel in San Francisco and a single-sex couple won't raise an eyebrow at check-in: some, like the *Queen Anne* and the *Archbishop's Mansion* (see above) attract equal numbers of gay and straight visitors. There are, however, a few places that especially cater to gay and lesbian travelers that we've singled out below.

24 Henry 24 Henry St at Sanchez, Castro ☎415/864-5686 or 1-800/900-5686, ⓦ www.24henry.com. This small blue-and-white home tucked away on a leafy residential street north of Market is a predominantly gay male guest house with five simple rooms, one with private bath. It makes a friendly bolthole from the cruisey Castro scene nearby. ❹

Inn on Castro 321 Castro St at Market, Castro ☎415/861-0321, ⓦ www.innoncastro2.com. This luxurious B&B is spread across two nearby houses. It has eight rooms and three apartments available, all of which are brightly decorated in individual styles and have private baths and phones. There's a funky lounge where you can meet other guests. Two-night minimum at weekends, three-night minimum on holidays. ❺

Monarch 1015 Geary St at Polk, Polk Gulch ☎415/673-5232 or 1-800/777-3210, ⓦ www.themonarchhotel.com. Large converted motel with nondescript, floral rooms that are clean if basic: a good base for exploring the bars of Polk Gulch. ❹

Noe's Nest 3973 23rd St, Noe Valley ☎415/821-0751. Seven-room bed and breakfast (six with private bath) on a quiet street in Noe Valley: all rooms have TV, VCR, and a private phone line. Lavish breakfasts are served each morning, and there's a hot tub, too. ❻

The Parker House 520 Church St at 18th, Castro ☎415/621-3222 or 1-888/520-7275, ⓦ www.parkerguesthouse.com. This converted Edwardian mansion is set in beautiful gardens and has a friendly vibe, thanks to its ample, large common areas: there's a sunny breakfast room and onsite sauna. ❻, ❺ without bath

The Renoir 45 McAllister St, at 7th, Civic Center ☎415/626-5200 or 1-800/576-3388, ⓦ www.renoirhotel.com. This wedge-shaped building is a historic landmark with 135 rooms that have recently been unexcitingly, if florally, refurbished. The superior rooms cost $20 more than standard – worth the extra if you can snag one of the oddly shaped large rooms at the building's apex. Especially popular during Gay Pride for its Market Street views along the parade route. ❺

California AIDS Hotline ☎415/863-2437. 24hr information and counseling.

Dignity 1329 7th Ave at Irving, Sunset ☎415/681-2491. Catholic worship and services.

Gay & Lesbian Medical Association ☎415/255-4547. Physician referral for gay and lesbian doctors.

Lesbian & Gay Freedom Band Info Line 1519 Mission St at 11th, SoMa/Mission ☎415/255-1355. Information on performances and how to join the band.

Lyon Martin Women's Health Services 1748 Market St at Gough, Suite 201, Hayes Valley ☎415/565-7667. Targets lesbian-bisexual-transgender community, but encourages all women to come for anonymous AIDS testing, gynecological care, pregnancy tests, counseling, and legal help. Nonprofit, and operating since 1979. Mon & Tues, Thurs & Fri 8.30am–5pm, Wed 11am–7pm.

Lyric Youth Talkline ☎415/863-3636. For gay and lesbian youth aged 23 and younger, discussion groups, movie nights, camping and sporting events, women's issues. Staffed Mon–Sat 6.30–9pm.

New Leaf 1853 Market St at Guerrero ☎415/626-7000. Outpatient mental health on a sliding fee scale.

Radical Women/Freedom Socialist Party New Valencia Hall, 1908 Mission St at 15th, Mission ☎415/864-1278. Socialist-feminist organization dedicated to building women's leadership and achieving full equality. Meetings, discussion groups, and poetry readings held on various issues: call for details.

San Francisco Sex Information ☎415/989-737. Free, anonymous, and accurate information. Staffed Mon–Fri 3–9pm, Sat 3–6pm.

Travel Alternatives Group ☎1-800/464-2987. Call to be routed to the nearest gay-friendly agent.

Information

The new **LGBT Community Center**, 1800 Market St at Octavia, Hayes Valley (☎415/865-5555, ⊛www.sfcenter.org), not only has plenty of resources at the first-floor information desk, but also regularly hosts performances by comedy and theater groups onsite – check the website or call for details. The **Golden Gate Business Association** promotes gay-owned businesses – check ⊛www.ggba.com for a list of members.

The *Lavender Pages*, a telephone-cum-resource book, is available at A Different Light (see p.581) and other gay bookstores. Otherwise, there are plenty of freesheets that provide entertainment and bar listings. For newspapers, check out the *San Francisco Spectrum*, a monthly community newsletter, as well as the better-known *Bay Times* and *Bay Area Reporter,* which has a thorough entertainment and reviews supplement. For nightlife, check the biweekly *Gloss*, or the weekly *Frontiers* (also online at ⊛www.frontiersweb.com). Alternatively, the website ⊛www.scum-online.com provides quirkier, more underground information.

Bars

San Francisco's **gay bars** are many and varied, ranging from cozy cocktail bars to no-holds-barred leather-and-chain hangouts. In the last few years, nearly every single lesbian bar has disappeared, with the notable exception of *Lexington Club* (see below). Otherwise, if you want exclusively female company you'll have to check out clubs that have lesbian nights. Many of the places in this section may turn up the music later and transform into mini-clubs: for hardcore dancing, though, check out "Clubs" below.

If you're tired of the gay bar circuit, check out Guerrilla Queer Bar (Ⓦwww.geocities.com/guerillaqueerbar), the mailing list for a roving monthly party that picks a straight bar (past candidates have included *XYZ* in the *W Hotel* and the *Edinburgh Castle* pub) and takes over with a mass queer invasion one evening.

Badlands 4131 18th St at Castro, Castro ℡415/626-9320, Ⓦwww.sfbadlands.com. Recently renovated, this video bar attracts a pretty, thirtysomething crowd and is usually packed at weekends. There's a wide selection of imported beer, and overall it's one of the less sceney places around the Castro.

Detour 2348 Market St at Castro, Castro ℡415/861-6053. The crowd here is young, buff, and cruisey, and oddly, the main floor is bisected by a chain link fence. There are go-go boys on Saturday and throbbing house DJs every night.

The Eagle Tavern 398 12th St at Harrison, SoMa ℡415/626-0880. This good, old-fashioned leather bar is particularly popular on Sundays, when it holds a late afternoon "beer bust" for charity.

Esta Noche 3079 16th St at Valencia, Mission ℡415/861-5757. A gay Latin drag bar, that's great fun and attracts a youngish, racially mixed clientele: there are shows nightly at 11.30pm, except on Sundays (7pm, 10.30pm, midnight).

Ginger's Trois 246 Kearny St at Bush, Financial District ℡415/989-0282. A charming, low-rent bar smack in the heart of downtown, with a group of diehard regulars who'll happily sing along with the showtunes occasionally played by the bartenders.

Hole in the Wall Saloon 289 8th St at Folsom, SoMa ℡415/431-4695. Formerly a rock'n'roll paradise, this divey bar is now part of the biker scene, and attracts hardcore, punky leather boys who want to play pool and pinball or hook up. Remember to dress accordingly, and don't be surprised to see an old man in diapers.

Lexington Club 3464 19th St at Lexington, Mission ℡415/863-2052, Ⓦwww.lexingtonclub .com. The only place in the city where the girls outnumber the boys (men must be accompanied by a woman to enter), this bustling lesbian bar attracts all sorts with its no-nonsense decor, friendly atmosphere, and excellent jukebox.

The Lone Star 1354 Harrison St at Tenth, SoMa ℡415/863-9999. One of the tamer biker bars in SoMa, the *Lone Star* attracts leather daddies, bears, cubs, and those who love them. It's large, friendly, and welcoming.

Martuni's 4 Valencia St at Market, Mission ℡415/241-0205, Ⓦwww.martunis.citysearch .com. This piano bar attracts a well-heeled, mid-

dle-aged crowd, all keen to sing along to classics from Judy, Liza, and Edith. There are regular open-mike evenings as well as a singles evening on Wed. Try a *martuni*, the signature cocktail, made from Bombay Sapphire gin and dry vermouth with a lemon twist.

Midnight Sun 4067 18th St at Castro, Castro ℡415/861-4186, Ⓦwww.midnightsunsf.com. Long, narrow video bar, always busy with well-dressed white boys checking out the movies shown on the monitors, as well as each other: it's not a place to strike up a casual conversation. The weekly showings of popular television programs are a big draw.

My Place 1225 Folsom St at 8th, SoMa ℡415/ 863-2329. Hardcore leather bar, sleazy and cruisey, with cheap drinks served to horny customers. There's a dark, smoky backroom.

Pendulum 4146 18th St at Castro, Castro ℡415/ 863-4441. Famous as the one place in the Castro that's popular among the black gay community, and there's a groovy, friendly atmosphere here. The women's night on Thursday, Alley Catz, is funky and great fun – plus there's no cover.

Pilsner Inn 225 Church St at Market, Castro ℡415/621-7058. The best neighborhood gay bar in the Castro, filled with a diverse, slightly older crowd playing pool and darts. There's a large, smoker-friendly patio out back, and a generally welcoming, open vibe.

Powerhouse 1347 Folsom St at Doré Alley, SoMa ℡415/861-1790. One of the prime pick-up joints in the city, this very cruisey old-school leather bar has plenty of convenient dark corners. The dress code (uniform, leather) is strictly enforced except on Thursday, which is underwear night.

Trax 1437 Haight St at Ashbury, Haight-Ashbury ℡415/864-4213, Ⓦwww.traxsf.com. The only gay bar in the Haight is a smoker's paradise, although it's been spiffed up slightly from its grungy heyday. There's a good mix of gays and straights, meaning it's much less cruisey than other bars.

Wild Side West 424 Cortland Ave at Wool, Bernal Heights ℡415/647-3099. Unpretentious, friendly lesbian pick-up joint, with a huge outdoor terrace – there are no heat lamps, though, so stay inside on a cold evening.

AIDS Candlelight Memorial March & Vigil (May) Procession from the Castro to Civic Center, commemorating all those who've died of AIDS (☎415/863-4676, ⓦwww.actupgg. org).

San Francisco LGBT Pride Parade (Late June) One of the largest Pride parades in the world – and also one of the longest (it can last up to four hours). Don't miss Pink Night, the evening when the Castro is virtually pedestrianized by thousands of revelers or the Dyke March that takes place on Friday night (☎415/864-3733, ⓦwww.sfpride.org).

GLBT Film Festival (June) Short films and features from amateurs and auteurs (☎415/703-8650, ⓦwww. frameline.org).

Up Your Alley Fair (Late July) Folsom Street Fair's little brother takes place on nearby Doré Alley: it's a more sex-driven event with fewer onlookers and plenty of S&M.

Folsom Street Fair (Late Sept) Hardcore leather fair, full of hairy-chested men in chaps. Surprisingly friendly and fun (☎415/861-3247, ⓦwww.folsomstreetfair.com).

Castro Street Fair (Oct) Food and craft stalls take over the Castro (☎415/467-3354, ⓦwww.castrostreetfair.org).

Clubs

Since the legendary *Club Townsend* (which was home to major gay parties like Club Q) closed in July 2002, there's been a void in queer-centric places to dance. Aside from the old favorites listed below, check local listings for up-to-date information and new venues for nights like Pleasuredome and Club Universe.

The Café 2367 Market St at Castro, Castro ☎415/861-3846. There's a DJ here seven nights a week, and for a long time, it was one of the few places to dance in the Castro, despite its postage stamp-sized dancefloor. The music's mainstream Hi-NRG and house, while the crowd is dominated by lesbians and their swishy gay male friends. There's still usually a long line at weekends, inspired no doubt by the free entrance.
Cat Club 1190 Folsom St at 8th, SoMa ☎415/431-3332. This dark, loud club is one of the lesbian hotspots of the city, mixing dancing and live performances. It's livelier the later you arrive. $5–10.
The EndUp 401 6th St at Harrison, SoMa ☎415/357-0827, ⓦwww.theendup.com. Open all night (though you can only drink until 2am), and attracting hardcore clubbers for after-hours dancing on its cramped dancefloor. If you want a break from the Beats, there's an outdoor patio with plen-

ty of seating. Club nights vary, but it's especially known for "Fag Fridays" (ⓦwww.fagfridays.com) for boys and "Kandy Bar" (ⓦwww.kandybar.com) for girls on Saturday. $5.
Liquid 2925 16th St at Capp, Mission ☎415/431-8889. This tiny, fun club is easy to miss as you walk by, but it's one of the city's best places to dance with a mixed, social gay-lesbian-straight crowd. Its best-known night is Monday for "Joy." Be aware that this is a grottier part of the Mission, so take care on the street. $2–10.
The Stud 399 Folsom St at 9th, SoMa ☎415/252-7883. Legendary gay club that's still as popular as ever, attracting a diverse, energetic and uninhibited crowd. Check out the fabulously freaky drag-queen cabaret at "Trannyshack" (Tues), or the younger alternative kids at "Reform Skool" (Thurs). "Sugar" on Saturday is one of the best underground gay dance nights in the city. $5–8.

Sex clubs

There are plenty of underground sex clubs and backrooms in bars across the city: those listed below are clean, secure, and promote safe sex.

7

SAN FRANCISCO AND THE BAY AREA | Gay and lesbian San Francisco

Eros 2051 Market St at Church, Castro ☎415/ 864-3767, ⓦwww.erossf.com. This clean, all-male sex club has a sauna and steam room and is open late most nights. $11.

Osento 955 Valencia St at 20th, Mission ☎415/ 282-6333, ⓦwww.osento.com. Women-only spa that's the closest the city comes to a lesbian bath-house. There's an indoor hot tub, as well as saunas and massages. Cover varies.

The Power Exchange 74 Otis St at Gough, Civic Center ☎415/487-9944, ⓦwww.powerexchange .com. Four-floor sexual playland, with themed rooms (leather, forest with tents, dancefloor). The top two floors are gay men only, the rest for men and women of every sexual orientation.

Shopping

Aside from the retail palaces around **Union Square** (including Macy's, Saks, and practically every major designer label), San Francisco's shopping scene is refreshingly edgy, peppered with one-off boutiques selling locally designed clothes and stylish homeware stores. There's also a brilliantly varied selection of **independent booksellers** (including the world-famous Beat poet favorite, City Lights) as well as terrific **music stores**, some focusing solely on rarities and others jammed with DJs rifling through the latest import 12" records from Europe. We've listed below some of the best shopping arteries in the city, as well as their main focus: it's worth remembering that, unlike many other American cities, stores in San Francisco close relatively early – 6pm Monday to Saturday and 5pm on Sunday isn't unusual – so start a major shopping expedition early in the day.

Shopping strips

Below we've given San Francisco's prime **shopping strips**, alphabetized according to the neighborhood in which each is situated – it's not an exhaustive list, as there are many other great places to browse, but should be useful for any shopaholic planning a day of retail therapy.

The Castro – Castro Street, between 17th and 19th streets & Market Street, between Castro and Church. Gay-oriented boutiques, clubwear, and shoes.

Cow Hollow – Union Street, between Steiner and Gough. Sweet if rather conservative boutiques (mostly for women), shoe stores, and cute home-wares.

The Haight-Ashbury – Haight Street, between Stanyan and Masonic. Clothing, especially vintage and secondhand.

Hayes Valley – Hayes Street, between Franklin and Laguna. Trendy but upscale, with edgy boutiques for men and women, as well as jewelry galleries and other gorgeous, high-end goodies.

Laurel Heights – Sacramento Street, between Arguello and Divisadero. Antique magnet of San Francisco, with vintage used clothes for women.

The Marina – Chestnut Street, between Broderick and Fillmore. Yuppified strip of health foods, wine shops, and women's clothing boutiques.

The Mission – Valencia Street, between 14th and 21st. The best choice for urban hipsters, with lots of used furniture and clothing stores, bookshops and avant garde designer gear.

North Beach – Grant Avenue between Filbert and Vallejo. Groovy boutiques, homewares, and divey cafés: one of the newest and freshest places to find cool clothes.

Bookstores

Unsurprisingly, for a city with such a rich literary history, San Francisco excels in terrific **specialty bookstores**: from the legendary City Lights in North Beach to the new literary hub in the Mission, home to some of the city's more energized – and politicized – bookstores. As for **secondhand booksellers**, there's a fine selection in the city, but rabid old book buyers should head across the Bay to Oakland and Berkeley for richer pickings (see p.603). Most bookstores tend to open every day, roughly 10am–8pm, though City Lights is open daily until midnight.

General bookstores

Books Inc 2251 Chestnut St at Pierce, The Marina ☎415/931-3663. Local chainlet of browsable bookstores, with several branches across the city and in the Bay Area: a standard selection, but a good alternative to the major names.

Borders Books and Music 400 Post St at Powell, Union Square ☎415/399-1633. Massive, emporium-style bookstore with some 160,000 books to chose from as well as CDs, videos, and software on four floors. There's also a café, popular with cruising singles, and a stage for performances and readings.

City Lights Bookstore 261 Columbus Ave at Broadway, North Beach ☎415/362-8193. Legendary bookstore, renowned as the first place in the country to stock only paperbacks and ground zero for the Beat era. Oddball and thoroughly browsable, where else could you find books filed under sections like "Stolen Continents" and "Anarchism"? Pity about the belligerent staff.

A Clean, Well Lighted Place for Books Opera Plaza, 601 Van Ness Ave at Golden Gate, Civic Center ☎415/441-6670. The stock here is now more mainstream and less impressively exhaustive than it once was, but it's worth checking out for the regular readings by authors.

Green Apple 506 Clement St at 6th Ave, Richmond ☎415/387-2272. Funky, browsable store with deft, eccentric touches like the regular section of "Books that will never be Oprah's picks." Not bargain prices, but a pleasure to rummage through the shelves. There's a smaller, less impressive music annex nearby.

Specialist and second-hand bookstores

Abandoned Planet Bookstore 518 Valencia at 16th, Mission ☎415/861-4695. Encouraging its customers to "Break the TV habit!" this eccentric and utterly San Francisco bookstore crams its black shelves with left-wing and anarchist volumes. A rebellious, oddball hold-out against the gentrification elsewhere on Valencia.

Black Oak Books 540 Broadway at Columbus Ave, North Beach ☎415/ 986-3872. Both new and used books together in a large, airily shambolic space; there's a particularly good selection of remaindered recent titles. Open until 11pm Sun–Thurs, midnight Fri–Sat.

A Different Light 489 Castro St at 18th, Castro ☎415/431-0891, ⊛www.adlbooks.com. Open 10am–10pm, this is a well-stocked bookshop featuring gay & lesbian titles, with an especially strong fiction section. Readings and events are held here regularly – check the website for up-to-date information.

Dog Eared Books 900 Valencia St at 20th, Mission ☎415/282-1901. Smallish corner bookstore with a snappy selection of budget-priced remainders as well as an eclectic range of secondhand titles, all in terrific condition. There's even one rack of low-priced secondhand CDs.

Forever After Books 1475 Haight St at Ashbury, Haight-Ashbury ☎415/431-8299. The windows of this store are blocked by the piles of accumulated paperbacks that have gradually grown up there for lack of space on the floor. Pick your way through mountains of haphazardly stocked books in this oddball, ramshackle store: it's worth rifling given the cheap prices.

Foto-Grafix Books 655 Mission St at 3rd, SoMa ☎415/495-7242. Formerly the in-house bookstore of the now-closed Ansel Adams Center, this store is now part of the Cartoon Art Museum and sells a smartly edited selection of photography, design, and art books, and cards.

Get Lost 1825 Market St at Valencia, Hayes Valley/Mission ☎415/437-0529. Tiny triangular travel book store, crammed with unusual titles alongside the standard guidebooks. It also stocks a decent assortment of maps and gear for the adventure traveler; the staff is especially helpful.

The Great Overland Bookstore Company 2848 Webster St at Union, Cow Hollow ☎415/351-1538. Cluttered with piles of books, this is a first-rate, old-fashioned store with mint-condition first-editions as well as cheap paperbacks. You can browse for hours listening to protest rock on the store's loudspeakers.

Kayo 814 Post St at Leavenworth, Theater District ☎415/749-0554. Glorious vintage paperback store, crammed with bargain classics including pulpy mysteries, sci-fi, and campy 1950s sleaze fiction. Closed Mon and Tues.

Kinokuniya 2nd floor, Japan Center, 1581 Webster St, Japantown ☎415/567-7625. Large stock of Japanese- and English-language books, but they really excel in art books.

Modern Times 888 Valencia St at 20th, Mission ☎415/282-9246. Hefty stock of Latin American literature and progressive political publications as well as small, but well-chosen selection of gay and lesbian literature and radical feminist magazines. Stages regular readings of authors' works.

Smoke Signals 2223 Polk St at Green, Polk Gulch ☎415/292-6025. Enormous newsstand stocking close to any magazine, domestic or foreign, that you can ask for.

Fashion

We've listed here a brief selection of the best **boutiques** in the city, selling funky clothes and groovy accessories. Don't miss the chance to trawl through a few thrift stores, either – San Francisco's a great place to pick up a vintage bargain.

Aaardvark's Odd Ark 1501 Haight St at Ashbury ☎415/621-3141. Haight-Ashbury outpost of this Californian thrift-store chain: expect plenty of glitz, glam, and day-glo colors, as well as a wide selection of vintage jeans.

ab fits 1519 Grant Ave at Union, Telegraph Hill ☎415/982-5726. Imaginative men's and women's boutique, offering directional clothing at moderate prices by the likes of J. Lindeberg and Rebecca Taylor as well as jewelry from local designer Janine Payer.

Clothes Contact 473 Valencia St at 16th, Mission ☎415/621-3212. Where the punkers come for bomber jackets. Pay by the pound ($8), as weighed at checkout on a vintage scale: be prepared to rummage and rifle through the endless racks, divided solely by type (shirt, coat, dress).

John Fluevog 1697 Haight St at Cole, Haight-Ashbury ☎415/436-9784. Clunky, chunky shoes for men and women; many designs are witty, clog-like shapes, which are fun if a little dated.

HRM Boutique 924 Valencia St at 20th, Mission ☎415/642-0841. Local labels HRM (for men) and House of Hengst (for women) are made and sold onsite at this boutique, with prices starting around $50. Menswear is simple, smart, and a little retro; while the womenswear is wittier and weirder, featuring hooded cardigans with built in-bunny ears.

Kweejibo Clothing Co. 541 Valencia St at 16th St, Mission ☎415/552-3888. This store sells laconic, ironically retro shirts for men in two fits (boxy or tailored) and dozens of fabrics. Named after an obscure reference to the *Simpsons* cartoon series; it's just a pity that the shrug-happy staff lacks Bart's sense of humor.

Levi's 300 Post St at Stockton, Union Square ☎415/501-0100. Four levels of jeans, tops, and jackets set against a thumping backdrop of club music. This flagship offers the Levi's "Original Spin" service, where customers can order customized denim, although many of the funkier offerings here (like a bath in which you could sit until your jeans had shrunk to fit) have been removed. Since this stocks the entire Levi's line, it carries edgier pieces in the Red line as well as retro-inspired Western wear.

Paolo Iantorno 524 Hayes St at Laguna, Hayes Valley ☎415/552-4580. Don't tell anyone but your best friends about this gem: designer Iantorno produces a limited edition (20–25 pairs) of his own men's and women's shoe designs in Italy, then sells them from his two stores here. Prices hover around $200, and every style is edgy but wearable. Branch at 1971 Sutter St, Fillmore ☎415/885-5701.

Retro Fit Vintage 910 Valencia St at 20th, Mission ☎415/550-1530. Poppy, kitschy selection of smart vintage clothes: don't expect bargains, but well worth it for a spot-on shirt or just-right jacket. Check out the DIY vintage tees: pick a style then flick through an enormous binder filled with retro transfers to customize the shirt, starting at $18.

Rolo 21 & 25 Stockton St at Market, Union Square ☎415/989-7656. There are five outposts of this funky retailer across the city selling sexy clothes for boys and girls by the likes of Miss Sixty and G-Star. Don't miss the outlet location in SoMa, where markdowns are up to 80 percent. Branches: 450 Castro St at Market, Castro ☎415/626-7171; 545 Castro St at 18th, Castro ☎415/864-0505; 2351 Market St at Castro, Castro ☎415/431-4545; 1301 Howard St at 9th, SoMa ☎415/861-1999; 535 Castro St at 19th, Castro ☎415/864-0505.

Subterranean Shoe Room 877 Valencia St at

20th, Mission ☎415/401-9504. Sneaker heaven. The front room holds classic styles form Nike, Asics, and Adidas; while the backroom stocks a few secondhand pairs as well as a seasonal selection of new designs. Great for retro bags and vegan athletes – animal-free shoes are marked with a "V."

Wasteland 1660 Haight St at Belvedere, Haight-Ashbury ☎415/863-3150. Smart, high-end vin-tage selection, sorted by style and color: you'll pay for the ease of browsing, but it's one of the best places to find top condition, fashionable vintage.

Worn Out West 582 Castro St at 19th, Castro ☎415/431-6020. Gay secondhand cowboy gear – a trip for browsing, and if you're serious about getting some Wild West kit, this is the least expensive place in town to pick out a good pair of boots, stylish Western shirts, and chaps.

Food and drink

Be sure to try such **local specialties** such as Boudin's sourdough bread (see p.557), Gallo salami, and Anchor steam beer – all of which are gourmet treats. If you're looking for everyday essentials, there are supermarkets across the city, including several branches of Safeway – the large, cruisey outpost on Market Street in the Castro is the most convenient for downtown. California alcohol laws are liberal: most stores carrying food sell alcohol too, provided you show ID proving you're at least 21 years of age.

Andronico's Market 1200 Irving St at 14th Ave, Sunset ☎415/753-0403. The California gourmet's answer to Safeway. Pricey but gorgeous produce: microbrews, good wine, craft breads, fancy cheeses, an olive bar, and a pretty good deli. Not the cheapest, but way better quality than your average supermarket.

Artisan Cheese 2413 California St at Steiner, Pacific Heights ☎415/929-8610. Gourmet cheese store that sells locally produced tangy cheeses as well as imported specials from Britain and France.

Castro Village Wine Co. 4121 19th St at Castro, Castro ☎416 /864-4411. Low-key, laid-back neighborhood winery at the heart of the Castro: prices are reasonable and the selection (especially of local wines) is enormous.

D & M Wine & Liquor Co. 2200 Fillmore St at Sacramento, Pacific Heights ☎415/346-1325. Great selection of Californian wines, but located as they are in Pacific Heights, their specialty is champagne; bargains abound.

Good Life Grocery 488 Cortland Ave at Andover, Bernal Heights ☎415/648-3221. There's a vast selection of organic or locally grown produce at this Bernal Heights gourmet grocery. Branch at 1524 20th St at Missouri, Potrero Hill ☎415/282-9204.

The Jug Shop 1567 Pacific Ave at Polk, Pacific Heights ☎415/885-2922. The Jug Shop is famous for its cheap Californian wines, but it also has more than 200 varieties of beer that are similarly well-priced. It's also known for stocking an interesting range of New World wines.

Molinari's 373 Columbus Ave at Vallejo, North Beach ☎415/421-2337. Bustling veteran North Beach deli, jammed to the rafters with Italian goodies both familiar and exotic. Pick the bread of your choice and order a sandwich to go.

PlumpJack Wines 3201 Fillmore St at Greenwich, Cow Hollow ☎415/346-9870. If you're looking for an obscure Californian vintage for an enophile relative, this is the place to come – it has an enormous, exhaustive selection of wines from across the state.

The Real Food Company 3060 Fillmore St at Filbert, Cow Hollow ☎415/567-6900. Smallish, artsy grocery store selling potions and vitamins alongside health foods. Excellent gourmet meat counter and whole-wheat pastries: grab a sandwich and sit outside on the terrace at one of the wrought-iron picnic tables.

Yum 1750 Market St at Gough, Hayes Valley ☎415/626-9001. Irresistible and fun hangar-like grocery store, whose slogan is "Have you played with your food today?" Gourmet selections of cookies are especially delicious and the friendly staff will let you sample most items before you buy. Head to the back of the store for its best feature: refrigerators filled with a vast selection of sodas from across the world.

Health and Beauty

For more information on drugstores, including those open 24 hours, see "Listings," on p.586.

Body Time 2072 Union St at Webster, Cow Hollow ⊤415/922-4076. Though this Bay Area-born company sold the original name to the UK-based Body Shop, they still put out a full range of aromatic natural bath oils, shampoos, and skin creams, and will custom-scent anything.
Branches: 1932 Fillmore St at Pine, Pacific Heights ⊤415/771-2431 and 1465 Haight St at Ashbury, Haight-Ashbury ⊤415/551-1070.
Common Scents 3920 24th St at Sanchez, Mission ⊤415/826-1019. Essential oils and bath salts, as well as hair and skincare products, stocked in bulk and sold by the ounce. They'll refill your empties.
Oui, Three Queens 225 Gough St at Oak, Hayes Valley ⊤415/621-6877. This tiny, cartoonish store produces custom-blended cosmetics, including lipsticks, at reasonable prices. The larger-than-life staff will make the process as well as the product utterly memorable, and the baroque, bejewled space is glorious.
Reflect 335 Powell St at Post, Union Square ⊤415/834-0932. Brick-and-mortar outpost of the online beauty retailer, offering customised cosmetics and lotions at affordable prices.
Scarlet Sage Herb Company 1173 Valencia St at 22nd, Mission ⊤415/821-0997. Organic herbal apothecary selling tinctures and treatments made from more than 300 herbs, as well as scented candles and bath oils: you can even arrange a tarot reading here.

Record stores

There are outposts of all the major **record stores** like Tower and Virgin in San Francisco but it's with its specialty stores that the city really shines: from old-school soul on vinyl to European 12" imports for local DJs, there are some superb **independent** and **collectors'** stores. And in Amoeba Records, Haight-Ashbury can lay claim to one of the best places to browse and buy music anywhere in the country.

Amoeba Records 1855 Haight St at Stanyan, Haight-Ashbury ⊤415/831-1200. This big sister to Berkeley's renowned emporium is one of the largest used-music retailers in America. Divided between new and used CDs, this massive warehouse space hums with bargain hunters rifling through an encyclopedic selection of modern music. Don't be put off by its rip-off location in the heart of the Haight: this is a treasure trove for any music fan. Branch at 2455 Telegraph, Berkeley ⊤510/549-1125.
Aquarius Records 1055 Valencia St at 21st, Mission ⊤415/647-2272. Friendly, ramshackle record store with hip, friendly staff: there's an emphasis on less mainstream music, including experimental, folk, and world. Store devotees can even buy logo'd underwear.
BPM 573 Hayes St at Laguna, Hayes Valley ⊤415/487-8680. One of the top DJ record stores in the city, with the latest UK imports from top-name British DJs and masses of flyers for upcoming events.
CD & Record Rack 3987 18th St at Castro, Castro ⊤415/552-4990. Castro emporium with a brilliant selection of dance music including a few Seventies 12" singles. The accent is definitely on stuff you can dance to.
Compound Records 597 Haight St at Steiner, Lower Haight ⊤415/864-8309. Throbbing, chic DJ-aimed store, known for its cutting edge selection of drum'n'bass and 2 Step, much of it imported from the UK.

Discolandia 2964 24th St at Mission, Mission ⊤415/826-9446. Join the snake-hipped groovers looking for the latest in salsa and Central American sounds in this Mission outlet.
Flat Plastic Sound 24 Clement St at 2nd, Richmond ⊤415/386-5095. Although this place claims to specialize in classical music, it's also known for its attentive, knowledgeable staff that can help customers (many of whom are local DJs) looking for obscure retro vinyl. Recommended.
Groove Merchant Records 687 Haight St at Pierce, Lower Haight ⊤415/252-5766. Come here for secondhand soul, funk, and jazz: the owner's passionate and knowledgeable, so don't be afraid to ask questions.
Hear Music 1314 Howard St at 9th, SoMa ⊤415/487-1822. Amazing selection of world music and indies, with dozens of listening stations.
Medium Rare 2310 Market St at Noe, Castro ⊤415/255-7273. Tiny store is crammed with CDs, ranging from camp classics like Peggy Lee and other Fifties cocktail lounge singers to throbbing hi-NRG stars like Donna Summer.
Mikado 1737 Post St (Japan Center), Japantown ⊤415/922-9450. Enormous Japanese record store sprawled across three units of the Japan Center: the staff will let you watch DVDs before you buy on the instore TV set and headphones.
Musica Latina/American Music Store 2653 Mission St at 22nd, Mission ⊤415/283-6033. Mission store selling music from all over the Latino

world, especially South America.

Recycled Records 1377 Haight St at Masonic, Haight-Ashbury ☎415/626-4075. Good all-round store, with a decent selection of music publications, American and imported.

Record Finder 258 Noe St at Market, Castro ☎415/431-4443. One of the best independents, with a range as broad as it's absorbing.

Virgin Megastore 2 Stockton at Market St, Union Square ☎415/397-4525. Three floors packed with music in a wide variety of styles. The third floor has a good stock of current, popular books, videos, and a café with windows overlooking Market Street.

Taiyodo Record Shop 1737 Post St (Japan Center), Japantown ☎415/885-2818. One of several record stores in the mall selling the latest releases by Japanese singers, whether bubblegum pop or Asian alt rock. Also great for hard-to-find *anime* DVDs.

Specialty stores

We've included here a variety of fun gift stores, funky offbeat outlets selling everything from vedic crystals to vibrators.

Flight 001 525 Hayes St at Octavia, Hayes Valley ☎415/487-1001. This sleek, futuristic travel store sells books, funky accessories (including chunky, dayglo luggage tags and all-in-one shaving kits), and dapper carry-on bags. The place to stock up on sundries if you only travel first class – or want to act like it.

Fredericksen Hardware 3029 Fillmore at Union, Cow Hollow ☎415/292-2950. Since 1896, this store has been selling everything from old clocks to kitchen gadgets – comprehensive, if not cheap.

Good Vibrations 1210 Valencia St at 23rd, Mission ☎415/974-8980. Gloriously sexy store, run by a co-op of men and women, that's designed to destigmatize sex shops and make browsing fun and comfortable for men, women, and couples. It's packed with every imaginable sex toy, plus racks of erotica and candy store-style jars of condoms. The co-op recently branched out into producing its own erotic videos in addition to the books it already publishes under the Down There Press imprint; all that, plus an onsite vibrator museum. Note that Good Vibrations is scheduled to

move to a larger location soon, so call ahead to check.

Happy Trails 1615 Haight St at Clayton, Haight-Ashbury ☎415/431-7232. Girlier and more inventive than most kitsch emporia, this massive trinket shop sells clothes and gimmickry as well as all the fixings to host your own retro Tiki bar. Browse slowly, or you'll miss things.

Lost Weekend Video 1034 Valencia St at Hill, Mission ☎415/643-3373. Video shop that's perfect for homesick Brits or Anglophiles, with a huge BBC section.

Mom's Bodyshop 1408 Haight St at Ashbury, Haight-Ashbury ☎415/864-MOMS. Tattoos for those who want to go home with a permanent souvenir. Large selection of Chinese, Celtic, and Tibetan scripts.

Psychic Eye 301 Fell St at Gough, Hayes Valley ☎415/863-9997. Pick up the roots and herbs you need to cast spells, or browse the books on ancient sexual positions. This is an enormous store packed with psychic paraphernalia: it's upscale and decidedly unhippie-ish, with prices to match.

Listings

American Express 455 Market St at 1st, Financial District (Mon–Fri 9am–5.30pm, Sat 10am–2pm; ☎415/536-2600). Also at 311 9th Ave at Clement, Richmond (Mon–Fri 9am–5pm; ☎415/221-6760).

Baby-sitting Bay Area Child Care (Mon–Wed 9.30am–6pm, Thurs–Sat 9.30am–8pm; ☎650/991-7474).

Car rental All the major firms have branches in the airport. Here we've listed their offices in town: Alamo, 687 Folsom St at 3rd, SoMa (☎415/882-9440); Avis, 675 Post St at Jones, Theater District (☎415/885-5011); Dollar, 364 O'Farrell St at Taylor, Theater District (☎415/771-5300); Enterprise, 1133

Van Ness Ave at Post, Tenderloin (☎415/441-3369); Hertz, 433 Mason St at Post, Union Square (☎415/771-2200); Reliable, 349 Mason St at Geary, Union Square (☎415/928-4414).

Children San Francisco is very much a place for adults – more so than, say, LA, where Disneyland and Universal Studios are major attractions. However, if you do have children with you, good options include the educational Exploratorium in the Marina as well as the Steinhart Aquarium in Golden Gate Park. There's also a merry-go-round and children's play area in Golden Gate Park that's a pleasant place to spend a sunny afternoon.

Consulates UK, 1 Sansome St at Market, Financial District (Mon–Fri 8.30am–5pm; ☎415/617-1300); Ireland, 100 Pine St at Front, Financial District (Mon–Fri 10am–noon, 2–3.30pm; ☎415/392-4214); Australia, 625 Market St at Montgomery, Financial District (Mon–Fri 8.45am–1pm, 2–4.45pm; ☎415/536-1970); New Zealand, One Maritime Plaza, Suite 400, Embarcadero (appointment only; ☎415/399-1255); Germany, 1960 Jackson St at Gough, Pacific Heights (Mon–Fri 9am–noon; ☎415/353-0300).

Dental treatment For a free referral to the nearest dentist, call the national Dental Society Referral Service (☎ 415/421-1435 or 1-800/511-8663).

Disabled visitors Steep hills aside, the Bay Area is generally considered to be one of the most barrier-free cities around, and physically challenged travelers are well catered for. Most public buildings have been modified for disabled access, all BART stations are wheelchair-accessible, and most buses have lowering platforms for wheelchairs – and, usually, understanding drivers. For more information, contact the Independent Living Resource Center (☎415/543-6222, ⓦwww.freed.org).

Drugstores Walgreens 24-hr pharmacies 498 Castro St at 18th, Castro (☎415/861-6276) or 3201 Divisadero St at Lombard, Marina (☎415/931-6415).

Ferries Golden Gate Ferry, commute-hours to Sausalito and Larkspur in Marin County, leaves from the Ferry Building, east end of Market Street (☎415/923-2000, ⓦwww.goldengate.org); Blue and Gold Fleet bay ferries to Sausalito, Tiburon, Vallejo, and the Alcatraz Island tour, from Pier 41 and 39, Fisherman's Wharf (info ☎415/773-1188, tickets ☎415/705-5555, ⓦwww.blueandgoldfleet.com).

Hospitals The San Francisco General Hospital, 1001 Potrero Ave at 23rd, Potrero Hill (☎415/206-8000 or 206-8111 emergency), has a 24-hr emergency walk-in service and rape treatment center (☎415/821-3222). Castro-Mission Health Center, 3850 17th St at Prosper, Mission (☎415/487-7500), offers a drop-in medical service with charges on a sliding scale depending on income, plus free contraception and pregnancy testing. California Pacific (formerly Davies) Medical Center, Castro and Duboce streets, Lower Haight (☎415/565-6060), has 24-hr emergency care and a doctors' referral service. Haight-Ashbury Free Clinic, 558 Clayton St at Haight, Haight-Ashbury (Mon 1–9pm, Tues & Wed 9am–9pm, Thurs & Fri 1–5pm; ☎415/487-5632), provides a general health care service with special services for women and detoxification, by appointment only.

Internet There's usually access at the hostels listed in the "Accommodation" section, but there's often a wait to get on a machine; likewise, the Public Library has 15 minutes' free access, often with a long wait. If you want a cup of coffee while surfing, there's free access with a purchase at *Caffè Sapore*, 790 Lombard St at Taylor, North Beach (☎415/626-4700), or *701 Café*, Yerba Buena Center for the Arts, 701 Mission St at 3rd, SoMa (☎415/243-0930). Otherwise, the following places all offer $3/per 20 mins and $7 per hr rates: *Blue Danube*, 306 Clement St at 5th, Richmond (☎415/221-9041), *Café International*, 508 Haight St at Fillmore, Lower Haight (☎415/552-7390), *Pendragon Bakery*, 400 Hayes St at Gough, Hayes Valley (☎415/552-7017), and *Yakkety Yak*, 679 Sutter St at Mason, Theater District (☎415/351-2090)). Finally, if you have your own laptop, you can plug into a phone line for a fee at the chic café *Circadia*, 2727 Mariposa St at Bryant, Mission (☎415/552-2649).

Legal advice Lawyer Referral Service, 465 California St at Montgomery, Financial District (Mon–Fri 8.30am–5.30pm; ☎415/989-1616).

Passport and visa office US Dept of Immigration, 630 Sansome St at Washington, Jackson Square (☎1-800/375-5283).

Post office You can collect general delivery mail (bring your ID) from the main post office, 101 Hyde St at Fulton, Civic Center (Mon–Fri 8.30am–5.30pm, Sat 10am–2pm; ☎1-800/275-8777), but letters will only be held for ten days before being returned to sender, so make sure there's a return address on the envelope. If you're receiving mail at someone else's address, it should include "c/o" and the regular occupant's name; otherwise it too is likely to be returned. San Francisco's two main post offices, with telephone and general delivery facilities, are at Sutter Street Station, 150 Sutter St at Montgomery, Financial District (Mon–Fri 8.30am–5pm), and Rincon Finance Station, 180 Steuart St at Mission, SoMa (Mon–Fri 7am–6pm, Sat 9am–2pm).

Public library Civic Center, 100 Larkin St at Grove (☎415/557-4400, ⓦwww.sfpl.lib.ca.us). Mon & Sat 10am–6pm, Tues–Thurs 9am–8pm, Fri noon–6pm, Sun noon–5pm.

Rape Crisis Center and Hotline (☎415/647-7273). 24-hr switchboard.

Religious Services Grace Cathedral on Nob Hill at 1051 Taylor St has an Episcopalian (Anglican) congregation (☎415/749-6300, ⓦwww.gracecathedral.org). Catholics can worship at St Mary's Cathedral, 600 California St at Grant (☎415/288-3800, ⓦwww.oldsaintmarys.org). The grandest synagogue is Congregation Emanu-El, 2 Lake St at

Arguello Blvd, at the eastern edge of the Richmond district by the Presidio (☏415/751-2535). **Sports** Advance tickets for all Bay Area sports events are available through Tickets.com (☏510/762-2277, ⓦwww.tickets.com) as well as from the teams themselves. **Baseball**: The San Francisco Giants play in the new Pac Bell Ballpark where homeruns over the rightfield fence will splash into the Bay (☏415/972-2000, ⓦwww.sfgiants.com). The Giants' East Bay counterparts, the Oakland's A's, play at the usually sunny Oakland Coliseum (☏510/638-0500, ⓦwww.oaklandathletics.com). Ticket prices range from $6 for bleacher seats to $125 for a field-side box, but promotions, like Wednesday Dollar Days, make seeing a baseball game the cheapest major sports event in town. **Basketball**: The Golden State Warriors play at the Oakland Arena (☏510/986-2222, ⓦwww.warriors.com). **Football**: The San Francisco 49ers appear at blustery 3COM Park on Candlestick Point, south of town (☏415/656-4900, ⓦwww.sf49ers.com).

Tickets start at $50 and are almost impossible to come by. The boisterous Oakland fans don silver and black to root on their Raiders, who knock helmets at the Coliseum. Tickets are also around $50, but are almost always available – call Tickets.com or check ⓦwww.raiders.com. **Ice hockey**: The Bay Area's newest sports team is the San Jose Sharks (☏ 1-800/888-2736, ⓦwww.sjsharks.com), based at their own arena in the South Bay, and tickets start at $16.

Suicide Crisis Hotline ☏415/781-0500. 24 hours.

Tax Sales tax is added to virtually everything you buy in a store, save for food, but isn't part of the marked price. In San Francisco and the East Bay the sales tax is 8.5 percent; hotel tax will add fourteen percent to your bill.

Telegrams Western Union has numerous locations around the Bay Area; call ☏1-800/325-6000 or check ⓦwww.westernunion.com to find the nearest.

The Bay Area

Of the six million people who make their home in the San Francisco **Bay Area**, only a lucky one in eight lives in the actual city of San Francisco. Everyone else is spread around one of the many less-renowned cities and suburbs that ring the Bay, either down the Peninsula or across one of the two impressively engineered bridges that span the chilly waters of the world's most exquisite natural harbor. There's no doubt about the supporting role these places play in relation to San Francisco – always "the city" – but each has a distinctive character and contributes to the range of people and landscapes that makes the Bay Area one of the most desirable places in the US to live or to visit.

Across the steel Bay Bridge, eight miles from downtown San Francisco, the **East Bay** is home to the lively, left-leaning cities of **Oakland** and **Berkeley**, which together have some of the best bookstores and restaurants, and most of the live music venues, in the greater Bay Area. The weather's generally much sunnier and warmer here too, and it's easy to reach by way of the BART trains that race under the Bay. The remainder of the East Bay is contained in Contra Costa County, which includes the short-lived early state capital of California, **Benicia**, as well as the former homes of writers John Muir and Eugene O'Neill.

South of the city, the **Peninsula** holds some of San Francisco's oldest and most upscale suburbs, spreading down through the computer-rich **Silicon Valley** and into **San Jose** – California's fastest-growing city, and now a larger one in both square mileage and population than San Francisco – though apart from a few excellent museums, there's not a lot to see. To the west, however, the **beaches** are excellent – sandy, clean, and uncrowded – and there's a couple of youth hostels in old lighthouses perched on the edge of the Pacific.

For some of the most beautiful land and seascapes in California, cross the Golden Gate Bridge or ride a ferry across the Bay to **Marin County**, a mountainous peninsula that's half wealthy suburbia and half unspoiled hiking country, with **redwood forests** rising sheer out of the thundering Pacific Ocean. A range of 2500-foot peaks divides the county down the middle, separating the yacht clubs and plush bay-view houses of **Sausalito** and **Tiburon** from the nearly untouched wilderness that runs along the Pacific Coast, through Muir Woods and the **Point Reyes National Seashore**. North of Marin County, at the top of the Bay, and still within an hour's drive of San Francisco, the Wine Country regions of the Sonoma and Napa valleys make an excellent day-trip; they're detailed in "Northern California," beginning on p.707.

The East Bay

The largest and most-traveled bridge in California, the **Bay Bridge** connects downtown San Francisco to the East Bay, part graceful suspension bridge and part heavy-duty steel truss. Built in 1933 as an economic booster during the Depression, the bridge is made from enough steel cable to wrap around the earth three times. Completed just seven months before the more famous (and better-loved) Golden Gate, it works a lot harder for a lot less respect: a hundred million vehicles cross the bridge each year, though you'd have to search hard to find a postcard of it. Local scribe Herb Caen dubbed it "the car-strangled spanner," a reflection of its often-clogged lanes. Indeed, the bridge's only claim to fame – apart from the much-broadcast videotape of its partial collapse during the 1989 earthquake – is that **Treasure Island**, where the two halves of the bridge meet, hosted the 1939 World's Fair. During World War II, the island became a Navy base, which, pending post-Cold War closures, it remains; just inside the gates there's a small **museum** (daily 10am–3pm; free) with pictures of the Fair amid maritime memorabilia. The island also offers great views of San Francisco and the Golden Gate so various plans are afoot to develop it as a tourist destination.

The Bay Bridge empties into **Oakland**, a hard-working, blue-collar city that is at the heart of the East Bay. The city traditionally earned its livelihood from shipping and transportation services, as evidenced by the enormous cranes in the massive Port of Oakland, but is in the beginning stages of a renaissance as it lobbies to attract businesses and workers from the information technology industry. Oakland spreads north along wooded foothills to **Berkeley**, an image-conscious university town that looks out across to the Golden Gate and collects a mixed bag of pinstriped Young Republicans, much-pierced dropouts, ageing 1960s radicals, and Nobel prize-winning nuclear physicists in its cafés and bookstores.

Berkeley and Oakland blend together so much as to be virtually the same city, and the hills above them are topped by a twenty-mile string of **regional parks**, providing much-needed fresh air and quick relief from the concrete grids below. The rest of the East Bay is filled out by Contra Costa County, a huge area that contains some intriguing, historically important waterfront towns – well worth a detour if you're passing through on the way to the Wine

Country region of the Napa and Sonoma valleys – as well as some of the Bay Area's most inward-looking suburban sprawl. Curving around the **North Bay** from the oil-refinery landscape of Richmond, and facing each other across the narrow **Carquinez Strait**, both **Benicia** and **Port Costa** were vitally important during California's first twenty years of existence after the 1849 Gold Rush; they're now strikingly sited but little-visited ghost towns. In contrast, standing out from the soulless dormitory communities that fill up the often baking hot **inland valleys**, are the preserved homes of an unlikely pair of influential writers: the naturalist John Muir, who, when not out hiking around Yosemite and the High Sierra, lived most of his life near **Martinez**, and playwright Eugene O'Neill, who wrote many of his angst-ridden works at the foot of **Mount Diablo**, the Bay Area's most impressive peak.

Arrival

You're most likely to be staying in San Francisco when you visit the East Bay, though it is as convenient and sometimes better value to fly direct to **Oakland Airport** (☎510/577-4015, automated flight info ☎1-800/992-7433, ⓦwww.oaklandairport.com), particularly if you're coming from elsewhere in the US. All major domestic airlines serve the facility, which is less crowded and more desirable than its San Francisco counterpart. It's an easy trip from the airport into town. The **AirBART** shuttle van (every 15min; $2; ☎510/577-4294) runs to the Coliseum BART station, from where you can hop on **BART** to Berkeley, Oakland, or San Francisco. There are numerous door-to-door **shuttle buses** that run from the airport to East Bay stops, such as Bridge Airporter Express (☎510/481-1050 or 1-800/300-1661); the fare to Oakland is $16 and expect to pay around $30 into San Francisco. **Taxis** run about $20 into Oakland and $40 into San Francisco.

The **Greyhound** station is in a dodgy part of northern Oakland alongside the I-980 freeway on San Pablo Avenue at 21st Street. **Amtrak** terminates at Second Street near Jack London Square in West Oakland, where a free shuttle bus heads across the Bay Bridge to the Transbay Terminal. A better option for heading into San Francisco is to get off at Richmond and change onto the nearby BART trains. The most enjoyable way to arrive in the East Bay is aboard an Alameda–Oakland **ferry** ($5 each way; ☎510/522-3300, ⓦwww.eastbayferry.com), which sails every hour from San Francisco's Ferry Building and Pier 39 to Oakland's Jack London Square. The fleet also runs a service to Angel Island via Pier 41, departing from Oakland (Sat & Sun May 18–Oct 27 9am, returning at 3.10pm; $12 round-trip, including park admission).

Getting around

The East Bay is linked to San Francisco via the underground BART Transbay **subway** (Mon–Sat 6am–midnight, Sun 9am–midnight). Three lines run from Daly City through San Francisco and on to downtown Oakland, before diverging to service East Oakland out to Fremont, north to Berkeley and Richmond, and northeast into Contra Costa County as far as Concord and Pittsburg/Bay Point. Fares range from $1.10 to $4.65, and the cost of each ride is deducted from the total value of the ticket, purchased from machines on the station concourse. If you're relying on BART to get around a lot, buy a **high-value ticket** ($5, $10, or $20) to avoid having to stand in line to buy a new ticket each time you ride. For $3.80, you can tour the entire system and get off at any of the 39 station platforms for up to three hours, so long as you enter and exit at the same station; the same charge is made for lost tickets. To phone BART from San Francisco, dial ☎415/989-BART; from the East Bay ☎510/465-BART, or check ⓦwww.bart .org; bikes are allowed on most trains.

From East Bay BART stations, pick up a **free transfer**, saving you 35¢ on the $1.35 fares of the revamped AC Transit (☎510/817-1717 ext 1111, ⓦwww.actransit.org), which provides a good **bus service** around the entire East Bay, especially Oakland and Berkeley. AC Transit also runs buses on a number of routes to Oakland and Berkeley from the Transbay Terminal in San Francisco. These operate all night and are the only way of getting across the Bay by public transit once BART has shut down. You can pick up excellent free maps of both BART and the bus system from any station. A smaller-scale bus company that can also prove useful, the Contra Costa County Connection (☎925/676-7500) runs buses to most of the inland areas, including the John Muir and Eugene O'Neill historic houses.

One of the best ways to get around the East Bay is by **bike**. A fine cycle route follows Skyline and Grizzly Peak boulevards along the wooded crest of the hills between Berkeley and Lake Chabot. Within Berkeley itself, the Ohlone Greenway makes for a pleasant cycling or walking route up through North Berkeley to El Cerrito. If you haven't got one, rent touring bikes or mountain bikes for $25 a day from Around World, 2416 Telegraph Ave in Oakland (☎510/835-8763), or from Cal Adventures, 2301 Bancroft Way on the UC Berkeley campus (☎510/642-4000). For those interested in **walking tours**, the City of Oakland sponsors free "discovery tours" (☎510/238-3234) of various neighborhoods; a popular excursion is the Oakland Historical Landmark Tour (Sun 1–3.30pm; free), beginning in front of the Oakland Museum at 10th and Fallon, and covering areas like Chinatown, Lake Merritt, Preservation Park, and Jack London Square.

If you're **driving**, allow yourself plenty of time to get there: the East Bay has some of California's worst traffic, with the Bay Bridge and I-80 in particular jam-packed sixteen hours a day. Car-pool lanes are becoming increasingly popular, so having more than one person in your vehicle can speed things up, slightly at least.

Information

The **Oakland CVB**, on the ground floor of a huge modern block at 475 14th St (Mon–Fri 8.30am–5pm; ☎510/839-9000, ⓦwww.oaklandcvb.com), is the best source of maps, brochures, and information on lodging and activities in the metropolitan area. In Berkeley, check in at the **Berkeley CVB**, 2015 Center St (Mon–Fri 9am–5pm; ☎510/549-7040, ⓦwww.visitberkeley.com). The **Berkeley TRiP Commute Store** (Tues–Fri noon–5.30pm, Thurs 9am–6pm; ☎510/644-7665, ⓦwww.berkeley.edu/transportation), almost next door to the visitor center, sells passes to all Bay Area transit systems and can help you figure out how to get just about anywhere in the area on public transportation; their satellite office is near campus at 2543 Channing Way (Mon–Fri 9am–2pm). The **University of California's Visitor Services**, 101 University Hall (Mon–Fri 8.30am–4.30pm; ☎510/642-5215), at the corner of Oxford and University, has plenty of info on the Berkeley campus, hands out free self-guided tour brochures, and conducts ninety-minute tours (see p.601). For information on hiking or horseriding in the many parks that top the Oakland and Berkeley hills, contact the **East Bay Regional Parks District**, 11500 Skyline Blvd (☎510/562-7275). The widely available *East Bay Express* (issued every Wed; free) has the most comprehensive listings of what's on in the vibrant

East Bay music and arts scene. The daily *Oakland Tribune* (50¢) is also worth a look for its coverage of local politics and sporting events.

Accommodation

The East Bay's **motels** and **hotels** are barely any better value for money than their San Francisco equivalents. However, they give visitors the chance to stay just outside of the city's hubbub whilst affording easy access to it. **Bed and breakfasts** often give the best value, tucked away as they are in Berkeley's leafy hills. Check with the *Berkeley & Oakland Bed and Breakfast Network* (☎510/547-6380, ⓦwww.bbonline.com/ca/berkeley-oakland) for a complete list, or get their brochure from the Berkeley CVB or UC's Visitor Services office. A few **campgrounds** and **dorm beds** are available in summertime.

Hotels, motels, and B&Bs

Bancroft Hotel 2680 Bancroft Way, Berkeley ☎510/549-1000 or 1-800/549-1002, ⓦwww .bancrofthotel.com. Small hotel with 22 rooms, a good location right by the campus, and fine service. Breakfast included. ⑥

Berkeley City Club 2315 Durant Ave, Berkeley ☎510/848-7800, ⓦwww.berkeleycityclub.com. Two blocks from the UC campus, this B&B was designed by Hearst Castle architect Julia Morgan, with indoor swimming pool and exercise room. Each of the spacious rooms has a private bath. ⑥

The Claremont Resort & Spa 41 Tunnel Rd, Berkeley ☎510/843-3000 or 1-800/551-7266, ⓦwww.claremontresort.com). Built in 1915, *The Claremont* is the lap of luxury among Berkeley hotels. Luxurious rooms come with coffeemakers, data ports for your laptop, hairdryers, cable TV, and big windows, some overlooking the large outdoor pool; spa sessions begin at $95 per hour for facials or massages. ⑧

Dean's Bed and Breakfast 480 Pedestrian Way, Rockridge ☎510/652-5024. A hidden gem with heated swimming pool (May–Oct) and Japanese garden, near a trendy shopping strip and the Rockridge BART stop. Tidy but simple rooms come with private bath, cable TV, and private phone line with answering machine. Highly recommended. ④

Hotel Durant 2600 Durant Ave, Berkeley ☎510/845-8981 or 1-800/238-7268, ⓦwww.hoteldurant.com. Upscale hotel at the heart of UC Berkeley, featuring large, airy rooms with refrigerators. Best location to stay if you can afford it. ⑦

East Brother Light Station 117 Park Place, Point Richmond ☎510/233-2385, ⓦwww.ebls.org. A handful of rooms in a converted lighthouse, on an island in the straits linking the San Francisco and San Pablo bays. Not a handy base for seeing the

sights, this is a retreat and adventure for an evening. Prices include highly rated gourmet dinners with wine as well as breakfast. Thursday to Sunday nights only. ⑧

Elmwood House 2609 College Ave, Berkeley ☎510/540-5123, ⓦwww.elmwoodhouse.com. Attractive 1902 house with small and sunny B&B rooms, not far from UC Berkeley. ④

Flamingo Motel 1761 University Ave, Berkeley ☎510/841-4242. No frills but adequate and with the lowest rates close to downtown Berkeley and the campus. ②

French 1538 Shattuck Ave, North Berkeley ☎510/548-9930. Small and comfortable hotel with 18 standard rooms in the heart of Berkeley's Gourmet Ghetto. ⑤

Golden Bear Inn 1620 San Pablo Ave, West Berkeley ☎510/525-6770 or 1-800/525-6770, ⓦwww.goldenbearinn.com. The most pleasant of the many motels in the "flatlands" of West Berkeley, though somewhat out of the way. ④

Holiday Inn Bay Bridge 1800 Powell St, Emeryville ☎510/658-9300 or 1-800/HOLIDAY, ⓦwww.holidayinn.com. Not outrageously pricey considering the great views to be had from the upper floors. Free parking. ⑥

Howard Johnson Express Inn 423 7th St, Oakland ☎510/451-6316 or 1-800/754-1115, ⓦwww.hojo.com/oakland. Spruced up ex-*Travelodge* providing one of the best deals downtown. ③

Jack London Inn 444 Embarcadero West ☎510/444-2032 or 1-800/549-8780. Kitschy motorlodge with a 1950s feel; located next to Jack London Square. ⑤

Hotel Mac 10 Cottage Ave, Point Richmond ☎510/ 235-0010, ⓦwww.hotelmachotel.bigstep.com. Built in 1907, the recently refurbished *Hotel Mac* boasts luxurious rooms with unbeatable prices. This was supposedly John Rockefeller's favorite place to stay when visiting his Standard Oil enterprise. ❹

Rose Garden Inn 2740 Telegraph Ave, Berkeley ☎510/549-2145 or 1-800/992-9005, ⊛www.rosegardeninn.com. Pleasant, if slightly dull, rooms with fireplaces in a pretty mock-Tudor mansion half a mile south of UC Berkeley. ❺

Hotel Shattuck Plaza 2086 Allston Way, Berkeley ☎510/845-7300 or 1-800/237-5359, ⊛www.hotelshattuckplaza.com. Comfortable good-value rooms in a central and well-restored older hotel, now under new management. ❹

Union Hotel and Gardens 401 First St, Benicia ☎707/746-0100, ⊛www.unionhotelbenicia.com. A bordello from 1882 until 1950, since converted into a comfortable bed and breakfast with twelve rooms. ❻

Waterfront Plaza Hotel 10 Washington St, Oakland ☎510/836-3800 or 1-800/729-3638, ⊛www.waterfrontplaza.com. Plush, modern hotel located on the best stretch of the Oakland waterfront. ❼

Hostels

Downtown Berkeley YMCA 2001 Allston Way at Milvia St, a block from Berkeley BART ☎510/848-9622, ⊛www.baymca.com. Berkeley's best bargain accommodation; rates, starting at $46 for a single, include use of gym and pool. No dorms. ❸

Haste-Channing Summer Visitor Housing 2601 Warring St, Berkeley ☎510/642-4444. Agency that can arrange summer-only rooms for a little over $50 in university accommodation such as Stern Hall. ❷

Campgrounds

Chabot Family Campground off I-580 in East Oakland ☎510/562-2267. Walk-in, tent-only places, with hot showers and lots of good hiking nearby; reservations wise in summer; $20.

Mount Diablo State Park 20 miles east of Oakland off I-680 in Contra Costa County ☎510/837-2525. RV and tent places; book through ParkNet ☎1-800/444-7275 in summer; $12.

Oakland

What was the use of me having come from Oakland, it was not natural for me to have come from there yes write about it if I like or anything if I like but not there, there is no there there.

Gertrude Stein, *Everybody's Autobiography*

As the workhorse of the Bay Area, **OAKLAND** is commonly known as a place of little or no play. One of the busiest ports on the West Coast and the western terminal of the rail network, it's also the spawning ground of some of America's most unabashedly revolutionary **political movements**, such as the militant **Black Panthers**, who gave a voice to the African-American population, and the **Symbionese Liberation Army**, who demanded a ransom for kidnapped heiress Patty Hearst in the form of free food distribution to the poor.

The city is also the birthplace of literary legends **Gertrude Stein** and **Jack London**, who grew up here at approximately the same time, though in entirely different circumstances – Stein was a stockbroker's daughter, while London was an orphaned delinquent. Most of the waterfront where London used to steal oysters and lobsters is now named in his memory, while Stein, who was actually born in East Oakland, is all but ignored here, not surprising given her unflattering quote above. Still, until very recently, locals found it hard to come up with anything better: Oakland businesses have a long history of deserting the place once the going gets good, and even the city's football team, the Raiders, defected to Los Angeles for thirteen years.

But residents who've stuck by the city through its duller and darker days recently elected a new mayor, former California governor and one-time presidential candidate **Jerry "Moonbeam" Brown**, who has promised to revitalize (some residents say gentrify) the town and slash its infamous crime rate. Advertising his city's lower rents and always sunny climate – consistently rated the best in the US – Brown is well on his way to meeting his promise of bringing 10,000 new residents downtown, an area being rapidly transformed despite the hiccough in the information age boom. Already, rents in the increasingly popular **Rockridge** and **Lake Merrit** districts are approaching San Francisco prices. The city has also attracted a significant number of lesbians, who've left San Francisco's Castro and Mission, as well as a great number of artists pushed from their SoMa lofts by sky-high rents into the warehouses of West Oakland.

Perhaps "Oaktown" (the local name for Oakland) is a better place in which to live than to visit. Locals call San Francisco "the city" and will point visitors to its myriad attractions before recommending those in the East Bay. But given it's a short hop on BART or quick drive across the Bay Bridge, a day-trip to Oakland is worth it to get a feel for the East Bay's diversity and changing times.

Downtown Oakland

Coming by BART from San Francisco, get off at the Twelfth Street–Civic Center station and you're at the new, open-air shopping and office space of **City Center** in the heart of **DOWNTOWN OAKLAND**. Oddly, the area can seem uncannily deserted outside of rush hours. Downtown's compact district of spruced-up Victorian storefronts overlooked by modern hotels and

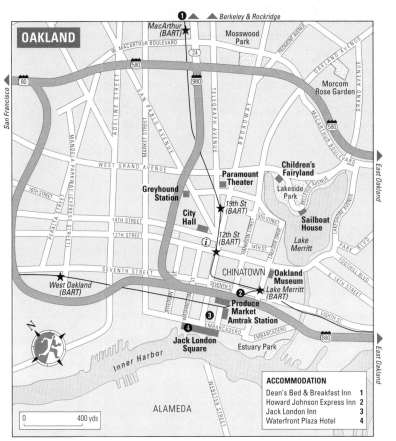

office buildings has been in the midst of an ambitious program of restoration and redevelopment for over a decade. Fraught with allegations of illegal dealings and incompetent planning, so far the program has been less than a complete success. To make way for the moat-like I-980 freeway – the main route through Oakland since the collapse of the Cypress Freeway in the 1989 earthquake – entire blocks were cleared of houses, some of which were saved and moved to **Preservation Park** at Twelfth Street and Martin Luther King Jr Way. The late-nineteenth-century commercial center along Ninth Street west of Broadway, now tagged **Old Oakland**, underwent a major restoration some years ago, and while some of the buildings are still waiting for tenants, others are occupied by architect and design firms, much like San Francisco's Jackson Square. By way of contrast to the subdued Old Oakland area, stroll a block east of Broadway, between Seventh and Ninth, to Oakland's **Chinatown**, whose bakeries and restaurants are neither as lively nor picturesque as those of its more famous cousin across the Bay.

Luckily, not all of downtown Oakland has the look of a permanent building site. The city experienced its greatest period of growth in the early twentieth century, and many of the grand buildings of this era survive a few blocks north along Broadway, centered on the gigantic grass triangle of **Frank Ogawa Plaza** and the awkwardly imposing 1914 **City Hall** on Fourteenth Street. Two blocks away at Thirteenth and Franklin stands Oakland's most unmistakable landmark, the chateauesque lantern of the **Tribune Tower**, the 1920s-era former home of the *Oakland Tribune* newspaper. A few blocks west at 659 14th St, the **African American Museum & Library** (Tues–Sat noon–5.30pm; free; ☏510/238-6716) is housed in an elegant Neoclassical building whose upper floor has a permanent display on the history of African-Americans in California from 1775 to 1900, and revolving art and photo exhibitions. Several blocks further on, the **Ebony Museum of Art**, 1034 14th St (Tues–Sat 11am–6pm, Sun noon–6pm; free; ☏510/763-0141), is another showcase for black artists and promotes greater appreciation of the African-American heritage.

Further north, around the Nineteenth Street BART station, are some of the Bay Area's finest early twentieth-century buildings, highlighted by the outstanding Art Deco interior of the 1931 **Paramount Theater** at 2025 Broadway (tours 10am first and third Sat of the month; $1; ☏510/465-6400). The West Coast's answer to New York's Radio City Music Hall, the Paramount shows Hollywood classics, and hosts occasional concerts by the likes of Tom Waits and Neil Young and performances by ballet troupes and the Oakland Symphony. Nearby buildings are equally flamboyant, ranging from the wafer-thin Gothic "flatiron" office tower of the **Cathedral Building** at Broadway and Telegraph, to the Hindu-temple-like facade of the magnificent 3500-seat **Fox Oakland** (now closed) on Telegraph at Nineteenth – the largest moviehouse west of Chicago at the time it was built in 1928 – and, across the street, the 1931 **Floral Depot**, a group of small modern storefronts faced in black-and-blue terracotta tiles with shiny silver highlights. If you're tired of walking, lace up skates at the nearby **Oakland Ice Center**, 519 18th St (☏510/268-9000, ⊛www.oaklandice.com). The facility is the finest in the Bay Area, evinced by the Olympians, such as Kristi Yamaguchi and Brian Boitano, who often practice here (Mon–Thurs noon–5pm, Fri–Sat 7–10pm, Sun noon–5pm; $10 skate rental and all-day use).

West of Broadway, the area around the Greyhound bus station on San Pablo Avenue is fairly seedy. San Pablo used to be the main route in and out of Oakland before the freeways were built, but many of the roadside businesses are now derelict, especially around the industrial districts of **Emeryville**. Some of the old warehouses have been converted by architects into artists' lofts and studios in an ongoing real-life workshop in an attempt to transform the area into a glitzy design centerpiece. Most intriguing is the new city hall, called **Civic Center**, at Park Avenue and Hollis Street, for which the 1902 town hall has been wrapped in a sheer glass box of 15,000 additional square feet of office space. Any gentrification here is diffused by the scenes on the street – prostitutes and drug dealers hang out under the neon signs of the dingy bars and gambling halls, such as the *Oaks Card Club*, where Oaktown rapper M.C. Hammer, who once made the city proud, used to work.

Lake Merritt and the Oakland Museum

Five blocks east of Broadway, the eastern third of downtown Oakland comprises **LAKE MERRITT**, a three-mile-circumference tidal lagoon that was bridged and dammed in the 1860s to become the centerpiece of Oakland's most desirable neighborhood. All that remains of the many fine houses that once circled the lake is the elegant **Camron–Stanford House**, on the southwest shore at 1418 Lakeside Drive, a graceful Italianate mansion whose sumptuous interior is open for visits (Wed 11am–4pm, Sun 1–5pm; $4; ☎510/444-1876). The lake is also the nation's oldest wildlife refuge, and migrating flocks of ducks, geese, and herons break their journeys here. **Lakeside Park** lines the north shore, where you can rent canoes and rowboats ($6 per hour), and a range of sailing boats and catamarans ($10–20 per hour) from the **Sailboat House** (summer daily 10am–5pm; winter Fri–Sun 10am–4.30pm; ☎510/238-2196) – provided you can convince the staff you know how to sail. A miniature Mississippi riverboat makes thirty-minute lake **cruises** ($1.50) on weekend afternoons, or you can splash out to be punted around and serenaded on the overpriced but romantic Gondola Servizio ($55 per hour; ☎510/663-6603). Kids will like the puppet shows and pony rides at the **Children's Fairyland** (summer daily 10am–5.30pm; winter Fri–Sun 10am–5.30pm; $4; ☎510/452-2259, ⓦwww.fairyland.org), along Grand Avenue on the northwest edge of the park. Every year, on the first weekend in June, the park comes to life during the **Festival at the Lake**, when all of Oakland gets together to enjoy nonstop music and performances from local bands and entertainers. At night, the lake's lit up by the "Necklace of Lights," an elegant source of local pride. Once you reach the north side of the lake, it's worth strolling under the MacArthur Freeway to soak up the relaxed atmosphere of the cafés and shops along gradually diverging Grand and Lakeshore avenues. Note the huge Art Deco-cum-mock-Classical facade of the still-functioning **Grand Lake Movie Theater**.

Two blocks south of the lake, or a block up Oak Street from the Lake Merritt BART station, the **OAKLAND MUSEUM**, 1000 Oak St (Wed–Sat 10am–5pm, Sun noon–5pm; $6, free every 2nd Sun of month; ☎510/238-2200, ⓦwww.museumca.org), is perhaps Oakland's most worthwhile stop, not only for the exhibits but also for the superb modern building in which it's housed, topped by a terraced rooftop sculpture garden that gives great views out over the water and the city. The museum covers many diverse areas: displays on the **ecology** of California, including a simulated walk from the seaside through various natural habitats up to the 14,000-foot summits of the Sierra Nevada mountains; state history, ranging from old mining equipment to the guitar that Berkeley-born Country Joe MacDonald played at the Woodstock Festival in 1969; and a broad survey of works by California artists and craftspeople, some highlights of which are pieces of turn-of-the-century **arts and crafts furniture**. You'll also see excellent **photography** by Edward Muybridge, Dorothea Lange, Imogen Cunningham, and many others. The museum also has a collector's gallery that rents and sells works by California artists.

Jack London Square, Alameda, and West Oakland

Half a mile down from downtown Oakland on AC Transit bus #51, at the foot of Broadway on the waterfront, **JACK LONDON SQUARE** is Oakland's sole concession to the tourist trade. An erratic voluntarily-manned information booth on Broadway between Water and Embarcadero streets can supply maps detailing what the square has to offer, if you find it open. Also accessible by direct ferry from San Francisco (see "Arrival," p.589), this somewhat anesthetic complex of harborfront boutiques and restaurants, anchored by a huge Barnes and Noble bookstore, was named after the self-taught writer who grew up pirating shellfish around here, but is about as distant from the spirit of the man as it's possible to get. Jack London's best story, *The Call of the Wild*, was written about his adventures in the Alaskan Yukon, where he carved his initials in a small cabin that has been reconstructed here. The one sight worth stopping at is **Heinold's First and Last Chance Saloon**, a slanting tiny bar at the eastern end of the promenade, built in 1883 from the hull of a whaling ship. Jack London really did drink here, and the collection of yellowed portraits of him on the wall are the only genuine thing about the writer you'll find on the square. Massive redevelopment plans, to the tune of $200 million, are afoot to revamp the square into a top-notch entertainment venue by 2005.

If you're not a keen fan of London (and if you are, you'd be better off visiting his Sonoma Valley ranch – see p.723), there are still a few worthwhile things to do here. On Sunday, the square bustles with the weekly farmers' market, where you can pick up all sorts of bargains and stock up on food. Otherwise, walk a few short blocks inland to the **Produce Market**, along Third and Fourth streets, where a couple of good places to eat and drink lurk among the rail tracks (see "Eating" on p.610). This bustling warehouse district has fruit and vegetables by the forklift load, and is at its most lively early in the morning, from about 5am. On the Embarcadero between Clay and Washington, **Yoshi's World Class Jazz House** is the Bay Area's, if not the West Coast's, premier jazz club (see "Nightlife," p.616).

AC Transit bus #51 continues from Broadway under the inner harbor to **ALAMEDA**, a quiet and conservative island of middle America dominated by a large, empty naval air station, one of the first to be closed by Bill Clinton in 1995 – although massive nuclear-powered aircraft carriers still dock here occasionally. Alameda, which has been hit very hard by post-Cold War military cutbacks, was severed from the Oakland mainland as part of a harbor improvement program in 1902. The fine houses along the original shoreline on Clinton Street were part of the summer resort colony that flocked here to the *contra costa* or "opposite shore" from San Francisco, near the now demolished Neptune Beach amusement park. The island has since been much enlarged by dredging and landfill, and 1960s apartment buildings now line the long, narrow shore of **Robert Crown Memorial Beach** along the Bay – a quiet, attractive spot.

WEST OAKLAND – an industrial district of warehouses, rail tracks, 1960s housing projects, and decaying Victorian houses – may be the nearest East Bay BART stop to San Francisco, but it's light years away from that city's prosperity. Despite the obvious poverty, it's quite a safe and settled place, but the only time anyone pays any attention to it is when something dramatic happens – in the double-whammy year of 1989, for example, when former Black Panther Huey Newton was gunned down here in a drugs-related revenge attack, and the double-decker I-880 freeway, which divided the neighborhood from the rest of the city, collapsed in on itself during the earthquake, killing dozens of commuters. Now the neighborhood is a magnet for artists and skate punks from across the Bay, who revel in its dirt-cheap rents and open spaces, though the first signs of its surprisingly tardy gentrification are finally afoot.

Local African-American leaders successfully resisted government plans to rebuild I-880, the old concrete eyesore which they asserted created an unsightly barrier within their community; the broad and potentially very attractive **Nelson Mandela Parkway** has replaced it. Otherwise, this remains one of the Bay Area's poorest and most neglected neighborhoods, and apart from a marvelous stock of turn-of-the-century houses, there's little here to tempt tourists. But locals – and Mayor Brown – say take a long look and buy now; given the district's proximity to San Francisco, West Oakland is bound to smarten up unrecognizably within five years.

East Oakland

The bulk of Oakland spreads along foothills and flatlands to the east of downtown, in neighborhoods obviously stratified along the main thoroughfares of Foothill and MacArthur boulevards. Gertrude Stein grew up here, though when she returned years later in search of her childhood home it had been torn down and replaced by a dozen Craftsman-style bungalows – the simple 1920s wooden houses that cover most of **EAST OAKLAND**, each fronted by a patch of lawn and divided from its neighbor by a narrow concrete driveway.

A quick way out from the gridded streets and sidewalks of the city is to take AC Transit bus #64 from downtown east up into the hills to **Joaquin Miller Park**, the most easily accessible of Oakland's hilltop parks. It stands on the former grounds of "The Hights," the misspelled home of the "Poet of the Sierras," Joaquin Miller, who made his name playing the eccentric frontier American in the literary salons of 1870s London. His poems weren't exactly acclaimed (his greatest poetic achievement was rhyming "teeth" with "Goethe"), although his prose account, *Life Amongst the Modocs*, documenting time spent with the Modoc people near Mount Shasta, does stand the test of time. It was more for his outrageous behavior that he became famous, wearing bizarre clothes and biting debutantes on the ankle. For years, Japanese poet Yone Noguchi also lived here, working the sprinkler as Miller impressed lady visitors with a rain dance he claimed to have learned from American Indians.

Perched in the hills at the foot of the park, the pointed towers of the **Mormon Temple**, 4766 Lincoln Ave, look like missile-launchers designed by the Wizard of Oz – unmissable by day or floodlit night. In December, speakers hidden in the landscaping make it seem as if the plants are singing Christmas carols. Though you can't go inside the main temple unless you're a confirmed Mormon, there are great views out over the entire Bay Area, and a small museum explains the tenets of the faith (daily 9am–9pm; free); expect to be greeted and offered a free personalised tour by one of the faithful upon entering. Several miles up in the hills behind the temple, the new **Chabot Space & Science Center**, 10000 Skyline Blvd (Tues–Sun 10am–5pm, Fri & Sat 7–9pm; $8; ☎510/336-7300, ⓦwww.chabotspace.org), is a state-of-the-art museum with interactive displays and a fine planetarium show at its **observatory** (summer dusk–11pm; winter 7–10pm; $8.75); it can be reached on AC Transit bus #53 from Fruitvale BART station.

Out past the airport in the suburb of San Leandro, **Oakland Zoo** (daily summer 9am–5pm; winter 10am–4pm; $7.50; ☎510/632-9525, ⓦwww .oaklandzoo.org) is home to over 300 species of animals, comfortably situated in the rolling hills of 525-acre Knowland Park; AC Transit bus #56 heads out there from Oakland, or it costs $3 to park. This is the only place of interest in the twenty miles of suburbs that stretch along the Bay southeast towards San Jose, apart from **Fremont**, at the end of the BART line, where the short-lived Essanay movie studios were based. Essanay, the first studios on the West Coast, made over 700 films in three years, including Charlie Chaplin's *The Tramp* in 1914. Not much remains from these pre-Hollywood days, however, and the only real sight is the **Mission San Jose de Guadalupe** on Mission Boulevard south of the I-680 freeway (daily 10am–5pm; donation), which in the best traditions of Hollywood set design was completely rebuilt in Mission style only a few years ago.

North Oakland and Rockridge

The horrific October 1991 Oakland **fire**, which destroyed 3000 homes and killed 26 people, did most of its damage in the high-priced hills of **NORTH OAKLAND**. It took the better part of two years, but most of the half-million -dollar houses have been rebuilt, and though the lush vegetation that made the area so attractive will never be allowed to grow back in order to prevent any more fires, things are pretty much back to normal. Which is to say that segregation is still in place; these bay-view homes, some of the Bay Area's most valuable real estate, look out across some of its poorest – the neglected flatlands below that in the 1960s were the proving grounds of Black Panthers Bobby Seale and Huey Newton.

Broadway is the dividing line between the two halves of North Oakland, and also gives access (via the handy AC Transit #51 bus) to most of what there is to see and do. One of Oakland's most neighborly streets, **Piedmont Avenue**, is lined by a number of small bookstores and cafés, and it makes for a nice stroll or day of hanging out. At the north end of Piedmont Avenue, the **Mountain View Cemetery** was laid out in 1863 by Frederick Law Olmsted (designer of New York's Central Park) and holds the elaborate dynastic tombs of San Francisco's most powerful families – the Crockers, the Bechtels, and the Ghirardellis. You can jog or ride a bike around the well-tended grounds, or just wonder at the enormous turtles in the pond. Next door, the columbarium, known as the **Chapel of the Chimes**, 4499 Piedmont Ave (daily 9am–5pm; free; ☎510/654-0123), was designed by Julia Morgan of Hearst Castle fame during her decade-long involvement with the chapel beginning in 1921. The structure is remarkable for its seemingly endless series of urn-filled rooms, grouped together around sky-lit courtyards, bubbling fountains, and intimate chapels – all connected by ornate staircases of every conceivable length. Morgan wanted the space to sing of life, not death, and she's succeeded – there's no better place in Oakland to wander about in peace, or even plop down with a book. Try and visit during one of the regular concerts held here for a completely unique – and distinctly Californian – experience.

Back on Broadway, just past College Avenue, Broadway Terrace climbs up along the edge of the fire area to **Lake Temescal** – where you can swim in summer – and continues on up to the forested ridge at the **Robert Sibley Regional Preserve**. This includes the 1761-foot volcanic cone of Round Top Peak and offers panoramas of the entire Bay Area. The peak has been dubbed the "Volcanic Witch Project" by the local media due to the five mysterious mazes, carved into the dirt and lined with stones, located in the canyons around the crater. Nobody knows where they came from, but navigating the designs leads to their center, where visitors add to the pile of diverse offerings ranging from trinkets to cigarettes to poetry. Skyline Boulevard runs through the park and is popular with cyclists, who ride the twelve miles south to Lake Chabot or follow Grizzly Peak Boulevard five miles north to Tilden Park through the Berkeley Hills.

Most of the Broadway traffic, and the AC Transit #51 bus, cuts off onto College Avenue through Oakland's most upscale shopping district, **ROCKRIDGE**. Spreading for half a mile on either side of the Rockridge BART station, the quirky stores and restaurants here, despite their undeniable yuppie overtones, are better than Piedmont's in variety and volume, and make for a pleasant afternoon's wander.

Berkeley

This Berkeley was like no somnolent Siwash out of her own past at all, but more akin to those Far Eastern or Latin American universities you read about, those autonomous culture media where the most beloved of folklores may be brought into doubt, cataclysmic of dissents voiced, suicidal of commitments chosen – the sort that bring governments down.

Thomas Pynchon, *The Crying of Lot 49*

More than any other American city, **BERKELEY** conjures up an image of 1960s student dissent. When college campuses across the nation were **protesting** against the Vietnam War, it was the students of the University of California, Berkeley, who led the charge – gaining a name as the vanguard of what was increasingly seen as a challenge to the authority of the state. Full-scale battles were fought almost daily here at one point, on the campus and on its surrounding streets, and there were times when Berkeley looked almost on the brink of revolution itself: students (and others) throwing stones and gas bombs were met with tear-gas volleys and truncheons by National Guard troops under the nominal command of then-Governor Ronald Reagan.

Such action was inspired by the mood of the time, and in an increasingly conservative America, Berkeley politics are nowadays far less confrontational. But despite an influx of conformist students, a surge in the number of exclusive restaurants, and the dismantling of the city's rent-control program, something of the progressive legacy manages to linger in the city's independent **bookstores** and at sporadic political demonstrations. In recent years, perhaps the biggest nationwide cause célèbre on campus was the plight of Naked Man, an undergrad who refused to wear clothing while attending class. More seriously, in 1999, the entire Berkeley community was outraged when Pacifica, the parent company of local leftist radio station KPFA 94.1 FM, decided to change the station's programs to less subversive themes in an attempt to draw funding. When staff members wouldn't play along, Pacifica sent in armed security guards to remove them and the ensuing standoff was broadcast live, leading to mass militant support marches in the ensuing weeks. KPFA remained on the air, as unrepentant as ever, though relationships with management are still strained. On the biggest issue of late, Berkeley has been a hub of protest against George W. Bush's war on terrorism, with posters, stickers, and badges on open sale along Telegraph Avenue questioning the bombing of Afghanistan and supporting Senator Barabara Lee, who cast the only vote against military action. Even more concerted opposition was evident to the government's plans to invade Iraq late in 2002.

The **University of California**, right in the center of town, completely dominates Berkeley and makes a logical starting point for a visit. Its many grand buildings and 30,000 students give off a definite energy, which spills down the raucous stretch of Telegraph Avenue that runs south from the campus and holds most of the student hangouts, including a dozen or so lively cafés, as well as a number of fine bookstores. Older students, and a good percentage of the faculty, congregate in the **Northside** area, the part of **North Berkeley** just above the campus, popping down from their woodsy hillside homes to partake of goodies from the Gourmet Ghetto, a stretch of Shattuck Avenue crammed with restaurants, delis, and bakeries. Of quite distinct character are the flatlands that spread through **West Berkeley** down to the Bay, a poorer but increasingly gentrified district that mixes old Victorian houses with builders' yards and light industrial premises. Along the Bay itself is the **Berkeley Marina**, where you can rent sailboards and sailboats or just watch the sun set behind the Golden Gate.

The University of California

Caught up in the frantic crush of students who pack the **UNIVERSITY OF CALIFORNIA** campus during the semesters, it's nearly impossible to imagine the bucolic learning environment envisaged by its high-minded founders.

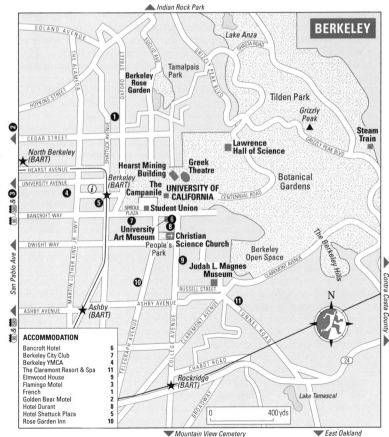

BERKELEY

Indian Rock Park

SOLANO AVENUE

Lake Anza

SHASTA ROAD

EUCLID AVE

GRIZZLY PEAK BLVD

THE ALAMEDA

OXFORD STREET

Tamalpais Park

Berkeley Rose Garden ❶

Tilden Park

HOPKINS STREET

Grizzly Peak

CEDAR STREET

SHATTUCK AVENUE

Steam Train

North Berkeley ★ (BART) ❷

GRIZZLY PEAK BLVD

HEARST AVENUE

Lawrence Hall of Science

UNIVERSITY AVENUE

Hearst Mining Building

Greek Theatre

Botanical Gardens

Berkeley (BART)

The Campanile

❹ ⓘ

❺

UNIVERSITY OF CALIFORNIA

CENTENNIAL ROAD

BANCROFT WAY

SPROUL PLAZA

■ Student Union

DWIGHT WAY

MARTIN LUTHER KING JR HWY

❼

University Art Museum

❻ ❽

Christian Science Church

The Berkeley Hills

People's Park

Berkeley Open Space

❾

Judah L. Magnes Museum

CLAREMONT AVENUE

Contra Costa County

❿

RUSSELL STREET

N

ASHBY AVENUE

ASHBY AVENUE

⓫

TUNNEL ROAD

Ashby (BART) ★

TELEGRAPH AVENUE

COLLEGE AVENUE

CLAREMONT AVENUE

San Pablo Ave

ACCOMMODATION

Bancroft Hotel	6
Berkeley City Club	7
Berkeley YMCA	4
The Claremont Resort & Spa	11
Elmwood House	9
Flamingo Motel	3
French	1
Golden Bear Motel	2
Hotel Durant	8
Hotel Shattuck Plaza	5
Rose Garden Inn	10

CHABOT ROAD

Rockridge (BART) ★

BROADWAY

24

Lake Temescal

0   400 yds

Mountain View Cemetery   East Oakland

When the Reverend Henry Durant and other East Coast academics decided to set up shop here in the 1860s, these rolling foothills were still largely given over to dairy herds and wheatfields, the last remnants of the Peralta family's Spanish land-grant rancho, which once stretched over most of the East Bay. In 1866, while surveying the land, a trustee recited "Westward the course of the empire takes its way," from a poem by George Berkeley. Moved by the moment, all assembled agreed to name their school after the bishop. Construction work on the two campus buildings – imaginatively named North Hall and South Hall – was still going on when the first 200 students, including 22 women, moved here from Oakland in 1873. Since then an increasing number of buildings have been squeezed into the half-mile-square main campus, and the state-funded university has become one of America's most prestigious, with so many Nobel laureates on the faculty that it's said you have to win one just to get a parking permit. University physicists built the first cyclotron, and plutonium was discovered here in 1941, along with thirteen other synthetic elements (including berkelium and californium). As such, sketches for the first atomic bomb began here. Nuclear weaponry and over-crowding aside, the beautifully landscaped campus, stepping down from the eucalyptus-covered Berkeley Hills toward the Golden Gate, is eminently stroll-able. With maps posted everywhere, you'd have to try hard to get lost – though enthusiastic students will show you around on a free ninety-minute **tour** (Mon–Sat 10am, Sun 1pm; free; ☎510/642-5215), explaining the campus's his-tory, architecture, and flavor. Be sure to take one if you want a fuller picture of Berkeley beyond looking at facades and the faces of passing students.

A number of footpaths climb the hill from the Berkeley BART station on Shattuck Avenue, but the best way to get a feel for the place is to follow Strawberry Creek from the top of Center Street across the southeast corner of the campus, emerging from the groves of redwood and eucalyptus trees at **Sproul Plaza**. It's the newest and largest public space on campus, enlivened by street musicians playing for quarters on the steps of the **Student Union** build-ing and conga drummers pounding away in the echoing courtyard below. Sather Gate, which bridges Strawberry Creek at the north end of Sproul Plaza, marks the entrance to the older part of the campus. Up the hill, past the impos-ing facade of Wheeler Hall, the 1914 landmark **Campanile** (Mon–Fri 10am–4pm, Sat & Sun 10am–5pm; $2) is modeled after the one in the Piazza San Marco in Venice; take an elevator to the top for a great view of the cam-pus and the entire Bay Area. At the foot of the tower stands the red-brick **South Hall**, the sole survivor of the original pair of buildings.

Inside the plain white building next door, the **Bancroft Library** (Mon–Fri 9am–5pm, Sat 1–5pm; ☎510/642-3781) displays odds and ends from its exhaustive accumulation of artifacts and documents tracing the history of California, including a fake brass plaque supposedly left by Sir Francis Drake when he claimed all of the West Coast for Queen Elizabeth I. It also contains an internationally important collection of manuscripts and rare books, from the works of Mark Twain to James Joyce – though to see any of these you have to show some academic credentials. Around the corner and down the hill, just inside the arched main entrance to Doe Library, you'll find the **Morrison Reading Room**, a great place to sit for a while and read foreign magazines and newspapers.

Also worth a look if you've got time to kill is the **Museum of Paleontology** (Mon–Sat 8am–5pm; free; ☎510/642-1821, ⓦwww.ucmp .berkeley.edu) in the nearby Valley Life Sciences Building, which details evolu-tionary concepts with hundreds of fossils, skeletons, and geological maps displayed along the corridors on the lower floors. From here it's a quick walk to the collection of cafés and restaurants lining Euclid Avenue and Hearst Avenue, and the beginning of the Northside (see below).

The Hearst family name appears with disturbing regularity around the Berkeley campus, though in most instances this is due not to the notorious newspaper baron William Randolph but to his altruistic mother, Phoebe Apperson Hearst. Besides inviting the entire senior class to her home every spring for a giant picnic, she sponsored the architectural competition that came up with the original campus plan and donated a good number of the campus buildings, including many that have since been destroyed. One of the finest survivors, the 1907 **Hearst Mining Building** (daily 8am–5pm; free), on the northeast edge of the campus, conceals a delicate metalwork lobby topped by three glass domes, above ageing exhibits on geology and mining – which is how the Hearst family fortune was originally made, long before scion W.R. took up publishing. Another Hearst legacy is the **Greek Theatre**, which hosts a summer season of rock concerts and is modeled after the amphitheater at Epidauros, Greece.

Higher up in the hills, above the 80,000-seat Memorial Stadium, the lushly landscaped **Botanical Garden** (daily 9am–5pm, 7pm in summer; free) defeats on-campus claustrophobia with its thirty acres of plants and cacti. Near the crest, with great views out over the Bay, a full-sized fiberglass sculpture of a whale stretches out in front of the space-age **Lawrence Hall of Science** (daily 10am–5pm; $8; ☎510/642-5132, ⓦwww.lawrencehallofscience.org), an excellent museum and learning center that features earthquake simulations, model dinosaurs, and a planetarium, plus hands-on exhibits for kids in the Wizard's Lab. Both the gardens and the Lawrence Hall of Science are accessible on weekdays via the free UC Berkeley Shuttle bus from the campus or the Berkeley BART station.

In the southeast corner of the campus, the **Phoebe Hearst Museum of Anthropology** in Kroeber Hall (Wed–Sat 10am–4.30pm, Sun noon–4.30pm; $2, free Thurs; ☎510/642-3682, ⓦwww.hearstmuseum.berkeley.edu) holds a variety of changing exhibits as well as an intriguing display of artifacts made by Ishi, the last surviving Yahi Indian who was found near Mount Lassen in Northern California in 1911. Anthropologist (and father of writer Ursula Le Guin) Alfred Kroeber brought Ishi to the museum (then located on the UC San Francisco campus), where he lived under the scrutiny of scientists and journalists – in effect, in a state of captivity – until his death from tuberculosis a few years later.

The brutally modern, angular concrete of the **Berkeley Art Museum** at 2626 Bancroft Way (Wed–Sun 11am–7pm; $6, free Thurs; ☎510/642-0808, ⓦwww.bampfa.berkeley.edu) is in stark contrast to the campus's older buildings. Its skylit, open-plan galleries hold works by Picasso, Cézanne, Rubens, and other notables, but the star of the show is the collection of Fifties American painter Hans Hofmann's energetic and colorful abstract paintings on the top floor. The museum is renowned for its cutting-edge, changing exhibitions: the main space hosts a range of major shows – such as Robert Mapplethorpe's controversial photographs – while the Matrix Gallery focuses on lesser-known, generally local artists. The new quarters of the **Pacific Film Archive**, diagonally opposite at 2575 Bancroft, feature nightly showings ($7) of classics, Third World, and experimental films. Call for listings (☎510/642-5249), or pick up a free monthly calendar around campus. The other rep house on campus is **UC Theatre**, 2036 University Ave (☎510/843-FILM), featuring funky theme-weeks of noir, melodrama, and other genres. Other artistic fare can be found at

Zellerbach Hall (☎510/642-9988), which showcases classical music, dance, and performances by modernists like Laurie Anderson and Phillip Glass.

Telegraph Avenue

Downtown Berkeley – basically two department stores, a few banks, a post office, and the City Hall building – lies west of the university campus around the Berkeley BART station on Shattuck Avenue, but the real activity centers on **TELEGRAPH AVENUE**, which runs south of the university from Sproul Plaza. This thoroughfare saw some of the worst of the Sixties riots and is still a frenetic bustle, especially the four short blocks closest to the university, which are packed with cafés and secondhand bookstores. Sidewalk vendors hawk

Berkeley's bookstores

Berkeley's **bookstores** are as exhaustive as they are exhausting – not surprising for a university town. Perfect for browsing and taking your time, you won't be made to feel guilty or obliged to buy a book you've been poring over for ages. The CVB has a useful list of over fifty shops, of which the following are a representative selection:

Black Oak Books 1491 Shattuck Ave ☎510/486-0698. Huge selection of secondhand and new books for every interest; also holds regular evening readings by internationally acclaimed authors.

Cody's Books 2454 Telegraph Ave ☎510/845-7852. The flagship of Berkeley booksellers, with an excellent selection of fiction, poetry, and literary criticism. There's a newer branch at 1730 4th St (☎510/559-9500).

Comics and Comix 2502 Telegraph Ave ☎510/845-4091. Great selection of comic books, especially fantasy and science fiction, both current and classic.

Comic Relief 2138 University Ave ☎510/843-5002. All the mainstream stuff, plus self-published mini-comics by locals.

Easy Going Travel Shop & Bookstore 1385 Shattuck Ave ☎510/843-3533. The essential bookstore for every traveler. Packed with printed travel paraphernalia, it offers a wide selection of guidebooks and maps for local, countrywide, and international exploration. Talks and slide shows by travel writers are also held on a regular basis.

Moe's Bookstore 2476 Telegraph Ave ☎510/849-2087. An enormous selection of new and used books on four floors with esoteric surprises in every

field of study; for academics, book collectors and browsers. There's also an excellent art section on the top floor.

Revolution Books 2425c Channing Way at Telegraph ☎510/848-1196. Wide range of books on political themes with, as you might expect, an emphasis on leftist and anarchist thought.

Serendipity Books 1201 University Ave ☎510/841-7455. This vast garage-like bookstore is off the loop of Berkeley bookstores, but an absolute must for collectors of first edition and/or obscure fiction and poetry, as well as black American writers. The prices are fair, and the owner – incredibly, given the towers of unshelved books – knows exactly where everything is to be found.

Shakespeare and Company 2499 Telegraph Ave ☎510/841-8916. Crammed with quality secondhand books at reasonable prices. The best place to linger and scour the shelves for finds.

Shambala Booksellers 2482 Telegraph Ave ☎510/848-8443. Have a transcendental out-of-body experience where eastern and western religious traditions meet in this cozy store near campus. Esoteric teachings a specialty.

handmade jewelry and brilliantly colored T-shirts, while down-and-outs hustle for spare change and spout psychotic poetry.

People's Park, now a seedy and partly overgrown plot of land half a block up from Telegraph between Haste Street and Dwight Way, was another battleground in the late Sixties, when organized and spirited resistance to the university's plans to develop the site into dormitories brought out the troops, who shot dead an onlooker by mistake. To many, the fact that the park is still a community-controlled open space (and outdoor flophouse for Berkeley's legions of pushers and homeless) symbolizes a small victory in the battle against the Establishment, though it's not a pleasant or particularly safe place to hang about, especially after dark. A mural along Haste Street recalls some of the reasons why the battles were fought, in the words of student leader Mario Savio: "There's a time when the operation of the machine becomes so odious, makes you so sick at heart, that you can't take part, you can't even tacitly take part. And you've got to put your bodies upon the gears and upon the wheels, upon the levers, upon all the apparatus, and you've got to make it stop" – ideals that can't help but be undermined by the state of the place these days. Efforts by the university to reclaim the space with volleyball and basketball courts in 1991 were met with violent protests: rioters trashed Telegraph Avenue storefronts, and a 19-year-old woman enraged at the university's plans for the park was shot dead by the police while trying to assassinate the chancellor with a knife in his home.

Directly across Bowditch Street from People's Park stands one of the finest buildings in the Bay Area, Bernard Maybeck's **Christian Science Church**. Built in 1910, it's an eclectic and thoroughly modern structure, laid out in a simple Greek Cross floor plan and spanned by a massive redwood truss with carved Gothic tracery and Byzantine painted decoration. The interior is only open on Sundays for worship and for tours at 11am, but the outside is worth lingering over, its cascade of gently pitched roofs and porticoes carrying the eye from one handcrafted detail to another. It's a clever building in many ways: while the overall image is one of tradition and craftsmanship, Maybeck also succeeded in inconspicuously incorporating such materials as industrial metal windows, concrete walls, and asbestos tiles into the structure – thereby cutting costs.

North Berkeley

NORTH BERKELEY is a subdued neighborhood of professors and post-graduate students, spreading from the flat leafy blocks around the BART lines to the steep, twisting streets that climb up the lushly overgrown hills north of the campus. At the foot of the hills, some of the Bay Area's finest **restaurants** and **delis** – most famously *Chez Panisse*, started and run by Alice Waters, the acclaimed inventor of California cuisine – have sprung up along **Shattuck Avenue** to form the so-called Gourmet Ghetto, a great place to pick up the makings of a tasty al fresco lunch. There are also a few **galleries**, most notably ACCI, 1652 Shattuck Ave (Tues–Thurs 11am–6pm, Fri 11am–7pm, Sat 10am–6pm, Sun noon–5pm; free; ☎530/843-2527), an arts-and-crafts co-operative designed to exhibit and sell the work of local artists.

Euclid Avenue, off Hearst and next to the north gate of the university, is a sort of antidote to Telegraph Avenue, a quiet grove of coffee joints and pizza parlors frequented by grad students, the focal point of the enclave known as **Northside**. Above Euclid (if you want to avoid the fairly steep walk, take the daily #65 bus or the weekdays-only #8), there are few more pleasant places for a picnic than the **Berkeley Rose Garden** (daily dawn–dusk; free), a terraced amphitheater filled with some three thousand varieties of roses and looking out across the Bay to San Francisco. Built as part of a WPA job-creation scheme during the Depression, a wooden pergola rings the top, stepping down to a small spring.

Along the crest of the Berkeley Hills, a number of enticing parks give great views over the Bay. The largest and highest of them, **Tilden Park**, spreads along the crest of the hills, encompassing some 2065 acres of near wilderness. Kids can enjoy a ride on the carved wooden horses of the carousel or the 1950s mini-steam train through the redwood trees. In the warmer months, don't miss a swim in **Lake Anza** (lifeguard on duty May–Oct daily 11am–6pm; $3).

Nearer to town at the north end of Shattuck Avenue and close by the shops and cafés along Solano Avenue, the gray basalt knob of **Indian Rock** stands out from the foot of the hills, challenging rock climbers who hone their skills on its forty-foot vertical faces. (Those who just want to appreciate the extraordinary view can take the steps around its back.) Carved into similarly hard volcanic stone across the street are the mortar holes used by the Ohlone to grind acorns into flour. In between, and in stark contrast, stands the rusting hulk of a Cold War-era air-raid siren.

West Berkeley and the Waterfront

From downtown Berkeley and the UC campus, **University Avenue** runs in an almost imperceptible gradient downhill toward the Bay, lined by increasingly shabby frontages of motels and massage parlors. The liveliest part of this **WEST BERKELEY** area is around the intersection of University and San Pablo avenues – the pre-freeway main highway north – where a community of recent immigrants from India and Pakistan have set up stores and restaurants that serve some of the best of the Bay Area's rare curries.

The area between San Pablo Avenue and the Bay is the oldest part of Berkeley, and a handful of hundred-year-old houses and churches – such as the two white-spired Gothic Revival structures on Hearst Avenue – survive from the time when this district was a separate city, known as Ocean View. The neighborhood also holds remnants of Berkeley's industrial past, and many of the old warehouses and factory premises have been converted into living and working spaces for artists, craftspeople, and computer software companies. The newly polished and yuppified stretch of **Fourth Street** between Gilman and University features upscale furniture outlets and quaint gourmet delis, as well as some outstanding restaurants (see p.610).

The I-80 freeway, and the still-used rail tracks that run alongside it, pretty well manage to cut Berkeley off from its **WATERFRONT**. The best way to get there is to take AC Transit bus #51, which runs regularly down University Avenue. Once a major hub for the transbay ferry services – to shorten journey times a three-mile-long pier was constructed, much of which still sticks out into the Bay – the **Berkeley Marina** is now one of the prime spots on the Bay for leisure activities, especially windsurfing and kayaking. People also stretch their own and their dogs' legs in the green confines of **Cesar Chavez Park**, north of the marina.

The North Bay and inland valleys

Compared to the urbanized bayfront cities of Oakland and Berkeley, the rest of the East Bay is sparsely populated, and places of interest are few and far between. The **North Bay** is home to some of the Bay Area's heaviest industry – oil refineries and chemical plants dominate the landscape – but also holds a few remarkably unchanged waterfront towns that merit a side-trip if you're passing by. Away from the Bay, the **inland valleys** are a whole other world of dry rolling hills dominated by the towering peak of **Mount Diablo**. Dozens of tract-house developments have made commuter suburbs out of what were once cattle ranches and farms, but so far the region has been able to absorb the numbers and still feels rural, despite having doubled in population in the past twenty years.

The North Bay

North of Berkeley there's not a whole lot to see or do. Off the Eastshore Freeway in **Albany**, Golden Gate Fields has **horse racing** from October to June, and beyond it, the **Albany Mud Flats** are a fascinating place to stroll; impromptu works of art made from discarded materials vie with wild irises to attract the passer-by's eye in this reclaimed landfill jutting out into the Bay. Back inland, San Pablo Avenue's strip of bars and clubs, including *Club Mallard* (no. 752), *The Ivy Room* (no. 858), and *The Hotsy-Totsy* (no. 601), are some of the best in the East Bay – that is, if you're looking for authentic, gritty saloons featuring live rock'n'roll on weekends, well-stocked jukeboxes, and pool tables reminiscent of San Francisco's Mission district. About a mile from Albany, **El Cerrito**'s main contribution to world culture was the band Creedence Clearwater Revival, who staged most of their *Born on the Bayou* publicity photographs in the wilds of Tilden Park in the hills above. The town is still home to one of the best record stores in California, Down Home Music, at 10341 San Pablo Ave, which stocks an amazing array of blues, gospel, Cajun, Tex-Mex, old time, jazz, world, and rock.

Depressing and rough **Richmond**, at the top of the Bay, was once a boom-town, building ships during World War II at the Kaiser Shipyards, which employed 100,000 workers between 1940 and its closure in 1945. Now it's the proud home to the gigantic Standard Oil refinery, the center of which you drive through before crossing the **Richmond–San Rafael Bridge** ($2) to Marin County. About the only reason to stop in Richmond is that it marks the north end of the BART line, and the adjacent Amtrak station is a better ter-minal for journeys to and from San Francisco than the end of the line in West Oakland.

Though not really worth a trip in itself, if you're heading from the East Bay to Marin County, **Point Richmond** merits a look. A cozy little town tucked away at the foot of the bridge between the refinery and the Bay, its many Victorian houses are rapidly becoming commuter territory for upwardly mobile professionals from San Francisco. Through the narrow tunnel that cuts under the hill stands the most obvious sign of this potential gentrification: "Brickyard Landing," an East Bay docklands development with modern bay-view condos, a private yacht harbor, and a token gesture to the area's industri-al past – disused brick kilns, hulking next to the tennis courts on the front lawn. The rest of the waterfront is taken up by the broad and usually deserted strand of **Keller Beach**, which stretches for half a mile along the sometimes windy shoreline.

The Carquinez Straits

At the top of the Bay some 25 miles north of Oakland, the land along the **CARQUINEZ STRAITS** is a bit off the beaten track, but it's an area of some natural beauty and much historic interest. The still-small towns along the waterfront seem worlds away from the bustle of the rest of the Bay Area, but how long they'll be able to resist the pressure of the expanding commuter belt is anybody's guess. AC Transit #74 runs every hour from Richmond BART north to **Crockett** at the west end of the narrow straits. This tiny town cut into the steep hillsides above the water seems entirely dependent upon the massive

C&H Sugar factory at its foot, whose giant neon sign lights up the town and the adjacent Carquinez Bridge.

From Crockett, the narrow Carquinez Straits Scenic Drive, an excellent cycling route, heads east along the Sacramento River. A turn two miles along drops down to **Port Costa**, a small town that was dependent upon ferry traffic across the straits to Benicia until it lost its livelihood when the bridge was built at Crockett. It's still a nice enough place to watch the huge ships pass by on their way to and from the inland ports of Sacramento and Stockton. If you don't have a bike (or a car), you can enjoy the view while riding on one of the Amtrak trains that run alongside the water from Oakland and Richmond, not stopping until Martinez at the eastern end of the straits, two miles north of John Muir's house (see p.608).

Benicia

On the north side of the straits, and hard to get to without a car, **BENICIA** is the most substantial of the historic waterfront towns, but one that has definitely seen better days. Founded in 1847, it initially rivaled San Francisco as the major Bay Area port and was even the state capital for a time. Despite Benicia's better weather and fine deep-water harbor, San Francisco, which is closer to the ocean, eventually became the main transportation point for the fortunes of the Gold Rush, and the town very nearly faded away altogether. Examples of Benicia's efforts to become a major city stand poignantly around the very compact downtown area, most conspicuously the 1852 Greek Revival structure that was used as the **first State Capitol** for just thirteen months. The building has been restored as a **museum** (Wed–Sun 10am–5pm; $2), furnished in the legislative style of the time, complete with top hats on the tables and shining spittoons every few feet.

A walking-tour map of Benicia's many intact Victorian houses and churches is available from the **tourist office**, 601 First St (Mon–Fri 8.30am–5pm, Sat & Sun 11am–3pm; ☎707/745-2120), including on its itinerary the steeply pitched roofs and gingerbread eaves of the **Frisbie–Walsh house** at 235 East L St. This prefabricated Gothic Revival building was shipped here in pieces from Boston in 1849. Across the City Hall park, the arched ceiling beams of **St Paul's Episcopal Church** look like an upturned ship's hull; it was built by shipwrights from the Pacific Mail Steamship Company, one of Benicia's many successful nineteenth-century shipyards. Half a dozen former brothels and saloons stand in various stages of decay and restoration along First Street down near the waterfront, from where the world's largest train ferries used to ply the waters between Benicia and Port Costa until 1930.

In recent years, Benicia has attracted a number of artists and craftspeople, and you can watch glassblowers and furniture makers at work in the **Benicia Glass Studios** at 675 East H St (Mon–Sat 10am–4pm, Sun in summer noon–5pm; free). Ceramic artist Judy Chicago and sculptor Robert Arneson are among those who have worked in the converted studios and modern light-industrial parks around the sprawling fortifications of the old **Benicia Arsenal**, whose thickly walled sandstone buildings east of the downtown area formed the main Army storage facility for weapons and ammunition from 1851 up to and including the Korean Conflict. One of the oddest parts of the complex is the **Camel Barn** in the **Benicia Historical Museum** (Wed–Sun 1–4pm; free; ☎707/745-5869, ⓦwww.beniciahistoricalmuseum.org). The structure used to house camels that the Army imported in 1856 to transport supplies across the deserts of the Southwestern US. The experiment failed, and the camels were kept here until they were sold off in 1864.

Vallejo and Six Flags Marine World

Across the Carquinez Bridge from Crockett, the biggest and dullest of the North Bay towns – **VALLEJO** – was, like Benicia, an early capital of California, though it now lacks any sign of its historical significance. In contrast to most of the other Gold Rush-era towns that line the Straits, Vallejo remained economically vital, largely because of the massive military presence here at the **Mare Island Naval Shipyard**, a sprawling, relentlessly gray complex that covers an area twice the size of Golden Gate Park. Closed in late 1997, Mare Island was once Vallejo's largest employer, and its less than glamorous history – the yard built and maintained supply ships and submarines, not carriers or battleships – is recounted in a small **museum** in the old city hall building at 734 Marin St (Tues–Sat 10am–4.30pm; $2), where the highlight is a working periscope that looks out across the Bay. Though no great thrill, it's worth a quick stop, situated in the center of town right on Hwy-29, the main route from the East Bay to the Wine Country (see Chapter Nine).

The best reason to come to Vallejo, however, is the newly renovated **SIX FLAGS MARINE WORLD** (daily May–Sept 10am–10pm; $43, $60 season pass; ℡707/643-ORCA, ℠www.sixflags.com), five miles north of Vallejo off I-80 at the Marine World Parkway (Hwy-37) exit. Billing itself as the nation's only wildlife park, oceanarium, and theme park, it offers a well-above-average range of performing sea lions, dolphins, and killer whales kept in approximations of their natural habitats. It also features waterski stunt shows and several newly constructed roller coasters, including the floorless Medusa, on which your legs dangle as you zoom through inversions at 65mph. The animals in the park seem very well cared for, their quarters are clean and spacious, and the shows are fun for all but the most jaded. The shark exhibit lets you walk through a transparent tunnel alongside twenty-foot Great Whites, and the tropical butterfly house is truly amazing. The most enjoyable way to get here from San Francisco is on the Blue and Gold Fleet **ferry** from Fisherman's Wharf, which takes an hour each way ($8 one way; ℡415/773-1188 for details). You can also take BART, getting off at the El Cerrito Del Norte stop where you catch the Vallejo BARTLink bus (℡707/648-4666) to the park.

The inland valleys

BART tunnels from Oakland through the Berkeley Hills to the leafy-green stockbroker settlement of **Orinda**, continuing east through the increasingly hot and dry landscape to **Concord**, site of a controversial nuclear weapons depot. In the mid-Nineties, a civilly disobedient blockade here ended in protester Brian Wilson losing his legs under the wheels of a slow-moving munitions train. The event raised public awareness – before it happened few people knew of the depot's existence – and earned Wilson a place in the Lawrence Ferlinghetti poem *A Buddha in the Woodpile;* but these days it's business as usual.

From the Pleasant Hill BART station, one stop before the end of the line, Contra Costa County Connection buses leave every thirty minutes for **MARTINEZ**, the seat of county government and a major Amtrak depot, passing the preserved home of naturalist **John Muir**, at 4202 Alhambra Ave (Wed–Sun 10am–4.30pm; $3; ℡925/228-8860), just off Hwy-4 two miles south of Martinez. Muir, an articulate, persuasive Scot whose writings and political activism were of vital importance in the preservation of America's wilderness, spent much of his life exploring and writing about the majestic Sierra Nevada mountains, particularly Yosemite. He was also one of the founders of the **Sierra Club** – a wilderness lobby and education organization still active today (see p.411 for more). Anyone familiar with the image of this thin, bearded man wandering the mountains with his knapsack, notebook, and packet of tea might be surprised to see his very conventional, upper-class Victorian home, now restored to its appearance when Muir died in 1914. Built by Muir's father-in-law, only those parts of the house Muir added himself reflect much of the personality of the man, not least the massive, rustic fireplace he had built in the East Parlor so he could have a "real mountain campfire." The bulk of Muir's personal belongings and artifacts are displayed in his study on the upper floor, and in the adjacent room an exhibition documents the history of the Sierra Club and Muir's battles to protect America's wilderness.

Behind the bell-towered main house is a large, still-productive orchard where Muir cultivated grapes, pears, and cherries to earn the money to finance his explorations (you can sample the fruits free of charge, pre-picked by staff gardeners). Beyond the orchard is the 1849 **Martinez Adobe**, homestead of the original Spanish land-grant settlers and now a small **museum** (same info as Muir House) of Mexican colonial culture. The contrast between Mexican and American cultures in early California is fascinating and, as a bonus, the building's two-foot-thick walls keep it refreshingly cool on a typically hot summer day.

At the foot of Mount Diablo, fifteen miles south, playwright **Eugene O'Neill** used the money he got for winning the Nobel Prize for Literature in 1936 to build a home and sanctuary for himself, which he named **Tao House**. It was here, before 1944 when he was struck down with Parkinson's disease, that he wrote many of his best-known plays: *The Iceman Cometh*, *A Moon for the Misbegotten*, and *Long Day's Journey into Night*. Readings and performances of his works are sometimes given in the house, which is open to visitors, though you must reserve a place on one of the free guided **tours** (Wed–Sun 10am & 12.30pm; ☎925/838-0249). There's no parking on site, so the tours pick you up in the tony town of **Danville**, whose richest neighborhood, **Blackhawk**, is the home of the **Blackhawk Automotive Museum**, 3700 Blackhawk Plaza Circle (Wed–Sun 10am–5pm; $8; ☎925/736-2277). Here you will find an impressive collection of classic cars from Britain, Germany, Italy, and the US, along with artwork inspired by them.

As for **Mount Diablo** itself, it rises up from the rolling ranchlands at its foot to a height of nearly four thousand feet, its summit and flanks preserved within **Mount Diablo State Park** (daily 8am–sunset; parking $2). North Gate, the main road through the park, reaches within three hundred feet of the top, so it's a popular place for an outing and you're unlikely to be alone to enjoy the marvelous view: on a clear day you can see over two hundred miles in every direction. There's no public transportation, though the Sierra Club sometimes organizes day-trips: see Basics, p.56.

Two main entrances lead into the park, both well-marked off I-680. The one from the southwest by way of Danville passes by the **ranger station**, where you can pick up a trail map ($1) which lists the best day-hikes. The other runs from the northwest by way of Walnut Creek, and the routes join together five miles from the summit. March and April, when the wildflowers are out, are the best times to come, and since mornings are ideal for getting the clearest view, you should drive to the top first and then head back down to a trailhead for a hike, or to one of the many picnic spots for a leisurely lunch. In summer it can get desperately hot and dry, and parts of the park are closed because of fire danger.

Livermore and Altamont Speedway

Fifteen miles southeast of Mount Diablo on the main road out of the Bay Area (I-580) or via WHEELS #12X from the Dublin/Pleasanton BART, the rolling hills around sleepy **LIVERMORE** are covered with thousands of shining, spinning, high-tech **windmills**, placed here by a private power company to take advantage of the nearly constant winds. The largest wind farm in the world, you'll probably have seen it used in a number of TV ads as a space-age backdrop to hype flashy new cars or sexy perfumes. Though the federal government provides no funding for this non-polluting, renewable source of energy, it spends billions of dollars every year designing and building nuclear weapons and other sinister applications of modern technology at the nearby **Lawrence Livermore National Laboratory**, where most of the research and development of the nuclear arsenal takes place. A small **visitor center** (Mon–Fri 1–4pm; free; ☎925/424-6575, ⓦwww.llnl.gov), one mile south of I-580 on Greenville Road, holds hands-on exhibits showing off various scientific phenomena and devices.

Up and over the hills to the east near the town of Tracy, before I-580 joins I-5 for the four-hundred-mile route south through the Central Valley to Los Angeles, stands the still-functioning **Altamont Speedway**, officially known as the Altamont Raceway Park, site of the nightmarish Rolling Stones concert in December 1969. The free concert, captured in the film *Gimme Shelter*, was intended to be a sort of second Woodstock, staged in order to counter allegations that the Stones had ripped off their fans during a long US tour. The event was a complete disaster: three people died, one kicked and stabbed to death by the Hell's Angels "security guards" – in full view of the cameras – after pointing a gun at Mick Jagger while he sang "Sympathy for the Devil." Needless to say, no historical plaque marks the site, yet if you wish to make the pilgrimage, the easiest way is by taking the Grant Line Road exit from I-580, then turning right after a mile or so onto Midway Road and continuing for a further mile and a half, crossing back over the freeway in the process.

East Bay eating

Official home of **California cuisine** and with some of the best restaurants in the state, Berkeley is an upmarket diner's paradise. But it's also a college town, and you can eat cheaply and well, especially around the southern end of the campus, along and around Telegraph Avenue. The rest of the East Bay is less remarkable, except for when it comes to **plain American food** such as barbecued ribs, grilled steaks, or deli sandwiches, for which it's unbeatable.

Budget food: diners and delis

Barney's 4162 Piedmont Ave, Oakland ☎510/655-7180; 5819 College Ave, Rockridge ☎510/601-0444; and 1591 Solano Ave, Berkeley ☎510/526-8185. The East Bay's most popular burgers – including meatless ones – smothered in dozens of different toppings.

Bette's Ocean View Diner 1807 4th St, Berkeley ☎510/644-3932. Named after the neighborhood, not after the vista, but serving up some of the Bay Area's best breakfasts and lunches. Very popular on weekends, when you may have to wait an hour for a table, so come during the week if possible.

Flint's Barbecue 3314 San Pablo Ave, Oakland ☎510/653-0593. Open until the early hours of the morning for some of the best ribs and link sausages west of Chicago, served at moderate prices.

Genova Delicatessen 5095 Telegraph Ave, Oakland ☎510/652-7401. Friendly deli complete with hanging sausages that serves up superb sandwiches for around $5.

Holy Land Kosher Food 677 Rand Ave, Oakland ☎510/272-0535. Casual diner-style restaurant just beyond the freeway north of Lake Merritt, serving moderately priced Israeli food, including excellent falafel.

Homemade Café 2454 Sacramento St, Berkeley ☎510/845-1940. Non-traditional inexpensive California-style Mexican and Jewish food served for breakfast and lunch at shared tables when crowded.

Lois the Pie Queen 851 60th St at Adeline, Oakland ☎510/658-5616. Famous around the Bay for its Southern-style sweet potato and fresh fruit pies, this cozy diner also serves massive, down-home breakfasts and Sunday dinners, all for under $10.

Rick & Ann's 2922 Domingo Ave, Berkeley ☎510/649-8538. Even in Berkeley sometimes folks want meatloaf and mashed potatoes instead of arugula, and the crowds line up outside this neighborhood diner every weekend.

Saul's Deli 1475 Shattuck Ave, Berkeley ☎510/848-3354. For pastrami, corned beef, *kreplach*, or knishes, this is the place. Great sandwiches and picnic fixings to take away, plus a full range of sit-down evening meals.

Top Dog 2534 Durant Ave, Berkeley ☎510/843-7450. OK, so the competition isn't exactly stiff, but when locals and starving college kids get a craving for the all-American treat, this dog always has its day.

Your Black Muslim Bakery 5836 San Pablo Ave, Oakland ☎510/658-7080 and 365 17th St, Oakland ☎510/839-1313. Pastries and pamphlets bringing together Oakland's diverse masses over some awesome sweet rolls.

American and California cuisine

Bay Wolf 3853 Piedmont Ave, Oakland ☎510/655-6004. Comfortable restaurant serving grilled meat, fish dishes, and specialties such as duck-liver flan on an ever-changing, expensive menu.

Café Fanny 1603 San Pablo, Berkeley ☎510/524-5447. Delicious and relatively cheap breakfasts and lunches in a small and unlikely space with a sparse industrial decor. Owned by Alice Waters of *Chez Panisse* fame (see below).

Cafe Rouge 1782 4th St, Berkeley ☎510/525-1440. Specializing in delicately prepared organic meats; they have their own butcher shop.

Chez Panisse 1517 Shattuck Ave, North Berkeley ☎510/548-5525. The California restaurant to which all others are compared. Chef Alice Waters is widely credited for first inventing California cuisine. Expect to pay at least $100 for a meal for two with delights like Monterey Bay sardine toast with arugula and fennel, or Sonoma County duck with roasted butternut squash, beets, and tatsoi, plus wine.

Citron 5484 College Ave, Rockridge ☎510/653-5484. Neighborhood gem that rivals San Francisco's best restaurants. Warm, unpretentious service and exquisite food, but expensive.

Fatapple's 1346 Martin Luther King Jr Way, Berkeley ☎510/526-2260. Crowded but pleasant family-oriented restaurant with excellent cheap American breakfasts and an assortment of sandwiches and burgers for lunch or dinner.

Grand Oaks Grill 736 Washington St, Oakland ☎510/452-1258. Moderately priced meat and seafood, cooked in a mixture of European and Asian sauces.

Lalime's 1329 Gilman St, North Berkeley ☎510/527-9838. A culinary dissertation on irony, as rich leftist Berkeley professors chow down on rich veal, pâté de foie gras, and other distinctly un-PC fare, in a casual setting.

Rivoli 1539 Solano Ave, Berkeley ☎510/526-2542. Delivering all that is wonderful about Berkeley dining: first-rate fresh food based on Italian and French cuisine, courteous service, and a casual, friendly atmosphere. All followed by a steep bill.

Spenger's 1919 4th St, West Berkeley ☎510/845-7771. With a spacious sit-down restaurant and cheap takeout counter, this is a local institution. As one of the largest chains in the Bay Area, *Spenger's* serves up literally tons of seafood to thousands of customers daily.

Asian, African, and Indian

Blue Nile 2525 Telegraph Ave, Berkeley ☎510/540-6777. Offering Ethiopian comfort food at the end of the teeming Telegraph Avenue strip, and just the place to flee the endless parade of bead merchants and incense burners.

Breads of India 2448 Sacramento St, Berkeley ☎510/848-7648. This gourmet curry house turns out delicious fresh daily specials for under $10.

Cha Am 1543 Shattuck Ave, Berkeley ☎510/848-9664. Climb the stairs up to this unlikely, always crowded small restaurant for deliciously spicy Thai food at moderate prices.

Jade Villa 800 Broadway, downtown Oakland ☎510/839-1688. For endless dim sum lunches or traditional Cantonese meals, this is one of the best places in Oakland's thriving Chinatown.

Kirala 2100 Ward St, Berkeley ☎510/549-3486. Many argue that *Kirala* serves the best sushi in the Bay Area. Others argue that it's the best in the world. Moderate pricing, too – expect to pay $10–$20 to get your fill.

Le Cheval 1007 Clay St, Oakland ☎510/763-8495. Serving simple Vietnamese the way it was meant to be, the chic, spacious surroundings and moderate prices here won't let you down.

Long Life Vegi House 2129 University Ave, Berkeley ☎510/845-6072. Vegetarian cooking (as the name suggests) that's perpetually popular with Cal students.

Nan Yang 6048 College Ave, Rockridge ☎510/655-3298. Burmese food served in colorful, large, palate-exciting portions. The political refugee owner/chef is willing to discuss all his esoteric delicacies.

New Star 526 8th St, Oakland ☎510/832-2888. No prizes for decor but this basic Chinese place serves a surprisingly good all-day buffet for $5.95.

O'Chame 1830 4th St, West Berkeley ☎510/841-8783. One of the very best Japanese restaurants in the US, with beautifully prepared sashimi and sushi as well as a full range of authentic Japanese specialties. A treat, in the $10–$20 range.

Sala Thai 807 1st St, Benicia ☎707/745-4331. Small-town, moderately priced Thai food can be just as delicious here as in any big city. Check out the enormous fish tank as your feet dangle in foot caves under the tables.

Steve's Barbeque in the Durant Center, 2521 Durant Ave, Berkeley ☎510/848-6166. Excellent, low-priced Korean food (*kimchee* to die for); other cafés in the center sell Mexican food, healthy sandwiches, deep-fried doughnuts, and slices of pizza – not to mention bargain pitchers of beer.

Vik's Chaat Corner 726 Allston Way at 4th, Berkeley ☎510/644-4412. A terrific lunchtime destination offering a wide array of Indian snacks – expect long queues at weekends. The ambience is minimal, leaving nothing to distract you from the delights of *masala dosa* or *bhel puri*. The small portions and low prices only open more possibilities for experimentation.

Italian

Angelina's 485 E 14th St, San Leandro ☎510/586-8646. Actually owned by a Greek, this friendly place serves up delicious pizza you can wash down with half-yards of ale. Not far from the airport or zoo.

Blondie's Pizza 2340 Telegraph Ave, Berkeley ☎510/548-1129. Delicious takeout New York-style pizza by the slice ($2.25, plus topping) or by the pie; it stays open until 2am and is always crowded.

Café Rustica 5422 College Ave, Oakland ☎510/654-1601. Intimate adobe-style, upscale eatery for designer pizza with a pesto and sun-dried tomatoes motif. If it's too expensive, try the tapas bar upstairs.

Cheese Board Pizza 1512 Shattuck Ave, Berkeley ☎510/549-3055. Tiny storefront selling some of the world's best "designer pizza" at very reasonable prices: $2.50 a slice, with a different topping every day. Worth searching out, but keeps irregular hours; usually Tues–Sat 11.30am–2pm & 4.30–7pm.

Garibaldi's on College 5356 College Ave, Rockridge ☎510/595-4000. Quality upmarket Italian with delicious pasta dishes and an emphasis on fine wines. Some of the sauces have a spicy Asian element.

LaVal's Pizza 1834 Euclid Ave, Berkeley ☎510/843-5617. Great graduate student hangout near the North Gate of campus. Pool table, wide-screen TV broadcasting sports, good selection of beers, and great pizza. Lunch special of a big slice and soda for $2.25.

Locanda Olmo 2985 College Ave, Berkeley ☎510/848-5544. Simple but discriminating menu at this tiny, intimate trattoria in the charming Elmwood neighborhood with moderate prices.

Oliveto 5655 College Ave, Rockridge ☎510/547-5356. With his back-to-basics recipes and dependence on home-grown ingredients, chef Paul Bertolli creates appetizing gourmet Italian cuisine. Expensive, but worth it.

Zachary's 5801 College Ave, Rockridge ☎510/655-6385 and 1853 Solano Ave, North Berkeley ☎510/525-5950. Zealously defended as the best pizza in the Bay Area, *Zachary's* is also one of the only places offering the rich, deep-dish Chicago-style pizza.

Mexican and Caribbean

Cancun Taqueria 2134 Allston Way, Berkeley ☎510/549-0964. Popular cheap downtown burrito joint with live music some nights of the week. Self-service.

Juan's Place 941 Carleton St, West Berkeley ☎510/845-6904. The original Berkeley Mexican restaurant, with cheap, great food (tons of it) and an interesting mix of people.

Mario's La Fiesta 2444 Telegraph Ave, Berkeley ☎510/540-9123. Always crowded with students and other budget-minded souls who flock here for the heaped portions of good, inexpensive Mexican food.

Picante Cocina Mexicana 1328 6th St, West Berkeley ☎510/525-3121. Good, inexpensive tacos with fresh salsa, plus live jazz on weekends.

Taqueria Morelia 4481 E 14th St, East Oakland ☎510/535-6030. Worth the long trip from downtown for the excellent burritos and more unusual but authentic *tortas*.

Tijuana Restaurant 1308 E 14th St, East Oakland ☎510/532-5575. Excellent and authentic Mexican food; famed for its *mariscada* – a plate piled high with garlicky seafood and fresh vegetables.

Tropix 3814 Piedmont Ave, Oakland ☎510/653-2444. Large portions of fruity Caribbean delicacies at reasonable prices, with authentic jerk sauce and thirst-quenching mango juice.

French and Spanish

Britt-Marie's Cafe and Wine Bar 1369 Solano Ave, Albany ☎510/527-1314. Along with a fine selection of mostly Californian wines by the glass, well-priced eclectic home cooking, plus outstanding chocolate cake, is also served.

César 1515 Shattuck Ave, Berkeley ☎510/883-0222. Perpetually crowded tapas bar serving small dishes overflowing with taste. Loosely affiliated with *Chez Panisse*, the combination of quality and a relaxed atmosphere has made it a cultish destination for locals. Gets expensive if you order too many of the diminutive dishes.

La Note 2377 Shattuck Ave, Berkeley ☎510/843-1535. The appropriately sunny, light cuisine of Provence isn't the only flavor you'll find in this petite dining room: students and teachers from the Jazzschool (sic) next door routinely stop in for casual jam sessions.

Ice cream and desserts

Dreyers Grand Ice Cream Parlor 5925 College Ave, Rockridge ☎510/658-0502. Oakland's own rich ice cream, which is distributed throughout California, is served at this small, slightly dull Rockridge café.

Fenton's Creamery 4226 Piedmont Ave, North Oakland ☎510/658-7000. A brightly lit 1950s ice cream and sandwich shop, open until 11pm on weeknights, midnight on weekends.

Yogurt Park 2433a Durant Ave, Berkeley ☎510/549-0570. Frozen yoghurt is the specialty here; open until midnight for the student throngs.

Specialty shops and markets

Acme Bread 1601 San Pablo Ave, West Berkeley ☎510/524-1327. Small bakery that supplies most of Berkeley's better restaurants; the house specialty is delicious sourdough baguettes.

Berkeley Bowl 2777 Shattuck Ave, Berkeley ☎510/841-6346. A converted bowling alley now an enormous produce, bulk, and health-food market. The least expensive grocery in town, with the largest selection of fresh food.

Cheese Board 1504 Shattuck Ave, North Berkeley ☎510/549-3183. Collectively owned and operated since 1967, this was one of the first outposts in Berkeley's Gourmet Ghetto and is still going strong, offering over 200 varieties of cheese and a range of delicious breads. Great pizzas a few doors down, too; see above.

La Farine 6323 College Ave, Rockridge ☎510/654-0338. Small but highly rated French-style bakery, with excellent *pain au chocolat*.

Monterey Foods 1550 Hopkins St, North Berkeley ☎510/526-6042. The main supplier of exotic produce to Berkeley's gourmet restaurants, this boisterous market also has the highest quality fresh fruit and vegetables available.

East Bay drinking: cafés and bars

One of the best things about visiting the East Bay is the opportunity to enjoy its many **cafés**. Concentrated most densely around the UC Berkeley campus, they're on a par with the best of San Francisco's North Beach for bohemian atmosphere – heady with the smell of coffee, and from dawn to near midnight full of earnest characters wearing their intellects on their sleeves. If you're not after a caffeine fix, you can generally also get a glass of beer, wine, or fresh fruit juice, though for serious drinking you'll be better off in one of the many **bars**, particularly in rough-hewn Oakland. Grittier versions of what you'd find in San Francisco, they're mostly blue-collar, convivial, and almost always cheaper. Not surprisingly, Berkeley's bars are brimming with students and academics.

Cafés and coffeehouses

Anna's 1801 University Ave at Grant, Berkeley ☎510/849-2662. A local institution, thanks to owner Anna de Leon's prominent involvement with city politics, not to mention her regular singing gig with the live jazz bands.

Brewed Awakenings 1807 Euclid Ave, Berkeley ☎510/540-8865. Spacious coffee and tea house near the North Gate of campus frequented by professors and grad students. Friendly staff, plenty of seating, and lovely artwork on the red-brick walls.

Annually confirmed as "Best Café to Study In" by the student press.

Café Intermezzo 2442 Telegraph Ave at Dwight, Berkeley ☎510/849-4592. Huge sandwiches on home-made sliced bread, even bigger salads, and great coffee – all very fresh and cheap.

Café Mediterraneum 2475 Telegraph Ave, Berkeley ☎510/841-5634. Berkeley's oldest café featuring sidewalk seating. Straight out of the Beat archives: beards and berets optional, battered paperbacks de rigueur.

Café Strada 2300 College Ave, Berkeley ☎510/843-5282. Upmarket, open-air café where art and architecture students cross paths with would-be lawyers and chess wizards.

Coffee Mill 3363 Grand Ave, Oakland ☎510/465-4224. Spacious room that doubles as an art gallery, and often hosts poetry readings.

Mama Bear's 6536 Telegraph Ave, Rockridge ☎510/428-9684. Mainly a women's bookstore, it doubles as a café and meeting place and has regular readings, often for women only, by lesbian and feminist writers.

Royal Ground 6255 College Ave, Rockridge ☎510/653-5458. Bright, modern, and relaxing spot in the Rockridge area, with outdoor seating. Perfect for a leisurely afternoon with the newspaper.

Bars

Albatross Pub 1822 San Pablo Ave, West Berkeley ☎510/THE-BIRD. Popular student superbar, replete with darts, pool, board games, and fireplace. Serves a large selection of ales from around the world, including a pretty good pint of Guinness. Live jazz, flamenco, and blues music on weekends (free–$3).

The Alley 3325 Grand Ave, North Oakland ☎510/444-8505. Ramshackle black-timber piano bar, decorated with business cards and with live old-time blues merchants on the keyboards.

Ben'n'Nick's 5612 College Ave, Rockridge ☎510/933-0327. Lively bar with good taped rock music and tasty food, if you're hungry.

Bison Brewing Company 2598 Telegraph Ave, Berkeley ☎510/841-7734. Eat and drink on the terrace, at great prices, where some of the best

Bay Area beers are brewed. The Honey Basil ale is highly recommended. Noisy bands on the weekend.

Cato's Alehouse 3891 Piedmont, Oakland ☎510/655-3349. Very local and casual alehouse with a good beer selection. Relax with a couple of beers and a pizza or sandwich.

Heinold's First and Last Chance Saloon 56 Jack London Square, Oakland ☎510/839-6761. Authentic waterfront bar that's hardly changed since the turn of the century, when Jack London was a regular. They still haven't bothered to fix the slanted floor caused by the 1906 earthquake.

Jupiter 2181 Shattuck Ave, Berkeley ☎510/THE-TAPS. Many types of beer to select from at this local favorite. Live jazz on weekends, an excellent atmosphere, wood-fired pizza, and an outdoor beer garden.

Pub (Schmidt's Tobacco & Trading Co) 1492 Solano Ave, North Berkeley ☎510/525-1900. Small, relaxed bar that attracts a mixture of bookworms and game players with a good selection of beers. Being in California, you can buy rare imported tobaccos but not consume them on the premises.

Pyramid Brewery 901 Gilman St, Berkeley ☎510/528-9880. Huge post-industrial space makes a surprisingly casual spot to sip the suds. Outdoor film screenings on weekend nights during summer.

Rickey's Sports Lounge 15028 Hesperian Blvd, San Leandro, near Bayfair BART ☎510/352-0200. With seven giant-screen TVs and 35 others spread around the cavernous room, this bar-cum-restaurant in a working suburb is the place to go to watch sports.

Triple Rock Brewery 1920 Shattuck Ave, Berkeley ☎510/843-2739. Buzzing, all-American beer bar: the decor is Edward Hopper-era retro, and the beers (brewed on the premises) are highly carbonated to suit the soda-pop palates of the studenty crowd, but it's still fun.

The White Horse 6560 Telegraph Ave at 66th St, Oakland ☎510/652-3820. Oakland's oldest gay bar – a smallish, friendly place, with mixed nightly dancing for men and women.

Nightlife

Nightlife is where the East Bay really comes into its own. Even more than in San Francisco, dancing to canned music and paying high prices for flashy decor is not the thing to do, which means that discos are virtually non-existent here. Instead there are dozens of **live music** venues, covering a range of musical tastes and styles – from small, unpretentious jazz clubs to buzzing R&B venues – of which Oakland's hot spots are unsurpassed. Berkeley's clubs tend more towards folk and world music, with occasional bouts of hardcore thrash, and the university itself holds two of the best medium-sized venues in the entire Bay Area, both of which attract touring big-name stars. **Tickets** for most venues are available at their box office or, for a $3 service charge, through BASS (☎510/762-2277).

Though not bad by US standards, the East Bay **theater** scene isn't exactly thriving, and shows tend to be politically worthy rather than dramatically innovative. By contrast, the range of **films** is first-class, with over a dozen movie theaters showing new releases and Berkeley's revamped Pacific Film Archive, one of the world's finest film libraries, filling its screens with obscure but brilliant art flicks. Check the free *East Bay Express* (ⓦwww.eastbayexpress.com) or the *SF Weekly* (ⓦwww.sfweekly.com) for details of who and **what's on**.

The large performance venues

Berkeley Community Theater 1930 Allston Way, Berkeley ☎510/845-2308. Jimi Hendrix played here, and the 3500-seat theater still hosts major rock concerts (Oasis to Tracy Chapman) and community events.

Center for Contemporary Music Mills College, 5000 MacArthur Blvd, Oakland ☎510/430-2191. One of the prime centers in the world for experimental music.

Oakland Coliseum Complex Coliseum BART, near the airport ☎510/639-7700, ⓦwww.oaklandcoliseum.com. Mostly stadium shows, inside the 18,000-seat arena or outdoors in the adjacent 55,000-seat coliseum. Used to be a favourite gig of the Grateful Dead's.

Paramount Theater 2025 Broadway, downtown Oakland ☎510/465-6400, ⓦwww.paramounttheater.com. Beautifully restored Art Deco masterpiece, hosting classical concerts, big-name crooners, ballets, operas, and a growing roster of rap and rock shows. Tickets $7–50. Some nights they play old Hollywood classics for $7.

Zellerbach Hall and the outdoor **Greek Theater** on the UC Berkeley campus ☎510/642-9988, ⓦwww.calperfs.berkeley.edu. Two of the prime spots for catching touring big names in the Bay Area. Zellerbach usually showcases classical music and dance, while the Greek welcomes popular acts like the Indigo Girls or Ben Harper. Tickets $20–50.

Live music venues

Ashkenaz 1317 San Pablo Ave, Berkeley ☎510/525-5054, ⓦwww.ashkenaz.com. World music and dance café. Acts range from modern Afro-beat to the best of the Balkans. Kids and under-21s welcome. Cover $5–10.

Blakes on Telegraph 2367 Telegraph Ave, Berkeley ☎510/848-0886, ⓦwww.blakesontelegraph.com. Student-patroned saloon with a funky roster of live music most nights of the week. Latin, funk, soul, hip hop, roots, rock, reggae, blues, and more. $3–8.

Eli's Mile High Club 3629 Martin Luther King Jr Way, North Oakland ☎510/655-6661. The best of the Bay Area blues clubs. Waitresses balance pitchers of beer on their heads to facilitate a safer passage through the rocking crowds. Cover $6–15.

Freight and Salvage 1111 Addison St, West Berkeley ☎510/548-1761, ⓦwww.freightandsalvage.org. Singer-songwriters in a coffeehouse setting. Cover averages $15.

Gilman Street Project 924 Gilman St, West Berkeley ☎510/525-9926. On the outer edge of the hard-core punk scene in a bare squat-like old warehouse. Weekends only; cover $5–10.

Jimmie's 1731 San Pablo Ave, Oakland ☎510/268-8445. Live blues, disco, ballads, and the occasional comedy act and fashion show at this lively bar. $5–30.

Kimball's East 4800 Shellmound St, Emeryville ☎510/658-2555, ⓦwww.kimballs.com. Fairly slick, high-style jazz and dancing venue. Cover $10–25.

La Peña Cultural Center 3105 Shattuck Ave, Berkeley, near Ashby BART ☎510/849-2568, ⓦwww.lapena.org. More folk than rock, often politically charged. Cover $8–24.

Maiko Dance Club 1629 San Pablo Ave, Berkeley ☎510/527-8226. Salsa and ballroom dance set to a live band. Very chic. Lessons available. $10–20.

Mr. E's 2286 Shattuck Ave, Berkeley ☎510/848-2009. Owned by salsa performer Pete Escovedo (the father of former Prince percussionist Sheila E), *Mr. E's* features a salsa-centric schedule to match. Free to $25.

Starry Plough 3101 Shattuck Ave, Berkeley, near Ashby BART ☎510/841-2082. Music ranges from noisy punk to alternative pop to country to traditional Irish folk, and the crowd is just as varied. Doubles as a friendly saloon and restaurant in the afternoon and early evening. Free to $5.

Yoshi's World Class Jazz House 510

Embarcadero West, Oakland ☎510/238-9200. If you only have time or money to visit one music venue, let it be this one. The West Coast's premier jazz club near Jack London Square regularly attracts a world-class roster of performers nightly. The place is almost always full. $5–40.

Cinemas

Act One and Act Two 2128 Center St, Berkeley ☎510/548-7200. Foreign films and non-mainstream American ones.

Grand Lake Movie Theater 3200 Grand Ave, Oakland ☎510/452-3556. The grand dame of East Bay picture palaces, right on Lake Merritt, showing the best of the current major releases.

Pacific Film Archive 2575 Bancroft at Bowditch St, Berkeley ☎510/642-5249. The archive's splendid new digs plays the West Coast's best selection of cinema. It features nightly showings of classics, third world, and experimental films, plus revivals of otherwise forgotten favorites. Call for listings or pick up a free monthly calendar around campus. Two films a night; tickets $7.

UC Theater 2036 University Ave, Berkeley ☎510/843-FILM. Popular revival house, with a huge auditorium and a daily double feature featuring funky theme-weeks of noir, melodrama, and other genres. Tickets $5 matinee, $7 thereafter.

Theatre

Berkeley Repertory Theater 2025 Addison St, Berkeley ☎510/845-4700, ⊛www.berkeleyrep .org. One of the West Coast's most highly respected theater companies, presenting updated classics and contemporary plays in an intimate modern theater. Tickets $10–30.

Black Repertory Group 3201 Adeline St, Berkeley ☎510/652-2120. After years of struggling, this politically conscious company moved into its own specially built home near Ashby BART in 1987, since when they've encouraged new talent with great success. Tickets $10–25.

California Shakespeare Festival Siesta Valley, Orinda ☎510/548-3422. After fifteen seasons in a North Berkeley park, this summer-long outdoor festival was forced to move to a larger home in the East Bay Hills. Tickets $15–50.

Julia Morgan Center for the Arts 2640 College Ave, Berkeley ☎510/84-JULIA, ⊛www.juliamorgan.org. A variety of touring shows stop off in this cunningly converted old church. Tickets $5–30.

The Peninsula

The city of San Francisco sits at the tip of a five-mile-wide neck of land commonly referred to as the **Peninsula**. Home of old money and new technology, the Peninsula stretches for fifty miles of relentless suburbia south from San Francisco along the Bay, past the wealthy enclaves of Hillsborough and Atherton, winding up in the futuristic roadside landscape of the **"Silicon Valley"** near **San Jose**, the fastest-growing city in California.

There was a time when the region was largely agricultural, but the computer boom – spurred by Stanford University in **Palo Alto** – has replaced orange groves and fig trees with office complexes and parking lots. Surprisingly, however, most of the land along the **coast** – separated from the bayfront sprawl by a ridge of redwood-covered peaks – remains rural and undeveloped; it also contains some excellent **beaches** and a couple of affably down-to-earth communities, all well-served by public transportation.

Getting around

BART only travels down the Peninsula as far as Daly City, from where you can catch SamTrans (☎1-800/660-4287) **buses** south to Palo Alto or along the coast to Half Moon Bay. For longer distances, **Caltrain** (☎650/817-1717 or 1-800/660-4287, ⊛www.caltrain.com) offers an hourly rail service from its terminal at Fourth and Townsend streets in downtown San Francisco, stopping at most bayside towns between the city and San Jose ($1–5); Greyhound runs regular buses along US-101 to and from their San Jose terminal at 70 S Almaden, on the corner of Santa Clara Street. Santa Clara Valley Transit

Authority (VTA) ($1.40, day-pass $4; ☎408/321-2300) runs buses and modern trolleys around metropolitan San Jose. If you're going to be spending most of your time there, most major American airlines fly direct into the newly renamed **Norman J. Mineta San Jose International Airport** (☎408/501-7600, ⓦwww.sjc.org), very close to downtown San Jose; the VTA SJC Airport Flyer bus runs to downtown San Jose and Santa Clara for $2.25 and there is the usual choice of taxis, limos, and shuttles for fancier rides to your destination.

Information

The **Palo Alto Chamber of Commerce**, 325 Forest Ave (Mon–Fri 9am–5pm; ☎650/324-3121, ⓦwww.paloaltochamber.com), has lists of local restaurants and cycle routes; for information on Stanford University, call its visitor center (Mon–Fri 8am–5pm, Sat & Sun 9am–5pm; ☎650/723-2560) in the Memorial Auditorium under Hoover Tower, or get a copy of the free *Stanford Daily*, published weekdays. To find out what's on in the area and where, pick up a free copy of the *Palo Alto Weekly*, available at most local shops or log onto ⓦwww.paloaltoonline.com, a well-organized, rich databank of everything from local bike shops and restaurants to history and movie times.

At the southern end of the Bay, the **San Jose Visitor Center** is at 125 S Market St (Mon–Fri 8am–5pm, Sat & Sun 11am–5pm; ☎408/295-9600 or 1-888/SAN-JOSE, ⓦwww.sanjose.org), or you can call in at their new **V.I.B.C.**, on the ground floor of the Convention Center at 150 W San Carlos St (same hours; ☎408/977-0900); both locations are more geared towards helping visiting businesspeople than the casual traveler though. For a better idea of local news and events pick up a copy of the excellent *San Jose Mercury* newspaper (ⓦwww.mercurycenter.com) or the free weekly *Metro* (ⓦwww.metroactive.com), although the latter usually lists as many events for San Francisco as it does for the South Bay. The website ⓦwww.sanjose.city-search.com also holds a treasure of reviews and features on the area.

Along the coast, the **Half Moon Bay Chamber of Commerce**, at 520 Kelly Ave (Mon–Fri 9am–4pm; ☎650/726-5202, ⓦwww.halfmoonbaychamber.org), gives out walking-tour maps and information on accommodation.

Accommodation

Many visitors to San Francisco choose to stay on the Peninsula rather than in the city. Dozens of $60-a-night motels line Hwy-82 – "El Camino Real," the old main highway – and, with a bit of advanced planning (and a car), sleeping here can save a lot of money. Also, if you're arriving late or departing on an early flight from SFO you might want to avail yourself of one of the many airport hotels. Perhaps the best reasons to spend the night down on the Peninsula are its low-priced, pleasant **hostels**, two of which are housed in old lighthouses right along the Pacific Coast. San Jose's **hotels** are grossly overpriced, catering more to the conventioning corporate world than the tourist or traveler, though it's possible to find the occasional decent deal, especially at weekends.

Motels and hotels

Cardinal Hotel 235 Hamilton Ave, Palo Alto ☎650/323-5101, ⓦwww.cardinalhotel.com. Affordable rates and comfortable rooms in the heart of downtown Palo Alto. The cheaper rooms have shared bathrooms. ❸

Craig Hotel 164 Hamilton Ave, Palo Alto ☎650/853-1133. Dumpy and threadbare, but right downtown and dirt cheap. Weekly rates work out at $30 a night. ❷

Days Inn Palo Alto 4238 El Camino Real, Palo Alto ☎650/493-4222 or 1-800/329-7466, ⓦwww.daysinn.com. Miles from anywhere, but the rooms are particularly clean and well kept. ❹

Hotel De Anza 233 W Santa Clara St, San Jose ☎408/286-0500 or 1-800/843-3700, ⓦwww.hoteldeanza.com. Plush business and conference orientated hotel with full amenities in one of the livelier sections of town. ❻

Executive Inn 1215 S 1st St, San Jose ☎408/280-5300 or 1-800/509-7666. Simple characterless rooms downtown near the few cafés in the city. ❹

Fairmont Hotel 170 S Market St, San Jose ☎408/998-1900 or 1-800/527-4727. San Jose's finest hotel and part of the luxury chain which began in San Francisco is located in the heart of downtown San Jose, on the Plaza. All the expected amenities, such as room service, swimming pool, lounge, and sparkling rooms. ❼

Pacifica Motor Inn 200 Rockaway Beach Ave, Pacifica ☎650/359-7700 or 1-800/522-3772. Large rooms just a block off the beach in a hamlet alongside Hwy-1. ❹

Ramada Inn 455 S 2nd St, San Jose ☎408/298-3500 or 1-888/298-2054, ⓦwww.ramada.com. Right in downtown San Jose, with pool and sauna. ❺

Sea Breeze Motel 100 Rockaway Beach Ave, Pacifica ☎650/359-3903. Beachfront hotel with attached restaurant, *Nick's*. Rooms are well kept, but standard motel style. ❹

Stanford Park Hotel 100 El Camino Real, Menlo Park ☎650/322-1234 or 1-800/368-2468, ⓦwww.stanfordparkhotel.com. Very pleasant and luxurious first-class hotel in extensive grounds near Stanford University. ❽

Valley Inn 2155 The Alameda, San Jose ☎408/241-8500, ⓦwww.valleyinnsanjose.com. Above-average motel not far from the Rosicrucian Museum. ❹

Bed and breakfast

Cowper Inn 705 Cowper St, Palo Alto ☎650/327-4475, ℱ650/329-1703. Restored Victorian house with pleasant parlor and attractive rooms close to University Avenue. ❹

Old Thyme Inn 779 Main St, Half Moon Bay ☎650/726-1616 or 1-800/720-4277, ⓦwww.oldthymeinn.com. Half a dozen incredibly quaint rooms, each with private bath, in a lovely Victorian house surrounded by luxuriant herb and flower gardens. ❻

San Benito House 356 Main St, Half Moon Bay ☎650/726-3425. Twelve restful B&B rooms in a hundred-year-old building, just a mile from the beach. Excellent restaurant downstairs. ❺

Hostels

HI-Hidden Villa 26807 Moody Rd, Los Altos Hills ☎650/949-8648, ⓦwww.norcalhostels.org. Located on an 1800-acre ranch in the foothills above Silicon Valley; closed June–Aug; members $15 per night, non-members $18.

HI-Pigeon Point Lighthouse Hwy-1, just south of Pescadero ☎650/879-0633, ⓦwww.norcalhostels .org. Worth planning a trip around, this beautifully situated hostel, fifty miles south of San Francisco, is ideally placed for exploring the redwood forests in the hills above or for watching the wildlife in nearby Año Nuevo State Reserve. Outdoor hot tub. Office hours 7.30–10am & 5.30–10pm; check-in from 4.30pm, doors locked at 11pm. Members $15 per night, non-members $18; reservations essential in summer. Private rooms $45–51, minimum two people.

HI-Point Montara Lighthouse 16th Street/ Hwy-1, Montara ☎650/728-7177, ⓦwww .norcalhostels.org. Dorm rooms in a converted 1875 lighthouse, 25 miles south of San Francisco and accessible by bike or SamTrans bus #1L or #1C (Mon–Fri until 5.50pm, Sat until 6.15pm). Outdoor hot tub. Office hours 7.30–10am & 4.30–9.30pm; doors locked 11pm. Members $15 per night, non-members $18; reservations essential in summer.

Sanborn Park Hostel 15808 Sanborn Rd, Saratoga ☎408/741-0166. Comfortable rooms in a beautiful wooded area fifteen minutes outside San Jose. Call from downtown Saratoga and they will arrange to pick you up. Open 7–9am & 5–11pm (curfew); members $10 per night, non-members $12.

Campgrounds

Butano State Park Pescadero ☎650/879-2040. RV and tent spaces in a beautiful redwood forest; reserve through ParkNet ☎1-800/444-7275; $12.

Half Moon Bay State Beach Half Moon Bay ☎650/726-8820. Tent sites in the woods behind the beach for $12.

South along the Bay

US-101 runs south from San Francisco along the Bay through over fifty miles of unmitigated sprawl lined by light-industrial estates and shopping malls to San Jose. One place along the freeway worth a visit is the **Coyote Point**

Museum (Tues–Sat 10am–5pm, Sun noon–5pm; $3), four miles south of the airport off Poplar Avenue in a large bayfront park, where examples of the natural life of the San Francisco Bay – from tidal insects to birds of prey – are exhibited in engaging and informative displays, enhanced by interactive computers and documentary films.

Six-lane freeways don't usually qualify as a scenic route, but an exception is **I-280**, one of the newest and most expensive freeways in California. It runs parallel to US-101 but avoids the worst of the bayside mess by cutting through wooded valleys down the center of the Peninsula. Just beyond the San Francisco city limits the road passes through **Colma**, a unique place filled with cemeteries, which, other than the military burial grounds in the presidio, are prohibited within San Francisco. Besides the expected roll call of deceased San Francisco luminaries like Levi Strauss and William Hearst, are a few surprises, such as Wild West gunman Wyatt Earp. If you're interested, contact the Colma Historical Association (℡650/757-1676) for free graveyard tour information.

Beyond Colma, the scenery improves quickly as I-280 continues past the **Crystal Springs Reservoir**, an artificial lake that holds the water supply for San Francisco – pumped here all the way from Yosemite. Surrounded by twenty square miles of parkland, hiking trails lead up to the ridge from which San Francisco Bay was first spotted by eighteenth-century Spanish explorers; it now overlooks the airport to the east, but there are good views out over the Pacific coast, two miles distant.

At the south end of the reservoir, just off I-280 on Canada Road near the well-heeled town of **Woodside**, luscious gardens surround the palatial **Filoli Estate** (mid Feb–late Oct Tues–Sat 10am–3.30pm, last admission 2.30pm; tours by reservation only; ℡650/364-8300 ext 507, ⓦwww.filoli.org). The 45-room mansion, designed in 1915 in neo-Palladian style by architect Willis Polk, may look familiar – it was used in the TV series *Dynasty* as the Denver home of the Carrington clan. It's the only one of the many huge houses around here that you can visit, although the gardens are what make it worth coming, especially in the spring when everything's in bloom.

Palo Alto and Stanford University

PALO ALTO, just south and three miles east of Woodside between I-280 and US-101, is a small, leafy community, and despite its proximity to Stanford, retains little of the college town vigor of its northern rival, Berkeley. In recent years, Palo Alto has become somewhat of a social center for Silicon Valley's nouveau riche, as evidenced by the trendy cafés and chic new restaurants that have popped up along its main drag, **University Avenue**. The computer industry boom job market made more than a few people rich, and this is where many of them came to spend their cash; small houses in the quaint neighborhoods surrounding the downtown area can cost close to a million dollars.

The town doesn't have a lot to offer in terms of sights other than Spanish Colonial homes, but it's a great place for a lazy stroll and a gourmet meal. Monthly historic tours of Palo Alto's neighborhoods take place during summer (℡650/299-8878), otherwise the best of the city's designs can be seen along **Ramona Street**. If you're feeling particularly energetic, or are tired of browsing in overpriced designer furniture stores, try cycling around the town's many well-marked bike routes; bikes are available for $15–30 a day from Action Sports Limited at 1047 El Camino Real (℡650/328-3180). Be aware, however, that **East Palo Alto**, on the Bay side of US-101, has a well-deserved reputation for gang- and drug-related violence, with one of the highest per capita murder rates of any US city. The area was founded in the 1920s as the utopian Runnymeade

Colony, an agricultural, poultry-raising co-operative, and the local preservation society (☎650/329-0294) can point out the surviving sites. East Palo Alto, where Grateful Dead guitarist Jerry Garcia grew up, is about as far as you can get off the San Francisco tourist trail.

STANFORD UNIVERSITY, spreading out from the west end of University Avenue, is by contrast one of the tamest places you could hope for. The university is among the top – and most expensive – in the US, though when it opened in 1891, founded by railroad magnate Leland Stanford in memory of his dead son, it offered free tuition. Ridiculed by East Coast academics, who felt that there was as much need for a second West Coast university (after UC Berkeley) as there was for "an asylum for decayed sea captains in Switzerland," Stanford was defiantly built anyway, in a hybrid of Mission and Romanesque buildings on a huge arid campus that covers an area larger than the whole of downtown San Francisco.

Stanford, whose reputation as an arch-conservative think-tank was enhanced by Ronald Reagan's offer to donate his video library to the school (Stanford politely declined), hasn't always been an entirely boring place, though you wouldn't know it to walk among the preppy future-lawyers-of-America that seem to comprise the majority of the student body. Ken Kesey came here from Oregon in 1958 on a writing fellowship, working nights as an orderly on the psychiatric ward of one local hospital, and getting paid $75 a day to test experimental drugs (LSD among them) in another. Drawing on both experiences, Kesey wrote *One Flew over the Cuckoo's Nest* in 1960 and quickly became a counterculture hero. The period is admirably chronicled by Tom Wolfe in *The Electric Kool-aid Acid Test*.

Approaching from the Palo Alto Caltrain and SamTrans bus station, which acts as a buffer between the town and the university, you enter the campus via a half-mile-long, palm-tree-lined boulevard which deposits you at its heart, the **Quadrangle**, bordered by the phallic **Hoover Tower**, whose observation platform (daily 10am–4.30pm; $2) is worth ascending, and the colorful gold-leaf mosaics of the **Memorial Church**. Free hour-long walking tours of the campus leave from here daily at 11am and 3.15pm, though it's fairly big and best seen by car or bike.

While Stanford isn't really on the tourist trail, visitors should seek out the area if only to experience one of the finest museums in the Bay Area. The **Iris and B. Gerald Cantor Center for Visual Arts** comprises 27 galleries (spread over 120,000 square feet) of treasures from six continents, dating from 500 BC to the present (Wed–Sun 11am–5pm, Thurs 11am–8pm; free; ☎650/723-3469, ⊛www.stanford.edu./dept/ccva). Housed in the old Stanford Museum of Art at the intersection of Lomita Drive and Museum Way, the Cantor Center is the result of a decade-long refubishing effort undertaken to repair damage caused by the Loma Prieta earthquake in 1989. The enchanting result incorporates the former structure with a new wing, including a bookshop and café. Visiting exhibitions have featured the work of such artists as Duchamp, Oldenburg, and Lucien Freud. One of the finest pieces in the permanent collection is the stunning *Plum Garden, Kameido*, by Japanese artist Hiroshige. Another reason to come to the museum is to have a look at its distinguished collection of over 200 **Rodin sculptures**, including a *Gates of Hell* flanked by a shamed *Adam and Eve*, displayed in an attractive outdoor setting on the museum's south side. There's a version of *The Thinker* here, as well, forming a sort of bookend with the rendition that fronts the Palace of the Legion of Honor Museum in San Francisco.

History buffs will enjoy the **Herbert Hoover Memorial Exhibit Pavilion**

(Tues–Sat 11am–4pm; free), which displays changing exhibits from the vast Hoover collection of posters, photographs, letters, and other documents. On the other hand, if you're more interested in keeping up on the latest trends in subatomic behavior, you won't want to miss the **Stanford Linear Accelerator** (Mon–Fri by appointment only; free; ℡650/926-2204), a mile west of the central campus on Sand Hill Road, where infinitesimally small particles are crashed into one another at very high speeds to see what happens. For a bird's-eye view of the campus and the rest of the Bay Area, head up one of the **hiking trails** that leads from the gate along Junípero Serra Boulevard at Stanford Avenue to Stanford's giant communications dish atop the foothills to the west of the campus.

San Jose

Burt Bacharach could easily find the way to **SAN JOSE** today – heading south from San Francisco, it's about an hour's drive (on those rare occasions when traffic is actually fluid) into the heart of the heat and smog that collects below the Bay. Sitting at the southern end of the Peninsula, San Jose has in the past 25 years emerged as the civic heart of Silicon Valley, spurred by the growth of local behemoths Apple, Cisco, Intel, and Hewlett-Packard. San Jose's current priority is the development of a culture outside the computer labs that surround the city, and new museums, shopping centers, restaurants, clubs, and performing-arts companies have mushroomed throughout the compact downtown area. However, the recent downturn in the economy has led to the ambitious multi-billion-dollar downtown renewal plan mooted by a consortium from New York to be shelved in favour of a more modest project still to be finalized by the city council. Still, while the nightlife and cultural scene here can't begin to compete with San Francisco, there are enough attractions around the city's clean and sunny streets to warrant a day-trip.

Downtown San Jose

Though now so rooted in the modern hi-tech world, San Jose's 1777 founding makes it one of the oldest settlements – and the oldest city – in California. The only sign of that downtown is the 1797 **Peralta Adobe**, at 184 W St John St (Tues–Sun noon–5pm; $6; ℡408/993-8182, ⓦwww.historysanjose.org), notable more for its having survived the encroaching suburbia than anything on display in its sparse, whitewashed interior. Admission includes a tour of the **Fallon House**, a Victorian mansion across the street, built by the city's seventh mayor in 1855, a one-time frontiersman in the Fremont expedition. The guided tours through the fifteen rooms furnished from the period also include a comprehensive video presentation on the home and adobe's relationship to the development of the cityscape.

The two blocks of San Pedro Street which run south of the adobe form a restaurant row known as **San Pedro Square**. There's no central plaza as such, just a collection of some of San Jose's best eateries (see "Peninsula eating," p.627). Further south, down Market Street, lies the pleasant and palm-dotted **Plaza de Cesar Chavez**. The Plaza is San Jose's town square and there is no better place to catch some rays on the grass, read while sitting on one of the many wooden benches, or play in the unique **fountain** whose shooting spumes are a favorite hangout for kids in the summer.

A block north of the plaza lies the **Cathedral Basilica of St Joseph**, which stands on the site of the first Catholic parish in California, circa 1803. The present building was dedicated in 1997, and it's worth entering to see its painted

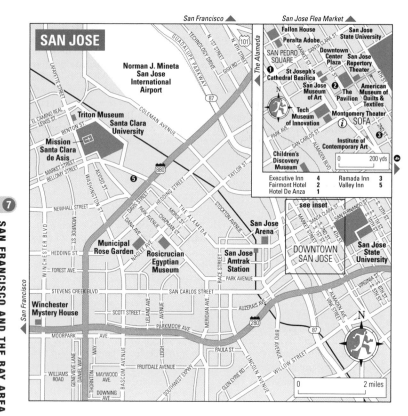

cupola, stained-glass windows, and stations of the cross. Masses are held daily, often in Spanish. Next door to the church at 110 Market is the fantastic **San Jose Museum of Art** (Tues–Sun 10am–5pm, Fri till 10pm; free; ⓦ www.sju-musart.org). Set in the old post office building built in 1892 (along with a new wing added in 1991), the museum contains more than one thousand twenti-eth-century works, with the spotlight falling on post-1980 Bay Area artists. A relationship with New York's Whitney Museum of American Art has recently been formed, allowing the museum to exhibit works from the Whitney's vast permanent collection. The sweeping, open galleries are flooded with light, as is the attached café, including its outdoor patio facing the Plaza.

Facing the southwest corner of the Plaza, downtown's biggest draw is the **Tech Museum of Innovation**, at 201 S Market St (daily 10am–5pm; $9; ⓣ 408/294-TECH, ⓦ www.thetech.org), with its hands-on displays of high-tech engineering. There are three floors of exhibits, as well as the inevitable IMAX theater ($9; combo ticket with museum entry $16). Highlights include a program that allows you to design a virtual roller coaster, regular demonstra-tions of state-of-the-art surgical instruments, and the chance to communicate with interactive robots. Unfortunately, the lines to access many of the best exhibits can seem like a virtual hell, and, unless you're a computer junkie, you may leave the museum feeling more like you've attempted to read an imper-vious software manual than visited a popular museum.

Aside from the attractions around the Plaza, San Jose's other area worth walking through is the up-and-coming **"SoFA"** entertainment district, short for South First Street. To get here from the southern tip of the Plaza, turn east on San Carlos Street and walk one block to First Street. SoFA forms the heart of San Jose's nightlife, with half a dozen clubs and discos along with a popular wine bar (see "Peninsula nightlife," p.628). There's plenty to see during the day as well, including the **Institute of Contemporary Art** (Tues–Sat noon–5pm; free) at 451 S First St. The ICA's large sunny room exhibits modern art, mainly Bay Area artists, but also work by international painters and sculptors. On the same street is downtown San Jose's **art cinema** house, the Camera 1, no. 366 (T408/998-3300), and at no. 490, one of its performing-arts companies, **The Stage** (T408/283-7142). Performances of contemporary work, like Steve Martin's *Picasso at the Lapin Agile*, regularly run Wednesday to Saturday, with tickets available for $20–25.

Walking north on First Avenue leads past the **Pavilion** shopping center, which has undergone a major renovation to become the anchor of commercial San Jose. The area needed it, having laid stagnant for decades as locals shopped at suburban malls. To combat this flight, city planners have zoned all of First and Second streets for the redevelopment mentioned earlier.

Around San Jose

Head four miles northwest of downtown and you'll come across two of San Jose's more intriguing, and relaxing, places to hang out. The first is the **Rosicrucian Museum**, 1342 Naglee Ave (Tues–Fri 10am–5pm, Sat & Sun 11am–6pm; $9; T408/947-3636, Wwww.rosicrucian.org), a grand structure that contains a brilliant collection of Assyrian and Babylonian artifacts, with displays of mummies, amulets, a replica of a tomb, and ancient jewelry. The museum consists of a dark and musty room befitting its contents. Don't miss the mummies of baboons, birds, and fish on the left-hand side of the tomb wing. Aside from the corpses and models within, the best part about the Rosicrucian is its garden grounds, featuring a replica of the Akhenaten Temple from Luxor. Across the street and two blocks west of the museum is the second relaxing locale, San Jose's **Municipal Rose Garden** (daily 8am–sunset; free). This beautiful expanse of green and rows of rose bushes is perfect for a picnic, and the fountain in the garden's center is a popular wading pool for local kids. Roll up your pants, soak your feet, and take in a nice view of the Santa Cruz Mountains to the west amidst the sweet scents.

Engulfed in the sprawl of northwestern San Jose, the small community of **Santa Clara** holds a few tourist attractions of its own. The late eighteenth-century **Mission Santa Clara de Asis**, just south of The Alameda (Route 82), is one of the least impressive structures in the mission chain that runs along the California coast on the traces of the El Camino Real. Hidden on the grounds of the Jesuit-run **University of Santa Clara**, there's not a lot to see of the original mission-era buildings here, though it can be interesting to note how their remnants have been subtly preserved, integrated into the overall campus design. The **de Saisset Museum** (Tues–Sun 11am–4pm; $1 donation suggested; T408/554-4528) on the grounds traces the history of the mission through a permanent display of objects recovered from its ruins – the mission burned in a 1926 fire – along with changing shows of contemporary art. The bell in the belfry is original, a gift from King Carlos IV of Spain in 1798. Overall, the university is a green, quiet place to stroll around and pass an afternoon.

A few miles south of here is a true American tourist trap, unmissable if you're into a good yarn. The **Winchester Mystery House**, 525 S Winchester Blvd, just off I-280 near Hwy-17 (daily 9am–5pm; $16.95; ☎408/247-1313, Ⓦwww.winchestermysteryhouse.com), belonged to Sarah Winchester, heiress to the Winchester rifle fortune, who was convinced upon her husband's death in 1884 that he had been taken by the spirits of men killed with his weapons. The ghosts told her that unless a room was built for each of them, the same fate would befall her. She took them so literally that the sound of hammers never ceased – 24 hours a day for the next thirty years. Now, unfinished, the house is a hodgepodge of extensions and styles: extravagant staircases lead nowhere and windows open onto solid brick walls. Today, the ghosts can't be much happier seeing that construction has stopped and the place has been converted into a shameless money maker, where visitors have to run a gauntlet of ghastly gift stores and soda stands to get in or out. If you're a real sucker for punishment you can take the extra Behind the Scenes tour for $13.95.

One other Peninsula place might exercise a certain attraction, particularly to those fond of rollercoasters, log rides, and all-American family fun; **Paramount's Great America** (summer daily 10am–10pm; rest of year Sat & Sun 10am–dusk; $44; ☎408/988-1776, Ⓦwww.pgathrills.com). This hundred-acre amusement park on the edge of San Francisco Bay, just off US-101 north of San Jose, may not be in the same league as Disneyland, but the range of high-speed thrills and chills available – from the looping Top Gun Jetcoaster and Stealth, which zooms over the rails at 65mph, to the fierce Delirium ride, unveiled in 2002 – should satisfy even the most hardcore adrenaline junkies.

The coast

The largely undeveloped **coastline** of the Peninsula south of San Francisco is worlds away from the inland valleys. A few small towns, countless beaches, and sea lions trace the way 75 miles south to the mellow summer fun of Santa Cruz and Capitola. Bluffs protect the many **nudist beaches** from prying eyes and make a popular launching pad for hang-glider pilots, particularly at **Fort Funston**, a mile south of the San Francisco Zoo – also the point where the earthquake-causing San Andreas Fault enters the sea, not to surface again until Point Reyes. **Skyline Boulevard** follows the coast from here past the repetitious tracts of proverbial ticky-tacky houses that make up Daly City, before heading inland toward Woodside at its intersection with Hwy-1, which continues south along the coast. Driving Hwy-1 can be a relaxing jaunt providing jaw-dropping views of the ocean, as long as you avoid the masses. Summer and weekend afternoons find the route clogged with campers creeping along at 30mph and few opportunities to pass. Try hitting the road early in the morning (as in at sunrise) and, provided the fog isn't obscuring everything, expect a magical ride.

Pacifica and around

San Pedro Point, a popular surfing beach fifteen miles south of San Francisco proper, and the town of **PACIFICA**, mark the southern extent of the city's suburban sprawl. Pacifica is a pleasant stopoff for lunch and wave gazing around Rockaway Beach. Stop in at the ultra-friendly **Chamber of Commerce**, 225 Rockaway Beach Ave (Mon–Fri 9am–5pm, Sat & Sun 10am–4.30pm; ☎650/355-4122, Ⓦwww.pacificachamber.com), for free maps of the area, including trail guides for **Sweeney Ridge**, from where Spanish explorer Gaspar de Portola discovered the San Francisco Bay in 1769. Pacifica's old

Ocean Shore Railroad Depot here, now a private residence, is one of the few surviving remnants of an ill-advised train line between San Francisco and Santa Cruz. Wiped out during the 1906 earthquake, the line was in any case never more than a third complete. Its few patrons had to transfer back and forth by ferry to connect the stretches of track that were built, the traces of which you can still see scarring the face of the bluffs. The continually eroding cliffs make construction of any route along the coast difficult, as evidenced a mile south by the **Devil's Slide**, where a new cement support has been added to lessen the regularity with which the highway is washed away by winter storms. The slide area was also a popular dumping spot for corpses of those who fell foul of rum-runners during Prohibition, and is featured under various names in many of Dashiell Hammett's detective stories.

Just south of the Devil's Slide, the sands of **Gray Whale Cove State Beach** (daily dawn–dusk) are clothing-optional. Despite the name, it's not an especially great place to look for migrating gray whales, but the stairway at the bus stop does lead down to a fine strand. Two miles south, the red-roofed buildings of the 1875 **Montara Lighthouse**, set among the windswept Monterey pine trees at the top of a steep cliff, have been converted into a youth hostel (see p.618). Just south of the hostel, on California Street, the **Fitzgerald Marine Reserve** (℡650/728-3584; free) has three miles of diverse oceanic habitat, peaceful trails, and, at low tide, the best tidal pools in the Bay Area. The ranger often gives free guided interpretive walks through the reserve at low tide, the best time to explore, so call ahead for low tide times. At the south end of the reserve, **Pillar Point** juts out into the Pacific; just to the east, along Hwy-1, fishing boats dock at Pillar Point Harbor. Mavericks Beach, just off Pillar Point beyond the enormous communications dish, with the largest waves in North America, attracts some of the world's best (and craziest) surfers when conditions are right – just watching them can be an exhilarating way to spend an hour or so, and hundreds of people do every day. There's a long breakwater you can walk out on, too, but remember never to turn your back to the ocean – rogue waves have crashed in and swept unsuspecting tourists to their deaths. The surrounding villages of **Princeton-By-The-Sea** and **El Grenada** have good roadside lunch stops serving freshly caught fish and hamburgers. Further along, more surfing is done just offshore from **Miramar Beach**; after a day in the water or on the beach, the place to head for is the beachfront Douglass Beach House (see p.628), an informal jazz club and beer bar that faces the sands.

Half Moon Bay

HALF MOON BAY, twenty miles south of the city and the only town of any size along the coast between San Francisco and Santa Cruz, takes its name from the crescent-shaped bay formed by Pillar Point. Lined by miles of sandy beaches, the town is surprisingly rural considering its proximity to San Francisco and Silicon Valley, and sports a number of ornate Victorian wooden houses around its center. The oldest of these, at the north end of Main Street, was built in 1849 just across a little stone bridge over Pillarcitos Creek. The **Chamber of Commerce** (see opposite for details) on Hwy-1 has free walking-tour maps of the town and information on the two annual festivals for which the place is well known. These are the **Holy Ghost and Pentecost Festival**, a parade and barbecue held on the sixth Sunday after Easter, and the **Pumpkin Festival**, celebrating the harvest of the area's many pumpkin farms, just in time for Halloween when the fields around town are full of families searching for the perfect jack-o'-lantern to greet the hordes of trick-or-treaters. If you fancy an equine experience, Friendly Acres Ranch, one mile north of town at 2150 N Cabrillo Hwy (☎650/726-9903, ⓦwww.friendly-acresinc.com) has trail **rides** for $30 per hour and ninety-minute beach rides for $40. Free, basic campgrounds line the coast in **Half Moon Bay State Park**, half a mile west of the town. Stop here if you're low on gas, as the fifty-mile stretch of Hwy-1 to Santa Cruz doesn't offer many places to fill up.

SamTrans bus #294 route ends in Half Moon Bay; to continue south, transfer here to route #15, which runs every three hours to Waddell Creek, twenty miles south. **San Gregorio State Beach**, ten miles south of Half Moon Bay, is at its best in the spring, after the winter storms, when flotsam architects construct a range of driftwood shelters along the wide beach south of the parking area. On hot summer days, the beach is packed with well-oiled bodies, but the sands around the bluffs to the north are quieter. You can bathe nude at San Gregorio Private Beach, though you pay to park and enter; follow Hwy-1 one mile north of San Gregorio Road and watch for the white gate that marks the turning. Just north of Half Moon Bay, Dunes Beach and Venice Beach are also beautiful expanses of sand and ocean.

The Butano redwoods and the Año Nuevo State Reserve

If you've got a car and it's not a great day for the beach, head up into the hills above, where the thousands of acres of the **Butano redwood forest** feel at their most ancient and primeval in the greyest, gloomiest weather. About half the land between San Jose and the coast is protected from development in a variety of state and county parks, all of which are virtually deserted despite being within a thirty-minute drive of the Silicon Valley sprawl. Any one of a dozen roads heads through endless stands of untouched forest, and even the briefest of walks will take you seemingly miles from any sign of civilization. Hwy-84 climbs up from San Gregorio through the Sam McDonald County Park to the hamlet of **La Honda**, where Ken Kesey had his ranch during the Sixties and once notoriously invited the Hell's Angels to a party. From here, you can continue on to Palo Alto, or, better, loop back to the coast via Pescadero Road. A mile before you reach the quaint town of **Pescadero**, Cloverdale Road heads south to **Butano State Park**, where you can hike and camp overlooking the Pacific. Tiny Pescadero itself has one of the best places to eat on the Peninsula – Duarte's (see below).

Back on Hwy-1, five miles south of Pescadero, you can stay the night in the old lighthouse keeper's quarters and soak your bones in a marvelous hot tub at the *HI-Pigeon Point Lighthouse Hostel* (see p.618). The calmest, most pleasant beach in which to wade is at **Bean Hollow State Beach**, a mile north of the hostel. If you're here during December through March, continue south another five miles to the **AÑO NUEVO STATE RESERVE** for a chance to see one of nature's most bizarre spectacles – the mating rituals of the **northern elephant seals**. These massive, ungainly creatures, fifteen feet long and weighing up to three tons, were once found all along the coast, though they were nearly hunted to extinction by whalers in the last century. During the mating season, the beach is literally a seething mass of blubbery bodies, with the trunk-nosed males fighting it out for the right to sire as many as fifty pups in a season. At any time of the year, you're likely to see a half dozen or so dozing in the sands. The reserve is also good for birdwatching, and in March you might even catch sight of migrating gray whales.

The slowly resurgent Año Nuevo seal population is still carefully protected, and during the breeding season the obligatory guided tours – designed to protect spectators as much as to give the seals some privacy – begin booking in September (hourly 8am–4pm; $4 per person, $2 parking; ☏650/879-2025 or 1-800/444-4445). Otherwise tickets are usually made available to people staying at the *Pigeon Point Hostel*, and SamTrans (☏650/656-4481 or 1-800/660-4287) sometimes runs charter bus tours for $12 per person from the town of **San Mateo** on the Bay side of the Peninsula. (See "The Central Coast" chapter for an account of the area from Año Nuevo south to Santa Cruz and Monterey.)

Peninsula eating

The **restaurants** on the Peninsula, particularly in pseudo-ritzy Palo Alto and newly yuppified Burlingame, on the east side of the Peninsula about four miles south of San Francisco Airport, are increasingly on a par with their San Franciscan counterparts. Many, filled with wealthy young computer executives, require dinner reservations every night of the week. In San Jose, consider dining around San Pedro Square for a good choice of cuisine. The following list concentrates primarily on establishments centrally located in the downtown areas of the various Peninsula cities, with a few others that are worth almost any effort to get to.

Restaurants

71 Saint Peter 71 N San Pedro St, San Jose ☏408/971-8523. Patio dining and oyster bar centered on a menu of filet mignon, pork loin, chicken and salads. Extremely hot with the in-crowd. Lunch Monday to Friday, dinner nightly.

AP Stump's 163 W Santa Clara St, San Jose ☏408/292-9928. Best place to go if you have an unlimited expense account. Pricey (entrées all over $20) California cuisine, but one of the places to be seen in Silicon Valley. Great wine list.

Barbara's Fish Trap 281 Capistrano Rd, off Hwy-1, Princeton-by-the-Sea ☏650/728-7049. Oceanfront seafood restaurant with good-value fish dinners and an unbeatable view.

Bistro Elan 448 S California Ave, Palo Alto ☏650/327-0284. Serving spiffy Cal cuisine to the cyber-elite. Prices are rather steep, so consider a lunchtime visit.

Bistro Vida 641 Santa Cruz Ave, Menlo Park ☏650/462-1686. Giving Silicon Valley a much-needed style infusion by serving delicious Left Bank Parisian bistro fare.

Blake's Steakhouse and Bar 17 N San Pedro St, San Jose ☏408/298-9221. Craving a New York strip or a steamed lobster, washed down with a fine martini? *Blake's* is the place. Entrées around $20, sandwiches also available.

Chateau des Fleurs 523 Church St, Half Moon Bay ☏650/712-8837. The exquisite flower garden in front welcomes you to this small, reasonably priced French restaurant.

Duarte's 202 Stage Rd, Pescadero ☏650/879-

0464. Platefuls of traditional American food (especially fish) for around $10 are served in this down-home find connected to a bar full of locals in cowboy hats. Famous for their artichoke soup.

E&O Trading Company 96 S First St, San Jose ☏408/938-4100. Upscale Southeast Asian grill featuring curried fish and other Vietnamese/Indonesian fare. Entrées approaching $20.

El Amigo Burrito 4485 Stevens Creek Blvd, Santa Clara ☏408/248-3113. Relaxed place serving huge portions of authentic Mexican food at very reasonable prices.

Eulipia 374 S First St, San Jose ☏408/280-6161. Stylish dinner spot featuring well-prepared versions of California cuisine staples like grilled fish and fresh pastas. Entrées from $11–26. Closed Mondays.

Evvia 420 Emerson St, Palo Alto ☏650/326-0983. California/Greek lamb and fish dishes with names like *paidakia arnisia* and *arni kapama* served in a cozy yet elegant dining room. Full bar.

Fresco 3398 El Camino Real, Palo Alto ☏650/493-3470. Wide selection of pastas, pizzas, and salads with palpably fresh ingredients in unusual combinations.

Il Forniao 327 Lorton Ave, Burlingame ☏650/375-8000. Part of an upscale chain serving reliably well-prepared Italian staple entrées and baked goods.

Joanie's Cafe 447 California Ave, Palo Alto ☏650/326-6505. Homestyle breakfasts and lunches in a comfortable neighborhood restaurant.

John's Market Town and Country Village,

Embarcadero at El Camino, Palo Alto ☎650/321-8438. Steer past the high school kids on lunch break to get one of the best (and biggest) deli sandwiches around. Located across the street from Stanford Stadium.

Krung Siam 423 University Ave, Palo Alto ☎650/322-5900. Classy but not too expensive restaurant serving beautifully presented traditional Thai fare.

L'Amie Donia 530 Bryant St, Palo Alto ☎650/323-7614. How do you simultaneously splurge and keep within your budget? A $34 three-course prix fixe menu from this classy French bistro serves you well.

Los Gallos Taqueria 3726 Florence St, Redwood City ☎650/369-1864. Simply put, they make the best burritos on the Peninsula. Take the Marsh Road exit from Hwy-101 and look for the Marsh Manor shopping center.

Mike's Cafe, Etc. 2680 Middlefield Rd, Palo Alto ☎650/473-6453. Unpretentious neighborhood restaurant hidden behind a hardware store. Excellent fresh salads, pastas, and simple meat dishes are sometimes brought to your table by Mike himself.

New India Palace 448 University Ave, Palo Alto ☎650/327-3455. Reasonable North Indian restaurant with a great-value lunch buffet.

Original Joe's 301 S First St, San Jose ☎408/292-7030. Grab a stool at the counter or settle into one of the comfy vinyl booths and enjoy a burger and fries or a plate of pasta at this San Jose institution, where $10 goes a long way. Open 11am–1am.

Peggy Sue's 29 N San Pedro St, San Jose ☎408/298-6750. Inexpensive milkshakes, burgers, and fries served in a 1950s setting. Also has a vegetarian and kids' menu. Popular with Sharks' fans before ice hockey games.

Rock'n'Rob's 450 Dundee Way, Rockaway Beach, Pacifica ☎650/359-3663. This new diner decorated in the old style churns out tons of burgers and fries all day, but no breakfast.

Spiedo 151 W Santa Clara St, San Jose ☎408/971-6096. Handmade pasta, pizza, calamari, salmon, and more delight the tastebuds at lunch and dinner daily. Entrées begin at $10.

St Michael's Alley 806 Emerson St, Palo Alto ☎650/326-2530. This former student café hangout has transformed itself into one of Palo Alto's hottest bistros and the "casual California" cuisine served at lunch and dinner couldn't be farther from the old fare of bagels and coffee. A fine wine list and weekend brunch ($10) keeps guests coming back for seconds.

Trieo Chau 325 S First St, San Jose ☎408/998-3306. Good inexpensive Chinese with authentic dishes from the southern Trieu Chau region and neighboring Cambodia.

Peninsula nightlife

For a serious night out on the town, you're better off heading up to San Francisco, though many San Jose residents may try to convince you otherwise. Nevertheless, there are several good **bars** and **clubs** on the Peninsula – particularly in San Jose's SoFA district, but also in the studenty environs of Palo Alto. If you're in the mood for quiet conversation rather than wild beer drinking, check out one of the **cafés** listed, many of which feature fresh sandwiches and salads along with the requisite microbrewed beers (Gordon Biersch originated in San Jose) and gourmet coffees.

Bars and clubs

Agenda 399 S First St, San Jose ☎408/287-3991. A bar/restaurant/lounge in SoFA which heralded the arrival of nightlife in San Jose. DJ dancing and live jazz nightly.

B-Hive 372 S First St, San Jose ☎408/298-2529. Upstairs dance club spinning hip hop, R&B, and reggae. Rhythm Records, below, keeps them supplied with loops. Over-21s only.

Blue Chalk Café 630 Ramona St, Palo Alto ☎650/326-1020. Yuppies and other young Siliconites have been flocking to this wildly successful bar/pool-hall/restaurant ever since it opened in 1993.

Brittania Arms Downtown 173 W Santa Clara St, San Jose ☎408/266-0550. Latest addition to the growing chain of British-themed pubs with fish'n'chips, real ale, footie (meaning soccer) on TV, and a trivia quiz night.

Cactus Club 417 S First St, San Jose ☎408/491-9300. One of the finest clubs in downtown San Jose, hosting some of the better up-and-coming bands with music ranging from roots reggae to hard-core thrash. More punk sensibility than attention to decor. Cover $5–10.

The Dance Plex 394 S First St, San Jose
☎408/280-1977. Retro joint in a disused Art Deco
cinema, featuring clubs like Polly Esther's 70s
disco and Culture Club 80s Night on different days.
Douglass Beach House Miramar Beach, two
and a half miles north of Half Moon Bay on Hwy-
1, go west down Medio Avenue ☎650/726-4143.
Two-story country beach house with fireplace
and outside deck hosting West Coast jazz performers.
Emma's Club Miami 177 W Santa Clara St, San
Jose ☎408/279-3670. Huge San Pedro Square
bar/Mexican restaurant with Latin music and
dancing on weekends. Great patio.
Gordon Biersch Brewery 640 Emerson St, Palo
Alto ☎650/323-7723. Among the first and still the
best of the Bay Area's microbrewery-cum-restau-
rants. Also in San Francisco (see p.567) and in
downtown San Jose at 33 E San Fernando St
☎408/294-6785.
Katie Bloom's 150 S First St, San Jose ☎408/294-
4408. Irish pub in the Pavilion shopping center that
also serves pub fare and occasionally has live acts.
Pictures of eminent Irishmen like James Joyce and
Flann O'Brien adorn the windows.
Kleidon's Cocktails 152 Post St, San Jose
☎408/293-2461. Old downtown San Jose dive
bar that's perfect if you get tired of drinking
amongst the beautiful people.
Moss Beach Distillery Beach and Ocean, Moss
Beach ☎650/728-0220. If you don't feel like paying out $20 per entrée at the popular restaurant,
snuggle up under a wool blanket, order a drink
and an appetizer, and watch the sunset from the
patio overlooking the ocean.
Tied House 65 N San Pedro St, San Jose
☎408/295-2739. San Pedro Square sports bar
and brewery which also serves burgers and the
like inside its gigantic space.
Toon's S Second St at Santa Clara, San Jose

☎408/292-7464. Downtown San Jose's hip-hop
dance club and pool bar. Sister club the *Voodoo
Lounge*, next door, is for 21-and-over only and
enforces a strict dress code of no hats, baggies, or
tennis shoes.
Trials Pub 265 N First St, San Jose ☎408/947-
0497. Longest established British pub in town,
with all the expected stouts, ales, and dartboards.
The Usual 400 S First St, San Jose ☎408/535-
0330. Live-music venue in SoFA featuring retro
Eighties acts and current artists of all stripes.
Waves Smokehouse and Saloon 65 Post St, San
Jose ☎408/885-WAVE. Huge sports screens dominate this spacious bar. Live country music on the
first Tuesday of each month.
Wine Galleria 377 S First St, San Jose
☎408/298-1386. Large wine bar with plush sofas
next to Café Matisse. Huge array of vintages for
sale by the glass, with specials such as five for
$20.

Cafés

Café Matisse 371 First St, San Jose ☎408/298-
7788. Modern 3-D art hangs on the walls of this
funky artist studio space, which serves fresh coffee and pastries.
Café at Printer's Inc 320 California Ave, Palo Alto
☎650/323-3347. Good food and coffees served
adjacent to Palo Alto's best bookstore.
Caffé Verona 236 Hamilton Ave, Palo Alto
☎650/326-9942. Relaxing hangout for Palo Alto's
intellectual crowd.
Global Village Café 172 N Main St, Sebastopol
☎650/829-4765. A popular breakfast gathering
spot for techie types – when they make time for
breakfast, that is.
M Coffee 522 Main St, Half Moon Bay
☎650/726-6241. Coffees, teas, sandwiches, and
ice cream in a small, homely eatery.

Marin County

Across the Golden Gate from San Francisco, **Marin County** (pronounced
"Ma-RINN") is an unabashed introduction to Californian self-indulgence: an
elitist pleasure zone of conspicuous luxury and abundant natural beauty, with
sunshine, sandy beaches, high mountains, and thick redwood forests. Often
ranked as the wealthiest county in the US, Marin has attracted a sizeable contingent of northern California's wealthiest young professionals, many of whom
grew up during the Flower Power years of the 1960s and lend the place its
New Age feel and reputation. Though many of the cocaine-and-hot-tub devotees who seemed to populate the swanky waterside towns in the 1970s have

traded in their drug habits for mountain bikes – which were invented here – life in Marin still centers on personal pleasure, and the throngs you see hiking and cycling at weekends, not to mention the hundreds of esoteric self-help practitioners – rolfing, rebirthing, and soul-travel therapists fill up the classified ads of the local papers – prove that Marinites work hard to maintain their easy air of physical and mental well-being. Indeed, early in 2002, George Bush Sr

△ One of the Bay Area's many murals

came in for some flak and had to back down after criticising the wealthy residents of Marin for having so many hot tubs and yet still voting Democrat.

Flashy modern ferry boats, appointed with fully stocked bars, sail across the Bay from San Francisco and give a good initial view of the county. As you head past desolate Alcatraz Island, curvaceous **Mount Tamalpais** looms larger until you land at its foot in one of the chic bayside settlements of **Sausalito** or **Tiburon**. **Angel Island**, in the middle of the Bay but accessible most easily from Tiburon, provides relief from the excessive style-consciousness of both towns, retaining a wild, untouched feeling among the eerie ruins of derelict military fortifications.

Sausalito and Tiburon (and the lifestyles that go with them) are only a small part of Marin. The bulk of the county rests on the slopes of the ridge of peaks that divides the Peninsula down the middle, separating the sophisticated harborside towns in the east from the untrammeled wilderness of the Pacific Coast to the west. The **Marin Headlands**, just across the Golden Gate Bridge, hold time-warped old battlements and gun emplacements that once protected San Francisco's harbor from would-be invaders, and now overlook hikers and cyclists enjoying the acres of open space and wildlife. Along the coastline that stretches north, the broad shore of **Stinson Beach** is the Bay Area's finest and widest stretch of sand, beyond which Hwy-1 clings to the coast past the rural village of **Bolinas** to seascapes around **Point Reyes**, where it is thought Sir Francis Drake may have landed in 1579 and claimed all of California for England. Whale and seal watchers congregate here year-round for glimpses of migrations and matings.

Inland, the heights of Mount Tamalpais, and specifically **Muir Woods**, are a magnet to sightseers and nature lovers, who come to wander through one of the few surviving stands of the native coastal redwood trees. Such trees covered most of Marin before they were chopped down to build and rebuild the wooden houses of San Francisco. The long-vanished lumber mills of the rustic town of **Mill Valley**, overlooking the Bay from the slopes of Mount Tam, as it's locally known, bear the guilt for much of this destruction; the oldest town in Marin County is now home to an eclectic bunch of art galleries and cafés. Further north, Marin's largest town, **San Rafael**, is best left alone, though its outskirts contain two of the most unusual attractions in the county: **Frank Lloyd Wright**'s peculiar Civic Center complex and the preserved remnants of an old Chinese fishing village in **China Camp State Park**. The northern reaches of Marin County border the bountiful wine-growing regions of the Sonoma and Napa valleys, detailed in Chapter 9, "Northern California."

Arrival and getting around

Just getting to Marin County can be a great start to a day out from San Francisco. Golden Gate Transit **ferries** (☎415/923-2000 in SF, ☎415/455-2000 in Marin, ⓦwww.goldengate.org) leave from the Ferry Building on the Embarcadero, crossing the Bay past Alcatraz Island to **Sausalito** and **Larkspur**; they run approximately every thirty minutes during the rush hour, less often the rest of the day, and every two hours on weekends and holidays (see box p.634 for details). Tickets cost $5.30 one way to Sausalito, $3.10 to Larkspur ($5.30 weekends); refreshments are served on board. The slightly more expensive Blue and Gold Fleet ($6.75 one way; ☎415/773-1188, ⓦwww.blueandgoldfleet.com) sail from Pier 41 at Fisherman's Wharf to Sausalito and Tiburon – from where the Angel Island ferry ($7 round-trip, $1 per bicycle; ☎415/435-2131) nips back and forth to **Angel Island State Park** daily in summer, weekends only in the winter. Blue and Gold Fleet provides an additional excursion service direct to Angel Island ($10.50 round-trip) from the Ferry Building, twice daily on weekdays, thrice at weekends.

Golden Gate Transit also runs a comprehensive **bus service** around Marin County and across the Golden Gate Bridge from the Transbay Terminal in San Francisco (same contacts as ferries above), and publishes a helpful and free system map and timetable, including all ferry services. Bus fares range from $1.50 to $6, with routes running every thirty minutes throughout the day, and once an hour late at night. Some areas can only be reached by GGT commuter services, which run only during the morning and evening rush hours (call ahead to check schedule). Also, San Francisco's MUNI bus #76 runs hourly from San Francisco direct to the Marin Headlands on Sundays only. Golden Gate Transit bus route #40, the only service available between Marin County and the East Bay, runs from the San Rafael Transit Center to the Del Norte BART station in El Cerrito ($5 each way).

If you'd rather avoid the hassle of bus connections, Gray Line ($37; ☎415/558-9400, ⍟www.grayline.com) offers four-hour guided **bus tours** from the Transbay Terminal in San Francisco, taking in Sausalito and Muir Woods (daily year-round 9am, check for increased services in summer); the Blue and Gold Fleet ferry also has a boat-and-bus trip to Muir Woods, via Tiburon (Mon–Fri 11am, weekends & holidays 9.45am & 11.30am; 4–5hr; $39).

One of the best ways to get around Marin is by **bike**, particularly using a mountain bike to cruise the many trails that crisscross the county, especially in the Marin Headlands. If you want to ride on the road, Sir Francis Drake Highway – from Larkspur to Point Reyes – makes a good route, though it's best to avoid weekends, when the roads can get clogged up with cars. All ferry services (except Alcatraz) allow bicycles.

Information

Three main on-the-spot sources can provide further information on Marin County: the **Marin County Visitors Bureau**, 1013 Larkspur Landing Circle,

Marin County bus services on Golden Gate Transit

#2: San Francisco–Marin Headlands–Marin City–Sausalito; weekdays.

#4: San Francisco–Mill Valley; weekdays.

#8: San Francisco–Tiburon–Sausalito; weekdays.

#10: Sausalito–Marin City–Mill Valley–Tiburon; daily.

#18: San Francisco–Corte Madera–College of Marin–Larkspur–San Anselmo; weekdays.

#20: San Francisco–Sausalito–Corte Madera–San Anselmo–San Rafael; daily.

#24: San Francisco–Greenbrea–San Anselmo–Fairfax–Lagunitas; weekdays.

#26: San Francisco–San Rafael–San Anselmo–Sleepy Hollow; weekdays.

#29: Larkspur Ferry–San Rafael; daily.

#30: San Francisco–Larkspur Ferry–San Rafael; weekdays.

#50: San Francisco–Sausalito–San Rafael–Novato–San Marin; daily.

#63: Marin City–Stinson Beach; weekends only.

#65: San Rafael–Point Reyes Station–Inverness; weekends only.

#80: San Francisco–San Rafael–Novato–Petaluma–Santa Rosa; daily.

#90: San Francisco–San Rafael–Sonoma Valley; weekdays.

#93: San Francisco Civic Center–Golden Gate Bridge; weekdays.

Larkspur (Mon–Fri 9am–5pm; ☎415/499-5000, ⊛www.visitmarin.org), the **Sausalito Visitor Center**, occupying a modest hut at 780 Bridgeway Ave (Tues–Sun 11.30am–4pm; ☎415/332-0505), and the **Mill Valley Chamber of Commerce**, 85 Throckmorton Ave (Mon–Fri 10am–noon & 1–4pm; ☎415/388-9700, ⊛www.millvalley.org), in the center of the town.

For information on hiking and camping in the wilderness and beach areas, depending on where you're heading, contact the **Golden Gate National Recreation Area**, Building 201, Fort Mason Center, San Francisco (Mon–Fri 9.30am–4.30pm; ☎415/561-3000); **Mount Tamalpais State Park**, 801 Panoramic Hwy, Mill Valley (daily 8am–5.30pm; ☎415/388-2070); or the Point Reyes National Seashore's **Bear Valley Visitors Center**, Point Reyes (Mon–Fri 9am–5pm, Sat & Sun 8am–5pm; ☎415/464-5100). Information on what's on in Marin can be found in the widely available local freesheets, such as the down-to-earth *Coastal Post* (⊛www.coastalpost.com), or the New-Agey *Pacific Sun* (⊛www.pacificsun.com).

Accommodation

You might prefer simply to dip into Marin County using San Francisco as a base, and if you've got a car or manage to time the bus connections right it's certainly possible, at least for the southernmost parts of the county. However, it can be nicer to take a more leisurely look at Marin, staying over for a couple of nights in some well-chosen spots. Sadly, there are few **hotels**, and those that there are often charge well in excess of $100 a night; **motels** tend to be the same as anywhere, though there are a couple of attractively faded ones along the coast. If you want to stay in a B&B, contact the **Bed and Breakfast Exchange**, 45 Entrata Drive, San Anselmo (☎415/485-1971), which can fix you up with rooms in comfortable private homes all over Marin County from $60 a night for two, ranging from courtyard hideaways on the beach in Tiburon to houseboats in Sausalito. The best bet for budget accommodation is a dorm bed in one of the beautifully situated **hostels** along the western beaches.

Motels and hotels

Casa Madrona 801 Bridgeway Ave, Sausalito ☎415/332-0502 or 1-800/567-9524, ⊛www.casamadrona.com. Deluxe hotel with a new extension spreading up the hill above the Bay. Spa facilities available. **7**

Colonial Motel 1735 Lincoln Ave, San Rafael ☎415/453-9188 or 1-800/554-9118. Quiet, well-furnished, and friendly motel with decent rates in a residential neighborhood. **4**

Grand Hotel 15 Brighton Ave, Bolinas ☎415/868-1757. Just two budget rooms in a funky, run-down old hotel above a secondhand shop. **2**

Mill Valley Inn 165 Throckmorton Ave, Mill Valley ☎415/389-6608 or 1-800/595-2100, ⊛www .millvalleyinn.co. By far the best hotel in Marin County. Gorgeous European-style inn with elegant rooms and two private cottages. **7**

Ocean Court Motel 18 Arenal St, Stinson Beach ☎415/868-0212, ⊛www.oceancourt.ws. Large simple rooms with kitchens, just a block from the beach and west of Hwy-1. **5**

Stinson Beach Motel 3416 Shoreline Hwy,

Stinson Beach ☎415/868-1712. Basic roadside motel right on Hwy-1, with tiny rooms. Five minutes' walk to the beach. **3**

Bed and breakfast

Blue Heron Inn 11 Wharf Rd, Bolinas ☎415/868-1102. Lovely double rooms in an unbeatable locale with ocean view. Now has its own fully operational restaurant. Friendly welcome. **5**

Lindisfarne Guest House Green Gulch Zen Center, Muir Beach ☎415/383-3134, ⊛www.sfzc.org. Restful rooms in a meditation retreat set in a secluded valley above Muir Beach. Price includes excellent vegetarian meals. **6**

Mountain Home Inn 810 Panoramic Hwy, Mill Valley ☎415/381-9000 or 1-877/381-9001, ⊛www.mtnhomeinn.com. Romantically located on Mount Tamalpais' crest, this bed and breakfast offers great views and endless hiking. Some rooms with hot tubs. **7**

Olema Inn 10000 Sir Francis Drake Blvd, Olema ☎415/663-9559 or 1-800/532-9252. Wonderful little B&B near the entrance to Point Reyes

San Francisco to Marin County ferries

Because ferry schedules change slightly four times a year, you should use the following timetable as an estimate of arrival and departure times. Current schedules are always available from the terminals. NB: All the Blue and Gold services below depart from Pier 41; they also run several commuter services between the San Francisco Ferry Building and Tiburon during weekday rush hours – call for details. All Golden Gate Transit ferries depart from the Ferry Building.

Golden Gate Transit ferries (☎415/923-3000)

San Francisco–Larkspur: Mon–Fri depart 6.35am, 7.20am, 7.55am, 8.20am, 9.15am, 10.15am, 10.50am, 12.05pm, 12.55pm, 1.50pm, 3.05pm, 3.35pm, 4.20pm, 4.45pm, 5.20pm, 5.50pm, 6.15pm, 7.05pm, 7.25pm, 8.15pm, 9.10pm & 11.45pm (Fri only); Sat, Sun & holidays 10.40am, 12.40pm, 2.40pm, 4.40pm & 6.40pm.

Larkspur–San Francisco: Mon–Fri depart 6am, 6.45am, 7.15am, 7.30am, 8.10am, 8.35am, 9.15am, 10.10am, 11.10am, 12.10pm, 12.55pm, 2.10pm, 2.40pm, 3.40pm, 4.25pm, 5.05pm, 5.30pm, 6.25pm, 6.30pm, 7.40pm, 8.15pm & 10pm (Fri only); Sat, Sun & holidays 9.40am, 11.40am, 1.40pm, 3.40pm & 5.40pm.

San Francisco–Sausalito: Mon–Fri depart 7.40am, 10.25am, 11.45am, 1.10pm, 2.35pm, 4.10pm, 5.30pm, 6.40pm & 8pm; Sat, Sun & holidays 11.30am, 1pm, 2.30pm, 4pm, 5.30pm & 6.55pm; also May–Sept 9.15am & 8.05pm.

Sausalito–San Francisco: Sat, Sun & holidays depart 7.05am, 8.15am, 9.15am (May–Sept only), 11.05am, 12.25pm, 1.55pm, 3.20pm, 4.45pm, 6.05pm & 7.20pm; Sat, Sun & holidays 10.50am, 12.15pm, 1.45pm, 3.15pm, 4.45pm, 6.10pm & 7.30pm (May–Sept only).

Blue and Gold Fleet ferries (☎415/773-1188)

San Francisco–Sausalito: Mon–Fri depart 11am, 12.15pm, 1.50pm, 3pm, 5pm; Sat, Sun & holidays 10.40am, 12.25pm, 1.50pm, 3.15pm, 4.45pm & 6.30pm; also May–Sept Fri & Sat 8.25pm.

Sausalito–San Francisco: Mon–Fri depart 11.50am, 1.05pm, 2.25pm, 3.35pm, 5.40pm & 8pm; also May–Sept Fri 8.50pm; Sat, Sun & holidays 11.20am, 1.05pm, 2.30pm, 3.55pm, 5.25pm & 7.10pm; also May–Sept Sat 9pm.

San Francisco–Tiburon: Mon–Fri depart 11am, 12.15pm, 1.35pm, 2.45pm, 4.05pm & 5pm; Sat, Sun & holidays 9.45am, 11.30am, 2pm, 4pm, 4.45pm & 6pm; also May–Sept Fri & Sat 8.25pm.

Tiburon–San Francisco: Mon–Fri depart 11.25am, 12.40pm, 1.55pm, 3.10pm, 6pm & 7.45pm; also May–Sept Fri 9.10pm; Sat, Sun & holidays 10.50am, 12.25pm, 2.35pm, 5.05pm, 5.50pm & 7.30pm; also May–Sept Sat 9.20pm.

National Seashore, on a site that's been a hotel since 1876. Features a gourmet restaurant serving seafood and a full bar with heady wine list. Comfy rooms and absolutely no nightlife or traffic noise to speak of; perfect if you want to really take a break from the city. ❻
Pelican Inn 10 Pacific Way, Muir Beach ☎415/383-6000, ⓦwww.pelicaninn.com. Very comfortable rooms in a romantic pseudo-English country inn, with good bar and restaurant downstairs, ten minutes' walk from beautiful Muir Beach. ❼

Ten Inverness Way 10 Inverness Way, Inverness ☎415/669-1648, ⓦwww.teninvernessway.com. Quiet and restful, with a hot tub and complimentary evening wine, in a small village of good restaurants and bakeries on the fringes of Point Reyes. ❺

Hostels

HI-Marin Headlands Building 941, Fort Barry, Marin Headlands; closed 9.30am–4.30pm; ☎415/331-2777, ⓦwww.norcalhostels.org. Hard to get to without a car – it's near Rodeo Lagoon just off Bunker Road, five miles west of Sausalito – but worth the effort for its setting, in cozy old army barracks near the ocean. On Sundays and holidays only, MUNI bus #76 from San Francisco stops right outside. Closed 10.30am–3.30pm, except for registration. Dorm beds $15 a night, double rooms $45.

HI-Point Reyes in the Point Reyes National Seashore; closed 9.30am–4.30pm; ☎415/663-8811, 🅦www.norcalhostels.org. Also hard to reach without your own transportation: just off Limantour Road six miles west of the visitor center and two miles from the beach, it's located in an old ranch house and surrounded by meadows and forests. Dorm beds $13–15 a night.

Campgrounds

China Camp State Park off N San Pedro Rd, north of San Rafael ☎415/456-0766. Walk-in plots (just 600ft from the parking lot) overlooking a lovely meadow. First-come-first-camped for $12 a night. Apr–Oct reserve through ParkNet ☎1-800/444-7275.

Marin Headlands just across the Golden Gate Bridge ☎415/331-1540. Five campgrounds, the best of which is very popular Kirby Cove (open April–Oct only), at the northern foot of the Golden Gate Bridge (reservations Tues–Thurs 10am–2pm; $20; ☎415/561-4304). Of the remaining sites, one is a group camp ($20), and the other three are free.

Mount Tamalpais State Park above Mill Valley ☎415/388-2070. Sixteen plots for backpackers on the slopes of the mountain ($5–16), and a few rustic cabins ($15 a night), along the coast at Steep Ravine. Reserve through ParkNet ☎1-800/444-7275.

Point Reyes National Seashore forty miles northwest of San Francisco ☎415/663-1092. A wide range of hike-in sites for backpackers, near the beach or in the forest. Reserve sites up to two months in advance (weekdays 9am–2pm; ☎415/663-8054; $10).

Samuel Taylor State Park on Sir Francis Drake Blvd, fifteen miles west of San Rafael ☎415/488-9897. Deluxe, car-accessible plots with hot showers, spread along a river for $15–16 a night, basic hiker/biker sites for $3. Don't miss the swimming hole or bat caves. In summer, reserve a place through ParkNet ☎1-800/444-7275.

Across the Golden Gate: Marin Headlands and Sausalito

The largely undeveloped **MARIN HEADLANDS** of the Golden Gate National Recreation Area, across the Golden Gate Bridge from San Francisco, afford some of the most impressive views of the bridge and the city behind. As the regular fog rolls in, the breathtaking image of the bridge's stanchions tantalisingly drifting in and out of sight and the fleeting glimpses of downtown skyscrapers will abide long in the memory. Take the first turn as you exit the bridge (Alexander Avenue) and follow the sign back to San Francisco – the one-way circle trip back to the bridge heads first to the west along Conzelman Road and up a steep hill. You'll pass through a largely undeveloped land, dotted by the concrete remains of old forts and gun emplacements standing guard over the entrance to the Bay, dating from as far back as the Civil War and as recent as World War II. The coastline here is much more rugged than it is on the San Francisco side, making it a great place for an aimless cliff-top hike or a stroll along one of the beaches dramatically situated near the crashing waves at the bottom of treacherous footpaths.

The first installation as you climb the steep hill up the headlands is **Battery Wallace**, the largest and most impressive of the artillery sites along the rugged coast here, cut through a hillside above the southwestern tip of the peninsula. The clean-cut military geometry survives, framing views of the Pacific Ocean and the Golden Gate Bridge. If you're interested in such things, come along on the first Sunday of the month and take a guided tour of an abandoned 1950s ballistic-missile launchpad, complete with disarmed nuclear missiles. Otherwise, continue along Conzelman for incredible views of the city from any of the many turnouts. For birdwatching, walk from the Battery Wallace parking lot through tunnels that lead 500 yards to the opposite bluff, overlooking **Rodeo Beach** and **Point Bonita Lighthouse** far below. To reach Point Bonita by vehicle, drive down the one-way lane that Conzelman becomes and keep winding down to the lighthouse. It stands sentry at the very end of the headlands and is often open for tours (Sat–Mon 12.30-3.30pm; free). Conzelman comes to a "T" in the road at the YMCA camp bunkhouse; turn left and park your car on the side of the road or at the parking lot 300 yards west, at the end of the drive. To reach the lighthouse, you have to walk the half-mile pathway down, a beautiful stroll that takes you through a tunnel cut into the cliff, and across a precarious suspension bridge.

Looping back around, you'll be heading northeast on Bunker Road. Stop off at the **Marin Headlands Visitor Center** (daily 9am–4.30pm; ☎415/331-1540), alongside Rodeo Lagoon, for free maps of popular hiking trails in the area. Across the road and a bit further along, the largest of **Fort Barry**'s old buildings has been converted into the spacious but homey *HI-Marin Headlands* hostel (see listings), an excellent base for more extended explorations of the inland ridges and valleys.

Turn off to the left where Bunker Road snakes down to wide, sandy Rodeo Beach (#76 MUNI bus from San Francisco: Sun & holidays only). The beach separates the chilly ocean from the marshy warm water of **Rodeo Lagoon**, where swimming is prohibited to protect nesting sea birds. North of the lagoon, the **Marine Mammal Center** rescues and rehabilitates injured and orphaned sea creatures, which you can visit while they recover; there's also a series of displays on the marine ecosystem and a bookstore that sells T-shirts and posters.

Sausalito

SAUSALITO, along the Bay below US-101, is a picturesque, snug little town of exclusive restaurants and pricey boutiques along a pretty waterfront promenade. Expensive, quirkily designed houses climb the overgrown cliffs above **Bridgeway Avenue**, the main road and bus route through town. Sausalito used to be a fairly gritty community of fishermen and sea-traders, full of bars and bordellos, and despite its upscale modern face it still makes a fun day out from San Francisco by ferry, the boats arriving next to the Sausalito Yacht Club in the center of town. Hang out in one of the waterfront bars and watch the crowds strolling along the esplanade, or climb the stairways above Bridgeway Avenue and amble around the leafy hills. If you have sailing experience, split the $157 daily rental fee of a four- to six-person sailboat at Cass's Marina, 1702 Bridgeway Ave (☎415/332-6789, ⓦwww.cassmarina.com). The other main diversion is sea kayaking, and Sea Trek (☎415/488-1000) rents single or double sea kayaks beginning at $25 for two hours' worth of paddling the Bay. They offer sit-on-top kayaks, lessons, and safe routes for first-timers or closed kayaks and directions around Angel Island for more experienced paddlers.

The old working wharves and warehouses that made Sausalito a haven for smugglers and Prohibition-era rum-runners are long gone; most have been taken over by dull steakhouses. However, some stretches of it have, for the moment at least, survived the tourist onslaught. A mile north of the town center along Bridgeway Avenue, an ad hoc community of exotic barges and houseboats, some of which have been moored here since the 1950s, are still staving off eviction to make room for yet another luxury marina. In the meantime, many of the boats – one looks like a South Pacific island, another like the Taj Mahal – can be viewed at Waldo Point, half a mile beyond the cavernous concrete **Bay Model Visitor Center**, 2100 Bridgeway Ave (Tues–Sat 9am–4pm; donation; ☎415/332-3870). Inside the huge building, elevated walkways lead you around a scale model of the Bay, surrounding deltas and its aquatic inhabitants, offering insight on the enormity and diversity of this area.

The Marin County Coast to Bolinas

The **Shoreline Highway**, Hwy-1, cuts off west from US-101 just north of Sausalito, following the old main highway towards Mill Valley (see p.639). The first turn on the left, Tennessee Valley Road, leads up to the less-visited northern expanses of the Golden Gate National Recreation Area. You can take a beautiful three-mile hike from the parking lot at the end of the road, heading down along the secluded and lushly green **Tennessee Valley** to a small beach along a rocky cove, or you can take a guided tour on horseback from Miwok Livery at 701 Tennessee Valley Rd ($45 per hour; ☎415/383-8048).

Hwy-1 twists up the canyon to a crest, where **Panoramic Highway** spears off to the right, following the ridge north to Muir Woods and Mount Tamalpais (see overleaf); Golden Gate Transit bus #63 to Stinson Beach follows this route every hour on weekends and holidays only. Be warned, however, that the hillsides are usually choked with fog until 11am, making the approach from San Francisco to Stinson Beach/Bolinas via Hwy-1 both dangerous and uninteresting. Two miles before you reach the crest, a small paved lane cuts off to the left, dropping down to the bottom of the broad canyon to the **Green Gulch Farm and Zen Center** (☎415/383-3134, ⓦwww.sfzc.org), an organic farm and Buddhist retreat, with an authentic Japanese teahouse and a simple but refined prayer hall. On Sunday mornings the center is opened for a public meditation period and an informal discussion of Zen Buddhism, after which you can stroll down to Muir Beach. If you already have some experience of Zen, inquire about the center's Guest Student Program, which enables initiates to stay from three days to several weeks at a time (it costs about $15 a night). Residents rise well before dawn for meditation and prayer, then work much of the day in the gardens, tending the vegetables that are eventually served in many of the Bay Area's finest restaurants (notably *Greens* in San Francisco – see p.562). If you just want a weekend retreat, you can also stay overnight in the far more upmarket attached *Lindisfarne Guest House* (see "Listings").

Beyond the Zen Center, the road down from Muir Woods rejoins Hwy-1 at **Muir Beach**, usually uncrowded and beautifully secluded in a semicircular cove. Three miles north, **Steep Ravine** drops sharply down the cliffs to a small beach, past very rustic cabins and a campground, bookable through Mount Tamalpais State Park (see "Listings"). A mile on is the small and lovely **Red Rocks** nudist beach, down a steep trail from a parking area along the highway. **Stinson Beach**, which is bigger, and more popular despite the rather cold water (it's packed on weekends in summer, when the traffic can be nightmarish), is a mile further. You can rent boogie boards for $10, surf boards for $25 and wetsuits for $12 a day from the Livewater Surf Shop (☎415/868-0333), 3448 Shoreline Hwy, or kayaks a bit further down the road at Off the Beach Boats, 15 Cal del Mar ($15 for two hours, $90 all weekend; ☎415/868-9445).

Bolinas and southern Point Reyes

At the tip of the headland, due west from Stinson Beach, is the village of **BOLINAS**, though you may have a hard time finding it – road signs marking the turnoff from Hwy-1 are removed as soon as they're put up, by locals hoping to keep the place to themselves. The campaign may have backfired, though, since press coverage of the "sign war" has done more to publicize the town than any road sign ever did; to get there, take the first left beyond the estuary and follow the road to the end. Another example of local eccentricity is the refusal to switch to daylight savings time. Bolinas is completely surrounded by federal property: the Golden Gate National Recreation Area and Point Reyes National Seashore. Even the lagoon was recently declared a National Bird Sanctuary. Known for its leftist hippy culture, the village itself has been home at different times to Grace Slick and Paul Kantner and a regular colony of artists, bearded handymen, stray dogs, and writers (the late trout-fishing author Richard Brautigan and basketball diarist Jim Carroll among them). There's not a lot to see apart from the small **Bolinas Museum**, 48 Wharf Rd (Fri 1–5pm, Sat & Sun noon–5pm; free; ☎415/868-0330, ⓦwww.bolinasmuseum.org), which has a few historical displays and works by local artists in a set of converted cottages around a courtyard. Mostly, it's just a case of people watching and taking in the laid-back atmosphere.

Beyond Bolinas, there's a rocky beach at the end of Wharf Road west of the village and, half a mile west at the end of Elm Road, **Duxbury Reef Nature Reserve** is well worth a look for its tidal pools, full of starfish, crabs, and sea anemones. Otherwise, Mesa Road heads north from Bolinas past the **Point Reyes Bird Observatory** (☎415/868-1221) – open for informal tours all day, though best visited in the morning. The first bird observatory in the US, this is still an important research and study center, and if you time it right you may be able to watch, or even help, the staff as they put colored bands on the birds to keep track of them. Beyond here, the unpaved road leads onto the **Palomarin Trailhead**, the southern access into the Point Reyes National Seashore (see p.642). The best of the many beautiful hikes around the area leads past a number of small lakes and meadows for three miles to **Alamere Falls**, which throughout the winter and spring cascade down the cliffs onto Wildcat Beach. **Bass Lake**, the first along the trail, is a great spot for a swim and is best entered from one of the two rope-swings that hang above its shore.

At the junction of Bolinas Road and Hwy-1, cross the highway and head due east. If there's no sign warning the road is closed (landslides and washouts are common), continue up this route, the **Bolinas–Fairfax Road**, for a superb, winding drive through redwoods and grassy hillsides. When you reach the "T" in the road, turn left to get to Fairfax, or right to scale Mount Tamalpais.

Mount Tamalpais and Muir Woods

MOUNT TAMALPAIS, fondly known as "Mount Tam", dominates the skyline of the Marin Peninsula, hulking over the cool canyons of the rest of the county and dividing it into two distinct parts: the wild western slopes above the Pacific Coast and the increasingly suburban communities along the calmer Bay frontage. Panoramic Highway branches off from Hwy-1 along the crest through the center of **Mount Tamalpais State Park** (☎415/388-2070, ⓦwww.mtia.net), which has some thirty miles of hiking trails and many campgrounds, though most of the redwood trees which once covered its slopes have long since been chopped down to form the posts and beams of San Francisco's Victorian houses. One grove of these towering trees does remain, however, protected as the **MUIR WOODS NATIONAL MONUMENT** (daily 8am–sunset; $3; ☎415/388-2595), a mile down Muir Woods Road from Panoramic Highway. It's a tranquil and majestic spot, with sunlight filtering through the 300ft trees down to the laurel- and fern-covered canyon below. The canyon's steep sides are what saved it from Mill Valley's lumbermen, and today it's one of the few first-growth redwood groves between San Francisco and the fantastic forests of Redwood National Park (see p.754), up the coast near the Oregon border.

Its proximity to San Francisco makes Muir Woods a popular target, and the paved trails nearest the parking lot are often packed with bus-tour hordes. However, if you visit during the week, or outside midsummer, it's easy enough to leave the crowds behind, especially if you're willing to head off up the steep trails that climb the canyon sides. Winter is a particularly good time to come, as the streams are gurgling – the main creek flows down to Muir Beach, and salmon have been known to spawn in it – and the forest creatures, including the colonies of ladybugs that spend their winter incubating in the rich undergrowth, are more likely to be seen going about their business. Keep an eye out for the various species of salamanders and newts that thrive in this damp environment; be warned, though, that some are poisonous and will bite if harassed.

One way to avoid the crowds, and the only way to get here on public transportation, is to enter the woods from the top by way of a two-mile hike from the **Pan Toll Ranger Station** (☎415/388-2070) on Panoramic Highway – which is a stop on the Golden Gate Transit #63 bus route. As the state park headquarters, the station has maps and information on hiking and camping, and rangers can suggest hikes to suit your mood and interests. From here the **Pan Toll Road** turns off to the right along the ridge to within a hundred yards of the 2571-foot summit of Mount Tamalpais, where there are breathtaking views of the distant Sierra Nevada, and red-necked turkey vultures listlessly circle.

Mill Valley

From the East Peak of Mount Tamalpais, a quick two-mile hike downhill follows the **Temelpa Trail** through velvety shrubs of chaparral to **MILL VALLEY**, the oldest and most enticing of Marin County's inland towns – also accessible every thirty minutes by Golden Gate Transit bus #10 from San Francisco and Sausalito. Originally a logging center, it was from here that the destruction of the surrounding redwoods was organized, though for many years the town has made a healthy living out of tourism. The **Mill Valley and Mount Tamalpais Scenic Railroad** – according to the blurb, "the crookedest railroad in the world" – was cut into the slopes above the town in 1896, twisting up through nearly three hundred tight curves in under eight miles. The trip proved so popular with tourists that the line was extended down into Muir Woods in 1907, though road-building and fire combined to put an end to the railroad by 1930. You can, however, follow its old route from the end of Summit Avenue in Mill Valley, a popular trip with daredevils on all-terrain bikes, which were, incidentally, invented here.

Though much of Mill Valley's attraction lies in its easy access to hiking and mountain-bike trails up Mount Tam, its compact yet relaxed center has a number of cafés and some good shops and galleries. The *Depot Bookstore and Café* (Mon–Sat 7am–10pm, Sun 8am–10pm; ☎415/383-2665) is a popular bookstore, café, and meeting place at 87 Throckmorton Ave, next door to the Chamber of Commerce (see p.633), which has free maps of Mount Tam and area hiking trails. Across the street, the **Pleasure Principle** is a reminder of the Northern California eclecticism hidden beneath a posh surface – the store, the self-declared UFO headquarters of Mill Valley, is also the proud purveyor of a large vintage porn collection. If in the area in early October, don't miss the **Mill Valley Film Festival**, a world-class event that draws a host of up-and-coming directors, as well as Bay Area stars like Robin Williams and Sharon Stone; for program information, call ☎415/383-5346, or check ⓦwww.finc.org.

Tiburon

TIBURON, at the tip of a narrow peninsula three miles east of US-101 and five miles from Mill Valley, is, like Sausalito, a ritzy harborside village to which hundreds of people come each weekend, many of them via direct Blue and Gold Fleet **ferries** from Pier 41 in San Francisco's Fisherman's Wharf. It's a relaxed place, less touristy than Sausalito, and if you're in the mood to take it easy and watch the boats sail across the Bay, sitting out on the sunny deck of one of the many cafés and bars can be idyllic. There are few specific sights to look out for here, but it's pleasant enough to simply wander around, browsing the galleries and antique shops. The best of these are grouped together in **Ark Row**, at the west end of Main Street, where the quirky buildings are actually old houseboats that were beached here early in the century. On a hill above the town stands **Old St Hilary's Church** (April–Oct Wed–Sun 1–4pm; ☏415/789-0066), a Carpenter Gothic beauty that is best seen in the spring, when the surrounding fields are covered with multicolored buckwheat, flax, and paintbrush.

Cyclists can cruise around the many plush houses of **Belvedere Island**, just across the Beach Road Bridge from the west end of Main Street, enjoying the fine views of the Bay and Golden Gate Bridge. More ambitious bikers can continue along the waterfront bike path, which winds from the bijou shops and galleries three miles west along undeveloped Richardson Bay frontage to a bird sanctuary at **Greenwood Cove**. The pristine Victorian house here is now the western headquarters of the National Audubon Society and open for tours on Sundays (10am–4pm); a small interpretive center has displays on local and migratory birds and wildlife.

Angel Island

However appealing, the pleasures of Tiburon are soon exhausted, and you'd be well advised to take the Angel Island Ferry (hourly 10am–4pm; $7 round-trip, plus $1 per bicycle; ☏415/435-2131) a mile offshore to the largest island in the San Francisco Bay, ten times the size of Alcatraz. **ANGEL ISLAND** is now officially a state park, but over the years it has served a variety of purposes, everything from a home for Miwok Native Americans to a World War II prisoner-of-war camp. It's full of ghostly ruins of old military installations but it's the nature that lures visitors to Angel Island, with its oak and eucalyptus trees and sagebrush covering the hills above rocky coves and sandy beaches, giving the island a feel quite apart from the mainland. Angel Island offers some pleasant biking opportunities: a five-mile road rings the island, and an unpaved track (and a number of hiking trails) leads up to the 800ft hump of **Mount Livermore**, with panoramic views of the Bay Area.

The ferry arrives at **Ayala Cove**, where a small snack bar selling hot dogs and cold drinks provides the only sustenance available on the island – bring a picnic if you plan to spend the day here. The nearby **visitor center** (daily 9am–4pm; ☏415/435-1915), in an old building that was built as a quarantine facility for soldiers returning from the Philippines after the Spanish–American War, has displays on the island's history. Around the point on the northwest corner of the island the **North Garrison**, built in 1905, was the site of a prisoner-of-war camp during World War II; while the larger **East Garrison**, on the Bay half a mile beyond, was the major transfer point for soldiers bound for the South Pacific.

Quarry Beach around the point is the best on the island, a clean sandy shore that's protected from the winds blowing in through the Golden Gate; it's also a popular landing spot for kayakers and canoeists who paddle across the Bay from Berkeley. **Camping** on Angel Island (☎415/435-1915; reserve through ParkNet ☎1-800/444-7275) costs $7 per night, incredible value considering the view of San Francisco and the East Bay at night. The nine sites fill up fast, so make reservations well ahead. For **tours** of Angel Island, contact Angel Island TramTours (☎415/897-0715, ⓦwww.angelisland.com), which rents mountain bikes ($25/day), gives tram tours ($11.50), and leads all-day kayak trips around the island (May–Oct weekends; $120).

Sir Francis Drake Boulevard and Central Marin County

The quickest route to the wilds of the Point Reyes National Seashore, and the only way to get there on public transportation, is by way of **SIR FRANCIS DRAKE BOULEVARD**, which cuts across central Marin County through the inland towns of **San Anselmo** and **Fairfax**, reaching the coast thirty miles west at a crescent-shaped bay where, in 1579, Drake supposedly landed and claimed all of what he called Nova Albion for England. The route makes an excellent day-long cycling tour, with the reward of good beaches, a youth hostel, and some tasty restaurants at the end of the road.

The Larkspur Golden Gate Transit **ferry**, which leaves from the Ferry Building in San Francisco, is the longest and, surprisingly, least expensive of the Bay crossings. Primarily a commuter route, it docks at the modern space-frame terminal at Larkspur Landing. The monolithic, red-tile-roofed complex you see on the bayfront a mile east is the maximum-security **San Quentin State Prison**, which houses the state's most violent and notorious criminals, and of which Johnny Cash sang so resonantly "I hate every stone of you." If you arrive by car over the Richmond–San Rafael Bridge, follow road signs off Hwy-101 for the **San Quentin Prison Museum**, Building 106, Dolores Way (Tues–Fri & Sun 11am–3pm, Sat 11.45am–3.15pm; $2).

San Anselmo, Fairfax, and Point Reyes Station

SAN ANSELMO, set in a broad valley two miles north of Mount Tam, calls itself "the antiques capital of Northern California" and sports a tiny center of specialty shops, furniture stores, and cafés that draws many San Francisco shoppers on weekends. The ivy-covered **San Francisco Theological Seminary** off Bolinas Avenue, which dominates the town from the hill above, is worth a quick visit for the view and architecture. At serene **Robson-Harrington Park** on Crescent Avenue you can picnic among well-tended gardens, and the very green and leafy **Creek Park** follows the creek that winds through the town center, but otherwise there's not a lot to do but eat and drink – or browse through fine bookstores, such as Oliver's Books, at 645 San Anselmo Ave (☎415/454-4421).

Center Boulevard follows the tree-lined creek west for a mile to **FAIRFAX**, a much less ostentatiously hedonistic community than the harborside towns, though in many ways it still typifies Marin lifestyles, with an array of whole-food stores and bookstores geared to a thoughtfully mellow crowd. From Fairfax, the narrow Bolinas Road twists up and over the mountains to the coast at Stinson Beach, while Sir Francis Drake Boulevard winds through a pastoral landscape of ranch houses hidden away up oak-covered valleys.

Ten miles west of Fairfax along Sir Francis Drake Boulevard, **Samuel Taylor State Park** has excellent camping (see p.635 for details); five miles more brings you to the coastal Hwy-1 and the hamlet of **Olema**, at the entrance to the park, which has good food and lodging. A mile north of Olema sits the tourist town of **POINT REYES STATION**, another good place to stop off for a bite to eat or to pick up picnic supplies before heading off to enjoy the wide open spaces of the Point Reyes National Seashore just beyond.

The Point Reyes National Seashore

From Point Reyes Station, Sir Francis Drake Boulevard heads out to the westernmost tip of Marin County at Point Reyes through the **Point Reyes National Seashore**, a near-island of wilderness surrounded on three sides by more than fifty miles of isolated coastline – pine forests and sunny meadows bordered by rocky cliffs and sandy, windswept beaches. This wing-shaped landmass, something of an aberration along the generally straight coastline north of San Francisco, is in fact a rogue piece of the earth's crust that has been drifting slowly and steadily northward along the San Andreas Fault, having started some six million years ago as a suburb of Los Angeles. When the great earthquake of 1906 shattered San Francisco, the land here – the quake's epicenter – shifted over sixteen feet in an instant, though damage was confined to a few skewed cattle fences.

The park's **visitor center** (see p.633 for details) two miles southwest of Point Reyes Station near Olema, just off Hwy-1 on Bear Valley Road, holds engaging displays on the geology and natural history of the region. Rangers dish out excellent hiking and cycling itineraries, and have up-to-date information on the weather, which can change quickly and be cold and windy along the coast even when it's hot and sunny here, three miles inland. They also handle permits and reservations for the various hike-in **campgrounds** within the park. Nearby, a replica of a native Miwok village has an authentic religious **roundhouse**, and a popular hike follows the Bear Valley Trail along Coast Creek four miles to **Arch Rock**, a large tunnel in the seaside cliffs that you can walk through at low tide.

North of the visitor center, Limantour Road heads west six miles to the *HI-Point Reyes Hostel* (see p.635), continuing on another two miles to the coast at **Limantour Beach**, one of the best swimming beaches and a good place to watch the sea birds in the adjacent estuary. Bear Valley Road rejoins Sir Francis Drake Boulevard just past Limantour Road, leading north along Tomales Bay through the village of **Inverness**, so named because the landscape reminded an early settler of his home in the Scottish Highlands. Eight miles west of Inverness, a turn leads down past **Johnson's Oyster Farm** (Tues–Sun 8am–4pm; ☎415/669-1149) – which sells the bivalves for around $6–7 a dozen, less than half the price you'd pay in San Francisco – to **Drake's Beach**, the presumed landing spot of Sir Francis in 1579 (his voyage journal makes the exact location unclear). Appropriately, the coastline here resembles the southern coast of England, often cold, wet, and windy, with chalk-white cliffs rising above the wide, sandy beach. The road continues southwest another four miles to the very tip of Point Reyes. A precarious-looking **lighthouse** (Thurs–Sun 10am–4.30pm; free) stands firm against the crashing surf, and the bluffs are excellent for watching migrating **gray whales** from mid-March to April and late December to early February. Just over a mile back from the lighthouse a narrow road leads to **Chimney Rock**, where you can often see basking **elephant seals** or **sea lions** from the overlook. Keep in mind the distance and slow speeds it takes to reach these spots, which is hard to judge on a map. From the visitor center, it's fifteen miles to Drakes Beach and 23 miles to the light-

SAN FRANCISCO AND THE BAY AREA | Marin County

house. Check with the rangers on weather conditions before setting out.

The northern tip of the Point Reyes National Seashore, **Tomales Point**, is accessible via Pierce Point Road, which turns off Sir Francis Drake Boulevard two miles north of Inverness. Jutting out into Tomales Bay, it's the least-visited section of the park and a refuge for hefty **tule elk**; it's also a great place to admire the lupins, poppies, and other wildflowers that appear in the spring. The best swimming (at least the warmest water) is at **Heart's Desire Beach**, just before the end of the road. Down the bluffs from where the road comes to a dead end, there are excellent tidal pools at rocky **McClure's Beach**. North of Point Reyes Station, Hwy-1 continues past the famed oyster beds of Tomales Bay north along the crashing surf and up the Northern California coast.

San Rafael and Northern Marin County

You may pass through **SAN RAFAEL** on your way north from San Francisco, but there's little worth stopping for. The county seat and the only big city in Marin County, it has none of the woodsy qualities that make the other towns special, though you'll come across a couple of good restaurants and bars along Fourth Street, the main drag. Its one attraction is the old **Mission San Rafael Arcangel** (daily 11am–4pm; free), in fact a 1949 replica that was built near the site of the 1817 original on Fifth Avenue at A Street. The real points of interest, however, are well on the outskirts: the Marin County Civic Center to the north and the little-known China Camp State Park along the Bay to the east.

The **Marin County Civic Center** (Mon–Fri 9am–5pm; tours Wed 10.30am; free; ☎415/499-6646), spanning the hills just east of US-101 a mile north of central San Rafael, is a strange, otherworldly complex of administrative offices, plus an excellent performance space that resembles a giant viaduct capped by a bright blue-tiled roof. These buildings were architect **Frank Lloyd Wright**'s one and only government project, and although the huge circus tents and amusement park at the core of the designer's conception were never built, it does have some interesting touches, such as the atrium lobbies that open directly to the outdoors.

From the Civic Center, North San Pedro Road loops around the headlands through **China Camp State Park** (☎415/456-0766), an expansive area of pastures and open spaces that's hard to reach without your own transportation. It takes its name from the intact but long-abandoned Chinese shrimp-fishing village at the far eastern tip of the park, the sole survivor of the many small Chinese communities that once dotted the California coast. The ramshackle buildings, small wooden pier, and old boats lying on the sand are pure John Steinbeck; the only recent addition is a chain-link fence to protect the site from vandals. On the weekend you can get beer and sandwiches from the old shack at the foot of the pier, but the atmosphere is best during the week at sunset, when there's often no one around at all. There's a hike-in **campground** ($12) with thirty primitive sites at the northern end of the park, about two miles from the end of the Golden Gate Transit bus #23 route.

Six miles north of San Rafael, the **Lucas Valley Road** turns off west, twisting across Marin to Point Reyes. Although he lives and works here, it was not named after Star Wars filmmaker George Lucas, whose sprawling **Skywalker Ranch** studios are well hidden off the road. Hwy-37 cuts off east, eight miles north of San Rafael, heading around the top of the Bay into the Wine Country of the Sonoma and Napa valleys (see p.710).

Eating

Marin's **restaurants** are as varied in personality as the people who inhabit the county – homey neighborhood cafés dish out nutritious portions to healthy mountain-bikers, well-appointed waterside restaurants cater to tourists, and gourmet establishments serve delicate concoctions to affluent executives. We have listed the best of the options below.

Restaurants

Bubba's Diner 566 San Anselmo Ave, San Anselmo ☎415/459-6862. Hip little old-fashioned diner with a friendly and casual atmosphere. Try a delicious biscuit with your meal.

Cactus Café 393 Miller Ave, Mill Valley ☎415/388-8226. Reasonably priced, small, and friendly restaurant serving fun Cal-Mex food flavored with home-made hot sauce.

Dipsea Café 200 Shoreline Hwy, Mill Valley ☎415/381-0298. Hearty pancakes, omelets, sandwiches, and salads, especially good before a day out hiking on Mount Tamalpais. Breakfast and lunch only.

Guaymas 5 Main St, Tiburon ☎415/435-6300. Some of the most unique, inventive Cal-Mex cuisine in the Bay Area (and priced accordingly), paired with a spectacular view of the city.

Hilda's 639 San Anselmo Ave, San Anselmo ☎415/457-9266. Great breakfasts and lunches in this down-home, cozy café.

The Lark Creek Inn 234 Magnolia Ave, Larkspur ☎415/924-7766. The place to go in Marin for fine dining. The contemporary American food at this classy restored Victorian is expensive, but not without reason: the food is exquisite, the service first rate, and the atmosphere charming.

Mikayla 801 Bridgeway Ave, Sausalito ☎415/331-5888. Mediterranean staples meet California cuisine in this expensive, but highly rated restaurant in the *Casa Madrona* hotel (see p.633). Romantic views of the harbor and excellent seafood. Huge Sunday brunch buffet offered.

Mountain Home Inn 810 Panoramic Hwy, above Mill Valley ☎415/381-9000. A place that's as good for the view as for the food, with broiled meat and fish dishes served up in a rustic lodge on the slopes of Mount Tamalpais.

New Morning Café 1696 Tiburon Blvd, Tiburon ☎415/435-4315. Lots of healthy wholegrain sandwiches, plus salads and omelets.

Olema Inn 10000 Sir Francis Drake Blvd, Olema ☎415/663-9559. Cozy nook of an eatery serving fresh fish and oysters at around $10 per person, on a patio looking into the woods. Quiet atmosphere and excellent service.

Orchid Thai 726 San Anselmo Ave, San Anselmo ☎415/457-9470. Family restaurant dishing up spicy fare, voted best Thai by *Pacific Sun* readers in 2002.

Piazza D'Angelo 22 Miller Ave, Mill Valley ☎415/388-2000. Good salads, tasty pasta, and affordable pizzas, served up in a lively but comfortable room right off the downtown plaza.

Rice Table 1617 Fourth St, San Rafael ☎415/456-1808. From the shrimp chips through the crab pancakes and noodles on to the fried plantain desserts, these fragrant and spicy Indonesian dishes are an excellent value and worth planning a day around. Dinners only.

Sam's Anchor Café 27 Main St, Tiburon ☎415/435-4527. This rough-hewn, amiable waterfront café and bar has been around for more than 75 years. Good burgers, sandwiches, and very popular Sunday brunches are best enjoyed on the outdoor deck.

Sartaj 43 Caledonia St, Sausalito ☎415/332-7103. Great, inexpensive Indian place that does a selection of meat and veggie dishes, including *thalis*, and, oddly enough, bagels for those who can't stomach a spicy breakfast.

Station House Café 11180 Hwy-1 (Main Street), Point Reyes Station ☎415/663-1515. Serving three meals daily, this friendly local favorite entices diners from miles around to sample their grilled seafood and great steaks.

Stinson Beach Grill 3465 Shoreline Hwy, Stinson Beach ☎415/868-2002. Somewhat pricey, but relaxed, with outdoor dining – look out for the bright-blue building right in the heart of town.

Sweet Ginger 400 Caledonia St, Sausalito ☎415/332-1683. Moderately-priced small Japanese restaurant that serves sushi, sashimi, and main courses like tempura and teriyaki.

Cafés, drinking, and nightlife

While the Marin County nightlife is never as charged as it gets in San Francisco, almost every town has at least a couple of **cafés** that are open long hours for a jolt of caffeine, and any number of saloon-like **bars** where you'll feel at home immediately. In addition, since most of the honchos of the Bay Area music scene and dozens of lesser-known but no less brilliant session musicians and songwriters live here, Marin's nightclubs are unsurpassed for catching big names in intimate locales.

Cafés

Caffè Trieste 1000 Bridgeway Ave, Sausalito ☏415/332-7770. This distant relative of San Francisco's North Beach institution serves good coffee, a wide menu of pastas and salads, and great gelati.

Depot Bookstore and Café 87 Throckmorton Ave, Mill Valley ☏415/383-2665. Lively café in an old train station, sharing space with a bookstore and newsstand. Weekly readings from local and nationally recognized authors.

Fairfax Café 33 Broadway, Fairfax ☏415/459-6404. Excellent Mediterranean food with occasional evening poetry readings.

Java Rama 546 San Anselmo Ave, San Anselmo ☏415/453-5282. Specialty coffees and pastries along with modern rock on the stereo attracts a young crowd.

Sweden House 35 Main St, Tiburon ☏415/435-9767. Great coffee and marvelous pastries on a jetty overlooking the yacht harbor, all for surprisingly reasonable prices.

Bars

19 Broadway 19 Broadway, Fairfax ☏415/459-0293. Live music every night, featuring a wide range of acts, some quite well known, others local or up-and-coming talent.

Café Amsterdam 23 Broadway, Fairfax ☏415/256-8020. Live alternative folk-rock nightly with an outdoor patio, microbrews, espresso drinks, and an extensive menu.

Fourth Street Tavern 711 Fourth St, San Rafael ☏415/454-4044. Gutsy, no-frills beer bar with free, bluesy music most nights.

Marin Brewing Company 1809 Larkspur Landing, Larkspur ☏415/461-4677. Lively pub opposite the Larkspur ferry terminal, with half a dozen tasty ales – try the malty Albion Amber or the Marin Hefe Weiss – all brewed on the premises.

No Name Bar 757 Bridgeway Ave, Sausalito ☏415/332-1392. An ex-haunt of the Beats, which hosts live jazz several times per week beginning at 8pm and on Sundays from 3–7pm.

Pelican Inn Hwy-1, Muir Beach ☏415/383-6000. Fair selection of traditional English and modern Californian ales, plus fish'n'chips (and rooms to rent in case you overdo it).

Smiley's Schooner Saloon 41 Wharf Rd, Bolinas ☏415/868-1311. The bartender calls the customers by name at one of the oldest continually operating bars in the state.

Sweetwater 153 Throckmorton Ave, Mill Valley ☏415/388-3820. Large, open room full of beer-drinking locals that after dark evolves into Marin's prime live-music venue, bringing in some of the biggest names in music, from jazz and blues all-stars to Jefferson Airplane survivors.

Travel details

Trains

A daily Amtrak shuttle bus departs from San Francisco from the San Francisco Shopping Center, 835 Market St (8am and 8.25pm); Pier 39 at Fisherman's Wharf (8.15am and 8.35pm); and the Ferry Building (8.40am 8.55pm) to the Emeryville depot, from where the *Coast Starlight* train departs at 10.15pm northeast to Sacramento, Portland, and Seattle and 8.20am south to San Jose, Santa Barbara, Los Angeles, and San Diego. The San Joaquin route operates four times daily to Stockton, Modesto, Fresno, and Bakersfield, where

there are Amtrak Thruway bus connections to Los Angeles. Amtrak's Capitol Corridor route links Oakland with San Jose (four daily; 1hr). San Francisco–San Jose commuters rely more on Caltrain (☏1-800/660-4287). Forty trains make the trip each way daily, taking 1hr30min or a little more ($5.25 each way). The San Francisco station is at 4th and King streets.

Buses

Greyhound unless specified otherwise; note the number of services can vary during the course of the year:

San Francisco to: Eureka (2 daily; 7hr–7hr 45min); Los Angeles (18 daily; 7hr 25min–12hr 45min; or 1 Green Tortoise weekly; 12hr); Redding (6 daily; 5hr 30min–10hr); Reno (19 daily; 5–7hr); Sacramento (22 daily; 2–3hr); San Diego (7 daily; 10hr 30min–14hr 40min); San Jose (13 daily; 1hr–1hr 45min); San Rafael (2 daily; 1hr); Santa Rosa (3 daily; 1hr 50min–3hr 10min).

The Gold Country
and Lake Tahoe

CHAPTER 8

Highlights

* **Sacramento Capitol building** The elegant Classical Revival building has some spectacular architectural detailing, and the comprehensive tours provide a glimpse of California's government innards. See p.657

* **Indian Grinding Rock** In this national park nine miles from Jackson, the Miwok Indians once carved hundreds of small cups into the limestone. See p.677

* **Jamestown's Railtown 1897 State Historic Park** Even if you're not a trainspotter, it's worth stopping by to see the old engines thanks to the enthusiastic, endlessly knowledgeable docents. See p.683

* **The Empire Mine State Park, Grass Valley** Now retired among thick stands of pine, the impressive array of mining equipment here opens an atmospheric window onto California's Gold Rush heyday. See p.668

* **Lake Tahoe** Beautiful scenery is guaranteed at any time of year around Lake Tahoe, whether you're skiing the slopes or paddling on the lake itself. See p.684

* **Virginia City, Nevada** A more obvious Wild West feel than most of its California contemporaries can be enjoyed in the mining town of Virginia City. See p.702

The Gold Country and Lake Tahoe

The gold of California is a touchstone which has betrayed the rottenness, the baseness, of mankind. Satan, from one of his elevations, showed mankind the kingdom of California, and they entered into a compact with him at once.

Henry David Thoreau, *Journal*, 1 February 1852

About 150 years before techies from all over the world rushed to California in search of Silicon Valley gold, the rough-and-ready forty-niners invaded the **GOLD COUNTRY** of the Sierra Nevada in search of the real thing. The first prospectors on the scene – about 150 miles east of San Francisco – sometimes found large nuggets of solid gold sitting along the river banks. While the dot-commers spend hours tied to computer screens, the miners worked all day in the hot sun, wading through fast-flowing, ice-cold rivers to recover trace amounts of the precious metal that had been eroded out of the hard-rock veins of the Mother Lode – the name given by miners to the rich sources of gold at the heart of the mining district.

The region ranges from the foothills near Yosemite National Park to the deep gorge of the Yuba River, two hundred miles north. In many parts throughout this area, little seems to have changed since the argonauts began their digging, and even in the air-conditioned comfort of your rental car – without one it's nearly impossible to navigate the area – distances from one town to the next may seem exponentially greater than they appear on the map: count on plenty of switchbacks and steep climbs.

The **Mother Lode** was first discovered in 1848 at Sutter's Mill in **Coloma**, forty miles east of **Sacramento**, the largest city in the Gold Country, and the state capital. Sacramento was once a tiny military outpost and farming community that boomed as a supply town for miners. The mining areas spread to the north and south of Sacramento and preserve distinct identities. The **northern mines**, around the twin towns of **Grass Valley** and **Nevada City**, were the richest fields, and today retain most of their Gold Rush buildings in an unspoiled, near-alpine setting halfway up the towering peaks of the Sierra Nevada mountains. The hot and dusty **southern mines**, on the other hand, became depopulated faster than their northern neighbors. These towns were the rowdiest and wildest of all, and it's not too hard to imagine that many of the abandoned towns sprinkled over the area once supported upwards of fifty

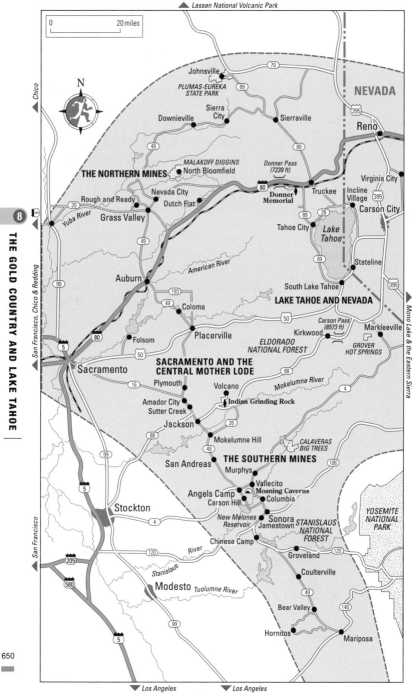

River rafting in the Gold Country

Although plenty of people come through the area to see the Gold Rush sights, at least as many come to enjoy the thrills and spills of **whitewater rafting** and **kayaking** on the various forks of the American, Stanislaus, Tuolumne, and Merced rivers, which wind down through the region from the Sierra crest towards Sacramento. Whether you just want to float in a leisurely manner downstream, or fancy careening through five-foot walls of water, contact one of the many river-trip operators, among them American River Recreation (☏1-800/333-7238, 🖳www.arrafting.com), CBOC Whitewater Raft Adventures (☏1-800/356-2262, 🖳www.cbocwhitewater.com), O.A.R.S., Inc. (☏1-800/ 346-6277, 🖳www.oars.com), Tributary Whitewater Tours (☏1-800/672-3846, 🖳www.whitewatertours.com), and Whitewater Adventures (☏1-800/977-4837, 🖳www.whitewater-adv.com). Trips run from late spring through early fall and start at about $70 per person.

saloons and gambling parlors, each with its own cast of cardsharps and thieves, as immortalized by writers like Bret Harte and Mark Twain.

Most of the mountainous forest along the Sierra crest is preserved as near-pristine wilderness, with excellent hiking, camping, and backpacking. There's great skiing in winter around the mountainous rim of **Lake Tahoe** – "Lake of the Sky" to the native Washoe – on the border between California and Nevada, aglow under the bright lights of the casinos that line its southeastern shore. East of the mountains, in the dry Nevada desert, sit the highway towns of **Reno**, famed for low-budget weddings and speedy divorces, and **Carson City**, the Nevada state capital and one-time boomtown of the Comstock silver mines.

Getting around

Hwy-49 runs north to south, linking most of the sights of the Gold Country; two main highways, US-50 and I-80, along with the transcontinental **railroad**, cross the Sierra Nevada through the heart of the region, and there is frequent Greyhound **bus** service to most of the major towns. To get a real feel for the Gold Country, however, and to reach the most evocative ghost towns, you'll need a **car**. Also, though it's all very scenic, **cycling** throughout the region is not a viable option: the distances between the sights are long, and the roads are far too hilly and narrow for comfort.

Sacramento and the Central Mother Lode

Before gold was discovered in 1848, the **area around Sacramento** belonged entirely to one man, John Sutter. He came here from Switzerland in 1839 to farm the flat, marshy lands at the foot of the Sierra Nevada mountains, which were then within Mexican California. Sacramento, the prosperous community he founded, became a main stopping place for the few trappers and travelers who made their way inland or across the range of peaks.Yet it was after the discovery of flakes of gold in the foothills forty miles east that things really took off and the small trading post was transformed.

Roughly midway between San Francisco and the crest of the Sierra Nevada, and well connected by Greyhound, Amtrak, and the arterial I-5 highway, **Sacramento** is likely to be your first stop in the Gold Country. It's the quintessential American state capital, with sleepy tree-lined streets fanning out from the elegant State Capitol building. The city's waterfront quarter, restored to the style of Pony Express days, contains the region's largest collection of Gold Rush-era buildings. From Sacramento, two main routes climb east through the gentle foothills of the Mother Lode: US-50 passes through the old supply town of **Placerville** on its way to Lake Tahoe, while I-80 zooms by **Auburn** over the Donner Pass into Nevada. Both towns have retained enough of their Gold Rush past to merit at least a brief look if you're passing through, and both make good bases for the more picturesque towns of the northern mines.

Sacramento

Until recently, **SACRAMENTO** had the reputation of being decidedly dull, a suburban enclave of politicians and bureaucrats surrounded by miles of marshes and farmland. The government looms large over the city, filling its streets on weekdays and emptying the center at weekends, although residential neighborhoods are slowly reawakening, especially around the Midtown area, thanks to the cafés and restaurants that have mushroomed on many of the leafier blocks. There's great local pride in the city's Gold Rush history, and this has led to important historic preservation and restoration projects, injecting a hefty, bludgeoning dose of tourist dollars into the local economy. The rise of the Sacramento Kings basketball team has also drawn sports-crazed tourists to town.

Sutter's 50,000 acre settlement, set at the confluence of the Sacramento and American rivers in the flatlands of the northern Central Valley, was granted to him by the Mexican government and he worked hard to build the colony into a busy trading center and cattle ranch. He was poised to become a wealthy man when his hopes were thwarted by the discovery of gold at a nearby sawmill. His workers quit their jobs to go prospecting, and many thousands more flocked to the goldfields, trampling over Sutter's lands: he was left a broken man. The small colony was soon overrun: since ships could sail upriver from the San Francisco Bay, Sacramento quickly became the main supply point for miners bound for the isolated camps in the foothills above. The city prospered, and in 1854 Sacramento snagged the title of California state capital, thanks to its equidistance between the gold mines, the rich farmlands of the Central Valley, and the financial center of San Francisco. As the Gold Rush faded, Sacramento remained important as a transportation center, first as the western terminus of the Pony Express and later as the western headquarters of the Transcontinental Railroad. Although its administrative role saved the city when mining dollars dwindled, it also smothered much of its rough, pioneer edges and, even now, it's only slowly developing a distinct, urban personality.

Arrival, information, and city transportation

At the intersection of the I-5, I-80, US-50, and Hwy-99 freeways, Sacramento is the hub for many long-distance transportation networks. Sacramento Metro

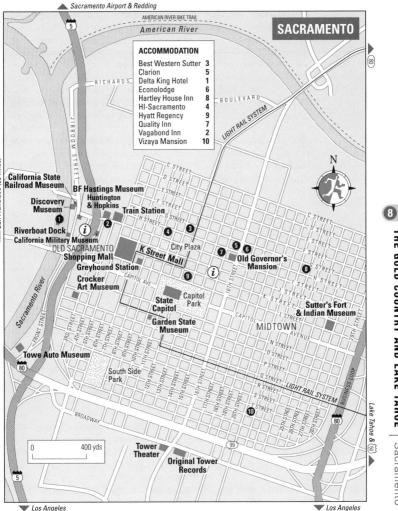

SACRAMENTO

ACCOMMODATION

Best Western Sutter	3
Clarion	5
Delta King Hotel	1
Econolodge	6
Hartley House Inn	8
HI-Sacramento	4
Hyatt Regency	9
Quality Inn	7
Vagabond Inn	2
Vizaya Mansion	10

AMERICAN RIVER BIKE TRAIL

American River

RICHARDS

BOULEVARD

LIGHT RAIL SYSTEM

JIBBOOM STREET

San Francisco (90 miles)

N

California State
Railroad Museum

BF Hastings Museum

Huntington
& Hopkins

Discovery
Museum

Train Station

Riverboat Dock

California Military Museum

OLD SACRAMENTO

Shopping Mall

Greyhound Station

Crocker
Art Museum

State
Capitol

Garden State
Museum

Towe Auto Museum

South Side
Park

K Street Mall

City Plaza

Old Governor's
Mansion

Capitol
Park

CAPITOL AVE

CAPITOL

MIDTOWN

AVENUE

Sutter's Fort
& Indian Museum

LIGHT RAIL SYSTEM

BUSINESS LOOP

BROADWAY

Sacramento River

FRONT STREET

0   400 yds

Tower
Theater

Original Tower
Records

Lake Tahoe & 50

THE GOLD COUNTRY AND LAKE TAHOE | Sacramento

8

airport (☎916/874-0700, ⊛www.sacairports.org), twelve miles northwest of downtown, is served by most major domestic airlines. SuperShuttle Sacramento vans (☎1-800-BLUEVAN) can take you directly to any downtown destination for $12. Thanks to its status as a governmental hub, public transport links are plentiful: **trains** from Los Angeles and Chicago stop at the Amtrak station at Fourth and I streets, near Old Sacramento (☎1-800/872-7245, ⊛www.amtrak.com), while the Capitol Corridor route has almost twenty daily services linking Sacramento with the Bay Area (☎1-800/872-7245, ⊛www.amtrakcapitols.com). From here, it's easy to catch a Thruway bus into the main Gold Country towns and the Lake Tahoe area. An almost continuous stream of Greyhound **buses** pulls into the bus depot at 715 L St, a block from the K Street Mall (☎1-800/231-2222).

There are two **visitors' centers**: one in the heart of tourist-clogged Old Sacramento in the basement of 1101 2nd St (daily 10am–5pm; ☎916/442-7644, ⓦ www.oldsacramento.org), and another close to K Street Mall downtown at 1303 J St (Mon–Wed 9am–4pm, Thurs–Fri 10am–5pm, Sat 10am–3pm; ☎916/264-4740; ⓦ www.sacramentocvb.org). Pick up a copy of the handy *Sacramento Visitors' Guide* (with maps and listings of accommodation and places to eat and drink in the city) at these offices or almost everywhere tourists congregate; the CVB also publishes an exhaustively informative self-guided walking tour of Sacramento's historic architecture. For the latest on **events and entertainment** in Sacramento, the best option is to check out the free *Sacramento News & Review;* otherwise, there's *Ticket,* the Friday supplement to the *Sacramento Bee* newspaper (50¢) or the free music listings publication *Alive and Kicking.* The city's gay and lesbian scene is lively enough to spawn two freesheets, *MGW* and *Outword,* which also contain general restaurant and events listings.

The city is compact, flat, and somewhat **walkable**, though many locals get around (especially along the 25-mile cycle path along the American River to Folsom Lake) by **bike** – rentals are available at The Bike Depot, 1028 2nd St (☎916/427-5844), or Bike Sacramento, 1050 Front St, Suite 110 in Old Sacramento (☎916/444-0200), both renting bikes starting around $15 an hour. The city center is criss-crossed with an extensive **bus and light rail** network – timetables and maps are available from the visitors' centers and the main transportation office, 1400 29th St at N Street (Mon–Fri 8am–5pm; ☎916/321-2877). The service you're most likely to use is the DASH shuttle (Route 30) connecting the Amtrak Station, K Street Mall, and Old Sacramento (50¢; ☎916/321-2877, ⓦ www.sacrt.com). The **riverboat tours** leaving from the L Street landing in Old Sacramento are popular if hokey: the paddle-wheel steamboats *Matthew McKinley* and *Spirit of Sacramento* offer varied trips along the Sacramento River ($10–35; ☎916/552-2933 or 1-800/433-0263, ⓦ www.spiritofsacramento.com). **Car rental agencies** include Budget, 6420 McNair Circle (☎916/9227317), Enterprise, 4515 Auburn Blvd (☎1-800/7368222), and Hertz, 1025 16th St (☎916/448-2228).

Accommodation

Sacramento has plenty of reasonably priced places to stay, all within easy walking distance of the center. A number of **motels** cluster around the old Governor's Mansion on the north side of town around 16th and H streets, a convenient walk to the trendy **Midtown** area, where much of the city's nightlife is centered. Dozens of other accommodation options line the highways on the outskirts, particularly Richards Boulevard, just off I-5. **Downtown**, choices are limited primarily to unexciting chains with a few B&Bs nearby – rates at weekends are often steeply discounted thanks to the exodus of government workers. There's no good **camping** anywhere within easy reach of Sacramento, though KOA runs the RV-heavy *Sacramento Metro* site, 3951 Lake Rd, West Sacramento (☎916/371-6771 or 1-800/562-2747, ⓦ www.koacampgrounds.com; ❶), four miles west of the center.

Amber House Bed & Breakfast Inn 1315 22nd St at N, Midtown ☎916/444-8085 or 1-800/755-6526, ⓦ www.amberhouse.com. The pick of the city's B&Bs, with luxurious rooms including marble baths, *Amber House* offers sumptuous breakfasts – with rates to match. A worthwhile treat to avoid the endless chain motels nearby. ❼

Best Western Suttter House 1100 H St, Downtown ☎916/441-1314 or 1-800/830-1314, ⓦ www.thesutterhouse.com. Low-rise hotel well located in the center of town, with large, comfy rooms set around an open-air pool and sun-baked courtyard. ❻

Clarion 700 16th St at H, Downtown ☎916/444-

8000 or 1-800/443-0880, Ⓦ www.clarion.com. Better than you might expect for a large chain motel thanks to its central location, excellent facilities, and modern rooms – the weekend rates are especially low if you book ahead. ⑤

Delta King Hotel 1000 Front St, Old Sacramento Ⓣ916/444-5464 or 1-800/825-5464, Ⓦ www.deltaking.com. A 1926 paddle-wheel river boat now permanently moored on the waterfront: although the rooms fail to justify their "stateroom" advertising, the vessel makes an enjoyably unusual place to stay. Be aware the area is usually throbbing with visitors at weekends, and prices rise accordingly. ⑤–⑦

Econo Lodge 711 16th St at H, Downtown Ⓣ916/443-6631 or 1-800/553-2666, Ⓦ www.econolodge.com. Best deal in town, with basic but comfortable rooms and complimentary continental breakfast. ②

Hartley House Inn 700 22nd St at H, Midtown Ⓣ916/447-7829 or 1-800/831-5806, Ⓦ www.hartleyhouse.com. B&B offering turn-of-the-century elegance in the heart of Sacramento's liveliest local neighborhood. ⑥

HI-Sacramento 925 H St at 10th, Downtown Ⓣ916/443-1691, Ⓦ www.norcalhostels.org. This hostel has recently reopened after a major spruce-up, which included moving the rambling 1885 mansion in which it's housed across the street from the original location. It has all the usual facilities, plus free bike rental, but there's a daytime lockout and 11pm curfew. $18 for members, $21 for others. There's a very limited number of private rooms ranging from $25–55, depending on size and private vs. shared bath. ①

Quality Inn 818 15th St at I, Downtown Ⓣ916/444-3980 or 1-800/228-5151, Ⓦ www.qualityinn.com/hotel/ca505. Refurbished rooms near the old Governor's Mansion, equipped with a pool. ③

Vagabond Inn 909 3rd St at J, Old Town Ⓣ916/446-1481 or 1-800/522-1555, Ⓦ www.vagabondinns.com. Motor-lodge style accommodation near the river and Old Sacramento: there's a pool and free shuttle to public transport hubs plus free continental breakfast. ⑤

Vizcaya Mansion 2019 21st St at T, Midtown Ⓣ916/455-5243 or 1-800/456-2019, Ⓦ www.sterlinghotels.com. A lavish, historic property with elegantly furnished rooms and marble-tiled bathrooms. ⑥

The Town

Most of the local attractions in Sacramento are close together, in one of the three main areas that comprise the city center: the I-5 highway quarantines **Old Sacramento** from the commercial hub of **Downtown**, centered on K Street Mall, as well as the funkier, residential **Midtown** district further east.

Old Sacramento and the riverfront

Sacramento grew up **along the riverfront**, where the wharves, warehouses, saloons, and stores of the city's historic core have been restored and converted into the novelty shops and theme restaurants of **OLD SACRAMENTO** (Ⓣ916/558-3912, Ⓦ www.oldsacramento.com). It's a shame that such a large collection of authentic Gold Rush-era architecture should be choked with such relentless fakery as the costumed sales staff hawking souvenirs, and tourist-chasing bars dressed up as faux Wild West saloons. In fact, although most of the buildings are original, some stood elsewhere until they were forcibly relocated here in the 1960s to make way for the massive I-5 highway that carves this area off from the rest of the city center. To avoid the stampede of tourists in search of taffy and souvenirs, it's best to avoid Old Sacramento completely at weekends, since that's when the place seems most inauthentic, its streets more like a Hollywood backlot than the real thing.

Three of the area's main historical attractions stand in a row along I Street: the smallest is the Huntington & Hopkins hardware store at no. 113. Here, the **Big Four** – Leland Stanford, Mark Hopkins, Collis P. Huntington, and Charles Crocker – held their first meeting to mastermind the Central Pacific and later Southern Pacific railroads (see box, p.658). It's now a **museum** (Tues–Sun 10am–5pm; free; Ⓣ916/323-7234) decked out as a spartan, 1840s supply store, highlighting the humble beginnings of the ruthless Huntington and the hen-pecked Hopkins, a meeker man who joined him as partner in his grocery store and later in the railroad. Upstairs there's a low-key homage to the men, with a re-creation of their boardroom and an archive of rail history.

One of the city's highlights is the **California State Railroad Museum** at 111 I St (daily 10am–5pm; $3; ℗916/445-7387, ⓦwww.californiastaterailroadmuseum.org), which brings together a range of lavishly restored 1860s locomotives with "cow-catcher" front grilles and huge bulbous smokestacks. Frankly, despite its exhaustive exhibits on early railroad technology, it's still a place for dedicated trainspotters rather than the casual tourist. Instead, catch a leisurely taste of railroad life by heading across to the old passenger station and freight depot a block south, which is also part of the museum. There, you can take a seven-mile, 45-minute jaunt beside the river on a vintage train (April–Sept Sat–Sun hourly 11am–5pm; $6).

A broader view of the area's history comes at the **Discovery Museum of History, Science and Technology** at 101 I St (Sept–May Tues–Sun 10am–5pm; June–Aug daily 10am–5pm; $5; ℗916/264-7057, ⓦwww.thediscovery .org). Here, you'll find a hands-on display about the early newspapers in California (including the *Sacramento Bee*, founded in 1857) as well as more recent history, like the Depression-era diner run by the pioneering African-American Dunlap family. The exhibits are hit and miss, but a better bet than the over-touted Railroad Museum.

Two smaller museums are really only worth a look if you're desperate to escape the souvenir shops. The **California Military Museum**, 1119 2nd St (Tues–Sun 10am–4pm; $3; ℗916/442-2883, ⓦwww.militarymuseum.org), provides an uninspiring chronicle – with documents, weaponry, and uniforms – of California's involvement in armed struggles from pre-statehood days to the present day; there's even a section on the 1992 race riots in Los Angeles. The **Wells Fargo Historical Museum**, 1000 2nd St at J (daily 10am–5pm; free; ℗916/440-4263), is one of the many corporate museums run by the bank across California. Unfortunately, it's not one of the best, with a tiny collection of unremarkable ephemera. In fact, most people only pass through to use the ATMs located inside this 1853 bank building, which also held the first State Supreme Court, the unassuming old chambers of which are sometimes open for public view on the top floor.

The **Crocker Art Museum** is close by, although you'll have to pass back under the highway to reach it, at 216 O St between Second and Third (Tues, Wed, Fri–Sun 10am–5pm, Thurs 10am–9pm; $6; ℗916/264-5423, ⓦwww .crockerartmuseum.org). Here exhibits of paintings collected by Supreme Court judge Edwin Crocker, brother of railroad baron Charles, are on display, in an odd complex of Renaissance Revival and modern buildings. Although there are a few pictures of early Californian life, otherwise its Eurocentric collection mainly old master paintings and drawings seems oddly incongruous in this city. More appropriate to its setting, in the shadow of the massive I-5 and I-80 interchange at 2200 Front St, the **Towe Auto Museum** (daily 10am–5pm; $6; ℗916/442-6802, ⓦwww.toweautomuseum.org) offers an impressive collection of antique cars and trucks, from Model Ts and As to classic '57 T-birds and "woody" station wagons.

Downtown

Running east from the riverfront and the Old Sacramento development, past the Greyhound and Amtrak stations, the **K Street Mall** is the commercial heart of **DOWNTOWN SACRAMENTO**, with the end of the modern suburban tramway running through the center of a pedestrianized shopping precinct. While its western reaches are rather forlorn, with plenty of empty storefronts, the street grows livelier the closer it gets to the massive, open-air **Downtown Plaza** shopping complex. There, you'll find every major retail name, a food court, plus an enormous cinema; at its western end, there's a time-warping tunnel that takes pedestrians under the highway to connect with Old Sacramento.

Northeast of the mall, at 16th and H, stands the old **Governor's Mansion** (tours daily on the hour 10am–4pm; $1; ⓦwww.parks.ca.gov/districts/goldrush/gmshp). Although built in 1877 as a private home, this enormous and elaborate Victorian house was home to California's governors for more than sixty years, until 1967, when then-governor Ronald Reagan abandoned its high ceilings and narrow staircases in favor of a ranch-style house on the outskirts of town. His excuse was that the structure had been condemned as a firetrap, although it's likely that he simply craved better creature comforts than the traditional building could offer. Today, the meringue-like mansion has been restored to its former glory, and is a perfect place to begin a self-guided **walking tour** of Sacramento's historic architecture with one of the detailed free brochures published by the Sacramento CVB.

The main building of the **State Capitol**, with its Classical Revival dome, was built in the 1860s, although there have been several significant, if insensitive, additions since then. It was restored to nineteenth–century opulence in 1976 in what was then the largest such project in US history; recently, it has undergone another heavy restoration, following a catastrophic incident in early 2001 when a mentally unstable truck driver ploughed his milk tanker into the southern facade and caused almost $15 million in damage, most of it smoke related. Unsurprisingly, security has been tightened, and you'll need a photo ID to enter the Capitol building: once inside, you're free to ramble around the main floor using the self-guided leaflets on offer in the rotunda. You'll see more, though, if you take one of the free **tours** (daily 9am–5pm, last tour 4pm; ☎916/324-0333) that leave hourly from Room B-27 on the lower ground floor. These tours will take you through administrative rooms set up as if it were April 1906, when the devastating San Francisco earthquake occurred. You'll also visit the salmon-pink Senate Gallery and lush green Assembly Room. Note the gargoyle's face in the egg-and-dart molding of the Assembly Room ceiling, sticking its tongue out at the speaker (illicitly added, it's claimed, by disgruntled artisans during construction). The park around the Capitol is delightful, filled with rowdy flowerbeds, enormous trees, and a plague of friendly squirrels; it's often crowded on weekday lunchtimes with office workers snacking in the sun.

The brand new **Golden State Museum**, 1020 O St (Tues–Sat 10am–5pm, Sun 12–5pm; $5; ☎916/653-7524, ⓦwww.goldenstatemuseum.org), is an enormous, cutting-edge facility that focuses on both the state's physical history and the development of the often ridiculed "California-ness" in its settlers. The layout's rather confusing, since each exhibit bleeds into the next, but don't miss the eye-catching re-creation of an early Chinese herbalist store or the perky TV montage showing Californians' own, often amusing, reflections on their home state.

Midtown

Sacramento's trendiest district is **MIDTOWN**, a pleasant neighborhood for a leisurely, leafy stroll – city planners planted trees on almost every street, so there's ample shade from the relentless sunshine. Here, although there are few

The Big Four and California's early railroads

Starting in 1861, the **Central Pacific** and **Southern Pacific railroads** monopolized transportation and dominated the economy and politics of California and the western US for over twenty years. These companies were the creation of just four men – Leland Stanford, Mark Hopkins, Collis P. Huntington, and Charles Crocker – known collectively as the **Big Four**.

For an initial investment of $15,000, the four financiers, along with the railroad designer and engineer Theodore Judah who died before its completion in 1883, received federal subsidies of $50,000 per mile of track laid – twice what it actually cost. On top of this, they were granted half the land in a forty-mile strip bordering the railroad: as the network expanded, the Southern Pacific became the largest landowner in the state, owning over twenty percent of California. An unregulated monopoly – caricatured in the liberal press as a grasping **octopus** – the railroad had the power to make or break farmers and manufacturers dependent upon it for the transportation of goods. In the cities, particularly Oakland and Los Angeles, it was able to demand massive concessions from local government as an inducement for rail connections. By the end of the nineteenth century, the Big Four had extracted and extorted a fortune worth over $200 million each and ran a network that stretched across the country to New Orleans. Although they all built fabulous mansions on San Francisco's swanky Nob Hill, those palaces were destroyed soon after the men's deaths by the 1906 earthquake and fire (see p.534). Perhaps the four's most enduring monument, though, is the prestigious university that vain Leland Stanford endowed in the honor of his namesake and only son after the boy's early death.

actual attractions, you'll find dozens of funky restaurants and cafés (see below) dotted among the old Victorian mansions, not to mention one of the city's best sights, **Sutter's Fort State Historic Park**. This re-creation of Sacramento's original settlement stands at 27th and L streets: the main entrance is on the south side (daily 10am–5pm; $1, free entry after 4.30pm; ☎916/445-4422, ⓦwww.parks.ca.gov/districts/goldrush/sfshp). With its low, starkly white-washed walls, the fort is strikingly simple amid the residential frippery of many Victorians nearby. Inside, motion-triggered audio commentary describes each room, like the Blacksmith's and the Bakery, and an adobe house exhibits relics from the Gold Rush; its empty stillness gives a vivid sense of early European life in California.

One block north, the small **Indian Museum** at 2618 K St (daily 10am–5pm; $1; ☎916/324-0971) displays tools, handicrafts, and ceremonial objects of the Native Americans of the Central Valley and the Sierra Nevada Mountains.

Out of the main city center, on the corner of 16th Street and Broadway, stands the original **Tower Records**. Technically, it's the second location as the chain started in what's now the Tower Theater (see opposite), where local entrepreneur Russ Solomon owned a drugstore in the 1940s and started selling used jukebox records for 10¢ each. The current location opened in 1965 and the chain began to spread in earnest, first across America and then around the world.

Eating

Dozens of fast-food stands, ice-cream shops, and pricey Western-themed **restaurants** fill Old Sacramento, but you'd do better to steer clear of these and search out the places we've listed below. Many of the restaurants Downtown cater primarily to office workers and are therefore closed in the evening; for dinner, it's better to stroll over to Midtown, around 20th Street and Capitol Avenue, where you'll also find the odd good bar.

Café Bernardo 28th St and Capitol Ave, Midtown ☎916/443-1180. Large, refectory-style restaurant, where you can order huge portions of healthy, cheap food from the walk-up counter and eat in the casual dining room that's reminiscent of a Tuscan farmhouse. The menu's mainly Italian, with pastas, salads, and small pizzas; it's also open for breakfast, when the food's more American with french toast and pancakes.

Centro Cocina Mexicana 2730 J St, Midtown☎916/442-2552. This innovative upscale Mexican restaurant offers regional cooking like delicious chicken and mole enchiladas from Oaxaca province. Lunch prices and dishes are lighter; the bar's especially impressive, since it stocks more than 50 aged tequilas.

Chipotle 1831 Capitol Ave, Midtown ☎916/444-8940. This funky café has a simple menu offering three kinds of burritos, including the deliciously tangy barbacoa (shredded spicy beef) for around $5.

Emma's Taco House 723 K St, Downtown ☎916/446-2122. One of the better choices on the patchy K Street Mall, this is a friendly, rather dilapidated restaurant that offers lavish portions of Cal-Mex food at budget prices.

Hukilau Island Grill 1501 16th St at O, Midtown ☎916/444-5850. Loud, garish, but fun restaurant, complete with cartoony Hawaiian decor and an eclectic, Pacific Rim menu: the simpler dishes, like grilled fish kebabs, are the most successful.

Jack's Urban Eats 20t St & Capitol Ave, Midtown ☎916/444-0307. Groovy bargain rotisserie, serving slab-like sandwiches of juicy herb chicken or steak for $5, with stylish, stark decor and local art on the walls. The urban-style fries, with blue cheese and spicy chili oil, are knockout.

Maharani 1728 Broadway at 18th St, Downtown ☎916/441-2172. Slightly pricey Californian-style Indian that's light on oil, but still heavy on all the traditional spices.

Megami 1010 10th St at J St, Downtown ☎916/448-4512. A functional, bargain Japanese restaurant with lunch and combination sushi plates for under $5. Try the sesame chicken. Mon–Fri only.

New Helvetia Roasters & Bakers 1215 19th St at Capitol Ave, Midtown ☎916/441-1106. One of the best, busiest cafés in town, this large, former firehouse has plenty of indoor and outdoor seating. The crowd's artsy and eclectic, and the place is especially popular with the city's gay community. Best of all, it's open until 11pm and is very single-traveler friendly.

Paesano's 1806 Capitol Ave at 18th St, Midtown ☎916/447-8646. Brick-walled pizzeria, serving hearty portions of pasta and oven-baked sandwiches at reasonable prices.

River City Brewing Company 545 Downtown Plaza ☎916/447-2745. One of the few acceptable places to stop off near Old Sacramento, this slick modern brew pub at the west end of the shopping mall serves standard food at regular prices, although the beers (some brewed onsite) are tasty.

Tapa the World 2115 J St at 20th St, Midtown ☎916/442-4353. Choose from twenty different tapas, or have a full meal of paella, lamb, or fresh fish, all while being serenaded by flamenco guitar.

Weatherstone Coffee & Trading Co 812 21st St at H, Midtown ☎916/443-6340. Sacramento's oldest coffeehouse has a massive courtyard that's pleasant on a sunny afternoon; the interior's a little dilapidated, but it's unpretentious and easygoing. Note that it can be hard to find, tucked away on a largely residential block.

Drinking and nightlife

Sacramento's **nightlife** can be rather flat, especially in the center of the city once the office workers have headed home to the suburbs. The best place to catch off-beat, live music is *Old Ironsides*, 1901 10th St (☎916/443-9751, ⓦwww.theoldironsides.com); another option is the *Capitol Garage*, 1427 L St at 14th (☎916/444-3633, ⓦwww.capitolgarage.com): this coffee bar-cum-performance space features local bands with a nominal cover. For bigger touring names, try the *Crest Theater*, a refurbished Art Deco gem on the K Street Mall at no. 1013, which also hosts short runs of edgy indie **movies** (☎916/442-7378, ⓦwww.thecrest.com). Otherwise, for arthouse films, try the *Tower Theater* at Broadway and 16th (☎916/442-4700).

The funky *Monkey Bar* adjacent to *Café Bernardo* (see above) (☎916/442-8940), with its mosaic decor and mixed preppy-indie crowd, is the best place to drink and serves bargain cocktails for less than $3. The biggest dance club in the city center is *Faces*, on the corner of K and 20th streets (☎916/448-7798, ⓦwww.facesnightclub.com), with two dancefloors and nine bars; the cover hovers around

$6, and there's a mixed gay/straight crowd. Opposite *Faces* is *The Depot*, a friend-ly gay video bar at 2001 K St (☎916/441-6823, ⓦwww.thedepot.net).

The Central Mother Lode

From Sacramento, US-50 and I-80 head east through the heart of the Gold Country, up and over the mountains past Lake Tahoe and into the state of Nevada. The roads closely follow the old stagecoach routes over the Donner Pass (named in honor of the gruesomely tragic exploration; see p.696). In the mid-1860s local citizens, seeking to improve dwindling fortunes after the Gold Rush subsided, joined forces with railroad engineer Theodore Judah to finance and build the first railroad crossing of the Sierra Nevada over much the same route – even along much of the same track – that Amtrak uses today. The area's less tourristed than the northern or southern mines: either **Placerville** or **Auburn** make good bases, with affordable accommodation and some local points of interest in each. And while the area's towns may not be nearly as post-card perfect as those elsewhere in the region, **Coloma** and **Folsom**, in between the two highways on the American River, are both worth exploring.

Folsom

In 1995, just as the **FOLSOM** powerhouse was gearing up for the centennial celebration of its pioneering efforts in long-distance electricity transmission, one of the sluice gates on the Folsom Dam gave way, sending millions of gal-lons of water down the American River towards Sacramento, twenty miles downstream. The levees held, but Folsom Lake had to be almost completely drained before repairs could be undertaken. The event sent shockwaves through California's extensive hydroelectric industry and brought a fame to Folsom unknown since Johnny Cash sang of being "stuck in Folsom Prison" after having "shot a man in Reno, just to watch him die." The stone-faced **Folsom State Prison**, two miles north of town on Green Valley Road, has an arts-and-crafts gallery (daily 8am–5pm) selling works by prisoners, who get the proceeds when released. It's more worthwhile stopping at the small **museum** across the road (daily 10am–4pm; donation; ☎916/985-2561), which is filled with grisly photographs, the medical records of murderers and thieves who were hanged for their crimes, and a whole armory of handmade escape tools recovered from prisoners over the years.

Folsom itself is attractive enough, with a single main street of restored homes and buildings that date from the days of the Pony Express. A reconstruction of the 1860 Wells Fargo office makes an imposing setting for the **Folsom History Museum**, 823 Sutter St (Wed–Sun 11am–4pm; $2; ☎916/985-2707, ⓦwww.folsomhistorymuseum.org), whose prized possessions include a work-ing-scale model of a steam-powered gold dredge, artifacts from the Chinese community that settled here in the 1850s, and a huge mural depicting the area's main Native American people, the Maidu.

In town, the Folsom **Chamber of Commerce**, 200 Wool St (Mon–Fri 9am–5pm, Sat–Sun 11am–4pm; ☎916/985-5555 or 1-800/377-1414, ⓦwww.folsomchamber.com), has plenty of the usual brochures. There are plenty of chain **eateries** around town; otherwise, a good choice is the *Balcony Restaurant*, 801 Sutter St (☎916/985-2605), where you can have a hearty meal while enjoying the view of the historic downtown. For **accommodation**,

El Dorado wine country

In the 1860s, when the now-famous Napa and Sonoma valleys were growing potatoes, **vineyards** flourished in El Dorado County. However, the fields were neglected
after the Gold Rush and killed off by phylloxera, a nasty yellow aphid that gorges
itself on vine roots; it wasn't until 1972 that vineyards were systematically re-established. Since then, however, the **wineries** in El Dorado County, especially around
Placerville, have rapidly gained a reputation that belies their diminutive size. Most
are low-key affairs where no charge is made for tasting or tours, and you're encouraged to enjoy a bottle out on the verandah. At quiet times, you may even be shown
around by the winemaker, a far cry from the organized tours and rampant commercialism of Napa and Sonoma (see p.710).

The differences in altitude and soil types throughout the region lend themselves to
a broad range of grape varieties, and the producers here are often criticized for
being unfocused; either way, in recent years local wineries have regularly snagged
awards. Zinfandel and Sauvignon Blanc are big, but it's the Syrah/Merlot blends that
attract the attention, and the Barbera (from a Piedmontese grape) is said to be one
of the best in the world.

If you're out for a relaxed day's tasting, avoid the **Passport Weekend** (①1-
800/306-3956, ⓦwww.eldoradowines.org; $50), usually the last weekend in March
or the first in April and booked out months in advance, when the purchase of said
passport entitles you to all manner of foodie extravagances to complement the tastings. Better to pick up the **El Dorado Wine Country Tour** leaflet from the El Dorado
Chamber of Commerce (see p.662) and make your way to the Boeger Vineyard,
1790 Carson Rd (daily 10am–5pm; ①530/622-8094, ⓦwww.boegerwinery.com),
less than a mile from the Greyhound stop (see p.662), where you can sit in an arbor
of apples and pears, or the Lava Cap Vineyard, 2221 Fruitridge Rd (daily 11am–5pm;
①530/621-0175, ⓦwww.lavacap.com), which in recent years has produced some
excellent Chardonnay and Muscat Canelli.

The quality of the local produce – not only grapes, but also apples, pears, peaches, cherries, and more – is widely celebrated around the district, especially during the
Apple Hill Festival (①530/644-7692, ⓦwww.applehill.com) in October, when a shuttle bus runs from Placerville to the majority of the orchards and wineries situated in
the Apple Hill region, along the winding country roads just north of I-50 and east of
town. At other times, you'll have to make your own way. The Chamber of Commerce
can also supply you with a *Cider Press Guide to Apple Hill* and a *Farm Trails Harvest
& Recreation Guide*, which has detailed information and maps leading to farms,
ranches, wineries, and historic country inns in the most remote areas of the county.

you'd do better heading back to Sacramento, though if you're particularly tired
and on a roomy budget, you might try the *Lake Natoma Inn*, 702 Gold Lake
Drive (①916/351-1500 or 1-800/808-5253, ⓦwww.lakenatomainn.com; ❺),
with full amenities, restaurant, and spa.

Placerville

PLACERVILLE, twenty miles east of Folsom, takes a perverse delight in having been known originally as Hangtown for its habit of lynching alleged criminals in pairs and stringing them up from a tree in the center of town. Despite
these gruesome beginnings, Placerville has always been more of a market than
a mining town and is now a major crossroads, halfway between Sacramento and
Lake Tahoe at the junction of US-50 and Hwy-49. For a time, it was the third-
largest city in California, and many of the men who went on to become the
most powerful in the state got their start here: railroad magnates Mark Hopkins

and Collis P. Huntington were local merchants, while car mogul John Studebaker made wheelbarrows for the miners.

The modern town spreads out along the highways in a string of fast-food restaurants, gas stations, and motels. The old Main Street, running parallel to US-50, retains some of the Gold Rush architecture, with an effigy dangling by the neck in front of the *Hangman's Tree* bar, which is built over the site where the town's infamous tree once grew. You'll also see many fine old houses scattered among the pine trees in the steep valleys to the north and south of the center. Nearby, one of the best of the Gold Country museums is located in the sprawling El Dorado County Fairgrounds, just north of US-50. This, the **El Dorado County Historical Museum**, 104 Placerville Drive (Wed–Sat 10am–4pm, Sun 12–4pm; free; ℡530/621-5865, ⓦwww.co.el-dorado.ca.us/generalsaervices/museum), gives a broad historical overview of the county from the Miwok to the modern day, including logging trains and a mock-up of a general store. For more on the days of the argonauts, head across US-50 to the **Gold Bug Mine Park** on Bedford Avenue (Nov–Feb Sat–Sun 12–4pm, weather permitting; Mar–April Sat–Sun 12–4pm; May–Oct daily 10am–4pm; $3, $1 audio tour; ℡530/642-5207, ⓦwww.goldbugpark.org), for a self-guided tour of a typical Mother Lode mine, including a hard-rock mining site as well as a stamp mill showing the ore extraction process.

Practicalities

Amtrak Thruway **buses** pull up twice daily outside the *Buttercup Pantry*, 222 Main St; while Greyhound buses on their way to South Lake Tahoe stop twice a day at 1750 Broadway, a mile and a half east of town. El Dorado Transit buses provide local transit service. Near the Greyhound stop are a number of **motels**, such as the *Mother Lode Motel*, 1940 Broadway (℡530/622-0895, ⓔlodgegoldcountry@aol.com; ➋), and the nicer but slightly pricier *National 9 Inn*, 1500 Broadway (℡530/622-3884; ➋). With more money, you're far better off at the *Chichester-McKee House*, 800 Spring St (℡530/626-1882 or 1-800/831-4008, ⓦwww.innlover.com; ➎), a historic B&B and a landmark in its own right, offering guestrooms with period furnishings and home-made baked breakfasts, and reached by turning north off US-50 onto Hwy-49 at the traffic lights in town.

The El Dorado County **Chamber of Commerce** office, 542 Main St (Mon–Fri 9am–5pm; ℡530/621-5885, ⓦwww.eldoradocounty.org), has local information and can help set up **river-rafting** trips in Coloma (see opposite).

For **eating**, try the local concoction, "the Hangtown Fry," an omelet-like mix-up of bacon, eggs, and breaded oysters. It's said to have been whipped up using ingredients that were scarce at the height of the Gold Rush for a wealthy miner who wanted the priciest dish on the menu: try one at *Chuck's Pancake House*, 1318 Broadway (closed Tues; ℡530/622-2858). *Sweetie Pies*, at 577 Main St (℡530/642-0128), serves great breakfasts and what could be the best cinnamon rolls on the planet. You can sip coffee, play chess, and listen to local folk and bluegrass inside the musty remnants of an actual gold mine at the bizarre *Placerville Coffee House*, 594 Main St (℡530/642-8481). Not to be missed if you've got a car is *Poor Red's Barbeque* (℡530/622-2901), housed in the old Adams and Co. stagecoach office on Hwy-49 three miles south of Placerville, which serves the Gold Country's best barbecued dinners for under $6, with $1 beers and two-fisted margaritas. If none of these appeal, *Lil' Mama D. Carlos*, 482 Main St (℡530/626-1612), serves up fine, affordable Italian food.

Coloma

Sights along Hwy-49 north of Placerville are few and far between, but it was here that gold fever began, when on January 24, 1848 James Marshall discovered flakes of gold in the tailrace of a mill he was building for John Sutter, along the south fork of the American River at **COLOMA**. By the summer of that year, thousands had flocked to the area, and by the following year Coloma was a town of ten thousand – though most left quickly following news of richer strikes elsewhere in the region, and the town all but disappeared within a few years. The few surviving buildings, including the cabin where Marshall lived and two Chinese stores, have been preserved as the **Marshall Gold Discovery State Historic Park** (daily 8am–5pm, museum daily 10am–4.30pm; $2 per car; ℡530/622-3470, ⓦwww.parks.ca.gov). A reconstruction of **Sutter's Mill** stands along the river within the park and working demonstrations are often held on weekends at 10am and 1pm. There's a small historical museum across the road, and on a hill overlooking the town a statue marks the spot where Marshall is buried. Marshall never profited from his discovery, and in fact it came to haunt him. At first, he tried to charge miners for access to what he said was his land along the river (it wasn't), and he spent most of his later years in poverty, claiming supernatural powers had helped him to find gold.

Whether or not you believe in ghosts, Coloma certainly has one attraction that will still turn your knuckles white: it's the best place to begin a **whitewater rafting** journey on the American River. Tours can be booked with Mariah Wilderness Expeditions (℡530/233-2303 or 1-800/462-7424, ⓦwww .mariahwe.com) or Rapid Descent Adventures (℡530/642-2370, ⓔrapidd@ pacbell.net): expect to pay around $100 for a half-day excursion; overnight trips start around $220. If you decide to stay for the night, the choicest **accommodation** is at the *Coloma Country Inn*, 345 High St (℡530/622-6919, ⓦwww .colomacountryinn.com; ❺), adjacent to the state park, with its antique-crammed rooms.

Auburn and Dutch Flat

Heading north thirty miles or so, the town of **AUBURN**, built into a hillside on three levels, manages to preserve its Gold Rush-era charm, even though it's right at the crossroads of Hwy-49 and I-80. Greyhound **buses** heading from Sacramento to Reno stop at 246 Palm Ave, and Amtrak **trains** depart from Nevada and Fulleiler streets. The outskirts are sprawling and modern, but the Old Town, on Auburn's lowest level just off Hwy-49, is one of the best-preserved and most picturesque of the Gold Rush sights, with antique stores and saloons clustered around a Spanish-style plaza. You'll also find California's oldest post office and the unmissable red-and-white tower of the 1891 **firehouse**. There are also a number of undervisited but informative museums like the **Gold Country Museum**, 1273 High St (Tues–Fri 10am–3.30pm, Sat–Sun 11am–4pm; free; ℡530/889-6500, ⓦwww.placer.ca.gov/museum/goldctry). More offbeat and unusual is the **Bernhard Museum Complex** at 291 Auburn-Folsom Rd (Tues–Fri 10.30am–3pm, Sat–Sun 12–4pm; free; ℡530/889-6500, ⓦwww.placer.ca.gov/museum/bernhard), which offers guided tours of an amateur viticulturist's 1851 home, as well as his carriage barn and modest winery.

For a free map and information on places to stay, stop by the **Placer County Visitor Center**, north of town at 13464 Lincoln Way (Mon–Fri 9am–5pm, Sat

9am–3pm; ☎530/887-2111, ⓦwww.sierraheritage.com/pcvb). If you're looking for a good **meal**, try either *Bootlegger's Old Town Tavern and Grill*, 210
Washington St (☎530/889-2229), where hearty meals are served in a stately
brick building, or *Latitudes*, 130 Maple Street (☎530/885-9535), for Californian
interpretations of multi-cultural cuisines. Affordable **accommodation** is available at the *Super 8 Motel* at 140 E Hillcrest Drive in Auburn, which offers comfort without the frills (☎530/888-8808 or 1-800/800-8000; ❸).

The twenty or so miles of Hwy-49 north of Auburn are a dull but fast stretch
of freeway to one of the best parts of the Gold Country – the twin cities of
Grass Valley and Nevada City (see p.669). For an interesting side trip on the
way there, or if you're heading for Lake Tahoe, take I-80 from Auburn 27 miles
east to the small town of **DUTCH FLAT**, where old tin-roofed cottages are
sprinkled among the pine- and aspen-covered slopes. Miners here used the
profitable, but very destructive, method of hydraulic mining (see p.672) to get
at the gold buried under the surface – with highly visible consequences.

The northern mines

The **northern section** of the Gold Country includes some of the most spectacularly beautiful scenery in California. Fast-flowing rivers cascade along the
bottom of steeply-walled canyons, whose slopes are covered in the fall with the
flaming reds and golds of poplars and sugar maples, highlighted against an evergreen background of pine and fir trees. Unlike the freelance placer mines of
the south, where wandering prospectors picked nuggets of gold out of the
streams and rivers, the gold here was (and is) buried deep underground and
had, therefore, to be pounded out of hard-rock ore. In spite of that, the **northern mines** were the most profitable of the Mother Lode – more than half the
gold that came out of California came from the mines of **Nevada County**,
and most of that from **Grass Valley**'s Empire Mine, now preserved as one of
the region's many excellent museums. Just north, the quaint Victorian houses
of **Nevada City** make it the most alluring Gold Rush town.

A few miles away, at the end of a steep and twisting backroad, the scarred yet
curiously beautiful landforms of the **Malakoff Diggins** stand as an exotic
reminder of the destruction wrought by overzealous miners, who, as gold
became harder to find, washed away entire hillsides to get at the precious metal.
Hwy-49 winds up further into the mountains from Nevada City, along the
Yuba River to the High Sierra hamlet of **Downieville**, at the foot of the towering Sierra Buttes, and even smaller **Sierra City** further along. From here
you're within striking distance of the northernmost Gold Rush ghost town of
Johnsville, which stands in an evocative state of arrested decay in the middle
of the forests of Plumas-Eureka State Park, on the crest of the Sierra Nevada.

You'll need a **car** to get to any of the outlying sights, but there is limited public transportation to Grass Valley and Nevada City in the form of four daily
Amtrak Thruway **buses**. You'll find a few inexpensive motels and a handful of
B&Bs, but there are no youth hostels; **camping** is an option too, often in
unspoiled sites in gorgeous mountain scenery.

△ Columbia State Historic Park

Grass Valley and Nevada City

Twenty-five miles north of Auburn and I-80, the neighboring towns of **GRASS VALLEY** and **NEVADA CITY** were the most prosperous and substantial of the gold-mining towns and are still thriving communities, four miles apart in beautiful surroundings in the lower reaches of the Sierra Nevada mountains. Together they make one of the better Gold Country destinations, with museums and many balconied, elaborately detailed buildings staggering up hills and hanging out over steep gorges.

Gold was the lifeblood of the area as recently as the mid-1950s, and both towns look largely unchanged since the Gold Rush. The locals have retained a bit of the fiery determination of their rough-and-ready ancestors, as evidenced by the booming downtown businesses that combine the Old West with big-city sophistication. Since the 1960s, a number of artists and craftspeople have also settled in the old houses in the hills around the area, tempering the rugged regional culture with a vaguely alternative feel that's reflected in the free weekly *Community Endeavor* newspaper, the non-commercial community radio station KVMR (99.3FM), the disproportionate number of bookshops, and in the friendly throngs that turn out for the annual Bluegrass Festival in the middle of June.

Both towns are very compact and connected every thirty minutes by the Gold Country Stage **minibus** (Mon–Fri 8am–5pm, Sat 9.15am–5.30pm; $1, $2 for a day-pass; ☏530/477-0103), which follows the same stretch of road that burro trains and stagecoaches frequented in the twin towns' heyday, when it was the busiest four-mile route in California. The four daily Amtrak Thruway **buses** from Sacramento and Auburn stop on Sacramento Street in Nevada City and on West Main Street in Grass Valley.

Accommodation

There is a scattering of cheapish **motels** around but if you can afford to fork out more for a **bed and breakfast**, Nevada City in particular has some excellent options. Otherwise, there are a couple of revamped old Gold Rush **hotels**. See box opposite for **camping** options.

Coach 'N' Four Motel 628 S Auburn St, Grass Valley ☏530/273-8009, ⓕ530/273-0827. Clean and comfortable motel with the best rates around. ❷

Flume's End 317 S Pine St, Nevada City ☏530/265-9665, ⓦwww.flumesend.com. Across the Pine Creek Bridge from the center of town, this small inn overlooks a pretty waterfall and features lovely gardens ranged along Deer Creek. ❺

Grandmere's Inn 449 Broad St, Nevada City ☏530/265-4660, ⓦwww.grandmeresinn.com. Nice friendly B&B with beautifully furnished rooms just up the hill from the center of town. ❻

Holbrooke Hotel 212 W Main St, Grass Valley ☏530/273-1353 or 1-800/933-7077, ⓦwww.holbrooke.com. Recently renovated and right in the center of town, this historic hotel, where Mark Twain once stayed, has great rooms and an opulent bar-cum-restaurant. ❹

Holiday Lodge 1221 E Main St, Grass Valley ☏530/2734406 or 1-800/742-7125. Comfortable, no-frills rooms in a lodge featuring a swimming pool, free breakfast, and free local calls. ❸

National Hotel 211 Broad St, Nevada City ☏530/265-4551. The oldest continuously operated hotel in the West and a state historic landmark, so plenty of character in the rooms and lobby, which is dominated by a grand staircase. ❹

Northern Queen Inn 400 Railroad Ave, Nevada City ☏530/265-5824, ⓦwww.northernqueeninn.com. Good-value hotel with a heated pool. Attractive woodland cottages and chalets, along with simpler rooms in another building. ❹

Outside Inn 575 E Broad St, Nevada City ☏530/265-2233, ⓦwww.outsideinn.com. Quiet, recently renovated 1940s motel with swimming pool, a 10min walk from the center of town. Credit cards not accepted. ❸

One of the best ways to get a feel for the day-to-day life of the miners is to "rough it" yourself, **camping** out in one of the many easily accessible campgrounds in the surrounding hills, which you can only reach by car. On Hwy-20, just east of Nevada City, *Gene's Pine-Aire Campground*, at Washington (℡530/265-2832), and *Scott's Flat Lake*, on Scott's Flat Road (℡530/265-5302), are privately operated and have the best facilities; seven miles on, *White Cloud* is more remote – for details, contact the ranger station (℡530/265-4531) in Nevada City on Coyote Street, a quarter of a mile north past the tourist office. Rates at all sites start at around $10, but can be more in the high season.

Piety Hill Cottages 523 Sacramento St, Nevada City ℡530/265-2245 or 1-800/443-2245, ⓦwww.pietyhillcottages.com. Cottages decorated in period furnishings with kitchenettes in a garden setting. ❺

Shady Rest Motel 10845 Rough and Ready Hwy, Grass Valley ℡530/273-4232. Ramshackle place a little way out of town, but a pleasant walk; good-value weekly rates available. ❷

Stagecoach Motel 405 S Auburn St, Grass Valley ℡530/272-3701. Decent rates and all the basic amenities, handily placed for the Empire Mine. ❸

Swan-Levine House 328 S Church St, Grass Valley ℡530/272-1873. Accommodation with the artist in mind; the friendly owners also give instruction in printmaking. Attractively decorated, sunny en-suite rooms in an old Victorian hospital. ❹

Grass Valley

There's nothing Gold Country folk love better than telling a long tale about their town's toughest days, making it virtually impossible to pass through **GRASS VALLEY** without getting at least one rendition of the **Lola Montez** story. This Irish dancer and entertainer – the former mistress of Ludwig of Bavaria, and friend of Victor Hugo and Franz Liszt – embarked on a highly successful tour of America in the 1850s, playing to packed houses from New York to San Francisco. Her provocative "Spider Dance," in which she wriggled about the stage shaking cork spiders out of her dress, didn't much impress the miners, but she liked the wild lifestyle of the town, gave up dancing, and retired to Grass Valley with her pet grizzly bear, which she kept tied up in the front yard. Max Ophüls' 1955 *Lola Montes*, which had the largest budget of any film in the history of French cinema at the time of its release, tells a surreal, fictionalized version of her life story.

A few mementos of Lola's life are displayed in the **Grass Valley Museum**, in the Old St Mary's Academy at the corner of Church and Chapel streets (June–Oct Tues–Sun; Nov–May Tues–Fri 12.30–3.30pm; donation suggested; ℡530/273-5509). The town's tourist office (Mon–Fri 9.30am–5pm, Sat 10am–3pm; ℡530/273-4667 or 1-800/655-4667, ⓦwww.gvncchamber.org) is housed in a replica of her home, on the south side of town at 248 Mill St. It also has reams of historical information, lists of accommodation, and a walking-tour map of the town, pointing out the oldest hardware store in California (which, sadly, closed in 1990 and has been converted into a tacky art gallery) among the wooden awnings and storefronts of the gas-lighted business district.

The North Star Mining Museum

The **North Star Mining Museum**, at the south end of Mill Street (May–Oct daily 10am–5pm, Nov–April closed; donation suggested; ℡530/273-4255), is one of the best of all the Gold Country museums, with enthusiastic guides and interesting exhibits, illustrating the days when Grass

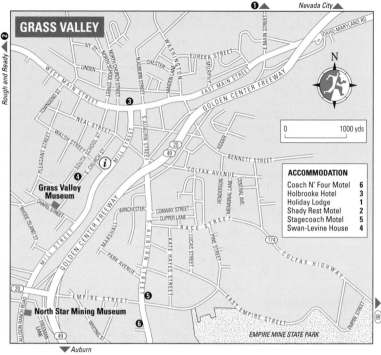

Valley was the richest and most important of all the California mining towns. Housed in what used to be the power station for the North Star Mine, the centerpiece is the giant **Pelton wheel**. Patented in 1878 and resembling nothing so much as a thirty-foot-diameter bicycle wheel, the wheel became one of the most important inventions to come out of the Gold Country. Many Pelton wheels were used to generate electricity, though the one here drove an air compressor that powered the drills and hoists of the mine.

A series of dioramas in the museum describe the day-to-day working life of the miners, three-quarters of whom had emigrated here from the depressed tin mines of Cornwall in England. Besides their expertise at working deep underground, the "Cousin Jacks," as they were called by the non-Cornish miners, introduced the **Cornish pump** (not to mention the Cornish pastie, a traditional pastry pie) to the mines. You can see a mock-up of one of these mammoth beasts here, as well as a replica of the old surface mechanism.

The great machines are now at peace, but when they were in action the racket could be heard for miles around. The noisiest offenders were the thundering stamp mills – a scaled-down version of which is operated upon request – which once mashed and pulverized the gold-bearing quartz ore.

The Empire Mine State Park

The largest and richest gold mine in the state was the **Empire Mine**, now preserved as a state park a mile southeast of Grass Valley, just off Hwy-174 at the top of Empire Street. The 800-acre park (daily Sept–May 10am–5pm: June–Aug 9am–6pm; $1) is surrounded by pines, amongst which are vast quantities of mining equipment and machinery, much of it only recently reinstated here after having been sold off for scrap after the mine closed in 1956. When standing among the machines, it is easy to imagine the din that shook the ground 24 hours a day, or the skips of fifty men descending the now-desolate shaft into the 350 miles of underground tunnels. After more than six million ounces of gold had been recovered, the cost of getting the gold out of the ground exceeded $35 an ounce – the government-controlled price at the time – and production ceased. Most of the mine has been dismantled, but there's a small, very informative **museum** at the entrance with a superb model of the whole underground system, built secretly to help predict the location of lucrative veins of gold. You can get some sense of the mine's prosperity by visiting the owner's house, the **Empire Cottage** at the north end of the park – a stone-and-brick, vaguely English manor house, with a glowing, redwood-paneled interior overlooking a formal garden.

Nevada City

Towns don't get much quainter than **NEVADA CITY**, four miles north of Grass Valley, with its crooked rows of elaborate Victorian homes set on the winding, narrow, maple-tree-lined streets, which rise up from Hwy-49. It gets away with all the quaintness, however, as it is one of the least changed of all the Gold Country towns with a cluster of excellent shops and restaurants in the town center – all in all, a good, if pricey, base for following the many steep streets up into the surrounding forest.

A good first stop is at the **tourist office** (Mon–Fri 9am–5pm, Sat 11am–4pm; ☎530/265-2692 or 1-800/655-6569, ⓦwww.nevadacitychamber.com) at 132 Main St, a block north of Hwy-49, where you can pick up a free walking-tour **map** of the town. It's hard to select specific highlights, but one place to start is the newly restored, lacy-balconied and bell-towered **Old Firehouse**, at 214 Main St, one block up from the tourist office, which houses a small **museum** (daily: May–Oct 11am–4pm; Nov–April Thurs–Sun 11am–4pm; donation suggested) describing the social history of the region. The heart of town is Broad Street, which climbs up from the highway past the 1854 **National Hotel** (see "Accommodation", p.666) and a number of antique shops and restaurants, all decked out in Gold Country balconies and wooden awnings. Almost the only exception to the rule of picturesque nostalgia is the Art Deco 1937 **City Hall**, near the top of Broad Street.

The **Miner's Foundry Cultural Center** (Mon–Fri 9am–5pm; free), close to the Deer Creek canyon at 325 Spring St, is an old tool foundry converted into a multi-use cultural center, art gallery, performance space, and KVMR radio studios. Immediately next door stands the **Nevada City Winery**, 321 Spring St (Mon–Sat 11am–5pm, Sun noon–5pm; ☎530/265-9463), where you can taste the produce of one of the state's oldest vineyards and take a free tour at 11.30am every Saturday. If you'd like to sample a different glass, stop by the **Indian Springs Winery**, which has its tasting room at 303 Broad St (11am–5pm; ☎530/478-1068 or 1-800/273-2550). Both wineries sell their product at very modest prices in comparison to those of the Wine Country.

Above the town at the top of Pine Street, a small plaque marks **Indian Medicine Stone**, a granite boulder with sunbeds worn into the hollows of the rock by Native Americans who valued the healing power of sunshine. Broad Street intersects Hwy-49 a block further on, and continues up into the mountains as the North Bloomfield Road, which twists up the hills to the Malakoff Diggins (below).

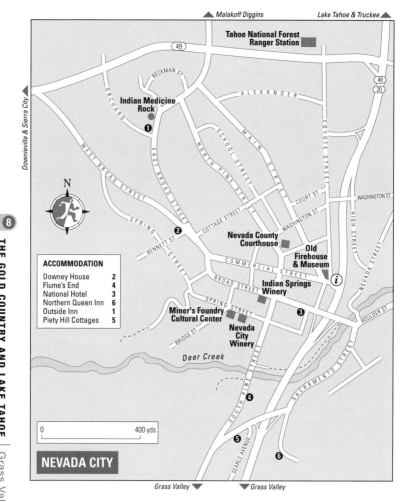

Tahoe National Forest
Ranger Station

BECKMAN ST

ALEXANDER

Indian Medicine
Rock ❶

Downieville & Sierra City ◀

ORCHARD

WEST BROAD STREET

EAST BROAD STREET

NORTH PINE STREET

SCHOOL STREET

MAIN STREET

COYOTE STREET

WASHINGTON ST

COURT ST

HIGH STREET

N

SPRING

BENNETT ST

COTTAGE STREET

WASHINGTON ST

❷

Nevada County
Courthouse

Old
Firehouse
& Museum

COMMERCIAL STREET

BROAD STREET

Indian Springs
Winery

ⓘ

NEVADA STREET

ACCOMMODATION

Downey House	2
Flume's End	4
National Hotel	3
Northern Queen Inn	6
Outside Inn	1
Piety Hill Cottages	5

SPRING STREET

Miner's Foundry
Cultural Center

❸

BOULDER ST

Nevada
City
Winery

BRIDGE ST

Deer Creek

SOUTH PINE STREET

SACRAMENTO STREET

❹

0 ————————— 400 yds

❺

NEVADA CITY

❻

SEARLS AVENUE

Eating and drinking

Both Grass Valley and Nevada City have some surprisingly sophisticated places
to **eat and drink**, including a few excellent **cafés**. Look out for pasties,
brought to the Gold Country by Cornish miners, and crisp-tasting Nevada
City beer, brewed locally and available at better establishments.

Cafés, restaurants, and bars

Apple Fare 121 Neal St, Grass Valley ☎530/272-
2555. Casual restaurant with an old hometown
diner feel, serving up generous portions at good
prices.

Broad Street Books 426 Broad St, Nevada City
☎530/265-4204. Pastries, light fare, and espresso
with wonderful tree-shaded outdoor seating.

Café Mekka 237 Commercial St, Nevada City
☎530/478-1517. Relaxed, fabulously decorated
coffee shop – from exposed piping to trompe l'oeil
wallpaper – popular with teenagers, trendies, and
ex-hippies. Open 8am–11pm weekdays, and until
1.30am on weekends.

Cirino's 309 Broad St, Nevada City ☎530/265-
2246. Good deli sandwiches for lunch and modest-
ly-priced Italian specialties at dinner, plus a full bar.

Citronée Bistro and Wine Bar 320 Broad St, Nevada City ☎530/265-5697. Upscale American-Mediterranean fusion cuisine in an elegant, yet unpretentious atmosphere.

Heavenly Espresso 154 Mill St, Grass Valley ☎530/274-2600. Centrally located café with a pleasant atmosphere and plenty of pastries, coffee drinks, and smoothies to choose from.

Jack's Internet Café 115 S Church St, Grass Valley ☎530/477-7873. Light meals, decadent desserts, and a pleasant atmosphere that help make checking your email less of a chore.

La Cucina Cirino 491 E Main St, Grass Valley ☎530/274-1337. An Italian delicatessen that doubles as a cooking school. Italian wines served.

Los Sombreros 311 Broad St, Nevada City ☎530/478-0275. Huge portions of tasty Mexican favourites in cheerful, colourful surroundings.

Mad Dogs and Englishmen 211 Spring St, Nevada City ☎530/265-8173. Pub-like bar with darts, good beer, and regular live, danceable blues and rock music. Open until 2am on weekends.

Main Street Café 213 W Main St, Grass Valley ☎530/477-6000. The best bet in the area for a really good meal, this casual but refined restaurant has an eclectic range of dishes – from pastas to

Cajun specialties – as well as good grilled meats and fresh fish, all at moderate prices. Also has a full wine and cocktail bar next door with live local musicians Thurs–Fri.

Marshall's Pasties 203 Mill St, Grass Valley ☎530/272-2844. Mind-boggling array of fresh filled Cornish pasties.

Moore's Café 216 Broad St, Nevada City ☎530/265-9440. Plain-looking, all-American diner with eggs for breakfast and burgers for lunch. Closed Mon.

Panoy Thai 210 Neal St, Grass Valley ☎530/272-6551. Simple canteen-style place serving authentic spicy Thai food at inexpensive prices. Good selection of veggie, meat, and seafood dishes.

Railroad Café 111 W Main St, Grass Valley ☎530/274-2233. Decent diner food accompanied by the clatter of a model railroad continuously operating overhead. Breakfast & lunch only Sun–Thurs, all three meals Fri & Sat.

Swiss House 535 Mill St, Grass Valley ☎530/273-8272. The Central European decor in the heart of the Sierra foothills warrants at least a grin, and you might even be tempted to stay for one of the hearty, reasonably priced Swiss-German meals.

Nevada County

Grass Valley, Nevada City, and the foothills of **NEVADA COUNTY** yielded more than half the gold that came out of California. Before the deep, hard-rock mines were established in the late 1860s, there were mining camps spread all over the northern Gold Country, with evocative names like "Red Dog" and "You Bet," that disappeared as soon as the easily recovered surface deposits gave out. **Rough and Ready**, five miles west of Grass Valley, survives on the tourist trade alone – visitors coming to take a look at the only mining town ever to secede from the United States, which Rough and Ready did in 1850. The band of veterans who founded the town, fresh from the Mexican–American War, opted to quit the Union in protest against unfair taxation by the federal government, and although they declared their renewed allegiance in time for that summer's Fourth of July celebrations, the conflict was not officially resolved until 1948. Now the place – little more than a handful of ramshackle buildings, including a gas station and a general store – isn't really worth visiting. If you must pass through, the **Chamber of Commerce** (☎530/272-4320) publishes a well-written brochure on the town's history that's about as long as the town's entire length; you can usually find one at the post office or general store. Every Sunday for most of the year from 10am to noon, visitors are welcome to join the Fruit Jar Pickers Band in an old-time singalong at the town's tiny square.

Six miles northwest of Rough and Ready, off the winding Bitney Springs Road in the **South Yuba River State Park**, stands the **Bridgeport covered bridge**, the longest single-span, wood-truss covered bridge in the world, spanning the Yuba River. The swimming spot underneath offers some relief from a hot summer's day, and the nearby visitors' center (☎530/432-2546) has plenty of information on the area's hiking trails, as well as guided wildflower, history, and birdwatching tours, as well as the inevitable gold-panning demonstrations.

Malakoff Diggins State Park

The waters of the Yuba River are now crisp and clear, but when the bridge was completed in 1862 they were being choked with mud and residue from the many **hydraulic mining** – or "hydraulicking" – operations upstream. Hydraulic mining was used here in the late 1850s to get at the trace deposits of gold that were not worth recovering by orthodox methods. It was an unsophisticated way of retrieving the precious metal: giant nozzles or monitors sprayed powerful jets of water against the gold-bearing hillsides, washing away tons of gravel, mud, and trees just to recover a few ounces of gold. It also required an elaborate system of flumes and canals – some still used to supply water to local communities – to collect the water, which was sprayed at a rate of over thirty thousand gallons a minute. Worst of all, apart from the obvious destruction of the landscape, was the waste it caused, silting up rivers, causing floods, impairing navigation, and eventually turning the San Francisco Bay, nearly 150 miles away, a muddy brown.

The worst offender, whose excesses caused hydraulic mining to be outlawed in 1884, was the **MALAKOFF DIGGINS**, sixteen miles up steep and winding North Bloomfield Road from Nevada City (or reachable via the sixteen-mile Tyler Foote Crossing Road, which turns off Hwy-49 twelve miles northwest of Nevada City). Here, a canyon more than a mile long, half a mile wide, and over six hundred feet deep was carved out of the red and gold earthen slopes. Natural erosion has softened the scars somewhat, sculpting pinnacles and towers into a miniature Grand Canyon, now preserved as a 3000-acre **state park** (summer daily, rest of year Sat & Sun dawn–dusk; $5; ☎530/265-2740). While the park may seem just a short detour from Hwy-49 on your map, its interminable unmarked gravel roads and snaking bends may give you the feeling you've landed in a sunny sequel to the *Blair Witch Project*. Inside the park, old buildings from ghost towns around the Gold Country are being moved to the restored town of **North Bloomfield**, where a small museum (June–Aug daily 10am–4pm; Sept–May Sat & Sun only, call ☎530/265-2740 for winter hours; free with park entry) shows a twenty-minute film on hydraulicking; there's a campground (ParkNet ☎1-800/444-7275; $12) near the eerie cliffs.

Downieville and the High Sierra towns

From Nevada City, Hwy-49 climbs up along the Yuba River Gorge into some of the highest and most marvelous scenery in the Gold Country, where waterfalls tumble over sharp, black rocks bordered by tall pines and maple trees. In the middle of this wilderness, an hour's drive from Nevada City, **DOWNIEVILLE**, the most evocatively situated of the Gold Rush towns, spreads out along both banks of the river, criss-crossed by an assortment of narrow bridges. Hwy-49 runs right through the center of town, slowing to a near-stop to negotiate tight curves that have not been widened since the stagecoaches passed through. Thick stone buildings, some enhanced with delicate wooden balconies and porches, others with heavy iron doors and shutters, face on to raised wooden sidewalks, as their backs dangle precipitously over the steep banks of the river.

For what is now a peaceful and quiet little hamlet of three hundred people, Downieville seems strangely proud of its fairly nasty history. It has the distinction of being the only mining camp ever to have hanged a woman, Juanita, "a fiery Mexican dancehall girl," who stabbed a miner in self-defense. A restored wooden gallows, last used in 1885, still stands next to the County Jail on the south bank of the river, to mark the ghastly heritage. Across the river and two blocks north, at the end of a row of 1850s storefronts, the Downieville Museum (May–Oct daily 11am–4pm; closed Nov–April; donation suggested; ☏530/289-3423) is packed full of odd bits and historical artifacts, including a set of snowshoes for horses and a scaled-down model of a stamp mill, "made by the boys of the shop classes 1947–8." Pick up a walking-tour map of the town from the phoneless and erratically opening **tourist kiosk** (May–Sept Sat & Sun only), which was about to relocate to a prime spot by the river as the town spruced itself up for its 150th anniversary in the summer of 2002.

Accommodation includes the *Riverside Inn* (☏530/289-1000 or 1-800/696-0310, ⓦwww.downiville.com; ❸) and the newly-done-up *Carriage House Inn* (☏530/289-3573, ⓦwww.downievillecarriagehouse.com; ❷), on opposite sides of the Yuba River where Hwy-49 crosses it, and the *Sierra Shangri-La* (☏530/289-3455, ⓦwww.sierrashangrila.com; ❹) two-and-a-half miles further northeast in a thick woods above the river, which has B&B rooms and fully fixtured cottages, the latter available weekly in summer. If the quainter places are full, try the decent motel lodgings at *Downieville Inn*, 117 Main St (☏530/289-3242, ⓦwww.downievilleinn.com; ❸).

Eating and **drinking** options can be found on Main Street at the family-style *Downieville Diner* (☏530/289-3616) or the *Riverview Pizzeria* (☏530/289-3540), and have your favorite café drink at the *Downieville Bakery & Café* (☏530/289-0108) on the corner of Commercial and Main streets.

The full-sized original of the stamp mill is maintained in working order at the **Kentucky Mine Museum** (summer Wed–Sun 10am–5pm; $1; ☏530/862-1310), a mile east of **Sierra City** further up Hwy-49, where a guided tour (11am & 2pm; $5) takes you inside a reconstructed miner's cabin, down a mineshaft, and gives you a look at various pieces of equipment used for retrieving the gold-bearing ore. Until the mine was shut down during World War II, the ore was dug out from tunnels under the massive **Sierra Buttes**, the craggy granite peaks that dominate the surrounding landscape.

Sierra City is full of rustic charm and can be a useful base for visiting the surrounding area. **Accommodation** is available year-round at *The Yuba River Inn* (☏530/862-1122, ⓦwww.yubariverinn.com; ❷), a rustic inn east on Hwy-49 by the river, and in town at the *Old Sierra City Hotel*, 212 Main St (☏530/862-1300, ⓔoschotel@inreach.com; ❷). Seasonal places include the *Busch & Heringlake Inn* B&B, 231 Main St (☏530/862-1501; ❸), and *Herrington's Sierra Pines* resort (☏530/862-1151; ❸), a little west of town. In the area you will also find some of the most remote and attractive **campgrounds** in the Gold Country, including the *Sierra Campground*, seven miles beyond Sierra City, and *Chapman Creek*, another mile upstream on the Yuba River. All sites are $10 and can be reserved by calling *High Sierra Campgrounds* (☏530/993-1410). The best place to eat is the English-run *Mountain Shadows Restaurant*, 224 Main St (☏530/862-1990), which serves genuine fish'n'chips and filling sandwiches.

Hwy-49 continues east through the **Tahoe National Forest**, passing over the 6700ft **Yuba Pass** on its way to join forces with Hwy-89 just north of Sattley at Bassett Junction. Here Hwy-89 heads north to Johnsville and south to Truckee and the Lake Tahoe area. Five miles south of the junction, there are basic facilities at **Sierraville**: at a pinch you could stay at the *Sierraville Motel &*

If all the twists and bends in Sierra County's stretch of Hwy-49 still aren't rugged enough for you, then consider a bumpy historical detour on the **HENNESS PASS**. Picked up just south of Sierraville or at Camptonville (southeast of Downieville near Grass Valley), the pass takes you along the route used by miners, freighters, immigrants, and highwaymen in their search for fame and riches. Today, the road is still largely unpaved and unvisited, though it includes sweeping views across the wooded river valleys typical of the area and a number of historic sites. The only town along the way is the all-but-abandoned **Forest City** – now home to a few Gold Rush-era buildings and a tiny museum (call the ranger stations below for hours). The road can take as little as an hour or up to half a day, depending on how much time you spend lingering at historic sights along the way. The **Mountain House**, the **Cornish House**, and the **Davis Station** were all of importance to miners negotiating the treacherous pass on horseback and in stagecoaches, while the **Kyburz Interpretive Area**, near Hwy-89, has Indian rock art and a reconstructed Basque bread oven. Four-wheel-drives are recommended for negotiating the pass today, though they are not necessary; a detailed brochure with a good map is available from the ranger stations in Sierraville (℡530/994-3401) or Camptonville (℡530/478-6253).

RV Park (℡530/994-3751;❷) or stop for a meal or drink at the *Stagecoach Café & Branding Iron Saloon* (530/994-3013), both by the right-angle turn where the two highways separate again in the middle of the tiny town.

Johnsville

Founded in 1870, **JOHNSVILLE** is, after Bodie (see p.362), the best-preserved and most isolated old mining town in California. Located 25 miles north of Bassett Junction, the ghost town is surrounded by over seven thousand acres of pine forest and magnificent scenery and lies at the center of the **Plumas–Eureka State Park** – which has $12 **camping** (reserve through ParkNet ℡1-800/444-7275) and miles of **hiking** trails. Johnsville's huge stamp mill and mine buildings are being restored; in the meantime, a small museum (daily 9am–5pm; $2) describes the difficult task of digging for gold in the High Sierra winters. For the rest of Plumas County and the Hwy-89 route north-west to Lassen Volcanic National Park, see p.767.

The southern mines

Though never as rich or successful as the diggings further north, the camps of the **southern mines** had a reputation for being the liveliest and most uproarious of all the Gold Rush settlements and inspired most of the popular images of the era: Wild West towns full of gambling halls, saloons, and gunfights in the streets. Certainly, the southern settlements were less segregated than those further north – Sonora, for instance, was established by Mexican immigrants and Chinese Camp was almost exclusively Asian. The mining methods here were also very different from those used further north. Instead of digging out gold-bearing ore from deep underground, claims here were more often worked by itinerant, roving prospectors searching for bits of gold washed out of rocks by rivers and streams, known as **placer** gold (from the Spanish word meaning both "sand bar," where much of the gold was found, and – appropriately – "pleasure"). Nuggets were sometimes found sitting on the riverbanks, though most of the gold had to be laboriously separated from mud and gravel using handheld pans or larger sluices. It wasn't a particularly lucrative existence: freelance miners roamed the countryside until they found a likely spot, and if and when they struck it rich quickly spent most of the earnings, either in celebration or buying the expensive supplies needed to carry on digging.

The boom towns that sprang up around the richest deposits were abandoned as soon as the gold ran out, but a few slowly decaying ghost towns have managed to survive more or less intact to the present day, hidden among the forests and rolling ranchland. Other sites were buried under the many **reservoirs** – built in the 1960s to provide a stable source of water for the agricultural Central Valley – that cover much of the lower elevations.

During spring, the hillsides are covered in fresh green grasses and brightly colored wildflowers, though by the end of summer the hot sun has baked everything a dusty golden brown. Higher up, the free-flowing rivers rush through steep canyons lined by oak trees and cottonwoods, and the ten-thousand-foot granite peaks in the Sierra Nevada mountains above offer excellent skiing in winter, and hiking and camping in the pine and redwood forests all year round. South from Placerville, Hwy-49 passes through **Jackson**, which makes a convenient, if unattractive, base for exploring the many dainty villages scattered around the wine-growing countryside of **Amador County**, continuing on through the mining towns of **Calaveras County**. The center of the southern mining district, then as now, is **Sonora**, a small, prosperous town of ornate Victorian houses set on ridges above steep gorges. Once an arch rival but now a ghost town, neighboring **Columbia** has a carefully restored Gold Rush-era Main Street. The gold-mining district actually extended as far south as **Mariposa**, but the mines here were comparatively worthless and little remains to make it worth the trip, except perhaps as a quick stop on the way to Yosemite National Park (see p.409).

You'll need your own **transportation** to see much of the southern Gold Country. Trains steer well clear of the hilly terrain and buses only pass through Mariposa on their way from Fresno and Merced to Yosemite. Drivers be warned – **speed traps** are rampant around the southern mines, particularly in Amador County and on any roads leading to Yosemite, where the speed limits tend to be a bit unrealistic and regional traffic police eagerly await to rake in some of that speedy tourist revenue.

Amador County

South from Placerville and US-50, the old mining landscape of **AMADOR COUNTY** has been given over to the vineyards of one of California's up-and-coming **wine-growing** regions, best known for its robust Zinfandel, a full-flavored vintage that thrives in the sun-baked soil. Most of the wineries are located above Hwy-49 in the Shenandoah Valley, near Plymouth on the north edge of the county. For a detailed map to all the local establishments, contact Amador Vintners in Plymouth (☎209/267-2297 or 1-888/655-8614, ⓦwww .amadorwine.com) or pick one up anywhere tourists congregate.

Amador City and Sutter Creek

About thirty miles east of Sacramento, Hwy-16 joins Hwy-49 at **AMADOR CITY**, whose short strip of antique shops gives it a cutesy, Old West look. The landmark *Imperial Hotel* at the northern edge dominates the town, its four-foot-thick brick walls standing at a sharp bend in Hwy-49. The hotel has recently been renovated, with sunny double **rooms** (℡209/267-9172 or 1-800/242-9172, Ⓦwww.imperialamador.com; ❹). Another option is the *Mine House Inn*, on the way to Sutter Creek (℡209/267-5900 or 1-800/646-3473, Ⓦwww.minehouseinn.com; ❺), and the secluded *Rancho Cicada B&B*, at 10001 Bell Rd near Plymouth (May–Oct only; ℡209/245-4841), which offers clothing-optional weekend retreats.

SUTTER CREEK, two miles south, is much larger than Amador City, but still little more than a row of tidy antique shops and restaurants catering to tourists along Hwy-49. Though there are a number of surprisingly large Victorian wooden houses – many styled after Puritan New England farmhouses – the town lacks the disheveled spontaneity that animates many of the other Gold Rush towns, perhaps because its livelihood was never based on independent prospectors panning for placer gold, but on hired hands working underground in the more organized and capital-intensive hard-rock mines. It was a lucrative business for the mine owners. The **Eureka Mine** operated until 1958. It was owned by one Hetty Green, the Warren Buffet of her day, who was at one time the richest woman in the world. At her death in 1916, her estate was worth $100m; she, however, was notorious for her cheapness, wearing old shabby clothes and giving nothing to charity. Hetty earned her nickname "The Witch of Wall Street" from fellow investors who envied her savvy ruthlessness. Leland Stanford was more generous with the money he made from the **Lincoln Mine**: he become a railroad magnate and governor of California, but used a chunk of his fortune to endow Stanford University (for more on Stanford and his cronies, see box on p.658).

Sutter Creek holds the bulk of Amador County's **accommodation** and **eating** places, with two central and very comfortable B&Bs: *The Foxes*, 77 Main St (℡209/267-5822, Ⓦwww.foxesinn.com; ❻), with well-appointed rooms and claw-foot baths; and the larger, more communally minded *Sutter Creek Inn*, 75 Main St (℡209/267-5606; ❹), with no TVs, no phones, and no fake Victoriana, but a nice garden with hammocks and a welcoming atmosphere. The *Bellotti Inn*, 53 Main St (℡209/267-5211; $45), has the cheapest accommodation in town and a decent **restaurant** serving full meals for $15 and pasta dishes for $7. *Susan's Place*, in the Eureka Street Courtyard, a half-block east of Hwy-49 (lunch only Wed–Sun, dinner Fri–Sat; ℡209/267-0945), serves sandwiches, soups, and salads under a shaded gazebo and, across the street, the *Sutter Creek Coffee Roasting Co.* (℡209/267-5550) serves the best coffee in town. For dessert, don't miss the *Sutter Creek Ice Cream Emporium*, 51 Main St (℡209/267-0543), where the friendly owner will play Scott Joplin tunes on the piano while you sip a milkshake.

Jackson

After Sutter Creek, the town of **JACKSON**, four miles south, can seem distinctly blue collar, mainly because of the huge Georgia Pacific lumber mill that serves as its northern gateway. Nevertheless, it's a more affordable base for exploring the surrounding countryside. Most of the well-preserved buildings in the small historic downtown area were erected after a large fire in 1862, and today are a bit drowned out by the encroaching modern businesses that surround it. There is a lovely, if architecturally inappropriate, 1939 Art Deco front on the **County Courthouse** at the top of the hill. Further along the crest, the **Amador County Museum**, 225 Church St (Wed–Sun 10am–4pm; free; ☎209/223-6386, ⓦwww.amadorarchive.org/museum), has displays of all the usual Gold Rush artifacts, but is worth a look most of all for its detailed models of the local hard-rock mines – with shafts over a mile deep – that were in use up until World War II. The headframes and some of the mining machinery are still standing a mile north of the museum on Jackson Gate Road, where two sixty-foot-diameter **tailing wheels** (8am–dusk; free), which carried away the waste from the Kennedy Mine, are accessible by way of short trails that lead up from a well-signposted parking area. The headframe of the six-thousand-foot shaft, the deepest in North America, stands out at the top of the slope, along Hwy-49. The other major mine in Jackson, the **Argonaut Mine** (of which nothing remains), was the scene of a tragedy in 1922, when 47 men were killed in an underground fire.

The **Amador County Chamber of Commerce**, 125 Peek St (daily 9am–5pm; ☎209/223-0350 or for lodging info 1-800/726-INNS, ⓦwww.amadorcountychamber.com), is rather awkwardly situated at the junction of Hwy-49 and Hwy-88, but offers a *Visitors Guide to Amador County*, full of the usual maps and historical information. The best place to stay is the friendly, if slightly run-down, *National Hotel*, 2 Water St (☎209/223-0500, Ⓔnationalhotel@volcano.net; ❷–❻), an 1860s hotel with individually decorated rooms, such as the "Bordello Room" with flock wallpaper, a four-poster bed and a free-standing bathtub on iron claw feet. If the *National* is full, try the *Amador Motel* (☎209/223-0970; ❶) on Hwy-49 north of town, or the nearby *Jackson Gold Lodge* (☎209/223-0486 or 1-888/777-0380; ❷). *Mel and Faye's Diner*, 211 Mountain View Drive (☎209/223-0835), on Hwy-49 near the town center, is open all day for **breakfasts and burgers**, while *Café Max Swiss Bakery*, 140 Main St (☎209/223-0174), serves pastries and a mean cup of coffee. For **drinking**, the *Pioneer Rex Saloon*, 28 Main St (☎209/223-3859), is the modern equivalent of a Wild West saloon, with cheap beers and all-night poker games behind swinging louvre doors.

Indian Grinding Rock and Volcano

Hwy-88 heads east from Jackson up the Sierra Crest, through hills that contain one of the most fitting memorials to the Native Americans who lived here for thousands of years before the Gold Rush all but wiped them out. Nine miles from Jackson, off Hwy-88, a side road passes by the **Indian Grinding Rock State Historic Park** (daily dawn–dusk; $2 per car; ☎209/296-7488, ⓦwww.sierra.parks.state.ca.us/igr/igr_main), where eleven hundred small cups – *Chaw'Se* in Miwok – were carved into the marbleized limestone outcropping to be used as mortars for grinding acorns into flour. It's the largest collection of bedrock mortar in North America, and if you arrive near dawn or dusk and look closely from the small elevated platform next to the biggest of the flat rocks, you can just detect the faint outline of some of the 360 **petroglyphs**. The state has developed the site into an interpretive center and has constructed replicas of Miwok dwellings and religious buildings with the close participation of tribal elders and community leaders. Descendants of the Miwok gather here during the weekend following the fourth Friday in September for **Big Time**, a celebration of the survival of their culture with traditional arts, crafts, and games. At the entrance to the site, the **Chaw'Se Regional Indian Museum** (Mon–Fri 11am–3pm, Sat–Sun 10am–4pm; ☎209/296-7488) explores the past and present state of the ten Sierra Nevada Native groups in a building said to simulate a Miwok roundhouse. The full process of producing acorn flour is covered, but the scant regard given to modern Miwok life is a sad testament to the extent of the devastation done to Miwok culture. If you'd like to spend the night, a **campground** in the surrounding woods costs $12 per pitch; space is not reservable and is on a first-come-first-served basis. Note that the campground is closed for Native American gatherings on the third weekend in May, third weekend in June, and last weekend in September.

Named after the crater-like bowl in which it sits, **VOLCANO**, a tiny village a mile and a half north once boasted over thirty saloons and dance halls. Today, it claims nearly as many historic sites as Jackson but has been mercifully bypassed by all the latter's development and traffic. The densely forested countryside around the village makes it well worth a visit, especially during spring (particularly mid-March to mid-April) when **Daffodil Hill**, three miles north of Volcano, is carpeted with more than 300,000 of the bobbing heads. Signs directing you there are only displayed when the flowers are in bloom. Its other notable attraction is the creaky cannon known as "Old Abe": locals threatened to fire it at a rebellious band of Southern sympathizers during the Civil War – this was the sole skirmish to take place in California even though not a single shot was actually exchanged. The only **accommodation** in the immediate area is the friendly *St George Hotel* on Main Street (℡209/296-4458, ⑩www .stgeorgehotel.com;④), offering bed and breakfast without the comforts of televisions, phones, or private bathrooms. Guests congregate in the restaurant and bar, whose walls are decked with every office poster and wisecrack bumper sticker imaginable.

Highway 88

Hwy-88 heads east beyond the Volcano turnoff to Pioneer, where it meets Hwy-26 from Mokelumne Hill (see below). Three miles east, the **Forest Ranger Station** (Mon–Fri 8am–4.30pm; ℡209/295-4251) supplies wilderness permits for overnighting in the **Mokelumne Wilderness**, a segment of the Stanislaus and Toiabe national forests south of Hwy-88, which closely follows the route of many early settlers. The ranger station also has details of camping and hiking in the **Eldorado National Forest**, beautiful in the fall, just before the winter snows turn the Sierra Nevada Mountains around the 8500-foot Carson Pass into *Kirkwood*, one of California's best cross-country ski resorts (see p.689). For more off-the-beaten-path recreation, try the **Bear River Lake Resort** (℡209/295-4868, ⑩www.bearriverlake.com; rooms $93.50, campsite $22), just south of Hwy-88 on the way to Kirkwood and Tahoe, which offers camping, hiking, fishing, swimming, and boating, without all the hype of the better-known resorts.

Calaveras County

CALAVERAS COUNTY lies across the Mokelumne River, eight miles south of Jackson, and is best known for being the setting of Mark Twain's first published story, *The Celebrated Jumping Frog of Calaveras County*. Today, precious few sights of historic interest remain, though there are plenty of options in the country for rugged outdoor recreation. The most northerly town in the county, **Mokelumne Hill**, or "Moke Hill," as it's called, was as action packed in its time as any of the southern Gold Rush towns, but tourism has been slower to take hold here, and today the town is an all-but-abandoned cluster of ruined and half-restored buildings, not without a certain melancholy appeal. The **Mokelumne Hill History Society**, 8367 East Center (summers, Sat–Sun 11am–3pm; donation suggested; ☎209/286-1770), has a modest exhibit on the history of the immediate area, once home to almost 10,000 people. The range of names and languages on the headstones of the **Protestant Cemetery**, on a hill a hundred yards west of town, gives a good idea of the mix of people who came from all over the world to the California mines.

San Andreas

Eight miles south, **SAN ANDREAS** hardly seems to warrant a second look: the biggest town for miles, it's now the Calaveras County seat, and has sacrificed historic character for commercial sprawl. The Calaveras County **Chamber of Commerce** (☎209/736-2580) publishes a handy map to the county that includes recreational activities in the area; it's available from the visitors' center in Angels Camp (see below). What remains of old San Andreas survives along narrow Main Street, on a steep hill just east of the highway, where the 1893 granite-and-brick County Courthouse has been restored and now houses an interesting collection of Gold Rush memorabilia in the **Calaveras County Museum**, 30 N Main St (daily 10am–4pm; $2; ☎209/754-4658). Local **nightlife** revolves around the *Black Bart Inn*, 35 N Main St (☎209/754-3808) across the street, which hosts bands on weekends. It is named after the gentleman stagecoach robber, **Black Bart**, who was captured and convicted here. Black Bart led a double life: in San Francisco he was a prominent citizen named Charles Bolton, who claimed to be a wealthy mining engineer. In the mining camps, though, he made his name by committing thirty robberies between 1877 and 1883, always addressing his victims as "Sir" and "Madam," never shooting anyone, and sometimes reciting bits of poetry before escaping with the loot. He was finally discovered after dropping a handkerchief at the scene of a hold-up – the police got him by tracing the laundry mark. He spent four years of a six-year sentence in San Quentin and, after his release, disappeared without trace.

Angels Camp and Carson Hill

The mining camps of southern Calaveras County were some of the richest in the Gold Country, both for the size of their nuggets and for the imaginations of their residents. The author Bret Harte spent an unhappy few years teaching in and around the mines in the mid-1850s and based his short story, *The Luck of Roaring Camp*, on his stay in **ANGELS CAMP**, thirty miles south of Jackson. There isn't much to see here these days, though the downtown feels mildly authentic. The **visitors' center** is located in a single-story clapboard building with a wide verandah at 1211 S Main St (Mon–Sat 9am–5pm, Sun 10am–4pm; ☎209/736-0049 or 1-800/225-3764, ⊛www.visitcalaveras.org) and has plenty of information on the surrounding area as well as copious frog-related memorabilia in honor of **Mark Twain**. The saloon in the *Angels Hotel* on Main Street is where 29-year-old Twain was told a tale that inspired him to write his famous story about a frog-jumping competition. It's now a discount tire store. Aside from the relentless onslaught of frog-themed souvenirs, the most unfortunate legacy of Twain's story is the **Jumping Frog Jubilee**, held on the third weekend in May each year and inexplicably attended by thousands of people. On the north side of town, the **Angels Camp Museum**, 753 Main St (Jan–Feb weekends only; March–Nov daily 10am–3pm; closed Dec; $1; ☎209/736-2963), presents a cornucopia of gold-

Limestone caverns in the Gold Country

Limestone caverns abound in the southern Gold Country: three that have been developed expressly for public tours, the largest of which is the **Moaning Caverns** in Vallecito, just south of Hwy-4 and five miles east of Angels Camp off Parrots Ferry Road (May–Sept daily 9am–6pm; Oct–April Mon–Fri 9.30am–5pm, Sat–Sun 9am–5pm; $10 walking tour, $45 rappel tour; ☏209/736-2708, ⊛www.caverntours .com). Although discovered by gold-miners in 1851, bones have been found here dating back 13,000 years. It didn't take long for locals to recognize the lucrative potential of the eerie, lacy rock formations here, and the caves were opened as a tourist attraction in 1919. The owners first inserted a 234-step spiral staircase to ease access and then corked the cavern's opening by building a gift shop on top of it: ironically, this wrecked the cave's natural acoustics and muted the moaning sounds after which it's named. The same company oversees **California Caverns** in Calaveras (May–Oct daily 10am–5pm; Nov–Dec & Apr 10am–4pm; closed Jan–March; $10; ☏209/736-2708 or 1-866/732-2837, ⊛www.caverntours.com), a horizontal network of caves that's a better choice for vertigo sufferers unwilling to brave the precipitous stairs at Moaning Caverns. Here, you can even take a four-hour Middle Earth Expedition ($99, reservations essential) wearing coveralls and a lighted helmet, and following a professional guide through miles of craggy recesses. The last of the local commercially developed sites, **Mercer Caverns** a mile north of Murphys on Sheep Ranch Road, is known for the spectacular stalagmite and stalactite formations in its 800-foot-long gallery, resembling swooping angels' wings and giant flowers (May–Oct Sun–Thurs 9am–5pm, Fri–Sat 9am–6pm; Nov–April Sun–Thurs 10am–4.30pm, Fri–Sat 9am–6pm; $10; ☏209/728-2101, ⊛www.mercercaverns.com).

excavating equipment and memorabilia, as well as a carriage barn filled with historic horse-drawn vehicles.

CARSON HILL, now a ghost town along Hwy-49 four miles south of Angels Camp, boasted the largest single nugget ever unearthed in California: 195 pounds of solid gold fifteen inches long and six inches thick, worth $43,000 when it was discovered in 1854 and well over a million dollars today. Nearby, **New Melones Reservoir** is the third largest reservoir in California and has all the camping ($14), swimming, hiking, boating, and other recreational possibilities you could hope for, not to mention spectacular, if manmade, views. It's seldom visited by the tourist throngs who fly through the Gold Country on their way to pricier recreational areas: for more information, stop at the **visitor center** (daily 10am–4pm; ☏209/536-9094 ext 22) located just past Carson Hill on Hwy-49.

Murphys

Nine miles east of Angels Camp, up the fairly steep Hwy-4, **MURPHYS**' one and only street is shaded by locust trees and graced by rows of decaying monumental buildings. One of the Gold Country's few surviving wooden water flumes still stands on Murphys' northern edge, while the oldest structure in town now houses the **Oldtimer's Museum** (Fri–Sun 11am–4pm; donation suggested; ☏209/728-1160), a small gathering of documents and a wall-full of rifles. If you want to **stay**, head across the street to the old *Murphys Hotel*, 457 Main St (☏209/728-3444 or 1-800/532-7684, ⊛www.murphyshotel.com; ❹), which hosted some of the leading lights of the boom days in its rustic double rooms. The **Calaveras Big Trees State Park** (visitors' center open Sept–April 11am–3pm; June–Aug 10am–4.30pm; ☏209/795-3840; $2 per car), fifteen miles east, covers six thousand acres of gigantic sequoia trees, threaded with trails. It makes for fine ski touring in winter, with **hiking** and **camping** (reserve mid-summer through ParkNet ℡1-800/444-7275; $16) the rest of the year.

Sonora, Columbia, Jamestown, and Chinese Camp

SONORA, fifteen miles southeast of Angels Camp, is the center of the southern mining district: it was the site of the **Bonanza Mine**, one of the most lucrative Gold Rush digs. Now a logging town, set on steep ravines, the town makes a good base for exploring the southern region: it's divided into Historic Sonora and the commercial district, known as East Sonora. There's little to see beyond the false-fronted buildings and Victorian houses on the main **Washington Street** and the Gothic **St James Episcopal Church** at its far end, but it's a friendly, animated place, worth spending an afternoon. There's also a superb bookstore, Sonora Used Books, at 21 S Washington St (℡209/532-1884), with a vast selection of cheap paperbacks in good condition. Pick up architectural and historical walking-tour **maps** (25¢) from the **Tuolumne** (rhymes with "you follow me") **County Visitors Bureau**, 542 W Stockton St (April–Sept Mon–Fri 9am–7pm, Sat 10am–6pm, Sun 10am–5pm; Oct–March Mon–Fri 9am–6pm, Sat 10am–6pm; ℡209/533-4420 or 1-800/446-1333, 🌐www.thegreatunfenced.com), or check in with the Tuolumne Chamber of Commerce, 22 S Shepherd St (Mon–Fri 8am–12pm, 1–5pm; ℡209/532-4212, 🌐www.tcchamber.com). The small **Tuolumne County Museum**, in the old County Jail at 158 W Bradford Ave (Mon–Fri & Sun 10am–4pm, Sat 10am–3.30pm; free; ℡209/532-1317) is worth a look for the restored cell block, if not for the collection of old clothes and photographs.

One of the best-value **hotel** options in Sonora is the old adobe *Gunn House* at 286 S Washington St (℡209/532-3421; ❷), which has large, slightly dark rooms; for a few dollars more, the *Sonora Days Inn*, 160 S Washington St, is more central although its decor is decidedly unloved (℡209/532-2400, 🌐www.sonoradaysinn.com; ❹). Otherwise, try the *Miner's Motel* (℡209/532-7850 or 1-800/451-4176; ❷) on Hwy-108, halfway to Jamestown. For **lunch** on Washington Street, try *The Pie Tin* at no. 51 (℡209/532-3663), where you can lounge on overstuffed sofas snacking on gourmet pies, muffins, and sandwiches. After dark, there are several good options along Washington Street. *Alfredo's*, at no. 123 (℡209/532-8332), is widely regarded as the best reasonably priced Mexican restaurant in these parts, serving standard burritos and enchiladas for $8 or so. Try the *Sonora Inn Restaurant and Steakhouse* at no. 160, for an old-fashioned, artery-clogging meat fest, with dishes around $14. *Carmela's*, at no. 301 (℡209/532-8858), is known for its home-made pastas and sauces. Of several **bars** on Washington, *The Brass Rail* at no. 131, and the retro *Iron Horse Lounge* at no. 97 (℡209/532-4482), are the best places to find a hint of the Wild West.

Columbia

Sonora's one-time arch rival, tourist-loving **COLUMBIA**, three miles north on Parrots Ferry Road, now passes itself off as a ghost town with a carefully restored Main Street that gives an excellent – if contrived – idea of what Gold Rush life might have been like, complete with period costumed staff in the local hotels and restaurants. The town experienced a brief burst of riches after a Dr Thaddeus Hildreth and his party picked up thirty pounds of gold in just two days in March 1850. Within a month, over five thousand miners were working claims limited by local law to ten square feet, and by 1854 Columbia was California's second-largest city, with fifteen thousand inhabitants supporting some forty saloons, eight hotels, and one school. The town missed becoming the state capital by two votes – just as well, since by 1870 the gold had run out and Columbia was abandoned, but only after over two and a half million ounces of gold (worth nearly a billion dollars at today's prices) had been taken out of the surrounding area.

Thanks to agitation from locals, the entire town of Columbia is now preserved as a **State Historic Park** (ⓦ www.sierra.parks.state.ca.us), though it's also a genuine town with an active main street and year-round residents. Most of the buildings that survive date from the late 1850s, built in brick after fire destroyed the town for a second time. Roughly half of them house historical exhibits – including a dramatized visit to the frontier dentist's office, complete with a two-hundred-proof anesthetic and tape-recorded screams. The rest have been converted into shops, restaurants, and saloons, where you can sip a sarsaparilla or munch on a hot dog. Two notable structures are the **Claverie Mason Building**, once the heart of Columbia's Chinatown, and the atmospheric ruins of the **Bixel Brewery**, a mile or so north along Main Street from downtown: although there's little to see now, it's an evocative change from the staged Victoriana in the center of town. As you might imagine, the park/town can be nightmarishly crowded, especially on **Living History Days** (early June) when volunteers dress up and act out scenes from the old days. If you want to escape the crowds, the hokey but fun stagecoach ride ($5) zips along the old mining trails around the town; it leaves hourly from the Wells Fargo Building. Alternatively, take a trip to the **Matelot Gulch gold mine**, where nuggets are still occasionally found: ninety-minute tours ($12; call for tour schedule ⓣ 209/532-9693, ⓔ hiddengoldmine@mlode.com) start from the shack at the south end of Main Street and are hosted by amusingly crabby former miners.

At the moment, the local visitors' center is undergoing major renovations, and is scheduled to reopen in 2005 in the Cheap Cash Store on Main Street as a full-scale museum and educational facility. In the interim, call the State Park for information (ⓣ 209/532-4301) or contact the local Chamber of Commerce about accommodation (ⓣ 209/536-1672).

If you want to **stay**, the *Columbia City Hotel* on Main Street (ⓣ 209/532-1479 or 1-800/532-1479, ⓦ www.cityhotel.com; ❺) is luxurious and central with a gourmet restaurant, while the *Columbia Inn Motel*, 22646 Broadway (ⓣ 209/533-0446, ⓦ www.columbiainnmotel.com; ❷) is basic but spotless, with a small pool and cheery staff. Alternatively, a mile south of town, the *Columbia Gem Motel*, 22131 Parrots Ferry Rd (ⓣ 209/532-4508, ⓦ www .columbiagemmotel.com; ❷), offers basic accommodation in rustic cabins or there are dorm beds on the college campus at the *HI-Sonora Hostel*, 11800 Columbia College Drive (ⓣ 209/533-2339, ⓦ www.hostels.com/sonora) for $12 (members) and $15 (non-members).

Jamestown

Three miles south of Sonora on Hwy-49, **JAMESTOWN** serves as the southern gateway to the Gold Country for drivers entering on Hwy-120 from the San Francisco Bay Area. Before 1966, when much of Jamestown burned down in a fire, it was used as location for many well-known Westerns: the classic TV series *Little House on the Prairie* spent several seasons filming in town, and Clint Eastwood shot scenes for his Oscar-winning *Unforgiven* here. The train from that movie – also used forty years earlier in *High Noon*, starring Gary Cooper – can be found among many other steam giants in the **Railtown 1897 State Historic Park**, Jamestown's biggest attraction, five blocks east of Main Street at Fifth and Reservoir (daily 9.30am–4.30pm; $6; ☏209/984-3953, ⓦwww.railtown1897.org). On summer weekends, you can ride one of the vintage trains for an additional fee (hourly 11am–3pm; $2). Along with its train collection, Jamestown is one of the few Gold Country towns that still has a **working mine** – the huge open-pit Sonora Mining Corporation west of town on Hwy-49 – and a number of outfits take visitors on gold-mining expeditions. Among them, Gold Prospecting Expeditions ($30 for 2hr; ☏209/984-4653 or 1-800/596-0009, ⓦwww.goldprospecting.com) gives brief instruction in the arts of panning, sluicing, and sniping, and allows you two hours to pan what you can from its local stream – although don't expect to strike it rich. Main Street is the town's central thoroughfare, with a few **accommodation** choices: the *National Hotel*, 77 Main Street (☏209/984-3446 or 1-800/252-8299, ⓦwww.national-hotel.com; ❹), has nine rooms and a casually elegant restaurant with a small bar. Nearby is the plush and historic *Palm Hotel B&B* at 10382 Willow St (☏209/984-3429 or 1-888/551-1849, ⓦwww.palmhotel .com; ❺). For **food** on Main Street, try the popular diner, *Mother Lode Coffee Shop*, at no. 18169, which is open for breakfast or lunch (☏209/984-3386), or grab a gooey sundae at the old-fashioned *Here's The Scoop* ice cream parlor, no. 18242 (☏209/984-4583). Nearby, there's also the *Smoke Café* (☏209/984-3733), which serves tasty Southwestern-style Mexican food and huge margaritas in a touristy atmosphere; lunch specials hover around $6, and there's live music most nights.

Chinese Camp

Hwy-49 winds south from Sonora through some sixty miles of the sparsely populated, rolling foothills of **Mariposa County**, but first it passes the scant remains of the town of **CHINESE CAMP**. It was here that the worst of the Tong Wars between rival factions of Chinese miners took place in 1856, after the Chinese had been excluded from other mining camps in the area by white miners. Racism was rampant in the southern Gold Rush camps, something which also accounts for its most enduring legend, the story of the so-called Robin Hood of the Mother Lode, **Joaquin Murieta**. Murieta was an archetype representing the dispossessed Mexican miners driven to banditry by violent racist abuse at the hands of newly arived white Americans and likely never existed. Now there's little evidence of this rural village's violent past amid the rundown shacks and trailers other than a historic marker on the main road.

Further south on Hwy-49 lie the southern Gold Rush towns of **Groveland**, **Coulterville**, and **Mariposa**. Owing to their proximity to Yosemite National Park, all three are covered in detail in Chapter Five (see pp.409–435).

Lake Tahoe, Truckee, and into Nevada

High above the Gold Country, just east of the Sierra ridge, **LAKE TAHOE** sits placidly in a dramatic alpine bowl, surrounded by high granite peaks and miles of thickly wooded forest. It's a big tourist area; the sandy beaches and surrounding pine-tree wilderness are overrun with thousands of fun-lovers (predominantly families) throughout the summer, and in winter, the snow-covered slopes of the nearby peaks are packed with skiers. The eastern third of the lake lies in Nevada and glows with light from the neon signs of the inevitable **Stateline casinos**.

TRUCKEE, fifteen miles north of Lake Tahoe, ranges along the Truckee River, which flows out of Lake Tahoe down into the desert of Nevada's Great Basin. It's a main stop on Greyhound and Amtrak cross-country routes, though apart from an influx of skiers in winter, is little-visited. **Donner Pass**, just west of town, was named in memory of the pioneer Donner family, many of whom lost their lives when trapped here by heavy winter snows.

Across the border in **NEVADA**, **Reno**, at the eastern foot of the Sierra Nevada, is a downmarket version of Las Vegas, popular with slot-machine junkies and elderly gamblers; others come to take advantage of Nevada's lax marriage and divorce laws. Though far smaller than Reno, **Carson City**, thirty miles south, is the Nevada state capital, with a couple of engaging museums that recount the town's frontier history. Heading deeper into Nevada, and up into the arid mountains to the east, the silver mines of the **Comstock Lode**, whose wealth paid for the building of much of San Francisco, are buried deep below the evocative, if touristy, **Virginia City**.

The two main trans-Sierra highways, **I-80** and **US-50**, head east from Sacramento and are kept open all year round, regardless of snowfall, passing by Truckee and Lake Tahoe respectively. Both places are served by Greyhound and there is a local bus route between the two, plus services from the Nevada cities to the Tahoe casinos.

Lake Tahoe

Fault-formed **LAKE TAHOE** is one of the highest, deepest, cleanest, coldest, and most beautiful lakes in the world. More than sixteen hundred feet deep, it is so cold – or so the story goes – that at its depths cowboys who drowned over a century ago have been recovered in perfectly preserved condition, gun holsters and all. The lake's position, straddling the border between California and Nevada, lends it a schizophrenic air, the dichotomy most evident at **South Lake Tahoe**, the lakeside's largest community, where ranks of restaurants, modest motels, and pine-bound cottages stand cheek by jowl with the high-rise gambling dens of **Stateline**, just across the border. **Tahoe City**, the hub of the lake's northwestern shore, does not escape the tourists but manages to retain a more relaxed – if somewhat exclusive – attitude. Expensive vacation homes and shabby family-oriented mini-resorts line much of the remainder of the lake.

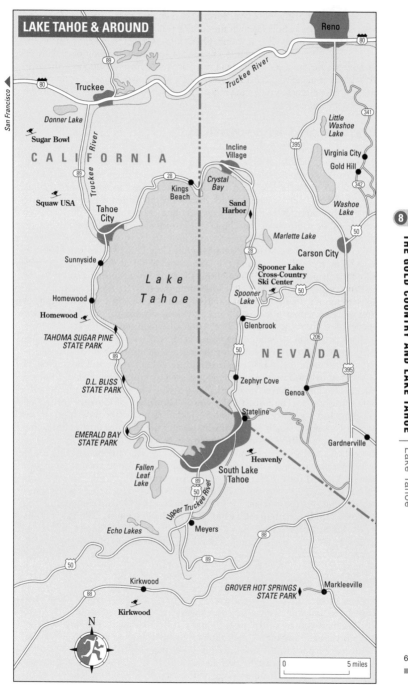

LAKE TAHOE & AROUND

Reno

80

San Francisco

89

80   Truckee

Truckee River

Donner Lake

341

Little
Washoe
Lake

Sugar Bowl

395

C A L I F O R N I A

Virginia City

Gold Hill

Truckee River

89

342

Squaw USA

28

Kings
Beach

Incline
Village

*Crystal
Bay*

Sand
Harbor

Washoe
Lake

Tahoe
City

50

Marlette Lake

Carson City

Sunnyside

28

L a k e
T a h o e

Spooner Lake
Cross-Country
Ski Center

Homewood

*Spooner
Lake*

50

Homewood

*TAHOMA SUGAR PINE
STATE PARK*

Glenbrook

206

89

*D.L. BLISS
STATE PARK*

50

N E V A D A

395

*EMERALD BAY
STATE PARK*

Zephyr Cove

Genoa

Stateline

*Fallen
Leaf
Lake*

Heavenly

Gardnerville

89
50

South Lake
Tahoe

Upper Truckee River

Echo Lakes

Meyers

88

50

89

88   Kirkwood

*GROVER HOT SPRINGS
STATE PARK*

Markleeville

Kirkwood

N

0   5 miles

8

Tahoe is never truly offseason, luring weekenders from the Bay Area and beyond with clear, cool waters in the summer, snow-covered slopes in the winter, and slot machines all year round. On holiday weekends, expect traffic in the area to reach maddening levels; packs of cars and trucks spilling over with ski equipment and mountain bikes will serve as your convoy throughout the area. To take advantage of the natural resources and still avoid at least some of the crowds, you might consider staying south of Tahoe near **Kirkwood**, though during peak times even that area can fill up quickly.

Arrival and information

One hundred miles east of Sacramento on both US-50 and US-80, Lake Tahoe is served by Greyhound **buses** and a number of coach **tours**, mainly catering to weekend gamblers. Several daily Greyhound buses from San Francisco and Sacramento use *Harrah's* casino in South Lake Tahoe as a terminus: Amtrak Thruway buses arrive several times daily from Sacramento on their way to Carson City, but they must be booked in conjunction with long-distance train routes. Tahoe Casino Express buses ($19 one-way; ☎775/785-2424 or 1-800/446-6128) run roughly every hour from 6.15am to 12.30am between Reno Airport and the Stateline casinos, while Gray Line (☎775/331-1147) has daily tours from Reno around the lake, stopping off at Virginia City – they even have "gambler's special" coach tours leaving from San Francisco. If you're **driving**, expect to get here in a little over three hours from San Francisco, unless you join the Friday night exodus in which case you can add an hour or two, more in winter when you'll need to carry **chains**; call the Caltrans road phone (☎1-800/427-7623) to check on road conditions before you depart.

There are booths claiming to be visitor centers all over South Lake Tahoe, but most are just advertising outlets for the casinos or fronts for timeshare agents. For slightly more useful **information**, you can obtain maps and brochures (all of them chock-full of advertisements), as well as limited help with finding a place to stay (if you haven't booked ahead, it won't be easy), at one of the official visitor centers. The **South Lake Tahoe Chamber of Commerce**, 13066 US-50 (Mon–Sat 9am–5pm; ☎530/541-5255, ⓦwww.tahoeinfo.com), is just west of El Dorado beach, where US-50 reaches the lake. Just north of Stateline in Nevada, the **Tahoe-Douglas Chamber & Visitor Center**, 195 Hwy-50 (Sept–May Mon–Sat 9am–5pm; June–Aug Mon–Sat 9am–6pm; ☎775/588-4591, ⓦwww.tahoechamber.org), will help with room reservations. The **North Lake Tahoe Chamber of Commerce**, 245 North Lake Blvd in Tahoe City (daily 9am–5pm; ☎530/581-6900 or 530/583-3494, ⓦwww.tahoefun.org) is the best bet for information on the North Lake region. And lastly, the **Incline Village/Crystal Bay Visitor Center**, 969 Tahoe Blvd (Mon–Fri 8am–5pm, Sat & Sun 10am–4pm; ☎775/832-1606 or 1-800/GO-TAHOE, ⓦwww.gotahoe.com), is another option on the Nevada side of the lake.

Getting around

STAGE **buses** (☎530/541-6328) run 24 hours a day all over the South Lake Tahoe area, and will take you anywhere within a ten-mile radius for a flat $1.25 fare ($2 buys you an all-day pass). Tahoe Casino Express (☎1-800/446-6128) runs northeast from South Lake Tahoe to Glenbrook, then east to Carson City and Reno Airport. In the north, TART buses (roughly 6am to 6pm; $1.25 flat fare, $3 for an all-day pass; ☎530/550-1212 or 1-800/736-6365) run between Sugar Pine Point and Incline Village, with a branch route from Tahoe City up to Truckee. Alternatively, the Tahoe Trolley ($1 flat fare, $3 day-pass; ☎530/550-1212) runs between Squaw Valley and Emerald Bay from 9am to 6pm and between Squaw Valley and Incline Village from 6pm to 11pm, with a short extra route between Tahoe City and Tahoma during those evening hours.

Car rental, starting at about $30 a day, is available through the Stateline outlets of most national chains – try Avis (☎775/588-4450 or 1-800/831-2847, ⓦwww.avis.com), Enterprise (☎775/586-1077 or 1-800/736-8222, ⓦwww .enterprise.com), and Hertz (☎775/586-0041 or 1-800/654-3131, ⓦwww .hertz.com) – as well as slightly cheaper local firms such as Empire Rent-a-car (☎530/544-4500 or 1-800/350-5741) at 4123 Laurel Ave, South Lake Tahoe. You could also **rent a bicycle** for around $20–25 a day from any of over a dozen lakeside shops in South Lake Tahoe – some of them offering a full range of **sports equipment rentals** – such as the Mountain Sports Center, Hwy-89 near the "Y" junction (☎530/542-6584), and Lakeview Sports, 3131 S Lake Blvd (☎530/544-0183), or the welter of outlets lining Ski Run Blvd on the way to Heavenly. In Tahoe City on North Lake Boulevard, try Olympic Bike Shop, no. 620 (☎530/581-2500), or The Back Country, no. 255 (☎530/581-5861).

Accommodation

Most of the hundred or so **motels** that circle the lake are collected together along US-50 in South Lake Tahoe. During the week, except in summer, many have bargain rates, from around $40 for a double; however, these rates can easily double on weekends or in summer, so be sure to confirm – bear in mind the price codes below are based on the lowest rates. Don't expect great deals at the **casinos**; there are fewer than in Las Vegas or Reno, and the casino hotels charge whatever the busy market will bear. If you're having trouble finding a room, the **Lake Tahoe Central Reservations**, 1156 Ski Run Blvd (☎530/583-3494 or 1-800/288-2463, ⓦwww.mytahoevacation.com), can book you a room anywhere on the lake for a one-off $12 fee.

Tahoe City lacks the range and competition of its southerly neighbor, South Lake Tahoe, so you can expect to pay slightly more for a room there, although the reprieve from the Stateline bustle may just make the extra cost worth it if you're looking for peace and quiet. There are also a few other pleasant options dotted around the lake. **Camping** (see box on p.692) is only an option during summer (Tahoe gets upwards of 20ft of snow every winter).

South shore

Camp Richardson Resort Hwy-89 between Emerald Bay and S Lake Tahoe ☎530/541-1801 or 1-800/544-1801, ⓦwww.camprichardson.com. Comfortable cabins with full kitchens on a 150-acre resort that also has campsites for $17–19. Cabins available for both nightly and weekly rentals. ❹

Caesars Tahoe Resort/Casino US-50, Stateline, Nevada ☎775/588-3515 or 1-800/648-3353, ⓦwww.caesars.com. Deluxe resort and upmarket casino; the best rooms overlook the lake. ❹

Doug's Mellow Mountain Retreat 3787 Forest Ave, S Lake Tahoe ☎530/544-8065. Essentially Doug's home, operating as a relaxed, if cramped, hostel with cooking facilities, cheap bike rental, and occasional barbecues. Beds are $15 a night and double rooms are available. A mile from the Greyhound stop, but Doug will pick you up. ❷

Driftwood Lodge 4115 Laurel Ave at Poplar, S Lake Tahoe ☎530/541-7400. The heated pool and private beach access make this otherwise very basic accommodation particularly appealing in summer. ❶

Inn by the Lake 3300 Lake Tahoe Blvd, S Lake Tahoe ☎530/542-0330 or 1-800/877-1466, ⓦwww.innbythelake.com. Nicely furnished rooms, a heated swimming pool and Jacuzzi, free breakfast, and use of bicycles make this relaxing spot good value for money. Free shuttle bus to the casinos. ❺

Lampliter Inn 4143 Cedar Ave, S Lake Tahoe
☎530/544-2936 or 1-888/544-4055,
ⓦwww.lampliterinn.com. Just off US-50, between
the casinos and the lakeshore, *The Lampliter* has a
hot tub with views of the ski field behind. ❶
Pine Cone Acre 735 Emerald Bay Rd, between
Emerald Bay and S Lake Tahoe ☎530/541-0375.
Pleasant, simple motel in wooded grounds with a
quieter location than most. ❷
Royal Valhalla 4104 Lakeshore Blvd, S Lake
Tahoe ☎530/544-2233 or 1-800/999-4104,
ⓦwww.tahoeroyalvalhalla.com. Balconied suites
with kitchenettes overlooking the lake, right opposite the beach. ❸
Seven Seas Inn 4145 Manzanita Ave, S Lake
Tahoe ☎530/544-7031 or 1-800/975-7653,
ⓦwww.sevenseastahoe.com. Another of the south
shore's countless small motels; a friendly place
offering clean, simple rooms and a hot tub. ❶
Super 8 3600 Lake Tahoe Blvd ☎530/544-3476
or 1-800/800-8000, ⓦwww.super8.com. National
chain outlet with simple rooms, but guaranteed
level of comfort and service, not always found in
other cheapies. ❷
Zephyr Cove Resort 760 Hwy-50, Zephyr Cove,
Nevada ☎775/588-6644, ⓦwww.tahoedixie2.com.
Run by the same management as the *MS Dixie II*
(see p.690), its simple lodge rooms and smarter
cabins are away from the hubbub in a quiet pine-
clad nook. ❷

North shore
Falcon Motor Lodge 8258 N Lake Blvd, Kings
Beach ☎530/546-2583 or 1-800/541-4631.
Ordinary but dependable budget accommodation,
right by the lake. ❶
Franciscan Lakeside Lodge 6944 N Lake Blvd,
Tahoe Vista ☎530/546-6300, ⓦwww.franciscan
lodge.com. Cosy cabins and some larger units,
right by one of north shore's best beaches. ❸
Inn at Incline 1003 Tahoe Blvd, Incline Village
☎775/831-1025 or 1-800/824-6391, ⓦwww
.innatincline.com. Nestled in a secluded forest setting, with private beach access, indoor pool, spa,
and sauna. ❸
Lake of the Sky Motor Inn 955 N Lake Blvd,
Tahoe City ☎530/583-3305. Justifiably a little
more expensive than the *Tahoe City Inn* for the
extra comfort and ambience. ❸

Mayfield House 236 Grove St, Tahoe City ☎1-
888/518-8898 or 530/583-1001, ⓦwww.may-
fieldhouse.com. Quality B&B with plush rooms in
the converted mansion and the sweet cottage
behind. ❻
Pepper Tree Inn 645 N Lake Blvd, Tahoe City
☎530/583-3711 or 1-800/624-8580,
ⓦwww.peppertreetahoe.com. Heated pool and
basic, affordable accommodation. ❷
River Ranch Hwy-89 & Alpine Meadows Road,
Alpine Meadows ☎530/583-4264 or 1-800/535-
9900, ⓦwww.riverranchlodge.com. Historic and
casual lodge on the Truckee River with one of the
lake's best restaurants. ❹
Sunnyside 1850 W Lake Blvd, 1 mile south of
Tahoe City ☎530/583-7200 or 1-800/822-2SKI,
ⓦwww.sunnysideresort.com. Large, comfortable
mountain lodge right on the lakeshore. Unbeatable
views of the lake from many rooms, and a popular
restaurant on the ground floor. ❺
Tahoe City Inn 790 N Lake Blvd, Tahoe City
☎530/581-3333 or 1-800/800-8246,
ⓦwww.tahoecityinn.com. These basic facilities are
centrally located and one of the better deals in the
area. ❷
Tahoma Meadows B&B 6821 W Lake Blvd,
Tahoma ☎530/525-1553, ⓦwww.tahomamead-
ows.com. Well-furnished rooms in a lovely setting
on the west shore, 7 miles south of Tahoe City. ❺
Tamarack Lodge 2311 N Lake Blvd, 1 mile northeast of Tahoe City ☎530/583-3350 or 1-888/824-
6323, ⓦwww.tamarackattahoe.com. Comfortable
and clean lodging that is one of the best deals
anywhere on the lake. ❷

Further out
Sierrawood Guest House 12 miles from the
south shore, Tahoe Paradise ☎530/577-6073 or
1-800/700-3802. For that romantic getaway, a
secluded chalet in the woods within a few minutes' drive of the casinos' glitter. Jacuzzi, exercise
room, fireplace, and free snowmobiling on premises. Popular with gay and lesbian couples. ❻
Sorensen's 14255 Hwy-88, Hope Valley
☎530/694-2203 or 1-800/423-9949. Nestled in
the aspens of Hope Valley about a half-hour drive
away from the south shore on the west fork of the
Carson River, *Sorensen's* features kitsch and cozy
cabins with a Bavarian ski lodge theme. ❺

South Lake Tahoe and Stateline

Almost all of Tahoe's lakeshore is developed in some way or another, but
nowhere is it as concentrated and overbearing as at the contiguous settlements
of **SOUTH LAKE TAHOE** and **STATELINE**. The latter is compact, a
clutch of gambling houses huddled, as you might expect, along the

Tahoe skiing and snowboarding

Lake Tahoe has some of the best **downhill skiing** in North America, and its larger resorts rival their Rocky Mountain counterparts. More than a few Bay Area residents head for the mountains at the first sign of snow, and, in a good year, many lifts continue to operate through the end of April. Although skiing is certainly not cheap – the largest ski areas charge over $50 for the privilege of using their mountain for a single day – many resorts offer decent-value rental/lift ticket/lesson packages or multiday discounts. **Snowboarding** has, of course, caught on in a big way, and the same resorts that once scoffed at the sport have now installed massive snow parks with radical half-pipes and jumps. The following list of ski resorts is not exhaustive, but highlights the best options for skiers of varying ability and financial standing. Skis can be rented at the resorts for about $25–28, and snowboards go for $32–37, but better deals for both can be found in the rental stores dotted around town. Pick up the *Reno–Tahoe Winter Vacation Guide for Skiers and Boarders* at any of the tourism information offices for a complete listing of resorts, along with prices and amenities.

Downhill skiing

Heavenly reachable by shuttle from Southshore, two miles from the casinos, (ⓣ775/586-7000 or 1-800/243-2836, ⓦwww.skiheavenly.com). Prime location and sheer scale (82 runs, 27 lifts, 3500 vertical feet) make this one of the lake's most frequented resorts. Non-skiers can take the aerial tram for the view from the 8200-foot summit ($20). Lift tickets are $57.

Homewood 6 miles north of Tahoe City on Hwy-89 (ⓣ530/525-2992 or 1-800/824-6348, ⓦwww.skihomewood.com). Smaller and more relaxed than its massive neighbors, Homewood boasts some surprisingly good skiing with unbeatable views of the lake and reasonable prices. Lift tickets go for $42. Beginner package costing $55 includes equipment, lesson, and beginner lift ticket.

Kirkwood Ski Resort south of Lake Tahoe on Hwy-88 (ⓣ209/258-6000 or 1-877/547-5966, ⓦwww.kirkwood.com). Kirkwood manages to escape the overdeveloped feel of many of the Tahoe resorts while still providing some amazing skiing. Lift tickets are $52.

Squaw Valley USA Squaw Valley Road, halfway between Truckee and Tahoe City (ⓣ530/583-6955 or 1-800/766-9321, ⓦwww.squaw.com). Thirty-one lifts service over 4000 acres of unbeatable terrain at the site of the 1960 Winter Olympics. Non-skiers can take the aerial tram ($16) and use the ice-skating/swimming pool complex for the day ($20 including tram). Lift tickets are $56, beginner package including equipment and 2hr lesson $65.

Sugar Bowl ten miles west of Truckee at the Soda Springs–Norden exit (ⓣ530/426-9000, ⓦwww.sugarbowl.com). The closest ski area to San Francisco has ten lifts and newly expanded terrain. Inexplicably, this excellent mountain is often less crowded than others in the area. Lift tickets cost $52.

Cross-country skiing

Kirkwood Cross Country Center south of Lake Tahoe on Hwy-88 (ⓣ209/258-7248, ⓦwww.kirkwood.com). More than 50 miles of groomed track and skating lanes for cross-country enthusiasts. Trail fee is $15.

Royal Gorge in Soda Springs, ten miles west of Truckee (ⓣ530/426-3871 or 1-800/500-3871, ⓦwww.royalgorge.com). The largest and best of Tahoe's cross-country resorts has 204 miles of groomed trails. $21.50–25 trail fee, $17.50 rental fee, and $20–30 for lessons.

Spooner Lake in Nevada at the intersection of Hwy-50 and Hwy-28 (ⓣ775/749-5349, ⓦwww.spoonerlake.com). The closest cross-country resort to South Lake Tahoe has lake views and 63 miles of groomed trails. Trail fees are $17.50, rentals $17, and lessons $38 including rental.

Nevada–California border. The dozen or so casinos compete for the attentions of the punters, almost all of whom base themselves in the much larger South Lake Tahoe on the California side. This is the best place to organize one of the many **outdoor activities** the lake has to offer. Power boating, water skiing, surfing, parasailing, scuba diving, canoeing, and mountain biking are just a few of the proposed activities on the menu of local sporting equipment rental offices (see p.687). If you happen to lose your vacation allowance at the tables and slot machines, you can always explore the beautiful hiking trails, parks, and beaches that adorn the surrounding area.

Though many stretches of the route around Lake Tahoe are stunning, the 72-mile **drive** is perhaps not the most beautiful in America, as at least one locally produced brochure touts. A better way to see the lake is to take a **paddlewheel boat cruise** on either the *Tahoe Queen* from South Lake Tahoe (three departures daily, call for times; $ 22–49; ℡530/541-3364 or 1-800/238-2463, ⓦwww.hornblower.com), or the *MS Dixie II* from Zephyr Cove (three departures daily, call for times; $24–49; ℡775/589-4906), reached on a free shuttle from South Lake Tahoe. Perhaps most impressive is the view of the lake from above. For those with no athletic ambition, the lazy way to ascend is in one of the neighboring ski resort's **aerial trams**. Finally, in lousy weather you can always visit the modest **Tahoe Museum**, next to the Chamber of Commerce at 3058 Hwy-50 (Tues–Sat 11am–4pm; free; ℡530/541-5458), which has a small collection of local artifacts and historical displays.

West around the lake

In summer, many enjoyable music and arts events take place at the **Tallac Historic Site** (April–Oct daily 10am–6pm; free; ℡1-888/631-9153), beside Hwy-89 on the western side of the lake just northwest of the "Y" (where Hwy-89 and Hwy-50 separate to the west and east of the lake). Even when there's nothing special going on, the historic site's sumptuous wooden homes – constructed by wealthy San Franciscans as lakeside vacation retreats in the late 1800s – are well worth a look. You can also see the remains of the lavish casino-hotel erected by Elias "Lucky" Baldwin, which brought the rich and famous to Lake Tahoe's shores until it was destroyed by fire in 1914. Inside the former Baldwin house, the **Tallac Museum** (daily 11am–3pm; free) records the family's impact on the region.

The prettiest part of the lake, however, is along the southwest shore, where **Emerald Bay State Park**, ten miles from South Lake Tahoe (daily dawn–dusk; $5 per vehicle), surrounds a narrow, rock-strewn inlet. In the park, at the end of a steep, mile-long trail from the parking lot, is **Vikingsholm**, an authentic reproduction of a Viking castle, believe it or not, built as a summer home in 1929 and open for half-hourly **tours** (summer daily 10am–4pm; $2). A short way out in the bay, diminutive **Fanette**, Lake Tahoe's only island, pokes pine-clad above the water. Its only structure is the defunct 1929 tea-house, built by Vikingsholm's original owner, Lara Knight. From Vikingsholm, the **Rubicon Trail** runs two miles north along the lakeside to **Rubicon Bay**, flanked by other grand old mansions, dating from the days when Lake Tahoe was accessible only to the most well-heeled of travelers. You can also drive here on Hwy-89 and enter through the **D.L. Bliss State Park** (extremely limited parking $2), just to the north. In the park, the 15,000-square-foot **Ehrman Mansion** here (guided tours daily 10am–4pm on the hour; free), decorated in a happy blend of 1930s opulence and backcountry rustic, is surrounded by extensive lakefront grounds, which were used as a location for the movie

Godfather II. Just under five miles further north, thickly-pined **Tahoma Sugarpine State Park** (day-use $2) offers more lakeside relaxation potential and has one of only two year-round campgrounds (see box, p.692).

Lake Kirkwood and Markleeville

About two dozen miles southwest of Tahoe, a dozen west of where Hwy-89 joins Hwy-88, **LAKE KIRKWOOD** is home to a popular ski resort (see box overleaf), and a destination in its own right, with plenty of **outdoor recreation** possibilities without all the Tahoe hype. Stop by the adventure center in Kirkwood Village (Mon–Fri 9am–5pm, Sat–Sun 9am–6pm; ☎209/258-6000 or 209/258-7357) for information on accommodation, equipment rentals, and hiking in the surrounding area, which includes nearly a dozen lakes, such as Winnemucca and Woods lakes. For accommodation, try the *Lodge at Kirkwood* in the Village, which must be booked through Kirkwood Central Reservations (☎1-800/9677500; ❾).

If you head a dozen miles southeast from the junction of Hwy-89 and Hwy-88, you'll come to **MARKLEEVILLE**, a town of two hundred people on the Sierra Crest. The major attraction here is the Grover Hot Springs State Park, four miles west (May to mid-Sept daily 9am–9pm; closed last two weeks in Sept; reduced hours through winter; $2; ☎530/694-2248), with two concrete, spring-filled tubs – one hot, one tepid – in which the water appears yellow-green due to mineral deposits on the pool bottom. There's a $12-a-night **campground** (reserve through ParkNet ☎1-800/444-7275) on site.

Tahoe City and around

TAHOE CITY, on the north shore, is less developed and more compact than South Lake Tahoe, and a close-knit population of permanent residents coupled with a family-oriented atmosphere give it a more relaxed, peaceful disposition. Still, you're never far from the maddening tourist crowds who flock here all year long.

At the western end of town, Hwy-89 meets Hwy-28 at Fanny Bridge, named for the body part that greets drivers as people lean over the edge to view the giant trout in the **Truckee River**. Flow-regulating sluice gates at the mouth of the river are remotely controlled from Reno, but were once operated by a gatekeeper who lived in what is now the **Gatekeeper's Museum** (mid-June–early Sept daily 11am–5pm; May–mid-June & early–late Sept Wed–Sun 11am–5pm; $2), containing a well-presented hodgepodge of artifacts from the last century, and a good collection of native basketware. Nearby, the **Truckee River Bike Trail** begins its three-mile waterside meander west to the River Ranch, which is also the end of a popular river-rafting route. **Rafting** down the Truckee is the thing to do on warm summer days, though it's really more of a relaxing social affair than a serious or challenging adventure. Several well-advertised boat-rental stands congregate along the river across from the Chevron Station, or call Tahoe Whitewater Tours (☎530/581-2441 or 1-800/442-7238, ⊛www.gowhitewater.com) for advance reservations. For a more relaxed excursion on the lake itself, you can take a **cruise** with the *Tahoe Gal* ($19–27; ☎530/583-0141 or 1-800/218-2464, ⊛www.tahoegal.com) from the jetty at 850 N Lake Blvd.

A couple of miles south along Hwy-89, 500 yards past the Kaspian picnic grounds, you'd be well advised to **hike** ten minutes up the unmarked trail to the top of **Eagle Rock** (see box below for more ambitious hiking suggestions). The amazing panoramic views that surround you as you look down on the expansive

Hiking, biking, and camping around Lake Tahoe

Of the many wonderful hikes in the Lake Tahoe area, only one – the 150-mile **Tahoe Rim Trail** – makes the circuit of the lake, some of it on the **Pacific Crest National Scenic Trail**, which follows the Sierra ridge from Canada to the Mexican border. Most people tackle only a tiny section of it, such as **Kingsbury Grade** to **Big Meadows** (22 miles), starting off Hwy-207 northwest of South Lake Tahoe and finishing on Hwy-50, south of Lake Tahoe.

There are also many **mountain-biking** trails around the lake: **Meiss County**, between Hwy-89 and Hwy-88 twenty miles south of South Lake Tahoe, is a favored area, where several beautiful lakes that escape most tourist itineraries are located. **Fallen Leaf Lake**, **Echo Lakes**, and **Angora Lake** are all pleasant, somewhat remote alternatives to the big T. Biking trails near the south shore include the three-mile loop of the **Pope-Baldwin Trail**, and you can pick up the popular **Marlett Lake/Flume Trail** in the Nevada State Park.

Ask at the **US Forest Service Visitor Center**, 870 Emerald Bay Rd (summer Mon–Thurs & Sat–Sun 8am–5.30pm, Fri 8am–7pm; ☏530/573-2674), three miles northwest of the junction where Hwy-89 and Hwy-50 separate to the west and east of the lake, for recommendations, free maps, and brochures on the entire area.

Camping

Lake Tahoe's best **campground** is *Campground by the Lake*, on the lakeshore three miles west of Stateline (☏530/542-6096, reserve through ParkNet ☏1-800/444-7275; $16). Other south shore sites include *Fallen Leaf* (☏530/573-2600, reserve through NRRS ☏1-877/444-6777; $16) and *Eagle Point* (☏530/541-3030, reserve through ParkNet ☏1-800/444-7275; $16). The north has several sites within striking distance of Tahoe City, including *Tahoe State Recreation Area* (☏530/583-3074, reserve through ParkNet ☏1-800/444-7275; $16) right in the center, and as crowded as you would expect. A mile and a half east, *Lake Forest* (☏530/581-4017; $10) is cheaper though far from the beach and cannot be reserved, and two miles southwest along Hwy-89, there's the large *William Kent* site (☏530/583-3642, reserve through NRRS ☏1-877/444-6777; $14). Halfway down the west shore, *Sugar Pine Point* (☏530/525-7982, reserve through ParkNet ☏1-800/444-7275; $14) has lovely sites in thick pine forest.

Along the western side of the lake, the Tahoe Rim Trail follows the Pacific Crest Trail through the glaciated valleys and granite peaks of the **Desolation Wilderness**. Here, **wilderness permits** ($5) are required by all users, though for day-users these are self-issued. For overnighters, a quota system operates in summer: fifty percent of these are first-come-first-served on the day of entry from the Forest Service visitor center, the remainder are reservable up to ninety days in advance (☏530/644-6048). Among the most strenuous trails here is the five-mile Bayview Trail to Fontanillis Lake. The other wilderness areas around Tahoe – Granite Chief to the northwest and Mount Rose to the northeast – are used much less and consequently no wilderness permits are needed, though campfire permits are.

royal-blue lake make this one of the world's greatest picnic spots. Several miles further south along Hwy-89 is **Chamber's Beach**, which, in summer, is as popular for sunning and **swimming** as it is for socializing.

You could also visit **Squaw Valley**, the site of the 1960 Winter Olympics, situated five miles west of Tahoe City off Hwy-89, although the original facilities (except the flame and the Olympic rings) are now swamped by the rampant development that has made this California's largest ski resort (see box, p.689). In the valley below, **hiking**, **horseback riding**, and **mountain–biking** are all popular summertime activities.

East from Tahoe City are some unremarkable settlements but decent stretches of beach at **Tahoe Vista** and **King's Beach**. Before you reach them, in the warmer months you can stop at the *Kayak Café*, 5166 N Lake Blvd (☎530/546-9337, ⓦ www.tahoepaddle.com) in **Carnelian Bay** for coffee or a spot of **kayaking**; rental is $15 per hour and $70 per day or you can take a guided kayaking tour for $70–90. As soon as you cross the Nevada state line from King's Beach into **Incline Village**, you are greeted by the predictable huddle of **casinos**, though they are not as numerous or in-your-face as at the south end of the lake. Consequently, the casual visitor might find having a flutter at the likes of the *Crystal Bay* or *Cal-Neva* somewhat less sordid and garish. Nearby is the **Ponderosa Ranch** (mid-April–Oct daily 9.30am–5pm; $11.50; ☎775/831-0691, ⓦ www.ponderosaranch.com), where *Bonanza* was filmed. If you loved the show as a kid, you'll probably find the museum fascinating for its behind-the-scenes glimpse at the filming of your favorite episodes; otherwise, give it a miss. Once you leave the buildings behind at the northeast corner of the lake and bear south, you enter one of the most appealing and quietest stretches. **Lake Tahoe Nevada State Park** boasts a great beach at **Sand Harbor**, though the water is always prohibitively cold, and has trails winding up through the backcountry to the Tahoe Rim Trail. Just south, **Secret Harbor** is an appropriate location for an idyllic nudist beach where gawkers are not tolerated.

Eating and drinking

Lake Tahoe has few exceptional **restaurants**; average burger-and-steak places, rustic in decor with raging fireplaces, are commonplace. Far better are the **buffets** at the Nevada **casinos**: *Harrah's*, for example, serves a wonderful spread, with good all-you-can-eat food for low rates. The casinos are also good places to **drink** and hold most of the region's entertainment options as well: low-budget Vegas-style revues, for the most part. For its size, Tahoe City has a good range of moderately priced places to eat as well as a couple of happening **bars**, all within a few minutes of each other.

South shore

The Brewery at the Lake 3542 Lake Tahoe Blvd, S Lake Tahoe ☎530/544-2739. Microbrewery with decent ales ranging from pale to porter and food specials such as beer-steamed shrimp.

Café Fiore 1169 Ski Run Blvd, S Lake Tahoe ☎530/541-2908. Small and intimate, *Café Fiore* serves innovative, upscale Italian meals, accompanied by an award-winning wine list.

Faces 270 Kingsbury Grade, Stateline ☎775/588-2333. The lake's main gay and lesbian bar – a bit frozen in time but friendly, with live DJs.

Heidi's Pancake House 3485 Lake Tahoe Blvd, S Lake Tahoe ☎530/544-8113. One in a local chain offering solid family-style meals at affordable prices.

Monument Peak at the top of the Heavenly tram ☎530/544-6263. Maybe a bit overpriced, but at 2000 feet above Lake Tahoe, it's more about the views than the food anyway.

Nephele's 1169 Ski Run Blvd, S Lake Tahoe ☎530/544-8130. Long-standing restaurant at the foot of Heavenly ski resort, with a great selection of fairly expensive California cuisine: grilled meat, fish, and pasta dishes. Hot tubs in back of restaurant.

New Emerald Palace 871 Emerald Bay Rd, S Lake Tahoe ☎530/542-4568. Authentic, inexpensive Chinese on the leafy outskirts towards Emerald Bay.

Red Hut Waffle Shop 2723 Lake Tahoe Blvd, S Lake Tahoe ☎530/541-9024. Ever-popular coffeeshop, justifiably crowded early winter mornings with carbo-loading skiers.

Six Bridges Bar & Grill 2500 Emerald Bay Rd, between S Lake Tahoe and the Emerald Bay ☎530/577-0788. Standard grill serving good portions of meaty fare in a quieter woody location.

Sprouts 3123 US-50 near Alameda Ave, S Lake Tahoe ☎530/541-6969. Almost, but not completely vegetarian, with good organic sandwiches, burritos, and smoothies.

Taj Mahal 3838 Lake Tahoe Blvd, S Lake Tahoe ☎530/541-6495. Basic Indian fare with a daily eleven-course lunch buffet for $6.99.

Tep's Villa Roma 3450 Lake Tahoe Blvd, S Lake Tahoe ☎530/541-8227. South shore institution that serves large portions of hearty Italian food, including several simple yet tasty vegetarian pasta dishes for about $10.

North shore

Bridgetender Bar & Grill 30 W Lake Blvd, Tahoe City ☎530/583-3342. Friendly rustic bar with good music, a fine range of beers, and huge portions of ribs, burgers, and the like.

Coyote's Mexican Grill 521 N Lake Blvd, Tahoe City ☎530/583-6653. Great-value burritos and enchiladas in a lively atmosphere.

Lakehouse Pizza 120 Grove St, Tahoe City ☎530/583-2222. In the Lakehouse Mall, Tahoe's best place for pizza is also a popular spot for cocktails on the lake at sundown. Be prepared to wait in winter.

Pierce Street Annex in the back of the Safeway complex, Tahoe City ☎530/583-5800. The place for drinking and dancing on the north shore. Packed with sunburned skiers or drunk beach-goers, depending on the season.

River Ranch Hwy-89 and Alpine Meadows Road, Tahoe City ☎530/583-4264. A trendy place to watch whitewater rafters return from their adventure on the Truckee River as you kick back on the deck nibbling mid-range Californian cuisine.

Soule Domaine just before the state line and casinos at 9983 Cove Ave, Crystal Bay ☎530/546-7529. Typical Tahoe "elegance": upscale cuisine in the cozy comfort of a real log cabin. Locals voted it "best place to take a date" six years in a row.

Spindleshanks 6873 N Lake Blvd, Tahoe Vista ☎530/546-2191. American bistro and wine bar, serving imaginative dishes like pan-roasted artichokes and chipotle lime-marinated brick chicken at moderate prices.

Sunnyside 1850 W Lake Blvd, Tahoe City ☎530/583-7200. One of the most popular places to have cocktails at sunset, on the deck overlooking the lake.

Tahoe House Bakery Hwy-89, half a mile south of Tahoe City ☎530/5831377. Family-style bakery and restaurant. Popular with locals.

Yama Sushi and Robata Grill 950 North Lake Blvd, Tahoe City ☎530/583-9262. Voted the best sushi bar on the north shore with prices to match.

Za's 395 North Lake Blvd, Tahoe City ☎530/583-1812. At the back of the friendly *Pete and Peter's* bar, this pizzeria also has a selection of pastas and a wide variety of sauces.

Truckee and around

Just off I-80, along the main transcontinental Amtrak train route, **TRUCKEE**, 15 miles north of Lake Tahoe, makes a refreshing change from the tourist-dependent towns around the lake. A small town lined up along the north bank of the Truckee River, it retains a fair amount of its late-nineteenth-century wooden architecture along the main section of Donner Pass Road, which many locals still refer to as Commercial Row; some of it appeared in Charlie Chaplin's *The Gold Rush*. The town is more of a stopoff than a destination in its own right, with a livelihood dependent on the forestry industry and the railroad. However, the town's rough, lively edge makes it as good a base as any from which to see the Lake Tahoe area, a fact that hasn't escaped the businesses beginning to exploit the commercial opportunities. There's even public transportation between the two (see below).

Practicalities

Greyhound **buses** from San Francisco stop in Truckee three times a day, where five daily TART buses connect to Tahoe City (daily 6.30am–6.30pm; $1.25; ☎530/581-6365 or 1-800/736-6365). Amtrak Thruway buses stop in each direction at the station on Commercial Row in the middle of town. The **Chamber of Commerce**, 10065 Donner Pass Rd (daily 8.30am–5.30pm; ☎530/587-2757, ⓦwww.truckee.com), has a few flimsy pamphlets and lots of advertisements; however, where Hwy-89 branches north off I-80, an easy to miss **Forest Service Ranger Station** (Mon–Fri 8am–4.30pm; ☎530/587-3558) has details of camping and hiking in the surrounding countryside. To get around, rent a mountain bike for $25 a day (as well as skiing and mountaineering equipment) from The Back Country, 11400 Donner Pass Rd (☎530/587-3933, ⓦwww.thebackcountry.net), or a car from Truckee Rent-a-Car at the Truckee Airport (☎530/587-2841); they'll deliver a car directly to you.

Truckee's cheapest **place to stay** is the *Cottage Hotel*, 10178 Donner Pass Rd (☎530/587-3108; ❶), central but a bit shabby with shared bathrooms. Much nicer is the *Truckee Hotel*, close to the train station at 10007 Bridge St (☎530/587-4444 or 1-800/659-6921, ⓦwww.thetruckeehotel.com; ❸), once decorated in the grand old railroad tradition, now decked out in Victorian B&B style, as is the quieter *Richardson House*, 10154 High St (☎530/587-5388 or 1-888/229-0365, ⓦwww.richardsonhouse.com; ❺). A mile east of town the *Best Western Truckee Tahoe Inn*, 11331 Hwy-267 (☎530/587-4525 or 1-800/824-6385, ⓦwww.bestwesterntahoe.com; ❹), is a reliable chain hotel. A number of low-priced **campgrounds** line the Truckee River between the town and Lake Tahoe, off Hwy-89, with sites starting at $10: the closest and largest is *Granite Flat*, three miles from Truckee; others are *Goose Meadows* and *Silver Creek*, five and nine miles south respectively (all three campgrounds can be contacted on ☎530/587-3558).

Commercial Row has several good **eating** options, especially the diner-style *Coffee And…* at 10106 Donner Pass Rd (☎530/587-3123), while omelets are the specialty at the *Squeeze Inn*, 10060 Donner Pass Rd (☎530/587-9814); both places are only open until 2pm. For cheap all-day meals, try *Andy's Truckee Diner*, on the other side of the tracks at 10144 W River St (☎530/582-6925), or *El Toro Bravo*, a standard taqueria at 10186 Donner Pass Rd (☎530/587-3557). The more expensive *Passage Restaurant* in the *Truckee Hotel* (☎530/587-7619) serves Pacific Rim-influenced American cuisine, and *Café Meridian*, 10118 Donner Pass Rd (☎530/587-0557), is a refreshingly modern place with a rooftop terrace, good light food, coffee and drinks. Though the old bucket-of-blood saloons of frontier lore are long gone, there are a few good places to stop for a **drink**, including the *Bar of America* (☎530/587-3110), downtown at the corner of Hwy-26 and Donner Pass Road, featuring free live music most nights, or *Ye Old Pastime*, 10096 Donner Pass Rd (☎530/582-9219), which features great live blues and jazz. *OB's*, at 10046 Donner Pass Rd (☎530/587-4164), is another relaxed pub with decent food. For chocolate so good that you might consider hibernating here through a brutal Truckee winter, try the award-winning cappuccino truffles at *Sweets*, 10118 Donner Pass Rd (☎530/587-6556 or 1-888/248-8840).

Donner Lake

Two miles west of Truckee, surrounded by alpine cliffs of silver-gray granite, **DONNER LAKE** was the site of one of the most gruesome and notorious tragedies of early California, when pioneers trapped by winter snows were forced to eat the bodies of their dead companions (see box).

The horrific tale of the Donner party is recounted in some detail in the small **Emigrant Trail Museum** (summer daily 10am–5pm; rest of year daily 10am–4pm; $1; ☎530/582-7892) – just off Donner Pass Road, three miles west of Truckee in **Donner Memorial State Park** – which shows a re-enactment of the events in the hourly 26min video that's so over-the-top most viewers will have a hard time choking back their chuckles. Outside, the **Pioneer**

The **Donner party**, named after one of the pioneer families among the group of 91 travelers, set off for California in April 1846 from Illinois across the Great Plains, following a shortcut recommended by the first traveler's guide to the West Coast (the 1845 *Emigrant's Guide to California and Oregon*), which actually took three weeks longer than the established route. By October, they had reached what is now Reno and decided to rest a week to regain their strength for the arduous crossing of the Sierra Nevada Mountains – a delay that proved fatal. When at last they set off, early snowfall blocked their route beyond Donner Lake, and the group was forced to stop and build crude shelters, hoping that the snow would melt and allow them to complete their crossing; it didn't, and they were stuck.

Within a month, the pioneers were running out of provisions, and a party of fifteen set out across the mountains to try and reach Sutter's Fort in Sacramento. They struggled through yet another storm and, a month later, two men and five women stumbled into the fort, having survived by eating the bodies of the men who had died. A rescue party set off from Sutter's Fort immediately, only to find more of the same: thirty or so half-crazed survivors, living off the meat of their fellow travelers.

Monument stands on a plinth as high as the snow was deep that fateful winter of 1846 – 22 feet. From the museum, an easy nature trail winds through the forest past a memorial plaque marking the site where the majority of the Donner party built its simple cabins. Nearby, on the southeastern shore of the lake, there's a $12-a-night summer-only **campground** (reserve through ParkNet ☎1-800/444-7275).

Above Donner Lake, the Southern Pacific railroad tracks climb west over the **Donner Pass** through tunnels built by Chinese laborers during the nineteenth century – still one of the main rail routes across the Sierra Nevada. For much of the way, the tracks are protected from the usually heavy winter snow by a series of wooden sheds, which you can see from across the valley, where Donner Pass Road snakes up the steep cliffs. On well-signposted Hwy-40, there's a scenic overlook where you can get that prize-winning photo of Donner Lake and possibly a glimpse beyond to Tahoe. Further on, rock climbers from the nearby Alpine Skills Institute (☎530/426-9108) can often be seen honing their talents on the 200-foot granite faces; the institute offers a variety of climbing and mountaineering courses and trips. At the crest, the road passes the Soda Springs, Sugar Bowl, and Royal Gorge **ski areas** before rejoining I-80, which runs east from Donner Pass to Reno, Nevada, and west to Sacramento.

Into Nevada: Reno and around

On I-80 at the foot of the Sierra Nevada, thirty miles east of Truckee, **RENO, NEVADA** has plenty of affordable places to stay and eat, making it a good stopoff, especially if you enjoy gambling, as many neighboring Californians do each weekend. The town itself, apart from the stream of blazing casino neon, may not be much to look at, having sprung up out of nowhere in the middle of the desert on the hopes that the gambling industry alone could sustain its existence. Nevertheless, its setting – with the snowcapped Sierra peaks as a distant backdrop and the Truckee River winding through – is nice enough, and unlike Las Vegas, to which it is most often compared, Reno maintains a small-

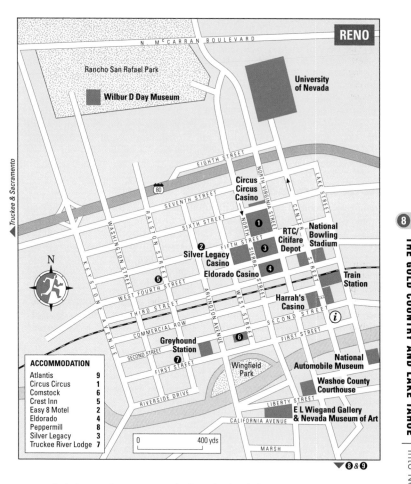

Rancho San Rafael Park

Wilbur D Day Museum

University
of Nevada

N McCARRAN BOULEVARD

Truckee & Sacramento

EIGHTH STREET

80

SEVENTH STREET

SIXTH STREET

FIFTH STREET

WEST FOURTH STREET

THIRD STREET

COMMERCIAL ROW

SECOND STREET

FIRST STREET

RIVERSIDE DRIVE

**Circus
Circus
Casino**

**Silver Legacy
Casino**

Eldorado Casino

**Harrah's
Casino**

**Greyhound
Station**

RTC/
Citifare
Depot

National
Bowling
Stadium

Train
Station

National
Automobile Museum

Washoe County
Courthouse

**E L Wiegand Gallery
& Nevada Museum of Art**

Wingfield
Park

LIBERTY STREET

CALIFORNIA AVENUE

MARSH

0   400 yds

ACCOMMODATION

Atlantis	9
Circus Circus	1
Comstock	6
Crest Inn	5
Easy 8 Motel	2
Eldorado	4
Peppermill	8
Silver Legacy	3
Truckee River Lodge	7

8 *THE GOLD COUNTRY AND LAKE TAHOE* | Into Nevada: Reno and around

town feel that residents are proud of. As the locals love to say – over and over
again – Reno is the biggest little town in the world. Even if you don't like to
gamble, you can still pass a pleasant afternoon here ambling in the dry desert
heat or visiting one of the mildly diverting museums. Reno is also another
good place from which to visit Lake Tahoe, and a good base for exploring the
evocative mining towns of **Carson City** and **Virginia City**.

Arrival and information

Reno's Cannon International **airport** (☎775/328-6400, ⓦwww.renoairport
.com) is served by most major domestic carriers. RTC/Citifare (6am–1am;
$1.25 flat fare, $3.75 day-pass; ☎775/348-0480, ⓦwww.citifare.com) bus #13
makes the twenty-minute journey from the terminals to Reno's downtown
Citicenter transit center, where you can connect to many of the company's
other routes. Greyhound **buses** from San Francisco, via Sacramento and
Truckee, and from LA, via the Owens Valley, use the terminal at 155 Stevenson

St, also used by KT Services (☎775/945-2282), which operates a daily bus to Las Vegas and Phoenix. The Amtrak *California Zephyr* **train** from Chicago stops in the center of town at 135 Commercial Row, as do Thruway buses from Sacramento. To **rent a car**, try Alamo (☎775/323-7940 or 1-800/327-9633), Avis (☎775/785-2727 or 1-800/831-2837), or Thrifty (☎775/329-0096 or 1-800/367-2277), all three at the airport.

The temporary **visitor center** is on the second floor of 1 E First St (Mon–Fri 8am–6pm; ☎775/827-7600 or 1-800/FOR-RENO, ⓦwww.reno-laketahoe.com), while new premises are being built. On the sixteenth floor of the same building, the **Chamber of Commerce** (Mon–Fri 9am–5pm; ☎775/337-3030, ⓦwww.reno-sparkschamber.org) can also dish out advice and brochures.

Accommodation

Inexpensive **accommodation** is plentiful, but if you arrive on a weekend you should book ahead and be prepared for rates to all but double. Usually, a two-nights' stay applies on weekends, especially at the **casinos**. You can also call the **Reno-Sparks Visitor and Convention Association**'s toll-free information and reservation line (☎1-800-FOR-RENO) for help with finding a place to stay. **Camping** is an RV experience in Reno; for tent sites, head west to the numerous campgrounds around Lake Tahoe (see p.692).

Atlantis 3800 S Virginia St ☎775/825-4700 or 1-800/723-6500, ⓦwww.atlantiscasino.com. Relatively new on the scene, this hotel's buffet, coffeeshop, and restaurant have all been voted the town's best by locals in recent surveys. Great rates and plush amenities for slightly less than casinos of the same class in the center of town. ❷

Circus Circus 500 N Sierra St ☎775/329-0711 or 1-800/648-5010, ⓦwww.circusreno.com. One of the largest and tackiest casinos, with over 1600 popular rooms. ❷

Comstock 200 W Second St ☎775/329-1880 or 1-800/COMSTOCK, ⓦwww.thecomstock.com. Centrally located casino that has passed its prime and consequently offers lower rates than some of the newer competitors. ❶

Crest Inn 525 W Fourth St ☎775/329-0808. Simple motel with few trimmings and low prices. ❶

Easy 8 Motel 255 W Fifth St ☎775/322-4588. Another basic motel just a stone's throw from the casinos. ❶

Eldorado 345 N Virginia St ☎775/786-5700 or 1-800/777-5325, ⓦwww.eldoradoreno.com. The nicer rooms are on the upper floors, those lower down are cheaper, in this bustling downtown casino. ❸

Peppermill 2707 S Virginia St ☎775/826-2121 or 1-800/648-6992, ⓦwww.peppermillreno.com. Another large new casino, slightly outside the center of town, with special rates offered frequently. ❸

Silver Legacy 407 N Virginia St ☎775/329-4777 or 1-800/687-7733, ⓦwww.silverlegacyreno.com. The flashiest of all the Reno casinos, and worth a tour even if you're not staying for its well-developed silver-mining theme, which brings the Gold and Silver rushes of yesterday right up to the present with plenty of technological wizardry. With the constant stampede of gawkers and gamblers, actually staying here entails negotiating the crowds. ❸

Truckee River Lodge 501 W First St ☎775/786-8888 or 1-800/635-8950. Non-smoking hotel with an emphasis on recreation. It has a fitness center and rents bikes from $20 a day. ❷

The Town

It may lack the glitz and the glamour that help make Vegas a global draw, but **Reno** is northern Nevada's number one **gambling** spot, offering a 24-hour diet of slot machines, blackjack, craps, keno, roulette, and many more ways to win and lose a fortune. Gaming was only legalized in Nevada in 1931, but silver miners in Virginia City and Gold Hill regularly tried their hands at fortune's wheel back in the mid-nineteenth century, when a deck of cards was an almost mandatory part of a miner's kit.

While nowhere near as grand as the Vegas gambling institutions to the south, most of Reno's **casinos** still warrant a quick tour. If you can only handle visiting a few, the best of the lot are: **Circus Circus**, 500 N Sierra St, where a small circus performs every half-hour, giving patrons a reason to look up from their dwindling savings; **Silver Legacy**, around the corner at 407 N Virginia St, which reveals a planetarium-style dome with a makeshift 120-foot mining derrick underneath, appearing to draw silver ore out of the ground and spilling cascades of coins in the process – it is joined onto *Eldorado* and you can quite unwittingly wander from one into the other; and **Harrah's**, a few blocks south at 219 N Center St, the classiest casino downtown with row upon row of high-stakes slot machines and the occasional famous entertainer. If touring the casinos solo doesn't teach you everything you want to know, contact the Reno–Tahoe Gaming Academy, 300 E First St (☎775/329-5665), for an overview of some of the rules of the major games followed by a behind-the-scenes **tour** of Reno's major gambling dens (hours vary; $10).

Once you're ready to cash in all the casino clatter and any remaining chips for some peace and quiet, take refuge in one of Reno's many **museums**. The largest and most significant among them is the **National Automobile Museum** (The Harrah Collection), at Mill and Lake streets (Mon–Sat 9.30am–5.30pm, Sun 10am–4pm; $7.50; ☎775/333-9300,ⓦwww.automuseum.org), which holds the most comprehensive public display of automobiles in the western hemisphere, with more than 200 vintage and classic cars, some of them artfully arranged along re-created city streets of bygone decades. The sheer scale of the collection can't help but impress, even if you think you'd rather be pulling on the arm of a slot machine than admiring the shine on an 1892 Philion. The one time it's guaranteed to get crowded is during the Hot August Nites classic cars festival. Art buffs should take a look at the inventive contemporary exhibitions at the **E.L. Weigand Gallery and Nevada Museum of Art**, 160 W Liberty St (Tues–Sun noon–6pm; $5; ☎775/329-3333, ⓦwww.nevadaart.org).

You'll find Reno's most curious trove, however, at the **Wilbur D. May Great Basin Adventure** (Mon–Sat 10am–5pm, Sun noon–5pm; ☎775/785-5961, ⓦwww.maycenter.com), which sits on the edge of **Rancho San Rafael Park**, a mile north of downtown Reno off North Sierra Street. The collection outlines the eventful life of Wilbur May – a traveler, hunter, military aviator, cattle-breeder, and heir to the May department store fortunes – with several rooms of furnishings, mounted animal heads, and plunder from his trips to Africa and South America; the museum also houses temporary exhibitions, hence admission fees vary. In summer only, the complex opens its **Great Basin Adventure** (Tues–Sat 10am–5pm, Sun noon–5pm; $3.50; ☎775/785-4319), where kids can pet animals, ride on ponies, shoot down a flume, and discover about Native Americans and dinosaurs.

On the other side of US-395, the University of Nevada campus hosts the **Nevada Historical Society Museum**, 1650 N Virginia St (Mon–Sat 10am–5pm; $2; ☎775/688-1190), full of items of local interest, especially Native American artifacts. Next door is the **Fleischmann Planetarium** (Mon–Fri 8am–8pm, Sat & Sun 11am–8pm; $6; ☎775/784-4811, ⓦwww .planetarium.unr.nevada.edu), where, amongst the telescopes and solar system galleries, OMNIMAX-style films (2–4 shows daily; ☎775/784-4811) are projected onto a huge dome; the museum contains all four meteorites recovered in Nevada and impressive six-foot globes of earth and moon.

If you've come to Reno to get **married**, you and your intended must be at least eighteen years old and able to prove it, swear that you're not already married, and appear before a judge at the **Washoe County Court** (daily 8am–midnight; ☎775/328-3275), south of the main casino district at South Virginia and Court streets, to obtain a **marriage license** ($50). There is no waiting period or blood test required. Civil services are performed for an additional $50 at the **Commissioner for Civil Marriages**, behind the Courthouse at 195 S Sierra St (☎775/328-3461). If you want something a bit more special, however, **wedding chapels** all around the city will help you tie the knot: over the crossroads from the courthouse, the Heart of Reno, 243 S Sierra St (☎775/786-6882), does the job quickly – "No Waiting, Just Drive In" – for around $80–100, providing a pink chintzy parlor full of plastic flowers. Fork out more cash, and you get the tux and frock, and can invite a few guests. Other chapels include the Park Wedding Chapel, 136 S Virginia St (☎775/323-1770), and the Silver Bells Wedding Chapel, 628 N Virginia St (☎775/322-0420 or 1-800/221-9336). If it doesn't work out, you'll have to stay in Nevada for another six weeks before you can get a **divorce**.

Eating and nightlife

All-you-can-eat buffets are the order of the day for tourists in Reno, and seemingly everyone goes out and stuffs themselves to bursting. The buffets can be fun and of surprisingly good quality; we list the best of them below along with the alternatives most favored by locals. Tourists tend to stick to the shows in the casinos for **nightlife**, but occasionally the city holds an art and/or music festival, and there are some popular venues downtown including *Reno Live*, at Sierra and Second streets (☎775/329-1952), which claims to be the largest nightclub complex in Nevada. Check Reno's free independent weekly *Reno News and Review* for listings. There are a number of **gay and lesbian bars** in town, including the popular *Patio Bar* at 600 W Fifth St (☎775/323-6565).

Buffets

Atlantis 3800 S Virginia St ☎775/825-4700. Consistently voted best buffet in town by locals. The casino's moderately priced *Café Alfresco* has wood-fired pizzas, and the decor of the more upscale *Seafood Steakhouse* may have all the class of the dining room on a tacky cruise ship, but the food and service are exceptional, as is the wine list.

Circus Circus 500 Sierra St. The place to go for a buffet meal if your budget is of greater concern than your stomach, with all-you-can-eat dinners for under $10.

Harrah's 219 N Center St ☎775/786-3232. The most lavish downtown casino buffet includes multiple entrees such as prime rib, crab leg, shrimp, and a fine Asian section for $9.99 most days. Their *à la carte Café Napa* is also recommended.

La Piñata 1575 Vassar St ☎775/323-3210. The best Mexican buffet in town, on a street running perpendicular to Virginia South, just south of casino central.

S.S. Super Indian Restaurant 1030 S Virginia St ☎775/322-5577. Fresh, primarily northern Indian specialties and a daily $6 lunch buffet.

Restaurants

Aloha Sushi in the Mervyns shopping center at 3338 Kietzke Lane ☎775/828-9611. A bit of a jump southeast from casino central, but reasonable and good; if you're staying for any length of time, you'll need to escape from the buffets eventually. Try their specialty mountain roll.

Bangkok Cuisine 55 Mt Rose St ☎775/322-0299. Cosy Thai family restaurant offering spicy dinners and filling lunch specials for $5.99.

Einstein's Quantum Café 6135 Lakeside Drive, near Virginia Lake Park ☎775/825-6611. An inexpensive new vegetarian café that's already a hit among locals.

La Vecchia Varese 130 West St ☎775/322-7486. Unfussy decor and an excellent, moderately priced selection of gourmet Italian dishes, with several vegetarian choices.

Liberty Belle Saloon & Restaurant 4250 S Virginia St ☎775/825-1776. Moderately priced

place famed for its prime rib with spinach salad and other meaty dishes. Established in 1958, it also houses a slot machine collection and other memorabilia.
Rickshaw Paddy 4944 S Virginia St ☎775/828-

2335. Mid-range Asian food combining influences from eight different countries, eaten, if you can believe it, to the accompaniment of Celtic background music.

Carson City

US-395 heads south from Reno along the jagged spires of the High Sierra past Mono Lake, Mount Whitney, and Death Valley (see Chapter Four). Just thirty miles south of Reno, it briefly becomes Carson Street as it passes through **CARSON CITY**, the state capital of Nevada. It is small compared to Reno, but despite the sprawling mess of fast-food joints, strip malls, and car dealerships that surround the town center, it is well worth a visit, especially if you are interested in the history of mining. The city has a number of elegant buildings, excellent historical museums, and a few world-weary casinos, populated mainly by old ladies armed with buckets of quarters.

Named, somewhat indirectly, after frontier explorer Kit Carson in 1858, Carson City is still redolent with Wild West history: you'll get a good introduction at the **Nevada State Museum** at 600 N Carson St (daily 8.30am–4.30pm; $3; ☎775/687-4811). Housed in a sandstone structure built during the Civil War as the Carson Mint, the museum's exhibits deal with the geology and natural history of the Great Basin desert region, from prehistoric days up through the heyday of the 1860s, when the silver mines of the nearby Comstock Lode were at their peak. Amid the many guns and artifacts, the two best features of the museum are the reconstructed **Ghost Town**, from which a tunnel allows entry down into a full-scale model of an **underground mine**, giving some sense of the cramped and constricted conditions in which miners worked. The brand new **North Building** is home to the **Under One Sky** exhibition, featuring material about cowboys and Indians, natural history, and children's interactive displays.

Four blocks from the museum, on the other side of Carson Street, the impressively restored **State Capitol**, 101 N Carson St (daily 9am–5pm; free), dating from 1871, merits a look for its stylish Neoclassical architecture and the commendable stock of artifacts relating to Nevada's past housed in an upper-floor room.

The **Nevada State Railway Museum**, 2180 S Carson St (daily 8.30am–4.30pm; $2; ☎775/687-6953), just a stone's throw away from the visitor center (see below), displays carefully restored locomotives and carriages, several of them from the long since defunct but fondly remembered Virginia & Truckee Railroad, founded in the nineteenth century.

Practicalities

Greyhound **buses** stop outside the *Frontier Motel* on North Carson Street. Amtrak Thruway services from Sacramento and South Lake Tahoe stop outside the *Nugget* casino at the junction of Robinson and Carson streets. The No Stress Express ($33 one-way; ☎1-800/426-5644) can be reserved in advance for transportation to Carson City from the Reno Airport. The **CVB**, on the south side of town at 1900 S Carson St (Mon–Sat 9am–5pm; ☎775/687-7410 or 1-800/NEVADA-1), can help with practical details, and sells the *Kit Carson Trail Map* ($2.50), a leaflet detailing a **walking tour** of the town, taking in the main museums, the state capitol, and many of the fine 1870s Victorian wooden houses and churches on the west side.

There are a number of reasonably priced **motels** in town, among them the

Nugget Motel & Inn at 555 N Stewart St (℡775/882-7711; ❷) behind the *Nugget* casino, and the more colorful *Plaza Hotel*, 801 S Carson St (℡775/883-9500 or 1-888/227-1499, ⓦwww.carsoncityplaza.com; ❷), not far from the Capitol; while a little further out is the plusher *Piñon Plaza Resort Hotel and Casino* at 2171 Hwy-50 (℡775/885-9000, ⓦwww.pinonplaza.com; ❹), a *Best Western* franchise. If exploring Carson City gives you an appetite, **places to eat** in town include *Heidi's Dutch Mill*, 1020 N Carson St (℡775/882-0486), which serves generous breakfasts and lunches, *Corina's Mexican Kitchen*, 1701 N Carson St (℡775/885-2248), or the *Whiskey Creek Steakhouse & Saloon* in the *Piñon Plaza Resort* (℡775/885-9000).

Virginia City and Genoa

Much of the wealth on which Carson City – and indeed San Francisco – was built came from the silver mines of the Comstock Lode, a solid seam of pure silver discovered in 1859 underneath Mount Hamilton, fourteen miles east of Carson City off US-50. Raucous **VIRGINIA CITY** grew up on the steep slopes above the mines, and a young writer named Samuel Clemens made his way west in the 1860s with his older brother, who'd been appointed acting secretary to the governor of the Nevada Territory, to see what all the fuss was about. His descriptions of the wild life of the mining camp, and of the desperately hard work men put in to get at the valuable ore, were published years later under his adopted pseudonym, **Mark Twain**. Though Twain also spent some time in the Gold Rush towns of California's Mother Lode on the other side of the Sierra – which by then were all but abandoned – his accounts of Virginia City life, collected in *Roughing It*, give a hilarious, eyewitness account of the hard-drinking life of the frontier miners.

The miners left, but Virginia City still exploits a rich vein, one which runs through the pocketbooks of tour parties bussed up here from Reno. But despite the camera-clicking throngs, there's a sense of authenticity to Virginia City missing from even the most evocative of the California mining towns. Perhaps it's the town's location, encircled by the barren Nevada Desert that so sharply contrasts with the diverse countryside of California's Gold Country, or perhaps it's the colorful advertisements that lure tourists to the many quirky museums. Then again, it could simply be the raucous spirit that seems to infect almost every sarsaparilla-sippin' tourist who sets foot here. Whatever the reason, it's hard not to get caught up in the infectious Wild West atmosphere and stay longer than you'd intended. Still, not everyone who floods into town is here for the Gold Rush nostalgia – many visitors are here to frequent the **legal brothels**, another reminder of the town's frontier days.

At the **Chamber of Commerce**, in the disused premises of the old *Crystal Bar Saloon* on the corner of Taylor and North C streets (daily 9am–5pm; ℡775/847-0311, ⓦwww.virginiacity-nv.org), you can pick up pamphlets and a self-guided walking-tour map, or you can just as easily wander around the town until you've bumped into all the sights in your own time. Historic highlights include the **Mackay Mansion Museum**, 129 South D St (daily 11am–6pm; $3; ℡775/847-0173), and **The Castle**, 70 South B St (daily late May–mid Oct 11am–5pm; closed Nov–early May; $3.50; ℡775/847-0766), both painstakingly preserved 1860s residences; and the **Nevada Gambling Museum**, 50 South C St (daily April–Sept 10am–6pm; Oct–March 10am–5pm; $1; ℡775/847-9022), with its historic roulette wheel and other period game-room accessories. You can also poke your head into the **Bucket of Blood Saloon**, which is delightfully crowded with period fixtures and crooked old furnishings. The mood of the era and current desire to cash in on it is summed up in **The Way It Was Museum**, 113 North C St (daily 10am–6pm; $2; ☎775/847-0766), with its collection of mining equipment, rare photos and maps, and fully stocked gift shop.

If you'd like to **stay in town**, there are a few decent options, but no Reno-style resorts. Right on the main drag, the *Silver Queen*, at 28 North C St (☎775/847-0468; ❷), and *Comstock Lodge*, at 875 South C St (☎775/847-0233; ❷), are two reasonable, if basic, options for spending the night on the main drag of an old boomtown. The converted 1861 *Chollar Mansion* B&B, 565 South D St (☎775/847-9777; ❹), provides greater comfort and amenities.

A 35-minute train ride ($5.50 round-trip) from the town center on the **Virginia & Truckee Railroad** will take you the short distance of little over a mile up to the all-but-extinct town of **Gold Hill**, which consists primarily of a hotel, restaurant, and tavern of the same name (☎775/847-0111; ❷); Nevada's oldest, with great rates and atmosphere, it also lets out half a dozen more expensive lodges in ex-miner houses around the tiny town.

South of Carson City in the Carson Valley lies another evocative Wild West scene, **GENOA**, the oldest town in Nevada. Slightly less stampeded by tourists than Virginia City, the main draw here is the curious **Mormon Station**, 2295 Main St (daily mid May–mid Oct; free; ☎775/782-2590), a replica of the original trading post and fort built on the site in 1851. For information on walking tours in town, stop by the information counter in the **Genoa Courthouse** at 2304 Main St (daily mid-May–mid-Oct 10am–4.30pm; ☎775/782-4325). You can stay in some comfort at *The Legend Country Inn*, 2292 Main St (☎775/783-0906, ⓦ www.thelegendcountryinn.com), part of a new complex mercifully built to blend in with the old architecture. Locals still congregate at the *Genoa Bar*, 2282 Main St (☎775/782-3870), which claims to be Nevada's oldest continuously operating watering hole.

Travel details

Trains

Oakland/Emeryville (for San Francisco Thruway service) **to**: Reno (5 daily; 5–8hr); Sacramento (10 daily; 2hr 10min).

Reno to: Oakland/Emeryville (5 daily; 5–8hr); Sacramento (5 daily; 3hr 30min–5hr 30min); Truckee (5 daily; 1hr).

Sacramento to: Oakland/Emeryville (10 daily; 2hr); Reno (5 daily; 3–5hr); Truckee (5 daily; 2hr–3hr 35min).

Buses

All buses are Greyhound unless otherwise stated.

Reno to: Las Vegas (5 daily; 9–10hr); Los Angeles (10 daily; 12–16hr); Sacramento (11 daily; 2hr 40min–3hr 50min); San Francisco (11 daily; 5hr

5min–6hr 55min).

Reno airport to: Stateline (14 daily Tahoe Casino Express; 1hr 45min).

Sacramento to: Auburn (3 daily; 1hr 20min); Grass Valley (4 daily Amtrak Thruway; 1hr 25min); Nevada City (4 daily Amtrak Thruway; 1 hr 35min); Placerville (2 daily; 1hr 30min); Reno (11 daily; 2hr 45min–4hr 10min); South Lake Tahoe (2 daily; 3hr); Truckee (3 daily; 3hr).

San Francisco to: Auburn (3 daily; 3hr 50min–4hr 15min); Reno (11 daily; 5hr 15min–7hr); Sacramento (15 daily; 2–3hr); South Lake Tahoe (2 daily; 5hr 25min–6hr 15min); Truckee (3 daily; 5hr 30min–6hr).

South Lake Tahoe to: Placerville (2 daily; 1hr 30min); Sacramento (2 daily; 2hr 55min); San Francisco (2 daily; 5hr 30min).

Northern California

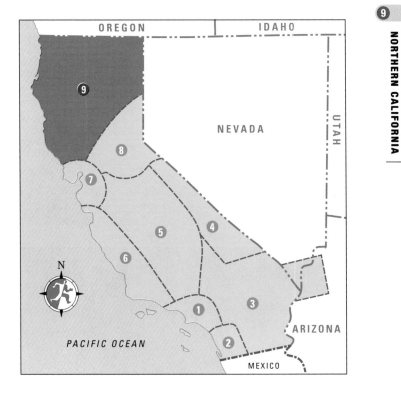

CHAPTER 9

Highlights

* **Russian River Valley wineries** The wine tasting here is more leisurely and less commercialized than in the Napa and Sonoma valleys just to the south. See p.732

* **Mendocino Art Center** Admire, purchase, or even participate in the creative output of this friendly community art center in the quaint seaside town of Mendocino. See p.740

* **Klamath Overlook** Where the Klamath River empties into the Pacific, this overlook affords marvelous vistas at this dramatic stop on the rugged Coastal Trail. See p.757

* **Lassen Volcanic National Park** Visit this top natural wilderness, which offers steaming geysers, high-altitude lakes, exhilarating walks, and bracing camping sites. See p.767

* **Mount Shasta** This huge volcanic peak is the focal point of many legends and a haven for cross-country skiing in winter and hiking or mountaineering in summer. See p.778

* **Lava Beds National Monument** Admire the black lavic rock, crawl through tubular caves, or indulge in a spot of bird-watching at California's northernmost attraction. See p.785

9

Northern California

The northern coast and interior of California covers about a third of the state, a gigantic area over 400 miles long and 300 miles wide, with a rugged rural landscape and ethic far removed from portions of the urbanized daydreams of the south. It's a schizophrenic region of a schizophrenic state, coupling volcanoes with vineyards, fog-shrouded redwoods with scorched olive trees, loggers with environmentalists, and legends of Bigfoot with movies of Ewoks. Northern Californians are tied to the land, and agriculture dominates the economy as well as the vistas. Deep-rooted logging, fishing, and cattle industries are also ever-present, even though the first two are in decline, along with the wild, crashing Pacific Coast and steady rain that supports a marijuana-farming region called the Emerald Triangle. Add only two major highways and the lack of a metropolis in favor of small, Main Street towns, and you have a region that has more in common with Oregon and Washington than Los Angeles or San Francisco. In that regard, Northern Californians have long rumbled about forming a state of their own. Indeed, in 1941 there was a proposal to form a state called Jefferson near Mount Shasta, an event that could have gained steam were it not for Japan's bombing of Pearl Harbor two days later, channeling collective energies into the war.

Immediately north of the Bay Area, the **Wine Country** might be your first – indeed your only – taste of Northern California, though it's by no means typical. The two valleys of **Napa** and **Sonoma** unfold in around thirty miles of rolling hills and premium real estate, home to the Californian wine barons and San Franciscan weekenders wanting to rough it in comfort. Napa is the reigning king of indulgence and high-caliber vintages, while Sonoma caters to a funkier set, with its interesting history and outdoor tours. The northwest corner of Sonoma County is Wine Country's other "grape escape," an area of six varieties and resorts clustered around the **Russian River** and its tributaries. Further north and towards the coast, the **Anderson Valley** in Mendocino County is gradually becoming established as the newest haven for vineyards. Another inland area that can be included in a longer itinerary is **Clear Lake**, to the north of the Wine Country.

It's the **northern coast** which provides the most appealing, and slowest, route through the region, beginning just north of Marin County and continuing for four hundred miles on Hwy-1 and US-101 along rugged bluffs and through forests as far as the Oregon border. The landscape varies little at first, but given time reveals tangible shifts from the flat oyster beds of **Sonoma County** to the seal and surfer breeding grounds around the coastal elegance of **Mendocino** and the big logging country further north in **Humboldt**. Trees are the big attraction up here: some thousands of years old and hundreds of feet

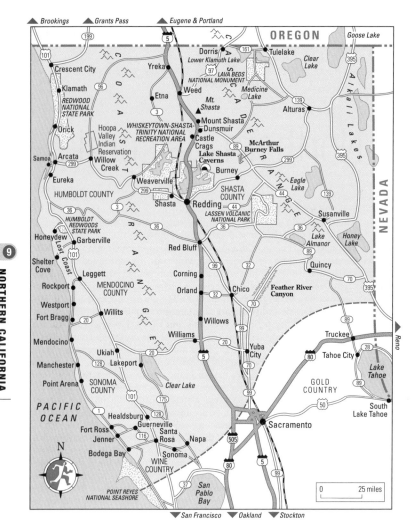

high, dominating a very sparsely populated landscape swathed in swirling mists. In summer, areas like the **Redwood National Park**, stretching into the most northerly **Del Norte** county, teem with campers and hikers, but out of season it can be an idyllic experience, co-existing with the area's woodland creatures, including, some say, Bigfoot. Although the nightlife is rarely swinging, the college town of **Arcata**, towards the top end of the northern coast, makes a lively refuge when the great outdoors begins to pall.

The **interior** is more remote still, an enchanting land whose mystery and sheer physical enormity can't help but leave a lasting impression. I-5 neatly divides the region, cutting through the forgettable Sacramento Valley north to the **Shasta Cascades**, a mountainous area of isolated towns, massive lakes, and a forbidding climate. In winter, much of this corner of the state is completely impassable, and the region's commercial activities are centered around the lower, warmer climes of the largest town and transportation hub of **Redding**. Redding, though of limited appeal itself, is a major crossroads serving **Whiskeytown–Shasta–Trinity National Recreation Area, Lassen Volcanic National Park, McArthur–Burney Falls State Park** and, northward, the railroad towns in the shadows of towering **Mount Shasta**. Up at the top of the interior, the eerie moonlike terrain of the **Lava Beds National Monument** rewards those who make the effort to get there, and the wetlands of the **Klamath Basin**, which straddles the Oregon border, are a must for birdwatchers. Unlike the Wine Country and the coast, locals all over the Shasta Cascades are actually glad to see tourists, and visitor centers take the time to explain the many outdoor recreational options. Food and lodging costs are cheap by California standards, and the efficient network of highways – byproducts of the logging industry – make travel easy. Parts of the region fill up in summer, but given the sheer enormity of the forests and the plethora of lakes, waterfalls, parks, and bird sanctuaries, escaping the masses and finding peace isn't much of a task. In the winter months, you may feel like you're the only one here at all.

Some history

As with elsewhere in California, the first inhabitants of the north were **Native Americans**, whose past has all but been erased, leaving only the odd desolate reservation or crafts museum. Much later, the **Russians** figured briefly in the region's history when they had a modest nineteenth-century settlement at Fort Ross on the coast, ostensibly to protect their interests in otter hunting and fur trading, though more likely to promote territorial claims. **Mexican** explorers and maintenance costs that exceeded revenues prevented them from extending their hunting activities further south, and in the 1840s they sold the fort to the **Americans**. It was the discovery of **gold** in 1848 that really put the north on the map, and much of the countryside bears the marks of this time, dotted with abandoned mining towns, deserted since the gold ran out. Not a lot has happened since, although in the 1980s New Ageism triggered a kind of future for the region, with low land prices drawing more and more devotees up here to sample the delights of a landscape they see as rich in rural symbolism. Hollywood has also been drawn to the region, using the north as a cost-effective way to travel to another place and time. *Robin Hood, Gone with the Wind, The Birds, The Return of the Jedi,* and *Jurassic Park: The Lost World* are just a few examples of movies filmed amongst the frozen-in-time beauty. In more recent years the spiralling rise in Bay Area property prices has led to a small but steady movement of more mainstream folk and retirees into some areas, searching for better value for money or a spacious second home. Many die-hard locals are fearful of this influx of new homes and lifestyles spoiling the coast in particular, though the Coastal Commission tightly controls development, and farmers, so far, have resisted selling out on a large scale.

Getting around

While most people see the Wine Country on a day-trip from San Francisco, it is also feasible to take the area in before encountering the less manicured territory further north, hooking up to the coast by bus from Santa Rosa. **Public transportation** is sparse all over Northern California, and to enjoy the region you'll need to be independently mobile. Infrequent Greyhound **buses** run from San Francisco and Sacramento up and down I-5, stopping in Chico, Redding, and Mount Shasta, and US-101, stopping in Garberville, Eureka, Arcata, and Crescent City. There is also one connection between the coast and interior in the shape of Greyhound's new Eureka–Redding service, though none of these routes solve the problem of actually getting around once you've arrived. Frankly, your best bet is a **driving tour**, fixing on a few points. Each of the three regions below can be covered, albeit sketchily, over an extended weekend, provided you have a reliable car. Only the largest of Northern California's towns have any local bus service although for some of the remoter spots you could, perhaps, consider an organized trip, notably Green Tortoise's one-week tours – see p.36 of Basics for details.

The Wine Country

"The coldest winter I ever spent was summer in San Francisco," quipped Mark Twain. Like Twain, many visitors to San Francisco can't get over the daily fog and winds that chill even the hottest August day. Heading into the golden, arid **Napa** and **Sonoma valleys**, less than an hour's drive north of San Francisco, can feel like entering another country. Here, 29,000 acres of vineyards feeding hundreds of wineries and their upscale patrons, make the area the heart of the American wine industry in reputation, if not in volume. In truth, less than five percent of California's wine comes from the region, but what it does produce is America's best.

Predictably, the region is also one of America's wealthiest and most provincial, a fact that draws – and repels – a steady stream of tourists. For every grape on the vine there seems to exist a bed and breakfast or spa, and tourism is gaining on wine production as the Wine Country's leading industry. Expect clogged highways and full hotels during peak season (May–Oct), as well as packed tastings. The main road through Napa, Hwy-29, can begin to feel like a monotonous chain of connecting towns anchored by rustic red-brick-facade antique stores.

However, there are two sides to the Napa and Sonoma valleys. There is, of course, its prominence for serious, quality **wine** experiences. Almost all of the region's many wineries offer tours and tastings, often free; when a fee is charged, it's usually small (around $5 or less), and includes the wineglass or a credit towards the purchase of a bottle, although tastings for some premium estate vintages can cost a lot more. But aside from the type and flavor of the drink, wineries all differ in what they offer visitors. Some delight enologists by explaining the process of growing grapes, some excite kids with tractor rides through the vineyard, and some please thirsty patrons with generous samples. A trip after the October crushing gives the added benefit of lower hotel rates and fewer tourists, allowing more time at tastings. The second reason to come to Wine Country is the **natural landscape**. Separated by the Mayacamas Mountains, the Napa and Sonoma valleys feature some of the most beautiful geography in the state, from the Valley of the Moon to Mount St Helena. Once you've tired of sipping, check out ballooning, biking, horse riding, hiking, and myriad historical sights, including Spanish missions and Jack London's homestead.

Around **Napa**, nothing is cheap, and the town itself can be quickly done with unless you want to board the over-hyped wine train. But many small towns

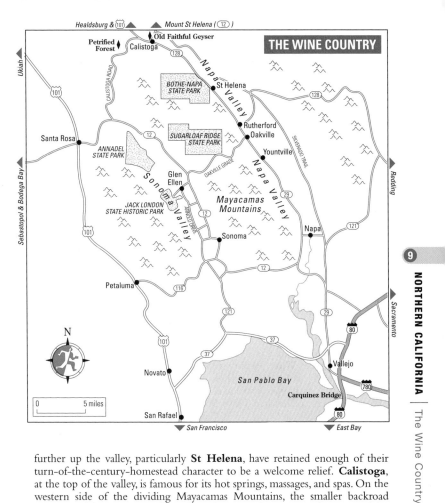

Healdsburg & 101 ▲ ▲ Mount St Helena (12)

Petrified Forest ▼ · Old Faithful Geyser
Calistoga
128
Napa Valley
Ukiah
CALISTOGA ROAD
BOTHE-NAPA STATE PARK · St Helena
128
Santa Rosa
ANNADEL STATE PARK
SUGARLOAF RIDGE STATE PARK
Rutherford
Oakville
12
OAKVILLE GRADE
Yountville
SILVERADO TRAIL
Napa Valley
Glen Ellen
Sonoma Valley
JACK LONDON STATE HISTORIC PARK
ARNOLD TRAIL
12
Mayacamas Mountains
101
29
Napa
121
Sonoma
12
Petaluma
116
121
29
N
101
37
80
37
Novato
San Pablo Bay
Vallejo
780
Carquinez Bridge
0 ____ 5 miles
San Rafael
80
▼ San Francisco   ▼ East Bay

Sebastopol & Bodega Bay
Redding
Sacramento

further up the valley, particularly **St Helena**, have retained enough of their turn-of-the-century-homestead character to be a welcome relief. **Calistoga**, at the top of the valley, is famous for its hot springs, massages, and spas. On the western side of the dividing Mayacamas Mountains, the smaller backroad wineries of the Sonoma Valley reflect the more down-to-earth nature of the place, which is both more beautiful and less crowded than its neighbor to the east. The town of **Sonoma** itself is by far the most attractive of the Wine Country communities, retaining a number of fine Mission-era structures around its gracious central plaza. **Santa Rosa**, at the north end of the valley, is the region's sole urban center, handy for budget lodgings but otherwise unremarkable.

Arrival and getting around

The Wine Country region spreads north from the top of the San Francisco Bay in two parallel, thirty-mile-long valleys, **Napa** and **Sonoma**. As long as you avoid the rush-hour traffic, it's about an hour's drive from San Francisco along either of the two main routes: through Marin County via the Golden Gate

Bridge and US-101, or through the East Bay via the Bay Bridge and I-80. Good highways ring the region, and a loop of the two valleys is conceivable in a day or so. Consider working against the flow of traffic by taking in Sonoma, Glen Ellen, and Santa Rosa first before crossing the Mayacamas and dropping into Calistoga, St Helena, and Napa.

As the Wine Country's attractions are spread over a fairly broad area, a **car** is pretty much essential. There are limited public bus options, however, from Golden Gate Transit (☎415/923-2000 or 707/541-2000), Greyhound (☎1-800/231-2222), Sonoma County Transit (☎707/576-RIDE), and the Mendocino Transit Authority (☎1-800/696-4MTA); see "Travel details", p.790, for routes. Another option for the car-less is to sign up for a Gray Line **guided bus tour** ($55; ☎415/558-9400, ⊛www.grayline.com) from San Francisco, which leaves from the Transbay Terminal at 9am. The tour covers both valleys, and visits three wineries, including favorites Sebastiani in downtown Sonoma and Sutter Home in St Helena, with a stop for lunch in pleasant Calistoga. To bypass San Francisco altogether, take the Sonoma Airporter (6 daily; 1hr 30min; $33; ☎707/938-4246 or 1-800/611-4246, reservations required) from the San Francisco airport directly to Sonoma City Hall. The bus also stops at the corner of Geary Boulevard and Park Presidio in San Francisco's Richmond District, and makes six return trips to the city daily.

Blue and Gold Fleet **ferries** travel from the Ferry Building (11 daily; $9 one-way, $14 day-pass; ☎415/773-1188, ⊛www.blueandgoldfleet.com) in San Francisco to Vallejo, and are met by hourly Napa Valley Transit buses (Mon–Sat; ☎1-800/696-6443), which continue on to the city of Napa and beyond. Blue and Gold also runs a Wine Country tour leaving daily from Pier 41 (weekdays 11am, weekends 9.30am; $53).

The three-hour **Wine Train** ($35 ticket only, $60–110 with meal; ☎707/253-2111 or 1-800/427-4124, ⊛www.winetrain.com) runs two or three times daily from Napa's station at 1275 McKinstry St, east of downtown. The ten-car train of restored 1950s Pullman cars chugs up the valley to St Helena, with a stop at Grgich Hills Cellar winery. The scenery en route is pleasant, but the ride is more of a wining-and-dining experience for older travelers than a means of transportation.

Cycling in the Wine Country

If you don't want to drive all day, **cycling** is a great way to get around. You can bring your own bike on Greyhound (though it costs $10, and the bike must be in a box), or rent one locally for around $25 per day and $120 per week. If renting, try Napa Valley Bike Tours, 4080 Byway East, Napa (☎707/255-3377 or 1-800/707-BIKE); Yountville Bike Rentals, Vintage 1870, Yountville (☎707/944-9080); St Helena Cyclery, 1156 Main St, St Helena (☎707/963-7736); Getaway Bike Shop, 1117 Lincoln Ave, Calistoga (☎707/942-0332 or 1-800/499-BIKE); or the Sonoma Cyclery, 20093 Broadway, Sonoma (☎707/935-3377).

Both valleys are generally flat, although the peaks in between are steep enough to challenge the hardiest of hill-climbers. If the main roads through the valleys are full of cars, as they are most summer weekends, try the smaller parallel routes: the **Silverado Trail** in Napa Valley and pretty **Arnold Drive** in Sonoma Valley. For the more athletically inclined, the **Oakville Grade** between Oakville in the Napa Valley and Glen Ellen in the Sonoma Valley has challenged the world's finest riders. Check with the Santa Rosa Cycling Club for itineraries, PO Box 11761, Santa Rosa, CA 95406 (☎707/544-4803).

Alternatively, plot your own route with the Bicycle Rider Directory (see Contexts, p.837).

Most local firms organize **tours**, providing bikes, helmets, food, and sag wagons in case you get worn out. In Calistoga, Getaway Adventures (☎707/942-0332 or 1-800/499-BIKE) offers trips of varying lengths, and Napa Valley Bike Tours (☎707/255-3377 or 1-800/707-BIKE, ⓦwww.napavalleybiketours.com) sets up more leisurely tours – highlighted by gourmet lunches – all over the Napa area. More ambitious (and quite expensive) overnight tours are run most weekends by Backroads Bicycle Tours, 1516 5th St, Berkeley (Mon-Fri 8am–5pm; ☎510/527-1555, ⓦwww.backroads.com).

The Wine Country by air

The most exciting way to see the region is on one of the widely touted **hot-air balloon rides**. These usually lift off at dawn, and last sixty to ninety magical minutes, winding up with a Champagne brunch. The most established of the operators is Napa Valley Balloons (☎707/253-2224 or 1-800/253-2224, ⓦwww.napavalleyballoons.com), who fly out of Yountville. Others include Balloons Above the Valley (☎707/253-2222 or 1-800/464-6824, ⓦwww.balloonsabovethevalley.com) in Napa and Sonoma County's Air Flambuoyant (☎1-800/456-4711, ⓦwww.airflambuoyant.com), who have the advantage of sending smaller groups of two to eight people aloft. The crunch comes when you realize the price – between $165 and $195 a head whichever company you use – but it really is worth every cent. Make reservations a week in advance, especially in summer, though with the increasing number of balloon companies, same-day drop-bys are a possibility.

If it's thrills you're looking for, consider taking to the air in a WWII-era propeller **biplane**. Vintage Aircraft Company, 23982 Arnold Drive, Sonoma (☎707/938-2444, ⓦwww.vintageaircraft.com), operates one- or two-person flights that take in the Sonoma Valley between loops and rolls. Choose from four stomach-churning flight patterns: Scenic, Aerobatic, Kamikaze, and Dawn Patrol. Flights take fifteen to forty minutes and cost $120–250.

Information

Not surprisingly for such a tourist-dependent area, the Wine Country has a well-developed network of **tourist information** outlets, though the rivalry between the two valleys makes it next to impossible to find out anything about Sonoma when you're in Napa, and vice versa. Both the **Napa Valley Visitors Bureau**, 1310 Napa Town Center off First Street in downtown Napa (daily 9am–5pm; ☎707/226-7459, ⓦwww.napavalley. com), and the **Sonoma Valley Visitors Bureau**, 453 1st St E at the center of Sonoma Plaza (daily 9am–5pm; ☎707/996-1090, ⓦwww.sonomavalley.com), should be able to tell you all you need to know about their respective areas; the smaller towns usually have a tourist office too. If you're keen on touring the wineries, both the above places sell handy **maps** ($3–4) giving the lowdown on the hundreds of producers.

Accommodation

Most people are content to visit the Wine Country as a day-trip from San Francisco, visiting a few of the wineries and maybe having a picnic or a meal before heading back to the city. But if you really want to absorb properly what the region has to offer, plan to spend at least one night here, pampering yourself in one of the many (generally pricey) **hotels** and **bed and breakfast inns** that provide the bulk of the area's accommodation options. In summer, the Sonoma Valley Visitors Bureau (see p.713) posts a daily list of available rooms in front of their downtown office. During summer weekends, prices can rise as much as fifty percent, so call ahead. And from November to March, lodging prices drop considerably, often up to half-off. At peak times, rooms of all descriptions get snapped up, so if you have a hard time finding a place, make use of one of the many **accommodation services**: B&B Style (☎1-800/995-8884) in Napa; Bed and Breakfast Inns of Napa Valley (☎707/944-4444); Inns of Sonoma Valley (☎707/996-INNS); Reservations Unlimited (☎707/252-1985); or the Napa Valley Visitors Bureau (☎707/226-7459, ⓦwww.napavalley.com).

Campers can find a pitch eight miles north of Sonoma at the Sugar Loaf Ridge State Park, 2605 Adobe Canyon Rd ($12; ☎707/833-5712); or outside Santa Rosa at the Spring Lake Regional Park, Newanga Avenue (May–Sept daily; Oct–April Sat & Sun; $15; ☎707/539-8092).

Hotels and motels

Astro Motel 323 Santa Rosa Ave, Santa Rosa ☎707/545-8555, ⓦwww.asterba.com/astro. No frills here, but some of the cheapest Wine Country rooms available. ❷

Calistoga Inn 1250 Lincoln Ave, Calistoga ☎707/942-4101, ⓦwww.calistogainn.com. Comfortable rooms with one bed, most with private bath, in a landmark building with its own restaurant and microbrewery right on the main street. ❹

Comfort Inn 1865 Lincoln Ave, Calistoga ☎ 707/942-9400 or 1-800/221-2222, ⓦwww.comfortinn.com. Quiet, modern motel on the edge of town with heated mineral pool, steam room, and sauna. ❸

Dr Wilkinson's Hot Springs 1507 Lincoln Ave, Calistoga ☎707/942-4102, ⓦwww.drwilkinson.com. Legendary health spa and hotel downtown. Choose from a variety of spacious, well-lit rooms with sparse furnishings, facing the courtyard or pool patio. Air conditioning and TV standard. ❺

El Bonita Motel 195 Main St, St Helena ☎707/963-3216 or 1-800/541-3284. Old roadside motel recently done up in Art Deco style, with a pool and hot tub. Surrounded by a 2.5-acre garden, the rooms here contain microwaves, refrigerators, and coffee makers. ❺

Harvest Inn 1 Main St, St Helena ☎707/963-9463 or 1-800/950-8466, ⓦwww.harvestinn.com. English Tudor cottages at the edge of a vineyard. The place to stay if you can afford it, as the rooms are huge and loaded with perks like a down feather bed, fireplace, and private terrace overlooking the garden or 14-acre vineyard. Two outdoor heated pools, whirlpool spas, and jogging/biking trails on-site make the just-completed $2 million renovation seem like money well spent. ❽

Hotel La Rose 308 Wilson St, Santa Rosa ☎707/579-3200 or 1-800/LAROSE-8, ⓦwww.hotellarose.com. Restored lodging on Railroad Square. Clean new rooms with two phone jacks in each room for Internet use. ❺

Hotel St Helena 1309 Main St, St Helena ☎707/963-4388 or 1-888/478-4355, ⓦwww.hotelsthelena.com. Slightly claustrophobic (or cozy, depending on your mood) country-style hotel right downtown. European breakfast included each morning. ❼

Jack London Lodge 13740 Arnold Drive, Glen Ellen ☎707/938-8510, ⓦwww.jacklondonlodge.com. Modern motel near the Jack London State Park, with a good restaurant and pool. A good place to try if Napa and Sonoma hotels are booked, or if you want a truly rural setting and fine stargazing. ❹

Metro Hotel 508 Petaluma Blvd S, Petaluma ☎707/773-4900, ⓦwww.metrolodging.com. Handily placed for both the Sonoma Valley and the coast, this newly renovated hotel offers unexpected touches of European style in its decor and French café at unbeatable rates. ❸

Motel 6 2760 Cleveland Ave, Santa Rosa ☎707/546-1500 or 1-800/466-8356,

△ The grapes of Wine Country

@ www.motel6.com. A little distant from the main wine areas, but good and cheap. There's another branch down the street at 3145 Cleveland Ave. ❷
Mount View Hotel and Spa 1457 Lincoln Ave, Calistoga ☎707/942-6877 or 1-800/816-6877. Lively Art Deco-style hotel with nightly jazz and a Cajun restaurant, *Catahoula*, on the ground floor. ❻, cottage with patio and hot tub ❽
Swiss Hotel 18 W Spain St, Sonoma ☎707/938-2884. A ninety-year-old landmark building situated right on the plaza with a fine restaurant. The five cramped rooms each have a view of either the garden patio or Sonoma's plaza, and come with a four-poster queen-sized bed. ❻
Triple-S Ranch 4600 Mount Home Ranch Rd, Calistoga ☎707/942-6730,
@ www.triplesranch.com. Up the hill from Calistoga, in the middle of the wilderness, these unpublicized cabins are decidedly no-frills, but clean and cheap, with a rustic steakhouse/bar on the premises. Take Hwy-128 north for one mile, turn left on Petrified Forest Road, follow it for five miles to Mount Home Road, turn right and continue one mile. ❸
Vintage Inn 6541 Washington St, Yountville ☎707/944-1112 or 1-800/351-1133, @ www .vintageinn.com. Huge luxury rooms in a modern hotel complex – all with fireplaces – plus swimming pool and free bike rental. Handy for Yountville's many fine restaurants, and great for romantic getaways. ❽
White Sulphur Springs 3100 White Sulphur Springs Rd, west of St Helena ☎707/963-8588. A relaxing retreat from the tourism of the Napa Valley – simple rooms in a rustic, newly remodeled 300-acre hillside resort, surrounded by hiking trails, with an outdoor sulphur pool, hot tub, and swimming pool. ❹
Wine Country Inn 1152 Lodi Lane, St Helena ☎707/963-7077 or 1-888/465-4608,
@ www.winecountryinn.com. Patios, strolling gardens, and vineyard-side swimming pool highlight this inn. The rooms are tasteful, open, and uncluttered with antiques. A fireplace comes with most rooms. ❼

Bed and breakfast

Ambrose Bierce Inn 1515 Main St, St Helena ☎707/963-3003, @ www.ambrosebiercehouse .com. Luxury accommodations in the 1872 house once inhabited by Bierce himself (see p.720).

Breakfast is washed down with complimentary Champagne. ❽
Christopher's Inn 1010 Foothill Blvd, Calistoga ☎707/942-0680, @ www.christophersinn.com. Small and friendly B&B with a lovely English-style garden and comfortable rooms, one block north of the center of town. ❼
Cottage Inn & Spa 302 1st St E, Sonoma ☎707/996-0719 or 1-800/944-1490, @ www .cottageinnandspa.com. A calm, downtown B&B owned by two interior designers, with hot tub and a relaxing courtyard. ❻
Churchill Manor 485 Brown St, Napa ☎707/ 253-7733, @ www.churchillmanor.com. Regal nineteenth-century mansion hidden on an unlikely suburban street. Antique furnishings, delicious breakfasts, and free tandem bikes. ❻
Cinnamon Bear 1407 Kearney St, St Helena ☎707/963-4653 or 1-888/963-4600. Quirky, sumptuously furnished inn that has long been a favorite. ❻
Gaige House Inn 13540 Arnold Drive, Glen Ellen ☎707/935-0237 or 1-800/935-0237,
@ www.gaige.com. Beautifully restored Queen Anne farmhouse in a quiet and contemporary country setting. No children under twelve permitted. ❼
Garnett Creek Inn 1139 Lincoln Ave, Calistoga ☎707/942-9797, @ www.garnettcreekinn.com. Lavishly and gaily decorated old house at the Hwy-29 end of the main street, recently converted into a B&B. Friendly and knowledgable innkeeper. ❼
Kenwood Inn & Spa 10400 Sonoma Hwy, Kenwood ☎707/833-1293 or 1-800/353-6966, @ www.kenwoodinn.com. Deluxe, beautiful, and secluded Italian-villa-style bed and breakfast with a fireplace in all suites. ❾
Ramekins Bed and Breakfast Inn 450 W Spain St, Sonoma ☎707/933-0452, @ www.ramekins .com. European-style lodging above a famous cooking school so you can bank on being fed a fine breakfast. ❻
Thistle Dew Inn 171 W Spain St, Sonoma ☎707/938-2909 or 1-800/382-7895, @ www .thistledew.com. Sonoma's most-raved-about B&B. The *Inn*, near Sonoma Plaza, features elegantly restored rooms, an amazing full breakfast and free bike rental, yet remains cheaper than many others. Some rooms come with a fireplace, private hot tub, and patio. ❻

The Napa Valley

A thirty-mile strip of gently landscaped corridors and lush hillsides, the **NAPA VALLEY** looks more like southern France than a near-neighbor of the Pacific Ocean. In spring, the valley floor is covered with brilliant wildflowers that mellow into autumnal shades by grape-harvest time. Local Native Americans named the fish-rich river which flows through the valley "Napa," meaning "plenty"; the name was adopted by Spanish missionaries in the early nineteenth century, but the natives themselves were soon wiped out. The few ranches the Spanish and Mexicans managed to establish were in turn taken over by Yankee traders, and by the 1850s, with California part of the US, the town of Napa soon became part of the Gold Rush. Its location also made it a thriving river port, sending agricultural goods to San Francisco and serving as a supply point for farmers and ranchers. The opening of White Sulphur Springs in 1852, California's first mineral springs resort, made Napa the vacation choice for San Francisco's elite. Settlers came, too, including Jacob Beringer in 1870. The rocky, well-drained soil he saw resembled that of his hometown, Mainz, Germany, and by 1875 he and his brother had established Beringer Vineyards, today America's oldest continually operating winery. Before long, Napa was bypassed by the railroads and unable to compete with other, deep-water Bay Area ports, but the area's fine climate saved it from oblivion.

Napa, Yountville, and Oakville

The town of **NAPA** itself, at the southern end of the valley, is the anomaly of the region. The highway sprawl that greets travelers is fair warning to what the rest of this 60,000-person city has to offer: but for a proud courthouse and some intriguingly decrepit old warehouses along the Napa River, it's rather lacking in character. That said, Napa is worth a quick stop to visit the **Napa Valley Visitors Bureau** (see p.713 for details). It's the most helpful in the whole valley and a good place to load up on free maps and brochures. Across the street, the Napa County Historical Society (☎707/224-1739) has free, informative materials on the region's pre-wine era. The other reason to visit is the smart new wine and arts center **COPIA**, built as the showcase for an organisation founded by Robert Mondavi, at 500 1st St (May–Sept Mon, Wed & Thurs 10am–5pm, Fri–Sun 10am–9pm; Oct–April Mon & Thurs–Sun 10am–5pm; $12.50; ☎707/259-1600, ⓦwww.copia.org). The somewhat steep entry-fee grants access to a thirty-minute video, the exclusively wine-or-food-themed art galleries, including an interesting wall display of spent matches ignited by one of the Mondavi clan, and some original Greek and Roman pottery, and the obligatory gift shop and restaurant. You can also sign up for classes and special events.

YOUNTVILLE, nine miles north on Hwy-29, is anchored by Vintage 1870, 6525 Washington St (daily 10.30am–5.30pm; ☎707/944-2451), a shopping complex in a converted winery that rents bikes, helmets, and a map of the Wine Country for $20 per day. Aside from antique shops and a few restaurants, nothing in town exerts enough pull to merit a long stop, so push on three miles to tiny **OAKVILLE**, further north along Hwy-29. Dominated by the massive Robert Mondavi winery (see box on p.719), Oakville features a dozen top-rated wineries, and almost all of them require an appointment and charge a tasting fee, ranging from $10 for a famous Silver Oak Cabernet Sauvignon to a whopping $25 for Opus One. Besides its high-caliber wines, Oakville is known for its wonderful Oakville Grocery, an unmissable deli packed with the finest local and imported foods.

Almost all of the Napa Valley's **wineries** offer tastings, though not all have tours. There are more than three hundred wineries in all, producing wines of a very high standard, so your taste should ultimately determine the ones you visit. The following selections, are some long-standing favorites, plus a few lesser-known hopefuls. Keep in mind that the intention is for you to get a sense of a winery's product, and perhaps buy some, rather than get drunk on the stuff, so don't expect more than a sip or two of any one sort – though some wineries do sell wines by the glass. If you want to buy a bottle, particularly from the larger producers, you can in fact usually get it cheaper in supermarkets than at the wineries themselves, unless you ship in bulk.

Beringer Vineyards 2000 Main St, St Helena ☏707/963-7115, ⓦwww.beringer .com. Napa Valley's most famous piece of architecture, the gothic "Rhine House," modeled on the ancestral Rhine Valley home of Jacob Beringer graces the cover of many a wine magazine. Expansive lawns and a grand tasting room, heavy on dark wood, make for a regal experience. Half-hourly 45min tours ($5) and complimentary tasting daily 9.30am–5pm, 6pm on Saturday.

Charles Krug Winery 2800 St Helena Hwy, St Helena ☏707/967-2297 or 1-888/747-5784, ⓦwww.charleskrug.com. Founded in 1861 by a Prussian immigrant, this winery was purchased by Cesare Mondavi in 1943 and is now owned by son Peter and family. Worth visiting to sample its array of wines, as Krug is renowned in Napa for its huge roster, including Chardonnay, Pinot Noir, Zinfandel, Merlot, and Cabernet. The Sangiovese Reserve is its best-rated. Tastings ($3–6) daily 10.30am–5pm.

Chateau Montelena 1429 Tubbs Lane, 2 miles north of Calistoga ☏707/942-9105, ⓦwww.montelena.com. Smaller but highly rated winery, nestled below Mount St Helena. The Cabernet Sauvignon, in particular, is gradually acquiring a fine reputation among connoisseurs. Tasting daily 10am–4pm, $10; in-depth tours with seated tasting 9.30am and 1.30pm, $25.

Clos Pégase 1060 Dunaweal Lane, Calistoga ☏707/942-4981, ⓦwww .clospegase.com. A flamboyant upstart at the north end of the valley, this high-profile winery emphasizes the links between fine wine and fine art, with a sculpture garden around buildings designed by postmodern architect Michael Graves. Tours daily at 11am and 2pm; tasting daily 10.30am–5pm, $2.50–5.

Domaine Chandon 1 California Drive, Yountville ☏707/944-2280, ⓦwww .chandon.com. Sparkling wines from this progeny of France's Moët & Chandon are known to challenge the authentic Champagnes from France. Enormous and modern, this winery and gallery is a standard to be toured by all visiting connoisseurs and features a highly regarded but expensive restaurant. Tasting summer daily 10am–6pm, winter Wednesday to Sunday 10am–6pm; tours 11am–5pm.

The Hess Collection 4411 Redwood Rd, Napa ☏707/255-1144, ⓦwww .hesscollection.com. A bit off the beaten track, this secluded winery features, in addition to its superior wines, a surprisingly good collection of modern art and a nice view of the valley. Self-guided tour. Tasting daily 10am–4pm; $3.

Mumm Napa Valley 8445 Silverado Trail, Rutherford ☏707/942-3434 or 1-800/686-6272, ⓦwww.mummnapavalley.com. Opened in 1986 by G.H. Mumm, France's renowned Champagne house, and Joseph E. Seagram & Sons, the sparkling wines from this beautifully situated winery are good, but the sweeping views of the surrounding valleys are the real reason to visit. The tours are particularly engaging and witty, and the informative guides never lose sight of the primary purpose:

fun. Tasting daily 10am–5pm, $3.50–6; hourly tours 10am–3pm, $4–12.

Napa Wine Company 7830-40 St Helena Hwy, Oakville ☎707/944-1710. Modeled after the co-operative wineries of France, the Napa Wine Company offers small-vineyard owners access to state-of-the-art crushing and fermentation machinery, and sells vintages of 50 small boutique wineries in the area. The result? Five of *Wine Spectator*'s recent "Top 10 wines." Their tasting room is one of the best – and certainly the broadest – in Wine Country; daily 10am–3.30pm; $5. Appointments recommended.

Niebaum-Coppola Estate Winery & Vineyards 1991 St Helena Hwy, Rutherford ☎707/968-1100, ⊛www .niebaum-coppola.com. In 1975, Francis Ford Coppola purchased this Inglenook estate, which was originally established by Gustav Niebaum in 1879. Memorabilia from Coppola's movie career is on display in the entryway to the massive new wine-tasting room, featuring their signature Rubicon wine. Tasting daily 10am–5pm; $7.50, includes glass; tours at 10.30am and 2.30pm.

Robert Mondavi 7801 St Helena Hwy, Oakville ☎707/251-4097 or 1-888/766-6328, ⊛www.robertmondavi.com. Long the standard-bearer for Napa Valley wines ("Bob Red" and "Bob White" are house wines at many California restaurants), they have one of the most informative and least hard-sell tours. Tours and tasting daily 10am–4.30pm, reservations recommended. Tastings from $5, tours from $10.

Silver Oak Cellars 915 Oakville Cross Rd, Oakville ☎1-800/273-8809, ⊛www .silveroak.com. Lovers of Cabernet Sauvignon mustn't miss a stop at Silver Oak, the crème de la crème of the heady red. At over $100 a bottle in the finest San Francisco restaurants, a tasting here in the fire-warmed stone-and-

wood room is not too outrageous at $10. (Plus, you get to keep the glass.) Bottle sales are limited to two per person ($60), but you can also buy a bottle of Meyer family port ($30). Tasting Mon–Sat 9am–4pm; tours Mon–Fri at 1.30pm. Reservations recommended.

Stag's Leap Wine Cellars 5766 Silverado Trail, east of Yountville ☎707/ 944-2020, ⊛www.stagsleapwinecellars .com. The winery that put Napa Valley on the international map by beating a bottle of Château Lafitte-Rothschild at a Paris tasting way back in 1976. Still quite highly rated. From Hwy-29, turn right on Yountville, then right on Silverado Trail. Tasting daily 10am–4.30pm; $5; tours by appointment.

Sterling Vineyards 1111 Dunaweal Lane, Calistoga ☎707/942-3344 or 1-800/726-6136, ⊛www.sterlingvineyards .com. Famous for the aerial tram ride that brings visitors up the 300-foot knoll to the tasting room, the view of Napa Valley from Sterling Vineyards is gorgeous. The extravagant white mansion, modeled after a monastery on the Greek island of Mykonos, is Napa's most recognizable. Tastings of their wide selection of reds and whites on the View Terrace, overlooking the spectacular scenery, is a memorable experience. Aerial tram, tasting, self-guided tour 10.30am–4.30pm, $10.

V. Sattui 1111 White Lane, St Helena ☎707/963-7774, ⊛www.vsattui.com. Small family-owned winery right off Hwy-29 with award-winning wines – the riesling and gamay rouge are particularly good. Sattui wines are only sold at the winery or through the mail. The adjoining gourmet deli has a large selection of cheeses and breads that can be enjoyed with a bottle of wine in the popular tree-shaded picnic grove. Lauded locally as the best small winery and decidedly not snobbish. Complimentary tasting daily summer 9am–6pm, winter 9am–5pm.

St Helena

The next town worth a stop is **ST HELENA**, eighteen miles from Napa, and the first of many antique-shop-filled villages you'll encounter heading north. Its main street, Hwy-29, is lined by some of the Wine Country's finest old buildings, many in pristine condition, and the town itself boasts some unlikely literary attractions. St Helena is also at the heart of a large concentration of wineries, and this combination of history and location make it the de facto tourism capital of Napa Valley, home to a large concentration of luxurious lodgings and restaurants, and with a chic appeal that you'll either love or hate.

If driving through, at least stop off to see the quaint Craftsman-style homes that line residential **Oak Avenue**, and also to see remnants of two unlikely past residents: Robert Louis Stevenson and Ambrose Bierce, both of whom lived in St Helena back in its days as a resort. The **Silverado Museum** (Tues–Sun noon–4pm; free), just off Main Street in the center of town, has a collection of over eight thousand articles relating to Stevenson, who spent just under a year in the area, honeymooning and recovering from an illness (see p.823). It's claimed to be the second most extensive collection of Stevenson artifacts in the US, though the only thing of interest to any but the most obsessed fan is a scribbled-on manuscript of *Dr Jekyll and Mr Hyde*. The other half of the building is taken up by the **Napa Valley Wine Library** (same hours), a briefly entertaining barrage of photos and clippings relating to the development of local viticulture. On the north side of town, at 1515 Main St, Bierce's former residence has been converted into the **Ambrose Bierce House** bed-and-breakfast inn (see p.716). The inn houses a very small collection of memorabilia relating to the misanthropic ghost-story writer and author of *The Devil's Dictionary*, who lived here for some fifteen years, before heading off to fight for Pancho Villa in the Mexican Revolution and mysteriously vanishing.

Calistoga and around

Beyond St Helena, towards the far northern end of the valley, the wineries become prettier and the traffic a little thinner. At the very tip of the valley, nestling at the foot of Mount St Helena, **CALISTOGA** is perhaps the most enjoyable Napa town, featuring nearly twenty wineries and some fancy bistros. The town, though, is better known for its mud baths and hot springs – and the mineral water that adorns every Californian supermarket shelf. Sam Brannan, a young Mormon entrepreneur who made a mint out of the Gold Rush, established a resort community here in 1860. In his groundbreaking speech he attempted to assert his desire to create the "Saratoga of California," modeled upon the Adirondack gem, but in the event got tongue-tied and coined the town's unique name.

Calistoga's main attraction, then as now, is the opportunity to soak in the soothing hot water that bubbles up here from deep in the earth. A multitude of **spas** and volcanic **mud baths**, together with a homely and health-conscious atmosphere, beckon city dwellers and tourists alike. The extravagant might enjoy *Dr. Wilkinson's Hot Springs*, 1507 Lincoln Ave (treatments from $65; ☎707/942-4102, ⓦwww.drwilkinson.com), a legendary health spa and hotel whose heated mineral water and volcanic ash tension-relieving treatments have been overseen by the same family for almost fifty years. *Mount View Spa*, 1457 Lincoln Ave (☎707/942-5789 or 1-800/772-8838, ⓦwww.mountviewspa.com), can soothe you with a variety of combined herbal and mud treatments for the best part of $100 and offers shorter but cheaper hydrotherapy sessions. If swaddled luxury isn't what you're after, a number of more down-to-earth establishments are spread along and off the mile-long main drag, Lincoln Avenue. *Golden Haven Hot Springs Spa and Resort*, 1713 Lake St (☎707/942-6793, ⓦwww.goldenhaven.com), for example, offers a one-hour mud bath, hot mineral Jacuzzi, and blanket wrap for $49–65 and *Calistoga Spa*, 1006 Washington St (☎707/942-6269 or 1-866/822-5772, ⓦwww .calistogaspa.com), has similar rates. If that's still too expensive, ask a local resident to spray you down with their garden hose – although even that might cost a few bucks given Calistoga water's restorative reputation.

Calistoga has one standard tourist attraction in the shape of the **Sharpsteen Museum and Sam Brannan Cottage**, 1113 Washington St (daily 11am–4pm; free; ☎707/942-5911). Founded by long-serving Disney producer Ben Sharpsteen, the quaint little museum contains some of his personal effects, including his Oscar for the pearl-diving film *Ama Girls*, as well as a model of the original resort and lots of biographical material on Sam Brannan, plus a full-size re-creation of his cottage. You can check what else is going on in town and get maps at the friendly **Chamber of Commerce**, 1458 Lincoln Ave (Mon–Fri 9am–5pm; ☎707/942-6333, ⓦwww.calistogafun.com).

Heading northwest out of town on Hwy-128 takes you up the ridge of the **Mayacamas**, a picturesque and steep drive that winds to the summit and spirals southwest, depositing you in Santa Rosa. More evidence of Calistoga's lively underground activity can be seen on this route at the **Old Faithful Geyser** (daily 9am–6pm; $6), two miles north of town on Tubbs Lane, which spurts boiling water sixty feet into the air at nine- to forty-minute intervals, depending on the time of year. The water source was discovered during oil-drilling here in the 1920s, when search equipment struck a force estimated to be up to a thousand pounds per square foot; the equipment was blown away and, despite heroic efforts to control it, the geyser has continued to go off like clockwork ever since. Landowners finally realized that they'd never tame it and turned it into a high-yield tourist attraction, using the same name as the famous spouter at Yellowstone National Park. Just south of the geyser, stylish Venetian artist Carlo Marchiori conducts weekly guided tours of his imaginatively decorated house, **Ca'Toga** (May–Oct Sat only 11am; $20). The Palladian villa is full of delicate whimsy – one room is painted as if you are a bird in a cage, another is adorned with painted cows – and the grounds secrete mock ruined temples, a Buddhist corner, and a shell-encrusted cave. An idea of his art can be gleaned, and tours arranged, through his gallery at 1206 Cedar St (☎707/942-3900).

The **Petrified Forest** (daily 10am–5pm; $5; ☎707/942-6667), located five miles west of Calistoga, is a popular local tourist trap, but there's little worth stopping here for unless you're a geologist or really into hardened wood. After an entire redwood grove was toppled during an eruption of Mount St Helena some three million years ago, the forest here was petrified by the action of the silica-laden volcanic ash as it gradually seeped into the decomposing fibers of the uprooted trees.

Mount St Helena

The clearest sign of the local volcanic unrest is the massive conical mountain that marks the north end of the Napa Valley, **MOUNT ST HELENA**, some eight miles north of Calistoga. The 4343-foot summit is worth a climb for its great views – on a very clear day you can see Point Reyes and the Pacific Coast to the west, San Francisco to the south, the towering Sierra Nevada to the east, and impressive Mount Shasta to the north. It is, however, a long steep climb (ten miles round-trip) and you need to set off early in the morning to enjoy it – take plenty of water (and maybe a bottle of local wine).

The mountain and most of the surrounding land is protected and preserved as the **Robert Louis Stevenson Park** (daily 8am–sunset; free), though the connection is fairly weak: Stevenson spent his honeymoon here in 1880 in a bunkhouse with Fanny Osborne, recuperating from tuberculosis and exploring the valley – a plaque marks the spot where his bunkhouse once stood. Little else about the park's winding roads and dense shrub growth evokes its former notoriety, though it's a pretty enough place to take a break from the wineries and have a picnic. In Stevenson's novel, *Silverado Squatters*, he describes the highlight of the honeymoon as the day he managed to taste eighteen of local wine baron Jacob Schram's Champagnes in one sitting. Quite an extravagance, especially considering that Schramsberg Champagne is held in such high esteem that Richard Nixon took a few bottles with him when he went to visit Chairman Mao.

The Sonoma Valley

On looks alone, the crescent-shaped **SONOMA VALLEY** beats Napa Valley hands down. This smaller, altogether more rustic valley curves between oak-covered mountain ranges from the small town of **Sonoma** a few miles north along Hwy-12 to the hamlet of **Glen Ellen** and **Jack London State Park**, and ends at the booming bedroom community of **Santa Rosa**. The area is known as the "Valley of the Moon," a label that's mined by tour operators for its connection to long-time resident Jack London, whose book of the same name retold a Native American legend about how, as you move through the valley, the moon seems to rise several times from behind the various peaks. The area has long been a favorite with visitors: Spain, England, Russia, and Mexico have all raised their flags in Sonoma, proclaiming it their own. The US took over in 1846 during the Bear Flag Revolt against Mexico in Sonoma's central plaza and annexed all of California.

The Bear Flag Revolt

Sonoma Plaza was the sight of the **Bear Flag Revolt**, the 1846 action that propelled California into independence from Mexico, and then statehood. In this much-romanticized episode, American settlers in the region, who had long lived in uneasy peace under the Spanish and, later, Mexican rulers, were threatened with expulsion from California along with all other non-Mexican immigrants. In response, a band of thirty armed settlers – including the infamous John Fremont and Kit Carson – descended upon the disused and unguarded *presidio* at Sonoma, taking the retired and much-respected commander, Colonel Mariano Guadalupe Vallejo, as their prisoner. Ironically, Vallejo had long advocated the American annexation of California and supported the aims of his rebel captors, but he was nonetheless bundled off to Sutter's Fort in Sacramento and held there while the militant settlers declared California an independent republic. The Bear Flag, which served as the model for the current state flag, was fashioned from a "feminine undergarment and muslin petticoat" and painted with a grizzly bear and single star. Raised on Sonoma Plaza, where a small plaque marks the spot today, the Bear Flag flew over the Republic of California for a short time. Three weeks later, the US declared war on Mexico and, without firing a shot, took possession of the entire Pacific Coast. While far from a frontier town now, the town once had a much wilder side and in fact gave the English language a slang word for prostitutes. Not long after the Bear Flag revolt, General Lee Hooker arrived, bringing along a group of ladies employed to cheer up the troops. The ladies soon became known as "Hooker's girls," and then simply, "hookers."

Sonoma Valley's **wineries** are generally smaller and more casual than their Napa counterparts, even though the Sonoma Valley fathered the wine industry from which Napa derives its fame. Colonel Agostin Haraszthy first started planting grapes here in the 1850s, and his Buena Vista Winery in Sonoma still operates today.

Sonoma

Behind a layer of somewhat touristy stores and restaurants, **SONOMA** retains a good deal of its Spanish and Mexican architecture. The town's charm emanates from the grassy square centering downtown, where wild chickens – escapees from an attempt to turn the bordering **Sonoma State Historic Park** into a living nineteenth-century exhibit – patrol the grounds. These feathered fugitives are indicative of the town's welcoming and relaxed feel, although as a popular retirement spot with a median age of about fifty, it's not exactly bubbling with action.

Today, a number of historic buildings and relics preserve history in the sprawling Sonoma State Historic Park ($1 combined entry to all sites; all daily 10am–5pm). The restored **Mission San Francisco Solano de Sonoma** was the last and northernmost of the California missions, and the only one established in Northern California by nervous Mexican rulers fearful of expansionist Russian fur traders. Half a mile west stands the **General Vallejo Home**, the leader's ornate former residence, dominated by decorated filigreed eaves and slender Gothic-revival arched windows. The chalet-style storehouse next door has been turned into a **museum** of artifacts from the general's reign.

There's more to Sonoma than historic buildings, though, and relaxing coffee shops, great restaurants, rare bookstores, and a 1930s-era movie house ring the plaza, making Sonoma a nice town to come back to after a day in the vineyards. To see Sonoma at its unspoiled best, get out of the car and ride across the Valley of the Moon on **horseback**. The Sonoma Cattle Co. (℡707/996-8566) offers two-hour rides, weather permitting, for $55.

Glen Ellen and Jack London State Park

Continuing north on Hwy-12, beautiful winding roads lead to the cozy hamlet of **GLEN ELLEN**, five miles from Sonoma, and more interestingly, **JACK LONDON STATE PARK** (daily 9.30am-6pm; $3 per car). A half-mile up London Ranch Road past the Benziger Family winery, the state park sits on the 140 acres of ranchland the famed author of *The Call of the Wild* owned with his wife Charmian. A mile walk through the woods leads to the ruins of the **Wolf House**, which was to be the London ancestral home: "My house will be standing, act of God permitting, for a thousand years," wrote the author. But in 1913, a month before they were to move in, the house burned to the ground, sparing only the boulder frame. Mounted blueprints point out the splendor that was to be: the mansion contained a manuscript room, sleeping tower, gun room, and indoor reflecting pool. Nearby lies the final resting place of London – a red boulder from the house's ruins under which his wife sprinkled his ashes. Just off the parking lot, the **House of Happy Walls** (daily 10am–5pm; free) is a jewel of a London museum, housing an interesting collection of souvenirs he picked up traveling the globe. Manuscripts, rejection letters (over 600 before he was published the first time), and the note explaining his and Charmian's resignation from the Socialist Party fill the exhibits, along with reproductions of the Londons' rooms and plenty of photographs. A nearby trail leads past a picnic ground to **London's Cottage** (daily, 10am–4pm; free),

NORTHERN CALIFORNIA | The Sonoma Valley

Around forty fine **wineries** are scattered all over the Sonoma Valley, but there's a good concentration in a well-signposted group a mile east of Sonoma Plaza, down East Napa Street. Some are within walking distance, but often along quirky back-roads, so take a winery map from the tourist office and follow the signs closely. If you're tired of driving around, visit the handy Wine Exchange of Sonoma, 452 1st St E (☎707/938-1794), a commercial tasting room where, for a small fee, you can sample the best wines from all over California. Local winemakers congregate here after 5pm for a change in beverage, enjoying the bar's selection of 300 beers.

Bartholomew Park Winery 1000 Vineyard Lane ☎707/935-9511, ⓦwww .bartholomewparkwinery.com. This lavish Spanish-colonial building is surrounded by some great topiary in the gardens and extensive vineyards. The wines are relatively inexpensive vintages that appeal to the pocket and palate alike; if you're looking to buy a case, this one's a safe bet. There's a good little museum, too, of regional history that also provides an introduction to local viticulture. The winery is set 100 yards from a replica of Haraszthy's Palladian villa (the original burned down) dating from 1862. Inside, the furnishings and fixtures give a sense of what being a wine-maker in Napa used to entail. The villa is open Wednesday, Saturday, and Sunday from 10am–4pm (☎707/938-2444). Self-guided tours of the winery and $3 tastings daily 10am–4.30pm.

Benziger Family Winery 1883 London Ranch Rd, Glen Ellen ☎707/935-3000, ⓦwww.benziger.com. Beautiful vineyard perched on the side of an extinct volcano next to Jack London State Park. $5 tram tours through the fields with emphasis on viticulture five or six times daily or self-guided tour introducing trellis techniques. Tastings daily 10am–5pm; free to $10, depending on wines sampled.

Buena Vista Winery 18000 Old Winery Rd ☎707/252-7117 or 1-800/926-1266, ⓦwww.buenavistawinery.com. Oldest and grandest of the wineries, established in 1857, whose wine is re-establishing a good reputation after some slim years. The tasting room, a restored state historical landmark, features a small art gallery. Free tasting daily 10am–5pm; tours daily at 11am and 2pm.

Chateau St Jean 8555 Sonoma Hwy, Kenwood ☎707/833-4134 or 1-800/ 543-7572, ⓦwww.chateaustjean.com.

Attractive estate with an overwhelming aroma of wine throughout the buildings. Quirky tower to climb from where you can admire the view. Self-guided tours. Free tasting daily 10am–5pm.

Gundlach-Bundschu 2000 Denmark St, Sonoma ☎707/938-5277 ⓦwww .gundlach-bundschu.com. Set back about a mile away from the main cluster, Gun-Bun, as it's known to locals, is highly regarded, having stealthily crept up from the lower ranks of the wine league to the point where it now regularly steals from the big names. The plain, functional building is deceptive – this is premium stuff and definitely not to be overlooked. The winery also hosts various theatrical, cinema, and musical events throughout the summer. Free tasting daily 11am–4.30pm; tours Saturday & Sunday only.

Ravenswood 18701 Gehricke Rd, Sonoma ☎707/933-2332 or 1-888/669-4679, ⓦwww.ravenswood-wine.com. Noted for their "gutsy, unapologetic" Zinfandel and advertising a "no wimpy" approach to the wine business, the staff at this unpretentious winery is particularly friendly and easygoing. The tasting room is well-known to locals for its summer barbecues. Tastings daily 10am–4.30pm; 10.30am tour by appointment. Tasting and/or tour $4.

Sebastiani Vineyards & Winery 389 4th St E, Sonoma ☎707/938-5532 or 1-800/888-5532, ⓦwww.sebastiani.com. One of California's oldest family wineries, only four blocks from central Sonoma, it now boasts a newly renovated hospitality center, while the rest of the estate is being returned to its original appearance. There is another tasting room on the central square at 103 W Napa St (☎707/933-3291). Free tasting and tours via tram every half-hour. Daily 10am–5pm.

where he died. A video display gives background to his life, his wife, and the era. West of the cottage, a trail leads one mile toward the mountains and into the woods, ending at the lake London had built so he and Charmian could fish and swim. Bring a bottle of wine and soak in the sunny charm; given the hoopla of the Wine Country, the usually uncrowded museum and lovely park grounds feel like an oasis of tranquility.

Santa Rosa

Sixty miles due north of San Francisco on US-101, and about twenty miles from Sonoma on Hwy-12, **SANTA ROSA**, the largest town in Sonoma County, sits at the top end of the Sonoma Valley and is more or less the hub of this part of the Wine Country. It's a very different world from the indulgence of other Wine Country towns, however; much of it is given over to shopping centers and roadside malls. In an attempt to form a central pedestrian-only hub, **Historic Railroad Square** – a strip of red-brick-facade boutiques – has been developed, but it will never be mistaken for St Helena's Main Street or Sonoma Plaza. With the real estate prices higher than ever in the Bay Area, Santa Rosa is exploding with growth, making it both a bedroom community for San Francisco and site of the Wine Country's cheapest lodging, with major hotel and motel chains located around town. It also has a decent selection of restaurants and bars. Full listings of what the town has to offer can be found at the **CVB**, 9 4th St (Mon–Fri 8.30am–5pm, Sat–Sun 10am–3pm; ☎707/577-8674 or 1-800/404-ROSE, ⓦwww.visitsantarosa.com).

Probably the most interesting thing about Santa Rosa is that it was the home-town of Raymond Chandler's fictional private eye Philip Marlowe. You can kill an hour or two at the **Luther Burbank Home and Gardens**, at the junction of Santa Rosa and Sonoma avenues (Tues–Sun 10am–3.30pm; free), where California's best-known horticulturist is remembered in the house where he lived and in the splendid gardens in which he created some of his most unusual hybrids. **The Redwood Empire Ice Arena**, 1667 W Steele Lane (☎707/546-7147), was built by *Peanuts* creator Charles Schulz as a gift to the community. The arena actually comprises two buildings: the ice skating rink and Snoopy's Gallery, a museum/gift shop of all things Peanuts (daily 10am–6pm; free; ☎707/546-3385) and a lasting tribute to the much-loved Schulz, who died at the turn of the millennium.

One enterprise few people would expect to find tucked away in the Wine Country is a full-blown **wildlife refuge**, yet spreading over four hundred acres of the pristine hills between the two valleys, five miles northeast of Santa Rosa, is **Safari West**, 3115 Porter Creek Rd (☎707/579-2551 or 1-800/616-2695, ⓦwww.safariwest.com). Set up in 1989 by Peter Lang, son of *Daktari* producer Otto, the refuge runs breeding programs for hundreds of rare mammal and bird species. Three-hour African-style **jeep tours** (daily 9am, noon & 3pm in summer; 10am & 2pm in winter; $48) take you through vast open compounds of herd animals, and you can wander at leisure past large cages of cheetah and primates or the leafy aviary, while expert guides supply detailed background on the furry and feathered inhabitants. You can even feed the giraffe, if you're lucky. Accommodation in genuine African luxury tents, hung on stilted wooden decks, is available for a princely $225 per unit and filling buffet meals are served in the mess tent.

Eating and drinking

Culinary satisfaction looms around every corner in the Wine Country. California cuisine is almost standard in both valleys, and freshness and innovative presentation are very much the order of the day. **Yountville**, in particular, is little more than a string of high-style restaurants, any of which is up there with the best San Francisco has to offer, with prices to match. **St Helena** and **Calistoga**, though more low-key, are both gourmet paradises. **Sonoma**, too, has its share and is strong on Italian food, while the size of **Santa Rosa** allows for a good deal of diversity. **Bars** are mostly locals' or immigrant Hispanic workers' hangouts, and nightlife nearly non-existent, perhaps a result of the free booze on offer from the wineries.

Inexpensive restaurants, cafés, and takeouts

Arrigoni's Deli 701 4th St, Santa Rosa ☏707/545-1297. The place to go for picnic supplies, serving an array of gourmet meats, cheeses, and other savories.

Bosko's Ristorante 1364 Lincoln Ave, Calistoga ☏707/942-9088. Standard Italian restaurant preparing moderately priced, fresh pasta dishes. Cheerful, and popular with families.

Café Citti 9049 Sonoma Hwy, Kenwood ☏707/833-2690. Small, inexpensive trattoria with great Italian food and an intimate, yet casual atmosphere.

Café Sarafornia 1413 Lincoln Ave, Calistoga ☏707/942-0555. Famous for delicious and enormous breakfasts and lunches with lines around the block on weekends. Let the owner talk your ear off.

The Coffee Garden 421 1st St W, Sonoma ☏707/996-6645. Fresh sandwiches are served on the back patio of this 150-year-old adobe, which was converted into a café with small gift shop.

The Diner 6476 Washington St, Yountville ☏707/944-2626. Start the day's wine-touring off right, with good strong coffee and brilliant breakfasts where locals and day-trippers mix. Open 8am–3pm for breakfast and lunch, and 5.30–9.30pm for flavorful Mexican dinners. Closed Mondays.

Ford's Café 22900 Broadway, Sonoma ☏707/938-9811. Hearty, working-class American food served to locals in this out-of-the-way diner. The generous breakfasts are worth the trip.

Gary Chu's 611 5th St, Santa Rosa ☏707/526-5840. Large helpings of high-quality Chinese at very reasonable prices.

La Casa 121 E Spain St, Sonoma ☏707/996-3406. Friendly, festive, and inexpensive Mexican restaurant just across from the Sonoma Mission. Enjoy an enchilada on the sunny outdoor patio.

Lo Spuntino 400 1st St E, Sonoma ☏707/935-5656. Spacious café and deli on the plaza; good for picnic supplies.

The Model Bakery 1357 Main St, St Helena ☏707/963-8192. Local hangout serving the best bread in Napa Valley, as well as sandwiches and pizza.

PJ's Café 1001 2nd St, Napa ☏707/224-0607. A Napa institution, open 8am to 10pm every day for pancakes, pasta, pizzas, and sandwiches.

Puerto Vallerta 1473 Lincoln Ave, Calistoga ☏707/942-6563. Heaps of tasty and genuine Mexican grub can be consumed in the shady courtyard of this establishment, tucked in beside the Cal-Mart supermarket.

Soo Yuan 1354 Lincoln Ave, Calistoga ☏707/942-9404. Good-value Mandarin and Szechuan cuisine in a small but friendly place on the main street.

The Spot One mile south of St Helena on Hwy-29 ☏707/963-2844. This tacky roadside diner is conveniently located for lunchtime on the cheap.

Upmarket restaurants

Brannan's Grill 1374 Lincoln Ave, Calistoga ☏707/942-2233. Pecan-stuffed quail, fresh steamed oysters, and a wonderful wooden interior make this rather expensive, high-profile eatery worth a visit.

Café LaHaye 140 E Napa St, Sonoma ☏707/935-5994. Only eleven tables, and always packed for its lovely, lively interior and tasty Italian food.

Celadon 1040 Main St, Napa ☏707/254-9690. Quality international nouvelle cuisine with dishes such as truffle and honey-glazed pork chops or Algerian-style lamb in an intimate setting.

Cole's Chop House 1122 Main St, Napa ☏707/224-6328. This is the place to come for huge chunks of well-prepared red meat. Very spacious inside and top service but rather a stilted atmosphere.

The General's Daughter 400 W Spain St, Sonoma ☎707/938-4004. Moderately priced California/Mediterranean hybrid dishes like wild mushroom ravioli, salmon and asparagus, and pork tenderloin in a Victorian building formally owned by General Vallejo's daughter.

The Girl & The Fig 110 W Spain St, Sonoma ☎707/938-3634. Recently moved from Glen Ellen to the ground floor of the *Sonoma Hotel*, this well-known restaurant offers French dinners and week-end brunch from a menu as eclectic as its name and pricey to match.

Glen Ellen Inn 13670 Arnold Drive, Glen Ellen ☎707/996-6409. Husband-and-wife team cook and serve slightly pricey gourmet dishes in an inti-mate, romantic dining room with half a dozen tables. Daily 5.30–9.30pm.

Mustards Grill 7399 St Helena (Hwy-29), Yountville ☎707/944-2424. Credited with starting the late-1980s trend toward "grazing" food, emphasizing tapas-like tidbits rather than main meals. Reckon on spending $15–20 a head and waiting for a table if you come on a weekend.

Pairs Parkside Cafe 1420 Main St, St Helena ☎707/963-7566. Tasty Cal-Asian cuisine in a funky and cozy café setting in the heart of St Helena. The chefs suggest a specific Napa Valley wine to go with every dish. Closed Tuesday.

Pinot Blanc 641 Main St, St Helena ☎707/963-6191. California fusion cuisine prepared by the famous chef Sean Knight, and a nearly California-exclusive wine list. Founded by Joachim Splichal, a noteworthy Los Angeles chef.

Rutherford Grill 1180 Rutherford Rd, Rutherford ☎707/963-1920. Large portions of basic contem-porary American food – the mash potatoes should not be missed – served in a handsome new dining room. Locals recently voted it both the home of the best martini and best place to meet a member of the opposite sex. A coincidence?

Tra Vigne 1050 Charter Oak Ave, St Helena ☎707/963-4444. Just north of town, but it feels as if you've been transported to Tuscany. Excellent food and fine wines, served up in a lovely vine-covered courtyard or elegant dining room, but you pay for the privilege. They also have a small deli, where you can pick up picnic goodies.

Wappo Bar Bistro 1226 Washington St, Calistoga ☎707/942-4712. Creative cuisine featuring unheard-of combinations like *chili rellenos* with walnut pomegranate sauce and roasted rabbit with potato gnocchi make this restaurant a culinary adventure.

Wine Spectator's Greystone Restaurant at the Culinary Institute of America 2555 Main St, St Helena ☎707/967-1010. California/ Mediterranean cuisine served in an elegant ivy-walled mansion just outside of town, with a taste-fully wacky Art Deco interior. Reasonably priced considering the delicious, large portions of chick-en, duck, fish, and venison.

Zuzu 829 Main St, Napa ☎707/224-5885. Not the place to come if ravenous, but this popular new tapas bar offers tasty fare and a good wine list in its trendy interior.

Bars

Amigos Grill and Cantina 19315 Sonoma Hwy, Sonoma ☎707/939-0743. Award-winning mar-garitas using your choice of one of 20 tequilas and a home-made mix.

Ana's Cantina 1205 Main St, St Helena ☎707/963-4921. Long-standing, down-to-earth saloon and Mexican restaurant with billiards and darts tournaments.

Compadres Bar and Grill 6539 Washington St, Yountville ☎707/944-2406. Outdoor patio seating and amazing martinis and margaritas, with free salsa and chips.

Downtown Joe's 902 Main St at Second, Napa ☎707/258-2337. One of Napa's most popular and lively spots for sandwiches, ribs, and pasta, with outdoor dining by the river and beer brewed on the premises. About the only place in town open until midnight and a good spot to meet locals.

Murphy's Irish Pub 464 1st St E, Sonoma ☎707/935-0660. Small bar with an eclectic interi-or and a few outdoor tables serving basic pub grub and European beers.

Third Street Aleworks 610 3rd St, Santa Rosa ☎707/523-3060. Frequent live music and hearty American grub like burgers and pizza, washed down with microbrewed beer, are the order of the day at this lively joint.

The northern coast

The fog-bound towns and windswept, craggy beaches of the **NORTHERN COAST** couldn't be farther removed from Southern California's sandy, sunny strip of ocean. Stretching north of San Francisco to the Oregon border, the northern coast is better suited for hiking than sunbathing, with a climate of cool temperatures year-round and a huge network of national, state, and regional **parks** preserving magnificent redwood trees. **Wildlife** thrives here and is always in view, from seals lounging on rocks around Goat Rock Beach in the south to elk chomping on berry bushes in the north, all against a backdrop of spectacular scenery. Far rarer fauna has been spotted up here as well: the legendary Bigfoot supposedly leaves footprints through the forest, and Ewoks once battled the Galactic Empire under the direction of Star Wars creator George Lucas, who used areas north of Orick as the set for *The Return of the Jedi*.

The only way to see the coast properly is on the painfully slow but visually magnificent Hwy-1, which hugs the coast for two hundred miles through the wild counties of **Sonoma** and **Mendocino**, before turning sharply inland at Legget to join US-101 and **Humboldt County**. The hundred miles of wild coastline Hwy-1 never reaches has become known, appropriately, as the **Lost Coast**, a virgin territory of campsites and trails. If you are heading for the coast from the Wine Country, a pleasant route is via the quieter wineries of the **Russian River Valley**, or you can take US-101 and detour inland further north to placid **Clear Lake**, before cutting across to Mendocino. North of here, the redwoods take over, blanketing the landscape all the way to Oregon, doubling as raw material for the huge logging industries (the prime source of employment in the area) and the region's prime tourist attraction, most notably in the **Redwood National Park**. **Eureka**, the coast's largest – and most boring – city, is neighbored by lively **Arcata**, home to **Humboldt State University** and thousands of Birkenstock sandals. The last stretch of redwood coast before the Oregon state line lies in **Del Norte County**, whose functional seat of **Crescent City** offers little to detain the visitor for long.

You'll need to be fairly independent to **get around** this region: only one Amtrak Thruway and two Greyhound buses a day travel the length of US-101, which parallels the coastal highway, but they don't link up with the coast until Eureka, far to the north. Otherwise most visitors travel by car and should, in summertime, expect legions of slow-moving campers trying to negotiate the two-lane road's hairpin curves.

The Sonoma Coast and Russian River Valley

Hwy-1 twists and winds along the edge of the **SONOMA COAST** through persistent fog that, once burned off by the sun, reveals oyster beds, seal breeding grounds, and twenty-foot-high rhododendrons. A spectacular introduction to the northern coast, Sonoma County's western rim is never short on visitors due to its proximity to San Francisco. But tourist activity is confined to a few narrow corridors at the height of summer, leaving behind a network of north coast villages and backwater wineries that for most of the year are all but asleep. The coast is colder and lonelier than the villages along the valley, and at some point most people head inland for a change of scene and a break from the pervasive fog. What both areas have in common, though, is a reluctance to change. As wealthy San Franciscans cast their eyes towards the north for potential second-home sites, the California Coastal Commission's policy of beach access for all keeps the architects at bay, making the Sonoma coast one of the few remaining undeveloped coastal areas in California; the southern third of the coast is almost entirely state beach.

At the tiny town of Jenner, Hwy-116 heads inland along the Russian River, leading to the **RUSSIAN RIVER VALLEY**, an affluent summer resort area popular for its canoeing, swimming, wineries, and gay resorts.

The Sonoma coast

Bodega Bay, about sixty-five miles north of San Francisco, is the first Sonoma County village you reach on Hwy-1. Pomo and Miwok Indians populated the area peacefully for centuries, until Captain Lt Juan Francisco de la Bodega y Quadra Mollineda anchored his ship in the bay and "discovered" it in 1775. Hitchcock filmed the waterside scenes for *The Birds* here; an unsettling number of them are still squawking down by the harbor. Not so long ago, a depleted fishing industry, a couple of restaurants, and some isolated seaside cottages were all there was to Bodega Bay, but in recent years San Franciscans have got wind of its appeal and holiday homes and modern retail developments now crowd the waterside.

If you're traveling the whole coast, Bodega Bay makes a tolerable first stop (although better beaches, weather, and services exist in Jenner, fourteen miles north). Of several **places to stay**, the *Bodega Harbor Inn*, 1345 Bodega Ave (☎707/875-3594, ⓦwww.bodegaharborinn.com; ❸), is the best value in town, while the extremely comfortable *Bodega Coast Inn*, 521 Hwy-1 (☎707/875-2217 or 1-800/346-6999, ⓦwww.bodegacoastinn.com; ❺), has newly renovated rooms with fireplaces. Reservations are pretty much essential in summer and on weekends throughout the year. If you don't have a reservation, the **Sonoma Coast Visitor Center** (Mon–Thurs 10am–6pm, Fri & Sat 10am–8pm, Sun 11am–7pm; ☎707/875-3866, ⓦwww.bodegabay.com), 850 Hwy-1, has information on room availability throughout the area. **Campsites** are available at the *Bodega Dunes Campground* (☎707/875-3483, reserve through ParkNet ☎800/444-7275; $12), two miles north of the village on Hwy-1 at the base of a windy peninsula known as **Bodega Head**, laid out across sand dunes that end in coastal cliffs behind the beach. There are **hiking** and **horseriding** trails around the dunes behind the beach – though in summer these tend to be packed with picnicking families, and for less crowded routes you should head up the coast.

If you are looking for a **restaurant**, *Breakers Café*, 1400 Hwy-1 (☎707/875-2513), serves nouvelle Californian seafood plates for little over $15, while *Brisas del Mar*, 2001 Hwy-1 (☎707/875-9190), does good inexpensive pastas and Mexican dishes, as well as seafood. *Lucas Wharf*, 595 Hwy-1 (☎707/875-3522), specializes in crab (mid-Nov–June) and salmon (mid-May–Sept) dishes at around $20, and has a good menu of local wines. As part of the upscale *Inn at the Tides*, the equally pricey *Tides Wharf and Restaurant*, 835 Hwy-1 (☎707/875-3652), gives a good viewpoint for watching fishing boats unload their catch. Breakfasts and lunches from $6 and rather costlier dinners can be enjoyed at the *Sandpiper Restaurant*, 1410 Bay Flat Rd (☎707/875-2278). Nearby, at 1580 Eastshore Rd, *The Seagull Café* (☎707/875-8871) offers a more limited menu of eggs and hot sandwiches. Bodega Bay Surf Shack in Pelican Plaza, 1400 Hwy-1 (☎707/875-3944), rents out bikes, kayaks, and windsurfing equipment at standard rates. For a **tour** of the bay, head over to Will's Fishing Adventures, 1580 Eastshore Rd (☎707/875-2323; $12), where boats leave daily at 6pm, and tour the locations where *The Birds* was filmed, the area where Sir Francis Drake supposedly really landed, and Bodega Rock, home to sea lions and oceanic birds.

North of Bodega Bay to Jenner

North of Bodega Bay, along the **Sonoma Coast State Beach** (actually a series of beaches separated by rocky bluffs), the coastline coarsens and the trails become more dramatic. It's a wonderful stretch to hike – quite possible in a day for an experienced hiker – although the shale formations are often unstable and you must stick to the trails, which are actually quite demanding. Of Sonoma's thirteen miles of beaches, the finest are surfer-friendly **Salmon Creek Beach**, a couple of miles north of Bodega Bay and site of the park headquarters, and **Goat Rock Beach**, at the top of the coast. The latter offers the chance to get close to harbor seals. For **horseback riding**, *Chanslor Guest Ranch*, 2660 Hwy-1 (☎707/875-3333, ⊛www.chanslor.com), requires a two-person minimum for their selection of rides, which range from a thirty-minute wetlands jaunt ($25 per person) to ninety-minute rides along Salmon Creek and on the beach of Sand Dune State Park (both $50 per person). Located on the same property is a B&B (☎707/875-/875-2721; ❺), and staying here takes ten percent off the price of a ride, and is worth it only if you plan on doing a lot of riding.

Campgrounds are dotted along the coast (call ☎707/875-3483 for information), but the best **places to stay** are in the tiny seaside village of **JENNER**, which marks the turnoff for the Russian River Valley – a small, friendly place where you can stay in the salubrious cabins and cottages of *The Jenner Inn*, 10400 Hwy-1 (☎707/865-2377 or 1-800/732-2377, ⊛www.jennerinn.com; rooms ❺, cottages ❻, and suites ❽), or the comfortable *River's End Resort* (☎707/865-2484; ❾). The **Russian River** joins the ocean in Jenner, and a massive sand spit at its mouth provides a breeding ground for harbor seals from March to June. The *Seagull Deli*, 10439 Hwy-1, provides wonderful clam chowder on a deck along the rivermouth to accompany your viewing.

Fort Ross and beyond

North of Jenner, the population evaporates and Hwy-1 turns into a slalom course of hairpin bends and steep inclines for twelve miles as far as **Fort Ross State Historic Park**, which houses the **Fort Compound** (daily 10am–4.30pm; free). At the start of the nineteenth century, San Francisco was still the northernmost limit of Spanish occupation in Alta California, and from 1812 to 1841 Russian fur traders quietly settled this part of the coast, clubbing the Californian sea otter almost to extinction, building a fort to use as a trading outpost, and growing crops for the Russian stations in Alaska. Officially they posed no territorial claims, but by the time the Spanish had gauged the extent of the settlement, the fort was heavily armed and vigilantly manned with a view to continued eastward expansion. The Russians traded here for thirty years until over-hunting and the failure of their shipbuilding efforts led them to pull out of the region. They sold the fort and chattels to one John Sutter in 1841, who moved them to his holdings in the Sacramento Valley, so all you see is an accomplished reconstruction built using the original tech-

niques. Among the empty bunkers and storage halls, the most interesting buildings are the Russian Orthodox Chapel and the Commandant's house, with its
fine library and wine cellar. At the entrance, a potting shed, which labors under
the delusion that it is a **museum**, provides cursory details on the history of the
fort, with a few maps and diagrams.

Fort Ross has a small beach and picnicking facilities, and you can **camp** here
(☎707/847-3286; $12) or in **Salt Point State Park** (☎707/847-3221, reserve
through ParkNet ☎1-800/444-7275; $12), six miles north on Hwy-1. Two rea-
sonable **hotel** options exist close to the two parks. *Fort Ross Lodge*, fifteen miles
north of Jenner at 20705 Hwy-1 (☎707/847-3333, ⓦwww.fortrosslodge.com;
❹), provides a VCR, microwave, coffeemaker, small refrigerator, patio, and barbecue in all rooms and some much pricier suites with a hot tub. A little further
north the *Timber Cove Inn*, 21780 Hwy-1 (☎707/847-3231 or 1-800/987-
8319, ⓦwww.timbercoveinn.com; ❺), is also comfortable, with splendid ocean
views and an intimate **restaurant**. The restaurant at the *Salt Point Lodge*, 23255
Hwy-1 (☎707/847-3234), also serves fine seafood and steak dinners for $13–20
but the rooms are reported to be noisy.

One of Sonoma County's most accessible and beautiful beaches is at **Gerstle
Cove**, which includes a paved, wheelchair-accessible path from the cove to Salt
Point, past kelp beds, wave-battered rocks, and lounging harbor seals. Salt Point
State Park's rainfall and habitat make mushrooms thrive and permits collecting,
and Gerstle Cove is also a popular place for **mushroom gatherers** to park
their cars and begin foraging. Ask the ranger for the sheet of guidelines when
you enter the lot. Just north of Salt Point, the **Kruse Rhododendron State
Reserve** (☎707/847-3221) is a sanctuary for twenty-foot-high rhododendrons, indigenous to this part of the coast and in bloom from April to June, and
you can drive through, or walk along a short trail. The beaches on this last
stretch of the Sonoma coastline are usually deserted, save for a few abalone fishermen, driftwood, and the seal pups who rest here. Again, they're good for hiking and beachcombing, but stick to the trails.

The Russian River Valley

Hwy-116 begins at Jenner (see above) and turns sharply inland, leaving behind
the cool fogs of the coast and marking the western entrance to a relatively
warm and pastoral area known as the **RUSSIAN RIVER VALLEY**. The tree-
lined highway follows the river's course through twenty miles of what appear
to be lazy, backwater resorts but in fact are the major stomping grounds for
partying weekenders from San Francisco. The valley's seat, **Guerneville**, has
the most nightlife and lodging, while **Healdsburg** serves as the gatekeeper for
the **wine area**, bordering US-101 and the Dry Creek and Alexander valleys.

The fortunes of the Russian River Valley have come full circle; back in the
Twenties and Thirties, it was a recreational resort for well-to-do city folk who
abandoned the area when newly constructed roads took them elsewhere.
Drawn by low rents, city-saturated hippies started arriving in the late Sixties,
and the Russian River took on a nonconformist flavor that lingers today. More
recently, an injection of affluent Bay Area property seekers, many of them gay,
has sustained the region's economy, and the funky mix of loggers, sheep farmers and wealthy weekenders gives it an offbeat cachet that has restored its former popularity.

The road that snakes through the valley is dotted with campgrounds every
few miles, most with sites for the asking, although during the first weekend
after Labor Day, when the region hosts the **Jazz on the River Festival**
(☎707/869-3940; $40), things can get a bit tight. The festival is something of

a wild weekend around here and a good time to come: bands set up on Johnson's Beach by the river and in the woods for impromptu jamming sessions as well as regular scheduled events. The new late-June **Russian River Blues Festival** has proven equally popular. Both events are now run by the same promoters in the East Bay (call ☏510/665-9471 for details).

Sonoma County Transit (☏707/576-7433) runs a fairly good weekday bus service (though patchy on weekends) between the Russian River resorts and Santa Rosa in the Wine Country, although to see much of the valley, you really need a car; or hire a **bike** or **kayak** from Russian River Kayak and Bicycle in Monte Rio (☏707/865-2141).

Russian River Valley wineries

The Guerneville Chamber of Commerce (see below) issues an excellent *Russian River Wine Road* map, which lists all the **wineries** that spread along the entire course of the Russian River. Unlike their counterparts in Napa and Sonoma, few of the wineries here either organize guided tours or charge for wine tasting. You can usually wander around at ease, guzzling as many and as much of the wines as you please. Some of the wines are of remarkably good quality, if not as well known as their Wine Country rivals. By car, you could easily travel up from the Sonoma Coast and check out a couple of Russian River wineries in a day, although the infectiously slow pace may well detain you longer.

Dry Creek Vineyard four miles northwest of Healdsburg at 3770 Lambert Bridge Rd, corner of Dry Creek Road ☏707/433-1000 or 1-800/864-WINE, ⓦwww.drycreekvineyard.com. This family-owned operation is well known for its consistently top-notch wines – particularly the Cabernet Sauvignon and Chardonnay. Picnic facilities. Tastings daily 10.30am–4.30pm.

Ferrari Carano 8761 Dry Creek Rd, six miles northwest of Healdsburg ☏707/433-6700 or 1-800/831-0381, ⓦwww.ferrari-carano.com. One of the smartest wineries in the region, Ferrari is housed in a Neoclassical mansion with beautiful landscaped grounds. They specialise in Italian-style wines. Tastings daily 10am–5pm; $3.

Hop Kiln 6050 Westside Rd, Healdsburg ☏707/433-6491, ⓦwww.hopkilnwinery.com. Recently established rustic winery with a traditional atmosphere but not a snobbish attitude. Tastings daily 10am–5pm.

Korbel Champagne Cellars 13250 River Rd, two miles east of Guerneville ☏707/824-7000, ⓦwww.korbel.com. The bubbly itself – America's best-selling premium Champagne – isn't anything you couldn't find in any supermarket, but the wine and brandy are sold only from the cellars, and are of such notable quality that you'd be crazy not to swing by for a glass or two. The estate where they are produced is lovely, surrounded by hillside gardens covered in blossoming violets, coral bells, and hundreds of varieties of roses – perfect for quiet picnics. A microbrewery and upscale deli are also on the premises.

Lake Sonoma 9990 Dry Creek Rd, Geyserville ☏707/473-2999, ⓦwww.lakesonomawinery.net. In a fine elevated setting at the far end of Dry Creek Valley from Healdsburg, there is a good range of wines and a particularly fine port, as well as a microbrewery on the premises. Tastings daily 10am–5pm.

Topolos at Russian River Vineyards 5700 Gravenstein Hwy, Forestville, five miles from Guerneville along Hwy-116 ☏707/887-1575 or 1-800/TOPOLOS, ⓦwww.topolos.com. One of the Russian River Valley's most accessible wineries, specializing in Zinfandels. The popular on-site restaurant (☏707/887-1562) serves Greek-inspired California dishes – dine on the patio and feast your eyes on the wildflower gardens. Tastings daily 11am–5.30pm; tours by appointment.

Guerneville

The main town of the Russian River Valley, **GUERNEVILLE**, has finally come out. No longer disguised by the tourist office as a place where "a mixture of people respect each other's lifestyles," it's quite clearly a **gay resort** and has been for the last fifteen years: a lively retreat popular with tired city dwellers who come here to unwind. Gay men predominate during the summer, except during two **Women's Weekends** (☎707/869-9000) – in early May and late September – when many of the hotels take only women.

If you don't fancy venturing along the valley, there's plenty to keep you busy without leaving town. Weekend visitors flock here for the canoeing, swimming, and sunbathing that comprise the bulk of local activities. **Johnson's Beach**, on a placid reach of the river in the center of town, is the prime spot, with canoes, pedal boats, and tubes for rent at reasonable rates. But Guerneville's biggest natural asset is the magnificent **Armstrong Redwoods State Reserve** (☎707/869-2015), two miles north at the top of Armstrong Woods Road ($2 parking) – 700 acres of massive redwood trees, hiking and riding trails, and primitive camping sites. Take food and water and don't stray off the trails: the densely forested central grove is quite forbidding and very easy to get lost in. One of the best ways to see it is on horseback; Horseback Adventures (☎707/887-2939) offers guided horseback tours that range from a half-day trail ride ($40) to a three-day pack trip ($450). A natural amphitheater provides the setting for the Redwood Forest Theater, once used for dramatic and musical productions during the summer but now simply a fine spot for rustic contemplations.

The newly combined **Chamber of Commerce & Visitor Center**, 16209 1st St (Mon–Fri 9am–5pm; 24-hr info line ☎707/869-9000 or 1-877/644-9001, @www.russianriver.com), is welcoming and has good free maps of the area plus **accommodation** listings. As with most of the valley, B&Bs are the staple; two luxurious choices are the comfortable *Creekside Inn and Resort*, 16180 Neely Rd (☎707/869-3623 or 1-800/776-6586, @www.creeksideinn.com; ❺), and *Applewood Inn & Restaurant*, 13555 Hwy-116 (☎707/869-9093, @www.applewoodinn.com; ❼), which also features a highly acclaimed gourmet restaurant. Lower rates can be found at the *New Dynamic Inn*, 14030 Mill St (☎707/869-1563, @www.newdynamicinn.com), a relaxed New-Age establishment where "cosmic energies unite with you." *Fife's*, 16467 River Rd (☎707/869-0656 or 1-800/7-FIFES-1, @www.fifes.com; ❸), is the original gay resort with a range of cabins right by the river, while *The Highlands*, 14000 Woodland Rd (☎707/869-0333), also caters primarily to the gay community; both have sites for camping too. Indeed a dearth of cheap motels (unless you head east to US-101) makes **camping** the economical answer: the *Austin Creek State Recreation Area*, Armstrong Woods Road (☎707/865-2391; $10), is guaranteed RV-free, while *Johnson's Beach and Resort*, 16241 1st St, also has cabins and rooms available ($16 camping; ☎707/869-2022, @www.johnsonsbeach.com; ❷). There are also a couple of free primitive sites, and $3 walk-in backcountry sites in the state reserve.

Guerneville has a good selection of reasonably priced, reliable **restaurants**, among them *Brew Moon*, 16248 Main St (☎707/869-0201), which serves tasty barbecued meats on paper plates in addition to cheap breakfasts and good coffees. *Burdon's Restaurant*, 15405 River Rd (☎707/869-2615), is slightly more upscale, with excellent gourmet meat and pasta dishes for around $15. Really, though, it's the **nightlife** that makes Guerneville a worthwhile stop. *Main Station*, 16280 Main St (☎707/869-0501), is a pizzeria with nightly live music, mostly jazz; while *Connolly's of West County*, 16129 Main St (☎707/869-1916),

The Sonoma coast and Russian River Valley

is a buzzing Irish pub showcasing more varied acts. Both the *Russian River Resort* ("*Triple R*"), 16390 4th St (☏707/869-0691), and *River Business, Inc*, 16225 Main St (☏707/869-3400), serve alcohol and food and are popular with the gay crowd – though you'd be hard pressed to find a place that isn't in Guerneville.

Monte Rio

The small town of **MONTE RIO**, three miles west along the river from Guerneville, is definitely worth a look: a lovely, crumbling old resort town with big Victorian houses in stages of graceful dilapidation. For years it has been the entrance to the 2500-acre **Bohemian Grove**, a private park that plays host to the San Francisco-based Bohemian Club. A grown-up summer camp, its membership includes a very rich and very powerful male elite – ex-presidents, financiers, politicians, and the like. Every year in July they descend for "Bohemian Week" – the greatest men's party on earth, noted for its hijinks and high-priced hookers, away from prying cameras in the seclusion of the woods.

The most reasonable of Monte Rio's pricey **places to stay** are the lovely *Rio Villa Beach Resort*, 20292 Hwy-116 (☏707/865-1143, ⓦwww.riovilla.com; ❹), in a beautiful spot on the banks of the Russian River, and the restored *Highland Dell Resort*, 21050 River Blvd (☏707/865-2300, ⓦwww.highland-dell.com; ❺). *Huckleberry Springs Country Inn and Spa* (☏707/865-2683 or 1-800/822-2683, ⓦwww.huckleberrysprings.com; ❼) is a deluxe women's retreat with massages and a spa, just outside of town at 8105 Old Beedle Rd. If you are hungry, *Northwood Restaurant and Lounge*, 19400 Hwy-116 (☏707/865-2454), serves up tasty Californian cuisine.

The lonely, narrow **Cazadero Highway** just to the west makes a nice drive from here, curving north through the wooded valley and leading back to Fort Ross on the coast. At the north end of the bridge over the Russian River in Monte Rio, **cyclists** can begin the world-renowned King Ridge–Meyers Grade ride, a 55-mile loop (and 4500 feet of climb) that heads along the Cazadero Highway and into the hills, finally descending to the coast and Hwy-1. Contact the Santa Rosa Cycling Club (☏707/544-4803) for a complete itinerary.

Healdsburg

The peaceful town of **HEALDSBURG** straddles the invisible border between the Wine Country and the Russian River Valley, and in a quiet way manages to get the best of both worlds. While **Veterans Memorial Beach**, a mile south of the plaza along the banks of the Russian River, is a popular spot for swimming, picnicking, and canoeing in the summertime, there are also some twenty wineries, most of them family owned, within a few miles of the center of town. Romantic bed and breakfasts have sprung up all over the area, including the neighboring village of **Geyserville**, and although the town's economic well-being is almost exclusively dependent on tourism, it still manages to maintain a relaxed, backcountry feel. The Healdsburg Area **Chamber of Commerce**, 217 Healdsburg Ave (Mon–Fri 9am–5pm, Sat & Sun 10am–2pm; ☏707/433-6935 or 1-800/648-9922), provides winery and lodging information.

If you have the money to spend it's hard to beat the *Madrona Manor*, 1001 Westside Rd (☏707/433-4231 or 1-800/258-4003, ⓦwww.madronamanor .com; ❽), a luxurious Victorian-style **bed and breakfast** mansion, crowning a hilltop, with meticulously maintained gardens and a gourmet restaurant. The best value is the *Best Western Dry Creek Inn*, 198 Dry Creek Rd (☏707/433-0300 or 1-800/222-5784, ⓦwww.drycreekinn.com; ❺).

Of several gourmet restaurants that circle the plaza, *Bistro Ralph*, 109 Plaza St (℡707/433-1380), with sparse modern decor and well-crafted dishes (around $20 per main course), is your best bet. If you want a cheaper meal, accompanied by fine local ale, look no further than *Bear Republic Brewing Co*, 345 Healdsburg Ave (℡707/433-2337). *Flying Goat Coffee Roastery and Café*, just off the main plaza at 324 Center St (℡707/433-9081), is a great place to unwind with a newspaper and a good cup of coffee.

Lake County and Clear Lake

An alternative route to the northern coast along Hwy-29 from the Wine Country or via Hwy-20, if coming from the I-5 north of Sacramento, is to take in often-neglected **LAKE COUNTY** and its centerpiece, **CLEAR LAKE**, the largest natural freshwater lake in California. With a basin that was lifted above sea level some fifty million years ago by the collision of the Pacific and North American crustal plates, it is also one of the most ancient lakes on the continent, possibly even the oldest. Its earliest inhabitants, attracted by the mild climate and abundance of fish, were the Pomo Indians, who traded peacefully with other tribes and remained here undisturbed until they were displaced by white settlers; now they number just two percent of the population. With a surface area of sixty-four square miles and over a hundred miles of shoreline, the lake is renowned among anglers as the best **bass fishing** territory in the country. Mostly surrounded by rolling hills, the lake is dominated by the green twin cone of **Mount Konocti**, a 4500ft dormant volcano, which looms above its south shore. The largest city, conveniently named **Clearlake**, which occupies the southeast corner of the lake, has plenty of tourist facilities but is rather modern and faceless, so it is better to concentrate on the lakefront areas around **Lakeport** to the west and along the **North Shore**.

Clear Lake

A popular playground for vacationing middle classes up until WWII, **CLEAR LAKE** is currently undergoing a drive to re-invent itself as a holiday destination after several slim decades during which it gained an unflattering reputation among many Californians as "white trash central." Evidence of this period can still be found in the rather dowdy motels that line parts of the lakeshore, some of which have been turned into recovery houses. However, the locals are once again trying to harness the lake's undoubted natural beauty, sunny climate, and its location a little over two hours from San Francisco in order to make it an attractive destination. This effort is bolstered by promoting its suitability for all sorts of **water activities**: watersports, boating, and fishing facilities are available all around the lake. Southeast of Lakeport, the adjacent attractions of **Clear Lake State Park** and **Soda Bay** provide ample opportunities to play or simply unwind, as do the string of small resorts on the lake's **North Shore**. As the revitalisation process is still in its early stages, the visitor can easily find great deals on accommodation, dining, and entertainment: check out the Lake County Resort and Restaurant Association website at ⓦwww .lakecountyrandr.com. It is also, by Northern Californian standards, relatively easy to spend time here without your own vehicle, thanks to decent **public transport** connections: a daily Greyhound service links Clearlake with San Francisco and the north coast, albeit slowly, and the efficient Lake Transit service (℡707/263-3334) runs frequent buses all round the lake and even operates a daily route to Calistoga and St Helena in the Napa Valley, with an onward service to Santa Rosa on Thursdays.

Lakeport and around

The county seat of **LAKEPORT** is the older and more picturesque of Clear Lake's two towns, dating from the latter part of the nineteenth century, when settlers moved into the picturesque area as gold fever began to wane. Although the suburban sprawl along the lakefront gives the impression of a larger town, it is home to less than five thousand people. If you arrive by Hwy-29, the first point of call is the smart new **Visitor Center**, perched on a green knoll right by the highway exit ramp at 875 Lakeport Blvd (Sept–May Mon–Fri 8.30am–5pm; June–Aug Mon–Sat 8.30am–5pm; ☎707/263-9544 or 1-800/525-3743, ⓦwww.lakecounty.com). As well as providing the usual brochures, maps, and helpful info, it affords a splendid view across the lake. Downtown Lakeport still retains a good deal of Victorian charm with the original 1871 brick courthouse standing imperiously on the gentle slopes of the grassy main square right in the heart of town. The building is now used to house the **Lake County Museum**, 255 N Main St (Oct–May Wed–Sat; June–Sept Wed–Sun 11am–4pm; free; ☎707/263-4555). Exhibits concentrate on the area's native Indian heritage with a full-size Pomo village diorama and large collection of baskets, arrowheads, and tools.

The dozen or so blocks of Main Street on either side of the square and the roads leading down from it to the waterfront contain most of the town's facilities. For **accommodation**, it's hard to beat *Mallard House*, 970 N Main St (☎707/262-1601, ⓦwww.mallardhouse.com; ❷), a friendly English-style inn, while the posher *Arbor House Inn*, 150 Clearlake Ave (☎707/263-6444; ❹), is the best of the B&B's around here. In the northern suburbs the *Rainbow Motel*, 2569 Lakeshore Blvd (☎707/263-4309, ⓦwww.rainbow-lakeport.com; ❸), is typical of the resort motels to be found in the vicinity. For **eating**, the nearby *Ma' Shauns Rainbow Restaurant*, 2599 Lakeshore Blvd (☎707/263-6237), does an imaginative array of seafood and meat appetizers, sandwiches and entrées for $6–20. Right downtown, *Park Place*, 50 3rd St (☎707/263-0444), is the place for filling pastas, burgers, and steaks. If you want to try your hand at **fishing**, go to The King Connection, 2470 Reeves Lane (☎707/263-8856), and for boat or jet ski rental contact Disney's Water Sports, 401 S Main St (☎707/263-0969, ⓦwww.disneywatersports.com).

About six miles southeast of Lakeport two adjacent areas are worthy of exploration. The first is **Clear Lake State Park**, whose visitor center (daily 9am–6pm; ☎707/279-4293) houses displays on the lake's cultural and natural history as well as a 700-gallon aquarium of indigenous fish. The park also offers forest trails, a swimming beach, and four developed campgrounds (book through ParkNet ☎1-800/444-7275; $12). Right below Mount Konocti, in the protected waters between the park and Buckingham Peninsula, which almost spans the lake, **Soda Bay** is another haven for swimming and watersports. The eastern shore of the bay is blessed with soda springs, hence the name, which bubble up from shafts over 100ft deep. Indian legend claims that the bubbling waters mark the spot where Chief Konocti's daughter Lupiyoma threw herself into the lake after her father and lover were killed in battle.

Mount Konocti

Majestic **MOUNT KONOCTI**, which is clearly visible from just about anywhere on Clear Lake's circumference, is a multiple volcano, which is estimated to have first erupted some 600,000 years ago but has now been inactive for several thousand years. Indeed, geologists have declared large parts of it officially extinct. Its name comes from the Pomo Indian words "kno" and "hatai," meaning "mountain" and "woman" respectively. Unfortunately, most of the mountain is under private ownership so you cannot wander its slopes at will. Visitors can, however, gain access by permission and guided tours are conducted on selected days; call ☎707/972-1990 for information and reservations. The nearest amenities can be found at **Kelseyville** on the lower western reaches. These include the biggest resort in the region, *Konocti Harbor Resort & Spa*, 8727 Soda Bay Rd (☎707/279-4281 or 1-800/660-LAKE, ⓦwww.konoctiharbor.com; ❸), which has accommodation ranging from motel-style rooms through beach cottages to VIP suites in excess of $300, as well as a spa, marina, sports facilities, restaurants, and a concert hall that attracts many famous acts.

Clearlake

Though somewhat anodyne and sprawling, with a population approaching twelve thousand, **CLEARLAKE** and the town of **Lower Lake** with which it merges do hold some interest and certainly offer plenty of amenities. Culturally speaking, the one place to see is the **Lower Lake Historical Schoolhouse Museum**, 16435 Morgan Valley Rd, Lower Lake (Wed–Sat 11am–3pm; free), which preserves one of the old grammar school classrooms just as it was during the late nineteenth century. For the less academic-minded, **Outrageous Waters**, on the south side of Clearlake at the corner of Old State Highway and Dam Road (May–Sept daily noon–8pm; $13.95; ☎707/995-1402 or 1-877/WE-BE-FUN, ⓦwww.outrageouswaters.com), is a family-orientated water park with race cars and other games to boot.

If you decide **to stay** in Clearlake, you shouldn't have any problem finding somewhere adequate and economical by the waterside. The *Lamplighter Motel*, 14165 Lakeshore Drive (☎707/994-2129; ❶), has basic rooms at rock-bottom prices, while the *Highlands Inn*, 13865 Lakeshore Drive (☎707/994-8982 or 1-800/300-8982, ⓦwww.high-lands.com; ❷), is a little more comfortable, and the *Clearlake Hostel & Cabins*, 14852 Lakeshore Drive (☎707/994-0978; ❷), offers dorm beds for $15. Decent breakfasts and simple **meals** are to be had inexpensively at the *Main Street Café*, 14084 Lakeshore Drive (☎707/994-6450), and good, filling Mexican fare at *Cabo's*, 14868 Olympic Drive (☎707/995-2162), several hundred yards back from the lakefront. Funtime Watersports at 6235 Old Hwy-53 (☎707/994-6267) rents out boats, fishing gear, and other equipment. The Greyhound **bus depot** is located about half a mile east of the lakefront at *The Caffiend*, Burns Valley Mall, 14828 Olympic Ave (☎707/994-3672).

North Shore

Some five miles north of Clearlake, Hwy-53 ends at Hwy-20, which continues northwest along the lake's **NORTH SHORE** past a series of small resorts under the shade of white oak and pepperwood trees. The first place you come to once the road hits the lake is **Clearlake Oaks**, where the *Lake Marina* resort/motel, 10215 E Hwy-20 (☎707/998-3787; ❸), offers reasonable waterfront rooms and has its own jetty. You can rent powered (4hr minimum, $32–38) or pedal boats ($11 per hr) from Blue Fish Cove, 10573 E Hwy-20 (☎707/998-1769, ⓦwww.bluefishcove.com). A couple of miles further west at **Glenhaven**, the *Sea Breeze Resort*, 9595 Harbor Drive (☎707/998-3327, ⓦwww.seabreeze-resort.com; ❹), has quaint, nicely decorated cottages; if you are seeking a **campsite**, try *Glenhaven Beach* at 9625 E Hwy-20 (☎707/998-3406), where sites cost $16–18.

There is more going on, however, up towards the lake's northwest corner, which also boasts the longest stretches of beach. Five miles beyond Glenhaven in the larger settlement of **Lucerne**, the *Riviera Motel*, 6900 E Hwy-20 (☎707/274-1032; ❷) offers bargain rooms, while *The Beachcomber Resort*, 6345 E Hwy-20 (☎707/274-6639, ⓦwww.beachcomberresort.net; ❷), has similar rates and you can fish from their own pier. Several miles further on, where Hwy-20 prepares to leave the lake as the shoreline dips south towards Lakeport, the pleasant town of **Nice** is the best base on the North Shore. Apart from more cheap cabins at *D&G's Last Resort*, 3796 Lakeshore Blvd (☎707/274-1289; ❸), there are a couple of attractive **B&Bs**: the unique railway-themed *Featherbed Railroad Company*, 2870 Lakeshore Blvd (☎707/274-8378 or 1-800/966-6322, ⓦwww.featherbedrailroad.com; ❺), where all the rooms are fashioned out of disused cabooses; and the more conventional *Gingerbread Cottages*, 4057 E Hwy-20 (☎707/274-0200, ⓦwww.gingerbread-cottages.com; ❺). Nice is also the most fruitful part of North Shore for **eating**: try the tasty and inexpensive American classics served all day at *Marina's Grill*, 3707 E Hwy-20 (☎707/274-9114), the fresh seafood, steaks, and pasta at the *Harbor Bar & Grill*, 4561 E Hwy-20 (☎707/274-1637), or the well-prepared fish at *The Boathouse*, 2685 Lakeshore Blvd (☎707/274-3534).

The Mendocino coast

The coast of **Mendocino County**, 150 miles north of San Francisco, is a dramatic extension of the Sonoma coastline – the headlands a bit sharper, the surf a bit rougher, but otherwise more of the same. Sea stacks form a dotted line off the coast, and there's an abundance of tidal pools, making the area a prime spot for diving and exploring on foot the secrets of the ocean. Surfers love it, too, for the waves and sandy beaches at **Gualala** and **Point Arena**, and March brings out droves of people to watch migrating **whales**. You can find out more about what the county has to offer at the Mendocino County Alliance's website ⓦwww.goMendo.com. Tourists tend to mass in charming **Mendocino** and gritty **Fort Bragg**, leaving the other small former logging towns along Hwy-1 preserved in the salt air and welcoming to visitors. The county also thrives as a location spot for the movie industry, having featured in such illustrious titles as *East of Eden*, *Frenchman's Creek*, *Same Time Next Year*, and *The Fog*. Occasionally such films are supposed to be set on the East Coast, making use of the New England-style architecture closer to Hollywood, so watch out for any suspicious sunsets over the ocean next time you're in the theater.

If you are already on the coast, you can continue to hug it all the way via Hwy-1 as far north as Rockport when it turns east to join US-101, the last thirty miles constituting the only true wilderness left on California's rim. The best direct route to Mendocino from the south, however, is to travel the length of the peaceful **Anderson Valley** by taking Hwy-128 north from US-101. **Willits**, forty miles inland from Fort Bragg, is served by Greyhound and Amtrak Thruway. From here, the Skunk Trains (see p.741) provide a **rail link** to the main towns of Mendocino and Fort Bragg. These coastal towns are also connected to each other and the interior towns of Willits and Ukiah by two local **bus** operators: Mendocino Stage (☎707/964-0167) and Mendocino Transit Authority buses (☎1-800/696-4MTA, ⓦwww.4mta.org), which has additional routes south to Gualala and Santa Rosa.

Mendocino

Once you leave Sonoma County, Hwy-1 winds for fifty miles along the wrinkled coast, past the communities of Gualala and Point Arena and the kelp forests of Van Damme State Park before you reach the coast's most lauded stop, the decidedly touristy village of **MENDOCINO**. The quaint town sits on a broad-shouldered bluff with waves crashing on three sides; it's hard to find a spot here where you can't see the ocean sparkling in the distance. New England-style architecture is abundant, lending Mendo, as the locals call it, a down-home, almost cutesy air. Its appearance on the National Register of Historic Places and reputation as something of an artists' colony draw the curious up the coastal highway, and a fairly extensive network of bed and breakfasts, restaurants, and bars are more than happy to cater to their every need.

Accommodation

Room rates in Mendocino are generally high, but provided you stay away from the chintzy hotels on the waterfront, it is possible to find adequate, reasonably priced hotels on the streets behind. The *Sea Gull Inn*, 44960 Albion St (☎707/937-5204 or 1-888/937-5204, ⦿www.mcn.org/a/seagull; ❸), is the best of the affordable options right in the center, though the antique-filled rooms at the *Mendocino Hotel*, 45080 Main St (☎707/937-0511 or 1-800/548-0513, ⦿www.mendocinohotel.com; ❺), are more luxurious and *The Agate Cove Inn*, 11201 N Lansing St (☎707/937-0551, ⦿www.agatecove.com; ❺), gets you closest to the ocean. The biggest of the many B&Bs is the *MacCallum House Inn*, 45020 Albion St (☎707/937-0289 or 1-800/609-0492, ⦿www.maccallum-house.com; ❺), while the *Joshua Grindle Inn*, 44800 Little Lake Rd (☎707/937-4143 or 1-800/GRINDLE, ⦿www.joshgrin.com; ❻), must rate as the friendliest and serves excellent gourmet breakfasts. The most romantic place to stay in the whole region is a tie. In Mendocino, *Reed Manor*, on Palette Drive (☎707/937-5446, ⦿www.reedmanor.com; ❼), is a five-bedroom mansion with canopied soaking tubs and in-room telescopes for whale watching. The other romantic choice is at **Albion**, a small fishing village ten miles south of Mendocino; the *Albion River Inn*, 3790 N Hwy-1 (☎707/937-1919 or 1-800/479-7944, ⦿www.albionriverinn.com; ❼), just beyond the junction with Hwy-128, perches on the edge of a cliff, and all the rooms except one have ocean views. The inn also has a first-class **restaurant**, serving pricey, wonderful food with a spectacular wine list and top service. *Mendocino Coast Accommodations* (☎707/937-5033 or 1-800/262-7801, ⦿www.mendocinova-cations.com) book rooms at B&Bs, hotels, cottages, and vacation homes for free. Just beyond blink-and-you'll-miss-it Caspar, halfway towards Fort Bragg on Hwy-1, *Jughandle Creek Farm* (☎707/964-4630, ⦿www.jughandle.creek.org; ❶) has dorm-style shared rooms ($20 per person), campsites ($9), and cabins; there's an extra $5 charge if you are unwilling to donate an hour's work. Staying there also allows you to explore the trails in the woods behind and participate in nature study programmes. There's $12 **camping** at Russian Gulch State Park and Van Damme State Park (reserve both through ParkNet ☎1-800/444-7275).

The Town

Like other small settlements along the coast, Mendocino was originally a mill site and shipping port, established in 1852 by merchants from Maine who thought the proximity to the redwoods and exposed location made it a good site for sawmill operations. The industry has now vanished, but the large community of artists has spawned craftsy commerce in the form of art galleries, gift shops, and boutique delicatessens. This preservation didn't come about by accident. The state of California traded a block of old-growth forest with the Boise–Cascade logging company in exchange for the headlands surrounding the town. The headlands became a state park, and Mendocino in turn became a living museum, with strict local ordinances mandating architectural design and upkeep.

The **visitor center**, 735 Main St (daily 11am–4pm; ☎707/937-5397), is located in **Ford House**, one of many mansions built by the Maine lumbermen in the style of their home state. **The Kelley House Museum**, 45007 Albion St (Fri–Mon 1–4pm; free; ☎707/937-5791), has exhibits detailing the town's role as a center for shipping redwood lumber to the miners during the Gold Rush, and conducts **walking tours** of the town on Saturday mornings at 11am – though you could do it yourself in under an hour, collecting souvenirs from the galleries as you go. Chief among them, the **Mendocino Art Center**, 45200 Little Lake St (daily 10am–5pm; ☎707/937-5818 or 1-800/653-3328, ⓦwww.mendocinoartcenter.org; free), has a revolving gallery for mainly Mendocino-based artists and runs workshops in ceramics, weaving, jewelry, and metal sculpture. The Mendocino Theater Company (☎707/937-4477) on the same premises puts on regular performances of both avant-garde and classic works.

Otherwise there's plenty to occupy you around the town, with a long stroll along the headlands topping the list. **Hiking** and **cycling** are popular, with bikes available for around $25 a day from Catch a Canoe & Bicycles, Too (☎707/937-0273 or 1-800/320-2453), just south of Mendocino at the corner of Hwy-1 and Compche–Ukiah Road. They also rent outriggers and kayaks. At the west end of Main Street, hiking trails lead out into the **Mendocino Headlands**, where you can explore the grassy cliffs and make your way down to the tidepools, next to the breaking waves. The **Russian Gulch State Park** ($3; ☎707/937-5804), two miles north of town, has bike trails, beautiful fern glens, and waterfalls. Just south of town, hiking and cycling trails weave through the unusual **Van Damme State Park** ($3; ☎707/937-5804), which has a **Pygmy Forest** of ancient trees, stunted to waist-height because of poor drainage and soil chemicals. The coast of the park is punctuated with sea stacks and caves, carved by the pounding surf. Two-hour sea cave tours are available through Lost Coast Kayaking (three times daily, $50; ☎707/937-2434). After a day of hiking and shopping, you may want to pamper yourself with a massage and a hot tub at one of the town's spas.

Abalone diving is extremely popular along the coast here, particularly just south of town in the small cove beside Van Damme State Park. In an attempt to thwart poaching, the practice is strictly regulated – the tasty gastropods are not available commercially, and you can only have three in your possession at any given time or collect a total of twenty-four in one season. In early October, 400 hungry judges pay a substantial fee for the opportunity to help choose the best abalone chef in the annual Abalone Cookoff. The Sub-Surface Progression Dive Center, 18600 Hwy-1 (☎707/964-3793) in Fort Bragg, leads all-inclusive half-day diving expeditions for $50.

Eating, drinking, and nightlife

Of Mendocino's **restaurants**, the best and most famous is *Café Beaujolais*, 961 Ukiah St (☎707/937-5614), whose founder wrote a book on organic California cuisine and which serves up a frequently changing menu of such fare nightly. Almost next door, *955 Ukiah Street* (☎707/937-1955; closed Tues) serves $15–$20 entrées that make it even more popular with many locals. For slightly cheaper fair, try the *Mendocino Café*, 10451 Lansing St (☎707/937-0836), serving an eclectic mix of salads, pastas, and sandwiches. *Tote Féte Bakery*, behind the deli of the same name at 10450 Lansing St (☎707/937-3383), produces delicious breads, pastries, and muffins, which you can eat outside on the tree-shaded deck. If you don't have time to visit any of the Anderson Valley wineries, Fetzer Vineyards Tasting Cellar, 45070 Main St (☎707/937-6191, Ⓦwww.fetzer.com), next to the *Mendocino Hotel*, sells its vintages and gives free tastings (daily 10am–6pm). If beer's your preferred tipple, *Dick's Place*, 45070 Main St, is Mendocino's oldest bar, with all the robust conviviality you'd expect from a spit-and-sawdust saloon, while *Patterson's Pub*, 10485 Lansing St (☎707/937-4782), is another friendly joint with fine ale.

The first weekend in March brings the **Mendocino Whale Festival** (☎1-800/726-2780), a celebration of food and headland views of whales returning back to the Arctic. They can also be spotted in November, on the trip to the warmer waters of the California Baja. Although the emphasis of the two-week **Mendocino Music Festival** (☎1-800/937-2044) in the second half of July is largely on classical music and opera, some blues and jazz bands from all over the state also perform. Since 1999 Mendocino has also hosted a twelve-day **Wine and Mushroom Fest** every November – check with the tourist authorities for details.

Fort Bragg, Willits, and Leggett

FORT BRAGG, a mere nine miles north of Mendocino, is very much the blue-collar flipside to its comfortable neighbor, although some trendier enterprises are beginning to spring up. Still, for the most part, where Mendocino exists on wholefood, art, and peaceful ocean walks, Fort Bragg brings you the rib-shack and tattoo parlor. The town sits beneath a perpetual cloud of steam choked out from the lumbermills of the massive Georgia Pacific Corporation, which monopolizes California's logging industry and to which Fort Bragg owes its existence. There was once a fort here, but it was only used for ten years until the 1860s when it was abandoned and the land sold off cheaply. The otherwise attractive **Noyo Harbor** (south of town on Hwy-1) is these days crammed full of as many pleasure boats as diminishing commercial fishing craft, and the billowing smog does little to add to the charm. Nevertheless, its proximity to the more isolated reaches of the Mendocino coast, an abundance of budget accommodation, and bevy of inexpensive restaurants make it a good alternative to Mendocino.

As for things to do, you can take a quick look at the historical exhibits of the **Guest House Museum** (☎707/964-4251), if you can catch it open; entry is free but hours are erratic. A worthwhile hour or two can be spent rummaging on **Glass Beach**, a ten-minute walk north of downtown at the end of Elm Street, below an attractive overgrown headland. Used as the town's dump until the Sixties, the disposed articles have been smoothed by the ocean into a kaleidoscopic beachcomber's paradise of broken glassware and crockery fragments. For a day-trip or convenient way of getting to or from the coast, you can amuse yourself on the **Skunk Trains** operated by the Californian Western Railroad ($29–39 one-way depending on the type of engine, $45 round-trip; ☎707/964-6371 or 1-800/77-SKUNK Fort Bragg depot, ☎707/459-5248 Willits depot), which run twice daily during the summer months and once the rest of the year from the terminus on Laurel Street forty miles inland to the town of **WILLITS** on US-101. Taking their name from the days when, piled up with timber from the redwood forests, they were powered by gas engines and could be smelt before they were seen, the trains now operate almost exclusively for the benefit of tourists. It's good fun to ride in the open observation car as it tunnels forty miles through mountains and rumbles across the thirty-odd high bridges on its route through the towering redwoods. Choose between a full eight-hour journey to Willits and back, or a four-hour ride that turns around half-way. Willits is the official county seat thanks only to its location in the center of Mendocino, and is no different from other strip-development, mid-sized American towns – disembark only to get a drink or to connect onto Greyhound or Amtrak.

A short drive or bus ride south of Fort Bragg will take you to the **Mendocino Coast Botanical Gardens**, 18220 N Hwy-1 (summer daily 9am–5pm; winter daily 9am–4pm; $6; ☎707/964-4352), where you can see more or less every wildflower under the sun spread across 47 acres of prime coastal territory. It is particularly renowned for the many varieties of **rhododendrons** that bloom in April and May. Heading north, the next stretch of Hwy-1 is the slowest, continuing for another twenty miles of road and windswept beach before leaving Mendocino County and the coastline to turn inland and head over the mountains to meet US-101 at **Leggett**. Redwood country begins in earnest here: there's even a tree you can drive through for $3, though you'd do better to stay on course for the best forests further north.

Practicalities

Fort Bragg's **Chamber of Commerce** (Mon–Fri 9am–5pm, Sat 9am–3pm; ☎707/961-6300 or 1-800/726-2780, ⊛www.mendocinocoast.com) is almost directly across the street from the **train station** at 332 N Main St. Most of the **motels** cluster along Hwy-1 close to the center of town, the lowest priced of which is the newly renovated *Chelsea Inn*, 763 N Main St (☎707/964-4787 or 1-800/253-9972; ❷). Other good options include the basic but clean *Tradewinds Lodge*, 400 S Main St (☎707/964-4761 or 1-800/524-2244; ❷), or the *Surf Motel*, 1220 S Main St (☎707/964-5361 or 1-800/339-5361, ⊛www.surfmotelfortbragg.com; ❷). **B&Bs** are naturally more upscale but cheaper than those in Mendocino: the *Grey Whale Inn B&B*, 615 N Main St (☎707/964-0640 or 1-800/382-7244; ❺), has great views from its rooms, while the *Colonial Inn*, 533 Fir St (☎707/964-1384 or 1-877/964-1384, ⊛www.colonialinnfortbragg.com; ❺), costs less and is tucked away down a quiet residential street. The *Old Coast Hotel*, 101 N Franklin (☎707/961-4488 or 1-888/468-3550, ⊛www.oldcoastinn.com; ❹), has comfortable rooms in a restored 1892 building with a steak-and-seafood restaurant attached. Finally, there's camping among six miles of sandy beach and coastal pines at **MacKerricher State Park** ($12; reserve through ParkNet ☎1-800/444-7275), three miles north of Fort Bragg.

Restaurants in Fort Bragg (of which there are plenty) tend to cater to the ravenous carnivore: *Jenny's Giant Burger*, 940 N Main St (☎707/964-2235), for example, is usually full of men from the mill scoffing large chunks of red meat. A more genteel option is the *Mendo Bistro*, upstairs in the converted old Union Lumber Store complex at 301 N Main St (☎707/964-4974), which serves excellent, imaginative international cuisine, including gourmet pasta dishes, at very moderate prices. Otherwise, *The Restaurant*, at 418 Main St (☎707/964-9800), has tasty fish entrées for around $20, and *Café Prima*, 124 E Laurel St (☎707/964-5814), does elegant Swahili dishes from the chef's native Kenya. Vegetarians can take refuge in the hearty Italian offerings at *Headlands Coffee*, 120 E Laurel St (☎707/964-1987), which also serves wine, along with a full menu of espressos. For big breakfasts, try *Egghead's*, at 326 N Main St (daily

7am–2pm), which lists 41 different omelets on their menu. If you're feeling thirsty, stop in for one of the "handmade ales" at the *North Coast Brewing Company*, 444 N Main St (℡707/964-3400), voted one of the ten best breweries in the world by the Beverage Testing Institute of Chicago as part of their year-long World Beer Championships. Try the Acme California Brown Ale and the Old Rasputin Russian Imperial Stout. Free tours of the brewery itself, on the opposite side of Main Street, are conducted at 2.30pm on Monday to Friday and 12.30pm on Saturday. If you want to work up a thirst first, Noyo Pacific Outfitters, 32400 N Harbor Drive (℡707/961-0559), can rent you a kayak (from $15 for 2hr) and organise guide trips upriver or off the coast, as well as abalone-diving expeditions.

The Anderson Valley

Running diagonally northwest for nearly twenty miles from just south of its small main town of **Boonville** to within a few miles of the coast is the fertile **ANDERSON VALLEY**, an amalgam of sunny rolling hills shaded by oaks and madrones that merge into dark redwood forest. Hwy-128, connecting US-101 near Cloverdale to the coast at Albion, is the sole artery through the valley, which has a longstanding reputation as a magnet for mavericks. The original settlers were sheep farmers who saw so few outsiders between the 1880s and 1920s that they even developed their own language, **boontling**, snippets of which still survive today. A good sixth of this odd dialect was known as "nonch harpin's," meaning "objectionable talk," and largely referred to the then

> ### Anderson Valley wineries
>
> There are already over a dozen **wineries** dotted along the Anderson Valley, and you can expect that number to increase dramatically in the coming years. The cooler temperatures, especially at the northwest end, which sees the coastal fogs roll in, are better suited mostly to white varieties such as Gewürtzraminer, Chardonnay, and Riesling, but the hardy Pinot Noir fares equally well. For further details you can contact the Mendocino Winegrowers Alliance in Ukiah (℡707/468-9886, ⓦwww.mendowine.com). Most wineries have **open tastings** and there is rarely a fee, as they remain for the time being far less commercialized than their cousins further south. Here are a handful that would repay a visit:
>
> **Christine Woods Vineyards** 3155 Hwy-128, less than a mile south of Navarro ℡707/895-2115, ⓦwww.christinewoods .com. The Chardonnay and Merlot from this family winery have received awards in Mendocino and San Francisco. All wines are made entirely from grapes grown on the estate, a relative rarity. Tastings daily 11am–5pm.
>
> **Husch Vineyards** 4400 Hwy-128, one mile south of Navarro ℡707/895-3216 or 1-800/55-HUSCH, ⓦwww.huschvineyards.com. Founded in 1971, this small family winery is the oldest in the valley, and you are assured of a warm welcome at its rustic tasting room. Tastings daily 10am–6pm, 10am–5pm in winter.
>
> **Navarro Vineyards** 5601 Hwy-128, two miles north of Philo ℡707/895-3686 or 1-800/537-WINE, ⓦwww.navarrowine .com. This small winery specializes in Alsatian-style wines, which it only sells directly to the consumer and select restaurants. It also concocts a wicked grape juice, so even the kids can enjoy a free sip or two here. Tastings daily 10am–6pm, 11am–5pm in winter.
>
> **Pacific Echo Cellars** 8501 Hwy-128, just north of Philo ℡707/895-2065, ⓦwww.pacific-echo.com. Established over twenty years ago, these cellars have employed the old European *méthode champenoise* to create a fine, creamy, sparkling wine as their flagship product. Tastings daily 10am–6pm.

taboo subjects of sexual activity and bodily functions. You can see examples of boontling in the names of local beers and establishments but if you want to know the full story, track down a copy of *Boontling, An American Lingo* in local stores. During the twentieth century, sheep farming gradually gave way to the cultivation of apples but, though many orchards still exist, they are fast being replaced by more lucrative vineyards, as the craze for Californian wine means this area is becoming a northern annexe of the Wine Country, along with the **Yorkville Highlands**, the southeastern extension of the valley. Most of the Anderson Valley's existing wineries line Hwy-128 between the tiny settlements of **Philo** and **Navarro**. The area is also famous for the excellent beer produced at the *Anderson Valley Brewing Co*, 17700 Hwy-253 (free tours daily 1.30 & 4pm; ☏1-800/207-BEER, ⓦwww.avbc.com), just east of the junction with Hwy-128 on the south side of Boonville. Their Hop Ottin' IPA (an example of boontling) and rich amber ales are especially delicious.

Boonville and Philo

Despite having a population of little over seven hundred, **BOONVILLE** still easily manages to be the largest town in the Anderson Valley. Strung along its widened half-mile section of Hwy-128 are some quaint shops, a hotel, and a few places to find sustenance. In terms of **accommodation**, the only place in town is the grand nineteenth-century *Boonville Hotel*, Hwy-128 at Lambert Lane (☏707/895-2210, ⓦwww.boonvillehotel.com; ④), although the *Anderson Creek Inn*, under two miles northwest of town just off Anderson Valley Way (☏707/895-3091 or 1-800/552-6202, ⓦwww.andersoncreekinn.com; ⑥) is an extremely comfy and quiet ranch-style B&B. Apart from the spicy Mexican-influenced California **cuisine** on offer at the *Boonville Hotel*, you can enjoy quality bar food and **drink** your way through the entire range of Boonville beers at the *Buckhorn Saloon*, 14081 Hwy-128 (☏707/895-3369). The boontling-named *Horn of Zeese Café*, 14025 Hwy-128 (☏707/895-3525), is a good spot for filling breakfasts and snacks.

Six miles beyond Boonville, as you head northwest towards the coast, the village of **PHILO** has alternative venues to spend the night or have a meal, although it's all rather cutesy. *The Philo Pottery Inn*, 8550 Hwy-128 (☏707/895-3069, ⓦwww.philopotteryinn.com; ⑤), is a plush **B&B** right in the village but the best deal to be had is at the nearby *Anderson Valley Inn*, 8480 Hwy-128 (☏707/895-3325, ⓦwww.avinn.com; ③). *Libby's Restaurant*, 8651 Hwy-128 (☏707/895-2646), serves up excellent inexpensive Mexican **food** and you can grab a sandwich or picnic ingredients from Lemon's Philo Market (☏707/895-3552), just down the road.

A great place to take your picnic is three miles northwest to **Hendy Woods State Park** (☏707/895-3141; $2 per car), clearly signposted off Hwy-128. The park features hiking trails through two sizeable redwood groves, fishing on the Navarro River and camping for $12 (reserve through ParkNet ☏1-800/444-7275). A mile or so beyond the park entrance another sign-posted left turn leads four miles up through more redwood-clad ridges to *Highland Ranch* (☏707/895-3600, ⓦwww.highlandranch.com; ⑨). The $285 per person overnight charge at this friendly guest ranch, set amidst a stunning 300 acres, includes a luxury detached cabin, three meals, plus all drinks and activities on offer, principally horse riding and clay-pigeon shooting.

The Humboldt coast

Of the northern coastal counties, **HUMBOLDT** is by far the most beautiful, and also the one most at odds with development. The biggest news story of 1999 concerned Eureka's decision to bar chainstore-behemoth WalMart from erecting an outlet, despite the company's offer to clean up and build on a now deserted, and very polluted, stretch of waterfront. This is logging land, and the drive up US-101 gives a tour of giant sawmills fenced in by stacks of felled trees. Yet Humboldt County also contains the largest preserves of giant redwoods in the world in **Humboldt Redwoods State Park** and, north, **Redwood National Park**. Both are peaceful, otherworldly experiences not to be missed, though the absence of sunlight within the groves and mossy surface can be eerie.

Indeed, many locals hope that the forests are too creepy for visitors. Tourism, while good for business, encroaches on a lifestyle far removed from the glitz of Mendocino and Sonoma counties. Locals are worried that as more people discover the area, the rugged serve-yourself mentality here could quickly turn into a service economy. Weekend visitors won't encounter any outright hostility, provided they tread lightly. Camping and communing with nature is considered cool, while expecting salad forks with dinner and a throbbing nightlife is not. The coastal highway's inability to trace Humboldt's southern coast formerly guaranteed isolation and earned the region the name of the **Lost Coast**. The area, while still isolated, is not quite as "lost" any more thanks to the construction of an airstrip in Shelter Cove and an infusion of hotels, restaurants, and new homes.

Humboldt is perhaps most renowned for its "Emerald Triangle," which produces the majority of California's largest cash crop, **marijuana**. As the Humboldt coast's fishing and logging industries slide, more and more people have been turning to growing the stuff to make ends meet and new hydroponic techniques ensure that the potency of the ultra-thick buds is extremely high. In the 1980s, the elder Bush's administration took steps to crack down on the business with CAMP (Campaign against Marijuana Planting), sporadically sending out spotter planes to pinpoint the main growing areas. Aggressive law enforcement and a steady stream of crop-poaching has been met with a defiant, booby-trapped, and frequently armed protection of crops, and production goes on – the camouflage netting and irrigation pipes you find on sale in most stores clearly do their job.

Apart from considerable areas of clandestine agriculture, the county is almost entirely forestland. The highway rejoins the coast at **Eureka** and **Arcata**, Humboldt's two major towns and both jumping-off points for the redwoods. These "ambassadors from another time," as John Steinbeck dubbed them, are at their 300-foot best in the **Redwood National Park**, which contains three state parks and covers some 106,000 acres of skyscraping forest.

Again, **getting around** is going to be your biggest problem. Although Greyhound and Amtrak Thruway buses run the length of the county along US-101, they're hardly a satisfactory way to see the trees, and you'll need a car to make the trip worthwhile. **Hitchhiking** still goes on up here, and you'll see gaggles of locals gathered at the gas stations and freeway entrances begging for rides. This is part necessity, as public transportation is scarce, and part lifestyle, as the region is a throwback to the kinder decades when hitching was a normal practice on American roads. Still, remember that stopping on the highways is illegal, and that no matter the kind appearance of a hitcher or driver, hitchhiking can be dangerous in the US. For information on **what's on** in

Humboldt, two excellent, free county newspapers, *The Activist* and *North Coast Journal* (@ www.northcoastjournal.com), detail the local scene and people, and where to go and what to do in the area. Look out, too, for the activist Arcata-based *Greenfuse* and *Econews*, which highlight the ecological plight of Northern California's wild country.

Southern Humboldt: Garberville and the Lost Coast

The inaccessibility of the Humboldt coast in the south is ensured by the **Kings Range**, an area of impassable cliffs that shoots up several thousand feet from the ocean, so that even a road as sinuous as Hwy-1 can't negotiate a passage through. To get there, you have to travel US-101 through deep redwood territory as far as **GARBERVILLE**, a one-street town with a few good bars and hotels that is the center of the cannabis industry and a lively break from the freeway. Each week, the local paper runs a "bust-barometer," which charts the week's pot raids, and every August, the town hosts the massive two-day **Reggae on the River** festival. Tickets cost around $110; call ☎707/923-4583 by early May to reserve them.

Practicalities

Amtrak Thruway **buses** stop twice daily outside the *Waterwheel Restaurant* on Redwood Drive, Garberville's main street, while the two daily Greyhound services connecting north to Eureka and south to San Francisco pull in around the corner on Church Street. The town's **Chamber of Commerce** (daily 10am–5pm; ☎707/923-2613 or 1-800/923-2613, @ www.garberville.org) is located at 773 Redwood Drive. For what you get, much of the town's accommodation is a bit overpriced. Of a couple you might try, the *Benbow Inn*, several miles south of town at 445 Lake Benbow Drive (☎707/923-2124 or 1-800/355-3301, @ www.benbowinn.com; ❻), is a flash place for such a rural location (former guests include Eleanor Roosevelt and Herbert Hoover); the *Humboldt House Inn*, 701 Redwood Drive (☎707/923-2771 or 1-800/862-7756, @ www.bestwestern.com/humboldthouse.inn; ❹), and the more basic *Motel Garberville*, 948 Redwood Drive (☎707/923-2422; ❷), round out the better options. The closest **campground** is seven miles south at **Benbow Lake State Recreation Area** (☎707/923-3238), while five miles further south on US-101 the **Richardson Grove State Park** in Piercy (☎707/247-3318) spreads over 1400 acres along the Eel River. Both cost $12 per site and can be reserved through ParkNet (☎1-800/444-7275).

Even if you don't intend to stay in Garberville, at least stop off to sample some of the town's **restaurants** and **bars**, which turn out some of the best live bluegrass you're likely to hear in the state. Redwood Drive is lined with bars, cafés, and restaurants: *The Galaxy* at no. 845 (☎707/923-2664), is the cheapest place for breakfast and also does some Japanese and fish'n'chips, while the *Woodrose Café*, at no. 911 (☎707/923-3191), serves organic lunches. *Treats Café*, at no. 764 (☎707/923-3554), offers snacks, drinks, and Internet access for 10¢ a minute. For an inexpensive eat-in or take-out meal, try *Calico's Deli and Pasta*, at no. 808 (☎707/923-2253). All the town bars tend to whoop it up in the evening; the noisiest of the lot is probably the *Branding Iron Saloon*, at no. 744 (☎707/923-2562), with a small cover for its nightly live music and a tell-tale "no patchouli" sign by the entrance. *The Riverwood Inn* (☎707/943-3333), in nearby Phillipsville, also showcases live bluegrass and other styles of music every Saturday and serves good Mexican food from Thursday to Sunday.

Shelter Cove and the Humboldt Redwoods State Park

From Garberville, via the adjoining village of **Redway**, where you can enjoy a gourmet meal on the terrace of the *Mateel Café*, 3342 Redwood Drive (☎707/923-3020), the Briceland and Shelter Cove roads wind 23 miles through territory populated by old hippies and New Agers beetling around in battered vehicles. You eventually emerge on the **Lost Coast** at **SHELTER COVE**, set in a tiny bay neatly folded between sea cliffs and headlands. First settled in the 1850s when gold was struck inland, its isolated position at the far end of the **Kings Range** kept the village small until recent years. Now, thanks to a new airstrip, weekenders arrive in their hordes and modern houses are indiscriminately dotted across the headland. Unfortunately, it's the closest real settlement to the **hiking** and **wildlife** explorations of the surrounding wilderness, which remains inhabited only by deer, river otter, mink, black bear, bald eagles, and falcons, so you might find yourself using either *Mario's Marina Motel*, 461 Machi Rd (☎707/986-7595, ✉emarios@saber.net; ④), or the *Beachcomber Inn*, 412 Machi Rd (☎707/986-7551 or 1-800/718-4789; ③), as a **base**; the former establishment also has an adequate restaurant (☎707/986-1401) with a sea view on its extensive grounds. The Cape Mendocino Lighthouse, on Upper Pacific Drive (late May–late Sept daily 10.30am–3.30pm; free), was reopened to the public in 1998 after being relocated from 25 miles further north, near Ferndale. The lighthouse operates limited hours during the rest of the year but you can call for a docent to come and open it up for you (☎707/986-7112) when it is closed. The 24-mile **Lost Coast Trail** runs along clifftops dotted with four primitive campgrounds ($9), all near streams and with access to black-sand beaches. Bring a tidebook, as some points of the trail are impassable at high tide. Another trail takes you to the top of **Kings Peak** which, at 4086ft, is the highest point on the continental US shoreline. Cape Mendocino can also lay claim to being the **westernmost point** of the lower 48 states.

The heart of redwood country begins in earnest a few miles north of Garberville, along US-101, when you enter the **HUMBOLDT RED-WOODS STATE PARK** (unrestricted entry; ☎707/946-2409, ⓦwww .humboldtredwoods.org): over 53,000 acres of predominantly virgin timber, protected from lumber companies, make this the largest of the redwood parks – though it is the least used. Thanks to the Save-the-Redwoods League, who have been acquiring land privately for the park, it continues to slowly expand year after year. At the Phillipsville exit, the serpentine **Avenue of the Giants** follows an old stagecoach road, weaving for 32 miles through trees which block all but a few strands of sunlight. This is the habitat of *sequoia sempervirens*, the coast redwood, with ancestors dating back to the days of the dinosaur. The avenue parallels US-101, adding at least thirty minutes to your travel time, but several exits to the freeway mean you won't get trapped here if traffic is intolerable. Pick up a free **Auto Tour** guide at the southern or northern entrances and, better still, stop at the **Visitor Center** (daily 9am–5pm; ☎707/946-2263), halfway along at **Weott**, which has fascinating interpretive exhibits highlighting the redwoods, other flora and fauna, logging history, and the catastrophic 1964 flood. All along the main road, small stalls selling lumber products and refreshments dot the course of the highway, chief among them the **Chimney Tree** (daily 9am–5pm; free), a wonderfully corny gift shop built into the burnt-out base of a still-living redwood. There are three campgrounds ($12; reserve through ParkNet ☎1-800/444-7275) within the park.

The Avenue follows the south fork of the Eel River, eventually rejoining US-101 at **Pepperwood**. Ten miles before this junction, Mattole Road peels off to the left and provides the best **backcountry** access to the towering trees, which most visitors neglect to explore. A few miles after the road emerges from the forest, it passes through **HONEYDEW**, into a region thin on even small settlements. Honeydew is a postage-stamp town popular with marijuana growers who appreciate its remote location – and the two hundred inches of annual rain that sustains the crops, making the town the wettest in California. If you continue up and over the treeless grazing country around **Petrolia**, you will descend to the ocean at a splendid driftwood-strewn beach just south of Cape Mendocino and are guaranteed that sheep and cattle will far outnumber fellow humans.

Back inland, any visitors awed by the majesty of the redwood forests can soon be brought back down to earth a few miles north of Pepperwood at **Scotia**, a one-industry town if ever there was one. In this case it is timber, and the stacks and stacks of logs that line the freeway are actually quite a sight. The Pacific Lumber Company has been here since 1869, but with the decline in the industry and the rise in environmental objections to clear-felling of native forests, the company is throwing itself at the tourist market and parts of the complex have already ceased active operations. Boasting of being "The World's Largest Redwood Mill," it attempts to win you over to the loggers' cause on self-guided **sawmill tours** (Mon–Fri 7.30am–2pm; ☎707/764-2222; free), starting at the Scotia Museum on Main Street.

Ferndale

Just over ten miles north of Scotia, you should definitely take a detour a few miles east to **FERNDALE**, unquestionably the Lost Coast's most attractive town, although with enough time on your hands an even better route is the stunningly scenic Mattole Road loop via Honeydew and Cape Mendocino. Promoting itself unabashedly as "California's best-preserved Victorian village," Ferndale certainly has its charms – for once the appealing architecture is not just confined to one quaint street but continues for blocks on either side of Main Street in a picturesque townscape of nineteenth-century houses and churches. Indeed, the entire town, which celebrated its 150th birthday in 2002, has been designated a State Historical Landmark. You can learn more about its history at the **Ferndale Museum**, 515 Shaw St (Wed–Sat 11am–4pm, Sun 1–4pm; $1), by perusing the old newspaper cuttings, documents, and photos, and trying to imagine exactly what people used to do with all the equipment on display that was once used in bygone occupations. The much more contemporary **Kinetic Sculpture Race Museum**, 393 Main St (daily 10am–5pm), contains vehicles from the peculiar annual competition that takes place between Arcata and Ferndale (☎707/786-9259; see p.752) every Memorial Day weekend. The museum also houses a small stall of brochures provided by the **Chamber of Commerce** (same hours; ☎707/786-7477, ⓦwww.victorianferndale.org/chamber). Ferndale supports an active artistic community, so there are a disproportionate number of galleries and antique shops to browse through.

As you might expect, most of Ferndale's **accommodation** comes in the shape of stylish hotels and B&Bs, though the remote location keeps prices very reasonable. The *Victorian Inn*, 400 Ocean Ave at the corner with Main Street (☎707/786-4558 or 1-888/589-1808, ⓦwww.a-victorian-inn.com; ❹), has comfortable rooms above its classy carpeted lobby and lounge. Almost directly opposite at 915 Main St, *The Ivanhoe* (☎707/786-9000, ⓦwww.hotel-ivanhoe.com; ❺), fully refurbished in 2001, claims to be the oldest hotel in town and westernmost in the country; it also has a decent restaurant. Further along, the *Francis Creek Inn*, 577 Main St (☎707/786-9611; ❸), offers hotel comforts at motel rates. *Curley's Grill* (☎707/786-9696), inside the *Victorian Inn*, serves quality California **cuisine** plus sandwiches and cocktails, while the *Candystick Fountain & Grill*, 361 Main St (☎707/786-9373), is the spot for a cheaper snack or whopping ice cream. The **entertainment** scene is appropriately low-key but you can drink in one of the hotel bars or catch a performance of the renowned Ferndale Repertory Theatre at 477 Main St (☎707/786-5483).

Eureka

Eureka may mean "I have found it!" but once you pull into the largest coastal settlement north of San Francisco you may wonder just what it was the first settlers were seeking. Near the top of the north coast of California between the Arcata and Humboldt bays, **EUREKA** feels – despite some rather attractive Victorian mansions – like an industrial, gritty, and often foggy lumbermill town, though its fishing industry carries the most economic weight, providing ninety percent of the state's catch of Pacific Ocean shrimp and Dungeness crab. There's a limited number of sights here, but the city has an abundance of cheap motels along Broadway, the type of mall-lined strip that's ubiquitous across America.

Downtown Eureka is fairly short on charm, lit by the neon of motels and generic chain restaurants, and surrounded by rail and shipyards, but the pretty, compact **Old Town**, bounded by C, G, First, and Third streets, at the edge of the bay, does its best to support a fledgling tourist economy. The peeling Victorian buildings and poky bars of the old sailors' district are pretty much rundown – though they do have a certain seedy appeal, along with a handful of lively, mostly Italian restaurants. What few sights there are include the **Carson Mansion**, 143 M St at Second, an opulent Gothic pile built in the 1880s by William Carson, who made and lost fortunes in both timber and oil. Carson designed the project to keep his millworkers busy during a slow

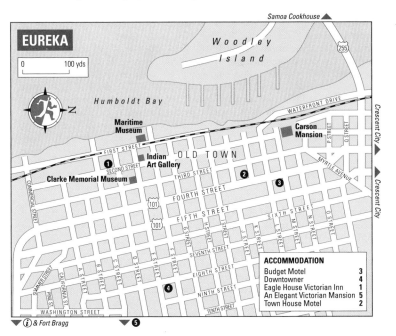

ACCOMMODATION

Budget Motel	3
Downtowner	4
Eagle House Victorian Inn	1
An Elegant Victorian Mansion	5
Town House Motel	2

period in the industry. It now operates as a private gentleman's club behind its gingerbread facade, and can only be enjoyed from the street. Nearby, at 1410 2nd St, the one-room **Maritime Museum** (daily noon–4pm; donation; ☎707/444-9440) is chock-full of photos, maps, and relics from the days when Eureka was a whaling port. **Fort Humboldt State Historic Park**, 3431 Fort Ave (daily 9am–5pm; free; ☎707/445-6567), gives a look at a restored army fort and not much else, disappointing given that the army general and future president Ulysses S. Grant used it for a headquarters in 1853.

The collection of Native American applied art at the **Clarke Memorial Museum**, Third and E streets (Tues–Sat noon–4pm; donation; ☎707/443-1947), can't hold a candle to the stuff at the **Indian Art Gallery**, 241 F St (Mon–Sat 10am–4.30pm; free; ☎707/445-8451), which affords a rare opportunity for Native American artists to show and market their works in a gallery setting, and an even rarer opportunity to get your hands on some incredibly good, inexpensive silver jewelry. If dragging yourself around town for these sights doesn't appeal, you might prefer the Eureka Health and Spa, 601 5th St (☎707/445-2992), with its salt-rubs, tranquility tanks, and saunas.

A few minutes by car from Eureka across the Samoa bridge, squashed against the Louisiana–Pacific plywood mill, the tiny community of **Samoa** is a company town that is the site of the last remaining cookhouse in the West. **The Samoa Cookhouse** (daily 6am–3.30pm & 5–9pm; ☎707/442-1659) was where the lumbermen would come to eat gargantuan meals after a day of felling redwoods, and although the oilskin tablecloths and burly workers have gone, the lumber-camp style remains, making the cookhouse somewhat of an institution. Eating massive portions of red meat at its long tables makes for an entertaining meal.

Practicalities

The collection of **motels** dotted around town, mostly on the busiest through streets, make Eureka bearable for a night, but nearby Arcata provides a much more laid-back environment. Try the *Town House Motel* at 933 4th St at K, which has clean rooms (☎707/443-4536 or 1-800/445-6888, ⓦwww .visithumboldt.com/townhouse; ❷); the slightly quieter *Downtowner*, 424 8th St (☎707/443-5061 or 1-800/862-4906, ⓦwww.eurekainn.com; ❷); or the rock-bottom *Budget Motel*, 1140 4th St (☎707/443-7321; ❶). The *Eagle House Victorian Inn*, at 139 2nd St (☎707/444-3344; ❸), is a strangely deserted and cavernous Victorian relic with surprisingly clean rooms. If you want more than just a bed and a shower, head for *An Elegant Victorian Mansion B&B*, 1406 C St at 14th St (☎707/444-3144; ❺), which, as the name suggests, recalls the opulence and splendor of a bygone era and even offers an architectural tour of the town in a Model "A" Ford. **Campgrounds** line US-101 between Eureka and Arcata; the best is the KOA (☎707/822-4243 or 1-800/562-3136; $18–20 per two-person tent, RV hook-ups $22–$28), a large site with copious amenities four miles north of town at 4050 N US-101.

One positive aspect of Eureka is that its **transportation** links are good: Greyhound, 1603 4th St, connects Eureka to San Francisco in the south and Portland in the north twice daily and recently introduced a twice-daily service inland to Redding, while Amtrak Thruway buses head out from outside *Stanton's Restaurant* on Fifth and L streets. For getting around town or up the coast as far as Trinidad and south as far as Scotia, Humboldt Transit Authority, 133 V St (☎707/443-0826, ⓦwww.hta.org), has a Monday to Saturday service. The Eureka Chamber of Commerce is on the southern approach to town at 2112 Broadway (June–Sept Mon–Fri 9am–7pm, Sat & Sun 10am–4pm;

Oct–May Mon–Fri 9am–5pm, Sat 10am–4pm; ☎707/442-3738 or 1-800 /356-6381, ⓦwww.eurekachamber.com).

In addition to the *Samoa Cookhouse* (see above), **eating** possibilities include the Italian restaurants in the Old Town, notably *Roy's*, 218 D St (☎707/442-4574), where complete meals cost around $20. *The Lost Coast Brewery and Café*, 617 4th St at G Street (☎707/445-4480), serves large, hearty dishes to a rambunctious crowd of microbrew drinkers and sports fans, and the *Six Rivers Brewing Co*, 325 2nd St (☎707/268-3893), also brews fine ale, rustles up tasty food, and has live bands at weekends. *Adel's*, south of downtown at 1724 Broadway, has basic meat-and-potato meals and salads for about $10, making it a local hangout, while on the north side *Samraat*, 1735 4th St (☎707/476-0930), is a good choice if you fancy a curry. The *Humboldt Bay Coffee Company*, 211 F St (☎707/444-3969), ranks as the coast's best coffee shop with its beautiful red-brick interior and sock-it-to-me roasts. It's open until around 9pm and often features live music. For delicious seafood and burgers, you might try *Café Waterfront*, 102 F St (☎707/443-9190), where entrées cost around $15. Eureka has a fair sprinkling of **nightlife** venues, apart from the breweries mentioned above; the most interesting is *The Vista*, tucked on the waterfront at 91 Commercial St (☎707/443-1491), which sporadically showcases hardcore and experimental punk bands from the local area and further afield. For full listings, check out the free weekly *North Coast Journal*.

Arcata

ARCATA, only seven miles up the coast from Eureka, is by far the more appealing of the two towns, centered on a grassy central plaza that flies an Earth flag under those of the US and California. Beards and Birkenstocks are the norm in this small college town, with a large community of rat-race refugees and Sixties throwbacks, whose presence is manifest in some raunchy bars and the town's earthy, mellow pace. The beaches north of town are some of the best on the north coast, white-sanded and windswept, and known for their easy hikeability and random parties. But think twice about diving headlong into the surf without a wetsuit, as the ocean in these parts remains frigid throughout the year.

The main square is the focal point of the town's shops and bars, with everything you're likely to want to see and do within easy walking distance. In the middle of the square rests a statue of President McKinley. Originally intended for nearby McKinleyville, it fell off the train on the way and stayed put in Arcata. Just east of the town center, **Humboldt State University** with its nationally known environmental education and natural resource management programs, attracts a decidedly liberal student body, which contributes considerably to Arcata's leftist feel. If you're interested in the college's history and programs, take a free student-led tour, which will give you much more insight than just wandering the campus's unflattering architecture. Free tours begin at the Plaza Avenue entrance on weekdays at 10am and 2pm and on Saturday at noon. Call ☎707/826-4402 for information.

At the foot of I Street, the **Arcata Marsh and Wildlife Sanctuary**, a restored former dump on 150 acres of wetland, is a peaceful place where you can lie on the boardwalk in the sun and listen to the birds. The Interpretive Center at the foot of South G Street (daily 1–5pm; ☎707/826-2359) runs **guided wildlife walks** (Sat 2pm), as does the Audubon Society, which meets at the very end of I Street at 8.30am every Saturday morning. For those who don't have time to explore the Redwood National Park, Arcata's own second-growth **community forest**, a 575-acre, beautiful spot with manageable trails and ideal picnic areas, is accessible by going east on 14th Street to Redwood Park Drive.

If you're around over Memorial Day weekend, don't miss the three-day **Kinetic Sculpture Race**, a spectacular event in which competitors use human-powered contraptions of their own devising to propel themselves over land, water, dunes, and marsh from Arcata to Ferndale; call ☎707/786-9259 for information.

Practicalities

Greyhound and Amtrak Thruway **buses** pull into the station at 925 E St, connecting with the Eureka services going north and south; there's also a Humboldt Transit Authority link with Eureka every day except Sunday. The brand new **California Welcome Center**, over a mile north of town just off US-101 at 1635 Herndon Rd (daily 9am–5pm; ☎707/822-3619, ⓦwww.arcatachamber.com), has free maps, brochures, and displays from all over the state, and lists of local accommodation and services.

Motels just out of town on US-101 are lower-priced than the increasingly popular **bed and breakfasts**, if a little less inviting, and can usually be found for under $50 per night. Trusty *Motel 6*, at 4755 Valley West Blvd (☎707/822-7061 or 1-800/4MOTEL6, ⓦwww.motel6.com; ❷), fills up with parents visiting for graduation at the adjacent university in May, but otherwise usually has space. You can get reasonable rooms at the *Fairwinds Motel*, 1674 G St (☎707/822-4824; ❷), though if you spend just a bit more money, the *Hotel Arcata*, 708 9th St (☎707/826-0217 or 1-800/344-1221, ⓦwww.hotelarcata.com; ❹), on the town's main square, is a far more stylish establishment. Of the B&Bs, try *The Lady Anne*, an Arcata favorite for years, located between the plaza and the college at 902 14th St (☎707/822-2797; ❺). There are several **campgrounds** north of Arcata along the coast, but none within easy reach of town unless you've got a car. The nearest and cheapest is at **Clam Beach County Park** (☎707/445-7651; day-use $2 per vehicle), eight miles north of town on US-101, where shower-less sites cost $8 per car or $3 per person walk-in, making it quite a party venue for dishevelled youngsters staying long-term. See the "Around Arcata" section below for options with better facilities.

Dotted around the plaza and tangential streets, Arcata's **bars** set the town apart. The best of the bunch, *Jambalaya* at 915 H St (☎707/822-4766), is more of a restaurant with an additional nightly diet of R&B, jazz, and rock bands. The *Humboldt Brewery*, 856 10th St (☎707/822-2739), is a working beer factory with its own bar and low-priced restaurant, where you can sample the preferred stronger, darker brews of Northern California. There's also the relaxed café at the Finnish County Sauna and Tubs (☎707/822-2228), on the corner of Fifth and J streets, with live acoustic sets at the weekend and tubs in the garden for $14.35 an hour. Facing US-101 on 1603 G St, *Muddy Waters Coffee Company* (☎707/826-2233) supports local music with weekly free concerts and is a pleasant place to relax and mingle with students. Good **restaurants** also abound – the *Wildflower Café and Bakery*, 1604 G St (☎707/822-0360), turns out good, cheap organic meals, while the *Big Blue Café*, 846 G St, is a great place to watch proceedings on the square over a fine leisurely breakfast, or you can try the excellent meat or veggie breakfast and lunch specials at *Crosswinds*, 860 10th St (☎707/826-2133). *Abruzzi*, 780 H St (☎707/826-2345), serves top-quality Italian dinners at moderate prices, while *Chan's*, a few blocks south at 359 G St (☎707/822-3922), makes delicious inexpensive Chinese and offers some American dishes.

Around Arcata

If you've got a car, take time to explore the coastline just north of Arcata along US-101. On the way, a short detour worth making east of the highway is through the modern strip-mall town of **McKinleyville**, near Clam Beach, in order to see the world's tallest **totem pole**. The gaily decorated 160ft ex-redwood stands proudly at the back of the McKinleyville Shopping Center halfway along Central Avenue near the junction with City Center Road. If you're peckish, you can't beat the gourmet sandwiches on offer the other side of the main road at *Tastebuds*, 2011 Central Ave (⊕707/839-2788).

Moonstone Beach, about twelve miles north of town, is a vast, sandy strip that, save for the odd beachcomber, remains empty during the day, and by night heats up with guitar-strumming student parties that rage for as long as the bracing climate allows. **Trinidad Harbor**, a few miles further on, is a good stop for a drink, nose around the small shops, or just sit down by the sea wall and watch the fishing boats being tossed about beyond the harbor. If you decide **to stay** in the area, there are two good options a little to the north: the *Trinidad Inn*, 1170 Patrick's Point Drive (⊕707/677-3349, ⊛www.trinidadinn.com; ❸), is a lovely motel in a quiet location, while the *Emerald Forest*, 733 Patrick's Point Drive (⊕707/677-3554, ⊛www.cabinsintheredwoods.com; ❹), offers secluded cabins and tent sites for $20. **Patrick's Point State Park**, five miles north of Trinidad, sports an agate beach atop rocky coastal bluffs and conducts tours of a recreated Yurok village by appointment (⊕707/677-3570), although you can wander alone at will. The park also offers reasonably secluded **camping** for $12 (reserve through ParkNet ⊕1-800/444-7275). Several miles further on, **Big Lagoon County Park** (⊕707/445-7651; day-use $2) has tent spaces for $12. Locals rave about the harbor's *Seascape Pier Restaurant* (⊕707/677-3762), whose menu of fresh fish, steaks, and pasta tastes all the more delicious given its waterfront location.

A more adventurous – some would say insane – destination is **Hoopa Valley Indian Reservation**, sixty miles inland. In past years the site of often violent confrontation between Native Americans and whites over fishing territory, Hoopa is now seen by some as the badlands of Humboldt and few take the time to check out the valley. There's a dead, lawless feel to the place, the locals hanging around listlessly outside their caravans or roaring up and down the dirt tracks on their Harley-Davidsons. Even the bar and bingo hall, once the lifeblood of the community, have been closed down as a result of alcohol-induced violence. The nervous will want to move on quickly, but if you're here in the last week in July you should make an effort to catch the All Indian Rodeo, which is held southwest of the village. Otherwise it is enough to visit the **Hoopa Tribal Museum** (Mon–Fri 8am–5pm, Sat 10am–4pm; donation suggested; ⊕530/493-2900) – full of crafts, baskets, and jewelry of the Hoopa (aka Natinixwe) and Yurok tribes.

The legend of Bigfoot

Reports of giant 350- to 800-pound humanoids wandering the forests of northwestern California have circulated since the late nineteenth century, fueled by long-established Indian legends, though they weren't taken seriously until 1958, when a road maintenance crew found giant footprints in a remote area near Willow Creek. Photos were taken and the **Bigfoot** story went worldwide. Since then there have been more than fifty separate sightings of Bigfoot prints. At the crossroads in Willow Creek stands a huge wooden replica of the prehistoric-looking apeman, who in recent years has added kidnapping to his list of alleged activities.

To get to the reservation, take Hwy-299 west out of Arcata for forty miles until you hit **Willow Creek** – self-proclaimed gateway to **"Bigfoot Country"** – then take Hwy-96, the "Bigfoot Scenic Byway," north. Beside the statue of Bigfoot, a small **Chamber of Commerce** (summer daily 9am–4pm; irregular hours rest of year; ☎530/629-2693, ⓦwww.willow-creekchamber.com) has details of Bigfoot's escapades, and information on the **whitewater rafting** that is done on the Smith, Klamath, and Trinity rivers near here. Among the numerous rafting companies in the area, two are based in Willow Creek – Aurora River Adventures (☎530/629-3843 or 1-800/562-8475) and Bigfoot Rafting Company (☎530/629-2263 or 1-800/722-2223), both offering guided trips from $40. Otherwise, the town comprises a handful of grocery stores, diners, and cheap motels such as the *Willow Creek Motel*, Hwy-96 (☎530/629-2115; ❶). Just north of town, the Lower Trinity Ranger Station (summer Mon–Sat 9am–4.30pm; rest of year Mon–Fri 9am–4.30pm; ☎530/629-2118) handles camping and wilderness permits for the immediate surroundings. Continue east on Hwy-299 and you'll arrive in the Weaverville/Shasta area (see p.776), where you can join the super-speedy I-5 highway.

The Redwood National and State parks

Way up in the top left-hand corner of California, the landscape is almost too spectacular for words, and the long drive up here is rewarded with a couple of tiny towns and thick, dense redwood forests perfect for hiking and camping. Some thirty miles north of Arcata, **Orick** marks the southernmost end of this landscape, a contiguous strip of forest jointly managed as the **REDWOOD NATIONAL AND STATE PARKS** (unrestricted access; free), a massive area that stretches up into Del Norte County at the very northernmost point of California, ending at the rather dull town of **Crescent City**. The fragmented Redwood National Park and the three state parks which plug the gaps – Prairie Creek Redwoods, Del Norte Coast Redwoods, and Jedediah Smith Redwoods – together contain some of the tallest trees in the world: the pride of California's forestland, especially between June and September when every school in the state seems to organize its summer camp here. Increasingly, and despite being designated a World Heritage Site and International Biosphere Reserve, it's becoming a controversial area where campers wake to the sound of chainsaws and huge lumber trucks roaring up and down the highway. Despite this and other sustained cutting, local loggers are still dissatisfied, claiming that they've lost much of the prime timber they relied on to make their living before the days of the parks.

One word of warning: **bears** and **mountain lions** inhabit this area, and you should heed the warnings in Basics on p.54.

Practicalities

The parks' 58,000 acres divide into distinct areas: **Redwood National Park**, southwest of the Orick Area; the Prairie Creek **Redwood State Park**, south of the riverside town of **Klamath**; and the area in the far north around the **Del Norte** and **Jedediah Smith** state parks, in the environs of Crescent City in Del Norte County. The park **headquarters** are in Crescent City, at 1111 2nd St (daily 9am–5pm; ☎707/464-6101, ⓦwww.nps.gov/redw), but the **visitor centers** and **ranger stations** throughout the parks are far better for maps and information, including up-to-date hiking conditions and the weather forecast. Most useful is the **Redwood National Park Information Center** (daily 9am–5pm; ☎707/464-6101 ext 5265), right by the southern entrance before you get to Orick.

The two daily Greyhound **buses** that run along US-101 to Crescent City will, if asked, stop (and if you're lucky can be flagged down) along forested stretches of the highway, and there's a twice-daily Redwood Coast Transit service looping out from Crescent City and back. Still, unless you want to single out a specific area and stay there (not the best way to see the parks), you'll be stuck without a **car**.

As for accommodation, **camping** is your best bet. You can stay at the many primitive and free campgrounds all over the parks; for more comfort, head for the sites we've mentioned in the text below (all $12), along with a hostel and a few **motel/B&B** recommendations. Failing that, get onto US-101 and look for motels around Crescent City.

Orick and Tall Trees Grove

As the southernmost and most used entrance to the Redwood National Park, the Orick area is always busy. Its major attraction is **TALL TREES GROVE**, home of one of the world's tallest trees – a mightily impressive specimen that stands at some 367 feet. The tallest tree in the world, by the way, less than a foot taller, was recently discovered in an inaccessible grove in Mendocino County. The easiest way to get to the Tall Trees Grove, avoiding too much picking amongst the lush undergrowth, is to drive yourself, although you will need to get a free access permit (limited to fifty cars per day – only a problem in high summer) at the visitor center. Here you can pick up a free trail guide that explains why some redwood cutting is being done to balance the damages inflicted on old growth in the past. When you reach the parking lot, it takes about half an hour to hike down the steep trail to the grove itself and, unless you're superfit, somewhat longer to get back up. The best view of the tallest redwood and its companions is to be had from the mostly dry riverbed nearby. Some people prefer to hike the 8.5-mile **Redwood Creek Trail** (permit needed if staying overnight in the backcountry) from near Orick: take a right off US-101 onto Bald Hills Road, then, 600 yards along, fork off to the picnic area where the trail starts. The bridge, 1.5 miles away, is passable in summer only. If you can make it from here, a bit further east another trail turns north off Bald Hills Road and winds for half a mile to **Lady Bird Johnson Grove** – a collection of trees dedicated to former US President LBJ's wife, "Lady Bird" Johnson, a big lover of flora and fauna. A mile-long self-guided trail winds through the grove of these giant patriarchs. On the western side of US-101, across from the entrance to the Redwood Creek Trail, begins the **Coastal Trail**, which follows the coastline and takes backpackers up the entire length of all three state parks. An unpaved road leads in for a few hundred yards before petering out into the hikers-only path.

In **ORICK** itself (actually two miles north of the entrance and ranger station), a couple of **stores** and **cafés**, along with two **motels**, string alongside US-101. On the right as you enter town from the south, the *Green Valley Motel* (☎707/488-2341; ❶) has bargain-rate rooms, while a little further along on the left the *Palm Motel & Cafe* (☎707/488-3381; ❷) also has adequate rooms and serves cheap burgers and sandwiches. You might also stop next door at the *Lumberjack* (☎707/488-5095) for a game of pool and an ice-cold beer. Three miles north of Orick, the narrow gravel Davison Road turns coastwards for a bumpy eight miles to **Gold Bluffs Beach** where you can camp surrounded by elk. The $2-per-vehicle fee also covers Fern Canyon, visited on an easy three-quarter-mile trail, its 45-foot walls slippery with mosses, fern, and lichen.

Prairie Creek State Park

Of the three state parks within the Redwood National Park area, **PRAIRIE CREEK** is the most varied and popular. Bear and elk often roam in plain sight, and you can take a ranger-led **tour** of the wild, solidly populated redwood forest. Check with the **ranger station** (summer daily 9am–5pm; rest of year daily 10am–4pm; ☎707/464-6101 ext 5300) for details. Whether you choose to go independently, or opt for a tour, main features of the park include the meadows of **Elk Prairie** in front of the ranger station, where herds of Roosevelt elk – massive beasts weighing up to four hundred pounds – roam freely, protected from poachers. Remember that elk, like all wildlife, are unpredictable and should not be approached. Day-use is $2 per vehicle but you can park beside the road and wander at will. There's a campground ($12) on the edge of Elk Prairie, at the hub of a network of hiking trails. If you're pressed for time, there are some car-accessible routes through the woods. Just south of the ranger station, on the east side of US-101, is the entrance to **Lost Man Creek**, an unpaved 1.5-mile round-trip drive into a grove that passes by a cascade. To enter Prairie Creek Redwoods State Park, take the **Newton B. Drury Scenic Byway** off US-101 north of Lost Man Creek. Even if you're just passing through, the eight-mile byway is a worthwhile trip deep into the trees. A mile north of the ranger station, the magnificent **Big Tree Wayside** redwood, more than three hundred feet tall and, at over 21ft in diameter, one of the fattest of the coastal redwoods, overlooks the road. North of the Big Tree Wayside and before the byway rejoins US-101, the rough gravel Coastal Drive branches off to the west following the Coastal Trail for 7.5 miles, leading to **High Bluff Overlook** and camping at **Flint Ridge**.

Prairie Creek also has a couple of **restaurants** on the southern approach on US-101. All do a good line in wild boar roasts, elk steaks, and the like, as well as a more traditional menu of burgers and breakfasts. *Rolf's Park Café* (☎707/488-3841; ❸), on US-101 by the Fern Canyon turnoff, is one of the best, with outdoor seating and German entrées as well as motel-style **accommodation**.

Klamath Area

KLAMATH, in Del Norte County, isn't technically part of the Redwood area nor, by most definitions, does it qualify as a town as most of the buildings were washed away when the nearby Klamath River flooded in 1964. Nonetheless, there are spectacular coastal views from trails where the Klamath River meets the ocean, famed salmon and steelhead fishing to be had in the river itself, a few decent accommodation options and, for a bit of fun, the **Trees of Mystery** (daily 9am–5pm; $15; ☎707/482-5971 or 1-800/638-3389, ⓦwww .treesofmystery.net) on US-101, where you'll notice two huge wooden sculptures of Paul Bunyan and Babe, his blue ox. Taped stories of Bunyan's adventures emanate periodically from within the redwood stands and ethereal choral music greets you at the most impressive specimen of all, the **Cathedral Tree**, where nine trees have grown from one root structure to form a spooky circle. Enterprising Californians hold wedding services here throughout the year. A recent addition to the site, which somewhat justifies the steep entry fee, is an aerial tram, which takes you from the top of the foot trail over the forest canopy to 750ft **Ted's Ridge**. Here you are provided with binoculars to enhance your enjoyment of the ocean views to the west and tree-clad ridges and valleys to the east – from March to October look out for the active osprey nest atop one distant redwood. Back down in the gift shop, the free **End of the Trail Museum** highlights artwork from a number of the region's Indian tribes. Further south, where Hwy-169 peels off from US-101, the 725-year-old living **Tour Thru Tree** on Terwer Valley Road (daylight hours; $2) provides a cute photo opportunity. Perhaps the most spectacular scenery in Klamath is not the trees, but the ocean: take Requa Road about three quarters of a mile down to the estuary, to a point known as the **Klamath Overlook**, from where, once the fog has burnt off, there is an awe-inspiring view of the estuary meeting the sea and the rugged coastline to the south. From here, you can pick up the Coastal Trail on foot, which leads north for ten miles along some of California's most remote beach, ending at Endert's Beach in Crescent City.

Practicalities

The newly refurbished *Requa Inn*, 451 Requa Rd (☎707/482-8205, ⓦwww.requainn.com; ❸), offers some of the best **accommodation** around. There are simple cabins at *Woodland Villa*, a mile and a half north of Requa (☎707/482-2081 or 1-888/866-2466, ⓦwww.klamathusa.com; ❷), and small cottages with kitchenettes at *Camp Marigold* (☎707/482-3585 or 1-800/621-8513; ❷), just over one mile south of the Trees of Mystery. Three miles southeast of Klamath down Hwy-275 the *Rhode's End*, 115 Trobitz Rd, Klamath Glen (☎707/482-1654; ❹), offers B&B accommodation along the Klamath River, and the beautifully situated, spotlessly clean, and friendly *HI-Redwood National Park Hostel* several miles north of Trees of Mystery at 14480 Hwy-101 (☎707/482-8265, ⓔetheredwoodhostel@earthlink.net), has dorm beds for $14, whether you are a member or not. A couple of miles yet further north is the free, primitive *DeMartin* campground. Two miles west of US-101 on Klamath Beach Road, *Riverwoods Campground* (☎707/482-5591) has shady tent sites for $13 on the south bank of the Klamath River towards its mouth. There are slim pickings in the **eating** department around Klamath, especially in the evening, but *Sis's Kitchen* (☎707/482-1408) on the southern edge of town at 301 Hwy-169 rustles up fine all-day breakfasts and other meals until the late afternoon. If you want to get into some river activity, Klamath River Jet Boat Tours, 17635 Hwy-101 S (☎707/482-7775 or 1-800/887-JETS, ⓦwww.jetboattours.com), runs four-hour ($30) and ninety-minute ($20) tours and can arrange guided fishing trips.

Crescent City

The northernmost outposts of the Redwood National Park, the Del Norte and Jedediah Smith state parks, sit either side of **CRESCENT CITY**, a rather forlorn place, whose most attractive buildings were wiped out by a typhoon over thirty years ago, leaving little to recommend it other than its proximity to the parks. That said, the city is the half-way point on US-101 between San Francisco (349 miles south) and Portland, Oregon (355 miles north), and is therefore often used as a rest stop so there are plenty of places to stay and eat. Greyhound buses stop at 1125 Northcrest Drive, and the visitor center is at 1001 Front St (Mon–Fri 9am–6pm; June–Oct daily 9am–7pm; ☎707/464-3174 or 1-800/343-8300, ⓦwww.northerncalifornia.net).

The most popular tourist attraction is **Ocean World** (daily 9am–7pm, later in summer; $7.95; ☎707/464-4900, ⓦwww.oceanworld.com), an unmissably large complex on US-101 south of town, which has a limited range of fish and other sea creatures, but the guided tours that run every fifteen minutes are informative and give you the opportunity to handle many of the inmates. So if you fancy picking up a starfish or stroking a shark or sea lion, this is the place for you. Take an hour to visit the **Battery Point Lighthouse** (April–Sept Wed–Sun 10am–4pm; tours sporadically during low tide; $2), reached by a causeway from the western end of town. The oldest working lighthouse on the West Coast, it houses a collection of artifacts from the *Brother Jonathan*, wrecked off Point St George in the 1870s. Because of this loss, the St George Lighthouse, the tallest and most expensive in the US, was built six miles north of Crescent City. Or you could visit the old-fashioned **Del Norte County Main Museum**, 577 H St (May–Sept Mon–Sat 10am–4pm; $2; ☎707/464-3922), whose dusty interior conceals some Indian artifacts, quilts, old musical instruments, the lens from St George Lighthouse, historical displays and, most interesting of all, original cells from the building's earlier incarnation as the **county jail**.

Of several passable **motels**, try the *Crescent Beach Motel*, on the beach two miles south of town at 1455 US-101 S (☎707/464-5436; ❸), or the ultra-cheap *Del Norte Motel*, 975 9th St (☎707/464-4321; ❶), which offers no frills but is in a more central location. If you want somewhere posher to stay, try *Lighthouse Cove*, 215 South A St (☎707/465-6565, ⓦwww.gocalif.com/bamboo; ❻), a smart B&B perched on a bluff overlooking the ocean – you might even spot a migrating whale from your room. For **eating**, try the pasta and vegetarian dishes at the upmarket *Bistro Gardens*, 938 K St (☎707/464-5627), or the excellent moderately priced Italian, steak, and seafood at *Da Luciana*, 575 Hwy-101 S (☎707/465-6566). Other fine ethnic choices are the Thai and Vietnamese dishes at *Thai House*, 105 N St (☎707/464-2427), the filling Chinese at *China Hut*, 928 9th St (☎707/464-4921), or *Los Compadres*, a cheap Mexican diner opposite the marina at 457 Hwy-101 S (☎707/464-7871).

Del Norte and Jedediah Smith state parks

DEL NORTE STATE PARK, seven miles south of Crescent City, is worth visiting less for its redwood forests (you've probably had enough of them by now anyway), than its fantastic beach area and hiking trails, most of which are an easy two miles or so along the coastal ridge where the redwoods meet the sea. From May to July, wild rhododendrons and azaleas shoot up everywhere, laying a floral blanket across the park's floor. The Mill Creek **campground** (reserve through ParkNet ☎1-800/444-7275; $12) here is in a lovely setting. **JEDEDIAH SMITH STATE PARK** (☎707/464-6101 ext 5113), nine miles east of Crescent City, is named after the European explorer who was the first white man to trek overland from the Mississippi to the Pacific in 1828, before being killed by Comanche tribes in Kansas in 1831. Not surprisingly, his name is everywhere: no less than eighteen separate redwood groves are dedicated to his memory. Sitting squatly on the south fork of the Smith River, the park attracts many people to canoe downstream or, more quietly, sit on the riverbank and fish. Of the hiking trails, the **Stout Grove Trail** is the most popular, a one-hour flat walk leading down to a most imposing Goliath – a 345-foot-tall, twenty-foot-diameter redwood.

If you're heading further east and can't face more highway, you could opt for the painfully slow, but scenic six-mile route that follows Howland Hill Road from Crescent City through the forest to the **Hiouchi Information Center** (May–Oct 9am–5pm; ☎707/458-3330) on Hwy-199, about five miles away. Branching off this are several blissfully short and easy trails (roughly half a mile) that are quieter than the routes through the major parts of the park. You can also access the **Little Bald Hills Trail** east of Hiouchi, which traces a strenuous ten-mile hike that should take about eight hours. You'll also find the Jedediah Smith Redwoods **campground** (reserve through ParkNet ☎1-800/444-7275; $12), and picnicking facilities at the end of the Howland Hill Road. Back on the main road at 2097 Hwy-199, the *Hiouchi Motel* (☎707/458-3041 or 1-866/HIOUCHI, ⓦwww.hiouchi.com; ❷) has decent rooms. About ten miles further on, shortly before you leave the redwoods behind, the *Patrick Creek Lodge & Historical Inn*, 13950 Hwy-199 (☎707/457-3323, ⓦwww.patrickcreeklodge.com; ❹), is the last place to stay in California on this route; there are good single rates on the stylish rooms and an excellent but pricey restaurant. The apparent detour into Oregon on Hwy-199 to connect with I-5 back south is actually by far the quickest way to connect to the interior of Northern California from the extreme north coast.

The northern interior

As big as Ohio, yet with a population of only 250,000, the **NORTHERN INTERIOR** of California is about as remote as the state gets. Cut off from the coast by the **Shasta Cascade** range, it's a region dominated by forests, lakes, some fair-sized mountains – and two thirds of the state's precipitation. It's largely uninhabited, and, for the most part, infrequently visited, which makes a spin up here all the more worthwhile. Locals take the time to chat and point out areas to explore, and the region's efficient network of hiking trails and roads usually remains empty of traffic jams.

I-5 leads through the very middle of this near wilderness, forging straight up the **Sacramento Valley** through acres of olive and nut trees, and past the college towns of **Chico** to **Redding**: the latter makes a useful base, with cheap lodging, from where you can venture out on loop trips a day or so at a time. Most accessible, immediately west and north of Redding, the **Whiskeytown-Shasta-Trinity National Recreation Area** is a series of three lakes and forests set aside for what can be heavily subscribed public use, especially in summer when it's hard to avoid the camper vans, windsurfers, jet-skiers, and packs of happy holidaymakers. A better bet lies east at **Lassen Volcanic National Park**, a stunning alpine landscape of sulphur springs and peaks, or in the scenic environs of **Plumas County** to the southeast, between Lassen and Lake Tahoe. Traveling on state highways north of Lassen through national forests reveals numerous roadside surprises, including towering **Burney Falls** and access points to the **Pacific Crest Trail**, the 1200-mile path from Canada to Mexico.

Further north, the crowds swell a bit in the shadows of **Mount Shasta**, a 14,000-foot volcano whose reputation as both spiritual convergence point and climbing challenge brings together an interesting cast of characters in the small town of the same name. Train buffs should stop in the historical railroad town of **Dunsmuir**, just south of Shasta, and anglers will find trout streams filled to the gills all around the area. North of Shasta, the mountains and pines give way to cattle and caves, the latter part of the stunning lava fields of **Lava Beds**

National Monument, the site of one of the saddest Indian wars in US history. Trails and monuments mark the battle's history, while all around the desolate plain, migrating birds rest up in the gigantic sanctuary of the **Klamath Basin** before resuming their journeys on the **Pacific Flyway**.

It's the usual story with sparse **public transportation**: reasonably frequent Greyhound and Amtrak Thruway buses connect San Francisco and Sacramento to Portland via I-5, stopping off at the Sacramento Valley towns and Redding on the way, and trains from Oakland stop in Redding and Chico. However, neither route provides anything close to comprehensive access to the area, and if you're going to come here at all it should be in a **car**. Anything worth seeing lies at least five miles from the nearest bus stop. The area is too big and the towns too far apart to make traveling by bus even faintly enjoyable.

The Sacramento Valley

The **Sacramento Valley** lays fair claim to being California's most uninteresting region; a flat, largely agricultural corridor of small, sleepy towns and endless vistas of wheat fields and fruit trees. By far the best thing to do is pass straight through on I-5 – the half-empty, straight, and speedy freeway cuts an almost two-hundred-mile-long swathe through the region, and you could forge right ahead to the more enticing far north quite painlessly in half a day. If you're coming from San Francisco, save time by taking the I-505 byway around Sacramento.

Chico

Charming little **CHICO**, about midway between Sacramento and Redding and some twenty miles east of I-5 from the Orland exit, is a good stopoff if you don't want to attempt to cover the whole valley from top to bottom in one day, or if you're here to visit Lassen Volcanic National Park (see p.767) and need somewhere to stay. Home to **Chico State University**, a grassy institution of sandal-wearing students named "Best Party School in the Country" by *Playboy* magazine a few years ago, Chico was once the grounds surrounding the mansion of General John Bidwell, one of the first men to cash in on the Gold Rush. As such, the city's traditional layout around a plaza, numerous college eateries, and surrounding expanse of parkland make it something of an oasis compared to the dusty fields and sleepy towns beyond.

Arrival, information, and getting around

Chico is right on Hwy-99. **Trains** (and Amtrak Thruway buses) stop at the unattended station at Fifth and Orange, as do Greyhound **buses**. The *Coast Starlight* train, from Los Angeles to Seattle, stops here once a day, though in the middle of the night. Greyhounds serving cities north and south along I-5 stop more frequently, three or four times a day. See schedules posted at the station.

Chico's **Chamber of Commerce**, 300 Salem St (Mon–Fri 9am–5pm, Sat 10am–3pm; ☎530/891-5556 or 1-800/852-8570, ⓦ www.chicochamber.com), has a terrific supply of information, from pamphlets outlining a historical walking tour through downtown to mountain bike trails and swimming hole locations nearby. They also publish updated lists of lodging options, with prices. To find out what's on, consult the free *Chico News & Review* (ⓦ www.newsreview .com), published every Thursday, or tune in to KZFR (90.1 FM) or The Point (107.5 FM), both broadcasting eclectic local community radio.

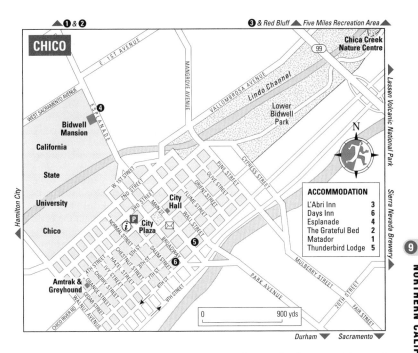

CHICO

3 & Red Bluff ▲ Five Miles Recreation Area ▲

Chica Creek
Nature Centre

Lassen Volcanic National Park

Sierra Nevada Brewery

Hamilton City

E. 1ST AVENUE

MANGROVE AVENUE

WEST SACRAMENTO AVENUE

ESPLANADE

VALLUMBROSA AVENUE

Lindo Channel

Lower
Bidwell
Park

Bidwell
Mansion

California

State

University

Chico

City
Hall

City
Plaza

Normal Street

Chestnut Street

Hazel Street

Salem Street

Broadway

Main Street

Wall Street

Flume Street

Orient Street

Olive Street

Pine Street

Cypress Street

Mulberry Street

Park Avenue

20th Street

Fair Street

Amtrak &
Greyhound

4th Street

5th Street

6th Street

7th Street

8th Street

9th Street

Ivy Street

Cherry Street

Orange Street

Cedar Street

Walnut Avenue

Chico River Rd

N

ACCOMMODATION

L'Abri Inn	3
Days Inn	6
Esplanade	4
The Grateful Bed	2
Matador	1
Thunderbird Lodge	5

0   900 yds

Durham ▼   Sacramento ▼

Parking is only 25¢ an hour downtown in the new lot between Salem and Broadway, near the Chamber of Commerce. The majority of places you are likely to want to visit are within walking distance of the town center, but the trails in Bidwell Park need to be biked to be appreciated. You can rent one for a rather steep $35 per day from Campus Bicycles right off the plaza at 330 Main St (☎530/345-2081). The shop also provides free maps for cyclists.

Accommodation

Chico has much more in the way of **accommodation** than it does in sights, though for **camping** you'll need to head to the Plumas National Forest to the east or Lassen Volcanic National Park. Motels are everywhere in town, particularly in the Main Street and Broadway area, and there are a couple of good B&Bs.

Days Inn 740 Broadway ☎530/343-3286 or 1-800/329-7466, ⓦwww.daysinn.com. Not the cheapest downtown motel but a safe bet chain franchise and just two blocks south of the Plaza, with refrigerators in rooms and a pool. ❸

The Esplanade 620 The Esplanade ☎530/345-8084, ⓦwww.now2000.com/esplanade. A particularly good-value B&B right across from the Bidwell Mansion. The beds are so high you almost need to pole-vault onto them, and tasty breakfasts are served on the back verandah. ❹

The Grateful Bed 1462 Arcadian Ave ☎530/342-2464, ⓔthegratefulbed@chico.com. No tie-dye linen but a laid-back atmosphere at this plush and friendly B&B two blocks west of the Esplanade. ❺

L'Abri Inn 4350 Hwy-99 ☎530/893-0824 or 1-800/489-3319, ⓦwww.now2000.com/labri. Five miles north of town, this place comprises three rooms in a ranch-style home with a serene country atmosphere. Enjoy a sumptuous breakfast, then go out and pet the barnyard animals. ❹

The Matador Motel 1934 The Esplanade ☎530/342-7543. A pretty Spanish Revival building ten blocks north of the Plaza; the tasteful rooms have individual tiling. Set around a courtyard, with palms shading one of Chico's largest pools, this is one of the town's best deals. ❷

Thunderbird Lodge 715 Main St ☎530/343-7911. Decent motel two blocks from the Plaza. Some rooms have refrigerators and coffee makers. ❷

The Town

Chico doesn't have much by way of sights, but strolling the leafy streets, college campus, and shady riverside feels great after the monotonous drive up I-5. The 1904 **Chico Museum**, housed in the former Carnegie Library at the corner of Second and Main streets (Wed–Sun noon–4pm; free; ☎530/891-4336), contains three distinct parts: a permanent historical section, a reconstruction of a Taoist temple altar, and a gallery for rotating shows. You might also try the three-story **Bidwell Mansion** at 525 The Esplanade, the continuation of Main Street (Wed–Sun noon–5pm; tours on the hour until 4pm; $1). Built in 1868, it's an attractive enough Italian country villa, filled with family paraphernalia visited on 45-minute anecdotal tours that are reasonably interesting, though Bidwell Park (most sections open daylight hours; free) is a more pleasurable place to spend your time. Extending from the center of the town for ten miles to the northeast, this is a tongue of semi-wilderness and oak parkland where, incidentally, the first Robin Hood film, starring Errol Flynn, was made, a fair hike from Sherwood Forest. No road runs right through the park, and it is too large to cover on foot, so cycling (see bike rental above) is by far the best way to explore. The most heavily used areas are around the recreation areas at One-Mile Dam and Five-Mile Dam, both reached off Vallombrosa Avenue, and Cedar Grove, reached off East Eighth Street, but a half-hour stroll into Upper Park will leave most of the regulars behind. Students frequent the **swimming holes** on Big Chico Creek in the Upper Park, including Bear Hole, Salmon Hole, and Brown's Hole, which has a small rope swing. For the holes, take Vallombrosa Avenue all the way east until it dead-ends into Manzanita Avenue. Turn left on Manzanita, and then right on Wildwood Avenue. Follow the road past the golf course, where it turns into gravel, and then on to the creek. Driving is the preferred method of getting out here, though biking the three miles from the center of town is rewarded with a cooling plunge into the creek.

Back in town, vintage American car fans will enjoy **Cruces Classic Auto Sales**, downtown on 720 Main St, a commercial showroom with a walk-through museum showing some of the really rare models that are brought here to be restored. The remodeled **Sierra Nevada Brewing Company**, 1075 E 20th St (☎530/893-3520, ⊛www.sierranevadabrewing.com), gives free and fairly cursory twenty-minute tours of the plant (Tues–Fri & Sun 2.30pm, Sat noon–3pm); there is no official tasting as such but you can sample the ten or so brews on tap for under $5 at the brewery's bar.

The **Farmers' Market** closes off downtown every summer Thursday at 5.30pm for three hours of produce sales. Come for the almonds and other fresh nuts grown nearby. The **Gold Cup Races** at the Silver Dollar Speedway (☎530/969-7484) brings Chico's biggest weekend. The stock car extravaganza, which takes place on the third weekend of September, fills all area hotels.

Ten miles outside Chico, south on Hwy-99 then east on Skyway to Humburg/Honey Run Road, the **Honey Run Covered Bridge** is one of the few remaining covered bridges in California. You can't drive on it, but its position in Butte Creek Canyon over a riffling river leads to peaceful walking and swimming opportunities. Further east, the apple orchards in Paradise were used as a location for *Gone with the Wind*.

Eating and nightlife

Chico also does itself proud when it comes to **food** and the listings below are just a sample of what is on offer. If you're here in early September look out for the one-day Taste of Chico **festival**; call ☎530/345-6000 for information.

Being a California State University town, there are many excellent places aimed at the younger customer, as well as a handful of lively **bars**, that feature live music by national acts. It's noticeably quieter when school's out, but on summer Friday evenings, **free concerts** by talented locals draw the crowds to the Downtown Park Plaza, beginning at 7pm.

The Brickworks 190 E 2nd St ☎530/895-7700. Chico's premier live music spot, hosting national touring acts and local bands. On nights without live music, sample the dance club with DJ music playing either country, progressive, or alternative music.

Chada Thai downstairs at 117b W 2nd St ☎530/342-7121. Authentic, and predominantly vegetarian, Thai cuisine at very reasonable prices, especially at lunchtime. Closed Sunday.

Chico Brewhouse 250 Cohasset Rd ☎530/894-2149. A winning combination of moderately priced California cuisine and fine beers microbrewed on site with a relaxed atmosphere and good rock soundtrack.

Cory's 230 W 3rd St ☎530/345-2955. Excellent breakfasts and lunches, featuring sandwiches served on freshly baked bread.

Franky's Fifth and Ivy sts ☎530/898-9948. Inexpensive freshly made pasta and pizza, a staple diet for students and locals alike.

Jack's Restaurant 540 Main St ☎530/343-8383. 24-hr diner, a bit on the greasy side, but good for breakfasts and late-night munchies.

Jasco's California Café 300 Broadway ☎530/899-8075. Salads, sandwiches, and gourmet pizza are all top-notch and reasonable at this second-floor café. The vegetarian sandwiches especially delicious. Lunch and dinner only.

Karim Restaurant 14066 Hwy-99 ☎530/343-0593. Five miles north of town, this is the place for tasty Arabian food such as kebabs and some spicier dishes from further east.

La Hacienda Inn 2635 Esplanade ☎530/893-8270. *Bon Appetit* and *Gourmet* magazines have done features on this Mexican restaurant's special pink sauce, known to locals as "Heroin Sauce" for its addictive sweet flavor. Try it on a tostada, but be warned, you may not be able to stop.

LaSalle's 229 Broadway ☎530/893-1891. The place in Chico to consume large quantities of beer, play pool, and listen to live rock bands.

Madison Bear Garden 316 W 2nd St ☎530/891-1639. A place for swigging beer with students from the nearby campus. Burgers, buffalo wings, and the like are also served.

Riley's 702 W 5th ☎530/343-7459. Catch the ballgame on one of the many TV screens and hang out with the excited students at the most popular sports bar in Chico.

Sierra Nevada Brewing Company 1075 E 20th St ☎530/893-3520. The bar food is unexceptional, but the pale ale, porter, stout, and seasonal brews are a strong draw. There's usually jazz on Mondays and good local bands some weekends.

Tres Hombres Long Bar and Grill 100 Broadway ☎530/342-0425. Large restaurant popular with students for the wide selection of margaritas. Reasonably priced burritos, quesadillas, tostadas, and tacos in a fun environment. Dinner until 10pm every night, drinks until 2am on weekends. Live jazz Sunday afternoons.

Red Bluff and Corning

The largest town in Tehama County, **RED BLUFF**, 45 miles north of Chico on Hwy-99, holds little of interest to travelers save for its proximity to Lassen Volcanic National Park. The Greyhound **bus** stops in front of the *Salt Creek Deli*, at the junction of Hwy-36 and Antelope Road (Hwy-99), but then heads into town for the junction with I-5, leaving no reliable form of public transportation into Lassen itself. Despite its favorable location on the Sacramento River, Red Bluff today is known more as a gas-and-lodging stop before the fifty-mile drive into Lassen along Hwy-36 or the push north to Redding and Mount Shasta on I-5. If you find yourself staying over, there's a reasonable selection of **motels** for $40 per night or less along Main Street – among them the *Crystal Motel*, 333 S Main St (☎530/527-1021, ⊛ www.crystalmotel.com; ❶), and the *Lamplighter Lodge*, 210 S Main St (☎530/527-1150; ❷) – and a handful of diners and burger joints in town. The one classier **restaurant** is the *Raging Fork*, 500 Riverside Way (530/529-9453), which serves great grilled steak and ribs on its patio overlooking the river by the bridge into town. You may consider visiting the **Kelly-Grigs House Museum**, 311 Washington St (Thurs–Sun 1–4pm; donation), where there's an exhibit on Ishi, "the last wild Indian," who appeared out of what is now the Ishi Wilderness in 1911 and was feted until his death in 1916. Pick up more information from the **Chamber**

△ Sequoia National Park

of **Commerce**, 100 Main St (Mon 8.30am–4pm, Tues–Thurs 8.30am–5pm, Fri 8.30am–4.30pm; ☎530/527-6220, or 1-800/655-6225, ⓦwww.red-bluffchamberofcommerce.com). There are a number of antique shops to browse in and Gaumer's, on the I-5 side of the bridge at 78 Belle Mill Rd (Mon–Fri 9am–5pm; free; ☎530/527-6166), is really a jeweller's with an onsite **gemology museum**, displaying hundreds of precious stones, mining equipment, a lapidary workshop, and collection of corals and ammonites. The star exhibit is a sparkly 4ft-tall amethyst cave from Brazil.

If you bypass Chico and enter Tehama County from the south on I-5, an alternative stop for gas and provisions is **CORNING**, home of the world-renowned **Olive Pit**, 2156 Solano St, just east off the Interstate (☎530/824-4667 or 1-800/654-8374, ⓦwww.olivepit.com). This only-in-America store and restaurant sells jars of olives, olive oil, garlic, almonds, and pickles, and has a good grill and ice-cream bar as well. Martini-lovers can get bottles of olive juice mixer, and a free tasting bar allows a trip around the world via olives – from Brine Greek wholes to Napa Valley Wine queens to French pitted and Sicilian cracked. The anchovy-stuffed greens are a must, and pint jars average $3.

Plumas County

Many visitors traveling between Lake Tahoe and the Lassen/Mount Shasta region bypass the Sacramento Valley altogether by using Hwy-89, which winds its way through sparsely populated and scenically exquisite **Plumas County**. Although it boasts no major set-piece attraction, with only one stoplight and constant vistas of pine-clad ridges, grassy valleys, sparkling lakes, and trout-rich rivers, the county is quintessential rural California at its best. Geographically it is significant as the meeting point of the lofty Sierra and volcanic Cascade mountain ranges. The area was home to the hunter-gatherer **Maidu Indians** before white settlers flooded into the valleys when gold frenzy took hold in the mid-nineteenth century, followed by a substantial number of Chinese. The veins of the precious metal were never as rich as those to the south, however, so the prospectors left and the **timber** industry soon took over as the prime economic factor. That too has since gone into decline, leaving farming as the prime source of income for the few inhabitants, along with a smattering of tourism.

Coming from the south, you pass through the missable golfing and retirement paradise of Graegle before Hwy-89 combines with Hwy-70 coming in from the east to form part of the **Feather River National Scenic Byway** and lead you to the county seat and commercial hub of **Quincy**, whose old town merits a wander. Further north Hwy-89 continues solo through the cattle-grazing land of the **Indian Valley**, past the lazy town of **Greenville** to the recreational area of **Lake Almanor**, within easy striking distance of Lassen Volcanic National Park, whose snow-capped peaks are clearly visible.

Quincy

Nestled on the lower western slopes of the northernmost reaches of the Sierra montains, **QUINCY** is a pleasant town, which falls into two distinct halves, divided by a hill. Modern and functional East Quincy is not especially appealing but the blocks surrounding West Main Street in Quincy proper present some fine examples of Victorian architecture and are worth stopping to look around. Behind the grand old Neoclassical **Courthouse**, which stands proudly near the junction where the highway through town veers from West Main St into Crescent Street, you can visit the **Plumas County Museum**, 500 Jackson St (Mon–Fri 8am–5pm, Sat & Sun 10am–4pm; $1; ℡530/283-6320, ⓦwww.countyofplumas.com). Inside you will find informative displays on the area's Indian culture, the story of its settlement, and on natural history, while the grounds contain an old buggy and an authentic 1890s gold-miner's cabin.

For information you have a choice between the **Chamber of Commerce**, 464 W Main St (Mon–Fri 9am–noon & 1–4.30pm; ℡530/283-0188, ⓦwww.psln.com/qchamber), and the more comprehensive **Plumas County Visitors Bureau** on the northern edge of town at 550 Crescent St (℡530/283-6345 or 1-800/326-2247, ⓦwww.plumascounty.com). Of several **motels** around town, the best choice in terms of location and comfort is the *Gold Pan Motel*, 200 Crescent St (℡530/283-3686 or 1-800/804-6541; ❷), while among the **B&Bs** in the old town *The Feather Bed*, 542 Jackson St (℡530/283-0102 or 1-800/696-8624, ⓦwww.featherbed-inn.com; ❹), and *Aspen Cottage*, 156 Coburn St (℡530/283-3375, ⓦwww.aspencottage.com; ❺), are both comfortable and suitably atmospheric. If you're hankering for a Wild West experience, horse-riding, fishing, and hiking are all included in the cost of a night's stay at *Greenhorn Creek Guest Ranch* (℡530/283-0930 or 1-800/33-HOWDY, ⓦwww.greenhornranch.com; ❽), twelve miles east of town, a mile and a half from the highway at 2116 Greenhorn Ranch Rd. **Eating** choices are not spectacular in Quincy but you can grab a filling breakfast or lunch at the *Courthouse Café*, 525 W Main St (℡530/283-3344), bang opposite – you guessed it – the Courthouse or enjoy a more upscale meal nearby at *Moon's* Italian steak house, 497 Lawrence St (℡530/283-0765). East Quincy offers a few cheap and cheerful joints such as *Round Table Pizza*, 60 E Main St (℡530/283-4545), and the *Mi Casita* Mexican, 875 E Main St (℡530/283-4755).

Northern Plumas County

Leaving Quincy behind, Hwy-70 soon peels off to the left and continues to follow the middle fork of the Feather River southwest, while Hwy-89 meanders in a northerly direction through the rich grassy meadows, ranches, and farms of the **Indian Valley** towards the old mining town of **Greenville**, 23 miles on from Quincy. A further nine miles brings you close to the western shore of **Lake Almanor**, an increasingly popular destination for boaters and families, and its main settlement of **Chester** at the northern end.

Greenville

Although it now depends more on cattle ranching and the felling of Christmas trees, **GREENVILLE** still celebrates its mining heritage every summer with the **Gold Digger Days** festival that takes place on the third weekend of July. For the rest of the year it remains in somewhat of a slumber but can still make a pleasant spot to break your journey. There's not much to see since the sole museum closed down several years ago, but just wandering along Main Street can give you a sense of the town's workaday past. If you stop for a bite to **eat**, the cheap diner-style meals at the *Coach House Restaurant* (℡530/284-0800) or bar food at the *Way Station Dinner House & Tiki Bar* (℡530/284-6018), on opposite corners of the central Hwy-89/Main Street junction, will suffice.

Lake Almanor and Chester

LAKE ALMANOR, created in 1914 by the Great Western Power Company damming the north fork of the Feather River, stands at an elevation of 4500ft and covers fifty-two square miles, making it the largest of Plumas County's many lakes. It is also here that the Cascades and the Sierras truly meet. The clear blue waters reach a comfortable seventy-five degrees in summer, rendering it ideal for all sorts of **watersports**. Numerous resorts ring the pine-forested shoreline of the lake and most rent equipment for all sorts of water-based activities from high-speed water-skiing to leisurely fishing, as well as providing a range of **accommodation** possibilities. Two such enterprises are *Plumas Pines Resort*, on the west shore at 3000 Almanor Drive West, Canyon Dam (℡530/259-4343, ⓦwww.plumaspinesresort.com; ➌), which has motel-style rooms, cabins, and RV slots ($22), as well as food at the *Boathouse Grill*, and, on the peninsula opposite, *Knotty Pine Resort*, 430 Peninsula Drive (℡530/596-3348; ➌), whose half-dozen cabins are nicely situated. The nearby *Peninsula Grill* at 401 Peninsula Drive (℡530/596-3538) does tasty seafood, steaks, and pasta. For **campers** there are simple sites all over the lake that are usually let on a first-come-first-served basis but some can be booked through the US Forest Service (℡1-800/280-CAMP, ⓦwww.ReserveUSA.com).

At the top of the lake, the only town, **CHESTER**, is a relaxed place with a splendid setting and a selection of amenities. Of the dozen places to **stay** the *Antlers Motel*, 268 Main St (℡530/258-2722; ➋), and *Seneca Motel*, 545 Martin Way (℡530/258-2815; ➋), are both fairly basic but reliable, while the *Cinnamon Teal* B&B, 227 Feather River Drive (℡530/258-3993; ➍), provides more ambience. Two miles east of town on Hwy-36, *North Shore Campground* (℡530/258-3376) is the biggest **campsite** on the lake with tent spaces for $16. By way of **restaurants** *Burger Depot*, 336 Main St (℡530/258-1880), serves pizza as well as the eponymous standard, while *Dan's Family Diner*, 300 Main St (℡530/258-2560), bashes out American classics and ice cream all day and *Ming's Dynasty*, 605 Main St (℡530/258-2420), provides copious portions of Chinese favorites.

Lassen Volcanic National Park

About fifty miles over gently sloping plains east from Red Bluff on Hwy-36, the 106,000 acres that make up the pine forests, crystal-green lakes, and boiling thermal pools of the **LASSEN VOLCANIC NATIONAL PARK** are one of the most unearthly parts of California. A forbidding climate, which brings up to fifty feet of snowfall each year, keeps the area pretty much uninhabited, with the roads all blocked by snow and (apart from a brief June to October season) completely deserted. It lies at the southerly limit of the Cascades, a low, broad range which stretches six hundred miles north to Mount Garibaldi in British Columbia and is characterized by high volcanoes forming part of the Pacific Circle of Fire. Dominating the park at over 10,000ft is a fine example, **Mount Lassen** itself, which – although quiet in recent years – erupted in 1914, beginning a cycle of outbursts which climaxed in 1915 when the peak blew an enormous mushroom cloud some seven miles skyward, tearing the summit into chunks that landed as far away as Reno. Although nearly ninety years of geothermal inactivity have since made the mountain a safe and fascinating place, scientists predict that of all the Californian volcanoes, Lassen is the likeliest to erupt again.

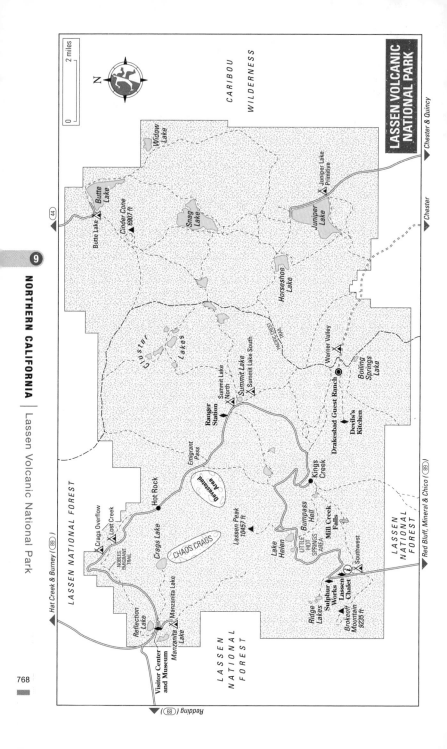

LASSEN VOLCANIC NATIONAL PARK

CARIBOU WILDERNESS

LASSEN NATIONAL FOREST

LASSEN NATIONAL FOREST

LASSEN NATIONAL FOREST

N

0   2 miles

Hat Creek & Burney (89)

Redding (89)

Red Bluff, Mineral & Chico (89)

Chester

Chester & Quincy

Widow Lake

Butte Lake

Butte Lake

Cinder Cone 6907 ft

Snag Lake

Juniper Lake

Juniper Lake Primitive

Horseshoe Lake

Cluster Lakes

Summit Lake North

Summit Lake

Summit Lake South

Ranger Station

Warner Valley

Boiling Springs Lake

Drakesbad Guest Ranch

Devil's Kitchen

Emigrant Pass

Hot Rock

Devastated Area

Crags Overflow

Lost Creek

NOBLES EMIGRANT TRAIL

Crags Lake

CHAOS CRAGS

Lassen Peak 10457 ft

Kings Creek

Bumpass Hell

Mill Creek Falls

Lake Helen

LITTLE HOT SPRINGS AREA

Southwest

Sulphur Works

Lassen Chalet

Ridge Lakes

Brokeoff Mountain 9235 ft

Reflection Lake

Manzanita Lake

Manzanita Lake

Visitor Center and Museum

44

9

Arrival and information

Lassen is always open ($10 per vehicle for seven days, $5 per hiker or biker), but you'll have a big job ahead of you if planning to get in or around without a car. During the winter, when the roads in the park are almost always shut down due to snow, a car won't do you much good either – snowshoes and cross-country skis are popular modes of transportation. Public transportation really isn't an option, seeing as the "mail truck" of Mount Lassen Motor Transit (Mon–Sat from 8am; ☎530/529-2722) from Red Bluff only reaches **Mineral**, some eight miles short of the park's southwestern entrance. From Mineral, Hwy-89 leads through Lassen to the northern entrance at the junction of Hwy-44 and Hwy-89 near Manzanita Lake.

The Park Service has its **headquarters** in Mineral (daily 8am–4.30pm; PO Box 100, Mineral, CA 96063; ☎530/595-4444, ⓦwww.nps.gov/lavo), where you can get free maps and information (there's a box outside when it's closed, and they'll leave your backcountry permits here if you arrive late), including the *Lassen Park Guide*. The main **visitor center** (June–Aug daily; May & Sept

Camping in and around Lassen

During the few months of the year when conditions are suitable for camping, this is by far the best accommodation option. All **developed campgrounds** in the park are listed below and operate on a first-come-first-served basis, not a problem except on midsummer weekends. Most remain open July to September. Remember that Lassen is **bear country**; follow the posted precautions for food and waste storage, and make your presence known when hiking.

Primitive camping requires a free **wilderness permit** obtainable in advance from the park headquarters in Mineral (see above), or in person from the visitor centers and entrance stations. There is no self-registration and chosen sites must be a mile from developed campgrounds and a quarter of a mile from most specific sites of interest. In the surrounding **Lassen National Forest**, camping is permitted anywhere, though you'll need a free permit to operate a cooking stove or to light a fire; these are sometimes refused in the dry summer months. In addition, there are a couple of dozen developed sites strung along the highways within thirty miles of Lassen, most charging between $8 and $12.

Butte Lake ($12; 6100ft). In the far northeast corner of the park, accessed by Hwy-44. Can accommodate trailers and has a boat launch.

Juniper Lake ($10; 6800ft). In the far southeastern corner of the park, with good hiking trails nearby and swimming in the lake. Drinking water must be boiled or treated.

Manzanita Lake ($14; 5900ft). By far the largest of the Lassen campgrounds and the only one with a camp store (8am–8pm), firewood for sale ($6), 24-hour showers (bring quarters), and a laundry. Trailers allowed and boat launch facilities available. Rangers run interpretive programs from here. Open May 23 to snow closure.

Southwest ($12; 6700ft). Small tent-only campground by the southwest entrance on Hwy-89 with walk-in sites, water, and fire rings. Open year-round if you are equipped to brave it.

Summit Lake ($12–14; 6700ft). The pick of the Hwy-89 campgrounds, right in the center of the park and at the hub of numerous hiking trails. It's divided into two sections, the northern half can take trailers and is equipped with flush toilets, the southern half only vaults. There's swimming in the lake for the brave.

Warner Valley ($12; 5700ft). Off Hwy-89 in the south of the park, this is a beautiful site, but its distance from the road makes it only worth heading for if you're planning extended hiking in the region.

Sat & Sun 9.30am–5.30pm; ☎530/595-4444 ext 5180) is at Manzanita Lake, just inside the northern entrance, and occupies the same building as the Loomis Museum (see opposite).

Accommodation

The only way to **stay** inside the Lassen park is to camp (see box), but even in August night temperatures can hover around freezing, and many people prefer to stay in one of the resorts and lodges that pepper the surrounding forest. To be sure of a room in the popular summer months, it pays to book well ahead.

Hat Creek Resort Hwy-89, Old Station, eleven miles northeast of the northern entrance ☎530/335-7121, ⓦ www.hatcreekresort.com. A complex of motel units and fancier cabins with kitchens (two-day minimum stay). ❷

Lassen Mineral Lodge Hwy-36, Mineral, nine miles southwest of the southwest entrance on Hwy-36 ☎530/595-4422, ⓦ www.minerallodge .com. Unspectacular base-rate rooms and considerably more comfortable family ones for not much more. There's a general store, restaurant, and bar on site, as well as tent sites for $16. ❸

Mill Creek Park Mill Creek Road, Shingletown, fifteen miles west of the northern entrance ☎530/474-5384. Set amid pines and cedars, simple cabins with cold-water kitchenettes cost $35,

those with hot water and bath around $10 more, and space at the campground is $10. ❶

Padilla's Rim Rock Ranch Resort 13275 Hwy-89, Old Station, eleven miles northeast of the northern entrance ☎530/335-7114. A collection of cabins of varying standards, the best sleeping up to six ($95), dotted around a meadow. Closed November to March. ❷

Weston House Red Rock Road, Shingletown, nineteen miles west of the northern entrance ☎530/474-3738, ⓦ www.westonhouse.com. One of the nicest B&Bs in all of California, with six elegant rooms beautifully sited on a volcanic ridge with pool and deck, overlooking the Ishi National Wilderness Area. ❻

The park

Unlike most other wilderness areas, you don't actually need to get out of the car to appreciate Lassen, as some of the best features are visible from the paved Hwy-89 that traverses the park. A thorough tour should take no more than a few hours. Pick up a copy of the *Road Guide: Lassen Volcanic National Park* ($5) in the visitor center.

Starting from the southwest entrance, you'll pass the trailhead to **Brokeoff Mountain**, a six-mile round-trip hike through wildflowers. Next is the **Lassen Chalet**, the only place to get food and, in winter, limited skiing facilities in the park. The first self-guiding trail is just up ahead – follow your nose and the **Sulphur Works** can be reached via a 200-foot boardwalk around its steaming fumaroles and burbling mud pots. The winding road climbs along the side of Diamond Peak before edging **Emerald Lake** and Lassen's show-stealer, **Bumpass Hell**, named after a man who lost a leg trying to cross it. This steaming valley of active pools and vents that bubbles away at a low rumble can be traversed on a flat, well-tended trail that loops three miles to boardwalks that put you right in the middle of the stinky action. Recall the fate of Mr Bumpass, however, and stay on the trails; the crusts over the thermal features are brittle and easy to break through, leaving you, literally, in hot water. Across the road from Bumpass Hell's parking lot, the trails around the icy-green glassy surface of Emerald Lake are also spectacular, though in much quieter fashion; the lake itself resembles a sheet of icy green, perfectly still and clear but for the snow-covered rock mound which rises from its center. The lake approaches swimmable temperatures only during summer.

Just north of here, the road reaches its highest point (8512 feet) at the trailhead for **Lassen Peak**. The road then winds down to the flat meadows around

King's Creek, whose trails along the winding water are popular for picnics. From roadmarker 32, a three-mile round-trip walk leads to the seventy-foot-tall Kings Creek Falls. At the halfway point you'll come to Summit Lake, a busy camping area set around a beautiful icy lake, from where you can start on the park's most manageable hiking trails. Press on further to the Devastated Area, where, in 1914, molten lava from Lassen poured down the valley, denuding the landscape as it went, ripping out every tree and patch of grass. Slowly the earth is recovering its green mantle, but the most vivid impression is still one of complete destruction. From here it's a gauntlet of pines to the northern entrance, site of Manzanita Lake and the Loomis Museum (June–Oct daily 9am–5pm; free), a memorial to Benjamin Loomis whose documentary photos of the 1914 eruption form the centerpiece of an exhibition strong on local geology – plug domes, composite cones, and cinder cones – and flora. An easy trail circles the lake, but so do many of the campers from the nearby campground: an early start is needed for any serious wildlife spotting.

Leaving Lassen, Hwy-44 heads forty miles west to Redding and I-5 or alternatively you can continue northwest on Hwy-89 one hundred miles to Mount Shasta, stopping halfway at the breathtaking McArthur–Burney Falls State Park ($2; ℡530/335-2777). The park's centerpiece is a 129-foot waterfall,

Hiking in Lassen Park

For a volcanic landscape, a surprisingly large proportion of the walking trails in the park are predominantly flat, and the heavily glaciated terrain to the east of the main volcanic massif is pleasingly gentle. Rangers will point you toward the hiking routes best suited to your ability – the park's generally high elevations will leave all but the most experienced walker short of breath, and you should stick to the shorter trails at least until you're acclimatized. For anything but the most tentative explorations, you should pick up a copy of Lassen Trails ($3.95) or the better, color Hiking Trails of Lassen ($14.95), which describe the most popular hikes.

Chaos Crags Lake (3.5 miles round-trip; 2–3hr; 800ft ascent). From the Manzanita Lake campground access road, the path leads gently up through pine and fir forest to the peaceful lake. An adventurous extension climbs a ridge of loose rock to the top of Chaos Crags, affording a view of the whole park.

Cinder Cone (13 miles round-trip; 1 day; 800ft ascent). Check with the rangers for the best seasonal starting point for this, Lassen's most spectacular hike, through the Painted Dunes and Fantastic Lava Beds before reaching Snag Lake. Can also be done as a 4hr hike from Butte Lake.

Lassen Peak (5 miles round-trip; 4hr; 2000ft ascent). A fairly strenuous hike from road marker 22 to the highest point in the park. Be prepared with water and warm clothing.

Manzanita Lake (1.5 miles; 1hr; flat). Easy trails on level ground make this one of the most popular short walks in the park.

Nobles Emigrant Trail (2.5 miles; 1–2hr; 200ft ascent). The most accessible and one of the more interesting sections of a trail forged in 1850 starts opposite the Manzanita Lake entrance station and meets Hwy-89 at marker 60. It isn't maintained, but is heavily compacted and easy going.

Paradise Meadows (3 miles round-trip; 3hr; 800ft ascent). Starting either at the Hat Creek parking area (marker 42) or marker 27, and passing Terrace Lake on the way, this hike winds up at Paradise Meadows, ablaze with wildflowers in the summer and a marvelous spot to pass an afternoon.

unique for the way the water spills over the rim from two different levels. A paved trail leads to the misty base and pool, and a 1.5-mile steep loop takes you downstream and then back up the other side of the pool to a bridge over the falls' headwater. The Pacific Crest Trail passes alongside nearby **Lake Briton**, and paddleboats, canoes, and rowboats can be rented at the park entrance. Plentiful **camping** amongst the black oaks is available for $12 a night.

Eating

For **food**, you don't have an awful lot to choose from in Lassen Volcanic National Park. There's a reasonable general store at *Manzanita Lake* campground (see box, p.771), and *Lassen Chalet* has a surprisingly good café (daily 9am–6pm), but beyond that you'll have to go outside the park.

Redding and around

With a sprawling expanse of strip malls along I-5, which have taken over from the ailing shopping center in its heart, and a concrete convention center at its

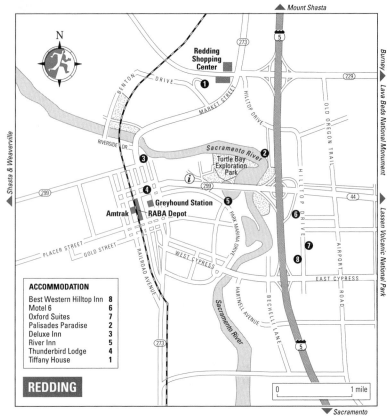

ACCOMMODATION

Best Western Hilltop Inn	8
Motel 6	6
Oxford Suites	7
Palisades Paradise	2
Deluxe Inn	3
River Inn	5
Thunderbird Lodge	4
Tiffany House	1

REDDING

0   1 mile

gate, **REDDING** first appears to be a bit of an anomaly amidst the natural splendor of the northern interior. The region's largest city, with over 70,000 people, it has acted as a northern nexus since the late nineteenth century, when the Central Pacific Railroad came through. Today it remains, essentially, a crossroads, bulging with cookie-cutter motels and diners that service traffic heading east to Lassen, west to Whiskeytown-Shasta-Trinity National Recreation Area, north to Mount Shasta, and south to San Francisco. The one annual event that does attract substantial crowds is the **Kool April Nites** classic-car meeting (℡1-800/874-7562, ⓦwww.koolaprilnites.com) on the third weekend of April, the only time you are likely to encounter problems finding a room.

Though fiercely hot in summer (100°F even in late September), the temperature drops forbiddingly in some of the surrounding areas in winter. Bear in mind that what looks like a mild day in Redding could turn out to be blizzard conditions a few miles up the road (and several thousand feet up a mountainside).

Arrival, getting around, and information

Considering its position at the crossroads of Northern California, **public transportation** in Redding is woefully inadequate, though at least the various modes of ground transport available all stop within easy walking distance of each other downtown. The Greyhound station is at 1321 Butte St (℡530/241-2070), while the local RABA **bus** system depot (℡530/241-2877) is on California Street, the other side of the deserted shopping center, and the Amtrak station is right beside it. If you are in a hurry to get to Northern California and want to bypass the Bay Area, there are at least six United Express (℡1-800/241-6522) **flight** connections daily from SFO to **Redding Municipal Airport** (℡530/224-4321), plus two daily from Seattle via Portland and sometimes Arcata with Horizon Air (℡1-800/547-9308). Typically, there is no public transportation from the airport and once here, you're not going to get to see much without a **car** anyway. Call Caltrans to check ahead for weather and road conditions (℡1-800/427-7623) and, if necessary, make extra provisions (de-icer, tire chains, and so on) in case of snowstorms.

The **Redding CVB**, 777 Auditorium Drive (Mon–Fri 8am–5pm, Sat 9am–5pm; ℡530/225-4100 or 1-800/874-7562, ⓦwww.visitredding.org), can give advice on accommodation in Redding, information on camping in the outlying areas, and details on where to rent camping equipment. For more specific information on the surrounding area and the whole of the northern interior and beyond, the brand new **California Welcome Center**, just off I-5 nine miles south of Redding at 1699 Hwy-273, Anderson (daily summer 9am–6pm; winter 9–5pm; ℡530/365-7500 or 1-800/474-2782, ⓦwww.shastacascade.com), has a huge collection of maps and information, well-organised displays, and is staffed by helpful outdoor experts. As a general rule, Lassen National Volcanic Park is for hardier and more experienced hikers, and novices are pointed in the direction of the Whiskeytown-Shasta-Trinity National Recreation Area, where there are warmer climes and easier trails.

Accommodation

Motels are concentrated along Redding's old main strip, Market Street (Hwy-273), and Pine Street, while the smarter chain hotels tend to be along Hilltop Drive, Redding's newer service area east of I-5. A few B&Bs dotted around town round out the options.

Best Western Hilltop Inn 2300 Hilltop Drive ☏530 /221-6100 or 1-800/336-4880, ⊛ www.bestwestern .com. This comfortable franchise – with its pool, sauna, and buffet breakfasts – succeeds in making you feel you are staying somewhere more personal than your average chain. ❹

Deluxe Inn 1135 Market St ☏530/243-5141. This ultra-cheapie is fine for a night but hardly lives up to its name. ❶

Motel 6 1640 Hilltop Drive ☏530/221-1800 or 1-800/4MOTEL6, ⊛ www.motel6.com. The most central of three outlets in the Redding area, as usual this one is basic but clean and efficient. ❷

Oxford Suites 1967 Hilltop Drive ☏530/221-0100 or 1-800/762-0133, ⊛ www.oxfordsuites.com. This great-value Californian chain offers smart and comfy suites at good rates. You can drink your two free happy-hour beverages in peace by the pool. ❹

River Inn 1835 Park Marina Drive ☏530/241-9500 or 1-800/995-4341, ⊛ www.reddin-griverinn.com. Glorified motel, perhaps a little overpriced for the area because of its prime river-side location. ❹

Palisades Paradise 1200 Palisades Ave ☏530/223-5305. Friendly B&B with a fabulous view of the Trinity Mountains to the west across a bend in the river. Only two rooms so book early. ❹

Tiffany House 1510 Barbara Rd ☏530/244-3225, ⊛ www.sylvia.com/tiffany.htm. Just over a mile north of downtown. Plush yet good-value B&B in a converted Victorian house, with a pricier detached cottage behind. ❹

The Town

Redding has been working hard of late on improving its image in order to tempt visitors to spend a day or two in its leafy urban environment before sampling the surrounding natural delights. Visitors are encouraged to stay in the newer areas near the freeway rather than in the dowdy old **downtown** area, which could really do with the proposed injection of cash to spruce it up. Though in no way unsafe, walking round it gives the distinct impression that it has seen better days. One place you might stop in at is the **Old City Hall Gallery**, 1313 Market St (Tues–Fri 9am–5pm, Sat 11am–3pm; free; ☏530/241-7320), which has rotating displays of works by local artists.

The centerpiece of the revitalisation process is the splendid new **Turtle Bay Exploration Park**, 800 Auditorium Drive (June–Sept daily 9am–6pm; Oct–May Tues–Sun 9am–5pm; $11; ☏530/243-8850 or 1-800/887-8532, ⊛ www.turtlebay.org), an ambitious $64 million project, the first part of which opened in June 2002 and has successfully combined the disparate exhibits from the site's two previous museums with plenty of new material into a fascinating interactive whole. The new glass-and-wood structure blends seamlessly into the riverside environment and contains permanent displays on native American culture, including a full-scale replica of an Indian bark-house, and the region's natural history and resources. The skilfully crafted **Visible River** exhibit, which allows you to enter a simulated limestone cave and view local water creatures in a 24ft tank, creates the impression you are below a river bank - a huge cottonwood tree even starts within the "river" and protrudes upwards into the museum. The River Lab enables you to play with natural materials and learn by experience how processes like erosion work on a large tilted table covered in sand, while the Exploration Hall and Art Gallery display changing cultural and artistic exhibitions. Also within the grounds Paul Bunyan's Forest Camp includes logging and ecological displays and a summer butterfly house, while the projected 220-acre McConnell Arboretum will conceal walking trails through oak savanna and wetlands when completed. The glass **café** at the west end of the main building gives uninterrupted views of the river bank, which forms part of the newly-extended **Sacramento River Trail**, a pleasant ten-mile loop designed for walkers and cyclists. Over the next couple of years you will also be able to watch the gradual erection of the unique **Sundial Bridge**, designed by top Spanish architect Santiago Calatrava. The tapered 218ft mast at the northern end of this slim, translucent, glass-floored footbridge will form a sundial and is anticipated to become a true icon for the region, even the state.

Eating

Restaurants are as ubiquitous as motels, some of them 24-hour, many of them greasy diners or fast-food outlets, limited in appeal. Here are some noble exceptions:

Chocolat de Nannette 1777 Market St ☎530/241-4068 A fairly chic but inexpensive bistro serving imaginative salads and main courses, combined with a quality bakery and café.

CR Gibbs American Grille 2300 Hilltop Drive ☎530/221-2335. Part of the *Best Western* complex, this relaxed place offers pizza or classic meat and seafood dishes, which you can wash down with good draught ale or local wine.

De Mercurio's 1647 Hartnell Ave ☎530/222-1307. Redding's most upscale restaurant with an eclectic seasonal menu of high-quality French, Italian, and American dishes. Most entrées over $20.

The Hatchcover 202 Hemsted Drive ☎530/223-5606. Tasty steak and seafood are served on the riverside terrace at the *Hatchcover*, and there's a comfortable cocktail lounge inside.

Jack's Grill 1743 California St ☎530/241-9705. Fine grilled steak, and shrimp and chicken dishes for $10–15. You'll probably have to wait for a table, which you cannot reserve, but it's worth the wait. Closed Sunday.

Pesce & Pasta 1790 Market St ☎530/246-3922. Excellent Italian eatery, providing mid-priced seafood and pasta specialties in a casual setting in the heart of town.

Taj Mahal 40 Hartnell Ave ☎530/221-4651. Authentic North Indian cuisine in a modern dining room; quite pricey dinner entrées but great lunch buffet seven days a week.

Shasta

Huddling four miles west of Redding, the ghost town of **SHASTA** – not to be confused with Mount Shasta (see p.778) – is about the only option for historic entertainment, and it's a slim option at that. A booming gold-mining town when Redding was an insignificant dot on the map, Shasta's fortunes changed when the railroad tracks were laid to Redding in the late nineteenth century. Abandoned since then, it remains today a row of half-ruined brick buildings that were once part of a runaway prosperity, and literally the end of the road for prospectors. All roads from San Francisco, Sacramento, and other southerly points terminated at Shasta; beyond, rough and poorly marked trails made it almost impossible to find gold diggings along the Trinity, Salmon, and Upper Sacramento rivers, and diggers contented themselves with the rich pickings in the surrounding area, pushing out the local Native Americans in a brutal territorial quest for good mining land.

The **Courthouse**, on the east side of Main Street, has been turned into a museum (Wed–Sun 10am–5pm; $1), full of mining paraphernalia and paintings of past heroes, though best are the gallows at the back and the prison cells below – a grim reminder of the daily executions that went on here. The miners were a largely unruly lot, and in the main room of the Courthouse a charter lays down some basic rules of conduct:

IV Thou shalt neither remember what thy friends do at home on the Sabbath day, lest the remembrance may not compare favorably with what thou doest here. VII Thou shalt not kill the body by working in the rain, even though thou shalt make enough money to buy psychic attendance. Neither shalt thou destroy thyself by "tight" nor "slewed" nor "high" nor "corned" nor "three sheets to the wind," by drinking smoothly down brandy slings, gin cocktails, whiskey punches, rum toddies and egg nogs.

From The Miners' Ten Commandments

The **Shasta State Historic Park** (unrestricted entry; ☎530/243-8194) straddles two blocks of Main Street, and is less grand than it sounds. Indistinguishable ruins of brick buildings are identified by plaques as stores and hotels, and the central area, not much bigger than the average garden really, features miscellaneous mining machinery and a picnic area, along with a trail that loops around the back. On the whole, the park is a place to stretch your legs before moving further west.

Whiskeytown-Shasta-Trinity National Recreation Area

To the west and north of Redding lies the **Whiskeytown–Shasta–Trinity National Recreation Area**. Assuming the roads are open – they often get blocked off due to bad weather in winter – this huge chunk of land is open for public use daily, year-round. Its series of three impounded **lakes** – **Whiskeytown**, **Trinity**, and **Shasta** – have artificial beaches, forests, and camping facilities designed to meet the needs of anyone who has ever fancied themselves as a water skier, sailor, or wilderness hiker. Sadly, during summer the area becomes completely congested, as windsurfers, motorboats, jet skis, and recreational vehicles block the narrow routes which serve the lakes. But in the winter, when the California weekenders have all gone, it can be supremely untouched, at least on the surface. In fact, there's an extensive system of tunnels, dams, and aqueducts directing the plentiful waters of the Sacramento River to California's Central Valley to irrigate cash crops for the huge agribusinesses. The lakes are pretty enough, but residents complain they're not a patch on the wild waters that used to flow from the mountains before the Central Valley Project came along in the 1960s.

Whiskeytown Lake

Of the three, **Whiskeytown Lake**, just beyond Shasta, is the smallest, easiest to get to, and inevitably the most popular. It is open all the time but day-use parking costs $5. Ideal for watersports, it hums with the sound of jet skis and powerboats ripping across the still waters. Those who don't spend their holiday in a wetsuit can usually be found four-wheel-driving and pulling action-man stunts on the primitive roads all around. The best place for **camping** and **hiking** is in the **Brandy Creek** area – a hairy five-mile drive along the narrow J.F. Kennedy Memorial Drive from the main entrance and **Whiskeytown Visitor Information Center** on Hwy-299 (daily summer 9am–6pm; winter 10am–4pm; ☎530/246-1225), where you can pick up permits for primitive camping sites (summer $10, winter $5) around the lake. There's a small store at the water's edge in Brandy Creek and three more developed campgrounds (summer $18, winter $8) about a mile behind the woods.

Trinity Lake and Weaverville

Northeast on Hwy-3 (off Hwy-299 forty miles west of Whiskeytown), **TRINITY LAKE** (officially called Clair Engle Lake, but not locally referred to as such) is much quieter, used by fewer in summer, and in winter primarily a picturesque stopoff for skiers on their way to the **Trinity Alps** area beyond, which in turn lead to the extensive **Salmon Mountains** range. There are several places to **stay** and enjoy the peaceful lapping waters or use as a base to get out onto them. Of these *Pinewood Cove*, 45110 Hwy-3 (☎530/286-2201 or 1-800/988-5253, ⓦwww.pinewoodcove.com; ❹), rents out boats of various sizes and has $20 campsites and luxury cabins, which are unfortunately only available by the week in summer, as are the slightly more modest cabins further north at *Trinity Lake Resorts*, 45810 Hwy-3 (☎530/286-2225 or 1-800/982-2279; ❸), which also has a full restaurant. At its southern end Lake Trinity squeezes through a narrow bottleneck to form the much slimmer and smaller Lewiston Lake, which can be reached by the backroad that cuts the corner between Hwy-299 and Hwy-3. You can camp for free on the grassy banks of the lake or stay in greater comfort at the *Old Lewiston Inn* (☎1-800/286-4441, ⓦwww.theoldlewistoninn.com; ❺) in the diminutive old mining town of Lewiston itself, on the same road.

Weaverville

Sadly, many people don't bother to stop in the small Gold Rush town of **WEAVERVILLE**, 43 miles west of Redding, where Hwy-3 branches north to Trinity Lake, while Hwy-299 continues a further one hundred miles west to Eureka (see p.749) and the coast. The town's distinctive brick buildings, fitted with exterior spiral staircases, were built to withstand fires – indeed, the fire station itself is particularly noteworthy. The main draw, though, is the **Joss House** on Main Street (Wed–Sun 10am–5pm; $1; ☎530/623-5284), a small Taoist temple built in 1874 by indentured Chinese mineworkers. A beautiful shrine, still in use today, it features a three-thousand-year-old altar and can be visited on a poor guided tour. Next door, the **J.J. Jake Jackson Museum** (daily: May–Oct 10am–5pm; Apr & Nov noon–4pm; free; ☎530/623-5211) exhibits artifacts from the Gold Rush. On the opposite side of the road look out for California's oldest still-functioning pharmacy, which still stocks a brilliant selection of remedies in glass jars within original glass and wood cabinets.

You can **stay** in some style at the newly refurbished *Weaverville Hotel*, 205 Main St (☎530/623-2222; ❺), a century-old building. Alternatives include the renovated *Gold Country Inn*, 718 Main St (☎530/623-4937; ❷). The friendly *Motel Trinity* (☎530/623-2129 or 1-877/623-5454; ❷) on Main Street just south of Hwy-3, has some rooms with hot tubs but they cost twice as much as the basic ones.

You can **eat** well-prepared chicken, steaks, and pasta for under $15 at the cozy *La Grange Café*, 315 Main St (☎530/623-5325), or delicious Chinese food in the dark-red interior of the *Red Dragon*, 401 Main St (☎530/623-30000), across from the Joss House, appropriately enough. The *New York Saloon*, 225 Main St (☎530/623-3492), is a great place to mingle with the friendly locals over a glass of beer. For more information, consult the **Chamber of Commerce**, 211 Trinity Lakes Blvd, off Hwy-299 in Weaverville (summer Mon–Sat 9am–5pm; rest of year Mon–Fri 9am–4pm; ☎530/623-6101 or 1-800/487-4648, ⓦwww.trinitycounty.com).

Shasta Lake

East of the other two, eight miles north of Redding, is **SHASTA LAKE**. The biggest of the three lakes – larger than the San Francisco Bay in fact – it's marred by the unsightly and enormous **Shasta Dam**, 465ft high and over half a mile long, bang in the middle. Built between 1938 and 1945 as part of the enormous Central Valley irrigation project, the dam backs up the Sacramento, McCloud, and Pit rivers to form the lake, the project's northern outpost. The best views of the millions of gallons of water gushing down the face of the giant structure are from marked vista points along the approach road (US-151, off I-5), especially since security concerns in the wake of September 11 knocked tours into the dam itself on the head, meaning the nearest you can get is the **powerhouse visitor center** (daily 9am–4pm) at the side.

On the north side of the lake, the massive limestone formations of the **Shasta Caverns** (daily 2hr tours: June–Aug every hour 9am–4pm; April, May, Sept hourly 9am–3pm; winter 10am, noon & 2pm; $17) are the largest in California, jutting above ground and clearly visible from the freeway. The interior, however, is something of a letdown – a fairly standard series of caves and tunnels in which stalactite and stalagmite formations are studded with crystals, flowstone deposits, and miniature waterfalls. The admission price covers the short ferry journey from the ticket booth across an arm of Shasta Lake and the bus transfer on the other side. If you turn west instead of east at the exit to the caverns, within a couple of miles you reach two great **places to stay**. First, in the small hillside settlement of **O'Brien**, the *O'Brien Mountain Inn* (☎530/238-8026 or 1-888/799-8026, ⓦ www.obrienmountaininn.com; ❺) is a welcoming country B&B, whose star room is the detached $225 Tree House Suite on stilts over the forest. A little further on the *Bridge Bay Resort*, 10300 Bridge Bay Rd (☎530/275-3021 or 1-800/752-9669; ❸), provides the only accommodation right on the lake in the shape of motel rooms, cabins, and larger suites; you can also dine with a view of the water at the resort's excellent *Tail of the Whale* restaurant. From Lake Shasta, I-5 crosses the world's highest double-deck bridge and races up towards Mount Shasta, an impressive drive against a staggering backdrop of mountains and lakes.

Mount Shasta . . . and Mount Shasta

When I first caught sight of it over the braided folds of the Sacramento Valley I was fifty miles away and afoot, alone and weary. Yet my blood turned to wine, and I have not been weary since.

John Muir, about Mount Shasta

The lone peak of the 14,162-foot **MOUNT SHASTA** dominates the landscape for a hundred miles all around, almost permanently snow-covered, hypnotically beautiful but menacing in its potential for destruction: it last erupted over two hundred years ago, but is still considered an active volcano. Summing up its isolated magnificence, Joaquin Miller once described it as "lonely as God and as white as a winter moon." Local lore is rich with tales of Lemurians – tall, barefoot men dressed in white robes – living inside the mountain, alongside their legendary neighbors the Yaktavians, who are said to be excellent bellmakers. Such tales have lent the mountain a bit of a Twilight Zone reputation, and numerous UFO sightings and other-worldly experiences have made Mount Shasta a center of the American spiritualism movement. This prominence was heightened in 1987 when 5000 people arrived to take part in the good vibes of the Harmonic Convergence, an attempt to channel the energies of sacred power spots into peace and harmony. Not all is peaceful on the mountain, however, as hundreds of climbers annually attempt to ascend its icy heights, an activity that has resulted in deaths, usually caused from falls or from the ever-changing weather.

Just below the shadow of the behemoth sits the historic railroad town of **Dunsmuir** and, right up against the mountain, pleasant **Mount Shasta City**, a small town of shops, outfitters, spiritual bookstores, and fantastic restaurants. To the southeast, also commanding wonderful views of the mountain, is pretty little **McCloud**, while on the northern flank of the peak rests **Weed**, another tiny town that offers better views of Mount Shasta in summertime and access to Lava Beds National Monument. Further north towards the Oregon

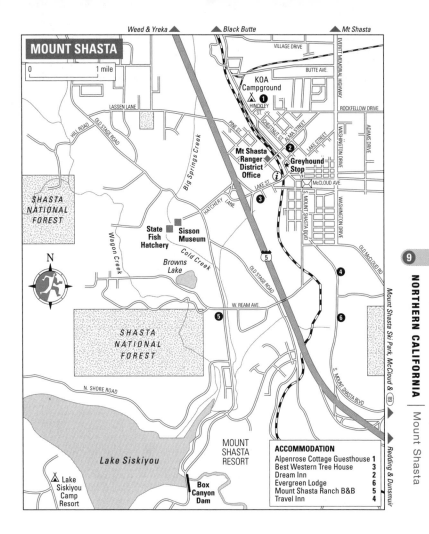

MOUNT SHASTA

Weed & Yreka ▲   ▲ Black Butte   ▲ Mt Shasta

0 |_____| 1 mile

VILLAGE DRIVE

BUTTE AVE.

KOA
Campground ❶

HINCKLEY ST.

ROCKFELLOW DRIVE

LASSEN LANE

HILL ROAD

OLD STAGE ROAD

PINE ST.

CHESTNUT ST.

ALMA STREET

LAKE STREET

WASHINGTON DRIVE

ADAMS DRIVE

EVERETT MEMORIAL HIGHWAY

Big Springs Creek

Mt Shasta
Ranger
District
Office ❷

Greyhound
Stop

LAKE ST.

McCLOUD AVE.

❸

S. MOUNT SHASTA BLVD.

WASHINGTON DRIVE

SHASTA
NATIONAL
FOREST

Wagon Creek

HATCHERY LANE

State
Fish
Hatchery

Sisson
Museum

Cold Creek

Browns
Lake

N

5

❹

OLD STAGE ROAD

OLD McCLOUD RD.

W. REAM AVE.

❺

❻

SHASTA
NATIONAL
FOREST

N. SHORE ROAD

S. MOUNT SHASTA BLVD

Mount Shasta Ski Park, McCloud & ⑧⑨

Redding & Dunsmuir

MOUNT
SHASTA
RESORT

Lake Siskiyou

Lake
Siskiyou
Camp
Resort

Box
Canyon
Dam

ACCOMMODATION
Alpenrose Cottage Guesthouse   1
Best Western Tree House   3
Dream Inn   2
Evergreen Lodge   6
Mount Shasta Ranch B&B   5
Travel Inn   4

⑨

NORTHERN CALIFORNIA | Mount Shasta

---

border, **Yreka** is more useful as an I-5 service stop than as a place to visit in its own right, unless you're a train buff.

Arrival and information

Merely getting to Mount Shasta City is a rewarding journey, easily accomplished on Greyhound **buses**, which connect the town with Redding to the south and stop on North Mount Shasta Boulevard, downtown across from Vet's Club, although the nearest ticketing office is seven miles north in Weed, 628 S Weed Blvd (Mon–Sat 8.30am–4pm; ☎530/938-4454 or 1-800/231-2222). Amtrak **trains** stop six miles south in Dunsmuir, unfortunately in the middle of the night; from there, six daily STAGE buses (☎530/842-8295 or 1-800/24-STAGE) run up to the Mount Shasta Shopping Center, next to the *Black Bear Diner*, although you'll have to wait at least three hours for the first bus. STAGE also operates five daily services to McCloud. The **Chamber of Commerce**, 300 Pine St (daily: May–Sept 9.30am–5.30pm; Oct–April 10am–4pm; ☎530/926-4865 or 1-800/926-4865, ⓦwww.mtshastachamber.com), has a rather limited selection of brochures; you can obtain more comprehensive information on the entire county from the **Siskiyou County Visitor Bureau** (☎1-877/847-8777, ⓦwww.visitsiskiyou.org), although there is no office to visit here.

Accommodation

Mount Shasta City has no shortage of **accommodation**, and reservations should only be necessary on weekends in the height of summer. **Campgrounds** abound in the surrounding area, but few have full amenities (hot showers are vital when the mercury drops).

Hotels, motels, and B&Bs

Alpenrose Cottage Guesthouse 204 E Hinckley St ☎530/926-6724, ⓦwww.snowcrest.net/alpenrose. A top-quality and friendly hostel-style guesthouse with a relaxed atmosphere and a great deck for watching the sunset over Mount Shasta immediately behind. Only double rooms, which are let out at $30 (half-price) to lone travelers, if you are prepared to share. Follow the KOA signs a mile north on North Mount Shasta Boulevard. ❸

Dream Inn 326 Chestnut St ☎530/926-1536 or 1-877/375-4744, ⓔedreaminn@jps.net. Very central and good-value B&B, a block east of Mount Shasta Boulevard, in a Victorian house with all the usual trappings. ❸

Evergreen Lodge 1312 S Mt Shasta Blvd ☎530/926-2143, ⓦwww.snowcrest.net/evergreenlodge. The smartest of the budget lodges lining the road in from the south, the *Evergreen Lodge* features well-maintained and nicely decorated rooms. ❸

Mount Shasta Cabins & Cottages 500 S Mount Shasta Blvd ☎530/926-5396 or 1-888/565-9422, ⓦwww.mtshastacabins.com. Agency office for a wide range of cabins and houses in and around Mount Shasta, rented by the night but particularly suited for longer stays. Most have kitchenettes, TVs, and wood stoves, and drop their rates substantially outside the summer season. ❷–❺

Mount Shasta Ranch B&B 1008 W A Barr Rd ☎530/926-3870, ⓦwww.stayinshasta.com. A stylish ranch house with spacious rooms and a great view of Mount Shasta. ❸

Travel Inn 504 S Mt Shasta Blvd ☎530/926-4617. Decent, clean motel with basic rooms at bargain rates. ❶

Camping

The most picturesque campground in the area is the woodland *Lake Siskiyou Camp Resort* ($18; ☎530/926-2618), four miles southwest of town on a lake of the same name, where you can picnic, bathe, and go boating. More **primitive sites** tend to be free if there is no piped drinking water, though creek water is often available. The most useful of these is the walk-in *Panther Meadows* (7400ft; closed in winter), high up on the mountain at the end of the Everitt Memorial Highway, though *McBride Springs* ($12; 5000ft), being lower down the same road, tends to be open for longer. The fully equipped *KOA*, 900 N Mount Shasta Blvd (☎530/926-4029 or 1-800/736-3617), a few blocks from downtown, charges $15 per tent site and has basic cabins from $40.

The Town and around

Quite rightly, few people come to Mount Shasta for its museums, but in bad weather you might visit the otherwise missable **Sisson Museum**, 1 N Old Stage Rd (June–Sept daily 10am–4pm; April, May & Oct–Dec daily 1–4pm; donation suggested; ☎530/926-5508), with a few examples of Native basketware, a fair bit on pioneering life in the region, and some more diverting material on the mountain itself. The brown, rainbow, and eastern brook trout in the **fish hatchery** outside (daily April–Sept 8am–4pm; free) can be fed on food from a vending machine.

A couple of New Age **bookstores** along North Mount Shasta Boulevard provide the key to some of the town's more offbeat activities. Golden Bough Books at no. 219 (☎530/926-3228 or 1-877/674-7282), for example, has active bulletin boards and stacks of publications exhorting you to visit a sweatlodge or get in touch with the ascended masters. The visitors center provides an ever-changing list of metaphysics, astrology, and alternative healing options as their practitioners and followers migrate in and out of the town. An increasing number of galleries and gift shops are sprouting up too.

Mainly, though, Mount Shasta is full of outfits hoping to help you into the **outdoors**, from trout fishing to dog sledding to, of course, mountain climbing. Competition keeps prices reasonable and the options wide open. Obviously, there are a thousand ways to climb Mount Shasta, and these are covered in the box on p.782. Otherwise, Shasta Mountain Guides, 1938 Hill Rd (☎530/926-3117, @www.shastaguides.com), arranges jeep trips up the mountain and conducts rock- and ice-climbing courses for all levels from $85 per day, as well as backcountry skiing trips for $75. For real thrills, whitewater rafting trips on the churning Upper Sacramento are offered by Turtle River Rafting (☎530/926-3223 or 1-800/726-3223, @www.turtleriver.com) and River Dancers (☎530/926-3517 or 1-800/926-5002, @www.riverdancers.com), both starting at $85 a day. Train enthusiasts should check out the elegant **Shasta Sunset Dinner Train**, which departs from the nearby town of McCloud (see p.783), nine miles southeast of Mount Shasta City on Hwy-89. Cars constructed in 1916 clack along east- and west-bound routes while you sit back and enjoy a full-course meal (3 hours; from $70; ☎530/964-2142 or 1-800/733-2141, @www.shastasunset.com).

Eating

Aside from a rash of fast-food outlets towards I-5, Mount Shasta's **eating** options are largely health-conscious, with vegetarian dishes featured on almost every menu. Hardy mountain types are amply catered for, too, with plenty of opportunities to stoke up on hearty fare before hitting the mountain heights.

The Bagel Café and Natural Bakery 315 N Mt Shasta Blvd ☎530/926-1414. A favorite with Mount Shasta's spiritual community, serving moderately priced soups, sandwiches, great huevos rancheros, and, of course, bagels.

Black Bear Diner 401 W Lake St ☎530/926-4669. Wholesome family diner, a great place for heaped breakfasts or classic American dinners.

Lily's 1013 S Mt Shasta Blvd ☎530/926-3372. Moderately priced and consistently good restaurant serving California cuisine, vegetarian, and Mexican dishes. Mains cost around $15, sandwiches around $6.

Mike and Tony's 501 S Mt Shasta Blvd ☎530/926-4792. It may not look like much, but this excellent Italian restaurant specializes in home-made ravioli. It offers good wines, figs, and goat cheese; great martinis. Dinner only; closed Tuesday and Wednesday.

Poncho & Lefkowitz 107 Chestnut St ☎530/926-6324. Inexpensive and tasty Mexican and American food is served in ample portions.

Serge's 531 Chestnut St ☎530/926-1276. Moderately priced and informal French dining at lunchtime and evenings. Several vegetarian plates are featured, and the Sunday brunch is something of a local tradition.

Trinity Café 622 N Mt Shasta Blvd ☎530/926-6200. The best place for quality international cuisine made from local produce. The menu changes weekly and fine microbrewed ales are available on tap.

Around Mount Shasta

Apart from Mount Shasta itself and the surrounding towns covered below, there are several other natural delights to explore, which you will certainly find less well-trodden in season than the main body of the mountain. Five miles north of town, the largely treeless cone of **Black Butte** (2.5 miles; 2–3hr;

1800ft ascent), offers a more modest alternative to climbing Mount Shasta. The switchback trail to this 6325ft volcanic plug dome is hard to find without the leaflet available from the ranger station or visitors center.

If you have time, you'd also be well advised to explore the beautiful trails that climb 4000ft up to the 225-million-year-old glacier-polished granite crags at the aptly named **Castle Crags State Park** (℡530/235-2684 or 1-800/444-7275), thirteen miles south of Mount Shasta along I-5. Campgrounds with full amenities are available for $12 per night in the often deserted 6200-acre forested park.

Mount Shasta Ski Park (℡530/926-8610 or 1-800/754-7478, ⓦwww.skipark.com), near McCloud on Hwy-89, has yet to establish itself on the

Climbing Mount Shasta

Even if you are only passing through the region, you'll be tempted to tackle Mount Shasta. Ambling among the pines of the lower slopes is rewarding enough, but the assault on the summit is the main challenge – and it can be done in a day with basic equipment and some determination.

Every year several deaths occur and numerous injuries are sustained through inexperience and over-ambition. The wise will stick to the routes prescribed by the **Mount Shasta Ranger District Office**, 204 W Alma St (June–Aug daily 8am–4.30pm; Sept–May Mon–Fri 8am–4.30pm; ℡530/926-4511), which will insist that you obtain a **wilderness permit** (also self-issued outside the office when closed and at the trailhead; $15) and enter your name in the voluntary **climbers' register** before and after your ascent.

The mountain's isolation creates its own **weather**, which can change with alarming rapidity. In early summer, when most novice attempts are made, the snow cover is complete, and crampons and an ice axe are a requirement to get a good grip; later during the season, as the snow melts, patches of loose ash and cinder appear, making the going more difficult and the chance of rockfall greater. Only at the end of summer, with most of the snow melted, is there a chance of climbing safely without equipment. There are countless equipment rental agencies in town, such as The Fifth Season, 300 N Mount Shasta Blvd (℡530/926-3606), which has the following rental prices for two/three-day trips: boots ($24), crampons and ice axe ($18), mountain tent ($50), and sleeping bag ($18). They also provide a mountain weather forecast on ℡530/926-5555. House of Ski & Board, 316 Chestnut St (℡530/926-2359, ⓦwww.shastaski.com), offers much the same at very competitive rates.

Even for fit, acclimatized climbers **the ascent**, from 7000ft to over 14,000ft, will take eight to ten utterly exhausting hours. The easiest, safest, and most popular way up is via **Avalanche Gulch** – just follow the footprints of the person in front of you. Drive up the mountain on the Everitt Memorial Highway to the **Bunny Flat** trailhead at 7000ft. A gentle hour's walk brings you to **Horse Camp**, 7900ft, a good place to acclimatize and spend the night before your ascent – there's drinking water, toilet facilities, and a knowledgeable caretaker who can offer good advice about your impending climb. The return trip is done in four or five hours, depending on the recklessness of your descent: Mount Shasta is a renowned spot for **glissading** – careering down the slopes on a jacket or strong plastic sheet – a sport best left to those proficient in ice-axe arrests, but wonderfully exhilarating nonetheless.

On the lower slopes, keep your eyes skinned for the inedible **watermelon snow**, its bright red appearance caused by a microbe which flourishes here. Most importantly, be prepared for **storms** on the mountain. Bring extra food, stove fuel, a good, wind-resistant shelter, and plenty of warm clothing. And if the weather does take a turn for the worst, don't hesitate to head back down the mountain – high elevation storms sometimes last for days, with little or no visibility.

ski circuit, so its lift tickets ($33) and rental charges for skis ($21), snowboards ($28), and snowshoes ($12) are quite reasonable. In summer, it transforms into some of the best **mountain-biking** territory in the region, with marked trails following the ski runs. A day-pass is $14, and bikes can be rented for $20 a day. There's also an artificial tower for climbing ($10 per day) and chairlift rides ($10).

After a day or two trudging around or up Mount Shasta, **Stewart Mineral Springs** (Mon–Thurs & Sun 10am–6pm, Fri & Sat 10am–8pm; ☎530/938-2222, Ⓦwww.stewartmineralsprings.com; ❷) at 4617 Stewart Springs Rd off I-5 just north of Weed, provides welcome relief. Individual bathing rooms in a cedar and pine forest glade soothe your aches away for $17–20, less if you stay in the very affordable cabins, tepees ($24), or campground ($13) here.

Dunsmuir

One example of how the Shasta area looked in the past can be seen in the hamlet of **DUNSMUIR**, which is even quainter than Mount Shasta City. Situated ten miles south of Mount Shasta on a steep hill sloping down from I-5, Dunsmuir's downtown was bypassed by the freeway, essentially freezing the community in time. Now it makes its living as a historic railroad town, and the main drag, **Dunsmuir Avenue**, is lined with restored hotels and shops, many of them taking the train theme a bit too far; expect to see shopkeepers dressed as train engineers and business names like Billy Puffer Suites. Amtrak stops at the very dilapidated railway station, its last California halt before continuing north to Oregon. The Visitors Bureau, near Amtrak at 4118 Pine St (Mon–Sat 10am–4pm, Sun noon–4pm; ☎530/235-2177 or 1-800/386-7684), has updated train and STAGE schedules; but if your interest in trains is more whimsical, Espee Dave's Trains-n-Things, 5815 Dunsmuir Ave, sells electric and model trains.

Dunsmuir used to bill itself as a day-trip from Shasta, but recently realized that it had a quietude and natural wonders of its own. Foremost among these are the Mossbrae and Hedge Creek **waterfalls**, along the Sacramento River Canyon, beautiful spots for walks and picnics. To reach **Mossbrae**, drive north on Dunsmuir Avenue to Scarlet Way, crossing the bridge and railroad tracks to the parking area. Follow the walking trail along the train tracks for one mile until you get to the railroad bridge. Don't cross, but continue along the tracks through the trees and the falls are ahead. **Hedge Creek Falls** are accessible via the parking area at the North Dunsmuir exit on I-5.

If you are planning **to stay**, several B&Bs ply their trade around town, the most central being *The Dunsmuir Inn*, 5423 Dunsmuir Ave (☎530/235-4543 or 1-888/386-7684; ❹). A good mile further north the *Cedar Lodge*, 4201 Dunsmuir Ave (☎530/235-4331, Ⓦwww.cedarlodgedunsmuir.com; ❷), is considerably cheaper and will do nocturnal Amtrak pickups for guests. The *Cornerstone Bakery Café*, 5759 Dunsmuir Ave (☎530/235-2620), sells all the fixings needed for a **picnic**, or you can grab a meal at the trendy *Gandy Dancer Café*, 5841 Sacramento Ave (☎530/235-9811).

McCloud

Home to the famous *Sunset Dinner Train* (see p.781 for details), **McCLOUD** is a delightful little town with stunning views of Mount Shasta and it can make another good base for the area, especially if you plan to spend much time in the Ski Park (see opposite). In the **accommodation** stakes the *McCloud Hotel*, right in town at 408 Main St (☎530/964-2822 or 1-800/964-2823, Ⓦwww.mccloudhotel.com), has smart rooms in a classy restored building, while two excellent B&B options just up the road are *Stoney Brook Inn*, 309 W Colombero Drive (☎530/964-2300 or 1-800/369-6118, ⓦwww.stoney-brookinn.com; ❸), which has particularly good single rates, and the *McCloud Guest House*, 600 W Colombero Drive (☎530/964-3160 or 1-877/964-3160, ⓦwww.mccloudguesthouse.com; ❺), beautifully situated in its own extensive wooded grounds. For a **meal** try the fine Italian food at *Raymond's*, 424 Main St (☎530/964-2009), or the tasty and filling Mexican dishes at the *Briar Patch Restaurant*, on the south side of Hwy-89 at 140 Squaw Valley Rd (☎530/964-2700). *Briar Patch* also has the town's main bar, and the owner occasionally plays live music for the customers himself.

There's not much to do in the town itself, but the nearby **McCloud River Falls**, five miles east on Hwy-89, is a great spot for a picnic or gentle stroll. The falls, set amidst thick woods, are divided into three distinct sections, each about one mile from the next and connected by a riverside walking trail, but also accessible by road. If you're short of time, head for the more dramatic Middle Falls; at *Fowlers*, near the Lower Falls, there is **camping**, often free because of problems with the water supply, while the Upper Falls boast a lovely picnic area. If you continue southeast on Hwy-89, you will eventually come to the more renowned and spectacular Burney Falls and, still further, Lassen Volcanic National Park (see p.767).

Weed

A gateway town to Klamath Falls, Oregon, and the Lava Beds National Monument, **WEED** can't compete with Mount Shasta City's hip charm. But, perhaps in a form of karmic justice, it gets the better view of the peak during the summertime. Too bad the tourism board couldn't leave it at that, instead of dressing up the place as a "historic lumber town" with the groaner of a slogan, "Weed love to see you." Despite this, there are a couple of good budget **motels** and **eateries** in town, as well as the College of the Siskiyous, which is certainly California's prettiest campus owing to its views of the peak. In town, the *Hi Lo Motel & Café*, 88 S Weed Blvd (☎530/938-2731, ⓦwww.hilomotel.com; ❷), has decent rooms and a café that slings hash and eggs. On the northern end of Weed Boulevard, at no. 466, the *Motel 6* branch includes a nice outdoor pool and stunning sunrise views of Mount Shasta (☎530/938-4101 or 1-800/4MOTEL6, ⓦwww.motel6.com; ❷). *Papa's Place*, 203 Main St (☎530/938-2277), is a friendly bar where you can drink beer with the locals and get a basic snack.

Five miles outside of town, north on US-97 on the way to Oregon and Lava Beds, the **Living Memorial Sculpture Garden** experience (unrestricted entry; donation) is an intriguing remembrance of the Vietnam War. Artist Dennis Smith has created ten metal sculptures illustrating different aspects of an American soldier's experience in the war. Surrounding the art are about 53,000 pine trees, one for every American killed in Vietnam. The trees, art, silence, and position under Mount Shasta add up to a very moving experience.

Yreka

There's little to justify more than an hour or two in quiet, leafy **YREKA** (pronounced "Why-reeka"), twenty-five miles north of Weed on I-5, but it makes a pleasant break. Most people come here to ride the Yreka Western Railroad, better known as the **Blue Goose** (mid-June to Aug Wed–Sun; late May to mid-June & Sept–Oct Sat & Sun only; ☎530/842-4146 or 1-800/973-5277, ⓦwww.yrekawesternrr.com), a 1915 Baldwin steam engine pulling attractive carriages to and from the nearby historic town of Montague; the three-hour excursion costs $12.25 and includes an hour in Montague – all very agreeable. The **Siskiyou County Museum**, 910 S Main St (summer Tues–Sat 9am–5pm; donation), deserves some attention, particularly the outdoor section (closes 4pm) with its historic buildings – church, houses, and shops – transported here from around the county. Finally, there's a paltry collection of gold nuggets in the **County Courthouse**, 311 4th St (Mon–Fri 8am–5pm; free).

The Chamber of Commerce, inside *Sue's Coffee and Cones* at 117 W Miner St (summer Mon 9am–5pm, Tues–Fri 9am–7.30pm, Sat 10am–6.30pm; rest of year Mon–Fri 9am–5pm; ℡530/842-1649 or 1-800/ON-YREKA, ⓦwww.yrekachamber.com), issues maps for a self-guided Historic Walking Tour around Yreka's numerous Victorian homes. It can also help you find accommodation, not that you'll need any with plenty of chain motels around the I-5 and independent ones such as the *Economy Inn*, 526 S Main St (℡530/842-4404, ⓔeprevia@snowcrest.net; ➋), or ultra-cheap *Ben Ber Motel*, 1210 S Main St (℡530/842-2791; ➊). **Eating** is best done along the street at *Nature's Kitchen*, 412 S Main St (℡530/842-1136; closed Sun), not at the cutesy *Grandma's House* which has an unfathomable, statewide appeal to elderly Americans whose RVs fill the parking lot. You can also get inexpensive Chinese and American food in the darkened dining room of the *China Dragon*, 520 Main St ℡530/842 3444). Yreka can be reached by STAGE **bus** (℡530/842-8295 or 1-800/24-STAGE) from Mount Shasta and Dunsmuir.

If you're here on a Saturday, fancy a drink, and don't mind backtracking a little, head twenty miles south of Yreka along Hwy-3 to charming, turn-of-the-century **Etna**, home to the Etna Brewing Company, 131 Callahan St (Sat 1–5pm; ℡530/467-5277), a tiny microbrewery producing just three hundred barrels a year for local distribution. There are usually four or five of the malty real ales and other beers available to taste, each and every one a beer drinker's dream. While here, check out the Fifties soda fountain in the Scott Valley Drugstore at the top of Main Street. And if you're really struck by the place, you can camp for free in the town park on Diggles Street.

Lava Beds National Monument and around

After seeing Mount Shasta, you should push on to the **LAVA BEDS NATIONAL MONUMENT**, which commemorates a war between the US and Modoc Indians in the far northeastern corner of the state. Carved out of the huge **Modoc National Forest**, it's actually a series of volcanic caves, which you can explore, and huge black lava flows with a history as violent as the natural forces that created it.

Lava Beds is one of the most remote and forgotten – and beautiful — of California's parks, with pungent yellow rabbit brush blooming around the burnt rocks in autumn. It's in the heart of Modoc country, a desolate outback where cowboys still ride the range, and where, as the territory of one of the last major battles with the Native Americans, there is still a suspicious relationship between the settlers and the native peoples. Until the 1850s Gold Rush it was home to the Modoc tribe, but after their repeated and bloody confrontations with the miners, the government ordered them into a reservation with the Klamath, their traditional enemy. After only a few months, the Modoc drifted back to their homeland in the Lava Beds, and in 1872 the army was sent in to return them by force to the reservation. It was driven back by 52 Modoc warriors under the leadership of one Kientpoos, better known as "Captain Jack," who held back an army of US regulars and volunteers twenty times the size of his for five months, from a stronghold at the northern tip of the park (see overleaf). Eventually Captain Jack was betrayed by a member of his tribe, captured, and hanged, and what was left of the tribe sent off to a reservation in Oklahoma, where most of them died of malaria.

Today the Lava Beds region is inhabited only by the wild deer and three million migrating ducks who easily outnumber the trickle of tourists that make it this far. To the west and north, the **Klamath Basin National Wildlife Refuge** spreads over the border into Oregon. This stop on the Pacific Flyway draws birders and hunters alike for its millions of migratory guests, hoping to catch sight of a rare eagle. In 2000–1, the area became the focus of a **controversy** that made national news after the Department of Fisheries banned the tapping of water from the basin for irrigation after a bottom-feeding fish that lives there was put on the endangered species list. This led to direct protests from farmers whose livelihood was in turn endangered, especially because the

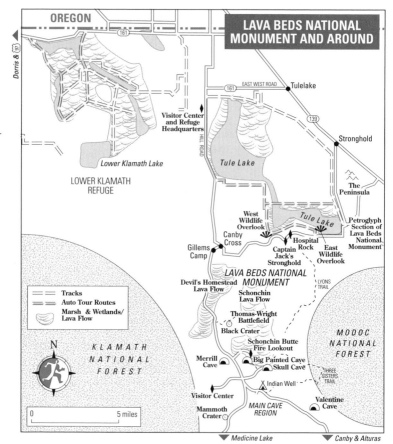

area had already been suffering from drought. Unsurprisingly, the anti-environmental new Bush administration came down on the side of the farmers by declaring that there needed to be an inquiry to decide if it was legal to withhold the water supply and the Deputy Secretary of the Interior even flew out to open the sluices.

Park practicalities

Lava Beds National Monument ($5 per vehicle for seven days) is 160 miles northeast of Redding, and inaccessible without a **car**. It's a day-trip from Mount Shasta, one-and-a-half hours away, but can be combined with camping, spelunking, and birdwatching for a much longer stay. The most tortuous route follows Hwy-89 to Bartle, then passes Medicine Lake (see p.789); the approach via Hwy-139 is easier, but the best and fastest is from Weed, following US-97 through Dorris and then via Hwy-161 through the Klamath Basin National Wildlife Refuge (see opposite).

Pick up an excellent **map** of the monument from the **visitor center**, just inside the southwestern entrance (daily summer 8am–6pm; rest of year 8am–5pm; ☎530/667-2282, ⓦwww.nps.gov/labe). Close by, at Indian Wells, is the park's one **campground** ($10 in summer, $6 in winter). All **wilderness camping** throughout the monument is free and no permits are necessary, but campers must pitch at least a quarter of a mile from any road, trail, or camping area, and fifty yards from any cave. Be warned, though, that elevation throughout the park ranges from 4000 to 5700 feet and there's snow and freezing nights for most of the year, which can make camping uncomfortable.

Tulelake

The only **accommodation** in the area, and the one place to pick up supplies (the monument can only muster a soda machine), is **TULELAKE**, fourteen miles north. The near-deserted Main Street holds the extremely friendly and good-value *Fe's Bed & Breakfast*, no. 660 (☎530/667-5145 or 1-877/478-0184, ⓔelucena@cot.net; ❷), while the only other option, the basic *Ellis Motel* (☎530/667-5342; ❶), is half a mile north on Hwy-139 but not much cheaper, and should only be used as a standby.

There are a couple of places to **eat** in town: *Mike and Wanda's*, just off Main Street at 423 Modoc Ave (☎530/667-3226) has filling meals in the café and bar sections and a more expensive menu in the dining room in between, while there is authentic inexpensive Mexican food at *Villapando's*, 337 Main St (☎530/667-2515). The area's top restaurant, however, is *Captain Jack's Stronghold* (☎530/664-5566), seven miles south on Hwy-139, which does good soups, steaks, and home-made pies. Nearby is the **Modoc Ranger Station** (Mon–Fri 8am–4.30pm; ☎530/667-2246) with general information on the Modoc National Forest. Even if you have your own car, and it's unlikely you'll be here if you don't, you might consider taking one of the expert guided **tours** ($50–60, including lunch) conducted by LuCena West Tours out of *Fe's B&B* (see above for contacts) in order to get the most out of the Lava Beds and Klamath Basin region.

There is one tourist attraction in town, the **Tulelake–Butte Valley Fair Museum of Local History**, which also houses the **Chamber of Commerce** information bureau, at 800 S Main St (daily 8am–4.30pm; $3; ☎530/667-5312, ⓦwww.tbvfair.com). The newly created complex contains excellent displays on geological features, wildlife, history (especially the Indian wars and WWII internment), Native American culture, and current issues. The entry fee includes a one-hour interpretive **audio tour** to enhance your visit. The fairgrounds host an enormous annual **fair** during the week following Labor Day in September. You can also camp on the grounds for $10 at any time.

The monument

A day spent in the **Lava Beds** is akin to exploring the innards of a volcano, scampering down hollow tubes through which molten lava once coursed. The youngest of them were formed 30,000 years ago when volcanic upwellings sent molten, basaltic magma careering across the Modoc Plateau. As the magma came into contact with cool air, it solidified, leaving a flowing molten core feeding the expanding lava field downhill. In time, the magma flow stopped and the molten lava drained out, leaving the world's largest concentration of such hollow tubes. Most remain unexplored, but where the casing has collapsed, access is possible and you are free to scramble through. Some of the caves are so small that you have to crawl along on all fours, while others are an enormous 75 feet in diameter. Some contain Native American **petroglyphs** – not to be confused with the names painted on the cave walls by J.D. Howard, one of the first white men to explore and name the caves.

Pick up the free loaner flashlights from the visitor center and begin your explorations of the caves just outside. Initially, though, entering the darkness alone can be an unnerving experience, so most people prefer to take the **free guided ranger walks** (daily Memorial Day–Labor Day). Two-to-three-hour morning walks (9am) leave from the visitor center and explore little-known sections of the monument; afternoon tours (2pm) concentrate on ninety-minute guided cave trips; and in the evening (9pm) rangers lead hour-long campfire talks and slide shows, which shift to Mushpot Cave in bad weather.

If you insist on eschewing ranger guidance, you must abide by a few **rules**. Don't go alone, wear decent shoes, and take two flashlights each. Borrowed flashlights must be returned by nightfall to ensure no one goes missing. For night explorations (the caves remain open), you'll need your own light source. Hard hats are strongly advised and can be purchased for $3.50 at the visitor center.

If caves don't do it for you, the other attraction of Lava Beds is its well-documented history. Begin at the visitor center for an exhibit on the Modoc War, including photos of its chief participants, including Modoc leader Captain Jack, and scathing editorials from national papers condemning the US Army over its mission. You'll need a car to get to the northern reaches of the park, around **Captain Jack's Stronghold**, a natural fortress of craggy lava flows and shallow caves on the shores of the Old Tule Lake. When you arrive, pick up a trail book ($.25) from the parking lot and enjoy one of two well-narrated **self-guided trails** (one half a mile, the other 1.5 miles) through a war that in many ways typified the conquest of the West. When you get here you'll see how the Modoc managed to hide and move around through the passageways of the hills. Two miles west, **Canby's Cross** marks a turning point in the war, when Captain Jack, coerced by the man who would later betray him, drew a gun during a council and murdered US General Canby and a pastor. Two miles east, the shallow lava bowl of **Hospital Rock** marks the point where one Lt Sherwood, wounded by the Modoc, was unsuccessfully tended in a makeshift field hospital towards the end of the siege on the stronghold.

Exploring the Lava Beds

Most of the interest in Lava Beds lies around the visitor center, where the largest concentration of caves can be visited on the short **Cave Loop** access road. For a confidence-building handle on your location in the twenty-five "developed" caves – less than a tenth of the known total – get the *Lava Caves Map* ($4.50) from the visitor center. New ones are discovered all the time, so the possibilities are almost endless, but for the moment, the tried and tested caves below should be enough to be going on with.

Catacombs Cave At over a mile long, this is the longest open tube in the monument, though you need perseverance, a slim body, and a cool head to get anywhere near the end. The profusion of interconnecting passageways make it one of the most confusing; keep track of whether you are heading up or downhill. On Cave Loop.

Golden Dome Cave The startling golden hues of the moist mossy roof lend the cave both its name and an otherworldly appearance. On Cave Loop.

Labyrinth Cave Striking geological features – lava pillars and lavacicles – and evidence of Native American habitation. At the entrance to Cave Loop.

Mushpot Cave Right by the visitor center near the start of Cave Loop, this is the most developed of the caves. It provides a good introduction, is lit during center opening hours, and has interpretive panels highlighting key features.

Skull Cave Named for Bighorn skulls found when the cave was discovered by early explorer E.L. Hopkins, this has the largest entrance of any of the lava tubes and contains ice all year round. About two miles north of Cave Loop.

Symbol Bridge and **Big Painted Cave** (1.5-mile round-trip; almost flat). Two very worthwhile caves adjacent to each other on a trail north of the visitor center. No flashlight is needed though one could come in handy. Some of the best examples of pictographs in the Monument – tentatively dated between 1000 AD and 1500 AD – show up as different angles of sunlight catch the rocks beside the entrance. Respecting Modoc sensibilities, make two clockwise turns before descending into a large cave, open at both ends (hence the "bridge" name), in which zigzags, squiggles, sunbursts, and human figures are picked out in grease and charcoal on pumice-washed background. Make a single anti-clockwise turn on departure for Big Painted Cave, where the pictographs are less impressive. In the mid-1920s, J.D. Howard excavated a small tunnel at the very back of the cave to reveal an ice flow in a cavity fifteen feet down: with a flashlight you can scramble down there. Two miles north of Cave Loop.

Valentine Cave Interesting because it combines various characteristic cave features, such as stalactites and catacombs. The ridges at the base of the walls leading down into the deep and wide chamber almost appear to be man-made, so even are their lines. About two miles southeast of Cave Loop.

Around the monument

Small volcanic craters, buttes, spatter cones, and chimneys dot Lava Beds, but the flows which produced most of the lava tubes came from **Mammoth Crater** on the southern perimeter of the monument, where a short path leads to a viewpoint overlooking the deep conical crater.

Underlying the most recent of Lava Beds' fabulous creations is a bed of basalt, the product of a huge shield volcano with a profile so flat it is barely noticeable. Its core is now filled by the sub-alpine **Medicine Lake**, ten miles southwest of Mammoth Crater. Formerly a Modoc healing center, the only therapies on offer today are fishing and swimming from the $7 campsites along the north shore. It's accessible via an unpaved road closed November to mid-May.

More volcanic spectacle lies just west at **Glass Mountain**, made almost entirely of glassy, black obsidian – source of Modoc arrowheads – but covered in fluffy, white pumice quarried for stonewashing jeans. A short and fairly easy trail leads in from the road. Just beyond the monument's northeast corner, a small outlier known as the Petroglyph Section contains **Petroglyph Point**, a three-hundred-yard-long cliff face made of "tuff," volcanic rock formed when lava flows hit Old Tule Lake. The soft rock offers some fine, but cryptic, examples of ancient art: shields, female figures, and a series of small circles thought to represent travel. The crevices are home to various bird species, especially horned owls. Pick up an interpretive leaflet at the visitor center.

East of the Petroglyphs Section, the road continues to Hwy-139 and the town of **Newell**, site of the **Tule Lake Camp**, where 110,000 people of Japanese descent, many of them American citizens, were interned without charge or trial between 1942 and 1946. There were as many as 18,000 inmates at any given time. Many of the camp buildings have been sold off to local farmers, but the wooden-sided police and military barracks remain. A simple plaque commemorates the disgraceful chapter and prays it will never be repeated, an all the more poignant message in the light of the current lengthy detention of some Islamic people for minor immigration infractions since the 2001 terrorist attacks. Nearby there was also a less-well-known camp for internees of German and Italian origin.

Perhaps the most rewarding excursion from the monument, though, is to the **Klamath Basin National Wildlife Refuge** (open daylight hours), just to the north along Hill Road (Hwy-161) leading to US-97 and spreading into Oregon. One of the last **wetlands** in California, with swathes of open water and emerging vegetation on the shoreline, it attracts an estimated eighty percent of birds following the Pacific Flyway, the major migration routes from Alaska and northern Canada to Baja California in Mexico. In spring and fall, almost a hundred species are present and the population tops a million. Bald eagles appear January to March, bringing out hundreds of photographers trying to navigate the snowy road. The most accessible reaches of the reserve are the **Lower Klamath Refuge** and **Tule Lake**, an open body of water surrounded by reeds (tule in Modoc). At the northwestern corner of the latter, the **visitor center** (Mon–Fri 8am–4.30pm, Sat & Sun 10am–4pm; ☎530/667-2231) issues free permits for the birdwatching and rents out hunting blinds ($5): call ahead to be sure of getting one. Surprisingly, the best way of spotting the wildlife is by driving along designated routes ($3): getting out of the car and walking scares the birds off.

Heading south back towards Mount Shasta on US-97, your car will be stopped in otherwise droll **Dorris** by agriculture agents checking to see if you're transporting fruit or vegetables from out of state. Say "No" and they'll give you a nice color map to welcome you to California.

Travel details

Trains

Oakland to: Chico (1 daily; 4hr 5min); Dunsmuir (1 daily; 7hr 14min); Redding (1 daily; 5hr 24min).
Fort Bragg to: Willits (1–2 daily; 4hr).

Buses

Schedules listed below are mostly Greyhound, combined with Amtrak Thruway where applicable. Some routes require a transfer. See text for additional connecting local services.

Arcata to: Crescent City (2 daily; 1hr 40min); Garberville (4 daily; 2hr 10min); San Francisco (2 daily; 8hr 30min); Santa Rosa (4 daily; 6hr).

Chico to: Mount Shasta (1 daily; 3hr 10min); Red Bluff (8 daily; 1hr); Redding (8 daily; 1hr 30min–1hr 55min); San Francisco (3 daily; 5hr 15min–6hr 30min); Santa Rosa (1daily; 7hr 35min).

Eureka to: Crescent City (2 daily; 2hr); Clearlake (1 daily; 11hr 5min); Garberville (4 daily; 1hr 30min); Redding (2 daily; 4hr); San Francisco (2 daily; 7hr 35min–8hr); Santa Rosa (4 daily; 5hr 30min).

Redding to: Chico (7 daily; 1hr 45min); Eureka (2 daily; 4hr); Mount Shasta (4 daily; 1hr 25min); Red Bluff (7 daily; 30–50min) Sacramento (11 daily; 2hr 40min–4hr 30min); San Francisco (7 daily; 5hr

15min–8hr 30min) Yreka (3 daily; 2hr 15min).

San Francisco to: Arcata (2 daily; 7hr 30min–8hr 25min); Chico (4 daily; 4hr 55min–6hr 5min); Clearlake (1 daily; 5hr 5min); Crescent City (2 daily; 9hr 10min–10hr 5min); Eureka (2 daily; 7hr–7hr 45min); Mount Shasta (2 daily; 8hr 10min–12hr 10min); Redding (5 daily; 5hr 30min–10hr 10min); Santa Rosa (3 daily; 1hr 50min–3hr 10min); Willits (2 daily; 4hr); Yreka (2 daily; 10hr 20min–13hr).

Santa Rosa to: Arcata (4 daily; 5hr 35min–6hr 30min); Crescent City (2 daily; 7hr 15min–8hr 10min); Eureka (4 daily; 5hr 5min–5hr 50min); Garberville (4 daily; 3hr 35min–4hr 20min); San Francisco (3 daily; 2hr–3hr 5min); Willits (4 daily; 2hr).

Contexts

Contexts

The historical framework

To many people, California seems one of the least historic places on the planet. Unburdened by the past, it's a land where anything seems possible, whose inhabitants live carefree lives, wholly in and for the present moment. Its very name, appropriately for all its idealized images, is a work of fiction, free of any historical significance. The word first appeared in a popular Spanish picaresque novel of the early 1500s, *Las Sergas de Esplandián* by García de Montalvo, as the name of an island, located "very near to the terrestrial paradise" and inhabited entirely by Amazons "without any men among them."

Native peoples

For thousands of years before the arrival of Europeans, the **aboriginal peoples** of California flourished in the naturally abundant land, living fairly peacefully in tribes along the coast and in the deserts and the forested mountains. Anthropologists estimate that nearly half the native population then living within the boundaries of the present-day US were spread throughout what's now California, in small, tribal villages of a few hundred people, each with a clearly defined territory and often its own distinct language. Since there was no political or social organization beyond the immediate level of the tribe, it was not difficult for the colonizing Spaniards to divide and to conquer, effectively wiping them out – though admittedly more died because of epidemics of disease than outright genocide.

Very little remains to mark the existence of the Californian Native Americans: they had no form of written language, relatively undeveloped craft skills, and built next to nothing that would last beyond the change of seasons. About the only surviving signs of the coastal tribes are the piles of seashells and discarded arrowheads that have been found, from which anthropologists have deduced a bit about their cultures. Also, a few examples of **rock art** survive, as at the Chumash Painted Cave, near Santa Barbara on the Central Coast. Similar sorts of petroglyph figures were drawn by the Paiute Native Americans, who lived in the deserts near Death Valley, and by the Miwok from the Sierra Nevada foothills.

Discovery and early exploration

The first Europeans to set foot in California were Spanish explorers, intent on extending their colony of New Spain, which, under the 1494 Treaty of Tordesillas, included all the New World lands west of Brazil and all of North America west of the Rocky Mountains. In 1535, **Hernán Cortés**, fresh from decimating the Aztecs, headed westward in search of a short cut to Asia, which he believed to be adjacent to Mexico. Though he never reached what's now California, he set up a small colony at the southern tip of the Baja (or lower) California peninsula. Thinking it was an island, he named it Santa Cruz, writing in his journals that he soon expected to find the imagined island of the Amazons.

The first explorer to use the name California, and to reach what's now the US state, was **Juan Cabrillo**, who sighted San Diego Harbor in 1542, and continued north along the coast to the Channel Islands off Santa Barbara. He died there six months later, persistent headwinds having made it impossible to sail any further north. His crew later made it as far north as what is now the state of Oregon, but were unable to find any safe anchorage and returned home starving and half-dead from scurvy. It was fifty years before another Spaniard braved the difficult journey: **Juan de Fuca**'s 1592 voyage caused great excitement when he claimed to have discovered the Northwest Passage, a potentially lucrative trade route across North America. It has long since turned out that there is really no such thing (de Fuca may have discovered the Puget Sound, outside Seattle), but Europeans continued to search for it for the next two hundred years.

The British explorer **Sir Francis Drake** arrived in the *Golden Hind* in 1579, taking a break from his piracy of Spanish vessels in order to make repairs. His landing spot, now called Drake's Bay, near Point Reyes north of San Francisco, had "white bancks and cliffes" that reminded him of Dover. Upon landing, he was met by a band of native Miwoks, who feted him with food and drink, and placed a feathered crown upon his head; in return, he claimed all of their lands – which he called Nova Albion (New England) – for Queen Elizabeth, supposedly leaving behind a brass plaque now on display in the Bancroft Library at the University of California.

Setting sail from Acapulco in 1602, **Sebastián Vizcaíno**, a Portuguese explorer under contract to Spain, made a more lasting impact than his predecessors, undertaking the most extensive exploration of the coast, and bestowing most of the place names that survive. In order to impress his superiors he exaggerated the value of his discoveries, describing a perfect, sheltered harbor, which he named **Monterey** in honor of his patron in Mexico. Subsequent colonizers based their efforts on these fraudulent claims (the windy bay did not live up to Vizcaíno's estimation), and the headquarters of the missions and military and administrative center of the Spanish government remained at Monterey, 100 miles south of San Francisco, for the next 75 years.

Colonization: The Spanish and the British

The Spanish occupation of California began in earnest in 1769, with a combination of military expediency (to prevent other powers from gaining a foothold) and Catholic missionary zeal (to convert the Native Americans). Father **Junípero Serra** and a company of three hundred soldiers and clergy set off from Mexico for Monterey, half of them by ship, the other half overland. In June 1770, after establishing a small mission and *presidio* (fort) at San Diego, the expedition arrived at Monterey, where another mission and small *presidio* were constructed.

The Spanish continued to build missions all along the coast, ostensibly to Catholicize the Native Americans, which they did with inquisitional fervor. The mission complexes were broadly similar, with a church and cloistered residential structure surrounded by irrigated fields, vineyards, and more extensive ranchlands. The labor of the Native American converts was co-opted: they were put to work making soap and candles, were often beaten and never educated. Objective accounts of the missionaries' treatment of the indigenous peoples are rare, though mission registries record twice as many deaths as they do births, and their cemeteries are packed with Native American dead. Not all of the Native Americans gave up without a fight: many missions suffered from raids, and the now-ubiquitous red-tiled roofs were originally a replacement for the earlier thatch to better resist arson attacks.

Most of the mission structures that survive today were built to the designs of Serra's successor, Father **Férmin de Lasuén**, who was in charge of the missions during the period of their greatest growth. By the time of his death in 1804, a chain of twenty-one missions, each a long day's walk from its neighbors and linked by the dirt path of **El Camino Real** (The Royal Road), ran from San Diego to San Francisco.

During this time the first towns, called **pueblos**, were established in order to attract settlers to what was still a distant and undesirable territory. The first was laid out in 1777 at San Jose, south of the new mission at San Francisco. Los Angeles, the second *pueblo*, was established in 1781, though neither had more than a hundred inhabitants until well into the nineteenth century.

One reason for Spain's military presence in California – which consisted of four *presidios* all told, with twelve cannon and only two hundred soldiers – was to prevent the expansion of the small **Russian** colony based in Alaska, mostly trappers collecting beaver and otter pelts in the northwestern states of Washington and Oregon. The two countries were at peace and relations friendly, and in any case the Spanish *presidios* were in no position to enforce their territorial claims. In fact, they were so short of supplies and ammunition that they had to borrow the gunpowder to fire welcoming salutes whenever the two forces came into contact. Well aware of the Spanish weakness, the Russians established the outpost of **Fort Ross** in 1812, sixty miles north of San Francisco. This further undermined Spanish sovereignty over the region, though the Russians abandoned the fort in 1841, selling it to John Sutter (who features prominently in later California history; see overleaf).

The Mexican era

While Spain, France, and England were engaged in the bitter struggles of the Napoleonic Wars, the colonies of New Spain rebelled against imperial neglect, with Mexico finally gaining independence in 1821. The Mexican Republic, or the United States of Mexico as the new country called itself, governed California as a territory. However, the fifteen distinct administrations it set up lacked the money to pay for improvements and the soldiers needed to enforce the laws, and they were unable to exercise any degree of authority.

The most important effect of the Mexican era was the final **secularization** in 1834, after years of gradual diminution, of the Franciscan missions. As most of the missionaries were Spanish, under Mexican rule they had seen their position steadily eroded by the increasingly wealthy, close-knit families of the *Californios* – Mexican immigrants who'd been granted vast tracts of ranchland. The government's intention was that half of the missions' extensive lands should go to the Indian converts, but this was never carried out, and the few powerful families divided most of it up among themselves.

In many ways this was the most lawless and wantonly wasteful period of California's history, an era described by **Richard Henry Dana** – scion of a distinguished Boston family, who dropped out of Harvard to sail to California – in his 1840 book *Two Years Before the Mast*. Most of the agriculture and cottage industries that had developed under the missionaries disappeared, and it was a point of pride amongst the *Californios* not to do any work that couldn't be done from horseback. Dana's Puritan values led him to heap scorn upon the "idle and thriftless people" who made nothing for themselves. For example, the large herds of cattle that lived on the mission lands were slaughtered for their hides and sold to Yankee traders, who turned the hides into leather which they sold back to the *Californios* at a tidy profit. "In the hands of an enterprising people," he wrote, "what a country this might be."

The first Americans

Throughout the Mexican and Spanish eras, foreigners were legally banned from settling, and the few who showed up, mostly sick or injured sailors dropped off to regain their health, were often jailed until they proved themselves useful, either as craftsmen or as traders able to supply needed goods. In the late 1820s, the first **Americans**, without exception males, began to make their way to California, tending to fit in with the existing Mexican culture, often marrying into established families, and converting to the Catholic faith. The American presence grew slowly but surely as more and more people emigrated, still mostly by way of a three-month sea voyage around Cape Horn. Among these was **Thomas Larkin**, a New England merchant who, in 1832, set up shop in Monterey, and later was instrumental in pointing the disgruntled *Californios* towards the more accommodating US; Larkin's wife Rachel was the first American woman on the West Coast.

The first people to make the four-month journey to California overland – in a covered wagon like in so many Hollywood Westerns – arrived in 1841, having forged a trail over the Sierra Nevada mountains via Truckee Pass, just north of Lake Tahoe. Soon after, hundreds of people each year were following in their tracks. In 1846, however, forty migrants, collectively known as the **Donner party**, died when they were trapped in the mountains by early winter snowfall. The immense difficulties involved in reaching California, over land and by sea, kept population levels at a minimum, and by 1846 just seven thousand people, not counting Native Americans but including all the Spanish and Mexicans, lived in the entire region.

The Mexican–American War

From the 1830s onwards – inspired by **Manifest Destiny**, the popular, almost religious, belief that the United States was meant to cover the continent from coast to coast – US government policy regarding California was to buy all of Mexico's land north of the Rio Grande, the river that now divides the US and Mexico. President Andrew Jackson was highly suspicious of British designs on the West Coast – he himself had been held as a (14-year-old) prisoner of war during the Revolutionary War of 1776 – and various diplomatic overtures were made to the Mexican Republic, all of which backfired. In April 1846, Jackson's protégé, President James Polk, offered forty million dollars for all of

New Mexico and the California territory, but his simultaneous annexation of the newly independent Republic of Texas – which Mexico still claimed – resulted in the outbreak of war.

Almost all the fighting of the **Mexican–American War** took place in Texas; only one real battle was ever fought on Californian soil, at San Pasqual, northeast of San Diego, where a roving US battalion was surprised by a band of pro-Mexican *Californios*, who killed twenty-two soldiers and wounded another fifteen before withdrawing south into Mexico. Monterey, still the territorial capital, was captured by the US Navy without a shot fired, and in January 1847, when the rebel *Californios* surrendered to the US forces at Cahuenga, near Los Angeles, the Americans controlled the entire West Coast.

Just before the war began, California had made a brief foray into the field of self-government: the short-lived **Bear Flag Republic**, whose only lasting effect was to create what's still the state flag, a prowling grizzly bear with the words "California Republic" written below. In June 1846, American settlers in the Sonoma Valley took over the local *presidio* – long abandoned by the Mexicans – and declared California independent, which lasted for all of three weeks until the US forces took command.

The Gold Rush

As part of the Treaty of Guadalupe Hidalgo, which formally ended the war in 1848, Mexico ceded all of the *Alta California* territory to the US. Nine days before the signing of the accord, in the distant foothills of the Sierra Nevada mountains, flakes of **gold** were discovered by workmen building a sawmill along the American River at Coloma, though it was months before this momentous conjunction of events became known.

At the time, California's non-Native American population was mostly concentrated in the few small towns along the coastal strip. Early rumors of gold attracted a trickle of prospectors, and, following news of their subsequent success, by the middle of 1849 – eighteen months after the initial find – men were flooding into California from all over, in the most madcap migration in world history. **Sutter's Fort**, a small agricultural community, trading post, and stage stop which had been established six years earlier by John Sutter on the banks of the American River, was overrun by miners, who headed up into the nearby foothills to make their fortune. Some did, most didn't, but in any case, within fifteen years most of the gold had been picked clean. The miners moved on or went home and their camps vanished, prompting Mark Twain to write that "in no other land, in modern times, have towns so absolutely died and disappeared as in the old mining regions of California."

Statehood

Following the US takeover after the defeat of Mexico, a **Constitutional Convention** was held at Monterey in the autumn of 1849. The men who attended were not the miners – most of whom were more interested in searching for gold – but those who had been in California for some time (about three years on average). At the time, the Territory of California extended all the way east to Utah, so the main topic of discussion was where to draw the eastern boundary of the intended state. The drawing up of a state constitution was also important, since it was the basis on which California applied for admission to the US. This constitution contained a couple of noteworthy inclusions – to protect the dignity of the manually laboring miners, **slavery** was prohibited; and to attract well-heeled **women** from the East Coast, California was the first state to recognize in legal terms the separate property of a married woman. In 1850, California was admitted to the US as the thirty-first state.

The Indian Wars

Though the US Civil War had little effect on California, many bloody battles were fought throughout the 1850s and 1860s by white settlers and US troops against the various Native American tribes whose lands the immigrants wanted. At first the government tried to move willing tribes to fairly large reservations, but as more settlers moved in the tribes were pushed onto smaller and smaller tracts. The most powerful resistance to the well-armed invaders came in the mountainous northeast of California, where a band of **Modoc** fought a long-running guerrilla war, using their superior knowledge of the terrain to evade the US troops.

Owing to a combination of disease and lack of food, as well as deliberate acts of violence, the Native American population was drastically reduced, and by 1870 almost ninety percent had been wiped out. The survivors were concentrated in small, relatively valueless reservations, where their descendants still live: the Cahuila near Palm Springs, the Paiute/Shoshone in the Owens Valley, and the Hupa on the northwest coast continue to reside near their ancestral homelands, and are naturally quite protective of their privacy.

The boom years: 1870–1900

After the Gold Rush, **San Francisco** boomed into a boisterous frontier town, exploding in population from 500 to 50,000 within five years. Though far removed from the mines themselves, the city was the main landing spot for ship-borne argonauts (as the prospectors were called), and the main supply town. Moreover, it was the place where successful miners went to blow their hard-earned cash on the whiskey and women of the **Barbary Coast**, then the raunchiest waterfront in the world, full of brothels, saloons, and opium dens. Ten years later, San Francisco enjoyed an even bigger boom as a result of the silver mines of the Comstock Lode in Nevada, owned mainly by San Franciscans, who displayed their wealth by building grand palaces and mansions on Nob Hill – still the city's most exclusive address.

The completion in 1869 of the **transcontinental railroad**, built using imported Chinese laborers, was a major turning point in the settlement of California. Whereas the trip across the country by stagecoach took at least a month, and was subject to scorching hot weather and attacks by hostile natives, the crossing could now be completed in just five days.

In 1875, when the Santa Fe Railroad reached Los Angeles (the railroad company having extracted huge bribes from local officials to ensure the budding city wasn't bypassed), there were just ten thousand people living in the whole of **Southern California**, divided equally between San Diego and Los Angeles. A rate war developed between the two rival railroads, and ticket costs dropped to as little as $1 for a one-way ticket from New York. Land speculators placed advertisements in East Coast and European papers, offering cheap land for homesteaders in towns and suburbs all over the West Coast that, as often as not, existed only on paper. By the end of the nineteenth century, thousands of people, ranging from Midwestern farmers to the East Coast elite, had moved to California to take advantage of the fertile land and mild climate.

Hollywood, the war, and after

The greatest boost to California's fortunes was, of course, the **film industry**, which moved here from the East Coast in 1911, attracted by the temperate climate in which directors could shoot outdoors year-round and by the incredibly cheap land on which large indoor studios could be built at comparatively little cost. Within three years, movies like D.W. Griffith's *Birth of a Nation* – most of which was filmed along the dry banks of the Los Angeles River – were being cranked out by the hundreds.

Hollywood, a suburb of Los Angeles that was the site of many of the early studios, and ever since the buzzword for the entire entertainment industry, has done more to promote the mystique of California as a pleasure garden landscape than any other medium, disseminating images of its glamorous lifestyles around the globe. Los Angeles still dominates the world film industry, and, increasingly, is an international center for the music business as well.

This widespread, idealized image had a magnetic effect during the **Great Depression** of the 1930s, when thousands of people from all over the country descended upon California, which was perceived to be – and for the most part was – immune to the economic downturn that crippled the rest of the US. From the dust bowl Midwest, entire families, who came to be known as **Okies**, packed up everything they owned and set off for the farms of the Central Valley, an epic journey captured by John Steinbeck's best-selling novel *The Grapes of Wrath*, in the photographs of Dorothea Lange, and in the baleful tunes of folksinger Woody Guthrie. Some Californians who feared losing their jobs to the incoming Okies formed vigilante groups and, with the complicity of local and state police, set up roadblocks along the main highways to prevent unemployed outsiders from entering the state.

One Depression-era initiative to alleviate the poverty, and to get the economy moving again, were the US government-sponsored **Works Progress Administration (WPA)** construction projects, ranging from restoring the California missions to building trails and park facilities, and commissioning art works like the marvelous Social Realist murals in San Francisco's Coit Tower.

Things turned around when **World War II** brought heavy industry to California, as shipyards and airplane factories sprang up, providing well-paid employment in wartime factories. After the war, most stayed on, and still today California companies – McDonnell Douglas, Lockheed, Rockwell, and General Dynamics, for example – make up the roll call of suppliers to the US military and space programs.

After the war, many of the soldiers who'd passed through on their way to the battlegrounds of the South Pacific came back to California and decided to stay on. There was plenty of well-paid work, the US government subsidized house purchases for war veterans and, most importantly, constructed the **freeways** and interstate highways that enabled land speculators to build new commuter suburbs on land that had been used for farms and citrus orchards.

The **Fifties** brought prosperity to the bulk of middle-class America (typified by President Dwight Eisenhower's goal of "two cars in every garage and a chicken in every pot"), and California, particularly San Francisco, became a nexus for alternative artists and writers, spurring an immigration of intellectuals that by the end of the decade had become manifest as the **Beat generation** – pegged "Beatniks," in honor of Sputnik, the Soviet space satellite, by San Francisco columnist Herb Caen.

The Sixties and Seventies

California remained at the forefront of youth and **social upheavals** into and throughout the **Sixties**. In a series of drug tests carried out at Stanford University – paid for by the CIA, who was interested in developing a "truth drug" for interrogation purposes – unwitting students were dosed with **LSD**. One of the guinea pigs was the writer Ken Kesey, who had just published the highly acclaimed novel *One Flew Over the Cuckoo's Nest*. Kesey quite liked the experience and soon secured a personal supply of the drug (which was still legal) and toured the West Coast to spread the word of "acid." In and around San Francisco, Kesey and his crew, the Merry Pranksters, turned on huge crowds at **Electric Kool-Aid Acid Tests** – in which LSD was diluted into bowls of the soft drink Kool-Aid – complete with psychedelic light shows and music by the Grateful Dead. The acid craze reached its height during the **Summer of Love** in 1967, when the entire Haight-Ashbury district of San Francisco seemed populated by barefoot and drugged flower children.

Within a year the superficial peace of Flower Power was shattered, as protests mounted against US involvement in the **Vietnam War**; Martin Luther King and Bobby Kennedy, heroes of left-leaning youth, were both gunned down – Kennedy in Los Angeles after winning the California primary of the 1968 presidential election. The militant **Black Panthers**, a group of black radical activists based in Oakland, terrorized a white population that had earlier been supporters of the Civil Rights Movement. By the end of the Sixties the "system," in California especially, seemed to be at breaking point, and the atrocities committed by **Charles Manson** and his "Family" seemed to signify a general collapse.

The antiwar protests, concentrated at the University of California campus in Berkeley, continued through the early **Seventies**. Emerging from the milieu of revolutionary and radical groups, the Symbionese Liberation Army, a small, well-armed, and stridently revolutionary group, set about the overthrow of the US, attracting media (and FBI) attention by murdering civil servants, robbing banks, and, most famously, kidnapping 19-year-old heiress **Patty Hearst**. Amid much media attention Hearst converted to the SLA's cause, changing her name to Tanya and for the next two years – until her capture in 1977 – she went underground, provoking national debate about her motives and beliefs.

Californian **politics**, after Watergate and the end of American involvement in Vietnam, seemed to lose whatever idealistic fervor it might once have had, and popular culture withdrew into self-satisfaction, typified by the smug harmonies of musicians like the Eagles and Jackson Browne. While the Sixties upheavals were overseen by California Governor Ronald Reagan, who was ready and willing to fight the long-haired hippies, the 1970s saw the reign of "Governor Moonbeam" Jerry Brown, under whose leadership California enacted some of the most stringent **anti-pollution** measures in the world. The state also actively encouraged the development of renewable forms of energy such as solar and wind power, and protected the entire coastline from despoliation and development. California also decriminalized the possession of under an ounce of **marijuana** (though it remains an offense to grow or sell it), and the harvesting of marijuana continues to account for over $1 billion each year, making it the number-one cash crop in the number-one agricultural region in the US.

The Eighties and Nineties

The easy-money **Eighties** of Reagonomics and the trickle-down economy, which naturally never trickled down as far as the state's poorest, crash-landed in a tangled mess. LA junk-bond king Michael Milkin was convicted of multi-billion-dollar fraud, and the S&L banking scandals enmeshed such high-ranking politicos as California Senator Alan Cranston. Consequently the **Nineties** kicked off with a stagnant property market and rising unemployment.

In **Los Angeles**, the videotaped beating of black motorist Rodney King by officers of the LA Police Department, and the subsequent acquittal of those officers, sparked off destructive **rioting** in April 1992. State and federal authorities, forced into taking notice of LA's endemic poverty and violence, promised all sorts of new initiatives but achieved few concrete results. Race also dominated the yearlong trial of black former football star **O.J. Simpson** – accused and finally acquitted of murdering his white ex-wife and her male friend – splitting public opinion into directly opposed camps of black and white.

All these factors combined to make the first five years of the 1990s perhaps the bleakest since the Great Depression, and **natural calamities** – regional flooding, Malibu fires and mudslides, and two dramatic earthquakes – only added to the general malaise. Mike Davis's *City of Quartz*, despite flaws and inaccuracies, served as a secular bible for the time, an artfully written work based on the inevitable doom LA was facing. And with LA's chronic inter-ethnic hatred, natural disasters, bureaucratic inaction, and general public pessimism, it seemed that Davis was probably right.

The latter half of the decade saw **Richard Riordan**, a multimillionaire technocrat who served as LA mayor from 1992 to 2000, preside over a major **revival** in the city's economic fortunes and a restructuring of its economic base – aerospace and automotive giving way to tourism, real estate and, as always, Hollywood. New property developments attempted to revitalize deprived areas, and even crime and violence tailed off marginally. However, these improvements probably owed more to the national upswing during the Clinton years than to purely local initiatives.

San Francisco also suffered in the early Nineties; on top of AIDS-related illnesses stretching health services, the area was hit by a series of natural disasters. An **earthquake** in October 1989 devastated much of the San Francisco Bay Area, followed two years later by a massive **fire** in the Oakland Hills which burned over two thousand homes and killed two dozen people – the third worst fire in US history.

But even more so than LA, San Francisco's economic upswing turned the city around, replacing pre-millennium jitters with Information Age optimism. The **Silicon Valley** industries boomed, with companies scrambling to find high-paid workers to fill their constantly growing rosters. San Jose, San Francisco's southern neighbor, surpassed the Golden Gate city in population, and even Oakland, the gritty East Bay port-town, started to receive a much needed facelift. Still, not everyone in the Bay Area was happy with the apparent prosperity. **Gentrification** threatened to turn San Francisco from a province of activism into a playground for Silicon Valley's rich young things. Housing prices rocketed sky high, and tenancy at 99 percent full, forcing out not only the city's poor, but the middle class as well.

Contemporary California

The optimism that had overidden many concerns at the tail end of the old millennium soon took a pummelling once the new one started. The world's computers may not have gone belly up at zero hour on Y2K, but the hi-tech industry had to come to terms with the fact it had outreached itself, becoming the biggest victim of a nationwide economic **recession** – the cause of it, in fact, according to many analysts. This immediately affected most Silicon Valley companies, which had expanded into global giants so rapidly, as they saw billions wiped off their stock values and had to offload employees faster than they had hired them. The silver lining for many who had not shared in the boom was that Bay Area **property prices** have slowed for the first time in a decade, though not imploded as some predicted.

More gloom, literally, struck California in 2001, when gross mismanagement of the state's energy supplies led to a series of third-world-type **power cuts**, as the ailing grid system was unable to meet the enormous demands for electricity. Long-term solutions have yet to be found for the energy crisis and, for the time being, California is having to fork out vast sums to import some of its shortfall in energy from other states.

While some of the blame for the crisis was heaped on Governor **Gray Davis**, he did manage to get re-elected in November 2002. In fact, Californian Democrats bucked the national trend in the mid-term elections by winning every constitutional office up for grabs in the state, emphasizing the state's liberal reputation. Somewhat impressively, at least for mainstream American poli-tics, the Green candidate for governor mustered five percent of the vote as well.

Also put to rest, at least for now, was an issue that has periodically surfaced in **Los Angeles**, when voters overwhelmingly rejected the proposition for Hollywood and the San Fernando Valley to **secede** from LA and create an independent city. Predictably, the proposed secession had the support of wealthy valley residents who are tired of having to fund projects in the more deprived parts of the metropolis, but it needed to gain a majority of all voters to pass. However, the much-publicized **Proposition 49**, to provide extra funding for after-school education, did pass, championed by archconservative **Arnold Schwarzenegger**, who, at the time of writing, is apparently positioning himself to follow in Reagan's gubernatorial footsteps.

Meanwhile, in San Francisco and Berkeley, there are strong signs that political activism is stirring once more in response to George W. Bush's hardline domestic and international policies. California Senator **Barbara Lee** bravely cast the sole vote against the resolution to use force in Afghanistan in 2001 and was one of the larger group of Democrats to vote against the Iraq resolution a year later. On the streets, San Francisco has hosted some of the largest antiwar demonstrations since the days of Vietnam, a beacon of progressive hope for the growing nationwide **Peace Movement** amidst all the flag waving and sabre rattling.

Throughout all of these changes, California still clings on to its aura as something of a Promised Land. Barring its complete destruction by the **Big One** (the earthquake that's destined one day to drop half of the state into the Pacific and wipe out the rest under massive tidal waves), the state seems set to continue much as it is, acting as the cornerstone of the mythical West and as the place where America reinvents itself.

Wildlife

Though popularly imagined as little more than palm trees and golden sand beaches, for sheer range of landscape, California is hard to beat. With glaciated alpine peaks and meadows, desolate desert sand dunes, and flat, fertile agricultural plains, it's no wonder that Hollywood film-makers have so often and successfully used California locations to simulate distant and exotic scenes. These diverse landscapes also support an immense variety of plant and animal life, much of which – due to the protection offered by the various state and national parks, forests, and wilderness areas – is both easily accessible and unspoiled by encroaching civilization.

Background: landscapes, geology, and earthquakes

California's landscape has been formed over millions of years through the interaction of all the main geological processes: Ice Age glaciation, erosion, earthquakes, and volcanic eruptions. The most impressive results can be seen in **Yosemite National Park**, east of San Francisco, where solid walls of granite have been sliced and shaped into unforgettable cliffs and chasms. In contrast, the sand dunes of **Death Valley** are being constantly shaped and reshaped by the dry desert winds, surrounded by foothills tinted by oxidized mineral deposits into every color of the spectrum.

Earthquakes – which earned Los Angeles the truck driver's nickname "Shakeytown" – are the most powerful expression of the volatile unrest underlying the placid surface. California sits on the Pacific "Ring of Fire," at the junction of two tectonic plates slowly drifting deep within the earth. Besides the occasional earthquake – like the 1906 quake which flattened San Francisco, or the 1994 tremor which collapsed many of LA's freeways – this instability is also the cause of California's many volcanoes. Distinguished by their symmetrical, conical shape, almost all of them are now dormant; though Mount Lassen, in Northern California, did erupt in 1914 and 1915, destroying much of the surrounding forest. Along with the boiling mud pools that accompany even the dormant volcanoes, the most attractive features of volcanic regions are the bubbling **hot springs** – pools of water that flow up from deep underground, heated to a sybaritically soothing temperature. Hot springs occur naturally all over the state, and though some have now been developed into luxurious health spas, most remain in their natural condition, where you can soak your bones *au naturel* surrounded by mountain meadows or wide-open deserts. The best of these are listed throughout the Guide.

Though some of the most fantastic **wildlife**, like the grizzly bear – a ten-foot-tall, two-ton giant that still adorns the state flag of California – and the California condor – one of the world's largest birds, with a wingspan of over eight feet – are now extinct in their natural habitats, plenty more are still alive and thriving, like the otters, elephant seals, and gray whales seen all along the coast, and the chubby marmots – shy mammals often found sunning themselves on rocks in higher reaches of the mountains. Plant life is equally varied, from the brilliant but short-lived desert wildflowers to the timeless Bristlecone pine trees, which live for thousands of years on the arid peaks of the Great Basin desert.

Below you will find details of the major **ecosystems** of California. The accounts are inevitably brief, as the area encompasses almost 320,000 square miles (ranging from moist coastal forests and the snow-capped Sierra Nevada peaks to Death Valley, 282 feet below sea level with an annual rainfall of two inches), and is inhabited by a multitude of species. Native to California are 54 species of cacti, 123 species of amphibians and reptiles, 260 species of birds, and 27,000–28,000 species of insects. See "Books" for recommendations of more specific habitat guides. Bear in mind, also, that museums all over the state examine and exhibit the natural world in depth, notably Monterey's superb Aquarium – see p.483 for details.

The ocean

The **Pacific Ocean** determines California's climate, keeping the coastal temperatures moderate all year round. During the spring and summer, cold nutrient-rich waters rise or well up to produce cooling banks of fog and abundant crops of phytoplankton (microscopic algae). The algae nourishes creatures such as krill (small shrimps), which in their turn provide baby food for juvenile fish. This food chain provides fodder for millions of nesting **sea birds**, as well as harbor and elephant **seals**, California **sea lions**, and whales. **Gray whales**, the most common species spotted from land, were once almost hunted to the point of extinction, but have returned to the coast in large numbers. During their southward migration to their breeding grounds off Mexico, from December to January, it is easy to spot them from prominent headlands all along the coast, and most harbors have charter services offering whale-watching tours. On their way back to the Arctic Sea, in February and March, the newborn whale pups can sometimes be seen playfully leaping out of the water, or "breaching." Look for the whale's white-plumed spout – once at the surface, it will usually blow several times in succession.

Tidepools

California's shoreline is composed of three primary ecosystems: tidepools, sandy beaches, and estuaries. To explore the **tidepools**, first consult a local newspaper to see when the low tides (two daily) will occur. Be careful of waves, don't be out too far from the shore when the tide returns, and also watch your step – there are many small lives underfoot. There are miles of beaches with tidepools, some of the best at Pacific Grove near Monterey. Here you will find **sea anemones** (they look like green zinnias), hermit crabs, purple-and-green shore crabs, red sponges, purple sea urchins, starfish ranging from the size of a dime to the size of a hubcap, mussels, abalone, and chinese-hat limpets – to name a few. You may also see black **oystercatchers**, their squawking easily heard over the surf, foraging for an unwary, lips-agape mussel. Gulls and black turnstones are also common, and during the summer brown pelicans dive for fish just offshore.

The life of the tidepool party is the **hermit crab**, who protects its soft and vulnerable hindquarters with scavenged shells, usually those of the aptly named black turban snail. Hermit crabs scurry busily around in search of a detritus snack, or scuffle with other hermit crabs over the proprietorship of vacant snail shells.

Pacific Grove is also home to large populations of **sea otters**. Unlike most marine mammals, sea otters keep themselves warm with a thick, soft coat rather than blubber. The trade in sea otter pelts brought entrepreneurial Russian and British fur hunters to the West Coast, and by the mid-nineteenth century the otters were virtually extinct. In 1938, a small population was discovered near Big Sur, and with careful protection otters have re-established themselves in the southern part of their range. They are charming creatures with big rubbery noses and Groucho Marx moustaches. With binoculars, it's easy to spot them amongst the bobbing kelp, where they lie on their backs opening sea urchins with a rock, or sleep entwined within a seat belt of kelp, which keeps them from floating away. The bulk of the population resides between Monterey Bay and the Channel Islands, but – aside from Pacific Grove – the best places to see them are Point Lobos State Park, the Seventeen-Mile Drive, and the Monterey Wharf, where, along with sea lions, they often come to beg for fish.

Many of the **seaweeds** you see growing from the rocks are edible. As one would expect from a Pacific beachfront, there are also **palms** – sea palms, with four-inch-long rubbery stems and flagella-like fronds. Their thick root-like holdfasts provide shelter for small crabs. You will also find giant **kelp** washed up on shore – harvested commercially for use in thickening ice cream.

Sandy beaches

The long, golden **sandy beaches** for which California is so famous may look sterile from a distance. However, observe the margin of sand exposed as a gentle wave recedes, and you will see jetstreams of small bubbles emerge from numerous clams and mole crabs. Small shore birds called **sanderlings** race amongst the waves in search of these morsels, and sand dollars are often easy to find along the high-tide line.

The most unusual sandy-shore bathing beauties are the **northern elephant seals**, which will tolerate rocky beaches but favor soft sand mattresses for their rotund torsos. The males, or bulls, can reach lengths of over six yards and weigh upwards of four tons; the females, or cows, are petite by comparison – four yards long, and averaging a mere two thousand pounds in weight. They have large eyes, adapted for spotting fish in deep or murky waters; indeed, elephant seals are the deepest diving mammals, capable of staying under water for twenty minutes at a time, reaching depths of over four thousand feet, where the pressure is over a hundred times that at the surface. They have to dive so deeply in order to avoid the attentions of the great white sharks who lurk offshore, for whom they are a favorite meal.

Like otters, elephant seals were decimated by commercial whalers in the mid-nineteenth century for their blubber and hides. By the turn of the century, less than a hundred remained, but careful protection has partially restored the California population, which is concentrated on the Channel and Farallon islands and at Año Nuevo State Park.

Elephant seals only emerge from the ocean to breed or molt; their name comes from the male's long trunk-like proboscis, through which it produces a resonant pinging sound that biologists call "trumpeting," which is how it attracts a mate. The Año Nuevo Beach is the best place to observe this ritual. In December and January, the bulls haul themselves out of the water and battle for dominance. The predominant, or alpha, male will do most of the mating, siring as many as fifty young pups, one per mating, in a season. Other males fight it out at the fringes, each managing one or two couplings with the hapless, defenseless females. During this time, the beach is a seething mass of ton upon ton of blubbery seals – flopping sand over their back to keep cool, squabbling with their neighbors while making rude snoring and belching sounds. The adults depart in March but the weaned pups hang around until May.

Different age groups of elephant seals continue to use the beach at different times throughout the summer for molting. Elephant seals are completely unafraid of people, but are huge enough to hurt or even kill you if you get in their way, though you're allowed to get close, except during mating season, when entry into the park is restricted to ranger-guided tours.

Estuaries

Throughout California, many **estuarine** or rivermouth habitats have been filled, diked, drained, "improved" with marinas, or contaminated by pollutants. Those that survive intact consist of a mixture of mud flats, exposed only at low tide, and salt marsh, together forming a critical wildlife area that provides nurseries for many kinds of invertebrates and fish, and nesting and wintering grounds for many birds. Cord grass, a dominant wetlands plant, produces five to ten times as much oxygen and nutrients per acre as does wheat.

Many interesting creatures live in the thick organic ooze, including the fat **innkeeper**, a revolting-looking pink hot-dog of a worm that sociably shares its burrow with a small crab and a fish, polychaete worms, clams, and other goodies. Most prominent of estuary birds are the **great blue herons** and **great egrets**. Estuaries are the best place to see wintering shore birds such as dunlin, dowitchers, eastern and western sandpipers, and yellowlegs. Peregrine falcons and osprey are also found here.

Important Californian estuaries include Elkhorn Slough, near Monterey, San Francisco Bay, and Bolinas Lagoon.

Coastal bluffs

Along the shore, **coastal meadows** are bright with pink and yellow sand verbena, lupines, sea rocket, sea fig, and the bright orange **California poppy**, the state flower. Slightly inland, hills are covered with coastal scrub, which consists largely of coyote brush. Coastal canyons contain broadleaf trees such as California laurel, alder, buckeye, and oaks – and a tangle of sword ferns, horsetail, and cow parsnip.

Common rainy-season canyon inhabitants include four-inch-long banana slugs and rough-skinned newts. In winter, orange-and-black **Monarch butterflies** inhabit large roosts in a few discreet locales, such as Bolinas, Monterey, and Pacific Grove. Coastal thickets also provide homes to weasels, bobcats, gray fox, racoons, black-tailed deer, California quail, and garter snakes. **Tule elk**, a once-common member of the deer family, have also been reintroduced to the wild; good places to view them are on Tomales Point at the Point Reyes National Seashore (see p.643), and inland at reserves near Bakersfield (p.370) and in the Owens Valley (p.337).

River valleys

Like most fertile **river valleys**, the Sacramento and San Joaquin valleys – jointly known as the Central Valley – have both been greatly affected by agriculture. Riparian (streamside) vegetation has been logged, wetlands drained, and streams contaminated by agricultural run-off. Despite this, the riparian habitat that does remain is a prime wildlife habitat. Wood ducks, kingfishers, swallows, and warblers are common, as are gray foxes, racoons, and striped skunks. The Sacramento National Wildlife Refuge has one of the world's largest concentrations of **snow geese** during winter months. Other common winter migrants include Canada geese, green-winged and cinnamon teals, pin-tail, shovelers, and wigeon. These refuges are well worth a visit, but don't be alarmed by large numbers of duck-hunters – the term "refuge" is a misnomer. However, most have tour routes where hunting is prohibited.

Vernal pools are a valley community unique to California. Here, hardpan soils prevent the infiltration of winter rains, creating seasonal ponds. As these ponds slowly evaporate in April and May, sharply defined concentric floral rings come into bloom. The white is meadowfoam, the blue is the violet-like downingia, and the yellow is goldfields. Swallows, meadowlarks, yellowlegs, and stilts can also be found. Jepson Prairie Nature Conservancy Reserve is the eas-iest to visit, south of Sacramento near the small town of Rio Vista.

Forests

Perhaps the most notable indigenous features of Californian forests are the wide expanses of **redwood** and **sequoia trees**. It's easy to confuse the coastal species, *Sequoia sempervirens*, or redwood, with the *Sequoiadendron giganteum*, or giant sequoia (pronounced *suk-oy-ah*), as both have the same fibrous reddish-brown bark. Redwoods are the world's tallest trees, sequoias have the greatest base circumference and are the largest single organisms on earth; for more on the latter, see the box on p.397. Both species can live for over two thousand years, and recent research now indicates a maximum age of 3500 years for the sequoia. Their longevity is partially due to their bark: rich in tannin, it protects the tree from fungal and insect attack and inhibits fire damage. In fact, fire is beneficial to these trees and necessary for their germination; prescribed fires are set and controlled around them. The wood of the redwoods in particular is much sought after both for its beauty – near any coastal forest you'll see signs advertising redwood burl furniture – and its resistance to decay (the bark con-tinues to protect the tree for several hundred years after felling).

They are the only surviving members of a family of perhaps forty species of trees which, fossil records show, grew worldwide 175 million years ago. Now just a few pockets remain, and a tremendous battle between environmentalists and loggers is being waged over the remaining acres. These **virgin forests** pro-vide homes to unique creatures such as the spotted owl and marbled murrelet.

Redwoods are a relict species, which means that they flourished in a moister climate during the Arcto-Tertiary (just after the golden age of the dinosaurs), and now occupy a much-reduced range. As the weather patterns changed, red-woods slowly retreated to their current near-coastal haunts. Today, they are found from the border with Oregon to just south of Monterey.

The floor of the redwood forest is a hushed place with little sunlight, the air suffused with a rufous glow from the bark, which gives the trees its name. One of the commonest ground covers in the redwood forest is the redwood sorrel, or oxalis, with its shamrock leaves and tubular pink flowers; ferns are also numerous. Birds are usually high in the canopy and hard to see, but you might hear the double-whistled song of the varied thrush, or the "chickadee" call from the bird of that name. Roosevelt elk, larger than the tule elk, also inhabit the humid northwest forests. Prairie Creek Redwoods State Park, near the border with Oregon, has a large herd.

Sequoias are found on the western slopes of the Sierra Nevada, most notably in Yosemite and Kings Canyon national parks – though saplings given as state gifts can be found growing all over the world.

The sequoia forest tends to be slightly more open than the redwood forest. Juvenile sequoias – say up to a thousand years old – exhibit a slender conical shape, which, as the lower branches fall away, ages to the classical heavy-crowned shape with its columnar trunk. For its bulk, its cones are astonishingly small, no bigger than a hen's egg, but they live on the tree for up to thirty years before falling.

The Sierra Nevada

In the late nineteenth century, the environmental movement was founded when John Muir fell in love with the **Sierra Nevada** mountains, which he called the Range of Light. Muir fought a losing battle to save Hetch Hetchy, a valley said to be as beautiful as Yosemite, but in the process the Sierra Club was born and the move to save America's remaining wilderness began.

The Sierra mountains, which run almost the entire length of the state, have a sharp, craggy, freshly glaciated look. Many of the same conifers can be found as in the forests further west, but ponderosa and lodge-pole pines are two of the dominants, and the forests tend to be drier and more open. Lower-elevation forests contain incense cedar, sugar pine (which has the longest pine cones – over eighteen inches – in the world), and black oak. The oaks, along with dogwood and willows, produce spectacular autumnal color. The east side is drier and has large groves of aspen, a beautiful white-barked tree with small round leaves that tremble in the wind. **Wildflowers** flourish for a few short months – shooting star, elephant's head, and wild onions in early spring, asters and yarrow later in the season.

The dominant campground scoundrels are two sorts of noisy, squawking bird: Steller's jays and Clark's nutcrackers. Black bears, who may make a raid on your campground, pose more danger to iceboxes than humans, but nonetheless you should treat them with caution. The friendly twenty-pound pot-bellied rodents that lounge around at the fringes of your encampment are **marmots**, who probably do more damage than bears: some specialize in chewing on radiator hoses of parked cars.

Other common birds include mountain chickadees, yellow-rumped warblers, white-crowned sparrows, and juncos. Deer, golden-mantled ground squirrels, and chipmunks are also plentiful.

The Great Basin

The little-known **Great Basin** stretches from the northernmost section of the state down almost to Death Valley, encompassing all of Nevada and parts of all the other bordering states. It's a land of many shrubs and few streams, and what streams do exist drain into saline lakes rather than the ocean.

Mono Lake, reflecting the 13,000-foot peaks of Yosemite National Park, is a spectacular example. Its salty waters support no fish but lots of algae, brine shrimp, and brine flies, the latter two providing a smorgasbord for nesting gulls (the term "seagull" isn't strictly correct – many gulls nest inland) and migrating phalaropes and grebes. Like many Great Basin lakes, Mono Lake has been damaged through diversion of its freshwater feeder streams to provide water for the city of Los Angeles.

Great Basin plants tolerate hot summers, cold winters, and little rain. The dominant Great Basin plant is **sagebrush**. Its dusky green leaves are wonderfully aromatic, especially after a summer thunderstorm. Other common plants include bitterbrush, desert peach, junipers, and piñon pines. Piñon cones contain tasty nuts that were a mainstay of the Paiute diet.

The **sage grouse** is one of the most distinctive Great Basin birds. These turkey-like birds feed on sage during the winter and depend on it for nesting and courtship habitat. In March and April, males gather at dancing grounds called leks, where they puff out small pink balloons on their necks, make soft drum-banging calls, and in general succeed in looking and sounding rather silly. The hens coyly scout out the talent by feigning greater interest in imaginary seeds.

Pronghorns are beautiful tawny-gold antelope seen in many places in the Great Basin. Watch for their twinkling white rumps as you drive.

Other Great Basin denizens include golden eagles, piñon jays, black-billed magpies, coyotes, feral horses and burros, black-tailed jackrabbits, and western rattlesnakes. Large concentrations of waterfowl gather at Tule Lake in northeastern California, where hundreds of wintering **bald eagles** gather in November before the cold really sets in.

The Mojave Desert

The **Mojave Desert** lies in the southeast corner of the state, near Death Valley. Like the Great Basin, the vegetation here consists primarily of drought-adapted shrubs, one of the commonest of which is creosote, with its olive-green leaves and puffy yellow flowers. Death Valley is renowned for its early spring wildflower shows. The alluvial fans are covered with desert trumpet, gravel ghost, and pebble pincushion. The quantity and timing of rainfall determines when the floral display peaks, but it's usually some time between mid-February and mid-April in the lower elevations, late April to early June higher up.

Besides shrubs, the Mojave has many interesting kinds of **cacti**. These include barrel, cottontop, cholla, and beavertail cactus, and many members of the yucca family. Yuccas have stiff, lance-like leaves with sharp tips, a conspicuous representative being the **Joshua tree** (see p.276), whose twisting, arm-like branches are covered with shaggy upward-pointing leaf fronds, which can reach to thirty feet high.

Many Mojave desert animals conserve body moisture by foraging at night, including the kit fox, wood rat, and various kinds of mice. The **kangaroo rat**, an appealing animal that hops rather than runs, has specially adapted kidneys that enable it to survive without drinking water. Other desert animals include mammals such as the Mojave ground squirrel, bighorn, and coyote; birds like the roadrunner, ash-throated flycatcher, ladder-backed woodpecker, verdin, and Lucy's warbler; and reptiles like the Mojave rattlesnake, sidewinder, and chuckwalla.

California on film

I n the early 1910s, attracted by endless sunshine, cheap real estate, and the rich variety of California landscapes, a handful of independent movie producers left the East Coast and the stranglehold monopoly of Thomas Edison's Motion Picture Patents Company, and set up shop in a small Los Angeles suburb called Hollywood. Within a decade Hollywood had become the movie capital of the world and Southern California became the setting for everything from Keystone Kop car chases to Tom Mix Westerns, not to mention the odd Biblical epic or historic romance shot on studio lots.

But, as the movie industry grew, Hollywood's films about California – as opposed to those that just happened to be set there – began presenting the state either as the kind of rustic arcadia beloved by the pioneers, or, more commonly, as a state of mind. Much has changed on the long road between John Farrow's **California** (1946), in which Ray Milland leads a wagon train to the Promised Land during the Gold Rush, and Dominic Sena's **Kalifornia** (1993), in which David Duchovny unwittingly invites a serial killer along for the cross-country ride, but both films posit California as the answer to everybody's problems. ("If it wasn't OK there, then it probably wouldn't be OK anywhere," says Duchovny).

Transcendence used to be what California was all about, and it's still a major theme in Californian films. But more and more California – or more specifically Los Angeles – is presented not as an answer, but simply a problem: the City of Dreams as City of Recurring Nightmares, a locus of vapid consumerism, rampant crime, and racial division, trembling on the verge of **apocalypse**. Or so the movies tell us.

Not surprisingly, the list of movies set in California, and especially LA, is endless. What follows are the most significant movies, those that make the most original use of Californian locations (from the vertiginous streets of San Francisco to the breakers of Monterey, from the dust bowls of the Mojave to the LA River), as well as those that reflect California's navel-gazing fascination with itself.

Hollywood does Hollywood

The Bad and the Beautiful (Vincente Minnelli 1952). Made just as the studio system was beginning to come apart at the seams, Minnelli's bitter insider tale of the rise and fall of a ruthless Hollywood producer (Kirk Douglas) is told in flashbacks by the star, the writer, and the director he launched and subsequently lost.

Barton Fink (Joel Coen 1991). Tinseltown in the 1940s is depicted by the Coen brothers as a dark world of greedy movie bosses, belligerent screenwriters, and murderers disguised as traveling salesmen.

The Big Knife (Robert Aldrich 1955). An incisive portrayal of Hollywood politics, in which a weak-willed actor can't get free from the tentacles of a hack director, despite the pleas of his wife. Based on a play by Clifford Odets and filmed like one as well.

Ed Wood (Tim Burton 1994). The ragged low-budget fringes of Fifties Hollywood are beautifully recreated in this loving tribute to the much-derided "auteur" of *Plan Nine from Outer Space* and *Glen or Glenda*. Gorgeously shot in black and white, and with a stunning performance by

Martin Landau as ailing Hollywood habitué Bela Lugosi.

Get Shorty (Barry Sonnenfeld 1995). When movie-loving Miami loan shark Chili Palmer (John Travolta) is sent to Hollywood to collect a debt from schlock-horror auteur Harry Zim (Gene Hackman), he sees his chance to pull a fast one on a gang of drug-smuggling mobsters and get his name in lights. Faithfully based on the Elmore Leonard novel.

Gods and Monsters (Bill Condon 1998). An interesting tale of the final days of 1930s horror-film director James Whale (masterfully portrayed by Ian McKellen), ignored by the Hollywood elite and slowly dying of malaise by his poolside. The title refers to a memorable Ernest Thesiger line from Whale's classic *The Bride of Frankenstein*.

Good Morning, Babylon (Paolo and Vittorio Taviani 1987). Two restorers of European cathedrals find themselves in 1910s Hollywood, working to build the monstrous Babylonian set for D. W. Griffith's *Intolerance*, in this Italian story of the contribution of immigrants in early Tinseltown. Oddly enough, that same set has now been partially rebuilt in Hollywood – as part of a mall.

Hurlyburly (Anthony Drazan 1998). David Rabe's acidic play about Hollywood players and hucksters is rendered in celluloid as a prattling pathos-fest, with much angst for Sean Penn and Chazz Palminteri and much ironic detachment for Kevin Spacey and Garry Shandling.

In a Lonely Place (Nicholas Ray 1950). A glamour-less Hollywood peopled with alcoholic former matinee idols, star-struck hat-check girls and desperate agents forms the cynical background for this devastating doomed romance between Humphrey Bogart's hot-tempered screenwriter and his Beverly Hills neighbor Gloria Grahame.

The Player (Robert Altman 1992). Tim Robbins is perfectly smug as an egocentric studio executive getting away with murder. Peopled with movie stars playing themselves, and packed with movie-biz in-jokes, Altman's tour-de-force is a wickedly accurate depiction of Hollywood's lowered expectations and diminishing returns.

Singin' in the Rain (Stanley Donen & Gene Kelly 1952). The eternally popular, lovingly made song-and-dance satire about Hollywood's fraught transition from silents to talkies. With great songs, perceptive gags, and the unforgettable title sequence, the film is pure pleasure.

A Star is Born (George Cukor 1954). The best of many versions of this classic Hollywood weepie, in which Judy Garland is given a hand up the ladder by James Mason, an alcoholic star very much on the way down.

Sunset Boulevard (Billy Wilder 1950). The darkest of the many mirrors Hollywood has held up to itself, Wilder's acerbic classic about an impoverished screenwriter (William Holden) who falls into the clutches of an aging silent-film star (Gloria Swanson) posits Hollywood as a nightmare world of vanity, illusion, and decline.

Who Framed Roger Rabbit? (Robert Zemeckis 1988). This eye-popping fusion of live action and animation imagines a Forties Hollywood in which cartoon characters inhabit the same universe as humans, but only as second-class citizens forced to live in the crime-ridden cartoon ghetto of Toontown.

LA crime stories

American Gigolo (Paul Schrader 1980). LA is at its glossiest and most vacuous in this arty, muted pulp thriller about a high-class, Armani-clad male prostitute (Richard Gere), framed for murder and searching for grace.

Chinatown (Roman Polanski 1974). One of the most memorable cinematic marriages of story and setting, Polanski's classic neo-noir stars Jack Nicholson as a private eye adrift in the moral desert of late Thirties LA, when real estate was booming, water scarce, and corruption at every level a given.

Devil in a Blue Dress (Carl Franklin 1995). Terrific modern noir, in which South Central detective Easy Rawlins (Denzel Washington) navigates the ethical squalor of elite 1940s white LA and discovers a few ugly truths about city leaders – most of which he already suspected.

Double Indemnity (Billy Wilder 1944). The definitive LA noir, in which traveling insurance salesman and all-round fall-guy Fred MacMurray provides us with an incidental tour of Forties LA as he winds himself ever more tightly into Barbara Stanwyck's devastating web of duplicity.

Heat (Michael Mann 1995). The urban architecture of LA has rarely been more beautifully filmed than in this criminally underrated face-off between Robert De Niro's master thief and Al Pacino's dogged detective, which plays out against a stunning Antonioni-esque backdrop of shimmering cityscapes, spaghetti-looped freeways, and the runways of LAX.

He Walked by Night (Alfred Werker 1948). This verité-style crime story set in "the fastest growing city in the nation" starts with a random cop-killing in Santa Monica and ends with a manhunt through the 700-mile subterranean city storm-drain system, stunningly shot by torch-light by peerless noir cinematographer John Alton.

Jackie Brown (Quentin Tarantino 1997). A glorious return to form for Pam Grier who, as a tough airline stewardess, plays the perfect foil for Samuel Jackson's smooth gangster. LA itself provides the dark, menacing backdrop.

The Killing of a Chinese Bookie (John Cassavetes 1976). Strange and self-indulgent, but perfectly evoking the sleazy charms of the Sunset Strip, Cassavetes' behavioral crime story about a club-owner (Ben Gazzara) in hock to the mob is just one of his many great LA-based character studies.

LA Confidential (Curtis Hanson 1997). A sizzling epic of police corruption and Tinseltown sleaze in Fifties Los Angeles – a city swarming with unscrupulous tabloid journalists, venal bureaucrats, racist cops, and movie-star-lookalike whores. Superbly done.

The Long Goodbye (Robert Altman 1973). Altman's masterpiece updates Raymond Chandler's shadowy Forties noir to sun-drenched Seventies me-generation LA. Elliot Gould's disheveled Philip Marlowe lives in the Hollywood Hills with a bevy of hippy chicks for neighbors and a bushel of problems that take him from Tijuana to Malibu and back.

Point Blank (John Boorman 1967). Though it begins and ends at Alcatraz, Boorman's virtuoso avant-garde thriller, in which a poker-faced Lee Marvin seeks revenge for an earlier betrayal, is most effective imagining Los Angeles as an impenetrable citadel of concrete and glass built on the wages of corporate crime.

To Live and Die in LA (William Friedkin 1985). The glossiest and flashiest of LA policiers, Friedkin's updating of his *French Connection* formula to the Eighties and the West Coast follows two FBI agents on the trail of a master counterfeiter, and features another of his trademark spectacular car chases – this time LA-style on a major freeway at rush hour.

Touch of Evil (Orson Welles 1958). Supposedly set at a Mexican border town, this noir classic was actually shot in a seedy, decrepit Venice. A bizarre, baroque master-piece with Charlton Heston playing a Mexican official, Janet Leigh as his beleaguered wife, and Welles himself as a bloated, corrupt cop addicted to candy bars.

Apocalyptic LA

1941 (Steven Spielberg 1979). "This isn't the State of California, this is a state of insanity," yells Robert Stack's General Stillwell as LA prepares for a Japanese invasion at the height of post-Pearl Harbor paranoia. Spielberg's joylessly frantic epic com-edy begins with John Belushi crash-landing in Death Valley and ends with a submarine attack on the Santa Monica Pier.

Blade Runner (Ridley Scott 1982). This brilliant combination of sci-fi and neo-noir envisions the Los Angeles of 2019 as a depopulated, crime-ridden metropolis of towering skyscrapers, sprawling street-markets, and perpetual darkness, where Harrison Ford's gumshoe tracks renegade replicants through the never-ending acid rain.

Earthquake (Mark Robson 1974). Watch the Lake Hollywood dam collapse, people run for their lives, and chaos hold sway in the City of Angels. Originally presented in "Sensurround!"

Escape from LA (John Carpenter 1996). In Carpenter's alternative vision of the future, Los Angeles has been cut off from the mainland by an earthquake and declared so "rav-aged by crime and immorality" that it has been turned into a deportation zone for undesirables. Sent in to uproot insurrection, Kurt Russell battles psychotic plastic surgeons in Beverly Hills and surfs a tsunami to a showdown in a netherworld Disneyland.

Falling Down (Joel Schumacher 1993). Mad as hell, and unable to tolerate the height-of-summer LA traffic jam in which he finds himself, Michael Douglas abandons his car and goes on the rampage through some of the city's less picturesque neighborhoods, railing at petty injus-tices and wreaking havoc with every step.

Kiss Me Deadly (Robert Aldrich 1955). Aldrich's no-holds-barred apocalypse-noir follows proto-fascist private eye Mike Hammer on a punch-drunk tour of LA in search of a deadly Maguffin – from boarding houses to the mansions of Beverly Hills to a Malibu beach house where, quite literally, all hell breaks loose.

Mulholland Drive (David Lynch 2001). A frightening take on the city by director Lynch, who uses non-linear storytelling to present a story of love, death, glamour, and doom – in which elfin cowboys mutter cryptic threats, elegant chanteuses lip- sync to phantom melodies, and a blue key can unlock a shocking dou-ble identity.

The Rapture (Michael Tolkin 1991). Mimi Rogers plays an LA telephone operator who abandons her hedonistic lifestyle when she hears a fundamentalist group talking about the impending "Rapture," and becomes born again, ultimately heading into the desert to await Armageddon. Michael Tolkin's wonderfully literal film takes his premise just as far as it can go, and then some.

Strange Days (Kathryn Bigelow 1995). In this visceral, millennial joyride by one of LA's most visionary auteurs, Angelenos party like it's 1999, and Ralph Fiennes' Lenny Nero fiddles while his racially sundered city burns. Surrogate thrills, in the form of virtual reality tapes of someone else's private heaven or hell, are the illegal drug of choice as the century goes out with a bang.

Terminator 2: Judgment Day (James Cameron 1991). As in Cameron's impressive first *Terminator* (1984), the machines in charge of the future have sent a cyborg back in time to assassinate a future resistance leader. This time, however, the film makes even more memorable use of LA locations, with a thrilling truck chase along the concrete bed of the Los Angeles River and a spectacular visualization of the city's apocalyptic destiny.

They Live (John Carpenter 1988). In this ludicrous but entertaining horror flick, a drifter living in a shanty town pitched on the outskirts of LA discovers a pair of sunglasses which allow him to see that skull-faced aliens in positions of wealth and power are subliminally encouraging the city's rampant consumerism.

Modern LA

Boyz N the Hood (John Singleton 1991). Singleton's influential debut film, a sober portrayal of life in South Central LA, highlights the odds against success or even survival in a community riddled with drugs, poverty, racism, and violence.

Clueless (Amy Heckerling 1995). As exemplary of LA in the Nineties as *Boyz N the Hood*, Heckerling's Girls in the Mall comedy made a star of Alicia Silverstone, who guides us through the empty heads of shopaholic Beverly Hills High schoolgirls and their Valley-inflected, rich-kid lingo.

Dogtown and Z-Boys (Stacy Peralta 2002). Even if you have no interest in skateboarding, this is a fun, high-spirited look at the glory times of the sport in the mid-1970s, when a daring group of LA kids took to using the empty swimming pools of the elite as their own private skate-parks.

The End of Violence (Wim Wenders 1997). Bill Pullman plays a successful schlock-movie producer obsessed with violence who finds redemption after he is nearly murdered himself. Wenders' existential thriller is preposterous and po-faced but his films end-of-the-millennium LA with a hypnotically otherworldly beauty and his typically quizzical outsider's gaze.

Ghost World (Terry Zwigoff 2001). An alienated teenager encounters LA (here, nameless) in all of its corporatized drabness, a soulless desert of identical mini-malls, cheap retro-50s diners, and desperate, lonely characters. Oddly enough, something of a dark comedy.

The Glass Shield (Charles Burnett 1995). Institutionalized racism in the LAPD is brought under the harsh glare of Charles Burnett, who, with his masterpieces *Killer of Sheep* (1977) and *My Brother's Wedding* (1983), has long been one of the great chroniclers of LA's black urban underclass.

Go (Doug Liman 1999). A kinetic joyride through LA's rave subculture told from three perspectives, including Sarah Polley's botching of an aspirin-for-Ecstasy drug sale, and Jay Mohr and Scott Wolf – as two TV soap stars – stuck in a police sting operation.

The Limey (Steven Soderbergh 1999). Gangster Terence Stamp wanders into a morally adrift LA looking for his daughter's killer, and finds the burned-out husk of former hippie Peter Fonda.

Magnolia (Paul Thomas Anderson 1999). Anderson's darkly affecting travelogue of human misery starring, amongst many others, Jason Robards and Tom Cruise. The San Fernando Valley serves as an emotional inferno of abusive parents, victimized children, haunted memories, plaintive songs, and a curious plague of frogs.

Mi Vida Loca (Alison Anders 1993). Depressing ensemble piece about the hard lives of Latinas in Echo Park girl-gangs and the central reason the director won a prestigious MacArthur Fellowship.

Pulp Fiction (Quentin Tarantino 1994). Tarantino's electrifying roundelay of stories about sudden deaths and second chances is set in a depopulated, down-at-heel Los Angeles of kitsch diners and low-rent motels, store basements, and funereal saloons – a deliberately bland backdrop against which his

fast-talking hustlers and half-hearted hit-men seem all the more vivid.

Short Cuts (Robert Altman 1993). Transposing the stories of Raymond Carver from Washington to LA, Altman's haunting, bluesy city symphony brilliantly knits together the parallel universes inhabited by a gaggle of suburban Angelenos whose lives are interlinked by small disasters and surprising moments of grace.

Speed (Jan De Bont 1994). In a city in which public transportation is little more than a utopian ideal, and in which bumper-to-bumper traffic clogs the freeways from morning till night, the idea of a city bus primed to explode if its speed drops below 50mph was the perfect LA joke, as well as the excuse for a thrilling travelogue of the city's transit system.

Star Maps (Miguel Arteta 1997). A *telenovela*-esque melodrama of immigrant life on the fringes of Hollywood. Carlos, who has grandiose dreams of movie stardom, is doing time in his father's prostitution ring, standing on street corners ostensibly selling maps to the homes of the stars, in reality selling his body for cash.

Swingers (Doug Liman 1996). Modern-day cocktail culture is skewered in this hilarious cult favorite about a couple of dudes who spend their nights in Sunset Boulevard lounges and swing clubs eyeing up the "beautiful babies" and shooting the breeze like Rat Pack-era Sinatras.

If you're going to San Francisco

Bullitt (Peter Yates 1968). In the minds of many filmgoers, *the* classic portrait of San Francisco, presented at breakneck speed in cinema's most famous car chase, ripping up and down the city's steep hills at a frenetic, still-amazing pace. No modern

special effects for this legendary sequence, either.

The Conversation (Francis Ford Coppola 1974). Opening with a mesmerizing sequence of high-tech eavesdropping in Union Square, Coppola's chilling character study of

San Francisco surveillance expert Harry Caul (Gene Hackman at his finest) is one of the best films of the paranoid Watergate era.

Dim Sum: A Little Bit of Heart (Wayne Wang 1985). Set among San Francisco's Chinese community, Wayne Wang's appealing comedy of manners about assimilation and family ties is a modest and rewarding treat. His earlier sleeper *Chan is Missing* (1982) also shows a Chinatown tourists don't usually see.

Dirty Harry (Don Siegel 1971). Based on the infamous case of the Bay Area Zodiac Killer, Siegel's morally debatable, sequel-spawning, catch-phrase-begetting thriller casts Clint Eastwood in his most famous role as a vigilante San Francisco cop who'll do anything to get his man and make his day.

Escape from Alcatraz (Don Siegel 1979). Though evocatively portrayed in *The Bird Man of Alcatraz*, *Point Blank*, *The Rock,* and many others, this is the ultimate movie about San Francisco's famously unbreachable offshore penitentiary. Starring Clint Eastwood (again) as a most resourceful con.

Gimme Shelter (Albert and David Maysles 1969). Excellent documentary about the ill-fated Rolling Stones' concert at Altamont. Its searing look at homegrown American violence and Vietnam-era chaos at the end of the 1960s also includes an on-camera stabbing.

Greed (Erich von Stroheim 1924). This legendary silent masterpiece about the downfall of Polk Street dentist Doc McTeague was shot mostly on location in the Bay Area, and remains, even in its notoriously truncated version, a wonderful time capsule of working-class San Francisco in the 1920s.

It Came from Beneath the Sea (Robert Gordon 1955). Apocalypse, San Francisco-style. One of the more memorable monster flicks of the 1950s, in which a super-sized octopus emerges from the waters of the Bay and begins scooping people up for lunch. Appealing special effects, for the time.

Petulia (Richard Lester 1968). Julie Christie is dazzling in this fragmented puzzle of a movie about a vivacious and unpredictable married woman who has an affair with a divorced doctor (George C. Scott). Set against the wittily-described background of psychedelic-era San Francisco, and superbly shot by Nicolas Roeg, *Petulia* is a forgotten Sixties masterpiece.

Play It Again, Sam (Herbert Ross 1972). A strike in Manhattan led to one of Woody Allen's rare visits to the West Coast, for this hilarious film about a neurotic San Francisco film critic in love with his best friend's wife and obsessed with Humphrey Bogart in *Casablanca*.

The Times of Harvey Milk (Robert Epstein 1984). This powerful and moving documentary about America's first openly gay politician chronicles his career in pre-Aids–era San Francisco and the aftermath of his 1978 assassination.

Vertigo (Alfred Hitchcock 1958). Hitchcock's somber, agonized, twisted, tragic love story is the San Francisco movie nonpareil. From James Stewart's wordless drives around the city to the film's climax at the San Juan Bautista Mission, Hitchcock takes us on a mesmerizing tour of a city haunted by its past.

What's Up, Doc? (Peter Bogdanovich 1972). This madcap homage to the heyday of Hollywood screwball comedy stars Ryan O'Neal as a hapless stuffed-shirt musicologist and Barbra Streisand as the kook who drives him around the bend, and features, next to Steve McQueen's *Bullitt*, one of the great vertiginous San Francisco car chases.

"Way out" West

The Big Lebowski (Joel Coen 1998). A bizarre Coen foray into LA, exploring the lower-class underbelly of the city – Jeff Bridges' "The Dude" and his pal John Goodman uncover mysteries, meet peculiar characters, and do lots of bowling.

Bob & Carol & Ted & Alice (Paul Mazursky 1969). This once-daring, now dated, but still funny zeitgeist satire about wife-swapping and bed-hopping in late Sixties Southern California, starring Natalie Wood, Robert Culp, Elliott Gould, and Dyan Cannon as the titular foursome.

Boogie Nights (Paul Thomas Anderson 1997). Eddie Adams from Torrance meets stroke-movie auteur Jack Horner in a San Fernando Valley nightclub and is reborn as porn star "Dirk Diggler" in this delirious ode to Seventies excess and Eighties redemption in sexy, swingin' Southern California.

California Suite (Herbert Ross 1978). "It's like paradise, with a lobotomy," snarls Jane Fonda's hard-bitten East Coast journalist when faced with ex-husband Alan Alda's new Californian lifestyle in the best of these four Neil Simon stories about out-of-towners at the Beverly Hills Hotel.

House on Haunted Hill (William Castle 1958). Not the clumsy remake, but the glorious Vincent Price original, with the King of Horror as a master of ceremonies for a ghoulish party thrown at his Hollywood Hills estate – actually, Frank Lloyd Wright's Ennis-Brown house (see p.114).

LA Story (Mick Jackson 1991). Steve Martin's sentimental, only-in-LA love story is laced with in-jokes about automobile dependence, health-obsession, and double-decaf lattes, and filmed by British director Jackson with an outsider's tolerant delight.

Modern Romance (Albert Brooks 1981). Brooks – the Woody Allen of the West Coast – stars in this hysterical comedy about a neurotic film editor who dumps his girlfriend and instantly regrets it. Full of early Eighties LA signifiers from quaaludes to jogging suits to off-Hollywood parties with B-movie stars.

Point Break (Kathryn Bigelow 1991). If any film captures the sun-drenched, free-spirited élan of California, it's this slightly preposterous but thrillingly kinetic crime story starring Patrick Swayze as a bank-robbing, sky-diving New Age surfer dude and Keanu Reeves as his straight-arrow FBI nemesis significantly named Johnny Utah.

Rebel Without a Cause (Nicholas Ray 1955). The seminal LA youth movie in which James Dean, at his most perfectly iconographic as the new kid in town, kicks over the traces at Hollywood High School and falls in with disaffected rich kid Sal Mineo and mixed-up school sweetheart Natalie Wood.

Repo Man (Alex Cox 1984). Emilio Estevez is a surly young punk who repossesses cars for Harry Dean Stanton. Very imaginative and fun, and darkly comic.

Safe (Todd Haynes 1995). In Haynes' brilliant tale of millennial unease and corporeal paranoia, Julianne Moore plays a San Fernando Valley homemaker with seemingly little inner-life and an opulent outer one, who is diagnosed with environmental sickness and finds refuge at a New Age desert retreat.

Sex: the Annabel Chong Story (Gough Lewis 1999) An unblinking documentary that reveals some of the seediest aspects of LA's porn business, starring Annabel Chong, porn star and avowed feminist who set out to break the world "gang bang" record by having sex with 251 men in front of a camera, all in the space of ten hours. A complex and riveting portrait, though not for the easily offended or disgusted.

Shampoo (Hal Ashby 1975). Great cast in a spot-on adult comedy, which sees LA as a big bed on the eve of the 1968 presidential election. Co-writer Warren Beatty has one of his best roles as an inarticulate, confused, priapic Beverly Hills hairdresser.

Slums of Beverly Hills (Tamara Jenkins 1998). Traveling back to the 1970s, troubled teen Natasha Lyonne deals with growing pains in a less glamorous section of town, far from Rodeo Drive, where a pill-popping cousin, manic uncle, weird neighbors, and her own expanding bustline are but a few of her worries.

Valley Girl (Martha Coolidge 1983). Southern Californian cultures clash in this sweet romance between the eponymous Valley Girl Deborah Foreman and "Hollyweird" punk Nicholas Cage. The *Clueless* of its day.

Off the beaten track

Bagdad Café (Percy Adlon 1988). Lovable, inspiring fable about a German tourist (the incomparable Marianne Sägebrecht), who arrives at a dusty roadside diner in the Mojave Desert and magically transforms the place with her larger-than-life charm.

The Birds (Alfred Hitchcock 1963). Set in Bodega Bay, just north of San Francisco, Hitchcock's terrifying allegory about a small town besieged by a plague of vicious birds, features indelible bird's-eye views of the Northern California coastline.

California (John Farrow 1946). Ray Milland leads a wagon train to the Land of Milk and Honey only to find the land ruled by greed and graft, in this elaborate paean to the pioneer spirit and the founding of the state. Worth seeing for its ecstatic opening montage of Californian vistas and aphorisms about the approaching Promised Land.

Citizen Kane (Orson Welles 1941). In this pinnacle of American film-making, director Welles successfully copies the baroque splendor and frightful vulgarity of William Randolph Hearst's legendary prison-like palace on the Central Coast, San Simeon (see p.463). Here, it's called "Xanadu."

Faster, Pussycat! Kill! Kill! (Russ Meyer 1965). Meyer's wonderfully lurid camp action flick unleashes a trio of depraved go-go girls upon an unsuspecting California desert. One of a kind.

Fat City (John Huston 1972). Stacy Keach and Jeff Bridges star in Huston's poignant, evocative, beautifully paced portrait of barflies, has-beens and no-hopers on the small-time boxing circuit in Stockton, Northern California.

High Plains Drifter (Clint Eastwood 1972). Spooky Mono Lake is one of the bleak, disturbing settings for this tale of a mysterious gunslinger who comes back to a dusty burg to avenge a wrongful death – before drenching the town in blood and renaming it "Hell."

One-Eyed Jacks (Marlon Brando 1961). Set, unusually for a Western, on the roaring shores of Monterey, where Brando tracks down Karl Malden – the bank-robbing partner who betrayed him five years earlier in Mexico – only to find him reformed and comfortably ensconced as sheriff.

Play Misty for Me (Clint Eastwood 1971). Another Monterey movie, Eastwood's directorial debut, a thriller about the consequences of a DJ's affair with a psychotic fan, was shot in Clint's home town of Carmel, and on his own two hundred acres of Monterey coastland.

Shadow of a Doubt (Alfred Hitchcock 1943). Urbane Uncle Charlie (Joseph Cotten) comes to stay with his sister's Santa Rosa family and seems to be the answer to his bored niece's prayers, until she starts to suspect that he might be a serial killer. Hitchcock's brilliantly funny and enthralling film is a perfect depiction of life in small-town Northern California.

Some Like It Hot (Billy Wilder 1959). The film some claim as the best comedy ever, set around a luxurious Florida resort that's actually San Diego's own *Hotel del Coronado* (see p.223), itself dripping with swank beachfront elegance.

Three Women (Robert Altman 1977). A fascinating, hypnotic, and utterly unique film in which Sissy Spacek and Shelley Duvall, co-workers at a geriatric center in Desert Springs, mysteriously absorb each other's identity. A film brilliantly imbued with the woozy spirit of Southern California.

Zabriskie Point (Michelangelo Antonioni 1970). Though it opens with student sit-ins at UCLA, Antonioni's gorgeous, too often derided, homage to Flower Power disaffection is most famous for its Death Valley love-in and the stunningly voluptuous explosion in the desert, that blows the lid off Southern Californian consumerism.

California in fiction

W hile California may be mythologized as the ultimate stimulant for the imagination, it has inspired comparatively few travel writers, an exception being Robert Louis Stevenson, whose lively description of the Napa Valley and Mount St Helena is printed below. In contrast, floods of fiction have poured out of the state, in particular Los Angeles, over the last few decades, not only shaping perceptions of the region, but often redefining the whole course of modern American writing.

The contemporary writers featured here – Amy Tan and T. Coraghessan Boyle – are both concerned with newcomers to the state: Amy Tan with the interaction of an older generation who grew up in China with their sophisticated San Francisco daughters, and T.C. Boyle with the explosion of the Mexican population in LA, and its uneasy impact on the white elite.

Robert Louis Stevenson

Robert Louis Stevenson was born in Edinburgh in 1850, and was educated at the academy and university there. He became an ardent traveler, writing *An Inland Voyage* and *Travels with a Donkey* about his journeys through France, where he fell in love with a married American woman, Fanny Osbourne. She obtained her divorce in 1879 and Stevenson, battling with ill health, sailed to America to marry her. They took their honeymoon in the mountains of San Francisco. The result of this happy period in Stevenson's life is *Silverado Squatters*, a charming, if occasionally slight, volume about the landscape and characters of the mountains, already inflected with Stevenson's vigorous descriptive powers – and love of a good yarn. In this extract, Stevenson sets the scene of his book, and interestingly prefigures how development will change the area.

The Silverado Squatters

The scene of this little book is on a high mountain. There are, indeed, many higher; there are many of a nobler outline. It is no place of pilgrimage for the summary globe-trotter; but to one who lives upon its sides, Mount Saint Helena soon becomes a centre of interest. It is the Mont Blanc of one section of the Californian Coast Range, none of its near neighbours rising to one-half its altitude. It looks down on much green, intricate country. It feeds in the spring-time many splashing brooks. From its summit you must have an excellent lesson of geography: seeing, to the south, San Francisco Bay, with Tamalpais on the one hand and Monte Diablo on the other; to the west and thirty miles away, the open ocean; eastward, across the cornlands and thick tule swamps of Sacramento Valley, to where the Central Pacific railroad begins to climb the sides of the Sierras; and northward, for what I know, the white head of Shasta looking down on Oregon. Three counties, Napa County, Lake County, and Sonoma County, march across its cliffy shoulders. Its naked peak stands nearly four thousand five hundred feet above the sea; its sides are fringed with forest; and the soil, where it is bare, glows warm with cinnabar.

Life in its shadow goes rustically forward. Bucks, and bears, and rattlesnakes, and former mining operations, are the staple of men's talk. Agriculture has only begun to mount above the valley. And though in a few years from now the whole district may be smiling with farms, passing trains shaking the mountain to the heart, many-windowed hotels lighting up the night like factories, and a prosperous city occupying the site of sleepy Calistoga; yet in the meantime, around the foot of that mountain the silence of nature reigns in a great measure unbroken, and the people of hill and valley go sauntering about their business as in the days before the flood.

To reach Mount Saint Helena from San Francisco the traveller has twice to cross the bay: once by the busy Oakland Ferry, and again, after an hour or so of the railway, from Vallejo junction to Vallejo. Thence he takes rail once more to mount the long green strath of Napa Valley.

In all the contractions and expansions of that inland sea, the Bay of San Francisco, there can be few drearier scenes than the Vallejo Ferry. Bald shores and a low, bald islet enclose the sea; through the narrows the tide bubbles, muddy like a river. When we made the passage (bound, although yet we knew it not, for Silverado) the steamer jumped, and the black buoys were dancing in the jabble; the ocean breeze blew killing chill; and, although the upper sky was still unflecked with vapour, the sea fogs were pouring in from seaward, over the hilltops of Marin County, in one great, shapeless, silver cloud.

South Vallejo is typical of many Californian towns. It was a blunder; the site had proved untenable; and, although it is still such a young place by the scale of Europe, it has already begun to be deserted for its neighbour and namesake, North Vallejo. A long pier, a number of drinking saloons, a hotel of a great size, marshy pools where the frogs keep up their croaking, and even at high noon the entire absence of any human face or voice – these are the marks of South Vallejo. Yet there was a tall building beside the pier, labelled the *Star Flour Mills*; and seagoing, full-rigged ships lay close along shore, waiting for their cargo. Soon these would be plunging round the Horn, soon the flour from the *Star Flour Mills* would be landed on the wharves of Liverpool. For that, too, is one of England's outposts; thither, to this gaunt mill, across the Atlantic and Pacific deeps and round about the icy Horn, this crowd of great, three-masted, deepsea ships come, bringing nothing, and return with bread.

The Frisby House, for that was the name of the hotel, was a place of fallen fortunes, like the town. It was now given up to labourers, and partly ruinous. At dinner there was the ordinary display of what is called in the west a *two-bit house*: the tablecloth checked red and white, the plague of flies, the wire hencoops over the dishes, the great variety and invariable vileness of the food and the rough coatless men devouring it in silence. In our bedroom, the stove would not burn, though it would smoke; and while one window would not open, the other would not shut. There was a view on a bit of empty road, a few dark houses, a donkey wandering with its shadow on a slope, and a blink of sea, with a tall ship lying anchored in the moonlight. All about that dreary inn frogs sang their ungainly chorus.

Early the next morning we mounted the hill along a wooden footway, bridging one marish spot after another. Here and there, as we ascended, we passed a house embowered in white roses. More of the bay became apparent, and soon the blue peak of Tamalpais rose above the green level of the island opposite. It told us we were still but a little way from the city of the Golden Gates, already, at that hour, beginning to awake among the sand-hills. It called to us over the waters as with the voice of a bird. Its stately head, blue as a sapphire on the paler azure of the sky, spoke to us of wider outlooks and the bright Pacific. For Tamalpais stands sentry, like a lighthouse, over the Golden Gates, between the bay and the open ocean, and looks down indifferently on both. Even as we saw and hailed it from Vallejo, seamen, far out at sea, were scanning it with shaded eyes; and, as if to answer to the thought, one of the great ships below began silently to clothe herself with white sails, homeward bound for England.

For some way beyond Vallejo the railway led us through bald green pastures. On the west the rough highlands of Marin shut off the ocean; in the midst, in long, straggling, gleaming arms, the bay died out among the grass; there were few trees and few enclosures; the sun shone wide over open uplands, the displumed hills stood clear against the sky. But by-and-by these hills began to draw nearer on either hand, and first thicket and then wood began to clothe their sides; and soon we were away from all signs of the sea's neighbourhood, mounting an inland, irrigated valley. A great variety of oaks stood, now severally, now in a becoming grove, among the fields and vineyards. The towns were compact, in about equal proportions, of bright, new wooden houses and great and growing forest trees; and the chapel bell on the engine sounded most festally that sunny Sunday, as we drew up at one green town after another, with the townsfolk trooping in their Sunday's best to see the strangers, with the sun sparkling on the clean houses, and great domes of foliage humming overhead in the breeze.

This pleasant Napa valley is, at its north end, blockaded by our mountain. There, at Calistoga, the railroad ceases, and the traveller who intends faring farther, to the Geysers or to the springs in Lake County, must cross the spurs of the mountain by stage. Thus, Mount Saint Helena is not only a summit, but frontier; and, up to the time of writing, it has stayed the progress of the iron horse.

Amy Tan

Amy Tan was born in Oakland in 1952, and first visited China in 1987. Her father, who was educated in Beijing and worked for the United States Information Service after the war, came to America in 1947. Her mother came to the United States in 1949, shortly before the Communists seized control of Shanghai. Amy Tan now lives in San Francisco and New York. Her first work of fiction, *The Joy Luck Club*, explores the nuances of Chinese-American identity through the relationships between four Chinese mothers and their American daughters, each of whom narrate their own stories, rich in detail and atmosphere. Each character's story carries inflections of their cultural identity, which is both a barrier to understanding between the two generations, and a source of shared strength. Here junior chess champion Waverly Jong takes a plunge into San Francisco's Chinatown.

The Joy Luck Club

My mother imparted her daily truths so she could help my older brothers and me rise above our circumstances. We lived in San Francisco's Chinatown. Like most of the other Chinese children who played in the back alleys of restaurants and curio shops, I didn't think we were poor. My bowl was always full, three five-course meals every day, beginning with a soup full of mysterious things I didn't want to know the names of.

We lived on Waverly Place, in a warm, clean, two-bedroom flat that sat above a small Chinese bakery specializing in steamed pastries and dim sum. In the early morning, when the alley was still quiet, I could smell fragrant red beans as they were cooked down to a pasty sweetness. By daybreak, our flat was heavy with the odor of fried sesame balls and sweet curried chicken crescents. From my bed, I would listen as my father got ready for work, then locked the door behind him, one-two-three clicks.

At the end of our two-block alley was a small sandlot playground with swings and slides well-shined down the middle with use. The play area was bordered by wood-slat benches where old-country people sat cracking roasted watermelon seeds with their golden teeth and scattering the husks to an impatient gathering of gurgling pigeons. The best playground, however, was the dark alley itself. It was crammed with daily mysteries and adventures. My brothers and I would peer into the medicinal herb shop, watching old Li dole out onto a stiff sheet of white paper the right amount of insect shells, saffron-colored seeds, and pungent leaves for his ailing customers. It was said that he once cured a woman dying of an ancestral curse that had eluded the best of American doctors. Next to the pharmacy was a printer who specialized in gold-embossed wedding invitations and festive red banners.

Farther down the street was Ping Yuen Fish Market. The front window displayed a tank crowded with doomed fish and turtles struggling to gain footing on the slimy green-tiled sides. A hand-written sign informed tourists, "Within this store, is all for food, not for pet." Inside, the butchers with their blood-stained white smocks deftly gutted the fish while customers cried out their orders and shouted, "Give me your freshest," to which the butchers always protested, "All are freshest." On less crowded market days, we would inspect the crates of live frogs and crabs which we were warned not to poke, boxes of dried cuttlefish, and row upon row of iced prawns, squid, and slippery fish. The sanddabs made me shiver each time; their eyes lay on one flattened side and reminded me of my mother's story of a careless girl who ran into a crowded street and was crushed by a cab. "Was smash flat," reported my mother.

At the corner of the alley was Hong Sing's, a four-table café with a recessed stairwell in front that led to a door marked "Tradesmen." My brothers and I believed the bad people emerged from this door at night. Tourists never went to Hong Sing's, since the menu was printed only in Chinese. A Caucasian man with a big camera once posed me and my playmates in front of the restaurant. He had us move to the side of the picture window so the photo would capture the roasted duck with its head dangling from a juice-covered rope. After he took the picture, I told him he should go into Hong Sing's and eat dinner. When he smiled and asked me what they served, I shouted, "Guts and duck's feet and octopus gizzards!" Then I ran off with my friends, shrieking with laughter as we scampered across the alley and hid in the entryway grotto of the China Gem Company, my heart pounding with hope that he would chase us.

My mother named me after the street that we lived on: Waverly Place Jong, my official name for important American documents. But my family called me Meimei, "Little Sister." I was the youngest, the only daughter. Each morning before school, my mother would twist and yank on my thick black hair until she had formed two tightly wound pigtails. One day, as she struggled to weave a hard-toothed comb through my disobedient hair, I had a sly thought.

I asked her, "Ma, what is Chinese torture?" My mother shook her head. A bobby pin was wedged between her lips. She wetted her palm and smoothed the hair above my ear, then pushed the pin in so that it nicked sharply against my scalp.

"Who say this word?" she asked without a trace of knowing how wicked I was being. I shrugged my shoulders and said, "Some boy in my class said Chinese people do Chinese torture."

"Chinese people do many things," she said simply. "Chinese people do business, do medicine, do painting. Not lazy like American people. We do torture. Best torture."

T. Coraghessan Boyle

PEN/Faulkner Award winner **T. Coraghessan Boyle** was born in Manhattan, but now lives in California; his sixth novel, *The Tortilla Curtain*, is pure LA. Its protagonist, prosperous and peaceable Delaney, lives on the leafy fringes of the city and spins out his nature column "Pilgrim at Topanga Creek," while his dynamic wife Kyra shifts real estate. Meanwhile another pilgrim has come to the creek: Cándido, an illegal Mexican immigrant, who is trying to protect his young pregnant wife América from the natural and unnatural forces around them. The initial violent encounter between the two men precipitates events that both tear at the veneer of Delaney's liberalism, satirized with easy precision by Boyle, and expose the vulnerability of LA's legions of have-nots. In this extract, Delaney's incipient fear of invasion is realized, in an unexpected and dramatic form.

The Tortilla Curtain

High up in the canyon, nestled in a fan-shaped depression dug out of the side of the western ridge by the action of some long-forgotten stream, lay the subdivision known as Arroyo Blanco Estates. It was a private community, comprising a golf course, ten tennis courts, a community center and some two hundred and fifty homes, each set on one-point-five acres and strictly conforming to the covenants, conditions and restrictions set forth in the 1973 articles of incorporation. The houses were all of the Spanish Mission style, painted in one of three prescribed shades of white, with orange tile roofs. If you wanted to paint your house sky-blue or Provençal-pink with lime-green shutters, you were perfectly welcome to move into the San Fernando Valley or to Santa Monica or anywhere else you chose, but if you bought into Arroyo Blanco Estates, your house would be white and your roof orange.

Delaney Mossbacher made his home in one of these Spanish Mission houses (floor plan #A227C, Rancho White with Navajo trim), along with his second wife, Kyra, her son, Jordan, her matching Dandie Dinmont terriers, Osbert and Sacheverell, and her Siamese cat, Dame Edith. On this particular morning, the morning that Cándido Rincón began to feel he'd lost control of his wife, Delaney was up at seven, as usual, to drip Kyra's coffee, feed Jordan his fruit, granola and hi-fiber bar and let Osbert and Sacheverell out into the yard to perform their matinal functions. He hadn't forgotten his unfortunate encounter with Cándido four days earlier – the thought of it still made his stomach clench – but the needs and wants and minor irritations of daily life had begun to push it into the background. At the moment, his attention was focused entirely on getting through the morning ritual with his customary speed and efficiency. He was nothing if not efficient.

He made a sort of game of it, counting the steps it took him to shut the windows against the coming day's heat, empty yesterday's coffee grounds into the mulch bucket, transform two kiwis, an orange, apple, banana and a handful of Bing cherries into Jordan's medley of fresh fruit, and set the table for two. He skated across the tile floor to the dishwasher, flung open the cabinets, rocketed the plates and cutlery into position on the big oak table, all the while keeping an eye on the coffee, measuring out two bowls of dog food and juicing the oranges he'd plucked from the tree in the courtyard.

Typically, he stole a moment out in the courtyard to breathe in the cool of the morning and listen to the scrub jays wake up the neighborhood, but today he was in a rush and the only sound that penetrated his consciousness was a strange excited yelp from one of the dogs – they must have found something in the fenced-in yard behind the house, a squirrel or a gopher maybe – and then he was back in the kitchen, squeezing oranges. That was what he did, every morning, regular as clockwork: squeeze oranges. After which he would dash round the house gathering up Jordan's homework, his backpack, lunch-box and baseball cap, while Kyra sipped her coffee and washed down her twelve separate vitamin and mineral supplements with half a glass of fresh-squeezed orange juice. Then it was time to drive Jordan to school, while Kyra applied her makeup, wriggled into a form-fitting skirt with matching jacket and propelled her Lexus over the crest of the canyon and into Woodland Hills, where she was the undisputed volume leader at Mike Bender Realty, Inc. And then, finally, Delaney would head back home, have a cup of herbal tea and two slices of wheat toast, dry, and let the day settle in around him.

Unless there was an accident on the freeway or a road crew out picking up or setting down their ubiquitous plastic cones, he would be back at home and sitting at his desk by nine. This was the moment he lived for, the moment his day really began. Unfailingly, no matter what pressures were brought to bear on him or what emergencies arose, he allotted the next four hours to his writing – four hours during which he could let go of the world around him, his fingers grazing lightly over the keyboard, the green glow of the monitor bathing him in its hypnotic light. He took the phone off the hook, pulled the shades and crept into the womb of language.

There, in the silence of the empty house, Delaney worked out the parameters of his monthly column for *Wide Open Spaces*, a naturalist's observations of the life blooming around him day by day, season by season. He called it "Pilgrim at Topanga Creek" in homage to Annie Dillard, and while he couldn't pretend to her mystical connection to things, or her verbal virtuosity either, he did feel that he stood apart from his fellow men and women, that he saw more deeply and felt more passionately – particularly about nature. And every day, from nine to one, he had the opportunity to prove it.

Of course, some days went better than others. He tried to confine himself to the flora and fauna of Topanga Canyon and the surrounding mountains, but increasingly he found himself brooding over the fate of the pupfish, the Florida manatee and the spotted owl, the ocelot, the pine marten, the panda. And how could he ignore the larger trends – overpopulation, desertification, the depletion of the seas and the forests, global warming and loss of habitat? We were all right in America, sure, but it was crazy to think you could detach yourself from the rest of the world, the world of starvation and loss and the steady relentless degradation of the environment. Five and a half billion people chewing up the resources of the planet like locusts, and only seventy-three California condors left in all the universe.

It gave him pause. It depressed him. There were days when he worked himself into such a state he could barely lift his fingers to the keys, but fortunately the good days outnumbered them, the days when he celebrated his afternoon hikes through the chaparral and into the ravines of the mist-hung mountains, and that was what people wanted – celebration, not lectures, not the strident call to ecologic arms, not the death knell and the weeping and gnashing of environmental teeth. The world was full of bad news. Why contribute more?

The sun had already begun to burn off the haze by the time Jordan scuffed into the kitchen, the cat at his heels. Jordan was six years old, dedicated to Nintendo, superheroes and baseball cards, though as far as Delaney could see he had no interest whatever in the game of baseball beyond possessing the glossy cardboard images of the players. He favored his mother facially and in the amazing lightness of his hair, which was so pale as to be nearly translucent. He might have been big for his age, or maybe he was small – Delaney had nothing to compare him to.

"Kiwi," Jordan said, thumping into his seat at the table, and that was all. Whether this was an expression of approval or distaste, Delaney couldn't tell. From the living room came the electronic voice of the morning news: *Thirty-seven Chinese nationals were drowned early today when a smuggler's ship went aground just east of the Golden Gate Bridge . . .* Outside, beyond the windows, there was another yelp from the dogs.

Jordan began to rotate his spoon in the bowl of fruit, a scrape and clatter accompanied by the moist sounds of mastication. Delaney, his back to the table, was scrubbing the counter in the vicinity of the stove, though any splashes of cooking oil or spatters of sauce must have been purely imaginary since he hadn't actually cooked anything. He scrubbed for the love of scrubbing. "Okay, buckaroo," he called over his shoulder, "you've got two choices today as far as your hi-fiber bar is concerned: Cranberry Nut and Boysenberry Supreme. What'll it be?"

From a mouth laden with kiwi: "Papaya Coconut."

"You got the last one yesterday."

No response.

"So what'll it be?"

Kyra insisted on the full nutritional slate for her son every morning – fresh fruit, granola with skim milk and brewer's yeast, hi-fiber bar. The child needed roughage. Vitamins. Whole grains. And breakfast, for a growing child at least, was the most important meal of the day, the foundation of all that was to come. That was how she felt. And while Delaney recognized a touch of the autocratic and perhaps even fanatic in the regimen, he by and large subscribed to it. He and Kyra had a lot in common, not only temperamentally, but in terms of their beliefs and ideals too – that was what had attracted them to each other in the first place. They were both perfectionists, for one thing. They abhorred clutter. They were joggers, nonsmokers, social drinkers, and if not full-blown vegetarians, people who were conscious of their intake of animal fats. Their memberships included the Sierra Club, Save the Children, the National Wildlife Federation and the Democratic Party. They preferred the contemporary look to Early American or kitsch. In religious matters, they were agnostic.

Delaney's question remained unanswered, but he was used to cajoling Jordan over his breakfast. He tiptoed across the room to hover behind the boy, who was playing with his spoon and chanting something under his breath. "Rookie card, rookie card," Jordan was saying, dipping into his granola without enthusiasm. "No looking now," Delaney warned, seductively tapping a foil-wrapped bar on either side of the boy's thin wilted neck, "right hand or left?"

Jordan reached up with his left hand, as Delaney knew he would, fastening on the Boysenberry Supreme bar just as Kyra, hunched over the weight of two boxes of hand-addressed envelopes – Excelsior, 500 Count – clattered into the kitchen in her heels. She made separate kissing motions in the direction of her husband and son, then slid into her chair, poured herself half a cup of coffee lightened with skim milk – for the calcium – and began sifting purposively through the envelopes.

"Why can't I have Sugar Pops or Honey Nut Cheerios like other kids? Or bacon and eggs?" Jordan pinched his voice. "Mom? Why can't I?"

Kyra gave the stock response – "You're not other kids, that's why" – and Delaney was taken back to his own childhood, a rainy night in the middle of an interminable winter, a plate of liver, onions and boiled potatoes before him.

"I hate granola," Jordan countered, and it was like a Noh play, timeless ritual.

"It's good for you."

"Yeah, sure." Jordan made an exaggerated slurping sound, sucking the milk through his teeth.

"Think of all the little children who have nothing to eat," Kyra said without looking up, and Jordan, sticking to the script, came right back at her: "Let's send them this."

Now she looked up. "Eat," she said, and the drama was over.

"Busy day?" Delaney murmured, setting Kyra's orange juice down beside the newspaper and unscrewing the childproof caps of the sturdy plastic containers that held her twelve separate vitamin and mineral supplements. He did the little things for her – out of love and consideration, sure, but also in acknowledgment of the fact that she was the chief breadwinner here, the one who went off to the office while he stayed home. Which was all right by him. He had none of those juvenile macho hang-ups about role reversal and who wore the pants and all of that – real estate was her life, and he was more than happy to help her with it, so long as he got his four hours a day at the keyboard.

Kyra lifted her eyebrows, but didn't look up. She was tucking what looked to be a small white packet into each of the envelopes in succession. "Busy?" she echoed. "Busy isn't the word for it. I'm presenting two offers this morning, both of them real low-ball, I've got a buyer with cold feet on that Calabasas property – with escrow due to close in eight days – and I'm scheduled for an open house on the Via Escobar place at one . . . is that the dogs I hear? What are they barking at?"

Delaney shrugged. Jordan had shucked the foil from his hi-fiber bar and was drifting toward the TV room with it – which meant he was going to be late for school if Delaney didn't hustle him out of there within the next two minutes. The cat, as yet unfed, rubbed up against Delaney's leg. "I don't know," he said. "They've been yapping since I let them out. Must be a squirrel or something. Or maybe Jack's dog got loose again and he's out there peeing on the fence and driving them into a frenzy."

"Anyway," Kyra went on, "it's going to be hell. And it's Carla Bayer's birthday, so after work a bunch of us – don't you think this is a cute idea?" She held up one of the packets she'd been stuffing the envelopes with. It was a three-by-five seed packet showing a spray of flowers and printed with the legend *Forget-Me-Not, Compliments of Kyra Menaker-Mossbacher, Mike Bender Realty, Inc.*

"Yeah, I guess," he murmured, wiping at an imaginary speck on the counter. This was her way of touching base with her clients. Every month or so, usually in connection with a holiday, she went through her mailing list (consisting of anyone she'd ever sold to or for, whether they'd relocated to Nome, Singapore or Irkutsk or passed on into the Great Chain of Being) and sent a small reminder of her continued existence and willingness to deal. She called it "keeping the avenues open." Delaney reached down to stroke the cat. "But can't one of the secretaries do this sort of thing for you?"

"It's the personal touch that counts – and moves property. How many times do I have to tell you?"

There was a silence, during which Delaney became aware of the cartoon jingle that had replaced the voice of the news in the other room, and then, just as he was clearing Jordan's things from the table and checking the digital display on the microwave for the time – 7:32 – the morning fell apart. Or no: it was torn apart by a startled breathless shriek that rose up from beyond the windows as if out of some primal dream. This was no yip, no yelp, no bark or howl – this was something final and irrevocable, a predatory scream that took the varnish off their souls, and it froze them in place. They listened, horrified, as it rose in pitch until it choked off as suddenly as it had begun.

The aftereffect was electric. Kyra bolted up out of her chair, knocking over her coffee cup and scattering envelopes; the cat darted between Delaney's legs and vanished; Delaney dropped the plate on the floor and groped for the counter like a blind man. And then Jordan was coming through the doorway on staccato feet, his face opened up like a pale nocturnal flower: "Delaney," he gasped, "Delaney, something, something—"

But Delaney was already in motion. He flung open the door and shot through the courtyard, head down, rounding the corner of the house just in time to see a dun-colored blur scaling the six-foot chainlink fence with a tense white form clamped in its jaws. His brain decoded the image: a coyote had somehow managed to get into the enclosure and seize one of the dogs, and there it was, wild nature, up and over the fence as if this were some sort of circus act. Shouting to hear himself, shouting nonsense, Delaney charged across the yard as the remaining dog (Osbert? Sacheverell?) cowered in the corner and the dun blur melded with the buckwheat, chamise and stiff high grass of the wild hillside that gave onto the wild mountains beyond.

He didn't stop to think. In two bounds he was atop the fence and dropping to the other side, absently noting the paw prints in the dust, and then he was tearing headlong through the undergrowth, leaping rocks and shrubs and dodging the spines of the yucca plants clustered like breastworks across the slope. He was running, that was all he knew. Branches raked him like claws. Burrs bit into his ankles. He kept going, pursuing a streak of motion, the odd flash of white: now he saw it, now he didn't. "Hey!" he shouted. "Hey, goddamnit!"

The hillside sloped sharply upward, rising through the colorless scrub to a clump of walnut trees and jagged basalt outcroppings that looked as if they'd poked through the ground overnight. He saw the thing suddenly, the pointed snout and yellow eyes, the high stiff leggy gait as it struggled with its burden, and it was going straight up and into the trees. He shouted again and this time the shout was answered from below. Glancing over his shoulder, he saw Kyra was coming up the hill with her long jogger's strides, in blouse, skirt and stocking feet. Even at this distance he could recognize the look on her face – the grim set of her jaw, the flaring eyes and clamped mouth that spelled doom for whoever got in her way, whether it was a stranger who'd locked his dog in a car with the windows rolled up or the hapless seller who refused a cash-out bid. She was coming, and that spurred him on. If he could only stay close the coyote would have to drop the dog, it would have to.

By the time he reached the trees his throat was burning. Sweat stung his eyes and his arms were striped with nicks and scratches. There was no sign of the dog and he pushed on through the trees to where the slope fell away to the feet of the next hill beyond it. The brush was thicker here – six feet high and so tightly interlaced it would have taken a machete to get through it in places – and he knew, despite the drumming in his ears and the glandular rush that had him pacing and whirling and clenching and unclenching his fists, that it was looking bad. Real bad. There were a thousand bushes out there – five thousand, ten thousand – and the coyote could be crouched under any one of them.

It was watching him even now, he knew it, watching him out of slit wary eyes as he jerked back and forth, frantically scanning the mute clutter of leaf, branch and thorn, and the thought infuriated him. He shouted again, hoping to flush it out. But the coyote was too smart for him. Ears pinned back, jaws and forepaws stifling its prey, it could lie there, absolutely motionless, for hours. "Osbert!" he called out suddenly, and his voice trailed off into a hopeless bleat. "Sacheverell!"

The poor dog. It couldn't have defended itself from a rabbit. Delaney stood on his toes, strained his neck, poked angrily through the nearest bush. Long low shafts of sunlight fired the leaves in an indifferent display, as they did every morning, and he looked into the illuminated depths of that bush and felt desolate suddenly, empty, cored out with loss and helplessness.

"Osbert!" The sound seemed to erupt from him, as if he couldn't control his vocal cords. "Here, boy! Come!" Then he shouted Sacheverell's name, over and over, but there was no answer except for a distant cry from Kyra, who seemed to be way off to his left now.

All at once he wanted to smash something, tear the bushes out of the ground by their roots. This didn't have to happen. It didn't. If it wasn't for those idiots leaving food out for the coyotes as if they were nothing more than sheep with bushy tails and eyeteeth . . . and he'd warned them, time and again. You can't be heedless of your environment. You can't. Just last week he'd found half a bucket of Kentucky Fried Chicken out back of the Dagolian place – waxy red-and-white-striped cardboard with a portrait of the grinning chicken-killer himself smiling large – and he'd stood up at the bimonthly meeting of the property owners' association to say something about it. They wouldn't even listen. Coyotes, gophers, yellow jackets, rattlesnakes even – they were a pain in the ass, sure, but nature was the least of their problems. It was humans they were worried about. The Salvadorans, the Mexicans, the blacks, the gangbangers and taggers and carjackers they read about in the Metro section over their bran toast and coffee. That's why they'd abandoned the flatlands of the Valley and the hills of the Westside to live up here, outside the city limits, in the midst of all this scenic splendor.

Coyotes? Coyotes were quaint. Little demi-dogs out there howling at the sunset, another amenity like the oaks, the chaparral and the views. No, all Delaney's neighbors could talk about, back and forth and on and on as if it were the key to all existence, was gates. A gate, specifically. To be erected at the main entrance and manned by a twenty-four-hour guard to keep out those very gangbangers, taggers and carjackers they'd come here to escape. Sure. And now poor Osbert – or Sacheverell – was nothing more than breakfast.

The fools. The idiots.

Delaney picked up a stick and began to beat methodically at the bushes.

Books

I n the following listing, wherever a book is in print, the publisher's name is given in parentheses after the title, in the format: UK publisher; US publisher. Where books are published in only one of these countries, we have specified which one; when the same company publishes the book in both, it appears just once.

Travel and impressions

Tim Cahill *Jaguars Ripped My Flesh* (Fourth Estate; Vintage). Adventure travel through California and the world, including skin diving with hungry sharks off LA and getting lost and found in Death Valley. Thoughtful and sensitive yet still a thrill a minute.

Umberto Eco *Travels in Hyperreality* (Harcourt Brace, US). A pointed examination of the still-potent concept of "simulacra," in which reality is denigrated in favor of its crass imitation, discussing such things as a now-closed museum in Orange County that re-created the great works of art as wax figurines.

Robert Koenig *Mouse Tales* (Bonaventure Press). All the Disneyland dirt that's fit to print: a behind-the-scenes look at the ugly little secrets – from disenchanted workers to vermin infestations – that lurk behind the happy walls of the Magic Kingdom.

Jan Morris *Destinations* (OUP). Of the essay on LA in this fine collection of essays written for *Rolling Stone* magazine, Joan Didion said, "A lot of people come here and don't get it. She got it."

Mark Twain *Roughing It* (Penguin; University of California Press). Vivid tales of frontier California, particularly evocative of life in the silver mines of the 1860s Comstock Lode, where Twain got his start as a journalist and storyteller.

John Waters *Crackpot* (Fourth Estate; Random House). Odds and ends from the Pope of Trash, the mind behind cult film *Pink Flamingos*, including a personalized tour of LA.

Edmund White *States of Desire* (Picador; Plume). Part of a cross-country sojourn that includes a rather superficial account of the gay scene in 1970s LA.

Tom Wolfe *The Electric Kool-Aid Acid Test* (Black Swan; Bantam). Take a trip with the Grateful Dead and the Hell's Angels on the magic bus of Ken Kesey and the Merry Pranksters as they travel through the early days of the psychedelic 1960s, on a mission to turn California youth on to LSD.

History

Oscar Zeta Acosta *Autobiography of a Brown Buffalo, Revolt of the Cockroach People* (Vintage). The legendary model for Hunter S. Thompson's bloated D. Gonzo, this author was in reality a trailblazing Hispanic lawyer who used all manner of colorful tactics to defend oppressed and indigent defendants. Two vivid portraits of late-1960s California, written just before the author mysteriously vanished in 1971.

Walton Bean *California: An Interpretive History* (McGraw-Hill, US). Blow-by-blow account of the history of California, including all the shady deals and back-room politicking, presented in accessible, anecdotal form.

H.W. Brands *The Age of Gold* (Doubleday). Excellent introduction to Gold Rush-era California, focusing on the immigrants from around the world who came to mine the ore, the unexpected fortunes of a lucky few, and the political and social repercussions of this unprecedented event – the first glimmer of the Gilded Age.

Gary Brechin *Imperial San Francisco* (University of California Press, US). A myth-shattering look at the genesis of the Golden Gate city, complete with close looks at the elite families who shaped San Francisco.

Daniel Boorstin *The Americas 2: The National Experience* (Random House; Cardinal, US o/p). Heavy going because of the glut of detail, but otherwise an energetic appraisal of the social forces that shaped the modern USA, with several chapters on the settlement of the West.

★ **Norman Klein** *A History of Forgetting* (Verso). A good selection to read with Mike Davis's *City of Quartz* (see below), uncovering some of the political ugliness and minority oppression that have characterized LA's past.

Carey McWilliams *Southern California: An Island on the Land* (Peregrine Smith, US). The bible of Southern Californian histories, focusing on the key years between the two world wars. Evocatively written and richly detailed.

Harris Newmark *Sixty Years in Southern California: 1853–1913* (Houghton Mifflin, US). One of the great nineteenth-century leaders of the Jewish community offers an insider's take on the region's politics as well as various secrets of the time.

Mark Reisner *Cadillac Desert* (Penguin). An essential guide to water problems in the American West, with special emphasis on LA's schemes to bring upstate California water to the metropolis. One of the best renderings of this sordid tale.

W.W. Robinson *Ranchos Become Cities* (San Pasqual Press, US). A chronicle of the changes that turned the old Mexican rancho system into subdivided plots of land fit for real estate speculation, urban growth, and massive profit taking.

★ **Kevin Starr** *Inventing the Dream* (OUP). One of a series of captivating books – the other two are *Material Dreams* (OUP) and *Americans and the Californian Dream* (OUP, US o/p) studying the phenomenon known as California. Cultural histories written with a novelist's flair.

Dale L. Walker *Bear Flag Rising: The Conquest of California, 1846* (Forge). An entertaining and painstakingly detailed account of how the US, in the name of Manifest Destiny, acquired California from Mexico.

Political, social, and ethnic

Jean Baudrillard *America* (Verso). Scattered thoughts of the trendy French philosopher, whose (very) occasionally brilliant but often overreaching exegesis of American pop culture, especially in LA, is undermined by factual inaccuracy.

★ **Mike Davis** *Ecology of Fear* (Picador; Vintage). As in his previous book, *City of Quartz: Excavating the Future of Los Angeles*, Davis writes a compelling account of LA's apocalyptic style, focusing on the gloom and doom in movies and literary fiction, the danger of earthquakes and fires, mountain lion attacks, and unrecognized threats like tornadoes.

★ **Joan Didion** *Slouching Towards Bethlehem* (Flamingo; Noonday Press). Selected essays from one of California's best journalists, taking a critical look at Sixties California, from the acid culture of San Francisco to a profile of American hero John Wayne. In a similar style, *The White Album* (Farrar Straus & Giroux, UK) traces the West Coast characters and events that shaped the Sixties and Seventies, including The Doors, Charles Manson, and the Black Panthers.

Frances Fitzgerald *Cities on a Hill* (Picador; Simon & Schuster). Intelligent and sympathetic exploration of four of the odder corners of American culture, including San Francisco's gay Castro district.

Lynell George *No Crystal Stair* (Anchor; Verso). A depressing reminder of the struggles of LA's African-American community, rendered in precise, painful detail.

★ **Maxine Hong Kingston** *China Men* (Picador; Vintage). A compelling history dealing with the various waves of Chinese immigrants to America, but specifically California. Interwoven with fact and myth, *China Men* examines the nature of being an American.

Russel Miller *Barefaced Messiah* (Sphere; Holt; both o/p). An eye-opening study of the rise and rise of L. Ron Hubbard and his Scientology cult, who have their HQ in LA and their devotees lurking everywhere.

Jay Stevens *Storming Heaven: LSD and the American Dream* (Flamingo; Groundwood Books). An engaging account of psychedelic drugs and their relationship with American society through the Sixties, with an epilogue to bring things up to date with "designer drugs" – Venus, Ecstasy, Special K, and others – and the inner space they apparently help some modern Californians chart.

Danny Sugarman *Wonderland Avenue* (Abacus; Bullfinch). Publicist for The Doors and other seminal US rock bands from the late Sixties on, Sugarman delivers a raunchy autobiographical account of sex, drugs, and LA rock'n'roll.

Architecture

Reyner Banham *Los Angeles: The Architecture of Four Ecologies* (Penguin). The most lucid account of how LA's history has shaped its present form; the author's enthusiasms are infectious.

★ **Federal Writers Project** *The WPA Guide to California* (Pantheon, US). Recently republished, this 1939 guide is a remarkable handbook to the architecture and neighborhoods of its time.

Philip Jodidio *Contemporary Californian Architects* (Taschen). This glossy trilingual (English, French, and German) book argues that the public and private buildings of Frank Gehry, Eric Owen Moss, Frank Israel, and Michael Routundi, among others, are strongly influenced by the state itself. The gorgeous photographs strengthen the case.

Sam Hall Kaplan *LA Lost and Found: An Architectural History of Los Angeles* (Random House, US). The text is informative but dull, though the outstanding photos vividly portray the city's growth and the trends in its design.

Esther McCoy *Five California Architects* (Hennessey and Ingalls, US). The still-relevant 1960s book that first drew attention to LA's Irving Gill, an early twentieth-century forerunner of the modern style, along with other important architects who practiced in Southern California.

Richard Meier *Building the Getty* (University of California Press; Knopf). If you're a fan of this hilltop art colossus in West LA, you'll want to pick up this highly readable account of the conception and creation of the Getty Center, as told by its architect, the high prince of modernism.

★ **Charles Moore** *The City Observed: Los Angeles* (Random House, US). The best book to guide you around the diffuse buildings and settings of LA, loaded with maps, illustrations, and historical anecdotes.

Elizabeth A.T. Smith *Blueprints for Modern Living: History and Legacy of the Case Study Houses* (MIT Press, US). An excellent compendium of essays and articles about the built and unbuilt homes of California's renowned Case Study Program, with descriptions, diagrams, and photographs of each.

Hollywood/The Movies

Kenneth Anger *Hollywood Babylon* (Arrow; Bantam). A vicious yet high-spirited romp through Tinseltown's greatest scandals, although the facts are bent rather too often. A rarer second volume covers more recent times, but was hurriedly put together and shoddily researched.

Robert Berger *The Last Remaining Seats* (Balcony Press; Princeton Architectural Press). An excellent photo guide to the extant movie palaces of Los Angeles, particularly along the Broadway corridor, including many shots of theaters that are now closed to the public.

Peter Bogdanovich *Who the Devil Made It* (Random House, US). Acclaimed book of conversations with the great Hollywood filmmakers.

David Bordwell, Janet Staiger and Kirstin Thompson *The Classical Hollywood Cinema* (Columbia UP). Academic handbook aimed at the serious student, but still a generally interesting account of the techniques used in the best-known Hollywood movies up to 1960.

Kevin Brownlow *Hollywood: The Pioneers* (Knopf, US). History of the founding of Hollywood by one of the great historians of the early days of cinema. (Brownlow and David

Gill's 1980 TV documentary *Hollywood* is available on video.)

★ **Otto Friedrich** *City of Nets* (Headline o/p; University of California Press). A rich and colorful social and cultural history of Hollywood during its golden age in the Forties.

Ephraim Katz *The Film Encyclopedia* (Harper). A massive tome that's the essential reference guide for anyone interested in the movies, providing valuable information on the old movie companies and countless studio-system bit players, along with more contemporary figures.

Clayton R. Koppes and Gregory D. Black *Hollywood Goes to War* (I.B. Tauris o/p; University of California Press). Masterly examination of the influence of World War II on the film industry – and vice versa.

Barry Norman *Talking Pictures: The Story of Hollywood* (Arrow; NAL-Dutton o/p). The most accessible mainstream outline of the growth of movies in Hollywood, informative and pleasantly irreverent in tone.

Julia Phillips *You'll Never Eat Lunch in This Town Again* (Mandarin; Signet). From the woman who became a Hollywood somebody by co-producing *The Sting*, a diary of drug abuse, spouse abuse, and film-business bitching.

Specific guides

Bicycle Rider Directory (Cycle America, US). Low-cost guide to do-it-yourself bicycle touring around the Bay Area and Napa and Sonoma valleys, with good fold-out route maps.

Tom Kirkendall and Vicky Spring *Bicycling the Pacific Coast* (Mountaineers Books). Detailed guide to the bike routes all the way along the coast from Mexico up to Canada.

John J. Lamb *San Diego Specters* (Sunbelt Publications). A different kind of travel guide, looking into the ghosts, poltergeists, and other assorted spooks that populate San Diego County. An intriguing counterpart to the usual sun-and-surf books about the city.

National Audobon Society Nature Guides: *Western Forests*; *Deserts*; *Pacific Coast*; *Wetlands*; and others (Random House; Knopf). California has six of the world's seven major ecosystem types, and between them, these immaculately researched and beautifully photographed field guides, though not specific to California, cover the lot.

National Geographic Society *A Field Guide to the Birds of North America* (National Geographic). Self-explanatory – and thoroughly useful.

Peterson Series Field Guides: *A Field Guide to Western Reptiles and Amphibians*; *A Field Guide to the Insects of America North of Mexico*; *A Field Guide to Pacific State Wildflowers* (Houghton Mifflin). Excellent general field guides to the flora and fauna of California and the West Coast.

★ **Ray Riegert** *Hidden Coast of California* (Ulysses Press). A detailed and interesting guide to the nooks and crannies along the California state beaches and parks, told from the perspective of a recreational enthusiast who tracks down all his favorite underrated beachside gems.

Jeffery Schaffer *The Pacific Crest Trail: California* (Wilderness Press). A guide to the southern section of the trail that leads all the way from Mexico to Canada through Sierra Nevada range.

David and Kay Scott *Guide to the National Park Areas: the Western States* (Globe Pequot). How to get around and camp in the West's national parks, including Yosemite and the Kings Canyon.

John R. Soares *100 Classic Hikes in Northern California* (Mountaineers Books). An engaging presentation of wilderness hiking in the northern side of the state, from the Bay Area up to the Oregon border.

Tom Steinstra and Ann Marie Brown *California Hiking: The Complete Guide* (Foghorn Press, US). Dense 700-page tome detailing over 1000 hikes, from hour-long strolls to the 1700 Californian miles of the Pacific Crest Trail. Unfortunately, the trail notes and maps are limited, and the text is hardly inspirational.

★ **Walking the West Series:** *Walking Southern California*; *Walking the California Coast*; *Walking California's State Parks*; and others (HarperReference). Well-written and -produced paperbacks, each covering over a hundred excellent day-walks from two to twenty miles. They're strong on practical details (maps, route descriptions, and so on), and boast-inspiring prose and historical background. Recommended.

For guidebooks of specific relevance to travelers with **disabilities**, see p.60 of Basics.

C

CONTEXTS | Books

California in fiction

James P. Blaylock *Land of Dreams* (Grafton o/p; Ace Books). A fantastic tale spun out as the twelve-year Solstice comes to a Northern Californian coastal town.

★ **T. Coraghessan Boyle** *The Tortilla Curtain* (Bloomsbury; Penguin). Set in LA, this novel boldly borrows its premise – a privileged white man running down a member of the city's ethnic underclass – from Tom Wolfe's *The Bonfire of the Vanities*, and develops its plot with a similar pacey intensity. See p.827 for an extract from the novel.

Ray Bradbury *The Martian Chronicles* (Flamingo; Bantam). Brilliant, lyrical study of colonization, of new worlds and new lands – it's very easy to read the Martian setting as a Californian one. Bradbury's first, and still best, book.

Scott Bradfield *What's Wrong With America* (Picador). Humor and idiosyncratic absurdity combine as Bradfield explores America's malaise through an elderly woman's slide towards mental breakdown. Southern California provides the backdrop and its people the caricatured bit players.

Richard Brautigan Born in Tacoma, Brautigan is more often associated with the California Beat writers of the Fifties and Sixties. His surreal fable-like work seems overtly simple, but is overlaid with cultural references that question the direction the country is traveling in. His most successful book, *Trout Fishing in America* (Vintage; Dell o/p), although designed as a fishing handbook, stealthily creates a disturbing image of contemporary life. Other novels include *A Confederate General from Big Sur* (Houghton Mifflin) and *In Watermelon Sugar* (o/p), and he also wrote a fine book of poems, *The Pill Versus the Springhill Mine Disaster* (Dell, US).

Charles Bukowski *Post Office*; *Women* (Black Sparrow). Three-hundred-hangovers-a-year Henry Chinaski (the author, thinly veiled) drinks and screws his way around downbeat LA, firstly as a misfit mailman, then as a moderately successful writer with his own tab at the local liquor store and an endless supply of willing female fans. Savage and quite unique. See also *Factotum* (Black Sparrow), which recounts Chinaski's early days.

James M. Cain *The Five Great Novels of James M. Cain* (Picador, UK); *Double Indemnity*; *The Postman Always Rings Twice*; *The Butterfly*; *Mildred Pierce*; *Love's Lovely Counterfeit* (all Vintage, US). Haunting stories of smoldering passion told with clipped prose and terse dialogue.

★ **Raymond Carver** *What We Talk About When We Talk About Love* (Harvil; Knopf); *Where I'm Calling From: New and Selected Stories* (Harvill; Vintage). Set mostly in the Northwest and Northern California, Carver's deceptively simple eye-level pictures of plain-dealing Americans, concise and sharply observed, are difficult to forget.

★ **Raymond Chandler** *Three Novels* (Penguin, UK); *The Raymond Chandler Omnibus* (Random House, US). Essential reading, some of the toughest and greatest LA crime fiction of the Thirties and Forties – including *The Big Sleep*, *The Lady in the Lake*, and *Farewell My Lovely*, to name only the best.

Michael Connelly *Angels Flight* (Little Brown; Orion). A sixth volume of contemporary detective fiction featuring the LAPD investigator Harry Bosch, whose appropriate moniker casts him as a keen observer of LA's blood-curdling mix of corruption, public scandals, and violence.

Philip K. Dick *A Scanner Darkly* (Voyager; Random House). Of all Dick's erratic but frequently brilliant books, this is the best evocation of California. Set in the mid-1990s, when society is split between the Straights, the Dopers, and the Narks, it's a dizzying study of individual identity, authority, and drugs. Among the pick of the rest of Dick's vast legacy is *Blade Runner* (*Do Androids Dream of Electric Sheep?*) (Voyager; Ballantine), set (unlike the movie) in San Francisco.

Joan Didion *Run, River* (Vintage, US). Focuses on the Sacramento Valley of the author's childhood and follows its change from agriculture into a highly charged consumer society. In contrast, but just as successfully done, *Play It as It Lays* (Flamingo; Farrar Straus & Giroux) is an electrifying dash through the pills, booze, and self-destruction linked with the LA film world.

★ **James Ellroy** *White Jazz* (Arrow; Fawcett). The final installment of Ellroy's quartet of LA books exploring, in nail-biting noir style, the mind-set of corrupt LA cops and psychotic criminals over three decades. The series began with *The Black Dahlia* and continued with *The Big Nowhere* and *LA Confidential* (all Arrow; Warner).

John Fante *Ask the Dust* (Black Sparrow; Rebel Inc.). The third and still the best of the author's stories of itinerant poet Arturo Bandini, whose wanderings during the Depression highlight California's faded glory and struggling residents.

★ **F. Scott Fitzgerald** *The Last Tycoon* (Penguin; Macmillan). Fitzgerald died before he completed his Hollywood novel, but what remains is executed in glittering prose, with passages of deep poignancy and tenderness, as well as Fitzgerald's trademark conjuring of glamorous decadence. The complex portrait of the brilliant, melancholy film producer Monroe Stahr is peculiarly memorable.

David Freeman *A Hollywood Education* (Michael Joseph o/p; Carroll & Graf). Cumulatively powerful collection of short stories concerning a writer's lot in Hollywood.

James Gardner *Fat City* (University of California Press). A beautifully precise, poignant account of small-time Stockton boxing, following the initiation and fitful progress of a young hopeful and the parallel decline of an old contender. Painfully exact on the confused, murky emotions of its men as their lives stagnate in the heat of the town and the surrounding country. Brilliantly filmed by John Huston, with a script by Gardner himself.

Molly Giles *Iron Shoes* (Scribner). A sobering but fascinating look into the life of a Northern California woman, busy caring for her dying mother while trying to juggle the alternately absurd and dismal characters in her life. Depressing, but rewarding.

Ursula le Guin *Always Coming Home* (Gollancz; Bantam). Impressive "archeology of the future," describing the lifestyles and culture of a mysterious race living in Northern California.

Dashiell Hammett *The Four Great Novels* (Picador; Vintage); *The Maltese Falcon* (Random House, US). The former is a volume of seminal detective novels starring Sam Spade, the private investigator working out of San Francisco; the latter is probably Hammett's best-known work. See also the absorbing biography of Hammett: Diane Johnson's *Dashiell Hammett: A Life* (Picador; Fawcett).

Joseph Hansen *The Dave Brandstetter Omnibus* (No Exit Press, UK o/p); *Death Claims* (Holt; No Exit Press); *Gravedigger* (Holt; No Exit Press); *Skinflick* (Holt; No Exit Press); *Troublemaker* (Holt; No Exit

Press). Entertaining tales of Dave Brandstetter, a gay insurance claims investigator, set against a vivid Southern California backdrop.

Chester Himes *If He Hollers Let Him Go* (Thunder's Mouth Press; Serpent's Tail). A fine literary introduction to mid-century race relations in LA, narrated by the ironically titled character Bob Jones, whose struggles mirrored those of author Himes, who eventually lived in exile in Spain.

Aldous Huxley *Ape and Essence* (Flamingo; I.R. Dee); *After Many a Summer Dies the Swan* (I.R. Dee, US). Huxley spent his last twenty years earning a crust as a Hollywood screenwriter, and both these novels are products of that time. The first chronicles moral degeneracy and Satanic rituals in post-apocalyptic Southern California; the latter, based on William Randolph Hearst, concerns a rich, pampered figure who surrounds himself with art treasures and dwells on the meaning of life.

Christopher Isherwood *Down There on a Visit* (Noonday Press; Minerva). Incisive, involving read by the British expatriate, who penned much of his later fiction in and on Southern California.

Helen Hunt Jackson *Ramona* (New American Library; Fisher Press). Ultra-romanticized depiction of mission life that rightfully criticizes the American government's treatment of Indians while showing the natives to be noble savages and glorifying the Spanish exploiters. Not particularly good reading, but a valuable period piece.

Jack Kerouac *Desolation Angels* (Flamingo; Riverhead); *The Dharma Bums* (Penguin). The most influential of the Beat writers on the rampage in California. See also his first novel *On the Road* (Penguin), which has a little of San Francisco and a lot of the rest of the US.

Elmore Leonard *Get Shorty* (Penguin; Bantam). Ice-cool mobster Chili Palmer is a Miami debt collector who follows a client to Hollywood, and finds that the increasing intricacies of his own situation are translating themselves into a movie script.

David Levien *Wormwood* (Allison & Busby; Hyperion) Get a glimpse of the seamier side of the contemporary movie biz, following an up-and-coming story editor through the corporate ranks until he achieved utter exhaustion, and curiously, an addiction to absinthe.

David Lodge *Changing Places* (Penguin). Thinly disguised auto-biographical tale of an English academic who spends a year teaching at UC Berkeley and finds himself bang in the middle of the late Sixties student upheaval.

Jack London *The Call of the Wild* (Penguin); *White Fang and Other Stories* (Penguin); *Martin Eden* (Penguin); *The Iron Heel* (Wordsworth Editions; Dugan). *The Call of the Wild*, a short story about a tame dog discovering the ways of the wilderness while forced to labor pulling sleds across the snow and ice of Alaska's Klondike, made London into the world's best-selling author almost overnight. Afterwards, frustrated by the emptiness of his easy fame and success, the young, self-taught author wrote the semi-autobiographical *Martin Eden*, in which he rails against the cultured veil of polite society. Besides his prolific fiction, London also wrote a number of somewhat sophomoric political essays and socialist tracts; the most effective was *The Iron Heel*, presaging the rise of Fascism.

Ross MacDonald *Black Money* (Allison & Busby; Vintage); *The Blue Hammer* (Allison & Busby; Vintage); *The Zebra-Striped Hearse* (Allison & Busby o/p; Knopf o/p); *The Doomsters*; *The Instant Enemy* (Allison

& Busby, US). Following in the footsteps of Sam Spade and Philip Marlowe, private detective Lew Archer looks behind the glitzy masks of Southern California life to reveal the underlying nastiness of creepy sexuality and manipulation. All captivating reads.

Armistead Maupin *Tales of the City; Further Tales of the City* (both Black Swan; HarperCollins); *More Tales of the City* (Corgi; HarperCollins). Lively and witty soap operas detailing the sexual antics of a select group of archetypal San Francisco characters of the late Seventies and early Eighties. See also *Babycakes* (Black Swan; HarperCollins) and *Significant Others*, which continue the story, though in more depth, and *Sure of You* (last two Black Swan; HarperCollins) – set several years later and more downbeat, though no less brilliant.

Brian Moore *The Great Victorian Collection* (Flamingo; Acacia Press). A professor dreams up a parking lot full of Victoriana, which becomes the biggest tourist attraction of Carmel, California.

Walter Mosely *Devil in a Blue Dress* (Pan; Pocket Books). The book that introduced Easy Rawlins, a black private detective in late-1940s South Central LA, the central character in an excellent portrayal of time and place. Easy gets further into his stride in the subsequent *A Red Death* and *White Butterfly* (both Pan; Pocket Books).

Kem Nunn *Tapping the Source* (Four Walls Eight Windows Press). One of the most unexpected novels to emerge from California beach culture, an eerie murder-mystery set among the surfing landscape of Orange County's Huntington Beach.

★ **Thomas Pynchon** *The Crying of Lot 49* (Vintage; HarperPerennial). Pynchon's celebrated – and most readable – excursion in modern paranoia follows the hilarious adventures of techno-freaks and potheads in Sixties California, and reveals the sexy side of stamp collecting. Fans will relish his later *Vineland* (Penguin), set in Northern California.

Richard Rayner *Los Angeles without a Map* (Flamingo; Mariner Book). An English non-driving journalist goes to LA on a romantic whim and lives out movie fantasies made even more fantastic by the city itself.

John Ridley *Love Is a Racket* (Knopf; Bantam). A delightful slice of Hollywood hell, in which protagonist Jeffty Kittridge, slumming through the dregs of local society and being abused by countless predators, leads us on a darkly comic journey through LA's many bleak corners.

Theodore Roszak *Flicker* (Bantam, US o/p). In a tatty LA movie house, Jonathan Gates discovers cinema, "like a bewildered neophyte wandering into the dark womb of an unformed faith." His particular obsession is the director Max Castle – a genius of the silent era who disappeared under mysterious circumstances in the Forties – and it leads Gates into a labyrinthine conspiracy with its roots in medieval heresy. Unlikely, disturbing, and immensely readable, *Flicker* deserves to be a Hollywood classic.

Danny Santiago *Famous All over Town* (New American Library, US). Coming-of-age novel set among the street gangs of East LA, vividly depicting life in the Hispanic community.

Vikram Seth *The Golden Gate* (Faber; Vintage). A novel in verse which traces the complex social lives of a group of San Francisco yuppies.

Mona Simpson *Anywhere But Here* (Faber; Vintage). Bizarre and unforgettable saga of a young girl and her ambitious mother as they pursue LA stardom for the daughter.

Upton Sinclair *The Brass Check* (Ayer Press o/p). The failed California gubernatorial candidate and activist author vigorously criticizes LA's yellow journalism and the underhanded practices of its main figures. Sinclair also wrote *Oil!*, about the city's 1920s oil rush, and *The Goose Step*, concerning collegiate life at USC.

★ **John Steinbeck** *The Grapes of Wrath* (Mandarin; Penguin). The classic account of a migrant family forsaking the Midwest for the Promised Land. For more localized fare, read the light-hearted but crisply observed novella, *Cannery Row*, capturing daily life on the pre-war Monterey waterfront, or the epic *East of Eden* (both Mandarin; Penguin), which updates and resets the Bible in the Salinas Valley and depicts three generations of familial feuding.

★ **Robert Louis Stevenson** *The Silverado Squatters* (Everyman; Tuttle). Stevenson vividly describes the splendor of the San Francisco hills and the cast of eccentrics and immigrants that populate them, as well as the strange atmosphere of Silverado itself, a deserted former Gold-Rush settlement, where the last trace of the mine is "a mound of gravel, some wreck of a wooden aqueduct, and the mouth of a tunnel, like a treasure grotto in a fairy story." For an extract, see p.823.

Amy Tan *The Joy Luck Club* (Mandarin; Putnam). The premise of this novel is that four Chinese women, new arrivals in San Francisco in the 1940s, come together to play mahjong, and tell their stories. They have four daughters, divided between Chinese and American identities, who also tell their stories, from childhood and from their often troubled present. The format of the novel is over-complex so that it often reads like a book of unconnected short stories, but there are passages of brilliant prose, and the evocation of childhood fears and perceptions is wonderful. For an extract, see p.825.

Erik Tarloff *The Man Who Wrote the Book* (Crown Publishing). An amusing look at the life of a frustrated college professor at a Fresno bible college, who finds himself immersed in the seedy world of Southern California's frenetic, libertine party culture.

Michael Tolkin *The Player* (Faber; Grove Atlantic). Convincing, multi-layered story of a movie executive using his power and contacts to skirt justice after committing murder.

Evelyn Waugh *The Loved One* (Little Brown). The essential literary companion to take with you on a trip to Forest Lawn – here rendered as Whispering Glades, the apex of funerary pretension and a telling symbol of LA's postmortem status mania.

★ **Nathanael West** *Complete Works* (Picador, UK o/p). Includes *The Day of the Locust*, an insightful and caustic tale that is *the* classic satire of early Hollywood.

Mexican-Spanish terms

California is bound to its Spanish colonial and Mexican past, a fact manifest in the profusion of Spanish place names, particularly in the south of the state. Today large numbers of people living in California speak Spanish as their first language, so it can be useful to know a few terms. Note that the double-L is pronounced like a "Y" and an "Ñ" sounds like an N and a Y run together.

abierto - open
agua - water
alta, alto - high
angeles - angels
arroyo - canyon or gully
avenida - avenue
buena, bueno - good
caliente - hot
calle - street, pronounced "ka-ye"
cerrado - closed
costa - coast
cruz - cross
de - of
del - of the
dorado - golden
el - the
escondido - hidden
fuego - fire
grande - big
hermosa - beautiful
jolla - jewel, pronounced "hoya"
las, los - the (plural)

mar - sea
mesa - high plateau, literally "table"
monte - mount(ain)
nevada - snowy
norte - north
obispo - bishop
oro - gold
parque - park
pescadero - fisherman
playa - beach
rey - king
rio - river
rojo - red
san, santa, santo - saint
sierra - mountain range
sol - sun
sur - south
taqueria - taco stall or shop
tienda - shop
tierra - land
tres - three
verde - green

For the basics, the most useful language book on the market is *Mexican Spanish: A Rough Guide Phrasebook* (Rough Guides), £3.99/$5, which covers the essential phrases and expressions, as well as dipping into grammar and providing a fuller vocabulary in dictionary format.

Index

and small print

Index

Map entries are in color

D

E

F

G

H

I

J

848

INDEX

I

INDEX

849

INDEX I

Twenty years of Rough Guides

In the summer of 1981, Mark Ellingham, Rough Guides' founder, knocked out the first guide on a typewriter, with a group of friends. Mark had been traveling in Greece after university, and couldn't find a guidebook that really answered his needs.There were heavyweight cultural guides on the one hand – good on museums and classical sites but not on beaches and tavernas – and on the other hand student manuals that were so caught up with how to save money that they lost sight of the country's significance beyond its role as a place for a cool vacation. None of the guides began to address Greece as a country, with its natural and human environment, its politics, and its contemporary life.

Having no urgent reason to return home, Mark decided to write his own guide. It was a guide to Greece that tried to combine some erudition and insight with a thoroughly practical approach to travelers' needs. Scrupulously researched listings of places to stay, eat, and drink were matched by careful attention to detail on everything from Homer to Greek music, from classical sites to national parks, and from nude beaches to monasteries. Back in London, Mark and his friends got their Rough Guide accepted by a farsighted commissioning editor at the publisher Routledge and it came out in 1982.

The Rough Guide to Greece was a student scheme that became a publishing phenomenon. The immediate success of the book – shortlisted for the Thomas Cook Award – spawned a series that rapidly covered dozens of countries. The Rough Guides found a ready market among backpackers and budget travelers, but soon acquired a much broader readership that included older and less impecunious visitors. Readers relished the guides' wit and inquisitiveness as much as the enthusiastic, critical approach that acknowledges everyone wants value for money – but not at any price.

Rough Guides soon began supplementing the "rougher" information – the hostel and low-budget listings – with the kind of detail that independent-minded travelers on any budget might expect. These days, the guides – distributed worldwide by the Penguin Group – include recommendations spanning the range from shoestring to luxury, and cover more than 200 destinations around the globe. Our growing team of authors, many of whom come to Rough Guides initially as outstandingly good letter-writers telling us about their travels, are spread all over the world, particularly in Europe, the USA, and Australia. As well as the travel guides, Rough Guides publishes a series of dictionary phrasebooks covering two dozen major languages, an acclaimed series of music guides running the gamut from Classical to World Music, a series of music CDs in association with World Music Network, and a range of reference books on topics as diverse as the Internet, Pregnancy, and Unexplained Phenomena. Visit **www.roughguides.com** to see what's cooking.

Rough Guide credits

Text editor: Richard Koss
Series editor: Mark Ellingham
Editorial: Martin Dunford, Jonathan Buckley, Kate Berens, Ann-Marie Shaw, Helena Smith, Olivia Swift, Ruth Blackmore, Geoff Howard, Claire Saunders, Gavin Thomas, Alexander Mark Rogers, Polly Thomas, Joe Staines, Richard Lim, Duncan Clark, Peter Buckley, Lucy Ratcliffe, Clifton Wilkinson, Alison Murchie, Matthew Teller, Andrew Dickson, Fran Sandham, Sally Schafer, Matthew Milton, Karoline Densley (UK); Andrew Rosenberg, Yuki Takagaki, Hunter Slaton (US)
Production: Link Hall, Helen Prior, Julia Bovis, Katie Pringle, Rachel Holmes, Andy Turner, Dan May, Tanya Hall, John McKay, Sophie Hewat

Cartography: Maxine Repath, Melissa Baker, Ed Wright, Katie Lloyd-Jones
Cover art direction: Louise Boulton
Picture research: Sharon Martins, Mark Thomas
Online: Kelly Martinez, Anja Mutic-Blessing, Jennifer Gold, Audra Epstein, Suzanne Welles, Cree Lawson (US)
Finance: Gary Singh
Marketing & Publicity: Richard Trillo, Niki Smith, David Wearn, Chloë Roberts, Demelza Dallow, Claire Southern (UK); Simon Carloss, David Wechsler, Megan Kennedy (US)
Administration: Julie Sanderson

Publishing information

This seventh edition published April 2003 by
Rough Guides Ltd,
80 Strand, London WC2R 0RL
345 Hudson Street, 4th Floor,
New York, NY 10014, USA
Distributed by the Penguin Group
Penguin Books Ltd,
80 Strand, London WC2R 0RL
Penguin Putnam, Inc,
375 Hudson St, NY 10014, USA
Penguin Books Australia Ltd,
487 Maroondah Hwy, PO Box 257,
Ringwood, Victoria 3134, Australia
Penguin Books Canada Ltd,
10 Alcorn Ave, Toronto, ON,
M4V 1E4 Canada
Penguin Books (NZ) Ltd,
182–190 Wairau Rd, Auckland 10,
New Zealand
Typeset in Bembo and Helvetica to an
original design by Henry Iles.

864pp includes index
A catalogue record for this book is available from the British Library

ISBN 1-84353-049-X

The publishers and authors have done their best to ensure the accuracy and currency of all the information in **The Rough Guide to California**; however, they can accept no responsibility for any loss, injury, or inconvenience sustained by any traveler as a result of information or advice contained in the guide.

SMALL PRINT

Help us update

We've gone to a lot of effort to ensure that the seventh edition of **The Rough Guide to California** is accurate and up-to-date. However, things change – places get "discovered," opening hours are notoriously fickle, restaurants and rooms raise prices or lower standards. If you feel we've got it wrong or left something out, we'd like to know, and if you can remember the address, the price, the time, the phone number, so much the better.

We'll credit all contributions, and send a copy of the next edition (or any other Rough Guide if you prefer) for the best letters. Everyone who writes to us and isn't already a subscriber will receive a copy of our full-color thrice-yearly newsletter. Please mark letters: **"Rough Guide California Update"** and send to: Rough Guides, 80 Strand, London WC2R 0RL, or Rough Guides, 4th Floor, 345 Hudson St, New York, NY 10014. Or send an email to **mail@roughguides.com**.

Have your questions answered and tell others about your trip at **www.roughguides.atinfopop.com**.

Acknowledgments

Jeff would like to thank his wife.

Mark would like to thank Lucy Steffens in Sacramento, Arianne Bautista and Julie Armstrong in Monterey County, the encyclopedically knowledgeable Ranee Ruble in Santa Cruz, Susan Carvalho in San Luis Obispo, and Dan Heller at Hearst Castle. Thanks, too, to Rachel Brown for company (and first-class map-reading skills).

Nick would like to thank the staff of the many tourist authorities, in particular all at Berkeley CVB; Bob Warren & Karen Whittaker at Shasta Cascades; Nancy Fuller at Sonoma County; Sharon Rooney & Heidi Cusick at Mendocino County; Joanne Steele of Siskiyou County; Sally Murray at Calistoga; Pettit Gilwee at Lake Tahoe; Katja Dahl for Squaw Valley skiing; and Bob Galeoto for the Lava Beds tour. Heartfelt gratitude to Heather Schlegel & Clint Marsh for the cozy nest in Berkeley, and warm thanks to Jim & Eleanor Reyner for hospitality in Santa Clara and to Nicki & Eric

Taylor in the wilds of Gold Country. Cheers to Greg Scott for sorting out the fun stay in Napa. Finally, much love to Maria and thanks for the wonderful transformation of the basement into RG and sports central.

Paul would like to thank everyone who shared experiences, opinions, and knowledge on various research trips over the years. For this update, special thanks go to Brett McGill for great company and different perspectives and to Ian Henderson for dangerous pursuits and positive outcomes. Thanks as always to Irene for unending support, holding the fort back home, and furnishing periodic back-garden snail reports.

Fervent thanks go out to Rachel Holmes for her indefatigable and adroit production work, Melissa Baker for her mapmaking ingenuity, Diane Margolis for her diligent proofreading, Eleanor Hill for her exquisite photo researching, Mark Ellwood for the judiciously compiled index, and, as ever, to Andrew Rosenberg for his guidance.

Readers' letters

Thanks to all the readers who took the trouble to write in with their comments and suggestions (and apologies to anyone whose name we've misspelt or omitted): Stephen Barnard, Reva Blau, Steven F. Ferndale, Randy Glessner, Gary Grice, Peter Licht, Martin Lievers, Diana Linden, Peter Martin, H.N. Mok, David Schaye, Gavin Scott, Peter and Susan Smith, Zoe Shore, John Song, and Michael Thaddeus.

Photo credits

06 Lower Klamath Falls National Wildlife Refuge © Corbis
07 Sequoia tree, Sequoia NP © Robert Harding/Gavin Hllier
08 Cable car, SF © Robert Harding/Nigel Francis
09 Casa de Balboa © Trip/J Greenberg
10 Red Rock Canyon petroglyphs © Paul Whitfield
11 Rafting on the Kern River © Corbis 5332
12 Uly the whale, SeaWorld © Seaworld
13 Overhead view of Sunset Boulevard © Dorling Kindersley
14 La Purisima Mission © Dorling Kindersley
15 Big Sur coastal scene – surf © Trip/S Grant
16 Museum in Nevada City (Firehouse No.1), California © Robert Holmes/C
17 Skiing in Lake Tahoe © Dorling Kindersley
18 Sand dunes of the Mojave National Preserve © Trip/V Greaves
19 Gay Pride float © Robert Harding/Alison Wright
20 Surfers on Swami Beach © Axiom/Conor Caffrey
21 Domaine Carneros/Sonoma © Jeff Greenberg/MR Trip
22 Burrito © Corbis
23 Amtrak Starlight © Amtrak
24 Mono Lake tufa towers © Paul Whitfield
25 Courtesy of Moe's Books/Erika Pino
26 View over the lava field © Dorling Kindersley
27 Hearst Mansion © Robert Harding/D Travers
28 Gray whale protruding above water © George D. Lepp/Corbis
29 Bridalveil Falls © Robert Harding/Roy Rainford
30 The exterior of the Getty Center © Trip/Amanda Edwards
31 Graumanns movie theater © Greg Evans
32 Tijuana's Centro Cultural © Trip/S Grant
33 Las Vegas: The Venetian © Dorling Kindersley
34 Hikers on Mount Whitney © Paul Whitfield

Black and whites

Rear view of skateboarder, Venice Beach © Corbis p.70
Traffic on Harbor Freeway, LA © Trip/S Grant p.76
Angels Flight funicular, LA © Trip/A Edwards p.159
Gaslamp Quarter banners on street light © Corbis p.200
Balboa Park, San Diego © Greg Evans p.218
Exterior of Luxor Hotel, Las Vegas © Trip/Viesti p.250
Joshua Tree and Rocks, evening, Joshua Tree NP © Robert Harding p.256
Salt evaporation flats, Death Valley © Axiom p.322
Bristlecone Pines, White Mountains, Owens Valley © Paul Whitfield p.331
Hikers at summit of Half Dome, Yosemite NP © Paul Whitfield p.366
Sequoia © Trip/T Mackie p.381
Memorial rose garden, Santa Barbara Mission © Travel Ink p.438
Sea Lions, California coast © Corbis p.447
Victorian-inspired houses in Haight-Ashbury © Corbis p.504
San Francisco mural © Axiom/C Caffrey p.630
San Francisco, view of downtown district © Travel Ink p.561
Lake Tahoe © Travel Ink p.648
Columbia State Historic NP © Corbis p.665
Bald Eagle, Lower Klamath Falls Wildlife Refuge © Corbis p.706
Grapes, Napa Valley vineyard © Trip/J Greenberg p.715
Sequoia tree, Sequoia NP © Robert Harding/Gavin Hllier p.764

SMALL PRINT

Visit us online
roughguides.com

Information on over 25,000 destinations around the world

- **Read** Rough Guides' trusted travel info
- **Share** journals, photos and travel advice with other readers
- Get exclusive Rough Guide **discounts** and travel **deals**
- Earn membership points every time you contribute to the Rough Guide **community** and get **free** books, flights and trips
- Browse thousands of CD reviews and artists in our **music** area

Rough Guides publishes new books every month

Rough Guides music, reference &

Music

Acoustic Guitar
Blues: 100 Essential
 CDs
Cello
Clarinet
Classical Music
Classical Music:
 100 Essential CDs
Country Music
Country: 100
 Essential CDs
Cuban Music
Drum'n'bass
Drums
Electric Guitar
 & Bass Guitar
Flute
Hip-Hop
House
Irish Music
Jazz
Jazz: 100 Essential
 CDs
Keyboards & Digital
 Piano
Latin: 100 Essential
 CDs
Music USA: a Coast-
 To-Coast Tour
Opera
Opera: 100 Essential
 CDs
Piano
Reading Music
Reggae
Reggae: 100
 Essential CDs
Rock
Rock: 100 Essential
 CDs
Saxophone
Soul: 100 Essential
 CDs
Techno
Trumpet & Trombone
Violin & Viola
World Music: 100
 Essential CDs

World Music Vol1
World Music Vol2

Reference

Children's Books,
 0–5
Children's Books,
 5–11
China Chronicle
Cult Movies
Cult TV
Elvis
England Chronicle
France Chronicle
India Chronicle
The Internet
Internet Radio
James Bond
Liverpool FC
Man Utd
Money Online
Personal Computers
Pregnancy & Birth
Shopping Online
Travel Health
Travel Online
Unexplained
 Phenomena
Videogaming
Weather
Website Directory
Women Travel

Music CDs

Africa
Afrocuba
Afro-Peru
Ali Hussan Kuban
The Alps
Americana
The Andes
The Appalachians
Arabesque
Asian Underground
Australian Aboriginal
 Music
Bellydance
Bhangra
Bluegrass

Bollywood
Boogaloo
Brazil
Cajun
Cajun and Zydeco
Calypso and Soca
Cape Verde
Central America
Classic Jazz
Congolese Soukous
Cuba
Cuban Music Story
Cuban Son
Cumbia
Delta Blues
Eastern Europe
English Roots Music
Flamenco
Franco
Gospel
Global Dance
Greece
The Gypsies
Haiti
Hawaii
The Himalayas
Hip Hop
Hungary
India
India and Pakistan
Indian Ocean
Indonesia
Irish Folk
Irish Music
Italy
Jamaica
Japan
Kenya and
 Tanzania
Klezmer
Louisiana
Lucky Dube
Mali and Guinea
Marrabenta
 Mozambique
Merengue & Bachata
Mexico
Native American
 Music
Nigeria and Ghana
North Africa

Nusrat Fateh Ali
 Khan
Okinawa
Paris Café Music
Portugal
Rai
Reggae
Salsa
Salsa Dance
Samba
Scandinavia
Scottish Folk
Scottish Music
Senegal
 & The Gambia
Ska
Soul Brothers
South Africa
South African Gospel
South African Jazz
Spain
Sufi Music
Tango
Thailand
Tex-Mex
Wales
West African Music
World Music Vol 1:
 Africa, Europe and
 the Middle East
World Music Vol 2:
 Latin & North
 America,
 Caribbean, India,
 Asia and Pacific
World Roots
Youssou N'Dour
 & Etoile de Dakar
Zimbabwe

Major Attractions, One Low Price!

Southern California   **$166.00** a $237.95 Value!

Includes: 3-Day Park Hopper to Disneyland® Park and Disney's California Adventure™
Plus 1-day admission to: Knott's Berry Farm® Theme Park • SeaWorld® San Diego • The World-Famous San Diego Zoo®

Hollywood   **$69.00** a $108.00 Value!

Includes: Universal Studios Hollywood • Starline Hollywood Movie Stars Homes Tour
Kodak Theater Tour • Hollywood Entertainment Museum • Autry Museum of Western Heritage

San Francisco   **$37.00** a $74.00 Value!

Includes: 7-Day Unlimited Use Cable Car & MUNI Transportation Pass
Plus admission to: Blue & Gold Fleet San Francisco Bay Cruise • S.F. Museum of Modern Art
Academy of Sciences and Steinhart Aquarium • Palace of the Legion of Honor • Exploratorium

CityPass is on sale at all of the above attractions. Ask for it at the first one you visit!
For more information visit **www.citypass.com** or call **(707) 256-0490.**